SOCIAL PERSPECTIVES IN LESBIAN AND GAY STUDIES

A READER

edited by

Peter M. Nardi
and
Beth E. Schneider

London and New York

First published 1998
by Routledge
11 New Fetter Lane, London EC4P 4EE

Simultaneously published in the USA and Canada
by Routledge
29 West 35th Street, New York, NY 10001

Typeset in Sabon by Solidus (Bristol) Limited
Printed and bound in Great Britain by The Bath Press

British Library Cataloguing in Publication Data
A catalogue record for this book is available from the British Library

Library of Congress Cataloging in Publication Data
Social perspectives in lesbian and gay studies: a reader / edited by
Peter M. Nardi and Beth E. Schneider.
p.   cm.
Includes bibliographical references and index.
(pbk.: alk. paper)
1. Gay and lesbian studies—United States.   2. Gay men—United
States—Social conditions.   3. Lesbians—United States—Social
conditions.   4. Homosexuality—United States—Philosophy.
I. Nardi, Peter M.   II. Schneider, Beth E.
HQ75.16.U6S63   1998
305.9'0664'07—dc21   97-2918
CIP

ISBN 0–415–16708–6 (hbk)
ISBN 0–415–16709–4 (pbk)

SOCIAL PERSPECTIVES IN LESBIAN AND GAY STUDIES

How the [...] principle of this c[...] begins in th[...] continues briefly in the 19[...] and begins to flourish by the late 1970s. Th[...] range from the earliest [...] the undergroun[...] the[...] worlds [...] gay men to feminist perspecti[...] identity, and to the em[...]

The f[...]undations of the cons[...] and the [...] empirical social res[...] [...] essays add a critical analy[...] Part 2 [...] *Locating The Sociological Baseline* [...] by looking at lesbian a[...] gay lives by sociologists [...] [...] sociology has for u[...] [...]sts made visible the [...] of homosexuality[...] [...]lars organized their co[...] [...] *Identities and Commu[...]* [...] [...]mmunity and iden[...] [...]ovement based on identity [...]

Part 3 [...] *Institutions [...] Socia[...]* [...] articles that look out from the [...] [...]tionships with the [...] and the hegemonic structure[...] [...] *[...] Ahead – Challe[...]* [...]s gay and lesbian s[...] [...]calism of Americ[...] [...] [...]; they urge the prod[...] [...]nces and how the[...] [...]eory and sociolog[...]

This [...] [...]lecting in one place the major social science articles from the past as well as providing challenges for future study.

Peter M. Nardi is Professor of Sociology at Pitzer College, The Claremont Colleges. **Beth E. Schneider** is Professor of Sociology at the University of California, Santa Barbara.

CONTENTS

2 LOOKING IN – IDENTITIES AND COMMUNITIES

Building Gay and Lesbian Communities

Building Identities

3 LOOKING OUT – INSTITUTIONS AND SOCIAL CHANGE

Creating Social Movements

Challenging Institutional Heterosexism

4 LOOKING AHEAD – CHALLENGES FOR FUTURE RESEARCH

Globalizing Gay and Lesbian Studies

Doing Race, Class, and Gender

Queering the Sociological

A NOTE ON THE EDITORS

Peter M. Nardi is Professor of Sociology at Pitzer College, one of the Claremont Colleges in the Los Angeles area. He is the co-editor of *In Changing Times: Gay Men & Lesbians Encounter HIV/AIDS* (Chicago), co-author/co-editor of *Growing Up Before Stonewall: Life Stories of Some Gay Men* (Routledge), and editor of *Men's Friendships* (Sage). He is the Book Review co-editor of *GLQ: A Journal of Lesbian and Gay Studies* and the Special Features co-editor of *Sexualities*, a new journal from Sage Publications. He has also published several op-ed pieces in the *Los Angeles Times* on gay/lesbian issues.

He is politically active in the gay community, having served as chair of the Sociologists' Lesbian & Gay Caucus of the American Sociological Association, co-chair of the Los Angeles Gay Academic Union, and co-president and board member of the Los Angeles chapter of the Gay & Lesbian Alliance Against Defamation (GLAAD). He received his BA from the University of Notre Dame and his Ph.D. from the University of Pennsylvania.

Beth E. Schneider is Professor of Sociology and Women's Studies at the University of California, Santa Barbara and editor of the journal, *Gender & Society*. She is the co-editor of both *The Social Context of AIDS* (Sage) and *Women Resisting AIDS: Feminist Strategies of Empowerment* (Temple University Press) and the Special Features co-editor of *Sexualities*. She has also written extensively on the sexualization of the workplace, lesbians' experiences at work and the contemporary women's movement. She served for four years as the President of the Board of the Gay and Lesbian Resource Center, the parent organization of the AIDS Counseling and Assistance Program of Santa Barbara County. She also served as the chair of the Sociologists' Lesbian and Gay Caucus of the American Sociological Association. She is currently the facilitator of the Queer Speakers Series and Symposia at UCSB and a member of Santa Barbara Community Pride. She received her BA from Hofstra University, her MA from the University of Michigan and her Ph.D. from the University of Massachusetts.

ACKNOWLEDGMENTS

Putting together a reader of classic and contemporary articles on lesbian and gay issues was made considerably easier with the assistance of some very capable people. Darcie Vandergrift helped us track down and copy many of the chapters and articles included in this collection. Ken Plummer, in addition to providing the Afterword, wrote some of the Introduction to Part 1 and contributed to our discussions of what might be included in the reader. Finally, the help that Mari Shullaw, our Routledge editor, and Geraldine Lyons, our desk editor, gave us in securing reprint rights and in encouraging us to complete this project, has been immeasurable.

The publishers would like to thank the following for permission to reprint their material:

From Evert van der Veen *et al.*, "Lesbian and Gay Rights in Europe: Homosexuality and the Law" in Aart Hendriks *et al.* (eds) *The Third Pink Book*, Prometheus Books. Copyright 1993. Reprinted with permission of the publisher. Gayle S. Rubin for "Thinking Sex: Notes for a Radical Theory of Sexuality" by Gayle S. Rubin in *Pleasure and Danger: Exploring Female Sexuality*, 1984, Routledge & Kegan Paul. The University of Chicago Press and Esther Newton for "The 'Queens'" in *Mother Camp*, 1979, pp. 20–39. Taylor and Francis Group and Dennis Altman for "The Emergence of a Non Government Response to Aids" in *Power and Community: Organizational and Cultural Responses to Aids*, 1994, pp. 13–35. Curtis Brown, Serpent's Tail and Dennis Altman for "Conclusion: the End of the Homosexual" in Altman and Weeks *Homosexual Oppression and Liberation*. Temple University Press for "Lesbian Involvement in the AIDS Epidemic" in *Women Resisting Aids* by Nancy Stoller and Beth Schneider (eds), pp. 270–85. Humphreys, Laud, *Tearoom Trade: Impersonal Sex in Public Places*, New York: Aldine de Gruyter. Copyright © 1970, 1975 R.A. Laud Humphreys. *differences: A Journal of Feminist Cultural Studies* for "Chicago Men: A Cartography of Homosexual Identity and Behavior" by Tomás Almaguer in *differences*, vol. 3, no. 2, Summer 1991: 75–100. New Society Publishers for "Bridge, Drawbridge, Sandbar or Island" by Anzaldúa in *Bridges of Power: Women's Multicultural Alliances*, 1990. University of California Press Journals and Joshua Gamson for "Silence, Death and the Invisible Enemy" in *Social Problems*, vol. 36: 4. University of California Press Journals and Maurice Leznoff for "The Homosexual Community" in *Social Problems*, vol. 3: 4. University of California Press Journals and Mary McIntosh for "The Homosexual Role" in *Social Problems*, vol. 16: 2. Barnes and Noble Books and Plummer for "Homosexual Categories" in *The Making of the Modern Homosexual*, edited by Barnes and Noble, pp. 55–75. Carol S. Vance for "Social Construction Theory: Problems in the History of Sexuality" in Anja van Kooten Niekerk and Theo Van Der Meer (eds) 1989 *Homosexuality, which Homosexuality?* Reprinted from Nardi and Bolton, "Gay Bashing" in *Targets of Violence and Aggression*, R. Baenninger (ed.) 1991. With kind permission from Elsevier Science B.V. Amsterdam, The Netherlands. The Society for the Scientific Study of Sexuality and Frederick Whitam for "The Homosexual Role: A Reconsideration" in *The Journal of Sexual*

Research, vol. 13, pp. 1–11. The Society for the Scientific Study of Sexuality and Nancy Achilles for "The Development of the Homosexual Bar as an Institution" in J. Gagnon and W. Simon (eds) 1967 *Sexual Deviance*. The Society for the Scientific Study of Sexuality and Martin P. Levine for "Gay Ghetto" in Levine (ed.) 1979 *Gay Men: the Sociology of Male Homosexuality*. Duke University Press and Lisa Duggan for "Queering the State" in *Social Text*, 39, Summer 1994, pp. 1–14. University of California Press and Joshua Gamson for "Must Identify Movements Self Destruct" in *Social Problems*, 42: 3, August 1995, pp. 390–407. © Society for the Study of Social Problems. University of California Press and Albert J. Reiss, Jr for "Social Integration of Queers and Peers" in *Social Problems*, 9: 2, August 1961, pp. 102–20. © Society for the Study of Social Problems. Routledge and Kegan Paul and Jeffrey Weeks for "The Meaning of Diversity" in Weeks (ed.) 1985 *Sexuality and its Discontents: Meanings, Myths and Modern Sensibilities*, pp. 108–20. "Gay Images and the Social Construction of Acceptability" reprinted from *Arresting Images: Impolitic Art and Uncivil Actions*, 1992, pp. 159–6. By permission of the publisher, Routledge, New York. © The Society for the Comparative Study of Society and History, Cambridge University Press and Barry Adam, 1985, for "Structural Foundations of the Gay World" in *Comparative Studies in Society and History*, 27 (4), pp. 658–71. Temple University Press for "An Identity Community" in *The Mirror Dance*, pp. 7–17. Reed Consumer Books for "A Concluding Overview" in *Homosexualities* by Alan Bell and Martin Weinberg, pp. 217–31. The Haworth Press, Inc, NY 13904 for "Introduction to Gay and Lesbian Youth" in *Journal of Homosexuality*, vol. 21 (1/2) pp. 19–46. Greenwood Publishing Group Inc. for "Social Construction of Lesbian Identities" by Barbara Ponse in *Identities in the Lesbian World*, 1978. Guilford Publications Inc. for "Coming out in the Gay World" in *Psychiatry*, 1971, vol. 34, May, pp. 60–77. General Hall Inc. for "A Model of Homosexual Identity Formation" by Richard Troiden in *Gay and Lesbian Identity: a sociological analysis*, 1988. Carol Warren for "Space and Time" in *Identity and Community in the Gay World*, pp. 17–43. Duke University Press for "Gay Politics, Ethnic Identity" by Steven Epstein in *Socialist Review*, 17: 3–4, May/August, 1987, pp. 93–4. Duke University Press for "Sisters and Queers" in *Socialist Review*, 22: 1, January–March, 1992, pp. 35–55. Yale University Press for "Collective Identity in Social Movement" by Morris and Meuller in *Frontiers in Social Movement Theory*.

INTRODUCTION

Lesbian and gay topics remain relatively invisible in the field of sociology. This is not surprising, given the silence that has greeted issues of sexuality within the classic studies and texts in sociology, and given the way homosexuality has been viewed as a social deviance. Yet, for decades a body of research has been growing, slowly making some impact on sociology and its views of the world. Sociologists are beginning to look at gay and lesbian issues and to consider the ways these issues affect important sociological theories and methodologies.

How sociology has looked at lesbian and gay issues is the organizing principle of this collection of articles. It is a journey that begins in the 1950s, continues briefly in the 1960s, and begins to flourish by the late 1970s. The articles range from the earliest research into the underground, marginal worlds of gay men, to feminist perspectives on lesbian and gay lives, to social constructionist debates on identity, and to the emerging queer theories of transgression and postmodern identities. Most are written by sociologists, though a few are by scholars in other fields who have contributed work that raises relevant social questions and provides salient sociological insights.

The earliest sociological studies set the stage for later research. The foundations of the constructional debate and the first collection of empirical research are presented in Part 1 *Looking – The Sociological Baselines*. The empirical articles suggest how limited the attention was to looking at lesbian and gay lives by sociologists, yet they indicate the enormous potential sociology has for understanding sexual diversity in contemporary society. Some of this is evident when reading the more extensive theoretical writing on sexuality and homosexuality, some of which is presented in the second section of Part 1 which focuses on the beginnings of the social constructionist debates. Here we are introduced to the first and most central articles about the making of the modern homosexual as a social category.

Once sociologists made visible the existence of homosexuality, focus began on how gays and lesbians organized their communities and established their identities. Looking into lesbian and gay worlds became the project of a good deal of the research in the 1970s. Part 2: *Looking In – Identities and Communities* collects articles emphasizing the building of lesbian and gay community and identity and the character and concerns of a growing social movement based on identity politics. Despite controversy about and the increased complexity of the concepts of identity and community, they are important both in sociology and in the social lives of gay men and lesbians.

Gay and lesbian issues, however, are not isolated social events; they exist in a cultural context and have impact on society. Some sociologists have studied the influence of gay and lesbian movements on society's core institutions and how these movements contributed to social change. Part 3: *Looking Out – Institutions and Social Change* presents articles that look out from the gay and lesbian communities and social worlds and assess their relationships with the larger society. Challenges to institutional heterosexism and the hegemonic structures of society are highlighted in many of these articles.

Despite the growth in sociological research, many important dimensions remain invisible. Most of the research has been conducted by and on white, gay American men. In order for sociology to progress from these limited perspectives, research must broaden its concerns and look at the multiplicity of identities and experiences. It must study homosexualities and the contested identities of difference. Part 4: *Looking Ahead – Challenges for Future Research* introduces more current research that pushes gay and lesbian studies in sociology in new directions. These articles question the localism of American viewpoints by raising more global and comparative perspectives; they urge the production of research that takes seriously racial, class, and gender differences and how they powerfully intersect; and they argue for a transformation of social theory and sociology through the development of and engagement with queer theory.

Sociology is being challenged to look ahead but also to make use of the work that has come before it. Some of these studies may now seem naive or simplistic in their methodologies and theoretical conceptualizations. Yet, they are included since they form the foundation upon which most of the later research has been built. What began as studies that looked at the role of the deviant, or looked into the isolated and contained world of (mostly white) gays and lesbians, have now become research projects assessing the complexities of identities and communities that are emergent and salient parts of both global and local societies.

This collection is a look at where lesbian and gay studies in sociology finds its roots. It is also an indication of where it can go and how it can take the lead in organizing the kinds of questions that need to be addressed sociologically. How sociology can do this is addressed in Ken Plummer's Afterword: "The Past, Present and Futures of the Sociology of Same-sex Relations." Here he discusses the limited role sociology played historically in the study of homosexuality, demonstrates how it helped shape some of the key research questions about gay and lesbian lives from the mid-1970s through the early 1980s, and proposes important ways sociology can contribute theoretically and empirically to the study of same-sex relations.

Looking – The Sociological Baselines

INTRODUCTION

For the first hundred and fifty years of its history, sociologists were mute on the subject of homosexuality. Only in the post-World-War-II period – and even then in a very modest way – were preliminary sociological speculations on homosexuality made. Ironically, the first major social statements came from a biologist and not a sociologist: the monumental Kinsey (1948, 1953) studies on the sexual behavior of the human male and the human female not only introduced the celebrated notion of a "continuum" (the 0–6 scale of heterosexuality–homosexuality) which helped to weaken the idea of homosexuality as a fixed condition, but – and perhaps more significantly – provided large-scale evidence about the differential social distribution and organization of same-sex experience.

In the 1950s the social psychological work of Evelyn Hooker (1958) attempted to demonstrate empirically the "normality" of the homosexual. Two "popular" books by Cory (1951) and Westwood (1960) turned attention in America and Britain, respectively, to the social lives of homosexuals. Both claimed that the "minority framework" used to study race was appropriate for studying homosexuals and both recognized the powerful role of prejudice in making the social experience of homosexuality a difficult and painful one. The first social surveys were conducted in the work of Schofield (1965) and suggested the importance of "the attitudes of other people" as significant in shaping the homosexual experience.

Although these early writers recognized different types of homosexual, they did not problematize the very concept. Even with these very few writings, no professional sociologist had yet tried to bring "the sociological imagination" to bear on an area that generally remained hidden from society. Slowly, a few scattered attempts were made. Part 1 includes some of these first studies.

Several sociologists attempted to approach homosexuality as an ethnographic phenomenon. Sometimes accused of being overly voyeuristic, they attempted to chart the inner meanings, social worlds and diversities of gay lifestyles and communities. The first section, *Researching Homosexualities*, includes five examples of the beginning empirical work on same-sex people. One of the earliest studies of a gay community is by Leznoff and Westley of a Canadian community which is marked by "overts" and "coverts." There soon followed Albert Reiss's classic study of male hustlers and the ways they construct an identity for themselves in an age when "queer" held a different meaning from the way it is used by contemporary "queer" theorists.

Also included is a chapter of Laud Humphrey's infamous study of men who cruised public toilets for impersonal sex, many of whom saw themselves and behaved as "straight married" men, and a striking ethnography of gay men and drag by Esther Newton. We offer these as instances of a particular style of work that developed during the 1950s and 1960s and, as is evident, one that was rooted in concepts of deviance. This section concludes with an excerpt from the first major survey research of gay men conducted in San Francisco in 1970 (but published in 1978) by Bell and Weinberg.

During the 1960s, sociology became a significant academic subject, and the sociology of deviance became increasingly one of its most studied specialities. Most notably, there was the development of labelling theory and a number of early papers attempted to apply this theory to homosexuality. It was indeed highly relevant since it stressed that (1) the societal reactions to deviance were critical variables in the understanding of deviance; (2) the focus of deviance research should be upon these societal reactions; and (3) deviance was not an absolute but a relative phenomenon which took many of its characteristics from the societal reactions towards it (Plummer 1979).

By the late 1960s, papers informed by labelling theory emerged. The second section, *Theorizing Homosexualities*, includes these articles as well as others that introduced the debates surrounding constructionist and essentialist perspectives. Work by John Gagnon and William Simon and an influential article by British sociologist Mary McIntosh set a much broader context for the analysis of same-sex relations: the themes of survey research, social epidemiology, and social prejudice give way to the need to reconceptualize sociologically the very problematic of study. Here, for the first time, there was no longer a sense that it was "the homosexual" who needed to be studied; instead the focus turned to placing same-sex experiences in a much wider social and historical context. No longer should "the homosexual" be seen as a universal entity, but instead the homosexual category should itself be analyzed and its relative historical, economic, and political base be scrutinized. Furthermore, "the homosexual" should not be studied in extraordinary ways: the focus now became to locate same-sex experiences within the much more casual social experiences of everyday life.

Many of the papers presented in this section helped to generate what eventually became known as "the essentialist–constructionist" controversy, an issue that dominated lesbian and gay studies through much of the 1980s, but which at last seems to have settled. Broadly, essentialists perceived homosexuality as a universal entity; constructionists argued that same-sex experiences were always socially mediated and historically transformable. Fred Whitam provides the classic essentialist critique of McIntosh; and Ken Plummer clarifies the problems of constructionism in a chapter from an influential anthology of the early 1980s, *The Making of the Modern Homosexual*. And Gayle Rubin challenges scholars to think politically about sexuality and to develop a theory of sexual stratification and social change.

Finally, Carole Vance's article presents a valuable overview, defense, and clarification of constructionism and Steve Epstein's paper establishes a more nuanced debate by successfully breaking down the somewhat crude polarization that had dominated the discussions. In the articles collected in Part 1, sociology took a first look at homosexuality and established a baseline for much future work.

REFERENCES

Cory, D. W. (1951), *The Homosexual in America* (New York: Greenberg).

Hooker, E. (1958), "Male Homosexuality in the Rorschach," *Journal of Projective Techniques* 22: 33–54.

Kinsey, A., W. Pomeroy and C. Martin (1948), *Sexual Behavior in the Human Male* (Philadelphia: W. B. Saunders).

Kinsey, A., W. Pomeroy, C. Martin and P. Gebhard. (1953), *Sexual Behavior in the Human Female* (Philadelphia: W. B. Saunders).

Plummer, K. (1979), "Misunderstanding Labelling Perspectives," in D. Downes and P. Rock (eds) *Deviant Interpretations*, (Oxford: Martin Robertson).

Schofield, M. (1965), *Sociological Aspects of Homosexuality*, (London: Longmans).

Westwood, G. (1960) *A Minority: A Report on the Life of the Male Homosexual in Great Britain* (London: Longmans).

MAURICE LEZNOFF and WILLIAM A. WESTLEY

"The Homosexual Community"

from *Social Problems* 3 (1956): 257–63

The significance of homosexuality in our society has been minimized and obscured by the force of social taboo. Yet there is evidence that homosexuals are distributed throughout all geographical areas and socio-economic strata.[1] Furthermore, the subjection of homosexuals to legal punishments and social condemnation has produced a complex structure of concealed social relations which merit sociological investigation. The psychological isolation of the homosexual from society, his dependence upon other deviants for the satisfaction of sexual needs and self-expression, the crystallization of social roles and behavior patterns within the deviant group, the reciprocal obligations and demands within the homosexual community, and their significance for the larger society in which they occur, are but a few of the areas of theoretical interest to the sociologist.

In this paper we shall confine our discussion to the social organization of one homosexual community and its constituent social groups: their function, etiology, and interrelationships.

The report is based upon an intensive study of sixty homosexuals in a large Canadian city. The data consist of four-hour interviews with forty homosexuals and briefer interviews with twenty others.[2] In addition, the data include information based on the observation of many homosexual parties and gatherings in bars and restaurants, and a series of thirty letters written by one homosexual to another.

FUNCTIONS OF HOMOSEXUAL GROUPS

The primary function of the homosexual group is psychological in that it provides a social context within which the homosexual can find acceptance as a homosexual and collective support for his deviant tendencies. Most homosexuals fear detection and are often insecure and anxious because of this. The following statement illustrates this:

> The thought that you are "gay" is always with you and you know it's there even when other people don't. You also think to yourself that certain of your mannerisms and your ways of expression are liable to give you away. That means that there is always a certain amount of strain. I don't say that it's a relief to get away from normal people, but there isn't the liberty that you feel in a gay crowd. When I associate with normal people I prefer very small groups of them. I don't like large groups and I think I try to avoid them when I can. You know, the only time when I really forget I'm gay is when I'm in a gay crowd.

To relieve this anxiety the deviant seeks collective support and social acceptance. Since the homosexual group provides the only social context in which homosexuality is normal, deviant practices moral, and homosexual responses rewarded, the homosexual develops a deep emotional involvement with his group, tending toward a ready acceptance of its norms and dictates, and subjection to its behavior patterns. The regularity with which he seeks the company of his group is a clear expression of this dependency.

A prohibition against sexual relationships within the group, in a manner suggestive of the incest taboo, indicates the extent to which the group culture is oriented to this function. The quotation which follows is indicative of this taboo:

As far as I know, people who hang around with each other don't have affairs. The people who are friends don't sleep with each other. I can't tell you why that is, but they just don't. Unless you are married[3] you have sex with strangers mostly. I think if you have sex with a friend it will destroy the friendship. I think that in the inner mind we all respect high moral standards, and none of us want to feel low in the eyes of anybody else. It's always easier to get along with your gay friends if there has been no sex. Mind you, you might have sex with somebody you just met and then he might become your friend. But you won't have sex with him any more as soon as he joins the same gang you hang around with.

Within these groups the narration of sexual experiences and gossip about the sexual exploits of others is a major form of recreation. The narration of sexual experiences functions to allocate prestige among the members because of the high evaluation placed upon physical attraction and sexual prowess. Yet it creates hostility and sexual rivalry. The intense involvement of homosexuals in the results of this sexual competition is illustrated in the following statement which was overheard in a restaurant:

Who wouldn't blow up. That bitch is trying to get her[4] clutches into Richard. She can't leave anybody alone. I wouldn't be surprised if she ended up with a knife in her back. I don't mean to say I'm threatening her. But she's not going to get away with that stuff forever ... playing kneesies under the table all night long. I had to get her away from Richard. That lousy bitch. From now on she better keep away from me.

An additional function is the provision of a social situation in which the members can dramatize their adherence to homosexual values. Thus, the gossip about sex, the adoption and exaggeration of feminine behavior, and the affectation of speech, represent a way of affirming that homosexuality is frankly accepted and has the collective support of the group. The extreme but not uncommon instance of this is the homosexual institution of the "drag" in which the members of the group dress and make themselves up as women. A good description of a drag is contained in the following letter:

Well, doll, last night was one to remember. Raymond of B. (city) gave me a letter of introduction to one of the local belles. He 'phoned yesterday and we arranged to go out in the evening. Met at my room and proceeded to the Frederick Hotel where I was introduced to my new acquaintances. It was decided to hold a party afterwards. Chez Norman, my new acquaintance. He told me they were supposed to be discontinued but we were going ahead in my honor. And in drag. One queen about 45–50 who is a window dresser brought some materials of fine nylon net, 2 yards wide and changing color across the width from yellow to flaming orange. There must have been about 25 yds. Well, he made his entrance wearing nothing but his shorts and this stuff wound around him and proceeded to do an exotic dance. Included in the costume was a blond wig from one of the store mannequins and artificial tropical fruits. It was something to see. It was very ludicrous to begin with and much more so when you realize that he is by no means graceful and has so much hair on him that I am smooth by comparison. Throughout the evening he kept on making variations of the costume – each becoming briefer until he was down to nothing. Really!

Another one, very slim, put on a pair of falsies, a turban hat to hide short hair, and a dress with a wide flair skirt. Other than hair on the chest which showed, the effect of feminity was so convincing (even his heels) that I promptly lost interest. Actually produced a beautiful effect – the kind of woman I would like if I could. Beautiful dancer, and performed all evening. Later borrowed some of the nylon net of the old queen and did a dance with flowing material and wearing *nothing*, but nothing else.

There were only three of us not in drag, including yrs. truly. But when it came time to leave (not alone, I might add) I couldn't resist flinging about my coat a fox fur which happened to be lying around. Really, my dear, it was quite an affair.

These functions reflect the common needs and problems which homosexuals face in hostile society.

ETIOLOGY: THE EVASION OF SOCIAL CONTROLS

In our society, homosexuality is defined both legally and socially as a criminal and depraved practice and the homosexual is threatened by powerful legal and social sanctions such as imprisonment, physical violence (Wesley 1953), social and occupational ostracism and ridicule. Therefore, all homosexuals face the problem of evading social controls. They do this in two predominant ways.

Some pass for heterosexuals on the job and in most of their social relationships. They mix regularly with heterosexuals for business, entertainment, and other social activities. They avoid situations and persons publicly recognized as homosexual for they fear that discovery will threaten their career and expose them to sanctions. This is illustrated in the following statement of a lawyer:

> I know a few people who don't care. They are really pitiful. They are either people who are in very insignificant positions or they are in good positions but are independent. I know of one who is in the retail business. He doesn't care. A lot of the artists don't care. For that reason I have never cultivated the friendship of artists. I just don't get along with anybody who doesn't care. That's why I really can't give you information about those who don't. It's just that I can't afford to get to know them very well, and I try to avoid them. Sometimes personal friends become this way. Then there is a mutual rejection of the friendship. From my point of view I am just no longer interested when they adopt that kind of attitude. From their point of view it means completely living outside of society and they are no longer interested in people who they consider hypocrites.

Others openly admit and practice homosexuality. They usually work in occupations where the homosexual is tolerated, withdraw from uncompromising heterosexual groups, and confine most of their social life to homosexual circles. This attitude is expressed in the following statement by a hairdresser:

> Rosenstein can go to hell as far as I care. She works you to the bone if she can get away with it. She told me I run around the place like a regular pansy. So I told her I am a pansy and if she doesn't like it she can get somebody else to do her dirty work for her. I knew she wouldn't fire me. All the ladies ask for me and I don't have to pretend to nobody.

While the problem of evasion is common to all homosexuals, the mechanisms of evasion present various alternatives. Most homosexuals find themselves compelled to conform outwardly to societal demands. They are conscious of their social position within society and seek such satisfactions as occupational mobility and prestige. They endeavor to retain intimate associations within the heterosexual community, and fear recognition as a status threat. Such homosexuals rely upon secrecy and the concealment of their deviant practices. They will therefore be referred to as "secret" homosexuals. A minority retreats from the demands of society and renounce societal goals. Such individuals will be referred to as "overt" homosexuals.

The mode of adaption is largely dependent upon the extent to which identification as a homosexual is a status threat. While economic status cannot be equated with social status, the individual's position within the work world represents the most significant single factor in the prestige scale. Therefore, the extent to which homosexuality is tolerated in various occupations determines to a great extent the mode of evasion chosen by the homosexual. Thus, there are many occupations, of which the professions are an obvious example, where homosexuals are not tolerated. In other areas, the particular occupation may have traditionally accepted homosexual linkages in the popular image or be of such low rank as to permit homosexuals to function on the job. The artist, the interior decorator, and the hairdresser exemplify the former type; such positions as counter man or bell-hop, the latter. Thus we find a rough relationship between form of evasion and occupation. The overt homosexual tends to fit into an occupation of low-status rank; the secret homosexual into an occupation with a relatively high status rank. The relationship is shown in Table 1.1.

DISTINCTIONS BETWEEN THE SECRET AND OVERT GROUPS

The chief distinctions between homosexual groups correspond to the differences in the general modes of evading social controls which homosexuals have developed. Thus, secret and overt homosexuals form distinctive groups.

The distinctions between these groups are maintained by the secret homosexuals who fear identification and refuse to associate with overt homosexuals. This statement by a secret homosexual is illustrative:

> If someone who is gay wanted to be spiteful they could say something in the wrong quarter. Nobody who cared about himself would say

Table 1.1 Occupation of forty secret and overt homosexuals

Occupation[1]	Secret[2]	Overt	Total
Professional & managerial	13	0	13
Clerical & sales	9	4	13
Craftsmen	2	1	3
Operatives	1	1	2
Service	0	6	6
Artists	0	3	3
Totals	25	15	40

Notes

1 Except for artists the categories and ranking are those established by the National Opinion Research Center. (1947) Artists have been listed as a separate category because they often represent a group which is apart from the status structure of the community.

2 The secret homosexuals gave the following reasons for concealment: (1) desire to avoid social ridicule – 22 cases; (2) fear of dismissal from the job, or, where self-employed, inability to get clients – 20 cases; (3) a desire to protect others such as family or friends – 18 cases.

anything. The trouble is that some don't care. I make it a rule to avoid anybody who is perfectly open about himself. It's easy not to become friendly with those people but it's hard to avoid them entirely. You certainly don't want to snub them because that might make them antagonistic. You just don't call them or see them at social gatherings. But you do meet them at bars and that's where you can be introduced to them. If they remember you and continue to say hello to you on the street, you have to acknowledge them or they might feel that you are trying to snub them.

As a result of this social distance a certain amount of reciprocal hostility has developed between the members of secret and overt groups. This hostility helps maintain the social distance and distinctions between these groups. This is demonstrated in the following statements by an overt and a secret homosexual respectively:

I know some of them because sometimes they stoop down and have an affair with somebody from our gang. They even come to a party over at Robert's once in a while but they never hang around for very long and then you don't see them again. They go over to the Red Room sometimes but we don't have much to say to each other and the same thing happens when we go over to the Burning Flame.[5] We just might say hello. But sometimes they will cruise us and try to take someone home to bed. I think you could say we mix sexually but not socially.

There are some people who I don't like and I wish these people didn't know about me. Then there are the people I don't know too well: people who are obvious or what I uncharitably call the riff-raff. I have always attempted to avoid them and I avoid them now. It is inevitable that you bump into a lot of people you would rather not know. Homosexuals are very democratic people. To achieve their own ends they overlook a lot they wouldn't overlook in other fields. People are bound to each other like a link of a chain. You try to avoid being a link in this chain by carefully choosing.

This poses serious problems for the homosexual who is socially mobile. He is forced to change his primary group affiliations within the homosexual community.

The following statement by the manager of an appliance shop shows how the homosexual tends to change his orientation from "overt" to "secret" as he becomes upwardly mobile.

My promotions have made me more conscious of the gang I hang around with. You see, for the first time in my life I have a job that I would really like to keep and where I can have a pretty secure future. I realize that if word were to get around that I am gay I would probably lose my job. I don't see why that should be, because I know that I'm the same person gay or not. But still that's the way it works. I don't want to hang around with Robert[6] any more or any of the people who are like Robert. I don't mind seeing them once in a while at somebody's house, but I won't be seen with them on the street any more.

Both types of groups were identified and observed in the course of this research. Each group consisted of fourteen members. The descriptions which follow are based on the study of these groups.

Secret groups

The secret homosexuals form groups which consist of a loose amalgamation of small cliques. Interaction within the cliques is frequent, with members meeting at each other's homes and in bars and restaurants. The clique's structure is a product of the diverse interests and occupations and of the desire to limit homosexual contacts which characterize secret homosexuals. The clique unites its several members in common specialized interests apart from the larger group.

Table 1.2 shows the clique structure and occupational composition of a secret homosexual group.

A secret homosexual group is generally characterized by: (1) informal standards of admission; (2) discretion in the manner in which homosexuality is practiced; (3) an attempt at concealment; (4) partial rather than complete involvement in the homosexual world.

Overt groups

Overt homosexuals gather in cohesive social groups which become the dominant focus of their lives. These groups are openly homosexual in character. The members make little effort to conceal their deviation, spend almost all their free time with the group, and tend to regard their other activities as peripheral.

These groups generally draw their members from persons of low socio-economic status who have jobs where concealment is not a prerequisite. Table 1.3 presents the occupational composition of the overt group identified in this study.

The members of the group met daily either at a bar, a restaurant or at the house of the acknowledged leader or "queen."[7] They spent their time in endless gossip about the sexual affairs of the members or other homosexuals known to them. Often they would go to bars and restaurants in the attempt to make a "pick-up," or spend the evening "cruising" individually or in groups of twos and threes.

The queen seems to characterize only "overt" groups. Functionally, the role of the queen is very important in the life of these groups. He provides a place where the group may gather and where its individual members may have their "affairs." He helps finance members in distress, functions as an intermediary in making sexual contacts, partially controls the entrance of new members, and warns the members of hoodlums who would prey upon them. Generally the queen is an older homosexual who has had wide experience in the homosexual world.

The following statement about the queen by a member of the overt group provides insight into the functioning of the queen and tells something of the way in which the individuals relate to him.

A queen really means the leader of the group. You see how that is in a small town where there are not many people who are gay and willing to admit it. She knows who's who and what's what. She will know every gay person in town and will arrange things just the way Roberta does.[8] The queen is always somebody pretty old and pretty much out of the game as far as getting anything for herself is concerned. But she doesn't have anything else to do, so she spends all her time on this. I don't know

---

Table 1.2 Clique structure and occupational composition of a secret homosexual group

Clique A	*Clique B*
Lawyer	Clerk-bookkeeper
Personnel Manager	Auditing clerk
University student	Assistant Office
Economist	Manager
	University student
	Secretary

Clique C	*Clique D*
Stenographer	Accountant
Store Manager	Interior Decorator
Manager of Statistical	
Dept	

Table 1.3 Occupational composition of an overt homosexual group

Occupation	Frequency
Manager of appliance shop[1]	1
School teacher	1
Hospital attendant	1
Hairdresser	4
Sales clerk	2
Foundry worker	1
Baker	1
Salesman	1
Waiter	1
Cashier	1
Total	14

Note
1 This individual had just been promoted and was beginning to leave the group. Both he and the school teacher retained for a time their affiliation with an overt group while at the same time concealing their homosexuality at work.

of any queen as commercial as Roberta. But that's because Roberta is so goddam crude. I know the queen in Hillsburg and she was a perfect lady if I ever saw one. She knows everything. She used to make quite a bit but it was always in the form of getting invitations for dinner or as a present. You feel grateful to somebody who does something for you and you pay off. It's like a debt.

Overt groups are characterized by: (1) no particular standards of admission; (2) unselfconscious and unrestrained practice of homosexuality; (3) little or no concealment; (4) high degree of social isolation with little involvement in heterosexual activities; (5) little concern with identification as a status threat or the sanctions of heterosexual society.

THE HOMOSEXUAL COMMUNITY

The diverse secret and overt homosexuals are linked together either through bonds of sex or of friendship. Within the primary group, the emphasis upon friendship rather than sex serves to eliminate excessive sexual competition and preserves group unity. However, this creates a sexual interdependency upon those outside the group with important social consequences.

In the first place, it forces the secret homosexual out into the open in an attempt to solicit sexual partners. He thus frequents the known homosexual meeting places within the city such as specific bars, hotel lobbies, street corners, and lavatories. These activities make him an increasingly familiar figure within the homosexual world.

Secondly, this solicitation leads to the interaction of secret and overt homosexuals on a sexual as opposed to a social basis. While these contacts occur in a spirit of anonymity, an approach to the other often requires an exchange of confidences.

Thirdly, this sexual interdependency increases the anxiety of secret homosexuals since it forces them to contact the overt ones whom they fear as a threat to their security.

Thus, it is the casual and promiscuous sexual contacts between the members of different categories of evasion (i.e. the secret and the overt) which weld the city's homosexuals into a community.

CONCLUSION

The homosexual community thus consists of a large number of distinctive groups within which friendship binds the members together in a strong and relatively enduring bond) and between which the members are linked by tenuous but repeated sexual contacts. The result is that homosexuals within the city tend to know or know of each other, to recognize a number of common interests and common moral norms, and to interact on the basis of antagonistic cooperation. This community is in turn linked with other homosexual communities in Canada and the United States, chiefly through the geographical mobility of its members.[9]

NOTES

1 Kinsey reports that 37 per cent of the total male population have at least some overt homosexual experience to the point of orgasm between adolescence and old age; 30 per cent of all males have at least incidental homosexual experience or reactions over at least a three year period between the ages of 16 and 55; 25 per cent of the male population have more than incidental homosexual experience or reactions for at least three years between the ages of 16 and 55; 18 per cent of the males have at least as much of the homosexual as the heterosexual in their histories for at least three years between the ages of 16 and 55; 4 per cent of the white males are exclusively homosexual throughout their lives, after the onset of adolescence. Homosexual practices are reported among all occupational groups with the percentage for professionals approximately 50 per cent lower than those of other groups. Further confirmation of the distribution of homosexuals among all social strata was obtained from police files and the testimony of homosexuals.

2 Access to this homosexual community was obtained through a client at a social welfare agency.

3 A stable social and sexual relationship between two homosexuals is frequently referred to as marriage.

4 The substitution of the female for the male

pronoun is a common practice within homosexual groups.

5 The Burning Flame refers to a bar which tended to draw its clientele from secret homosexuals; the Red Room was the acknowledged gathering place of overt homosexuals.

6 Robert is the leader of an overt group of which the respondent was a member at the time he was contacted.

7 Our data with respect to the prevalence of this role are incomplete. However, homosexuals regularly refer to the queens of other cities, suggesting that the practice is widespread.

8 The adoption of feminine names is a widespread practice among all homosexuals interviewed.

9 The queen of the overt group studied maintained an address book containing the names of approximately three thousand homosexuals scattered across North America.

REFERENCES

Westley, William A., "Violence and the Police," *American Journal of Sociology* 59 (July 1953).

National Opinion Research Center, *Opinion News* 9 (September 1947): 3–13.

ALBERT J. REISS, Jr

"The Social Integration of Queers and Peers"

from *Social Problems* 9 (1961): 102–20

Sex delinquency is a major form of behavior deviating from the normative prescriptions of American society. A large number of behaviors are classified as sex delinquency – premarital heterosexual intercourse, pederasty, and fellation, for example.

Investigation of sex behavior among males largely focuses on the psychological structure and dynamic qualities of adult persons who are described as "sexual types" or on estimating the incidence, prevalence, or experience rates of sex acts for various social groups in a population. There is little systematic research on the social organization of sexual activity in a complex social system unless one includes descriptive studies of the social organization of female prostitution.

An attempt is made in this paper to describe the sexual relation between "delinquent peers" and "adult queers"[1] and to account for its social organization. This transaction is one form of homosexual prostitution between a young male and an adult male fellator. The adult male client pays a delinquent boy prostitute a sum of money in order to be allowed to act as a fellator. The transaction is limited to fellation and is one in which the boy develops no self-conception as a homosexual person or sexual deviator, although he perceives adult male clients as sexual deviators, "queers" or "gay boys."

There has been little research on social aspects of male homosexual prostitution; hence the exploratory nature of the investigation reported here and the tentative character of the findings. Although there are descriptions of "marriage" and of the "rigid caste system of prison homosexuality"[2] which contribute to our understanding of its social organization in the single sex society of deviators, little is known about how homosexual activity is organized in the nuclear communities of America.

A few recent studies discuss some organizational features of male prostitution.[3] Ross distinguishes three types of male homosexual prostitutes on the basis of the locus of their hustling activity:[4] (1) the *bar-hustler* who usually visits bars on a steady basis in search of queer clients; (2) the *street-hustler*, usually a teenaged boy who turns "tricks" with older men; (3) and, the *call-boy* who does not solicit in public. The street-hustler has the lowest prestige among hustlers, partly because his is the more hazardous and less profitable form of activity. One might expect their prestige status in the organized "gay world" to be low since they apparently are marginal to its organization. Street-hustlers, therefore, often become bar-hustlers when they are able to pass in bars as of legal age.

The boys interviewed for this study could usually be classified as street-hustlers, given the principal locus of their activity. Yet, the street-hustlers Ross describes are oriented toward careers as bar-hustlers, whereas none of the boys I studied entered hustling as a career. For the latter, hustling is a transitory activity, both in time and space.

There apparently are crucial differences among hustlers, however, in respect to the definition of the hustler role and the self-concept common to occupants in the role. The hustlers Ross studied are distinguished by the fact that they define themselves as both prostitute and homosexual. The boys I studied *do not define themselves either as hustlers or as homosexual*. Most of these boys see themselves as "getting a queer" only as a substitute activity or as part of a versatile pattern of delinquent activity.[5] The absence of a shared definition of one another as hustlers together with shared definitions of when one "gets a queer" serve to insulate these boys from self-definitions either as street-hustlers or as homosexual.

The boys interviewed in this study regard hustling as an acceptable substitute for other delinquent earnings or activity. Although the sexual transaction itself may occur in a two person *or* a larger group setting, the prescribed norms governing this transaction are usually learned from peers in the delinquent gang. Furthermore, in many cases, induction into the queer–peer transaction occurs through participation in the delinquent group. They learn the prescribed form of behavior with adult fellators and are inducted into it as a business transaction by means of membership in a group which carries this knowledge in a common tradition and controls its practices. In particular, it will be shown that the peer group controls the amount of activity and the conditions under which it is permitted. Finally, it is postulated that this is a shared organizational system between peer hustlers and adult fellators.

There apparently exist the other possible types of males who engage in homosexual sex acts based on the elements of self-definition as homosexual and hustler. John Rechy in several vignettes describes a third type who conceive of themselves as hustlers but do not define themselves as homosexual.[6]

> the world of queens and male-hustlers and what they thrive on, the queens being technically men but no one thinks of them that way – always "she" – their "husbands" being the masculine vagrants – fruithustlers – fleetingly sharing the queens' pads – never considering they're involved with another man (the queen), and as long as the hustler goes only with queens – and with fruits only for scoring (which is making or taking sexmoney, getting a meal, making a pad) *he is himself not considered queer.* (italics mine)[7]

The importance of being defined as non-homosexual while acknowledging one's role as a hustler is brought forth in this passage:

> Like the rest of us on that street – who played the male role with other men – Pete was touchy about

one subject – his masculinity. In Bickford's one afternoon, a good looking masculine young man walked in, looking at us, walks out again hurriedly. "That cat's queer," Pete says, glaring at him. "I used to see him and I thought he was hustling, and one day he tried to put the make on me in the flix. It bugged me, him thinking I'd make it with him for free. I told him to f... off, go find another queer like him." He was moodily silent for a long while and then he said almost beligerently: "No matter how many queers a guy goes with, if he goes for money, that don't make him queer. You're still straight. It's when you start going for free, with other young guys, that you start growing wings."[8]

The literature on male homosexuality, particularly that written by clinicians, is abundant with reference to the fourth possible type – those who define themselves as homosexual but not as hustlers.

THE DATA

Information on the sexual transaction and its social organization was gathered mostly by interviews, partly by social observation of their meeting places. Though there are limitations to inferring social organization from interview data (particularly when the organization arises through behavior that is negatively sanctioned in the larger society), they provide a convenient basis for exploration.

Sex histories were gathered from 18.6 per cent of the 1008 boys between the ages of 12 and 17 who were interviewed in the Nashville, Tennessee, standard metropolitan area for an investigation of adolescent conforming and deviating behavior. These represent all of the interviews of one of the interviewers during a two-month period, together with interviews with all Nashville boys incarcerated at the Tennessee State Training School for Boys.

As Table 2.1 discloses, the largest number of interviews was taken with lower-class delinquent boys. There is a reason for this: when it was apparent that delinquents from the lowest social class generally had some contact with adult male fellators, an attempt was made to learn more about how this contact was structured and controlled. Sex histories, therefore, were obtained from all of the white Nashville

Table 2.1 Type of sex experience by conforming–deviating type of boy (Per cent by conforming–deviating type)

Type of sex experience	Lower class				Middle class				All classes		
	Org. career delinquent	Peer-oriented delinquent	Conforming non-achiever	Conforming achiever	Peer-oriented delinquent	Conforming non-achiever	Conforming achiever	Hyper-conformer	Non-conforming isolate	Conforming isolate	Total
Total	73	166	250	81	38	86	193	56	24	41	1008
Queers, masturbation, and heterosexual	32.5	27.3	5.1	20.0	–	10.0	–	–	37.5	–	17.6
Queers, masturbation, hetero and animal	30.2	4.5	–	–	5.0	–	–	–	–	–	8.5
Heterosexual only	4.7	11.4	–	–	70.0	30.0	–	–	12.5	–	13.4
Heterosexual and masturbation	25.6	34.1	33.3	40.0	15.0	10.0	40.0	–	25.0	–	27.3
Masturbation only	2.3	15.9	48.7	40.0	–	10.0	40.0	57.1	25.0	100.0	21.9
Denies sex experience	4.7	6.8	12.8	–	10.0	40.0	20.0	42.9	0.0	–	11.2
Subtotal	43	44	39	5	20	10	10	7	8	1	187
No sex history	41.1	73.5	84.4	93.8	47.4	88.4	94.8	87.5	66.7	97.6	81.4

Note
1 Includes three cases of heterosexual, masturbation, and animal (2 lower-class organized career delinquent and 1 peer-oriented delinquent).

boys who were resident in the Tennessee State Training School for Boys during the month of June, 1958.

The way sex history information was obtained precludes making reliable estimates about the incidence or prevalence of hustling within the Nashville adolescent boy population. Yet the comparisons among types of conformers and deviators in Table 2.1 provide an informed guess about their life chances for participation in such an activity.[9]

Only two middle-class boys report experience in the peer–queer transaction. In one case, the boy acquiesced once to solicitation; in the other, the boy had acquired experience and associations in the State Training School for Boys which led to continued participation following his release. Within the lower-class group, it seems clear that the career-oriented delinquent is most likely to report sex experiences with fellators. Roughly three of every five boys report such experiences as contrasted with the peer-oriented delinquent, the type with the next highest relative frequency, where only about one in three report such experiences.

Taking into account the proportional distribution of types of conformers and deviators in a school population of adolescent boys and applying in a very rough way the proportional distribution for type of sex deviation set forth in Table 2.1, the experience rate with fellators is quite low in a population of all adolescent boys. The peer–queer relationship seems almost exclusively limited to lower-class delinquent boys – particularly career-oriented delinquent boys, where the experience rate is probably very high.

While not of direct concern here, it is of interest that the conformers in Table 2.1 seem to consist about equally of boys who either report a history of heterosexual and masturbation experience, or masturbation only experience, while hyperconformers either report no sex experience or that they masturbate only.

It might also be inferred from Table 2.1 that the adolescent conforming boy of lower-class origins in our society is very unlikely to report he never masturbates, though a substantial proportion of middle-class conforming boys maintain they never masturbate and never have

masturbated. Although there may be age differences among the class levels in age of onset of masturbation, the class difference may yet be genuine. It is possible, of course, that this difference in masturbation experience reflects only a difference in willingness to report masturbation to a middle-class investigator, i.e., middle-class boys are more likely to hide their sexual experience, even that of masturbation, from others. Nevertheless, there may be class differences in the social organization of sexual experiences, since lower-class boys reported masturbating in groups when they first began to masturbate, while this experience was reported much less frequently by middle-class boys, for whom it is more likely a private matter. The same thing is true for heterosexual experience: lower-class boys, particularly delinquent ones, frequently report they participate in group heterosexual activity in "gang-bangs," while heterosexual experience appears to be a more private experience for the middle-class boy, who does not share his sexual partner with peers. All of this may reflect not only greater versatility in the sex experience of the lower-class male but perhaps a greater willingness to use sex as a means to gratification.

HOW PEERS AND QUEERS MEET

Meetings between adult male fellators and delinquent boys are easily made, because both know how and where to meet within the community space. Those within the common culture know that contact can be established within a relatively short period of time, if it is wished. The fact that meetings between peers and queers can be made easily is mute evidence of the organized understandings which prevail between the two populations.

There are a large number of places where the boys meet their clients, the fellators. Many of these points are known to all boys regardless of where they reside in the metropolitan area. This is particularly true of the central city locations where the largest number of contact points is found within a small territorial area. Each community area of the city, and certain fringe areas, inhabited by substantial numbers of lower-class persons, also have their meeting places, generally known only to the boys residing in the area.

Queers and peers typically establish contact in public or quasi-public places. Major points of contact include street corners, public parks, men's toilets in public or quasi-public places such as those in transportation depots, parks or hotels, and "second" and "third-run" movie houses (open around the clock and permitting sitting through shows). Bars are seldom points of contact, perhaps largely because they are plied by older male hustlers who lie outside the peer culture and groups, and because bar proprietors will not risk the presence of under-age boys.

There are a number of prescribed modes for establishing contact in these situations. They permit the boys and fellators to communicate intent to one another privately despite the public character of the situation. The major form of establishing contact is the "cruise," with the fellator passing "queer-corners" or locations until his effort is recognized by one of the boys. A boy can then signal – usually by nodding his head, a hand gesticulation signifying OK, following, or responding to commonly understood introductions such as "You got the time?" – that he is prepared to undertake the transaction. Entrepreneur and client then move to a place where the sexual activity is consummated, usually a place affording privacy, protection and hasty exit. "Dolly," a three-time loser at the State Training School, describes one of these prescribed forms for making contact:

> Well, like at the bus station, you go to the bathroom and stand there pretendin' like ... and they're standin' there pretendin' like ... and then they motions their head and walks out and you follow them, and you go some place. Either they's got a car, or you go to one of them hotels near the depot or some place like that ... most any place.

Frequently contact between boys and fellators is established when the boy is hitchhiking. This is particularly true for boys' first contacts of this nature. Since lower-class boys are more likely than middle-class ones to hitch rides within a city, particularly at night when such contacts are most frequently made, they perhaps are most often solicited in this manner.

The experienced boy who knows a "lot of queers," may phone known fellators directly from a public phone, and some fellators try to establish continued contact with boys by giving them their phone numbers. However, the boys seldom use this means of contact for reasons inherent in their orientation toward the transaction, as we shall see below.

We shall now examine how the transaction is facilitated by these types of situations and the prescribed modes of contact and communication. One of the characteristics of all these contact situations is that they provide a *rationale* for the presence of *both* peers and queers in the *same* situation or place. This rationale is necessary for both parties, for were there high visibility to the presence of either and no ready explanation for it, contact and communication would be far more difficult. Public and quasi-public facilities provide situations which account for the presence of most persons since there is relatively little social control over the establishment of contacts. There is, of course, some risk to the boys and the fellators in making contact in these situations since they are generally known to the police. The Morals Squad may have "stake-outs," but this is one of the calculated risks and the communication network carries information about their tactics.

A most important element in furnishing a rationale is that these meeting places must account for the presence of delinquent boys of essentially lower-class dress and appearance who make contact with fellators of almost any class level. This is true despite the fact that the social settings which fellators ordinarily choose to establish contact generally vary according to the class level of the fellators. Fellators of high social class generally make contact by "cruising" past street-corners, in parks, or the men's rooms in "better" hotels, while those from the lower class are likely to select the public bath or transportation depot. There apparently is some general equation of the class position of boys and fellators in the delinquent peer–queer transaction. The large majority of fellators in the peer–queer transaction probably are from the lower class ("apes"). But it is difficult to be certain about the class position of the fellator clients since no study was made of this population.

The absence of data from the fellator population poses difficulties in interpreting the contact relationship. Many fellators involved with delinquent boys do not appear to participate in any overt or covert homosexual groups, such as the organized homosexual community of the "gay world."[10] The "gay world" is the most visible form of organized homosexuality since it is an organized community, but it probably encompasses only a small proportion of all homosexual contact. Even among those in the organized homosexual community, evidence suggests that the homosexual members seek sexual gratification outside their group with persons who are essentially anonymous to them. Excluding homosexual married couples, Leznoff and Westley maintain that there is a prohibition against sexual relationships within the group.[11] Ross indicates that young male prostitutes are chosen, among other reasons, for the fact that they protect the identity of the client.[12] Both of these factors tend to coerce many male fellators to choose an anonymous contact situation.

It is clear that these contact situations not only provide a rationale for the presence of the parties to the transaction but a guarantee of anonymity. The guarantee does not necessarily restrict social visibility as both the boys and the fellators may recognize cues (including, but not necessarily, those of gesture and dress) which lead to mutual role identification.[13] But anonymity is guaranteed in at least two senses: anonymity of presence is assured in the situation and their personal identity in the community is protected unless disclosed by choice.

There presumably are a variety of reasons for the requirement of anonymity. For many, a homosexual relationship must remain a secret since their other relationships in the community – families, business relationships, etc. – must be protected. Leznoff and Westley refer to these men as the "secret" as contrasted with the "overt" homosexuals,[14] and in the organized "gay world" they are known as "closet fags." For some, there is also a necessity for protecting identity to avoid blackmail.[15] Although none of the peer hustlers reported resorting to blackmail, the adult male fellator may nonetheless hold such an expectation, particularly if he is older or of high social class. Lower-class ones, by contrast, are more likely to face the threat of violence from adolescent boys since they more often frequent situations where they are likely to contact "rough trade."[16] The kind of situation in which the delinquent peer–queer contact is made and the sexual relationship consummated tends to minimize the possibility of violence.

Not all male fellators protect their anonymity; some will let a boy have their phone number and a few "keep a boy." Still, most fellators want to meet boys where they are least likely to be victimized, although boys sometimes roll queers by selecting a meeting place where by prearrangement their friends can meet them and help roll the queer, steal his car or commit other acts of violence. Boys generally know that fellators are vulnerable in that they "can't" report their victimization. Parenthetically, it might be mentioned that these boys are not usually aware of their own institutional invulnerability to arrest. An adolescent boy is peculiarly invulnerable to arrest even when found with a fellator since the mores define the boy as exploited.[17]

Situations of personal contact between adolescent boys and adult male fellators also provide important ways to *communicate intent* or to carry out the transaction *without* making the contact particularly visible to others. The wall writings in many of these places are not without their primitive communication value, e.g., "show it hard," and places such as a public restroom provide a modus operandi. The entrepreneur and his customer in fact can meet with little more than an exchange of non-verbal gestures, transact their business with a minimum of verbal communication and part without a knowledge of one another's identity. In most cases, boys report "almost nothing" was said. The sexual transaction may occur with the only formal transaction being payment to the boy.

INDUCTION INTO THE PEER–QUEER TRANSACTION

The peer–queer culture operates through a delinquent peer society. Every boy interviewed in this study who voluntarily established contacts with fellators was also delinquent in many other respects. The evidence shows that contact with fellators is an institutionalized aspect of the organization of lower-class delinquency oriented groups. This is not to say that boys outside these groups never experience relationships with adult male fellators: some do, but they are not participants in groups which sanction the activity according to the prescribed group standards described below. Nor is it to say that all delinquent groups positively sanction the peer–queer transaction since its distribution is unknown.

How, then, do lower-class delinquent boys get to meet fellators? Most boys from the lowest socioeconomic level in large cities are prepared for this through membership in a delinquent group which has a knowledge of how to make contact with fellators and relate to them. This is part of their common culture. Often, too, the peer group socializes the boy in his first experiences or continuing ones with fellators. The behavior is apparently learned within the framework of differential association.

The peer group actually serves as a school of induction for some of its members. The uninitiated boy goes with one or more members of his peer group for indoctrination and his first experience. Doy L., a lower-class boy at a lower-class school and a two-time loser at the State Training School, explains how he got started:

> I went along with these older boys down to the bus station, and they took me along and showed me how it was done ... they'd go in, get a queer, get blowed and get paid ... if it didn't work right, they'd knock him in the head and get their money ... they showed me how to do it, so I went in too.

In any case, boys are socialized in the subcultural definitions of peer–queer relations by members of their group and many apply this knowledge when an opportunity arises. Within the group, boys hear reports of experiences which supply the cultural definitions: how contacts are made, how you get money if the queer resists, how much one should expect to get, what kind of behavior is acceptable from the queer, which is to be rejected and how. Boys know all this *before* they have any contact with a fellator. In the case of street gangs, the fellators often pass the neighborhood corner; hence, even the preadolescent boy learns about the activity as the older boys get picked up. As the boy enters adolescence and a gang of his own which takes over the corner, he is psychologically and socially prepared for his first experience, which generally occurs when the first opportunity presents itself. Lester H illustrates this; his first experience came when he went to one of the common points of convergence of boys and fellators – The Empress Theatre – to see a movie. Lester relates:

> I was down in the Empress Theatre and this gay came over and felt me up and asked me if I'd go out ... I said I would if he'd give me the money as I'd heard they did, and I was gettin' low on it ... so he took me down by the river and blew me.

In a substantial number of cases, a brother introduces the boy to his first experience, much as he introduces him to other first experiences. Jimmie M. illustrates this pattern. Jimmie describes how he was led into his first heterosexual experience:

> When I was almost 14, my younger brother said he'd screwed this woman and he told me about it, so I went down there and she let me screw her too.

His induction into the peer–queer transaction also occurred through his younger brother:

> Well, my younger brother came home and told me this gay'd blowed him and he told me where he lived ... And, I was scared to do it, but I figured I'd want to see what it was like since the other guys talked about it and my brother'd done it. So I went down there and he blowed me.

Not all boys belonging to groups which sanction peer hustling accept the practice. Some boys reject the peer–queer transaction while retaining membership in the group. It is not too surprising that such exceptions occur. Although in most delinquent groups some forms of sex activity confer status, it is rarely an absolute requisite for participation in such groups. Some boys in gangs which frequently gang shag, for example, refuse to participate in these activities: "I don't like my meat that raw" appears to be an acceptable "out." Exemption appears possible so long as the boy is acceptable in all, if not most, other respects. A lower-class delinquent boy apparently doesn't "chicken-out" or lose his "rep" if he doesn't want to engage in sex behaviors which most of his peers practice. (The same condition may hold for other practices, such as the use of narcotics.) Jerry P. from a lower-class school in a group where all the other boys go with fellators; but he refuses to become involved, though he goes so far as to ride in the car with one of the gang's "regular queers." Jerry is in a gang which often gets picked up by a well known "local gay," a David B. Jerry admits: "I ride with B. a lot, but he's never done anything to me; I just can't go for that." When asked how he knew B. was a queer, he replied, "Oh, all the guys say so and talk about doin' it with him ... I could, but I just don't want to." Joe C., at a school which crosscuts the class structure, was asked if he had any other kind of sex experiences. His reply shows his rejection of his peer group's pattern of behavior with fellators. "You mean with queers?" "Uh huh." "I don't go with any. Most of my friends queer-bait, but I don't." A friend of his, Roy P., also rejects the activity: "Ain't no sense in queer-baitin'; I don't need the money that bad."

The impression should not be gained that most lower-class boys who are solicited by fellators accept the solicitation. A majority of all solicitations are probably refused when the initial contact is made unless several other conditions prevail. The first is that the boy must be a member of a group which permits this form of transaction, indoctrinates the boy with its codes and sanctions his participation in it. Almost all lower-class boys reported they were solicited by a queer at least once. A majority refused the solicitation. Refusal is apparently easy since boys report that queers are seldom insistent. There apparently is a mutual willingness to forgo the transaction in such cases, perhaps because the queer cannot afford the risk of exposure, but perhaps also because the probability of his establishing contact on his

next try is sufficiently high so that he can "afford" to accept the refusal. Looked at another way, there must be a set of mutual gains and expectations for the solicitation to be accepted and the transaction to proceed. Boys who refuse to be solicited are not vulnerable for another reason: they usually are members of groups which negatively sanction the activity. Such groups generally "bug" boys who go out with fellators and use other techniques of isolation to discourage the transaction. There also are gangs which look upon queers as "fair game" for their aggressive activity. They beat them, roll, and otherwise put upon them. A third condition that must prevail is that the boy who accepts or seeks solicitation from fellators must view the offer as instrumental gain, particularly monetary gain (discussed below).

There are boys, however, particularly those who are quite young, who report a solicitation from a man which they were unable to refuse but which they subsequently rejected as neither gratifying nor instrumentally acceptable. It is these boys who can be said to be "exploited" by adult fellators in the sense that they are either forced into the act against their will, or are at least without any awareness of how to cope with the situation. One such instance is found in the following report:

> This guy picked me up down at Fourth and Union and said he was going over to East Nashville, so I got in ... but he drove me out on Dickerson Pike. (What'd he do?) ... Well, he blowed me and it made me feel real bad inside ... but I know how to deal with queers now ... ain't one of 'em gonna do that to me again ... I hate queers.... They're crazy.

There is an important admission in the statement, "But I know how to deal with 'em now." The lower-class boy as he grows older learns how to deal with sexual advances from fellators. Boys exchange experiences on how they deal with them and it becomes quite difficult to "exploit" a lower-class boy who is socialized in a peer group. It is perhaps largely the very young boy, such as the one in the case above, or those isolated from peer groups, who are most vulnerable to solicitation without previous preparation for it.

Lower-class boys, as we have seen, have the

highest probability of being in situations where they will be solicited by fellators. But, *the lower-class boy who is a member of a career-oriented gang which positively sanctions instrumental relationships with adult male fellators and which initiates members into these practices, and a boy who at the same time perceives himself as "needing" the income which the transaction provides, is most likely to establish personal contact with adult male fellators on a continuing basis.*

It is suggested that the peer–queer transaction is behavior learned through differential association in delinquent gangs. This cannot be demonstrated without resort to a more specific test of the hypothesis. But, as Sutherland has pointed out,

> Criminal behavior is partially a function of opportunities to commit special classes of crimes . . . It is axiomatic that persons who commit a specific crime have the opportunity to commit that crime . . . While opportunity may be partially a function of association with criminal patterns and of the specialized techniques thus acquired, it is not entirely determined in this manner, and consequently differential association is not a sufficient cause of criminal behavior.[18]

Middle-class boys are perhaps excluded from the peer–queer transaction as much through lack of opportunity to commit this special class of crime in their community of exposure as through any criterion of differential association. The structure of the middle-class area is incompatible with the situational requirements for the peer–queer transaction.

NORMS GOVERNING THE TRANSACTION

Does the peer society have any norms about personal relations with fellators? Or, does it simply induct a boy into a relationship by teaching him how to effect the transaction? The answer is that there appear to be several clear-cut norms about the relations between peers and queers, even though there is some deviation from them.

The first major norm is that *a boy must undertake the relationship with a queer solely as a way of making money: sexual gratification cannot be actively sought as a goal in the relationship.* This norm does not preclude a boy from sexual gratification by the act; he simply must not seek this as a goal. Put another way, a boy cannot admit that he failed to get money from the transaction unless he used violence toward the fellator and he cannot admit that he sought it as a means of sexual gratification.

The importance of making money in motivating a boy to the peer–queer transaction is succinctly stated by Dewey H:

> This guy in the Rex Theatre came over and sat down next to me when I was 11 or 12, and he started to fool with me. I got over and sat down another place and he came over and asked me, didn't I want to and he'd pay me five bucks. I figured it was *easy money* so I went with him . . . I didn't do it before that. That wasn't too long after I'd moved to South Nashville. I was a pretty good boy before that . . . not real good, but I never ran with a crowd that got into trouble before that. But, I met a lot of 'em there. (Why do you run with queers?) It's *easy money* . . . like I could go out and break into a place when I'm broke and get money that way . . . but that's harder and *you take a bigger risk* . . . with a queer it's *easy money*.

Dewey's comments reveal two important motivating factors in getting money from queers, both suggested by the expression, "easy money." First, the money is easy in that it can be made quickly. Some boys reported that when they needed money for a date or a night out, they obtained it within an hour through the sexual transaction with a queer. All a boy has to do is go to a place where he will be contacted, wait around, get picked up, carried to a place where the sexual transaction occurs, and in a relatively short period of time he obtains the money for his service.

It is easy money in another and more important sense for many of these boys. Boys who undertake the peer–queer transaction are generally members of career-oriented delinquent groups. Rejecting the limited opportunities for making money by legitimate means or finding them inaccessible, their opportunities to make money by illegitimate means may also be limited or the risk may be great. Theft is an available means, but it is more difficult and involves greater risk than the peer–queer transaction.

Delinquent boys are not unaware of the risks they take. Under most circumstances, delinquents may calculate an act of stealing as "worth the risk." There are occasions, however, when the risk is calculated as too great. These occasions occur when the "heat" is on the boy or when he can least afford to run the risk of being picked up by the police, as is the case following a pick-up by the police, being put on probation or parole, or being warned that incarceration will follow the next violation. At such times, boys particularly calculate whether they can afford to take the risk. Gerald L., describing a continuing relationship with a fellator who gave him his phone number, reflects Dewey's attitude toward minimizing risk in the peer–queer transaction: "So twic'd after that when I was gettin' real low and couldn't risk stealin' and gettin' caught, I called him and he took me out and blowed me." Here is profit with no investment of capital and a minimum of risk in social, if not in psychological, terms.

The element of risk coupled with the wish for "easy money" enters into our understanding of the peer–queer relationship in another way. From a sociological point of view, the peer–queer sexual transaction occurs between two major types of deviators – "delinquents" and "queers." Both types of deviators risk negative sanctions for their deviant acts. The more often one has been arrested or incarcerated, the more punitive the sanctions from the larger social system for both types of deviators. At some point, therefore, both calculate risks and seek to minimize them, at least in the very short run. Each then becomes a means for the other to minimize risk.

When the delinquent boy is confronted with a situation in which he wants money and risks little in getting it, how is he to get it without working? Illegitimate activities frequently provide the "best" opportunity for easy money. These activities often are restricted in kind and number for adolescents and the risk of negative sanctions is high. Under such circumstances, the service offered a queer is a chance to make easy money with a minimum of risk.

Opportunities for sexual gratification are limited for the adult male fellator, particularly if he wishes to minimize the risk of detection in locating patrons, to avoid personal involvement and to get his gratification when he wishes it. The choice of a lower-class male, precisely because of his class position somewhat reduces the risk. If the lower-class male also is a delinquent, the risk is minimized to an even greater degree.

This is not to say that the parties take equal risks in the situation. Of the two, the fellator perhaps is less able to minimize his risk since he still risks violence from his patron, but much less so if a set of expectations arise which control the use of violence as well. The boy is most able to minimize his risk since he is likely to be defined as "exploited" in the situation if caught.

Under special circumstances, boys may substitute other gratifications for the goal of money, provided that these gratifications do not include sexual gratification as a major goal. These special circumstances are the case where an entire gang will "make a night (or time) of it" with one or more adult male fellators. Under these circumstances, everyone is excepted from the subcultural expectations about making money from the fellator because everyone participates and there is no reason for everyone (or anyone) to make money. For the group to substitute being given a "good time" by a "queer" for the prescribed financial transaction is, of course, the exception which proves the rule.

Several examples of group exemption from the prescribed norm of a financial gain were discovered. Danny S., leader of the Black Aces, tells of his gang's group experiences with queers:

> There's this one gay who takes us to the Colonial Motel out on Dickerson Pike ... usually it's a bunch of us boys and we all get drunk and get blowed by this queer ... we don't get any money then ... it's more a drinking party.

The Black Aces are a fighting gang and place great stress on physical prowess, particularly boxing. All of its members have done time more than once at the State Training School. During one of these periods, the school employed a boxing instructor whom the boys identified as "a queer," but the boys had great respect for him since he taught them how to box and was a game fighter. Danny refers to him in accepting terms:

> He's a real good guy. He's fought with us once or twice and we drink with him when we run into him ... He's taken us up to Miter Dam a coupla times; he's got a cabin up there on the creek and he blows us ... But mostly we just drink and have a real good time.

These examples illustrate the instrumental orientation of the gang members. If the expense of the gang members getting drunk and having a good time are borne by a "queer," each member is released from the obligation to receive cash. The relationship in this case represents an exchange of services rather than that of money for a service.

The second major norm operating in the relationship is that *the sexual transaction must be limited to mouth–genital fellation. No other sexual acts are generally tolerated.*[19] The adult male fellator must deport himself in such a way as to re-enforce the instrumental aspects of the role relationship and to insure affective neutrality.[20] For the adult male fellator to violate the boy's expectation of "getting blowed," as the boys refer to the act, is to risk violence and loss of service. Whether or not the boys actually use violent means as often as they say they do when expectations are violated, there is no way of knowing with precision. Nevertheless, whenever boys reported they used violent means, they always reported some violation of the subcultural expectations. Likewise, they never reported a violation of the subcultural expectations which was not followed by the use of violent means, unless it was clearly held up as an exception. Bobby A. expresses the boys' point of view on the use of violent means in the following exchange: "How much did you usually get?" "Around five dollars; if they didn't give that much, I'd beat their head in." "Did they ever want you to do anything besides blow you?" "Yeh, sometimes ... like they want me to blow them, but I'd tell them to go to hell and maybe beat them up."

Boys are very averse to being thought of in a queer role or engaging in acts of fellation. The act of fellation is defined as a "queer" act. Most boys were asked whether they would engage in such behavior. All but those who had the status of "punks'" denied they had engaged in behavior associated with the queer role. Asking a boy whether he is a fellator meets with strong denial and often with open hostility. This could be interpreted as defensive behavior against latent homosexuality. Whether or not this is the case, strong denial could be expected because the question goes counter to the subcultural definitions of the peer role in the transaction.

A few boys on occasion apparently permit the fellator to perform other sexual acts. These boys, it is guessed, are quite infrequent in a delinquent peer population. Were their acts known to the members of the group, they would soon be defined as outside the delinquent peer society. Despite the limitation of the peer–queer sexual transaction to mouth–genital fellation, there are other sexual transactions which the peer group permits members to perform under special circumstances. They are, for example, permitted to perform the *male* roles in "crimes against nature," such as in pederasty ("cornholing" to the boys), bestiality (sometimes referred to as buggery) and carnal copulation with a man involving no orifice (referred to as "slick-legging" among the boys) provided that the partner is roughly of the same age and not a member of the group and provided also that the boys are confined to a single-sex society of incarcerated delinquent boys. Under no circumstances, however, is the female role in carnal copulation acceptable in any form. It is taboo. Boys who accept the female role in sexual transactions occupy the lowest status position among delinquents. They are "punks."

The third major norm operating on the relationship is that *both peers and queers, as participants, should remain affectively neutral during the transaction.* Boys within the peer society define the ideal form of the role with the fellator as one in which the boy is the entrepreneur and the queer is viewed as purchasing a service. The service is a business deal where a sexual transaction is purchased for an agreed upon amount of money. In the typical case, the boy is neither expected to enjoy or be repulsed by the sexual transaction; mouth–genital fellation is accepted as a service offered in exchange for a fee. It should be kept in mind that self-gratification is permitted in the sexual act. Only the motivation to sexual gratification in the transaction is tabooed. But self-gratification must occur without displaying either positive or negative affect toward the queer. In the prescribed form of the role relationship, the boy sells a service for profit and the queer is to accept it without show of emotion.

The case of Thurman L., one of three brothers who are usually in trouble with the law, illustrates some aspects of the expected pattern of affective neutrality. Thurman has had a continuing relationship with a queer, a type of relationship in which it would be anticipated that affective neutrality would be difficult to maintain. This relationship continued, in fact, with a 21-year-old "gay" until the man was "sent to the pen." When queried about his relationship with this man and why he went with him, Thurman replied:

> Don't know ... money and stuff like that I guess. (What do you mean? ... stuff like that?) Oh, clothes ... (He ever bought you any clothes?) Sure, by this one gay ... (You mind being blowed?) No. (You like it?) Don't care one way or the other. I don't like it, and I don't not like it. (You like this one gay?) Nope, can't say that I liked anythin' about him. (How come you do it then?) Well, the money for one thing ... I need that. (You enjoy it some?) Can't say I do or don't.

More typical than Thurman's expression of affective neutrality is the boy who accepts it as "OK" or, "It's all right; I don't mind it." Most frequent of all is some variant of the statement: "It's OK, but I like the money best of all." The definition of affective neutrality fundamentally requires only that there be no positive emotional commitment to the queer *as a person*. The relationship must be essentially an impersonal one, even though the pure form of the business relationship may seldom be attained. Thus, it is possible for a boy to admit self-gratification without admitting any emotional commitment to the homosexual partner.

Although the peer group prescribes affective neutrality toward the queer in the peer–queer transaction, queers must be regarded as low prestige persons, held in low esteem, and the queer role is taboo. The queer is most commonly regarded as "crazy, I guess." Some boys take a more rationalistic view "They're just like that, I guess" or, "They're just born that way." While there are circumstances under which one is permitted to like a particular fellator, as in the case of all prejudices attached to devalued status, the person who is liked must be the exception which states the rule. Though in many cases both the boy and the fellator are of very low-class origins, and in many cases both are altogether repulsive in appearance, cleanliness and dress by middle-class standards, these are not the standards of comparison used by the boys. The deviation of the queers from the boy's norms of masculine behavior places the fellator in the lowest possible status, even "beneath contempt." If the fellator violates the expected affective relationship in the transaction, he may be treated not only with violence but with contempt as well. The seller of the service ultimately reserves the right to set the conditions for his patrons.

Some boys find it difficult to be emotionally neutral toward the queer role and its occupants; they are either personally offended or affronted by the behavior of queers. JDC is an instance of a boy who is personally offended by their behavior; yet he is unable to use violence even when expectations governing the transaction are violated. He does not rely very much on the peer–queer relationship as a source of income. JDC expresses his view: "I don't really go for that like some guys; I just do it when I go along with the crowd ... You know ... That, and when I do it for money.... And I go along ... But ... I hate queers. They embarrass me." "How?" "Well, like you'll be in the lobby at the theatre, and they'll come up and pat your ass or your prick right in front of everybody. I just can't go for that – not me." Most of the boys wouldn't either, but they would have resorted to violent means in this situation.

Two principal types of boys maintain a continuing relationship with a known queer. A few boys develop such relationships to insure a steady income. While this is permitted within peer society for a short period of time, boys who undertake it for extended periods of time do so with some risk, since to the words of the boys, "queers can be got too easy." The boy who is affectively involved with a queer or his role is downgraded in status to a position, "Ain't no better'n a queer." There are also a few boys affectively committed to a continuing relationship with an adult male homosexual. Such boys usually form a strong dependency relationship with him and are kept much as the cabin boys of old. This type of boy is clearly outside the peer society of delinquents and is isolated from participation in gang activity. The sociometric pattern for such boys is one of choice into more than one gang, none of which is reciprocated.

Street-hustlers are also downgraded within the peer society, generally having reputations as "punk kids." The street-hustler pretty much "goes it alone." Only a few street-hustlers were interviewed for this study. None of them was a member of an organized delinquent group. The sociometric pattern for each, together with his history of delinquent activity, placed them in the classification of non-conforming isolates.

A fourth major norm operating on the peer–queer relationship serves as a primary factor in stabilizing the system. This norm holds that *violence must not be used so long as the relationship conforms to the shared set of expectations between queers and peers.* So long as the fellator conforms to the norms governing the transaction in the peer–queer society, he runs little risk of violence from the boys.

The main reason, perhaps, for this norm is that uncontrolled violence is potentially disruptive of any organized system. All organized social systems must control violence. If the fellator clients were repeatedly the objects of violence, the system as it has been described could not exist. Most boys who share the common expectations of the peer–queer relationship do not use violent means unless the expectations are violated. To use violence, of course, is to become affectively involved and therefore another prescription of the relationship is violated.

It is not known whether adult male fellators who are the clients of delinquent entrepreneurs share the boys' definition of the norm regarding the use of violence. They may, therefore, violate expectations of the peer society through ignorance of the system rather than from any attempt to go beyond the set of shared expectations.

There are several ways the fellator can violate the expectations of boys. The first concerns money: refusal to pay or paying too little may bring violence from most boys. Fellators may also violate peer expectations by attempting to go beyond the mouth–genital sexual act. If such an attempt is made, he is usually made an object of aggression as in the following excerpt from Dolly's sex history:

> (You like it?) It's OK. I don't mind it. It feels OK. (They ever try anything else on you?) They usually just blow and that's all. (Any ever try anything else on you?) Oh sure, but we really fix 'em. I just hit 'em on the head or roll 'em ... throw 'em out of the car.... Once a gay tried that and we rolled him and threw him out of the car. Then we took the car and stripped it (laughs with glee).

Another way the fellator violates a boy's expectations is to introduce considerable affect into the relationship. It appears that affect is least acceptable in two forms, both of which could be seen as "attacks on his masculinity." In one form, the queer violates the affective neutrality requirement by treating the adolescent boy as if he were a girl or in a girl's role during the sexual transaction, as for example, by speaking to him in affectionate terms such as "sweetie." There are many reasons why the feminine sex role is unacceptable to these lower-class boys, including the fact that such boys place considerable emphasis on being "tough" and masculine. Walter Miller, for example, observes that:

> The almost compulsive lower class concern with "masculinity" derives from a type of compulsive reaction-formation. A concern over homosexuality runs like a persistent thread through lower class culture – manifested by the institutionalized practice of "baiting queers," often accompanied by violent physical attacks, an expressed contempt for "softness" or frills, and the use of the local term for "homosexual" as a general pejorative epithet (e.g., higher class individuals or upwardly mobile peers are frequently characterized as "fags" or "queers").[21]

Miller sees violence as part of a reaction-formation against the matriarchal lower-class household where the father often is absent. For this reason, he suggests, many lower-class boys find it difficult to identify with a male role, and the "collective" reaction-formation is a cultural emphasis on masculinity. Violence toward queers is seen as a consequence of this conflict. Data from our interviews suggests that among career-oriented delinquents, violation of the affective-neutrality requirement in the peer–queer relationship is at least as important in precipitating violence toward "queers." There are, of course, gangs which were not studied in this investigation which "queer-bait" for the express purpose of "rolling the queer."

The other form in which the fellator may violate the affective-neutrality requirement is to approach the boy and make suggestive advances to him when he is with his age-mates, either with girls or with his peer group when he is not located for "business." In either case, the sexual advances suggest that the boy is not engaged in a business relationship within the normative expectations of the system, but that he has sexual motivation as well. The delinquent boy is expected to control the relationship with his customers. He is the entrepreneur "looking" for easy money or at the very least he must appear as being merely receptive to business; this means that he is receptive only in certain situations and under certain circumstances. He is not in business when he is with girls and he is not a businessman when he is cast in a female role. To be cast in a female role before peers is highly unacceptable, as the following account suggests:

This gay comes up to me in the lobby of the Empress when we was standin' around and starts feelin' me up and callin' me Sweetie and like that ... and, I just couldn't take none of that there ... what was he makin' out like I was a queer or somethin' ... so I jumps him right then and there and we like to of knocked his teeth out.

The sexual advance is even less acceptable when a girl is involved:

I was walkin' down the street with my steady girl when this gay drives by that I'd been with once before and he whistles at me and calls, "hi Sweetie" ... And, was I mad ... so I went down to where the boys was and we laid for him and beat on him 'til he like to a never come to ... ain't gonna take nothin' like that off'n a queer.

In both of these instances, not only is the boys' masculinity under attack, but the affective-neutrality requirement of the business transaction is violated. The queer's behavior is particularly unacceptable, however, because it occurs in a peer setting where the crucial condition is the maintenance of the boy's status within the group. A lower-class boy cannot afford to be cast in less than a highly masculine role before lower-class girls nor risk definition as a queer before peers. His role within his peer group is under threat even if he suffers *no* anxiety about masculinity. Not only the boy himself but his peers perceive such behavior as violating role expectations and join him in violent acts toward the fellator to protect the group's integrity and status.

If violence generally occurs only when one of the major peer norms has been violated, it would also seem to follow that *violence is a means of enforcing the peer entrepreneurial norms of the system.* Violence or the threat of violence is thus used to keep adult male fellators in line with the boys' expectations in his customer role. It represents social control, a punishment meted out to the fellator who violates the cultural expectation. Only so long as the fellator seeks gratification from lower-class boys in a casual pick-up or continuing relationship where he pays money for a "blow-job," is he reasonably free from acts of violence.

There is another, and perhaps more important reason for the use of violence when the peer defined norms of the peer–queer relationship are violated. The formally prescribed roles for peers and queers are basically the roles involved in all institutionalized forms of prostitution, the prostitute and the client. But in most forms of prostitution, whether male or female, the hustlers perceive of themselves in hustler roles, and furthermore the male hustlers also develop a conception of themselves as homosexual whereas *the peer hustler in the peer–queer relationship develops no conception of himself either as prostitute or as homosexual.*

The fellator risks violence, therefore, if he threatens the boy's self-conception by suggesting that the boy may be homosexual and treats him as if he were.

Violence seems to function, then, in two basic ways for the peers. On the one hand, it integrates their norms and expectations by controlling and combatting behavior which violates them. On the other hand, it protects the boy's self-identity as non-homosexual and reinforces his self-conception as "masculine."

The other norms of the peer society governing the peer–queer transaction also function to prevent boys in the peer–queer society from defining themselves as homosexual. The prescriptions that the goal is money, that sexual gratification is not to be sought as an end in the relationship, that affective neutrality be maintained toward the fellator and that only mouth–genital fellation is permitted, all tend to insulate the boy from a homosexual self-definition. So long as he conforms to these expectations, *his "significant others" will not define him as homosexual*; and this is perhaps the most crucial factor in his own self-definition. The peers define one as homosexual not on the basis of homosexual *behavior* as such, but on the basis of participation in the homosexual *role*, the "queer" role. The reactions of the larger society, in defining the *behavior* as homosexual is unimportant in their own self-definition. What is important to them is the reactions of their peers to violation of peer group norms which define roles in the peer–queer transaction.

TERMINATING THE ROLE BEHAVIOR

Under what circumstances does a boy give up earning money in the peer–queer transaction? Is it altogether an individual matter, or are there group bases for abandoning the practice? We have little information on these questions since interviews were conducted largely with boys who were still participants in the peer–queer culture. But a few interviews, either with boys who had terminated the relationship or spoke of those who had, provide information on how such role behavior is terminated.

Among lower-class adolescent boys, the new roles one assumes with increasing age are important in terminating participation in the peer–queer relationship. Thus older boys are more likely to have given up the transaction as a source of income. Several boys gave as their reason, "I got a job and don't need that kind of money now." An older boy, who recently married, said that he had quit when he was married. Another responded to the question, "When do you think you'll quit?" with, "When I quit school, I reckon . . . I don't know a better way to make money afore then." A few boys simply said that they didn't care to make money that way any more, or that since they got a steady girl, they had quit.

The reasons older boys have for giving up the peer–queer transaction as a means of making money is perhaps different for the career-oriented than for the peer-oriented delinquent boy. As career-oriented delinquents get older, the more serious crimes direct their activity and the group is more actively involved in activities which confer status. The boy has a "rep" to maintain. The peer hustler role clearly contributes nothing to developing or maintaining a reputation, and the longer one gets money this way, the more one may risk it. The older career-oriented delinquent boy perhaps gives up peer hustling activity, then, just as he often gives up petty theft and malicious destruction of property. These are activities for younger boys.

As peer-oriented delinquents get older, they enter adult groups where a job becomes one of the acceptable ways of behaving. Many of them may also move out of the "tight little island" of the peer group which inducted them into the activity. If one gets enough money from a job, there is no socially acceptable reason for getting money in the peer–queer transaction. One risks loss of status if one solicits at this age, for this is the age to move from one steady girl to another and perhaps even settle on one and get married, as often one "has to."

Regardless of the reasons for moving out, it seems clear that most boys do move out of their roles as peer hustlers and do not go on to other hustling careers. The main reason perhaps that most boys do not move on in hustling careers is that they never conceived of themselves in a hustling role or as participants in a career where there was a status gradation among hustlers. Hustling, to the peer hustler, is simply another one of the activities which characterizes a rather versatile pattern of deviating acts. It is easier, too, to move out when one has never defined oneself as homosexual. It is in this sense, perhaps, that we have reason to conclude that these boys are not involved in the activity primarily for its homosexual basis. Peer hustlers are primarily oriented toward either delinquent, and later criminal, careers, or toward conventional conformity in lower-class society. They become neither hustlers nor queers.

SUMMARY

This paper explores a special form of male prostitution in American society, a homosexual relationship between adult male fellators and delinquents. It is seen as a financial transaction between boys and fellators which is governed by delinquent peer norms. These norms integrate the two types of deviators into an institutionalized form of prostitution and protect the boys from self-definitions either as prostitutes or as homosexuals.

The conclusions offered in this paper must be regarded as tentative, because of limitations inherent in the data. Study of the fellator population might substantially change the conclusions. Cross-cultural studies also are necessary. Discussion of these findings with criminologists in Denmark and Sweden and exploratory investigations in several larger American cities, however, suggest that the description and explanation offered in this paper will hold for other American cities and for some other social systems.

NOTES

1 The word "queer" is of the "straight" and not the "gay" world. In the "gay" world it has all the qualities of a negative stereotype but these are not intended in this paper. The paper arose out of the perspective of boys in the "straight" world.
2 Arthur V. Huffman, "Sex Deviation in a Prison Community," *The Journal of Social Therapy* 6 (Third Quarter, 1960): 170–81; Joseph E. Fishman, *Sex in Prison* (New York: The Commonwealth Fund, 1930); Donald Clemmer, *The Prison Community* (Boston: The Christopher Publishing House, 1940): 260–73.
3 William Marlin Butts, "Boy Prostitutes of the Metropolis," *Journal of Clinical Psychopathol-*

ogy 8 (1946–7): 673–81; H. Laurence Ross, "The Hustler in Chicago," *The Journal of Student Research* 1 (September, 1959): 13–19; Jens Jersild, *Boy Prostitution* (Copenhagen: C. E. Gad, 1956) (translation of *Den Mandlige Prostitution* by Oscar Bojesen).
4 Ross: 15.
5 The distinction made here is not intended to suggest that other types of hustlers do not also define themselves in other deviant roles. Hustlers may occupy a variety of deviant roles which are classified as delinquent or criminal; they may be "hooked," blackmailers, thieves, etc.
6 I am indebted to Ned Polsky for bringing Rechy's stories to my attention.
7 John Rechy, "The Fabulous Wedding of Miss Destiny," *Big Table* 1: 3 (1959): 15.
8 John Rechy, "A Quarter Ahead," *Evergreen Review* 5: 19 (July–August 1961): 18.
9 For a definition of the types of conformers and deviators see Albert J. Reiss, Jr, "Conforming and Deviating Behavior and the Problem of Guilt," *Psychiatric Research Reports* 13 (December 1960): 209–10, and Albert J. Reiss, Jr and Albert Lewis Rhodes, "The Distribution of Juvenile Delinquency in the Social Class Structure," *American Sociological Review* 26: 5 (October 1961): 720–32.
10 See, for example, Maurice Leznoff and William A. Westley, "The Homosexual Community," *Social Problems* 4 (April 1956): 257–63.
11 Leznoff and Westley: 258.
12 Ross: 15.
13 The cues which lead to the queer–peer transaction can be subtle ones. The literature on adult male homosexuality makes it clear that adult males who participate in homosexual behavior are not generally socially visible to the public by manner and dress. Cf. Stearn: chapters 1 and 3.
14 Leznoff and Westley: 260–1.
15 Ross notes that, failing in the conman role, some hustlers resort to extortion and blackmail since they provide higher income. See Ross: 16. Sutherland discusses extortion and blackmail of homosexuals as part of the practice of professional thieves. The "muzzle" or "mouse" is part of the role of the professional thief. See Edwin Sutherland, *The Professional Thief* (Chicago: University of Chicago Press, 1937): 78–81. See also the chapter on "Blackmail" in Stearn: chapter 16.
16 Stearn: 47.
17 Albert J. Reiss, Jr, "Sex Offenses: The Marginal Status of the Adolescent," *Law and Contemporary Problems* 25 (spring 1960): 322–4 and 326–7.
18 Albert Cohen, Alfred Lindesmith and Karl Schuessler (eds), *The Sutherland Papers* (Bloomington: University of Indiana Press, 1956): 31.
19 It is not altogether clear why mouth–genital

fellation is the only sexual act which is tolerated in the peer–queer transaction. The act seems to conform to the more "masculine" aspects of the role than do most, but not all possible alternatives. Ross has suggested to me that it also involves less bodily contact and therefore may be less threatening to the peers' self-definitions. One possible explanation therefore for the exclusiveness of the relationship to this act is that it is the most masculine alternative involving the least threat to peers' self-definition as nonhustler and non-homosexual.

20 Talcott Parsons in *The Social System* (Glencoe: The Free Press, 1951): chapter 111, discusses this kind of role as "the segregation of specific instrumental performances, both from expressive orientations other than the specifically appropriate rewards and from other components of the instrumental complex" (p. 87).

21 Walter Miller, "Lower-Class Culture as a Generating Milieu of Gang Delinquency," *The Journal of Social Issues* 14: 3 (1958): 9.

LAUD HUMPHREYS

"The Breastplate of Righteousness"

from *Tearoom Trade: Impersonal Sex in Public Places* (Chicago: Aldine, 1970): chapter 7

From one viewpoint, tearoom [public toilet] encounters may be analyzed as structured interaction that evolves from the need for information control: signals and strategies are developed to exclude the potentially threatening and uninitiated intruder, while informing potential partners of one's willingness to engage in sex; silence serves to protect participants from biographical disclosure; and locales are chosen for an ease of access that keeps wives, employers and others from discovering the deviant activity. Scott has made just this sort of analysis of horse racing as an "information game."[1]

In considering the types of participants in these encounters, information control has again appeared as a crucial variable for those who engage in sexually deviant activity. Married men with dependent occupations have more to fear – and less to enjoy – from their clandestine behavior because they are deficient in means of countering exposure when compared with men of greater autonomy. The ambisexuals, along with single men in unthreatened occupations, have access to information sources that facilitates their activity in the restroom settings.

The unmarried man who is able to cross over into the world of overt homosexuality is not obsessed with guarding data. His moral history is, in most cases, already public – at least in the sense that his parents, customers, and close friends have been made aware of it. This gives him greater resistance to being discredited. Even arrest and publicity (if not accompanied by severe penalties) on a morals charge would not be disastrous. The degree of resistance, then, refers to the relative ability of a person to withstand the shock of exposure.

The overt single man also has better recep-

tion than other types of participants. He is in a better position to receive information that may be of use to him in locating, performing, and safeguarding his chosen brand of deviant action. Thievery, pot-smoking, or homosexual activity – almost any sort of deviance – is made both easier and safer by the communication networks that are built into deviant subcultures. Participants in the homosexual subculture do not have to depend, as does the researcher, on repeated excursions or the observation of physical traces to discover where the action is. They learn of the popular spots in any season at all sorts of homosexual gatherings. By the same channels, they will be informed of hidden cameras or decoys in the public restrooms that might result in arrest.

Of all tearoom participants, those who might be labeled homosexuals in the secondary or subcultural sense are least susceptible to arrest. The professional, experienced, well-informed criminal is in far less danger of being a "loser" than the man who dabbles in deviance. This irony is illustrated in an interview with Tim, the former police decoy:

INTERVIEWER: Was there publicity about people being arrested?
TIM: No, they kept it quiet. There was so much bullshit!
INTERVIEWER: Don't things usually get around in the gay circles?
TIM: Well, see, the gay circles were the younger people.
INTERVIEWER: The men [in the tearooms] weren't organized in groups or anything like that? The men were just individuals?
TIM: Yes, the men who were arrested in the tearooms were just individuals who hadn't gotten into a group – or who were businessmen who couldn't get into a group.

INTERVIEWER: Because they were married or something like that?

TIM: Yes, most of them were married.

Once learned, the rules and strategies of the game, like other means of avoiding entrapment and exposure, become part of the skills an actor has on tap. Socialization in the deviant subculture thus adds to the reservoir of defense and adaptation that is essential in transforming drudgery into adventure. Such resources include both capital and skill. What the gay men lack in capital they make up in skill. The ambisexuals are apt to have a good deal of both: a learned ability to manipulate the game to their advantage, accompanied by the means to buy and bluff their way out of danger.

As both occupation and marital status combine to lower resistance, restrict reception, and limit skill and capital, the deviant actor is increasingly frightened and desperate. His stigmatized behavior becomes more furtive and less enjoyable. Lacking control of information, threatened with exposure, the Georges and Arnolds are moved from tearoom to tearoom by a double nightmare of flight from fear and pursuit of satisfaction.

Under these adverse conditions, with such high costs, the trade and closet queens might be expected to withdraw altogether from the sexual market of public restrooms. The data indicate, however, that this is seldom the case – tearoom behavior is not easily extinguished. At least two methods of minimizing costs tend to preserve a margin of profit sufficient to sustain such activity for years. The first of these methods is the structuring of interaction so as to minimize revelation. The second is a process whereby the threatened deviant supplements his resistance. As socioeconomic factors and poor reception limit resources – and resistance is decreased – the covert participant engages in a strategy of information control that is designed to increase resistance by detracting from his deviance.

Ball, in his discussion of the management of respectable appearances, refers to this phenomenon as "misdirection," a substrategy of "concealment": "The basic technique here is to present information or activity of a sufficiently engrossing nature that the performer is able to carry on other affairs unnoticed."[2] Whether one interprets such misdirection as a method of achieving concealment or of building up resistance depends largely on his view of the intentions of the actor. "Concealment" has certain negative connotations, implying a degree of dishonest or deceptive intent, which I should like to avoid.

The emphasis of psychoanalytic theory on unconscious motivation (always a convenient evasion of the question of intent) has resulted in the development of the theory of reaction formation, which may also provide a suitable conceptualization for description of this strategy. I am no more convinced of the unconscious or nonrational nature of this method of information control, however, than I am of its deceptive intent. I propose, therefore, to direct our thinking toward a fresh vocabulary and conceptualization.

REFULGENT RESPECTABILITY

What is needed here is a term that implies the taking on of a protective covering, the assumption of a defensive shield to ward off social disapproval. There is also a positive aspect to the phenomenon observed. These men are not only concerned with avoiding trouble but are involved, as well, in the creation of a social image, in presenting themselves as respectable members of society.

In the process of getting to know the secret deviant, the researcher soon realizes that he must first penetrate a thick nimbus of propriety. The person who is easily discredited because of an occasional hidden act seldom appears so apart from that act. He zips his pants and straightens his tie before leaving the tearoom and, in a short period of time, has resumed life as the respectable next-door neighbor, homemaker, and businessman.

For lack of more appropriate conceptualization, I suggest the use of a biblical phrase which, having suffered from misleading translation in the King James version and a subsequent history of theological misuse, might be put to more constructive use in the sociology of deviant behavior. I refer to a portion of "the armour of

God" that the author of the letter to the Ephesians would have us put on: "the breastplate of righteousness" (Ephesians 6:14).

In donning the breastplate of righteousness, the covert deviant assumes a protective shield of superpropriety. His armor has a particularly shiny quality, a refulgence, which tends to blind the audience to certain of his practices. To others in his everyday world, he is not only normal but righteous – an exemplar of good behavior and right thinking. However much the covert participant may be reacting to guilt in erecting this defensive barrier, he is also engaging in a performance that is part and parcel of his being. Goffman remarks that "there is often no reason for claiming that the facts discrepant with the fostered impression are any more the real reality than is the fostered reality they embarrass."[3] The secret offender may well believe he is more righteous than the next man – hence his shock and outrage, his disbelieving indignation, when he is discovered and discredited.

Motivated largely by his own awareness of the discreditable nature of his secret behavior, the covert deviant develops a presentation of self that is respectable to a fault. His whole life style becomes an incarnation of what is proper and orthodox. In manners and taste, religion and art, he strives to compensate for an otherwise low resistance to the shock of exposure.[4]

The breastplate of righteousness is most evident – and most easily measured – in the respondents' views on social and political issues. Early in the analysis of data from the interview sched-ules, indices of liberal opinion were constructed for each of four sets of social issues on which the views of research subjects were sought: measures of economic reform, police practices, the civil rights movement, and the Vietnamese war. From these indicators, a composite liberalism index was constructed, which facilitated ranking the subjects in terms of their scores on these questions and their classification as conservatives, moderates, or liberals.

Answers to eleven questions on social and economic issues revealed the sharpest differences observed between the control and participant samples. As shown in Table 3.1, the orientations on these issues differ markedly between the two samples, the participants in homosexual acts being more conservative in each of the areas. Among the participants, 16 were ranked as conservatives, 26 as moderates, and only 7 as liberals. In the control sample, only 4 might be called conservatives, 31 moderates, and 15 liberals. For the total scores on the composite liberalism index, the median for the participants was 14; that of the non-deviants was 20.

By comparing the mean scores on the liberalism indices for each of the participant types with those of their matched partners from the control sample, it is possible to discern the degree to which the various participant types supplement their resistance by putting on the breastplate of righteousness. Such compensation, along with other resources for information control, is illustrated in Table 3.2. The ambisexual and gay men have little or no need for the

Table 3.1 Mean scores on liberalism indices by type of tearoom participants, compared with control sample scores (in parentheses)

	Type I "Trade"	Type II "Ambisexual"	Type III "Gay"	Type IV "Closet queens"	Total participants	Total controls "Straights"
Economic	4.4	2.3	6.3	4.2	4.2	(6.2)
Police	2.0	4.0	6.6	3.3	3.4	(4.3)
Civil Rights	2.0	1.9	5.3	1.7	2.4	(3.3)
Vietnam	3.7	6.2	8.3	5.3	5.3	(6.7)
Totals	12.1	14.4	26.5	14.5	15.3	(20.5)
(Controls)	(18.3)	(18.2)	(28.0)	(22.3)		

breastplate of righteousness and are thus only slightly more conservative than those in the control sample with whom they are matched.

In order to check for social factors that might explain differences on these indices between the groups because of disproportionate representation in the samples, a number of cross-tabulations were run. Variables of socio-economic status, race, age, education, type of military service, and religion were all tabulated against the scores of the composite liberalism index for both samples. As was expected from care taken in matching the samples, few differences were found for the statistics of these variables between the two groups. The only major differences were evident in regard to the variables of age, education and religious affiliation. There was a higher proportion of men in their thirties in the participant sample, twice as many persons with graduate education in the control sample, and a disproportionately high representation of Roman Catholics and Episco-

palians in the participant sample.

Analysis of the data casts doubt on the possibility that differences in these social characteristics explain away the disparity in social outlooks. If, for instance, the relatively small number of men with graduate education among the participants had evidenced a degree of liberalism consonant with those in the control sample, this might have explained some of the between-sample difference. But persons with this degree of education in the participant sample included *no* liberals.

On the other hand, had the proportion of conservatives among Roman Catholics or men in their thirties in the control sample been consistent with those in the deviant group, it might have been possible to attribute the differences in social views to the variation in age and religion representation between samples. Again, this does not hold. There are no conservatives among the men in their thirties in the straight sample (as contrasted with eight conservatives

Table 3.2 Relative resources for information control by participant types

	MARRIED Type II "Ambisexual" (Dwight)	UNMARRIED Type III "Gay" (Ricky)

INDEPENDENT OCCUPATION	Moderate Reception
	High Skills
	High Capital
	Moderate Resistance
	(Some Need for Breastplate)
	Mean Liberalism Score:
	    Observed 14.4
	    Expected 18.2[1]
	    —3.8
		High Reception
		High Skills
		Low Capital
		High Resistance
		(No Need for Breastplate)
		Mean Liberalism Score:
		    Observed 26.5
		    Expected 28.0[1]
		    —1.5

DEPENDENT OCCUPATION	Type I
	"Trade" (George)
	Low Reception
	Low Skills
	Low Capital
	Low Resistance
	(Breastplate Essential)
	Mean Liberalism Score:
	    Observed 12.1
	    Expected 18.3[1]
	    —6.2
		Type IV
		"Closet Queens" (Arnold)
		Some Reception
		Some Skills
		Low Capital
		Low Resistance
		(Breastplate Needed)
		Mean Liberalism Score:
		    Observed 14.5
		    Expected 22.3[1]
		    —7.8

Note
1 "Expected" scores are the mean scores on the Composite Liberalism Index for members of the control sample matched with these types.

in that age range among the participants) and only one who took a comparable position among the Roman Catholics in the control group.

Such specification, then, does not enable us to discern any causal factors among the social variables considered. This is not to say that age, race, education, and religion are unimportant in determining the outlook of these respondents on social issues; rather, what is indicated here is that at least one other intervening variable serves to distort and intensify the effects of characteristics which would normally be expected to influence social and political views.

AFRAID OF BEING LIBERAL

Turning directly to the interviews, it becomes apparent that the fear of exposure and stigmatization serves as an intervening lens through which the effects of other social characteristics are filtered and distorted. Social conservatism is revealed as a product of the illegal roles these men play in the hidden moments of their lives. An example is found in the case of Marvin, a young Negro in his mid-twenties:

INTERVIEWER: Have you ever participated in a civil rights march, picket line or other such demonstration?
MARVIN: Look, I'm black and I'm gay! Isn't that asking for enough trouble without getting mixed up in this civil rights stuff, too?

This man shares a very neat, if modest, apartment with another unmarried man of the same race. He drives a late-model economy car – not flashy but well cared for. He works forty-eight hours each week as a salesman of men's clothing. In reply to questions about his activities and interests, he says: "I just work, go to church, come home, go out to a movie occasionally." Marvin's concern with projecting a non-stigmatizing image crops up throughout the interview. When asked about his good points, he says: "I try to respect other people's feelings and stay by myself to keep out of trouble." Most of his social activities center on his church, a fundamentalist congregation, which he serves as organist on a part-time basis. He rates

himself at ten on a ten-point scale of participation in church activities. "I go to church whenever the doors are open."

Marvin does not know who his father was. His mother, who later married a laborer, raised him in a city ghetto. She always suffered from bad health, and both of her other children died at childbirth. Marvin left high school in the eleventh grade. He doesn't like living in his declining neighborhood and feels that it is not safe there.

Although many of those with whom he was raised may be prime candidates for riot participation, Marvin comes closer to qualifying for membership in the John Birch Society. Concerning the "civil rights movement, as a whole," he believes it has "stirred up people to commit criminal acts." He replied, "Definitely not!" when asked if citizens should participate in demonstrations against the war.

On the composite liberalism index, with a range from three to thirty-seven points, Marvin scored thirteen – two points below the median for his sample of fifty men. For purposes of analysis, he was thus ranked with the moderates. His liberalism on economic questions kept him from joining the ranks of conservatives in the study.

The black man matched with him in the control sample was rated as a liberal by his score of twenty-eight. Although this non-deviant is nearly thirty years older than Marvin (controls for age not being permitted by the sampling technique), there is little difference in socioeconomic background between the two men. The liberal also ranked himself at ten in terms of his religious activity.

A white, upper class participant who, like Marvin, scored below the median of his sample on the composite liberalism index reflected the same concern with exposure. In one of the lengthy, open-ended interviews with this man, I asked why he wasn't active in politics like another member of his family. "With my clandestine activities," he replied, "who wants to get involved in politics? The last thing I need is to get my picture in the papers or on television!"

One of the trade, when questioned about his attitude toward war protestors, says: "We ought to send the bastards over there! They'd see what it's like!" Another Type I participant, a minister, thinks "we should give our whole-hearted support to those who fight godless Communism." This same man believes the civil rights movement has "made people dissatisfied with what the Lord has given them ... God made the races separate – we shouldn't inter-fere!"

Knowing of the constant threat to the trade from members of the vice squad, I expected these participants to evidence some anti-police sentiment in that portion of the interviews. Quite the opposite was true. The minister quoted above felt that the police should not give as much regard as they do to the rights of citizens. Vice squad activity, he insisted, should be increased: "This moral corruption must be stopped!" One young closet queen had this to say about vice squad activity: "They should be more strict. I can think of a lot of places they ought to raid."

So consistent were the replies of trade and closet queens (the participants most apt to be arrested in tearooms) in encouraging more vice squad activity that a portrait emerges of these men as moral crusaders. This at least suggests the ironic possibility of a type of moral entrepre-neur who contributes to his own stigmatiza-tion.[5] Homosexual folklore insists that "there is a witch behind every witch hunt." These data suggest not only the truth underlying that per-ception but that deviant behavior may be plagued by a sort of moral arms race, in which the deviant is caught in the cycle of establishing new strategic defenses to protect himself from the fallout of his own defensive weapons. It is not necessary to adopt a psychoanalytic view-point in order to discern the self-hatred behind such a punishment process.

Karl, a closet queen whom I have interviewed repeatedly, is a member of the John Birch Society. His parents are prosperous and well-educated people who "never really accepted" him as an equal with his brother. "They have always thrown him at me as an example and deeply resent my remaining unmarried. Father has also criticized me for not being a famous athlete ... I've never seemed to be good enough for them." Although slight of build, this

respondent showed the greatest interest in ath-letics of any person in his sample.

In his search for acceptance and masculinity on his parents' terms, Karl has driven himself in work and play, study and religious orthodoxy, at a determined and nervous pitch. It was his idea to spend his adolescent years in a military prep school and to join the Marines at the time of the Korean war. Like Mack in *The Author-itarian Personality*, this man reveals a tendency to displace his hostility on to outgroups:

> The frustrating, punishing, persecutory features which had to be denied in the father were seen as originating in outgroups who could then be hated in safety, because they were not strong in actuality, and in good conscience, because the traits ascribed to them were those which the in-group authorities would condemn.[6]

Karl speaks of Negroes as "those damned Ethiopians" and claims that they are "taking over the church and the country."

It is possible that this respondent's con-servatism and his tearoom activities both arise from a common, psychological source. He rates his father at one (very cold) on a six-point scale of warmth of relationship with him as a child. His mother was rated at six. Both parents received a one for strictness. He looks back on his childhood as "not too happy." On the other hand, there is much evidence of feedback from his deviant sexual activity into the motivational network behind Karl's intense concern with social respectability, orthodoxy, and masculine image. Highly critical of most others in the homosexual "fraternity," he speaks disparag-ingly of those who patronize the bars and coffeehouses of the gay community. For the sake of his job and social position, he fears being identified with the more obvious of his kind.

This man, like another closet queen whom I shall call John, will not turn to psychiatric help, although both expressed a belief that they were on the verge of a "nervous breakdown" at the time of the interviews. Karl's response to nerv-ousness and depression is to "throw myself into activity." John, who doesn't want to see a physi-cian or psychiatrist "because they can't change me," finds solace with his friends. The important point is that these men are both strong con-servatives: highly moralistic, supportive of stronger police activity and intensification of the war in Vietnam, and derogatory in speaking of Negroes. They are defensive and uneasy about their own sexual tendencies and highly motivated toward the maintenance of their images of occupational and political respectability.

GAY LIBERALS

It is interesting to note that five of the eight liberals in the participant sample are classified as Type III, gay participants. In talking of their homosexual activity, these men seemed more accepting of their own sexual natures and more intent upon establishing love relationships with others. One high-scoring liberal insists that he is looking for a "permanent lover" among those whom he fellates in the tearooms. Frenkel-Brunswick found that those men scoring low on the Fascism Scale manifest a "fusion of sex and affect, a tendency to more personalized sex relations."[7] My interviews give strong support to these findings by the Adorno group.

An interesting parallel between changing social views and sexual adjustment was traced in an interview with David:

DAVID: When I was first in college, the thing that stands out in my mind most was my attitude towards Negroes. Oh, I believed in civil rights, but civil rights meaning separate but equal. On the war, I just wanted to get it over with – drop a couple of atomic bombs! And then, I was much more religiously orthodox than now.

I first started coming out of this whole morass of conservatism shortly after I came here. I had had a series of very bad love affairs. Then my priest demanded I quit being gay or be denied the sacraments. I quit going to church altogether for the entire summer . . . and began to come to terms with myself as a sexual person.

At this point, I met [Rodger]. It had been a bad week – a number of very sordid one-night-stands, tearooms and bar hopping. Through him, I started on a course of changing churches and working out a meaningful pattern of life. I had been experimenting with a semi-Bohemian type of life – but scared to death of drugs of any sort. Was carrying on a respectable daytime job and playing the Bohemian part at night, but didn't accept the philosophy behind the life. It was more a way of having some sort of sex without any obligations attached.

INTERVIEWER: What sort of attitudes did you have then toward your own sexual orientation?

DAVID: Strictly a "numbers" attitude.[8] I was a typical tearoom type. Used to stand on the street until three or four in the morning looking for a trick. But I was playing it straight in the daytime. I was working with straights down at the office. Doing my best to pass with them, I strictly played the masculine bit, telling dirty jokes, trying to date girls. I kept a pretty conventional apartment – regular bed, sofa, hi-fi, chairs, and such.

My ideas on politics were completely nil in those days. I was so busy trying *not* to do something that I could never develop a valid spiritual life or social consciousness. It wasn't until I met [Roddy] that I really turned on to who I was or what was going on in the world.

The three highest scorers among participants – the three most liberal deviants – were the men of this sample whom I would consider the best adjusted of the tearoom clientele. In this connection, it should be noted that the average score on the index for the five men from the combined samples who admit to having undergone psychiatric therapy was twenty-three – a score well above the mean for even the control group. The highest scoring liberals in each sample were men who have had psychiatric help. This finding calls to mind Bay's hypothesis that "the better the individual has been able to resolve his own anxieties, the more likely that he will empathize with others less fortunate than himself."[9]

THE COVERT LIFESTYLE

The secret offender's breastplate of righteousness is not limited to right-wing social and political attitudes. His performance of duties as husband, father, neighbor, and friend is likewise bent in a direction that might give credence to his life of respectability. He is apt to earn more money than his straight counterpart and to spend more hours each week at his work. From the standpoint of surface appearance, at least, the participant marriages are "smoother" than those of the control sample.

One of the early impressions formed from research among these men was the remarkable neatness and propriety of their style of life. The automobiles that cluster around the tearoms are almost uniformly clean and well polished and generally of a late-model vintage. Moreover, the personal attire and grooming of the participants was noteworthy for its neatness. "Impeccable" was a word frequently used in description: well-tailored suits, conservative ties, clean work clothes appear to be almost mandatory for tearoom activity.

The condition of their residences was striking. In 50 per cent of the cases, my descriptions included such comments as "very neat," "well kept," "nicest house (or apartment building) in the neighborhood." New awnings, a recent coat of paint, or an exceptionally well-trimmed yard became trademarks that often enabled me to single out the home of a respondent from others down the block. More of these men listed devoting time to their families and homes as their chief interest in life than did those in the control sample. Twice as many expressed an interest in arts and crafts (excluding the fine arts) and in improving the appearance of their homes.

Whereas eight of those in the non-deviant group manifested a Bohemian (or hip) life style, as seen in furnishings or personal attire, this was true of only four of the participants. The general antipathy of covert deviants toward hippies is illustrated by negative reactions in the "Letters" column of a San Francisco-based homophile magazine, following the publication of a "hippie" issue. The following letter is representative:

> To identify the homosexual community with any adjunct of the hippie mentality is as gross a distortion as identifying all Birchers as anti-Semites. There may be a few "gays" in the Haight Street scene, and there may be a few "kooks" in the Birch Society, but, for the main, the bulk of responsible adults in both are ashamed of the harmful image created by an irresponsible few. I speak first hand being both a homosexual and a Bircher, and I for one am speaking out against any equation which your July issue might have created as between the "homo" and the "hip."[10]

For those participants with less autonomy, the trade and closet queens, the breastplate of righteousness is thick and almost blinding with the polish of frequent use. It might be said of the covert deviant that he takes on "the whole armour of God." This is true in an almost literal sense, his religious orientation tending to the more authoritarian bodies. Eighteen of these men are Roman Catholics, most of whom express some resentment over changes taking place in the Church. Another is a fundamentalist minister, some of whose views have already been quoted. Most other trade and closet queens belong to no organized religion but are quick to add that they have "strong religious convictions." These men indicate bitterness at "the direction in which the churches are moving."

Two covert participants informed me that they are members of the John Birch Society, although there were no questions aimed at acquiring such data on the interview schedule. After interviews with them, the researcher gains the impression that "the Bible on the table and the flag upon the wall" may be signs of secret deviance more than of "right thinking."

There appear to be two variables that interact with other social characteristics to determine the lifestyle and sociopolitical position of any type of deviant actor: first, the intensity of anticipated sanctions against the particular deviant behavior; second, the degree of autonomy governing the control of information. As anticipated sanctions increase and autonomy decreases, the more elaborate and encompassing will be the breastplate of righteousness the deviant assumes for his overt performances in life. This hypothesis should be seen as cognate to that of Bay: "To the extent that a person is deeply worried about his popularity, his career prospects, his financial future, his reputation, etc., he will utilize his political opinions not for achieving realistic insight but for impressing his reference groups and his reference persons favorably."[11]

In this light, I would suggest that another factor be added to a recent hypothesis of Horowitz and Liebowitz.[12] Because I regard as important their argument that "the line between the social deviant and the political marginal is fading," I would suggest they qualify this theory by adding the word overt in order to make the thesis supportable. Not only for homosexuals but for other deviants as well there is a growing body of evidence that the more overt (autonomous) social deviants are becoming political deviants. However, for the vast majority, the unseen deviants, the breastplate of righteousness replaces the offensive weapons of all but the most conservative political action.

Because I have not engaged in research with other types of marginal people in our society, I am thrown back upon the literature and ten years of experience in the pastoral ministry in order to extend the applicability of my hypothesis to other than participants in homosexual encounters. I recall years of puzzlement over the striking respectability of the visible lives of so many of those who came to my pastoral attention: the countless alcoholics with exceptionally neat apartments and tidy houses; the highly respected businessmen arrested in tearooms; the hyper-orthodox clergymen with extracurricular sex lives. In one pastorate, three of my laymen were active in the John Birch Society. One of these was a secret alcoholic who beat his wife, another was a tearoom habitué, and the third stole from his employer with regularity. I use these illustrations (which, as isolated cases, can prove nothing) to underline my point that the secret alcoholic, the embezzler, the tearoom customer, may appear to his neighbors as the paradigm of propriety, the finest of citizens. It is not at all unlikely that he will be a moral entrepreneur, serving on the vice squad or heading the local League for Decent Literature.

At home, a Mafia leader "is the soul of respectability – an affectionate husband, a kind father, usually temperate and a faithful worshipper at his church."[13] Centuries of experience as a population of covert deviants has taught the Mafia to incorporate the breastplate of righteousness into its code of behavior. Only when deviants achieve relative autonomy, when information control becomes less problematic, can they afford to be different.

NOTES

1 Marvin B. Scott, *The Racing Game* (Chicago: Aldine, 1968): 159. "In *information games*, the participants seek to conceal and uncover certain kinds of knowledge."

2 Donald W. Ball, "The Problematics of Respectability," to appear in Jack D. Douglas (ed.), *Deviance and Respectability: The Social Construction of Moral Meanings* (New York: Basic Books, forthcoming), p. 50 of the unpublished manuscript.

3 Erving Goffman, *The Presentation of Self in Everyday Life* (Garden City, New York: Doubleday Anchor, 1959): 65.

4 My thanks to Irving Horowitz, who suggested that this phenomenon might best be expressed in terms of compensation.

5 For a discussion of moral entrepreneurship, see Howard S. Becker, *Outsiders* (New York: The Free Press, 1963): 147–63.

6 R. Nevitt Sanford, "Genetic Aspects of the Authoritarian Personality: Case Studies of Two Contrasting Individuals," in T. Adorno and others, *The Authoritarian Personality* (New York: Harper, 1950): 805–6.

7 Else Frenkel-Brunswick, "Sex, People, and Self as Seen Through the Interviews," in Adorno and others, *The Authoritarian Personality*: 397.

8 Here the respondent is referring to John Rechy, *Numbers* (New York: Grove Press, 1967). In this novel, a former hustler engages in a compulsive search for impersonal sexual contacts.

9 Christian Bay, "Political and Apolitical Students: Facts in Search of Theory," *Journal of Social Issues* 23: 3 (July 1967): 90.

10 From a letter to the editor, published in the August 1967 issue of *Vector*.

11 Bay "Political and Apolitical Students,": 87.

12 Irving Louis Horowitz and Martin Liebowitz, "Social Deviance and Political Marginality: Toward a Redefinition of the Relation between Sociology and Politics," *Social Problems* 15: 3 (winter 1968): 285.

13 Frederic Sondern, Jr, *Brotherhood of Evil: The Mafia* (New York: Farrar, Straus and Cudahy, 1959): 55.

ESTHER NEWTON

"The 'Queens'"

from *Mother Camp: Female Impersonators in America* (Chicago: University of Chicago Press, 1972): chapter 2

THE "GAY WORLD"

Female impersonators are both performing homosexuals and homosexual performers. The juxtaposition of the nouns indicates that, whether one considers impersonators in the context of show business or in the context of the homosexual subculture, the reverse qualifying adjective will apply. In whatever order one chooses to emphasize them, the two terms of the equation cannot be separated. This chapter describes certain features of drag queens' homosexual world.

Female impersonators are an integral part of the homosexual subculture, and yet collectively they are a separate group within it. Many of the most distinctive characteristics and problems of female impersonators as a group spring from their membership in the homosexual subculture on the one hand, and their special relationship to it on the other.

Homosexuals, like many other American social groups, do not constitute a traditional "community." The concept is useful though, because it clearly contrasts with the notion that homosexuals are simply a category of deviant people. As Kinsey has pointed out, the general public and many so-called scholarly writers tend to classify as homosexual anyone who has had *any* homosexual experience, and as heterosexual only those who have had *no* homosexual experience.[1] Since the publication of the Kinsey statistics on the frequency of homosexual occurrence in the American male (1948), even some optimistic homosexuals have used the "one out of six" statistic as a population base for the number of homosexuals in this country. While the use of this figure as part of ideology may in

future change social reality, it does not represent social reality now, nor in practice do homosexuals identify themselves and their group by means of Kinsey's definition.

Not all self-defined homosexuals belong to the homosexual community, however. The community is an on-going social reality in, around, and against which people align themselves according to their own self-definitions. Many kinds and degrees of participation in the community are possible and available, and people move in and out of various statuses at different times in their lives.

The community centers on formal voluntary associations (Mattachine Society, Daughters of Bilitis, etc.), informal institutions (bars, baths, parks) and most of all, informal social groups, such as those described by Sonenschein and by Leznoff and Westley, which have their most characteristic expression in parties and living arrangements.[2]

All of these institutions and groupings collectively are called "the gay world," and participation in them is termed "gay life." The separation of the gay world and its inclusiveness as a mode of existence were much emphasized by my informants who stated that it was a "walk of life"; that one is not a "homosexual" but that one "lives homosexuality."[3]

In Kansas City and Chicago, both overt and covert homosexuals were found to "live homosexuality."[4] The overts live their *entire* lives within the context of the community; the coverts live their entire *non-working* lives within it. That is, the coverts are "straight" during working hours, but most social activities are conducted with and with reference to other homosexuals. These overts and coverts together form the core of the homosexual community. They may constitute approximately 3 per cent of the American population and are located almost exclusively in large- and medium-sized urban centers.

Homosexual *communities* are entirely urban and suburban phenomena.[5] They depend on the anonymity and segmentation of metropolitan life. Potential recruits to "gay life" migrate to cities so much so that in San Francisco the Mattachine Society describes the in-migration of young homosexuals as a major "social problem," especially for the central city.[6] In the cities, the hard core (that is, the most active participants) of the homosexual community tend to favor special residential areas, and these areas become focal orientation points even for the many members who do not live there. The homosexual inhabitants of these areas of great concentration generally give the area a name such as "fairy heights," or "lesbian row." In a large city there will be several such concentrations differing in rental prices and social status. For instance, in Chicago the middle-class residential core is in Oldtown and environs, the working-class core is on the West Side, and the lower-class in the near and far North Sides.[7]

A similar breakdown for New York City might be: upper and middle-class: East Sixties to Eighties and Brooklyn Heights; middle and lower class: Greenwich Village; lower class: West Seventies, Times Square area, lower East Side. Bars are usually located in or near these cores. The residential cores, while they are geographical focal points, do not circumscribe or confine the homosexual community of any city. Not only do people move in and out of these cores, change cores and so on, but the social network extends to people who live in every part of the city (including the suburbs and even exurbs), people who live with their parents, people who are stationed at nearby army bases, and so on.

The principal mode of communication between homosexual communities is through individual mobility, although lately guidebooks of homosexual bars and institutions, the printed matter of the homosexual organizations, as well as homosexual fiction have augmented social networks. Homosexuals boast that they can be quickly "at home" in any city in the world. It is not unusual to see groups of German, English and French homosexuals on the "gay" beaches adjacent to residential cores in Chicago, and the homosexual community in New York City especially is probably extremely cosmopolitan.

All people who define themselves as "gay" are placing themselves with other homosexuals as opposed to heterosexuals. However, this by no means implies that homosexuals are united, or that they are prepared to act in unison on any issue whatsoever, be it moral, political, religious, or economic. Indeed, the *only* thing they *all* share is the name itself, together with the agreement that they are deviant. Although one can discern the beginnings of a homosexual movement, the fragmenting differences between homosexuals still outweigh any potential solidarity.[8]

Some homosexuals consider themselves essentially normal members of society, deviating *only* in the choice of a sexual partner, a deviance that they conceptually minimize. At the other extreme, some homosexuals see themselves as *completely* outside conventional society. Those who minimize their deviance are likely to reject most contact with the gay world. They may live quietly with a lover who is passed off to the straight friends as a roommate. An alternative style is to live socially in the straight world with a wife and family, refuse all gay social contacts, and participate in the gay world by anonymous sexual contacts in public toilets. These people are connected with, but marginal to, the homosexual community. At the other extreme, many homosexuals organize their entire lives, including their working lives, around the self-definition and the deviance. They are, in the fullest sense, what Lemert has called "secondary deviants."

Secondary deviation refers to a special class of socially defined responses which people make to problems created by the societal reaction to their deviance. These problems are essentially moral problems which revolve around stigmatization, punishments, segregation, and social control. Their general effect is to differentiate the symbolic and interactional environment to which the person responds, so that early or adult socialization is categorically affected. They become central facts of existence for those experiencing them, altering psychic structure, producing specialized organization of social roles and self-regarding attitudes. Actions which have these roles and self attitudes as their referents make up secondary deviance. The secondary deviant, as opposed to his actions, is a person whose life and identity are organized around the facts of deviance.[9]

Even people who consider themselves fully part of the homosexual community, or "in" gay life, are internally subdivided in ways that profoundly affect their identities and patterns of social interactions. The two most fundamental divisions are the overt–covert distinction and the male–female gender division.

Overt–covert distinctions correlate to some extent with social class, but by no means invariably. I met a number of homosexuals who were construction and factory workers, sailors, waiters, and so on, who were just as covert as people working in upper-status jobs. Covert means only that one cannot be publicly identified by the straight world and its representatives, such as bosses, co-workers, family, landladies, teachers, and the man of the street. One hides, or attempts to hide, one's homosexual identity *from straight people*. In Goffman's terminology, one attempts to manage one's discreditability through control of personal front and restriction of information about one's personal life.[10]

The desire to avoid "guilt by association" on the part of covert homosexuals causes the most fundamental division in homosexual social life. But it must not be seen as a fixed principle that categorically places individuals on one side of the fence or the other. Rather it is a dynamic principle, one that continually causes tension and the redrawing of social lines. Of course, at the extremes there are individuals who are loud, aggressive, and declarative about their homosexualilty at almost all times and in an immediately recognizable manner, and at the other pole, those whose behavior almost never incriminates them and whose sexual and social lives are a closed book. But the great majority fall somewhere in between; any given person's "obviousness" is largely relative and situational. Joe may feel that John is "too obvious" to be seen with publicly, while Bill may not feel that John is "too obvious" at all. Furthermore,

if John himself feels that he is not "obvious," he will bitterly resent Joe's avoidance. The resentment will be compounded because the avoidance contains an accusation. If I belong to a secret society and a member is threatening to give out knowledge of his and my membership, he is guilty of disloyalty or indiscretion. But the overt homosexual is accused of a more degrading crime, that of being "too nellie," that is roughly, "too effeminate," or, in the lesbian case, "too butch," "too masculine." In effect, I will not associate with you because you are too stigmatized. I saw this principle in action again and again:

1   Jane is furious with Judy because Judy said hello to her on the street when she was walking with a straight couple. Jane says, "Judy is too butch-looking. My straight friends said, 'How do you know *her*?' and I had to make up a big story. Judy should have known better than that. I told her never to recognize me on the street unless I was alone." But Jane often goes to the opera with Judy.

2   Gus is very fond of Tim personally, and has used his influence as leader of a respectable group to get Tim invited to parties where Tim is appreciated as a clown. However, Gus considers Tim "too nellie" to be seen with publicly. One of Gus's friends relates to me with great relish how Tim once approached Gus on Wells Street and walked down the whole length of it with him. The friend says that Gus was squirming and looking down at the sidewalk out of embarrassment, but didn't have the heart to snub Tim completely. The friend says this shows how much Gus really likes Tim, because Gus is usually the soul of discretion and carefulness, and looks out only for himself.

The point here is that overtness is not in fact a fixed quality that invariably divides the sheep from the goats, but is rather a continuum, and that people vary a great deal as to how they fall on it situationally, and relative to comparison with others. However, these are groups that are consistently placed near one pole or the other. This may be viewed as a hierarchy of stigmatization, or "obviousness." Any particular group will tend to draw the line just below itself. For instance, female impersonators are considered by most homosexuals to be too overt. They are consistently placed on the low end of the continuum of stigmatization, and one of the first things that female impersonators must learn is not to recognize anyone on the street or in any other public place unless they are recognized first. Yet female impersonators who believe themselves to be less overt try to avoid public association with female impersonators whom they consider "too obvious," and very few female impersonators will associate publicly with "street fairies," boys who wear make-up on the street, because "there's no point in wearing a sign. I believe I can pass." Those on the low end resent those above them.

The question of the gender division among homosexuals could be the subject of another book. The questions of political, normative, social, and ideological relations between homosexual men and homosexual women are debated by both. Although the men are in the majority and set the overall tone of "gay life," the women are an integral part of the scene. It is said that the degree to which the men and women socialize with each other varies from city to city. It certainly does from group to group within any one city, such as Chicago. For instance, two groups of middle-class "respectables," one male and the other female, center their bar life in an Oldtown bar that caters about equally to men and women. In this bar the men and women mingle and socialize freely, sit at the same tables, dance together, and so on. Many small and all large parties and social events sponsored by members of each group are integrated, so much so that both men and women belonging to each group speak of themselves sometimes collectively as "the Oldtown crowd." Male and female members of the Oldtown crowd very frequently go out to restaurants, the opera, symphonies, antique shows, and office parties in pairs or foursomes. Not only are personal friendships formed, but members approve of this policy in principle, saying that it makes good "cover." However, another group of lower middle-class girls who form the membership of the Daughters of Bilitis (a lesbian organization) apparently associate with men very little, although they have some personal links with women in the "Oldtown crowd."

Numerically, most homosexual bars in Chicago are exclusively or largely male, and females are not welcomed. Two bars are mostly female, although men are tolerated. At all status levels, a person's greatest interaction and allegiance is with his or her same sex group, but a complex social network exists between the sex groups. There is, however, a great deal of latent tension which can always be mobilized. This is nicely reflected in linguistic usage. When a person wants to emphasize solidarity between the sex groups, he (or she) refers to the opposites as "the gay boys (guys)," conversely "the gay girls," and all collectively as "the gay kids"[11] or "gay people." When he (or she) wants to emphasize differences, usually with a negative tone, he refers to the opposites as "faggots" or conversely, "dykes" or "lesbians." Male homosexual informants who do not like women consistently use "gay kids" or "homosexuals" to refer *only* to men and use the term "lesbian" to refer to women. At the extreme, some individuals completely repudiate commonality with homosexual women:

EN: Why don't you like X (a lesbian?)
I: Because I don't like women, (or worse) "broads" (or even worse) fish."

The ratio of male homosexuals has been debated in the literature and among homosexuals themselves. Whatever the ratio may be between those of each sex who have engaged in homosexual *acts* or even who *define themselves* as homosexuals, there can be no doubt that men far outnumber the women *in gay life*. My impression over a two-year period was that men outnumber women by a ratio of at least four to one. The males considered as a group, have a much more elaborate subculture and contribute disproportionately to distinctively homosexual concepts, styles, and terminology. Although the women distinguish among themselves in roughly the way the men do as to overt–covert, masculine–feminine, race, age, and social class, they are not as intricately subdivided along one dimension: specialized subtype of sexual deviance. There are no feminine counterparts of the male SM queens, tearoom queens, chicken queens, park queens, brownie queens, butch hustlers, dinge queens, hormone queens, and so on.[12] This difference surely reflects the more restrictive conception and expression of sexuality that lesbians share with heterosexual women.[13]

Of course age, race, and social class distinctions are important in the homosexual community. Age sets are much more apparent among the men than the women. The men place an extreme value on youth. A person of thirty is considered old. Men over forty are seen as desexualized and are often referred to as "aunties." Aging is seen as a paramount and agonizing life problem. There is a definite tendency for primary and reference groups to be of similar age. The segregation is roughly by decades: "chickens" under twenty; the "young crowd," twenties; the older crowd, thirties; and "aunties," forty and over.

In Chicago, racial segregation among homosexuals is not enforced. There is a good deal of segregation based on residence, that is, there is said to be a distinct homosexual subcommunity in the black ghetto. It is apparently easy, however, for individual Negroes to cross this line and frequent bars, parties, and so on, in white residential areas; at least many of them do so. In Hyde Park, a residentially integrated area, the homosexual social groups of both men and women are integrated, as is the one gay bar. While I heard disparaging remarks about homosexuals who preferred Negro sex partners (dinge queens), social discrimination against Negroes is generally discouraged: "We can't afford that," or "We should know better," were typical replies to my questions about racial prejudice. In Kansas City, on the other hand, I seldom met a black homosexual, and I assume that they tend to be confined to the ghetto.

Finally, social class distinctions are important. As in the heterosexual world, one of the most important methods of "placing" any given individual, of hooking him into his place in the social structure, is his work. For instance, people with upper-status professions tend not to associate with minor clerical workers, who in turn tend not to associate with menial laborers.

That is to say, a person's social status is primarily based on his supposed or demonstrated social class membership in the straight world. This makes sense because gay life is not based on productive relationships: it has an economics but no economy. Strictly speaking, the gay world has no class system. Nevertheless, gay life has recognizable social strata that are accorded differential value. People speak about "high-class," "middle-class," and "low-class" bars, parties, clothes, and people. Social status is seen in the usual American way as personal attributes or life style, and the money that supports it.

Two differences in addition to the lack of an economy are worth noting. Both operate to telescope social class distinctions, particularly within the three major classes. Homosexuals are drawn from the full range of American social classes, but there are not enough homosexuals to recreate the whole complexity of the American system. So, for instance, while in the straight world the difference between a college professor and a high school teacher might seem major, in the male homosexual world it is relatively unimportant, and the two men might be in the same primary group. Second, there are no families in the gay world, and there is no class of persons classified as non-competing sexual objects (women). This makes for much less stability (or rigidity) in the social structure. My impression is that social networks more often extend across barriers that would be formidable in the straight world.

Homosexuals who belong to professions that include a relatively large number of homosexuals tend to form subgroups built on common membership in the profession. In Chicago there are whole occupational groups that are considered part of the gay world, such as the "hairburners" (hairdressers), the "window dressers," and subgroups built on some professional institution or business: "the Art Institute crowd," the "Marshall Field crowd," the "theatre crowd." These are exceptions, however. Most job-based and professional groups are explicitly or implicitly heterosexual, and the individual homosexual passes or accommodates as best he can. The other kind of exception is found among certain highly sophisticated urban occupational groups whose occupations form subcultures of their own, and where the members do not care about each other's sexual preferences: the art world, the theatre world, the fashion world, where homosexuals may sometimes participate openly *as* homosexuals.

The structure of the gay world is closely related to its flavor, quality, or style, which is nearly as distinctive as that of urban Negroes, and probably now more distinctive than that of urban Jews. To talk about homosexual style, it is necessary to bear in mind the broad distinctions among lower-, middle-, and upper-status homosexuals. These groups are different because their members are drawn from the lower, middle, and upper classes of heterosexual society. But they are also different because they each have distinctive life problems as homosexuals. Another way of looking at this is to say that the kinds of problems that are posed by being homosexual vary with social class.

Distinctive homosexual styles issue principally from the upper- and lower-status groups. The "uppers" seem to be composed mainly of men (and women) in the arts and related fields, including both commercial arts (acting, photography, advertising, fashion, etc.) and non-commercial or "pure" arts (painting, dancing, etc.). The uppers are in direct or indirect contact with the wealthy and sophisticated segments of the straight world, i.e., the upper and upper-middle classes; these gay uppers are the artistic and taste specialists for the rich. As a consequence, the rich, the sophisticated, and the cultural leaders are heavily influenced by the taste and ideas of the uppers, who in turn are themselves influenced. There is probably a lot of overlap; some homosexual uppers seem to be people from straight upper-class backgrounds who have become artists. The taste and style of the homosexual uppers is strenuously imitated by the middle- and to some extent lower-status groups. This is possible because social networks and interpersonal contacts are much more fluid than in the straight world. Another factor probably is the widespread belief that homosexuals are especially sensitive to matters of aesthetics and refinement. I know a good many homosexuals who admit that they knew nothing about "culture" until they became involved in the gay world, where such knowledge is valued and "pushed." A very widespread characteristic of the homosexual community is attempted assumption of upper patterns of speech, taste, dress, and furnishings – patterns that are not at all commensurate with income or status, as this is generally understood in the heterosexual world. It is found most intensely in the essentially lower-middle-class young men who were referred to by my informants as "ribbon clerks," those who were "paying for their Brooks Brothers suit on time."

At the other extreme are the low-status homosexuals who are socially avoided and morally despised by the middles and uppers, but who, in their flamboyant stylization and distinctive adaptations to extreme alienation, rival and even surpass the uppers. This applies especially to the low-status queens, who represent a role model of extraordinary coherence and power.[14]

While many of the lowers and uppers may be openly homosexual, the distinctive characteristic of the middles is the necessity to hide, to live a double life.[15] This limits their development of a public style.[16] Their private style, however, resembles the more open and expressive styles developed by the uppers and lowers. The common concern of the middles as a group is secrecy, recognition, and the conscious manipulation of roles that will allow them to maintain two quite separate and conflicting life spheres. Individuals in the middle-status group form the backbone of the homosexual audience for female impersonators. In the female impersonator show, the covert homosexual can see the homosexual identity acted out openly, and this he evidently regards with mixed proportions of disapproval, envy, and delight.

THE DEVIANT CAREER

Many studies of homosexuals and other communal deviants, such as prostitutes and criminals, have discussed the etiology of the individual deviant, but very few have attempted to describe or understand what happens to the deviant once he has joined the community of his peers. The social structure of the homosexual community can be described from the point of view of the individual as being what Merton calls a status-sequence:

Considered as changing in the course of time, the

succession of statuses occurring with sufficient frequency as to be socially patterned will be designated as a *status-sequence*, as in the case, for example, of the statuses successively occupied by a medical student, intern, resident, and independent medical practitioner.[17]

A related concept is that of the "deviant career" that postulates a culturally patterned status-sequence for individual deviants within the deviant community.[18] Of course, status-sequences within the homosexual community are much more flexible and open to variation than those in Merton's institutionalized and formalized example above, as are all non-institutionalized "career" patterns.

The status of female impersonator has two fundamental and inseparable parts, show business and homosexuality. Just as "blues singer" is a status in the context of black culture,[19] "female impersonator" is a status in the context of the gay world. This is simply to say that becoming a female impersonator is a status choice in the deviant career of the homosexual in the homosexual community, or that the status is one of those offered by the community. Every informant I questioned had entered the homosexual community and become in Lemert's terms, a "secondary deviant," that is, one whose identity is based on deviance, before becoming a female impersonator. I never heard of one for whom the status-sequence was reversed, who became a female impersonator and then a homosexual. This is not to deny that some female impersonators hold show business jobs before becoming impersonators, and in this sense the status can be seen as part of a show business career. But the peculiar skills involved in being a female impersonator were learned in the gay world, not in show business.

The first stage in the process of becoming a female impersonator is, therefore, the recognition of oneself as homosexual and entry into the homosexual community. Unfortunately, I wasn't able to get much detail about this part of the informants' past; the impersonators preferred not to talk about it. I had the general impression that for most this had been an intensely painful experience that they wanted to forget. No matter how hard I tried to make clear that my questions were not psychological, they

were interpreted and resisted as such. I saw and learned enough, however, to place female impersonators in a general framework of "entry" problems.

Some people sneak into the gay world; others burst in. At one polar extreme, the covert homosexual makes a precipitous distinction between his roles in the straight world and his roles in the gay world. The former typically include his working roles, and the professional and the social roles derived from work; his family roles, which can be with his parents and siblings, or even with a wife and children; and his social roles with friends who knew him before his entry into the gay world, i.e., his "straight friends." In addition to these more intimate situations, he preserves a "straight face" on things in any public situation. His participation in the gay world is kept completely separate from his public roles. The distinguishing mark of the covert homosexual is the double life, wherever the line may fall between the two worlds. But, most crucially, that line must fall between work and social life.

The overt homosexual, as an ideal type, withdraws from *any participation* in the straight world. All his contact with it (and some contact is unavoidable), is in the nature of *confrontation*. The extreme overt homosexual is unwilling or unable to present a heterosexual "front" to anyone at any time. His entire social life is conducted with other homosexuals and heterosexuals who "know." He does not participate in the "straight" working world, but rather finds some means of support that does not take him out of the gay world. This can mean being kept by another man, hustling, pushing narcotics, pimping, or it can mean a job in the gay world, such as bartending or waiting tables in a gay bar or restaurant, or female impersonation. A compromise position is to take a job that does not involve direct services to the gay world, but in which open homosexuality is tolerated, such as hairdressing or window-trimming. (A different solution is "passing," that is, participating in the working world as the other sex.) If the characteristic mark of the covert homosexual is the double life, that of the overt homosexual is the single fused identity marked by complete absorption into the gay world and constant confrontation with the straight one. Stage impersonators try to model themselves on the covert plan, while street impersonators are overt. The overt–covert distinction is directly related to a second polarity, that between "butch" and "nellie." These terms can be roughly translated as masculine (butch) and feminine (nellie). They are central to the expressive and social styles of the homosexual subculture.[20]

Here I am interested in butch and nellie styles as aspects of the management of personal front, in Goffman's terms. All homosexuals have personal styles that will be described by their fellows as either butch or nellie or some composite of the two. The nellie male homosexual and the butch lesbian who attempt to participate in the straight world must usually either counteract the information given by their styles (for instance by being married, divorced, or by talking conspicuously about relations with the opposite sex), or they must manage these deviant styles so as to suppress them in straight company, and express them only in the appropriate homosexual context. So, for instance, many covert male homosexuals attempt to present a butch front in straight situations, but become quite nellie in homosexual situations.[21] The covert homosexual hopes that he cannot be "spotted" in heterosexual social contexts, and one of the major elements of cover or "the mask" is the suppression of nellie style.[22] The overt homosexual, on the other hand, makes no attempt to cover his nellie style in public situations and may, on the contrary, positively flaunt and accentuate his nellie behavior as part of his confrontation with the straights.

All of this is basic to the situation of the proto-female impersonator who is just entering gay life. Obviously all homosexuals have faced the entry crisis somehow, and yet only a very few become female impersonators. But becoming a female impersonator seems often to evolve out of an entry experience that is shared by many, but by no means all homosexuals. This can be conveniently termed "the drag phase":

the point in some homosexuals' lives at which they go through a siege of intensely public and exhibitionistic behavior during which they flaunt strongly feminine types of behavior. Few homosexuals enter into an exclusive wearing of female clothing even for commercial purposes (impersonation or prostitution), but many homosexuals have had to manage a "drag" phase.[23]

For the basically covert homosexual, entry into the gay world means acquiring a second life that must be kept separate from the first. Outwardly, there may be very little change in his life patterns. Gradually his straight relationships may be attenuated, as he becomes more and more involved in and committed to gay life, but important working and family relationships may remain outwardly unchanged if he can hide his other life. On the other hand, the person who bursts into gay life by entering a public drag phase is risking or even inviting "social suicide." All pre-entry relationships, including familial ones, will be broken unless the heterosexuals can tolerate the change in a way that is acceptable to the new homosexual. In such cases it is frequently found that the new homosexual previously had weak ties in the heterosexual world.

There are two distinct types of entry (which in practice are not so cleanly defined): the process of becoming a covert homosexual, and the process of becoming an overt homosexual. The former is associated with the development of a double life, the cultivation of a butch public style that may or may not contrast with a "nellie" homosexual style, and continuity in pre-entry life situation. The latter is associated with total withdrawal from the butch styles necessary to participate in the "normal" world, and total immersion in the gay world built around a fused nellie style and identity.

My impression is that the proto-female impersonator almost always tends toward overt entry, and that the "social suicide" and nellie style are important pre-conditions to the assumption of the extremely deviant status of female impersonator. Every informant who told me how he got into female impersonation described himself as a person who (1) was already committed to and knowledgeable about the homosexual community, and (2) already had done "drag" as part of this commitment.

Being gay and doing drag are not the same. The relationship between homosexuality and sex role identification is complicated. The ability to impersonate women is not widely learned by males in American culture. Any serious (as opposed to farcical) attempt to impersonate the opposite sex is not part of the approved male (or female) role. However, the skills involved in female impersonation are widely known in the homosexual subculture and, in certain contexts, the use of these skills is subculturally approved. There are many opportunities for the male homosexual who is so inclined to "get in drag" in a social context. The most formal of these is the annual Halloween "drag ball," which is traditional in most large cities. Since the central event of most of these balls is a beauty contest, most of the participants make a serious attempt at impersonation through the use of "high drag," that is, very formal female attire and all that goes with it – high heels, elaborate hair-do (usually a wig), feminine make-up, and formal accessories, and, if possible, a male escort in formal men's evening wear. The Halloween balls are, moreover, not the only formal events that provide opportunities for drag. For instance, the homosexual community on Fire Island, New York, sponsors a drag ball and contest during the summer; some cities have New Year's balls as well.

There are also numerous parties given in the homosexual community at which guests are encouraged or at least permitted to wear drag. These may be private parties of small cliques or large relatively open parties. Depending on the context and the social group, this may range from "high drag" to simple clowning in a woman's hat and a little make-up. All of this can be done in the privacy of the home. The limiting condition on drag in public places is its illegality. Thus on Halloween, drag is legal as a masquerade, and in predominantly homosexual communities such as Cherry Grove (Fire Island), the police are not always stringent. But under any other conditions, the person who wants to wear drag must be able to pass for a woman on the street or else risk arrest. My own impression from having seen a great deal of amateur drag is that very few homosexuals can pass successfully. This stops people from wearing drag in public, and it limits going to homosexual parties and bars in drag because one has to pass through public places to get there. In spite of this, I have occasionally spotted men in full drag on city streets.

At the most informal level, a great deal of "camping" goes on wherever gay people congregate at parties, bars, and beaches, in which female identification of one sort of another is a large component. This is equivalent to saying that homosexual gatherings do not discourage, and frequently encourage, by means of an appreciative audience, the expression of this identification. Much of this "camping" is highly imaginative drag with few props:

In a small, racially mixed homosexual bar in Chicago, I saw a tall, thin Negro do a perfect imitation of a middle-aged Negro matron at a Gospel church to the accompaniment of a gospel-type song on the juke box. He was wearing slacks, a sports shirt, and no make-up or conspicuous jewelry. His only prop was a small but fantastic feathered hat, which had come into his hands while being passed around the bar. Using his bar stool as a base, he jumped up and down in time to the musical climaxes, waving his arms in the air, swooning, and shouting "Amen" and "Jesus loves me," until he had approximated "getting the spirit," which was indicated by flailing arms, rolled-back eyes, and twitching muscular movements. The crowd at the bar, and especially the Negroes, who presumably had had opportunity to witness this phenomenon in its original context, were convulsed with enthusiastic laughter, and shouted "Amen" back at the appropriate choral points to encourage him.

In a small homosexual bar in Chicago, I saw a young white homosexual do a burlesque imitation with no props at all. He was wearing light eye make-up, slacks, and a red and black ski sweater. He was sitting on a bar stool at the end of the bar when the band began to play a burlesque type song. He pulled his legs up onto the stool, so that his feet were resting on the seat and his knees were pulled up to his chest *underneath* the sweater and slightly apart. This created a strong suggestion of two large and pendulous breasts. By moving these "breasts" in time to the burlesque music, he imitated the unmistakable chest movements of a stripper. Those sitting around the bar laughed and clapped, encouraging the young man to greater efforts. The female impersonator sitting next to me said, "Watch what that queen [the young man] does. That is fine camp."

Now it is highly likely that many or most proto-female impersonators have worn female attire before they ever became involved in the homosexual community. It is logical to suppose that an underlying psychological conflict in sex role identification has been a major factor in pushing the proto-female impersonator toward the homosexual community (as it probably is a strong factor for many homosexuals), and that many of them will have acted out this conflict in private. But the point is that membership in the homosexual community *socializes* this conflict by providing it with a form and an audience. There is no communication between performer and audience without shared meanings. In fact *the* distinguishing characteristic of drag, as opposed to heterosexual transvestism, is its group character; *all* drag, whether formal, informal, or professional, has a theatrical structure and style. There is no drag without an actor and his audience, and there is no drag without drama (or theatricality). Men who become female impersonators have all, as far as I could determine, undergone this socialization of their deviance in the homosexual community *first*. In this context, the decision to become a female impersonator, whether tentative or abrupt, is simply a professionalization of an informally learned social skill.

By whatever particular route a young man (beginning drag queens are usually in their late teens or early twenties) takes his first steps in a drag career, he will always have learned the rudiments of female impersonation as it is understood to the homosexual community. The "drag phase" may be acted out in strictly homosexual settings, such as bars, parties, and balls. The support and encouragement of other homosexuals apparently figures strongly in the decision to try professional female impersonation. The experiments of the pre-professional drag phase not only give the opportunity simply "to try on drag for size," but to receive (or not receive; this is, after all, a selection process) the applause of various informal audiences. The drag queen looks in the mirror of the audience and sees his female image reflected back approvingly. It is through the process of group support and approval that the drag queen creates himself. The transformation culminates in the female impersonator's first job, where the approval of the mirror is ratified by the payment of cold, hard cash, an event of tremendous symbolic importance:

EN: Did you do any drag before you started working?

I: I did, back home . . . I used to go . . . there's one gay club in Covington, Kentucky. I did shows there. I did 'em just for my own self-satisfaction. At parties, I used to entertain, and like this. I went to one place in Cleveland. They had just this one-night affair, a big buffet supper. And this one kid from Dayton was gonna drive down and work there as a waiter or something and asked if I would be interested in going down, that they would pay me well. And I went down. I did three songs. They paid me seventy-five dollars and flew me back home. So I think . . . if you're that good, I certainly would call myself just as professional a performer as anyone else.

Some informants indicated that they had gone through a "street-fairy" phase as a prelude to professional female impersonation. Street fairies are the pariahs of the homosexual subculture. They are young homosexual men who do not work, who flaunt an aggressively nellie style in public (penciled eye-brows, facial make-up, long teased hair, fingernail polish, charm bracelets, exaggeratedly effeminate body postures, etc.). The distinguishing characteristics of the street fairy are (usually) his poverty and his public assumption of a modified drag style. Among his heroes, if he recognizes any, will be the professional drag queens, who, from his point of view, are street fairies who have "made it." The impersonators make money on a regular basis for "easy work," they can wear full drag legitimately and often, they have a guaranteed audience whose approval is symbolized by the cover charge or price of a drink, and they have a certain prestige and status.

The young street fairy who wants to work will begin by hanging around bars where drag is performed with the aim of "crashing" the drag queen set socially, meeting the management, and learning how to perform drag for a paying audience. It is through the bar or the established drag queens that he will get his first break. Somehow he must impress the manager sufficiently to get hired. If he can make friends with someone who already works in the show, this person may suggest that he be given a trial, the trial generally consisting of an audition during some slow night of the week. In some drag bars an entire evening may be given over to these auditions, which are often called "talent nights." In others, the regular show will feature guest spots, and these are more difficult because the neophyte must perform in direct comparison with the established professionals. Informants who spoke about their professional beginning generally stated that the manager had approached them, rather than the other way around:

> When I first started ... it started like, I used to go to this bar all the time. And business ... they were in a slump. And so, we used to dance around there a lot, and the manager came up ... 'course I knew him well 'cause I was in there a lot, he says, "Terry, how would you like to uh ..." He said he was thinking about putting in a show. I said, "Well, what kind of show?" He said, "Well, female impersonators. How would you like to be one?" I said, "Me?" And he said, "Yes." I said, "Well, I've never done it before," and at the time I wasn't working, and so I said, "Well, how much you going to pay me?" So he told me how much he was going to pay me. So I said, "You know I don't have anything to wear." He said, "I'll buy that."

In the first stages of a drag career, the commitment is often gradual or sporadic. The informal drag queen becomes a week-end or part-time drag queen:

> [The informant is explaining how he accumulated his drag wardrobe.] When I started, uh, here in Chicago, I had a couple of dresses that I used to use for parties back home, or I would entertain a lot. That's kind of how I got my start, got used to people watching me and so forth. [This is difficult for informant to get out. His voice is strained and embarrassed, but then plunges on, more confidently. He watches my reactions closely.] And I had these dresses, and I worked at the Back Cover on weekends, which is called the Microphone now. And I used to earn a little extra pennies, plus I was working my other job [clerical work]. And when I found that I liked doing it, and I had a possible chance of maybe doing this more often, I invested some money in some wardrobe and had it made up.

The story related by another informant contains a number of typical elements including a strong interest in show business and performing, prior socialization in the homosexual community, and a street phase:

EN: You say you've only been in drag about three and a half years. How'd you get started in it?
I: [informant is white]: Well, that's a long story.

Actually, what happened was, I was in L.A. and I was staying with this colored queen who wanted to work in drag. So we used to go around and try to get jobs, but you can't work in drag in L.A.
EN: Yeah, so I hear.
I: So I worked in some straight clubs in records, and I did things like Spike Jones and Sammy Davis, Jr., and things like that, at colored clubs in L.A. And then once in a while we would get brave, and put on drag and all this, you know, and do some wild drag numbers, but we never would announce it, so we'd just do like the one night, and that was it. And everybody knew who we were, so they would just go along with it. And have a ball. I had bought this wig. I still have it in fact, for I think thirty dollars or something like that, and it was a very natural looking wig, and I loved it. We used to go out in drag and everything ...
EN: On the street?
I: On the street, yes. Because that was in the colored areas, and they never bother you. You could walk around nude, and they probably wouldn't say anything. But I came to San Francisco, and I decided, well, I might as well work in drag, just to see what it was like.
EN: Had you been in theatre before, performing somehow?
I: Little bit of theatre, but never professional.
EN: What did you do before you –
I: I worked in offices, and I used to work in nightclubs on weekends. Emcee in rock and roll shows with people like—. On Halloween night, I emceed in drag.
EN: But still, as far as drag went, it was still pretty much amateur?
I: Oh, yeah. Until I got to San Francisco, and then it was even more so, even though I was getting paid for it.
EN: Well, how did you break into the business? There you are in San Francisco, and you decide, well, I'd like to try it out ...
I: I just went to a club, the 220 Club that had a record show, and I sat in the audience for four days and watched the show. I thought, "I can do better than that," and on the fifth day, I went in and I did.

NOTES

1 Alfred Kinsey, W. Pomeroy, C. Martin and P. Gebhard, *Sexual Behavior in the Human Female* (Philadelphia: Saunders, 1953): 69. The similarity here to American folk racial classification, whereby any person who is "Negro" to the slightest degree is black, and only "pure" whites are white is not coincidental. The "badness" of a sitgma can often be judged from its power of contamination.

2 David Sonensehein, "A Typology of Homosexual Relationships" (unpublished manuscript, 1966) and "The Ethnography of Male Homosexual Relationships" (paper read at the meetings of the Central States Anthropological Society, Chicago, Illinois, 1967). Maurice Leznoff and W. A. Westley, "The Homosexual Community," *Social Problems* 3 (1956): 257–63.

3 Gay life is rather like the early Christian Church: it exists wherever and whenever two gay people gather together.

4 The overt–covert dichotomy was made by Leznoff and Westley (*ibid.*). They found a strong correlation of covertness with high occupational status. Gay people recognize this correlation. Homosexuals who participate in gay life with extreme discretion are sometimes referred to as "closet queens" meaning that they are hiding. Readers of *Come Out!*, the newspaper of the radical Gay Liberation Front in New York, are urged to "come out of the closet."

5 Places such as Fire Island's Cherry Grove are not part of rural social systems, but are isolated vacation extensions of metropolitan culture.

6 Rechy's semifictional account, *City of Night* (New York: Grove Press, 1963) describes the situation of these young men.

7 This does not include the specifically Negro cores, which are located in Hyde Park and probably in the ghetto.

8 I do not mean to underestimate the emotional and symbolic power of the category. As a perception of commonality, it overrides *in the first instance*, distinctions of race, sex, class, generation, and even nationality. Homosexuals are much closer to constituting a political force today than they were in 1968. The younger generation of homosexuals have been politicized and are pushing for political unity within the framework of radical politics.

9 Edwin Lemert, "The Concept of Secondary Deviation," in *Human Deviance, Social Problems and Social Control*, 2nd ed. (Englewood Cliffs, N.J.: Prentice-Hall, 1972): 73.

10 Erving Goffman, *Stigma* (Englewood Cliffs, N.J.: Prentice-Hall, Inc., 1963). A number of politically militant homosexuals are now overt as a matter of principle, that is, they wear homosexual lapel buttons and/or verbally announce their homosexuality publicly. It is of interest that many of these people are not overt in the older sense; they don't look or act like homosexuals.

11 The widespread use of these juvenile nouns among homosexuals is certainly significant.

12 The noun "queen," denoting male homosexual (and connoting much more), admits of numerous imaginative modifiers. Many of these modifiers refer to sexual practices: SM = sado-masochist sex; tearoom = toilet (public) sex; chicken = young boy, therefore, chicken queen = likes sex with young boys; park queen = likes sex in parks; brownie queen = desires sexual intercourse through his anus; dinge queen = likes sex with Negroes; hormone queen = someone who takes female hormone shots or pills.

Some of these terms, such as SM queens and butch hustlers (male prostitutes who are masculine, as opposed to nellie hustlers), denote whole social subgroups, that is, a social commonality and distinct social roles have been built up around the common sexual role or interest. Other terms denote individual sexual preference, may have moral and value overtones, but do not provide the basis for distinct social roles or groupings, e.g., dinge queens, brownie queens. The few equivalent feminine distinctions are in this category, e.g., muff-diver = likes to perform cunnilingus.

13 William Simon and John Gagnon, "The Lesbians: A Preliminary Overview" (Unpublished manuscript, 1967).

14 The "queen" is the central homosexual role at every level, but has somewhat different content in each. Lower-status queens have been intensively fictionalized. See, for instance, "The Queen is Dead" (Hubert Selby, *Last Exit to Brooklyn* (New York, Grove Press, 1957): 23–81) and "Miss Destiny: The Fabulous Wedding" (Rechy 1963: 102–29). A good comparison can be made with Genet's French queens, especially "Devine" in *Our Lady of the Flowers* (1963).

15 There are probably many men who are uppers in respect to power and money whose need to hide is greater than that of the middles, in that they have more to lose. The case of Roy Jenkins during the Johnson administration shows that uppers who do need to hide may not participate, except very marginally, in the homosexual subculture. Ironically, this marginal participation is the most degrading and dangerous, from the point of view of capture by the police, blackmail, and so on.

16 Interestingly enough, even the public style of confessed middle-status homosexuals, such as the leaders of Mattachine Society, is very subdued and "straight." This may be because these organizations represent the middle-status respectables who want to make the "straights" believe that homosexuals differ from them only in the matter of sexual preference. To do this, they have to contradict the heterosexual perception (represented in stereotypical thinking) that homosexuals look and act very differently from straights.

17 Robert K. Merton, *Social Theory and Social Structure* (New York: Free Press, 1957): 370.

18 Lemert, "The Concept of Secondary Deviation": 50.

19 Recently the blues singing style has been "lifted" by young white singers, but many attributes of the status cannot be reproduced in the context of white youth culture. For a good discussion of the black blues singer, see Charles Keil, *The Urban Blues* (Chicago: University of Chicago Press, 1966).

20 Female homosexuals also make a distinction between "butch" and "fem" that is equally important to them. But, of course, the signs are reversed, since in contrast to the "butch" man, the "butch" lesbian is the more "deviant." Oddly enough, "butch" and "nellie" as applied to males can only be used as adjectives: "He is butch," but not "He is *a* butch" or "He is *a* nellie." This holds true even when the gender of the pronoun is reversed, as it often is in referring to male homosexuals. You cannot say "She is a nellie" (using "nellie" as a noun), although you can say "She is a queen" and be referring to a male. "Butch" and "fem" as applied to lesbians can be used as either adjectives or nouns, however: "She is fem (or butch)," or "She is *a* fem (or butch)." Male homosexuality, therefore, makes a linguistic distinction between expressive style "nellie" (adjective) and essential identity "queen" (noun), whereas female homosexuality makes "butch" cover both.

21 For the purposes of this discussion it is useful to equate butch front and style with socially acceptable masculine style. Homosexuals themselves often make this comparison by saying that the butch homosexuals are the ones who look and act like "normal" men. However, for distinctions within the homosexual community, butch becomes an element of style on a distinctively homosexual scale. Leather clothing, for example, is described as butch even though "leather queens" do not look like straight men.

22 Effective cover has its opposite problem, that one may not be identifiable as a homosexual even when one wants to be. At the extreme, one is thought to be straight even in homosexual contexts. At the least, one may sometimes want to make oneself known to another homosexual or suspected homosexual in a public situation. It is generally assumed that other homosexuals will pick up cues that heterosexuals will miss. Many homosexuals boast that they "can always spot one." However, in situations of ambiguous identity, homosexuals have developed extremely subtle and elaborate systems of recognition, which, however, are not sufficiently shared to be failure-proof. The process of sending out subtle cues or "feelers" is called "dropping the hairpin." (This phrase is also used when one has made an outright admission of homosexuality.) This expression is clearly related to "letting your hair down," which has connotations of both frankness and femininity.

23 Personal communication from William Simon and John Gagnon, 1965.

ALAN P. BELL AND MARTIN S. WEINBERG

"Homosexualities: A Concluding Overview and Epilogue"

from *Homosexualities: A Study of Diversity Among Men and Women* (New York: Simon & Schuster, 1978)

We are pleased at the extent to which the aims of our investigation of homosexual men and women have been realized. Homosexual adults are a remarkably diverse group. Seldom do we find the vast majority of a given sample responding to a particular question in exactly the same way. Whether they were reporting about an aspect of their sexual lives, their social adjustment or their emotional feelings, our respondents tended to say widely different things. This, of course, accounts for the many useful response distributions to be found in connection with almost every item. Needless to say, if we had not obtained samples from so many different sources, or if our respondents had been very similar demographically or only men or only women, the diversity of homosexual experience would not have been so evident. Again and again our data have demonstrated the need for specifying the race, sex, age, and sometimes educational or occupational level of homosexual adults before drawing any particular conclusions about them.

In addition, we were able to delineate our respondents beyond what their demographic characteristics would suggest. Initially based on differences in how they experienced and expressed their homosexuality, our typology proved to be more comprehensive. The types demonstrate important relationships between homosexual adults' sexually related behavior and feelings and their social and psychological adjustment. These relationships, evident in the more comprehensive typologies described below, make it clear that the sexual, social and psychological spheres of human life are inevitably related to each other, that experiences in one sphere frequently coincide with and influence

what occurs in another. An important lesson to be learned from our data is that homosexual men and women are best understood when they are seen as whole human beings, not just in terms of what they do sexually, despite the connection between sex and other aspects of their lives.

Another lesson our data provide is that future research in this area should attend increasingly to differences among homosexual adults. Researchers must be made keenly aware of the necessity to develop more precise typologies than the one in the present study, and for heterosexuals as well. These should refer not only to the sexual features of people's lives but also to the variety of contexts in which sexual feelings and impulses are expressed and to their social and psychological correlates.

Our data show that using a typology of homosexual experience helps to clarify whatever differences there might be between homosexual and heterosexual adults. In many instances a much greater amount of the variance was accounted for when the heterosexual group was compared with various types of homosexuals than when the comparisons involved simply the two undifferentiated groups. In some cases, if we had not distinguished one type of homosexual male or female from another and had not been able to compare each type with those in the heterosexual group, we would have concluded that homosexual men and women in general are quite different from their heterosexual counterparts, both socially and psychologically. In fact, however, the Close-Coupled homosexual men and women, similar perhaps to many of the married men and women in the heterosexual group, hardly differed at all from the heterosexual sample and in some cases actually appeared better adjusted; the same was true of the Functional homosexuals. Usually it was the Dysfunctional and Asexual homosexuals who differed from the heterosexual respondents, and often in much the same way that they differed from other homosexual respondents. There is no question but that the heterosexual population has its share of types equivalent to those found among homosexuals and that if we had been in a position to develop a corresponding heterosexual typology, we might have concluded that the chief difference between the two groups involves only the nature of their sexual preference.

Returning to the *raison d'être* of our study, it should be clear by now that we do not do justice to people's sexual orientation when we refer to it by a singular noun. There are "homosexualities" and there are "heterosexualities" each involving a variety of different interrelated dimensions. Before one can say very much about a person on the basis of his or her sexual orientation, one must make a comprehensive appraisal of the relationships among a host of features pertaining to the person's life and decide very little about him or her until a more complete and highly developed picture appears.

In what follows we present composite pictures of the types of homosexual men and women that emerged from our samples, involving their standings on the various measures of sexual experience and social and psychological adjustment. The descriptions are based on comparisons reported throughout this book and, in those instances where additional comparisons were made in order to determine differences between particular types (the Close-Coupleds versus the Functionals, the Dysfunctionals versus the Asexuals, etc.), on our multivariate analysis of variance. Each composite picture will include descriptions of some of the actual respondents assigned to the particular type. These descriptions are excerpts of "thumbnail sketches" prepared for each respondent by his or her interviewer, who, of course, did not know we would be "typing" the homosexual respondents.

CLOSE-COUPLEDS

We resisted the temptation to call this group "happily married," though some of its members described themselves that way, because we did not want to imply that heterosexual relationships and marriage in particular are standards by which to judge people's adjustment. Instead, we use the word "close" in two senses. First, the partners in this kind of relationship are closely bound together. Second, the partnership is closed in that the Close-Coupleds tend to look to each other rather than to outsiders for sexual and interpersonal satisfactions.

The ways in which the Close-Coupleds differ from respondents in other homosexual groups bear out this description. They were the least likely to seek partners outside their special relationship, had the smallest amount of sexual problems, and were unlikely to regret being homosexual. They tended to spend more evenings at home and less leisure time by themselves, and the men in this group seldom went to such popular cruising spots as bars or baths. Although the Close-Coupleds did not have the highest level of sexual activity, they reported more than most respondents, and their sexual lives were evidently gratifying to them. They were likely to have engaged in a wide variety of sexual techniques and tended not to report the kinds of problems that might arise from a lack of communication between partners.

The Close-Coupleds' superior adjustment is demonstrated in other aspects of their lives. The men in this group had rarely experienced difficulties related to their sexual orientation such as being arrested, trouble at work, or assault and robbery. They were less tense or paranoid and more exuberant than the average respondent. The Close-Coupled lesbians were the least likely of all the groups ever to have been concerned enough about a personal problem to have sought professional help for it. Both the men and the women were more self-accepting and less depressed or lonely than any of the others, and they were the happiest of all.

Our interviewers described some of the Close-Coupled respondents as follows:

There was an obvious warmth and caring between him and his roommate. Altogether I felt that he had his life in better order than the vast majority of people I've met.

Although he and his roommate do not think of themselves as husband and wife, there seemed to be some consistent division of roles. For example, his roommate does most of the cooking and serving, while he does more about keeping their finances in order. They seem to have a very good relationship. Although they did not display physical affection in my presence, they clearly like each other.

She was very friendly, interested, talkative, and open. I felt like I was a friend whom she was inviting in to share part of her life. I liked her paintings, her roommate's photographs of the Bay Area, and the warm togetherness of their home. She and her roommate were obviously very much in love. Like most people who have a good, stable, five-year relationship, they seemed comfortable together, sort of part of one another, able to joke, obviously fulfilled in their relationship. They work together, have the same times off from work, do most of their leisure activities together. She is helping her roommate to learn to paint, while her roommate is teaching her about photography. They sent me home with a plateful of cookies, a good symbolic gesture of the kind of welcome and warmth I felt in their home.

The apartment which he shares with his lover is very clearly "their" home. A lot of love went into fixing it up. Interestingly, when I asked him questions about his own siblings, he called in his roommate to help him out with the answers!

The room was filled with *their* things – paintings her roommate had done, their books and records, etc. The relationship seemed quite stable and satisfying to them both.

She lives in a nice modern home with her girl-friend, who is in real estate. They really have a loving, happy thing going together. Although she's had previous relationships, she says she's really happy for the first time.

I got the feeling that both were warm and loving people and had their heads together as to what they were doing and wanted.

The salience of a viable "coupled" relationship among our homosexual respondents is evident in comparisons between the Close-Coupled and the next group to be described, the Open-Coupleds. The latter are not as fully committed to their special partner, placing more reliance on a large circle of homosexual friends and less stress on the importance of their relationship with their partner. They are also less happy, self-accepting, and relaxed than the Close-Coupleds. These differences seem to suggest that the Open-Coupled relationship reflects a conflict between the ideal of fulfilled monogamy and dissatisfactions within the partnership.

OPEN-COUPLEDS

Like their Close-Coupled counterparts, the men and women in this group were living with a special sexual partner. They were not happy with their circumstances, however, and tended (despite spending a fair amount of time at home) to seek satisfactions with people outside their partnership. For example, the Open-Coupled men did more cruising than average, and the lesbians in this group cruised more than any of the other female respondents. Concomitantly, the Open-Coupleds worried about their cruising, especially about the possibility of being arrested or otherwise publicly exposed – perhaps because of their partner's ignorance of their cruising activities. In addition, the Open-Coupleds reported more sexual activity than the typical homosexual respondent and broader sexual repertoires, but the men tended to have trouble getting their partner to meet their sexual requests, and the women had the greatest worry about their partner wanting to do unwelcome sexual things or about being unable to carry on a conversation with her.

In most respects of their social and psychological adjustment, the Open-Coupleds could not be distinguished from the homosexual respondents as a whole. For example, they were not notable in how they spent their leisure time, how often they had experienced various social difficulties connected with homosexuality, or how many other people knew about their sexual orientation. Psychologically, they were about as happy, exuberant, depressed, tense, paranoid, or worrisome as the average homosexual respondent. However, the Open-Coupled lesbians were less self-accepting than any of the other groups.

He tries to give the appearance of happiness with his roommate but cruises continually, feels grave guilt about this, and says that it contributes to his domestic travail. He stopped me from introducing myself to his roommate, as if I were a pickup he wanted to keep secret.

At first he wanted his roommate to sit in on the interview but later acknowledged that he was glad I hadn't allowed this, since his roommate doesn't know he cruises.

He indicated that he has never had moral qualms about his homosexuality, but he is upset about his promiscuity.

As she talked, I discovered that her lover is very jealous and that she (the respondent) would like to date men and explore her own sexual orientation further, but that her lover was demanding a long-term commitment and she was not free to try out other relationships.

He is having a serious problem with his lover right now. The latter jumped off a third-floor porch on Christmas Day in an alcoholic stupor.

His partner is eleven years older than he and has begun slowing down sexually, which is a problem for them both. He has another friend with whom he's sexually compatible, but he doesn't want to end his present relationship. He appears troubled by this dilemma.

In discussing her current affair, she said that they had had sex twice and that she doesn't care to again and that she is not involved emotionally with her partner.

He was disappointed that he and his lover do not have sex anymore.

He said that he could not say whether he was in love with his roommate because he did not know what love really is.

It should be noted that the Open-Coupleds were the modal type among the males but relatively rare among the females, many more of whom were Close-Coupled. Whether lesbians find it easier than do homosexual males to achieve a stable and satisfying relationship with just one person, or whether they are more strongly motivated by romantic feelings than the men are, is not clear. However, our analysis of variance did show that the Open-Coupled males expressed more self-acceptance and less loneliness than the females did. This kind of relationship, then, is apparently more trying for the lesbian than for her male counterpart.

Compared with members of the other groups, the Open-Coupleds are intermediate in their adjustment. They went out more often and also spent more time alone than the Close-Coupleds did, and among the males, felt more lonely. On the other hand, the Open-Coupled males appear much better off than the Dysfunctional males do. The latter were less likely to have many homosexual friends or to value having a special partner, and the Open-Coupleds were significantly better adjusted psychologically, reporting more happiness and self-acceptance and less worry, paranoia, tension, or depression. Since the Open-Coupled lesbians did not differ from their Dysfunctional counterparts in these ways, it seems possible that managing a less than exclusive homosexual relationship is more difficult for women than for men.

FUNCTIONALS

If Close- and Open-Coupled respondents are in some respects like married heterosexuals, the Functionals come closest to the notion of "swinging singles." These men and women seem to organize their lives around their sexual experiences. They reported more sexual activity with a greater number of partners than did any of the other groups, and the Functional lesbians had been married more times than the rest of the female respondents. The Functional men and women were least likely to regret being homosexual, cruised frequently, and generally displayed a great deal of involvement in the gay world. They were not particularly interested in finding a special partner to settle down with, engaged in a wide variety of sexual activities, considered their sex appeal very high, and had few if any sexual problems. They were particularly unlikely to complain about not getting enough sex or difficulties in their sexual performance. Of all the groups, they were the most interested in sex, the most exuberant, and the most involved with their many friends. In addition, the Functional men had the fewest psychosomatic symptoms. They were also the most likely ever to have been arrested, booked, or convicted for a "homosexual" offense; this may be related to their greater overtness, their high attendance at gay bars, and perhaps as well their relative lack of worry or suspicion of others – or even a certain degree of recklessness.

> He lived in a very neat apartment. A music lover, he must have had close to a thousand blues and jazz records on the shelf. He also had three motorcycle trophies.

> He seemed very self-assured, and it was enjoyable interviewing him.

> He was a very energetic and open kid, looking much younger than twenty-seven. He seemed to be feeling very happy, likes his job in the Merchant Marine, and enjoys being back for just short stays. Although this militates against long-term relationships, he really enjoys his feelings of independence.

> Just a warm, lovely lady.

> She was friendly and completely comfortable during the interview. She had a very pleasant, lively personality.

> A very calm, well-adjusted "man's man" type. His social skills were most evident.

> He is a crusty but likeable old Yankee from Maine, a warm, friendly person who lives in a renovated Victorian house full of gay roomers. He has plenty of money and seems beautifully adjusted.

> He is a well-adjusted, confident, relaxed homosexual male: obvious but not flamboyant.

The Functionals' good adjustment seems to be a function of their particular personalities. They were energetic and self-reliant, cheerful and optimistic, and comfortable with their highly emphasized sexuality. One should not conclude, however, that Functionals are an ideal type as regards coping with a homosexual orientation. It is rather the Close-Coupled men and women who have made the best adjustment. For example, while the Functionals had few sexual problems and were not very depressed or unhappy, the Close-Coupleds surpass them in these respects. When the two groups are compared directly, we see that the Functionals understandably spend less time at home and see their friends more often, but the males are more tense, unhappy, and lonely than their Close-Coupled counterparts.

DYSFUNCTIONALS

The Dysfunctionals are the group in our sample which most closely accords with the stereotype of the tormented homosexual. They are troubled people whose lives offer them little gratification, and in fact they seem to have a great deal of difficulty managing their existence. Sexually, socially, and psychologically, wherever they could be distinguished from the homosexual respondents as a whole, the Dysfunctionals displayed poorer adjustment.

In terms of their sexual lives, the Dysfunctionals were the most regretful about their homosexuality. They reported more sexual problems than any other groups, and they were especially prone to worry about their sexual adequacy, how they could maintain affection for their partner, and whether they or their partner would attain orgasm. Despite fairly frequent cruising (among the males) and a relatively high number of partners, they tended to complain about not having sex often enough and were most likely of all the groups to report that they and their partner could not agree on what kind of sexual activity should take place. In addition, the men had trouble finding a suitable partner and were the most likely ever to have experienced impotence and premature ejaculation. Not surprisingly, with all these difficulties, the Dysfunctionals tended to think they were sexually unappealing.

Other aspects of the Dysfunctionals' lives were similarly problematic for them. Among the men in this group, there were more reports of robbery, assault, extortion, or job difficulties due to their being homosexual; they were also more likely ever to have been arrested, booked, or convicted regardless of the reason. The Dysfunctional lesbians were the least exuberant and the most likely to have needed long-term professional help for an emotional problem, and their male counterparts were more lonely, worrisome, paranoid, depressed, tense, and unhappy than any of the other men.

> He is a bookkeeper type, prim and a little stuffy, not a warm person. He lives alone with his ledgers.

> He has a languid, apathetic manner.

He seems to have an adolescent religious hang-up. I see his admission to being a "chicken queen" as a way for him to relive or act out his lost youth. He drives to the Tenderloin "meat rack," picks up young hustlers, drives them to Redwood City, and then pays them for sex.

He tends to project his own inadequacies onto others. For example, he claims that others are shallow and not desirous of lasting relationships, and yet he's had more than a thousand partners in the past two years.

He lives in an ugly, bleak two-room apartment, where he seems to devote most of his time to watching TV. He has no close friends, and those he has he seldom sees. All relationships seem casual and unimportant to him.

He wanted very much to be an Episcopal priest, but his moral conflict over his homosexuality stood in his way. He seemed very depressed and low in self-esteem.

I felt a horrible sense of resignation about him of surrender to a dead-end fate.

She seemed quiet, somewhat stiff, almost cold.

He says he enjoys drinking more than sex. He kept referring to his drinking when I asked a question about sex.

She seemed very well put together for someone with two psychotic breaks to her record.

Direct comparisons of the Dysfunctionals with other groups strengthen the impression of their general distress. The Dysfunctional men differ significantly from both the Functionals and the Open-Coupleds on virtually every measure of psychological adjustment. If we had numbered only Dysfunctionals among our respondents, we very likely would have had to conclude that homosexuals in general are conflict-ridden social misfits.

ASEXUALS

The most prominent characteristic of the Asexual men and women in our samples is their lack of involvement with others. They scored the lowest of all the groups in the level of their sexual activity, reported few partners, had narrow sexual repertoires, rated their sex appeal very low, and tended to have a fair number of sexual problems. In this regard, the Asexual males tended to mention trouble finding a partner and not having sex often enough, but they were also less interested in sex than the other men. The Asexuals were the least likely of all the groups to describe themselves as exclusively homosexual, and, among the males, they were less overt about their homosexuality and had fewer same-sex homosexual friends. Both the men and the women in this group tended to spend their leisure time alone and to have infrequent contact with their friends. They described themselves as lonely and (among the men) unhappy; the Asexual lesbians were most apt to have sought professional help concerning their sexual orientation but also to have given up counseling quickly, and they had the highest incidence of suicidal thoughts (not necessarily related to their homosexuality).

This woman now lives alone, has had no sexual experience with a partner in the past year, and seems never to have had any deep commitments to anyone. I can't imagine her really responding with warmth to any person or any need.

Quite subdued and reticent, he lives alone in his apartment with five cats. There are five different cat food bowls on the floor in the kitchen. One for each cat.

When the interview came to an end, he asked me why he had difficulty relating to people and why people didn't like him, exclaiming "I'm always clean, neat, polite, proper ..." He seems very lonely to me.

He seemed like a totally ineffectual, frightened, withdrawn sort of person. He was desperately shy and seemed very afraid of me for the first part of the interview. The house was a fantastic state of rubble, full of boxes of junk, files, and furniture. He explained them by saying simply, "I collect things."

He has to be one of the saddest, most forlorn human beings I've ever met. He said to me, "Here I've made it financially and professionally. I could travel anywhere or do anything, but why bother? I'm more lonesome away than I am at home, and I'm desperately lonesome at home." He has a big dog named Chipper who is very important in his life.

She says no one has ever loved her. Indubitable!

She was a bit cool and businesslike. Her difficulties with interpersonal relations were hinted at when she said she tends to be suspicious of people who are "too nice." When the interview was over she was pleasant, but it felt superficial.

He lives alone in a run-down Nob Hill apartment. He's over fifty years old and engages only in solitary masturbation with male fantasies. This has been the case for over four years.

He was a very soft-spoken and shy person. I couldn't imagine this short, timid little guy driving a big bus around the city.

The Asexual life-style is a solitary one. Despite their complaints of loneliness, Asexuals are not very interested in establishing a relationship with a special partner or in any of the rewards the gay world might offer them. For example, in addition to their lack of involvement with friends, the Asexual men seldom went to gay bars and did less cruising than any of the other groups except the Close-Coupleds When compared directly with the Dysfunctionals, the Asexuals differed from them chiefly in terms of their disengagement from others. Nevertheless, since the Asexuals of either sex did not differ from the sample as a whole in many respects of psychological adjustment or in the extent to which being homosexual had caused them difficulty, it seems reasonable to infer that these people's quiet, withdrawn lives are the inevitable product of an underlying apathy toward the panoply of human experience.

EPILOGUE

It would be unfortunate to conclude this study of homosexual men and women without making its meaning more explicit and urging serious attention by those for whom our findings have special import. Such persons include state legislators involved in debates over the decriminalization of homosexual conduct, community leaders addressing themselves to the matter of civil rights for gays, governmental and business executives charged with the responsibility of hiring and firing personnel, educators and lay people dealing with sex education, religious leaders who are reexamining their churches' sexual beliefs and values, counselors with homosexual clients, and, finally, homosexual men and women themselves.

Until now, almost without exception, people in general, as well as those above, have been outraged, fearful, or despairing toward homosexuality because of the stereotypes they hold. Not only have they believed that homosexuals are pretty much alike, but that this similarity necessarily involves irresponsible sexual conduct, a contribution to social decay, and, of course, psychological pain and maladjustment. Given such a stereotype, it is little wonder that the heterosexual majority has seen fit to discourage the acceptance of homosexuality by criminalizing homosexual behaviors and ferreting out people who engage in them, refusing to employ homosexuals, withholding from homosexual men and women the civil rights enjoyed by the majority and by a growing number of other minority groups, trying to cure homosexuals of their "aberration," and feeling grief or shame at the discovery that a loved one is "afflicted" by homosexual propensities. Reactions such as these to the millions of homosexual men and women in America and elsewhere are understandable in the light of common notions about what it means to be homosexual.

The present investigation, however, amply demonstrates that relatively few homosexual men and women conform to the hideous stereotype most people have of them. In addition, it is reasonable to suppose that objectionable sexual advances are far more apt to be made by a heterosexual (usually, by a man toward a woman) than a homosexual. In the same vein, seduction of an adolescent girl by a male teacher is probably more frequent than the seduction of young people by homosexual teachers, who are more apt to regard the class as a surrogate family than as a target for their sexual interests. And outside the classroom, the seduction of "innocents" far more likely involves an older male, often a relative, and a pre- or postpubescent female. Moreover, rape and sexual violence more frequently occur in a heterosexual than a homosexual context. Rape (outside of prisons) generally involves sexual attacks made by men upon women, while the relatively rare violence occurring in a homosexual context is usually the result of male youth "hunting queers" or a man's guilt and disgust over a sexual episode just concluded. Finally, with respect to homosexuals' sexual activity itself, as our study notes, it commonly begins with highly cautious pursuits in places not normally frequented by heterosexuals or in more public surroundings where heterosexuals are not aware of what is taking place. Most often it is consummated with the full consent of the persons involved and in the privacy of one of the partners' homes. Even this description, however, disregards the numerous instances in which homosexual contact occurs solely between persons whose commitment to each other includes sharing a household.

As for homosexuals' social and psychological adjustment, we have found that much depends upon the type of homosexual being considered. Many could very well serve as models of social comportment and psychological maturity. Most are indistinguishable from the heterosexual majority with respect to most of the non-sexual aspects of their lives, and whatever differences there are between homosexuals' and heterosexuals' social adjustment certainly do not reflect any malevolent influence on society on the part of the homosexuals concerned. Close-Coupleds and Open-Coupleds behave much like married heterosexuals. Functionals draw on a host of support systems and display joy and exuberance in their particular life-style. To be sure, Dysfunctionals and Asexuals have a difficult time of it, but there are certainly equivalent groups among heterosexuals. Clearly, a deviation from the sexual norms of our society does not inevitably entail a course of life with disastrous consequences. The homosexual who is afraid that he might end up a "dirty old man," desperately lonely, should be assured that such a plight is not inevitable and that, given our society's failure to meet the needs of aging people, heterosexuality hardly guarantees well-being in old age. Between the time of their "coming out" and whatever years remain, homosexual men and women must become increasingly aware of the array of options they have in their lives.

Perhaps the least ambiguous finding of our investigation is that homosexuality is not necessarily related to pathology. Thus, decisions about homosexual men and women, whether they have to do with employment or child custody or counseling, should never be made on the basis of sexual orientation alone. Moreover, it should be recognized that what has survival value in a heterosexual context may be destructive in a homosexual context, and vice versa. Life-enhancing mechanisms used by heterosexual men or women should not necessarily be used as the standard by which to judge the degree of homosexuals' adjustment. Even their personality characteristics must be appraised in the light of how functional they are in a setting that may be quite different from the dominant cultural milieu. It must also be remembered that even a particular type of homosexual is never entirely like others categorized in the same way, much less like those whose life-styles barely resemble his or her own. And while the present study has taken a step forward in its delineation of types of homosexuals, it too fails to capture the full diversity that must be understood if society is ever fully to respect, and ever to appreciate, the way in which individual homosexual men and women live their lives.

WILLIAM SIMON and JOHN H. GAGNON

"Homosexuality: The Formulation of a Sociological Perspective"

from *Journal of Health and Social Behavior* 8 (1967): 177–85

The study of homosexuality today, except for a few rare and relatively recent examples, suffers from two major defects: it is ruled by a simplistic and homogeneous view of the psychological and social contents of the category "homosexual," and at the same time it is nearly exclusively interested in the most difficult and least rewarding of all questions, that of etiology. While some small exceptions are allowed for adolescent homosexual experimentation, the person with a major to nearly exclusive sexual interest in persons of the same sex is perceived as belonging to a uniform category whose adult behavior is a necessary outcome and, in a sense, reenactment of certain early and determining experiences. This is the prevailing image of the homosexual and the substantive concern of the literature in psychiatry and psychology today.[1]

In addition to the fact that sexual contact with persons of the same sex, even if over the age of consent, is against the law in forty-nine of the fifty states, the homosexual labors under another burden that is commonly the lot of the deviant in any society.[2] The process of labeling and stigmatizing behavior not only facilitates the work of legal agencies in creating a bounded category of deviant actors such as the "normal burglar" and the "normal child molester" as suggested by Sudnow, but it also creates an image of large classes of deviant actors all operating from the same motivations and for the same etiological reasons.[3] The homosexual, like most significantly labeled persons (whether the label be positive or negative), has *all* of his acts interpreted through the framework of his homosexuality. Thus the creative activity of the playwright or painter who happens to be homosexual is interpreted in terms of his homosexu-

ality rather than in terms of the artistic rules and conventions of the particular art form in which he works. The plays of the dramatist are scanned for the Albertine Ploy and the painter's paintings for an excessive or deficient use of phallic imagery or vaginal teeth.

It is this nearly obsessive concern with the ultimate causes of adult conditions that has played a major role in structuring our concerns about beliefs and attitudes toward the homosexual. Whatever the specific elements that make up an etiological theory, the search for etiology has its own consequences for research methodology and the construction of theories about behavior. In the case of homosexuality, if one moves beyond those explanations of homosexual behavior that are rooted in constitutional or biological characteristics – that is, something in the genes or in the hormonal system – one is left with etiological explanations located in the structure of the family and its malfunctions.[4] The most compelling of these theories are grounded ultimately in Freudian psychology, where the roots of this as well as the rest of human character structure is to be found in the pathological relationships between parents and their children.[5]

As a consequence of our preliminary work and the work of others, such as Hooker, Reiss, Leznoff and Westley, Achilles, and Schofield,[6] we would like to propose some alternative considerations in terms of the complexity of the life cycle of the homosexual, the roles that mark various stages of this cycle, and the kinds of forces, both sexual and non-sexual that impinge on this individual actor. It is our current feeling that the problem of finding out how people become homosexual requires an adequate theory of how they become heterosexual; that is, one cannot explain homosexuality in one way and leave heterosexuality as a large residual category labeled "all other." Indeed, the explanation of homosexuality in this sense may await the explanation of the larger and more modal category of adjustment.

Further, from a sociological point of view, what the original causes were may not even be very important for the patterns of homosexuality observed in a society. Much as the medical student who comes to medicine for many reasons, and for whom the homogenous character of professional behavior arises from the experiences of medical school rather than from the root causes of his occupational choice, the patterns of adult homosexuality are consequent upon the social structures and values that surround the homosexual after he becomes, or conceives of himself as, homosexual rather than upon original and ultimate causes.[7]

What we are suggesting here is that we have allowed the homosexual's sexual object choice to dominate and control our imagery of him and have let this aspect of his total life experience appear to determine all his products, concerns, and activities. This prepossessing concern on the part of non-homosexuals with the purely sexual aspect of the homosexual's life is something we would not allow to occur if we were interested in the heterosexual. However, the mere presence of sexual deviation seems to give the sexual content of life an overwhelming significance. Homosexuals, moreover, vary profoundly in the degree to which their homosexual commitment and its facilitation becomes the organizing principle of their lives. Involved here is a complex outcome that is less likely to be explained by originating circumstances than by the consequences of the establishment of the commitment itself.

Even with the relatively recent shift in the normative framework available for considering homosexuality – that is, from a rhetoric of sin to a rhetoric of mental health – the preponderance of the sexual factor is evident. The change itself may have major significance in the way homosexual persons are dealt with; at the same time, however, the mental health rhetoric seems equally wide of the mark in understanding homosexuality. One advance, however, is that in place of a language of optimum man which characterized both the moral and the early mental health writings, we find a growing literature concerned with the psychological characteristics necessary for a person to survive in some manner within specific social systems and social situations.[8] In this post-Freudian world, major psychic wounds are increasingly viewed as par for the human condition and, as one major psychiatric theoretician observes, few survive the relationship with their parents without such wounding.[9] The problem becomes then, whether these wounds become exposed to social situations that render them either too costly to the individual or to the surrounding community. Accompanying this trend toward a reconceptualization of mental health has been a scaling-down of the goals set for men; instead of exceedingly vague and somewhat utopian goals, we tend to ask more pragmatic questions: Is the individual self-supporting? Does he manage to conduct his affairs without the intervention of the police or the growing number of mental health authorities? Does he have adequate sources of social support? A positively-balanced and adequately-developed repertoire for gratification? Has he learned to accept himself? These are questions we are learning to ask of nearly all men, but among the exceptions is found the homosexual. In practically all cases, the presence of homosexuality is seen as prima facie evidence of major psychopathology. When the heterosexual meets these minimal definitions of mental health, he is exculpated; the homosexual – no matter how good his adjustment in nonsexual areas of life – remains suspect.

Recent tabulations drawn from a group of 550 white males with extensive histories of homosexuality, interviewed outside institutions by Kinsey and his associates, suggest that most homosexuals cope fairly well, and even particularly well, when we consider the stigmatized and in fact criminal nature of their sexual interests.[10] Of this group, between 75 and 80 per cent reported having had no trouble with the police, the proportion varying by the exclusivity of their homosexual commitment and their educational attainment (see Table 6.1). Following this same pattern, trouble with their

Table 6.1 Reported incidence of social difficulties by education and exclusivity of homosexual commitment (%)

	High School		College	
	Exclusive homosexual	*Mixed homosexual and heterosexual*	*Exclusive homosexual*	*Mixed homosexual and heterosexual*
Trouble with:				
Police	31	22	24	17
Family of origin	25	16	19	11
Occupation	10	8	7	8
(N)	(83)	(83)	(283)	(101)

families of origin tended to occur in a joint relationship with level of education and degree of homosexual commitment, with the less educated and the more homosexual reporting a greater incidence of difficulties. Only about ten per cent of the group reported trouble at work and less than five per cent at school as a result of their homosexuality. Of those who had military experience, only one fifth reported difficulties in that milieu. In the military, possibly more than in civilian life, homosexuality is a difficulty that obliterates all other evaluations made of the person.

We do not wish to say that homosexual life does not contain a great potential for demoralization, despair, and self-hatred. To the contrary, as in most deviant careers, there remains the potential for a significant escalation of individual psychopathology. This potential is suggested by some other aspects of these same data. About one half of these males reported that 60 per cent or more of their sexual partners were persons with whom they had sex only one time. Between 10 and 20 per cent report that they often picked up their sexual partners in public terminals, and an even larger proportion reported similar contacts in other public or semipublic locations. Between a quarter and a third reported having been robbed by a sexual partner, with a larger proportion characteristically having exclusively homosexual histories. Finally, between 10 and 15 per cent reported having been blackmailed because of their homosexuality (see Table 6.2).

There were further indicators of alienation and difficulty in the findings. For two-fifths of

Table 6.2 Selected negative aspects of a homosexual career by education and exclusivity of homosexual commitment (%)

	High School		College	
	Exclusive homosexual	*Mixed homosexual and heterosexual*	*Exclusive homosexual*	*Mixed homosexual and heterosexual*
Proportion with 60% or more of sexual partners with whom had sex only once	49	43	51	45
Often pickup partners in public terminals	19	18	17	7
Ever been rolled	37	26	34	29
Ever been blackmailed	16	6	12	15
(N)	(83)	(83)	(283)	(101)

the respondents the longest homosexual affair lasted less than one year, and for about one quarter kissing occurred in one third or less of their sexual contacts. In addition, about 30 per cent reported never having had sex in their own homes. Accumulatively, such conditions add up to the two fifths of these men who indicated some serious feelings of regret about being homosexual, giving such reasons as fear of social disapproval or rejection, inability to experience a conventional family life, feelings of guilt or shame, or fear of potential trouble with the law. These figures require a more detailed analysis, and there are also uncertainties about sample bias that must be considered. However, it is our feeling that these proportions would not be substantially changed, given a more complete exploration of these factors. These data, then, suggest a depersonalized character, a driven or compulsive quality of the sexual activity of many homosexuals, which cannot be reckoned as anything but extremely costly to them.

Obviously, the satisfaction of a homosexual commitment – like most forms of deviance – makes social adjustment more problematic than it might be for members of a conventional population. What is important to understand is that consequences of these sexual practices are not necessarily direct functions of the nature of such practices. It is necessary to move away from an obsessive concern with the sexuality of the individual, and attempt to see the homosexual in terms of the broader attachments that he must make to live in the world around him. Like the heterosexual, the homosexual must come to terms with the problems that are attendant upon being a member of society: he must find a place to work, learn to live with or without his family, be involved or apathetic in political life, find a group of friends to talk to and live with, fill his leisure time usefully or frivolously, handle all of the common and uncommon problems of impulse control and personal gratification, and in some manner socialize his sexual interests.

There is a seldom-noticed diversity to be found in the life cycle of the homosexual, both in terms of solving general human problems and in terms of the particular characteristics of the life cycle itself. Not only are there as many ways of being homosexual as there are of being heterosexual, but the individual homosexual, in the course of his everyday life, encounters as many choices and as many crises as the heterosexual. It is much too easy to allow the label, once applied, to suggest that the complexities of role transition and identity crises are easily attributable to, or are a crucial exemplification of, some previously existing etiological defect.

An example of this is in the phase of homosexuality called "coming out," which is that point in time when there is self-recognition by the individual of his identity as a homosexual and the first major exploration of the homosexual community. At this point in time the removal of inhibiting doubts frequently releases a great deal of sexual energy. Sexual contacts during this period are often pursued nearly indiscriminately and with greater vigor than caution. This is very close to that period in the life of the heterosexual called the "honeymoon," when coitus is legitimate and is pursued with a substantial amount of energy. This high rate of marital coitus, however, declines as demands are made on the young couple to take their place in the framework of the larger social system. In these same terms, during the homosexual "honeymoon" many individuals begin to learn ways of acting out a homosexual object choice that involve homosexual gratification, but that are not necessarily directly sexual and do not involve the genitalia.

It is during this period that many homosexuals go through a crisis of femininity; that is, they "act out" in relatively public places in a somewhat effeminate manner; and some, in a transitory fashion, wear female clothing, known in the homosexual argot as "going in drag." During this period one of the major confirming aspects of masculinity – that is, non-sexual reinforcement by females of masculine status – has been abandoned, and it is not surprising that the very core of masculine identity should not be seriously questioned. This crisis is partially structured by the already existing homosexual culture in which persons already in the crisis stage become models for those who are newer to their homosexual commitment. A few males retain this pseudo-feminine commitment, a few others emerge masquerading as female prostitutes to males, and still others pursue careers as female impersonators. This adjustment might be more widely adapted if feminine behavior by men – except in sharply delimited occupational roles – was not negatively sanctioned. Thus the tendency is for this kind of behavior to be a transitional experiment for most homosexuals, an experiment that leaves vestiges of "camp" behavior, but traces more often expressive of the character of the cultural life of the homosexual community than of some overriding need of individual homosexuals. Since this period of personal disorganization and identity problems is at the same time highly visible to the broader community, this femininity is enlisted as evidence for theories of homosexuality that see, as a central component in its etiology, the failure of sexual identification. The homosexual at this point of his life cycle is more likely to be in psychotherapy, and this is often construed as evidence for a theory which is supported by a mis-sampling of the ways of being homosexual.

Another life cycle crisis that the homosexual shares with the heterosexual in this youth-oriented society is the crisis of aging. While American society places an inordinate positive emphasis on youth, the homosexual community, by and large, places a still greater emphasis on this fleeting characteristic. In general, the homosexual has fewer resources with which to meet this crisis. For the heterosexual there are his children whose careers assure a sense of the future and a wife whose sexual availability cushions the shock of declining sexual attractiveness. In addition, the crisis of aging comes later to the heterosexual, at an age when his sexual powers have declined and expectations concerning his sexuality are considerably lower. The management of aging by the homosexual is not well understood, but there are, at this point in his life, a series of behavioral manifestations (symptoms) attendant to this dramatic transition that are misread as global aspects of homosexuality. Here, as with "coming out," it is important to note that most homosexuals, even with fewer resources than their heterosexual counterparts, manage to weather the period with relative success.

A central concern underlying these options

and the management of a homosexual career is the presence and complexity of a homosexual community, which serves most simply for some persons as a sexual market place, but for others as the locus of friendships, opportunities, recreation, and expansion of the base of social life. Such a community is filled with both formal and informal institutions for meeting others and for following, to the degree the individual wants, a homosexual life style. Minimally, the community provides a source of social support, for it is one of the few places where the homosexual may get positive validation of his own self-image. Though the community often provides more feminine or "camp" behavior than some individuals might desire, in a major sense "camp" behavior may well be an expression of aggregate community characteristics without an equal commitment to this behavior on the part of its members. Further, "camp" behavior may also be seen as a form of interpersonal communication characteristic of intracommunity behavior and significantly altered for most during interaction with the larger society. The community serves as a way of mediating sexuality by providing a situation in which one can know and evaluate peers and, in a significant sense, convert sexual behavior into sexual conduct.[11] Insofar as the community provides these relationships for the individual homosexual, it allows for the dilution of sexual drives by providing social gratification in ways that are not directly sexual. Consequently, the homosexual with access to the community is more protected from impulsive sexual "acting out" than the homosexual who has only his own fear and knowledge of the society's prohibitions to mediate his sexual impulses.

It should be pointed out that in contrast to ethnic and occupational subcultures the homosexual community, as well as other deviant subcommunities, has very limited content.[12] This derives from the fact that the community members often have only their sexual commitment in common. Thus, while the community may reduce the problems of access to sexual partners and reduce guilt by providing a structure of shared values, often the shared value structure is far too narrow to transcend other areas of value disagreement. The college-trained professional and the bus boy, the WASP and the Negro slum dweller, may meet in sexual congress, but the similarity of their sexual interests does not eliminate larger social and cultural barriers.[13] The important fact is that the homosexual community is in itself an impoverished cultural unit. This impoverishment, however, may be only partially limiting, since it constrains most members to participate in it on a limited basis, reducing their anxiety and conflicts in the sexual sphere and increasing the quality of their performance in other aspects of social life.

Earlier we briefly listed some of the general problems that the homosexual – in common with the heterosexual – must face; these included earning a living, maintaining a residence, relations with family, and so on. At this point we might consider some of these in greater detail.

First there is the most basic problem of all: earning a living. Initially, the variables that apply to all labor force participants generally apply to homosexuals also. In addition there are the special conditions imposed by the deviant definition of the homosexual commitment. What is important is that the occupational activity of homosexuals represents a fairly broad range. The differences in occupational activity can be conceptualized along a number of dimensions, some of which would be conventional concerns of occupational sociology, while others would reflect the special situation of the homosexual. For example, one element is the degree of occupational involvement, that is, the degree to which occupational activity, or activity ancillary to it, is defined as intrinsically gratifying. This would obviously vary from professional to ribbon clerk to factory laborer. A corollary to this is the degree to which the world of work penetrates other aspects of life. In terms of influence upon a homosexual career, occupational involvement very likely plays a constraining role during the acting-out phase associated with "coming out" as well as serving as an alternative source of investment during the "crisis of aging." Another aspect bears directly upon the issue of the consequences of having one's deviant commitment exposed. For some

occupational roles disclosure would clearly be a disaster – the school teacher, the minister, and the politician, to mention just three. There are other occupations where the disclosure or assumption of homosexual interests is either of little consequence or – though relatively rare – has a positive consequence. It should be evident that the crucial question of anxiety and depersonalization in the conduct of sexual activity can be linked to this variable in a rather direct way.

A second series of questions could deal with the effects of a deviant sexual commitment upon occupational activity itself. In some cases the effect may be extremely negative, since the pursuit of homosexual interests may generate irresponsibility and irregularity. Some part of this might flow from what we associate with bachelorhood generally: detachment from conventional families and, in terms of sex, constant striving for what is essentially regularized in marriage. Illustrations of these behaviors include too many late nights out, too much drinking in too many taverns, and unevenness in emotional condition. On the other hand, several positive effects can be observed. Detachment from the demands of domestic life not only frees one for greater dedication to the pursuit of sexual goals, but also for greater dedication to work. Also, the ability of some jobs to facilitate homosexual activity – such as certain marginal, low-paying, white-collar jobs – serves as compensation for low pay or limited opportunity for advancement. There may be few simple or consistent patterns emerging from this type of consideration, yet the overdetermination of the sexual element in the study of the homosexual rests in our prior reluctance to consider these questions which are both complex and pedestrian.

Similarly, just as most homosexuals have to earn a living, so must they come to terms with their immediate families. There is no substantial evidence to suggest that the proportion of homosexuals for whom relatives are significant persons differs from that of heterosexuals. The important differences rest in the way the relationships are managed and, again, the consequences they have for other aspects of life. Here also one could expect considerable variation containing patterns of rejection, continuing involvement without knowledge, ritualistically suppressed knowledge, and knowledge and acceptance. This becomes more complex because several patterns may be operative at the same time with different members of one's family constellation. Here again it is not unreasonable to assume a considerable degree of variation in the course of managing a homosexual commitment as this kind of factor varies. Yet the literature is almost totally without reference to this relationship. Curiously, in the psychiatric literature – where mother and father play crucial roles in the formation of a homosexual commitment – they tend to be significant by their absence in considerations of how homosexual careers are managed.

This order of discussion could be extended into a large number of areas. Let us consider just one more: religion. As a variable, religion (as both an identification and a quality of religiosity) manifests no indication that it plays an important role in the generation of homosexual commitments. However, it clearly does, or can, play a significant role in the management of that commitment. Here, as in other spheres of life, we must be prepared to deal with complex, interactive relations rather than fixed, static ones. Crucial to the homosexual's ability to "accept himself" is his ability to bring his own homosexuality within a sense of the moral order as it is projected by the institutions surrounding him as well as his own vision of this order. It may be that the issue of including homosexuality within a religious definition is the way the question should be framed only part of the time, and for only part of a homosexual population. At other times and for other homosexuals, to frame the question in terms of bringing religiosity within the homosexual definition might be more appropriate. The need for damnation (that rare sense of being genuinely evil) and the need for redemption (a sense of potentially being returned to the community in good standing) can be expected to vary, given different stages of the life cycle, different styles of being homosexual, and varying environments for enactment of the homosexual commitment. And our sense of the relation suggests that, more than asking about the homosexual's reli-

gious orientation and how it expresses his homosexuality, we must also learn to ask how his homosexuality expresses his commitment to the religious.

The aims, then, of a sociological approach to homosexuality are to begin to define the factors – both individual and situational – that predispose a homosexual to follow one homosexual path as against others; to spell out the contingencies that will shape the career that has been embarked upon; and to trace out the patterns of living in both their pedestrian and their seemingly exotic aspects. Only then will we begin to understand the homosexual. This pursuit must inevitably bring us – though from a particular angle – to those complex matrices wherein most human behavior is fashioned.

NOTES

1 Irving Bieber et al., *Homosexuality, A Psychoanalytic Study* (New York: Basic Books, 1962).
2 Sex law reform occurred in the State of Illinois as part of a general reform of the criminal code in 1961. For the manner in which the law's reform was translated for police officials, see Claude Sowle, *A Concise Explanation of the Illinois Criminal Code of 1961* (Chicago: B. Smith, 1961).
3 David Sudnow, "Normal Crimes," *Social Problems* 12 (Winter 1965): 255–76.
4 A. C. Kinsey, "Criteria for the Hormonal Explanation of the Homosexual," *The Journal of Clinical Endocrinology* 1 (May 1941): 424–8; F. J. Kallman, "Comparative Twin Study on the Genetic Aspects of Male Homosexuality," *Journal of Nervous and Mental Disorders* 115 (1952): 283–98; F. J. Kallman, "Genetic Aspects of Sex Determination and Sexual Maturation Potentials in Man," in George Winokur (ed.), *Determinants of Human Sexual Behavior* (Springfield: Charles C. Thomas, 1963): 5–18; and John Money, "Factors in the Genesis of Homosexuality," in George Winokur (ed.), *Determinants of Human Sexual Behavior* (Springfield: Charles C. Thomas 1963): 19–43.
5 The work of Bieber *op. cit.*, is the most recent of these analytic explorations, the central finding of which is that in a highly selected group of male homosexuals there was a larger proportion of males who had mothers who could be described as close-binding and intimate and fathers who were detached and hostile. The argument proceeds that the mother has selected this child for special overprotection and seductive care. In the

process of childrearing, sexual interest is both elicited and then blocked by punishing its behavioral manifestations. As a result of the mother's special ties to the child, the father is alienated from familiar interaction, is hostile to the child, and fails to become a source of masculine attachment.

Regardless of the rather engaging and persuasive character of the theory, there are substantial complications. It assumes that there is a necessary relationship between the development of masculinity and femininity and heterosexuality and homosexuality. There is the assumption that homosexuals play sexual roles that are explicitly modeled upon those of the heterosexual and that these roles are well-defined and widespread. This confusion of the dimensions of sexual object choice and masculinity and femininity is based on two complementary errors. The first is that the very physical sexual activities of the homosexual are often characterized as passive (to be read feminine) or active (to be read masculine) and that these physical activities are read as direct homologues of the complex matters of masculinity and femininity. The second source of the confusion lies in the two situations in which homosexuality can be most easily observed. One is the prison, where the characteristics of homosexuality do tend to model themselves more closely on the patterns of heterosexuality in the outside community, but where the sources and the character of behavior are in the service of different ends. The second situation is that of public homosexuality characterized by the flaunted female gesture which has become stereotypic of homosexuality. This is not to say that such beliefs about the nature of homosexuality on the part of the heterosexual majority do not influence the homosexual's behavior; however, just because stereotypes are held does not mean that they play a role in the etiology of the behavior that they purport to explain.

Another major problem that exists for etiological theories of homosexuality based on family structure is the difficulty one finds in all theories that depend on the individual's memories of his childhood and that call upon him for hearsay evidence not only about himself, but about his parents. We live in a post-Freudian world and the vocabulary of motives of the most psychologically illiterate is replete with the concepts of repression, inhibition, the oedipus complex, and castration fears. The rhetoric of psychoanalysis permeates the culture as a result of a process that might best be called the democratization of mental health. One of the lessons of existentialism is that our biographies are not fixed quantities but are subject to revision, elision, and other forms of subtle editing based on our place in the life cycle, our audience, and the mask that we are currently wearing. Indeed, for many persons the rehearsed past and the real past become so intermixed that there is only the present. Recent research in childrearing practices suggests that two years after the major events of childrearing, weaning and toilet training mothers fail to recall accurately their previous conduct and hence sound a good deal like Dr. Spock. An important footnote here is that persons do not always edit the past to improve their image in the conventional sense. Often the patient in psychotherapy works very hard to bring out more and more self-denigrating materials to assure the therapist that he, the patient, is really working hard and searching for his true motives.

6 Evelyn Hooker, "The Homosexual Community," James C. Palmer and Michael J. Goldstein (eds), *Perspectives in Psychopathology* (New York: Oxford University Press, 1966) 354–64; Albert J. Reiss, "The Social Integration of Queers and Peers," *Social Problems* 9 (Fall 1961) 102–20; M. Leznoff and W. A. Westley, "The Homosexual Community," *Social Problems* 3 (April 1956): 257–63; N. Achilles, "The Development of the Homosexual Bar as an Institution," in J. H. Gagnon and W. Simon (eds) *Sexual Deviance* (New York: Harper and Row, 1967); and Michael Schofield, *Sociological Aspects of Homosexuals* (Boston: Little Brown, 1965).

7 Howard S. Becker, "Change in Adult Life," *Sociometry* 27 (March 1964), 40–53; Howard S. Becker, Blanche Geer and Everett C. Hughes, *Boys in White: Student Culture in the Medical School* (Chicago: University of Chicago Press, 1961).

8 Marie Jahoda, "Toward a Social Psychology of Mental Health," in Arnold M. Rose (ed.), *Mental Health and Mental Disorder* (New York: Norton, 1955): 556–77; F. C. Redlich, "The Concept of Health in Psychiatry," in A. H. Leighton, J. A. Clausen and R. N. Wilson, *Explorations in Social Psychiatry* (New York: Basic Books, 1957): 138–64.

9 Lawrence Kubie, "Social Forces and the Neurotic Process," in A. H. Leighton, J. A. Clausen and R. N. Wilson, *Explorations in Social Psychiatry* (New York: Basic Books, 1957), pp. 77–104.

10 Extensive homosexuality is here defined as a minimum of 51 or more times and/or contact with 21 or more males.

11 Ernest W. Burgess makes this useful distinction in his article, "The Sociologic Theory of Psychosexual Behavior," in Paul H. Hoch and Joseph Zubin (eds), *Psychosexual Development in Health and Disease* (New York: Grune and Stratton, 1949): 227–43. Burgess says, "Accurately speaking the various forms of sexual outlet for man are not behavior, they are con-

duct. Conduct is behavior as prescribed or evaluated by the group. It is not simply external observable behavior, but behavior that expresses a norm or evaluation."

12 For descriptions of the content of other deviant subcultures see Harold Finestone, "Cats Kicks and Color," *Social Problems* 5 (July 1957) 3–13; Howard S. Becker, *The Outsiders* (New York: The Free Press, 1963); James H. Bryan, "Apprenticeships in Prostitution," *Social Problems* 12 (Winter 1965): 278–97.

13 The homosexual community does provide for an easing of strain by training essentially lower-class types in middle-class lifestyles and even middle-class occupational roles to a greater extent than most people realize. In contrast, for those for whom homosexuality becomes the salient organizing experience of their lives there may be a concomitant downward mobility as their ties with commitments to systems of roles that are larger than the homosexual community decrease.

MARY McINTOSH

"The Homosexual Role"

from *Social Problems* 16 (Fall 1968): 182–92

Recent advances in the sociology of deviant behavior have not yet affected the study of homosexuality, which is still commonly seen as a condition characterizing certain persons in the way that birthplace or deformity might characterize them. The limitations of this view can best be understood if we examine some of its implications. In the first place, if homosexuality is a condition, then people either have it or do not have it. Many scientists and ordinary people assume that there are two kinds of people in the world: homosexuals and heterosexuals. Some of them recognize that homosexual feelings and behavior are not confined to the persons they would like to call "homosexuals" and that some of these persons do not actually engage in homosexual behavior. This should pose a crucial problem, but they evade a crux by retaining their assumption and puzzling over the question of how to tell whether someone is "really" homosexual or not. Lay people too will discuss whether a certain person is "queer" in much the same way as they might question whether a certain pain indicated cancer. And in much the same way they will often turn to scientists or to medical men for a surer diagnosis. Thus one psychiatrist, discussing the definition of homosexuality, has written:

> I do not diagnose patients as homosexual unless they have engaged in overt homosexual behavior. Those who also engage in heterosexual activity are diagnosed as bisexual. An isolated experience may not warrant the diagnosis, but repetetive [*sic*] homosexual behavior in adulthood, whether sporadic or continuous, designates a homosexual.[1]

Along with many other writers, he introduces the notion of a third type of person, the "bisexual," to handle the fact that behavior patterns cannot be conveniently dichotomized into heterosexual and homosexual. But this does not solve the conceptual problem, since bisexuality too is seen as a condition (unless as a passing response to unusual situations such as confinement in a one-sex prison). In any case there is no extended discussion of bisexuality; the topic is usually given a brief mention in order to clear the ground for the consideration of "true homosexuality."

To cover the cases where the symptoms of behavior or of felt attractions do not match the diagnosis, other writers have referred to an adolescent homosexual phase or have used such terms at "latent homosexual" or "pseudo homosexual." Indeed one of the earliest studies of the subject, by Krafft-Ebing,[2] was concerned with making a distinction between the "invert" who is congenitally homosexual and others who, although they behave in the same way, are not true inverts.

A second result of the conceptualization of homosexuality as a condition is that the major research task has been seen as the study of its aetiology. There has been much debate as to whether the condition is innate or acquired. The first step in such research has commonly been to find a sample of "homosexuals" in the same way that a medical researcher might find a sample of diabetics if he wanted to study that disease. Yet after a long history of such studies, the results are sadly inconclusive, and the answer is still as much a matter of opinion as it was when Havelock Ellis's *Sexual Inversion* was published seventy years ago. The failure of research to answer the question has not been due to lack of scientific rigour or to any inadequacy of the available evidence; it results rather from the fact that the wrong question has been asked. One might as well try to trace the aetiology of "committee chairmanship" or "Seventh Day Adventism" as of "homosexuality."

The vantage point of comparative sociology enables us to see that the conception of homosexuality as a condition is, in itself, a possible object of study. This conception and the behavior it supports operate as a form of social control in a society in which homosexuality is condemned. Furthermore the uncritical acceptance of the conception by social scientists can be traced to their concern with homosexuality as a social problem. They have tended to accept the popular definition of what the problem is, and they have been implicated in the process of social control.

The practice of the social labeling of persons as deviant operates in two ways as a mechanism of social control.[3] In the first place it helps to provide a clear-cut, publicized and recognizable threshold between permissible and impermissible behavior. This means that people cannot so easily drift into deviant behavior. Their first moves in a deviant direction immediately raise the question of a total move into a deviant role with all the sanctions that this is likely to elicit. Second, the labeling serves to segregate the deviants from others, and this means that their deviant practices and their self-justifications for these practices are contained within a relatively narrow group. The creation of a specialized, despised and punished role of homosexual keeps the bulk of society pure in rather the same way that the similar treatment of some kinds of criminals helps keep the rest of society law-abiding.

However, the disadvantage of this practice as a technique of social control is that there may be a tendency for people to become fixed in their deviance once they have become labeled. This too is a process that has become well-recognized in discussion of other forms of deviant behavior, such as juvenile delinquency and drug taking, and indeed of other kinds of social labeling, such as streaming in schools and racial distinctions. One might expect social categorizations of this sort to be to some extent self-fulfilling prophecies: if the culture defines

people as falling into distinct types – black and white, criminal and non-criminal, homosexual and normal – then these types tend to become polarized, highly differentiated from each other. Later in this paper I shall discuss whether this is so in the case of homosexuals and "normals" in the United States today.

It is interesting to notice that homosexuals themselves welcome and suppose the notion that homosexuality is a condition. For just as the rigid categorization deters people from drifting into deviancy, so it appears to foreclose on the possibility of drifting back into normality and thus removes the element of anxious choice. It appears to justify the deviant behavior of the homosexual as being appropriate for him as a member of the homosexual category. The deviancy can thus be seen as legitimate for him and he can continue in it without rejecting the norms of the society.[4]

The way in which people become labeled as homosexual can now be seen as an important social process connected with mechanisms of social control. It is important therefore that sociologists should examine this process objectively and not lend themselves to participation in it, particularly since, as we have seen, psychologists and psychiatrists on the whole have not retained their objectivity but have become involved as diagnostic agents in the process of social labeling.[5]

It is proposed that the homosexual should be seen as playing a social role rather than as having a condition. The role of "homosexual," however, does not simply describe a sexual behavior pattern. If it did, the idea of a role would be no more useful than that of a condition. For the purpose of introducing the term "role" is to enable us to handle the fact that behavior in this sphere does not match popular beliefs: that sexual behavior patterns cannot be dichotomized in the way that the social roles of homosexual and heterosexual can.

It may seem rather odd to distinguish in this way between role and behavior, but if we accept a definition of role in terms of expectations (which may or may not be fulfilled), then the distinction is both legitimate and useful. In modern societies where a separate homosexual role is recognized, the expectation, on behalf of those who play the role and of others, is that a homosexual will be exclusively or very predominantly homosexual in his feelings and behavior. In addition there are other expectations that frequently exist, especially on the part of non-homosexuals, but affecting the self-conception of anyone who sees himself as homosexual. These are the expectation that he will be effeminate in manner, personality, or preferred sexual activity, the expectation that sexuality will play a part of some kind in all his relations with other men, and the expectation that he will be attracted to boys and very young men and probably willing to seduce them. The existence of a social expectation, of course, commonly helps to produce its own fulfillment. But the question of how far it is fulfilled is a matter for empirical investigation rather than *a priori* pronouncement. Some of the empirical evidence about the chief expectation – that homosexuality precludes heterosexuality – in relation to the homosexual role in America is examined in the final section of this paper.[6]

In order to clarify the nature of the role and demonstrate that it exists only in certain societies, we shall present the cross-cultural and historical evidence available. This raises awkward problems of method because the material has hitherto usually been collected and analyzed in terms of culturally specific modern Western conceptions.

THE HOMOSEXUAL ROLE IN VARIOUS SOCIETIES

To study homosexuality in the past or in other societies we usually have to rely on secondary evidence rather than on direct observation. The reliability and the validity of such evidence is open to question because what the original observers reported may have been distorted by their disapproval of homosexuality and by their definition of it, which may be different from the one we wish to adopt.

For example, Marc Daniel[7] tries to refute accusations of homosexuality against Pope Julian II by producing four arguments: the Pope had many enemies who might wish to blacken his name; he and his supposed lover, Alidosi, both had mistresses; neither of them was at all effeminate; and the Pope had other men friends about whom no similar accusations were made. In other words Daniel is trying to fit an early sixteenth-century pope to the modern conception of the homosexual as effeminate, exclusively homosexual and sexual in relation to all men. The fact that he does not fit is, of course, no evidence, as Daniel would have it, that his relationship with Alidosi was not a sexual one.

Anthropologists too can fall into this trap. Marvin Opler, summarizing anthropological evidence on the subject, says:

> Actually, no society, save perhaps ancient Greece, pre-Meiji Japan, certain top echelons in Nazi Germany, and the scattered examples of such special status groups as the *berdaches*, Nata slaves and one category of Chuckchee shamans, has lent sanction in any real sense to homosexuality.[8]

Yet he goes on to discuss societies in which there are reports of sanctioned adolescent and other occasional "experimentation." Of the Cubeo of the North West Amazon, for instance, he says "*true* homosexuality among the Cubeo is rare if not absent," giving as evidence the fact that no males with persistent homosexual patterns are reported.[9]

Allowing for such weaknesses, the Human Relations Area Files are the best single source of comparative information. Their evidence on homosexuality has been summarized by Ford and Beach,[10] who identify two broad types of accepted patterns: the institutionalized homosexual role and the liaison between men and boys who are otherwise heterosexual. The recognition of a distinct role of *berdache* or transvestite is, they says, "the commonest form of institutionalized homosexuality." This form shows a marked similarity to that in our own society, though in some ways it is even more extreme. The Mojave Indians of California and Arizona, for example, recognized both an *alyha*, a male transvestite who took the role of the woman in sexual intercourse, and a *hwame*, a female homosexual who took the role of the male.[11] People were believed to be born as *alyha* or *hwame*, hints of their future proclivities occurring in their mothers' dreams during pregnancy. If a young boy began to behave like a girl and take an interest in women's things instead of men's, there was an initiation ceremony in which he would become an *alyha*. After that he would dress and act like a woman, would be referred to as "she" and could take "husbands."

But the Mojave pattern differs from ours in that, although the *alyha* was considered regrettable and amusing, he was not condemned and was given public recognition. The attitude was the "he was an *alyha*, he could not help it." But the "husband" of an *alyha* was an ordinary man who happened to have chosen an *alyha*, perhaps because they were good housekeepers or because they were believed to be "lucky in love," and he would be the butt of endless teasing and joking.

This radical distinction between the feminine, passive homosexual and his masculine, active partner is one which is not made very much in our own society,[12] but which is very important in the Middle East. There, however, neither is thought of as being a "born" homosexual, although the passive partner, who demeans himself by his feminine submission, is despised and ridiculed while the active one is not. In most of the ancient Middle East, including among the Jews until the return from the Babylonian exile, there were male temple prostitutes.[13] Thus even cultures that recognize a separate homosexual role may not define it in the same way as our culture does.

Many other societies accept or approve of homosexual liaisons as part of a variegated sexual pattern. Usually these are confined to a particular stage in the individual's life. Among the Aranda of Central Australia, for instance, there are long-standing relationships of several years' duration between unmarried men and young boys, starting at the age of 10 to 12 years.[14] This is rather similar to the well-known situation in classical Greece, but there, of course, the older man could have a wife as well. Sometimes, however, as among the Siwans of North Africa[15] all men and boys can and are expected to engage in homosexual activities, apparently at every stage of life. In all of these societies there may be much homosexual behavior, but there are no "homosexuals."

THE DEVELOPMENT OF THE HOMOSEXUAL ROLE IN ENGLAND

The problem of method is even more acute in dealing with historical material than with anthropological, for history is usually concerned with "great events" rather than with recurrent patterns. There are some records of attempts to curb sodomy among minor churchmen during the medieval period,[16] which seem to indicate that it was common. At least they suggest that laymen feared on behalf of their sons that it was common. The term "catamite," meaning "boy kept for immoral purposes" was first used in 1593, again suggesting that this practice was common then. But most of the historical references to homosexuality relate either to great men or to great scandals. However, over the last seventy years or so various scholars have tried to trace the history of sex,[17] and it is possible to glean a good deal from what they have found and also from what they have failed to establish.

Their studies of English history before the seventeenth century consist usually of inconclusive speculation as to whether certain men, such as Edward II, Christopher Marlowe, William Shakespeare, were or were not homosexual. Yet the disputes are inconclusive not because of lack of evidence but because none of these men fits the modern stereotype of the homosexual.

It is not until the end of the seventeenth century that other kinds of information become available, and it is possible to move from speculations about individuals to descriptions of homosexual life. At this period references to homosexuals as a type and to a rudimentary homosexual subculture, mainly in London, being to appear. But the earliest descriptions of homosexual do not coincide exactly with the modern conception. There is much more stress on effeminacy and in particular on transvestism, to such an extent that there seems to be no distinction at first between transvestism and homosexuality.[18] The terms emerging at this period to describe homosexuals – Molly, Nancy-boy, Madge-cull – emphasize effeminacy. In contrast the modern terms – like fag, queer, gay, bent – do not have this implication.[19]

By the end of the seventeenth century, homosexual transvestites were a distinct enough group to be able to form their own clubs in London.[20] Edward Ward's *History of the London Clubs* (1896), first published in 1709, describes one called "The Mollie's Club" which met "in a certain tavern in the City" for "parties and regular gatherings." The members "adopt[ed] all the small vanities natural to the feminine sex to such an extent that they try to speak, walk, chatter, shriek and scold as women do, aping them as well in other respects." The other respects apparently included the enactment of marriages and childbirth. The club was discovered and broken up by agents of the Reform Society.[21] There were a number of similar scandals during the course of the eighteenth century as various homosexual coteries were exposed.

A writer in 1729 describes the widespread homosexual life of the period:

> They also have their Walks and Appointments, to meet and pick up one another, and their particular Houses of Resort to go to, because they dare not trust themselves in an open Tavern. About twenty of these sort of Houses have been discovered, besides the Nocturnal Assemblies of great numbers of the like vile Persons, what they call the Markets, which are the Royal Exchange, Lincoln's Inn, Bog Houses, the south side of St James's Park, the Piazzas in Covent Garden, St Clement's Churchyard, etc.
>
> It would be a pretty scene to behold them in their clubs and cabals, how they assume the air and affect the name of Madam or Miss, Betty or Molly, with a chuck under the chin, and "Oh you bold pullet, I'll break your eggs," and then frisk and walk away.[22]

The notion of exclusive homosexuality became well established during this period:

> Two Englishmen, Leith and Drew, were accused of paederasty ... The evidence given by the plaintiffs was, as was generally the case in these trials, very imperfect. On the other hand the defendants denied the accusation, and produced witnesses to prove their predeliction for women. They were in consequence acquitted.[23]

This could only have been an effective argument in a society that perceived homosexual behavior as incompatible with heterosexual tastes.

During the nineteenth century there are further reports of raided clubs and homosexual brothels. However, by this time the element of transvestism had diminished in importance. Even the male prostitutes are described as being of masculine build, and there is more stress upon sexual licence and less upon dressing up and play-acting.

THE HOMOSEXUAL ROLE AND HOMOSEXUAL BEHAVIOR

Thus a distinct, separate, specialized role of "homosexual" emerged in England at the end of the seventeenth century, and the conception of homosexuality as a condition which characterizes certain individuals and not others is now firmly established in our society. The term role is, of course, a form of shorthand. It refers not only to a cultural conception or set of ideas but also to a complex of institutional arrangements which depend upon and reinforce these ideas. These arrangements include all the forms of heterosexual activity, courtship and marriage as well as the labeling processes – gossip, ridicule, psychiatric diagnosis, criminal conviction – and the groups and networks of the homosexual subculture. For simplicity we shall simply say that a specialized role exists. How does the existence of this social role affect actual behavior? And, in particular, does the behavior of individuals conform to the cultural conception in the sense that most people are either exclusively heterosexual or exclusively homosexual? It is difficult to answer these questions on the basis of available evidence because so many researchers have worked with the preconception that homosexuality is a condition, so that in order to study the behavior they have first found a group of people who could be identified as "homosexuals." Homosexual behavior should be studied independently of social roles, if the connection between the two is to be revealed. This may not sound like a particularly novel programme to those who are familiar with Kinsey's contribution to the field. He, after all, set out to study "sexual behavior;" he rejected the assumptions of scientists and laymen:

that there are persons who are "heterosexual" and persons who are "homosexual," that these two types represent antitheses in the sexual world and that there is only an insignificant class of "bisexuals" who occupy an intermediate position between the other groups ... that every individual is innately – inherently – either heterosexual or homosexual ... [and] that from the time of birth one is fated to be one thing or the other.[24]

But although some of Kinsey's ideas are often referred to, particularly in polemical writings, surprisingly little use has been made of his actual data.

Most of Kinsey's chapter on the "Homosexual Outlet" centers on his "heterosexual–homosexual rating scale." His subjects were rated on this scale according to the proportion of their "psychologic reactions and overt experience" that was homosexual in any given period of their lives. It is interesting, and unfortunate for our purposes, that this is one of the few places in the book where Kinsey abandons his behavioristic approach to some extent. However, "psychologic reactions" may well be expected to be affected by the existence of a social role in the same way as overt behavior. Another problem with using Kinsey's material is that although he gives very full information about sexual behavior, the other characteristics of the people he interviewed are only given in a very bald form.[25] But Kinsey's study is undoubtedly the fullest description there is of sexual behavior in any society, and as such it is the safest basis for generalizations to other Western societies.

The ideal way to trace the effects on behavior of the existence of a homosexual role would be to compare societies in which the role exists with societies in which it does not. But as there are no adequate descriptions of homosexual behavior in societies where there is no homosexual role, we shall have to substitute comparisons within American society.

Polarization

If the existence of a social role were reflected in people's behavior, we should expect to find that relatively few people would engage in bisexual behavior. The problem about investigating this empirically is to know what is meant by "relatively few." The categories of Kinsey's rating scale are, of course, completely arbitrary. He has five bisexual categories, but he might just as well have had more or less, in which case the number falling into each would have been smaller or larger. The fact that the distribution of his scale is U-shaped, then, is in itself meaningless (see Table 7.1).

It is impossible to get direct evidence of a

Table 7.1 Heterosexual–homosexual rating: active incidence by age

Age	% of each age group having each rating								
	(1) X	(2) 0	(3) 1	(4) 2	(5) 3	(6) 4	(7) 5	(8) 6	(9) 1–6
15	23.6	48.4	3.6	6.0	4.7	3.7	2.6	7.4	28.0
20	3.3	69.3	4.4	7.4	4.4	2.9	3.4	4.9	27.4
25	1.0	79.2	3.9	5.1	3.2	2.4	2.3	2.9	19.8
30	0.5	83.1	4.0	3.4	2.1	3.0	1.3	2.6	16.4
35	0.4	86.7	2.4	3.4	1.9	1.7	0.9	1.6	12.9
40	1.3	86.8	3.0	3.6	2.0	0.7	0.3	2.3	11.9
45	2.7	88.8	2.3	2.0	1.3	0.9	0.2	1.8	8.5

Note
X = unresponsive to either sex; 0 = entirely heterosexual; 1 = largely heterosexual but with incidental homosexual history; 2 = largely heterosexual but with a distinct homosexual history; 3 = equally heterosexual and homosexual; 4 = largely homosexual but with distinct heterosexual history; 5 = largely homosexual but with incidental heterosexual history; 6 = entirely homosexual.
Source
Based on Kinsey *et al.* (1948): 652, table 148.

polarization between the homosexual and the heterosexual pattern, though we may note the suggestive evidence to the contrary that at every age far more men have bisexual than exclusively homosexual patterns. However, by making comparisons between one age group and another and between men and women, it should be possible to see some of the effects of the role.

Age comparison

As they grow older, more and more men take up exclusively heterosexual patterns, as Table 7.1, column 2 shows. The table also shows that *each* of the bisexual and homosexual categories, columns 3–8, contains fewer men as time goes by after the age of 20. The greatest losses are from the fifth bisexual category, column 7, with responses that are "almost entirely homosexual." It is a fairly small group to begin with, but by the age of 45 it has almost entirely disappeared. On the other hand, the first bisexual category, column 3, with only "incidental homosexual histories" has its numbers not even halved by the age of 45. Yet at all ages the first bisexual category represents a much smaller proportion of those who are almost entirely heterosexual (columns 2 and 3) than the fifth category represents of those who are almost entirely homosexual (columns 7 and 8). In everyday language it seems that proportionately more "homosexuals" dabble in heterosexual activity than "heterosexuals" dabble in homosexual activity and such dabbling is particularly

common in the younger age groups of 20 to 30. This indicates that the existence of the despised role operates at all ages to inhibit people from engaging in occasional homosexual behavior, but does not have the effect of making the behavior of many "homosexuals" exclusively homosexual.

On the other hand, the overall reduction in the amount of homosexual behavior with age can be attributed in part to the fact that more and more men become married. While the active incidence of homosexual behavior is high and increases with age among single men, among married men it is low and decreases only slightly with age. Unfortunately the Kinsey figures do not enable us to compare the incidence of homosexuality among single men who later marry and those who do not.

Comparison between men and women

The notion of a separate homosexual role is much less well developed in women than it is for men, and so too are the attendant techniques of social control and the deviant subculture and organization. So a comparison with women's sexual behavior should tell us something about the effects of the social role on men's behavior (Table 7.2).

Fewer women than men engage in homosexual behavior. By the time they are 45, 26 percent of women have had *some* homosexual experience, whereas about 50 percent of men have. But this is probably a cause rather than an

Table 7.2 Comparison of male and female heterosexual–homosexual ratings: active incidence at selected ages

	Age	(1) X	(2) 0	(3) 1	(4) 2	(5) 3	(6) 4	(7) 5	(8) 6	(9) 1–6
		\multicolumn{9}{c}{*% of each age group having each rating*}								
Male	20	3.3	69.3	4.4	7.4	4.4	2.9	3.4	4.9	27.4
Female		15	74	5	2	1	1	1	1	11
Male	35	0.4	86.7	2.4	3.4	1.9	1.7	0.9	2.6	12.9
Female		7	80	7	2	1	1	1	1	13

Source
Based on Kinsey *et al.* (1948): 652, table 148, and Kinsey *et al.* (1953): 499, table 142. For explanation of the ratings, see table 7.

effect of the difference in the extent to which the homosexual role is crystallized, for women engage in less non-marital sexual activity of any kind than men. For instance, by the time they marry, 50 percent of women have had some pre-marital heterosexual experience to orgasm, whereas as many as 90 percent of men have.

The most revealing contrast is between the male and female distributions on the Kinsey rating scale, shown in Table 7.2. The distributions for women follow a smooth U-shaped pattern, while those for men are uneven with an increase in numbers at the exclusively homo-sexual end. The distributions for women are the shape that one would expect on the assumption that homosexual and heterosexual acts are ran-domly distributed in a ratio of 1 to 18.[26] The men are relatively more concentrated in the exclusively homosexual category. This appears to confirm the hypothesis that the existence of the role is reflected in behavior.

Finally, it is interesting to notice that although at the age of 20 far more men than women have homosexual and bisexual patterns (27 percent as against 11 percent), by the age of 35 the figures are both the same (13 percent). Women seem to broaden their sexual experi-ence as they get older whereas more men become narrower and more specialized. None of this, however, should obscure the fact that, in terms of behavior, the polarization between the heterosexual man and the homosexual man is far from complete in our society. Some polarization does seem to have occurred, but many men manage to follow patterns of sexual behavior that are between the two, in spite of our cultural preconceptions and institutional arrangements.

CONCLUSION

This paper has dealt with only one small aspect of the sociology of homosexuality. It is, never-theless, a fundamental one. For it is not until he sees homosexuals as a social category, rather than a medical or psychiatric one, that the sociologist can begin to ask the right questions about the specific content of the homosexual role and about the organization and functions of homosexual groups.[27] All that has been done here is to indicate that the role does not exist in many societies, that it emerged in England only towards the end of the seventeenth century, and that, although the existence of the role in modern America appears to have some effect on the distribution of homosexual behavior, such behavior is far from being monopolized by persons who play the role of homosexual.

NOTES

1 Irving Bieber, "Clinical Aspects of Male Homo-sexuality," in Sexual Inversion: The Multiple Roots of Homosexuality, ed. J. Marmor (New York: Basic Books, 1965): 248.

2 Richard von Krafft-Ebing, Psychopathia Sex-ualis: A Medico-Economic Study, trans. M. E. Wedeck (New York: G. P. Putnam's and Sons, 1965).

3 This is a grossly simplified account. Edwin Lemert provides a far more subtle and detailed analysis in his Social Pathology (New York: McGraw-Hill, 1951): chapter 4, "Sociopathic Individuation."

4 For discussion of situations in which deviants can lay claim to legitimacy, see Talcott Parsons, The Social System (New York: Free Press, 1951): 292–3.

5 The position taken here is similar to that of Erving Goffman in his discussion of becoming a mental patient in Asylums: Essays on the Social Situation of Mental Patients and Other Inmates (New York: Anchor Books, 1961): 128–46.

6 For evidence that many self-confessed homo-sexuals in England are not effeminate and many are not interested in boys, see Michael Schofield, Sociological Aspects of Homosexuality (Boston: Little, Brown, 1965).

7 Marc Daniel, "Essai de Methodologie pour l'étude des aspects homosexuals de l'historie," Arcadie 133 (January 1965): 31–7.

8 Marvin Opler, "Anthropological and Cross Cul-tural Aspects of Homos," in Sexual Inversion: 174.

9 Ibid.: 117.

10 C. S. Ford and F. Beach, Patterns of Sexual Behavior (New York: Harper, 1951).

11 G. Devereux, "Institutional Homosexuality of the Mohave Indians," Human Biology 9 (1937): 498–627.

12 The lack of cultural distinction is reflected in behavior. Gordon Westwood found that only a small proportion of his sample of British homo-sexuals engaged in anal intercourse, and many of these had been active and passive and did not

have a clear preference. See Westwood [alias for Michael Schofield], *A Minority Report on the Life of the Male Homosexual in Great Britain* (London: Longmans, 1960): 127–34.

13 G. R. Taylor, "Historical and Mythological Aspects of Homosexuality," in *Sexual Inversion* and F. Henriques, *Prostitution and Society*, vol. 1 (London: MacGibbon and Kee, 1962): 341–3.

14 *Patterns of Sexual Behavior*: 132.

15 *Ibid.*: 131–2.

16 G. May, *Social Control of Sex* (New York: Morrow and Company, 1931): 65, 101.

17 See especially H. Ellis, *Studies in the Psychology of Sex*, vol. 2: *Sexual Inversion* (New York: Random House, 1936); I. Bloch (F. Uuhren, pseud.), *Sexual Life in England: Past and Present* (London: Francis Adler, 1938); G. R. Taylor, *Sex in History* (New York: Vanguard, 1954); N. I. Garde, *Jonathan to Gide: The Homosexual History* (New York: Vantage, 1964).

18 Evelyn Hooker has suggested that in a period when homosexual grouping and a homosexual subculture have not yet become institutionalized, homosexuals are likely to behave in a more distinctive and conspicuous manner because other means of making contact are not available. This is confirmed by the fact that lesbians are more conspicuous than male homosexuals in our society, but does not seem to fit the seventeenth century, where the groups are already described as "clubs."

19 However, "fairy," and "pansy," the commonest slang terms used by non-homosexuals, have the same meaning of effeminate as the earlier terms.

20 Bloch, *Sexual Life in England: Past and Present*: 328, gives several examples, but attributes their emergence to the fact that "the number of homosexuals increased."

21 *Sex in History.*

22 *Ibid.*: 142.

23 *Sexual Life in England: Past and Present*: 334.

24 A. C. Kinsey, W. B. Pomeroy and C. E. Martin, *Sexual Behavior in the Human Male* (Philadelphia, W. B. Saunders, 1948): 636–7.

25 The more general drawbacks of Kinsey's data, particularly the problem of the representativeness of his sample, have been thoroughly canvassed in a number of places; see especially W. G. Cochran, F. Mosteller and J. W. Tukey, *Statistical Problems of the Kinsey Report* (Washington, DC.: American Statistical Society, 1954).

26 This cannot be taken in a rigorously statistical sense, since the categories are arbitrary and do not refer to numbers, or even proportions, of actual sexual acts.

27 But an interesting beginning has been made by Evelyn Hooker, "The Homosexual Community" in *Sexual Deviance*, eds J. H. Gagnon and W. S. Simon (New York: Harper & Row, 1967) and "Male Homosexuals and Their 'Worlds'" in *Sexual Inversion: The Multiple Roots of Homosexuality*: 83–107; there is much valuable descriptive material in D. W. Cory (pseud. for Edward Saqarin), *The Homosexual Outlook: A Subjective Approach* (New York: Greenberg, 1951) and in *A Minority Report on the Life of the Male Homosexual in Great Britain*, as well as elsewhere.

FREDERICK L. WHITAM

"The Homosexual Role: A Reconsideration"

from *The Journal of Sex Research* 13: 1 (February 1977): 1–11

Sociologists, in keeping with a tradition of sympathy for deviants, have been more charitable in their theoretical treatment of the "homosexual" than many other social scientists, notably psychiatrists and psychoanalysts. In the last few years as the medical model – which all too often influenced sociological theorizing – has been shaken, the concept "role" has emerged as dominant in sociological reinterpretations of homosexuality. McIntosh for example has staunchly argued that "the homosexual should be seen as playing a social role rather than having a condition" (McIntosh 1968). More recently, a study emanating from the Institute for Sex Research advocates that "homosexuality be conceptualized in terms of social statuses and roles rather than as a condition" (Weinberg and Williams 1974).

While the use of the concept role may serve the commendable end of loosening the grip of often bizarre theories, it is argued here that, as reasonable and harmless as it may appear, the application of the concept "role" to explain homosexuality is quite inappropriate and serves to further confound a theoretical issue which already has a somewhat confusing history.

Homosexuality should not be regarded as a role for two important reasons: (1) When applied to the homosexual, the concept *role* violates the prevailing definitions and conventional usage of this concept in sociology; (2) the application of the term *role* to an interpretation of the homosexual is inconsistent with basic and significant characteristics of the nature of homosexuality and the homosexual subculture. Empirical data utilized here are part of a larger study of male homosexuality and were gathered during the past two years primarily in Phoenix,

Arizona, New York City, and the homosexual summer community of Cherry Grove, Fire Island, New York. Cross-cultural data on homosexuality are currently being gathered in Guatemala City, Guatemala.

In short it will be argued that homosexuality is not suitable for productive analysis in terms of role theory and such analysis should not be forced no matter how laudable the ideological purpose. Homosexuality is neither a pathological condition nor a role, but rather a sexual orientation and no useful purpose can be served by regarding it as anything else.

While there may be few concepts in sociology upon which there is general agreement, the concept "role" is perhaps one of the least controversial, at least with respect to its most essential elements. There is general agreement among sociologists upon at least the following three basic elements of role: (1) a role is a prescription for behavior which has a prior existence in the social structure; (2) a role may be ascribed in the sense of age or sex roles, in which case individuals are socialized into such roles; (3) a role may be achieved in the sense of occupation, in which case an individual chooses to enact such roles. Interpretations which argue that homosexuality is best understood in terms of role violate all three basic tenets of this most ordinary definition of role.

In the first place homosexuality does not, at least in Western societies, have a prior existence in the social structure in the way in which role is ordinarily understood. McIntosh argues that the homosexual role "emerged in England at the end of the seventeenth century." What is apparent here is that in her analysis *homosexuality* as a sexual orientation has been confused with the homosexual subculture. The confusion is perhaps forgiveable in that the relationship between homosexuality as a sexual orientation and the homosexuality subculture is complex and subtle, and there are, to be sure certain kinds of role behavior within the homosexual subculture. The crucial misconception here is the implication that it is the existence of a homosexual subculture which creates homosexuality. However close the relationship between homosexuality and the homosexual subculture, it is patently clear that the homosexual subculture does not create homosexuality but rather is a response to it. This point may be easily misunderstood because subcultural theory – so influential in sociology in the past two decades – has generally emphasized the reverse relationship – that is, that deviant subcultures produce and/or perpetuate deviancy: the delinquent subculture produces and perpetuates delinquency; the drug subculture proselytizes and initiates new drug users, etc. This direction of the relationship between subculture and deviancy has been so influential that a sociologist might be excused for extending the logic to homosexuality. McIntosh writes for example

> there may be a tendency for people to become fixed in their deviancy once they have become labeled. This, too, is a process that has become well-recognized in discussions of other forms of deviant behavior such as juvenile delinquency and drug taking and indeed of other kinds of social labeling such as streaming in schools and racial distinctions. One might expect social categorizations of this sort to be some extent self-fulfilling prophecies: if the culture defines people as falling into distinct types – black and white, criminal and non-criminal, homosexual and normal – then these types will tend to become polarized, highly differentiated from each other.
>
> (McIntosh 1968)

Data in Table 8.1 are derived from a questionnaire administered to a group of 206 males who regard themselves as predominantly homosexual and a group of 78 males who regard themselves as predominantly heterosexual.

It is apparent from an examination of Table 8.1 that the homosexual orientation begins to emerge quite early and generally parallels the emergence of heterosexual feelings. By the age 17 all of the heterosexual respondents and roughly 91 percent of the homosexual respondents have experienced attraction to females or males as the case may be. Thus, by age 17 nearly all homosexuals have already experienced awareness of attraction to other males. These findings are consistent with those of Dank (1971) who found that, by the age of 19, 93 percent of his homosexual respondents had experienced attraction to the same sex. Tentative results of a study of homosexuality in Guatemala City, presently being conducted by the author, suggest that such findings may be valid cross-culturally. In interviews with twenty-five homosexuals in Guatemala City, all twenty-five reported feelings of attraction toward males by the age 17. While quantifiable evidence is not available on this point, most homosexuals

Table 8.1 Age at which respondents were first aware of attraction to males (homosexuals) or females (heterosexuals)

Age	Exclusively homosexual		Non-exclusively homosexual		Non-exclusively heterosexual		Exclusively heterosexual	
	N	(%)	(N)	(%)	(N)	(%)	(N)	(%)
0–4	5	4.7	9	9.1	1	10.0	8	11.8
5–6	15	14.0	14	14.1	3	30.0	12	17.6
7–9	19	17.8	18	18.2	0	0	15	22.1
10–13	33	30.8	31	31.3	6	60.0	26	38.2
14–17	26	24.3	18	18.2	0	0	7	10.3
18–25	8	7.5	7	7.1	0	0	0	0
26–35	1	1.0	2	2.0	0	0	0	0
35+	0	0	0	0	0	0	0	0
Total	107	100.0	99	100.0	10	100.0	68	100.0

report that they did not come into contact with the homosexual subculture until late adolescence – usually after the high school years. It should also be noted that some homosexuals experienced a "delayed reaction" with respect to discovery of their homosexuality. That is, a few homosexuals did not become aware of homosexual attractions until their twenties or in rare instancies their early thirties. This phenomenon of the late bloomer is probably not due to contact with the homosexual subculture but to the fact that Western societies – rather than providing for a homosexual role – emphatically *do not* provide a homosexual role nor do they provide the emerging homosexual any way of conceptualizing or dealing with his homosexuality. Dank has commented on this point:

> It is sometimes said that the homosexual minority is just like any other minority group; but in the sense of early childhood socialization it is not, for the parents of a Negro can communicate to their child that he is a Negro and what it is like to be a Negro, but the parents of a person who is to become homosexual do not prepare their child to be homosexual – they are not homosexual themselves, and they do not communicate to him what it is like to be a homosexual.

(Dank 1971)

The crucial fact here is that, despite the absence of a homosexual role in society, by age 17 most homosexuals are already aware of attraction to other males. There are undoubtedly role aspects within the homosexual subculture as numerous articles and studies have pointed out– the "hustler," "the drag queen," the "auntie" – yet these "roles" do not create homosexuality. By the time most homosexuals have contact with the homosexual subculture they already have well-defined homosexual orientations.

It should also be emphasized that, while a considerable number of homosexuals do in fact find their way to the homosexual subculture, there are many who for one reason or another do not. Some homosexuals live out their lives without active involvement in the homosexual subculture, although they may be vaguely aware of its existence. Others – and perhaps this is rarer – never even learn of its existence. A young French-Canadian respondent related a story which illustrates the latter point. The respond-

ent worked for two years as a government employee in an isolated village of Quebec's Gaspé peninsula. While there, he boarded with a married couple in their early sixties. Eventually the husband confessed his love for the young boarder and his desire to have sexual relations. No sexual relationship resulted but the two men became friends and began to talk about homosexuality. For the older man this was the first time in his life of some sixty years that he had ever had such a discussion with another homosexual. Moreover, he was astounded to learn that in Quebec city and Montreal there were hundreds perhaps thousands, of other homosexuals and a homosexual subculture which included bars, steambaths, and gay parties. Throughout his life he had believed that there were only a handful of people with such desires in all of Canada. While his sexual interest in females was minimal, he had married and had thus lived out most of his life. While a homosexual subculture existed in Victorian and Edwardian England, access to it was perhaps more difficult than in contemporary society. There are several interesting accounts dating from this era which describe the struggle against homosexual desires in the absence not only of access to the homosexual subculture, but the absence of terminology with which to conceptualize one's own sexuality. A prominent Victorian, John Addington Symonds, married to "cure" himself – a practice not uncommon in Victorian society – and discovered the homosexual subculture after the emergence of his homosexuality and after his marriage (Grosskurth 1964). Forster's autobiographical novel *Maurice*, written in 1913 but not published until after the author's death in 1970, is an interesting account of a struggle to understand one's homosexuality in the absence of knowledge of a homosexuality subculture (Forster 1971). It is clear then, that not only does homosexuality as a sexual orientation usually precede knowledge of the homosexual subculture, but that it is possible to achieve a homosexual orientation without contact with or knowledge of the homosexual subculture.

The use of role theory to interpret homosexuality violates a second widely accepted tenet of the sociologist's definition of role – that of ascription. Little boys in all societies are socialized into male sex-ways and little girls in female sex-ways. There is no society (and certainly not American society) which socializes children into a homosexual role. American parents, after years of careful socialization into heterosexual roles, are usually shocked and disappointed when they discover that they have reared a homosexual child. Ford and Beach summarize their findings based on analysis of the Human Relations Area files:

> Homosexual behavior is never the predominant activity for adults in any of the societies covered by this book. Heterosexual coitus is the dominant sexual activity for the majority of the adults in every society. But some homosexual behavior occurs in nearly all the societies comprising our sample.
>
> (Ford and Beach 1951)

There are a few societies, such as the traditional Mohave, which give official recognition to the existence of homosexuals through ritual, but it is clear from anthropological reports (Devereux 1963) that the Mohave society did not socialize children into homosexual patterns. Mohave families which had homosexual children were not particularly pleased, and the ritual is one in which homosexuality is recognized as inevitable though not desirable and through which the homosexual adolescent is given a legitimate place in society and in which the parents are relieved of guilt for having produced a homosexual child.

The most pressing theoretical problem for the sociologist, then, would seem to be – rather than asserting that homosexuality is role behavior – to account for the apparent universal emergence of homosexuality given the apparent universal absence of a homosexual role.

Table 8.2 presents data which speak to another dimension of this theoretical problem. Not only are there no homosexual roles nor role models in Western societies, but feelings of attraction to one's own sex often precede knowledge that such relations exist in the adult world. Data in Table 8.2 reveal that the emergence of homosexual feelings of sexual attraction parallels that of heterosexuals. Nearly half of the homosexual respondents reported feeling sexually attracted to males before they learned of the existence of such sexual relations in the adult world. These data suggest only one of many reasons why labeling theory, often invoked in connection with role theory, is inappropriate for explaining homosexuality: feelings of homosexual attraction often begin to emerge before any kinds of labels or terminology are relevant. Respondents frequently reported knowing that they were or would become homosexuals without having heard the term *homosexual* or its equivalents and without knowing that such behavior existed in the adult world.

I recently conducted an interview with a 14-year-old Guatemalan youth who was unaware of the existence of a homosexual subculture, unaware of the term *homosexual*, had never been labeled "homosexual" by parents or

Table 8.2 Feelings of attraction to males (homosexuals) or females (heterosexuals) relative to learning of the existence of homosexual or heterosexual sexual relations

	Exclusively homosexual		Non-exclusively homosexual		Non-exclusively heterosexual		Exclusively heterosexual	
	N	(%)	(N)	(%)	(N)	(%)	(N)	(%)
Felt attraction before learning of adult sexual relations	53	49.5	49	49.5	5	50.0	27	39.7
Felt attraction about the same time as learning of adult sexual relations	40	37.4	38	38.4	3	30.0	25	36.8
Felt attraction after learning of adult sexual relations	14	13.8	12	12.1	2	20.0	16	23.5
Total	107	100.0	99	100.0	10	100.0	68	100.0

friends, and yet who had had a full-blown homosexual orientation. He is strongly attracted to males, feels that his attraction is more than adolescent sex-play, has had homosexual sex-fantasies since early childhood, enjoys and expects to continue his homosexuality, is not at all attracted to women and does not expect to marry.

Most homosexuals in the US, even with the advent of the Gay Liberation movement, probably have never been publicly labeled as homosexuals. Labels do exist in society – faggot, queer, etc. – but it is highly doubtful (no convincing empirical data have been presented thus far) that the use of such labels is sufficiently potent to determine the nature of one's sexuality. There is no doubt that public labeling in a society which is repressive towards homosexuality may have deleterious effects upon one's life – Oscar Wilde, as is well known, was destroyed by the labeling process in Victorian England. However, it was not labeling which created Wilde's homosexuality.

While it is true that some labeling is conferred upon homosexuals by the straight world, it is the homosexual world itself which has devised an even more complex system of labels and terminology. The term "chicken hawk," for example, refers to someone who is exclusively attracted to teenagers. Yet the term does not create the reality. The term emerged to call attention to a form of behavior within the homosexual subculture. It is doubtful that by eliminating the label we would eliminate the behavior even if we assumed it were desirable to do so. Not only is it the gay world which often confers labels, but this system of labeling is probably more highly elaborated than in the straight world. Equivalent behavior often exists in the gay and straight worlds; that is, there are heterosexual adults who are attracted to teenagers. But in the straight world no label is ordinarily used, unless of course such activity is discovered in which case the term "child molester" is invoked. The homosexual world has labels for almost every form of "sub-deviancy," all of which probably have behavioral analogies, without labels, in the straight world. There are undoubtedly white heterosexuals who are attracted to black females (and

vice versa). A white homosexual attracted to blacks is called a "dinge queen." No such label exist in the straight world. Simon and Gagnon argue that "sexual behavior is socially scripted behavior and not the masked or rationalized expression of some primordial drive. The individual learns to be sexual as he or she learns scripts, scripts that invest actors and situations with erotic content" (Simon and Gagnon 1971). Yet for the pre-homosexual child there is no script. He is not socialized into a role-with-script. On the contrary one of the most amazing aspects of homosexuality is that it emerges without a script. Children seem to be sexual beings who invest others and situations with their own childish eroticism.

Sociologists generally agree that a role has prior existence in the social structure, that it may be ascribed, in which case an individual is socialized into the role or that it is achieved, in which case an individual chooses the role. If one is not socialized into the role of homosexual, then it stands to reason that one chooses it. While there is not consensus in the social sciences upon how one's sexual orientation is determined, it does not appear likely that one's sexuality is chosen – despite the current use of terms such as "alternative lifestyles," which suggest a choice in this matter. While there is perhaps a degree of flexibility and choice in various aspects of sexuality it is unlikely that homosexuals choose a "homosexual role." In the first place, for most children and young adolescents, the homosexual subculture is largely invisible. The popular image of the homosexual as an old man who sits in the park and does nasty things to teenage boys is likely to be the pre-homosexual's first knowledge of the homosexual world – hardly an appealing role-model. In the second place, it is doubtful that most homosexuals would willingly choose a "homosexual role," not because it is socially repugnant, but because it is terribly inconvenient. The world is by and large constructed by heterosexuals for heterosexuals. For more compelling reasons, however, those having to do with the psychodynamics of human sexuality, homosexuals do not choose a "homosexual role." It is simply that one's fundamental sexual orientation lies outside one's ability to decide. A bisexual respondent recently told me that he felt that we should love whomever we should – be it male or female, that one should not be bound to one sex or the other. This is perhaps a commendable sexual philosophy; however, it is feasible only if one is bisexual. In a heterosexual world, most homosexuals have been exposed to some form of heterosexual experimentation. Many male homosexuals have had women fall in love with them, try to seduce them, and make themselves available. For the bisexual his perception of making a choice with respect to the object of his sexual orientation is an illusion. Someone who is predominantly homosexual cannot will himself to become heterosexual just as someone who is predominantly heterosexual cannot will himself to become homosexual.

Space does not permit a more detailed analysis of this view of the psychodynamics of homosexuality. It is clear, however, that one's sexual orientation begins to emerge very early – long before the age at which one is able to make a "rational" choice about the object of one's sexuality. Money, Hampson, and Hampson, for example feel that gender role is usually set by a little after two years of age (Gagnon and Simon 1973). Data in Table 8.3 suggest a very close connection between one's first – usually childhood – sexual contact and one's adult sexual orientation. The first sexual contact of nearly all homosexuals is with other males. The first sexual contact of nearly all heterosexuals is with females. While learning theorists might argue otherwise, I am inclined to believe on the basis of interviews with homosexuals that one's emerging sexual orientation exists prior to the first sexual contact and determines that contact. Popular and even sometimes scientific view

regards childhood sexuality as random and meaningless. For example, Kathadourian and Lunde, authors of a widely used text in human sexuality, write

> Much prepubescent sex play is motivated by curiosity and is influenced by the availability and sex of companions. To the extent that a child's companions are of the same sex, his sex play will likely to be "homosexual." And, when a boy lies on top of a girl, it is often viewed as coital play. As children are often quite unaware of the significance of such acts, we should refrain from ascribing adult sexual motives to them. These activities are largely experimental, imitative, exploratory play, sexual only in a general sense ... It is particularly important not to label the sex play of children as deviant or perverse, no matter what it entails.
>
> (Katchadourian and Lunde 1972)

While it is not possible to extrapolate precisely from observations of childhood sex play, childhood sexual feelings and experiences cannot be summarily dismissed as meaningless for future sexual orientation.

Homosexuals frequently report very strong homosexual interests at a very early age, often reporting themselves as sexually aggressive with other little boys. One respondent reported that at the age of five he performed fellatio on his 6-month-old brother. Data in Table 8.4 lend further support to his notion. This table shows responses to the question, "In childhood sex play were you more interested in and excited by playing around with other boys than with girls?"

It is argued here then that while the concepts of role and the related labeling theory, now enjoying considerable popularity in sociology, may have utility for interpreting certain forms of deviant behavior, they do not constitute, whatever else

Table 8.3 Gender of first sexual contact

Gender	Exclusively homosexual		Non-exclusively homosexual		Non-exclusively heterosexual		Exclusively heterosexual	
	N	(%)	N	(%)	N	(%)	N	(%)
Male	90	84.1	66	66.7	3	30.0	9	13.2
Female	15	14.0	21	21.2	7	70.0	56	82.5
Mixed group	2	1.9	12	12.1	0	0	3	4.4
Total	107	100.0	99	100.0	10	100.0	68	100.0

Table 8.4 Sexual interest in children of same sex, in answer to question "Were you more interested in and excited by other boys than with girls?"

	Exclusively homosexual		Non-exclusively homosexual		Non-exclusively heterosexual		Exclusively heterosexual	
	N	(%)	N	(%)	N	(%)	N	(%)
Yes	83	77.6	69	69.7	1	10.0	8	11.8
No	21	19.6	27	27.3	6	60.0	56	82.4
Other	3	2.8	3	3.0	3	30.0	4	5.9
Total	107	100.0	99	100.0	10	100.0	68	100.0

may be their merits, a sound theoretical basis for a general interpretation of homosexuality and their use toward this aim should be abandoned. Homosexuality is neither a condition nor a role, but rather a sexual orientation. As sociologists pursue the elusive quest for a final work on the nature of homosexuality it is likely that we will be pushed toward a more adequate theoretical formulation of the nature of man's total sexuality. As Simon and Gagnon have aptly suggested, "The problem of finding out how people become homosexual requires an adequate theory of how they become heterosexual" (Simon and Gagnon 1967).

REFERENCES

Dank, Barry, "Coming out in the Gay World," *Psychiatry* 34 (May 1971), 180–97.

Devereux, George, "Institutionalized Homosexuality of the Mohave Indians," in Hendrik M. Ruitenbeek, *The Problem of Homosexuality in Modern Society*: 183–226 (New York: E. P. Dutton, 1963).

Dinitz, Simon, Russell R. Dynes, and Alfred C. Clarke, *Deviance* (New York: Oxford University Press, 1975).

Ford, Cellan S. and Frank A. Beach, *Patterns of Sexual Behavior* (New York: Harper and Row, 1951).

Forster, E. M., *Maurice* (New York: W. W. Norton, 1971) (London: Longmans, 1964).

Gagnon, John H. and William Simon, *Sexual Conduct* (Chicago: Aldine, 1973).

Grosskurth, Phyllis, *John Addington Symonds* (London: Longmans, 1964).

Katchadourian, Herant A. and Donald T. Lunde, *Fundamentals of Human Sexuality* (New York: Holt, Rinehart and Winston, 1972).

McIntosh, Mary, "The Homosexual Role," *Social Problems* 16: 2 (Fall 1968) 182–92.

Simon, William and John H. Gagnon (eds) *Sexual Deviance* (New York: Harper and Row, 1967).

Simon, William and John H. Gagnon, "On Psychosexual Development," in Donald L. Grummon and Andrew M. Barclay (eds), *Sexuality: A Search for Perspective* (New York: Van Nostrand Reinhold Co., 1971).

Simon, William and John H. Gagnon, "Homosexuality: The Formulation of a Sociological Perspective," *Journal of Health and Social Behavior* 8: 3 (September 1967), 177–85.

Weinberg, Martin S. and Colin J. Williams, *Male Homosexuals* (New York: Oxford University Press, 1974).

Whitam, Frederick L. "Homosexuality as Emergent Behavior," paper presented at Pacific Sociological Meetings, Victoria, British Columbia, April 1975.

KENNETH PLUMMER

"Homosexual Categories: Some Research Problems in the Labelling Perspective of Homosexuality"

from Kenneth Plummer (ed.), *The Making of the Modern Homosexual* (London: Hutchinson, 1981): 53–75

This article is primarily concerned with a cluster of recently invented categorizations that purport to locate coherent phenomena. To the scientist such categorizations include "the inverts", whether "absolute", "amphigenic" or "contingent" (Freud 1977) and "the homosexual", whether "pre-oedipal", "oedipal", or "pseudo" (Socarides 1978). To the lay person such categorizations include "queer", "bender", "dyke", "pansy" and "faggot". To a small group of people the category now is "gay". There is a considerable difference between the first two – which are largely negative and "other-created" – and the latter – which is positive and "self-created"[1] – but they all nevertheless point to an external empirical referent which is supposed to be identifiable. I am not at all sure that it exists. Certainly the categories exist; they are applied now (willingly or unwillingly to millions of people throughout the world, and indeed are also today applied to large numbers of people throughout history. Certainly there is considerable political intent behind the making of such categorizations – to order, control and segregate in the name of benevolence (Gaylin 1978). Certainly too these categories have rendered – in the main – whole groups of people devalued, dishonourable or dangerous, and have frequently justified monstrous human atrocities and the denial of human rights.[2] But these certainties about the categories should not be confused with certainties about the phenomena to which the category refers.

In this article my concern lies with presenting some research suggestions for studying the category *not* the phenomena, and in doing this I am drawing heavily from the labelling *perspective*.

Thus four broad questions need detailed exploration:

1 What is the nature of the homosexual categorizations?
2 When and how did such categorizations emerge?
3 How do they come to be bestowed upon certain behaviours and people?
4 What kind of impact do they have on people once bestowed?

These are large and significant questions which signpost a dramatic turn away from clinical concerns with the phenomena itself. In what follows, I can only treat each question selectively.

THE NATURE OF THE "HOMOSEXUAL" CATEGORY

The starting point of all labelling research must lie with rendering the very categories we use as a problem. In this case we need to know the nature of the diverse and ever changing meanings which people bestow upon "same sex emotional and erotic encounters",[3] from those who are formally and informally engaged in their control through to those who find the meanings applied to them. What meanings are imputed by specific groups? How do such meanings change in different contexts? What part do such general features as "stigma" (the devaluation of people) and "essentializing" (the translation of doing into being) play in the assembling of such meanings? What is the relationship between what people *say* about "homosexuals" and what people do to them? Answering such questions will turn the researcher away from an oversimplified version of both uniform hostility and identifiable "types" to a view of the world that is more empirically valid, because it will highlight the multi-tiered, changing, conflicting, confused and contrasting social meanings surrounding same-sex experiences. What is called for here, then, is an ethnography of societal reactions to same sex experiences, a task that has hardly begun.

The issue from above that I would like to consider more fully here concerns the problem of "essentializing" – of the ways in which "doing" and "experiencing" can become consolidated into "being" through categoric labelling. For two recent trends can be discerned in the clarification of homosexual categories: an essentializing trend from homosexuals themselves and an opposite trend from social scientists.

Essentialism and the gay movement

Most agree that a distinct "homosexual role" now exists in Western capitalist societies which did not exist in earlier historical periods and which does not exist in other cultures now; they differ primarily on *when* that role emerged, *what* its precise content is and *how* it gets translated into people's actual lives. Thus McIntosh sees it emerging in the late seventeenth century, Weeks in the late nineteenth century and Marshall in the mid twentieth. McIntosh focuses on the expectations that "homosexuals" would be sex-focused, boy-molesting effeminates, Weeks highlights the medicalization of homosexuals and Marshall links medicalization with the separation of gender from sex.

None of these discussions, however, considers the role and its constitution in the 1970s (although this is Blachford's concern). Yet this is a curious omission for something unusual is happening: the expectations of homosexuality being a "condition", which were generated in the past by clinicians, are today being sustained and reinforced by gay radicals. It is true liberationists would reject the effeminate, boy-seeking, "sick" expectations of earlier role portraits, but they still sustain the view that gays

are types of being. Indeed Dank has even argued – rightly I believe – that

> the reality constructions created by persons overtly committed to homosexual liberation perform the same functions as the reality constructions of the traditionalists. Specifically, their reality constructions function to homogenise and dehumanise homosexually oriented persons often through the process of deification and at the same time they construct *the* heterosexual as an alien being. Just as the traditionalists have created *the* homosexual and *the* heterosexual so have other persons done so while invoking the rhetoric of homosexual liberation.
>
> (Dank 1976: 14–15)

Here, then, Dank extends the McIntosh–Weeks–Marshall argument by showing that the liberationists themselves have started to become key definers of a homosexual role and hence ironically have started to become their own source of regulation. "Homosexuals" were once regulated and defined by "experts"; now these experts need no longer do it, for the homosexual has assumed that role for himself or herself. Ghettoized and reified, "the homosexual" remains firmly under control in "liberated" capitalism. He and she are being "pushed" further and further down from the mainstream of society – establishing their own colonies and ghettos (see Levine 1979; Humphreys 1979),[4] rendering their "gay identities" as increasingly pivotal to their personal world and creating a proliferation of separatist groups, until both mentally and spatially "the homosexual" exists as a highly restricted and confined species. And even within this world, "gays" cut themselves off further from each other through the construction of further types: "men" with "men", "women" with "women", "effeminates" with "effeminates" "SMs" with "SMs". It forms a heady spiral of ever-increasing *self*-categorization as types anticipate an ever increasing self-imposed segregation.[5]

I do not want to be too pessimistic about this trend, for it can be rightly counter-argued that this increasing categorization and segregation, far from being harmful, may have very positive consequences for "homosexuals" because it is *self*-created and *self*-controlled. Better to live in a self-imposed ghetto than a state-imposed concentration camp! However valid this may be, one should at least be aware that the history of many labels has shown a passage from a benevolent origin to a malevolent consequence, where ostensible humanitarianism has led to a straitjacketing and closure of opportunities to whole groups of people (Gaylin 1978).

The research questions generated by these brief observations are especially crucial for "radical/critical" criminologists. For they remind us, sociologically, that "radical" and "liberating" social movements are never just that; they will always bring their own forms of control. "Total" freedom and "total" liberation can exist only in the revolutionary's mind; they are sociological nonsense. And the question that needs asking is whether these movement-based forms of control can be seen to complement or even extend the wider societal forms of control. In this case, as homosexuality appears to be entering a new phase of "liberation" and "acceptance" in the Western world, could it be that the control processes prevalent earlier are simply being more firmly extended – only now in a more private manner – by "homosexuals" themselves?

Decategorization and deconstruction

Along with this invention, classification and expansion of the "homosexual role" first by clinicians and latterly by homosexuals themselves, another process has been taking place which perpetually aims to subvert the idea that homosexuality is a condition or type of person. It is an underground tradition, yet it is rooted in both classical thinking (which highlighted free will) and more recent sex research. While the "condition" viewpoint is completely congruent with the mainstream criminological positivism which dominated thinking from the mid nineteenth century to the mid twentieth, this alternative aims to subvert that kind of viewpoint by stressing that *homosexuality is a complex, diffuse experience that anyone may have*. A number of strategies can be located which attempt to reconstruct homosexuality in this fashion. Four such processes can be briefly identified:

1 polymorphous perversity
2 the continuum
3 the normalization
4 the pluralization of identity

Human nature and polymorphous perversity

Although Freud's writings helped in the constitution of "perverted" types, his underlying imagery – of bisexuality and polymorphus perversity – helps subvert them. For it provides a portrait of people who at least initially are open to a broad range of experiences, who harbour the potential for masculine and feminine conduct, as well as a diffuse sexual pleasure seeking with multiple aims and objects. Of course in Freud's account it is necessary for such world-openness to become canalized, but in the writings of others such restrictions of experience are too high a price to pay (Brown 1959; Marcuse 1969; Altman 1971). In this imagery homosexuality is one component of a more general "desire" that exists in us all: "Desire emerges in a multiple form, where components are only divisible *a posteriori*, according to how we manipulate it. Just like heterosexual desire, homosexual desire is an arbitrarily frozen frame in an unbroken and polyvocal flux" (Hocquenghem 1978: 36). The belief in this "diffuse desire" constantly strains against the view that homosexuality is a condition, since this desire is present in us all (see Stambolian and Marks 1979).

The homosexual continuum and homosexualities

It was Kinsey who first clearly argued that "the world is not to be divided into sheep and goats" and stressed the need to view homosexuality as a seven-point continuum with the scaling classification running from zero (exclusive heterosexuality) to six (exclusive homosexuality). The baseline for such a continuum was Kinsey's own empirical findings – based on sixteen thousand white Americans living in the first decades of this century – who clearly showed the mix of homosexual and heterosexual experiences found in many people's lives. Thus while only 4 per cent of his male population was exclusively homosexual from puberty onwards, 37 per cent experienced homosexuality leading to orgasm at least once in the period between puberty and old age. Further, 30 per cent had at least accidental homosexual experience or reactions during a period of at least three years between the ages of 16 and 55; 25 per cent had more than incidental homosexual experience or reaction during a period of at least three years between the ages of 16 and 55; 18 per cent recollected at least equal amount of homosexual and heterosexual experience during a period of at least three years between the ages of 16 and 55; 13 per cent had more homosexual than heterosexual experience over a period of at least three years; 10 per cent of the men were more or less predominantly homosexual during a period of at least three years between 16 and 55 years, and 8 per cent were exclusively homosexual during a period of at least three years between the ages of 16 and 55. These figures – despite weaknesses – are of homosexual experiences at a time when they were strongly taboo, but they convey the flux, change and diversity of homosexual experiences in human life very well (Kinsey *et al.* 1948 and 1953). Not surprisingly, the more recent "Kinsey study", specifically focused on homosexuals in the early 1970s in California, reasserts and strengthens this diversity. Bell writes

> In regard to how they [adult homosexuals] rated themselves during adolescence, less than a third of the males rated themselves exclusively homosexual in their sexual behaviours during this entire period; about one third of them were predominantly *heterosexual* in their behaviours at that time. About a third of the males classified themselves as exclusively homosexual in their feelings during the adolescent period, and more than a quarter of them were predominantly *heterosexual* in their feelings at that time. 40 per cent of the males had changes in their feelings and behaviour ratings during adolescence and about one half of them recorded some degree of discrepancy between the two different ratings ... Clearly a homosexual is not a homosexual when it comes to their past and present sexual feelings and behaviours. Again, going back to the adolescent career, almost two thirds of both males and females experienced heterosexual arousal; smaller but still relatively large numbers of them did not know

what it was like to be aroused sexually by a person of the opposite sex. Among the males who reported both homosexual and heterosexual sexual arousal prior to young adulthood, 54 per cent were sexually aroused by males before they experienced sexual arousal by females; about a quarter of them experienced both forms of arousal during the same year; and a similar number were sexually aroused by a female before they were ever sexually aroused by a male. About two thirds of the white homosexual females were sexually aroused by another female before they experienced heterosexual sexual arousal ... a lengthy and detailed explanation of a person's self ratings on the Kinsey scale over the course of his or her lifetime can provide rich dividends. It enables both the clinician and the client to get a sense of the ebb and flow of homosexual versus heterosexual experience, to challenge the commonly held assumption that one is *either* homosexual or heterosexual, to consider and to compare the conditions under which homosexual and heterosexual arousal first occurred, to explore a person's reaction to such arousal as well as its behavioural consequences, and to delve into the nature of the client's masturbatory fantasies, cognitional rehearsals, romantic attachments and sexual dreams.

> (Bell 1976: 8–9)

It should be noted that this continuum highlights the diversity at any moment in time *and* across the life cycle, and leads the authors to advocate the term "homosexualities" rather than homosexuality.

The "normalization" of homosexuality

One of the key forces in shaping a "homosexual type" has been the process of medicalization. In declaring homosexuality a "disease" and a "sickness" – albeit in diverse ways – the psychiatrists and physicians effectively found a way of separating out and controlling homosexuality. It became a diagnostic category used to identify a species of person.

But all the time this massive medicalization process has been occurring, another subordinate one has been arguing the reverse. From Freud onwards, a great many psychiatrists, anthropologists, sociologists and psychologists have been arguing that homosexuality "cannot be classified as an illness" (Freud 1951: 787; Crompton 1969; Freedman 1971; Green 1972), and indeed by

1973 this became the considered opinion of the American Psychiatric Association (Freedman and Mayers 1976). There are many good examples of early and recent social scientists trying to break down the idea of homosexuality as a clinical diagnosis and to pin-point the overlaps between homosexualities and heterosexualities. Indeed most recently leading practitioners from all scientific spheres have converged on the position that homosexuality is not a sickness. Thus alongside the recent work of the Kinsey Institute referred to above, the founding "fathers" of sex therapy – Masters and Johnson – have also been studying homosexuality, both highlighting the functional equivalence of homosexuality and heterosexuality and stressing that "therapists must realize homosexuality is not a disease" (Masters and Johnson 1979: 272).

A further, very lucid discussion is provided in the work of Robert Stoller, who crucially distinguishes between labels as social forces and psychiatric diagnoses, and then proceeds to consider whether homosexual categories are valid in the second sense. He suggests a psychiatric diagnosis should, at the least, specify a syndrome (a cluster of visible signs and symptoms), an underlying dynamic and a coherent aetiology from which this dynamic originates. Using such criteria he concludes that:

> homosexuality is not a diagnosis; there is only a sexual preference, not a uniform constellation of signs and symptoms; different people with this sexual preference have different psychodynamics underlying their sexual behaviour; quite different life experiences can cause these dynamics and this behaviour.
>
> (Stoller 1975: 199)

There remain many psychiatrists who would firmly reject the work of those like Masters and Johnson, Stoller or the Kinsey Institute and insist that homosexuality is a gross pathology; Socarides's updated text, for instance, does not even consider the possibility that it is anything other than a disease (1978). Nevertheless the lobby to demedicalize homosexuality is both highly visible and highly influential, and is increasingly becoming the dominant "professional" mode of viewing homosexuality.[6]

The pluralization of identities

Much wider processes – nothing to do with homosexuality *per se* – can also be seen to contribute to this move to "break down" the constructed homosexual role. At base it is suggested that since industrialization there has been a steady retreat from a public world to a private world of self, family, relationships. A split, which did not formerly exist, has occurred, and individuals who can no longer find support, sustenance or meaning from the public symbols "retreat" to their own private worlds for "life-enhancing meanings" (see Sennet 1974; Lasch 1979; Berger *et al.* 1973; Zaretsky 1976; Zijderveld 1971; Brittan 1977; Zurcher 1977). This complex argument – which takes many forms – suggests that in this transition our sense of identities become less stable and more negotiable; we are involved in a "quest for identity" and part of that quest inevitably entails a view of the open-endedness of identity formation. In the past we were *given* our identities; now we *make* them ourselves (see Berger *et al.* 1973: 73).

Such a process takes us full circle for it would seem to hold contradictory implications for the homosexual experience. On the one hand, it suggests that people may experience homosexuality without it becoming a "masteridentity" since all identities are options; on the other, it implies that if individuals elect to call themselves "homosexuals" in their private worlds, they could then erect this into a lifesustaining "hero system" (see Becker 1973) around which to organize their lives. It is this peculiar tension which needs much more sustained analysis.

THE ORIGINS OF HOMOSEXUAL CATEGORIES

The standard "causal" question in the study of homosexuality has for a long time been: what makes people homosexual? The labelling perspective inverts this causal problem and asks: what makes people respond as they do to homosexuality? Partly the issue is why they should bother to invent a concern for homosexuality at all – why the experience should be recognized as an "issue" and in our culture translated into a "way of being". But the bigger and more central question is why it should often be invested with so much fear, hostility and rage. It is this question that I wish to address here.

At root, there are two main approaches to understanding the origins of the fear of "homosexuals"; one focuses upon individuals and seeks to explain "homophobia", and the other focuses upon society and seeks to explain "the homosexual taboo". The concept of "homophobia" – though far from new[7] – was first explicitly discussed by George Weinberg in the early 1970s. In his book *Society and the Healthy Homosexual* (1973) he defined homophobia as a phobic disease whereby there is a "dread of being in close quarters with homosexuals" and went on to identify the kind of panic reaction which this phobia can generate, usually in heterosexuals, but sometimes in oppressed homosexuals. Through the use of this concept it is the oppressors of homosexuals who come to be seen as sick, not the homosexuals themselves.[8]

Now as a tactical weapon in the gay movement I think the concept of homophobia contains a number of splendid ironies. At root it employs all the same pseudo-scientific weapons that are used to condemn homosexuality. Thus whereas once it was only the homosexual who was viewed as sick, it is now the heterosexual who is charged with pathology. Whereas once the homosexual was identified by a long series of character traits, it is now possible to identify the traits of the homophobe: authoritarian, cognitively restricted, with gender anxieties (MacDonald and Games 1974). Whereas once the diffuseness of homosexual experiences became channelled down into the idea of the homosexual person, it is now the homophobe who is seen as a special person. Whereas once the homosexual could be discovered by submitting him to a long battery of psychological tests, now the homophobe can be located by the use of homophobe scales – a social distance measure which asks respondents to write their agreement with such statements as "if a homosexual sat next to me on a bus I would get nervous" and "a

homosexual could be a good president of the United States" (Lumby 1976). Further, whereas once it was the homosexual who got treated for his problem, it is now the sick homophobe who needs a therapist.

While the concept of homophobia may have a symbolic rallying value within the gay movement, as a social science concept it does raise a number of difficulties. Indeed its ironic twist – that it uses the same weapons which used to be employed in attacking homosexuality and applies them to heterosexuality – serves to reinforce much that current social science would now seek to reject. Most notably, four worries can be raised with the current use of the concept: that it reinforces the idea of mental illness, that it neglects women, that it directs attention away from sexual oppression in general and that it individualizes the entire problem.

First, then, it ratifies and strengthens the notion of mental illness. It is curious that in the same year as the American Psychiatric Association struck homosexuality off its sickness nomenclature classification, an American psychologist should create the new disease of homophobia (Weinberg 1973). Now whatever one may think about the current view propounded by the American psychiatrist Szasz[9] – that all mental illness is a myth – it is fair, I think, to say that *certain* problems are better viewed as problems in living rather than sickness. There may be some behavioural variations where notions of sickness are helpful. But the inability of some people to get along with homosexuals hardly seems one of these. If homosexuality is not inherently a sickness, and I obviously don't think it is, then homophobia should not be seen as one either.

A second problem flows from the misogyny frequently embedded in the term. "Homophobia" is nearly always "fear of *male* homosexuals", and it is frequently explained as having its origins in threats to masculinity (see Lehne 1976). Not much attention is given to either the "lesbian threat" (Stanley 1976) or women's responses to gays, thereby reinforcing the persistent male bias of gay research.

Third, "homophobia" directs attention to the attack on homosexuals to the detriment of other sexual minority groups, for homosexuals may actually be the least oppressed of all sexual minorities. Our wrath and anger become even greater when confronted with the paedophile, the incestuous father, the sado-masochist and the fetishist. Are we to produce a whole series of new words – "sadophobia", "paedophobia", "fetophobia" – for each of these fears and hostilities, or could they all in some fashion be connected? To focus upon homophobia is to reveal one's own myopia and to do a disservice to the more general attitudes of sexual negativism in society.

Fourth, and most important, the notion of homophobia individualizes the entire problem of homosexual hostility, making it a problem of personalities rather than societies. The approach is reminiscent of that used to study the authoritarian, anti-Semitic, fascist personality by social scientists after World War II (Adorno *et al.* 1950). They too saw the problem of minority persecution as the outcome of thwarted personality types, rather than the social generation of a problem which subsequently gets justified through a learned ideology of racism.

While there are a number of difficulties with such a concept it does highlight one critical feature of some homosexual hostility: its fear-based irrationality. To reduce public hostility to homosexuality cannot simply be seen as a matter of more education or more information, because much of the hostility appears to be a personal defence erected to conceal and keep at bay some terrifying fears and anxieties. How else can one account for some of its public manifestations – all the way from homosexual murder through queer-bashing to media mockery? These responses seem to be thinly veiled responses to fear (sometimes so terrifying that they traumatize the person to murder), and the research issue here is to get at the basis of it. Among the solutions suggested have been the fear of one's own homosexuality (Cory 1953), fear of one's own sex (Lehne 1976), fear of a loss of immortality (Weinberg 1973; Becker 1973) and fear of a loss of status (see Zurcher and Kirkpatrick 1976).

These notions of "fear" and "threat" also provide, I believe, a bridge into a wider social explanation – what I have referred to as "The homosexual taboo" (Plummer 1976) – where the hostility is seen as a widespread social taboo (akin to the incest taboo) rather than as an individualistic phobia. Since few, if any, societies have accepted homosexuality as the major or dominant form of sexual experience, the problem cannot be reduced to the quirks of a few ill-informed or prejudiced individuals; it is more probably that the hostility is bound up with fears about widespread threats to social order, and this hostility becomes more intense under certain forms of social organization.

At the most general (and hence historically non-specific) level of social order, same sex experiences can come under attack because they act as a threat to a society's dominant set of symbols, which provides the overarching canopy of meaning for most of its members: the "natural order". People are born into a possibly meaningless universe with an enormous range of potentials and capacities; they could organize and experience the world in a vast assortment of different ways. They could change their identities, values, beliefs, friends, roles and perceptions of the world from day to day; nobody *has* to ritualize and routinize their worlds – everybody *could* do anything. But of course should everybody choose to, the world would become chaotic – a buzzing centre of booming confusion. Confronted with the possibility of new experiences at every minute of the waking day and the likelihood that nobody would know what to expect of anyone, the world would tumble away into chaos (see Scott 1972).

In our minds then we have to cast out these possibilities or else each day would be a Kafkaesque nightmare of unpredictability. To ward off this potential pandemonium, we come to believe that the world could not be otherwise – that it is "natural" or "God-given". We thus make sense of our predicaments by imposing master schemes (symbols) of order upon the world; anything that arises outside of these symbols therefore comes to be seen as a threat to our own personal security and must be either explained away or expelled. We may explain them away by rendering them as anomalies or perversions of the system; calling homosexuals "sick" serves to neutralize their threat. But when this fails, they need to be ejected from society (imprisoned, deported or killed).

Now in many societies, but notably ours, same-sex experiences are one such threat; they shatter much common sense thinking and render the everyday world highly vulnerable. Thus many members of our society have learnt that it is natural "to fall in love with a person of the opposite sex": "homosexuals" imply that love need not be so narrowly channelled. Many members come to believe that the "family is natural": "homosexuals" imply that people do not have to make families and can live without them. Many members believe that the differences between men and women are instinctive: "homosexuals" make gender much more ambiguous – men can be gentle and women can be assertive. Many members take it for granted that the lynchpin of morality is "proper" sexual conduct: "homosexuals" violate that assumed morality. Many members seek some meaning for their lives and find it in the idea of having children, providing a focus for one's life and a vicarious immortality: "homosexuals" imply that life can be led without children.

On all these scores, then, and others, "homosexuals" are devastatingly threatening to the "natural order". They do not live in families, often cannot have children, muddle up the two gender system and stand in conflict to the assumed morality. "Homosexuals" are hated because they violate the orderly "natural world" that is taken for granted by many people.

Of course "natural orders" are symbolic worlds which differ across cultures and – it can reasonably be argued – within cultures once industrialization, bureaucratization and urban diversity have set in (Berger *et al.* 1973). So to say that homosexuality constitutes a threat to the "natural order" is not to say it constitutes the same threat to all such orders. Indeed it is, likely that the more diffuse, complex, divergent and ambiguous the symbolic order (in other words, the less simple and rigid), the greater the potential for homosexual experiences to be more acceptable.

The weakness of this view – and indeed all symbolic analyses – is that it fails to explain *why* the existing order is as it is. It looks at the consequences of existing arrangements; it rarely looks at how the order emerged. It can therefore be conservative rather than critical, descriptive rather than explanatory, and concerned with the present rather than unfolding changes from the past. Yet if homosexuals are attacked because they do not fit into the prevailing familial, gender and moral systems of today, we have to understand how these systems came about, how they relate to the wider society, whose interests – if any – they serve and what alternative arrangements are possible. Questions like these need much more examination in the future.

These questions demand a scrupulous search of historical and anthropological materials; there are no easy answers. Some studies have already been made of certain areas – Bailey, for instance, examined in detail the impact of Judeo-Christian culture on homosexual oppression and reached the somewhat surprising conclusion that it did not play such a significant part as is often imagined (Bailey 1955). As well as looking at religious interests, historical studies should also consider the interests of lawmakers, doctors and psychiatrists, moralists, pressure groups and the like (see Spector 1977; Morrison and Tracey 1979). The trouble with such materials is that they would still fail to locate gay hostility in much wider contexts; they do not show how hostility may be linked to increasing rationalization and bureaucratization (Greenberg and Bystryn 1978), the Protestant ethic (Rotenberg 1979) and the changing nature of family, gender and class systems (Weeks 1977).

Once we start doing this another important possibility arises: that gay oppression is not the *intended* outcome of specific groups who hate gays for various reasons. Rather it is the *unintended* price that has to be paid for organizing society in certain ways. Thus attention should be directed not to why "individuals suffer from homophobia" but rather to why we have societies built around strong families, clear gender roles, rigid class and status structures, and a belief system which equates morality with sexuality.

THE CONDITIONS OF CATEGORIZATIONS: HOMOSEXUAL CAREERS AND HOMOSEXUAL IDENTITIES

A third set of research directions generated by the labelling perspective centres around the ways in which individuals come to be categorized as "homosexuals". This is by no means the same as asking why people become homosexuals – the standard aetiological problem – for this question prejudices the issue in assuming homosexuality to *be* a state of condition. It is perfectly possible – and, from existing accounts, quite common – for people to have same-sex fantasies, to engage in same-sex behaviour or to have flirtations with the same sex and for these same people *not* to see themselves as "homosexuals". Likewise it is not at all unusual for people to spend large portions of their lives behaving and feeling "heterosexually" only to adopt the label of "homosexual" at a much later stage in their life.[10] Further, it is possible that some people apply the label "homosexual" to themselves without ever meeting other homosexuals or having a same-sex experience. There is, in short, no absolute "fit" or congruency between doing, thinking or feeling, and there is no necessary fit between any of these and the act of labelling oneself as "a homosexual".[11] What is it then that prompts the adoption of the category for some people and not others?

The crudest answer to this question is to suggest that it is *imposed* by formal control agents – police, psychiatrists – on unsuspecting victims, "more sinned against than sinning" (see Gouldner 1968). But this view is now recognized as wholly inadequate; *self-constructed, symbolic self-labelling* is a much more fundamental theoretical and empirical problem (see Warren 1974; Plummer 1975; Rotenberg 1979). We need to ask about the ways in which individuals come to categorize themselves as certain kinds of sexual (or non-sexual) beings, how they come to hook themselves on to both wider societal and narrower community definitions, and how such definitions are used in fashioning subsequent lifestyles.

There are two broad ways of approaching the problem of building a homosexual identity:

the *sexual orientation model* and the *identity construct model*. The orientation model is found among geneticists, clinicians and behaviourists alike and suggests that a person's sexual orientation is firmly established by mid childhood.[12] For the geneticists it is there at birth; for the others it is shaped in early family experiences. Either way, our sexual attractions are firmly and irrevocably set up *before* we reach puberty. Money, for instance, argues that a core gender identity (the sense of being a man or a woman) is set up by the age of three and that sexual orientation is established in relationship to this a few years later:

> Because the erotic preferences usually reveal themselves at puberty, it is often assumed that they were instilled by a first sexual experience at that time, or caught from exposure to erotic pictures, books or films, an assumption that is responsible for much of today's judicial panic about pornography. On the contrary, each person's turn-on has rather fixed boundaries which are set before puberty. Whether the boundaries are orthodox or unorthodox, conventional or unconventional, they were established in childhood as part of a differentiation of gender identity, by the coding of the schemers, and by any quirks or oddities that were incorporated into the schemers. Boundaries may first show themselves at puberty, but they are not set in puberty and they don't change much, at puberty or later. Their relative unchangability helps to explain such phenomena as why a second spouse so often resembles the first. Their persistence also explains why adult obligative homosexuals can be fond of and behave affectionately towards a member of the other sex, especially if the other is older, but can never fall in love with her or him. Tales of sex degenerates who go from one form of depravity to another, sampling everything, are only fiction: even so-called sex degenerates stick to their particular preferences.
>
> (Money and Tucker 1977: 123)

Side by side with this view of the development of sexual orientation is the idea that sexual identity emerges simultaneously. Thus either the identity emerges unproblematically, so that the child en route to becoming a heterosexual *being* also learns the heterosexual *identity*, or a disjunction may occur between the orientation (being) that is built up in childhood and the identity that developed. Thus, for instance, in the category of the "latent homosexual", the being – that of "a homosexual" – is set up in childhood, but the identity that is acquired is inappropriate; the homosexual person comes (falsely and maybe because of heterosexual coercion) to view himself or herself as a "heterosexual". This model would assume that the category of "heterosexual identity" is inappropriate in this case; the person's *actual* identity is that of a homosexual.

In sharp contrast to this "orientation model", the "identity-construct" view – favoured by symbolic interactionists[13] – focuses upon the cognitive processes by which members of a society interpret their sexual selves by scanning their past lives (their bodies, group involvements, feelings and behaviours) and connecting these to "accounts" available in their contemporary worlds (through friends, family, psychiatrists, media). The focus here is not upon childhood determinations and permanent "real" orientations; rather it is upon the process of building identities throughout life through significant encounters.

As Blumstein and Schwartz (1976) have noted, the issues I have referred to here derive from the sociology of knowledge. Basically the problem is to explain how the existing given social categories – the heterosexual, the homosexual, the pederast, the bisexual – come to be filled: how do individuals scan their life history (at different moments) and identify themselves as certain kinds of sexual people (at different moments)? The orientation model answers this by saying that the individual experiences a deep erotic attraction to members of the same sex, and thereby comes to define himself or herself as homosexual. The constructionist approach suggests that perhaps initially our experiences are much more random, unstructured and uncrystallized than we choose to believe, and that it is through the definitional process that this randomness becomes channelled into stable sexual identities.

At first sight these models seem mutually exclusive. One says that identities are fixed by childhood; the other says they are flexible and negotiated in adult life. One raises the spectre of "latency", of having a true sexual identity of which one may be unaware; the other denies such a "realist" epistemology. The immediate problem, however, of trying to decide which

might prove more valid is compounded by discovering that there is certainly evidence available to support both models.

Thus most social surveys suggest that homosexual responses are "already determined and established very early in life" (Saghir and Robins 1973: 44). The Spada report (with its undoubtedly heavily biased sample) unequivocally reports that "35 per cent of the respondents report their first homosexual attraction before the age of ten, and another 41 per cent place it between the ages of ten and fourteen" (Spada 1979: 23). Further, Whitam, in his critique of the homosexual role, comments that:

> Nearly half of the homosexual respondents reported feeling sexually attracted to males before they learned of the existence of such sexual relations in the adult world ... Respondents frequently reported knowing that they were or would become homosexuals without having heard the term *homosexual* or its equivalent and without knowing that such behaviour existed in the adult world.
>
> (Whitam 1977: 7)

It seems that for *some* homosexuals, an orientation – independent of social labelling – is firmly seen to be fixed in childhood.

But if this is true of some, there is certainly other evidence which shows the flux and sway of adult homosexual identity (and often this comes from the same survey). Many "homosexuals" lead a heterosexual lifestyle at some point in their history and do not construct a homosexual identity till later in life. Dank (1974), for instance, in his study of 377 self-identified male homosexuals, found the age at which they constructed a homosexual identity varied greatly. Thus 45 (or 12.2 per cent) of his sample saw themselves as gay before the age of 15; another 130 (35.3 per cent) saw themselves as gay before the age of 20; a further 113 (30.7 per cent) saw themselves as homosexual by the time they were 25; and another 80 (21.8 per cent) saw themselves as gay once they were over the age of 25. Now this study is not talking about the emergence of homosexual behaviours or homosexual orientations, but rather the self-labelling as a homosexual. It may therefore be that there is a very real separation between the development of an *orientation* in a person and the development of an *identity* in a person. Likewise a small scale study by T. Weinberg (1978) distinguished between homosexual activities ("doing"), homosexual identities ("being") and suspicions of being a homosexual, and charted the order of their emergence in thirty male homosexuals. He found four patterns:

1 E → S → L   Engaged in activity → suspected himself to be homosexual → labelled self as a homosexual
2 E → L   Engaged in activity → labelled a homosexual
3 S → E → L   Suspicious of being homosexual → engaged in activity → labelled as a homosexual
4 S → L → E   Suspicious, labelled, engaged

Of these thirty men, "only four definitely thought of both their behaviour and themselves as homosexual at the time they were first engaging in sex with other males" (151). Unless one regards this as a purely "fluke" sample, the study must be taken to indicate the complexity of linking "doing" with "being". There is no one pattern.

There is then evidence to support the orientation model, since it seems well established that for some individuals orientation is set up in early childhood; but there is also evidence to support the construct model, since people's identities do empirically shift and swap very much in adult life. Confronted with such evidence, the "sexual orientation" theorists would say that although men and women may not become "aware" of their identities till later in life, until that time they were "latent", for their orientation was set up earlier. Likewise the "identity construct" theorists would say that the significance of childhood experiences was a reconstructed "vocabulary of motive" used as a legitimation of contemporary homosexuality.[14] Argument and counter-argument leave us undecided and in confusion.

For me, the problem is an important one demanding conceptual and empirical clarification. At present I believe a synthesis of the two views is required – a synthesis which acknowledges the importance of childhood experiences in the restricting of our sexual possibilities and the importance of adult experiences in moulding, further limiting and sometimes transcending this childhood base. Such a synthesis is often seen to be a contradictory nonsense: the irreconcilable cannot be reconciled. But empirically both *are* true; what is wrong is not the person's "contradictory" lived experience but the social scientists' theoretical debates which fail to incorporate such lived confusions.

But such apparent confusions are in effect only confusions if we seek simple, uniform answers to questions of identity and orientation. *Orientations* are – in all likelihood – set up in childhood; but while some people develop restrictive and rigid orientations, others may be open and flexible, while still others may develop no "orientations" at all. Further, underlying emotional predispositions are not cognitions, and many individuals may not – indeed may never throughout their life – be aware of them. If this is so, they are outside the participant's own world of meaning and should not therefore be given *too* much importance. Likewise *identities* are – in all likelihood – highly variable throughout social encounters; but while for some people this may mean drastic restructuring of self-conceptions at critical turning points in life, others may develop relatively stable identities at early moments in life and use these as foci to orientate most future conduct. Even if such stable identities are out of harmony with underlying orientations, they have to be taken very seriously as how people define their situations.

THE IMPACT OF LABELLING

This area is the one that sociologists have most frequently studied in the past, and hence only a little need be said here. The core idea highlights the negative consequences for homosexual experiences which flow from stigma. Elsewhere I have outlined how stigma may give rise to problems in at least three areas: in the process of becoming a homosexual, in the daily interactional problems and in the collective problems of the subculture. In the first area the situation of stigma gives rise to a series of engulfing problems – of guilt, identity and access to partners – for potential homosexuals as they move into the first stages of their homosexual career. In the second area the day-to-day life of homosexuals may become more problematic through such matters as conceal-ment, passing, and the heightened self-awareness that at any moment one may slip from a discreditable into a discredited person (see Goffman 1963). In the third area some of the characteristics of the gay sub-culture and the gay world flow from hostility. Hoffman (1968) has described many of the characteristics of the homosexual community and has tried to show how these characteristics flow out of the hostil-ity of society. Other, such as Schur (1965) and Williams and Weinberg (1971), have dealt with the more objective consequences of negative sanctions – matters like blackmail, police har-assment, work discrimination and even sexual murder.

Now although I think these three areas constitute a major and important research pro-gramme in the sociology of homosexuality, they are not without their problems. One important problem has been voiced by Sagarin and Kelly (1976). They critically note an irony that runs through the work of many labelling theorists whereby two divergent strands of thought may be found. On the one hand, there is a strong statement in most labelling studies about the normality of deviants: deviants are not dis-turbed, sick or pathological. On the other hand, there is a strand in labelling theory that suggests that negative sanctions create stressful and diffi-cult situations which in turn must lead to pathology, disturbance and even sickness. Now it is very clear in the labelling perspective on homosexuality that both these strands exist side by side, and as Sagarin and Kelly rightly com-ment *"pathology cannot be denied, and at the same time accounted for, in terms of social hostility"* (1976: 262). There is no doubt that the writings of Gagnon and Simon, Hooker and most notably Freedman suggest that "homo-sexuals" are very frequently psychologically well-adjusted individuals. As Freedman says:

> Homosexuality is compatible with positive psy-chological functioning. Studies demonstrate that most of the homosexually oriented individuals evaluated in the studies of adjustment function as well as comparable groups of heterosexually ori-

ented individuals; that their functioning could be typically characterised as normal; and that in some cases, their functioning even approximates that of self-actualising people. Cumulatively these studies (reviewed by Freedman) dealt with more than six hundred homosexually oriented subjects, whereas the studies with negative or mixed results had only about a hundred and fifty homosexual oriented subjects in all.

> (1971: 87)

Likewise Gagnon and Simon, in their review of 550 Kinsey subjects, "suggest that most homo-sexuals cope fairly well, and even particularly well when we consider the historical period involved and the stigmatized and, in fact, crimi-nal nature of their sexual interests" (1973: 138).

However, while theorists do place a great deal of emphasis upon the psychologically nor-mal functioning of many "homosexuals", they acknowledge that disturbance, pathology and tragedy may be also found. Gagnon and Simon in fact comment:

> We do not wish to say that homosexual life does not contain a great potential for demoralisation, despair and self-hatred. To the contrary, as in most unconventional careers there remains the poten-tial for a significant escalation of individual psycho-pathology.

> (1973: 139)

This issue then may be simply put. Labellists seem to be saying that, on the one hand, homosexuals are normal – just like everybody else. On the other hand, they seem to be saying that stigmatization processes create the poten-tial for pathology, despair and tragedy. The findings suggest that some homosexuals are well adjusted and that others are not. Sagarin and Kelly, however, seem to be producing a straw man in their criticism of labelling theory for *both* positions are tenable; there are both "pathological" and "non-pathological" homo-sexualities. The important variables to take into account are the *stage* of the homosexual career and the *nature* of the surrounding significant others. Thus in the early stages of the homo-sexual career, it is very likely that the stigmatiz-ing context of the wider society will create an enormous potential for demoralization and despair. The problems of guilt, secrecy, access, identity and so forth may lead to a pivotally engulfing, depressive experience; and these experiences just may lead "homosexuals" straight to the psychiatric couch. But as they work out solutions to these various problems, and in particular gain access to a supportive sub-culture ("gay", "feminist" or just "tolerant"), so the identity begins to change. Dank, for instance, has clearly demonstrated how access to other homosexuals serves to give one a more positive identity. Here then the "labelling others" are those people who provide positive support rather than destructive and negative attack. Hence under these circumstances one would not predict a high potential for demoralization and despair, but indeed would predict a better psychologically functioning "homosexual". This is precisely what empirical work has so far found. Homosexuals in prisons and under psychiatric treatment tend to show more disturbed signs than homosexuals in the gay community at large (Schofield 1965).

While in the early stages of the homosexual career negative sanctions may lead to problems and pathology, and in the middle stages of the homosexual career the positive reference group of other homosexuals may lead to a positive identity, there comes perhaps a later stage for some homosexuals where, far from functioning poorly or just averagely, they actually begin to function better than many people in society. Freedman suggests that when male homosexuals learn to overcome the oppression and difficulties that confront them in a hostile society, they become more "centred" people. They fight off the oppressive straitjacketing of gender roles, the oppressive restrictions of emotional expression given to most men and rigid controls of monogamous sex. Through an active, self-conscious working out of one's personal problems, the person comes to be more sensitive, aware and creative, able to control and master life more adequately. This position of course is also compatible with labelling theory. Here it is no longer a simple matter of hostile society leading to problems, or supportive reference group giving stable identities, but now a self-defined positive evaluation which gives rise to higher levels of psychological functioning. Positive self-esteem leads to positive self-functioning.

The Sagarin and Kelly argument therefore seems to be misconceived. By taking into account the different stages of the career process of the homosexual and by allowing for the differential responses instead of the uniformly hostile responses that some theorists seem to suggest, differential modes of adjustment and response can be predicted. It is precisely of course this reason why the findings of Weinberg and Williams on homosexuals in New York, San Francisco, Copenhagen and Amsterdam seem to refute the labelling theory. In fact they do no such thing; they merely provide evidence for the argument that in tolerant, supportive cultures, homosexuals who are involved in the gay world will not show the signs of pathology and disturbance predicted by some of the propositions in labelling theory.

CONCLUSION

In this paper I have argued for the study of homosexual categorizations rather than for the study of homosexuals. The need is to grasp the ways in which specifiable, historically produced meanings shape – and often damage – human experiences. It is not an easy area for investigation, since while it raises some very broad worries (the four questions outlined on p. 84), it also raises a seemingly irresolvable question: does the "category" mirror or construct the phenomena? We have had nearly a hundred years of assuming that "categories" simply mirror; the sociologist's task now is to analyse the alternative "constructionist" view.

NOTES

1 This shift from derogatory terms to positive self-constructed ones is discussed in Berzon and Leighton (1979) and in Morin and Schultz (1978).

2 The denial of civil liberties is being slowly documented in England by the Campaign for Homosexual Equality (1979), and in America by the Center for Homosexual Education, Evaluation and Research through the pages of the *Journal of Homosexuality* (see Petersen and Licata 1979). The "atrocities" delivered on "homosexuals" in other times are only slowly

coming to light but see, for example, Katz (1976) and the Martin Sherman play, *Bent*.

3 I use this phrase only in the most general sensitizing way; I do not wish to imply the discovery of a rigid definition which would negate the central thesis of this chapter.

4 While both authors – Levine and Humphreys – see aspects of this segregation as arising from social hostility, Humphreys at least sees the formation of a gay "satellite culture" as a very positive development for gay men, and does not contemplate its control role.

5 John Alan Lee (1979: 179–80) vividly described this "institutional completeness" of the Toronto gay scene. He writes:

> A gay citizen of Toronto can buy a home through a gay real estate agent familiar with the types of housing and neighborhoods most suitable to gay clients. He can close the deal through a gay lawyer, and insure with a gay insurance agent. If he is new to the community and cannot ask acquaintances for the names of these agents, he can consult the Gay Yellow Pages, a listing of businesses and services which is available in many larger cities. Or he can approach a typical source of connection with the gay community, such as a gay bookstore, or he can consult a local gay newspaper or periodical. From any of these sources of information he will also learn where he can buy lumber and renovating supplies from a company catering to a gay clientele. He will find gay suppliers of furniture, houseplants, and interior decorating. He will find gay sources of skilled labour or gay cleaning services.
>
> Having moved in, our gay citizen can clothe himself at gay-oriented clothing stores, have his hair cut by a gay stylist, his spectacles made by a gay optician. He can buy food at a gay bakery, records at a gay phonograph shop, and arrange his travel plans through gay travel agents. He can buy newspapers and books at a gay bookstore, worship in a gay church or synagogue, and eat at gay restaurants. Naturally he can drink at gay bars and dance at gay discotheques. He can obtain medical care from a gay physician or if he prefers, a gay chiropractor. If he wishes to remain entirely within the gay culture, he can seek work at many of these agencies and businesses, but he will have to bank his earnings at a nongay bank, though he may be able to deal with a gay credit union. He can contribute money to tax-deductible gay foundations, participate in gay political groups, and enjoy gay-produced programs on cable television. To keep him up to date on everything happening in his gay community he can telephone the Gay Line, which is updated weekly. If he feels the need for counselling to adjust his lifestyle to the nongay environment, he can get help anonymously, or in person, as he prefers.

6 An illuminating interactionist account of this lobby is to be found in Spector and Kitsuse (1977).

7 The term seems to hail from Wainwright Churchill's "homoerotophobia" (1967).

8 Sections of the following are reproduced from Plummer (1976).

9 Szasz has discussed homosexuality in a number of places, but see especially Szasz (1979).

10 The literature which supports these statements is now quite vast. See Bell and Weinberg (1978), Dank (1974), Ovesey (1969), Reiss (1962), Humphreys (1972), Blumstein and Schwartz (1976), T. Weinberg (1978)

11 I will discuss this non-congruency much more fully in a forthcoming book.

12 The orientation model implies people become "types of being". This is akin to Sagarin's "tyranny of isness" (1975), a view which has been criticized by Humphreys (1979).

13 This model is primarily allied to symbolic interactionist theory, but variants of it connect to the sociology of knowledge (Blumstein and Schwarz 1976), interpersonal congruency theory (Cass 1979) and existential sociology (Warren and Ponse 1977).

14 The standard source of this argument is C. W. Mills (1940).

REFERENCES

Adorno, T. W. *et al.* (1950), *The Authoritarian Personality* (London: Harper and Row).

Altman, D. (1971) *Homosexuals: Oppression and Liberation* (London: Outerbridge & Dienstfrey).

Bailey, P. D. Sherwin (1955) *Homosexuality and the Western Christian Tradition* (London: Longmans).

Becker, E. (1973) *The Denial of Death* (New York: Free Press).

Bell, A. P. (1976) "The Appraisal of Homosexuality", paper given at Kinsey Summer Conference, 1976.

Berger, P. L., Berger, B and Kellner, H. (1973), *The Homeless Mind* (London: Penguin).

Blumstein, P. and Schwartz, P. (1976) "The Acquisition of Sexual Identity: The Bisexual Case", unpublished paper for ASA Conference.

Brittan, A. (1977) *The Privatised World* (London: Routledge and Kegan Paul).

Brown, N. (1959), *Life Against Death* (Connecticut: Wesleyan University Press).

Cory, D. W. (1953) *The Homosexual Outlook: A Subjective Approach* (London: Nevill).

Crompton, L. (1969) "Homosexuality and the Sickness Theory", *Albany Trust Talking Point* (London: Albany Trust Publication).

Dank, B. (1974) "The Homosexual", in E. Goode and R. Troiden, *Sexual Deviance & Sexual Deviants* (New York: William Morrow).

Dank, B. (1976) "The Social Construction of the Homosexual", unpublished paper, California State University, Long Beach.

Ellis, H. (1920) *Studies in the Psychology of Sex*, vol. 2, *Sexual Inversion*, 3rd edn (Pennsylvania: F. A. Davis).

Freedman, M. (1971) *Homosexuality and Pyschological Functioning* (California: Wadsworth).

Freedman, M. and Mayers, J. (1976) *Loving Men: A Photographic Guide to Gay Love-Making* (New York: Hark Publishing Co.).

Freud, S. (1951) "Letter to an American Mother", *American Journal of Psychiatry* (April): 787.

Freud, S. (1977) *On Sexuality*, Penguin Freud Library, vol. 7 (London: Penguin).

Gagnon, J. H. and Simon, W. S. (1973) *Sexual Conduct: The Social Sources of Human Sexuality* (Chicago: Aldine).

Gaylin, W. (ed.) (1978) *Doing Good: The Triumph of Benevolence* (New York: Pantheon).

Goffman, E. (1963) *Stigma: Notes on the Management of Spoiled Identity* (New Jersey: Prentice-Hall).

Gouldner, A. W. (1968) "The Sociologist as Partisan: Sociology and the Welfare State", *American Sociologist* 3: 103–16.

Green, R. (1972) "Homosexuality as Mental Illness", *International Journal of Psychiatry* (10 March): 77–128.

Greenberg D. F. and Bystryn, M. H. (1978) "Social Sources of the Prohibition against Male Homosexuality", unpublished paper presented at the annual meeting of the SSSP, September.

Hocquenghem, G. (1978) *Homosexual Desire* (London: Allison & Busby).

Hoffmann, M. (1968) *The Gay World: Male Homosexuality and the Social Creation of Evil* (New York: Basic Books).

Humphreys, L. (1979) "Exodus and Identity: The Emerging Gay Culture", in M. P. Levine (ed.), *Gay Men: The Sociology of Male Homosexuality* (London: Harper & Row),

Kinsey, A. C. Pomeroy, W. B. and Martin, C. E. (1948) *Sexual Behavior in the Human Male* (Philadelphia: W. B. Saunders).

Kinsey, A. C., Gebhard, P., Pomeroy, W. B. and Martin, C. E. (1953) *Sexual Behavior in the Human Female* (Philadelphia: W. B. Saunders).

Lasch, C. (1979) *The Culture of Narcissism: American Life in an Age of Diminishing Experience* (New York: W. W. Norton).

Lehne, G. K. (1976) "Homophobia among Men", in D. S. David and R. Brannon (eds), *The Forty-Nine Percent Majority: the Male Sex Role* (London: Addison-Wesley): 66–88.

Levine, M. P. (1979) "Gay Ghetto", in M. P. Levine (ed.), *Gay Men: The Sociology of Male Homosexuality* (London: Harper & Row).

Lumby, M. E. (1976) "Homophobia: The Quest for a Valid Scale", *Journal of Homosexuality* 2: 39–47.

MacDonald, A. P. and Games, R. G. (1974) "Some Characteristics of Those who Hold Positive and Negative Attitudes towards Homosexuals", *Journal of Homosexuality* 1: 9–28.

Marcuse, H. (1969) *Eros and Civilization* (London: Sphere).

Masters, W. and Johnson, V. (1979) *Homosexuality in Perspective* (Massachusetts: Little, Brown).

Money, J. and Tucker, P. (1977) *Sexual Signatures* (London: Abacus).

Morrison, D. and Tracey M. (1979) *Whitehouse* (London: Macmillan)

Plummer, K. (1975) *Sexual Stigma: An Interactionist Account* (London: Routledge & Kegan Paul).

Plummer, K. (1976) "The Homosexual Taboo", *Gay News* 106.

Rotenberg, M. (1979) *Damnation and Deviance* (London: Free Press).

Sagarin, E. and Kelly R. J. (1976) "Sexual Deviance and Labeling Perspectives", in W. Gove (ed.), *The Labeling of Deviance* (New York: Wiley): 243–72.

Saghir, M. T. and Robins, E. (1973) *Male and Female Homosexuality: A Comprehensive Investigation* (Maryland: Williams and Wilkins).

Schofield, M. (1965) *Sociological Aspects of Homosexuality* (London: Longman).

Schur, E. M. (1965) *Crimes Without Victims – Deviant Behavior and Public Policy: Abortion, Homosexuality, Drug Addiction* (New Jersey: Prentice-Hall).

Scott, R. A. (1972) "A Proposed Framework for Analyzing Deviance as a Property of Social Order", in R. A. Scott and J. D. Douglas (eds) *Theoretical Perspectives on Deviance* (London: Basic Books), pp. 9–35.

Sennett, R. (1974) *The Fall of Public Men* (Cambridge: Cambridge University Press).

Socarides, C. W. (1978) *Homosexuality* (London: Jason Aronson).

Spada, J. (1979) *The Spada Report* (New York: Signet).

Spector, M. (1977) "Legitimizing Homosexuality", *Society* (July/August): 52–6.

Stambolian, G. and Marks, E. (eds) (1979) *Homosexualities and French Literature* (New York: Cornell University Press).

Stanley, L. (1976) "On the Receiving End", *Out* (Che magazine), 1: 6–7.

Stoller, R. J. (1975) *Sex and Gender, vol. II: The Transsexual Experiment* (London: Hogarth Press).

Warren, C. A. (1974) *Identity and Community in the Gay World* (London: Wiley).

Weeks, J. (1977) *Coming Out: Homosexual Politics in Britain from the 19th Century to the Present* (London: Quartet).

Weinberg, G. (1973) *Society and the Healthy Homosexual* (New York: Anchor).

Weinberg, T. (1978) "On 'Doing' and 'Being' Gay: Sexual Behavior and Homosexual Male Self Identity", *Journal of Homosexuality* 4: 143–56.

Whitam, F. (1977) "The Homosexual Role: A Reconsideration", *Journal of Sex Research* 13; 1–11.

Williams, C. and Weinberg, M. (1971) *Homosexuals and the Military* (New York: Harper & Row).

Zaretsky, E. (1976) *Capitalism, the Family and Personal Life* (London: Pluto Press).

Zijderveld, A. (1971) *The Abstract Society* (London: Penguin).

Zurcher, L. A. (1977) *The Mutable Self: A Self Concept for Social Change* (London: Sage).

Zurcher, L. A. Jnr and Kirkpatrick, R. G. (1976) *Citizens for Decency: Anti-Pornography Crusades, a State of Defence* (Austin: University of Texas Press).

GAYLE S. RUBIN

"Thinking Sex: Notes for a Radical Theory of the Politics of Sexuality"

first published in Carole S. Vance (ed.) *Pleasure and Danger: Exploring Female Sexuality* (1984); this revised and extended version from H. Abelove, M. Borale and D. Helperin, *The Lesbian and Gay Studies Reader* (New York: Routledge, 1993)

THE SEX WARS

> Asked his advice, Dr. J. Guerin affirmed that, after all other treatments had failed, he had succeeded in curing young girls affected by the vice of onanism by burning the clitoris with a hot iron ... I apply the hot point three times to each of the large labia and another on the clitoris ... After the first operation, from forty to fifty times a day, the number of voluptuous spasms was reduced to three or four ... We believe, then, that in cases similar to those submitted to your consideration, one should not hesitate to resort to the hot iron, and at an early hour, in order to combat clitoral and vaginal onanism in little girls.
>
> (Demetrius Zambaco)[1]

The time has come to think about sex. To some, sexuality may seem to be an unimportant topic, a frivolous diversion from the more critical problems of poverty, war, disease, racism, famine, or nuclear annihilation. But it is precisely at times such as these, when we live with the possibility of unthinkable destruction, that people are likely to become dangerously crazy about sexuality. Contemporary conflicts over sexual values and erotic conduct have much in common with the religious disputes of earlier centuries. They acquire immense symbolic weight. Disputes over sexual behavior often become the vehicles for displacing social anxieties, and discharging their attendant emotional intensity. Consequently, sexuality should be treated with special respect in times of great social stress.

The realm of sexuality also has its own internal politics, inequities, and modes of oppression. As with other aspects of human behavior, the concrete institutional forms of sexuality at any given time and place are products of human activity. They are imbued with conflicts of interest and political maneuvering, both deliberate and incidental. In that sense, sex is always political. But there are also historical periods in which sexuality is more sharply contested and more overtly politicized. In such periods, the domain of erotic life is, in effect, renegotiated.

In England and the United States, the late nineteenth century was one such era. During that time, powerful social movements focused on "vices" of all sorts. There were educational and political campaigns to encourage chastity, to eliminate prostitution and to discourage masturbation, especially among the young. Morality crusaders attacked obscene literature, nude paintings, music halls, abortion, birth control information and public dancing.[2] The consolidation of Victorian morality, and its apparatus of social, medical and legal enforcement, was the outcome of a long period of struggle whose results have been bitterly contested ever since.

The consequences of these great nineteenth-century moral paroxysms are still with us. They have left a deep imprint on attitudes about sex, medical practice, child-rearing, parental anxieties, police conduct, and sex law.

The idea that masturbation is an unhealthy practice is part of that heritage. During the nineteenth century, it was commonly thought that "premature" interest in sex, sexual excitement, and, above all, sexual release, would impair the health and maturation of a child. Theorists differed on the actual consequences of sexual precocity. Some thought it led to insanity, while others merely predicted stunted growth. To protect the young from premature arousal, parents tied children down at night so they would not touch themselves; doctors excised the clitorises of onanistic little girls.[3] Although the more gruesome techniques have been abandoned, the attitudes that produced them persist. The notion that sex *per se* is harmful to the young has been chiseled into extensive social and legal structures designed to insulate minors from sexual knowledge and experience.

Much of the sex law currently on the books also dates from the nineteenth-century morality crusades. The first federal anti-obscenity law in the United States was passed in 1873. The Comstock Act – named for Anthony Comstock, an ancestral anti-porn activist and the founder of the New York Society for the Suppression of Vice – made it a federal crime to make, advertise, sell, possess, send through the mails, or import books or pictures deemed obscene. The law also banned contraceptive or abortifacient drugs and devices and information about them.[4] In the wake of the federal statute, most states passed their own anti-obscenity laws.

The Supreme Court began to whittle down both federal and state Comstock laws during the 1950s. By 1975, the prohibition of materials used for, and information about, contraception and abortion had been ruled unconstitutional. However, although the obscenity provisions have been modified, their fundamental constitutionality has been upheld. Thus it remains a crime to make, sell, mail, or import material which has no purpose other than sexual arousal.[5]

Although sodomy statutes date from older strata of the law, when elements of canon law were adopted into civil codes, most of the laws used to arrest homosexuals and prostitutes come out of the Victorian campaigns against "white slavery." These campaigns produced the myriad prohibitions against solicitation, lewd behavior, loitering for immoral purposes, age offenses, and brothels and bawdy houses.

In her discussion of the British "white slave" scare, historian Judith Walkowitz observes that "Recent research delineates the vast discrepancy between lurid journalistic accounts and the reality of prostitution. Evidence of widespread entrapment of British girls in London and abroad is slim."[6] However, public furor over this ostensible problem

forced the passage of the Criminal Law Amendment Act of 1885, a particularly nasty and pernicious piece of omnibus legislation. The 1885 Act raised the age of consent for girls from 13 to 16, but it also gave police far greater summary jurisdiction over poor working-class women and children ... it contained a clause making indecent acts between consenting male adults a crime, thus forming the basis of legal prosecution of male homosexuals in Britain until 1967 ... the clauses of the new bill were mainly enforced against working-class women, and regulated adult rather than youthful sexual behaviour.[7]

In the United States, the Mann Act, also known as the White Slave Traffic Act, was passed in 1910. Subsequently, every state in the union passed anti-prostitution legislation.[8]

In the 1950s, in the United States, major shifts in the organization of sexuality took place. Instead of focusing on prostitution or masturbation, the anxieties of the 1950s condensed most specifically around the image of the "homosexual menace" and the dubious specter of the "sex offender." Just before and after World War II, the "sex offender" became an object of public fear and scrutiny. Many states and cities, including Massachusetts, New Hampshire, New Jersey, New York State, New York City and Michigan, launched investigations to gather information about this menace to public safety.[9] The term "sex offender" sometimes applied to rapists, sometimes to "child molesters," and eventually functioned as a code for homosexuals. In its bureaucratic, medical, and popular versions, the sex offender discourse tended to blur distinctions between violent sexual assault and illegal but consensual acts such as sodomy. The criminal justice system incorporated these concepts when an epidemic of sexual psychopath laws swept through state legislatures.[10] These laws gave the psychological professions increased police powers over homosexuals and other sexual "deviants."

From the late 1940s until the early 1960s, erotic communities whose activities did not fit the postwar American dream drew intense persecution. Homosexuals were, along with communists, the objects of federal witch hunts and purges. Congressional investigations, executive orders, and sensational exposés in the media aimed to root out homosexuals employed by the government. Thousands lost their jobs, and restrictions on federal employment of homosexuals persist to this day.[11] The FBI began systematic surveillance and harassment of homosexuals which lasted at least into the 1970s.[12]

Many states and large cities conducted their own investigations, and the federal witch-hunts were reflected in a variety of local crackdowns. In Boise, Idaho, in 1955, a schoolteacher sat down to breakfast with his morning paper and read that the vice-president of the Idaho First National Bank had been arrested on felony sodomy charges; the local prosecutor said that he intended to eliminate all homosexuality from the community. The teacher never finished his breakfast. "He jumped up from his seat, pulled out his suitcases, packed as fast as he could, got into his car, and drove straight to San Francisco ... The cold eggs, coffee, and toast remained on his table for two days before someone from his school came by to see what had happened."[13]

In San Francisco, police and media waged war on homosexuals throughout the 1950s. Police raided bars, patrolled cruising areas, conducted street sweeps and trumpeted their intention of driving the queers out of San Francisco.[14] Crackdowns against gay individuals, bars, and social areas occurred throughout the country. Although anti-homosexual crusades are the best-documented examples of erotic repression in the 1950s, future research should reveal similar patterns of increased harassment against pornographic materials, prostitutes, and erotic deviants of all sorts. Research is needed to determine the full scope of both police persecution and regulatory reform.[15]

The current period bears some uncomfortable similarities to the 1880s and the 1950s. The 1977 campaign to repeal the Dade County, Florida, gay rights ordinance inaugurated a new wave of violence, state persecution, and legal initiatives directed against minority sexual populations and the commercial sex industry. For the last six years, the United States and Canada have undergone an extensive sexual repression in the political, not the psychological, sense. In the spring of 1977, a few weeks before the Dade County vote, the news media were suddenly full of reports of raids on gay cruising areas, arrests for prostitution, and investigations into the

manufacture and distribution of pornographic materials. Since then, police activity against the gay community has increased exponentially. The gay press has documented hundreds of arrests, from the libraries of Boston to the streets of Houston and the beaches of San Francisco. Even the large, organized and relatively powerful urban gay communities have been unable to stop these depredations. Gay bars and bath houses have been busted with alarming frequency, and police have gotten bolder. In one especially dramatic incident, police in Toronto raided all four of the city's gay baths. They broke into cubicles with crowbars and hauled almost 300 men out into the winter streets, clad in their bath towels. Even "liberated" San Francisco has not been immune. There have been proceedings against several bars, countless arrests in the parks, and, in the fall of 1981, police arrested over 400 people in a series of sweeps of Polk Street, one of the thoroughfares of local gay nightlife. Queerbashing has become a significant recreational activity for young urban males. They come into gay neighborhoods armed with baseball bats and looking for trouble, knowing that the adults in their lives either secretly approve or will look the other way.

The police crackdown has not been limited to homosexuals. Since 1977, enforcement of existing laws against prostitution and obscenity has been stepped up. Moreover, states and municipalities have been passing new and tighter regulations on commercial sex. Restrictive ordinances have been passed, zoning laws altered, licensing and safety codes amended, sentences increased and evidentiary requirements relaxed. This subtle legal codification of more stringent controls over adult sexual behavior has gone largely unnoticed outside of the gay press.

For over a century, no tactic for stirring up erotic hysteria has been as reliable as the appeal to protect children. The current wave of erotic terror has reached deepest into those areas bordered in some way, if only symbolically, by the sexuality of the young. The motto of the Dade County repeal campaign was "Save Our Children" from alleged homosexual recruitment. In February 1977, shortly before the Dade County vote, a sudden concern with "child pornography" swept the national media. In May, the *Chicago Tribune* ran a lurid four-day series with three-inch headlines, which claimed to expose a national vice ring organized to lure young boys into prostitution and pornography.[16] Newspapers across the country ran similar stories, most of them worthy of the *National Enquirer*. By the end of May, a congressional investigation was under way. Within weeks, the federal government had enacted a sweeping bill against "child pornography" and many of the states followed with bills of their own. These laws have re-established restrictions on sexual materials that had been relaxed by some of the important Supreme Court decisions. For instance, the Court ruled that neither nudity nor sexual activity *per se* were obscene. But the child pornography laws define as obscene any depiction of minors who are nude or engaged in sexual activity. This means that photographs of naked children in anthropology textbooks and many of the ethnographic movies shown in college classes are technically illegal in several states. In fact, the instructors are liable to an additional felony charge for showing such images to each student under the age of 18. Although the Supreme Court has also ruled that it is a constitutional right to possess obscene material for private use, some child pornography laws prohibit even the private possession of any sexual material involving minors.

The laws produced by the child porn panic are ill-conceived and misdirected. They represent far-reaching alterations in the regulation of sexual behavior and abrogate important sexual civil liberties. But hardly anyone noticed as they swept through Congress and state legislatures. With the exception of the North American Man/Boy Love Association and the American Civil Liberties Union, no one raised a peep of protest.[17]

A new and even tougher federal child pornography bill has just reached House–Senate conference. It removes any requirement that prosecutors must prove that alleged child pornography was distributed for commercial sale. Once this bill becomes law, a person merely possessing a nude snapshot of a 17-year-old lover or friend may go to jail for fifteen years, and be fined $100,000. This bill passed the House 400 to 1.[18]

The experiences of art photographer Jacqueline Livingstone exemplify the climate created by the child porn panic. An assistant professor of photography at Cornell University, Livingstone was fired in 1978 after exhibiting pictures of male nudes which included photographs of her 7-year-old son masturbating. *Ms. Magazine*, *Chrysalis* and *Art News* all refused to run ads for Livingston's posters of male nudes. At one point, Kodak confiscated some of her film, and for several months, Livingstone lived with the threat of prosecution under the child pornography laws. The Tompkins County Department of Social Services investigated her fitness as a parent. Livingstone's posters have been collected by the Museum of Modern Art, the Metropolitan, and other major museums. But she has paid a high cost in harassment and anxiety for her efforts to capture on film the uncensored male body at different ages.[19]

It is easy to see someone like Livingston as a victim of the child porn wars. It is harder for most people to sympathize with actual boy-lovers. Like communists and homosexuals in the 1950s, boy-lovers are so stigmatized that it is difficult to find defenders for their civil liberties, let alone for their erotic orientation. Consequently, the police have feasted on them. Local police, the FBI, and watchdog postal inspectors have joined to build a huge apparatus whose sole aim is to wipe out the community of men who love underaged youth. In twenty years or so, when some of the smoke has cleared, it will be much easier to show that these men have been the victims of a savage and undeserved witch-hunt. A lot of people will be embarrassed by their collaboration with this persecution, but it will be too late to do much good for those men who have spent their lives in prison.

While the misery of the boy-lovers affects very few, the other long-term legacy of the Dade County repeal affects almost everyone. The success of the anti-gay campaign ignited long-simmering passions of the American right, and sparked an extensive movement to compress the boundaries of acceptable sexual behavior.

Right-wing ideology linking non-familial sex with communism and political weakness is nothing new. During the McCarthy period, Alfred Kinsey and his Institute for Sex Research were attacked for weakening the moral fiber of Americans and rendering them more vulnerable to communist influence. After congressional investigations and bad publicity, Kinsey's Rockefeller grant was terminated in 1954.[20]

Around 1969, the extreme right discovered the Sex Information and Education Council of the United States (SIECUS). In books and pamphlets, such as *The Sex Education Racket: Pornography in the Schools* and *SIECUS: Corrupter of Youth*, the right attacked SIECUS and sex education as communist plots to destroy the family and sap the national will.[21] Another pamphlet, *Pavlov's Children (They May Be Yours)*, claims that the United Nations Educational, Scientific and Cultural Organization (UNESCO) is in cahoots with SIECUS to undermine religious taboos, to promote the acceptance of abnormal sexual relations, to downgrade absolute moral standards, and to "destroy racial cohesion," by exposing white people (especially white women) to the alleged "lower" sexual standards of black people.[22]

New Right and neo-conservative ideology has updated these themes, and leans heavily on linking "immoral" sexual behavior to putative declines in American power. In 1977, Norman Podhoretz wrote an essay blaming homosexuals for the alleged inability of the United States to stand up to the Russians.[23] He thus neatly linked "the anti-gay fight in the domestic arena and the anti-communist battles in foreign policy."[24]

Right-wing opposition to sex education, homosexuality, pornography, abortion, and pre-marital sex moved from the extreme fringes to the political center stage after 1977, when right-wing strategists and fundamentalist religious crusaders discovered that these issues had mass appeal. Sexual reaction played a significant role in the right's electoral success in 1980.[25] Organizations like the Moral Majority and Citizens for Decency have acquired mass followings, immense financial resources, and unanticipated clout. The Equal Rights Amendment has been defeated, legislation has been passed that mandates new restrictions on abortion, and funding for programs like Planned Parenthood and sex education has been slashed. Laws and regulations making it more difficult for teenage girls to obtain contraceptives or abortions have been promulgated. Sexual backlash was exploited in successful attacks on the Women's Studies Program at California State University at Long Beach.

The most ambitious right-wing legislation initiative has been the Family Protection Act (FPA), introduced in Congress in 1979. The Family Protection Act is a broad assault on feminism, homosexuals, non-traditional families, and teenage sexual privacy.[26] The Family Protection Act has not passed and probably will not pass, but conservative members of Congress continue to pursue its agenda in a more piecemeal fashion. Perhaps the most glaring sign of the times is the Adolescent Family Life Program. Also known as the Teen Chastity Program, it gets some 15 million federal dollars to encourage teenagers to refrain from sexual intercourse, and to discourage them from using contraceptives if they do have sex, and from having abortions if they get pregnant. In the last few years, there have been countless local confrontations over gay rights, sex education, abortion rights, adult bookstores, and public school curricula. It is unlikely that the anti-sex backlash is over, or that it has even peaked. Unless something changes dramatically, it is likely that the next few years will bring more of the same.

Periods such as the 1880s in England, and the 1950s in the United States, recodify the relations of sexuality. The struggles that were fought leave a residue in the form of laws, social practices, and ideologies which then affect the way in which sexuality is experienced long after the immediate conflicts have faded. All the signs indicate that the present era is another of those watersheds in the politics of sex. The settlements that emerge from the 1980s will have an impact far into the future. It is therefore imperative to understand what is going on and what is at stake in order to make informed decisions about what policies to support and oppose.

It is difficult to make such decisions in the absence of a coherent and intelligent body of radical thought about sex. Unfortunately, progressive political analysis of sexuality is relatively underdeveloped. Much of what is available from the feminist movement has simply added to the mystification that shrouds the subject. There is an urgent need to develop radical perspectives on sexuality.

Paradoxically, an explosion of exciting scholarship and political writing about sex has been generated in these bleak years. In the 1950s, the early gay rights movement began and prospered while the bars were being raided and anti-gay laws were being passed. In the last six years, new erotic communities, political alliances, and analyses have been developed in the midst of the repression. In this essay, I will propose elements of a descriptive and conceptual framework for thinking about sex and its politics. I hope to contribute to the pressing task of creating an accurate, humane, and genuinely liberatory body of thought about sexuality.

SEXUAL THOUGHTS

"You see, Tim," Phillip said suddenly, "your argument isn't reasonable. Suppose I granted your first point that homosexuality is justifiable in certain instances and under certain controls. Then there is the catch: where does justification end and degeneracy begin? Society must condemn to protect. Permit even the intellectual homosexual a place of respect and the first bar is down. Then comes the next and the next until the sadist, the flagellist, the criminally insane demand their places, and society ceases to exist. So I ask again: where is the line drawn? Where does degeneracy begin if not at the beginning of individual freedom in such matters?"
(Fragment from a discussion between two gay men trying to decide if they may love each other, from a novel published in 1950[27])

A radical theory of sex must identify, describe, explain, and denounce erotic injustice and sexual oppression. Such a theory needs refined conceptual tools which can grasp the subject and hold it in view. It must build rich descriptions of sexuality as it exists in society and history. It requires a convincing critical language that can convey the barbarity of sexual persecution.

Several persistent features of thought about sex inhibit the development of such a theory. These assumptions are so pervasive in Western culture that they are rarely questioned. Thus, they tend to reappear in different political contexts, acquiring new rhetorical expressions but reproducing fundamental axioms.

One such axiom is sexual essentialism – the idea that sex is a natural force that exists prior to social life and shapes institutions. Sexual essentialism is embedded in the folk wisdoms of Western societies, which consider sex to be eternally unchanging, asocial, and transhistorical. Dominated for over a century by medicine, psychiatry, and psychology, the academic study of sex has reproduced essentialism. These fields classify sex as a property of individuals. It may reside in their hormones or their psyches. It may be construed as physiological or psychological. But within these ethnoscientific categories, sexuality has no history and no significant social determinants.

During the last five years, a sophisticated historical and theoretical scholarship has challenged sexual essentialism both explicitly and implicitly. Gay history, particularly the work of Jeffrey Weeks, has led this assault by showing that homosexuality as we know it is a relatively modern institutional complex.[28] Many historians have come to see the contemporary institutional forms of heterosexuality as an even more recent development.[29] An important contributor to the new scholarship is Judith Walkowitz, whose research has demonstrated the extent to which prostitution was transformed around the turn of the century. She provides meticulous descriptions of how the interplay of social forces such as ideology, fear, political agitation, legal reform, and medical practice can change the structure of sexual behavior and alter its consequences.[30]

Michel Foucault's *The History of Sexuality* has been the most influential and emblematic text of the new scholarship on sex. Foucault criticizes the traditional understanding of sexuality as a natural libido yearning to break free of social constraint. He argues that desires are not preexisting biological entities, but rather, that they are constituted in the course of historically specific social practices. He emphasizes the generative aspects of the social organization of sex rather than its repressive elements by pointing out that new sexualities are constantly produced. And he points to a major discontinuity between kinship-based systems of sexuality and more modern forms.[31]

The new scholarship on sexual behavior has given sex a history and created a constructive alternative to sexual essentialism. Underlying this body of work is an assumption that sexuality is constituted in society and history, not biologically ordained.[32] This does not mean the biological capacities are not prerequisites for human sexuality. It does mean that human sexuality is not comprehensible in purely biological terms. Human organisms with human brains are necessary for human cultures, but no examination of the body or its parts can explain the nature and variety of human social systems. The belly's hunger gives no clues as to the complexities of cuisine. The body, the brain, the genitalia, and the capacity for language are all necessary for human sexuality. But they do not determine its content, its experiences, or its institutional forms. Moreover, we never encounter the body unmediated by the meanings that cultures give to it. To paraphrase Lévi-Strauss, my position on the relationship between biology and sexuality is a "Kantianism without a transcendental libido."[33]

It is impossible to think with any clarity about the politics of race or gender as long as these are thought of as biological entities rather than as social constructs. Similarly, sexuality is impervious to political analysis as long as it is primarily conceived as a biological phenomenon or an aspect of individual psychology. Sexuality is as much a human product as are diets, methods of transportation, systems of etiquette, forms of labor, types of entertainment, processes of production, and modes of oppression. Once sex is understood in terms of social analysis and historical understanding, a more realistic politics of sex becomes possible. One may then think of sexual politics in terms of such phenomena as populations, neighborhoods, settlements patterns, migration, urban conflict, epidemiology, and police technology. These are more fruitful categories of thought than the more traditional ones of sin, disease, neurosis, pathology, decadence, pollution, or the decline and fall of empires.

By detailing the relationships between stigmatized erotic populations and the social forces which regulate them, work such as that of Allan Bérubé, John D'Emilio, Jeffrey Weeks, and Judith Walkowitz contains implicit categories of political analysis and criticism. Nevertheless, the constructivist perspective has displayed some political weaknesses. This has been most evident in misconstructions of Foucault's position.

Because of his emphasis on the ways that sexuality is produced, Foucault has been vulnerable to interpretations that deny or minimize the reality of sexual repression in the more political sense. Foucault makes it abundantly clear that he is not denying the existence of sexual repression so much as inscribing it within a large dynamic.[34] Sexuality in Western societies has been structured within an extremely punitive social framework, and has been subjected to very real formal and informal controls. It is necessary to recognize repressive phenomena without resorting to the essentialist assumptions of the language of libido. It is important to hold repressive sexual practices in focus, even while situating them within a different totality and a more refined terminology.[35]

Most radical thought about sex has been embedded within a model of the instincts and their restraints. Concepts of sexual oppression have been lodged within that more biological understanding of sexuality. It is often easier to fall back on the notion of a natural libido subjected to inhumane repression than to reformulate concepts of sexual injustice within a more constructivist framework. But it is essential that we do so. We need a radical critique of sexual arrangements that has the conceptual elegance of Foucault and the evocative passion of Reich.

The new scholarship on sex has brought a welcome insistence that sexual terms be restricted to their proper historical and social contexts, and a cautionary scepticism towards sweeping generalizations. But it is important to be able to indicate groupings of erotic behavior and general trends within erotic discourse. In addition to sexual essentialism, there are at least five other ideological formations whose grip on sexual thought is so strong that to fail to discuss them is to remain enmeshed within them. These are sex negativity, the fallacy of misplaced scale, the hierarchical valuation of sex acts, the domino theory of sexual peril, and the lack of a concept of benign sexual variation.

Of these five, the most important is sex negativity. Western cultures generally consider sex to be a dangerous, destructive, negative force.[36] Most Christian tradition, following Paul, holds that sex is inherently sinful. It may be redeemed if performed within marriage for procreative purposes and if the pleasurable aspects are not enjoyed too much. In turn, this idea rests on the assumption that the genitalia are an intrinsically inferior part of the body, much lower and less holy than the mind, the "soul," the "heart," or even the upper part of the digestive system (the status of the excretory organs is close to that of the genitalia).[37] Such notions have by now acquired a life of their own and no longer depend solely on religion for their perseverance.

This culture always treats sex with suspicion. It construes and judges almost any sexual practice in terms of its worst possible expression. Sex is presumed guilty until proven innocent. Virtually all erotic behavior is considered bad unless a specific reason to exempt it has been established. The most acceptable excuses are marriage, reproduction, and love. Sometimes scientific curiosity, aesthetic experience or a long-term intimate relationship may serve. But the exercise of erotic capacity, intelligence, curiosity, or creativity all require pretexts that are unnecessary for other pleasures, such as the enjoyment of food, fiction, or astronomy.

What I call the fallacy of misplaced scale is a corollary of sex negativity. Susan Sontag once commented that since Christianity focused "on sexual behavior as the root of virtue, everything pertaining to sex has been a 'special case' in our culture."[38] Sex law has incorporated the religious attitude that heretical sex is an especially heinous sin that deserves the harshest punishments. Throughout much of European and American history, a single act of consensual anal penetration was grounds for execution. In some states, sodomy still carries twenty-year prison sentences. Outside the law, sex is also a marked category. Small differences in value or behavior are often experienced as cosmic threats. Although people can be intolerant, silly, or pushy about what constitutes proper diet, differences in menu rarely provoke the kinds of rage, anxiety and sheer terror that routinely accompany differences in erotic tastes. Sexual acts are burdened with an excess of significance.

Modern Western societies appraise sex acts according to a hierarchical system of sexual value. Marital, reproductive heterosexuals are alone at the top of the erotic pyramid. Clamoring below are unmarried monogamous heterosexuals in couples, followed by most other heterosexuals. Solitary sex floats ambiguously. The powerful nineteenth-century stigma on masturbation lingers in less potent, modified forms, such as the idea that masturbation is an inferior substitute for partnered encounters. Stable, long-term lesbian and gay male couples are verging on respectability, but bar dykes and promiscuous gay men are hovering just above the groups at the very bottom of the pyramid. The most despised sexual castes currently include transsexuals, transvestites, fetishists, sado-masochists, sex workers such as prostitutes and porn models, and the lowliest of all, those whose eroticism transgresses generational boundaries.

Individuals whose behavior stands high in this hierarchy are rewarded with certified mental health, respectability, legality, social and physical mobility, institutional support, and material benefits. As sexual behaviors or occupations fall lower on the scale, the individuals who practice them are subjected to a presumption of mental illness, disreputability, criminality, restricted social and physical mobility, loss of institutional support, and economic sanctions.

Extreme and punitive stigma maintains some sexual behaviors as low status and is an effective sanction against those who engage in them. The intensity of this stigma is rooted in Western religious traditions. But most of its contemporary content derives from medical and psychiatric opprobrium.

The old religious taboos were primarily based on kinship forms of social organization. They were meant to deter inappropriate unions and to provide proper kin. Sex laws derived from Biblical pronouncements were aimed at preventing the acquisition of the wrong kinds of affinal partners: consanguineous kin (incest), the same gender (homosexuality) or the wrong species (bestiality). When medicine and psychiatry acquired extensive powers over sexuality, they were less concerned with unsuitable mates than with unfit forms of desire. If taboos against incest best characterized kinship systems of sexual organization, then the shift to an emphasis on taboos against masturbation was more apposite to the newer systems organized around qualities of erotic experience.[39]

Medicine and psychiatry multiplied the categories of sexual misconduct. The section on psychosexual disorders in the *Diagnostic and Statistical Manual of Mental and Physical Disorders (DSM)* of the American Psychiatric Association (APA) is a fairly reliable map of the current moral hierarchy of sexual activities. The APA list is much more elaborate than the traditional condemnations of whoring, sodomy, and adultery. The most recent edition, *DSM-III*, removed homosexuality from the roster of mental disorders after a long political struggle. But fetishism, sadism, masochism, transsexuality, transvestism, exhibitionism, voyeurism, and pedophilia are quite firmly entrenched as psychological malfunctions.[40] Books are still being written about the genesis, etiology, treatment, and cure of these assorted "pathologies."

Psychiatric condemnation of sexual behaviors invokes concepts of mental and emotional inferiority rather than categories of sexual sin. Low-status sex practices are vilified as mental diseases or symptoms of defective personality integration. In addition, psychological terms conflate difficulties of psycho-dynamic functioning with modes of erotic conduct. They equate sexual masochism with self-destructive personality patterns, sexual sadism with emotional aggression, and homoeroticism with immaturity. These terminological muddles have become powerful stereotypes that are indiscriminately applied to individuals on the basis of their sexual orientations.

Popular culture is permeated with ideas that erotic variety is dangerous, unhealthy, depraved, and a menace to everything from small children to national security. Popular sexual ideology is a noxious stew made up of ideas of sexual sin, concepts of psychological inferiority, anti-communism, mob hysteria, accusations of witchcraft, and xenophobia. The mass media nourish these attitudes with relentless propaganda. I would call this system of erotic stigma the last socially respectable form of prejudice if the old forms did not show such obstinate vitality, and new ones did not continually become apparent.

All these hierarchies of sexual value – religious, psychiatric, and popular – function in much the same ways as do ideological systems of racism, ethnocentrism, and religious chauvinism. They rationalize the well-being of the sexually privileged and the adversity of the sexual rabble.

Figure 10.1 diagrams a general version of the sexual value system. According to this system, sexuality that is "good," "normal," and "natural" should ideally be heterosexual, marital, monogamous, reproductive, and non-commercial. It should be coupled, relational, within the same generation, and occur at home. It should not involve pornography, fetish objects, sex toys of any sort, or roles other than male and female. Any sex that violates these rules is "bad," "abnormal," or "unnatural." Bad sex may be homosexual unmarried, promiscuous, non-procreative, or commercial. It may be masturbatory or take place at orgies, may be casual, may cross generational lines, and may take place in "public," or at least in the bushes or the baths. It may involve the use of pornography, fetish objects, sex toys, or unusual roles (see Figure 10.1).

Figure 10.2 diagrams another aspect of the sexual hierarchy: the need to draw and maintain an imaginary line between good and bad sex. Most of the discourses on sex, be they religious, psychiatric, popular, or political, delimit a very small portion of human sexual capacity as sanctifiable, safe, healthy, mature, legal, or politically correct. The "line" distinguishes these from all other erotic behaviors, which are understood to be the work of the devil, dangerous, psychopathological, infantile, or politically reprehensible. Arguments are then conducted over "where to draw the line," and to determine what other activities, if any, may be permitted to cross over into acceptability.[41]

All these models assume a domino theory of sexual peril. The line appears to stand between sexual order and chaos. It expresses the fear that if anything is permitted to cross this erotic DMZ, the barrier against scary sex will crumble and something unspeakable will skitter across.

Most systems of sexual judgment – religious, psychological, feminist, or socialist – attempt to determine on which side of the line a particular act falls. Only sex acts on the good side of the line are accorded moral complexity. For

THE CHARMED CIRCLE
Good, Normal, Natural, Blessed Sexuality

Heterosexual
Married
Monogamous
Procreative
Non-commercial
In pairs
In a relationship
Same generation
In private
No pornography
Bodies only
Vanilla

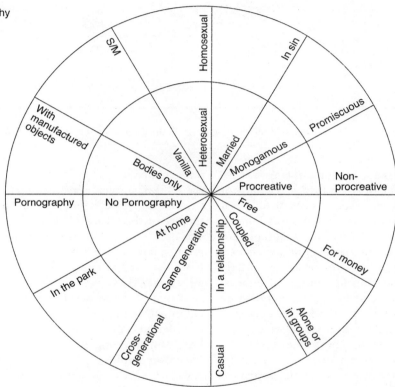

THE OUTER LIMITS
Bad, Abnormal, Unnatural,
Damned Sexuality

Homosexual
Unmarried
Promiscuous
Non-procreative
Commercial
Alone or in groups
Casual
Cross-generational
In public
Pornography
With manufactured objects
Sadomasochistic

Figure 10.1 The sex hierarchy: the charmed circle vs. the outer limits

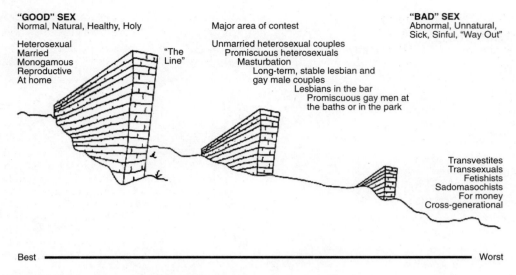

"GOOD" SEX
Normal, Natural, Healthy, Holy

Heterosexual
Married
Monogamous
Reproductive
At home

"The
Line"

Major area of contest

Unmarried heterosexual couples
Promiscuous heterosexuals
Masturbation
Long-term, stable lesbian and
gay male couples
Lesbians in the bar
Promiscuous gay men at
the baths or in the park

"BAD" SEX
Abnormal, Unnatural,
Sick, Sinful, "Way Out"

Transvestites
Transsexuals
Fetishists
Sadomasochists
For money
Cross-generational

Best ————————————————————— Worst

Figure 10.2 The sex hierarchy: the struggle over where to draw the lime

instance, heterosexual encounters may be sublime or disgusting, free or forced, healing or destructive, romantic or mercenary. As long as it does not violate other rules, heterosexuality is acknowledged to exhibit the full range of human experience. In contrast, all sex acts on the bad side of the line are considered utterly repulsive and devoid of all emotional nuance. The further from the line a sex act is, the more it is depicted as a uniformly bad experience.

As a result of the sex conflicts of the last decade, some behavior near the border is inching across it. Unmarried couples living together, masturbation and some forms of homosexuality are moving in the direction of respectability (see Figure 10.2). Most homosexuality is still on the bad side of the line. But if it is coupled and monogamous, the society is beginning to recognize that it includes the full range of human interaction. Promiscuous homosexuality, sadomasochism, fetishism, transsexuality and cross-generational encounters are still viewed as unmodulated horrors incapable of involving affection, love, free choice, kindness, or transcendence.

This kind of sexual morality has more in common with ideologies of racism than with true ethics. It grants virtue to the dominant groups, and relegates vice to the underprivileged. A democratic morality should judge sexual acts by the way partners treat one another, the level of mutual consideration, the presence or absence of coercion, and the quantity and quality of the pleasures they provide. Whether sex acts are gay or straight, coupled or in groups, naked or in underwear, commercial or free, with or without video, should not be ethical concerns.

It is difficult to develop a pluralistic sexual ethics without a concept of benign sexual variation. Variation is a fundamental property of all life, from the simplest biological organisms to the most complex human social formations. Yet sexuality is supposed to conform to a single standard. One of the most tenacious ideas about sex is that there is one best way to do it, and that everyone should do it that way.

Most people find it difficult to grasp that whatever they like to do sexually will be thoroughly repulsive to someone else, and that whatever repels them sexually will be the most treasured delight of someone, somewhere. One need not like or perform a particular sex act in order to recognize that someone else will, and that this difference does not indicate a lack of good taste, mental health, or intelligence in either party. Most people mistake their sexual preferences for a universal system that will or should work for everyone.

This notion of a single ideal sexuality characterizes most systems of thought about sex. For religion, the ideal is procreative marriage. For psychology, it is mature heterosexuality. Although its content varies, the format of a single sexual standard is continually reconstituted within other rhetorical frameworks, including feminism and socialism. It is just as objectionable to insist that everyone should be lesbian, non-monogamous, or kinky, as to believe that everyone should be heterosexual, married, or vanilla – though the latter set of opinions are backed by considerably more coercive power than the former.

Progressives who would be ashamed to display cultural chauvinism in other areas routinely exhibit it towards sexual differences. We have learned to cherish different cultures as unique expressions of human inventiveness rather than as the inferior or disgusting habits of savages. We need a similarly anthropological understanding of different sexual cultures.

Empirical sex research is the one field that does incorporate a positive concept of sexual variation. Alfred Kinsey approached the study of sex with the same uninhibited curiosity he had previously applied to examining a species of wasp. His scientific detachment gave his work a refreshing neutrality that enraged moralists and caused immense controversy.[42] Among Kinsey's successors, John Gagnon and William Simon have pioneered the application of sociological understandings to erotic variety.[43] Even some of the older sexology is useful. Although his work is imbued with unappetizing eugenic beliefs, Havelock Ellis was an acute and sympathetic observer. His monumental *Studies in the Psychology of Sex* is resplendent with detail.[44]

Much political writing on sexuality reveals complete ignorance of both classical sexology and modern sex research. Perhaps this is because so few colleges and universities bother to teach human sexuality, and because so much stigma adheres even to scholarly investigation of sex. Neither sexology nor sex research has been immune to the prevailing sexual value system. Both contain assumptions and information which should not be accepted uncritically. But sexology and sex research provide abundant detail, a welcome posture of calm, and a well-developed ability to treat sexual variety as

something that exists rather than as something to be exterminated. These fields can provide an empirical grounding for a radical theory of sexuality more useful than the combination of psychoanalysis and feminist first principles to which so many texts resort.[45]

SEXUAL TRANSFORMATION

> As defined by the ancient civil or canonical codes, sodomy was a category of forbidden acts; their perpetrator was nothing more than the juridical subject of them. The nineteenth-century homosexual became a personage, a past, a case history, and a childhood, in addition to being a type of life, a life form, and a morphology, with an indiscreet anatomy and possibly a mysterious physiology ... The sodomite had been a temporary aberration; the homosexual was now a species.
>
> (Michel Foucault[46])

In spite of many continuities with ancestral forms, modern sexual arrangements have a distinctive character which sets them apart from preexisting systems. In Western Europe and the United States, industrialization and urbanization reshaped the traditional rural and peasant populations into a new urban industrial and service workforce. It generated new forms of state apparatus, reorganized family relations, altered gender roles, made possible new forms of identity, produced new varieties of social inequality, and created new formats for political and ideological conflict. It also gave rise to a new sexual system characterized by distinct types of sexual persons, populations, stratification and political conflict.

The writings of nineteenth-century sexology suggest the appearance of a kind of erotic speciation. However outlandish their explanations, the early sexologists were witnessing the emergence of new kinds of erotic individuals and their aggregation into rudimentary communities. The modern sexual system contains sets of these sexual populations, stratified by the operation of an ideological and social hierarchy. Differences in social value create friction among these groups, who engage in political contests to alter or maintain their place in the ranking. Contemporary sexual politics should be reconceptualized in terms of the emergence and on-going development of this system, its social relations, the ideologies which interpret it, and its characteristic modes of conflict.

Homosexuality is the best example of this process of erotic speciation. Homosexual behavior is always present among humans. But in different societies and epochs it may be rewarded or punished, required or forbidden, a temporary experience or a life-long vocation. In some New Guinea societies, for example, homosexual activities are obligatory for all males. Homosexual acts are considered utterly masculine, roles are based on age and partners are determined by kinship status.[47] Although these men engage in extensive homosexual and pedophile behavior, they are neither homosexuals nor pederasts.

Nor was the sixteenth-century sodomite a homosexual. In 1631, Mervyn Touchet, Earl of Castlehaven, was tried and executed for sodomy. It is clear from the proceedings that the earl was not understood by himself or anyone else to be a particular kind of sexual individual. "While from the twentieth-century viewpoint Lord Castlehaven obviously suffered from psychosexual problems requiring the services of an analyst, from the seventeenth century viewpoint he had deliberately broken the Law of God and the Laws of England, and required the simpler services of an executioner."[48] The earl did not slip into his tightest doublet and waltz down to the nearest gay tavern to mingle with his fellow sodomists. He stayed in his manor house and buggered his servants. Gay self-awareness, gay pubs, the sense of group commonality, and even the term *homosexual* were not part of the earl's universe.

The New Guinea bachelor and the sodomite nobleman are only tangentially related to a modern gay man, who may migrate from rural Colorado to San Francisco in order to live in a gay neighborhood, work in a gay business, and participate in an elaborate experience that includes a self-conscious identity, group solidarity, a literature, a press, and a high level of political activity. In modern, Western, industrial societies, homosexuality has acquired much of the institutional structure of an ethnic group.[49]

The relocation of homoeroticism into these quasi-ethnic, nucleated, sexually constituted communities is to some extent a consequence of the transfers of population brought about by industrialization. As laborers migrated to work in cities, there were increased opportunities for voluntary communities to form. Homosexually inclined women and men, who would have been vulnerable and isolated in most pre-industrial villages, began to congregate in small corners of the big cities. Most large nineteenth-century cities in Western Europe and North America had areas where men could cruise for other men. Lesbian communities seem to have coalesced more slowly and on a smaller scale. Nevertheless, by the 1890s, there were several cafés in Paris near the Place Pigalle which catered to a lesbian clientele, and it is likely that there were similar places in the other major capitals of Western Europe.

Areas like these acquired bad reputations, which alerted other interested individuals of their existence and location. In the United States, lesbian and gay male territories were well established in New York, Chicago, San Francisco, and Los Angeles in the 1950s. Sexually motivated migration to places such as Greenwich Village had become a sizable sociological phenomenon. By the late 1970s, sexual migration was occurring on a scale so significant that it began to have a recognizable impact on urban politics in the United States, with San Francisco being the most notable and notorious example.[50]

Prostitution has undergone a similar metamorphosis. Prostitution began to change from a temporary job to a more permanent occupation as a result of nineteenth-century agitation, legal reform, and police persecution. Prostitutes, who had been part of the general working-class population, became increasingly isolated as members of an outcast group.[51] Prostitutes and other sex workers differ from homosexuals and other sexual minorities. Sex work is an occupation, while sexual deviation is an erotic preference. Nevertheless, they share some common features of social organization. Like homosexuals, prostitutes are a criminal sexual population stigmatized on the basis of sexual activity. Prostitutes and male homosexuals are the primary prey of vice police everywhere.[52] Like gay men, prostitutes occupy well-demarcated urban territories and battle with police to defend and maintain those territories. The legal persecution of both populations is justified by an elaborate ideology which classifies them as dangerous and inferior undesirables who are not entitled to be left in peace.

Besides organizing homosexuals and prostitutes into localized populations, the "modernization of sex" has generated a system of continual sexual ethnogenesis. Other populations of erotic dissidents – commonly known as the "perversions" or the "paraphilias" – also began to coalesce. Sexualities keep marching out of the *Diagnostic and Statistical Manual* and on to the pages of social history. At present, several other groups are trying to emulate the successes of homosexuals. Bisexuals, sado-masochists, individuals who prefer cross-generational encounters, transsexuals, and transvestites are all in various states of community-formation and identity-acquisition. The perversions are not proliferating as much as they are attempting to acquire social space, small businesses, political resources, and a measure of relief from the penalties for sexual heresy.

SEXUAL STRATIFICATION

An entire sub-race was born, different – despite certain kinship ties – from the libertines of the past. From the end of the eighteenth century to our own, they circulated through the pores of society; they were always hounded, but not always by laws; were often locked up, but not always in prisons; were sick perhaps, but scandalous, dangerous victims, prey to a strange evil that also bore the name of vice and sometimes crime. They were children wise beyond their years, precocious little girls, ambiguous schoolboys, dubious servants and educators, cruel or maniacal husbands, solitary collectors, ramblers with bizarre impulses; they haunted the houses of correction, the penal colonies, the tribunals, and the asylums; they carried their infamy to the doctors and their sickness to the judges. This was the numberless family of perverts who were on friendly terms with delinquents and akin to madmen.

(Michel Foucault[53])

The industrial transformation of Western Europe and North America brought about new forms of social stratification. The resultant inequalities of class are well known and have been explored in detail by a century of scholarship. The construction of modern systems of racism and ethnic injustice has been well documented and critically assessed. Feminist thought has analyzed the prevailing organization of gender oppression. But although specific erotic groups, such as militant homosexuals and sex workers, have agitated against their own mistreatment, there has been no equivalent attempt to locate particular varieties of sexual persecution within a more general system of sexual stratification. Nevertheless, such a system exists, and in its contemporary form it is a consequence of Western industrialization.

Sex law is the most adamantine instrument of sexual stratification and erotic persecution. The state routinely intervenes in sexual behavior at a level that would not be tolerated in other areas of social life. Most people are unaware of the extent of sex law, the quantity and qualities of illegal sexual behavior, and the punitive character of legal sanctions. Although federal agencies may be involved in obscenity and prostitution cases, most sex laws are enacted at the state and municipal level, and enforcement is largely in the hands of local police. Thus, there is a tremendous amount of variation in the laws applicable to any given locale. Moreover, enforcement of sex laws varies dramatically with the local political climate. In spite of this legal thicket, one can make some tentative and qualified generalizations. My discussion of sex law does not apply to laws against sexual coercion, sexual assault, or rape. It does pertain to the myriad prohibitions on consensual sex and the "status" offenses such as statutory rape.

Sex law is harsh. The penalties for violating sex statutes are universally out of proportion to any social or individual harm. A single act of consensual but illicit sex, such as placing one's lips upon the genitalia of an enthusiastic partner, is punished in many states with more severity than rape, battery, or murder. Each such genital kiss, each lewd caress, is a separate crime. It is therefore painfully easy to commit multiple felonies in the course of a single evening of illegal passion. Once someone is convicted of a sex violation, a second performance of the same act is grounds for prosecution as a repeat offender, in which case penalties will be even more severe. In some states, individuals have become repeat felons for having engaged in homosexual love-making on two separate occasions. Once an erotic activity has been proscribed by sex law, the full power of the state enforces conformity to the values embodied in those laws. Sex laws are notoriously easy to pass, as legislators are loath to be soft on vice. Once on the books, they are extremely difficult to dislodge.

Sex law is not a perfect reflection of the prevailing moral evaluations of sexual conduct. Sexual variation *per se* is more specifically policed by the mental-health professions, popular ideology and extra-legal social practice. Some of the most detested erotic behaviors, such as fetishism and sado-masochism, are not as closely or completely regulated by the criminal justice system as somewhat less stigmatized practices, such as homosexuality. Areas of sexual behavior come under the purview of the law when they become objects of social concern and political uproar. Each sex scare or morality campaign deposits new regulations as a kind of fossil record of its passage. The legal sediment is thickest – and sex law has its greatest potency – in areas involving obscenity, money, minors, and homosexuality.

Obscenity laws enforce a powerful taboo against direct representation of erotic activities. Current emphasis on the ways in which sexuality has become a focus of social attention should not be misused to undermine a critique of this prohibition. It is one thing to create sexual discourse in the form of psychoanalysis, or in the course of a morality crusade. It is quite another to depict sex acts or genitalia graphically. The first is socially permissible in a way the second is not. Sexual speech is forced into reticence, euphemism, and indirection. Freedom of speech about sex is a glaring exception to the protections of the First Amendment, which is not even considered applicable to purely sexual statements.

The anti-obscenity laws also form part of a group of statutes that make almost all sexual commerce illegal. Sex law incorporates a very strong prohibition against mixing sex and money, except via marriage. In addition to the obscenity statutes, other laws impinging on sexual commerce include anti-prostitution laws, alcoholic beverage regulations, and ordinances governing the location and operation of "adult" businesses. The sex industry and the gay economy have both managed to circumvent some of this legislation, but that process has not been easy or simple. The underlying criminality of sex-oriented business keeps it marginal, underdeveloped, and distorted. Sex businesses can operate only in legal loopholes. This tends to keep investment down and to divert commercial activity towards the goal of staying out of jail rather than the delivery of goods and services. It also renders sex workers more vulnerable to exploitation and bad working conditions. If sex commerce were legal, sex workers would be more able to organize and agitate for higher pay, better conditions, greater control, and less stigma.

Whatever one thinks of the limitations of capitalist commerce, such an extreme exclusion from the market process would hardly be socially acceptable in other areas of activity. Imagine, for example, that the exchange of money for medical care, pharmacological advice, or psychological counseling were illegal. Medical practice would take place in a much less satisfactory fashion if doctors, nurses, druggists, and therapists could be hauled off to jail at the whim of the local "health squad." But that is essentially the situation of prostitutes, sex workers, and sex entrepreneurs.

Marx himself considered the capitalist market a revolutionary, if limited, force. He argued that capitalism was progressive in its dissolution of pre-capitalist superstition, prejudice and the bonds of traditional modes of life. "Hence the great civilizing influence of capital, its production of a state of society compared with which all earlier stages appear to be merely local progress and idolatry of nature."[54] Keeping sex from realizing the positive effects of the market economy hardly makes it socialist.

The law is especially ferocious in maintaining the boundary between childhood "innocence" and "adult" sexuality. Rather than recognizing the sexuality of the young, and attempting to provide for it in a caring and responsible manner, our culture denies and punishes erotic interest and activity by anyone under the local age of consent. The amount of law devoted to protecting young people from premature exposure to sexuality is breath-taking.

The primary mechanism for insuring the separation of sexual generations is age of consent laws. These laws make no distinction between the most brutal rape and the most gentle romance. A 20-year-old convicted of sexual contact with a 17-year-old will face a severe sentence in virtually every state, regardless of the nature of the relationship.[55] Nor are minors permitted access to "adult" sexuality in other forms. They are forbidden to see books, movies, or television in which sexuality is "too" graphically portrayed. It is legal for young people to see hideous depictions of violence, but not to see explicit pictures of genitalia. Sexually active young people are frequently incarcerated in juvenile homes, or otherwise punished for their "precocity."

Adults who deviate too much from conventional standards of sexual conduct are often denied contact with the young, even their own. Custody laws permit the state to steal the children of anyone whose erotic activities appear questionable to a judge presiding over family court matters. Countless lesbians, gay men, prostitutes, swingers, sex workers, and "promiscuous" women have been declared unfit parents under such provisions. Members of the teaching professions are closely monitored for signs of sexual misconduct. In most states, certification laws require that teachers arrested for sex offenses lose their jobs and credentials. In some cases, a teacher may be fired merely because an unconventional lifestyle becomes known to school officials. Moral turpitude is one of the few legal grounds for revoking academic tenure.[56] The more influence one has over the next generation, the less latitude one is permitted in behavior and opinions. The coercive power of the law ensures the transmission of conservative sexual values with these kinds of controls over parenting and teaching.

The only adult sexual behavior that is legal in every state is the placement of the penis in the vagina in wedlock. Consenting adults statutes ameliorate this situation in fewer than half the states. Most states impose severe criminal penalties on consensual sodomy, homosexual contact short of sodomy, adultery, seduction, and adult incest. Sodomy laws vary a great deal. In some states, they apply equally to homosexual and heterosexual partners and regardless of marital status. Some state courts have ruled that married couples have the right to commit sodomy in private. Only homosexual sodomy is illegal in some states. Some sodomy statutes prohibit both anal sex and oral–genital contact. In other states, sodomy applies only to anal penetration, and oral sex is covered under separate statutes.[57]

Laws like these criminalize sexual behavior that is freely chosen and avidly sought. The ideology embodied in them reflects the value hierarchies discussed above. That is, some sex acts are considered to be so intrinsically vile that no one should be allowed under any circumstance to perform them. The fact that individuals consent to or even prefer them is taken to be additional evidence of depravity. This system of sex law is similar to legalized racism. State prohibition of same-sex contact, anal penetration, and oral sex make homosexuals a criminal group denied the privileges of full citizenship. With such laws, prosecution is persecution. Even when they are not strictly enforced, as it usually the case, the members of criminalized sexual communities remain vulnerable to the possibility of arbitrary arrest, or to periods in which they become the objects of social panic. When those occur, the laws are in place and police action is swift. Even sporadic enforcement serves to remind individuals that they are members of a subject population. The occasional arrest for sodomy, lewd behavior, solicitation, or oral sex keeps everyone else afraid, nervous, and circumspect.

The state also upholds the sexual hierarchy through bureaucratic regulations. Immigration policy still prohibits the admission of homosexuals (and other sexual "deviates") into the United States. Military regulations bar homosexuals from serving in the armed forces.[58] The fact that gay people cannot legally marry means that they cannot enjoy the same legal rights as heterosexuals in many matters, including inheritance, taxation, protection from testimony in court, and the acquisition of citizenship for foreign partners. These are but a few of the ways that the state reflects and maintains the social relations of sexuality. The law buttresses structures of power, codes of behavior and forms of prejudice. At their worst, sex law and sex regulation are simply sexual apartheid.

Although the legal apparatus of sex is staggering, most everyday social control is extra-legal. Less formal, but very effective social sanctions are imposed on members of "inferior" sexual populations.

In her marvelous ethnographic study of gay life in the 1960s, Esther Newton observed that the homosexual population was divided into what she called the "overts" and the "coverts." "The overts live their *entire* working lives within the context of the [gay] community; the coverts live their entire *nonworking* lives within it."[59] At the time of Newton's study, the gay community provided far fewer jobs than it does now, and the non-gay work world was almost completely intolerant of homosexuality. There were some fortunate individuals who could be openly gay and earn decent salaries. But the vast majority of homosexuals had to choose between honest poverty and the strain of maintaining a false identity.

Though this situation has changed a great deal, discrimination against gay people is still rampant. For the bulk of the gay population, being out on the job is still impossible. Generally, the more important and higher-paid the job, the less the society will tolerate overt erotic deviance. If it is difficult for gay people to find employment where they do not have to pretend, it is doubly and triply so for more exotically sexed individuals. Sado-masochists leave their fetish clothes at home, and know that they must be especially careful to conceal their real identities. An exposed pedophile would probably be stoned out of the office. Having to maintain such absolute secrecy is a considerable burden. Even those who are content to be secretive may be exposed by some accidental event. Individuals who are erotically unconventional risk being unemployable or unable to pursue their chosen careers.

Public officials and anyone who occupies a position of social consequence are especially vulnerable. A sex scandal is the surest method for hounding someone out of office or destroying a political career. The fact that important people are expected to conform to the strictest standards of erotic conduct discourages sex perverts of all kinds from seeking such positions. Instead, erotic dissidents are channeled into positions that have less impact on the mainstream of social activity and opinion.

The expansion of the gay economy in the last decade has provided some employment alternatives and some relief from job discrimination against homosexuals. But most of the jobs provided by the gay economy are low-status and low-paying. Bartenders, bathhouse attendants, and disc jockeys are not bank officers or corporate executives. Many of the sexual migrants who flock to places like San Francisco are downwardly mobile. They face intense competition for choice positions. The influx of sexual migrants provides a pool of cheap and exploitable labor for many of the city's businesses, both gay and straight.

Families play a crucial role in enforcing sexual conformity. Much social pressure is brought to bear to deny erotic dissidents the comforts and resources that families provide. Popular ideology holds that families are not supposed to produce or harbor erotic nonconformity. Many families respond by trying to reform, punish, or exile sexually offending members. Many sexual migrants have been thrown out by their families, and many others are fleeing from the threat of institutionalization. Any random collection of homosexuals, sex workers, or miscellaneous perverts can provide heart-stopping stories of rejection and mistreatment by horrified families. Christmas is the great family holiday in the United States and consequently it is a time of considerable tension in the gay community. Half the inhabitants go off to their families of origin; many of those who remain in the gay ghettos cannot do so, and relive their anger and grief.

In addition to economic penalties and strain on family relations, the stigma of erotic dissidence creates friction at all other levels of everyday life. The general public helps to penalize erotic nonconformity when, according to the values they have been taught, landlords refuse housing, neighbors call in the police, and hoodlums commit sanctioned battery. The ideologies of erotic inferiority and sexual danger decrease the power of sex perverts and sex workers in social encounters of all kinds. They have less protection from unscrupulous or criminal behavior, less access to police protection, and less recourse to the courts. Dealings with institutions and bureaucracies – hospitals, police, coroners, banks, public officials – are more difficult.

Sex is a vector of oppression. The system of sexual oppression cuts across other modes of social inequality, sorting out individuals and groups according to its own intrinsic dynamics. It is not reducible to, or understandable in terms of, class, race, ethnicity, or gender. Wealth, white skin, male gender, and ethnic privileges can mitigate the effects of sexual stratification. A rich, white male pervert will generally be less affected than a poor, black, female pervert. But even the most privileged are not immune to sexual oppression. Some of the consequences of the system of sexual hierarchy are mere nuisances. Others are quite grave. In its most serious manifestations, the sexual system is a Kafkaesque nightmare in which unlucky victims become herds of human cattle whose identification, surveillance, apprehension, treatment, incarceration, and punishment produce jobs and self-satisfaction for thousands of vice police, prison officials, psychiatrists, and social workers.[60]

SEXUAL CONFLICTS

The moral panic crystallizes widespread fears and anxieties, and often deals with them not by seeking the real causes of the problems and conditions which they demonstrate but by displacing them on to "Folk Devils" in an identified social group (often the "immoral" or "degenerate"). Sexuality has had a peculiar centrality in such panics, and sexual "deviants" have been omnipresent scapegoats.

(Jeffrey Weeks[61])

The sexual system is not a monolithic, omnipotent structure. There are continuous battles over the definitions, evaluations, arrangements, privileges, and costs of sexual behavior. Political struggle over sex assumes characteristic forms.

Sexual ideology plays a crucial role in sexual experience. Consequently, definitions and evaluations of sexual conduct are objects of bitter contest. The confrontations between early gay liberation and the psychiatric establishment are the best example of this kind of fight, but there are constant skirmishes. Recurrent battles take place between the primary producers of sexual ideology – the churches, the family, the shrinks, and the media – and the groups whose experience they name, distort, and endanger.

The legal regulation of sexual conduct is another battleground. Lysander Spooner dissected the system of state-sanctioned moral coercion over a century ago in a text inspired primarily by the temperance campaigns. In *Vices Are Not Crimes: A Vindication of Moral Liberty*, Spooner argued that government should protect its citizens against crime, but that it is foolish, unjust, and tyrannical to legislate against vice. He discusses rationalizations still heard today in defense of legalized moralism – that "vices" (Spooner is referring to drink, but homosexuality, prostitution, or recreational drug use may be substituted) lead to crimes, and should therefore be prevented; that those who practice "vice" are *non compos mentis* and should therefore be protected from their self-destruction by state-accomplished ruin; and that children must be protected from supposedly harmful knowledge.[62] The discourse on victimless crimes has not changed much. Legal struggle over sex law will continue until basic freedoms of sexual action and expression are guaranteed. This requires the repeal of all sex laws except those few that deal with actual, not statutory, coercion; and it entails the abolition of vice squads, whose job it is to enforce legislated morality.

In addition to the definitional and legal wars, there are less obvious forms of sexual political conflict which I call the territorial and border wars. The process by which erotic minorities form communities and the forces that seek to inhibit them lead to struggles over the nature and boundaries of sexual zones.

Dissident sexuality is rarer and more closely monitored in small towns and rural areas. Consequently, metropolitan life continually beckons to young perverts. Sexual migration creates concentrated pools of potential partners, friends, and associates. It enables individuals to create adult, kin-like networks in which to live. But there are many barriers which sexual migrants have to overcome.

According to the mainstream media and

popular prejudice, the marginal sexual worlds are bleak and dangerous. They are portrayed as impoverished, ugly, and inhabited by psychopaths and criminals. New migrants must be sufficiently motivated to resist the impact of such discouraging images. Attempts to counter negative propaganda with more realistic information generally meet with censorship, and there are continuous ideological struggles over which representations of sexual communities make it into the popular media.

Information on how to find, occupy, and live in the marginal sexual worlds is also suppressed. Navigational guides are scarce and inaccurate. In the past, fragments of rumor, distorted gossip, and bad publicity were the most available clues to the location of underground erotic communities. During the late 1960s and early 1970s, better information became available. Now groups like the Moral Majority want to rebuild the ideological walls around the sexual undergrounds and make transit in and out of them as difficult as possible.

Migration is expensive. Transportation costs, moving expenses, and the necessity of finding new jobs and housing are economic difficulties that sexual migrants must overcome. These are especially imposing barriers to the young, who are often the most desperate to move. There are, however, routes into the erotic communities which mark trails through the propaganda thicket and provide some economic shelter along the way. Higher education can be a route for young people from affluent backgrounds. In spite of serious limitations, the information on sexual behavior at most colleges and universities is better than elsewhere, and most colleges and universities shelter small erotic networks of all sorts.

For poorer kids, the military is often the easiest way to get the hell out of wherever they are. Military prohibitions against homosexuality make this a perilous route. Although young queers continually attempt to use the armed forces to get out of intolerable hometown situations and closer to functional gay communities, they face the hazards of exposure, court martial, and dishonorable discharge.

Once in the cities, erotic populations tend to nucleate and to occupy some regular, visible territory. Churches and other anti-vice forces constantly put pressure on local authorities to contain such areas, reduce their visibility, or to drive their inhabitants out of town. There are periodic crackdowns in which local vice squads are unleashed on the populations they control. Gay men, prostitutes, and sometimes transvestites are sufficiently territorial and numerous to engage in intense battles with the cops over particular streets, parks, and alleys. Such border wars are usually inconclusive, but they result in many casualties.

For most of this century, the sexual underworlds have been marginal and impoverished, their residents subjected to stress and exploitation. The spectacular success of gay entrepreneurs in creating a variegated gay economy has altered the quality of life within the gay ghetto. The level of material comfort and social elaboration achieved by the gay community in the last fifteen years is unprecedented. But it is important to recall what happened to similar miracles. The growth of the black population in New York in the early part of the twentieth century led to the Harlem Renaissance, but that period of creativity was doused by the Depression. The relative prosperity and cultural florescence of the gay ghetto may be equally fragile. Like blacks who fled the South for the metropolitan North, homosexuals may have merely traded rural problems for urban ones.

Gay pioneers occupied neighborhoods that were centrally located but run down. Consequently, they border poor neighborhoods. Gays, especially low-income gays, end up competing with other low-income groups for the limited supply of cheap and moderate housing. In San Francisco, competition for low-cost housing has exacerbated both racism and homophobia, and is one source of the epidemic of street violence against homosexuals. Instead of being isolated and invisible in rural settings, city gays are now numerous and obvious targets for urban frustrations.

In San Francisco, unbridled construction of downtown skyscrapers and high-cost condominiums is causing affordable housing to evaporate. Megabuck construction is creating pressure on all city residents. Poor gay renters are visible in low-income neighborhoods; multimillionaire contracters are not. The specter of the "homosexual invasion" is a convenient scapegoat which deflects attention from the banks, the planning commission, the political establishment, and the big developers. In San Francisco, the well-being of the gay community has become embroiled in the high-stakes politics of urban real estate.

Downtown expansion affects all the territorial erotic underworlds. In both San Francisco and New York, high investment construction and urban renewal have intruded on the main areas of prostitution, pornography, and leather bars. Developers are salivating over Times Square, the Tenderloin, what is left of North Beach, and South of Market. Anti-sex ideology, obscenity law, prostitution regulations, and the alcoholic beverage codes are all being used to dislodge seedy adult businesses, sex workers, and leathermen. Within ten years, most of these areas will have been bulldozed and made safe for convention centers, international hotels, corporate headquarters, and housing for the rich.

The most important and consequential kind of sex conflict is what Jeffrey Weeks has termed the "moral panic." Moral panics are the "political moment" of sex, in which diffuse attitudes are channeled into political action and from there into social change.[63] The white slavery hysteria of the 1880s, the anti-homosexual campaigns of the 1950s, and the child pornography panic of the late 1970s were typical moral panics.

Because sexuality in Western societies is so mystified, the wars over it are often fought at oblique angles, aimed at phony targets, conducted with misplaced passions, and are highly, intensely symbolic. Sexual activities often function as signifiers for personal and social apprehensions to which they have no intrinsic connection. During a moral panic, such fears attach to some unfortunate sexual activity or population. The media become ablaze with indignation, the public behaves like a rabid mob, the police are activated, and the state enacts new laws and regulations. When the furor has passed, some innocent erotic group has been decimated, and the state has extended its power into new areas of erotic behavior.

The system of sexual stratification provides easy victims who lack the power to defend themselves, and a preexisting apparatus for controlling their movements and curtailing their freedoms. The stigma against sexual dissidents renders them morally defenseless. Every moral panic has consequences on two levels. The target population suffers most, but everyone is affected by the social and legal changes.

Moral panics rarely alleviate any real problem, because they are aimed at chimeras and signifiers. They draw on the pre-existing discursive structure which invents victims in order to justify treating "vices" as crimes. The criminalization of innocuous behaviors such as homosexuality, prostitution, obscenity, or recreational drug use, is rationalized by portraying them as menaces to health and safety, women and children, national security, the family, or civilization itself. Even when activity is acknowledged to be harmless, it may be banned because it is alleged to "lead" to something ostensibly worse (another manifestation of the domino theory).[64] Great and mighty edifices have been built on the basis of such phantasms. Generally, the outbreak of a moral panic is preceded by an intensification of such scapegoating.

It is always risky to prophesy. But it does not take much prescience to detect potential moral panics in two current developments: the attacks on sado-masochists by a segment of the feminist movement, and the right's increasing use of AIDS to incite virulent homophobia.

Feminist anti-pornography ideology has always contained an implied, and sometimes overt, indictment of sado-masochism. The pictures of sucking and fucking that comprise the bulk of pornography may be unnerving to those who are not familiar with them. But it is hard to make a convincing case that such images are violent. All of the early anti-porn slide shows used a highly selective sample of S/M imagery to sell a very flimsy analysis. Taken out of context, such images are often shocking. This shock value was mercilessly exploited to scare audiences into accepting the anti-porn perspective.

A great deal of anti-porn propaganda implies that sado-masochism is the underlying and essential "truth" towards which all pornography tends. Porn is thought to lead to S/M porn which in turn is alleged to lead to rape. This is a just-so story that revitalizes the notion that sex perverts commit sex crimes, not normal people. There is no evidence that the readers of S/M erotica or practicing sado-masochists commit a disproportionate number of sex crimes. Anti-porn literature scapegoats an unpopular sexual minority and its reading material for social problems they do not create.

The use of S/M imagery in anti-porn discourse is inflammatory. It implies that the way to make the world safer for women is to get rid of sado-masochism. The use of S/M images in the movie *Not a Love Story* was on a moral par with the use of depictions of black men raping white women, or of drooling old Jews pawing young Aryan girls, to incite racist or anti-Semitic frenzy.

Feminist rhetoric has a distressing tendency to reappear in reactionary contexts. For example, in 1980 and 1981, Pope John Paul II delivered a series of pronouncements reaffirming his commitment to the most conservative and Pauline understandings of human sexuality. In condemning divorce, abortion, trial marriage, pornography, prostitution, birth control, unbridled hedonism, and lust, the pope employed a great deal of feminist rhetoric about sexual objectification. Sounding like lesbian feminist polemicist Julia Penelope, His Holiness explained that "considering anyone in a lustful way makes that person a sexual object rather than a human being worthy of dignity."[65]

The right wing opposes pornography and has already adopted elements of feminist anti-porn rhetoric. The anti-S/M discourse developed in the women's movement could easily become a vehicle for a moral witch-hunt. It provides a ready-made defenseless target population. It provides a rationale for the recriminalization of sexual materials which have escaped the reach of current obscenity laws. It would be especially easy to pass laws against S/M erotica resembling the child pornography laws. The ostensible purpose of such laws would be to reduce violence by banning so-called violent porn. A focused campaign against the leather menace might also result in the passage of laws to criminalize S/M behavior that is not currently illegal. The ultimate result of such a moral panic would be the legalized violation of a community of harmless perverts. It is dubious that such a sexual witch-hunt would make any appreciable contribution towards reducing violence against women.

An AIDS panic is even more probable. When fears of incurable disease mingle with sexual terror, the resulting brew is extremely volatile. A century ago, attempts to control syphilis led to the passage of the Contagious Diseases Acts in England. The Acts were based on erroneous medical theories and did nothing to halt the spread of the disease. But they did make life miserable for the hundreds of women who were incarcerated, subjected to forcible vaginal examination, and stigmatized for life as prostitutes.[66]

Whatever happens, AIDS will have far-reaching consequences on sex in general, and on homosexuality in particular. The disease will have a significant impact on the choices gay people make. Fewer will migrate to the gay meccas out of fear of the disease. Those who already reside in the ghettos will avoid situations they fear will expose them. The gay economy, and the political apparatus it supports, may prove to be evanescent. Fear of AIDS has already affected sexual ideology. Just when homosexuals have had some success in throwing off the taint of mental disease, gay people find themselves metaphorically welded to an image of lethal physical deterioration. The syndrome, its peculiar qualities, and its transmissibility are being used to reinforce old fears that sexual activity, homosexuality, and promiscuity led to disease and death.

AIDS is both a personal tragedy for those who contract the syndrome and a calamity for the gay community. Homophobes have gleefully hastened to turn this tragedy against its victims. One columnist has suggested that AIDS has always existed, that the Biblical prohibitions on sodomy were designed to protect people from AIDS, and that AIDS is therefore an appropriate punishment for violating the Levitical codes. Using fear of infection as a rationale, local right-wingers attempted to ban the gay rodeo from Reno, Nevada. A recent issue of the *Moral Majority Report* featured a picture of a "typical" white family of four wearing surgical masks. The headline read: "AIDS: HOMOSEXUAL DISEASES THREATEN AMERICAN FAMILIES."[67] Phyllis Schlafly has recently issued a pamphlet arguing that passage of the Equal Rights Amendment would make it impossible to "legally protect ourselves against AIDS and other diseases carried by homosexuals."[68] Current right-wing literature calls for shutting down the gay baths, for a legal ban on homosexual employment in food-handling occupations, and for state-mandated prohibitions on blood donations by gay people. Such policies would require the government to identify all homosexuals and impose easily recognizable legal and social markers on them.

It is bad enough that the gay community must deal with the medical misfortune of having been the population in which a deadly disease first became widespread and visible. It is worse to have to deal with the social consequences as well. Even before the AIDS scare, Greece passed a law that enabled police to arrest suspected homosexuals and force them to submit to an examination for venereal disease. It is likely that until AIDS and its methods of transmission are understood, there will be all sorts of proposals to control it by punishing the gay community and by attacking its institutions. When the cause of Legionnaires' Disease was unknown, there were no calls to quarantine members of the American Legion or to shut down their meeting halls. The Contagious Diseases Acts in England did little to control syphilis, but they caused a great deal of suffering for the women who came under their purview. The history of panic that has accompanied new epidemics, and of the casualties incurred by their scapegoats, should make everyone pause and consider with extreme scepticism any attempts to justify anti-gay policy initiatives on the basis of AIDS.[69]

THE LIMITS OF FEMINISM

We know that in an overwhelmingly large number of cases, sex crime is associated with pornography. We know that sex criminals read it, are clearly influenced by it. I believe that, if we can eliminate the distribution of such items among impressionable children, we shall greatly reduce our frightening sex-crime rate.

(J. Edgar Hoover[70])

In the absence of a more articulated radical theory of sex, most progressives have turned to feminism for guidance. But the relationship between feminism and sex is complex. Because sexuality is a nexus of the relationships between genders, much of the oppression of women is born by, mediated through, and constituted within, sexuality. Feminism has always been vitally interested in sex. But there have been two strains of feminist thought on the subject. One tendency has criticized the restrictions on women's sexual behavior and denounced the high costs imposed on women for being sexually active. This tradition of feminist sexual thought has called for a sexual liberation that would work for women as well as for men. The second tendency has considered sexual liberalization to be inherently a mere extension of male privilege. This tradition resonates with conservative, anti-sexual discourse. With the advent of the anti-pornography movement, it achieved temporary hegemony over feminist analysis.

The anti-pornography movement and its texts have been the most extensive expression of this discourse.[71] In addition, proponents of this viewpoint have condemned virtually every variant of sexual expression as anti-feminist. Within this framework, monogamous lesbianism that occurs within long-term, intimate relationships, and which does not involve playing with polarized roles, has replaced married, procreative heterosexuality at the top of the value hierarchy. Heterosexuality has been demoted to somewhere in the middle. Apart from this change, everything else looks more or less familiar. The lower depths are occupied by the usual groups and behaviors: prostitution, transsexuality, sado-masochism, and cross-generational activities.[72] Most gay male conduct, all casual sex, promiscuity, and lesbian behavior that does involve roles or kink or non-monogamy are also censured.[73] Even sexual fantasy during masturbation is denounced as a phallocentric holdover.[74]

This discourse on sexuality is less a sexology than a demonology. It presents most sexual behavior in the worst possible light. Its descriptions of erotic conduct always use the worst available example as if it were representative. It presents the most disgusting pornography, the most exploited forms of prostitution, and the least palatable or most shocking manifestations of sexual variation. This rhetorical tactic consistently misrepresents human sexuality in all its forms. The picture of human sexuality that emerges from this literature is unremittingly ugly.

In addition, this anti-porn rhetoric is a massive exercise in scapegoating. It criticizes non-routine acts of love rather than routine acts of oppression, exploitation, or violence. This demon sexology directs legitimate anger at women's lack of personal safety against innocent individuals, practices, and communities. Anti-porn propaganda often implies that sexism originates within the commercial sex industry and subsequently infects the rest of society. This is sociologically nonsensical. The sex industry is hardly a feminist utopia. It reflects the sexism that exists in the society as a whole. We need to analyze and oppose the manifestations of gender inequality specific to the sex industry. But this is not the same as attempting to wipe out commercial sex.

Similarly, erotic minorities such as sado-masochists and transsexuals are as likely to exhibit sexist attitudes or behavior as any other politically random social grouping. But to claim that they are inherently anti-feminist is sheer fantasy. A good deal of current feminist literature attributes the oppression of women to graphic representations of sex, prostitution, sex education, sado-masochism, male homosexuality, and transsexualism. Whatever happened to the family, religion, education, child-rearing practices, the media, the state, psychiatry, job discrimination, and unequal pay?

Finally, this so-called feminist discourse recreates a very conservative sexual morality. For over a century, battles have been waged over just how much shame, distress, and punishment should be incurred by sexual activity. The conservative tradition has promoted opposition to pornography, prostitution, homosexuality, all erotic variation, sex education, sex research, abortion, and contraception. The opposing, pro-sex tradition has included individuals like Havelock Ellis, Magnus Hirschfeld, Alfred Kinsey and Victoria Woodhull, as well as the sex education movements, organizations of militant prostitutes and homosexuals, the reproductive rights movement, and organizations such as the Sexual Reform League of the 1960s. This motley collection of sex reformers, sex educators, and sexual militants has mixed records on both sexual and feminist issues. But surely they are closer to the spirit of modern feminism than are moral crusaders, the social purity movement, and anti-vice organizations. Nevertheless, the current feminist sexual demonology generally elevates the anti-vice crusaders to positions of ancestral honor, while condemning the more liberatory tradition as anti-feminist. In an essay that exemplifies some of these trends, Sheila Jeffreys blames Havelock Ellis, Edward Carpenter, Alexandra Kollantai, "believers in the joy of sex of every possible political persuasion," and the 1929 congress of the World League for Sex Reform for making "a great contribution to the defeat of militant feminism."[75]

The anti-pornography movement and its avatars have claimed to speak for all feminism. Fortunately, they do not. Sexual liberation has been and continues to be a feminist goal. The women's movement may have produced some of the most retrogressive sexual thinking this side of the Vatican. But it has also produced an exciting, innovative, and articulate defense of sexual pleasure and erotic justice. This "pro-sex" feminism has been spearheaded by lesbians whose sexuality does not conform to movement standards of purity (primarily lesbian sado-masochists and butch/femme dykes), by unapologetic heterosexuals and by women who adhere to classic radical feminism rather than to the revisionist celebrations of femininity which have become so common.[76] Although the anti-porn forces have attempted to weed anyone who disagrees with them out of the movement, the fact remains that feminist thought about sex is profoundly polarized.[77]

Whenever there is polarization, there is an unhappy tendency to think the truth lies somewhere in between. Ellen Willis has commented sarcastically that "the feminist bias is that women are equal to men and the male chauvinist bias is that women are inferior. The unbiased view is that the truth lies somewhere in between."[78] The most recent development in the feminist sex wars is the emergence of a "middle" that seeks to evade the dangers of anti-porn fascism, on the one hand, and a supposed "anything goes" libertarianism, on the other.[79] Although it is hard to criticize a position that is not yet fully formed, I want to draw attention to some incipient problems.[80]

The emergent middle is based on a false characterization of the poles of the debate, construing both sides as equally extremist. According to B. Ruby Rich, "the desire for a language of sexuality has led feminists into locations (pornography, sadomasochism) too narrow or overdetermined for a fruitful discussion. Debate has collapsed into a rumble."[81] True, the fights between Women Against Pornography (WAP) and lesbian sado-masochists have resembled gang warfare. But the responsibility for this lies primarily with the anti-porn movement, and its refusal to engage in principled discussion. S/M lesbians have been forced into a struggle to maintain their membership in the movement, and to defend themselves against slander. No major spokeswoman for lesbian S/M has argued for any kind of S/M supremacy, or advocated that everyone should be a sadomasochist. In addition to self-defense, S/M lesbians have called for appreciation for erotic diversity and more open discussion of sexuality.[82] Trying to find a middle course between WAP and Samois is a bit like saying that the truth about homosexuality lies somewhere between the positions of the Moral Majority and those of the gay movement.

In political life, it is all too easy to marginalize radicals, and to attempt to buy acceptance for a moderate position by portraying others as extremists. Liberals have done this for years to communists. Sexual radicals have opened up the sex debates. It is shameful to deny their contribution, misrepresent their positions and further their stigmatization.

In contrast to cultural feminists, who simply want to purge sexual dissidents, the sexual moderates are willing to defend the rights of erotic non-conformists to political participation. Yet this defense of political rights is linked to an implicit system of ideological condescension.[83] The argument has two major parts. The first is an accusation that sexual dissidents have not paid close enough attention to the meaning, sources, or historical construction of their sexuality. This emphasis on meaning appears to function in much the same way that the question of etiology has functioned in discussions of homosexuality. That is, homosexuality, sadomasochism, prostitution, or boy-love are taken to be mysterious and problematic in some way that more respectable sexualities are not. The search for a cause is a search for something that could change so that these "problematic" eroticisms would simply not occur. Sexual militants have replied to such exercises that although the question of etiology or cause is of intellectual interest, it is not high on the political agenda and that, moreover, the privileging of such questions is itself a regressive political choice.

The second part of the "moderate" position focuses on questions of consent. Sexual radicals of all varieties have demanded the legal and social legitimation of consenting sexual behavior. Feminists have criticized them for ostensibly finessing questions about "the limits of consent" and "structural constraints" on consent.[84] Although there are deep problems with the political discourse of consent, and although there are certainly structural constraints on sexual choice, this criticism has been consistently misapplied in the sex debates. It does not take into account the very specific semantic content that consent has in sex law and sex practice.

As I mentioned earlier, a great deal of sex law does not distinguish between consensual and coercive behavior. Only rape law contains such a distinction. Rape law is based on the assumption, correct in my view, that heterosexual activity may be freely chosen or forcibly coerced. One has the legal right to engage in heterosexual behavior as long as it does not fall under the purview of other statutes and as long as it is agreeable to both parties.

This is not the case for most other sexual acts. Sodomy laws, as I mentioned above, are based on the assumption that the forbidden acts are an "abominable and detestable crime against nature." Criminality is intrinsic to the acts themselves, no matter what the desires of the participants. "Unlike rape, sodomy or an unnatural or perverted sexual act may be committed between two persons both of whom consent, and, regardless of which is the aggressor, both may be prosecuted."[85] Before the consenting adults statute was passed in California in 1976, lesbian lovers could have been prosecuted for committing oral copulation. If both participants were capable of consent, both were equally guilty.[86]

Adult incest statutes operate in a similar fashion. Contrary to popular mythology, the incest statutes have little to do with protecting children from rape by close relatives. The incest statutes themselves prohibit marriage or sexual intercourse between adults who are closely related. Prosecutions are rare, but two were reported recently. In 1979, a 19-year-old Marine met his 42-year-old mother, from whom he had been separated at birth. The two fell in love and got married. They were charged and found guilty of incest, which under Virginia law carries a maximum ten-year sentence. During their trial, the Marine testified, "I love her very much. I feel that two people who love each other should be able to live together."[87] In another case, a brother and sister who had been raised separately met and decided to get married. They were arrested and pleaded guilty to felony incest in return for probation. A condition of probation was that they not live together as husband and wife. Had they not accepted, they would have faced twenty years in prison.[88]

In a famous S/M case, a man was convicted of aggravated assault for a whipping administered in an S/M scene. There was no complaining victim. The session had been filmed and he was prosecuted on the basis of the film. The man appealed his conviction by arguing that he had been involved in a consensual sexual encounter and had assaulted no one. In rejecting his appeal, the court ruled that one may not consent to an assault or battery "except in a situation involving ordinary physical contact or blows incident to sports such as football, boxing, or wrestling."[89] The court went on to note that the "consent of a person without legal capacity to give consent, such as a child or insane person, is ineffective," and that "It is a matter of common knowledge that a normal person in full possession of his mental faculties does not freely consent to the use, upon himself, of force likely to produce great bodily injury."[90] Therefore, anyone who would consent to a whipping would be presumed *non compos mentis* and legally incapable of consenting. S/M sex generally involves a much lower level of force than the average football game, and results in

far fewer injuries than most sports. But the court ruled that football players are sane, whereas masochists are not.

Sodomy laws, adult incest laws, and legal interpretations such as the one above clearly interfere with consensual behavior and impose criminal penalties on it. Within the law, consent is a privilege enjoyed only by those who engage in the highest-status sexual behavior. Those who enjoy low-status sexual behavior do not have the legal right to engage in it. In addition, economic sanctions, family pressures, erotic stigma, social discrimination, negative ideology, and the paucity of information about erotic behavior, all serve to make it difficult for people to make unconventional sexual choices. There certainly are structural constraints that impede free sexual choice, but they hardly operate to coerce anyone into being a pervert. On the contrary, they operate to coerce everyone toward normality.

The "brainwash theory" explains erotic diversity by assuming that some sexual acts are so disgusting that no one would willingly perform them. Therefore, the reasoning goes, anyone who does so must have been forced or fooled. Even constructivist sexual theory has been pressed into the service of explaining away why otherwise rational individuals might engage in variant sexual behavior. Another position that is not yet fully formed uses the ideas of Foucault and Weeks to imply that the "perversions" are an especially unsavory or problematic aspect of the construction of modern sexuality.[91] This is yet another version of the notion that sexual dissidents are victims of the subtle machinations of the social system. Weeks and Foucault would not accept such an interpretation, since they consider all sexuality to be constructed, the conventional no less than the deviant.

Psychology is the last resort of those who refuse to acknowledge that sexual dissidents are as conscious and free as any other group of sexual actors. If deviants are not responding to the manipulations of the social system, then perhaps the source of their incomprehensible choices can be found in a bad childhood, unsuccessful socialization, or inadequate identity formation. In her essay on erotic domination, Jessica Benjamin draws upon psychoanalysis and philosophy to explain why what she calls "sado-masochism" is alienated, distorted, unsatisfactory, numb, purposeless, and an attempt to "relieve an original effort at differentiation that failed."[92] This essay substitutes a psycho-philosophical inferiority for the more usual means of devaluing dissident eroticism. One reviewer has already construed Benjamin's argument as showing that sado-masochism is merely an "obsessive replay of the infant power struggle."[93]

The position which defends the political rights of perverts but which seeks to understand their "alienated" sexuality is certainly preferable to the WAP-style bloodbaths. But for the most part, the sexual moderates have not confronted their discomfort with erotic choices that differ from their own. Erotic chauvinism cannot be redeemed by tarting it up in Marxist drag, sophisticated constructivist theory, or retro-psychobabble.

Whichever feminist position on sexuality – right, left or center – eventually attains dominance, the existence of such a rich discussion is evidence that the feminist movement will always be a source of interesting thought about sex. Nevertheless, I want to challenge the assumption that feminism is or should be the privileged site of a theory of sexuality. Feminism is the theory of gender oppression. To assume automatically that this makes it the theory of sexual oppression is to fail to distinguish between gender, on the one hand, and erotic desire, on the other.

In the English language, the word "*sex*" has two very different meanings. It means gender and gender identity, as in "the female sex" or "the male sex." But sex also refers to sexual activity, lust, intercourse, and arousal, as in "to have sex." This semantic merging reflects a cultural assumption that sexuality is reducible to sexual intercourse and that it is a function of the relations between women and men. The cultural fusion of gender with sexuality has given rise to the idea that a theory of sexuality may be derived directly out of a theory of gender.

In an earlier essay, "The Traffic in Women," I used the concept of a sex/gender system, defined as a "set of arrangements by which a society transforms biological sexuality into products of human activity."[94] I went on to argue that "Sex as

we know it – gender identity, sexual desire and fantasy, concepts of childhood – is itself a social product."[95] I did not distinguish between lust and gender, treating both as modalities of the same underlying social process.

"The Traffic in Women" was inspired by the literature on kin-based systems of social organization. It appeared to me at the time that gender and desire were systemically intertwined in such social formations. This may or may not be an accurate assessment of the relationship between sex and gender in tribal organizations. But it is surely not an adequate formulation for sexuality in Western industrial societies. As Foucault has pointed out, a system of sexuality has emerged out of earlier kinship forms and has acquired significant autonomy:

> Particularly from the eighteenth century onward, Western societies created and deployed a new apparatus which was superimposed on the previous one, and which, without completely supplanting the latter, helped to reduce its importance. I am speaking of the deployment of *sexuality* ... For the first [kinship], what is pertinent is the link between partners and definite statutes; the second [sexuality] is concerned with the sensations of the body, the quality of pleasures, and the nature of impressions.[96]

The development of this sexual system has taken place in the context of gender relations. Part of the modern ideology of sex is that lust is the province of men, purity that of women. It is no accident that pornography and the perversions have been considered part of the male domain. In the sex industry, women have been excluded from most production and consumption, and allowed to participate primarily as workers. In order to participate in the "perversions," women have had to overcome serious limitations on their social mobility, their economic resources, and their sexual freedoms. Gender affects the operation of the sexual system, and the sexual system has had gender-specific manifestations. But although sex and gender are related, they are not the same thing, and they form the basis of two distinct arenas of social practice.

In contrast to my perspective in "The Traffic in Women," I am now arguing that it is essential to separate gender and sexuality analytically to reflect more accurately their separate social existence. This goes against the grain of much contemporary feminist thought, which treats sexuality as a derivation of gender. For instance, lesbian feminist ideology has mostly analyzed the oppression of lesbians in terms of the oppression of women. However, lesbians are also oppressed as queers and perverts, by the operation of sexual, not gender, stratification. Although it pains many lesbians to think about it, the fact is that lesbians have shared many of the sociological features and suffered from many of the same social penalties as have gay men, sadomasochists, transvestites, and prostitutes.

Catherine MacKinnon has made the most explicit theoretical attempt to subsume sexuality under feminist thought. According to MacKinnon, "Sexuality is to feminism what work is to Marxism ... the molding, direction, and expression of sexuality organizes society into two sexes, women and men."[97] This analytic strategy in turn rests on a decision to "use sex and gender relatively interchangeably."[98] It is this definitional fusion that I want to challenge.[99]

There is an instructive analogy in the history of the differentiation of contemporary feminist thought from Marxism. Marxism is probably the most supple and powerful conceptual system extant for analyzing social inequality. But attempts to make Marxism the sole explanatory system for all social inequalities have been dismal exercises. Marxism is most successful in the areas of social life for which it was originally developed – class relations under capitalism.

In the early days of the contemporary women's movement, a theoretical conflict took place over the applicability of Marxism to gender stratification. Since Marxist theory is relatively powerful, it does in fact detect important and interesting aspects of gender oppression. It works best for those issues of gender most closely related to issues of class and the organization of labor. The issues more specific to the social structure of gender were not amenable to Marxist analysis.

The relationship between feminism and a radical theory of sexual oppression is similar. Feminist conceptual tools were developed to detect and analyze gender-based hierarchies. To the extent that these overlap with erotic stratifications, feminist theory has some explanatory power. But as issues become less those of gender and more those of sexuality, feminist analysis becomes misleading and often irrelevant. Feminist thought simply lacks angles of vision which can fully encompass the social organization of sexuality. The criteria of relevance in feminist thought do not allow it to see or assess critical power relations in the area of sexuality.

In the long run, feminism's critique of gender hierarchy must be incorporated into a radical theory of sex, and the critique of sexual oppression should enrich feminism. But an autonomous theory and politics specific to sexuality must be developed.

It is a mistake to substitute feminism for Marxism as the last word in social theory. Feminism is no more capable than Marxism of being the ultimate and complete account of all social inequality. Nor is feminism the residual theory which can take care of everything to which Marx did not attend. These critical tools were fashioned to handle very specific areas of social activity. Other areas of social life, their forms of power, and their characteristic modes of oppression, need their own conceptual implements. In this essay, I have argued for theoretical as well as sexual pluralism.

CONCLUSION

these pleasures which we lightly call physical
(Colette[100])

Like gender, sexuality is political. It is organized into systems of power, which reward and encourage some individuals and activities, while punishing and suppressing others. Like the capitalist organization of labor and its distribution of rewards and powers, the modern sexual system has been the object of political struggle since it emerged and as it has evolved. But if the disputes between labor and capital are mystified, sexual conflicts are completely camouflaged.

The legislative restructuring that took place at the end of the nineteenth century and in the early decades of the twentieth was a refracted response to the emergence of the modern erotic system. During that period, new erotic communities formed. It became possible to be a male homosexual or a lesbian in a way it had not been previously. Mass-produced erotica became available, and the possibilities for sexual commerce expanded. The first homosexual rights organizations were formed, and the first analyses of sexual oppression were articulated.[101]

The repression of the 1950s was in part a backlash to the expansion of sexual communities and possibilities which took place during World War II.[102] During the 1950s, gay rights organizations were established, the Kinsey reports were published, and lesbian literature flourished. The 1950s were a formative as well as a repressive era.

The current right-wing sexual counter-offensive is in part a reaction to the sexual liberalization of the 1960s and early 1970s. Moreover, it has brought about a unified and self-conscious coalition of sexual radicals. In one sense, what is now occurring is the emergence of a new sexual movement, aware of new issues and seeking a new theoretical basis. The sex wars out on the streets have been partly responsible for provoking a new intellectual focus on sexuality. The sexual system is shifting once again, and we are seeing many symptoms of its change.

In Western culture, sex is taken all too seriously. A person is not considered immoral, is not sent to prison, and is not expelled from her or his family, for enjoying spicy cuisine. But an individual may go through all this and more for enjoying shoe leather. Ultimately, of what possible social significance is it if a person likes to masturbate over a shoe? It may even be non-consensual, but since we do not ask permission of our shoes to wear them, it hardly seems necessary to obtain dispensation to come on them.

If sex is taken too seriously, sexual persecution is not taken seriously enough. There is systematic mistreatment of individuals and communities on the basis of erotic taste or behavior. There are serious penalties for belonging to the various sexual occupational castes. The sexuality of the young is denied, adult sexuality is often treated like a variety of nuclear waste, and the graphic representation of sex takes place in a mire of legal and social circumlocution. Specific populations bear the brunt of the current system of erotic

power, but their persecution upholds a system that affects everyone.

The 1980s have already been a time of great sexual suffering. They have also been a time of ferment and new possibility. It is up to all of us to try to prevent more barbarism and to encourage erotic creativity. Those who consider themselves progressive need to examine their preconceptions, update their sexual educations and acquaint themselves with the existence and operation of sexual hierarchy. It is time to recognize the political dimensions of erotic life.

ACKNOWLEDGMENTS

This paper owes a great deal to many people. Its roots go back to my graduate study at the University of Michigan in the early 1970s, particularly a course on the urbanization of Europe taught by Charles Tilly in 1973, and courses by Kent Flannery on Near Eastern pre-history (1971) and Mesoamerican Archeology (1972). It developed further in a rich conversation about sexuality, politics, and history that took place in the San Francisco area in the late 1970s and early 1980s, particularly in the Lesbian and Gay History Project and a feminist study group on sexuality and history. Among those participating at various points in this conversation were Allan Bérubé, Jeffrey Escoffier, Ellen Dubois, Amber Hollibaugh, Mary Ryan, Judith Stacey, Kay Trimberger, Pat Califia, Martha Vicinus, Eric Garber, Estelle Freedman, Willie Walker, Carole Vance, and John D'Emilio. Other people who contributed insights or information were Rayna Rapp, Judith Walkowitz, Daniel Tsang, Cynthia Astuto, David Sachs, Ralph Bruno, Kent Gerard, Barbara Kerr, and Michael Shively. Commenting on the manuscript at various points were Jeanne Bergman, Sally Binford, Lynn Eden, Laura Engelstein, Jeff Escoffier, Mark Leger, and Carole Vance. I owe special thanks to Ellen Willis, whose surgically precise and unerringly brilliant editorial skills were lavished on this essay, to its immense benefit and improved clarity. None of these individuals should be held responsible for my opinions and comments, but I am profoundly grateful to them all for inspiration, information, and assistance.

A NOTE ON DEFINITIONS

I want to clarify the use in this essay of terms such as homosexual, sex worker, and pervert. Contrary to much contemporary usage which restricts "homosexual" to males, I use "homosexual" to refer to both women and men. If I want to be more specific, I use "lesbian" or "gay male." "Sex worker" is intended to be more inclusive than "prostitute," in order to encompass the many jobs of the sex industry. Sex worker thus includes erotic dancers, strippers, porn models, nude women who will talk to a customer via telephone hook-up and can be seen but not touched, phone sex partners, and the various other employees of sex businesses such as receptionists, janitors, and barkers. Obviously, it also includes prostitutes, hustlers, and "male models." I use the term "pervert" as a shorthand for all the stigmatized sexual orientations. It used to commonly include male and female homosexuality as well but as these become less disreputable, the term has increasingly referred to the other "deviations." Terms such as "pervert" and "deviant" have, in general use, a connotation of disapproval, disgust, dislike or which I do not share. I am using these terms in a denotative fashion, and do not intend them to convey any disapproval on my part.

NOTES

1 Demetrius Zambaco, "Onanism and Nervous Disorders in Two Little Girls," in François Peraldi (ed.), *Polysexuality, Semiotext(e)* IV: (1981): 31, 36.
2 Linda Gordon and Ellen Dubois, "Seeking Ecstasy on the Battlefield: Danger and Pleasure in Nineteenth Century Feminist Sexual Thought," *Feminist Studies* 9: 1 (spring 1983); Steven Marcus, *The Other Victorians* (New York: New American Library, 1974); Mary Ryan, "The Power of Women's Networks: A Case Study of Female Moral Reform in America," *Feminist Studies* 5: 1 (1979); Judith R. Walkowitz, *Prostitution and Victorian Society*, (Cambridge, Cambridge University Press, 1980); Judith R. Walkowitz, "Male Vice and Feminist Virtue: Feminism and the Politics of Prostitution in Nineteenth-Century Britain," *History Workshop Journal*, 13 (spring 1982); Jeffrey Weeks, *Sex, Politics and Society: The Regulation of Sexuality Since 1800* (New York: Longman, 1981).
3 G. J. Barker-Benfield, *The Horrors of the Half-Known Life* (New York: Harper Colophon, 1976); Marcus, op. cit.; Weeks, op. cit. especially pp. 48–52; Zambaco, op. cit.
4 Sarah Senefield Beserra, Sterling G. Franklin and Norma Clevenger (eds), *Sex Code of California* (Sacramento: Planned Parenthood Affiliates of California, 1977): 113.
5 *Ibid*: 113–17.
6 Walkowitz, "Male Vice and Feminist Virtue", op. cit.: 83. Walkowitz's entire discussion of the *Maiden Tribute of Modern Babylon* and its aftermath (83–5) is illuminating.
7 Walkowitz, "Male Vice and Feminist Virtue": 85.
8 Beserra *et al.*, op. cit.: 106–7.
9 Commonwealth of Massachusetts, *Preliminary Report of the Special Commission Investigating the Prevalence of Sex Crimes*, 1947; State of New Hampshire, *Report of the Interim Commission of the State of New Hampshire to Study the Cause and Prevention of Serious Sex Crimes*, 1949; City of New York, *Report to the Governor on a Study of 102 Sex Offenders at Sing Sing Prison*, 1950; Samuel Hartwell, *A Citizen's Handbook of Sexual Abnormalities and the Mental Hygiene Approach to Their Prevention*, State of Michigan, 1950; State of Michigan, *Report of the Governor's Study Commission on the Deviated Criminal Sex Offender*, 1951. This is merely a sampler.
10 Estelle B. Freedman, "'Uncontrolled Desire': The Threat of the Sexual Psychopath in America, 1935–1960," paper presented at the Annual Meeting of the American Historical Association, San Francisco, December 1983.
11 Allan Bérubé, "Behind the Spectre of San Francisco," *Body Politic* (April 1981); Allan Bérubé, "Marching to a Different Drummer," *Advocate* (October 15, 1981); John D'Emilio, *Sexual Politics, Sexual Communities: The Making of the Homosexual Minority in the United States, 1940–1970* (Chicago: University of Chicago Press, 1983); Jonathan Katz, *Gay American History* (New York: Thomas Y. Crowell, 1976).
12 D'Emilio, op. cit.: 46–7; Allan Bérubé, personal communication.
13 John Gerassi, *The Boys of Boise* (New York: Collier, 1968: 14. I am indebted to Allan Bérubé for calling my attention to this incident.
14 Allan Bérubé, personal communication; D'Emilio, op. cit.; John D'Emilio, "Gay Politics, Gay Community: San Francisco's Experience," *Socialist Review* (January–February 1981).
15 The following examples suggest avenues for additional research. A local crackdown at the University of Michigan is documented in Daniel Tsang, "Gay Ann Arbor Purges," *Midwest Gay Academic Journal*: 1 (1977); and Daniel Tsang, "Ann Arbor Gay Purges," part 2, *Midwest Gay Academic Journal* 1: 2 (1977). At the University of Michigan, the number of faculty dismissed for alleged homosexuality appears to rival the number fired for alleged communist tendencies. It would be interesting to have figures comparing the number of professors who lost their positions during this period due to sexual and political offenses. On regulatory reform, many states passed laws during this period prohibiting the sale of alcoholic beverages to "known sex perverts" or providing that bars which catered to "sex perverts" be closed. Such a law was passed in California in 1955, and declared unconstitutional by the state Supreme Court in 1959 (Allan Bérubé, personal communication).

It would be of great interest to know exactly which states passed such statutes, the dates of their enactment, the discussion that preceded them, and how many are still on the books. On the persecution of other erotic populations, evidence indicates that John Willie and Irvin Klaw, the two premier producers and distributors of bondage erotica in the United States from the late 1940s through the early 1960s, encountered frequent police harassment and that Klaw, at least, was affected by a congressional investigation conducted by the Kefauver Committee. I am indebted to personal communication from J. B. Rund for information on the careers of Willie and Klaw. Published sources are scarce, but see John Willie, *The Adventures of Sweet Gwendoline* (New York: Belier Press, 1974); J. B. Rund, "Preface," *Bizarre Comix* 8 (New York: Belier Press, 1977); J. B. Rund, "Preface," *Bizarre Fotos* 1 (New York: Belier Press, 1978); and J. B. Rund, "Preface," *Bizarre Katalogs* 1 (New York: Belier Press, 1979). It would be useful to have more systematic information on legal shifts and police activity affecting non-gay erotic dissidence.

16 "Chicago is Center of National Child Porno Ring: The Child Predators," "Child Sex: Square in New Town Tells it All," US Orders Hearings On Child Pornography: Rodino Calls Sex Racket an "Outrage," "Hunt Six Men, Twenty Boys in Crackdown," *Chicago Tribune* (May 16, 1977); "Dentist Seized in Child Sex Raid: Carey to Open Probe," "How Ruses Lure Victims to Child Pornographers," *Chicago Tribune* (May 17, 1977); "Child Pornographers Thrive on Legal Confusion," "US Raids Hit Porn Sellers," *Chicago Tribune* May 18, 1977).

17 For more information on the "kiddie porn panic" see Pat Califia, "The Great Kiddy Porn Scare of '77 and Its Aftermath," *Advocate* October 16, 1980); Pat Califia, "A Thorny Issue Splits a Movement," *Advocate* (October 30, 1980); Mitzel, *The Boston Sex Scandal* (Boston: Glad Day Books, 1980); Gayle Rubin, "Sexual Politics, the New Right, and the Sexual Fringe," in Daniel Tsang (ed.), *The Age Taboo* (Boston: Alyson Publications, 1981). On the issue of cross-generational relationships, see also Roger Moody, *Indecent Assault* (London: Word Is Out Press, 1980); Tom O'Carroll, *Paedophilia: The Radical Case* (London: Peter Owen, 1980); Tsang, *The Age Taboo*; and Paul Wilson, *The Man They Called a Monster* (New South Wales: Cassell Australia, 1981).

18 "House Passes Tough Bill on Child Porn," *San Francisco Chronicle* (November 15, 1983): 14.

19 George Stambolian, "Creating the New Man: A Conversation with Jacqueline Livingstone," *Christopher Street* (May 1980); "Jacqueline Livingstone," *Clothed With the Sun* 3: 1 (May 1983).

20 Paul H. Gebhard, "The Institute," in Martin S. Weinberg (ed.), *Sex Research: Studies from the Kinsey Institute* (New York: Oxford University Press, 1976).

21 Phoebe Courtney, *The Sex Education Racket: Pornography in the Schools (An Exposé)* (New Orleans: Free Men Speak, 1969); Dr. Gordon V. Drake, *SIECUS: Corrupter of Youth* (Tulsa, Oklahoma: Christian Crusade Publications, 1969).

22 *Pavlov's Children (They May Be Yours)* (Los Angeles: Impact Publishers 1969).

23 Norman Podhoretz, "The Culture of Appeasement," *Harper's* (October 1977).

24 Alan Wolfe and Jerry Sanders, "Resurgent Cold War Ideology: The Case of the Committee on the Present Danger," in Richard Fagen (ed.), *Capitalism and the State in US–Latin American Relations* (Stanford: Stanford University Press, 1979).

25 Jimmy Breslin, "The Moral Majority in Your Motel Room," *San Francisco Chronicle* (January 22 1981): 41; Linda Gordon and Allen Hunter, "Sex, Family, and the New Right," *Radical America* (Winter 1977–8); Sasha Gregory-Lewis, "The Neo-Right Political Apparatus," *Advocate* (February 8, 1977); Sasha Gregory-Lewis, "Right Wing Finds New Organizing Tactic," *Advocate* (June 23, 1977); Sasha Gregory-Lewis, "Unravelling the Anti-Gay Network," *Advocate* (September 7, 1977); Andrew Kopkind, "America's New Right," *New Times* (September 30, 1977); Rosalind Pollack Petchesky, "Anti-abortion, Anti-feminism, and the Rise of the New Right," *Feminist Studies* 7: 2 (Summer 1981).

26 Rhonda Brown, "Blueprint for a Moral America," *Nation* (May 23, 1981).

27 James Barr, *Quatrefoil* (New York: Greenberg, 1950): 310.

28 This insight was first articulated by Mary McIntosh, "The Homosexual Role," *Social Problems* 16: 2 (fall 1968); the idea has been developed in Jeffrey Weeks, *Coming Out: Homosexual Politics in Britain from the Nineteenth Century to the Present* (New York: Quartet, 1977), and in Weeks, *Sex, Politics and Society*; see also D'Emilio, *Sexual Politics, Sexual Communities*; and Gayle Rubin, "Introduction" to Renée Vivien, *A Woman Appeared to Me* (Weatherby Lake, MO: Naiad Press, 1979).

29 Bert Hansen, "The Historical Construction of Homosexuality," *Radical History Review* 20 (spring/summer 1979).

30 Walkowitz, *Prostitution and Victorian Society*; and Walkowitz, "Male Vice and Female Virtue."

31 Michel Foucault, *The History of Sexuality*, (New York: Pantheon, 1978).

32 A very useful discussion of these issues can be found in Robert Padgug, "Sexual Matters: On Conceptualizing Sexuality in History," *Radical History Review* 20 (spring/summer 1979).

33 Claude Lévi-Strauss, "A Confrontation," *New Left Review* 62 (July–August 1970). In this conversation, Lévi-Strauss calls his position "a Kantianism without a transcendental subject."

34 Foucault, op. cit.: 11.

35 See the discussion in Weeks, *Sex, Politics and Society*: 9.

36 See Weeks, *Sex, Politics and Society*: 22.

37 See, for example, "Pope Praises Couples for Self-Control," *San Francisco Chronicle* (October 13, 1980): 5; "Pope Says Sexual Arousal Isn't a Sin If It's Ethical," *San Francisco Chronicle* (November 6, 1980): 33; "Pope Condemns 'Carnal Lust' As Abuse of Human Freedom," *San Francisco Chronicle* (January 15, 1981): 2; "Pope Again Hits Abortion, Birth Control," *San Francisco Chronicle* (January 16, 1981): 13; and "Sexuality, Not Sex in Heaven," *San Francisco Chronicle* (December 3, 1981): 50. See also note 65 below.

38 Susan Sontag, *Styles of Radical Will* (New York: Farrar, Straus, & Giroux, 1969: 46.

39 See Foucault, op. cit.: 106–7.

40 American Psychiatric Association, *Diagnostic and Statistical Manual of Mental and Physical Disorders*, 3rd edn (Washington, DC: American Psychiatric Association).

41 Note 1992: Throughout this essay I treated transgender behavior and individuals in terms of the sex system rather than the gender system, although transvestites and transsexuals are clearly transgressing gender boundaries. I did so because transgendered people are stigmatized, harassed, persecuted, and generally treated like sex "deviants" and perverts. But clearly this is an instance of the ways in which my classificatory system does not quite encompass the existing complexities. The schematic renderings of sexual hierarchies in Figures 10.1 and 10.2 were oversimplified to make a point. Although the point remains valid, the actual power relationships of sexual variation are considerably more complicated.

42 Alfred Kinsey, Wardell Pomeroy, and Clyde Martin, *Sexual Behavior in the Human Male* (Philadelphia: W. B. Saunders, 1948); Alfred Kinsey, Wardell Pomeroy, Clyde Martin, and Paul Gebhard, *Sexual Behavior in the Human Female* (Philadelphia: W. B. Saunders, 1953).

43 John Gagnon and William Simon, *Sexual Deviance* (New York: Harper & Row, 1967); John Gagnon and William Simon, *The Sexual Scene* (Chicago: Transaction Books, Aldine, 1970); John Gagnon, *Human Sexualities* (Glenview, ILL: Scott, Foresman, 1977).

44 Havelock Ellis, *Studies in the Psychology of Sex*, (2 vols), (New York: Random House, 1936).

45 Note 1992: The intention of this section was not to appeal to scientific authority, not to claim scientific objectivity for sexology, and certainly was not to privilege biological models as "tools [for] social inquiry" (Mariana Valverde, "Beyond Gender Dangers and Private Pleasures: Theory and Ethics in the Sex Debates," *Feminist Studies* 15: 2 (summer 1989): 237–54). It was to suggest that sexology would be a rich vein to mine for analyses of sexuality, although it never occurred to me that those who did so would fail to subject sexological texts to analytic scrutiny. I did intend the claim that sexological studies have more direct relevance than the endless rehashings of Freud and Lacan on which so much feminist thought on sex has been based. Such topographies are a bit like European maps of the world before 1492. They suffer from empirical deprivation. I am not a believer in "facts" unmediated by cultural structures of understanding. However, I do believe that social science theories which fail to recognize, assimilate and account for the relevant information are useful primarily as calisthenics. Outside of mathematics most theory is anchored in some set of privileged data, and psychoanalytic feminism is hardly an exception. For an exemplary feminist history of twentieth-century American sexology see Janice Irvine, *Disorders of Desire* (Philadelphia: Temple University Press, 1990).

46 Foucault, op. cit: 43.

47 Gilbert Herdt, *Guardians of the Flutes* (New York: McGraw-Hill, 1981); Raymond Kelly, "Witchcraft and Sexual Relations," in Paula Brown and Georgeda Buchbinder (eds), *Man and Woman in the New Guinea Highlands* (Washington, DC: American Anthropological Association, 1976); Gayle Rubin, "Coconuts: Aspects of Male/Female Relationships in New Guinea," unpublished MS, 1974; Gayle Rubin, review of *Guardians of the Flutes*, *Advocate* (December 23, 1982); J. Van Baal, *Dema* (The Hague: Nijhoff, 1966); F. E. Williams, *Papuans of the Trans-Fly* (Oxford: Clarendon, 1936).

48 Caroline Bingham, "Seventeenth-Century Attitudes Toward Deviant Sex," *Journal of Interdisciplinary History* (spring 1971): 465.

49 Stephen O. Murray, "The Institutional Elaboration of a Quasi-Ethnic Community," *International Review of Modern Sociology* (July–December 1979).

50 For further elaboration of these processes, see: Bérubé, "Behind the Spectre of San Francisco"; Bérubé, "Marching to a Different Drummer"; D'Emilio, "Gay Politics, Gay Community"; D'Emilio, *Sexual Politics, Sexual Communities*; Foucault; Hansen; Katz; Weeks, *Coming Out*; and Weeks, *Sex, Politics and Society*.

51 Walkowitz, *Prostitution and Victorian Society*.

52 Vice cops also harass all sex businesses, be these gay bars, gay baths, adult book stores, the producers and distributors of commercial erotica, or swing clubs.

53 Foucault, op. cit.: 40.

54 Karl Marx, in David McLellan (ed.), *The Grundrisse* (New York, Harper & Row, 1971): 94.

55 Clark Norton, "Sex in America," *Inquiry* (October 5, 1981). This article is a superb summary of much current sex law and should be required reading for anyone interested in sex.

56 Bessera *et al.*, op. cit.: 165–7.

57 Sarah Senefeld Beserra, Nancy M. Jewel, Melody West Matthews and Elizabeth R. Gatov (eds), *Sex Code of California*, Public Education and Research Committee of California (1973): 163–8. This earlier edition of the *Sex Code of California* preceeded the 1976 consenting adults statute and consequently gives a better overview of sodomy laws.

58 1992: For a wonderful history of the relationship between gays and the United States military, see Allan Bérubé, *Coming Out Under Fire: The History of Gay Men and Women in World War II* (New York: The Free Press, 1990).

59 Esther Newton, *Mother Camp: Female Impersonators in America* (Englewood Cliffs, NJ: Prentice-Hall, 1972): 21, emphasis in the original.

60 D'Emilio, *Sexual Politics, Sexual Communities*: 40–53, has an excellent discussion of gay oppression in the 1950s which covers many of the areas I have mentioned. The dynamics he describes, however, are operative in modified forms for other erotic populations, and in other periods. The specific model of gay oppression needs to be generalized to apply, with appropriate modifications, to other sexual groups.

61 Weeks, *Sex, Politics and Society*: 14.

62 Lysander Spooner, *Vices Are Not Crimes: A Vindication of Moral Liberty* (Cupertino, CA: Tanstaafl Press, 1977).

63 I have adopted this terminology from the very useful discussion in Weeks, *Sex, Politics and Society*: 14–15.

64 See Spooner, op. cit.: 25–9. Feminist anti-porn discourse fits right into the tradition of justifying attempts at moral control by claiming that such action will protect women and children from violence.

65 "Pope's Talk on Sexual Spontaneity," *San Francisco Chronicle* (November 13, 1980): 8; see also note 37 above. Julia Penelope argues that "we do not need anything that labels itself purely sexual" and that "fantasy, as an aspect of sexuality, may be a phallocentric 'need' from which we are not yet free" in "And Now For the Really Hard Questions," *Sinister Wisdom* 15 (fall 1980): 103.

66 See especially Walkowitz, *Prostitution and Victorian Society*, and Weeks, *Sex, Politics and Society*.

67 *Moral Majority Report* (July 1983). I am indebted to Allan Bérubé for calling my attention to this image.

68 Cited in Larry Bush, "Capitol Report," *Advocate* (8 December, 1983): 60.

69 1992: The literature on AIDS and its social sequelae has mushroomed since this essay was published. A few of the important texts are Douglas Crimp, *AIDS: Cultural Analysis, Cultural Activism* (Cambridge, MA: MIT Press, 1988); Douglas Crimp with Adam Rolston, *AIDS Demographics* (Seattle Bay Press, 1990); Elizabeth Fee and Daniel M. Fox, *AIDS: The Burdens of History* (Berkeley: University of California Press, 1988); Elizabeth Fee and Daniel M. Fox, *AIDS: The Making of a Chronic Disease* (Berkeley: University of California Press, 1992); Cindy Patton, *Sex and Germs: The Politics of AIDS* (Boston: South End Press, 1985); Cindy Patton, *Inventing AIDS* (New York: Routledge, 1990); Simon Watney, *Policing Desire: Pornography, AIDS, and the Media* (Minneapolis: University of Minnesota Press, 1987); Erica Carter and Simon Watney, *Taking Liberties: AIDS and Cultural Politics* (London: Serpent's Tail, 1989); Tessa Boffin and Sunil Gupta, *Ecstatic Antibodies* (London: Rivers Oram Press, 1990); and James Kinsella, *Covering the Plague: AIDS and the American Media* (New Brunswick: Rutgers University Press, 1989).

70 Cited in H. Montgomery Hyde, *A History of Pornography* (New York: Dell, 1965): 31.

71 See for example Laura Lederer (ed.), *Take Back the Night* (New York: William Morrow, 1980); Andrea Dworkin, *Pornography* (New York: Perigee, 1981). The *Newspage* of San Francisco's Women Against Violence in Pornography and Media and the *Newsreport* of New York Women Against Pornography are excellent sources.

72 Kathleen Barry, *Female Sexual Slavery* (Englewood Cliffs, NJ: Prentice-Hall, 1979); Janice Raymond, *The Transsexual Empire* (Boston: Beacon, 1979); Kathleen Barry, "Sadomasochism: The New Backlash to Feminism," *Trivia* 1 (fall 1982); Robin Ruth Linden, Darlene R. Pagano, Diana E. H. Russell and Susan Leigh Starr (eds), *Against Sadomasochism* (East Palo Alto, CA: Frog in the Well, 1982); and Florence Rush, *The Best Kept Secret* (New York: McGraw-Hill, 1980).

73 Sally Gearhart, "An Open Letter to the Voters in District 5 and San Francisco's Gay Community," 1979; Adrienne Rich, *On Lies, Secrets, and Silence* (New York, W. W. Norton, 1979): 225. ("On the other hand, there is homosexual patriarchal culture, a culture created by homosexual men, reflecting such male stereotypes as dominance and submission as modes of relationship,

and the separation of sex from emotional involvement – a culture tainted by profound hatred for women. The male 'gay' culture has offered lesbians the imitation role-stereotypes of 'butch' and 'femme,' 'active' and 'passive,' cruising, sado-masochism, and the violent, self-destructive world of 'gay' bars"); Judith Pasternak, "The Strangest Bedfellows: Lesbian Feminism and the Sexual Revolution," *Woman-News* (October 1983); Adrienne Rich, "Compulsory Heterosexuality and Lesbian Existence," in Ann Snitow, Christine Stansell, and Sharon Thompson (eds), *Powers of Desire: The Politics of Sexuality* (New York: Monthly Review Press, 1983).

74 Julia Penelope, op. cit.

75 Sheila Jeffreys, "The Spinster and Her Enemies: Sexuality and the Last Wave of Feminism," *Scarlet Woman* 13: 2 (July 1981): 26; a further elaboration of this tendency can be found in Judith Pasternak, op. cit. Note 1992: These trends have become much more fully articulated. Some of the key texts are Sheila Jeffreys, *The Spinster and Her Enemies: Feminism and Sexuality 1880–1930* (London: Pandora Press, 1985); Sheila Jeffreys, *Anti-Climax* (London: The Women's Press, 1990); Lal Coveney, Margaret Jackson, Sheila Jeffreys, Leslie Kay and Pat Mahony, *The Sexuality Papers: Male Sexuality and the Social Control of Women* (London: Hutchinson, 1984); and Dorchen Leidholdt and Janice G. Raymond, *The Sexual Liberals and the Attack on Feminism* (New York: Pergamon, 1990).

76 Pat Califia, "Feminism vs. Sex: A New Conservative Way," *Advocate* (February 21, 1980); Pat Califia, "Among Us, Against Us – The New Puritans," *Advocate* (April 17, 1980); Califia, "The Great Kiddy Porn Scare of 77 and Its Aftermath"; Califia, "A Thorny Issue Splits a Movement"; Pat Califia, *Sapphistry* (Tallahassee, FA: Naiad, 1980); Pat Califia, "What Is Gay Liberation," *Advocate* (June 25, 1981); Pat Califia, "Feminism and Sadomasochism," *Co-Evolution Quarterly* 33 (spring 1981); Pat Califia, "Response to Dorchen Leidholdt," *New Women's Times* (October 1982); Pat Califia, "Public Sex," *Advocate* (September 30, 1982); Pat Califia, "Doing It Together: Gay Men, Lesbians, and Sex," *Advocate* (July 7, 1983); Pat Califia, "Gender-Bending," *Advocate* (September 15, 1983); Pat Califia, "The Sex Industry," *Advocate* (October 13, 1983); Deirdre English, Amber Hollibaugh, and Gayle Rubin, "Talking Sex," *Socialist Review* (July–August 1981); "Sex Issue," *Heresies* 12 (1981); Amber Hollibaugh, "The Erotophobic Voice of Women: Building a Movement for the Nineteenth Century," *New York Native* (September 26–October 9, 1982); Maxine Holz, "Porn: Turn On or Put Down,

Some Thoughts on Sexuality," *Processed World* 7 (spring 1983); Barbara O'Dair, "Sex, Love, and Desire: Feminists Struggle Over the Portrayal of Sex," *Alternative Media* (spring 1983); Lisa Orlando, "Bad Girls and 'Good' Politics," *Village Voice*, Literary Supplement (December 1982); Joanna Russ, "Being Against Pornography," *Thirteenth Moon* VI: 1 and 2 (1982; Samois, *What Color Is Your Handkerchief* (Berkeley: Samois, 1979); Samois, *Coming to Power* (Boston: Alyson, 1982); Deborah Sundahl, "Stripping For a Living," *Advocate* (October 13 1983); Nancy Wechsler, "Interview with Pat Califia and Gayle Rubin," part I, *Gay Community News*, Book Review (July 18, 1981), and part II, *Gay Community News* (August 15, 1981); Ellen Willis, *Beginning to See the Light* (New York: Knopf, 1981). For an excellent overview of the history of the ideological shifts in feminism which have affected the sex debates, see Alice Echols, "Cultural Feminism: Feminist Capitalism and the Anti-Pornography Movements," *Social Text* 7 (spring and summer 1983).

77 Lisa Orlando, "Lust at Last! Spandex Invades the Academy," *Gay Community News* (May 1982); Ellen Willis, "Who Is a Feminist? An Open Letter to Robin Morgan," *Village Voice*, Literary Supplement (December 1982).

78 Ellen Willis, *Beginning to See the Light*: 146. I am indebted to Jeanne Bergman for calling my attention to this quote.

79 See, for example, Jessica Benjamin, "Master and Slave: The Fantasy of Erotic Domination," in Snitow *et al.*: 297; and B. Ruby Rich, review of *Powers of Desire*, *In These Times* (November 16–22, 1983).

80 1992: The label "libertarian feminist" or "sexual libertarian" continues to be used as a shorthand for feminist sex radicals. The label is erroneous and misleading. It is true that the Libertarian Party opposes state control of consensual sexual behavior. We agree on the pernicious quality of state activity in this area, and I consider the Libertarian program to repeal most sex legislation superior to that of any other organized political party. However, there the similarity ends. Feminist sex radicals rely on concepts of systemic, socially structured inequalities and differential powers. In this analysis, state regulation of sex is part of a more complex system of oppression which it reflects, enforces and influences. The state also develops its own structures of interests, powers, and investments in sexual regulation.

As I have explained in this essay and elsewhere, the concept of consent plays a different role in sex law than it does in the social contract or the wage contract. The qualities, quantity and significance of state intervention and regulation of sexual behavior need to be analyzed in context, and not crudely equated with analyses drawn from economic theory. Certain basic freedoms which are taken for granted in other areas of life do not exist in the area of sex. Those that do exist are not equally available to members of different sexual populations and are differentially applied to various sexual activities. People are not called "libertarian" for agitating for basic freedoms and legal equality for racial and ethnic groups; I see no reason why sexual populations should be denied even the limited benefits of liberal capitalist societies.

I doubt anyone would call Marx a liberal or libertarian, but he considered capitalism a revolutionary, if limited, social system. The failure to support democratic sexual freedoms does not bring on socialism; it maintains something more akin to feudalism.

81 B. Ruby Rich, op. cit.: 76.

82 Samois, *What Color Is Your Handkerchief*; Samois, *Coming To Power*; Pat Califia, "Feminism and Sadomasochism"; Pat Califia, *Sapphistry*.

83 1992: A recent example of dismissive ideology condescension is this: "The Sadomasochists are not entirely 'valueless,' but they have resisted any values that might limit their freedom rather than someone else's judgement; and in this they show themselves as lacking in an understanding of the requirements of common life." It appears in Shane Phelan, *Identity Politics: Lesbian Feminism and the Limits of Community* (Philadelphia: Temple University Press, 1989): 133.

84 Lisa Orlando, "Power Plays: Coming to Terms with Lesbian S/M," *Village Voice* (July 26, 1983); Elizabeth Wilson, "The Context of 'Between *Pleasure and Danger*': The Barnard Conference on Sexuality," *Feminist Review* 13 (spring 1983): especially 35–41.

85 *Taylor* v. *State*, 214 Md. 156, 165, 133 A. 2d 414, 418. This quote is from a dissenting opinion, but it is a statement of prevailing law.

86 Bessera, Jewel, Matthews and Gatov: 163–5. See note 57 above.

87 "Marine and Mom Guilty of Incest," *San Francisco Chronicle* (November 16, 1979): 16.

88 Norton: 18.

89 *People v. Samuels*, 250 Cal. App. 2d 501, 513, 58 Cal. Rptr. 439, 447 (1967).

90 *People v. Samuels*, 250 Cal. App. 2d. at 513–514, 58 Cal. Rptr. at 447.

91 Mariana Valverde, "Feminism Meets Fist-Fucking: Getting Lost in Lesbian S & M," *Body Politic* (February 1980); Wilson, op. cit.: 38.

92 Benjamin, op. cit.: 292, but see also 286, 291–7.

93 Barbara Ehrenreich, "What Is This Thing Called Sex," *Nation* (September 24, 1983): 247.

94 Gayle Rubin, "The Traffic in Women," in Rayna R. Reiter (ed.), *Toward an Anthropology of Women* (New York: Monthly Review Press, 1975): 159.

95 Rubin, "The Traffic in Women": 166.

96 Foucault, op. cit.: 106.

97 Catherine MacKinnon, "Feminism, Marxism, Method and the State: An Agenda for Theory," *Signs*: 3 (spring 1982): 515–16.

98 Catherine MacKinnon, "Feminism, Marxism, Method, and the State: Toward Feminist Jurisprudence," *Signs* 8 (summer 1983): 635.

99 1992: MacKinnon's published oeuvre has also burgeoned: Catherine A. MacKinnon, *Toward a Feminist Theory of the State* (Cambridge, MA: Harvard University Press, 1989); Catherine A. MacKinnon, *Feminism Unmodified: Discourses on Life and Law* (Cambridge, MA: Harvard University Press, 1987).

100 Colette, *The Ripening Seed*, trans. and cited in Hannah Alderfer, Beth Jaker and Marybeth Nelson, *Diary of a Conference on Sexuality* (New York: Faculty Press, 1982): 72.

101 John Lauritsen and David Thorstad, *The Early Homosexual Rights Movement in Germany* (New York: Times Change Press, 1974).

102 D'Emilio, *Sexual Politics, Sexual Communities*; Bérubé "Behind the Spectre of San Francisco"; Bérubé, "Marching to a Different Drummer."

STEVEN EPSTEIN

"Gay Politics, Ethnic Identity: The Limits of Social Constructionism"

from *Socialist Review* 93/94 (May–August 1987): 9–54

I seem to be surrounded at all times in all ways by who I am ... It goes with me wherever I go ... and my life is gay and where I go I take my gay life with me. I don't consciously sit and think while I'm eating soup that I'm eating this "gayly," but, you know, it surrounds me.

To me being gay is like having a tan. When you are in a gay relationship, you're gay. When you're not in a gay relationship, you're not gay.

As I sit at a concert or engage volubly in a conversation in the office or at home, or as I look up from my newspaper and glance at the people occupying the seats of the bus, my mind will suddenly jump from the words, the thoughts, or the music around me, and with horrible impact I will hear, pounding within myself, the fateful words: *I am different*. I am different from these people, and I must always be different from them. I do not belong to them, nor they to me.

There's nothing in me that is not in everybody else, and nothing in everybody else that is not in me. We're trapped in language, of course. But homosexual is not a noun. At least not in my book.

What does it mean to be gay? Do lesbians and gay men constitute a "deviant subculture"? A "sexual minority"? A privileged "revolutionary subject"? Is homosexuality a "preference" (like a taste for chocolate ice cream)? Or perhaps an "orientation" (a fixed position relative to the points of a compass)? Or maybe it's a "life-style," like being a "yuppie" or a surfer? Is being gay something that has some importance? Or is it a relatively inconsequential difference?

The gay men and women quoted above are undoubtedly not a representative sample, but the range of contradictory opinions certainly testifies to the difficulties involved in answering these questions.[1] And the types of disagree-

ments observed in these quotes are present not only between individuals, but also within them. Most people who identify as gay or practice homosexuality adopt some variety of relatively inconsistent positions regarding their identity over the course of time, often depending on the needs of the moment. These contradictions are paralleled by the attitudes of homophobic opponents of the gay moment, which are typically even less consistent; for example, one frequently hears the belief that homosexuality is an "illness" combined with a simultaneous concern that youngsters can be "seduced" into it. The whole issue, it seems, is a terminological and conceptual minefield. Yet given the startling newness of the idea of there being such a thing as a "gay identity" – neither that term, nor "lesbian identity," nor "homosexual identity" appeared in writing by or about gays and lesbians before the mid-1970s – the confusion is hardly surprising.[2]

This article does not address the question of what "causes" homosexuality, or what "causes" heterosexuality. Instead what I seek to explore is how lesbians and gay men, on a day-to-day basis, interpret their sexual desires and practices so as to situate themselves in the world; how these self-understandings relate to social theories about homosexuals, and how both the theories and the self-understandings can shape – or block – different varieties of political activism by gays.[3] I take as given that power inheres in the ability to name, and that what we call ourselves has implications for political practice. An additional assumption is that lesbians and gay men in our society consciously seek, in a wide variety of ways, to *legitimate* their forms of sexual expression, by developing explanations, strategies, and defenses. These legitimations are articulated both on an individual level ("This is who I am, and this is why I am that way") and on a collective level ("This is what we are, and here is what we should do"). Legitimation strategies play a mediating function between self-understanding and political programs, and between groups and their individual members.

Existing theories of sexuality fail to address these concerns adequately. For some time now, sexual theory has been preoccupied with a debate between "essentialism" and "constructionism" – a debate which despite its importance in reorienting our thinking about sexuality, may well have outlived its usefulness. "Essentialists" treat sexuality as a biological force and consider sexual identities to be cognitive realizations of genuine, underlying differences; "constructionists," on the other hand, stress that sexuality, and sexual identities, are social constructions, and belong to the world of culture and meaning, not biology. In the first case, there is considered to be some "essence" within homosexuals that makes them homosexual – some gay "core" of their being, or their psyche, or their genetic make-up. In the second case, "homosexual," "gay," and "lesbian" are just labels, created by cultures and applied to the self.

Both essentialist and constructionist views are ingrained in the folk understandings of homosexuality in our society – often in a highly contradictory fashion. In a recent letter to Ann Landers, "Worried in Montana" expresses concern that her 14-year-old son may be "seduced" into homosexuality (folk constructionism) by the boy's friend, who she has "no question" is gay, because of his "feminine mannerisms" (folk essentialism). Ann reassures the mother that the only way her son would turn out to be gay is if "the seeds of homosexuality were already present" (folk essentialism). At the same time, she questions the mother's certainty about the sexual orientation of the friend, claiming that it is "presumptuous" to label a 14-year-old as "gay" (folk constructionism).[4] But if such inconsistent views can at times exist side by side, it is equally true that at other times they clash violently. Homosexuals who are advised to "change" and become

straight, for example, might have more than a passing investment in the claim that they've "always been that way" – that their gayness is a fundamental part of who they "really are."

This debate is not restricted to the field of sexuality; it parallels similar ones that have taken place in many other domains, including gender, race and class. For example, while some feminists have proposed that qualities such as nurturance constitute a feminine "essence," others have insisted that any differences between men and women, beyond the strictly biological, are the products of culture and history: men and women have no essential "nature."[5] But while the issues may be generalizable, they have a special salience for contemporary gay politics, because of a peculiar historical irony. With regard to sexuality, the constructionist critique of essentialism has become the received wisdom in left academic circles. And yet, curiously, the historical ascendancy of the new constructionist orthodoxy has paralleled a growing inclination within the gay movement in the United States to understand itself and project an image of itself in ever more "essentialist" terms.

As many observers have noted, gays in the 1970s increasingly came to conceptualize themselves as a legitimate minority group, having a certain quasi- "ethnic" status, and deserving the same protections against discrimination that are claimed by other groups in our society.[6] To be gay, then, became something like being Italian, black or Jewish. The "politics of identity" have crystallized around a notion of "gayness" as a real, and not arbitrary, difference. So while constructionist theorists have been preaching the gospel that the hetero/homosexual distinction is a social fiction, gays and lesbians, in everyday life and in political action, have been busy hardening the categories. Theory, it seems, has not been informing practice. Perhaps the practitioners are misguided; or perhaps there is something about the strict constructionist perspective which neither adequately describes the experiences of gays and lesbians nor speaks to their need to understand and legitimate their places in the world.[7]

To address these questions, my analysis will proceed as follows. First, I will recapitulate the constructionist–essentialist debate and discuss why neither side proves altogether useful in understanding or guiding contemporary gay politics. Then, I will argue that other theoretical perspectives on identity and ethnicity can provide valuable help in understanding recent political trends and in defending some version of an "ethnic/minority group model." In the process, I will return to the theoretical debate, examine some more subtle expressions of it, and show that the "ethnic" model is congruent with a modified constructionist position. Finally, I will explore the implications of this analysis for the future directions of gay politics.

THE DEBATE

At heart, the theoretical debate is located on the all-too-familiar terrain of nature versus nurture. As against the essentialist position that sexuality is a biological force seeking expression in ways that are preordained, constructionists treat sexuality as a blank slate, capable of bearing whatever meanings are generated by the society in question. In addition, the debaters line up on opposite sides of an old epistemological argument concerning categorization.[8] Essentialists are "realists" in their insistence that social categories (e.g., "homosexual," "heterosexual," "bisexual") reflect an underlying reality of difference; constructionists are "nominalists" in their contrary assertion that such categories are arbitrary, human-imposed divisions of the continuum of experience – categories create social types, rather than revealing them.

"Essentialism" is often equated with "traditional" views on sexuality in general, but can be linked specifically to the work of nineteenth-century "sexologists," such as Havelock Ellis and Krafft-Ebing; to certain aspects of Freud's work; and to deterministic theories such as sociobiology.[9] Essentialist views stress the "natural" dimensions of sex; and essentialist conceptions of homosexuality seek to account for such persons on the basis of some core of difference, whether that difference be hormonal, or medical, or a consequence of early child-rearing, or "just the way we are."

The constructionist critique of sexual essentialism has played an important role in debunking this traditional view. Much like essentialism, though constructionism should not be thought of as a specific school, but rather as a broader tendency of thinking that has found representations in a number of disciplines. At the risk of oversimplifying, it can be said that recent historical and sociological work on gays and lesbians in Western societies[10] traces its roots to two schools of sociology: *symbolic interactionists*, particularly the pathbreaking work of John Gagnon and William Simon on "sexual conduct"; and *labeling theorists*, especially Mary McIntosh's analysis of the "homosexual role" and Kenneth Plummer on "sexual stigma."[11] To a lesser degree, analyses of sexual constructionism in Western societies have also been influenced by the cross-cultural work of constructionist anthropology; these studies of "sex/gender systems" trace a somewhat different history from the mid-century cultural anthropology of Boas, Benedict, and Mead.[12] Finally, in the 1980s, the work of Michel Foucault has become a new rallying point for sexual constructionism and has served as the impetus for further investigations.[13] I will briefly discuss some of these sources of constructionism, in order to describe the main contours of the perspective as it has evolved.

In keeping with the central thrust of symbolic interactionism, constructionists propose that sexuality be investigated on the level of subjective meaning. Sexual acts have no inherent meaning, and in fact, no act is inherently sexual. Rather, in the course of interactions and over the course of time, individuals and societies spin webs of significance around the realm designated as "sexual." People *learn* to be sexual, Gagnon and Simon stress, in the same way they learn everything else: "Without much reflection, they pick up direction from their social environment."[14] As actors attribute subjective meanings to their interactions with others, they begin to develop "sexual scripts" which guide them in their future sexual interactions. Unlike "drives," which are understood as fixed essences destined to seek a particular expression, "scripts" are highly variable and fluid, subject to constant revision and editing.[15]

Central to the constructionist critique of

essentialist "drive theory" is a repudiation of the popular imagery of sex. In this view we tend to see sex as

> an overpowering, instinctual force, whose characteristics are built into the biology of the human animal, which shapes human institutions and whose will will out, either in the form of direct sexual expression, or if blocked, in the form of perversion or neuroses.[16]

In this view which preceded but was popularized by Freud, "society" must restrain "sexuality," and social order depends on the proper channeling of sexual energy. In the left-wing version of the same ideology, "sex radicals" such as Wilhelm Reich and Herbert Marcuse have treated sexual repression as the liberator from bondage.[17] More generally, in the popularizations of this imagery, the sex drive is treated as some sort of magical energy; hence the idea that athletes shouldn't have sex before the big game, or that masturbation constitutes a waste of one's potency. In all these views the sex drive is credited "with enormous – almost mystical – power."[18]

While symbolic interactionists debunked the notion of a "natural" sexuality, it was labeling theory that first provided the means to challenge essentialist views of "the homosexual" as a natural, transhistorical category. This challenge, which lies at the very crux of the constructionists argument about homosexuality, can be expressed in the following claim: although every known society has examples of homosexual *behavior*, only recently has there arisen a conception of "the homosexual" as a distinct type of *person*. In Mary McIntosh's important essay on the modern "homosexual role," her immediate target was the medical conception of the homosexual person. McIntosh argued vehemently against the prevailing medical logic:

> Many scientists and ordinary people assume that there are two kinds of people in the world: homosexuals and heterosexuals. Some of them recognize that homosexual feelings and behaviour are not confined to the persons they would like to call "homosexuals" and that some of these persons do not actually engage in homosexual behaviour. This should pose a crucial problem, but they evade the crux by retaining their assumption and puzzling over the question of how to tell whether someone is "really" homosexual or not.

> Lay people too will discuss whether a certain person is "queer" in much the same way as they might question whether a certain pain indicated cancer. And in much the same way they will often turn to scientists or to medical men for a surer diagnosis.[19]

In place of this essentialism, McIntosh argues that "the homosexual" has come to occupy a distinct "social role" in modern societies. Since homosexual *practices* are widespread but socially threatening, a special, stigmatized category of *individuals* is created so as to keep the rest of society pure. By this means, a "clear-cut, publicized and recognizable threshold between permissible and impermissible behaviour" is constructed; anyone who begins to approach that threshold is immediately threatened with being labeled a full-fledged deviant: one of "them."[20] A homosexual identity, then, is created not so much through homosexual activity *per se* (what labeling theorists would call "primary deviance"), but through the reactions of the deviant individual to being so described, and through the internalization of the imposed categorization ("secondary deviance").

These sociological theories were employed by historians who, in empirical studies, have traced the genesis of the modern homosexual.[21] More recently, the work of Foucault has helped us to theorize a historical dimension to the constructionist arguments. According to Foucault, sexuality in the modern Western world has been the site of an explosion of discourses of power and knowledge; sexual meanings, sexual doctrines, and sexual beings have been generated incessantly by a culture that has come to be obsessed with the significance of the sexual, has elevated it to unprecedented dimensions, and has sought in it "the truth of our being."[22]

Foucault has tried to use this perspective to account for the origin of "the homosexual." In Foucault's view, the transformation from sexual behavior to sexual personhood is attributable to three factors: the increasing importance attached to sexuality in general; a more widespread transformation in structures of social control, from control that operates through sanctions against specific acts to control based on highly individualized discipline; and the growing power of professionals, and especially doctors, to define social problems and enforce social norms. In an oft-cited passage, Foucault argues:

> As defined by the ancient civil or canonical codes, sodomy was a category of forbidden acts; their perpetrator was nothing more than the juridical subject of them. The nineteenth-century homosexual became a personage, a past, a case history, and a childhood, in addition to being a type of life, a life form, and a morphology ... Homosexuality appeared as one of the forms of sexuality when it was transposed from the practice of sodomy onto a kind of interior androgyny, a hermaphrodism of the soul. The sodomite has been a temporary aberration; the homosexual was now a species.[23]

As summarized in this brief sketch, constructionism posed a serious challenge to the prevailing essentialist orthodoxy concerning homosexuality. Where essentialism took for granted that all societies consist of people who are either heterosexuals or homosexuals (with perhaps some bisexuals), constructionists demonstrated that the notion of "the homosexual" is a sociohistorical product, not universally applicable, and worthy of explanation in its own right. And where essentialism would treat the self-attribution of a "homosexual identity" as unproblematic – as simply the conscious recognition of a true, underlying "orientation" – constructionism focused attention on identity as a complex development outcome, the consequence of an interactive process of social labeling and self-identification. Finally, by refusing to privilege any particular expression of sexuality as "natural," constructionism shifted the whole framework of debate on the question of homosexuality: instead of asking, why is there homosexuality? the constructionists took variation for granted and asked, why is there homophobia?[24]

Unfortunately, while constituting a significant advance in our understanding of sexuality and homosexuality, constructionism also posed some inherent difficulties. However, before attempting a critique of constructionism, it is important to situate the debate within a social and political context. Rather than juxtaposing ideas in the abstract, we need to examine the politics of gay communities during the postwar period and the connection between those politics and the evolving theoretical stances.

THE POLITICAL CONTEXT

As Foucault notes, the labeling practices of the nineteenth-century doctors who invented the term *homosexual* created the possibility for a "reverse affirmation," by which the stigmatized could gradually begin to organize around their label and assert the legitimacy of that identity.[25] Focault, however, neglects the material bases for these practices. As Jeffrey Weeks and John D'Emilio have argued, the medical categorization itself presupposed certain social conditions, including changes in family structure that were linked to the Industrial Revolution, and urbanization, which provided the social space for a homosexual subculture to develop.[26] By mid-century, such subcultures were firmly established in most major cities in the United States.

Homosexual politics in the 1950s and early 1960s preached liberal tolerance and stressed the goal of integration into the larger society.[27] The birth of the gay liberation movement marked a radical break with these accommodationist politics. When American gay liberation burst out of quiescence with the Stonewall riot in Greenwich Village in 1969, the politics that were espoused represented a mixture of the new-left ideology and the left Freudian arguments that anticipated constructionism.[28] Activists with groups such as the Gay Liberation Front portrayed homosexuals as revolutionary subjects who were uniquely situated to advance the cause of sexual liberation for society as a whole. However, the notion of "the homosexual" as a distinct type of person was specifically repudiated in favor of a left Freudian view of human sexuality as "polymorphously perverse." In utopian fashion, activists prophesied the disappearance of both "the homosexual" and "the heterosexual" through the abolition of constraining categories.

> The reason so few of us are bisexual is because society made such a big stink about homosexuality that we got forced into seeing ourselves as either straight or nonstraight ... We'll be gay until everyone has forgotten that it's an issue. Then we'll begin to be complete people.[29]

Or in the words of a lesbian activist:

I will tell you what we want, we radical homosexuals: not for you to tolerate us, to accept us, but to understand us. And this you can do only by becoming one of us. We want to reach the homosexuals entombed in you, to liberate our brothers and sisters, locked in the prisons of your skulls ... We will never go straight until you go gay. As long as you divide yourselves, we will be divided from you – separated by a mirror trick of your mind.[30]

Perhaps the most sophisticated expression of this ideology is Dennis Altman's, whose *Homosexual: Oppression and Liberation* (1971) remains the classic statement of early post-Stonewall gay male politics. In the final chapter, entitled "The End of the Homosexual?", Altman looks forward to not only the abolition of sexual categorization but also the elimination of "masculinity" and "femininity," along with the creation of a "new human" for whom such distinctions would simply be irrelevant.[31]

While such arguments are not exactly "constructionist" – Gagnon and Simon, after all, would criticize the lingering essentialism of the left Freudians such as Marcuse – they resonated fairly closely with the gay and lesbian constructionist history that began to be written soon afterward; this history, in fact, was inspired by the events of the early gay liberation movement, and many of the historians had been active in it from the start. What the liberationist position shared with the constructionist arguments was an insistence that sexual typologies are social, rather than natural facts; that these categories are highly fluid; and that they need to be transcended. Both shared a sense of the openness of historical possibilities that was inspired by the political climate of the day.

Needless to say, the radical liberationist politics did not achieve its goals. However, the greater irony is that, to the extent that the activists did succeed in advancing the situation of gays and lesbians, they undermined the logical supports for their own arguments. That is, simply by advancing the cause of gay liberation, the liberationists helped to further the notion, among both gays and straights, that gays constitute a distinct social group with their own political and social interests. This is a familiar dilemma, and one that is by no means peculiar to the gay movement: How do you protest a socially imposed categorization, except by organizing around the category? Just as blacks cannot fight the arbitrariness of racial classification without organizing *as blacks*, so gays could not advocate the overthrow of the sexual order without making their gayness the very basis of their claims.

The 1970s witnessed a phenomenal growth in the institutionalization of a gay identity as "deviant subcultures" gave way to "gay communities." And contrary to the "proto-constructionist" perspective that had been espoused by the early liberationists, the next generation of gay activists embraced a conception of gay identity that was significantly essentialist. To some extent, these essentialist notions had been around from the start; and in the political climate of the late 1970s, one can imagine why they would have more appeal than the utopian vision of the early liberationism, with its focus on historical openness. What this meant, however, is that a disjuncture developed between theory and practice: in place of the rough congruence between early gay liberation politics and evolving constructionist theory, we now find a growing tension between an evolving essentialist politics and a constructionist theory that is firmly in place.

Each variant of essentialism is based on some sort of legitimation strategy. In some cases, activists have legitimated their claims with reference to the trans-historical unity of homosexuals or their trans-cultural functional role. Perhaps most prominently, Adrienne Rich has proposed the existence of a "lesbian continuum" which links the resisters of heterosexist patriarchy across cultures and throughout history.[32] In a somewhat analogous vein, a male activist claimed: "We look forward to regaining our ancient historical role as medicine people, healers, prophets, shamans, and sorcerers."[33] Others have sought legitimations of a more "scientific" sort, making reference to a biological or genetic basis for homosexuality. Most typically, and far more usefully, gays and lesbians have adopted what Altman has in recent writings characterized as an "ethnic" identification.[34]

This "ethnic" self-characterization by gays and lesbians has a clear political utility, for it has permitted a form of group organizing that is particularly suited to the American experience, with its history of civil-rights struggles and ethnic-based, interest-group competition. In fact, an irony that Altman points out is that, by appealing to civil rights, gays as a group have been able to claim a legitimacy that homosexuals as individuals are often denied:

> One of the paradoxes of the present situation is that even where the old laws defining homosexual behavior as a major crime remain, there is a growing de facto recognition of a gay minority, deserving of full civil and political rights *as a minority*. Thus for years the mayor of New York could proclaim an official Gay Pride Week while the very people being honored remained criminals under state law.[35]

Gay people's sense of themselves as belonging to a "minority group" was not altogether new; this view had been stated publicly at least as early 1951, when Donald Webster Cory discussed the "invisible minority" in *The Homosexual in America*.[36] However, this self-conception could not really take root at a time when the institutional and cultural content of the gay subculture was so relatively impoverished. By the late 1970s, however, the "ethnic" self-understanding truly seemed to correspond to the reality of the burgeoning gay male communities, which had become, at least in New York and San Francisco, wholly contained cities-within-cities (or "ghettos," as they were not infrequently called). Inhabitants of these "urban villages" need never leave them to satisfy their desires, whether those desires be sexual, recreational, cultural, or commercial. There were gay churches, gay banks, gay theaters, gay hiking clubs, gay bookstores, and gay yellow pages listing hundreds of gay-owned businesses. While lesbian communities were neither as visible nor as territorially based, they, too, provided a variety of cultural supports and institutions, fostering a sense of minority-group identity that was furthered by separatist tendencies. Little wonder, then, that lesbians and gay men began to be seen as, and to think of themselves as, almost a distinct type of being, on an ontological par with "Irish-Americans" or "Japanese-Americans."[37] Gone were the dreams of liberating society by releasing "the

homosexual in everyone." Instead, homosexuals concentrated their energies on social advancement *as homosexuals*.

It should be noted that the "ethnic" self-understanding is a much looser form of essentialism than, say, a strict genetic or hormonal theory of homosexuality. Based on an analogy that is not necessarily intended literally, this form of group identification is peculiarly vague about where the essential "core" of gayness resides. Nonetheless, the notion does tend toward a reification of the category "homosexual," implying that lesbians and gay men are in some fundamental sense different from heterosexuals. Such viewpoints can be quite dangerous: they can lend support to eugenicist arguments and are also disturbingly compatible with the contemporary understanding of AIDS as a "gay disease."

Moreover, there are a number of questions that can be raised, from a progressive standpoint, about the political manifestations of "ethnicity." It would be unfortunate to reduce the politics of gay liberation to nothing more than the self-interested actions of an interest group, in competition with other such groups for various resources; such a model would imply that gays have no interests in common with other oppressed groups, and would almost entirely abandon any notion of a broader role for the gay movement in radical politics. In addition, such a move would further separate gay men from gay women, by questioning whether even they have sufficient common interests to overcome their senses of difference. Finally, as many critics have noted, the politics of gay "ethnicity" have tended to foster the hegemonic role in community-building played by white males within the gay movement,[38] and have been articulated to an uncomfortable extent through capitalist enterprise and the commodification of sexual desire.[39]

Given the problems posed by "ethnic" essentialism, one might think that the role of gay and lesbian theorists should be to continue promoting a constructionist critique. In a certain sense, I think this is true; but it is a project that needs some rethinking. Is constructionism to be defended unproblematically? If so, the defenders must grapple with the problem that their theoretical perspective is "out of sync" with the self-understandings of many gay people. From the standpoint of the defenders of constructionism, lesbians and gay men must be seen as victims of "false consciousness," unaware of the constructedness of their identities. Moreover, we might predict that constructionists would experience considerable difficulties in leading the gay masses to a state of "true consciousness," given that constructionism poses a real and direct threat to the ethnic legitimation: people who base their claims to social rights on the basis of a group identity will not appreciate being told that that identity is just a social construct; and people who see their sexual desires as fixed – as "just the way we are" – are unlikely to adopt a viewpoint that presents "sexual scripting" as a fluid, changeable process open to intentional redefinition. Altman has recognized this dilemma:

> Few arguments have caused as much controversy among gay audiences as the assertion of a universal bisexual potential. I was once interrupted during a taping of a gay radio program in Los Angeles by a producer very concerned by this position, which he said justified Anita Bryant's claim that all homosexuals could be "cured." He was only partially mollified by my pointing out that the reverse was equally true.[40]

While it is important to challenge essentialism, particularly in its most insidious forms, we need not do so by reverting to a dogmatic constructionism. A strict constructionist position of the kind outlined above not only poses a threat to contemporary legitimations of lesbians and gay men: it is also theoretically unsound and analytically incomplete. Having situated the essentialists–constructionist debate within contemporary politics, I would now like to return to the examination of constructionism and spell out its shortcomings.

CONSTRUCTIONIST PITFALLS

For all its radical potential, constructionism has trapped itself in the basic dualisms of classic liberalism. Liberal discourse goes back and forth between two extreme views of the relation between the individual and society: either it asserts that individuals are free to create themselves, rise above their environments and take control over their lives; or it sees individuals as simply the product of their environment (or their genes, or what have you), molded like clay into various shapes.[41] Similarly, constructionism vacillates between a certain type of libertarian individualism (the left Freudian variant is the best example here)[42] in which sexual categories may be appropriated, transcended, and deconstructed at will; and just the opposite conception of the individual's sexual identity as created for him or her by the social and historical context (a strand of thinking best represented by Foucault). In either case, the "individual" is pitted against "Society"; and what is missing is any dynamic sense of how society comes to dwell within individuals or how individuality comes to be socially constituted.

Put more simply, constructionism is unable to theorize the issue of determination. This is true both on the societal level and on the level of individual lives. As Jeffrey Weeks has acknowledged, though constructionism would predict an infinite variety of sexual identities, sexual acts, and sexual scripts, practical experience indicates that only the tiniest fraction of these possibilities are realized.[43] Stephen Murray points out that if we take the constructionist assumption that gender identity, gender roles, sexual identity, sex roles, and object choice can all vary independently of each other, and if we assume that each feature might take on one of three possible values (e.g., "masculine," "feminine," and neither/both), then there are 243 potential permutations of sexual beings. Needless to say, even if we combed through the entire history of human civilization, we would not find anywhere near that many variations.[44] Each society seems to have a limited range of potential storylines for its sexual scripts – and constructionists have surprisingly little to say about how that limiting process takes place. Moreover, strict constructionism implies a lack of determination in the sexual histories of *individuals* as well: their scripts are assumed to be in a constant state of revision. While this is no doubt true to a point, it would seem to belie most people's experiences of a relatively fixed sexual identity. It may be that we're all acting out scripts – but most of us seem to be typecast.

It is precisely this perceived non-voluntary component of identity that cannot be accounted for within a strict constructionist perspective. Constructionism has no theory of the intra-psychic; it is unable to specify the ways in which desire comes to be structured over the course of people's lives. While it asserts that people are social products, it has no way of explaining how it is that social meanings come to resonate with the core of who people are.[45] Falling into the dualistic traps of liberal theory, constructionism then lends itself to further misunderstanding on the part of those who encounter the theory. A "folk constructionism" comes to be disseminated: the view that sexual identities are willful self-creations. And in reaction against this folk constructionism, which denies the experience of a non-voluntary component to identity, lesbians and gays operating within the liberal discourse slide to the opposite extreme: they assert that there is something "real" about their identity, and then try to locate that felt reality in their genes, or their earliest experiences, or their mystical nature. In this way, constructionism becomes its own worst enemy, driving its potential converts into the enemy camp.

A final point can be made about the theoretical inadequacies of constructionism as well as essentialism. If such theories are to be politically useful, then they should provide some means of evaluating concrete political strategies. In fact, the debate can at times appear quite beside the point, for there are many gay political strategies which cannot be cleanly conceptualized as either "essentialist" or "constructionist." For example, consider the situation of "political lesbians" living in separatist communities of women. Such women have consolidated an (essentialist) conception of group difference to a significant extent – but the emphasis on identity as a conscious political choice would seem to place them squarely within the constructionist camp. Alternately, we might examine the politics of the pre-Stonewall homophile movement in the United States in the 1950s and 60s. The leaders of this integrationist movement stressed in no uncertain terms that homosexuality was not a consequential difference, and that homosexuals were really just the same as straights and wanted to be treated as such. But this more-or-less constructionist viewpoint was mixed with an equally rigid essentialist insistence that homosexuals could not help being the way they were, and should therefore not be asked or forced to "change."[46]

It seems that when we scrutinize the essentialist–constructionist debate closely, it immediately unravels into two underlying dual-isms: "sameness" versus "difference," and "choice" versus "constraint." Constructionism insists that homosexuals and heterosexuals are basically the same, and not fundamentally distinct types of beings; and it emphasizes the possibilities for the self-conscious creation of sexual identities ("choice"). Essentialism, conversely, stresses the politics of difference and presumes the existence of constraint on one's sexual identity: sexual desires are not a "preference" but a fixed "orientation."

However, when we separate out the two dimensions, we find that there are four logical possibilities (Figure 11.1), rather than the two presumed by the constructionist–essentialist debate. First, there is *sameness–choice*, which is exemplified by the early 1970s gay liberationist perspective, as well as by certain civil-libertarian arguments. Gay liberationists of the early 1970s, for example, thought that all people were bisexual and hence fundamentally similar; and they stressed the role of volition in identity-formation. Next, there is *sameness–constraint*, the position of the pre-Stonewall homophile movements. Then, there is *difference–constraint*, best exemplified by the ethnic/civil rights model. Actors within such a model possess a strong sense of group difference and a notion of sexual identity as a fixed orientation. Finally, there is *difference–choice*, which would characterize "political lesbians" as well as certain expressions of cultural radicalism within the gay male community.[47] Each box, then, has its political embodiments, and each box also implies specific legitimating strategies which would need to confront specific ideological challenges (Figure 11.2). The problem, though, is that the politics of only two of the boxes (sameness–choice and difference–constraint) are explicable within the context of the constructionist–essentialist debate. That is,

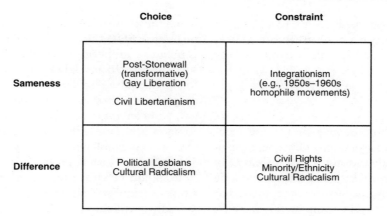

	Choice	**Constraint**
Sameness	Post-Stonewall (transformative) Gay Liberation Civil Libertarianism	Integrationism (e.g., 1950s–1960s homophile movements)
Difference	Political Lesbians Cultural Radicalism	Civil Rights Minority/Ethnicity Cultural Radicalism

Figure 11.1 Political embodiments of a deconstructed debate

sameness–choice can be seen as pure constructionist, while difference–constraint is pure essentialist. The other two boxes would seem to indiscriminately criss-cross the bounds of the argument – and yet they are no less logically defensible or worthy of theoretical attention. It follows that, to explore systematically the essentialist–constructionist debate, we really need to delve more deeply into these two oppositions – choice versus constraint, and sameness versus difference – and see if they are really so opposing.

In order to build up a stronger constructionist position, my strategy will be as follows. First, I will examine more closely the idea of a gay "ethnic identity," exploring, from the standpoint of theories of identity and of ethnicity, the

historical conjuncture in which this idea appeared. I will argue that the debates on identity and ethnicity have been bogged down by certain polar oppositions that parallel the essentialism–constructionism divide. By staking out an alternative position in these debates, I will further argue that it is reasonable, with certain qualifications, to accept the "ethnic" model – both as a relatively accurate characterization of contemporary gay identity formation, and as a politically defensible starting point from which the gay movement can evolve in a progressive direction. In the course of this analysis, I will return to the oppositions that undergird the essentialism–constructionism debate – choice versus constraint, and sameness versus difference – and once again seek some

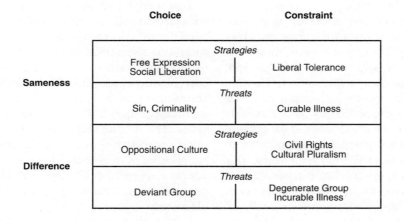

	Choice	**Constraint**
Sameness	*Strategies*	
	Free Expression Social Liberation	Liberal Tolerance
	Threats	
	Sin, Criminality	Curable Illness
Difference	*Strategies*	
	Oppositional Culture	Civil Rights Cultural Pluralism
	Threats	
	Deviant Group	Degenerate Group Incurable Illness

Figure 11.2 Corresponding legitimation strategies and delegitimating threats

way of transcending the dualisms, in a way that helps sexual theory to resonate more closely with the politics of gay "ethnic" identity.

IDENTITY

The concept of "homosexual identity," as mentioned earlier, is a surprisingly new one; though the term is now ubiquitous, it first appeared in the relevant literature little more than a decade ago.[48] Perhaps it is not so surprising, then, that the term has been used in a consistently haphazard fashion. In her survey of the literature on homosexual identity, Vivienne Cass has found that

> in these articles it is possible to infer diverse meanings such as (1) defining oneself as gay, (2) a sense of self as gay, (3) image of self as homosexual, (4) the way a homosexual person *is*, and (5) consistent behavior in relation to homosexual-related activity.[49]

General definitions of identity are equally problematic. In an interesting "semantic history" of the term, Philip Gleason notes that it, too, is a new concept, having entered the general social-science literature only in the 1950s. Popularized initially by psychoanalyst Erik Eriskon, "identity" then wound its way through various sociological "feeder streams," including role theory, reference-group theory, and symbolic interactionism. By the mid-1960s, the term "was used so widely and so loosely that to determine its provenance in every context would be impossible."[50]

Nevertheless, Gleason observes that most definitions tend to fall toward one or the other pole of an opposition between two conceptions of identity, one a psychological reductionism, the other a sociological reductionism. The first conception of identity – which might be called "intrapsychic" – treats identity as a relatively fixed and stable characteristic of a person, which, from a developmental standpoint, more or less unwinds from within. In a word, this sense of identity is essentialist: it is the type of "identity" that we mean when we speak of identity as describing who someone *really is*. Quite distinct is the sense of "identity" which I will call "acquired" (although the term "constructionist" would not be inappropriate). In this sense, identity is the internalization or conscious adoption of socially imposed or socially constructed labels or roles. According to the "acquired" definition, identity is not so deeply entrenched in the psyche of the individual, and can vary considerably over the course of one's life. This is the type of "identity" that we have in mind when we say that someone "identifies as" a such-and-such.[51]

It should be clear that not all psychologists adopt a simplistic intrapsychic definition, nor do all sociologists see identity as purely acquired. Erikson, for example, was quite specific on the point that identity emerged through an interactive developmental process between self and others.[52] Conversely, the symbolic interactionsts Berger and Luckmann argue that "identity is a phenomenon that emerges from the dialectic between individual and society."[53] Nonetheless, these two polar senses have each become prevalent, and it is not uncommon to encounter fairly pure expression of either type.[54]

Mediating between the poles of intrapsychic and acquired identity is Habermas's useful discussion of identity:

> [Ego] identity is produced through *socialization*, that is, through the fact that the growing child first of all integrates itself into a specific social system by appropriating symbolic generalities; it is later secured and developed through *individuation*, that is, precisely through a growing independence in relation to social systems.[55]

Ego identity, then, is a *socialized sense of individuality*, an internal organization of self-perceptions concerning one's relationship to social categories, that also incorporates views of the self perceived to be held by others. At its core, identity is constituted relationally, through involvement with – and incorporation of – significant others and integration into communities. The relationship of ego identity to subsidiary identities (such as occupational, class, racial, gender, or sexual identities) is an interactive one, in which all subsidiary identities are integrated into a relatively coherent and unique life history.[56]

Where then do these subsidiary identities come from, and in what circumstances can they be appropriated and incorporated? As Berger and Luckmann maintain, it is important to recognize that such identities are, at the same time, both human self-creations and constraining structures. To paraphrase Marx, people make their own identities, but they do not make them just as they please. Identities are phenomena that permit people to become acting "subjects" who define who they are in the world, but at the same time identities "subject" those people to the controlling power of external categorization.[57]

In this regard, it is vital to note that identity has increasingly come to be seen as something quite important. In modern, fluid, "mass" society, the relationship of the individual to the social whole is rendered problematic; as part of a continual "quest for identity," we go through "identity crises"; we seek to "find ourselves." It is not surprising that group identities – occupational, racial, ethnic, sexual – become increasingly attractive, since they provide an intermediate link between the individual and the mass.[58] As we accept more and more identities, it does indeed begin to seem that they are all somewhat arbitrary, tried on like hats and discarded for next year's style. And yet the fundamental irony of this apparent freedom to define ourselves is that in a world where identity has been transformed into a problem – where identity "crises" must be resolved, and where we all search for our identities – external cues and definitions become increasingly authoritative. The more we feel impelled to discover our "true" identity, the more we are likely to grasp at the reassurance provided by the adoption of available identity types.

The pressure to define oneself *sexually* is particularly keenly felt. This is true in part because labels such as "homosexual" are powerfully charged, carrying with them the risk of strong social disapproval. But beyond that, a Foucaultian argument can be made about the increasing importance of sex, in general, to the constitution of identity. As Dennis Altman notes,

sex remains one of the few areas of life where we feel able to be more than passive spectators. It is a feature of modern society that we increasingly define achievement in terms of immediate gratifi-

cation, and the move to burden sexuality with greater expectations is closely related to the stress on ideas of "self-fulfillment" and "personal actualization."[59]

In a similar vein, Jeffrey Weeks observes:

As divorce rates rise, fertility declines, and the distinction between married and unmarried tends to blur, "the couple" rather than marriage emerges as the one seeming constant of western life. But sex becomes even more central to its success ... Sex has become the cement that binds people together.[60]

Gay, lesbian, and bisexual identities must be understood as arising out of this historical conjuncture.[61] Their emergence reflects a world in which group identity has assumed paramount importance, and where sexuality has become a central dimension of identity formation in general. In addition, as already suggested, these identities constitute "reverse affirmations" of social labels, adoptive contestations of imposed stigma categories. As labeling theory indicates, deviant identities are particularly likely to assume totalizing dimensions: *all* behavior of persons so categorized becomes interpreted by others through the prism of the perceived difference: "One will be identified as a deviant first, before other identifications are made."[62] And as Erving Goffman points out, the need for the stigmatized to "manage" their stigma in social situations – to tell or not to tell, to confront or to excuse – causes the stigma-identity to assume substantial proportions within the overall ego identity – to become, in some cases, an all-consuming preoccupation.[63] Attempts to assert the legitimacy of one's position and claim that one's stigma is not grounds for social exclusion tend to have the ironic effect, also noted by Goffman, of furthering the process by which the particular identity consumes the overall ego.[64]

Finally, the emergence of various types of sexual identity as important components of ego identity presumes the existence of individuals who are in some loose sense qualified to fill the categories – people who are capable of interpreting their erotic and emotional desires and actions as corresponding to their understanding of the meaning of these social terms.[65] This is the point at which both labeling theory and symbolic interactionism falter, for they have nothing to say about how such people come to exist. The rigid temporal sequence laid down by labeling theory is particularly inadequate. In that model, the individual commits an act of "primary" deviance (in this case, a homosexual act), is in consequence met with a stigmatizing label ("You're a queer"), and by internalizing this label becomes fixed in a "secondary" deviant identity ("I'm a homosexual").[66] But in the real world, the developmental sequences vary tremendously. Interview data suggest, in fact, the relationship among the processes of engaging in homosexual identity, being labeled a homosexual, and having suspicions that one is a homosexual can come in various orders; typical patterns seem to include "engaged, suspicious, labeled," "engaged, labeled," "suspicious, engaged, labeled," "suspicious, labeled, engaged." As Plummer has pointed out in his review of several studies, some gay men and lesbians report a fixity and clarity of sexual preferences dating to early childhood; others experience several shifts in sexual identity and the structure of desire over the course of their lives.[67] Research into the lives of homosexuals increasingly suggests that there is no "homosexuality," but rather "homosexualities."[68]

A theory of sexual identity formation, therefore, must be able to identify a wide range of potential developmental strategies by which individuals, in relation with significant others, compare (or fail to compare) their experiences and feelings against their comprehension (or lack of comprehension) of existing sexual and gender typologies.[69] As a result of these processes, individuals arrive (or fail to arrive) at consistent or variable interpretations of their sexual identity.[70] This is a complex and never-ending activity, involving both conscious and unconscious dimensions. Consciously, people perform what Barbara Ponse has called "identity work": they actively seek to organize into a coherent whole their thoughts, motivations, and experiences with others – to create a consistent biography which legitimates their places in the world.[71] Critical phases, such as the "coming out" process, may represent cognitive strategies for handling breaks and discontinuities in these biographies. To the extent that such processes remain unconscious, people are often subject to

constraints that they but dimly perceive; their needs, desires, actions, cognitions and self-concepts may all be out of sync with one another, and a consistent biography may not be achieved.

This discussion sheds new light on the polarity between "choice" and "constraint," which was observed to be one dimension underlying the essentialist–constructionist debate. If the question is, "Are sexual identities the outcome of choice or constraint?", then the whole thrust of the preceding argument is to suggest that the only possible answer is "neither and both." Choice and constraint constitute a false opposition; and the way to transcend this dualism, I think, is with some form of psychoanalytic theory. Such a perspective can account for the ways that sexual and emotional desires can be structured, developmentally, into relatively well-defined directions. In particular, the "object relations" school of psychoanalysis, with its focus on relational experience, and with its theory of the ego as possessing a "relational core," might be usefully applied to an analysis of sexual identity.[72] Object relations theory describes, in a vivid way, how from a child's earliest moments onward a sense of self is constituted through "introjections" of significant others. The child's needs and desires, which can only be satisfied externally, come to be mediated and shaped through these encounters; while aspects of these desires may remain highly fluid and subject to what constructionists want to call scripting, other dimensions may be sharply structured and come to comprise fundamental parts of the ego core.[73] Without displacing the symbolic interactionist focus on conscious, adult experience, psychoanalysis also permits us to conceptualize the unconscious and to appreciate the formative element of early childhood experiences. From such a perspective, identity becomes more than just a serial enactment of roles; it takes on a socially constituted reality.

In light of this discussion, the organization of the gay community around the "politics of identity" would seem to have strong social roots. Once we abandon both the strict essentialist notion of identity as forever fixed within the psyche, as well as the strict constructionist conception of identity as an arbitrary acquisition, we can recognize that a gay or lesbian identity might have a clear resonance for individuals without necessarily binding them to any specific definition of what that identity "means." An intermediate position between the poles of intrapsychic and acquired identity allows us to recognize that these sexual identities are *both inescapable and transformable*, and are capable of giving rise to a variety of political expressions. The question that must now be asked is why the contemporary gay identity in the United States has particularly assumed an "ethnic" dimension, and what this implies for gay politics.

ETHNICITY

How can we speak seriously of gays and lesbians as an "ethnic" group – or even a minority group? After all, there would seem to be some rather fundamental differences between gays and the other groups that we normally associate with these terms. In the first place, ethnic or racial identifications are normally conferred at birth and transmitted through the family. In place of this "primary socialization" into a racial or ethnic identity, the entrance into a gay community constitutes a "secondary socialization," occurring later in life.

A process of secondary socialization is typically seen as less formative than primary socialization, because "it must deal with an already formed self and an already internalized world. It cannot construct subjective reality *ex nihilo*."[74] In particular, it is unclear what sort of coherent cultural content can be transmitted through a secondary socialization into a gay community, and whether this cultural distinctiveness corresponds with the kinds of cultural differences that we normally consider to be ethnic. Ethnic culture is presumed to be handed down through the generations; gay "culture" lacks both the historical roots and the standard transmission devices. This problem is compounded by the fact that individuals being socialized into a gay community will already possess a variety of cross-cutting identities – ethnic, racial, class, gender, religious, occupational and so on –

which may claim much greater allegiance and inhibit the secondary socialization process.[75]

The treatment of these objections rest ultimately on the particular definition of "ethnicity" that is adopted. And once again, an investigation into the existing definitional possibilities reveals a debate between two polar opposite conceptions. Lining up on one side are the "primordialists," who treat ethnicity as an inescapable given, an absolute ascription. And in opposition to this traditional view has arisen the "optionalist" (a.k.a. "circumstantialist") critique, which in its most vulgar manifestations argues that "ethnicity may be shed, resurrected, or adopted as the situation warrants."[76] It should be clear that a "primordialist" conception of ethnicity implies an "intrapsychic" notion of ethnic identity; while conversely, an understanding of ethnicity in the "optionalist" sense is quite compatible with a definition of ethnic identity as "acquired."[77]

Once again, we need to transcend a false dualism: on the one hand, it seems ridiculous to claim that we can shed or adopt ethnicities as we please. Clearly, there are major constraints on this process. But on the other hand, it is quite true that racial and ethnic categories are historical products that are subject to extensive redefinition over time. Omi and Winant give an interesting example of the definitional crisis surrounding the influx of Mexicans and Chinese into the United States in the mid-nineteenth century. Confused over what sort of racial/legal status to accord these groups, courts eventually ruled that Mexicans were "white" but that Chinese were "Indian."[78] Even in the lives of individuals, racial designations can change. In South Africa, where race, of course, is of paramount importance, there is a special government agency responsible for adjudicating claims about one's racial classification; and each year many people officially "upgrade" their racial identity.[79]

Donald Horowitz strikes a good intermediate note between primordialism and optionalism:

> Ascription is, of course, the key characteristic that distinguishes ethnicity from voluntary affiliation. *Ethnic identity is generally acquired at birth. But this is a matter of degree.* In the first place, in greater or lesser measure, there are possibilities for

changing individual identity. Linguistic or religious conversion will suffice in some cases, but in others the changes may require a generation or more to accomplish by means of intermarriage and procreation. In the second place, collective action, in the sense of conscious modification of group behavior and identification, may effect shifts of boundaries ... It is, therefore, a putative ascription, rather than an absolute one, that we are dealing with ... Ethnicity thus differs from voluntary affiliation, not because the two are dichotomous, but because they occupy *different positions on a continuum*.[80]

This definition brings us a step closer to feeling comfortable with the idea that the ethnic analogy is a reasonable one for gays and lesbians. If ethnicity does not necessarily begin at birth, and if ethnicity involves some combination of external ascription and chosen affiliation, then a gay identity as described above seems not wholly unlike an ethnic identity. But we can better understand the adoption of the ethnic model by gays and lesbians if we spell out the particular ways in which ethnicity has come to be understood in the contemporary United States.

In the 1970s, social scientists announced that the United States was in the throes of an "ethnic revival" – a "resurgence" of ethnicity.[81] Though heavily influenced by the cultural and political assertiveness of racial minorities in the late 1960s, the revival was essentially a phenomenon of white European ethnic groups, manifesting a rediscovered pride in their heritage.[82] It was quickly observed that, despite the implications of a turn toward the past, there was something quite new about this form of ethnicity. As Frank Parkin notes,

the nature of collective action mounted by ethnic groups has undergone a significant change in recent times. Originally dedicated to fighting rearguard actions of cultural preservation, they have now adopted more combative forms of activity expressly designed to alter the distribution of rewards in their members' favour.[83]

The "new ethnicity" differs from traditional ethnicity in a variety of respects. First, as Daniel Bell points out, the new ethnicity combines an affective tie with the pursuit of explicitly sociopolitical goals in "interest group" form: ethnic groups become "instrumental" and not just "expressive."[84] Second, the new ethnicity

places ethnic-group activity firmly on the terrain of the state.[85] Third, and as a corollary to the preceding arguments, the new ethnicity is "forward-looking," seeking to expand the group's social position, while the old ethnicity was "backward-looking," aimed at "preserv[ing] the past against the encroachments of centralization and 'modernization.'"[86] Fourth, as a reaction against "mass society," the new ethnicity is not so much a new form of aggregation as a "disaggregation" or "de-assimilation" from the mass.[87] Fifth, lacking the type of structural power possessed by subordinate social classes (i.e., the ability to disrupt production), the new ethnic groups are increasingly inclined to press their demands by appealing to, and manipulating, hegemonic ideologies (such as "equal rights").[88] And finally, neo-ethnic politics frequently take on a localist character, organized around specific geographic space or community, leading to a distinctively ethnic involvement in urban political affairs.[89] While to some extent a general feature of contemporary Western politics, the "new ethnicity" manifested itself most prominently in the United States, where the political possibilities for organizing around ethnicity were the greatest (and, conversely, class-based organizing had proven relatively ineffective).[90]

Of course, it would be a mistake to exaggerate the changes that have occurred and ignore either the continuities between the "old" and the "new" ethnicity, or the extent to which both varieties have always been present. Nonetheless, it seems that a somewhat new understanding of what ethnicity is all about emerged in the United States in the 1970s -- that is to say, at the very same time that gay and lesbian identity was taking on an ethnic cast.[91] And indeed, on the basis of the preceding discussion, this notion of gay ethnic identity seems increasingly comprehensible and plausible. Like the archetypal "new ethnicity," gay ethnicity is a "future-oriented" identity linking an affective bond with an instrumental goal of influencing state policy and securing social rewards on behalf of the group. Like the other ethnic groups, gay ethnicity functions typically through appeals to the professed beliefs of the dominant culture, emphasizing traditional American values such as equality, fairness, and freedom from persecution. And finally, in neo-ethnic fashion, gay identity (in this case, gay *male* identity in particular) operates by using the control of a specific geographic space to influence urban political decision-making.[92]

The final question that must be addressed, to understand and assess the gay community's adoption of an ethnic self-understanding, has to do with the issue of culture and tradition. No matter how much ethnicity may now be articulated in the sociopolitical realm, most conceptions of ethnicity would certainly still include some sense of a unique ethnic culture heritage; indeed, one manifestation of the new ethnicity that was frequently alluded to in the 1970s was the resurgence of pride in one's ethnic cuisine, ethnic costume, and so on. And no matter how much ethnic groups may now be "forward-looking," many of the legitimations for group allegiance are focused on the past and argue for the preservation of traditional forms. Can the lesbian and gay communities claim to be ethnic, given these considerations?

The answer is that the analogy holds. On the one hand, gay communities have developed a variety of cultural forms which, despite the considerable internal variation, serve to unify those communities.[93] And on the other hand, the cultural potency of at least the European ethnic groups would seem to be much less than it's often cracked up to be. In an interesting twist on the "new ethnicity" argument, Stephen Steinberg has characterized the recent "ethnic fever" as sort of a Freudian reaction-formation: an assertion that ethnicity is still culturally and psychologically meaningful, voiced with such rigid insistence as to imply that even the proponents themselves are not convinced. He quotes Irving Howe to this effect:

> These ethnic groups now turn back – and as they nervously insist, "with pride" – to look for fragments of a racial or national or religious identity that moves them to the extent that it is no longer available. Perhaps, also, *because* it is no longer available.[94]

Because ethnicity no longer provides the institutional supports capable of integrating individuals into the community and providing them with a sense of belonging, individuals futilely attempt to re-create that sense of belonging by grasping at a *psychological* affiliation. In the process, they fail to observe that the ground has fallen away beneath their feet:

> Indeed, it is precisely because the real and objective basis for ethnic culture is rapidly disappearing that identity has been elevated to a "symbolic" plane and a premium is placed on the subjective dimensions of ethnicity. People desperately wish to "feel" ethnic precisely because they have all but lost the prerequisites for "being" ethnic.[95]

Steinberg's analysis would lead one to characterize the gay community's adoption of an ethnic identity as profoundly ironic. It would seem to be precisely the fact that ethnic culture has been *evacuated of content* that has permitted the transposition of the category of "ethnicity" onto a group that, in the traditional sense of the term, clearly would not qualify for the designation. Thus it is true that lesbians and gay men don't really fit the original definition of what an ethnic group is: but then, neither really, do contemporary Jews, or Italian-Americans, or anyone else. In this way, the decline of the old ethnicity permits and encourages new groups to adopt the mantle and revive the phenomenon. Indeed, to the extent that the gay community has succeeded in creating new institutional supports that link individuals into the community and provide their lives with a sense of meaning, gays may now be more "ethnic" than the original ethnic groups.[96] And in any event, as the term progressively loses its original significations and acquires a more future-oriented, sociopolitical connotation, there is a diminishing tendency to assume that an ethnic group needs to provide those original functions anyway.

Now that we have explored the historical conjuncture in which the idea of a "gay ethnicity" made its appearance, we can see that the term is more than a simple catch-phrase, as it appears in Altman's analysis. Rather, it is at the very least a compelling analogy, and perhaps even the most accurate designation we can come up with.[97]

This discussion of the particular sense in which "gay identity" has come to resemble an "ethnic" identity also sheds light on the "sameness–difference" dichotomy that underlies the essentialism–constructionism debate. Just as "choice" and "constraint" proved to be a false polarity with regard to gay *identity*, so are "sameness" and "difference" an unhelpful analytical distinction with regard to gay *ethnicity*: it makes little sense to quarrel over whether homosexuals and heterosexuals are fundamentally the same or fundamentally different. First, we need to rethink what we mean by the terms, and escape a sense of "sameness" as meaning a coercive uniformity, or "difference" as the clash of opposites. As Chodorow argues in the analogous case of gender difference, a rigid assertion of differentness reflects a defensive need to separate: it stems from anxieties about one's sense of self that are manifested in a refusal to recognize the other as also a "self" – as an active subject. It is possible to be differentiated, she argues, "without turning the cognitive fact into an emotional, moral, or political one."[98]

In this regard, it may be useful to talk about the relationship between gay "ethnic" communities and the larger society in terms of varying combinations of "sameness-in-difference," or "difference-in-sameness." This is true in several senses. First, the adoption of a neo-ethnic form of social closure combined with a civil-rights political strategy implies that gays are asserting their difference partly as a way of gaining entry into the system. By consolidating as a group, they are essentially following the rules of the modern American pluralist myth, which portrays a harmonious competition among distinct social groups. Neither "sameness" nor "difference" would seem to capture the peculiar ambiguity of this political expression.

Second, as many commentators have noted, the more coherent an ethnic group in the United States becomes, the greater its cultural influence upon the larger society. That is, at the time when Jews, or blacks, have been most "separatist," the diffusion of those cultures has also been the greatest. In the areas of sexual practices and urban lifestyles, lesbians and gays have indeed had an influence on the general culture in opening up possibilities for new forms of sexual and aesthetic expressions.[99]

This leads to another point, which is that the "lifestyles" of homosexuals and heterosexuals (at least among the white middle class) would seem in some ways to be moving closer together, even as the identity categories congeal. Once again, neither "sameness" nor "difference" seems to adequately characterize the phenomenon. As D'Emilio indicates, the conventional nuclear family is less and less the norm; the variety of living arrangements has multiplied; and sexuality has been increasingly divorced from a procreative intent: "As the life cycle of heterosexuals exhibits greater variety and less predictability, they have come to face many of the choices and experiences that gay men and women confront."[100] And conversely, D'Emilio argues that homosexuals are moving closer to heterosexuals:

> The gay liberation movement allowed many lesbians and homosexuals to break out of the ideological prison that confined them to a sexual self-definition. It also began the transformation of a sexual subculture into an urban community. The group life of gay men and women came to encompass not only erotic interaction but also political, religious, and cultural activity. Homosexuality and lesbianism have become less of a sexual category and more of a human identity.[101]

D'Emilio would seem to be exaggerating somewhat the convergence that has taken place; moreover, his endorsement of a "desexualized" lesbian and gay identity is certainly controversial.[102] Nonetheless, to the extent that there is some truth in the argument, it would seem that gays are becoming "the same" as straights to the extent that they are "different."

A final point in this regard relates to the potency of sexual classification itself. Jeffrey Weeks points out that the consolidation of typologies of sexual "persons" can have the paradoxical effect of challenging the whole system of categorization. Initially, labels such as "homosexual" were applied by doctors and sex researchers to describe deviations from a presumed norm. But once the people so labeled, in a "reverse" affirmation, began to assert the legitimacy of their sexual identity – and once that legitimacy began to be more widely recognized – then the whole classificatory scheme began to lose its cultural force:

> For the elaborate taxonomies and distinctions

existed in the end only to explain the variations in relationship to an assumed norm. Once the norm itself was challenged, then the category of the perverse became redundant, and with them the whole elaborate edifice of "sexuality" – the belief that the erotic is a unified domain, governed by its own laws, organized around a norm and its variations – began to crumble.[103]

Weeks's argument is misleading because it presumed that categorization can be abolished – that the elimination of one set of norms somehow precludes the installation of others. In fact, as Weeks himself has noted elsewhere, not only is categorization a never ending process, but gays and lesbians have increasingly become the new categorizers, subdividing and stratifying their communities into a variety of new types.[104] But clearly Weeks has a point. By consolidating their sense of difference *and* asserting their legitimacy, lesbians and gays may be helping to usher in a world where they no longer seem to be different. But neither an essentialist claim of basic difference, nor a constructionist insistence on fundamental similitude, alone seems adequate to capture this ambiguous process.

CONCLUSION

In making sense of the notion of "gay 'ethnic' identity," I have deliberately steered clear of both the strict essentialist and the strict constructionist understandings of ethnicity as well as identity. The constitution of a gay identity is not something that simply unwinds from within, nor is it just an amalgam of roles that proceed according to scripts; only an intermediate, and dialectical, definition makes sense in this case. Similarly, if "ethnicity" is to serve even as an analogy for comprehending gay and lesbian group identity, then ethnicity must be understood as something that is neither an absolutely inescapable ascription nor something chosen and discarded at will; as something neither there from birth, nor something one joins like a club; as something that makes one neither fundamentally different from others, nor fundamentally the same. It is in the dialectics between choice and constraint, and

between the individual, the group, and the larger society, that "identities," "ethnic identities," and "gay and lesbian identities" emerge.

Neither strict constructionism nor strict essentialism are capable of explaining what it means to be gay. The fact that contemporary gay self-understandings and political expressions are inexplicable within the bounds of these theoretical perspectives therefore should come as no surprise. No sexual theory can inform sexual practice without transcending the limitations imposed by aligning oneself on either fringe of a bootless philosophical argument between "nature" and "society." This whole discussion so far has really been a series of variations on that theme, since all the oppositions that have been described can be located at one or the other pole of what is basically the same debate:

essentialist	constructionist
realist	nominalist
constraint	choice
difference	sameness
intrapsychic	acquired
primordialist	optionalist
nature	society
internal	external
real	fictive

The fact that, in seeking to transcend these oppositions, I have ended up quoting the arguments of many constructionists, is not incidental. Constructionists have become increasingly aware of the complexities of these debates, and have continued to provide the most insightful analyses of the changing character of the gay community and gay identity. But what constructionists have failed to acknowledge are the way in which their own observations are increasingly at odds with the basic premises of the theoretical perspective. Plummer, in an interesting article aimed at a "synthetic" position, has gone so far as to embrace the possibility of the existence of fixed sexual "orientations" – while carefully skirting the question of how such a concept accords with his general theoretical stance.[105] Altman, one of the most subtle chroniclers of the gay ethnic experience, can never seem to quite escape his own suspicion that ethnicity rests on an illusion that is also a trap. Weeks, who is perhaps the most sensitive to the theoretical limitations of strict contructionism, and who provides the most insightful discussions of both the limitations and the possibilities inherent in gay identities, is also capable of lapsing into the most utopian constructionist arguments about the abolition of sexual categories. The hold of strict constructionism remains tenacious; and its expositors seem unwilling to clarify their relationship to the doctrine.[106]

Clarification would require a number of modifications to strict constructionism, yet would in no way amount to an endorsement of essentialism. First, there is a need to understand the issue of determination: out of the range of potential forms of sexual expression, how are limitations created on that expression, both socially and within the individual psyche? On the individual level, this implies the systematic introduction of psychoanalytic conceptions of needs and desire and of the development of the self in relation to others. On the social level, it implies a more comprehensive understanding of power, and of the dialectical relationship between identities as self-expressions and identities as ascriptive impositions. Anthropological analyses of "sex/gender systems" in kinship-based societies have something to offer here. As Harriet Whitehead has pointed out, "To say that gender definitions and concepts pertaining to sex and gender are culturally variable is not necessarily to say that they can vary infinitely or along any old axis." Analyses such as hers have attempted to connect cultural meanings about gender and sexuality with specific social–structural relations, so as to show how culture can structure the possibilities for personhood in distinctive ways.[107]

An example of how such an analysis might proceed for Western societies is offered by Michael Omi and Howard Winant's analysis of a different domain, "racial formation":

> Racial formation ... should be understood as a *process*: (1) through which an unstable and contradictory set of social practices and beliefs are articulated in an ideology based fundamentally on race; (2) through which the particular ideology thus generated is enforced by a system of racial subjection having both institutional and individ-

ual means of reproduction at its disposal; and (3) through which new instabilities and contradictions emerge at a subsequent historical point and challenge the pre-existing system once more.[108]

Substitute "sexuality" for "race" in the above quote, and its relevance to the present discussion would be apparent. It is "subjection" to be understood in the dual sense discussed earlier: both the creation of political *subjects*, and their simultaneous *subjection* to structural and ideological controls. For as Omi and Winant point out in their evaluation of the black movement:

> Probably the greatest triumph of the movement was not its legislative accomplishments or even the extent of this mass mobilization. The social movement for racial equality had its greatest success in its ability to create new racial "subjects," in its ability to *redefine the meaning of racial identity*, and consequently, of race *itself*, in American society.[109]

Similarly, the creation of a positive identity, and the simultaneous redefinition of legitimate sexual and affectional possibilities, is the overriding accomplishment of the lesbian and gay movements to date.

Beyond the issue of determination, a second requirement for the reinvigoration of constructionism is a better understanding of the "collectivization of subjectivity." We must be able to speak of sexually based group identities without assuming *either* that the group has some mystical or biological unity *or* that the "group" doesn't exist and that its "members" are indulging in a dangerous mystification. "Ethnicity" is a metaphor; but the relationships that it entails can come to be internalized as a fundamental part of the self. To the extent that this is consciously recognized – to the extent that "ethnicity" can be seen as both strategy and reality – then the dangers of it being misunderstood in a rigidly essentialist sense becomes greatly reduced. Furthermore, this sense of what it means to be part of a distinctive community can rescue us from investing "difference" with moral implications. Rather than reifying difference into a defensive separatism or dissolving it into a false vision of homogeneity, we need to acquire an appreciation for difference as harmless, perhaps synergistic.[110]

A modified constructionist perspective of this sort would address the deficiencies of constructionism that were noted earlier in this paper. Not only would it permit a fuller description of the complex experiences of being homosexual, but it might also permit lesbians and gay men to feel that constructionism described the world and themselves as they experience it, rather than inducing them to flee from constructionism and into the arms of essentialism.

A modified constructionism could also allow theory to play a more helpful role in the analysis of the contemporary political expressions of gays and lesbians. In fact, the preceding analysis of the complexities and ironies of gay identity and ethnicity raises several important political dilemmas. The first of these has to do with the political manifestations of ethnicity. As I indicated, the gay movement's (and in this case, particularly the gay male movement's) subscription to the tenets of pluralism – its attempt to simply get its "piece of the pie" by appealing to hegemonic ideologies – raises questions about its potential (or desire) to mount a serious challenge to the structural roots of inequality – whether that be sexual inequality or any other kind. However, we might be better off avoiding facile distinctions between "reformist" and "revolutionary" strategies. As Omi and Winant note, civil-rights movements have an inherently radical dimension: "By asserting that society denied minorities their rights as *groups*, they challenged the overall legitimacy of a hegemonic social order whose political logic and cultural coherence was based fundamentally in ideologies of competitive individualism."[111]

Moreover, rights movements that are organized around the politics of identity tend, by their nature, to imbue political actors with the capacity to make radical demands that they may not even intend. When the leader of the New York Gay Men's Chorus proclaims: "We show the straight community that we're just as normal as they are,"[112] this would seem on the face of it to be a rather conservative proposition, reminiscent of the accommodationist politics of the 1950s homophile movements. And yet in fact the comparison is inappropriate. When the members of homophile organizations stressed their "normality," they meant: We're the same

as you, so please stop excluding us. But the sense of the above quote is quite different; it is saying: We're different from you, and that doesn't make us any less human. In this sense, it would seem that the modern adherents of identity politics are engaged, willy-nilly, in a process of changing the very bounds of the normal.

Gay "ethnic" politics, therefore, certainly have capacities for moving in a more radical direction. Part of what would be required, however, is a recognition that the freedom from discrimination of homosexual *persons* is an insufficient goal, if homosexuality as a *practice* retains its inferior status. The disjuncture that Altman has noted between "homosexuality" and "the homosexual" – whereby the former remains stigmatized while the latter increasingly is awarded civil rights and civil liberties – presents an opportunity, in the short run, and a hurdle to be leaped, in the long run. Overcoming this obstacle would entail the adoption of political methods beyond those appropriate for electoral and established institutional politics.

But part of what may determine the political direction in which gays move is the particular model of minority-group organizing and political consciousness that is employed. Despite the adoption of a goal of civil rights, gay collective identity is at present close in form to that of the white ethnic groups than to those of racial minorities. Movement away from a political consciousness based on white "ethnicity" and toward a "sexual minority" self-understanding might increase the gay movement's capacity to pose a more fundamental challenge to the sociosexual order.

This, however, raises other dilemmas, regarding both the internal composition of the gay movement and its leadership, and the relationship of the gay movement to other social movements. The adoption of a "white ethnic" model, in other words, is not unexpected in a movement dominated by white, middle-class males. An adequate discussion of these issues is beyond the scope of this essay; however, it seems clear enough that the gay movement will never be able to forge effective alliances with other social movements unless it can address the inequalities that plague its internal organization. In this light it is worth noting a peculiar paradox of identity politics: while affirming a distinctive group identity that legitimately differs from the larger society, this form of political expression simultaneously imposes a "totalizing" sameness *within* the group: it says, this is who we "really are."[113] A greater appreciation for internal diversity – on racial, gender, class, and even sexual dimensions – is a prerequisite if the gay movement is to move beyond "ethnic" insularity and join with other progressive causes.[114] The obvious first step in that direction would be improved understandings between lesbians and gay men – and a better articulation of feminist theory with theoretical perspectives on sexuality.

Finally, in considering the political dilemmas confronting lesbians and gays, it is vital to discuss the most serious crisis that the movement has yet faced, namely, AIDS. The "moral panic" surrounding AIDS demonstrates some of the inherent fragility of identity politics. By hardening a notion of group difference, identity politics present a highly visible target. Those social groups who see their understandings of the world as called into question by changing conceptions of sexuality, gender, and morality more broadly defined, have found in the consolidated notion of "gayness" a potent and available symbol upon which they can easily discharge their anxieties – and vent their wrath. And if there is perceived to be such a thing as a "homosexual person," then it is only a small step to the conclusion that there is such a thing as a "homosexual disease," itself the peculiar consequence of the "homosexual lifestyle."[115]

Thus the ideological and practical consequences of a complete solidification of identity into a reified notion of " the gay person" would seem to be quite grave. But to reiterate, this is not an argument for the maintenance of a strict-constructionist pose; for both the "politics of constructionism" and the "politics of essentialism" present legitimating possibilities as well as dangers of delegitimation. The task of melding theory with practice will involve creatively capitalizing on the most effective legitimations of the moment, while still remaining true both to theoretical insights and to the contemporary self-understandings of the women and men who populate the movement.

NOTES

1 The four quotes are, in order, (1) an unnamed lesbian, interviewed by Barbara Ponse in *Identities in the Lesbian World: The Social Construction of Self* (Westport, Conn.: Greenwood Press, 1978): 178; (2) a different lesbian interview subject, quoted Ponse: 189; (3) Donald Webster Cory, pseud., *The Homosexual in America* (New York: Castle Books, 1951): 9; (4) James Baldwin, interviewed by Richard Goldstein, "Go the Way Your Blood Beats: An Interview with James Baldwin," *Village Voice*, (June 26, 1984): 14.

2 Vivienne C. Cass, "Homosexual Identity: A Concept in Need of a Definition," *Journal of Homosexuality* 9 (winter 1983/spring 1984): 105.

3 This analysis does not systematically explore the self-understandings or politics of people who identify as bisexuals, though the category "bisexual" itself is important to the discussion. For an analysis of bisexuality that touches on many of the issues explored here, see Lisa Orlando, "Bisexuality: Loving Whom We Chose," *Gay Community News* (February 25, 1984): 6. At times, I will discuss gay men separately from lesbians; at other points, the analysis will refer to both at the same time. While this may be confusing from an analytic standpoint, it seems unavoidable if one wants to avoid simplistic assumptions of parallelism between experiences of gay men and women.

4 *Oakland Tribune* (March 6, 1987): F-7.

5 See Nancy Chodorow, "Feminism and Difference: Gender, Relation, and Difference in Psychoanalytic Perspective," *Socialist Review* 46 (July–August 1979): 51–69. For an analogous discussion in the domain of race, see Michael Omi and Howard Winant, *Racial Formation in the United States: From the 1960s to the 1980s* (New York: Routledge and Kegan Paul, 1986): 68 and *passim*. For class, see Ernesto Laclau and Chantal Mouffe, *Hegemony and Socialist Strategy: Towards a Radical Democratic Theory of Politics* (London: Verso, 1985) or Pierre Bourdieu, "The Social Space and the Genesis of Groups," *Theory and Society* 14:6 (November 1985), 723–44. Similar arguments have taken place with regard to mental illness, alcoholism, and drug addiction.

6 See, in particular, Dennis Altman, *The Homosexualization of America* (Boston: Beacon Press, 1982).

7 I do not mean to suggest that constructionism is the *only* theoretical perspective on homosexuality proposed by left academics. Clearly, feminist theory has played a significant role in informing debates on sexual politics. However, feminism has often been guilty of "gender reduction" by

treating questions of sexual identity as epiphenomena of gender debates. To the extent that there is a coherent theoretical perspective on homosexuality *as* homosexuality, it is constructionism. For a discussion of the contributions and limitation of feminist theory (and, somewhat analogously, Marxism) to the study of sex, see Gayle Rubin, "Thinking Sex: Notes for a Radical Theory of the Politics of Sexuality," in *Pleasure and Danger: Exploring Female Sexuality*, ed. Carole Vance (Boston: Routledge and Kegan Paul, 1974): 300–9.

8 This argument about "nominalism" and "realism" is taken from John Boswell, "Revolutions, Universals and Sexual Categories," *Salmagundi* 58–9 (1982–3): 89–113. See also Ian Hacking, "Making Up People," in *Reconstructing Individualism: Autonomy, Individuality, and the Self in Western Thought*, eds. Thomas Heller, Morton Sosna and David Wellbery (Stanford: Stanford University Press, 1986): 222–36.

9 Gay and lesbian exponents of essentialist positions include John Boswell, *Christianity, Social Tolerance and Homosexuality* (Chicago: University of Chicago Press, 1980) and Adrienne Rich, "Compulsory Heterosexuality and Lesbian Existence," in *Powers of Desire: The Politics of Sexuality*, eds. Ann Snitow *et al.* (New York: Monthly Review Press, 1983): 177–206.

10 Prime examples of this recent scholarship would be Jeffrey Weeks, *Coming Out: Homosexual Politics in Britain from the Nineteenth Century to the Present* (London: Quartet Books, 1977), John D'Emilio, *Sexual Politics, Sexual Communities: The Making of a Homosexual Minority in the United States, 1940–1970* (Chicago: University of Chicago Press, 1983) and the essays in Kenneth Plummer (ed.), *The Making of the Modern Homosexual* (Totowa, NJ: Barnes and Noble, 1981). Many other examples could be added. In the bibliography to *Coming Out*, Weeks identifies the main influences on his thinking as Plummer, McIntosh, and Gagnon and Simon (239); in later essays, he has testified to the importance of Foucault. D'Emilio, p. 4n, cites the same casts of characters, with a few additions, such as Jonathan Katz and Estelle Freedman.

11 John Gagnon and William Simon, *Sexual Conduct* (Chicago: Aldine, 1973), Mary McIntosh, "The Homosexual Role," *Social Problems* 17 (fall 1968): 262–70 and Ken Plummer, *Sexual Stigma* (London: Routledge and Kegan Paul, 1975).

12 The phrase "sex/gender system" is from Gayle Rubin, "The Traffic in Women: Notes on the 'Political Economy' of Sex," in *Towards an Anthropology of Women*, ed. Rayna Reiter (New York: Monthly Review, 1975): 157–210. Good examples of anthropological studies in

this vein include the essays in Sherry B. Ortner and Harriet Whitehead (eds), *Sexual Meanings: The Cultural Construction of Gender and Sexuality* (Cambridge: Cambridge University Press, 1981). Anthropological constructionism escapes some, but not all, of the problems I identify in the sociological and historical forms, for reasons I return to in the conclusion.

13 Michel Foucault, *The History of Sexuality, Volume I: An Introduction*, trans. Robert Hurley (New York: Pantheon, 1978).

14 John Gagnon, *Human Sexualities* (Chicago: Scott, Foresman and Co., 1977): 2, quoted in Kenneth Plummer, "Symbolic Interactionism and Sexual Conduct," in *Human Sexual Relations*, ed. Mike Brake (New York: Pantheon, 1982): 226.

15 Gagnon and Simon, *Sexual Conduct*: 19.

16 Jeffrey Weeks, "The Development of Sexual Theory and Sexual Politics," in *Human Sexual Relations*: 294.

17 Wilhelm Reich, *The Sexual Revolution* (New York: Farrar, Straus and Giroux, 1969) and Herbert Marcuse, *Eros and Civilization* (Boston: Beacon Press, 1966).

18 Weeks, "Development of Sexual Theory": 295.

19 McIntosh, "Homosexual Role": 182.

20 *Ibid.*: 183–4.

21 The first and most influential of these was Weeks's study of Britain, *Coming Out*.

22 Foucault, *History of Sexuality*.

23 *Ibid.*: 43.

24 Tomás Almageur, "Conceptualizing Sexual Straticaton: Notes Toward a Sociology of Sexuality" (unpublished essay, 1986): 8.

25 *History of Sexuality*: 101.

26 Weeks, *Coming Out*: 2 and parts I–III; D'Emilio, *Sexual Politics*: 9–22; also D'Emilio, "Capitalism and Gay Identity," in *Powers of Desire*: 100–13.

27 Jeffrey Escoffier, "Sexual Revolutions and the Politics of Gay Identity," *Socialist Review* 82–3 (July–October 1985): 119–53 and *Sexual Politics*: chapters 5–7.

28 The most influential of the left Freudians was Herbert Marcuse, *Eros and Civilization*.

29 Carl Wittman, "Refugees from Amerika: A Gay Manifesto," in *The Homosexual Dialectic*, ed. Joseph A. McCaffrey (Englewood Cliffs, NJ: Prentice-Hall, 1972): 159.

30 Quoted in Ponse, *Identities*: 95.

31 Dennis Altman, *Homosexual: Oppression and Liberation* (New York: Avon, 1971). Altman's radical Freudian views can be seen in the frequent references to Marcuse.

32 Rich, "Compulsory Heterosexuality." Other forms of lesbian essentialism are actually gender essentialism, stressing the superiority of the intrinsic qualities of women. For a striking example, see Karla Jay, "No Man's Land," in

Lavender Culture, eds Karla Jay and Allen Young (New York: Jove, 1978): 48–68.

33 Quoted in Altman, *Homosexualization of America*: 161.

34 This is one of the prime arguments made by Altman in *Homosexualization of America*, written a decade after his earlier "liberationist" book.

35 Altman, *Homosexualization of America*: 9.

36 Cory, *The Homosexual in America*. It is interesting to note that while the term "minority" is indexed frequently, "identity" does not appear.

37 Granted, the majority of self-identified gays and lesbians did not live in these communities, but many of them did make their pilgrimages to the "Gay Mecca" or were exposed to it through the mass media. And beyond that, to use a different religious metaphor, San Francisco came to symbolize for gays around the United States what Israel represents for Jews around the world: a focal point for cultural identity, that functions even for those who are not firmly integrated into the culture. It should be clear, of course, that there is no *single* gay or lesbian "culture" but rather a variety of them that are loosely integrated.

38 Almaguer, "Conceptualizing Sexual Stratification": 25, and Frances Fitzgerald, *Cities on a Hill: A Journey through Contemporary American Cultures* (New York: Simon and Schuster, 1986): 58.

39 Jeffrey Weeks, *Sexuality and Its Discontents: Meanings, Myths and Modern Sexuality* (London: Routledge and Kegan Paul, 1985): 21–5 and Altman, *Homosexualization of America*: chapter 3.

40 *Homosexualization of America*: 45.

41 On the dualism of liberal thought, see Roberto M. Unger, *Knowledge and Politics* (New York: Free Press, 1975): esp. chapter 5. I want to thank Steve McMahon for pointing out this argument to me.

42 For a discussion of the underlying asocial individualism in Marcuse, see Nancy Chodorow, "Beyond Drive Theory: Object Relations and the Limits of Radical Individualism," *Theory and Society* 14:3 (May 1985): 271–319.

43 Jeffrey Weeks, "Discourse, Desire and Sexual Deviance: Some Problems in a History of Homosexuality," in *The Making of the Modern Homosexual*: 94–5.

44 Stephen O. Murray, *Social Theory, Homosexual Realities* (New York: Gay Academic Union, 1984): 19–20.

45 In a more recent revision that deserves attention, Gagnon and Simon speak of three levels of scripting: "cultural scenarios," "interpersonal scripts," and "intrapsychic scripts." While this is a drastic improvement over the original definition of scripts, it still does not go far enough. The intrapsychic is conceptualized primarily as the realm in which the self "rehearses" for interpersonal experience; there is no real dynamic theory of intrapsychic processes in relation to actions in the external world. Also, a conception of unconscious mental processes, as opposed to conscious ones, is missing from their version of intrapsychic scripts. See Simon and Gagnon, "Sexual Scripts," *Society* 22:1 (November–December 1984): 53–60.

46 On the politics of the homophile movement, see D'Emilio, *Sexual Politics*: chapters 5–7 and Escoffier, "Sexual Revolution."

47 It should be clear that groups or individuals can be "located" within these boxes only in a highly ideal-typical fashion. In the real world, at some point or another, most of us are all over the map.

48 Cass, "Homosexual Identity": 107–8. A comparison of the indexes of Altman's *Homosexual: Oppression and Liberation* (1971) and *The Homosexualization of America* (1982) is instructive. In the earlier book, the term *identity* does not appear in any form in the index. In the more recent book, "Identity, homosexual" has eleven direct page references, and six subheadings with further page references.

49 Cass, "Homosexual Identity,": 108.

50 Philip Gleason, "Identifying Identity: A Semantic History," *Journal of American History* 69:4 (March 1983): 910–31. The quote is from p. 918.

51 *Ibid.*: 918–19.

52 *Ibid.*

53 Peter Berger and Thomas Luckmann, *The Social Construction of Reality* (New York: Anchor Books, 1967): 174.

54 Lee Rainwater, for example, has used a definition of identity as something completely acquired, treating identities as things that people "try on," like hats: "Individuals are led to announce a particular identity when they feel it is congruent with their needs, and the society influences these needs by its willingness to validate such announcements by a congruent placement ... Each individual tries on identities that emerge from the cultural material available to him and tests them by making appropriate announcements." See Lee Rainwater, *Behind Ghetto Walls: Black Families in a Federal Slum* (Chicago: Aldine, 1970): 375; quoted in Laud Humphreys, "Exodus and Identity: The Emerging Gay Culture," in *Gay Men: The Sociology of Male Homosexuality*, ed. Martin Levine (New York: Harper and Row, 1979): 144.

55 Jürgen Habermas, "Moral Development and Ego Identity," in *Communication and the Evolution of Society* (Boston: Beacon Press, 1979): 74.

56 *Ibid.*: 90–1; Cass, "Homosexual Identity": 110; Unger, *Knowledge and Politics*: 195, and Chodorow, "Feminism and Difference:" 60.

57 Louis Althusser, "Ideology and Ideological State Apparatuses," in *Lenin and Philosophy* (New York: Monthly Review, 1971): 183.

58 Kenneth Plummer, "Homosexual Categories: Some Research Problems in the Labelling Perspective of Homosexuality," in *Making of the Modern Homosexual*: 60–1.

59 *Homosexualization of America*, p. 82.

60 Weeks, *Sexuality and Its Discontents*, p. 28. See also Simon and Gagnon, "Sexual Scripts," a recent discussion of how "the erotic" historically has come to be separated out as a distinct realm of human experience.

61 In a somewhat different, though clearly related sense, the notion of "straight" identity emerges out of the same historical conjuncture. The idea of a "heterosexual" person is also quite new, and has been created in some sense by its opposite. See Michael Omi and Howard Winant, "By the Rivers of Babylon: Race in the United States (Part 2)," *Socialist Review* 72 (November–December 1983): 45, for a discussion of the changing concepts of "white" identity through redefinitions of "black" identity.

62 Howard Becker, *Outsiders: Studies in the Sociology of Deviance* (New York: Free Press, 1963): 33–4.

63 Erving Goffman, *Stigma: Notes on the Management of Spoiled Identity* (Englewood Cliffs, NJ: Prentice-Hall, 1963): 14, 88.

64 *Ibid*: 114.

65 Cass, "Homosexual Identity,": 10, 114.

66 See, for example, Becker, *Outsiders*. A notable exception to this presumption of a standard sequence of deviant identity-formation is Goffman's discussion of the "moral career" of the stigmatized individual, which can unfold in several distinctive fashions, depending upon the relative timing of (1) developing of stigma and (2) learning that the world considers this to *be* a "stigma." Goffman, *Stigma*: 32–4.

67 Plummer, "Homosexual Categories": 66–72. See also the critique of the "stages" theory in labeling theory as applied to homosexual identity development, in Murray, *Social Theory*: 17.

68 Alan Bell and Martin Weinberg, *Homosexualities: A Study of Diversity Among Men and Women* (New York: Simon and Schuster, 1978).

69 I would like to thank Ellyn Kestenbaum for substantially helping me to clarify and rethink the discussion that follows.

70 To complicate the above discussion even further, it should probably be added that, to the extent that sexual identity and gender identity are ideologically linked, the individual's perception of his or her relationship to the gender categories (e.g., gender "conformity" or "nonconformity") can influence the developmental understanding of sexual identity.

71 Ponse, *Identities*. This much underrated book may be the best symbolic interactionist study of identity and legitimacy; the discussion of methods of biographical reconstruction, drawing on Berger and Luckmann, is particularly excellent. Still, the notion of identity never really sneaks beneath the level of "roles"; Ponse has no conception of the intrapsychic, or of conscious processes. Also, she focuses almost exclusively on adult life, to the exclusion of childhood.

72 See Nancy Chodorow, *The Reproduction of Mothering: Psychoanalysis and the Sociology of Gender* (Berkeley: University of California Press, 1978); also Chodorow, "Feminism and Difference": 54–60. For differences between the object–relations school and the appropriation of Freud by Marcuse that has influenced gay liberation so far, see Chodorow, "Beyond Drive Theory."

73 It may even be useful to reintroduce a concept of "drives" – stripped of its essentialist Freudian baggage. Rather than treat drives as pre-social and biological, Chodorow (following Edith Jacobson) suggests that "the infant is born with undifferentiated drive potentials, which are transformed and used in the process of development, in the interest of internal and external relationships, to become aggressive and libidinal drives." Chodorow, "Beyond Drive Theory,": 308. From this perspective, it might be possible to conceptualize a developmental organization of drives that results in a homosexual "object choice." However, it could be argued that the term "drive" has been so contaminated by Freud's biologism, ahistoricism, prescriptive claims about "normality," and assumptions that drives serve to "channel" sexuality in order to stabilize the moral and social order, that it would be best to avoid the term altogether.

74 Berger and Luckmann, *Social Construction of Reality*: 140 and Escoffier, "Sexual Revolution": 127.

75 Almaguer, "Conceptualizing Sexual Stratification": 27.

76 Peter K. Eisenger, "Ethnicity as a Strategic Option: An Emerging View," *Public Administration Review* 38 (January–February 1978). The terms *primordialist* and *circumstantialist* are used by Nathan Glazer and Daniel P. Moynihan in their introduction to *Ethnicity: Theory and Experience* (Cambridge, MA: Harvard University Press, 1975): 19–20. *Optionalist* is used in place of *circumstantialist* by Eisenger and Gleason.

77 This point is made by Gleason, "Identifying Identity": 919–20.

78 Omi and Winant, "By the Rivers of Babylon: Race in the United States (Part 1)," *Socialist Review* 71 (September–October 1983): 52.

79 *Ibid*.: 47.

80 Donald L. Horowitz, "Ethnic Identity," in *Ethnicity*: 113–114, emphasis added.

81 *Ethnicity.*

82 This occurrence posted a bit of a puzzle to social scientists, many of whom had previously adopted the assumptions of the "melting pot" theory, or who, following the predictions of classical social theorists such as Karl Marx and Max Weber, had assumed that "irrational," "communal" ties such as ethnicity would be progressively swept away by the advance of capitalism and the inexorable process of rationalization. See Stephen Steinberg, *The Ethnic Myth: Race, Ethnicity, and Class in America* (Boston: Beacon Press, 1981): 3–4; also Frank Parkin, *Marxism and Class Theory: A Bourgeois Critique* (New York: Columbia University Press, 1979): 32.

83 Parkin, *Marxism and Class Theory*: 33–4.

84 Daniel Bell, "Ethnicity and Social Change," in *Ethnicity*: 169–70.

85 *Ethnicity*: 9–10 and *Marxism and Class Theory*: 95.

86 Eisenger, "Ethnicity as a Strategic Option,": 90. The quote is from Altman, *Homosexualization in America*: 223.

87 Glazer and Moynihan discuss ethnic "disaggregation," *Ethnicity*: 9. Murray makes a parallel argument about gay "de-assimilation," *Social Theory*: 38.

88 *Marxism and Class Theory*: 85–6.

89 Ira Katznelson, *City Trenches: Urban Politics and the Patterning of Class in the United States* (New York: Pantheon, 1981).

90 *Ibid.*

91 Other countries that have gay political movements have failed to develop gay "ethnicity." French activist Guy Hocquenghem, for example, has commented that France does not have a "gay community." Mark Blasius, "Interview with Guy Hocquenghem," *Christopher Street*, (April 1980): 36. This would tend to support the argument that the United States has structural spaces for "ethnic" organizing that other countries lack.

92 On the last point, see Manuel Castells, *The City and the Grassroots* (Berkeley: University of California Press, 1983): chapter 14.

93 Michael Bronski, *Culture Clash: The Making of Gay Sensibility* (Boston: South End Press, 1984).

94 Irving Howe, "The Limits of Ethnicity," *New Republic* (June 25, 1977): 18; quoted in Steinberg, *Ethnic Myth*: 73.

95 Steinberg, *Ethnic Myth*: 63.

96 This process is limited, of course, by the extensive variation within and among the gay communities and the fact that integration of individuals into those "communities" is often extremely partial.

97 Purists who wish to preserve a more conventional sense of the term *ethnicity* that would be applicable outside of the contemporary American context might instead prefer to call the gay community a "status group" of a "communal" character, organized around sexual expression. While Parkin does not discuss sexual minorities, it would not be hard to incorporate them into his neo-Weberian argument on "communal" forms of usurpationary social closure. See Parkin, *Marxism and Class Theory*: 67 and Almaguer, "Conceptualizing Sexual Stratification."

98 Chodorow, "Feminism and Difference": 57.

99 *Homosexualization of America*: 223–4.

100 D'Emilio, *Sexual Politics*: 248.

101 *Ibid.*

102 Much of the early panic surrounding AIDS within the gay male community would seem to cast doubts on the viability of a "desexualized" notion of gay identity. The view was frequently expressed that if gay men couldn't have sex with each other, they would lose their identity altogether and the community would fall apart. Clearly, sex is unlikely ever to become an incidental part of gay male sexuality. Conversely, the general public seems unprepared to grant gays a "desexualized" gay identity, even if gays want it. Here again, AIDS is a good example: much of the "moral panic" surrounding AIDS can be interpreted as an attempt to "re-sexualize" gay (male) identity, by asserting that "the homosexual" (as a person) is inherently diseased, due to the diseased nature of his sexuality. Similarly, for lesbians, the issue of a "desexualized" identity has been controversial. While some lesbian-feminists have proposed "desexualized" definitions of *lesbian* that would be more inclusive of feminists in general, others have protested against these "women-loving-women" definitions, which too often hide the genital homophobia of an otherwise purified and cleansed reconstruction of the term." Jacquelyn Zita, "Historical Amnesia and the Lesbian Continuum," *Signs* 7 (autumn 1981): 173.

103 Weeks, *Sexuality and Its Discontents*: 244.

104 Weeks, "Development of Sexual Theory": 305–7. See also Plummer, "Homosexual Categories": 55–7 and Jacquelyn N. Zita, "Historical Amnesia": 173.

105 Plummer, "Homosexual Categories": 71–2.

106 And on the other side of the divide are scholars such as John Boswell, who rightly claim the need to develop some sort of middle ground, but continue to conceive of "gay history" in fundamentally essentialist terms. See Boswell, "Revolutions."

107 Harriet Whitehead, "The Bow and the Burden Strap: A New Look at Institutionalized Homosexuality in Native America," in *Sexual Meanings*: 80–115 (quote is from p. 110). The idea that culture structures the possibilities of per-

sonhood is developed more generally in Clifford Geertz, *The Interpretation of Cultures* (New York: Basic Books, 1973): chapter 2. See the analogous argument by Hacking, "Making Up People."

108 Omi and Winant, "By the Rivers of Babylon: Race in the United States (Part 1): 50. See also their *Racial Formation*.

109 Omi and Winant, "By the Rivers of Babylon: Race in the United States (Part 2): 35, emphasis in the original.

110 This implies a greater degree of acceptance among the gay community of those who stand at the "boundary," namely, bisexuals. See Lisa Orlando, "Bisexuality: Loving Whom We Chose."

111 "By the Rivers of Babylon": 53.

112 Altman, *Homosexualization of America*: viii.

113 Escoffier, "Sexual Revolution": 148–9 and Weeks, *Sexuality and Its Discontents*: 187.

114 On sexual intolerance *within* the gay community, see Rubin, "Thinking Sex."

115 See Steven Epstein, "Moral Contagion and the Medicalizing of Gay Identity: AIDS in Historical Perspective," *Research in Law, Deviance, and Social Control* 9 (1987).

CAROLE S. VANCE

"Social Construction Theory: Problems in the History of Sexuality"

from A. van Kooten Nierkerk and T. Van Der Meer (eds),
Homosexuality, Which Homosexuality? (Amsterdam: An Dekker,
1989): 13–34.

Social construction theory in the field of sexuality proposed an extremely outrageous idea. It suggested that one of the last remaining outposts of the "natural" in our thinking was fluid and changeable, the product of human action and history rather than the invariant result of the body, biology or an innate sex drive.

Empirical and theoretical work on history of sexuality has grown dramatically in the last twenty years, for which social construction approaches plus the invigorating questions raised by social movements like feminism and lesbian and gay liberation are largely responsible. Indeed, the links between social construction theory and gay activism run very deep. Efforts to transform society inevitably raised questions about the past and the future, as they also called into question prevailing ideological frameworks for examining the "facts" about sex and gender.

This attempt to historicize sexuality has produced an innovative body of work to which historians, anthropologists, sociologists, and others have contributed in an unusual interdisciplinary conversation. Social construction theory has become the influential, some charge orthodox, framework in the new sex history. Its advantages (lest you've forgotton) can be immediately recognized through comparison with contemporary mainstream literature in sexology and biomedicine, seemingly archaic kingdoms in which the body and its imperatives still rule.

The very real advantages of social construction theory, however, and the enthusiasm it has generated make it all the more neccessary to identify and explore current problems in social construction. In doing so, this paper attempts to differentiate between problems which are generated by common misunderstandings of social construction theory – and thus which are more easily resolved – and intellectual problems embedded in the social construction framework for which no quick and easy solution can be found.

TRUE CONFESSIONS OF A SOCIAL CONSTRUCTIONIST

In the sometimes heated debates that have gone on about essentialism and social construction, the word "essentialist", to some ears, sounds increasingly pejorative – a dirty word, a contemptuous put-down, a characterization of being hopelessly out of date. Yet we need to start this discussion by recognizing that we have all been brought up to think about sexuality in essentialist ways.

Essentialism can take several forms in the study of sexuality: a belief that human behavior is "natural", predetermined by genetic, biological, or physiological mechanisms and thus not subject to change; or the notion that human behaviors which show some similarity in form are the same, an expression of an underlying human drive or tendency. Behaviors that share an outward similarity can be assumed to share an underlying essence and meaning.

The development of science and social science in Euro-America in the past century can be characterized by a general movement away from essentialist frameworks toward perspectives that, although called by various names, are contructionist. These new frameworks have challenged the "natural" status of many domains, presenting the possibility of a truly *social* inquiry as well as suggesting that human actions have been and continue to be subject to historical forces and, thus, to change. Gender and sexuality have been the very last domains to have their natural, biologized status called into question. For all of us, essentialism was our first way of thinking about sexuality and still remains the hegemonic one in the culture.

The novelty of constructionist approaches in sexuality explains several things: the volatile reaction to it (among heterosexuals, too, not just lesbians and gays); the residual essentialism in all of us, even those trying to work in a social construction frame; and the difficulty in adopting a consistent rather than a partial constuctionist approach. Some use the words "social construction", yet their analytic frames show – unbeknownst to them – many remaining essentialist elements. This leads to the phenomenon of somewhat unattractive, if triumphant, "essentialist tendencies" in their colleagues' work. Seen in a more generous light, this scrutiny is an attempt to clarify the assumptions we use in doing our work and make them explicit.

The dominance of essentialist approaches also explains why there a few self-proclaimed essentialists. Only those who depart from the dominant system have cause to label themselves; those who work within it remain more unselfconscious. For the same reasons that heterosexuals do not classify themselves or have a developed awareness of "heterosexual identity", essentialists have had less reason to name themselves and reflect on their practice than social constructionists.

The chief virtue of social construction theory is the new questions it encourages us to ask. Social construction is not a dogma, a religion, or an article of faith. If and when in the course of these discussions it becomes reified, its value is lost. Social construction theory does not predict a particular answer: whether something we call "gay identity" existed in the seventeenth or nineteenth century, in London or in Polynesia, or whether nineteenth-century female romantic friendship or crossing-women are properly called "lesbian", is a matter for empirical examination. Contemporary gay identity might exist in other times and cultures or it might not; its construction could be the same as we know it now, or radically different. Construction theory does not have a stake in the answer, but it is committed to asking the questions and to challenging assumptions which impair our ability to even imagine these questions. Construction theory is against premature closure, and its price is tolerating ambiguity.

UNHELPFUL CRITICISMS OF SOCIAL CONSTRUCTION THEORY

The ways in which social construction theory intersects with sexual politics and our daily social and personal lives gives the discussion surrounding it a special volatility and charge, often disguised in more intellectual, though still legitimate, concerns. It is evident that many problems with social construction theory remain to be worked out. However, there is a class of criticisms of social construction theory which is based on a misunderstanding and even possibly intentional misreading of it. These criticisms do not advance the development of our discussion, because they set up false problems and draw attention from legitimate questions. Before moving on to genuine problems in social constuction theory, I would like to identify unhelpful and misguided ways of phrasing the issues.

Some critics contend that social construction theory implies that sexual identity, or more to the point, lesbian and gay identity is somehow fictional, trivial, unimportant, or not real, because it is socially constructed. The punch line "it's *only* socially constructed" is a characteristic remark of these critics, revealing their belief that only biologically determined phenomena could have any significance in human social life. This is an odd position for historians and social scientists to take. Social construction approaches call attention to the paradox between the historically variable ways in which culture and society construct seemingly stable reality and experience: here, the ways in which the prevailing sexual system seems natural and inevitable to its natives, and for many individuals the expression of some deeply felt essence.

To explain how reality is constructed does not imply that it is not real for the persons living it – or trivial, unimportant, or ephemeral, though it is also true that the insight of construction, when absorbed by the natives (that is, us) has the potential to subvert the natural status of the sexual system and cause us to question and rethink our experience of essential identity.

Other variants of this misreading suggest that individual sexual identity is easily changeable, much like a new outfit plucked from the closet at whim; that individuals have conscious control over sexual identity; and that large scale cultural formations regarding sexuality are easily changed. Since social constructionists have said nothing of the kind, one is at first puzzled by the enormity of this misunderstanding, but the explanation for it is perhaps to be found in the special status of sex in our culture and our thought.[1]

An analogy from anthropology is useful here. It is commonplace for anthropologists to say that human behavior is socially or culturally constructed, by which we mean that human behavior is learned and not intrinsic or essentially determined. But to suggest that any feature of human life, for example, national or ethnic identity, is socially constructed is not to say that it is trivial. Nor is it to say that entire cultures can transform themselves overnight, or that individuals socialized in one cultural tradition can acculturate at whim to another.

This criticism of social construction confuses the individual level with the cultural level: that sexuality is constructed at the level of culture and history through complex interactions which we are now trying to understand does not mean that individuals have an open-ended ability to construct themselves, or to reconstruct themselves multiple times in adulthood. (This is not to deny individuals' experiences of sexual malleability and change, which are probably considerably more extensive than our cultural frames and our own biographical narratives admit.) The specialness of sex is highlighted by this comparison, since a quite ordinary and accepted insight about cultural construction in most areas of human life seems very difficult to understand without distortion when applied to sexuality. When we come to sex, our minds grind to a halt: normal distinctions become incomprehensible, and ordinary logic flies out of the window.

A third major misreading of construction theory concerns continuity and change. In contrast to essentialism's assumption of continuity in behavior and subjective meaning, social construction appears much more receptive to the possibility of change, discontinuity and rupture. Some critics have exaggerated this characterization, claiming that constructionist theory predicts only discontinuity and, thus, any demonstration of historical or social continuity proves that construction theory is wrong.

The openness to recognizing difference in behavior and subjective meaning, however, in no way commits the researcher to always finding it, nor does it rule out the discovery of similarity. The very nature of historical and cultural change makes it likely that peoples closely related by time and space will show many continuities.

We should be especially attentive to these types of criticisms of social construction theory (especially signaled by the comment "it's *only* socially constructed"), because the continual demand to address misreadings of the theory is unhelpful and needs to be put to rest. Energy would be better spent in exploring three genuine and difficult theoretical issues: (1) degrees of social construction theory; (2) the instability of sexuality as a category; and (3) the role of the body.

DIFFERENT DEGREES OF SOCIAL CONSTRUCTION

The widespread use of social construction as a term and as a paradigm obscures the fact that constructionist writers have used this term in diverse ways. It is true that all reject transhistorical and transcultural definitions of sexuality and suggest instead that sexuality is mediated by historical and cultural factors. But a close reading of constuctionist texts shows that social construction spans a theoretical field of what might be constructed, ranging from sexual acts, sexual identities, sexual communities, the direction of sexual desire (object choice) to sexual impulse or sexuality itself.

At minimum, all social construction approaches adopt the view that physically identical sexual acts may have varying social significance and subjective meaning depending on how they are defined and understood in different cultures and historical periods. Because a sexual act does not carry with it a universal social meaning, it follows that the relationship between sexual acts and sexual identities is not a fixed one, and it is projected from the observer's time and place to others at great peril. Cultures provide widely different categories, schemata, and labels for framing sexual and affective experiences. The relationship of sexual act and identity to sexual community is equally variable and complex. These distinctions, then, between sexual acts, identities, and communities are widely employed by constructionist writers.

A further step in social construction theory posits that even the direction sexual desire itself, for example, object choice or hetero/homosexuality, is not intrinsic or inherent in the individual but is constructed. Not all constructionists take this step; for some, the direction of desire and erotic interest are fixed, although the behavioral *form* this interest takes will be constructed by prevailing cultural frames, as will the subjective experience of the individual and the social significance attached to it by others.

The most radical form of contructionist theory[2] is willing to entertain the idea that there is no essential, undifferentiated sexual impulse, "sex drive" or "lust", which resides in the body due to physiological functioning and sensation. Sexual impulse itself is constructed by culture and history. In this case, an important contructionist question concerns the origins of these impulses, since they are no longer assumed to be intrinsic or, perhaps, even neccessary. This position, of course, contrasts sharply with more middle-ground constructionist theory which implicitly accepts an inherent sexual impulse which is then constructed in terms of acts, identity, community, and object choice. The contrast between middle-ground and radical positions makes it evident that constructionists may well have arguments with each other, as well as with essentialists. Each degree of social construction points to different questions and assumptions, possibly to different methods, and perhaps to different answers.

The increasing popularity (perhaps even faddishness in some circles) of the term "social construction", however, made it appear that social construction is a unitary and singular approach and that all social construction writers share the same paradigm. But a review of social construction literature, which makes its first distinct appearance in the mid-1970s, as well as its forerunners in the 1960s, shows a gradual development of the ability to imagine that sexuality is constructed. The intellectual history of social construction is a complex one, and the moments offered here are for purposes of illustration, not comprehensive review.[3]

Intellectual precursors to constructionist approaches, for example, include anthropologists doing cross-cultural work on sexuality in the 1960s.[4] They assumed that culture encouraged or discouraged the expression of specific sexual acts and relationships. Oral–genital contact, for example, might be a part of normal heterosexuality in one group but taboo in another; female homosexuality might be severely punished in one tribe yet tolerated in another. However, these anthropologists accepted without question the existence of universal categories like heterosexual and homosexual, male and female sexuality and sex drive. Culture shaped sexual expression and customs, but the basic material to work with – a kind of sexual Play Doh – was the same everywhere, a naturalized category and thus never open to investigation. Although we can recognize this work as a precursor to social construction theory, it clearly contains many essentialist elements.

The struggle to move away from essentialist and naturalizing ways of thinking about sexuality was a difficult one. Mary McIntosh's 1968 essay on the homosexual role appears to us as a landmark article, offering many suggestive insights about the historical construction of sexuality in England.[5] But her observations vanished like pebbles in a pond, until they were engaged with by mid-1970s writers, clearly motivated by the questions of feminisim and gay liberation. An identifiably constructionist approach dates from this period, not before.

Early work in lesbian and gay history attempted to retrieve and revive documents (and lives) which had been lost or been made invisible. These lives were first conceived of as lesbian or gay, and the enterprise akin to a search for historical roots, an attempt to document the existence of gay people and experience. This was history against the grain, against the heterosexist narrative: in short, activist history and history as political work. To their credit, researchers who had started this enterprise from a firm point of fixed sexual categories began to consider other ways of looking at their material and more expansive questions to ask. Jonathan Katz's work is one example of this process, since his first book, *Gay American History*, is very much in the "gay ancestors" tradition.[6] In the course of researching his second book, *Gay/Lesbian Almanac*, he began to consider that sexual acts reported in American colonial documents from the seventeenth century, for example sodomy, might not be equivalent to contemporary homosexuality.[7] Sodomy – then understood as any unnatural, non-reproductive sexual act – was a temptation and sin to which anyone, male or female, could fall victim, as to envy or theft. Although the documents amply show discovery and punishment, colonial society did not seem to conceive of a unique type of person – a homosexual – who engaged in these acts, nor did it provide a homosexual identity on a cultural level or anything resembling a homosexual subculture on a social level.

Katz's second book marks a sharp departure from the first, in that records or accounts that document same-sex emotional or sexual relations are not taken as evidence of "gay" or "lesbian" people, but are treated as jumping off points for a whole series of questions about the meanings of these acts to the people who engaged in them and to the culture and time in which they lived.

The intellectual development reflected in Katz's work is not unique to him, but appears in many others' as well. And from this work came an impressive willingness to imagine: had the category "homosexual" or "lesbian" always existed? And if not, what was its point of origin and the conditions for development? If identical physical acts had different subjective meanings, how was sexual meaning constructed? If sexual subcultures come into being, what leads to their formation? In these and other questions, researchers imagined what has become the foundation of lesbian and gay history.[8]

The intellectual history of social construction is a complex one. The point of briefly noting a few moments in its history here is simply to illustrate that social construction theorists and writers differ in their willingness to imagine *what* was constructed. For us, their differences suggest that we should avoid using "social construction" in such an undifferentiated way. As readers we should try to be clear about what each theorist or author imagines to be constructed. As writers and speakers, we should try to indicate more exactly what we mean by social construction in our own work.

THE INSTABILITY OF SEXUALITY AS A CATEGORY

Because they were tied to essentialist assumptions which posited biological and physiological factors as influential in determining the contours of sexuality, sexological and biomedical paradigms of sexuality nevertheless offered one advantage: sexuality enjoyed the status of a stable, ongoing, and cohesive entity. The constructionist paradigm more flexibly admits variability in behavior and motive over time and place. But to the extent that social construction theory grants that sexual acts, identities and even desire are mediated by cultural and historical factors, the object of study – sexuality – becomes evanescent and threatens to disappear. If sexuality is constructed differently at each time and place, can we use the term in a comparatively meaningful way? More to the point in lesbian and gay history, have constructionists undermined their own categories? Is there an "it" to study?

We have attempted to address the problem of false universalism by exercising more care in our terminology and conceptual categories: thus, in examining fellatio among Sambia adult men and teenage boys in the New Guinea highlands,[9] it may be more appropriate to speak of "same-sex" rather than "homosexual" acts or relations. The first term attempts to describe sexual behavior without assuming that its social and affective meaning is equivalent to that of contemporary society: New Guinea is not Amsterdam or Greenwich Village. This term and others like it encourage openness rather than premature closure in our thinking about the historical and cultural meaning of diverse sexual acts and identities. However, even with my care, I've already called these acts "sexual".

Here we may detect, despite genuine efforts toward conceptual and definitional openness, that even the new sex history has an ambivalent and more complex relationship to the idea of sexuality as a coherent category. Some social constructionists explicitly encourage the total deconstruction of the category of the sexual, for example, Foucault. Others have not taken this theoretical position, though it remains implicit in their work. For, if sexuality is constituted differently in different times and places, it follows that behaviors and relations seen as sexual by contemporary Euro-Americans may not be by others, and vice versa.[10]

Questioning the very category of sexuality, however, proves difficult. A student of mine agreed that it would be incorrect to call Sambia male intiation rites involving fellatio between older men and younger boys "homosexuality", but he was nevertheless convinced that this was experienced as a sexual act by those engaging in it. How did he know it was sexual, I asked? "Their cosmology posits that young boys grow to adulthood only through the ingestion of semen," he replied, "but you don't see them eating it with a bowl and a spoon." The move to question the category "sexuality" remain counterintuitive, therefore, and thus often results in an intellectual stance that can only be inconsistently or unconvincingly maintained. The attempt to deconstruct sexuality as a meaningful universal construct has also generated considerable backlash for reasons we will describe later.

Many other social constuctionists assume, as perhaps it is easier to, that specific, core behaviors and physical relations are reliably understood as sexual, even though they occur in diverse cultures or historical periods. The knowledge or assumption that behavior is indeed sexual serves as a guide to what must be studied or what might be safely ignored. To give up this assumption considerably widens the field of what might be the object of study, with both good and bad results. The often implicit assumptions about the sexual nature of physical acts or relations depend in turn on deeply embedded cultural frameworks that we use to think about the body.

THE ROLE OF THE BODY

Social construction's greatest strength lies in its violation of our folk knowledge and scientific ideologies that would frame sexuality as "natural", determined by biology and the body. This violation makes it possible, indeed compels us to raise questions that a naturalizing discourse would obscure and hide. Social constructionists have been even-handed in this endeavor, dethroning the body in all fields – in heterosexual history as well as in lesbian and gay history. At first, we greeted this development with good cheer, happy to be rid of the historical legacy of nineteenth-century spermatic and ovarian economies, women's innate sexual passivity, and the endless quest to find the hormonal cause of homosexuality. Yet the virtue of social construction may also be its vice.

Has social construction theory, particularly variants which see "sexual impulse", "sex drive", or "lust" as created, made no room for the body, its functions, and physiology? As sexual subjects, how do we reconcile constructionsist theory with the body's visceral reality and our own experience of it? If our theory of sexuality becomes increasingly disembodied, does it reach the point of implausibility, even for us? And if we wish to incorporate the body within social construction theory, can we do so without returning to essentialism and biological determinism?

Let me discuss these points more concretely by giving an example from my own work in female circumcision. Although not a specifically lesbian or gay topic, it illuminates the difficulty of thinking about the relationship of sexuality to the body and has much to offer for other body issues.

Briefly, female circumcision[11] is an umbrella term for traditional customs carried out in various Middle Eastern and African countries. These customs involve the surgical alteration and removal of female genital tissue, usually performed by midwives and female kin. The procedures vary in severity and range from removing part or all of the clitoris (simple circumcision) to removing the labia (excision). In infibulation, the most radical form of surgery, the clitoris and labia are excised, and the vaginal opening is sutured to reduce its circumference, making heterosexual penetration impossible and thus guaranteeing virginity. These operations are done at different ages and for different reasons – to promote hygiene and fertility, to render women aesthetically more feminine and thus marriageable, and to promote virginity. It is important to understand that these procedures are widespread and in local terms thought to be required by religion or custom.[12]

In the past ten years, an intense conversation has developed between Western and Third-World feminists over these practices. It is not my goal here to thoroughly describe this debate, or to suggest, by examining Western views, that we enjoy a privileged vantage point or right to intervene. What interests me here is how we think about these practices and the body in less guarded moments.

First, we tend to think about the effect of these customs, particularly on sexual functioning. We draw on a physiological model of Masters and Johnson, which places the clitoris at the center of female sexual response and orgasm.[13] We reason that removal of part or all of the clitoris interferes with orgasm, perhaps making it impossible. That is, we are universalizing a physiological finding made on American subjects without much thought.[14] Could Sudanese women's responses be different?

If we are willing to consider that sexual response is more than physiology, we might ask what is known about female sexual experience in these cultures. The answer is not clear cut, in part due to the small number of studies done and the difficulty of doing them. A Sudanese gynecologist compared women with different degrees of circumcision in Khartoum, finding that women with milder degrees of circumcision

reported orgasm whereas women with severe degrees did not.[15] But even this inquiry depends in eliciting a response to terms like "orgasm", whose subjective meaning is what is at issue. A highly-educated Sudanese woman who had been infibulated mused on this problem during our conversation in New York. Familiar with the Masters and Johnson framework which would suggest orgasm was unlikely, she asked me if she had experienced an orgasm. But how could I know?, short of resorting to the clearly inappropriate American adage: "if you have to ask, you haven't." She struggled to navigate the boundaries of culture and language, saying that perhaps she did, since she enjoyed sex with her husband and found the experience pleasurable.

Our response is complicated: still tied to a physiological frame, we think about different degrees of tissue removed, the possible nerves remaining under the excised clitoris, the transferral of sexual response from one body zone to another. We strain to imagine a different scenario of pleasure, still plausible within our framework. Western feminists also think of what is familiar to us: women's accommodation to the lack of sexual pleasure and even active displeasure – rationalizations, protestations of satisfaction, low expectations. In viewing these customs, we oscillate between imagining the sexually familiar and the unfamliar. Nor are we alone in our efforts to compare and contrast: another Sudanese woman famliar with Western culture found her situation far from unique. "You circumcise women, too," she said, "but you do it through Freudian theory, not through surgery. You are not so different from us."

If we give up physiological frames of thinking about circumcision and acknowledge that in these countries it is a culturally normative practice, we begin to entertain unsettling questions. Is female orgasm constructed? What are the conditions for it? Is it neccessary? Is it a physiological potential, whose expression may be facilitated or curtailed? If curtailed, is that repression and injustice? Or is the construction of female orgasm open-ended, with no imperative for it to happen? Can sexual pleasure be constructed totally without orgasm for women? (And here I mean, can women in an entire culture experience sexual pleasure, though they rarely or never experience orgasm?, not the more customary question we might ask in our own culture: can a single sexual episode be pleasurable, even though the women has not experienced orgasm? These are very different qustions.)

By now, even social constructionists, particularly women, are disturbed and upset. Abandoning or even detaching from a physiological frame makes us feel – to the extent that we questioned this practice – that we are now losing ground to object to it. It points up the tendency, even among social constructionists, to defend sexuality and sexual pleasure in terms of an essential right and the functioning of the body. More importantly, the discomfort we experience as the body slips away, or threatens to, in this particular case suggests that we need to explore the limitations of sexual theory which has no room for the body. As we consider restoring the body to social construction theory, we wonder if it is possible to be a materialist without sliding into essentialism? Are there ways to integrate bodily sensation and function into a social construction frame, while still acknowleding that human experience of the body is always mediated by culture and subjectivity, and without elevating the body as determinative? The answer will not be found in a return to essentialism, whether frank or disguised, but in exploring more sensitive and imaginative ways of considering the body.

As difficult as these problems may be, social constructionists do not grapple with theoretical issues about degrees of social construction, the object of study, or the meaning of the body in a vacuum. The new sex history is indebted to feminism and gay liberation for many of its insights, for non-academic settings which nurtured this work during the early stages of its development when the university disapproved, and for its intellectual urgency. These popular political movements created an audience of activist and self-reflective individuals who very much wanted to know and to use the knowledge to inform their activism. I mention this because some of the problems in social construction theory, particularly the critical reaction to it in the last few years in lesbian and gay political circles, originate in the meaning of this theory to

members of oppressed groups in the contemporary sexual hierarchy.[16]

THE SEXUAL SUBJECT'S DESIRE FOR HISTORY

A common motivation for fans of lesbian and gay history was a desire to reclaim the past and to insist on lesbian and gay visibility in every place and at every time. But the discoveries of the new sex historians have sometimes proved disturbing as researchers gave up their initial certainty about the existence of "gay people" and embarked on a more complicated discussion about the origins of gay identity in the seventeenth to nineteenth centuries. In these discussions, sexual acts could not be read as unproblematic indicators of homosexuality; and rather than an unchanging essence which defied legal and religious prohibitions, homosexuality increasingly came to be seen as a variable experience whose boundaries and subjectivity were shaped through complex negotiations between state institutions, individuals, and subcultures.

Variability, subjectivity, negotiation and change often violated the wish for a continuous history. If the point of gay history was to document an ancestry, a gay *Roots*, then for many activists this kind of gay history was frustrating, even a failure. The disappointment and anger at not being able to see oneself reflected in the mirror of history has fueled some of the criticism of social construction theory in the belief that a more essentialist perspective would permit the development of group history and solidarity.

In addition, it is common for mainstream lesbian and gay political and lobbying groups in the United States to use essentialist argument and rhetoric in advancing their case. Lesbians and gays are deserving of civil rights, they say, much like women, ethnic, and racial groups. This argument derives less from a self-conscious theoretical commitment to essentialism and more from the pervasiveness of essentialist frames in American culture, particularly in regard to race and ethnicity. In an ideological system that defines these groups as natural, real, and organized according to relatively unchanging biological features, one obvious and powerful symbolic strategy is to claim an equal status for lesbians and gays. In this ideological and political context, it is to the advantage of all groups struggling for resources to stress not only group unity and historical privilege (buttressed by and documented through histories of the ancestors), but their status as an essential group to which members have no choice in belonging. Fundamentalists and conservatives are fond of ridiculing the analogy between gay rights and minority rights: minorities are "real" groups to which members can't help but belong through their racial features, whereas no one has to be gay, if he or she simply refrains from sin and lust. Gays and lesbians do not constitute a natural group, right-wingers insist; they are just a bunch of perverts.

In such an arena, gay politicos and lobbyists find it helpful in the short run to respond with assertions about gays through the ages, to assert a claim to a natural group status, and to insist that being gay is an essential, inborn trait about which there is no choice. And, indeed, essentialist arguments about sexual identity can be extended to heterosexuals and used to good advantage: if sexual identity is inborn, or at least fixed by age three, then lesbian or gay schoolteachers pose no threat to students in terms of influencing their identity or development (in an undesirable way, the argument would seem to concede). By dint of repetition, ideas about gay essentialism were reinforced in the contemporary gay movement (though they were hardly unknown in American culture) and, more importantly, linked to group advancement, success, and self-affirmation. Therefore, arguments which opposed or undercut essentialist rhetoric about gay identity were increasingly unfamiliar and heretical, even perceived as damaging to gay interests. Within the lesbian and gay community's internal discussions and self-education, the failure to make a distinction between politically expedient ways of framing and argument and more complex descriptions of social relations promoted an increasingly rigid adherence to essentialism as an effective weapon against persecution.

THE RELATIONSHIP OF MARGINAL GROUPS TO DECONSTRUCTION

In a similar vein, it is ironic to note that in the war of ideas against heterosexual hegemony, social construction theory has become most influential only in the intellectual circles of oppositional groups. Social construction theory may be the new orthodoxy in feminist, progressive, and lesbian and gay history circles, but it has made a minimal impact on mainstream authorities and literatures in sexology and biomedicine. These groups continue their investigation and theorizing from the assumption that sexuality is essential. At most, the deviant status of homosexuality calls for inquiry into its etiology (whether hormonal, psychological, or sociological), but the causes of heterosexuality have attracted little interest. In traditional sexual science, heterosexuality remains an unexamined and naturalized category, and little in popular culture causes heterosexuals to consider their sexual identity or its origins and history.

In contrast, the social constructionist framework common in lesbian and gay history has become disseminated to a larger lesbian and gay public. Some wonder whether this constructionist perspective is helpful. What are its implications? Why should lesbians and gays have a developed consciousness that their sexual identities have been "constructed", when heterosexuals do not? Does this intellectual sophistication lead to a sense of group frailty instead of robustness? And does any history of construction inevitably pose the theoretical possibility of a future deconstruction, even disappearance, which is alarming and uncomfortable? The retorts of Dorothy Allison and Esther Newton at recent conferences – "deconstruct heterosexuality first!" and "I'll deconstruct when they deconstruct – reflect in their immediacy and robustness both anxiety about group dissolution and the improbability of such a development.

The tension here is identical to a tension felt within feminism, which simultaneously holds two somewhat contradictory goals. One goal is to attack the gender system and its primacy in organizing social life, but the second goal is to defend women as a group. Defending women or advancing their interest (in equal pay, abortion rights, or child care, for example) emphasizes their status as a special group with a unique collective interest, distinct from men, thus replaying and perhaps reinforcing the very gender dichotomy crucial to the system of gender oppression.

The same irresolvable tension exists within the lesbian and gay movement, which on the one hand attacks a naturalized system of sexual hierarchy which categorizes and stabilizes desires and privileges some over others, and on the other hand defends the interest of "lesbian and gay people", which tends to reify identity and essential nature in a political process I've described. There is no solution here, since to abandon either goal for the other would be foolish. Real, live lesbians and gays need to be defended in an oppressive system, and the sexual hierarchy, which underlies that oppression, needs to be attacked on every level, particularly on the intellectual and conceptual levels where naturalized systems of domination draw so much of their energy. There is no easy solution here, but even an awareness of this tension can be helpful, since it powerfully contributes to the larger political and emotional climate in which social construction theory is received, and rightly so.

CONCLUSION

Social construction theory offered many radical possibilities in theorizing about sexuality. To take the next steps, we need to continue and deepen our discussions about its very real problems. These problems will not be resolved through discussions alone, though such discussion offer clarification, but through the course of continued research and investigation.

To the extent social construction theory strives for uncertainty through questioning assumptions rather than seeking closure, we need to tolerate ambiguity and fluidity. The future is less closed than we feared, but perhaps more open than we hoped. All movements of sexual liberation, including lesbian and gay, are built on imagining: imagining that things could be different, other, better than they are. Social construction shares that imaginative impulse and thus is not a threat to the lesbian and gay movement, but very much of it.

Clearly, the tension between deconstructing systems of sexual hierarchy and defending lesbians and gays will be an ongoing one. In that case, we need to find a way to acknowledge more openly and respond more appropriately to the emotional responses social construction theory engenders, deeply felt responses about identity, community, solidarity, politics, and survival – in short, our lives.

ACKNOWLEDGMENTS

I am pleased to acknowledge my debts in writing this paper, most especially to the researchers, writers, and activists (too many to acknowledge by name) whose work in the past twenty years originated and refined social construction approaches in sexuality.

This paper was originally given as a keynote address at the International Scientific Conference on Gay and Lesbian Studies in Amsterdam, December 15 1987. I've remained faithful to the talk format rather than convert my remarks into a formal paper. Many thanks to those responsible for this stimulating and productive conference; the hardworking Conference Organizing Committee; the Schorer Foundation; and the Research Group for Gay and Lesbian Studies of the Interdisciplinary Centre for the Study of Science, Society, and Religion, Free University of Amsterdam. I am especially grateful to Anja van Kooten Niekerk and Rick Stienstra for their dedication and vision. Thanks also to participants in the conference for their helpful comments and criticisms.

While writing and revising this paper, I benefited from the comments and conversation of Alan Berube, Frances Doughty, Lisa Duggan, Jeffrey Escoffier, Janice Irvine, Jonathan Katz, Lou McDonald, Esther Newton, Gayle Rubin, Ann Snitow, David Schwartz, and Gilbert Zicklin. I appreciated the encouragement of Lisa Duggan, Frances Doughty, and Alan Berube at crucial moments.

NOTES

1 Gayle Rubin, "Thinking Sex", in Carole S. Vance (ed.), *Pleasure and Danger: Exploring Female Sexuality* (London: Routledge & Kegan Paul, 1984): 267–319.

2 There is no suggestion here that the most radical forms of social construction theory are neccessarily the best, although the exercise of totally

deconstructing one of the most essential categories, sexuality, often has an electrifying and energizing effect on one's thinking. Whether this degree of deconstruction can be plausibly maintained is another question, explored in a later section of this essay.

3 A more comprehensive account is offered in my review "An Intellectual and Political History of Social Construction Theory", unpublished manuscript.

4 For typical examples of this approach, see: Robert C. Suggs, *Marquesan Sexual Behavior* (New York: Harcourt, Brace, & World, 1966); Marvin K. Opler, "Anthropological and Cross-Cultural Aspects of Homosexuality" in Judd Marmor (ed.), *Sexual Inversion* (New York: Basic Books, 1965): 108–23; William Davenport, "Sexual Patterns and their Regulation in a Society of the Southwest Pacific" in Frank A. Beach (ed.), *Sex and Behavior* (New York: Wiley & Sons, 1965): 164–207.

5 Mary McIntosh, "The Homosexual Role", *Social Problems* 16 (1968): 182–91. Reprinted in Kenneth Plummer (ed.), *The Making of the Modern Homosexual* (London: Hutchinson, 1981).

6 Jonathan Katz, *Gay American History* (New York: Thomas Y. Crowell, 1976).

7 Jonathan Katz, *Gay/Lesbian Almanac* (New York: Harper & Row, 1983).

8 One interesting question concerns the differential manifestation of social construction, theory in lesbian versus gay male history. The most contentious battles between essentialists and social constructionists have been conducted in gay, not lesbian history. At first glance, one might think this is so because social construction theory has had less impact on lesbian history and, indeed, there is less self-conscious invocation of constructionist frameworks in some of this work

An examination of the actual content, however, suggests widespread adherence to constructionist approaches in lesbian history. And essentialism, when it appears, often takes a different form, focusing less on the universality of sexual acts, as is the case in gay male history, and more on the universality of emotion and interpersonal relations. The reasons for these differences would be interesting to explore.

9 For an ethnographic account of these practices, see Gilbert Herdt, *Guardians of the Flutes* (New York: McGraw Hill, 1981).

10 We have been sensitized to the dangers and limitations of imposing our categories and systems of meaning. The commitment to avoid ethnocentric readings of non-Western behavior, however, encounters another problem: the tendency in the cross-cultural literature to withhold and dismiss data about homosexuality, from combined motives of sexual reticence and homophobia. Similar problems occur in history. Knowing this, the alert reader is reluctant to accept the glib and formulaic dismissals that the behavior in question does not constitute homosexuality, and instead leaps at suggestive evidence, treating data which can only be seen as clues as definitive evidence instead. We need to chart a course between these extremes.

11 Although "female circumcision" is perhaps the most common Western term for these practices, many researchers in the field prefer the terms "female genital surgery" or "female genital operations". Female circumcision too easily suggests an analogy to male circumcision, whereas the procedures performed on women are usually far more serious in terms of the degree of bodily tissue removed and in the physical and psychological consequences.

12 For more detailed description and discussion of female circumcision, see: Asma El Dareer, *Women, Why Do You Weep? Circumcision and Its Consequences* (London: Zed Press, 1982); Olayinka Koso-Thomas, *The Circumcision of Women: A Strategy for Eradication* (London: Zed Press, 1987); A. Verzin, "Sequelae of Female Circumcision", *Tropical Doctor* 5 (1975): 163–9; World Health Organization, Eastern Mediterranean Regional Office, *Traditional Practices Affecting the Health of Women and Children* (Khartoum, February 1979); R. Cook, *Damage to Physical Health from Pharaonic Circumcision (Infibulation) of Females: A Review of the Medical Literature* (World Health Organization, Office for the Eastern Mediterranean, 1976); Fran P. Hosken, *The Hosken Report: Genital and Sexual Mutilation of Females*, 3rd rev. ed. (Lexington, MA.: Women's International Network News, 1982).

13 William Masters and Virginia Johnson, *Human Sexual Response* (New York: Bantam Books, 1966).

14 Constructionists might well question whether the sexual response among even American women should be viewed as a function of physiology.

15 Ahmed Abu-el-Futuh Shandall, "Circumcision and Infibulation of Females: A General Consideration of the Problem and a Clinical Study of the Complications in Sudanese Women", *Sudan Medical Journal* 5 (1967): 178–207.

16 For a discussion of the concept of sexual hierarchy, see Gayle Rubin: 279–83 (in the original of "Thinking Sex").

Looking In – Identities and Communities

PART TWO

INTRODUCTION

As lesbian and gay lives increasingly became more public and political following the years after the Stonewall rebellion, interest developed among some sociologists to study the emerging communities and the rise of identity politics. By the early 1970s, a series of important empirical and theoretical studies documented the ways lesbians and gay men lived and the ways identity began to be conceptualized and politicized. The focus was on looking into the world of gays and lesbians and seeing how they created their own meaning, identity, and communities within the context of the larger social system dominated by heterosexuality.

Within lesbian and gay studies, issues of identity and community have often been an organizing theme. Yet, the development of gay community and gay identity have remained marginal topics within sociology, even though many theories and research studies in sociology have centered on these same basic themes. By understanding the issues raised over the past thirty years by observers of gay and lesbian lives, sociologists can enhance their own work on the sociology of communities and identities.

The emergence of gay/lesbian identity and community and the implications for a social movement based on identity politics clearly have characterized much of the popular and academic literature on the topic. However, the so-called "gay community" and "gay identity" are limiting concepts. Beginning in the 1970s and into the 1980s, what has been described as gay community has been predominantly an American male, urban, middle-class, and white culture. People of color, working-class gays, lesbians, and rural and suburban residents cannot always claim shared identities and communities.

While a search for any single entity called "gay community" or "gay identity" is an impossible quest, the study of the multiple ways lesbians and gay men organize their public and private lives is rich with information and insights. The articles in Part 2 offer sociologists and students of gay and lesbian life a look into the ideas, concepts, and theories used to study the numerous ways gays and lesbians have built communities and identities.

The articles are organized into two parts. The first section, *Building Gay and Lesbian Communities*, includes articles which capture the historic shift from focusing, as Nancy Achilles does, on a single gay institution – the gay bar – around which much of gay community life was organized, to analyzing the very concept of community and residential neighborhood, as Stephen Murray discusses. This section includes a selection from Carol Warren's ethnography about the development of a gay community around the time of Stonewall, an article about the emergence of a particular style of masculine urban community and identity as viewed by Martin Levine, and a discussion of the complex problems of building a lesbian community by Susan Krieger. Finally, Barry Adam's important article analyzes the structural traits that make possible the contemporary social organization of homosexuality.

Since an underlying theme in the papers on community is the development of an identity and political consciousness that are historically and culturally based, the second section, *Building Identities*, focuses on the topic of lesbian and gay identities. Included are a classic statement by

Barry Dank on the coming out process and Richard Troiden's ideal-typical model of identity formation. In an article by Gilbert Herdt and a chapter from Barbara Ponse's work, how identity is built around age and gender, respectively, is explored.

Despite these attempts at understanding identities and communities, sociologists have only started to study the complexities of today's more diverse lesbian and gay worlds. With a growing recognition of the way lives are organized around social class, race, ethnicity, rural/urban location, age, and gender, in future years the study of gay community, culture, and identity must seriously look into these differences. The relative absence of information on rural and suburban gay lives is evident, not to mention the lack of social histories of urban communities outside New York, San Francisco, and Los Angeles. We also need good ethnographies of communities and studies of identities based on age and social class. For example, given the youth-oriented aspects of visible gay urban culture, how do elder lesbians and gay men create communities and shared identities? And what can we learn about identity and community by studying the world of working-class lesbians and gay men?

These are the challenges for the next generation of researchers. There remains much work to be done before we can fully comprehend the multiple ways sexual orientation identity is constructed and community is built, and how these intersect with other identity constructions. Looking into gay and lesbian lives for insights about identity politics and the power of community becomes an important sociological project.

NANCY ACHILLES

"The Development of the Homosexual Bar as an Institution"

from John Gagnon and William Simon (eds), *Sexual Deviance* (New York: Harper & Row, 1967): 228–44

An institution must arise from a particular social situation, when the individuals concerned feel that there is a need for a change in the existing order or a need for the creation of a new order. Thus it may be that all institutions have their origins in deviance.

When an individual experiences strain in the social system, he may become motivated toward deviance. When this occurs, three basic alternatives are available to the potential deviate. He may continue to participate in his environment, finding conformance to its norms frustrating, but less painful than deviance and separation. He may alter his environment through an alliance with others who share his dissatisfaction, in the formation of a subculture, or in joining an already existing subculture. The final choice open to him is to alienate himself from his environment altogether and attempt to chart his own life course.

If the second alternative is adopted, and the individual becomes a participant in a subculture, he may find moral legitimatization for his deviance and satisfaction of his socioemotional needs. Socio-emotional gratification, however, is not sufficient. When the individual pulls away from his former reference group, he is also apt to pull away from the established system of goods and services with which his former institutionalized group was connected. According to Cohen:

> The important point is that the consequences of an act in terms of want satisfaction depend upon the way in which it articulates with the established systems of interaction through which goods and services are produced and distributed. Families, businesses, fraternal organizations, churches ... are such systems. To obtain the goods and services

they offer, the individual must participate in them on their own terms.[1]

The act of joining a deviant group may force the individual to break away from these systems, wholly or in part. A new reference group may satisfy his social wants and needs, but not his non-social ones. For this an institution must be created, a system which can supply goods and services as well as social interaction. When such an institution is established, the individual may remain completely and comfortably within his subculture, maintaining only minimal ties with the larger society.

The goods and services provided by the bar are well adapted to the needs of the homosexual Community. Its most important service is the provision of a setting in which social interaction may occur; without such a place to congregate, the group would cease to be a group. The milieu of this institution is both permissive and protective, necessary conditions for the continued functioning of the group. It provides the social stimulus and diversion of alcohol and entertainment especially created for the homosexual. Articulating with various commercial and political institutions in the larger society, the bar may obtain legitimate and illegitimate goods and services for its clientele. As each bar develops a "personality" of its own and becomes an institution in its own right, it fulfills more specialized social and non-social functions. A particular bar, for example, may serve as a loan office, restaurant, message reception center, telephone exchange, and so forth.

The bar was naturally adopted as the institution serving the homosexual Community for several reasons. For the most part, participation in the Community is a leisure-time activity, albeit the participants' most important activity. Therefore, the institution serving the Community must be one adapted to sociability and leisure. Homosexuals, subject to pressure from law enforcement agencies, require a gathering place which is as mobile and flexible as possible, that is, a place which can open, close, and open again without great alteration or loss. The bar is sufficiently flexible, as it can be situated almost anywhere, and requires little space and few material embellishments. The Community's main institution must be one which provides some degree of anonymity and segregation from the larger society. The bar renders this service well, because it is such a common type of establishment that there is no great pressure from members of the larger society to gain access to any particular bar. Bars located in the outlying districts of the city, with inconspicuous façades, may appear quite innocent and unenticing to all but the cognoscenti.

An essential service which this institution must render is to permit yet control, the formation of sexual relationships. Sexual contacts may be made on the street, in the park, or on the bench, but as Cory states:

> From the gay street to the gay bar may be but a few steps, or several miles, but an aura of respectability is to be found at the latter that is lacking at the former ... in the final analysis, it may be that the bar provides a superstructure behind which the libidinous impulses can hide, whereas on the street the passions are denuded, deprived of an aura of romance and culture. In one place it is fun, in the other it is lust ... the drinks, the music and the atmosphere of friendliness give a far less outlawed aspect to sex.[2]

The bar is the only place where these contacts, necessary to those concerned and illegal according to the law, can be made with a reasonable degree of safety and respectability. The individual may feel much less anxiety and guilt if he is able to carry on this aspect of his life in an organized framework of social norms and values. The bar is the homosexual equivalent of the USO or the youth club, where the rating and dating process may unfold in a controlled and acceptable manner.

Despite the efforts of management and clientele alike, the bar cannot, by its very nature, remain a totally private and segregated institution. It must be open to the public, and, if outsiders choose to enter, they may do so. The bar, therefore, becomes both the center of the private activities of the Community and its liaison with the larger society.

Perhaps the most frequent, and certainly the most frequently discussed, contact between the bar and its surroundings occurs via the police force. While the bar generally protects its patrons from the hazards of "going it alone," it exposes them to the risk of becoming involved in a police action directed against the bar itself. "Disorderly conduct," "lewd and obscene behavior," and "running a disorderly house" are the most common charges brought against the gay bars, and encompass behavior ranging from homosexual dancing to brief and incidental physical contact. Should the owner of the bar be found guilty of these charges, which is usually the case, the bar may be closed or the liquor license revoked.

The fear of a "raid" is always present in a gay bar, and stories of past raids on now defunct bars are part of the group tradition. It becomes rather a badge of honor to have been involved in such an escapade and have survived. Stories of what one did and how one escaped identification and/or arrest are passed on in full detail to newcomers to the group, accompanied by advice as to what one should do in such situations. The owners and employees, however, are fully aware of the consequences of such police action, and take great care to see that their customers toe the mark. A few bars have the extra precaution of warning lights or bells which signal an approaching officer, at which sign all customers are to make certain that no one is standing too close to his neighbor.

The question of "payoff" always arises in such situations, with many rumors and few substantiations. It is unlikely, however, that such arrangements occur frequently in San Francisco for several reasons. The "gay life" in San Francisco is more visible and more a matter of public knowledge than it is in many other cities. As the president of the LCE [a homophile reform group – eds.] described it:

> Another thing that makes San Francisco unique is that the gay life is very open – everyone knows it goes on, where a lot of the bars are, and so on. But

the practices are closed – nobody can get away with anything, anyone trying to make propositions or making out or even dancing in most places gets thrown out. The owners stick together on this, they're a pretty close group. This makes people from out of town make mistakes sometimes, they think that because the gay life is so evident they can just cut loose and have a ball – and they find out they can't. Bars in Chicago and LA, for example, are hard to find, but once you get in you can do almost anything.

This openness makes the gay bars less subject to underworld control and, therefore, less likely to be involved in police bribery. Secrecy is almost impossible, as the homosexual communication network reaches almost every corner of the city, and the homosexual "problem" receives considerable attention from the press. Furthermore, most of the bars are owned by residents of the city and represent their entire business investment. There is seldom enough capital to make bribery practical. The bar owners, as the preceding quote indicates, are a cohesive group, and are generally opposed to illegitimate dealings with the law. It is interesting to note, however, that only three of the thirty-seven San Francisco bars considered in this study were owned by persons who were not residents of the city. These three were all large, successful, and inclined to be rather lax in enforcing behavioral standards. Although all three have been in existence for an unusual length of time, according to gay bar standards, none has ever been troubled by the police.

Several respondents in this study reported having had direct experience with the method of "entrapment" used by law officers in gathering evidence against the homosexual collectivity, the gay bars, and their patrons. Entrapment is a system whereby an officer learns the language, behavior, and dress of the homosexual group, enters a bar or walks down a street frequented by homosexuals, and pretends he is one of them in order to elicit a sexual "pass." He may then use the behavior he calls forth as evidence against the individual or against the owner of the bar in which it occurred. Needless to say, the reaction against this method as expressed by the homosexual organizations and by individuals is rather strong. One respondent recalled his experience as follows:

I remember I was sitting in the ——— one night, a week night, and it was quiet. Only about five other people there. I was by myself, having a beer and about to go home. A young guy with a crew cut comes up and sits next to me. He had on a bright shirt and slacks and tennis shoes, the whole bit. He started a conversation and was real friendly and all, and kind of cute, so I talked to him. Then he started pressing his knee against mine, which you don't do in a bar with only five people in it unless you're asking to get 86'd.[3] I should have known, but hell, you can't suspect everybody! He went out after me when I left, and walked with me to my apartment. So what the hell, naturally I invited him up, and then I find out he's a cop. He took me downtown and said I should be booked for a sex crime.

Another respondent:

I was walking down the street and a man started to follow me. I went faster, and he kept pace, right behind me. Then he came up to me and mumbled something that sounded like he was asking me what I liked to do. I wasn't going to have any part of that, so I kept on walking. He went with me about two more blocks, until he saw he wasn't going to get to add me to his arrest quota. Then he said, "I'm a police officer, and you'd better stop wandering around the streets or I'll arrest you for vagrancy."

If there is one particular issue which calls forth a unified protest from the homosexual Community, it is that of police activity. Many homosexuals remain passive until a favorite bar or a close friend is threatened by the police; then all the latent hostility is fully expressed. A manifestation of hostility from the representative of the larger society calls forth a similar response from the homosexual Community.

It's a police state, I'm telling you. They make me so goddamn mad sometimes. Like the ———, no one had made any trouble there and it was a nice place. But they wanted to get something on it, just for the record, so they parked a police car in front of the door every night for two weeks. That usually scares people off, but it didn't this time. So they put a cop in uniform right inside the door every night, with a dog yet! It got to be kind of a kick after a while, people would come in and bring things to feed the dog, and pet him and everything. It got so the dog was friends with everyone in the place. Not the cop, just the dog.

The cops are fantastic, really. Before they finally closed ———'s, there was one that used to come in every night for a drink. But he wouldn't drink out of the same glasses that all those dirty fairies used, he had to keep his own glass under the bar!

The greatest sense of group cohesion in the homosexual Community is expressed in reaction to the police. The homosexual organizations, apparently aware of this fact and seeking to further develop a sense of unity, give police activity maximum coverage in their publications. The homosexual's relationship to the law and the police, however, may be viewed as latently functional for the group, and this may explain why the group is often reluctant to express its resentment in action as well as words. The homosexual's legal status enables him to see himself as wronged and persecuted, which relieves his own feeling of guilt. The police are a target upon which he may center his hostility; they are the enemy and he is the underdog. It is in large part due to the police that the homosexual can, and often does, regard himself as a member of an unfairly treated minority group.

In addition to the latent functions they provide for the homosexual group, police "brutality" and "persecution" rally some support from the larger society on behalf of the group. Reports of brutality against any group, even if they are exaggerated, tend to stimulate the traditional American spirit of "rooting for the underdog."

It is often the bars themselves which make the most salient plea for the homosexual's civil rights, for it is most often the bars which undertake a defense in cases involving the law. The attorneys hired to defend the bars serve as intermediaries between the institutions of the homosexual group and those of the larger society.

The case of the Black Cat in San Francisco illustrates both the arousal of some degree of public support for the homosexual collectivity and the attempt to legalize it through institutionalized channels. The Black Cat has long been a part of San Francisco tradition, and is well known to the city's inhabitants. It began as a meeting place for literary Bohemia, and developed into one of the few places in the city where homosexuals, tourists, bohemians, and socialites congregated together. Its reputation, however, was as a "gay" bar.

Over a period of fifteen years, the Alcoholic Beverage Control Board brought various complaints against the owner of the Black Cat, who hired one of the city's most renowned civil rights lawyers in his defense. The case went to the California Supreme Court in 1954, with the ruling that homosexuals, if properly behaved, had the legal right to congregate. However, a change in the administration of the liquor control board and a charge of "lewd and indecent acts" ended the bar's career in October of 1963.

The state liquor agents elected to close the Black Cat on Hallowe'en, the night of the traditional costume party at the bar. This brought a response of protest from many quarters, so the agents altered their plans and revoked the license on the preceding evening. The Black Cat, however, remained open on Hallowe'en, serving only coffee and soft drinks. The party that evening was attended by a crowd of some two thousand persons, including a large representation from the homosexual Community, and "college students, business men, matrons with mink coats and jewelry, tee-shirted men in boots, and couples who looked as if they had just come to town for a big night out."[4] The crowd lined the sidewalks, and television cameras were present to record the entrance of the costumed "drag queens." Toward the end of the evening, the bartender led the entire congregation in a rendition of "God Save the Nellie Queen."

The coverage accorded the occasion by the press included three feature columns and several articles. One article quoted the partner of the Black Cat's attorney as saying, "That place is like an institution. This is like closing the cable cars or the Golden Gate Bridge." The same story presented the views of the bar's owner: "I know it's an unpopular cause. The Black Cat has been the symbol of a fight that has benefited the gay people to a degree. That's why they want to knock us out."[5]

The public response, while it manifested more amusement and curiosity than actual sympathy, seemed an illustration of the sophisticated and liberal attitude upon which San Franciscans base their city's image. As a bystander proudly remarked, "It could only happen here." This self-conscious liberalism may be one reason why San Francisco has attracted such a large homosexual population and why the gay life in the city is unusually visible. San Franciscans seem rather ambivalent toward the homosexual collectivity, at times defending it as something of a tourist attraction, and at other times demanding that "something be done about the problem." What effect this type of attitude has had in making the San Francisco homosexual collectivity different from that of other cities cannot be determined without comparative data, which are not yet available.

It is through the bars that members of the larger society may become acquainted with the homosexual Community. The tourist, the reporter, the researcher, the heterosexual who enters a bar by mistake or out of curiosity, and the straight person with friends in the gay Community, all are potential means of interchange between the world of the homosexual and that of the heterosexual.

The official attitude of the larger society toward any deviant group is determined to a great extent by what is contained in the statutes, and the law is often the last institution to adapt to changes in public opinion. Although homosexuality may be considered a form of mental disorder in some quarters and a fashionable peccadillo in others, legally it remains a crime. The police, as the society's official agents, are required to apprehend anyone committing a homosexual act, in private or in public. In practice, however, such legalities are difficult to enforce. A police officer described the situation as follows:

> We can't get rid of them, there's too many of them. You close one bar and another one opens somewhere else. As long as they behave themselves you might as well have the bars, at least it keeps them off the streets. People complain about so many bars for that kind of people in the city, but they'd probably complain a lot more if they were all running around in public. All we can do is keep an eye on them, try to keep them in line.

Police relations with the gay bars are closely linked to the politics of city government. When a change of administration is due or there are reports in the press about sex crimes or the increasing crime rate, the pressure on the homosexual bars is intensified. The closing of a bar tends to pacify the public demand for action, and makes it appear that the administration is doing a fine job of cleaning up the city. Much of the evidence gathered in the constant police surveillance of the bars is held in abeyance until political expediency requires it. The bar owners, aware of the shifting patterns of police pressure, often have a fairly good idea of when the "heat" will be most intense.

In the final analysis, little is resolved in the contest between the gay bars and the police, but important latent functions emerge from the situation. The homosexual collectivity develops a greater unity, its societal position is brought to public attention, and it gains support and sympathy from some sectors of the larger society. On the other hand, those so inclined may vicariously vent their feelings of hostility toward the homosexual group.

OPENING AND CLOSING OF THE BARS

A gay bar does not develop by accident; it is the result of careful and systematic planning. Homosexuals rarely infiltrate an already established bar and make it their own; a gay bar is gay from the beginning. Opening such a bar is a calculated risk; the owner is virtually assured of many customers and a good income, but his successful enterprise is apt to be short-lived.

The most important factor to be considered in opening a gay bar is attracting the type of clientele desired. This again is not a matter of chance. The location of the bar determines its clientele to some extent, but the personal characteristics of the owner and his employees are most significant.

The gay bars of San Francisco comprise a closely knit social system. The individual bars may open and close rapidly and regularly, but the system and its participants remain the same. As familiar bars close and new ones replace them, the employees and customers move in a steady flow from one to another. In this shifting system, a particular owner may have operated several bars, and a particular bartender may have been employed in a dozen. These individuals become well known in the Community and acquire personal "followings." The character of a bar often reflects the personality of its owner, and will attract a certain type of customer as a result. According to the president of the LCE:

I think the owner's personality makes a lot of difference. That's another thing about San Francisco gay bars that's different from anywhere else in the country. The owner is always around, and everyone who goes to the bar knows him by name. That really puts a stamp on a place, and you either like it or you don't. There are only three major bars whose owners live out of town, and any gay person could tell you which ones they are. Take Bill out at the ———, for example, he puts everything he has into that bar, and he's a wonderful guy. They only serve beer there, but it's packed every night. It's a matter of the owner's personality, Bill never lets anyone feel he doesn't belong.

The personality of the bartender is even more important than that of the owner in drawing a particular group or type of customer. A successful bartender attracts a personal following, a large number of people who come to a bar because he is employed there. It may be his personality, his looks, his wit, or his style that brings the customers, but whatever it is, he becomes the bar's most valuable asset. If a bartender with a large following leaves one bar and goes to work in another, his retinue usually accompanies him. The services of the most popular bartenders, known to everyone in the homosexual Community, are sought by many owners. A classified advertisement to this effect appeared in the *LCE News*: "Bartender – Liquor bar, must be experienced and either have a following or the personality to build a following."[6]

The gay world is one marked by a galaxy of social types, each one comprising a subgroup within the Community. Often a bar will cater to one particular subgroup, and the bartender will be representative of its social type. For example, one bar will be known as a "leather bar,"[7] where the customers are the exaggeratedly masculine type, sporting motorcycle jackets and boots. Another bar may be popular with the effeminate "queens." The bartender has an important symbolic function, serving as a mark of identification. One swift glance at the bartender, and the initiate knows what kind of a bar he is in and what kind of people he is likely to find there. The bartender in the leather bar will be a rough looking individual, dressed accordingly; in the "faggot"[8] bar, the person mixing the drinks does so with a limp wrist. A female behind the bar indicates a primarily lesbian clientele. The same applies to more subtle distinctions; in the discreet gilt and mahogany bars of the financial district, the bartenders wear black ties and speak with Oxford accents; in the neighborhood bars, slacks and sport shirts are the rule.

Someone who intends to open a gay bar may intentionally try to attract a particular subgroup, hoping to reduce competition by catering to those other bars exclude. This goal is accomplished by hiring a bartender who personifies the subgroup's social type.

There aren't many faggot bars in town, really, mainly because no one can stand to have them around. Also because most of them aren't old enough to drink. So Carl opened the ———, as a coffee place. It's full of them, running around like a bunch of crazy parrots. That bartender has got fingernails long enough to reach across the bar. I don't know if it'll stay that way long though, it's so near ———'s that that crowd, the general gay crowd, may start going there for coffee after closing time.

Once a bar's character has been established and a suitable bartender installed, a regular clientele builds up and becomes its own attraction. One goes to a particular bar because his friends meet there, or because he is "cruising" that night and wants a "butch"[9] bar.

Occasionally the process of invasion and succession occurs, and one group begins to frequent a bar which was the stronghold of another or which was merely "gay" and catered to no particular subgroup. In this case, the owner may make it clear that he does not care for the new patronage or he may change the "identity" of the bar. The latter is done quite simply; he hires a new bartender. A respondent outlined the history of a bar with a distinctly protean character.

It's in transition now, I guess it always has been. They've had more trouble down there, and none of it their fault. It was a leather bar, and then somebody started pushing pills, which always seems to bring Hell's Angels.[10] They're not very popular anywhere, so the owner hired a real faggot. That got the motorcycle boys out, and for a while it was all swish. Then the hustlers moved in, and there was a lot of that going on, so they closed for a while. A new owner has it now, and it's a nice place. Some of the girls are going there now, it's mostly a mixed crowd.

A grand opening almost always launches a

new bar into the gay world. This usually means a party, with gifts and prizes, entertainment, and food and drinks either gratis or greatly reduced in price. Members of the Community are advised of the event through various channels. If the owner is well known, it is likely that his future plans are also, and the opening of his new bar will be eagerly anticipated. If a popular bartender is to be employed at a new bar, his following will certainly be present at the opening, and his friends will bring their friends. In some instances, the owner will send announcements of the opening to members of the Community, a procedure described by the president of the Mattachine Society as follows:

> Someone may decide to open a bar, and he sends out announcements to everyone on a gay mailing list. There are several of these around, I have one – not the Mattachine membership list, that's confidential, but one of people I know who go to the bars. The owners get them by having guest books where people sign, or by selling tickets to things, on which people put their names and addresses, or just by knowing a lot of people. Often people ask to be put on mailing lists. I have about 900 names on mine. Then the bar sends printed announcements, and offers a party or a special price on drinks, or something similar to attract customers.

Ecological factors

The location of a bar is another important factor in determining the nature of its clientele. The bar situated in one of the residential areas will almost always be a neighborhood bar, which those who live nearby use as a social meeting place. Unless the owner or bartender is particularly well known or the bar has a unique attraction, its business will be limited primarily to those who live within a short distance. It is this type of neighborhood bar which most often performs extra services for its patrons, such as taking messages, lending money, or providing a bottle of milk for the cat.

Bars in the outlying areas of the city, away from the main business and entertainment districts, are not as unified in character. For the most part, however, they too have a clublike atmosphere, and often cater to those who come to the city from other parts of the Bay Area or to a particular group of city residents who have adopted it as their own.

Several bars are located in the Tenderloin district of San Francisco, and several others in the industrial section and its adjacent waterfront. The nature of these bars varies widely, and they include some which serve the subgroups within the Community. In general, they tend to be large and rather impersonal places, where people come for entertainment, to "cruise," or for a change of scenery.

Bars are often intentionally situated in a particular area or type of area, in order to draw a desired clientele.

> It's not going to have any alcohol at all, just dinners and short-orders, from eight until four in the morning. It's near the ——— and ———, so it'll get those people after the bars close. What she [the owner] wants most are the bartenders, after they get off work. I think they'll come, they want a clean place where they can unwind after work. They're a particular group, and if they like it, it'll go.
>
> I'm going to have it out along the avenues, not near the downtown area. A nice quiet bar, just beer and wine and maybe some games and singing. I don't want anyone there who might make trouble. If it's out there, I think the Sausalito crowd will come.

Patrons go to a specific bar for a specific purpose, and a bar's locale may be an important factor in determining the purpose for which it is used.

> Bars where everyone knows everyone else are hard to cruise in, so if that's what you have in mind, you don't go to the neighborhood bar. You want to see some new faces, and you don't want your sisters[11] coming up and slapping you on the back and saying "Hi Mary"[12] when you're trying to make an impression.
>
> A big shift happens right before the bars close. If all you want is a bed partner, there's no use hanging around a bar all night waiting, so you sit around in the early hours with your friends, and maybe go find someone later on at ———'s or the ———. The big bars are always jammed right before closing time, especially on weekends. If someone doesn't make it then, maybe you'll find him in one of the coffee places that stay open all night.

The purely physical characteristics of an area also influence the nature of a bar's patronage.

> A lot of how a bar gets to be a certain way or draws a certain crowd depends on the area. People with cars like to go away from around where they live, and it can depend on whether the roads between their homes and the bars are hilly, or

whether there's a lot of stoplights, or if there's parking. The bars in the industrial area off Market have acres of parking after five o'clock, and the streets are empty then too, so people don't have to worry about being seen.

The internal layout of the bar is an additional factor.

> The actual layout of the bar may have something to do with who goes to it, depending on what they're looking for. A well-lit place will get a different crowd than a dark place. Some of the bars in the Tenderloin have johns arranged so that there's a lot of traffic by them. A dark bar like ——'s, with long narrow passages is a paradise for the hustlers and such.

Economic factors

In a city with a homosexual population the size of San Francisco's, a gay bar is a lucrative enterprise. To operate such an establishment is a gamble, as no gay bar lives for long, but the income one produces far exceeds that usually obtained from a "straight" bar. According to one bartender:

> ——'s brings in more money than any bar in the city. The only place that sells more beer is the Red Garter, and beer's all they sell there. On a week night there will always be at least 75 guys in there, and on a weekend it always reaches 250 capacity.

The probability of financial success often means that an owner will receive some assistance in opening a gay bar and need invest less of his own capital at the outset.

> The gay bars are so sure to be a success that the juke box company or the beer supplier will give an owner all he needs to begin, if they know he's opening a gay bar. Or they'll pay his expenses if he gets in trouble, just so he keeps buying from them.

Thus the gay bar articulates with commercial institutions in the larger society, to the profit of both. These economic factors often outweigh the dangers inherent in an operation which borders on illegality.

Closing of the bars

Due to its inimical relations with the police force, the gay bar has a brief life expectancy. A bar may be closed or its license revoked for any one of the many reasons previously discussed, and these legal complaints account for the highest percentage of the mortality rate. Other

pressures may be brought to bear, however; the gay bar is in the path of an urban renewal project, or the Health Department finds a leaky pipe, or the neighbors complain of the noise.

The bars come and go, like a chain of lights blinking on and off over a map of the city, but the system remains constant. When a bar closes, its patrons shift their activities elsewhere. In he new bar, the same music comes out of the jukebox, the same bartenders mix drinks, the same faces appear, and the conversation repeats the same themes. And often, the same policeman is standing by the door.

NOTES

1. Albert Cohen, "The Study of Social Disorganization and Deviant Behavior" in Robert Merton, Leonard Broom and Leonard Cottrell (eds) *Sociology Today* (New York: Basic Books, 1959): 471.
2. Donald W. Cory, *The Homosexual in America* (New York: Castle Books, 1951): 120.
3. 86'd means to be evicted from some public place, usually a bar.
4. *San Francisco Chronicle*, November 1, 1963: 4.
5. *San Francisco Chronicle*, October 25, 1963: 2.
6. *LCE News*, April 3, 1963: 3.
7. A leather bar is one where the patrons wear motorcycle clothes, often made of leather. This type of bar is sometimes associated with sadomasochism.
8. Faggot is a derogatory term for an extremely effeminate male homosexual, who flagrantly displays his effeminacy.
9. Butch means having a masculine appearance or character or the playing of a masculine role. When applied to the male, it is a complimentary term indicating a lack of effeminacy. Applied to the female, it connotes a masculine appearance, demeanor, and the playing of the masculine role.
10. Hell's Angels is a group of motorcyclists and their girl friends who often invade the less genteel gay bars. Their habitual attire is leather jackets, ragged pants, gold hoop earrings, and bandanas wrapped about the head, pirate fashion. Members of the Community firmly maintain that the Hell's Angels are not gay, but hang around the bars as perennial troublemakers.
11. A male homosexual's "sisters" are his good friends, with whom he has an asexual relationship. The term is used infrequently and always jokingly.
12. Mary is an affectionate, but slightly deprecating, nickname which male homosexuals use in addressing one another.

CAROL WARREN

"Space and Time"

from _Identity and Community in the Gay World_ (New York: Wiley, 1974): chapter 2

Space and time are the concrete boundaries of a community, in a not quite metaphorical sense. A community that is secret and stigmatized must quite literally have walls: places and times set apart from other places and times in which the community can celebrate itself. Although gay places are always specific and can be found, gay time may be spent internally, invisible from the world around, as well as externally, within gay places.

Walls imply walling out as well as walling in; gay people learn to wall themselves out of straight places. Whereas straight people may find companionship, sex, and lifetime love in all kinds of settings, from church to the workplace, secret gay people may neither find others like themselves there, nor be gay in those settings. Gay people who cannot find gay settings remain isolated, outside the straight world and not within the gay one:

KIM: Before I found the gay bar[1] I knew that I was a homosexual but there was nowhere for me to go and meet others. I would often just roam the streets, riding on buses and walking, looking for a face that might be sympathetic. I literally did not know what to do.

(Conversation)

Gay time may be spent within gay spaces or inside the self, walled off from the surrounding straight setting. Externally, and beyond the general boundaries of our social calendar and twenty-four-hour time clock, social time in our society is divided into experience phases: worlds of work and leisure and sleep. It is characteristic of the twentieth century that leisure time expands as work lessens.

The gay community exists within leisure time, since the contexts of stigma and secrecy prevent its extension into work time. The gay world, then, is a world of leisure time, structured by the concept of leisure and play, and giving a value to leisure beyond simple relaxation. By confinement to leisure time, and through the centrality of the gay experience, sociability and play become the most significant of life's tasks.

The stigmatization of the gay world ensures that all gay space and time will tend toward secrecy. Gay inner time and gay interaction are protected from the invasion of outsiders by other kinds of walls: the refusal of entry to strangers, the concealment of gay bar entrances, and the palpable change that happens in a gay crowd on the entry of straights. In this way, gay time spent within gay spaces gains a highly exclusive, trusting, and valuable character by its very secrecy.

SPACE

There are both public and private gay places where gay identity may be exposed in every town and probably every village of the nation. Private spaces are primarily people's homes and a few private clubs, and there are public bars, streets, parks, beaches, baths, gyms, movie houses, motels, tearooms,[2] and bars. Just about every community has at least one gay or mixed[3] bar, since bars are the most important public community places.

Gay community members know about the types of places likely to be gay, and they find specific gay places by word-of-mouth recommendations and, especially when they are traveling, from published gay guides. There are several of these, published yearly, covering various territories of the United States and other countries. International bar guides list gay bars, baths, and other institutions in countries where the police are lenient to the gay community (most of Western Europe), and also good cruising spots,[4] from parks to hotel lobbies. In Roman Catholic and Eastern European countries, where specifically gay places are discouraged, entries list only cruising spots and places where gays congregate (always Hilton hotels and Dennys). In the nations of Asia and Africa, gays are told where to find such specialities as male brothels and male children.

Other guides cover the United States as a whole, geographical regions of the west or north, or individual states. Since particular bars shift in clientele from gay to straight, go broke, disappear, or change in atmosphere, the bar guides are always out of date and often prove less useful than recommendations:

> We searched for bars listed in last year's San Francisco gay guide entry. The first one was just not there; the area's buildings were being torn down. The second had become a straight bar with go-go entertainment. The third was still there and still gay, but the guide designated it as "elegant," and it certainly wasn't.
>
> (From field notes)

The gay guides not only list the addresses of bars and other places but also give some indication of the type of atmosphere and clientele. In one guide, bars are classified by the following symbols:

D Dancing
R Restaurant
G Gay girls' bar
M Mixed straight and gay
H Hippie or collegiate; young crowd
E Elegant; coat and tie may be required
C Coffee bar only
L Liquor bar
B Beer, or beer and wine only served
SM Sado-masochist or leather crowd[5]
W Western-type attire[6]
* Popular

In many cities, including "Sun City," gay bars and homes are clustered in the same areas. Some areas have so many gay people that the gay community gives them special names, like the "Swish Alps" for one particular part of Los Angeles; some streets and apartment buildings become all-gay or have a majority of gay dwellers. In Sun City there are several major areas of gay residence: downtown among the city's gay and straight night life, an upper-middle-class suburb, and an adjacent beach area, all of which have gay bars.

Gay bars

Gay bars are most significant for community activity for many reasons. First, they are sexually defining spaces. Anyone inside them is presumed to be gay, and, if male, a legitimate object for a sexual advance.[7] There are few other places in our society where this is true for homosexuals; settings of work, family or church seem dangerous to secret gays in search of sex:

JASON: I've always had a hang-up against approaching anyone unless they were in a gay context so that the context would do the definition for me ... I've never revealed my preferences to anyone who wasn't gay – well, with a couple of exceptions – with a very few exceptions – and I really get uptight about the prospect of doing that, and trying to approach people in a straight situation, where, you don't know about them, might lay you open to that kind of exposure which – which I just wouldn't like to do.

(Tape-recorded interview)

Bars are used not only to make sexual contacts, but to expand the circle of sociability:

CAROL: What is your motivation to go to gay bars?
JASON: The motivation is – to – to – meet people, it's not to drink, or it's not to, you know, must go out for the sake of going out. It always has a purpose behind it – the purpose is not necessarily looking for sex either, but it's, you know, to meet new people, and, you know, have these acquaintances lead where they may, whether you might have sex that night, or get to meet someone who's a friend, or whatever.

(Tape-recorded interview)

OLIVER: When I want to pick up a trick I go to the Den, but the Flyover is best to meet new people.

(Conversation)

Bars are also places to greet members of the

clique networks to which gay people belong and continue sociable relations. This function is in tension with sexual and sociable searching, since talking to acquaintances can prevent meeting new people, and talking to new people in front of cronies can be embarrassing:

JASON: Gay circles can be sort of gossipy and closed, and there tends to be a great deal of talk and gossip outside the bars about – "well, I saw so-and-so in the bar, and he picked up on a certain type of guy, and that's his hang up" or something like that, or – you're talked about all the time, people try to construct patterns out of your behavior and so forth which, you know, I dislike – there's a great deal of emphasis placed on making it, you know, and finding an attractive guy to go with, and so forth, and, er, as I say it's a thing which you're being tested so to speak in front of everybody else, and you know I just don't like to feel that way.

(Tape-recorded interview)

Because of their multiple functions, gay bars become specialized. As Oliver said, the Den is a cruising bar and the Flyover is a bar popular with people from out of town; other bars are popular with blacks, or sailors, and still others are home territory bars for particular cliques.[8]

Whatever their particular clientele and reputation, however, gay bars are places in which gay identities are created and sustained for the self and others, by the self and others. People in gay bars who know where they are (and most of them do) assume that the others present are gay, which means that many people in professional or business occupations are fearful about going to gay bars because of the possible violation of their secrecy. Contextual labeling of this kind is particularly likely in mixed bars that have a reputation in straight circles (such as bars featuring drag shows[9]), where a secret gay may run into straight business acquaintances out on the town.

Members of the secret gay community vary in the degree to which they boycott gay bars in fear of exposure. Gary, for example, says:

Although I sometimes go to Christophers, I never go to Midlands or Kenos (drag show bars) because I might run into other faculty there, or parents, or students who graduated. I sometimes go to the Flyover, but it makes me uncomfortable. In that part of town, anybody might walk in.

(Conversation)

But Peter, who is also a teacher, disagrees: "I go everywhere, I say, if they are there, it's for the same reason I am." Although a few members refuse to go to any bar, most do so from time for time, and some indeed have had the experience of running into straight acquaintances:

BRENTON: Oh sure I have run into people I know in gay bars – it's too small a town not to. Particularly when you teach high school. I've seen lots of kids in there, and usually I've already picked them out.

(Conversation)

Labeling is not just done by others in bars, it is done by the self. Many people "come out" in the sense of identifying themselves as gay people, in gay bars. Hooker calls this the "socialization function" of gay bars, and, as important as the bars are for coming out, they would be more so if the drinking age were lower (Hooker 1967; Dank 1971). In Dank's study, although 50 per cent reported that they had come out through association with other gay people, only 19 per cent of his sample had done so in bars. Most had come out before they were 21 years old, in other kinds of places (Dank 1971: 181–4.)

As Hooker adds, "the bar system is relatively stable" (1967: 173). Gay bars are found in most sizable cities, and they open and close generally in areas where previous gay bars have attracted gay homes. Rarely are gay bars opened in areas of the city not having gay colonies, and rarely do gay people take over an existing straight bar as their own (Achilles 1967: 228–44). Hooker points out that, although the system is stable, the actual bars are not, but that was in Los Angeles. In Sun City, both the system and the bars are stable: of the approximately thirteen gay bars operating in 1968, nine were still in operation in 1973. Some had closed, and there were some new ones too.

There are mixed bars as well as gay bars in most cities, although not as many, because for secret gays the mixing of worlds can be uncomfortable. Some mixed bars are predominantly gay but have some straight clientele, such as the Sun City drag bars Midlands and Kenos. Others are predominantly straight but are patronized by a few gay people on a regular basis. Sometimes bars change in character from straight to gay, gay to straight, or mixed to straight or gay exclusively, but this is difficult because of the period of transition (see Lyman and Scott 1970: 92–3):

> Barbara's had been not just a go-go bar but a famous one until it was bought by a gay business and turned into a gay bar a few months ago. As the bartender commented "the sailors are always walking in here looking for the girls, and boy do they get freaked out."
>
> (From field notes)

The maintenance of a mixed bar is, if anything, even more difficult than the transition from straight to gay and back. In my observation, it can really only be accomplished with a drag bar, for reasons suggested by Sherri Cavan (1965: 155–60). In a bar with a show, the focus of eye attention is the stage, and interaction is suspended. In such a situation, two potentially colliding worlds can stay out of collision, and more or less ignore one another.

Kenos and Midlands started as gay bars and advertised for straight clients to make more money. In only one instance I encountered did the management open a bar specifically to attract both gays and straights, and in this instance it wasn't even a drag bar:

> The ID checker at the door quickly scrutinized the incoming crowd to ascertain the sexual characteristics of each entering person or couple. Straight people were sent to the large main restaurant, gay men to a somewhat smaller room, and gay women to a still smaller back room. I asked the checker how he knew; he said "I just know." People stayed where they were put; the few who did wander around were cooled out by those who belonged. The manager walked around attempting to sell private club membership to the gay people; for $15 a month they would get a key to the proposed gay club upstairs. To reach this club they would have to walk through the main dining room, which was to be predominantly straight.
>
> (Field notes)

This was not a popular idea with the gay community, and within a few months only the straight crowd patronized the bar-restaurant. The gays did not like the idea of the membership fee, or walking through the main dining room (which is hardly conducive to the keeping of a secret), or the stigmatization implied in the segregation of the gay group.

As this indicates, bar owners and managers have various problems in running a successful bar. The gay crowd, as many of the members point out, is basically fickle, and there are fashions in bar going. A bar which is full one week is empty the next, then full again some months later (if it hasn't closed) without a reason. This happens to both home territory and cruising bars; cruising bars because new faces quickly become old, and home territory bars because the communications network is so rapid that a whole group can shift from bar to bar with little trouble.

There is of course a variation in bar life, from a few that open and close with hardly a trace to bars that attract the same people for months and even years, and everything in between. In Sun City, Christophers (located in the upper-middle-class suburb of El Sol) is the most stable, with a changeless clientele of middle-class, middle-aged people who hardly vary with the decades. At the opposite extreme is the Flashlight, which has changed many times during the past four years from a gay men's to a gay women's bar and back, from a popular to an unpopular place and back.

One of the reasons for such fickleness, as Cavan points out, is that bars are used for various purposes, from sexual contacts to entertainment, so habit is not always the major factor. As already indicated, some bars are known for cruising, others for drag shows; still others are funky beer bars where lower-class tricks[10] can be picked up:

OLIVER: I go to the Flyover, which is – over a few blocks – when I want to have a quick beer after work and see my friends, then on weekends when I don't have to get up I'll mostly go to the Den downtown – all those cute young things to pick from, and me such an old man.

CAROL: The Den? That's a new one … do you ever go to Kenos?

OLIVER: No never. I don't care for the drag shows. When you're footloose and single you have other things on your mind.

(Conversation)

CAROL: What did you do last night?

OLIVER: I went to the Flyover and ran into George – you know, this guy I had a thing with years ago, and I'd really like to get something going again – and then we went to the Casket –

CAROL: (interrupts, surprised, since the Casket is a

gay women's bar): – What on earth were you doing there?

OLIVER: Frankly, I took him there because I didn't want any competition. No danger of him running into a cute trick at the Casket.

(Conversation)

Bar owners and mangers are aware of the problems they face in running a predictable and profitable business; successful bars can make a fortune, although unsuccessful ones have lost everything for their owners. They try all kinds of inducements to increase their patronage. One type of inducement is financial, like happy hours with drinks for 40 cents, or Tuesday meals for $1.25, or parties with food "on the house." Other inducements are atmospheric, like a live band, a dance floor with a light show, or a pool table.

Very important, too, is the bar's personnel; its managers, bartenders, and cocktail waiters and waitresses (and food waiters and waitresses if it is also a restaurant). As Achilles points out, "A particular owner may have operated several bars, and a particular bartender may have been employed by a dozen" (1967: 239); this is not necessarily because of bar closures, but because bars raid one another for personnel. The importance of personnel popularity, especially the bar-tender, is great, since he may take his following with him to the new bar; they say "Let's go see Bill," rather than "Let's go to the Den":

> I was surprised to see Charles tending night bar at Kenos, since he had for years been the day bartender at Christophers, and everyone was used to him. Kenos had also raided Midlands for some of their top drag performers, and their cocktail waitress, Katharine, who had also been at Christophers some years back. A few months later Charles was back at Christophers, saying that he couldn't stand the pace or the straight people.
>
> (From field notes)

Owners are as often straight as gay; for example, the owners of Christophers are a straight couple, and the owners of Midlands are a gay couple. Bartenders and cocktail and food waiters are almost always attractive young gay men, whereas the cocktail and food waitresses are almost always straight, and sometimes middle-aged and motherly (like Katharine) rather than young and pretty. Whether bar personnel are gay or straight, the important thing is that they relate well to the gay community and do not stigmatize them (see also Cavan 1965: 226–7):

> "Ernie's"[11] ... a good place not to go. Why should we support an establishment that has for so many years taken money and support of the gay clientele and yet never put a thing back into it, other than rotten service and sarcasm. Support your own!!!
>
> (*Exodus*, 1970: 13)

Not only must bar personnel be supportive, it helps if they are well known in the local gay community. Most bars that opened between 1968 and 1973 were opened by established bar owners and succeeded fairly well, at least for a time; the two or three bars that were opened by out-of-towners did not do well at all:

> Flower Field opened near where I lived, and I went in a few times. It was a routine beer bar, with 24-cent draft, pool, and a small dance floor. There was never more than one person in there at any time, and several times there was just the bartender, watching his color television. He was from Los Angeles, and had opened the bar as a business venture. Within three months it had been sold and was a straight bar.
>
> (Field notes)

Gay homes

Whereas the bars are the most important gay public places, the owned and rented homes of the gay community are the most important private spaces. Younger gay people do a lot of their socializing in gay bars; when they get older they entertain more in their own homes, which increasingly become the focus of their attention. The younger men claim that the older men drift into this pattern because they are no longer able to compete sexually in the marketplace of the gay bar, but the older men say it is because home entertainment is more intimate and rewarding:

TIMOTHY (age 24): You know why these older guys say they don't go to the bars? They don't make out in the bars, that's why. The only place they can go is Christophers, there's no competition because they're all old.

(Conversation)

JOHN (age 40): ... but I prefer the gay crowd now, particularly my particular kind of people.

CAROL: What do you mean by your particular kind of people?

JOHN: Uh – socializing on a home basis. Entertaining for cocktails in the home, going to people's houses for parties. I like to go to the bars, periodically, but – er – I'm not that interested in that particular socialization. I have more fun in a closer relationship with people rather than going and sitting in a bar all evening long and maybe talking to someone that you don't even know.

CAROL: Yes.

JOHN: Regardless of whether you want to take them home or not – but – at least at my age. It might be different if was younger.

(Tape-recorded interview)

Home socialization requires that the homes of gay people be of a particular style and (depending on the particular clique) of a certain scope. Older couples, in their late twenties, thirties, forties, and fifties, spend a large portion of their incomes in obtaining, decorating, and maintaining their homes for lifestyle and entertainment purposes, and, although many live in rented apartments and houses, the ideal is to own a home. Types of home include very expensive owned ($40,000 and on up); expensive owned ($30,000–45,000); less expensive owned ($15,000–30,000) and rentals of various shapes and sizes:

Samuel and Dawson's house is in the newly developed part of Cahuenga, just north of Sun City, overlooking mountains and ocean. Its cost was probably somewhere in the $80,000 range, and I have no way of estimating the additional cost of the decoration. There is an Olympic size pool, surrounded by marble statuary, with a small guest house – cabana. Inside the house are three bedrooms and two bathrooms, all large. The dining room and kitchen have marble floors, while the enormous living room is furnished with at least three furniture groupings, all antiques or elaborate approximations. The green carpeting is soft and deep throughout.

Frederick and Darrell just moved into their new condominium, which cost around $35,000. Frederick is building a marble fountain in the backyard, and they are busy putting down new shag carpeting (deep red). The old carpeting looks new; they tell me "we like to lie naked on the floor." They, like the other separate-dwelling owners, have use of the gardenlike grounds, a pool, sauna and tennis courts. Their house has two bedrooms and two baths, and a good-size living room. The dining room is an angled corner of the living room with a small chandelier to designate the spot for the table, and the kitchen is visible from the dining room (they plan to mirror the opening and hide it). They move into a house like this, fix it up with marble fountains, landscaping and new rugs, then sell it for hundreds of dollars more than they paid, and buy a new one.

Justin lives in a small house in the fashionable part of El Sol, which he rents but is trying to buy. It is small, but has a fireplace in the living room and a lovely enclosed patio. He has fixed it up in vivid yellows, black and white with very little money; yellow vinyl cushions, chairs and black and white animals, a gleaming dining room table of black that is actually a painted picnic set, topped by heavy silver chandeliers. There is a huge round cocktail table with some very elegant crystal, and fresh flowers.

(From field notes)

Although these homes are quite different in scope, they show similarities in style. The style is one of subdued elegance and neatness, with exact placement of objects and combinations of colors, textures, and surfaces; idiosyncratic and personal touches; and great care, cleanliness, and tidiness. The scope of this style, of course, varies from the cleverly painted picnic tables and stools of the yellow, black and white living room to the most opulent elegance of Samuel and Dawson. But the thread is there throughout.

Gay men, especially couples, will save and make sacrifices to own a home. One reason for this is that home ownership is the best way to preserve secrecy and privacy. Nosy neighbors cannot spy, and watchful landlords cannot evict. For the same reasons, those who do rent prefer houses to apartments.

Often, though, gay men make payments on homes which appear to be quite large in terms of their incomes. Moreover, the fixing up of these houses, with the kind of styles involved, also costs a lot of money, so many gay men learn to do their own gardening, plumbing, roofing, and even fountain building. The attractiveness, and especially the orderliness of gay men's homes never ceased to amaze me; the time spent in sociability is considerable, but the time spent setting the stage must also be great.

Spaces and masks

Whatever the gay space, however, the function is the same – a place where the expression of the true self can be allowed. This was most often expressed as "letting down my hair" or "being myself":

JEROME: You get in a gay bar, I think, it gives you a chance to really let your hair down, and say, you know that you don't have to put on any kind of a façade, no one there is looking for you to be any one else but yourselves.

(Conversation)

Restating the near-metaphor of the wall, gay places are where the walls can be allowed to fall, where the mask worn in straight interactions can be dropped, and where the secret gay can quite literally be himself:

JOHN: At the present time I no longer work for the company that I used to, and my association now with people is almost literally – with the gay set of people, and as far as straight people are concerned, I see some of my friends periodically, and I call them, but I – er – I very seldom have any social obligations with them.
CAROL: Do you prefer this?
JOHN: Yes. It's much more comfortable for me now. It's very difficult leading a double set of standards, where you have to switch on and off so fast – and particularly in your home.

(Tape-recorded interview)

What Simmel describes quite concertedly may be taken symbolically with reference to the gay community: "an outstanding expert suggested that the presence of masks among a nature people should at once make one suspect the existence of secret societies. It is ... in the nature of the secret order for the members to conceal themselves." (Simmel 1950: 373). Although "nature people" wear quite real physical masks to conceal their identities, secret gay people wear quite real role-playing masks, which must be worn in all straight spaces, and can only be dropped in gay ones.

Territorial invasion

Even the most secret spaces are not completely protected from what Lyman and Scott call "territorial invasion ... where those not entitled to entrance or use nevertheless cross the boundaries and interrupt, halt, take over or change the social meaning of the territory." Reactions to this are varied: ignoring the newcomers, routing them, or being overpowered by them (Lyman and Scott 1970: 99–102). In the gay world, territorial invasion may be by gay people into straight places or by straight people into gay places, and either can be unwitting or deliberate. Public places are most likely to be invaded, but homes are not inviolate:

A couple entered Kenos. He was young and crewcut; she was clinging closely to his neck. They sat down, and watched the drag show, which had just started, with an air of grim determination and an occasional nervous laugh. "Midwest tourists" murmured my neighbor.

Gerald invited two gay guys to come to dinner at his house and added "Alice and Tom will be there." To their quizzical looks he replied. "It's OK. They're straight, but they're wise, and they love the gay scene."

Oliver was recounting his recent dinner party with Bill and his wife Ann. Bill had been gay for years and a good friend of Oliver's, but a year ago, in his mid-thirties, he had married Ann. Ann was aware of Bill's past and of Oliver's homosexuality, but no one apparently wanted to talk about it. Oliver said "We couldn't talk about old times, or what the crowd was doing, or who was going with whom, or anything. We just sat there."

The Hi-Tide was crowded with people, and there were many couples on the dance floor – men with men, women with women, and men with women. Two heterosexual middle-aged couples came in, obviously left over from the time when the Hi-Tide was a straight restaurant. They headed for a table. Suddenly the lead man wheeled around and flailed his arms at his companions, shouting, "Oh my god, oh my god, we're got to get out of here – quick – hurry – oh my god!" They all rushed out.

Donald was relating how his mother had gone to the Warmup Room with another elderly lady who had known the Room when it was a popular Chinese restaurant. They found out that food was no longer served, so stayed only for a couple of pre-dinner cocktails. Donald related: "She said it seemed kind of strange – she couldn't say exactly why. When I think I was there the previous evening, I almost died!"

JOHN: I was having a party one evening, and I was living alone at the time, it was when I first moved out to the beach, and I had about, oh, eight or ten people over at the house for dinner and as usual, when you get – uh – a few drinks under your belt, the talking gets very loud, and everyone's camping and carrying on, and suddenly the doorbell rings, and its a very close friend of mine and his wife – happened to be in the area and stopped by, and – you just – it's like a shot of adrenalin to you, you just don't know what to do, but you'd like to put tape over everyone's mouth for a few minutes, but you don't.

As these examples show, different circumstances lead to different reactions to territorial invasion. In Kenos, Midlands, and other drag bars, straight couples like the "Midwest tourists" are part of the setting, and gay people who want to go there get used to them. At the other end of the spectrum, Christophers has many tactics to prevent the entry of straight people, and to cool them out if they do enter:

I was having dinner with a friend at Christophers, and noticed that the waiter was setting up the table next to us for three people. He put a "reserved" sign on it. I asked if that meant that three people I knew who dined frequently at Christophers were coming in, and he said: "No, no one's coming, but it keeps the straight people out."

(Field notes)

A man and wife that lived in the apartment building where I lived came into Christophers and sat down at a table. The bartender looked at them, but didn't ask them what they wanted, and they did not go up to the bar. After twenty minutes of sitting and being ignored, they got up and left.

(Field notes)

In other instances, the invaders may refuse to leave, and possibly even rout the habitués:

There were four women and a man in Casket when five men in leather jackets, boots, and caps came in. They clustered around the end of the bar close to the girls, and stood behind them shouting their drinks orders to the woman bartender. They talked and horsed around loudly for a few minutes as they were served. The women had been talking quietly when the five entered; now all were silent, and two moved to the other end of the bar. The man got up and left.

(Field notes)

There is a possibly apocryphal story in the community that one night some years ago a group of men wielding baseball bats rushed into Christophers shouting "let's kill the queers," utterly routing the middle-aged patrons.

(Anecdote)

Although gay people live in straight as well as gay worlds, they also sometimes invade straight space in the same ways. Gays may be secret tourists in the straight world, pretending to be straight but inwardly, or quietly together, laughing at all that the straights represent:

The group of two gay men and two gay women were planning a trip to a performance of the Soroptimists' club in El Sol. Noreen said: "What shall we wear?" They all agreed on very lavish and elegant clothing, and Jeremiah added: "We'll go and watch the straights do their thing. It should be good for a laugh. We'll look better than any of them."

(Field notes)

Clearly, this kind of invasion retains the secrecy of the group; their activities are what Goffman calls "backstage." What distinguishes backstage gay invasions from simple interaction in the straight world is that the group would not pretend to be straight at the Soroptimists' performance, they would go as a group of gay people, cut off from the others by a wall of secrecy.

Lyman and Scott refer to this kind of backstage behavior as "time out," "a respite of the activities related to the time track ... a period when roles and rules relating to the ongoing time track are relaxed or revoked" (Lyman and Scott 1970: 204). Gay people in straight settings, when they take time out, quietly drop the mask of straightness and relax with other gays. This kind of thing happens quite a lot, and it helps cement community relationships even within the straight context. For example, at a Sun City community college there are several gay teachers who, although they do not all socialize on a regular basis in the gay world, meet as often as they can for lunch or coffee in the straight world, quietly turning a corner of the cafeteria into a gay backstage.

Not all gay time out in straight spaces is backstage or quiet, however. There are two kinds of frontstage gay invasion of straight space: overt and dramaturgical. Overt invasions, where gay people in straight places act in a way that will get them labeled, is sometimes deliberate (and of course secret gays don't do this) and sometimes accidental (usually a result of drunkenness):

We all came together at Denny's for a very gay breakfast. The waitress can never be the same. We can't begin to tell you all the remarks that were made, but among the things that we noticed was an additional $20, added on to ———'s tab for the busboy.

(*The Prodigal* 1971: 5)

Eight people (including teachers and social welfare workers) from the secret gay community went into a Mexican restaurant, all very drunk from a cocktail party they had just left. Soon, they were loudly quarreling, shouting, some kissing. Kim sat on Darrell's knee, and their chair broke; Darrell threw it against the wall where it shattered. The group was thrown out and told never to come back.

(Field notes)

Needless to say, they would not have done this in a purposeful way to freak out the restaurant – and, to my knowledge, none of them has ever been back.

Sometimes gay people may use the frontstage of a straight setting exactly as a stage, for the playing of a part, acting as a woman. This role gives the person a sense of freaking out the straights, but only through an inward satisfaction, since none of them knows that the "woman" is really a man. Thus, although overt and frontstage, passing as a woman has all the advantages of secrecy:

JEROME: It's more or less a game – and as I said again – possibly with a little bit of sarcasm, you know, you're saying to the people you have no idea – would that I stood up right now and took off this wig, and I said here I am a man, you now, you would have everything from giggles to laughs, you know, a complete variety of social reactions to this. But with them not knowing they're actually not looking for it, and if you're a decent looking drag it's even that much better – as I said, I have honestly no desire to be a woman so of course I feel like a man. It's more like I suppose an actor on a stage – it's a game – because when you're an actor and you're on a stage you're putting yourself into someone else's place and you're convincing the audience that you are what you are really not ... most kids have been in drag before.

CAROL: You have?

JEROME: It's sort of a kick, it's sort of a panic, you know, something different to do – to go socially out, which I have done, completely in drag, and go and mix with society in the nicest of restaurants and have no one have any idea that I'm a man, it's different, you know, it gives you sort of a feeling you can say, OK, now,

because conventionally I look like a woman, here I am sitting here eating, and I'm being totally – er – accepted.

(Tape-recorded interview)

Space is a most proprietory thing. Invasion of space in both contexts can increase the feeling of community among gay people. In the act of keeping others out of gay bars and homes, gay people reinforce the in-group–out-group division of the gay world, without challenging the stigma or the secrecy behind such actions. In the act of treating straight spaces either as unreal worlds or as stage settings for the invasion of outsiders, gay people continue to define themselves as outsiders, and as strangers to the straight world. As Robert Frost once said, walling in and walling out are aspects of one act.

TIME

Time is both internal and external. Take a man in the work world, performing a routine task and daydreaming about another world – his home. He may be thinking about his wife, his bills, his children; if a colleague interrupts and asks him what he is thinking, he says "Oh, about my wife and family." If he is gay, he may be thinking about his home too – his lover, and perhaps the new carpeting they are putting down in the living room. If he is interrupted, he becomes flustered and does not know what to say, or perhaps, adeptly, he says "I was thinking about the great chick I met last night." For gay people, internal gay worlds cannot be shared with straights in other worlds even in casual conversation, because the gay world is secret.

External time, divided by the calendar and by the clock, has the characteristic of what Lyman and Scott call "time tracks ... temporal periods employed by individuals, groups and whole cultures to designate the beginnings or the termination of things" (1970: 189). As they indicate, "time tracks are defined by events, activities, thoughts, or typifications of events, activities or thoughts, and movements from track to track may be marked by symbolism or rites of passage" (1970: 190). Time tracks are the external measurement of worlds.

Secret gay people often experience a kind of time schizophrenia. Time spent in worlds other than the straight one may be experienced both as unreal time and as split from the kind of time experienced in the gay world. The gay time track is leisure; the times spent at work, with one's family, and simply walking around the city have a different character and meaning for the gay person, since he can never externally "be himself" at these times. Gay time and leisure itself become of primary importance.

The split between gay and other times is a kind of splitting of the self, which can have emotional consequences for the gay person. Although some do not mind alternately wearing a mask and letting one's hair down (metaphors often used for the experience of self in straight and gay settings), others do. Whereas some do not mind relating to others dishonestly, fearfully, or impersonally in straight settings, others do. In either case, what might be one world is divided into two by stigma and secrecy, connected by tiny time tracks in which one self is exchanged for another:

JOHN: You've got to be able to make instant changes – you can be flitting[12] around in one instant and just absolutely have to stop dead in the next. Uh – it's like putting on a mask and taking it off and you have to do it instantaneously you – and – literally you nave to change your method of speech and everything else – your vocabulary changes – there's a lot of things that you would say in one instance that you would not say in the next, and you have to be able to turn it off and on just like you would a light switch. You get at home, you get in a leisure world – er leisure world after hours, and your vocabulary does change, you have a tendency to – to – socialize like the rest of the people do.

(Tape recorded interview)

For secret gay people, the only time they can really be themselves is in gay spaces, on the gay leisure world time track:

JEROME: You get into a gay bar, I think, it gives you a chance to – to really let your hair down, and say, you know, use the lingo, let the – you know, you don't have to put on any kind of a façade, because no one there is looking for you to be anything else but yourselves.

(Tape-recorded interview)

The segmentation of time and space in this way is not a simple matter, however. Extreme secrecy and separation lie at one end of the continuum: openness and lack of concealment form the other:

Isadore, who is a wealthy married man, flies to another city in order to have sexual and social relationships with the gay community.

(Anecdote)

ANTOINE: Everyone knows about me – how could they miss it. A hairdresser. Everyone at the salon knows too, but they don't say anything because they know if they did I would go somewhere else. My family knows too and they are very good about it. I act the same everywhere.

(Conversation)

Most gay people operate somewhere in between, sometimes easily, and sometimes most uncomfortably.

Consciousness and identity

Internal time, or consciousness, is vital in the search for identity characteristic of industrial society in general, and of those making the leap into a stigmatized community in particular. People about to make or break fundamental commitments to themselves or others, to answer the questions Who am I? and Where do I belong? in a way that will fatefully structure their lives, need time for reflection.

Consciousness and reflectivity are the essential psychic conditions for the building of an identity, just as space and external time tracks are the essential physical conditions. In quite different contexts, Merle Miller and Helen Merill Lynd have given us insights into the relationship between states of consciousness and the growth of identity.

Writing on shame, Helen Lynd describes the experience of engaging in stigmatized behavior in terms of guilt and shame. Whereas guilt is a sense of responsibility to others, shame reflects responsibility to the self, and it is out of shame that a changed identify can come. In the act of feeling ashamed, the newly sexual adolescent – or the homosexually awakened adult – reflects upon the experience as a previously unknown possibility.

Merle Miller, a novelist who came out publicly as a homosexual after years of secrecy, also discusses the importance of conscious reflection and of internal and divided time for the process of identity. In *On Being Different*, he indicates that when inner time becomes separated from outer time, the self is made aware that there is "something to hide" and opens to conscious exploration of what is being hidden and why. Ultimately, conscious reflection in inner time enables the development and taking of a homosexual identity. After this identity is assumed, the continuing division of inner and external time deepens the division between worlds and reinforces the sense of "being different" (Miller 1971).

NOTES

1 A bar whose patronage is predominantly homosexual, and which is gay in atmosphere and reputation.
2 Men's rest rooms noted for homosexual activity (see, for example, Humphreys 1970).
3 Bars with some gay patronage.
4 Places known for homosexual pick-ups.
5 A gay person who is "leather" is either sadomasochistic by sexual preference or wears the kind of clothes popular among S&Ms: leather jackets and pants, or motorcycle gear.
6 In some bars, the men costume themselves in Western attire: boots and spurs, breeches, cowboy hats. This does not indicate a sexual act preference.

7 Contrary to public stereotypes, such advances usually take the form of glances, not instant attack.
8 A home territory bar is patronized by the same people over long periods of time (see Cavan 1965).
9 Shows with female impersonators.
10 Pick-up for casual sex purposes.
11 A downtown mixed bar.
12 Behaving in a camp, effeminate or flamboyant manner.

REFERENCES

Achilles, Nancy, "The Development of the Homosexual Bar as an Institution," in *Sexual Deviance*, eds John H. Gagnon and William Simon, (New York: Harper and Row, 1967: 228–44.

Cavan, Sherri, *Liquor License* (Chicago: Aldine, 1965).

Dank, Barry, "Coming Out in the Gay World," *Psychiatry* 34 (May 1971).

Hooker, Evelyn "The Homosexual Community," in *Sexual Deviance*, eds John H. Gagnon and William Simon (New York: Harper and Row, 1967): 1167–84.

Humphreys, Laud, *Tearoom Trade: Impersonal Sex in Public Places* (Chicago: Aldine, 1970).

Lyman, Stanford and Marvin Scott, *A Sociology of the Absurd* (New York: Appleton-Century Crofts, 1970).

Lynd, Helen Merrill, *On Shame and the Search for Identity* (London: Routledge and Kegan Paul, 1958).

Miller, Merle, *On Being Different: What It Means to be a Homosexual* (New York: Random House, 1971).

Simmel, Georg, *The Sociology of Georg Simmel*, ed. and trans. Kurt H. Wolf, (Glencoe, ILL: Free Press, 1950).

MARTIN P. LEVINE

"Gay Ghetto"

from Martin P. Levine (ed.), *Gay Men: The Sociology of Male Homosexuality* (New York: Harper & Row, 1979): 182–204

We are refugees from Amerika. So we came to the ghetto.

(Carl Wittman)

Gays have claimed that there exist within major cities "gay ghettos," neighborhoods housing large numbers of gays as well as homosexual gathering places, and in which homosexual behavior is generally accepted, designating as such certain sections of Boston, New York, Chicago, San Francisco and Los Angeles (Aiken 1976; Altman 1971: 42; Brill 1976; Chicago Gay Liberation, 1970: 3–4; Kantrowitz 1975: 48; Nassberg 1970: 1; Russo 1975; Shilts, 1977: 20; Whitmore 1975: 45; Wittman, 1972: 167–8). Sociologists have picked up the term, repeatedly using it in homosexual research. For example, Humphreys (1972a: 80–1) labels as "gay ghetto" a neighborhood characterized by marked tolerance of homosexuality and a clustering of gay residences and bars. Weinberg and Williams (1974: 43) use the term "lavender ghetto" for districts with large numbers of homosexuals and their institutions.[1] Typically, however, these authors offer no observations to support their use of the term.

This paper analyzes the validity of "gay ghetto" as a sociological construct, limiting the discussion to the male homosexual community.

THE GHETTO

The term "ghetto" has been employed by sociologists in varied and sometimes inconsistent ways. Most sociologists consider a ghetto to be an area of the city housing a segregated cultural community, but there is marked disagreement about the particular features of the community that qualify it as a ghetto. The term was first used in accordance with its historical connotation, as applicable only to the Jewish community (Wirth 1928: 4). In the 1920s, sociologists from the Chicago School, notably Robert E. Park (1928: vii–ix) and Louis Wirth (1928: 1–10), began to use it to describe any urban neighborhood inhabited by a people socially segregated from the larger society and bearers of a distinctive culture. Noting that the circumstances of immigrant groups often did fit these requisites, Park and Wirth applied the term to neighborhoods inhabited by Jews, Poles, blacks, and Italians. They also suggested its suitability as a depiction of areas dominated by such moral deviants as bohemians, hobos, and prostitutes (Park, 1928: vii–viii; Wirth 1928: 6, 20, 286). Disregarding Park's and Wirth's more general formulation, contemporary usage of the term has in some instances restricted the concept to communities inhabited by racial and ethnic groups, particularly those that are poverty stricken and socially disorganized (Butler 1977: 121; Kerner Commission, 1968: 12). In other cases, the word "ghetto" is applied to any area inhabited by a minority group (Fischer 1976: 13; Theodorson and Theodorson 1969: 174). Even affluent minority communities are said to live in ghettos, these being called "gilded ghettos" (Michelson 1970: 65).

Park's and Wirth's notion is superior to the other formulations because it removes "ghetto" from its historical connotation and translates it into a construct useful to the study of urban ecology. Wirth (1928: 6) recognizes this advantage when he notes that a ghetto epitomized ecological segregation in the sense that it is a spatial indicator of the extent to which a community is isolated from the surrounding society. Unfruitfully grounded in the ghetto's historical meaning, the other formulations limit the term to racial and ethnic communities, obscuring the generalizability of its features and thus hiding its important implication for urban ecology. For these reasons, I will use Park's and Wirth's conceptualization.

The classic exposition of Park's and Wirth's formulation appears in Wirth's well-known study *The Ghetto*. In the book's foreword, Park (vii) defines a ghetto as an area of the city that houses a segregated cultural community. Wirth develops the concept further by specifying as key elements of a ghetto four features: institutional concentration, culture area, social isolation, and residential concentration. Institutional concentration denotes the centralization of the ghettoized people's gathering places and commercial establishments in the ghetto. For example, in the Jewish ghetto are concentrated large numbers of synagogues, religious schools, ritual bathhouses, kosher butchers and restaurants, and Yiddish theaters and bookstores.

Wirth (286) means by "culture area" that the culture of a particular people dominates the geographic area, a dominance reflected in the spatial centralization of the ghettoized people's cultural traits. Inside the Hebrew quarter, for example, Wirth observes a concentration of Jewish traits. He finds mainly Yiddish written on store signs, restaurant menus, and billboards; he hears mainly Yiddish spoken in conversations and speeches. The distinctive attire of the Jews also prevails in this neighborhood. Most of the men have long sidelocks and flowing beards, and wear long black coats and hats or skullcaps. Most of the women wear kerchiefs, long dresses, aprons, and shawls. Wirth also records the widespread adherence to the special customs of the Jewish people, such as the closing of stores on the Sabbath and high holy days.

The third key element of the ghetto, social isolation, denotes the segregation of the ghettoized people from meaningful social relations with the larger community. To Wirth (287), this isolation is produced by the prejudice that is typically heaped upon the ghettoized people or by the social distance different cultural practices create between the group and the larger community. Wirth (222–6) illustrates this type of social isolation by showing how anti-Semitism and/or the social distance caused by Jewish subcultural practices are responsible for the restriction of the ghettoized Jews' social lives to other Jews.

Residential concentration, the last key element, signifies that the ghetto is a residential area with a concentration of the homes of the ghettoized people. Wirth (205–10) demonstrates, with population statistics, that the majority of the people living in Chicago's Jewish ghetto are Jewish.

Following Park and Wirth, an urban neighborhood is a "gay ghetto" if it possesses the attributes Park and Wirth have put forth. It must contain gay institutions in number, a conspicuous and locally dominant gay subculture that is socially isolated from the larger community, and a residential population that is substantially gay. The rest of the paper presents exploratory research findings which show that some metropolitan subcommunities are indeed "gay ghettos." To prove this, I used a multifaceted research strategy. First I limited my inquiry to metropolises commonly reputed to have large numbers of homosexuals. Then I developed procedures to demonstrate the degree to which gay institutions concentrate in each metropolis, to measure the extent of concentration, and to determine the boundaries and the names of the areas in which the institutions cluster. Finally I carried out exploratory fieldwork in the areas of concentration to study the degree to which they fulfilled the other requisites.

PARK'S AND WIRTH'S FIRST REQUISITE: INSTITUTIONAL CONCENTRATION

This section locates neighborhoods with large numbers of homosexual institutions. My strategy for the research was the ecological method (Michelson 1970: 11). I first plotted the location of gay institutions on maps of five cities. I then studied the maps for concentrations of these institutions, and ascertained the names and boundaries of the districts in which they occur.

The data used in constructing the maps came

from a national directory of gay gathering places, *Bob Damron's 1976 Address Book*. This directory contains the names and addresses of bars, bookstores, steam baths, churches, restaurants, and movie theaters catering to the gay community. It also lists cruising locations, indoor or outdoor places such as beaches, parks, or street corners where homosexuals go to meet each other, often to set up sexual encounters. Places listed within this directory are coded as to the type of patrons who frequent them (e.g., youths, hustlers, Western) and as to the kinds of activities available there (e.g., dancing, entertainment, overnight accommodations).[2] *Bob Damron's Address Book* is one of several available gay directories, all of which vary in the accuracy of their listings. *Bob Damron's* is the most current and accurate, according to the personnel of New York's Oscar Wilde Memorial Bookshop, the nation's oldest, largest, and best-known gay bookstore.[3]

Cities selected for study were Boston, New York, Chicago, San Francisco, and Los Angeles. They were chosen because the available literature makes reference to areas in these cities housing large numbers of homosexuals and their institutions.

Maps were constructed by plotting the location of the directory listings on city street maps. The street maps used contain street indexes and are labeled by neighborhood and house number. The plotting was done city by city, by locating with the street index and the house numbers the position of every directory listing on each map. This procedure placed each listing on its appropriate block. The institutional listings such as bars, restaurants, and steam baths are indicated by solid black dots. The cruising areas are represented by solid black lines. The street maps were then simplified and reduced into spot maps.

The spot maps (see maps) indicate a definite distribution pattern of gay gathering places in these cities.[4] They show that large numbers of these places are concentrated in small areas, usually in the inner city, and that none or very few are found in other city areas. Owing to the social construction of community, there is no precise way of determining the names and boundaries of these areas of concentration

(Suttles 1972). Therefore, I decided to ask this of several informants, in some cases sociologists, who had lived or were currently living in each of these cities. From the information they gave me, the names that appear on the legends of the maps were attached to the areas of institutional concentration, and two measures of the extent of concentration, based on the boundaries of the concentrated areas, were developed.[5]

The first concentration measure represents the proportion of gay institutions and cruising places within the concentrated areas compared to the total number of such places in each city. This measure was calculated by totaling the number of gay institutions and cruising places in the concentration areas and then calculating the percentage this sum is of the total number of such locations for a particular city. The second measure represents the ratio of the total sum of the land mass of each concentrated area to the total land mass of each city. This ratio was calculated by (1) turning each concentrated area into a rectangular form by connecting the outermost gay places; (2) figuring the area of each rectangle; (3) summing all these areas; and (4) computing the percentage of each city's total land mass represented by this sum.

I found, using these measures of concentration, that in Boston, 83 per cent of the gay locations are situated on less than 2 per cent of the city's total land mass. Similarly, in New York, 86 per cent of gay locations are situated in less than 2 per cent of this city's total land mass; in Chicago, 64 per cent in less than 1 per cent; in San Francisco, 64 per cent in less than 1 per cent; and in Los Angeles, 78 per cent in less than 3 per cent. The spot maps thus clearly demonstrate that gay institutions and cruising areas are not randomly distributed but in each case are concentrated in specific city districts.

Areas of concentration revealed by these maps also tend to vary as to what kinds of establishments are housed within them. The majority of these districts are comprised mainly of restaurants, cruising areas, and bars. A few, however, shelter places that cater to a specialized interest within the gay community. Gay-oriented movie theaters and bookstores and bars or street corners frequented by male prostitutes tend to concentrate only in one of these districts, usually in the downtown public entertainment districts, e.g., Times Square or the Tenderloin. Bars catering to Western or sado-masochistic gays also are centralized in a particular district, usually an industrial warehouse area, e.g. Folsom Street.

The maps demonstrate the existence of gay institutional concentration in areas of each city. This is one indicator that there may indeed be gay ghettos.

PARK'S AND WIRTH'S OTHER REQUISITES: CULTURE AREA, SOCIAL ISOLATION, RESIDENTIAL CONCENTRATION

To determine the extent to which the twenty-seven districts on the spot maps fulfill Park's and Wirth's other criteria for a ghetto, I conducted exploratory research, which entailed informal fieldwork and a literature survey. Fieldwork was carried out in New York and to

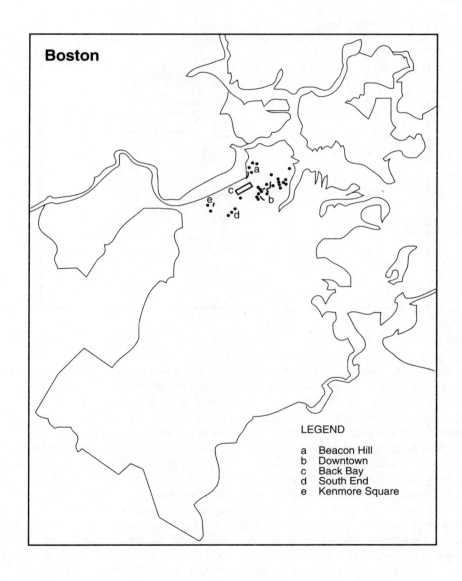

LEGEND

a   Beacon Hill
b   Downtown
c   Back Bay
d   South End
e   Kenmore Square

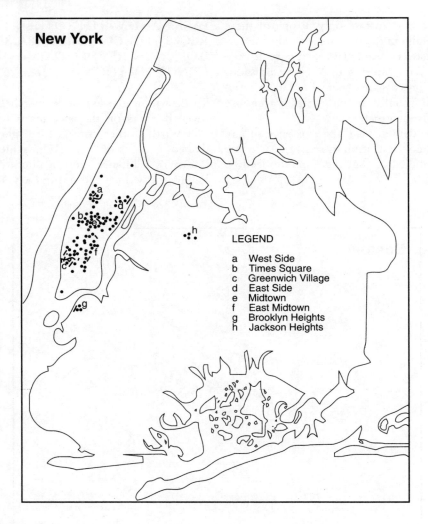

New York

LEGEND

a   West Side
b   Times Square
c   Greenwich Village
d   East Side
e   Midtown
f   East Midtown
g   Brooklyn Heights
h   Jackson Heights

a lesser degree in Boston, Chicago, San Francisco, and Los Angeles. The fieldwork was conducted in each of the neighborhoods indicated in the five cities' spot maps as housing a large number of gay locations. It included informal and formal interviews as well as observations made in the course of lengthy walks. Walks were oriented toward discovering the social characteristics of these areas by noting the types of institutions, land use, and populations within each community. The interviews were conducted with gay residents of each city. In interviews, questions were asked concerning the residence of the interviewee and his gay friends and the character of the interviewee's social network. Observations were conducted on main thoroughfares, from a place where I could both see and hear street activity, usually a street corner or in front of the popular bars, as well as in restaurants and stores.

The survey of the literature included both the professional literature and a national publication of the gay community, *The Advocate*. The professional literature search was confined mainly to literature on homosexuality and produced material that was generally impressionistic. *The Advocate* was utilized because it is widely recognized as a leading gay publication (Humphreys 1972a: 133; Warren 1974: 178). A scan of issues dated from September 1975 to

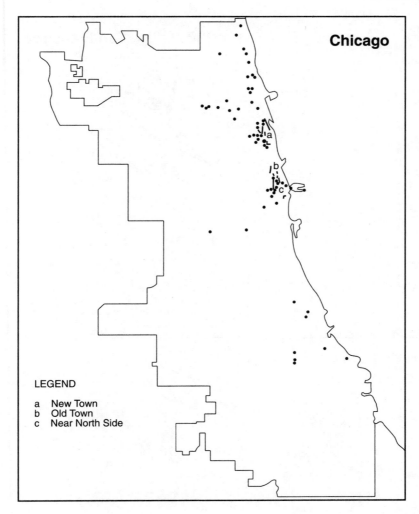

June 1977 uncovered articles on the gay community in each of the five cities under consideration, all written by local correspondents.[6] The results of this research are presented below, broken down in terms of Wirth's other requisites of the ghetto – culture area, social isolation, and residential concentration.

Culture area

The culture of these districts was partially determined in the course of the fieldwork and literature search. The method used to ascertain this has been employed by many other sociologists (Park 1925: 6; Zorbaugh 1929: 4). This technique determines the culture of an area by examining the cultural traits that appear within it. A neighborhood's culture, according to this method, is that of a group whose cultural traits are most prevalent in the area.

The results of this research indicate that only certain sections – those sheltering places of the local gay scene – of seven of these districts are homosexual culture areas. The districts in which these sections occur are the West Side, Greenwich Village, New Town, Polk Street, Folsom Street, Castro Village, and West Hollywood. The boundaries of the homosexual cultural areas within these districts are ambiguous

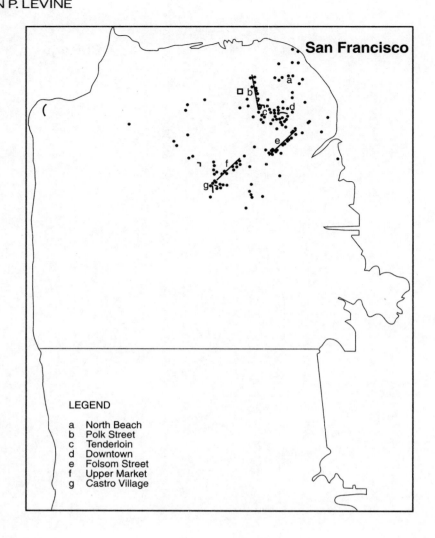

San Francisco

LEGEND

a   North Beach
b   Polk Street
c   Tenderloin
d   Downtown
e   Folsom Street
f   Upper Market
g   Castro Village

because of the social construction of community (Suttles 1972). Generally, these sections consist of the streets housing a cluster of gay locations and the blocks proximate to them. For example, on New York's West Side, the homosexual culture area is comprised on the blocks surrounding the concentration of gay places between Broadway and Central Park in the low West Seventies. Similarly, in Greenwich Village, the homosexual culture area consists of the blocks encircling the cluster of gay establishments in the vicinity of the West Village's Christopher Street; in New Town, the intersection of Broadway and Clark Street; in Polk Street, Polk between Eddy and Broadway; in

Folsom Street, Folsom between 4th and 12th Streets; in Castro Village, the intersection of Castro and 18th Streets; and in West Hollywood, Santa Monica Boulevard between Doheny Drive and La Cienega Boulevard.

These homosexual culture areas are typified by an extraordinarily high concentration of gays and their culture traits. This concentration is so extensive that the scene on many of the major commercial streets in these areas seems predominantly gay. Large numbers of gay men are present on the street, while women and children are conspicuously absent. Streets are lined with bars, bookstores, restaurants, and clothing stores catering to homosexuals, and many stores are

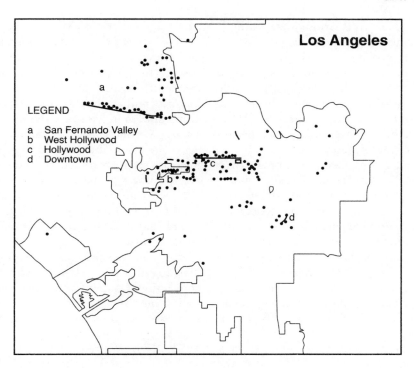

gay-owned (Shilts 1977; Thompson 1976).

The most prevalent culture traits in these sections are those of the homosexual community. Gay language is widely used in these places.[7] For example, I frequently overheard conversations between gay men in which they referred to each other or other men with female names and pronouns. Many billboards, posters, and store signs also utilize this argot. Two oversized billboards towering over the intersection of Christopher Street and 7th Avenue South advertise a homosexual steam bath (Weinberg and Williams 1975) by showing a drawing of the head of the cowboy and the message, "Come! to Man's Country." The billboards use knowledge common to gay men, the sexual implications of the word "come," and the Western motif (Humphreys 1972b) to imply that sex with desirable partners is available at the steam bath. There are also bars called Boot Hill, Numbers, Chaps, and stores called Boys' Market and Spike Liquors.

Gay fashion is a ubiquitous element of homosexual culture in these sections. The vast majority of men on the streets are dressed in the fashion currently favored by gays. This style, called "butch" in homosexual argot, includes four major looks: working man, lower-class tough, military man and athlete (St. Clair 1976). To illustrate, one variant of the lower-class tough look entails a tight black T-shirt, faded, skin-tight, straight-legged Levis, work boots, and a black leather motorcycle jacket. All of these looks call for short hair, muscular bodies, mustaches, closely cropped beards, and such accessories as key chains and handkerchiefs. These looks are so prevalent on these blocks that for a minute one gets the distinct impression of being in a union hall, army camp, or locker room. A few men in these areas wear the attire of sado-masochists – complete black leather outfits. Gay fashion is also sold in many of the local retail establishments, several specializing in it.[8]

Many social conventions within these areas are distinctly homosexual. Gestures of affection are exchanged openly between men, as well as eye contact and other gestures of sexual interest. For example, two men are frequently seen walking with their arms around each other's waists or holding hands. These open displays of affection rarely evoke sanctions; for the most part, people either accept or ignore them. Even police patrols through these sections pay little attention to such behavior. In light of the societal aversion to homosexuality, this tolerance is remarkable. In other places, such behavior quickly elicits harsh sanctions.

The scene in the homosexual culture areas shifts with the time of day. On weekday mornings and afternoons, bars and streets are relatively quiet. At night and on weekends, however, streets and bars are crowded, because participation in the gay world, for most homosexuals, occurs after normal working hours (Achilles 1967; Hooker 1967; Warren 1974). At such times the areas are flooded with resident gays, as well as gays from surrounding neighborhoods and suburbs who come in to participate in the scene.

Gays recognize the culture areas as their quarters. These sentiments are reflected in the special names they give each area, names that are part of gay argot. For example, the homosexual culture area in West Hollywood is called Boy's Town (Stone 1977). They are also reflected in the following statements made by gay residents of these areas (field notes): "I feel like an alien in other places. But in the Castro, I feel like I belong because I do." "For me, leaving the Village means pulling myself together and straightening up my act."

Social isolation

The literature on homosexuality reveals that most homosexuals are socially isolated (Gagnon 1977: 244; Hooker 1967; Humphreys, 1972a: 13–41; Leznoff and Westley 1967; Warren 1974; Weinberg and Williams 1974: 18–30). Americans, strongly prejudiced against homosexuality, perceive it as a loathsome deviation (Levitt and Klassen 1974; Weinberg and Williams 1974: 19–21). This societal antipathy creates an "intolerable reality" for gays, a reality in which homosexuals are confronted with a host of stringent sanctions (Humphreys 1972a: 13). Gays are discrimi-

nated against in employment and often fired upon discovery of their sexual orientation; they are criminals under various laws and thus subject to police surveillance; and they are frequently treated by those with whom they interact with ridicule, condemnation, ostracism, and even violence (Humphreys 1972a: 13–41; Weinberg and Williams 1974: 17–30). This prejudice and accompanying sanctions make it extremely difficult for homosexuals and heterosexuals to be socially and emotionally involved with each other. Gays, whether their condition is known or hidden, are always aware that most heterosexuals regard them as socially unacceptable. As a reaction to this, many homosexuals have withdrawn from meaningful social relations with members of conventional society and have restricted their social life and primary relations to other homosexuals (Hooker 1967: 180–1; Leznoff and Westley 1967: 193–5; Saghir and Robins 1973: 170; Warren 1974). Thus, gays are socially isolated from the larger society.

My research indicates that this is the case for many of the homosexuals I encountered. Some of my informants told me that their interaction with heterosexuals was restricted to their jobs or sporadic family visits. Aside from this, social relations were confined mainly to other homosexuals. Their friends and acquaintances were usually gay residents of the district in which they lived. Roommates, if they had them, were also homosexuals. A few informants told me they had even less contact with the heterosexual world. These individuals managed to live within an almost exclusively gay world by limiting their social relations to fellow homosexuals and working in either stereotypical gay jobs or businesses catering to gays. The extent of some gay men's social isolation is underscored in the following remarks (field notes):

The people at work are real friendly, always asking me out for drinks or inviting me to parties. I never go. It's too much of a hassle. They don't know I am gay, so I avoid seeing them outside of work. I'd much rather spend my free time with other gay men, hanging out on Polk Street.

I live on the West Side with two gay men, work in a gay restaurant, and spend my summers on Fire Island. I never relate to straight people.

Residential concentration

Normally, the determination of residential segregation patterns is a relatively simple affair. Data are collected, usually from the census, on the addresses of all the members of the group under consideration. The residential location of the group is then ascertained by analyzing data through one of three possible methods: spot maps, social area analysis, and factorial ecology (Timms 1971). These procedures cannot be used for homosexuals because the data upon which they are based are lacking, namely, the addresses of all homosexuals. The census does not supply such information because it fails to ask questions about sexual orientation. Other potential sources of homosexual addresses (e.g., police files, psychiatrists' records, homophile organizations) are inadequate because they are patently misrepresentative of gays (Kitsuse and Cicourel 1963: 9; Weinberg 1970). My inability to approach this problem with traditional measures prompted utilization of informal fieldwork and literature search.

The information obtained from the research indicates that only certain of these districts house significant numbers of homosexuals. In *The Advocate* articles of gay life in the cities under consideration, references are made to the large gay populations in a few of these districts. The article on Boston, for example, asserts that large numbers of homosexuals live in Beacon Hill, Back Bay, and South End (Brill 1976). Similarly, articles on New York imply that substantial numbers of gays reside on the East Side, West Side, Greenwich Village, and Brooklyn Heights (Kantrowitz 1975: 48; Russo 1975; Stoneman 1975; Whitmore 1975); on Chicago, Near North Side, Old Town, New Town (Aiken 1976); on San Francisco, Castro Valley (Shilts 1977: 21); and on Los Angeles, West Hollywood (Stone 1977).

Several sociologists concur with these observations (Bell and Weinberg 1978: 233–5, Newton 1972: 22; Starr and Carns 1973: 282). In addition Weinberg and Williams (1974: 46, 60) find similar concentrations in New York's East Midtown and Jackson Heights, and on San Francisco's Polk Street. Similar results were found in the fieldwork. The overwhelming majority of my informants stated that they and most of their friends lived in these neighborhoods.

Greenwich Village's subarea the West Village, Castro Village, and the Boy's Town area of West Hollywood seem to have the largest concentrations of homosexual residents. In fact, judging from the available material, the latter two areas may even be predominantly homosexual (Shilts 1977; Stone 1977). The gay concentration in all these areas is so extensive that entire blocks and buildings are inhabited exclusively by gays, many of whom own the buildings in which they live (Shilts: 21; Stone 1977)[9] "Almost everyone in the West Village Houses [a large housing development in Greenwich Village's homosexual culture area] is gay, my neighbors across the hall, upstairs, downstairs." [Field notes].

CONCLUSION

This paper examined the validity of "gay ghetto" as a sociological concept. I have argued that its validity is contingent upon the existence of urban homosexual communities that meet Park's and Wirth's requisites for a ghetto.

Three communities in the cities studied, the West Village, Castro Village, and Boy's Town, fulfill all these requisites. All communities are characterized by large numbers of gay institutions and cruising places, a marked gay culture, socially isolated gay residents, and a substantially gay population. The West Village, Castro Village, and Boy's Town are thus gay ghettos. Their existence, in turn, validates "gay ghetto" as a sociological construct.

Twelve communities are partially developed gay ghettos. These communities partly satisfy the ghetto requisites. Three of them (West Side, New Town, Polk Street) house a concentration of gay locations, a homosexual culture area, and socially isolated gay residents. Their lack of a markedly gay population prevents them from being fully developed ghettos. Nine of the communities (Beacon Hill, Back Bay, South End, East Side, Brooklyn Heights, East Midtown, Jackson Heights, Old Town, Near North

Side) are marked by large numbers of gay institutions and socially isolated residents. These communities are not fully developed gay ghettos because they lack a salient homosexual culture area and a substantially gay populace. The remaining twelve spot map districts are probably not ghettos because they meet only one requisite – institutional concentration.

When considered together, it is possible that these communities represent different stages in ghetto development. Societal antipathy toward homosexuality sets the stage for their formation. Conditions of total suppression and zealous persecution inhibit ghetto development, but with a modicum of tolerance, the process begins. At first gay institutions and cruising places spring up in urban districts known to accept variant behavior, resulting in a concentration of such places in specific sections of the city, as shown on the spot maps. This concentration attracts large numbers of homosexuals, causing a centralization of gay culture traits, turning the districts into homosexual culture areas. Tolerance coupled with institutional concentration make the areas desirable residential districts for gays. Many homosexuals, especially those publicly labeled as gay or open about their orientation, settle in these areas. At this point, the areas have become partially developed gay ghettos.

Recent modifications of social attitudes toward homosexuals explain the transformation of the West Village, Castro Village, and Boy's Town into fully developed gay ghettos. A growing acceptance of homosexuality in the more liberal parts of the country signifies that gays can now practice an openly gay lifestyle without fear of penalization. Once out of the closet, gays may be drawn to the partially developed ghettos, to be near others like them and the places of gay life, increasing the number of gay residents in such districts. In cities like New York, San Francisco, and Los Angeles, with large gay populations, this increase coupled with a possible "heterosexual flight" (withdrawal from the community) may turn the areas into markedly gay neighborhoods, that is, fully developed gay ghettos.

This discussion of the development of gay ghettos is speculative. The actual process by which gay ghettos evolve can only be ascertained through longitudinal research of fully developed ghettos. Further research is thus needed on the West Village, Castro Village, and Boy's Town.

NOTES

1   The color lavender has been traditionally used to symbolize homosexuality.
2   "Western" denotes, in gay argot, that patrons dress in Western attire: chaps, cowboy hats, leather vests (Warren 1974: 20).
3   This opinion is shared by Weinberg and Williams (1974: 41n, 58n). Warren (1974: 19) is of the opinion that all the directories are out of date. Harry (1974: 241) formed a different guide, the *Guild Guide*, to be the most current and up to date.
4   The map of New York City omits Staten Island because the directory contains no listings there.
5   Other authors have noted similar concentrations in these areas. Newton (1972: 22) observed institutional concentrations in the same areas shown by the spot maps of New York and Chicago. Weinberg and Williams (1974: 41–6, 56–61) cite as areas housing large numbers of gay locations the districts shown on the spot maps of New York and San Francisco. Although Hooker (1967) and Warren (1974: 20) do not specify areas in which institutional concentration occurs, they state that this happens in the cities they studied.
6   I was informed of this in a conversation with Mr. Joe Richards, director of public information at *The Advocate*, on June 7, 1977.
7   Warren's (1974: 100–21) conceptualization of gay language is used in this paper. She sees it as the linguistic aspect of the gay world, including vocabulary, ideology, mythology, and a symbolic universe.
8   In these culture areas are found stores specializing in leather clothes, work clothes, Western outfits or military gear. West Hollywood's Intermountain Logging Company is an example of a store that caters to the Western look; Greenwich Village's The Leather Man, the sadomasochist look.
9   I noted this in my fieldwork in Castro Village. My informants and Roy Tacker, owner of Paul Langley Real Estate, a major real estate agency in the area, concurred with this observation. Hooker (1967: 172) and Warren (1974: 20) also discovered predominantly gay blocks but they fail to specify their location.

REFERENCES

Achilles, Nancy, "The Development of the Homosexual Bar as an Institution," in John H. Gagnon and William Simon (eds), *Sexual Deviance* (New York: Harper & Row, 1967).

Aiken, David, "Chicago," *The Advocate* 198 (September 8, 1976): 27–8.

Altman, Dennis, *Homosexual Oppression and Liberation* (New York: Avon Books, 1971).

Bell, Alan P. and Martin S. Weinberg, *Homosexualities: A Study of Diversity Among Men and Women* (New York: Simon & Schuster, 1978).

Brill, David. "Boston," *The Advocate* 184 (February 25, 1976): 27.

Butler, Edgar W., *The Urban Crisis: Problems and Prospects in America* (Santa Monica, Cal.: Goodyear Publishing Company, 1977).

Chicago Gay Liberation, "Working Paper for the Revolutionary Peoples Constitutional Convention," Gay Flames Pamphlet no. 13 (New York: Gay Flames, 1970).

Fischer, Claude S., *The Urban Experience* (New York: Harcourt Brace Jovanovich, 1976).

Gagnon, John H., *Human Sexualities* (Oakland, N.J.: Scott, Foresman, 1977).

Harry, Joseph, "Urbanization and the Gay Life," *The Journal of Sex Research* 10 (August 1974): 238–47.

Hooker, Evelyn, "The Homosexual Community," in John H. Gagnon and William Simon (eds), *Sexual Deviance* (New York: Harper & Row, 1967).

Humphreys, Laud, *Out of the Closets: The Sociology of Homosexual Liberation* (Englewood Cliffs, N.J.: Prentice-Hall, 1972a).

—— "New Styles in Homosexual Manliness," in Joseph A. McCaffrey (ed.), *The Homosexual Dialectic* (Englewood Cliffs, N.J.: Prentice-Hall, 1972).

Kantrowitz, Arnie, "I'll Take New York," *The Advocate* 175 (October 22, 1975): 48–51.

Kerner Commission, *Report of the National Advisory Commission on Civil Disorders* (New York: Bantam Books, 1968).

Kitsuse, John I. and Aaron V. Cicourel, "A Note on the Use of Official Statistics," *Social Problems* 11 (Fall 1963): 131–9.

Levitt, Eugene E. and Albert D. Klassen, Jr. "Public Attitudes Toward Homosexuality: part of the 1970 National Survey by the Institute for Sex Research," *Journal of Homosexuality* 1 (Fall 1974): 29–43.

Leznoff, Maurice, and William A. Westley. "The Homosexual Community," in John H. Gagnon and William Simon, (eds), *Sexual Deviance* (New York: Harper & Row, 1967).

Michelson, William, *Man and His Urban Environment: A Sociological Approach* (Reading, Mass.: Addison-Wesley, 1970).

Nassberg, Guy, "An Introduction to Gay Liberation," in *Revolutionary Love*, Gay Flames Pamphlet no. 11 (New York: Gay Flames, 1970).

Newton, Esther, *Mother Camp: Female Impersonators in America*, (Englewood Cliffs, N.J.: Prentice-Hall, 1972).

Park, Robert E., "The City: Suggestions for the Investigation of Human Behavior in the Urban Environment," in Robert E. Park and Ernest W. Burgess, *The City*, (Chicago: University of Chicago Press, 1925).

——"Foreword," in Louis Wirth, *The Ghetto* (Chicago: University of Chicago Press, 1928).

Russo, Vito, "The Village," *The Advocate* 175 (October 22, 1975): 47.

Saghir, Marcel T., and Eli Robins, *Male and Female Homosexuality: A Comprehensive Investigation* (Baltimore: Williams & Wilkins, 1973).

Starr, Joyce R., and Donald E. Carns, "Singles and the City: Notes on Urban Adaptation," in John Walton and Donald E. Carns, (eds), *Cities in Change: Studies on the Urban Condition* (Boston: Allyn & Bacon, 1973).

St Clair, Scott, "Fashion's New Game: Follow the Gay Leader," *The Advocate* 186 (March 26, 1976): 18–19.

Shilts, Randy M. 'Mecca or Ghetto? Castro Street," *The Advocate* 209 (February 9, 1977): 20–3.

Stone, Christopher, "West Hollywood. Where the Boys Are," *The Advocate* 214 (April 20, 1977): 23–4.

Stoneman, Donnell, "East Side," *The Advocate* 175 (October 22, 1975): 44–5.

Suttles, Gerald D., *The Social Construction of Communities* (Chicago: University of Chicago Press, 1972).

Theodorson, George A. and Achilles G. Theodorson, *A Modern Dictionary of Sociology* (New York: Thomas Y. Crowell, 1969).

Thompson, Mark, "Small Business Owners Experiencing a Natural Progression of Liberated Consciousness," *The Advocate* 192 (June 16, 1976): 12–13.

Timms, Duncan, *The Urban Mosaic: Towards a Theory of Residential Differentiation* (New York: Cambridge University Press, 1971).

Warren, Carol A. B., *Identity and Community in the Gay World*, (New York: Wiley, 1974).

Weinberg, Martin S. "Homosexual Samples: Differences and Similarities," *The Journal of Sex Research* 6 (November 1970): 312–25.

Weinberg, Martin S. and Colin J. Williams, *Male Homosexuals: Their Problems and Adaptations* (New York: Oxford University Press, 1974).

—— "Gay Baths and the Social Organization of Impersonal Sex," *Social Problems* 23 (December 1975): 124–36.

Whitmore, George, "West Side," *The Advocate* 175

(October 22, 1975): 44–5.

Wittman, Carl, "Refugees from Amerika: A Gay Manifesto," in Joseph A. McCaffrey, (ed.), *The Homosexual Dialectic* (Englewood Cliffs, NJ: Prentice-Hall, 1972).

Wirth, Louis, *The Ghetto* (Chicago: University of Chicago Press, 1928).

Zorbaugh, Harvey Warren, *The Gold Coast and the Slum* (Chicago: University of Chicago Press, 1929).

STEPHEN O. MURRAY

"The Institutional Elaboration of a Quasi-ethnic Community"

from *International Review of Modern Sociology*
9 (July 1979): 165–77

Several scholars have claimed it is not meaningful to speak of a "gay community" (Simon and Gagnon 1967; Sweet 1968; Stanley 1970, 1974; Sagarin in various fulminations). However, insofar as "community" is a technical term in the social sciences and insofar as there can be said to be "communities" in North American cities,[1] there are "gay communites."

Like other basic terms in social sciences, *community* is used in a variety of ways. There is no consensus about what many of the basic terms mean. Thus, the *uses* of elementary concepts become topics for systematic scrutiny and critical rethinking – e.g. culture (Kroeber and Kluckhohn 1952), norm (Gibbs 1962), role (Goodenough 1965), social control (Gibbs 1972), power (Lukes 1974; Murray 1978). In a content analysis of definitions of community in sociological literature Sutton and Munson (1976) extracted 125 definitions from 395 works published since an earlier collation of community definitions (Hillery 1959), and reduced those definitions to eighteen basic types. Such convergence as there was in the use of the term was to declare "community" an "entity." Sixty-one per cent of the definitions could be so classified, but this super-class included definitions of community as "social system," "a social group," "a population or set of people" or "a territory." Of these, "social system" was the most common, but "social system" is not more empirically applicable than the term supposedly specified. If anything, the criteria for deciding what is or is not a "social system" are less clear than those advanced for "community," and, unsurprisingly, there were eleven different components of "comunity as a social system" in recent sociological literature.

Given this dissensus about the term, there are no clear-cut criteria with which to decide whether there is a "community." Here, how closely the gay community in one city fits the various conceptualizations advanced will be considered by a contrast to ethnic communities in the same city. Since there are more institutionally elaborated and distinct ethnic communities in Toronto than in most other North American cities, this is a fairly stringent test.

The formal analysis which follows is based on participant observation in the social, cultural and political life of gay[2] Toronto, residence in two of the city's ethnic neighborhoods, retrospective interviews of persons long involved with several Toronto communities and scrutiny of such fugitive materials as membership rolls of gay organizations and listings of gay facilities.

COMMUNITY AS AN ENTITY

Territory

The first, commonsense component of "community" is territory. The mythical "traditional" rural village is supposed to have been geographically distinct. However, except for those communities with formidable geological barriers, rural villages throughout the world have some persons who are oriented to larger entities. This is true even in the rugged mountains of Chiapas (Vogt 1972). In general, rural villages are not completely isolated from each other, because demands for taxes, soldiers and labor are levied from outside. In the North American prairies, villages are exogamous to a large extent, and in "Kansas and Nebraska, where there are no physical barriers to communication, neighboring relations tend to trace out a vast network without any clear boundaries" (Suttles 1972: 28). Geographical distinctness must be supplemented by endogamy, restriction of trade, local cults and other such *social* creations in order to make communities of geographical aggregates. Isolation and propinquity do not automatically produce solidarity, or even interaction, as myriad studies of Mexican peasants show (e.g. Selby 1974). On the other hand, seemingly trivial commonalities such as living in red units rather than white units in a housing project inhabited entirely by blacks may serve as a basis for differentiation (Suttles 1972). Thus, geographical barriers must be reinforced by social ones (Decamp 1961). Territory itself must be socially constituted, and boundaries are never absolute. There are no walled-in ghettos in North American cities, nor are there government-run checkpoints to impede the flow of persons. One can travel from predominantly Italian territory to predominantly gay territory to predominantly Greek territory without physical obstruction.

Although there are no hermetically sealed, separate territories, there are, nevertheless, areas recognized as predominantly West Indian, Croatian, Greek, Italian, Portuguese, Chinese, Jewish, or gay in Toronto. Residents of the city can tell an investigator where most of these communities are – at least where the centers are, for boundaries are hazy and vary on different cognitive maps of the city. In general, human perception is organized in terms of "fuzzy sets": "colors and probably most reference classes are not proper sets at all, not sets in which membership is an all-or-none matter" (Brown 1976: 135). Perceptions of neighborhoods similarly fade away from a clear center, especially since no area is ethnically totally distinct. Even the Jewish ghetto within the Pale was not (Wirth 1928: 3), nor were the "defended neighborhoods" in the city on which the ecological approach to urban communities was based. Park claimed, "Our great cities turn out, upon examination, to be a mosaic of segregated peoples" (1928: vii), but

> Very few of the defended neighborhoods in Chicago which Park, Burgess and their followers described seem to have been exclusively or almost exclusively occupied by a single ethnic group. Moreover, many of the defended neighborhoods reported by Park and Burgess retained their identities and their boundaries despite continuous shifts in ethnic composition.
>
> (Suttles 1972: 27)

While areas are perceived as "Chinatown" or "Little Italy," none is homogeneous. However, certain facilities are frequented exclusively by persons of one ethnic derivation. Intruders are made to feel they "don't belong" in the pool halls and bars, clubs and apartment buildings of various groups (cf. Cavan 1963; Lee 1978b on techniques used to make outsiders feel out of place). Urban territories are most distinct nocturnally, when there is more choice in where one goes.

In Toronto, most recognizable communities have recreational centers in a single area. While many participants live nearby, others do not. The social center of gay Toronto is the Yonge/Wellesley area. Almost all of the gay facilities and gay organizations of the city are within walking distance of that corner, and there is a residential concentration in that area. Some indication of this is provided by mapping where members of Toronto homophile organizations live. These men constitute a biased sample of the total and unknown population engaging in homosexual activities, but they form an acceptable sample of the part of that larger population who identify themselves as gay and who participate in the gay community. As can be seen in Table 16.1 and Figure 16.1, members of the gay organizations tend to reside in the borough of Toronto, and, within Toronto, in two neighborhoods. More than half these active participants in the gay community live in less than 2 per cent of the total land mass of Metropolitan Toronto. Such a pattern of unifocal recreational territory and less than random residential dispersion holds for Toronto ethnic communities and for the "gay ghettos" of five US cities studied by Levine (1977).

Of course, many gay Torontonians who consider themselves part of its gay community live outside the self-proclaimed ghetto, and many persons who are not gay live within it. The

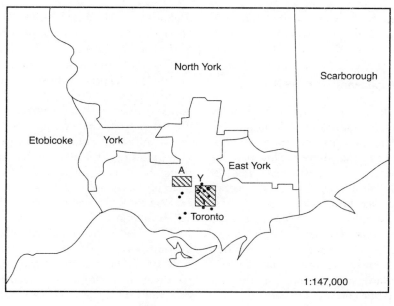

KEY

•	Gay facilities (organizations, bars, discos)
▨	Residential concentrations
A	Annex (Bathurst to Avenue Road, Bloor to Dupont)
Y	Yonge Street (Bay to Parliament, Bloor to Dundas)

Figure 16.1 Scatter of Toronto homophile organizations and members

Table 16.1 Residential concentration (%) of members of two Toronto Homophile organizations

Area	CHAT[1] members resident	GAY[2] members resident
East York	1	1
Etobicoke	1	0
North York	11	5
Scarborough	3	1
Toronto: Yonge/Wellesley[3]	33	31
Toronto: Annex[4]	17	27
Toronto: Other	33	35
York	1	0
Total	100 (109)	100 (78)

Notes

1 Community Homophile Association of Toronto (a moderate, service-oriented organization), membership data mapped in 1976 by John Firth.
2 Gay Academic Union (a liberationist organization promoting gay studies), membership data mapped in 1978 by author.
3 Area bounded by Bay and Parliament, Bloor and Dundas.
4 Area bounded by Bathurst and Avenue Road, Bloor and Dupont, plus Palmerston Boulevard between Bloor and College.

Toronto gay community has a territorial base. It is more than territory, but it has and holds territory.

Institutional completeness

The existence of distinctive facilities is more salient to the identification of a community – both for insiders and for others – than is residential segregation. Here again, the gay community deserves the appelation as much as other Toronto communities. Those gay meccas, New York and San Francisco, may be more institutionally complete, but within the last decade a fairly complete set of basic social services and facilities has developed. In addition to the profitable and venerable facilities of the sexual marketplace such as bars, baths and discos, other facilities oriented to a gay clientele have emerged. These include bookstores, churches, travel agencies, hair-styling shops, realtors, doctors, lawyers, clinics, stores, periodicals, tours, a lumber yard specializing in do-it-yourself rennovations, plus religious and political groups. Practically the only institution missing is a gay bank. This lack is a function of the centralization of banking in Canada. There are branches of the great national banks that have predominantly gay clients and are served by gay bankers, just as there are branches catering to particular ethnic groups elsewhere in the city. Many of the facilities catering to gay persons are located in the vicinity of Yonge and Wellesley.

In introducing the conception "institutional completeness" to distinguish the degree of community development, Breton (1964) stated that it "would be at its extreme whenever the ethnic community could perform all the services required by its members. Members would *never have to* make use of native institutions for the satisfaction of any of their needs" (emphasis added). He added, "In contemporary North American cities very few, if any, ethnic communities showing full institutional completeness can be found" (1964: 194).

The Toronto gay community includes all three types of institutions Breton used to construct an index of institutional completeness – religious organization, periodicals and welfare

organizations – and would be classified as "high" in institutional completeness by his criteria. The importance of institutional completeness is that the existence of a full range of institutions makes it possible to concentrate social relations within the group. Breton suggested the degree of in-group sociation could be predicted from the extent of formal organizations, and in his study of "gay ghettos" Levine (1977) found in the cities with many gay institutions there were numbers of gay men whose meaningful social relations were more or less exclusively with other gay men (cf. also Warren 1974; Covelli 1976).

The near-institutional completeness in the Toronto gay community is remarkable in that *none* of the factors stimulating the elaboration of distinct institutions presented by Breton operates.[3] These were (1) group distinctiveness, separate language in particular; (2) low level of resources commanded by the group members; and (3) systematic (chain) migration. Immigrants often need services rendered in their native language, but all gays speak languages served by existing institutions. Furthermore, most gay persons can "pass" and need not be confined to interacting with their "own kind." Second, affluent strata of the population engaged in homosexual activity patronize distinctively gay facilities. Third, gay immigration to urban centers is the result of discrete decisions by individuals, rather than the group response Breton saw as facilitating institutional elaboration of ethnic communities. Despite the irrelevance of these factors, gay Torontonians developed a panoply of gay institutions. Residents of high-rise complexes in the heart of the city can live entirely in a gay world, consulting "The Gay Yellow Pages" as new needs arise.

Collective action and solidarity

Like class-consciousness or ethnic consciousness, gay consciousness is not an automatic correlate of an objective characteristic. Homosexual behavior need not be the basis for a gay identity (Weinberg 1978),[4] just as Italian derivation does not spontaneously produce an Italian self-identity. From the pool of persons with such an attribute, there are some who do not consider themselves to be defined by it in any way and others who deny the existence of the attribute. Among those who do consider themselves x (gay or Italian, etc.) are some who do not have any commitment to a group defined by sharing attribute x, and some who do not interact with other x persons. Even those who do have the feeling of being x and part of a group may still not join in collective action. Collective action is rarely – if ever – characteristic of any broadly defined population.

Communities are *potential bases* for collective action in the same way "objective class position" was seen by Marx and Weber to be a potential basis for class consciousness and class action. Actual participation is characteristic of only a minority of any class, ethnic group, or community. Surely, if measures were available, intra-group variance would be much greater than inter-group variance. Collective action by a community is sporadic at best, regardless of what kind of community is considered. Unified action by rural communities is also rare, even during "peasant revolution" (Wolf 1969). Particularly during the 1970s, the Toronto gay population began to assert itself politically. It is one of the most politically active Toronto communities at present.

Temporal aspects

Despite the lack of primary socialization into gay communities, distinctive gay areas, institutions, lifestyles, terms and folklore have existed for decades in urban centers. Recovering a proud past is typically important in the formation of a group identity, as the most superficial examination of the emergence of nation states reveals. In recent years efforts to learn about the history of subordinated groups have gained momentum (Genovese 1974; Haley 1976; Howe 1976; Adam 1978). The quest for forerunner heroes – what one informant called "the Jonathan to Gide syndrome" – has been supplemented by serious historical research on the everyday life of oppression and on suppressed gay history including incidents of rebellion (Katz 1976; Steakley 1975; gay journals). Historical narratives have always served as a

rationale by emerging peoples for the independence they seek (Murray 1979b).

In addition to symbolic affirmation of links with famed and oppressed homosexuals of the past, members of the contemporary gay community have their own personal histories of engagement with the gay community. Participation in the community varies in intensity and duration, and there are clear generational differences in self-identification, public openness, and use of particular facilities (Lee 1978a, 1978b). Thus, there is a continuity with the past and ongoing social change.

Shared values and norms

Within the gay community there are norms of appropriate speech and behavior (Murray 1979a; Lee 1978a, 1978b). These are *learned*. Not everyone who considers himself gay knows them (Stanley 1970) and there are violations (reportable as such).

In all communities there is intra-group variation in values. Even nuclear families contain diversity without denying that families exist (Suttles 1972: 35).

Primary groups

For some gay persons the primary group consists of other gay persons. Levine (1977) reported

> Most of my informants in these areas told me that their interactions with heterosexuals were restricted to their jobs or sporadic visits with their families. Aside from these, they stated that their social relations were confined mainly to other homosexuals. Their friends and acquaintances were usually gay residents of the district in which they lived.

Homophily is characteristic of friendship generally, and studies of friendship networks have shown a strong tendency for persons who are homosexual to be homosocial as well (Sonenschein 1968).

In ethnic communities, kinship is frequently the basis for group loyalty and the central constituent of an ethnic "we." This is a resource not available to gay communities, since very few members of the gay community have been raised by gay parents. The gay community, like occupational communities, is based on secondary socialization and membership in it is an achieved characteristic. The gay community is more consciously created than other communities claiming a basis in shared "blood."[5]

Manages conflict

The final, very functionalist identifying characteristic of "community as a social system" is one that "manages conflict." There are several ways to apply this, including the following: (1) there are normative patterns of dealing with competition for resources (Lee 1978b); (2) aggression is turned back on other group members so that it does not challenge the overall society and the structures of repression (Adam 1978; Murray 1979a); (3) gay reference groups bring about compliance (Sweet 1968); (4) community leaders bring murderers to the law (as in the Emile Jacques case).

COMMUNITY AS A PROCESS

Having reviewed the components of the usual view of a community as an entity/social system, we have seen that only in terms of a familistic orientation is there a difference between the urban gay community and urban ethnic communities. For most practitioners of what Mullins (1973) labeled "standard American sociology" (structural functionalism and the original Chicago School) community was an entity. For some of the other groups within sociology Mullins discussed – symbolic interactionists, ethnomethodologists and structuralists – community is a creation or process. Consciousness of kind (analogously to class consciousness) is fundamental in this view, and "is not an automatic product of an abstract 'homogeneity' nor of 'common territory,' but comes from a sense of participating in the same history ... Communities might almost be defined as people *who see themselves* as having

a common history and destiny different from others" (Gusfield 1975: 32, 35; emphasis added). Consciousness of kind is an emergent quality, not at all innate. Collective identity may crystallize in the gaze of others (Shibutani and Kwan 1965), although it seems there is often a concerted effort to "divide and conquer" and to blame the victim on an individual basis. But dominant groups also ignore the diversity within stigmatized groups (Adam 1978; Genovese 1974). Gross categories may not be experienced as meaningful by those to whom they are applied so that a Cantonese is Chinese (Glick 1942) or a Sicilian is Italian only in the eyes of others. But such perception by others can have real consequences for life chances.

Suttles (1972: 50) argued that communities "come into existence with the aid of adversaries and advocates." Anita Bryant and John Briggs pushed homosexual men to become publicly gay and galvanized Miami and California gay communities into collective action to unprecedented degrees. Police raids caused the Stonewall riot of 1969 in New York and gay barricades in the Montréal gay territory in 1977. The gay liberation movement grew out of the former and the latter led almost directly to Québec including sexual orientation in its human rights code. In such well-publicized instances and on a smaller scale in organizing self-protection patrols and gay political groups, gay men have fought for their territories and their rights. "It is in their 'foreign relations' that communities come into existence," Suttles (1972: 13) suggested, and only in the past decade have there been gay Torontonians willing to undertake foreign policy in the public glare.

There is, then, a sense in which it is unfair to fault earlier writers for denying the existence of a gay community, because only in the 1970s has a community with a panoply of institutions, collective action, and a willingness to fight back developed. There were organizations devoted to improving the treatment of homosexuals and combating the stigmas (Sweet 1968; Wolf 1979), but collective action requires a willingness to affirm gayness in public that was lacking before (Lee 1978a). Rather than deny they are homosexual, gay liberationist men and lesbians of the "post-Stonewall generation" deny the validity of the "queer" stigma by their personal example. So long as there were only friendship networks of homosexually inclined men or women and systems of delivering sex, it was possible to argue there was not a "community." Since a more complete social system has emerged, however, there remains no rational basis for invidious distinctions between gay communities and other kinds of urban communities. Institutions, group consciousness and collective action have developed and membership in the gay community has become a salient identification for many.

In the usual complicated dialectic of self-affirmation of groupness and the perception of a group by others, a realization has come that emergent communities are potential lucrative markets: a profit can be made from groups in seach of an identity and of a heritage. When repression gives way to repressive tolerance, minority groups become special markets and have commodities symbolizing group membership tailored for them – yet another way in which a "people" and a group identity are produced by the definition of others.[6]

There are close, primary, enduring relationships within the gay community, structured exchange relations, some co-operation and some conflict – all of the modes of "social relations" Sutton and Munson (1976) found in community definitions. The Toronto gay community fits the criteria for community as an entity at least as well as Toronto ethnic communities. Since much of the elaboration of gay institutions, collective action, challenge to stigma and claim to gay identity has occurred during the 1970s, "gay community" is emerging over time rather than being a fixed entity.

Because there is "no well-defined and widely shared model of the local urban community ... so compelling that it can be applied authoritatively" (Suttles 1972: 45), to assess whether it is meaningful to speak of a "gay community" required consideration of a range of extant conceptualizations. By all offered, "community" is applicable to gays. While some may be driven by the conceptual dissensus to abandon the term "community," so long as it is retained, there is no basis to argue that "gay community" is not an appropriate locution.

NOTES

1   A rigid and absolute dichotomy between traditional, rural *gemeinschaften* and modern, urban *gesellschaften* held considerable sway in American sociology as an explanation of social change. What were ideal types for Tonnies frequently reified simple-minded theories of modernization or enlisted in romantic visions of a mythic golden age or quest for communion in contrast to which all existing social relationships are devalued. Schmalenbach's distinction between community (*gemeinschaft*) and communion (*bund*) is crucial in cutting through confusion. Beyond that, case studies have shown *gesellschaft* characteristics in rural areas and *gemeinschaft* characteristics in cities of capitalist states. On the applicability of the term "community" to urban settings, cf. Suttes (1972).

2   At the time of the fieldwork (1975–7) lesbian separatism was at a height and lesbian participation in organizations or socialization with gay men infrequent. The attacks of Bryant, Briggs, and Toronto police fostered greater co-operation and perception of common oppression than had existed. The description here refers to gay males. Lesbian institutions were developing and geographically dispersed, so the components of community of territory and institutional completeness were debatable (but see Wolf (1979) on San Francisco lesbian community).

3   Breton (1964) presented institutional completeness as a negative indicator of synchronic assimilation to the majority community. One of the sociologically most interesting features of gay communities is that assimilation decreases with the passage of time after migration (cf. Murray 1979b).

4   A parallel examination of the concept *identity* would reveal a similar ideological double standard when it is applied to gay people. Identity is regarded as a social process usually, but somehow requires an innate biological basis to be applied to "gay identity."

5   The folk belief that homosexuality is a biologically determined datum is widespread, so the contrast should not be exaggerated, especially since blood ties must be mobilized and are not automatic sources of community.

6   Individual coming out does not seem to be connected to having been labeled (Dank 1971; Lee 1978a). Openly gay men are invariably aware of the negative stereotypes held about gay men and are often combating such stereotypes by their public example. The importance of labels of groups, and the theory of individual "secondary deviance" as a response to being labeled are separate problems, and emphasis on the former should not be read as a "labeling theory" explanation of individuals.

REFERENCES

Adam, Barry D. (1978),*The Survival of Domination* (New York: Elsevier).

Breton, Raymond (1964), "Institutional Completeness of Ethnic Communities," *American Journal of Sociology* 70: 195–205.

Brown, Roger (1976), "Reference," *Cognition* 4: 125–33.

Cavan, Sherri (1963), "Interaction in Home Territories," *Berkeley Journal of Sociology* 7: 17–32.

Covelli, Lucille H. (1976), "Gay Friendship Networks," MS.

Dank, Barry (1971), "Coming out in the Gay World," *Psychiatry* 34: 188–97.

Decamp, David (1961), "Social and Geographical Factors in Jamaican Dialects," in R. Le Page (ed.), *Proceedings of the Conference on Creole Language Studies*: 61–84 (London: Macmillan).

Genovese, Eugene D. (1974), *Roll, Jordan, Roll* (New York: Pantheon).

Gibbs, Jack P. (1962), "Norms," *American Journal of Sociology* 70: 56–74.

—— (1972), "Social Control," *Warner Module* 1.

Glick, Clarence (1942), "The Relation between Position and Status in the Assimilation of the Chinese in Hawaii," *American Journal of Sociology* 47: 667–79.

Goodenough, Ward H (1965), "Rethinking 'Status' and 'Role,'" in Banton (ed.), *The Relevance of Models for Social Anthropology*, pp. 1–14 (London: Tavistock).

Gusfield, Joseph R. (1975), *Community* (Oxford: Blackwell).

Haley, Alex (1976), *Roots* (New York: Dell).

Hillery, George A. Jr (1959), "A Critique of Selected Community Concepts," *Social Forces* 37: 237–42.

Howe, Irving (1976), *World of Our Fathers* (New York: Simon and Schuster).

Katz, Jonathan (ed.) (1976), *Gay American History* (New York: Crowell).

Kroeber, Alfred L. and Clyde Kluckhohn (1952), *Culture* (Cambridge, MA: Harvard).

Lee, John Alan (1978a) "Going Public," *Journal of Homosexuality* 3: 47–78.

—— (1978b) *Getting Sex* (Toronto: General).

Levine, Martin P. (1977), "Gay Ghetto," paper presented at the American Sociological Association meetings, Chicago.

Lukes, Steven (1974), *Power* (Toronto: Macmillan).

Mullins, Nicholas C. (1973), *Theories and Theory Groups in American Sociology* (New York: Harper & Row).

Murray, Stephen O. (1978), "The Second Face of Power in Micro-perspective," MS.

—— (1979a), "Stigma Transformation and the Emergence of Quasi-ethnic Communities," paper presented at the Canadian Sociology and Anthropology Association meetings, Saskatoon, Saskatchewan.

—— (1979b), "The Art of Gay Insulting," *Anthropological Linguistics* 21: 211–22.

Park, Robert E. (1928), "Introduction," in Louis Wirth, *The Ghetto*, pp. vii–x.

Selby, Henry (1974), *Zapotec Deviance* (Austin: University of Texas Press).

Shibutani, Tomatsu and Kian Kwan (1965), *Ethnic Stratification* (New York: Macmillan).

Simon, William and John H. Gagnon (1967), "Homosexuality," *Journal of Health and Social Behavior* 8: 177–85.

Sonenschein, David (1968), "The Ethnography of Male Homosexual Relationships," *Journal of Sex Research* 4: 69–83.

Stanley, Julia P. (1970), "Homosexual Slang," *American Speech* 45: 45–59.

—— (1974), "Gay Slang/Gay Culture," paper presented at the American Anthropological Association Meetings, Mexico, D.F.

Steakley, James (1975), *The Homosexual Emancipation Movement in Germany* (New York: Arno).

Suttles, Gerald D. (1972), *The Social Construction of Communities* (Chicago: University of Chicago).

Sutton, Willis A. and Thomas Munson (1976), "Definitions of Communities: 1954–73," paper presented at the American Sociological Association meetings, New York.

Sweet, Roxanne Thayer (1968), *Political and Social Action in Homophile Organizations*. Doctor of Criminology dissertation. University of California (reproduced in 1976: New York: Arno).

Vogt, Evon (1972), *Zinacantan* (Cambridge, MA: Harvard).

Warren, Carol A. B. (1974), *Identity and Community in the Gay World*, (New York: Wiley).

Weinberg, Thomas S. (1978), "On 'Doing' and 'Being' Gay," *Journal of Homosexuality* 4: 143–56.

Wirth, Louis (1928), *The Ghetto* (Chicago: University of Chicago).

Wolf, Deborah Goleman (1979), *Lesbian Community* (Berkeley: University of California).

Wolf, Eric (1969), *Peasant Revolutions of the Twentieth Century* (New York: Harper & Row).

SUSAN KRIEGER

"An Identity Community"

from *The Mirror Dance* (Philadelpia: Temple University Press, 1983): chapter 2

She saw several different lesbian communities in town, said Ruth, though she understood what people meant when they said "the community." It was definitely the most out, the most woman-identified. It was a group of women who were almost exclusively lesbians, who had been out or around for just about as long as she had been here, which was about five years, or longer than that. These were women who were the lesbian community almost because it was important to them and because they found a sense of being, belonging, fellowship, and sharing that way.

By and large, they had known each other for a number of years, many of them, or at least the nucleus; they were people who had chosen to remain here. They were mostly older than student age, professionals, people who had life ties here, and if they were students, they were graduate students. That was basically the core of the group that was meant as the lesbian community. As a claim to being "the community" they probably had it, she thought, because they named themselves in such a way and wanted it.

They were a real tight-closed group, felt Norah, a group that was closed until they knew for sure that you were a lesbian for one thing. And she didn't think that you could just go meet them, go hang out with them. She thought you had to join them, which happened if you knew somebody.

They were basically a social network, felt Irene. The common denominator was people who defined themselves as lesbians. The community was a social entity that had its own rules, its own membership, its own qualifications. It was primarily devoted to itself rather than a proselytizing organization (like a church

or Rape Crisis). It had functions: it gave its members a group identity: it gave them support for their life style and a sense of security and affirmation: for some people who didn't have a strong identity other than the fact of their lesbianism, it was crucial. It was also exclusive. The membership qualifications were pretty narrowly defined: a woman had to be either sexually involved with another woman, or planned to be, or had a good strong history of having been.

But more than that was that the most important thing in 85 per cent of the cases was a person's affectional life, or the way a person dealt with her relationship with other people. It focused, the community focused, Irene felt, on how somebody was in relation to somebody else. It had a lot to do with the other and how the individual developed herself in an abstract sense: how she developed in terms of ideas she had about herself in relation to others.

The community consisted, said Valerie, of a loose federation of support groups and the women's service organizations that were linked to these groups (the Women's Shelter, The Rape Crisis Center, the Women's Information Network), plus activity groups like the choir and the sports teams and the newsletter. Then there were women who were not in any of these groups but who related to people who were as friends or lovers and participated in community events: the coffeehouse, the parties, the Seder, the May Day, and Sapphic Plains Collective events like the square dance. And then there were the Arts Festival Collective people.

It didn't seem to be just any women in the larger community who happened to be lesbian, Bronwyn believed. It was a particular group of women who were lesbians and a few who were not, a group of women whose lives touched, who came in contact socially and emotionally.

It was basically women who chose to relate to other women sexually, felt Madeleine, who generally were in relationships with other women, although some were not. But it was the idea of community as opposed to single women relating sexually. There was a whole culure, a camaraderie, a support system, a network, shared understanding, shared vision. Then within that there were strong friendships and people who met each other in cluster arrangements.

They were, felt Lillian – the group that she had observed – many of them were "Ain't it awful." Everybody kept dumping on them. She saw many sick people. It was like you gained your support and identity by putting youself in a bunch of people who were equally oppressed. She had chosen not to actively identify with them.

It was women who identified as lesbians and feminists so that they had a consciousness of wanting to be part of a community, felt Carol. She thought there had to be an idea of wanting a community for it to exist. Then that was built on by the shared activities, the newsletter, the coffeehouses. She wasn't sure, but she thought there were maybe fifty to a hundred people in it on different levels: a core group and those who were more peripheral.

Right now the lesbian community for her, said Jill, was the potential for being what she would call home.

She came to it six years ago through the Women's Shelter support group, recalled Gayle. That was how the so-called elite group in the community got started. The people in that group all met each other through working on forming the Women's Shelter. Being thirty years old before you met another lesbian, that was where she was then. Going to the Women's Shelter and meeting all these lesbians and finding people saying all these daring radical statements, she just felt her whole life had come together. It was Melissa and Elinor. They were the core of it for her. The daring radical statements ranged from Elinor sitting on the kitchen table doing self-examination, to daring

to say the word "lesbian" out loud, to doing a demonstration in support of a woman who didn't wear a bra. It was like she had spent her whole life looking for this one little living room of people arguing.

She was around then too, recalled Ruby, and for her the community was people who identified themselves as lesbians or women-identified women. They came to events of a social nature, maybe sponsored by one of the support groups, some kind of activity that was larger than just friends, and they had some commitment to helping women in a social service sense; so they worked at the Women's Shelter, or babysat for a lesbian mother, or wrote about women. They also usually would talk about the community and not be terribly uncomfortable about not being able to define it.

The community itself, she felt, was changing all the time. It already had gone through several stages. There was a time when it hadn't been as solidified as now, so going outside it wasn't an issue. But now there was much more available. You had all these choices: there was a party every weekend at least, you could have musical activity, you could have sports activity, you could dance at the bar, you could play pool at the bar, you could have religious services, you could carry out your politics with your friends, you could have your job with your friends, you could make love with your friends, you could die with them, everything.

Most of the women she saw were 20 to 35; they had some education beyond high school, were heavily academic for the most part, were middle class and real interested, probably, in exploring the relationship between who they were and the roles they had been playing. That was the larger community in which there were, she would say, about fifty.

Within it there were smaller communities: women who had agency bonds like Rape Crisis or the Women's Shelter; women who had the bond of planning to spend their lives here, who were trying to organize a community in part so it would be there when they were old for survival reasons. Then there was another group that was made up of people who were going to school and wanted to identify with a lesbian community while they were in school, but they were transients. There were also a lot of people who just dropped in and out, like they only came to choir and you never saw them anywhere else. Or they only came to Chip and Jessica's parties. They probably didn't have enough bonds to enough people or groups to make it worth their while to come more often.

These women were the majority community in terms of race, felt Edwina, although their numbers were small. They were predominantly white women; they were growing in ideas and size, so they were a very hungry-minded group of women, a very strong group of women.

They were an anti-intellectual group, said Hollis, very hedonistic, self-interested in that sense of being self-maintaining, very inward-looking. If she wasn't one of them, she didn't think she would find their community admirable. If she didn't need these people socially, she would not have had anything to do with them. What was the community exactly? It was everybody in town she knew, the ones she saw regularly, whose faces were in it. It rested on face-to-face knowledge of one another. She didn't see it as a community really. It was mainly a social network. She thought it was much more a reference group than a community.

Right now, said Nikki, the community she saw was a sexually identified group of women, but she wasn't comfortable with that as a base of much of anything really. It was all women in town who were able to identify a community and include themselves as members. That included some straight women and ruled out some lesbian women who couldn't identify a community, or who could and who didn't want to consider themselves members.

It was mostly very young women, nineteen to thirty, felt Vivian. There seemed to be a broad spectrum of interests. The women tended to be poor. They were much more affectionate, warm or affectionate, than the average acquaintance you might have. They were not necessarily more open or friendly, but they tended to be willing to express their feelings. She kept wishing that everybody in it would get to be about twenty years older, so then she would feel more part of it.

It was a group, said Martha, she had found a few years ago that she really wanted to be part

of for the first time in her life. She felt she could count on people here in ways she had never thought of before.

She felt, said Aurora, that this was a group of women who she could call on to have her needs met in whatever way: physical needs or psychological needs, basic needs like moving, a place to sleep if she was having trouble with her own space. It was people who were willing to be open around each other, sharing with each other, sharing feelings.

There were fifteen to twenty women in it, said Pat. These were the most active, the core. They represented no cross-section of anything really, which was a problem she had with the whole thing.

There were thirty to forty, she would guess, said Stephanie, an estimate which came from the fact that you usually didn't see more than thirty to forty of the women in one place at one time.

There were a hundred or more, thought Ellen, a number which came from the number of names on the newsletter mailing list. The list had about 140 names on it the last time she mailed it and about a third of them didn't have local addresses.

The number varied, said Maria, depending on how you defined it.

There were other lesbian groups in town, said Ruth, but defining them got tenuous because the farther away you got from this particular group that called itself "the community," the more reluctant women were to name themselves. There was, for example, the P.E. Department at the university. She could probably go through a list of names and tell you who they were, meaning the faculty, and it was funny because they were mostly closeted. Yet everybody knew who was living with who and probably why. "Everybody" was mainly people who were close enough: the P.E. students. They were a kind of community too. They were also fairly closety. There were more than just a few she knew among the students who'd had four or five sexual experiences with women who would nonetheless say they were not gay, who refused the title or the label or even the idea.

There were people in town like Emmy and Priss, felt Alison, who never even went to the bar. They just saw themselves and a couple of other people. They wouldn't be involved in the community. There were people like Nan and Cherry, said Cynthia. Nan drove a truck for UPS. Cherry was from a family of three daughters, two of whom were gay. They lived in a trailer a half-mile down the road. They had a different kind of relationship: a division of labor along traditional male–female lines. Nan worked days. Cherry went to school, high school, and took care of the house. Nan worked funny hours because she drove out in the country. They didn't have a university association or any tie to the community.

There was the trailer park circle, noted Connie, some lesbians who lived in trailers off I-28 north-west of town. There were about six couples out there. They kept mostly to themselves and didn't have to do with the community.

There were the people who lived in the Rose Street house behind where she did, said Norah. You'd see them at the bar. They had their own group. They had identified her with the community, she felt, so they didn't talk to her.

There was this women in Math, recalled Nell, who parked her car near where she, Nell, did at the university, but who never said anything about it. There was also a dean of something, an old dyke from way back who had short hair and walked tough. Then there were the two women out on McDermid Road who were in Public Health and in their late fifties. Vivian said that if you called them, they'd probably hang up on you. There were probably a lot of people like them who wouldn't have anything to do with the community, who just had six friends.

There were the women at the bar, said Earth, some of whom sometimes came to community events: but mostly they didn't. That was a whole different world. It was the second most visible lesbian community in town.

Then there were those, felt Edwina, who hadn't even come to awareness yet, who going to the bar would be terrifying for, who didn't even know it.

Generally speaking there were "the farm lesbians" who just came in on weekends, noted Judith, as different from "the bar crowd" who used to frequent Leo's all the time, who were just apart from "the intellectual lesbian community." And then there were "the jocks" who could be broken into those who did things with the community and those who had no relationship to it.

She had a lot of trouble, said Millicent, because there were all the lesbians in the area, and then there was a group of people who thought that there was a *community*. It seemed to her that these people perceived themselves as the be-all and end-all of lesbianism in the four-county area. In ways, they tried to define the lesbian population and make a lesbian feel either part of or not part of the community. These people defined what it was to be a really good lesbian or a really good dyke. For example: you needed to be articulate or aggressive (socially aggressive, party aggressive, like, "Hi, how are you, I have heard about you. Aren't you the one who . . .?"). You either needed to be a university or a community college person, or a real sincere and hardworking blue collar. If you were from one of the outlying towns, you had a black mark against you in the first place, because you were not likely to be a clever person. For herself, she had been all the way on the inside with them and now she was on the outside.

She was not in the particular group known as the community, said Norah, but she knew them and they knew her. How did she know they knew her? Because they said "Hi" to her on the street. She felt she was probably identified more as Kitty's lover (Kitty was one of them for a while) or Hollis's friend than as herself. But she said "Hi" to them too and she didn't know them. She mainly knew what she heard from Hollis and Kitty's conversations. From that, from all the gossip, she had decided that she didn't want to get involved with them. She didn't want to be part of an organization. She just didn't think there was any way she could be judged as an individual with that group.

She had gone to one of the Arts Festival concerts last year and looked around for people who had a similar age, education, and socio-economic level as herself, recalled Lillian, and she had seen a bunch of very overweight, very sloppy, and rather obnoxious people with whom she preferred not to be identified. Opal, her lover, had gone too and Opal thought there were some nice songs in there that talked about life in general, but if there was a line in them about men, it was totally negative, She had problems with that because she considered herself to be a humanist.

She did at times have a yearning to be part of the community, said Opal, but she felt, and she knew by the grapevine, that she would be rejected. She understood that she was seen as snobby. That was based on her occasional appearance at a social gathering where she didn't know anybody well enough to be part of a group so she sat and talked with a few friends and didn't appear for another year; and her involvements were with people who were closety. She was not seen putting up posters.

She had kept a distance from them, said Terry, because she feared an involvement would jeopardize her career and she felt that she simply didn't share that many interests with people in the community.

She hadn't joined, said Joan, because of feeling that she didn't need that kind of group. Also, she didn't buy the line that just being lesbian tied people together.

She came from a poor family, said Leslie. To break into a group that was on the upper level of classism, professionalism, and all that – which was how she saw this community – you needed basically to have confidence in yourself, and she was feeling sometimes, "Only a year of college." But then she thought she had the same skills as any of the others; she just didn't have the categories and the numbers. Finally, by being with these people, by associating with Gloria, she came to feel, "They don't have anything on me."

She first got involved through Aurora, said Roxanne, and she got the feeling that there were certain rules in this community: like you should be a vegetarian and not like red meat or pork and prefer shopping at the natural foods store. These were people who preferred whole wheat bread, wore Earth Shoes, drove small cars, and didn't use paper products. They believed mostly in triangles, like fidelity in a relationship was almost a negative value. Also you couldn't shave your legs. It was an anti-cigarette culture. You had to go canoeing. You had to know about the moon.

It was hard to capture because all that was implicit, felt Carol – the sense that this community did have these strong rules. Examples of the rules: there was a dress code. Levis had always been acceptable. No make-up. Hiking boots and track shoes, tee shirts and work shirts (or man's shirt kind of thing). Certainly the T-shirt was predominant. Overalls. That was your basic uniform. There were variations, like India blouses. But you had to make a conscious decision to do that, a conscious decision, for example, about what you were going to say when people said, "You're all dressed up tonight." But people did that, dressed up. People even wore dresses and skirts on occasion.

The community, felt Harriet, was made up of people who found solidarity and comfort in participating. She did think you had to consciously join it, but she didn't think there were any rules about being in it. It was basically an open association, except for the one requirement: that you had to be supportive of women who were trying to build healthy relationships with other women.

The community for her, said Jenny, was a place of belonging. At the same time she thought of it as very distant and hard-to-know. It was what she was supposedly part of, yet she didn't feel part of it.

BARRY D. ADAM

"Structural Foundations of the Gay World"

from *Comparative Studies in Society and History* 27:4
(October 1985): 658–71

In recent years, there has been a growing realization that the contemporary social organization of homosexuality into lesbian and gay worlds is a socially and historically unique development and that the traditional academic constructure of "the homosexual" has participated in this reifying process (Foucault 1978; Hocquenghem 1978; McIntosh 1981; Weeks 1981; Plummer 1981; Faderman 1981). This article seeks to contribute to this understanding by proposing a set of structural characteristics seen as preconditions to the existence of the gay world and by exploring theoretical leads, especially Marxist feminist initiatives, to make sense of these structures. The study of homosexuality has been so long dominated by psychiatry, biology, and theology that the usual tools of analysis provided by political economy (construed broadly) have not been employed to analyze it. This essay puts forward some structural linkages which set homosexuality within the contex of the larger histories of gender, family, and production.

I contend that the structural traits outlined below make the lesbian and gay worlds possible and, indeed, largely define the lesbian/gay manifestation of same-sex bonding apart from other social constructions of homosexuality.

- Homosexual relations are released from the strictures of the dominant, heterosexual kinship system.
- Exclusive homosexuality becomes possible for both partners.
- Sex-role definitions fade from interpersonal bonding.
- People discover each other and form large-scale social networks because of their homosexual interests and not only as a result of already existing social relationships.

- Homosexual bonds make up an "endogamous" and autonomous social formation with sufficient collective self-awareness to act as an historical force.

Historical and anthropological examples of socially recognized homosexual relationships show how different the modern form is. The evidence from precapitalist societies reveals little opportunity for divergence from kinship codes (Adam 1985); in age-graded systems prevalent in such diverse areas as Melanesia (Herdt 1984), Amazonia (Lévi-Strauss 1969: 446), central Africa (Evans-Pritchard 1970: 1430), Siwa ('Abd Allah 1917), and Ancient Greece (Dover 1978; Foucault 1984), kin rules order homosexual relations as directly as heterosexual ones, prescribing tabooed and preferred categories of sexual combination. Though exclusive homosexuality appears in certain circumstances, the general rule in age-graded systems is toward transitory (usually adolescent) exclusive homosexuality followed by adult hetero- or bisexuality. Homosexuality in the context of gender "crossing" or mixing is prevalent in anthropological studies from the Americans (see Callender and Kochems 1983: 443), Polynesia (Levy 1971), Indonesia (Geertz 1960: 291–8), and the Palco-Asiatic (Bogoras 1909: 449–55) regions. *Trans*genderist models typically assimilate same-sex sexuality into kinship codes through the social redesignation of the gender of one partner. Finally, both the intra- and transgenderist systems embed homosexuality within cultural complexes of existing family, gender, and sexual meanings, whereas the modern gay world has become sufficiently disarticulated from its antecedents to begin to generate some of its own cultural institutions.

KINSHIP

The social dynamics that shaped the modern conjugal family also reorganized bonding patterns among individuals of the same sex. Despite the Judeo-Christian inheritance, which regards homosexuality as the irretrievable Other and provides the elements from which medical and legal discourses evolved, same- and cross-sex mateship forms show similar origins and mutual influence. Of central importance is the transition to capitalism, which profoundly reorganized the significance of kinship and family, thereby opening new possibilities in personal bonding. It is in advanced capitalist societies and the major metropolises in the semiperipheries of the modern world system that gay/lesbian worlds have emerged, while rural, "folk," and precapitalist pockets have, to varying degrees, maintained radically different articulations of homosexual desire and relations.

First among the historical changes that allowed for the emergence of lesbian and gay worlds in modern capitalist societies was the expansion of the wage-labor sector that accompanied the rise of capitalism. When a kinship code allocates the new generation to productive land, there is little room for sexual or other subjective concerns to find independent expression; location within a lineage strongly influences chances of future economic well-being. With mobilization of labor in a free-market system, kinship can, to some degree, be made irrelevant in securing a livelihood.

Having said this, it must be noted that the gay and lesbian worlds of today are not simply "caused" outcomes of a supposed general breakdown of family relationships. Focus upon the structural antecedents of the gay world necessarily emphasizes the options that became available to and were seized by those already uncomfortable with institutionalized prescriptions for domestic life. For homosexually interested people, the issue is not one of family decline but of the development of other hidden and unintended possibilities that loosened the monopoly of traditional arrangements and make opting out of the system more viable.

Much of the current evidence (see Bray 1982: 43–51) suggests that homosexual relationships of the preindustrial period came about in households and local communities, emerging from already existing associations between master and servant or apprentice, as well as neighbors and friends. Public institutions such as monasteries, armies, and colleges seem also to have engendered limited homosexual networks. The expansion of the public realm through mobilization of labor in capitalist production, however, provided regular opportunities for previously unacquainted men to make contact and thus begin to constitute a gay world. A largely male public world of pubs, coffeehouses, public parks, and railway stations gained a new significance for urbanized workers (Steakley 1975: ch. 1). Here new friendships could arise and social networks develop. Despite attempts by the state to order and control these public places (attempts that continue today with increasingly sophisticated surveillance technology), they functioned as free zones where new social and political ideas could circulate (Ariès 1977) and new alliances be forged.

At least as early as the 1700s, reports from London (Bray 1982: 82) speak of about twenty gay coffeehouses, as well as plazas, parks, and latrines frequented by gay men. At that time, notes Randolph Trumbach (1977: 15), "the prosecuting activities of the Societies for the Reformation of Manners" turned up a gay world of wage laborers and small businessmen complete with its own gestural semiology and language (Taylor 1965: 142; Bullough 1976: 480). They maintained a precarious foothold subject to intermittent attacks by moral entrepreneurs (cf. Bray 1982: 87–97) throughout the eighteenth century.

A distinctive gay world originated at the moment when homosexuality became an organizing principle of social behavior under which homosexually interested men came in contact with each other because of their homosexuality and not simply as an outgrowth of existing social relations. Men with homosexual interests carved out semiclandestine places in the public realm – places that inevitably fell under the surveillance of the moral entrepreneurs and police.

GENDER: FEMALE

David Levine (1977: 28) points out that early capitalist relations penetrated the domestic sphere through a "putting-out" system wherein women (and often children) were paid a piece rate for goods produced at home from materials supplied centrally. While men were being transformed from peasants to agricultural wage laborers, women were being integrated into the monetary economy through domestic production for the market. This economic innovation brought about a lowering of the marriage age as the younger generation no longer had to wait to inherit land in order to support itself but came to reply upon a wage income. An immediate outcome of this change was a higher birth rate stimulated by the lower marriage age and by the prospect of the additional labor services that children could offer to the household (Levine 1977: 146; Fischer 1973; Braun 1966).

The prospective augmentation of women's economic power thus opened by capitalist production proved short-lived. By the mid-eighteenth century, production was becoming centralized in factories; cottage industry was declining into obsolescence. The fading of domestic production prompted women, like men, to accept wage labor in industry. As Joan Scott and Louise Tilly (1975) remark, women went out to take advantage of the new employment opportunities unhampered by Victorian ideas of womanhood, which appeared only later.

The entry of women into wage labor was detoured through state intervention. In Great Britain, the Factory Acts of 1847 and 1850 restricted the employment of women (and children) in industry, effectively returning women from the factory to the home (Curtis 1980: 127; McDonough and Harrison 1978: 35; Pearce and Roberts 1973: 55). The domestic sphere to which women now returned was outside the monetary economy and dependent upon the wages of husbands and fathers. In the words of Heidi Hartmann (1976: 152 and see 1981),

> women became more dependent on men economically ... English married women, who had supported themselves and their children, became the domestic servants of their husbands. Men increased their control over technology, production, and marketing, as they excluded women from industry, education, and political organization.

Women's work in the reproduction and maintenance of laborers became a socially necessary form of production for use, but not for exchange (Himmelweit and Mohun 1977: 15; Gardiner 1975: 47; Coulson, Magas, and Wainwright 1975: 62; Secombe 1973: 3).

A few very brave women took the extraordinarily difficult route of migrating to the other gender to avail themselves of men's opportunities, and, passing as men, some married women (Katz 1976: ch. 3). This is not to deny the vast network of female "romantic friendships" well described by Carroll Smith-Rosenberg (1975: 1), Nancy Sahli (1979: 17), Blanche Cook (1978: 718), Lillian Faderman (1981), and others, but only to point out the differences between the histories of the lesbian and male gay worlds. Lesbian and gay relationships (keeping in mind the structural criteria listed in the opening of this article) presuppose a degree of free choice which wage laborers could exercise but housewives could not, a distinction in relations of production which corresponds to the gender divide through much of the nineteenth century. Only when women began to trickle back into wage labor did a lesbian world begin to emerge, toward the end of the century.

An intriguing contrast is offered by reports about prewar silk workers in southern China (Yang 1953: 198; Smedley 1976: 103). Where women were able to enter wage labor on a massive scale, lesbian subcultures, as alternatives to traditional kin arrangements, became possible in China and elsewhere. When the kinship code did not provide for homosexual relationships, homosexuality arose in a new structural location with the changing mode of production. The opening of alternatives to kin relations for gaining access to the means of production permitted workers, in turn, to experiment with alternative domestic and sexual arrangements.

In a century which set the sexuality of men in opposition to the purity of women (Cott

1978: 219), lesbianism could scarcely exist. Where Victorian semiology located sexuality in the phallic signifier, intimacy between women had no place in sexual discourse. Unlike modern lesbianism, these romantic friendships were (1) almost always subordinate to the dominant heterosexual kinship system, (2) almost never realized as an exclusive or alternative relationship in place of marriage and family, and (3) therefore not the basis for a cultural or personal identity. In Faderman's (1981: 152) words,

> Because throughout much of the nineteenth century in Britain and America, sex was considered an activity in which virtuous women were not interested and did not indulge unless to gratify their husbands and to procreate, it was generally inconceivable to society that an otherwise respectable woman could choose to participate in a sexual activity that had as its goal neither procreation nor pleasing a husband.

The irony of this social mapping of intimacy which opposed male carnality to female purity is that same-sex bonds took on radically different meanings. Romantic friends could then participate in the Victorian women's movement which in England, the United States, and, to some degree, Germany, occupied itself with morality legislation, anti-prostitution campaigns, and temperance, along with right-to-work and right-to-vote issues. The English Labouchère Amendment, which recriminalized male homosexuality, was tacked onto an anti-prostitution bill, thereby ranging male homosexuality and female homosexuality (to project a more modern term back in time) on opposite ends of a moral spectrum. The logic of the Victorian era cannot be ignored: it is only because of the powerlessness of Victorian women that the patriarchal hegemony could afford to trivialize women's relationships and tolerate them as being not very serious. It is when women first began to achieve financial independence in wage labor that romantic friendship was able to divest itself of the constraints of marriage and heterosexuality (see Ferguson 1981: 11). And it is at this moment, when women threatened to escape male control, that lesbianism crystallized as a suppressed and reviled identity.

GENDER: MALE

The changing structural conditions that made lesbian and gay worlds increasingly possible also generated new forms of opposition. Much of the scholarly treatment of homophobia, in noting antihomosexual trends in both medieval and modern societies, has relied on "inertia" to explain the continuity of the resistance. But dependence on the element of tradition alone in explaining public campaigns against same-sex bonding fails to address how homophobia is reproduced in succeeding social systems.

While femininity was being reshaped in the image of the privatized family, masculinity was undergoing changes in the wage-labor economy. Men, more than women, were on the front line of the new production system and were forced to conform to its demands in order to secure employment. Karl Marx, in the *German Ideology* (Tucker 1978: 186), laments that competitiveness isolated workers from one another, thereby inhibiting class-consciousness – the labor market pitted man against man to exhibit a requisite personality type. Masculinity was reconstituted to reflect the machine, the motions of which the worker was required to adapt. The industrial system sought to discipline and regularize workers as steady, reliable, emotionless, hard, and instrumental. Even fashion reflected the revaluation of male purpose as the flamboyance of the aristocracy gave way to the "fastidious austerity" of the businessman and sober practicality of the male worker (see Ewen and Ewen 1982: 132).

Homosexuality as a manifestation of tenderness and a road to male bonding was cast, by the terms of the capitalist discourse, as a violation and failure, a betrayal of masculine virtues necessary for success. Any male temptation toward sexual polymorphism would be contained by the monogamous family. A dependent wife and children ensured that men would be "'good'" workers who would not risk unemployment and loss of wage through industrial rebellion (Horkheimer 1972: 120; Rapp 1978: 286). Corporate executives continue to believe that "'being a family man' is a clear sign of stability and maturity and is taken into account in promotion decisions" (Kanter 1977: 28). In this way, most men are innoculated against homosexual activity and convinced of its inutility. Male bonding is to be counteracted by competitiveness and mediated by the "team." Even the male gestural repertoire of affection needed to be dressed in the language of aggression: touching between males could occur legitimately only as mock punches, slaps, and jabs.

Yet the history of the gay world is an ironic realization of the Marxian critique of capitalism. "Male sex role ideology, which embodies the competitive egocentricity of the capitalist market system, militates against the homoerotic bond which threatens the atomizing methods of domination" (Adam 1978: 56). It is not accidental that psychiatrists who insist upon "curing" homosexuality prescribe rivalry and competition with "male figures" as the "solution" to homosexual relationships. At the same time, homosexual choice is consistent with the ascendant revaluation of mateship as being a reflection of personal desires and an aspiration for emotional fulfillment rather than a pragmatic productive relationship or union of lineages. With the rise of "voluntary" mateship and the increased currency of "romantic love" and "companionate marriage" as ideological constructs, same-sex ties could be made meaningful in similar terms. For those whose emotional lives were most caught up in same-sex relationships, the ascendance of such a discourse could provide a code for organizing homoerotic experience. Marx's analysis foresaw a new revolutionary solidarity which would overcome the alienation of worker from worker as they were thrown en masse into factory production. In this entirely unexpected way, the lesbian and gay worlds developed with the rise of industrial capitalism, providing solutions on an individual, personal level to worker atomization.

THE STATE

With its now more indirect relationship to production, the family became yet another social institution shaped and buoyed by the state which, in association with middle-class philanthropic societies, set out to enroll the masses in legally bound marriages (Donzelot 1979) in the eighteenth and ninetenth centuries. The English Marriage Act of 1753 instituted the state as guarantor of marriages and enforcer of its obligations (Weeks 1981: 24). Other professions joined medicine and law to define and administer family ideals and to discipline those who strayed from its confines.

Charles Rosenberg (1973: 35) remarks:

> Authorities of the 18th and early 19th centuries routinely indicted "sexual excess"; yet their injunctions have a calm, even bland tone.... Beginning with the 1830s, however, the ritualized prudence of their traditional admonitions became sharpened and applied far more frequently, while for some authors sexuality began to assume an absolutely negative tone ... only the need for propagating the species, some authors contended, could justify so dangerous an indulgence.

Work by Vern Bullough, Jonathan Katz (1983: pt. 2), Peter Conrad and Joseph Schneider (1980: ch. 7) documents the accumulating weight of medical opinion which first identified masturbation as a source of mental and physical degeneration and later assimilated homosexuality into the masturbation paradigm. By the late 1800s, a cascade of medical and professional writings had produced a veritable antimasturbation hysteria, a surveillance system directed at children, and a technology of sexual repression (Bullough 1976: 542; Demos and Demos 1969: 632; Neuman 1975: 2; Gilbert 1975: 220; Parsons 1977: 66). A series of increasingly restrictive anti-abortion laws was enacted throughout the United States, especially in the 1860s and 1870s in the midst of a campaign in which physicians played a central role (Mohr 1978).

Traditional antipathy to nonreproductive sexuality became reactivated in new, virulent forms in nineteenth-century England, the United States and, to a lesser degree, Germany. Similar trends were disrupted in France by the Franco-Prussian War and the German occupation of 1870–1 which resulted in the Paris Commune. In England, the freedom to distribute information on contraception succumbed to the purity crusades by the 1880s (Bristow 1977: 126). In 1889, the Indecent Advertisements Act suppressed advertisements for venereal disease remedies. In 1898 flogging was instituted as punishment for "Soliciting for immoral purposes," a penalty imposed primarily on persons making homosexual propositions (Bristow 1977: 204, 193).

The purity campaigns, stimulated by tales of white-slave traffic, succeeded in raising the age of consent, extended police surveillance over prostitutes, and recriminalized homosexuality (Weeks 1981: 106; Pearce and Roberts 1973; Judith Walkowitz (1980: 130, and see 1983) remarks: "Begun as a libertarian struggle against the state sanction of male vice, the repeal campaign helped to spawn a hydra-headed assault against sexual deviation of all kinds. The struggle against state regulation evolved into a movement that used the instruments of state for repressive purposes."

Several theorists have linked the Victorians' preoccupation with masturbation with the accumulative ideologies of the day. Anita Fellman and Michael Fellman (1981: 240) stress that semen, like capital, was seen as a resource to be hoarded for productive investment. Mark Poster (1978: 169) observes:

> Literary evidence points consistently to the view that sex was the model of impulsive, incautious action to the Victorian businessman. A gospel of thrift was applied to semen as well as to money. The act of sex, with its connotations of lust, rapture and uncontrolled passion, was the epitome of unbusinesslike behavior.

Whatever the links may have been between the interests of capitalists and the state proscription of nonreproductive sexuality, it is worth noting that pro-reproductivist campaigns proved functional for the expanding labor needs of nineteenth-century capitalism, especially in the face of declining fertility.

Just as the state stepped in to mold the modern family, it multiplied an institutional apparatus of hospitals disciplining the sick, the mad, and the immoral; prisons confining the recalcitrant; schools supervising the young; military training the masses; and factories controlling the workers. As Michael Foucault (1980: 41, and see 1979) remarks, a regime of supervision and control was established to protect the means of production while it was in workers' hands through a "formidable layer of moralisation deposited on the nineteenth-century population."

Early industrialists showed no reluctance in examining the "moral lives" of workers and did not hesitate to dismiss those who violated Victorian ideals of sexual propriety (see Baritz 1960: 33). In North America, a number of industrial towns were founded, built, and governed by a single capitalist family that enforced moral standards. Antonio Gramsci (1971: 297, 302, 304–5; see Poster 1978: 169) observes:

> The new industrialism wants monogamy: it wants the man as worker not to squander his nervous energies in the disorderly and stimulating pursuit of occasional sexual satisfaction ... The exaltation of passion cannot be reconciled with the timed movements of productive motions connected with the most perfected automatism.

Though the rise of capitalism opened new avenues for homosexual expression, it also laid the groundwork for the reorganization and rejuvenation of older doctrines proscribing it. As John Boswell (1980) points out, the consolidation of the Christian church around an antihomosexual dogma is a product of the twelfth to fourteenth centuries – the height of feudalism – an era that stands in marked contrast to the ancient recognition of homosexual relationships. The sexual repression of the nineteenth century, in turn, stands in contrast to the apparent sexual liberalism of twentieth-century state-regulated corporate capitalism (to use Jürgen Habermas's terms), a transition that merits further analysis.

THE NINETEENTH-CENTURY GAY WORLD

> The competitive labor market of the strengthening capitalist economic system created a negative common equality for all the dispossessed. The ground was laid for the idea of civil equality in a "public" sphere, weakening the moral divisions among people of the feudal period and "privatizing" religious, cultural, and erotic distinction.
> (Adams 1978: 28)

Wage labor challenged church values by asserting a new norm for personal worth: competence at one's job became the pre-eminent criterion for survival (an ideal invoked today by oppressed minorities who have yet to benefit fully from its logic). Religion, ethos, and sex, once integral components of the societal code, began to recede into personal preferences contained by the private sphere. Like kinship, religion declined as a determiner of life-chances, partially opening the public world to greater tolerance and variability.

Early capitalism contained and reworked religious tenets while nurturing the liberal, individualist ethic that was flourishing in the competitive marketplace. It should come as no surprise, then, that the French Revolution broke with medieval doctrine in decriminalizing homosexual relations at the same time as it liberated the Jews from ghettos and cleared the way for later battles of national independence among European peoples.

There can be no doubt that "by the mid-nineteenth century, ... the male homosexual subculture a least had characteristics not dissimilar to the modern, with recognized cruising places and homosexual haunts, ritualised sexual contact and a distinctive argot and 'style'" (Weeks 1977: 166). By this same period, the gay world had begun to produce its own intelligentsia (Adam 1979; Adam 1986), which articulated the idea of a homosexual identity, at first in terms of a third-sex theory (Kennedy 1981: 106). Karl Ulrich's formulation of a "third sex" of "feminine souls confined by masculine bodies" attracted not to each other but to "normal" men, shows the signs of its origins in heterosexist discourse. The theory now seems quaint and archaic. What is new in the third-sex thesis is the idea that homosexually interested men are a people with a distinct identity and culture. By the 1920s, Marcel Proust (1963: 286, 289) refers to gay men in *Remembrance of Things Past* as "a race accursed, persecuted like Israel, and finally, like Israel, under a mass opprobrium of undeserved abhorrence, taking on mass characteristics, the physiognomy of a nation." Gay men formed an "Oriental colony" in a diaspora from Sodom. In this early period of gay self-awareness molded by anti-homosexual environs (Adam 1978: ch. 2), there is a search for a new language and new names to consolidate the homosexual experience. The word *gay* achieved predominance only in the 1970s; at the turn of the century early writers experimented with such words as *Urning/Uranian*, *third sex* and *intermediate sex*, *homosexual/homogenic/homophile*, and *adhesive comrades*.

When physicians and jurists began to report on homosexuals in the late nineteenth century, they were observing a social formation that had been evolving for more than two centuries. Jeffrey Weeks (1981: 101) points out:

As late as 1871, concepts of homosexuality were extremely undeveloped both in the Metropolitan Police and in high medical and legal circles, suggesting the absence of any clear notion of a homosexual category or of any social awareness of what a homosexual identity might consist of.

Naive nineteenth-century observers were astounded by the complexity and completeness of the gay world. Lydston, writing in the United States in 1889, remarked:

There is in every community of any size a colony of male sexual perverts; they are usually known to each other, and are likely to congregate together. At times they operate in accordance with some definite and concerted plan in quest of subjects wherewith to gratify their abnormal sexual impulses.
(quoted in Burnham 1973: 41)

Francis Anthony, in a paper read before the Massachusetts Medical Society in 1898, stated:

I have been told – and I am informed that the fact is true of nearly every centre of importance – a band or urnings, men of perverted tendencies, men known to each other as such, bound by ties of secrecy and fear and held together by mutual attraction. This band ... embraces, not as you might think, the low and vile outcasts of the slums, but men of education and refinement, men gifted in music, in art and in literature, men of professional life and men of business and affairs.
(quoted in Katz 1983: 293)

The German Social Democrat W. Herzen (1977: 37) wrote in 1898:

The homosexuals of Berlin, Hamburg, London are certainly not less numerous than those of Paris or Brussels. There are places here where homosexuals hold their gatherings, baths they frequent, premises where they hold their dances, streets in which male prostitutes offer themselves to homosexuals. Homosexuals have their *Cafe National* in Berlin.

CONCLUSION

The modern gay and lesbian worlds, then, present a unique set of structural characteristics unparalleled by historical and anthropological examples of socially recognized and institutionalized forms of homosexuality. The very term *homosexuality* is, of course, problematic. A nineteenth-century innovation, it is part of the process of separation which reconstituted those having same-sex bonds as a people apart, and it paved the way for the modern encoding of intrasex intimacy as yet another "ethnic" group to be assigned a place in liberal, pluralist ideology. Far more common in precapitalist societies are kinship codes which articulate homosexuality *within* kin logic, either as age-defined, transitory, masculine relationships or as the relationships of a minority of gender-reassigned persons with gender-consistent persons. Exclusive homosexuality for both partners presumes a complex division of labor and most typically appears in gender-defined occupations such as the military or clergy. Though intergenerational and transgenderist homosexuality is by no means unknown in the modern gay world (though far less common than popularly imagined), they tend to continue as "little traditions" within the "big tradition" defined by the structural criteria presented at the beginning of this essay.

REFERENCES

'Abd Allah, Mahmud Mohammad (1917), "Siwan Customs," *Harvard African Studies* 1: 7.

Adam, Barry D. (1978), *The Survival of Domination: Inferiorization and Everyday Life* (New York: Elsevier/Greenwood).

——(1979), "A Social History of Gay Politics," in *Gay Men: The Sociology of Homosexuality*, ed. Martin P. Levine (New York: Harper and Row).

——(1985), "Age, Sex, and Structure," *Journal of Homosexuality* 11: 314.

——(1986), *The Rise of a Gay and Lesbian Movement*, Twayne Series on Social Movements (Boston: G. K. Hall).

Ariès, Philippe (1977), "The Family and the City," *Daedalus* 102:2: 227.

Baritz, Loren (1960), *The Servants of Power* (Middletown: Wesleyan University Press).

Bogoras, W. (1909), "The Chukchee," *Memoirs of the American Museum of Natural History* 11 (New York: American Museum of Natural History).

Boswell, John (1980), *Christianity, Social Tolerance, and Homosexuality* (Chicago: University of Chicago Press).

Braun, Rudolf (1966), "The Impact of Cottage Industry on an Agricultural Population," in *The Rise of Capitalism*, ed. David Landes (New York: Macmillan).

Bray, Alan (1982), *Homosexuality in Renaissance England* (London: Gay Men's Press).

Bristow, Edward (1977), *Vice and Vigilance* (Dublin: Gill and Macmillan).

Bullough, Vern (1976), *Sexual Variance in Society and History* (New York: Wiley).

Burnham, James (1973), "Early References to Homosexual Communities in American Medical Writings," *Medical Aspects of Human Sexuality*, 7:8: 34.

Callender, Charles and Kochems, Lee (1983), "The North American Berdache," *Current Anthropology* 23:4: 443.

Conrad, Peter and Schneider, Joseph (1980), *Deviance and Medicalization* (St. Louis, Missouri: Mosby).

Cook, Blanche (1978), "Women Alone Stir My Imagination," *Signs* 4:4: 718.

Cott, Nancy (1978), "Passionlessness," *Signs* 4:2: 219.

Coulson, Margaret, Magas, Branka and Wainwright, Hilary (1975), "The Housewife and Her Labour under Capitalism – A Critique," *New Left Review* 89: 59.

Curtis, Bruce (1980), "Capital, the State, and the Origins of the Working-Class Household," in *Hidden in the Household*, ed., Bonnie Fox, pp. 101–34 (Toronto: Women's Press).

Demos, John and Demos, Virginia (1969) "Adolescence in Historical Perspectives," *Journal of Marriage and the Family* 31:4: 632.

Donzelot, Jacques (1979) *The Policing of Families*, trans. Robert Hurley (New York: Pantheon).

Dover, K. J. (1978), *Greek Homosexuality* (New York: Vintage).

Evans-Pritchard, E. E. (1970), "Sexual Inversion among the Azande," *American Anthropologist* 72:6: 1430.

Ewen, Stuart and Ewen, Elizabeth (1982), *Channels of Desire* (New York: McGraw-Hill).

Faderman, Lillian (1981), *Surpassing the Love of Men* (New York: Morrow).

Fellman, Anita and Fellman, Michael (1981), "The Rule of Moderation in Late Nineteenth-Century American Sexual Ideology," *Journal of Sex Research* 17:3: 238.

Ferguson, Ann (1981), "Pariarchy, Sexual Identity, and the Sexual Revolution," *Signs* 7:1: 11.

Fischer, Wolfram (1973), "Rural Industrialization and Population Change," *Comparative Studies in Society and History* 15:2: 158.

Foucault, Michel (1978), *The History of Sexuality* (New York: Pantheon).

——(1979), *Discipline and Punish* (New York: Vintage).

——(1980) *Power/Knowledge* (New York: Pantheon).

——(1984), *L'usage des plaisirs* (Paris: Gaillimard).

Gardiner, Jean (1975), "Women's Domestic Labour," *New Left Review*, 89: 47.

Geertz, Clifford (1960), *The Religion of Java* (New York: Free Press of Glencoe).

Gilbert, Arthur (1975), "Doctor, Patient, and Onanist Diseases in the Nineteenth Century," *Journal of the History of Medicine and Allied Sciences* 30:3: 217.

Gramsci, Antonio (1971), *The Prison Notebooks of Antonio Gramsci* (New York: International).

Hartmann, Heidi (1976), "Capitalism, Patriarchy, and Job Segregation by Sex," *Signs* 3:2: 137.

——(1981), "The Family as the Locus of Gender, Class and Political Struggle," *Signs* 6:3: 366.

Herdt, Gilbert (1984), *Ritualized Homosexuality in Melanesia* (Berkeley: University of California Press).

Herzen, W. (1977) "Antithetical Sexual Sentiment and Section 175 of the Imperial Penal Law, 1898," in *Bernstein on Homosexuality*, trans. Angela Clifford (Belfast: Athol Books).

Himmelweit, Susan and Mohun, Simon (1977), "Domestic Labour and Capital," *Cambridge Journal of Economics* 1:1: 15.

Hocquenghem, Guy (1978), *Homosexual Desire* (London: Allison and Busby).

Horkheimer, Max (1972), *Critical Theory* (New York: Seabury).

Kanter, Rosabeth (1977), *Men and Women of the Corporation* (New York: Basic Books).

Katz, Jonathan (1976), "Passing Women," in *Gay American History* (New York: Crowell).

——(1983), *The Gay/Lesbian Almanac* (New York: Morrow).

Kennedy, Hubert (1981), "The 'Third Sex' Theory of Karl Heinrich Ulrich," *Journal of Homosexuality* 6 (Winter): 103.

Levine, David (1977), *Family Formation in an Age of Nascent Capitalism* (New York: Academic Press).

Lévi-Strauss, Claude (1969), *The Elementary Structures of Kinship* (Boston: Beacon).

Levy, Robert (1971), "The Community Function of Tahitian Male Transvestitism," *Anthropological Quarterly* 44:1: 12.

McDonough, Roisin and Harrison, Rachel (1978), "Patriarchy and Relations of Production," in *Feminism and Materialism*, eds. Annette Kuhn and AnnMarie Wolpe, pp. 11–41 (London: Routledge and Kegan Paul).

McIntosh, Mary (1981), "The Homosexual Role," in *The Making of the Modern Homosexual*, ed. Kenneth Plummer, pp. 30–43 (Totowa, New Jersey: Barnes and Noble).

Mohr, James (1978), *Abortion in America* (New York: Oxford University Press).

Neuman, R. P. (1975) "Masturbation, Madness, and the Modern Concepts of Childhood and Adolescence," *Journal of Social History* 8 (spring): 1.

Parsons, Gail (1977), "Equal Treatment for All," *Journal of the History of Medicine and Allied Sciences*, 32:1: 55.

Pearce, Frank and Roberts, Andrew (1973), "The Social Regulation of Sexual Behaviour and the Development of Industrial Capitalism in Britain," in *Contemporary Social Problems in Britain*, eds Roy Bailey and Jock Young (Westmead: Saxon House).

Plummer, Kenneth (ed.) (1981), *The Making of the Modern Homosexual* (Totowa, New Jersey: Barnes and Noble).

Poster, Mark (1978), *Critical Theory of the Family* (New York: Seabury).

Proust, Marcel (1963), Excerpts from *Cities of the Plain* and *By Way of Sainte-Beuve*, in *Eros: An Anthology of Male Friendship*, eds. Alistair Sutherland and Patrick Anderson (New York: Citadel).

Rapp, Rayna (1978), "Family and Class in Contemporary America," *Science and Society* 42 (fall): 278.

Rosenberg, Charles (1973), "Sexuality, Class, and Role in 19th-Century America," *American Quarterly* 25:2: 131.

Sahli, Nancy (1979), "Smashing," *Chrysalis*, 8 (summer): 17.

Scott, Joan and Tilly, Louise (1975), "Women's Work and the Family in Nineteenth-Century Europe," *Comparative Studies in Society and History* 17: 1: 42.

Secombe, Walley (1973), "The Housewife and Her Labour under Capitalism," *New Left Review* 83: 3.

Smedley, Agnes (1976), *Portraits of Chinese Women in Revolution* (Old Westbury, NY: Feminist Press).

Smith-Rosenberg, Carroll (1975), "The Female World of Love and Ritual," *Signs* 1:1: 1.

Steakley, James (1975), *The Homosexual Emancipation Movement in Germany* (New York: Arno).

Taylor, Gordon Rattray (1965), "Historical and Mythological Aspect of Homosexuality," in *Sexual Inversion*, ed. Judd Marmor (New York: Basic Books).

Trumbach, Randolph (1977) "London's Sodomites: Homosexual Behavior and Western Culture in the Eighteenth Century," *Journal of Social History* 11:1: 1.

Tucker, Robert (ed.) (1978), *The Marx–Engels Reader: Second Edition* (New York: Norton).

Walkowitz, Judith (1980), "The Politics of Prostitution," *Signs* 6:1: 123.

——(1983), "Male Vice and Female Virtue," in *Powers of Desire*, eds Ann Snitow, Christine

Stansell and Sharon Thompson (New York: Monthly Review Press).

Weeks, Jeffrey (1977), *Coming Out* (London: Quartet).

——(1981), *Sex, Politics, and Society* (London: Longman).

Yang, C. K. (1953), *The Chinese Family in the Communist Revolution* (Cambridge, MA: MIT Press).

BARRY M. DANK

"Coming Out in the Gay World"

from *Psychiatry* 34 (May 1971): 60–77

In spite of the recent sociological interest in the study of the transition from primary to secondary deviance,[1] few empirical studies have been addressed to this question.[2] It is in essence posited that at one point in time the actor can be described as being at the "primary stage," in which he engaged in rule-breaking behavior and still regards himself as "normal"; at a later point in time he may reach the secondary stage, in which he may engage in overtly the same behavior but regard himself as "deviant," or at least in some way different from the average, ordinary person. For example, at one point in time a person may furtively take goods from a store and regard himself as a borrower, but at a later time he may take similar goods and regard himself as a thief (Cameron 1964). This paper is devoted to exploring the emergence of a particular deviant identity – the male homosexual identity.

There is almost no sociological literature on "becoming" homosexual. There is a vast literature on the etiology of homosexuality – that is, the family background of homosexuals[3] – but little is known concerning how the actor learns that he is a homosexual, how he decides that he is a homosexual. In terms of identity and behavior, this paper is concerned with the transition to a homosexual identity, not in the learning of homosexual behavior *per se*, or the antecedent or situational conditions that may permit an actor to engage in a homosexual act. One may engage in a homosexual act and think of oneself as being homosexual, heterosexual, or bisexual. One may engage in a heterosexual act and think of oneself as being heterosexual, homosexual, or bisexual, or one may engage in no sexual acts and still have

a sexual identity of heterosexual, homosexual, or bisexual. This study is directed toward determining what conditions permit a person to say, "I am a homosexual."[4]

RESEARCH METHOD

This report is part of a study that has been ongoing for over two years in a large metropolitan area in the United States. The analysis is based on data obtained from lengthy interviews with fifty-five self-admitted homosexuals, on observations of and conversations with hundreds of homosexuals and on the results of a one-page questionnaire distributed to three hundred self-admitted homosexuals attending a meeting of a homophile organization. The statistical data are based on the 182 questionnaires that were returned.

The four- to five-hour interviews with the fifty-five self-admitted homosexuals were generally conducted in the subject's home, and in the context of a "participant-observation" study in which the researcher as researcher became integrated into friendship networks of homosexuals. The researcher was introduced to this group by a homosexual student who presented him correctly as being a heterosexual who was interested in doing a study of homosexuals as they exist in the "outside world." He was able to gain the trust of the most prestigious person in the group, which enabled him, on the whole, to gain the trust of the rest of the group. The guidelines employed in the study were based on those outlined by Polsky (1967) for participant-observation studies.

There is no way of determining whether the

sample groups studied here, or any similar sample, would be representative of the homosexual population. Thus it remains problematic whether the findings of this study can be applied to the homosexual population in general or to other samples of homosexuals.[5] Since age is a critical variable in this study, the questionnaire sample was used in the hope that the replies to a questionnaire would represent a fairly wide age range. The age distribution of the questionnaire sample is shown on Table 19.1.

COMING OUT

The term "coming out" is frequently used by homosexuals to refer to the identity change to homosexual. Hooker (1965) states:

> Very often, the debut, referred to by homosexuals as the coming out, of a person who believes himself to be homosexual but who has struggled against it will occur when he identifies himself publicly for the first time as a homosexual in the presence of other homosexuals by his appearance in a bar.
>
> (p. 99)

Gagnon and Simon refer to coming out as that "point in time when there is self-recognition by the individual of his identity as a homosexual and the first major exploration of the homosexual community" (1968: 356).

In this study it was found that the meaning that the informant attached to this expression was usually directly related to his own experiences concerning how he met other gay[6] people and how and when he decided he was homosexual. For purposes of this study the term "coming out" will mean identifying oneself as being homosexual.[7] This self-identification as being homosexual may or may not occur in a social context in which other gay people are present. One of the tasks of this paper is to identify the social contexts in which the self-definition of homosexual occurs.

THE SOCIAL CONTEXTS OF COMING OUT

The child who is eventually to become homosexual in no sense goes through a period of anticipatory socialization (Merton 1957); if he does go through such a period, it is in reference to heterosexuality, not homosexuality. It is sometimes said that the homosexual minority is just like any other minority group (Cory 1951;

Table 19.1 Age characteristics of sample

Age	Age distribution		Age of first sexual desire toward same sex		Age at which decision was made that respondent was a homosexual	
	N	(%)	N	(%)	N	(%)
0–4	0	0	1	0.5	0	0
5–9	0	0	28	15	1	0.5
10–14	0	0	83	46	27	15
15–19	13	7	54	29	79	44
20–24	36	20	14	8	52	29
25–29	39	22	1	0.5	11	6
30–34	28	16	1	0.5	4	2
35–39	21	12	0	0	3	2
40–44	18	10	0	0	1	0.5
45–49	6	3	0	0	0	0
50–59	11	6	0	0	0	0
60–69	8	4	0	0	1	0.5
Total	180	100	182	99.5	179	99.5
	$\bar{X} = 32.5, S = 11.3$		$\bar{X} = 13.5, S = 4.3$		$\bar{X} = 19.3, S = 6.4$	

Westwood 1960); but in the sense of early childhood socialization it is not, for the parents of a Negro can communicate to their child that he is a Negro and what it is like to be a Negro, but the parents of a person who is to become homosexual do not prepare their child to be homosexual – they are not homosexual themselves, and they do not communicate to him what it is like to be a homosexual.[8]

The person who has sexual feelings or desires toward persons of the same sex has no vocabulary to explain to himself what these feelings mean. Subjects who had homosexual feelings during childhood were asked how they would have honestly responded to the question, "Are you a homosexual?" at the time just prior to their graduation from high school. Some typical responses follow:

SUBJECT 1: I had guilt feelings about this being attracted to men. Because I couldn't understand why all the other boys were dating, and I didn't have any real desire to date.
INTERVIEWER: Were you thinking of yourself as homosexual?
SUBJECT 1: I think I did but I didn't know how to put it into words. I didn't know it existed. I guess I was like everybody else and thought I was the only one in the world … I probably would have said I didn't know. I don't think I really knew what one was. I would have probably asked you to explain what one was.
SUBJECT 2: I would have said, "No. I don't know what you are talking about." If you had said "queer," I would have thought something about it, this was the slang term that was used, although I didn't know what the term meant.
SUBJECT 3: I don't think I would have known then. I know now. Then I wasn't even thinking about the word. I wasn't reading up on it.

Respondents were asked the age at which they first became aware of any desire or sexual feeling toward persons of the same sex; subsequently they were asked when they decided they were homosexual. Results are presented in Table 19.1. On the average, there was a six-year interval between time of first sexual feeling toward persons of the same sex and the decision that one was a homosexual. The distribution of the differing time intervals between a person's awareness of homosexual feelings and the decision that he is homosexual is presented in Table 19.2. As Table 19.2 indicates, there is

Table 19.2 Time interval between first homosexual desire and the decision that one is a homosexual

Time interval (years)	Distribution	
	N	%
0	29	16
1–4	66	37
5–9	49	27
10–14	21	12
15–19	7	4
20–29	5	3
30–39	1	0.5
40–49	0	0
50–59	1	0.5
Total	179	100

$$\bar{X} = 5.7, S = 6.4$$

considerable variation in this factor.[9]

The fact that an actor continues to have homosexual feelings and to engage in homosexual behavior does not mean that he views himself as being homosexual. In order for a person to view himself as homosexual he must be placed in a new social context, in which knowledge of homosexuals and homosexuality can be found; in such a context he learns a new vocabulary of motives, a vocabulary that will allow him to identify himself as being a homosexual. This can occur in any number of social contexts – through meeting self-admitted homosexuals, by meeting knowledgeable straight persons, or by reading about homosexuals and homosexuality. Knowledge of homosexuals and homosexuality can be found in numerous types of physical settings: a bar, a park, a private home, a psychiatrist's office, a mental hospital, and so on (see Table 19.3). It is in contexts where such knowledge tends to be concentrated that the actor will be most likely to come out. It is therefore to be expected that an actor is likely to come out in a context in which other gay people are present; they are usually a ready and willing source of knowledge concerning homosexuals and homosexuality. In the questionnaire sample, 50 per cent came out while associating with gay people.

It is also to be expected that a likely place for an actor to come out would be in one-sex situations or institutions. Sexually segregated environments provide convenient locales for

Table 19.3 Social contexts in which respondents came out

Social contexts	N	(%)
Frequenting gay bars	35	19
Frequenting gay parties and other gatherings	46	26
Frequenting parks	43	24
Frequenting men's rooms	37	21
Having a love affair with a homosexual man	54	30
Having a love affair with a heterosexual man	21	12
In the military	34	19
Living in a YMCA	2	1
Living in all-male quarters at a boarding school or college	12	7
In prison	2	1
Patient in a mental hospital	3	2
Seeing a psychiatrist or professional counselor	11	6
Read for the first time about homosexuals and/or homosexuality	27	15
Just fired from a job because of homosexual behavior	2	1
Just arrested on a charge involving homosexuality	7	4
Was not having any homosexual relations	36	20

Note

[1] Total N of social contexts is greater than 180 (number of respondents) because there was overlap in contexts.

knowledge of homosexuality and homosexual behavior. Examples of these one-sex environments are mental institutions, YMCAs, prisons, the military, men's rooms, gay bars, and school dormitories. The first six case histories below illustrate the influence of such milieux.

The first example of an actor coming out in the context of interacting with gay persons concerns a subject who came out in a mental hospital. The subject was committed to a mental hospital at age 20; his commitment did not involve homosexuality and the hospital authorities had no knowledge that the subject had a history of homosexual behavior. Prior to commitment he had a history of heterosexual and homosexual behavior, thought of himself as bisexual, had had no contact with self-admitted homosexuals, was engaged to marry, and was indulging in heavy petting with his fiancée. In the following interview excerpt the subject reports on his first reaction to meeting gay persons in the hospital:

SUBJECT: I didn't know there were so many gay people, and I wasn't use to the actions of gay people or anything, and it was quite shocking walking down the halls, going up to the ward, and the whistles and flirting and everything else went on with the new fish, as they called it.

And there was this one kid who was a patient escort and he asked me if I was interested in going to church, and I said yes ... and he started escorting me to church and then he pulled a little sneaky to see whether I'd be shocked at him being gay. There was this queen[10] on the ward, and him and her, he was looking out the hall to see when I'd walk by the door and they kissed when I walked by the door and this was to check my reaction. And I didn't say a word. So he then escorted me to the show, and we were sitting there and about half-way through the movie he reaches over and started holding my hand, and when he saw I didn't jerk away, which I was kind of upset and wondering exactly what he had in mind, and then when we got back to the ward, he wrote me a long love letter and gave it to me; before we knew it we were going together, and went together for about six months.

[After 3 weeks] he had gotten me to the point where I'd gotten around the hospital, where I picked up things from the other queens and learned how to really swish and carry on and got to be one of the most popular queens in the whole place. [About that same time] I'd gotten to consider myself – I didn't consider myself a queen. I just considered myself a gay boy; we sat down, a bunch of us got together and made out the rules about what was what as far as the joint was concerned, drew definitions of every little thing ... if someone was completely feminine, wanted to take the female role all the time, then they were a "queen," if they were feminine but butchy, then they were a "nellie-butch," and I was considered a "gay boy" because I could take any role, I was versatile.

INTERVIEWER: Before this bull session were you considering yourself gay?

SUBJECT: Yes, I had definitely gotten to be by this time; after three months my folks came down to see me and I told them the whole thing point blank.

INTERVIEWER: What would you say was the most important effect the hospital had on you?

SUBJECT: It let me find out it wasn't so terrible ... I met a lot of gay people that I liked and I figured it can't be all wrong. If so and so's a good Joe, and he's still gay, he can't be all that bad ... I figured it couldn't be all wrong, and that's one of the things I learned. I learned to accept myself for what I am – homosexual.

This subject spent a year and a half in the mental hospital. After release he did not engage in heterosexual relations, and has been actively involved in the gay subculture for the past four years.

The above example clearly demonstrates how a one-sex environment can facilitate the development of a homosexual identity. Although some one-sex environments are created for homosexuals, such as gay bars, any one-sex environment can serve as a meeting and recruiting place for homosexuals, whether or not the environment was created with that purpose in mind.

The YMCA is a one-sex environment that inadvertently functions as a meeting place for homosexuals in most large urban areas in the United States.[11] The following subject came out while living and working at a YMCA. He was 24 when he first visited a Y, never had had a homosexual experience, and had just been separated from his wife.

> I became separated from my wife. I then decided to go to Eastern City. I had read of the Walter Jenkins case and the name of the YMCA happened to come up, but when I got to the city it was the only place I knew of to stay. I had just $15.00 in my pocket to stay at the Y, and I don't think I ever had the experience before of taking a group shower. So I went into the shower room, that was the first time I remember looking at a man's body and finding it sexually enticing.[12] So I started wondering to myself – that guy is good-looking. I walked back to my room and left the door open and the guy came in, and I happened to fall in love with that guy.

After this first experience, the subject became homosexually active while living and working at the Y and became part of the gay subculture that existed within the Y.

> I found that the kids who were working for me, some of them I had been to bed with and some of them I hadn't, had some horrible problems and trying to decide the right and wrong of homosexuality. . . . and they would feel blunt enough or that I had the experience enough to counsel them along the lines of homosexuality or anything else . . . Part of this helped me realize that one of the greatest things that you can do is to accept what you are and if you want to change it, you can go ahead and do it.

This subject spent six months living in this Y; by the end of three months he had accepted himself as being homosexual and has been exclusively homosexual for the last two years.

The prison is another one-sex environment in which homosexual behavior is concentrated. Although there have been studies of situational homosexuality in prison (Giallombardo 1966; Sykes 1958; Tittle 1969; Ward and Kassebaum 1965), and of how homosexual activities are structured in prison, there have been no studies that have looked at the possible change of the sexual identity of the prisoner. In the following case the subject was sentenced to prison on a charge of sodomy at the age of 32, and spent five years in prison. He had been homosexually active for 22 years, and before his arrest he had been engaging predominantly in homosexual behavior, but he had not defined himself as being a homosexual. He had had only peripheral contacts with the gay subculture before his arrest, largely because he was married and held a high socioeconomic position.

INTERVIEWER: In prison did you meet homosexuals?
SUBJECT: Yes.
INTERVIEWER: I'm not talking about people who are just homosexual while in prison.
SUBJECT: People who are homosexual, period. I became educated about the gay world, how you can meet people and not lay yourself open to censure, and how to keep from going to prison again. And still go on being homosexual. While in prison I definitely accepted myself as being homosexual . . . I had frequent meetings with psychiatrists, various social workers. We were all pretty much in tacit agreement that the best thing to do would be to learn to live with yourself. Up until then, I rationalized and disillusioned myself about a lot of things. As I look back on it, I was probably homosexual from ten years on.

After his release from prison, this subject became involved in the gay subculture and has been exclusively homosexual for the last eight years.

The military is a one-sex environment that is a most conducive setting for homosexual behavior. In the military, a large number of young men live in close contact with one another and are deprived of heterosexual contacts for varying periods of time; it is not surprising that a homosexual subculture would arise. Given the young age of the military population, it should also be expected that a certain proportion of men would be entering military service with homosexual desires and/or a history of homosexual behavior, but without a clearly formulated homosexual identity. Approximately 19 percent of the sample came out while in military service. The following subject had a history of homosexual desires and behavior previous to joining the Navy, but came out while in military service.

INTERVIEWER: How did you happen to have homosexual relations while in the Navy?

SUBJECT: We were out at sea and I had heard that one of the dental technicians was a homosexual, and he had made advances toward me, and I felt like masturbation really wouldn't solve the problem so I visited him one night. He started talking about sex and everything. I told him I had never kissed a boy before. And he asked me what would you do if a guy kissed you, and I said you mean like this and I began kissing him. Naturally he took over then ... There were other people on the ship that were homosexual and they talked about me. A yeoman aboard ship liked me quite a bit, was attracted to me; so he started making advances toward me, and I found him attractive, so we got together, and in a short period of time, we became lovers. He started to take me to the gay bars and explain what homosexuality was all about. He took me to gay bars when we were in port.

SUBJECT: Did you start to meet other gay people aboard ship?

SUBJECT: The first real contact with gay people was aboard ship....

INTERVIEWER: Was it while you were in the Navy that you decided you were a homosexual?

SUBJECT: Yes. Once I was introduced to gay life, I made the decision that I was a homosexual.

Public restrooms, another part of society which is sexually segregated, are known in the gay world as T-rooms, and some T-rooms become known as meeting places for gay persons and other who are looking for homosexual contacts (Humphreys 1970). Sex in T-rooms tends to be anonymous, but, since some nonsexual social interaction also occurs in this locale, some homosexuals do come out in T-rooms. In the sample studied here 21 percent came out while frequenting T-rooms for sexual purposes. The following subject came out in the context of going to T-rooms when he was 15. Previously he had been homosexually active,

but had not thought of himself as being a homosexual.

> I really didn't know what a homosexual was. In the back of my mind, my definition of a homosexual or queer was someone who wore girls' clothes and women's shoes, 'cause my brothers said this was so, and I knew I wasn't.

At the age of 15 this subject had a sexual relationship with a gay man.

> And he took me out and introduced me to the gay world. I opened the door and I went out and it was a beautiful day and I accepted this whole world, and I've never had any guilt feelings or hang-ups or regrets ... I was young and fairly attractive and I had men chasing me all the time ... He didn't take me to bars. We went to restrooms, that was my outlet. He started taking me to all the places they refer to in the gay world as T-rooms, and I met other people and I went back there myself and so on.

After meeting other gay persons by going to T-rooms, this subject quickly discovered other segments of the gay world and has been exclusively homosexual for the last nine years.

Gay bars are probably the most widespread and well-known gay institutions (Achilles 1967; Hooker 1965). For many persons who become homosexual, gay bars are the first contact with organized gay society and therefore a likely place to come out. In this sample 19 percent came out while going to gay bars. Since gay bars apparently are widespread throughout the nation, this could be viewed as a surprisingly low percentage. However, it should be remembered that generally the legal age limit for entering bars is 21. If the age limit is enforced, this would reduce the percentage of persons coming out in gay bars. T-rooms and gay private parties and other gatherings perform the same function as gay bars, but are not hampered by any age limit. Thus, it is not really surprising that the percentages of persons who came out in several other ways are higher than the percentage coming out in gay bars.

The following subject came out in the context of going to gay bars. He had been predominantly homosexual for a number of years and was 23 at the time he came out.

SUBJECT: I knew that there were homosexuals,

queers and what not; I had read some books, and I was resigned to the fact that I was a foul, dirty person, but I wasn't actually calling myself a homosexual yet . . . I went to this guy's house and there was nothing going on, and I asked him, "Where is some action?," and he said, "There is a bar down the way." And the time I really caught myself coming out is the time I walked into this bar and saw a whole crowd of groovy, groovy guys. And I said to myself, there was the realization, that not all gay men are dirty old men or idiots, silly queens, but there are some just normal-looking and acting people, as far as I could see. I saw gay society and I said, "Wow, I'm home."

INTERVIEWER: This was the first time that you walked into this gay bar that you felt this way?

SUBJECT: That's right. It was that night in the bar. I think it saved my sanity. I'm sure it saved my sanity.

This subject has been exclusively homosexually active for the last thirteen years.

Even after an introduction to gay bars, labeling oneself as homosexual does not always occur as rapidly as it did in the previous example. Some persons can still, for varying periods of time, differentiate themselves from the people they are meeting in gay bars. The following subject came out when he was 22; he had been predominantly homosexual before coming out. He interacted with gay people in gay bars for several months before he decided he was a homosexual. He attempted to differentiate himself from the other homosexuals by saying to himself, "I am not really homosexual since I am not as feminine as they are."

Finally after hanging around there for so long, some guy came up to me and tried to take me for some money, and I knew it, and he said, "You know, you're very nellie,"[13] And I said I wasn't, and he said, "Yes, you are, and you might as well face facts and that's the way it is, and you're never going to change." And I said, "If that's the case, then that's the way it's going to be." So I finally capitulated.

This subject has been predominantly homosexually active for the last twenty-one years.

It should be made clear that such a change in sexual identity need not be accompanied by any change in sexual behavior or any participation in homosexual behavior. It is theoretically possible for someone to view himself as being homosexual but not engage in homosexual relations just as it is possible for someone to view himself as heterosexual but not engage in heterosexual relations. Approximately 20 percent of this sample came out while having no homosexual relations. The following subject is one of this group; he came out during his late twenties even though he had his last homosexual experience at age 20.

I picked up a copy of this underground newspaper one day just for the fun of it . . . and I saw an ad in there for this theatre, and after thinking about it I got up enough nerve to go over there . . . I knew that they had pictures of boys and I had always liked boys, and I looked at the neighborhood and then I came home without going in . . . I went back to the neighborhood again and this time I slunk, and I do mean slunk through the door . . . and I was shocked to see what I saw on the screen, but I found it interesting and stimulating and so I went back several more times.

Eventually this subject bought a copy of a gay publication, and subsequently he went to the publication's office.

I visited with the fellows in the office and I had time on my hands and I volunteered to help and they were glad to have me. And I have been a member of the staff ever since and it was that way that I got my education of what gay life is like . . . For the last ten years, I had been struggling against it. Back then if I knew what homosexuality was, if I had been exposed to the community . . . and seen the better parts, I probably would have admitted it then.

This subject has been very active socially but not sexually in the gay subculture for the last year.

In contrast to the previous examples, there are cases in which the subject has no direct contact with any gay persons, but yet comes out in that context. Fifteen percent (27) of the sample came out upon first reading about homosexuals or homosexuality in a book, pamphlet, etc.; ten of these (about 6 percent of the sample) were not associating with gay people at the time they came out. The following subject came out in this context. He was 14 at the time, had just ended a homosexual relationship with a person who considered himself to be straight, and had had no contact with gay society.

I had always heard like kids do about homosexuals and things, but that never really entered my mind, but when I read this article, when I was in the 8th grade, and it had everything in it about them sexually, not how they looked and acted and where they go. It was about me and that was what I was thinking. I just happen one day to see a picture of a guy, and thought he was kind of cute, so I'll read the article about him. But before that I didn't realize what was happening. I didn't even realize I wasn't right as far as heterosexuals were concerned. I didn't realize that what I was thinking wasn't kosher ... If people don't like it I'll keep my mouth shut. The article said people wouldn't like it, so I decided to keep my mouth shut. That's the way I was, so I accepted it.

This subject has been active sexually and socially in the gay subculture for the last five years.

Another context in which a subject can come out is that of having a homosexual relationship with a person who defines himself as being heterosexual; 12 percent (21) of the sample came out in such a context. Of these, 12 (about 7 percent of the sample) had never met any self-admitted homosexuals and had never read any material on homosexuality. The following case involves a subject who came out in such a context. At the age of 21 he was having an intense love affair with a serviceman who defined himself as straight. The subject also became involved in a triangular relationship with the serviceman's female lover.

> This got very serious. I told him I loved him ... He wanted me for a sex release; I didn't admit it then, but now I see, through much heartbreak. He liked me as a person ... At the same time he was dating a married woman; he was dating her and having sex with her ... She couldn't admit to having a relationship with him 'cause she was married, but he told me and I was extremely jealous of her. [We worked together] and privately she was a very good friend of mine. So I started feeling hatred toward her because she was coming between he and I, competition. I was strong competition, 'cause I frankly dominated it, and she sensed this; so one day she said, "I bet he'd be very good in bed." So I said, "You know he is." She said, "What did you say?" and I said, "Oh, I guess he would be." And I wanted to tell her; so I finally acted like I just broke down and I told her everything in order to make her not like him. So she got on his tail and told him to stop seeing me or she wouldn't have anything to do with him ... I taped all their phone conversations and told her if she wouldn't leave him alone, I'd play them for her husband. She got furious, so

she said if I tried to blackmail her she would go to the police with the whole thing ... it all backfired on me and I really didn't want to hurt her, but my love for him was so strong; I'd hurt anybody to keep him, so I erased the tape. And later I bawled and bawled and cried about it to her because I was very sensitive at this time and I told her I was sorry, didn't want to hurt her, but I loved him so much ... After I fell in love with him I knew I was homosexual. I talked to my brother about it and he said I wasn't really in love. He said you're just doing it cause you want to; it's not right, boys don't fall in love with boys. He wasn't nasty about it ... I really loved him; he was my first love; I even dream about him once in a while to this very day ... It was during this time that I came out, and I was extremely feminine, not masculine in any way. I wore male clothing, but dressed in a feminine way, in the way I carried myself, the way I spoke ... I realized that I was homosexual because I loved him. I was afraid of gay people; heard they did all kinds of weird things from straight people talking about them.

Before this relationship, the subject had engaged in both homosexual and heterosexual petting. Shortly after the relationship terminated the subject became involved in the gay subculture and had been almost exclusively homosexual since that time.

COGNITIVE CHANGE

What is common to all the cases discussed is that the subject placed himself in a new cognitive category (McCall and Simmons 1966), the category of homosexual. In some cases, such placement can occur as soon as the person learns of the existence of the category; an example of this is the boy who placed himself in that category after reading about homosexuals in a magazine. However, probably most persons who eventually identify themselves as homosexuals require a change in the meaning of the cognitive category *homosexual* before they can place themselves in the category.

The meaning of the category must be changed because the subject has learned the negative stereotype of the homosexual held by most heterosexuals, and he knows that he is no queer, pervert, dirty old man, and so on (Simmons 1965). He differentiates himself from the homosexual image that straight society has presented to him. Direct or indirect contact with the gay subculture provides the subject with information about homosexuals that will challenge the "straight" image of the homosexual. The subject will quite often see himself in other homosexuals, homosexuals he finds to be socially acceptable. He now knows who and what he is because the meaning of the cognitive category has changed to include himself. As one subject said: "Wow, I'm home"; at times that is literally the case since the homosexual now feels that he knew where he really belongs.

A person's identification of himself as being homosexual is often accompanied by a sense of relief, of freedom from tension. In the words of one subject:

> I had this feeling of relief; there was no more tension. I had this feeling of relief. I guess the fact that I had accepted myself as being homosexual had taken a lot of tensions off me.

Coming out, in essence, often signifies to the subject the end of a search for his identity.

IDENTIFICATION AND SELF-ACCEPTANCE

Identifying oneself as being homosexual and accepting oneself as being homosexual usually come together, but this is not necessarily the case. It can be hypothesized that those who identify themselves as being homosexual but not in the context of interacting with other homosexuals, are more likely to have guilty feelings than those who identify themselves as being homosexual in the context of interacting with other homosexuals. Interaction with other homosexuals facilitates the learning of a vocabulary that will not simply explain but will also justify the homosexual behavior.

Identifying oneself as homosexual is almost uniformly accompanied by the development of certain techniques of neutralization (Sykes and Matza 1957).[14] In this self-identification, it would be incorrect to state that the homosexual accepts himself as being deviant, in the evaluative sense of the term. The subject may know he is deviant from the societal standpoint but often

does not accept this as part of his self-definition. Lemert has defined secondary deviation as the situation in which "a person begins to employ his deviant behavior or a role based upon it as a means of defense, attack or adjustment to the overt and covert problems created by the consequent societal reaction to him" (1951: 76). Once the subject identifies himself as being homosexual, he does develop means, often in the process of the change in self-definition, of adjusting to the societal reaction to the behavior. The means employed usually involve the denial, to himself and to others, that he is really deviant. Becker (1963: 1–2) explained the situation when he stated:

> But the person thus labeled an outsider may have a different view of the matter. He may not accept the rule by which he is being judged and may not regard those who judge him as either competent or legitimately entitled to do so.

The societal reaction to homosexuality appears to be expressed more in a mental health rhetoric (Bieber 1965; Hadden 1967; Ovesey 1969; Socarides 1970; Szasz 1970), than in a rhetoric of sin and evil or crime and criminal behavior. In order to determine how the subject adjusted to this societal reaction to homosexuality, they were asked to react to the idea that homosexuals are sick or mentally ill. With very few exceptions, this notion was rejected.

SUBJECT 1: I believe this idea to be very much true, if added that you are talking from society's standpoint and society has to ask itself why are these people sick or mentally ill . . . In other words, you can't make flat statements that homosexuals are sick or mentally ill. I do not consider myself to be sick or mentally imbalanced.

SUBJECT 2: That's a result of ignorance; people say that quickly, pass quick judgments. They are not knowledgeable, fully knowledgeable about the situation.

SUBJECT 3: I don't feel they are. I feel it's normal. What's normal for one person is not always normal for another. I don't think it's a mental illness or mental disturbance.

SUBJECT 4: Being a homosexual does not label a person as sick or mentally ill. In every other capacity I am as normal or more normal than straight people. Just because I happen to like strawberry ice cream and they like vanilla, doesn't make them right or me right.

It is the learning of various ideas from other

homosexuals that allows the subject to in effect say, "I am homosexual, but not deviant," or, "I am homosexual, but not mentally ill." The cognitive category of *homosexual* now becomes socially acceptable, and the subject can place himself in that category and yet preserve a sense of his self-esteem or self-worth.

It should be emphasized that coming out often involves an entire transformation in the meaning of the concept of homosexual for the subject. In these cases the subject had been entirely unaware of the existence of gay bars or an organized gay society, of economically successful homosexuals, of homosexually "married" homosexuals, and so on. In the words of one subject:

> I had always thought of them as dirty old men that preyed on 10-, 11-, 12-year-old kids, and I found out that they weren't all that way; there are some that are, but they are a minority. It was a relief for me 'cause I found out that I wasn't so different from many other people. I had considered consulting professional help prior to that 'cause at the time I thought I was mentally ill. Now I accept it as a way of life, and I don't consider it a mental illness. It's an unfortunate situation . . . I consider myself an outcast from general society, but not mentally ill.

PUBLIC LABELING

It should be made clear that the self-identification as a homosexual does not generally take place in the context of a negative public labeling, as some labeling theorists imply that it does (Garfinkel 1956; Lemert 1951; Scheff 1966). No cases were found in the interview sample in which the subject had come out in the context of being arrested on a charge involving homosexuality or being fired from a job because of homosexual behavior. In the questionnaire sample, 4 percent (7) had just been arrested and 1 percent (2) had just been fired from a job. A total of 8 respondents or 4.5 percent of the sample came out in the context of public exposure.

It can be hypothesized that the public labeling of an actor who has not yet identified himself as being homosexual will reinforce in his mind the idea that he is not homosexual.

This is hypothesized because it is to be expected that at the time of the public labeling the actor will be presented with information that will present homosexuals and homosexuality in a highly negative manner. For example, the following subject was arrested for homosexual activities at the age of 11. Both before and after the arrest he did not consider himself to be a homosexual. His reaction to the arrest was:

SUBJECT: The officer talked to me and told me I should see a psychiatrist. It kind of confused me. I really didn't understand any of it.
INTERVIEWER: And were you thinking of yourself at that time as a homosexual?
SUBJECT: I probably would have said I wasn't. 'Cause of the way the officer who interrogated me acted. It was something you never admit to. He acted as if I were the scum of the earth. He was very rude and impolite.

If the actor has not yet identified himself as being homosexual, it can probably be assumed that to a significant degree he already accepts the negative societal stereotype; the new information accompanying the public labeling will conform to the societal stereotype, and the actor consequently will not modify his decision not to place himself in the homosexual category. This is not to say that public labeling by significant others and/or official agents of social control does not play a significant role in the life of the homosexual; all that is hypothesized is that public labeling does not facilitate and may in fact function to inhibit the decision to label oneself as being homosexual.

THE CLOSET QUEEN

There are some persons who may continue to have homosexual desires and may possibly engage in homosexual relations for many years, but yet do not have a homosexual identity. Self-admitted homosexuals refer to such persons as "closet queens."[15] Such persons may go for many years without any contact with or knowledge of self-admitted homosexuals. The subject previously cited who came out in prison was a closet queen for twenty years.

An interval of ten or more years between first awareness of sexual attraction toward males and the decision that one is a homosexual, would probably classify one as having been a closet queen. As Table 19.2 shows, the questionnaire sample included thirty-five respondents (20 percent of the sample) who at one time were closet queens.

It is the closet queen who has most internalized the negative societal stereotype of the homosexual societal stereotype of the homosexual. It is to be expected that such persons would suffer from a feeling of psychological tension, for they are in a state of cognitive dissonance (Festinger 1957) – that is, feelings and sometimes behavior are not consistent with self-definition.

The following subject was a closet queen for over fifty years. He had his first homosexual experience at the age of 12, has had homosexual desires since that time, and has been exclusively homosexual for fifty-three years. At the time the subject was interviewed, he expressed amazement that he had just come out during the last few months. Over the years, his involvement with the gay subculture was peripheral; at the age of 29 for about one year he had some involvement with overt homosexuals, but otherwise he had had only slight contact with them until recently. During that earlier involvement:

> I was not comfortable with them. I was repressed and timid and they thought I was being high hat, so I was rejected. It never worked out; I was never taken in. I felt uncomfortable in their presence and I made them feel uncomfortable. I couldn't fit in there, I never wanted to, never sought to; I was scared of them. I was scared of the brazen bitches who would put me down.

During the years as a closet queen he was plagued with feelings of guilt; for varying periods of time he was a patient in over twenty mental hospitals. His social life was essentially nil; he had neither gay friends nor straight friends. His various stays in mental hospitals relieved continuing feelings of loneliness. At the age of 65 he attended a church whose congregation was primarily homosexual. It was in the context of interacting with the gay persons who were associated with this church that after fifty-three years this subject came out.

SUBJECT: I had never seen so many queens in one place; I was scared somebody would put me down, somebody would misunderstand why I was there. I had this vague, indescribable fear. But all this was washed away when I saw all were there for the one purpose of fellowship and community in the true sense of the term ... I kept going and then I got to be comfortable in the coffee hour ... Then out in the lobby a young fellow opened his heart to me, telling me all his troubles and so forth, and I listened patiently, and I thought I made a couple of comforting remarks. Then I went out to the car, and when I got in the car I put my hand out to shake hands and he kissed my hand ... it's hard for you to understand the emotional impact of something like this – that I belong, they love me, I love them.

Until the last few weeks, in all my life I had never been in a gay bar for more than a few minutes, I was acutely uncomfortable. But now I can actually go into it; this is the most utterly ludicrous transformation in the last few weeks ... there's no logic whatsoever. I'm alive at 65.

It's a tremendous emotional breakthrough. I feel comfortable and relieved of tensions and self-consciousness. My effectiveness in other fields has been enhanced 100 percent. I have thrown off so many of the prejudices and revulsions that were below the surface ... I'm out of the closet. In every way, they know, where I work, in this uptight place where I work; I've told them where I live; I've written back east. What more can I do?

INTERVIEWER: Do you think you are now more self-accepting of yourself?

SUBJECT: Brother! I hope you're not kidding. That's the whole bit. How ironical it would come at 65. The only thing that I wouldn't do now is to go to the baths. I told the kids the other day; it's the only breakthrough I cannot bring myself to.

One can only speculate why after all these years this subject came out. The reason may have been that he had had a very religious upbringing and could not conceive of homosexuals in a religiously acceptable manner. The church he attended for the first time at age 65 presented homosexuals as being religiously acceptable, and presented to the subject highly religious homosexuals.[16] Contact with this church may have helped change the meaning of the category homosexual so that he could now include himself.[17]

In a sense the closet queen represents society's ideal homosexual, for the closet queen accepts the societal stereotype of the homosexual and feels guilt because he does the same sort of things that homosexuals do, yet believes he is really different from homosexuals in some significant way. This inability of the closet queen to see himself in other homosexuals prevents him from placing himself in the cognitive category of *homosexual*, and he will not come out until some new information is given to him about homosexuals which permits him to say, "There are homosexuals like myself" or "I am very much like them."

There may be significant differences between ex-closet-queens and those closet queens who never come out. Of course, I had contact only with ex-closet queens, and they uniformly reported that their own psychological adjustment has been much better since coming out. Their only regret was that they had not come out sooner. Possibly the closet queen who remains a closet queen reaches some sort of psychological adjustment that ex-closet queens were unable to reach.

THE ROLE OF KNOWLEDGE

The change of self-identity to *homosexual* is intimately related to the access of knowledge and information concerning homosexuals and homosexuality. Hoffman (1968: 195) has observed:

> Society deals with homosexuality as if it did not exist. Although the situation is changing, this subject was not even discussed and was not even the object of scientific investigation until a few decades ago. We just didn't speak about these things; they were literally unspeakable and so loathsome that nothing could be said in polite society about them.

The traditional silence on this topic has most probably prevented many persons with homosexual feelings from identifying themselves as being homosexual. Lofland has noted that the role of knowledge in creating a deviant identity is an important one. If significant others or the actor himself does not know of the deviant category, his experience cannot be interpreted in terms of that category; or if his experience appears to be completely alien from that category he will not interpret his experience in terms of that category. If the societal stereotype of

homosexuals is one of dirty old men, perverts, Communists, and so on, it should not be surprising that the young person with homosexual feelings would have difficulty in interpreting his experience in terms of the homosexual category.

The greater tolerance of society for the freer circulation of information concerning homosexuality and homosexuals has definite implications in reference to coming out. The fact that there is greater overt circulation of homophile magazines and homophile newspapers, that there are advertisements for gay movies in newspapers, and that there are books, articles and movies about gay life, permits the cognitive category of homosexuals to be known to a larger proportion of the population and, most importantly, permits more information to be circulated that challenges the negative societal stereotype of the homosexual.

Since there has been a freer circulation of information on homosexuality during the past few years, it can be hypothesized that the development of a homosexual identity is now occurring at an increasingly earlier age. Indeed, older gay informants have stated that the younger homosexuals are coming out at a much earlier age. In order to test this hypothesis, the sample was dichotomized into a 30-and-above age group and a below-30 age group. It can be seen that in Table 19.4. that the below-30 mean age for developing a homosexual identity was significantly lower (at the 0.01 level) than the above-30 mean age; the drop in mean age was from approximately 21 to 17.[18]

Indications are that the present trend toward greater circulation of information that is not highly negative about homosexuals and homosexuality will continue. The fact that a mass circulation magazine such as *Time* gave its front cover to an article entitled "The Homosexual in America" (Oct. 31, 1969) and that this article was not highly negative represents a significant breakthrough. The cognitive category of homosexual is now being presented in a not unfavorable manner to hundreds of thousands of people who previously could not have been exposed to such information through conventional channels. This is not to say that more information about homosexuals and homosexuality will

Table 19.4 Relationship of respondent age to age at homosexual self-identification

Age at homosexual self-identification	Age of respondents			
	30 and above		Below 30	
	N	(%)	N	(%)
5–9	0	0	1	1
10–14	8	9	19	22
15–19	35	38	44	50
20–24	29	32	23	21
25–29	10	11	1	1
30–39	7	8	0	0
40–49	1	1	0	0
50–59	0	0	0	0
60–69	1	1	0	0
Total	91	100	88	100
Mean	21.4[1]		17.2[1]	
Standard deviation	7.7		3.8	

Note
1 Means significantly different at 0.01 level.

lead to a significantly greater prevalence of persons engaging in homosexuality. What is being asserted is that a higher proportion of those with homosexual desires and behavior will develop a homosexual identity, and that the development of that identity will continue to occur at an increasingly younger age.

CONCLUSION

This study has suggested that the development of a homosexual identity is dependent on the meanings that the actor attaches to the concepts of homosexual and homosexuality, and that these meanings are directly related to the meanings that are available in his immediate environment; and the meanings that are available in his immediate environment are related to the meanings that are allowed to circulate in the wider society. The commitment to a homosexual identity cannot occur in an environment where the cognitive category of homosexual does not exist. Hoffman (1968: 138) in essence came to the same conclusion when he hypothesized that the failure to develop a homosexual identity is due to a combination of two factors:

the failure of society to make people aware of homosexuality as an existent way of life (and of the existence of the gay world), and the strong repressive forces that prevent people from knowing what their real sexual feelings are. One might consider this a psychological conspiracy of silence, which society insists upon because of its belief that it thereby safeguards existent sexual norms.

In an environment where the cognitive category of homosexual does not exist or is presented in a highly negative manner, a person who is sexually attracted to persons of the same sex will probably be viewed and will probably view himself as sick, mentally ill, or queer.

It can be asserted that one of the main functions of the viewpoint that homosexuality is mental illness is to inhibit the development of a homosexual identity. The *homosexuality-as-mental-illness* viewpoint is now in increasing competition with the *homosexuality-as-way-of-life* viewpoint. If the homosexuality-as-way-of-life viewpoint is increasingly disseminated, one would anticipate that the problems associated with accepting a homosexual identity will significantly decrease, there will be a higher proportion of homosexually oriented people with a homosexual identity, and this identity will develop at an earlier age.[19]

If the homosexuality-as-way-of-life philosophy does become increasingly accepted, the nature of the homosexual community itself may undergo a radical transformation. To have a community one must have members who will acknowledge to themselves and to others that they are members of that community. The increasing circulation of the homosexuality-as-way-of-life viewpoint may in fact be a self-fulfilling prophecy. It may lead to, and possibly is leading to, the creation of a gay community in which one's sex life is becoming increasingly less fragmented from the rest of one's social life.

NOTES

1 See Becker 1963; Erikson 1962; Goffman 1961, 1963; Lemert 1951, 1967; Lofland 1969; Matza 1969; Scheff 1966.
2 See Becker 1953; Bryan 1965; Cameron 1964; Chambliss 1967; Feldman 1968; Goffman 1961;

Lemert 1962; Scheff 1966; Wertham and Pilia-vin 1967.

3 See Bergler 1951; Bieber 1965; Freud 1962; Gebhard *et al.* 1965; Hooker 1969; Krich 1954; Ovesey 1965; Ruitenbeek 1963; Schofield 1965; West 1959; Westwood 1960.

4 It should also be pointed out that from the subjective viewpoint of the actor, it becomes problematic exactly at which point a "homo-sexual" act should be viewed as such. A male actor may have a sexual contact with another male, but fantasize during the sexual act either that the other male is a female or that he himself is a female; in either case he may view the act as being heterosexual. Or a male actor may have a sexual contact with a female, but fantasize the female as being a male or himself as being a female; in such a case he might view the act as being homosexual (Stoller 1968).

5 In addition, it should be pointed out that the sample employed may be skewed in an unknown direction since the questionnaire response rate was approximately 60 percent. In the interview sample, the researcher received excellent coop-eration from both those who viewed themselves as being psychologically well-adjusted and those who did not; those more reluctant to participate tended to occupy high socioeconomic positions.

6 In homosexual argot, "gay" means homosexual and "straight" means heterosexual. These terms are acceptable to homosexuals whether used by gay or straight persons.

7 Sometimes homosexuals use the expression "to bring out" or "bringing out." The meaning attached to these expressions varies; they are sometimes used interchangeably with "coming out." However, as used by my informants, they usually refer to the first complete homosexual act which the subject found enjoyable. The statement. "He brought me out," usually means, "He taught me to enjoy real homosexual acts."

8 Some homosexuals are parents. In the homo-sexual social networks that I am involved in, there are many persons who once played the role of husband and father – generally before they decided they were homosexual (Dank). In addi-tion, there are homosexual couples who are raising children they adopted or children from a former heterosexual marriage; however, such couples tend to be lesbian. In some cases one parent has decided that he or she is homosexual, but both parents have remained together as husband and wife. "Front" marriages also occur, in which a male homosexual marries a female homosexual and they adopt children or have children of their own; such marriages are generally for purposes of social convenience. What the effects are, if any, of being raised by at least one homosexual parent have not been determined. In this sample, there were no cases in which a subject had a homosexual mother or father.

9 First sexual desire toward persons of the same sex was chosen instead of first sexual contact with persons of the same sex since it is quite possible for one to have homosexual desires, fight against those desires, and have no homo-sexual contacts of any type for an extensive period of time. The mean age of first homosexual contact of any type was 13, which was not significantly different at the 0.01 level from age of first homosexual desire. In reference to which came first, homosexual act or homosexual desire, 31 per cent (56) had desire before the act; 49 per cent (87) had act before desire; 20 per cent (36) had first homosexual desire and first homosexual act at approximately the same time.

10 In gay argot, the meaning of the term "queen" is variable. Depending on the context, it can mean any homosexual or a homosexual on the femi-nine side.

11 YMCAs have not been studied in their relation to homosexual society. It appears that YMCAs function as meeting places for homosexuals and for those desiring homosexual relations but defining themselves as straight. This is not a regional phenomenon but is, according to my informants, true for almost all YMCAs in large metropolitan areas. YMCAs are often listed in gay tourist guides.

12 This subject later admitted that he had pre-viously been attracted to other males.

13 In gay argot, "nellie" means feminine or feminine-appearing. The word is not usually used in a complimentary manner.

14 Particularly, denial that there is a victim and denial of injury.

15 In gay argot, the meaning of the term "closet queen" varies, but usually it is applied to one who does not admit to being homosexual. How-ever, the term is sometimes used to refer to a self-admitted homosexual who does not like to associate with other homosexuals, or who may be trying to pass as being straight most of the twenty-four hours of the day.

16 It may be that among closet queens, or those who have been closet queens for many years, one would find a disproportionately high number of very religious persons; the traditional negative religious reaction would probably prevent highly religious persons from easily placing themselves in the homosexual category. It would therefore be expected that clergymen who have homosexual feelings would tend to be closet queens for many years. Not only do clergymen have a more difficult time in resolving problems of guilt, but also interaction with other homo-sexuals could lead to their losing their jobs. In this sample, there were ten respondents who were ministers or who were studying for the

ministry at the time they came out. Their mean age for coming out was 22, and the mean time interval between first homosexual desire and the homosexual self-identification was 10.4 years. I hope to publish a report in the near future on the social life of homosexual ministers.

17 There have been some recent actions that challenge the traditional religious reaction against homosexuality and homosexuals. Particularly see: John Dart, "Church for Homosexuals," *Los Angeles Times*, Dec. 8, 1969, part 2: 1–3; Edward B. Fiske, "Homosexuals in Los Angeles . . . Establish Their Own Church," *New York Times*, Feb. 15, 1970, sec. 1: "The Homosexual Church," *Newsweek*, Oct. 12, 1970: 107. Some churches have openly accepted homosexuals; I am currently preparing an article on such a church.

18 It can be argued that this was not a meaningful test because of sample bias, since the sample could not include subjects of the younger generation who had still not come out. However, the age of 30 was chosen as the dividing point because only nine respondents (5 percent) had come out after the age of 30. Any remaining bias in the sample from this source should presumably be insignificant.

19 Weinberg (1970) has recently reported that younger homosexuals have on the whole a worse psychological adjustment than older homosexuals. As the age for the development of a homosexual identity drops, the psychological adjustment of younger homosexuals may significantly improve.

REFERENCES

Achilles, Nancy, "The Development of the Homosexual Bar as an Institution," in John H. Gagnon and William Simon (Eds), *Sexual Deviance* (Harper & Row, 1967).

Becker, Howard S., "Becoming a Marihuana User," *Amer. J. Sociology* 59 (1953): 235–42.

——, *Outsiders: Studies in the Sociology of Deviance* (Free Press, 1963).

Bergler, E., *Neurotic Counterfeit-Sex* (Grune & Stratton, 1951).

Bieber, Irving *et al. Homosexuality. A Psychoanalytic Study of Male Homosexuals* (Vintage Books, 1965).

Bryan, J. H., "Apprenticeships in Prostitution," *Social Problems* 12 (1965): 287–97.

Cameron, Mary O., *The Booster and the Snitch: Department Store Shoplifting* (Free Press, 1964).

Chambliss, William J., "Two Gangs: a Study of Societal Responses to Deviance and Deviant Careers," unpublished manuscript, 1967.

Cory, Donald W., *The Homosexual in America* (New York: Greenberg, 1951).

Dank, Barry M., "Why Homosexuals Marry Women," in *Medical Aspects of Human Sexuality*, in press.

Erikson, Kai T., "Notes on the Sociology of Deviance," *Social Problems* 9 (1962): 307–14.

Feldman, H. W., "Ideological Supports to Becoming and Remaining a Heroin Addict," *J. Health and Social Behavior* 9 (1968): 131–9.

Festinger, Leon, *Theory of Cognitive Dissonance* (Harper & Row, 1957).

Freud, Sigmund, *Three Contributions to the Theory of Sex* (Dutton, 1962).

Gagnon, John H. and Simon, William, "Homosexuality: The Formulation of a Sociological Perspective," in Mark Lefton *et al.* (eds), *Approaches to Deviance* (Appleton-Century-Crofts, 1968).

Garfinkel, Harold, "Conditions of Successful Degradation Ceremonies," *Amer. J. Sociology* 61 (1956): 420–24.

Gebhard, Paul, *et al.*, *Sex Offenders, An Analysis of Types* (Hoeber-Harper, 1965).

Giallombardo, Rose, *Society of Women: A Study of a Women's Prison* (Wiley, 1966).

Goffman, Erving, *Asylums* (Doubleday Anchor, 1961).

——, *Stigma* (Prentice-Hall, 1963).

Hadden, Samuel, B., "A Way Out for Homosexuals," *Harper's Magazine* (March 1967): 107–20.

Hoffman, Martin, *The Gay World, Male Homosexuality and the Social Creation of Evil* (Basic Books, 1968).

Hooker, Evelyn, "Male Homosexuals and Their 'Worlds'," in Judd Marmor (ed.), *Sexual Inversion: The Multiple Roots of Homosexuality* (Basic Books, 1965).

——, "Parental Relations and Male Homosexuality in Patient and Non-Patient Samples," *J. Consulting and Clin. Psychology* 33 (1969): 140–2.

Humphreys, Laud, *Tearoom Trade* (Aldine, 1970).

Krich, A. M. (ed.), *The Homosexuals* (Citadel Press, 1954).

Lemert, Edwin, M., *Social Pathology* (McGraw-Hill, 1951).

——, "Paranoia and the Dynamics of Exclusion," *Sociometry* 25 (1962): 2–20.

——, *Human Deviance, Social Problems and Social Control* (Prentice-Hall, 1967).

Lofland, John, *Deviance and Identity* (Prentice-Hall, 1969).

Matza, David, *Becoming Deviant* (Prentice-Hall, 1969).

McCall, C. J. and Simmons, J. L. *Identities and Interactions* (Free Press, 1966).

Merton, Robert, *Social Theory and Social Structure* (rev. ed.) (Free Press, 1957).

Ovesey, Lionel, *Homosexuality and Pseudohomosexuality* (Science House, 1969).

Polsky, Ned, *Hustlers, Beats and Others* (Aldine, 1967).

Ruitenbeek, Hendrik (ed.), *The Problem of Homosexuality in Modern Society* (Dutton, 1963).

Scheff, Thomas, *Being Mentally Ill* (Aldine, 1966).

Schofield, Michael, *Sociological Aspects of Homosexuality* (Little Brown, 1965).

Simmons, J. L. "Public Stereotypes of Deviants," *Social Problems* 13 (1965): 223–32.

Socarides, Charles W., "Homosexuality and Medicine," *J. Amer. Med. Assn* 212 (1970): 1199–202.

Stoller, Robert, *Sex and Gender* (Science House, 1968).

Sykes, Gresham M., *Society of Captives* (Princeton Univ. Press, 1958).

Sykes, Gresham M. and Matza, David, "Techniques of Neutralization: A Theory of Delinquency," *Amer. Sociol. Review* 22 (1957): 664–70.

Szasz, Thomas, *The Manufacture of Madness* (Harper & Row, 1970).

Time, "The Homosexual in America," (Oct. 31 1969): 56, 61–2, 64–7.

Tittle, Charles R., "Inmate Organization: Sex Differentiation and the Influence of Criminal Subcultures," *Amer. Sociol. Review* (1969): 492–505.

Ward, David A. and Kassebaum, Gene G., *Women's Prison: Sex and Social Structure* (Aldine, 1965).

Weinberg, Martin S., "The Male Homosexual: Age-Related Variations in Social and Psychological Characteristics," *Social Problems* 17 (1970): 527–37.

Wertham, C. and Piliavin, I., "Gang Members and the Police," in David Bordua (ed.), *The Police: Six Sociological Essays* (Wiley, 1967).

West, Donald J., "Parental Figures in the Genesis of Male Homosexuality," *Internat. J. Social Psychiatry* 5 (1959): 85–97.

Westwood, Gordon, *A Minority: A Report on the Life of the Male Homosexual in Great Britain* (London, Longmans Green, 1960).

BARBARA PONSE

"The Social Construction of Identity and its Meanings within the Lesbian Subculture"

from *Identities in the Lesbian World: The Social Construction of Self* (Westport, CT: Greenwood Press, 1978): chapter 5

The integration of groups within the lesbian subculture provides the basis for the emergence of alternate meanings of lesbian identity. The content of these alternate meanings is the first focus of this chapter. The second is a description of the way lesbian identity is socially constructed within the gay subculture, summarized in what I call the *trajectory of gay identity*.

THE MEANINGS OF IDENTITY WORDS IN THE LESBIAN WORLD

In the lesbian world, the terms *lesbian*, *homosexual*, and *gay* have special meanings in the context of identity. The way these terms are used is important in distinguishing the lesbian subculture from the larger society and in making distinctions within the subculture itself. As commonly used, outside the lesbian world, these terms assume an equation between lesbian activity and lesbian identity. In the lesbian world, too, the terms might be used interchangeably in the course of conversation by many woman-related women. However, in the lesbian world these terms do have a variety of specific meanings and may connote political identity and personal stances.

Usage of the terms *gay*, *female homosexual*, *lesbian*, and *bisexual* as identity labels or descriptive terms is related to several interacting dimensions of an individual's involvement with the subculture. These include a woman's chronological age, her age of entry into the community, the historical time in which she enters lesbian life, the extent of her integration into the community, her degree of politicization, as well as the particular sector of the community with which she is affiliated.

Gay, *homosexual*, and *lesbian* are commonly perceived within both the lesbian community and the larger society as referring to essential identities[1] rather than as describing mere behavior. Extending in meaning beyond a mere equation between sexual object choice and sexual behavior, the words *lesbian*, *homosexual*, *gay* and, occasionally, *butch* and *femme*, signify an orientation, a way of being, or the essence of the person so designated. In the perspective of the lesbian subculture these terms refer to *ontological status*, or a state of being. Thus one does not change into a lesbian or become one, according to this logic: one simply recognizes what has been there all along.

In some instances women in the lesbian community use identity words not only to designate themselves but also to indicate solidarity with other lesbians. For example, in political, radical, and self-help groups some women use these terms with reference to themselves in an effort to destigmatize and neutralize their meanings. Other women in groups with a feminist orientation may retain private definitions of themselves as not really lesbian and yet use lesbian as a public identity statement for political reasons. To some women referring to themselves as lesbian connotes the acceptance of an essential self. Yet other women in the lesbian community, particularly those connected with bisexual groups or groups that are permissive about the identity designations of their members, call themselves bisexual or sexual to indicate their difference from lesbians.

Warren observes that words serve to demarcate the gay world from the straight world: "In the absence of any distinction between straight and gay, say in a society where bisexuality is the rule, there would be no gay world."[2] Berger and Luckmann note the crucial role of language in elaborating a particular world of meaning by stating that incipient legimation of a world view may inhere in meanings and connotations of worlds. Special vocabularies not only serve a nomic or ordering function but may serve to legitimate the phenomena to which they refer.[3] The repetition and acceptance of gay terms within the subculture inherently serves to normalize and legitimate that world for its members.

LESBIAN

The term *lesbian* has a historical tradition stemming from the days of the poet Sappho, who wrote odes celebrating love between women on the isle of Lesbos.[4] Some women have a sense of connection with this historical tradition and have used the term *lesbian* to designate themselves for many years. However, most of the women over 40 years old whom I met use the term *homosexual* or *gay* when referring to themselves.

> I have always called myself a *lesbian*. To me it has always been a beautiful word and describes what I am – I occasionally use the term *Sapphist*, which I also like. I think it's important for lesbians to know that they have a history. The word *gay* seems silly to me, and *homosexual* doesn't fit quite – oh, I suppose in a strict sense. But *lesbian* suits me and is who I am.
>
> (Tape-recorded interview)

The political use of the term *Lesbian*

At the present time, the term *lesbian* is having a renaissance; in certain political and feminist groups, it is the preferred term for all women-related women. *Lesbian*, in its traditional sense, has the connotation of essence and of primary and ontological orientation toward women. As used in political circles, *lesbian* describes a total life-style and solidarity with the women's community. Several of the women I interviewed and many whom I met were involved with feminism to some extent and had come to adopt the word

lesbian – after many years of calling themselves gay or homosexual – as a political statement. These women consider *lesbian* to be an unequivocal statement about the self that affirms their alliance with women, and may consider *homosexual* and *gay* to be male terms. Political lesbians see the usage of the term *lesbian* as a move toward destigmatization and demystification of the word and the social category – in short, as a consciousness-raising device.

In some feminist, gay liberation, radical, and self-help circles, *lesbian* is used as a self-designation to signify support of and solidarity with lesbians not only by women who consider themselves to be gay but by women who privately refer to themselves as bisexual or heterosexual as well, as the following account illustrates:

I: Do you define yourself as a lesbian?
R: I think so. I define myself publicly as a lesbian. Privately I think I might be a bisexual.
I: What's the difference? Why the dichotomy between the public and private?
R: Because I feel it's a cop-out to call myself bisexual publicly. It's like a way of evading the stigma attached to being a lesbian. So I don't want to do a cowardly thing. In terms of accuracy about my feelings, I am involved with women right now and really expect to be involved with women in the future. But it's not inconceivable to me at all that I could also be involved with a man you know, if things were right.

(Tape-recorded interview)

The position of such women – who define themselves publicly as lesbian but who privately define themselves as bisexual or heterosexual and continue to have sexual–emotional affiliations with men – is somewhat equivocal in the view of other lesbians. On the one hand, they are viewed favorably, as supportive toward the community of lesbians. At the same time their continued personal and sexual relationships with men may be seen by some lesbians as puzzling, if not disloyal.

In the subculture, as in the larger society, lesbianism is regarded as an essential identity, though with a meaning quite different from that which the heterosexual world attributes to the essentiality. The idea of choice about lesbianism is incompatible with a notion of the essentiality or ontological status of lesbianism. The self-labeled political lesbian who is bisexual or heterosexual in practice is somewhat of a mystery to women who have always defined themselves as lesbians and see this as not something one chooses to be but something one simply is.

> I must say that I do have some problem understanding women who *decide* to become a lesbian. Somehow I don't see how a woman can *decide to become* a lesbian. She can find out maybe late in life, early or late, she can find out that this was potential in her and she didn't know about it, but that's not *becoming* a lesbian, do you think? It's just finding out what has been repressed or suppressed. To make a political decision to become a lesbian, this seems to me a little farfetched, not to say arbitrary.
>
> (Tape-recorded interview)

HOMOSEXUAL

The terms *female homosexual* and *homosexual* are prevalent usage in groups whose members are over 40 years old and whose socialization into gay life took place early in their own lives. These terms are virtually unused among younger women. Those who entered gay life relatively recently – during the late 1960s and early 1970s – consider *homosexual* to be a technical or medical term or a word that is more appropriately applied to men. But among the women who use *homosexual* as a designation of identity, it is similar in connotation to the term *lesbian*, referring to a primary sexual orientation and to an ontological status. Women who call themselves *homosexual* tend to view themselves as having been "born that way" and are likely to invoke a hormonal or genetic explanation for their orientation. For example, in the following account, a 42-year-old woman-related woman posits an endocrinological explanation of her homosexuality:

> I was actually having homosexual affairs before I was aware of the word *homosexual*. So when I became aware of the word as it pertained to me, I was a freshman in college ... I think it's a matter of different endocrinal pattern between homosexuals and straights. They don't know what comes first, the emotions that produce the pattern or the pattern producing the emotions ...

> I think with some homosexuals it's related to endocrine patterns.
>
> (Tape-recorded interview)

Whether the individual invokes an endocrinological or cosmological explanation to account for homosexuality, *homosexual* is similar to *lesbian* in its centrality and reference to individual essence.

GAY

The word *gay* is probably the most widely used of the three terms. *Gay* derives from the French, *gaie* – meaning a homosexual man. Transmuted into English, *gay* came to refer to a prostitute; its meaning then changed to connote once again a homosexual man. It has now come to refer to the elaboration of homosexuality into a subculture.[5] Its use is common in self-help and gay liberation groups and among younger women in the secretive lesbian community, while it is relatively less common in radical feminist lesbian groups.

Gay is frequently used in a generic and adjectival sense to describe the subculture, persons, lifestyles, communities, relationships, places, and situations. *Gay* may also be used to connote an aspect of the self, as contrasted to an essential identity, among some women who are in gay relationships but do not have gay or lesbian identities.

Although *gay* is widely used in the community as a sort of slang or shorthand expression, it is perceived by some older women-related women as an inappropriate and not un-ironical term that does not truly reflect their life-styles or identities. *Gay* has a connotation that is not without pain for these women, because for them being a homosexual has meant isolation, secrecy, and a fear of discovery – which are in no sense gay. Nonetheless, *gay* has a wide currency among women-related women, particularly among younger women. *Gay*, like *homosexual*, is a term applicable to both men and women and many woman-related women consider gay to be milder and less stigmatizing a term than is *lesbian*.

In addition, some women use this term as an identity label to distinguish or differentiate themselves from what they consider to be real lesbians. A 44-year-old therapist exemplifying this view stated that she distinguishes herself from true lesbians and uses the term *gay* only as conversational shorthand so as not to disrupt the expectation of mutual gayness when she is with gay friends.

> I call myself gay when I'm with my gay friends; otherwise, I don't ... Sometimes I think of myself as not exclusively gay, but as kind of playing a gay game. Like I'm not really gay... that ... I'm really heterosexual, no really bisexual, I would say, and I don't really feel myself as exclusively gay as those lesbian women that I meet. Especially with the younger, more militant lesbians. I don't identify with them at all ... *Lesbian* itself has an old-fashioned, last-generation connotation to it, so I hardly every use that word about myself ... I sort of do fit the word *gay*, but I sort of don't. Because I still have my whole adult history essentially being married and having children, which a lot of lesbians don't. And so that puts a whole other dimension to it, and the ones that are younger and exclusively gay, I can't identify with them any more than I identify with any other single, younger woman.
>
> (Tape-recorded interview)

Gay is used by other woman-related women, however, as a statement of identity in much the same sense as *lesbian* and *homosexual* are used. *Lesbian, gay,* and *homosexual* are not the only major identity tags in the lesbian world. "*Butch*" and "*femme*" are also ways of describing both the essential self, the activities and the apparent identities of others.

BUTCH AND FEMME

Earlier it was mentioned that the term *role playing*, as used in the lesbian world, involves the adaptation of masculine and feminine roles, modeled after typifications of these roles in the heterosexual world. The woman who plays he masculine role is called the butch, while the femme plays the stereotypical traditional female role.

Butch and femme are interpreted by some women simply in terms of a role that one plays. Other women-related women interpret these roles as the external manifestation of the char-

acter of the self and thus see butch and femme in terms of identities.

Role playing is characteristic of a minority of women in the lesbian subculture today. Although it was more prevalent in the past, even then, as reported by respondents, it was practiced by only a small proportion of the women in the community. However, role playing is a prevailing stereotype of lesbian behavior in the heterosexual world and as such has importance as a kind of negative standard in the perception of the lesbians I met. It remains an issue that women in the lesbian subculture may take into account in the formulation of their own identities. Therefore, the following discussion of role playing deals with it as an image rather than as a practice.

Notions of what constitutes butch and femme vary among different groups in the subculture.[6] Many of the characteristics thought of as masculine are attributed to and expected from the butch. Such qualities as being logical (as opposed to emotional), factual, directive, capable of decision-making, as well as being able to take care of tasks outside the home and to handle emergency situations are likewise expected of the butch. In some instances, the butch is expected to be the breadwinner although, according to the women interviewed, usually both butch and femme work.

In its most fully elaborated form the femme role embodies qualities of wifely virtue such as passivity, docility, and nurturance – the panoply of characteristics that comprise the expectations for stereotypical femininity in the heterosexual community. Not infrequently, the femme is described by respondents in disparaging terms as an exaggeration of a stereotypical female role.

> Having been a role player for many years, I would have to say that role playing is where one assumes a more aggressive, more domineering, more masculine kind of role and the other assumes a more passive, more subservient kind of role. Not necessarily in terms of household duties or whatever but in terms of how you relate to one another. Somebody is the boss and somebody is not the boss. Femme is the woman who sees herself in the societal pattern of wife. Femme is the more – I hate to use the word *feminine* – I'll

try and find a better word than that – the societal sense of the ultra-feminine woman, the kind that has to put out that she's not too bright, though she may be very bright. But in her head she's got to let the butch be brighter and stronger than she is; less in the limelight, she takes more of a back seat, more of a "back" role and is sexually passive.

(Tape-recorded interview)

Various aspects of role playing are emphasized among different groups of lesbians. Some lesbian groups stress the importance of appearance and clothing styles. According to respondents, some butches adopt male clothing, wear close-cropped hair and approximate a male physique by such measures as binding their breasts and padding the genital area, though none of the women I interviewed had done this. The more prevalent trend, however, is simply that the butch should affect a more tailored style than the femme:

Well, I tend to be the more feminine. I like make-up and pretty feminine clothes, not your frilly feminine, but more softer looking. And H tends to be somewhat butchy, not really masculine, but more tailored than I am, and she was always into sports and that type of thing when she was younger.

(Tape-recorded interview)

Among most middle-class role-playing lesbians, the modification of dress codes for butch and femme are not necessarily expected to be apparent to heterosexual audiences. In other role-playing lesbian groups, however, women are expected to be identifiably gay in the straight world as well as among other lesbians. A 56-year-old lesbian recounted the range of role-playing expectations that were made of her in various groups:

[Some crowds] that one got into expected more role playing and some were very, very conservative, where everyone was very hard to identify. And then there were groups where there was a great deal of group pressure to be easier to identify – and there was a kind of daring – did you dare be that easy to identify all the time? I dared during the war, when I worked in an aircraft plant. I enjoyed it, but it puts an awfully big strain on you, you know. You have to decide how much you are willing to risk.

(Tape-recorded interview)

MODES AND MEANINGS OF ROLE PLAYING

Some groups, mostly in the secretive world, exert pressures with regard to role playing: some proscribe it and others expect it. Respondents in this study engaged in role playing with varying degrees of commitment both in the context of the community and as isolated individuals. They attributed a range of meanings to the roles they assumed – from roles being mere play to being an expression of the true self.

Role playing as play

A sense of playfulness, fun, and experimentation characterized the role adaptations of some women. They would quite consciously adapt the semblances of role playing with little or no sense of role commitment, exemplifying what Goffman has called *role distance*. That is, women participated in playing a role but with an ironical sense, as this account illustrates.

Role playing? Oh sure, I was into that. You know, I'm really a green country kid. I was. I didn't know anything about anything. All I knew was how I felt, and from adolescence on I felt inclined toward women. By the time I was 24 and ready to get involved with a woman, I went there [to a bar] not realizing that I had to be other than me. When I got there, to that bar, I saw that there was a very definite division. Some women looked very masculine and some looked very feminine, and I really felt that I looked kind of in-between, but people took me to be feminine, and I was *assigned* a role because of my appearance. It doesn't mean that I was overly feminine. It just means that I wasn't overly masculine. So I was classified. That was on the Missouri side in Kansas City. Uh – I got into realizing that I was restricted. I was limited in the kinds of people I could relate to, and I found the kinds of people that I was willing to relate to me as a femme were people that I was not really interested in . . . It restricted me to a class of people that considered themselves butches, butches in the sense of how they look and how they dress. They were not really appealing to me. I had been on the receiving end of aggression from men for years, and I wasn't interested . . . You know, it wasn't really that comfortable for me, and so it was a time when I really didn't know what to do . . . So when I went to the Kansas side, I decided to experiment a little, and I got to the point where I cut off my hair, and so I would go the Kansas side, and I would dress very masculine in terms of men's pants, men's clothes, and men's sweatshirts and things like that, just jeans not really anything else, you know. Uh I would go to the Kansas side, and I would slick my hair back, and I'd be a butch, and I could pursue more feminine women, as we see them, you know, and that was a little more satisfying, and I – so since that time – and people were calling me the "it" because, you know, they'd see me on one side and I'd be a butch, and in Missouri I'd look like a femme, but I didn't want to be restricted. I didn't want to put restrictions on who I could relate to.

(Tape-recorded interview)

The one-way butch

In some groups in the lesbian community, specific sexual expectations for the butch role are normative. For example, the expectations for the butch role sometimes include sexual self-denial. In the argot of the community – referring to the fact that they did not permit reciprocity in love making – such women are called one-way butches or "untouchables." By the logic of role stereotypes the expectations of passivity for the femme and aggressiveness for the butch, taken to an extreme, preclude both sexual initiating behavior and reciprocity on the part of the femme, which would be construed as aggressive on her part. At the same time, the expectations that the butch be the aggressor preclude her from being sexually receptive. The butch was expected to be the lover but not the beloved: she would make love to femmes but not expect love-making in return.

Sexual self-denial, though practiced by some butch lesbians, is considered an anathema by other butches and is never practiced by them. The reasoning behind the self-denial is interesting. Most of the women who said that they played the untouchable in the past stated that they accepted that part of the role because they felt frightened to allow someone to make love to them. Others emphasized that it would have destroyed their ersatz maleness to allow reciprocity. In addition, the heterosexual logic of inversion – "If I like women, I must be masculine" – was operative in several instances.

The experience of one woman echoes the above themes in her account of playing a one-way butch role:

I: What about sexual role playing? Were you into that?
R: Yeah, I was. And I think it was, I think I cheated myself.
I: Are you familiar with the term *one-way butch*?
R: Yes, I'm familiar with the term, I was one. I didn't really like it, because, I again, I feel that I was cheated out of something that I should be getting, more than what I was getting. Somehow I felt frightened because I felt that if I tore down that particular barrier and had a freer sexual exchange with people, they might be frightened, they might be frightened away.
I: What would frighten them?
R: Well, a lot of the people that I know, well, if I tried to have a freer – well, that would frighten them. Oh dear, what would frighten them was that I wasn't really a man and we were putting up a beautiful illusion, and that it wasn't real, and it wasn't true. And I was afraid that if we did anything other than the one-way butch trip that they would be frightened away and not – want – want me anymore.

The majority of the women with whom I spoke disparaged the one-way butch role. Even women, such as the one just quoted, who had engaged in this role in the past had come to feel that they had played it out of a sense of personal insecurity. The following respondent, however, presented a uniquely positive view of the one-way butch role, which she periodically plays:

I've been in relationships like that, where I suppose it sounds kind of weird and far out, but I don't believe that's so entirely the way it sounds – you can become so identified and so empathetic in making love that you can and do come. It's not a wild orgasm, but it certainly doesn't leave you wanting. There is something so exciting and gratifying and climactic about the orgasm of a person you love, it's like, as if you were to pick up on how people feel three or four minutes after an orgasm, that tremendous peace and serenity. So if you can leave out the moment of orgasm and move on a few minutes, that's a very possible thing. I've experienced it, so it isn't quite the same thing as the partner being left in wild need. It can be a very loving thing. I can understand how one could go through a series of relationships like that. I think if you are so empathetic to the other, that's when that happens, only if you love and adore the person who you were with – and then again there are some people who are so inhibited about their gayness that that they may be the only thing they're about to do. Now people that run from one person to another, I think they're on a male trip.

(Tape-recorded interview)

Most lesbians with whom I spoke emphasized the mutuality and reciprocity of lovemaking in lesbian relationships. Most women who had played a butch role among my respondents expressed a disassociation from the one-way butch role, as evidenced in the following:

I have some friends like that, and I think that's very strange, too ... And I used to say to them. "You don't know what you're missing, you know. I think you're missing something here." I don't see it. There again is role playing in some respects, and for some reason or another even the people that are – live a very butch and femme life. If the butch thought that I thought for a minute that maybe they enjoyed some femme making love to them, they would die of mortification.

(Tape-recorded interview)

As indicated earlier, for some women role-playing behavior was a short-lived adaptation to the patterns of relations they saw in gay bars. Interestingly, there is suggestive evidence that isolation from the community of lesbians may have tended toward role-playing behavior among self-labeled lesbians. One respondent remarked:

You have to remember that a lot of the women you are talking to now are urban women, sophisticated women. But twenty years ago, particularly rural women, farm women, country women who had no contact with any kind of gay community, these women tended to be very masculine, male-identified. They didn't have any other models to follow and so when they found themselves attracted to women, they really thought they must be like men. And this was true for some urban women like myself who were young and didn't know what was happening and had no gay community around. You knew you were gay or something, but you weren't even sure what that meant, apart from thinking that you were like a man. It's really meeting other lesbians and being in the community that teaches you that you don't have to be masculine to love another woman.

(Conversation from field notes)

The majority of the women interviewed were disinclined to play roles at all. For example, women whose lesbianism had the meaning, to some degree, of disaffiliation with traditional women's and men's role found the role options of the gay world equally unattractive. Some women, in light of the expectations of role-playing groups, purposely adopted a middle-of-the-road stance, refusing to conform to the expectations of either role. Among role players such women were called "Ki-Ki."[7] Being Ki-Ki – being unwilling to choose a role – was somewhat stigmatized in role-playing crowds. In a taped interview one woman remarked with regard to her Ki-Ki status. "No self respecting butch would have anything to do with you if you were Ki-Ki."

For other women this activity had implications for identity: role playing, particularly the butch role, seemed to satisfy their conceptions of themselves. Martin and Lyon refer to such women as having a "heterosexual consciousness."[8] That is, they perceive themselves as being really masculine in accounting for their attraction to women. Conversely, the femme conceives of herself as a really feminine woman who relates to man-like women. There is some evidence in the accounts of respondents that role-playing styles also characterized women who were isolated from an urban gay community. Rural women, they reported, were much more likely to model themselves after heterosexual standards. Role playing among lesbians would tend to be a more prevalent style in groups where male–female roles are perceived as dichotomous. For many women, role playing was simply a *modus operandi* in certain social (and sometimes sexual) situations. For others, butch and femme roles were enacted as identities in much the same way.

Role playing is clearly on the wane in today's lesbian community and was characteristic in the past of a minority of lesbians as a continuing pattern of behavior. For the respondents in this study, role playing was a temporary pattern of behavior, engaged in either playfully or seriously, in light of expectations they encountered in particular groups or relationships. Thus, it was a passing phase of becoming socialized into the life of the lesbian world.

In the past, more than is true today, the novice lesbian's avenue of access to the lesbian community was through lesbian bars, where role playing expectations frequently prevailed. The greater access to the community provided by political groups, the widespread questioning of the legitimacy of stereotyped sex roles in both straight and gay worlds, and the influence of feminism have served as forces toward diminishing and even proscribing role-playing expectations.

BISEXUAL

The identity status of bisexual is problematic in the lesbian community. Although women with whom I spoke call themselves bisexual when referring to their personal identities and in fact have or have had sexual and emotional relationships with men as well as women, bisexuality is a rather stigmatized identity label in the lesbian community. First of all, it is considered a "cop-out," an evasion of stigma, an attempt to keep one foot in the door of heterosexual respectability. Even more significantly, within the lesbian world as in the heterosexual world, lesbianism in whatever degree is considered more definitive of the self than is heterosexual activity or association. Bisexuality is thus considered an inauthentic identity statement in most parts of the secretive community. Identifying oneself as bisexual is seen as evidence of having problems in accepting "true" lesbian identity in the activist community.

> Bisexual – it is a difficult term for me to believe. It's hard for me to understand how a person can truly relate personally, sexually, emotionally to members of the same sex and the opposite sex. I think you are one way or the other. It's like a child of mixed blood. Even those people who say they are bisexual *must* have something in them that relates to one sex more than the other ... I can't believe it's the same with both ... I can't understand it. I think people have the responsibility to make up their minds and not try and play both sides of the street at the same time. All I can say is, God help the lesbian that gets involved with one, and God help the straight man, too.
>
> (Tape-recorded interview)

As these comments illustrate, the bisexual is considered by many lesbians to be in an impossible position. An implicit assumption about bisexuality in the lesbian community is that the bisexual woman is untrustworthy and lacking in commitment in her relationships, particularly relationships with women. Further, the bisexual

is frequently considered as really a lesbian who is caviling at the stigma involved in identifying herself as such.

> You know, I think bisexual women should shit or get off the pot – they're ripping off lesbians. You know, they have a love affair with a woman and then go revert to status become heterosexual – when things get a little hot ... and it's so easy for women to say they're bisexual. And it's very easy to say that.
>
> (Tape-recorded interview)

Perceptions of bisexuals in the lesbian subculture

The experiences of some lesbians who have been emotionally involved with bisexual women have lent support to the negative valuation of bisexuals in the community. Accounts such as the one that follows become part of subcultural lore, particularly among lesbian activists, and ultimately serve to support polar definitions of heterosexuality and lesbianism and a continuing distrust of bisexuals.

> I got involved with a few bisexual women which I felt really fucked over about, because I felt really put down because they would be with me one night, and they would be with men the next day, and I felt really put down by that. I felt like – I guess anybody can go to bed with them. And I didn't want to be used that way, and there were a lot of lesbians, especially when the woman's movement first started off, there were a lot of what I call political lesbians, not really lesbians but women who did it as a political statement. Like, "Now I've made it with a woman, I'm liberated." Really! And I felt used by those kind of women because they weren't really gay women, as far as emotional – as far as *really* being identified with lesbianism. They were like bisexual women, or they were liberated women. And I felt really oppressed by the, because I was really – I knew I definitely was gay ... But women that are into a big trip where they go back and forth, and they really hurt the lesbians, because emotionally the lesbian might get involved with them ... It makes me feel like I was just an experience; like, "I went to bed with a dyke last night."
>
> (Tape-recorded interview)

The assertion of bisexual identity while engaging in lesbian relationships is regarded by some lesbians with extreme disapprobation and, not infrequently, fear. A lesbian who becomes involved with a bisexually identified woman might experience the ending of such a relationship in terms of a fundamental betrayal, implying a rejection of the lesbian above and beyond personal incompatibility, such as is evinced in the preceding remarks. Relationships between bisexuals and lesbians frequently carry the connotation of the lesbian being objectified as an experience or as an experiment in the course of the bisexual's "liberation."

The status of the bisexual: a paradox in the subculture

Despite the disapprobation received in parts of the lesbian subculture, women-related women who do not identify themselves as lesbians most frequently assert that they are bisexuals. Two general conditions typically underlie the assertion of bisexual identity. First, the woman's past or present experience or future expectations of heterosexual relationships provide a legitimating rationale for bisexual identity. Second, and less frequently, some women maintain the idea of universal bisexuality, asserting that "everyone is a bisexual."

Within the lesbian subculture, the status of the woman who identifies herself as a bisexual is somewhat paradoxical. Bisexuality as an "ideal state," one of which all humans are capable "by nature," is an ideologically legitimate position among activist lesbians. Calling oneself a bisexual, however, is considered to be an evasion of stigma and a denial of one's real self by these same movement-allied, lesbian-identified women. Accepting bisexuality as an ideal while rejecting it in practice is a contradiction in gay ideology as expressed by gay movement people. This contradiction has its apologists, who maintain that emphasizing the differences between heterosexuals and homosexuals makes it possible to build a sense of unity or a collective consciousness among gays. The practical rejection of bisexuality is clearly acknowledged to be a political tactic, one seen as necessary because of the present oppression of gays. According to this logic, separatism is a necessary step in building a strong sense of gay pride.

Other women assert that basically everyone is bisexual but with the proviso that living a bisexual lifestyle is not practicable, given their perception of the disadvantageous position of women in relation to men.

THE SOCIAL CONSTRUCTION OF IDENTITY IN THE LESBIAN WORLD

Sexual behavior is only one criterion for imputing a homosexual identity to the self or others in the lesbian community. In addition to sexual behavior, and ultimately more important than behavior, are feelings of sexual–emotional attraction to the same sex, *whether or not these feelings have been acted upon.*[9] Assumed motivations and feelings may be the basis for the attribution of lesbian or homosexual identity within the gay community, paralleling the notion of latency within the psychiatric community.

Within the lesbian subculture the emergence of lesbian-related identity, irrespective of the terms used and of its specific content, is interpreted within the framework of what I call the *gay trajectory* and the process of coming out. The gay trajectory and coming out constitute basic underlying images of the social construction of identity within the lesbian world. The term *trajectory* is used in a special sense to describe a set of trajectories of identities. Each one of four elements of the gay trajectory may be the starting point of a projected path that leads to the most critical element – the assumption of lesbian identity.

The trajectory of gay identity, the principle of identity construction in the lesbian world, functions similarly to the principle of consistency, the underlying assumption of the social construction of sex-related identities in the larger society. It is construed as a relationship among five elements of subjective experience and behavior, an atemporal series of elements. The first element is that the individual has a subjective sense of being different from heterosexual persons and identifies this difference as feelings of sexual–emotional attraction to her own sex. Second, an understanding of the homosexual or lesbian significance of these feelings is acquired. Third, the individual accepts these feelings and their implication for identity – that is, the individual comes out or accepts the identity of lesbian. Fourth, the individual seeks a community of like persons. Fifth, the individual becomes involved in a sexual–emotional lesbian relationship. Given one of these elements, irrespective of their order in time, it is commonly assumed in the lesbian world that the others will logically come to pass.

The first three – the subjective experience of sexual–emotional attraction to one's same sex, an understanding of the lesbian significance of these feelings, and the acceptance of lesbian identity – are considered primary elements in the subculture's perspective. Though the search for a community of like persons and an actual sexual relationship are expected to co-vary with the other elements, their absence can be circumstantially explained. It is presumed, however, that given the first three elements, the individual will experience a sense of strain toward the other two. Such individuals are presumed to be in search of community. With respect to a woman who has not had a sexual–emotional relationship but who conforms to other elements of the trajectory, again it is assumed that, were she to have such relationships, by definition they would be with women.

These identity experiences are usually located separately in time, and their specific order of occurrence varies widely among individuals. In the experience of some lesbians, these elements are reported as occurring simultaneously. In these instances, it can be presumed that the lesbian significance of these behaviors and experiences is part of the individual's stock of knowledge.

The gay trajectory, as the assumption underlying the social construction of lesbian identity, functions as a biographic norm of the community.[10] Moreover, its normative power is most clearly manifested when rule breaking occurs – when an individual reports experiencing all the elements outlined above, save the acceptance of lesbian identity. For example, certain women with whom I spoke had subjective feelings of attraction for their same sex that they define as lesbian, were in the lesbian world, had lesbian relationships, and yet stated that they were not really lesbians but were bisexuals or heterosexuals. Such women do not accept the essentiality of their lesbian behavior. In the community's terms a bisexual would be explained as "having trouble dealing with her gayness." The self-definition would not be considered legitimate or authentic within the lesbian world, given that the individual has lesbian feelings and relationships. In brief, when women claim (or are thought to have) attractions to women, or have sexual relations with women, or are present in the lesbian community over time, or acknowledge a subjective sense of difference from heterosexual others, then the acceptance and acknowledgment of lesbian identity (at least in the company of other lesbians) are expected to follow.

Being in the community

Unattached females who associate with gay groups by going to gay meeting places such as bars and clubs will probably have gayness ascribed to them. A vocabulary of motives is implicit in the way in which identities are socially construed within the lesbian community that leads to assumptions about persons who seem attracted to gay company.[11] The exceptions to these expectations are persons who are considered wise by the community, a status that is facilitated by membership in a heterosexual couple. Once established, the status of the wise straight person may not be suspect, but for some it may be difficult to achieve. For example, a single or unattached woman who seeks out and seems to prefer the company of gay women is likely to have gayness attributed to her or she may be said to be in the process of realizing her gayness, whether she acknowledges it or not. Protestations of a non-gay identity are likely to be interpreted in terms of having problems facing gayness, while counterclaims about identity are explained in terms of being in a transitional period in the gay trajectory.

Blumstein and Schwartz comment in their study of bisexuals and lesbians that

since most lesbians have had some heterosexual experience, and all have suffered some emotional strain from the process of "coming out" as homosexual, it is widely believed in the lesbian community that a "bisexual phase" really is only a manifestation of the ambivalent feelings associated with "coming out." Hence, a bisexual is often defined simply as a homosexual who has not yet been able to accept her true identity. In the extreme, some lesbians refuse to believe that true bisexuality (or even ambisexuality) exists ... Hence, women who claim a bisexual identity receive not only hostility from their lesbian peers, but are in a sense told that the identity they are claiming is not real, but rather a fantasy or a phase which will not endure experience.[12]

However, a woman may engage in sexual relations with another woman without having the motives that are deemed appropriate by the lesbian community and thus may not have lesbian identity assigned to her by lesbians. An example would be a woman who is perceived as experimenting with lesbian relationships, a practice considered reprehensible.[13] A certain seriousness in motivation and a transitional commitment to lesbian relationships are expected to obtain.

EXPLAINING DEVIATIONS FROM THE GAY TRAJECTORY

Deviations from the expectations of the gay trajectory are explained in terms of having difficulty accepting gayness or in terms of programming by the larger society, such as explanations employing the concept of repression. For example, a woman may have a sexual–emotional relationship with a woman and "not be aware" of previous feelings of attraction for her own sex. During the process of learning to acknowledge her lesbian identity, she may learn to reinterpret her biography in such a way that previously "unrecognized" feelings are brought to light. Such reinterpretations are supported by subcultural rhetorics of repression and oppression. Subcultural ideology also provides explanations for events that seem incongruous or contradictory with lesbianism, such as lesbians having current heterosexual attractions as well as heterosexual pasts, which might tend to call into question the essentiality and pervasiveness of a gay identity. These feelings are explained in terms of programming by the larger society that results in superficial conformity to heterosexual standards. In this regard, Blumstein and Schwartz note that "lesbians who have spent a long time in the homosexual community often socialize younger ones to treat any heterosexual feelings as delusions."[14]

The following 45-year-old respondent, for example, accounted for her twenty-five-year heterosexual marriage and other relationships with men to her lack of knowledge about approaching women sexually:

> I've been attracted to girls sexually since I was fourteen. I was such a chicken shit that we always did minimal things. We'd neck and pet. It was never – I didn't know how to take it past that. I was hemmed in by convention so I could never find anybody who would go along with what I wanted. So I was forced to have sex with men, and to release with them what was stimulated by being with women, and the fact [is] that in this culture we aren't allowed or even know how to do these things with women.
>
> (Tape-recorded interview)

Identity lag

Members of the gay community recognize that the acceptance of gay identity may be problematic for the individual. Such problems may be expressed in the term *identity lag*, that is, there may be a lapse of time between experiencing feelings of difference from heterosexual others, labeling the feelings, engaging in sexual behavior, and accepting and acknowledging lesbian identity. Dank notes in his observations of the male gay community that there is an average lapse of six years between an initial sense of attraction to persons of the same sex and the assumption of gay identity.[15] Identity lag has been institutionalized in the gay community. In the argot of the community, it is called coming out.

Coming out

The initial process of indicating to the self that one is gay is called coming out. Another significant meaning of the term in the lesbian world relates to the interaction between gay actors and their audiences. In addition to indicating gayness to the self, coming out refers to disclosing a gay self before an expanding series of audiences. This second use is more characteristic of political groups, for whom disclosure is a political and ideological stance. But both secret lesbians and activists refer to coming out before various audiences; for example, "I came out with my parents" or "She came out with her straight friends at work."[16]

Coming out is conceived of as a process that takes place over time – a series of acknowledgments and self-labelings. The self is the first audience to the coming out process. Later the individual comes out to an ever expanding audience of people. One is virtually "all the way out" when most others with whom the individual is in contact are aware of her gay identity.

Full membership as a lesbian is often extended to participants whose identity status is problematic, under the rationale of coming out. It is expected in the gay community that some persons may have lesbian feelings and engage in lesbian acts and maintain a heterosexual or a bisexual identity for some time. Even though there is an expected congruence between acts and identity on the one hand and feelings and identity on the other hand, these breaches of expectations of the gay trajectory are explained in terms of the process of coming out, unless the individual is deemed an experimenter.

The community gives permission for a period of transition in which the individual's identity may not have caught up with her feelings and behavior. But one is not expected to tarry too long in the transitional phase. If a person continues to assert an identity that is perceived as incongruent with feelings and behavior, sanctions ranging from mild disapproval to public denouncement (the latter in highly political circles) may ensue. Explanations for the person's identity lag will move from the rationale and permission of the coming out process to accusations of inauthenticity, stigma evasion, or fence-sitting. Thus although the elements of the gay trajectory may vary in their temporal order, the trajectory does include implicit time norms.

The following conversation with a lesbian refers to a woman that I had seen in gay settings many times over a period of two and one-half years.

I: Well, how is K? I usually expect to see her when I see you.
R: Oh, my god! She's such a closet case![17] It gets to be a real pain in the ass. She'll have a little to drink and then try and be affectionate. I'm no damned experiment! She's always getting crushes and then getting angry with the woman because she can't handle her own feelings. She's so scared about what someone will say. You know, she's been my friend for years, but it's gotten ridiculous lately. I just can't stand her lying and denying. I wish she'd just come out and get it over with. It's getting boring already.
(Conversation condensed from field notes)

Thus, if over the course of time a woman "talks differently than she walks" – if she is perceived as being "long overdue" with respect to realizing her gay identity – she may become unwelcome in gay circles.

INDIVIDUAL RESPONSES TO THE GAY TRAJECTORY

Individual women within the lesbian community have a range of responses to the expectations of the gay trajectory as well as to the process of coming out. These responses can be typified in three general forms: rejection of lesbian identity, public conformity with private reservations, and acceptance of the group's definition of identity, thus rendering social identity and personal identity congruous.

Some persons continue to construct individualistic conceptualizations of themselves and to reject the validity of the gay trajectory: they refuse to come out. In so doing, they implicitly reject the essentiality of gayness altogether.

I think that a person can love and relate sexually to a man or a woman – *if* they'll let themselves. It's so arbitrary to have to put some label on it. I suppose that there are some people who really are at the ends of the continuum and, like, who are really lesbian who never cared about men – ever – and I guess never ever would be attracted to men, and I suppose they are *really* lesbians, but even there it could be learning, don't you think? I mean they are *used* to relating to women and not men.
(Tape-recorded interview)

Women who are in lesbian relationships but do not consider themselves to be lesbians may handle the expectations implied in the gay trajectory by publicly (that is, with other gay people) stating that they are gay or by not disrupting the homosexual assumption and yet maintaining their private interpretations of their personal identity.

Some women state that they believe gayness is an essential identity for real lesbians but that they are not real lesbians themselves. They often make this claim by virtue of either past heterosexual experience or projected plans for heterosexual experience in the future. Alternatively, they may feel that lesbian identity does not correspond to their experiences of themselves. A 50-year-old woman distinguishes her use of the term *lesbian* with reference to herself from her concept of real lesbians:

> At my age I consider it expedient to be a lesbian. It's a smart choice for me. The chances of my meeting a man my own age aren't great, and I'm not interested in being involved in a "mother–son" relationship. My best chances, being realistic, for a good relationship are with a woman. So when I say I'm a lesbian, I'm saying that I choose to relate to women at this time in my life and that I'll probably continue to do so. But I'm not closed to relating to a man again. I'm certainly not. At the same time women who have always been lesbians, real lesbians, absolutely fascinate me. I believe they have a real different culture like X and her friends – so conventional in so many ways and yet really unconventional in their sexuality. You may not agree with me, but I think there is really something different about them. For me it's a choice, and I think a smart one looking at the world around me. I don't call myself a bisexual because it's a cop-out, but I guess that's how I'd describe myself.
> (Conversation condensed from field notes)

It should be pointed out that identity statements vary over time, not simply in response to perceived pressures from others but also in response to varying interpretations of the self and the meaning of lesbianism to the individual. The fact that sexual object choices vary over time for many individuals stimulates efforts to interpret the meaning of sexuality and self. Obviously, women who have had subjectively meaningful experiences with both men and women might be expected to be in the most conflicted position, given the stigma accruing to lesbianism and the presumptions of essentiality of lesbianism in both the heterosexual and lesbian communities as well as the gay trajectory as an expectation in the gay community.

Acceptance of lesbian identity

Many women involved in the lesbian world over time come to accept the subculture formulation of identity and to embrace the logic of the gay trajectory. Further, most of the women who do come to designate themselves as lesbians reinterpret their biographies in conformity with the gay trajectory. For many of these women contact with the lesbian subculture is experienced as finding one's own, finally having a framework for understanding themselves and placing themselves in the world.

> Coming out was an absolute relief. I always knew I was different, but I didn't know what it was. It was like suddenly I was home. Searching for years, in this difference. Knowing I was different and not knowing how I could relate to this difference, and it was like all of a sudden someone lifted a whole load off me. I felt like I finally found a structure, an awareness of myself where I suddenly knew where I belonged in the world, as compared to constantly searching and knowing that no matter where I was, I didn't quite fit. Not knowing, not being sure where I was in relationship to the people I was around.
> (Tape-recorded interview)

Recognition and acknowledgment of gayness as the true self frequently involves attributing inauthenticity to acts and behaviors that do not conform to gay identity. Previous identity statements may come to be viewed as instances of mistaken identity, as indicated by the following remarks:

> Coming out means that I used to *think* I was straight and now I *know* that I'm gay.
> (Tape-recorded interview)

> As I became close to the [women's] movement, I thought every time I have these love feelings, it's always towards a man; you know, I took them as I didn't question them, because I they seemed so genuine. It was soft and loving and so seemed so much a part of me, but only because this part [the lesbian part] was all squashed down.
> (Tape-recorded interview)

> Now I'm not the person I was before I got embroiled in this marriage trip [an eighteen-year marriage]. When I was married, I didn't even

know who I was. When I left, I found that part of being my own person has to do with loving women.

(Tape-recorded interview)

SUMMARY

The gay trajectory and coming out provide a framework for interpreting the meaning of gayness and its relationship to identity. Coming out is experienced by many women as a process of conversion within the self and as a resolution of identity.

Ideological features of the lesbian subculture tend toward the adaptation of a lesbian identity as the essential and true self. Not having a lesbian identity when one does have other lesbian elements is perceived in the community in terms of difficulties in acknowledgment and acceptance of lesbian identity. Recognition of these difficulties has been institutionalized in the community in the process of coming out.

It is worthwhile to note the parallels between the conceptualizations and theories about lesbianism and homosexuality in the heterosexual and lesbian communities. The attribution of essentiality is an important element in formulations about lesbianism in both communities, for the belief in its essentiality reinforces the polarization of lesbian and heterosexual identities and conceptualizations about them. The principle of consistency is matched in its inexorability by the biographic norms suggested in the gay trajectory and in the coming out process. Of course, the positive value placed on lesbianism or gayness within the lesbian community radically distinguishes its theories from those of the heterosexual community. Nonetheless, both the stigmatizing perspective of the larger society and the idealizing perspective of the lesbian world are similar in conceptions about the pervasiveness of gayness and its relation to identity.

The trajectory of gay identity in the gay world is similar to the principle of consistency in the heterosexual world as both are used as a standard in terms of which variations in sexual identities are explained. The gay trajectory also provides a method for locating the true self, because here again gayness is considered definitive of the self in an essential way. The gay trajectory presumes the existence of the true self and presumes to know the character of the true self of individuals who supply the cues of feelings, sexual attractions, interests or associations with gay people.

NOTES

1. Cf. Jack Katz, "Deviance, Charisma, and Role-Defined Behavior," *Social Problems* 20 (1972): 186–202; Jack Katz, "Essences as Moral Identities."
2. Warren, *Identity and Community*: 101.
3. Berger and Luckmann, *Social Construction of Reality*, 92–4.
4. Klaich, *Woman + Woman*: 129–60.
5. Bruce Rodgers, *The Queen's Vernacular* (San Francisco: Straight Arrow Books, 1972): 93.
6. There is some suggestive evidence from respondents' reports that the adaptation of role playing styles may vary inversely with social class. One would thus expect a greater degree of role playing behavior and commitment to that behavior in groups whose members derive from heterosexual groups or milieus that dichotomize strongly between male and female roles. Hedblom's work suggests regional variations in the adaptation of role-playing styles – the Midwest being the most conservative (that is, participating in role playing) and the two coasts displaying considerably less role playing. See Jack H. Hedblom and John J. Hartman, "Comparative Dimensions of Lesbianism Over Time, Place and Data Collection Techniques" (paper read at the Annual Meeting of the Midwest Sociological Society, 1976).
7. "Ki-Ki" means a lesbian who will not adopt or declare a masculine or feminine role. See Sidney Abbott and Barbara Love, *Sappho Was a Right-On Woman: A Liberated View of Lesbianism* (New York: Stein & Day Publishers, 1972): 93–4.
8. Martin and Lyon, *Lesbian/Woman*.
9. Cf. Warren, *Identity and Community*.
10. Warren, "Observing the Gay Community," 144.
11. Cf. C. W. Mills, "Situated Actions and Vocabularies of Motive," *American Sociological Review* 5 (December 1940): 904–13.
12. Philip W. Blumstein and Pepper Schwartz, "Lesbianism and Bisexuality" (manuscript, University of Washington, 1974): 17.
13. Experimentation may be perceived essentially in two ways depending on the motives attributed to

the experimenter – the first in conformance with the gay trajectory and the coming out process. A woman may be seen as experimenting as an expression of her underlying true lesbian identity, of which she is unaware. On the other hand, a woman may be seen as a heterosexual whose experiments example callousness – who in effect is "using" lesbians for her own pleasure with no sense of commitment to relationship.

14 Blumstein and Schwartz, "Lesbianism and Bisexuality": 18.

15 Barry Dank, "Coming Out in the Gay World," *Psychiatry* 34 (May 1971): 180–97.

16 For an elaboration of the many meanings of "coming out," see Dank, "Coming Out in the Gay World."

17 "Closet case" means someone who is assumed to be gay but will not acknowledge it.

RICHARD TROIDEN

"A Model Of Homosexual Identity Formation"

from *Gay and Lesbian Identity: A Sociological Analysis* (New York: General Hall, 1988): chapter 4

This chapter develops an ideal-typical model that describes how committed homosexuals – men and women who have defined themselves as homosexual and adopted homosexuality as a way of life – recall their arrival at perceptions of self as homosexual in relation to romantic and sexual settings. More specifically, the chapter describes ideal types, reviews models for homosexual identity formation that influenced the present work, present a four-stage ideal-typical model of homosexual identity formation in both lesbians and gay males, and calls attention to the variables that influence rates of homosexual identity formation.

IDEAL TYPES

Ideal types represent abstractions based on concrete observations of the phenomena under investigation. They are heuristic devices – ways of organizing materials for analytical and comparative purposes. These types are not real; nothing and nobody fits them exactly (Theodorson and Theodorson 1969).

Ideal types are used as benchmarks against which to describe, compare, and test hypotheses relating to empirical reality (Theodorson and Theodorson 1969); they are frameworks for ordering observations logically. Ideal types are similar to stereotypes except that they are examined and refined continuously to correspond more closely to the empirical reality that they try to represent. At best, ideal models capture general patterns encountered by many individuals; variations are expected and explained, and often lead to revisions of ideal types.

The four-stage model of homosexual identity

formation outlined here describes only general patterns encountered by committed homosexuals – women and men who see themselves as homosexual and adopt corresponding lifestyles. Often repeated themes in the life histories of lesbians and gay males, clustered according to life stages, provide the content and characteristics of each stage. Progress though the various stages increases the probability of homosexual identity formation, but does not determine it fully. A shifting effect is involved; some men and women "drift away" at various points before the fourth and final stage and never adopt homosexual identities or lead homosexual lifestyles.

THEMES OF MODELS

During the past decade, several investigators have proposed theoretical models that attempt to explain the formation of homosexual identities (Cass 1979, 1984; Coleman 1982; Lee 1977; Minton and McDonald 1983/4; Plummer 1975; Ponse 1978; Schäfer 1976; Sophie 1985/6; Troiden 1977, 1979; Weinberg 1977, 1978). Although the various models suggest different numbers of stages to explain homosexual identity formation, they describe strikingly similar patterns of growth and change as major hallmarks of homosexual identity formation.

First, nearly all the models view homosexual identity formation as taking place against a backdrop of stigma. The stigma surrounding homosexuality affects both the formation and management of homosexual identities. Second, homosexual identities are described as developing over a protracted period and involving a number of "growth points or changes" that may be ordered into a series of stages (Cass 1984). Third, homosexual identity formation involves increasing acceptance of the label "homosexual" as applied to the self. Fourth, although "coming out" begins when individuals define themselves to themselves as homosexual, lesbians and gay males typically report an increased desire over time to disclose their homosexual identity to at least some members of an expanding series of audiences. Thus, coming out, or identity disclosure, takes place at a number of levels: to self, to other homosexuals, to heterosexual friends and family, to co-workers, and to the public at large (Coleman 1982; Lee 1977). Finally, lesbians and gays develop "increasingly personalized and frequent" social contacts with other homosexuals over time (Cass 1984).

MAJOR WORKS

The four-stage model developed later in this chapter is a revision of my earlier work, which synthesized and elaborated on Plummer's (1975) model of "becoming homosexual." The revised model incorporates insights provided by Barbara Ponse's (1978) and Vivienne Cass's (1979, 1984) theorizing and research on homosexual identity formation. Because the works of Plummer, my earlier research, and the investigations by Ponse and Cass influenced my revised model of homosexual identity formation, I discuss each prototype briefly.

Plummer

According to Plummer (1975), homosexual identity formation is part of the larger process of "becoming homosexual," that is, adopting homosexuality as a way of life. Becoming homosexual involves the decision to define oneself as homosexual, the learning of homosexual roles and the decision to live one's adult life as a practicing homosexual. Plummer believes that males who adopt homosexuality as a way of life pass through a "career" consisting of four stages.

In the *sensitization* stage, boys gain childhood experiences that may later serve as bases for defining themselves as homosexual. These experiences are gained in three areas: *social* (gender-inappropriate interests), *emotional* (same-sex emotional attachments), and *genital* (same-sex genital activities). Childhood experiences sensitize boys to interpret past events as indicating a homosexual potential.

Signification and disorientation occur during adolescence. During this stage, boys begin to speculate that their interests and feelings "might" be homosexual. Their awareness of homosexuality and its potential relevance to self is subsequently heightened (signified). The homosexual implications of their activities, feelings, or interests produce anxiety and confusion (disorientation).

Boys establish contact with other homosexuals, self-define as homosexual, and begin to learn homosexual roles during the *coming-out* stage, which typically begins at some point during middle to late adolescence. Finally, *stabilization* occurs when they become comfortable with homosexuality and committed to it as a way of life.

Further research and theorizing on homosexual identity formation has revealed some problems with Plummer's theoretical account. First, his analysis focuses on men who adopt homosexuality as a way of life, but neglects homosexual identity formation in lesbians. Second, he does not define homosexual identity or indicate its relationship to self-concept. Third, his account is theoretical rather than empirical; he did not test his model against the experiences of a sample of gay males.

Troiden

My own research (Troiden 1977, 1979) on acquisition of gay identity, using a sample of 150 homosexual men, provides empirical support for a theoretical framework similar to Plummer's. This formulation also consists of four stages: sensitization, dissociation and signification, coming out, and commitment.

The sensitization and coming-out stages are comparable to those described by Plummer, but *dissociation* consists of the conscious partitioning of sexual feelings or activity from sexual identity. Rather than diminish the awareness of possible homosexual feelings, dissociation has the unintended and ironic effect of signifying or highlighting the feelings. Finally, *commitment* presupposes a reluctance to abandon the homosexual identity even in the face of an opportunity to do so. Happiness and satisfaction with the homosexual identity and lifestyle also characterize the commitment stage.

This model also has its shortcomings. It focuses only on males, fails to give a clear definition of homosexual identity, and neglects to distinguish between, and relate, the concepts of self-concept and identity (Cass 1983/4).

Ponse

Barbara Ponse's (1978) sociological study of identities in the lesbian world focused on how lesbian identities are formed in relation to the norms of the lesbian community. She contacted informants in her observational study through self-help organizations of overt homosexual women and friendship networks among lesbians. Seventy-five informants took part, thirty-six of whom were interviewed in depth (Ponse 1984).

Ponse's research identified a "gay trajectory" consisting of five elements that serve as possible steps toward assuming lesbian identities. The first element is a subjective sense of difference from heterosexuals, which is identified as an emotional or sexual preference for other women. Next, women gain an understanding of the lesbian or homosexual significance of their sexual or romantic feelings. The third element is the assumption of a lesbian identity. Fourth, these women seek the company of similarly situated women. Fifth and last, they become involved in lesbian emotional or sexual relationships.

The first three steps are of primary importance from the perspective of the lesbian community. Given these three elements, "the individual will experience a sense of strain toward the other two" (Ponse 1978: 125). Ponse found wide variations in the order in which her informants encountered elements of the gay trajectory. I shall return to this point.

Ponse's study led her to conclude that it is difficult to define who "really is" lesbian; a certain amount of independence exists between identity and activity. She identified four combinations of identity and activity and determined that women can and do shift from one to another: lesbian identity and lesbian activity; lesbian identity without lesbian activity (e.g., celibacy or heterosexual activity); lesbian activity without lesbian identity (e.g., heterosexual or bisexual identity); and heterosexual activity and heterosexual identity. Similar distinctions have been drawn for gay males (Troiden 1977; Warren 1974) as well as for lesbians (Blumstein and Schwartz 1974).

A majority of the women interviewed by Ponse fell into the category of lesbian identity and activity, and saw the lesbian identity as "an emanation from the essential self: lesbianism is a totality of which sexuality is a mere part" (Ponse 1978: 171). The gay males observed by Carol Warren (1974) drew a similar distinction between "being" gay and "doing" homosexual activity.

Ponse also distinguishes between *primary* lesbians, *elective* lesbians and women with *idiosyncratic* identities. For primary lesbians, memories of sexual or emotional attractions to the same sex predated puberty, and few of these women reported heterosexual experiences. Elective lesbians, in contrast, generally identified their feelings as homosexual at much later ages, and most reported heterosexual experiences. Bell, Weinberg, and Hammersmith (1981a: 201) make the same point when they distinguish between exclusive homosexuals and bisexuals. Finally, women with idiosyncratic identities generally viewed themselves as heterosexual or bisexual, even though they were involved in meaningful lesbian relationships or participating actively in the lesbian subculture.

Ponse's analysis of lesbian identity suffers a few limitations. First, her work details the range of identities and roles available to women in the lesbian community instead of describing how women came to assume their lesbian identities in the first place. Second, although the women in her sample encountered the elements making up the gay trajectory in somewhat different orders, some of this variation may be explained by her small sample size and the fact that her analysis includes all four combinations of identity and activity described above. Third, she did not ask her informants standardized questions to determine, for example, the age at which they recalled first becoming aroused by the same sex, or the age of first homosexual activity. Thus she had no way of determining the model pattern for her informants. Fourth, had she focused only on women with lesbian identities and activities, as in the present study, she might have found less variation along the gay trajectory.

Cass

Vivienne Cass's (1979) theoretical account of homosexual identity formation was the first attempt at explaining homosexual identity development in both lesbians and gay males. Her original formulation cast homosexual identity development into a mold involving six stages.

Before stage 1, according to Cass, people believe thay are heterosexual and never question this assumption. During the first stage, *identity confusion*, they begin to think they might possibly be homosexual. In the second stage, *identity comparison*, people begin to believe they are probably homosexual. Women and men define themselves as homosexual during the *identity tolerance* stage, but remain uncomfortable with their homosexual identities. "Contacting other homosexuals is viewed as 'something that *has* to be done' in order to counter the felt isolation and alienation from others" (Cass 1979: 229; italics added). The fourth stage, *identity acceptance*, occurs in the wake of positive contacts with other lesbians and gays who provide neophytes with information and justifications that "normalize" homosexuality as an identity and a lifestyle.

During the fifth stage, *identity pride*, gays and lesbians are proud to be homosexual and enjoy their homosexual lifestyles. They do not hide their homosexuality, but frequently disclose it to others. Moreover, they become angry when exposed to the anti-homosexual attitudes held by many heterosexuals, and vigorously defend homosexuality in their presence. For this reason, lesbians and gay males prefer to mix socially with other homosexuals during this stage.

During *identity synthesis*, gay males and lesbians are prepared to tell anyone they are homosexual, although they no longer perceive their homosexual identities as the most important part of themselves. Although occasionally angered by anti-homosexual sentiments, they have learned through experience that many heterosexuals accept homosexuals comfortably. In this final stage, gay males and lesbians mix socially with both homosexuals and heterosexuals.

Cass (1984) tested her theoretical model with a specially developed questionnaire. Analysis of results obtained from 103 gay males and sixty-three lesbians revealed no clear-cut boundaries between stages 1 and 2 (identity confusion, identity comparison) and stages 5 and 6 (identity pride, identity synthesis); the hypothesized differences between these stages are indistinct. Cass concluded that homosexual identities may be formed in four stages: identity confusion, identity tolerance, identity acceptance, and identity synthesis.

Although Cass's (1979, 1983/4, 1984) scholarship on homosexual identity formation is theortically and empirically rigorous, critical evaluation of her work reveals some shortcomings. First, her model ignores the role of childhood genital, emotional and social experiences in creating alienation and perceptions of difference that contribute to initial feelings of identity confusion. Second, her conceptualization of homosexuality identity equates identity *development* with identity *disclosure*. For Cass, a homosexual identity is "fully evolved" only when individuals disclose the identity to "*all* others constituting the individual's social environment" (1983/4, 111). An identity option – degree of openness about the homosexual identity – becomes a prerequisite for full identity development. Because most homosexuals do not disclose their identities to most people (as is demonstrated later in this chapter), Cass's model would characterize them as "developmentally arrested."

Identity disclosure is more a matter of identity management than identity development. Strictly speaking, homosexual identities are developed when individuals define themselves as such, but a shift of emphasis does occur in the wake of homosexual self-labeling. Questions about sexual identity are replaced by concerns about managing the stigma attached to homosexual identities and lifestyles.

Identity disclosure, however, is an overt indication of commitment to homosexuality as a way of life. To the extent that people routinely present themselves as homosexual in most or all social settings, their homosexual identities are realized – brought into concrete existence – more frequently than those of people who disclose their identities less frequently, if at all.

Third, when Cass asserts that the homosexual identity (a cognition) is not developed fully without full self-disclosure in all settings (a behavior), she mixes cognitive and behavior elements within the same construct, something she claims must be avoided for the sake of conceptual clarity.

Fourth, although Cass conceptualizes identity tolerance and identity acceptance as two different stages, identity tolerance may be viewed as the beginning, and identity acceptance as the end, of a single stage. During this stage, people define themselves as homosexual, begin to associate with other homosexuals, learn homosexual roles, and acquire a series of "accounts" (Scott and Lyman 1968) or "vocabularies of motives" (Mills 1940) that excuse, justify or legitimize homosexual feelings and behavior. In this way, they neutralize the negative views of homosexuality absorbed from the wider, stigmatizing society.

AN IDEAL-TYPICAL MODEL

Sensitization, the first stage in my four-stage model, is borrowed from Plummer. Stage 2, identity confusion, combines insights borrowed from Plummer, Cass, and my earlier model. The third stage, identity assumption, incorporates Cass's hypothesized stages of identity tolerance and acceptance and the "coming out" stage from my earlier model. The fourth stage, commitment, builds on my earlier model; it posits

identity disclosure (from Cass) as an identity option rather than a separate stage, and as an external indicator of commitment to homosexuality as a way of life. Theoretical insights borrowed from Ponse are incorporated throughout the model.

Sociological analysis of homosexual identity formation begins with an examination of the social contexts and patterns of interaction that lead individuals to accumulate a series of sexual meanings, which predispose them to identify themselves subsequently as homosexual (Plummer 1975). The meanings of feelings or activities, sexual or otherwise, are not self-evident. Before people can indentify themselves in terms of a social condition or category, they must learn that a social category representing the activity or feelings exists (e.g., homosexual preferences or behavior); learn that other people occupy the social category (e.g., that homosexuals exist as a group); learn that their own socially constructed needs and interests are more similar to those who occupy the social category than they are different; begin to identify with those included in the social category; decide that they qualify for membership in the social category on the basis of activity and feelings in various settings; elect to label themselves in terms of the social category, that is, define themselves as "being" the social category in contexts where category membership is relevant; and incorporate and absorb these situationally linked identities into self-concepts over time (Lofland 1969; McCall and Simmons 1966; Simmons 1965).

A word of warning: From an interactionist perspective, although identities develop over time in a series of stages, identity formation is not conceptualized as a linear, step-by-step process, in which one stage follows and builds on another, with fluctuations written off as regression. Instead, the process of homosexual identity formation resembles a horizontal spiral, like a spring lying on its side. Progress through the stages occurs in a back-and-forth, up-and-down fashion; the stages overlap and recur in somewhat different ways for different people (McWhirter and Mattison 1984). In many instances, stages are encountered in consecutive order, but sometimes they are merged, glossed over, bypassed, or realized simultaneously. In particular, the approximate ages outlined for each stage are rough guidelines. Because these ages are based on averages, variations are to be expected and should not be treated as regressions. People also vary somewhat in the order in which they encounter homosexual events (e.g., age at first homosexual activity).

Stage 1: Sensitization

The *sensitization* stage occurs before puberty. At this time, most lesbians and gay males do not see homosexuality as personally relevant; that is, they assume they are heterosexual, if they think about their sexual status at all. Lesbians and gay males, however, typically acquire social experiences during their childhoods that serve later as bases for seeing homosexuality as personally relevant, lending support to emerging perceptions of themselves as possibly homosexual. In short, childhoood experiences sensitize lesbians and gays to subsequent self-definition as homosexual. Sensitization parallels Minton and McDonald's (1983/4) "egocentric" stage.

Sensitization is characterized by generalized feelings of marginality, perceptions of being different from same-sex peers. The following comments illustrate the forms these childhood feelings of difference assumed for lesbians: "I wasn't interested in boys"; "I was more interested in the arts and in intellectual things"; "I was very shy and unaggressive"; "I felt different: unfeminine, ungraceful, not very pretty, kind of a mess"; "I was becoming aware of my homosexuality. It's a staggering thing for a kid that age to live with"; "I was masculine, more independent, more aggressive, more outdoorish"; "I didn't express myself the way other girls would. For example, I never showed my feelings. I wasn't emotional" (Bell, Weinberg, and Hammersmith 1981a: 148, 156).

Similar themes of childhood marginality are echoed in the comments of gay males: "I had a keener interest in the arts"; "I couldn't stand sports so naturally that made me different. A ball thrown at me was like a bomb"; "I never learned to fight"; "I wasn't interested in laying girls in the cornfields. It turned me off completely"; "I just didn't feel I was like other boys. I was very fond of pretty things like ribbons and flowers and music"; "I began to get feelings I was gay. I'd notice other boys' bodies in the gym and masturbate excessively"; "I was indifferent to boys' games, like cops and robbers. I was more interested in watching insects and reflecting on certain things"; and "I was called the sissy of the family. I had been very pointedly told that I was effeminate" (Bell, Weinberg, and Hammersmith 1981a: 74, 86).

Research by Bell, Weinberg, and Hammersmith (1981a) found that homosexual males (N=573) were almost twice as likely (72 per cent vs. 39 per cent) as heterosexuals controls (N=284) to report feeling "very much or somewhat" different from other boys during grade school (grades 1–8). Lesbians (N=229) were also more likely than heterosexual controls (N=101) to have felt "somewhat or very much" different from other girls during grade school (72 per cent vs. 54 per cent).

During sensitization, childhood social experiences play a larger role than emotional or genital events in generating perceptions of difference. Both lesbians and gay males in the Bell, Weinberg, and Hammersmith sample saw gender-neutral or gender-inappropriate interests or behaviors as generating their feelings of marginality (the social realm). Only a minority of the lesbians and gay males felt different because of same-sex attractions (the emotional realm) or sexual activities (the genital realm).

More specifically, lesbians in the Bell, Weinberg, and Hammersmith study were more likely than heterosexual controls to say they felt different because they were more "masculine" than other girls (34 per cent vs. 9 per cent), because they were more interested in sports (20 per cent vs. 2 per cent), or because they had homosexual interests or lacked heterosexual interests (15 per cent vs. 2 per cent). Moreover, fewer lesbian than heterosexual controls (13 per cent vs. 55 per cent) reported having enjoyed typical girls' activities (e.g., hopscotch, jacks, playing house), but lesbians were much more likely (71 per cent vs. 28 per cent) to say they enjoyed typical boys' activities (e.g., baseball, football).

In a similar vein, homosexual males were

more likely than heterosexual controls to report that they felt odd because they did not like sports (48 per cent vs. 21 per cent), because they were "feminine" (23 per cent vs. 1 per cent), or because they were not sexually interested in girls or were sexually interested in other boys (18 per cent vs. 1 per cent). Gay males were also significantly more likely than heterosexual controls (68 per cent vs. 34 per cent) to report having enjoyed solitary activities associated only indirectly with gender (e.g., reading, drawing, music). Moreover, homosexual males were much less likely than heterosexual controls (11 per cent vs. 70 per cent) to report having enjoyed boys' activities (e.g., football, baseball) "very much" during childhood.

Although a sense of being different and set apart from same-sex age mates is a persistent theme in the childhood experiences of lesbians and gay males, research indicates that only a minority of gay males (20 per cent) and lesbians (20 per cent) begin to see themselves as *sexually* different before age 12 and fewer still – only 4 per cent of the females and 4 per cent of the males – label this difference as "homosexual" while they are children (Bell, Weinberg, and Hammersmith 1981b: 82–3). It is not surprising that "pre-homosexuals" used gender metaphors rather than sexual metaphors to interpret and explain their childhood feelings of difference; the mastery of gender roles rather than sexual scripts is emphasized during childhood (Doyle 1983; Tavris and Wade 1984). Although they may have engaged in heterosexual and/or homosexual sex play, children do not appear to define their sexual experimentation in heterosexual or homosexual terms. The socially created categories of homosexual, heterosexual, and bisexual hold little or no significance for them. Physical acts become meaningful only when thay are embedded in sexual scripts, which are acquired during adolescence (Gagnon and Simon 1973). For these reasons, pre-homosexuals rarely wonder, "Am I a homosexual?" or believe that homosexuality has anything to do with them personally while they are children.

The significance of sensitization resides in the meanings attached *subsequently* to childhood experiences, rather than the experiences themselves. Because sociocultural arrangements in American society articulate linkages between gender-inappropriate behavior and homosexuality, gender-neutral or gender-atypical activities and interests during childhood provide many women and men with a potential basis for subsequent interpretations of self as possibly homosexual. Childhood experiences gained in social, emotional, and genital realms come to be invested with homosexual significance during adolescence. The reinterpretation of past events as indicating a homosexual potential appears to be a neccessary (but not sufficient) condition for the eventual adoption of homosexual identities.

Stage 2: Identity confusion

Lesbians and gay males typically begin to personalize homosexuality during adolescence, when they begin to reflect upon the idea that their feelings or behaviors could be regarded as homosexual. The thought that they are potentially homosexual is dissonant with previously held self-images. The hallmark of this stage is *identity confusion* – inner turmoil and uncertainty surrounding their ambiguous sexual status. The sexual identities of lesbians and gay males are in limbo; they can no longer take their heterosexual identities as given, but they have yet to develop perceptions of themselves as homosexual. Minton and McDonald (1983/4) draw a similar portrait in their "sociocentric" stage, and Sophie (1985/6) calls this the "first awareness" stage of lesbian identity formation.

Cass (1984: 56) describes the early phase of identity confusion in the following way:

> You are not sure who you are. You are confused about what sort of person you are and where your life is going. You ask yourself the questions "Who am I?" "Am I a homosexual?" "Am I really a heterosexual?"

By middle or late adolescence, a perception of self as "probably" homosexual begins to emerge. In retrospective studies involving adults, gay males begin to suspect that they "might" be homosexual at an average age of 17 (Troiden 1979; Troiden and Goode 1980), lesbians at an average age of eighteen (Schäfer 1976).

Cass (1984: 156) describes the later phase of identity confusion as follows:

> You feel that you *probably* are a homosexual, although you're not definitely sure. You feel distant or cut off from [other people]. You are beginning to think that it might help to meet other homosexuals but you're not sure whether you really want to or not. You prefer to put on a front of being completely heterosexual.

Several factors are responsible for the identity confusion experienced during this phase: altered perceptions of self, the experience of heterosexual and homosexual arousal and behavior, the stigma attached to homosexuality, and inaccurate knowledge about homosexuals and homosexuality.

Altered perceptions of self are partly responsible for the identity confusion experienced during this phase. Childhood perceptions of self as different crystallize into perceptions of self as sexually different after the onset of adolescence. Whereas only 20 per cent of the lesbians and gay males in the Bell, Weinberg, and Hammersmith (1981a) study saw themselves as sexually different before age 12, 74 per cent of the lesbian and 84 per cent of the gay males felt sexually different by age 19, as compared to only 10 per cent of the heterosexual female and 11 per cent of the heterosexual male controls. For both homosexual women and men, the most frequently cited reasons for feeling sexually different were homosexual interests and/ or the lack of heterosexual interests. Gender atypicality was mentioned, but not as frequently. Thus genital and emotional experiences, more than social experiences, seem to precipitate perceptions of self as sexually different during the stage of identity confusion.

Another source of identity confusion is found in sexual experience itself. Recent investigation of homosexuality have revealed consistently that homosexuals exhibit greater variability in their childhood and adolescent sexual feelings and behaviors than heterosexuals (Bell and Weinberg 1978; Bell, Weinberg, and Hammersmith 1981b; Saghir and Robins 1973; Schäfer 1976; Weinberg and Williams 1974). By early to middle adolescence, most lesbians and gay males have experienced both heterosexual and homosexual arousal and behavior. Only a minority of the Bell, Weinberg, and Hammersmith sample, for example – 28 per cent of the gay males and 21 per cent of lesbians – were *never* sexually aroused by the opposite sex, and only 21 per cent of the males and 12 per cent of the females reported never having an opposite-sex encounter that they or others considered sexual. Thus significant majorities of lesbians and gay males experience heterosexual and homosexual arousal and behavior before age 19. Since American society portrays people as either homosexual or heterosexual, it is not surprising that adolescent lesbians and gay males are uncertain and confused regarding their sexual orientations.

As a general rule, gay males are aware of their same-sex attractions at earlier ages than lesbians. Males report awareness of their same-sex feelings at an average age of 13 (Bell, Weinberg, and Hammersmith 1981a; Dank 1971; Kooden *et al.* 1979; McDonald 1982). The corresponding average age for lesbians is between 14 and 16 (Bell, Weinberg, and Hammersmith 1981a; Riddle and Morin 1977). Gay males first act on their sexual feelings at an average age of 15 (Bell, Weinberg, and Hammersmith 1981a; Kooden *et al.* 1979; McDonald 1982; Troiden 1979; Troiden and Goode 1980), whereas lesbians first act on their sexual feelings at an average age of 20, four to six years after first awareness of their same-sex attractions (Bell, Weinberg, and Hammersmith 1981a; Riddle and Morin 1977; Schäfer 1976).

The stigma surrounding homosexuality also contributes to identity confusion because it discourages adolescent (and some adult) lesbians and gay males from discussing their emerging sexual desires and/or activities with either age mates or families. As Plummer (1975) has noted, the societal condemnation of homosexuality creates problems of guilt, secrecy, and difficulty in gaining access to other homosexuals. Moreover, the emphasis placed on gender roles and the privatization of sexuality compounds identity confusion and aloneness.

Ignorance and inaccurate knowledge about homosexuality also contribute to identity confusion. People are unlikely to identify themselves in terms of social category as long as they are unaware that the category exists, lack accurate information about the kinds of people who occupy the category, or believe they have nothing in common with category members (Lofland 1969). In other words, before they can see themselves as homosexual, people must realize that homosexuality and homosexuals exist, learn what homosexuals are actually like as people, and be able to perceive similarities between their own desires and behaviors and those of people labeled socially as homosexual. Today, accurate information about homosexuality has been circulated and distributed throughout society, making it easier to identify homosexual elements in feelings and activities (Dank 1971; Troiden 1979; Troiden and Goode 1980). Lesbian and gay males first understand what the term *homosexual* means at approximately the same time, at the average age of 16 or 17 respectively (Riddle and Morin 1977). Knowledge about the term *homosexual* may be acquired more rapidly in urban areas than in rural areas, where homosexuality is less likely to be discussed.

Lesbians and gay males typically respond to identity confusion by adopting one or more of the following strategies: denial (Goode 1984; Troiden 1977); repair (Humphreys 1972) avoidance (Cass 1979); redefinition (Cass 1979; Troiden 1977); and acceptance (Cass 1979; Troiden 1977).

Gay males and lesbians who use *denial* disclaim the homosexual component to their feelings, fantasies, or activities. *Repair* involves wholesale attempts to eradicate homosexual feelings and behaviors. Professional help is sought to eliminate the sexual feelings, fantasies, or activities considered unacceptable.

Avoidance is a third overall strategy for dealing with identity confusion (Cass 1979). Although avoidant women and men recognize that their behavior, thoughts, or fantasies are homosexual, they regard them as unacceptable, something to be avoided.

Avoidance may assume at least one of several forms. Some teenaged (and adult) men and women *inhibit* the behaviors or interests they have learned to associate with homosexuality: "I thought my sexual interest in other girls would go away if I paid more attention to boys and concentrate more on being feminine"; "I

figured I'd go straight and develop more of an interest in girls if I got even more involved in sports and didn't spend much time on my art" (author's files).

Some adolescent men and women *limit* their *opposite-sex exposure* to prevent peers or family from learning about their relative lack of heterosexual responsiveness: "I hated dating. I was always afraid I wouldn't get erect when we petted and made out and that the girls would find out I was probably gay." "I felt weird compared to the other girls. I couldn't understand why they thought guys were so great. I dated only to keep my parents off my back" (author's files).

Other gay males and lesbians *limit* their *exposure to information* about homosexuality during adolescence because they fear that the information may confirm their suspected homosexuality: "Your first lecture on homosexuality awakened my fears of being homosexual. I cut class during the homosexuality section and skipped the assisted readings. I just couldn't accept the idea of being a lesbian" (author's files); "One ingenious defense was to remain as ignorant as possible on the subject of homosexuality. No one would ever catch *me* at the 'Ho' drawer of the New York Public Library Card Catalog" (Reid 1973: 40).

Another avoidance strategy is to assume *anti-homosexual postures*. Some teenaged (and adult) men and women distance themselves from their own homoerotic feelings by attacking and ridiculing homosexuals: "At one time I hated myself because of sexual feelings for men. I'm ashamed to admit that I made a nellie guy's life miserable because of it"; "I really put down masculine acting women until I came out and realized that not all lesbians act that way and that many straight women do" (author's files).

Heterosexual immersion is another strategy for avoidance. Some adolescent lesbians and gay males establish heterosexual involvements at varying levels of intimacy in order to eliminate their "inappropriate" sexual interests: "I thought my homosexual feelings would go away if I dated a lot and had sex with as many women as possible"; "I thought my attraction to women was a passing phase and would go away once I started having intercourse with my boyfriend" (author's files). In some instances, an adolescent girl may purposely become pregnant as a means of "proving" that she could not possibly be homosexual.

Another avoidance strategy is *escapism*. Some adolescent lesbians and gay males avoid confirming their homosexual erotic feelings through the use and abuse of chemical substances. Getting high on drugs provides temporary relief from feelings of identity confusion and may be used to justify sexual feelings and behavior ordinarily viewed as unacceptable.

A fourth general means of reducing identity confusion is to *redefine* behavior, feelings, or context along more conventional lines. (Plummer [1984] calls redefinition "neutralization".) Redefinition is reflected in the use of special-case, ambisexual, temporary-identity (Cass 1979), or situational strategies.

In the *special-case* strategy, homosexual behavior and feelings are seen as an isolated case, a one-time occurrence, part of a special, never-to-be repeated relationship: "I never thought of my feelings and our love-making as lesbian. The whole experience was too beautiful for it to be something so ugly. I didn't think I could ever have those feelings for another woman" (author's files).

Defining the self as *ambisexual* (bisexual) is another redefinitional strategy: "I guess I'm attracted to both women and men" (author's files). People who adopt *temporary-identity* strategies see their homosexual feelings and behavior as stages or phases of development that will pass in time: "I'm just passing through a phase, I'm not really homosexual" (author's files). Finally, those who adopt situational strategies define the situation, rather than themselves, as responsible for the homosexual activity or feelings: "It only happened because I was drunk"; "It never would have happened if I hadn't been sent to prison."

A fifth overall strategy is *acceptance*. With acceptance, men and women acknowledge that their behavior, feelings, or fantasies may be homosexual, and seek out additional sources of information to determine the nature of their sexual preferences. For adolescent men and women who always felt different because they felt that their thoughts, feelings, and behavior

were at odds with others of their sex, their sense of isolation is diminished by the gradual realization that homosexuals exist as a social category and that they are "probably" homosexual. The homosexual category provides them with a label for their difference. "From the time I was quite young I felt different from other girls and I felt more masculine than feminine. When I learned that lesbians existed I had a word that explained why I was different from other girls" (author's files). "The first name I had for what I was, was 'cocksucker'. 'Cocksucker' was an awful word the way they used it, but it meant that my condition was nameable. I finally had a name for all those feelings. I wasn't nothing" (Reinhart 1982: 26).

Perceptions of self anchored in the strategies of denial, repair, avoidance, or redefinition may be sustained for months or years or permanently. Ambisexual perceptions of self, for example – a redefinitional strategy – may be maintained or undermined by a person's social roles, social structures, and relationships, and by the perceived stength, persistence, and salience of the homosexual feelings. Although individuals may use several different strategies for stigma management, they characteristically use some more than others.

Whether the etiology of homosexuality is anchored in biological predispositions or social learning, "the evidence now available suggests that, at least for some individuals, childhoood and adolescent experiences may serve as the basis for adult homosexual identity" (Minton and McDonald 1983/4: 97).

Stage 3: Identity assumption

Despite differences in stigma-management strategies, a significant number of men and women progress to *identity assumption*, the third stage of homosexual identity formation, during or after late adolescence. In this stage, the homosexual identity becomes both a self-identity and a presented identity – at least to other homosexuals. Defining the self as homosexual and presenting the self as homosexual to other homosexuals are the first stages in a larger process of identity disclosure called *coming out*

(Coleman 1982; Lee 1977). The hallmarks of this stage are self-definition as homosexual, identity tolerance and acceptance, regular association with other homosexuals, sexual experimentation, and exploration of the homosexual subculture.

Homosexual self-definition occurs in contexts that vary between the sexes. Lesbians typically arrive at homosexual self-definition in contexts of intense affectionate involvements with other women (Cronin 1974; Schäfer 1976). Seventy-six per cent of the lesbians interviewed by Cronin, for example, defined themselves in contexts of meaningful emotional involvements with other women. Gay males, in contrast, are more likely to arrive at homosexual self-definition in social/sexual contexts where men are reputed to gather for sexual purposes – gay bars, parties, parks, YMCAs, and men's rooms (Dank 1971; Troiden 1979; Warren 1974). Only a minority of males appear to define themselves in contexts of same-sex love relationships (Dank 1971; McDonald 1982; Troiden 1979). Today, I suspect that young men are more likely to arrive at homosexual self-definitions in romantic or fantasized contexts than in sexual settings. For many men, the possibility of contracting AIDS has reduced the perceived desirability of sexual experimentation.

Patterns laid down during sex-role socialization explain why lesbians define themselves in emotional contexts, gay males in social/sexual contexts. "Male sexuality is seen as active, initiatory, demanding of immediate gratification, and divorced from emotional attachment; female sexuality emphasizes feelings and minimizes the importance of immediate sexual activity" (de Monteflores and Schultz 1978). For males, admitting a desire for homosexual activity implies the label of homosexual; for females, intense emotional involvement with the same sex has similar implications.

Lesbians and gay males also typically define themselves as homosexual at different ages. Retrospective studies of adult homosexuals suggest that gay males arrive at homosexual self-definitions between the ages of 19 and 21, on the average (Dank 1971; Harry and Devall 1978; Kooden et al. 1979; McDonald 1982; Troiden 1979). Retrospective studies involving small samples of adolescent gay males indicate a younger age at the time of self-identification as homosexual: age 14, on the average (Remafedi 1987). Adult lesbians recall reaching homosexual self-definitions slightly later, between the average ages of 21 and 23 (Califia 1979; Riddle and Morin 1977; Schäfer 1976; Smith 1980).

Self-definition as homosexual may occur just before, at the same time as or shortly after first social contact with other homosexuals (Cronin 1974; Dank 1971; Ponse 1978; Troiden 1979). Initial contacts may have been engineered consciously (e.g., by deciding to go to a homosexual bar) or accidentally (e.g., by learning that a friend is homosexual). Only a minority of lesbians and gay males appear to define themselves as homosexual without having direct contact with one or more homosexuals. Self-designation as homosexual in the absence of affiliation with other homosexuals (e.g., as a consequence of reading about homosexuality) has been referred to as *disembodied affiliation* (Ponse 1978).

Although homosexual identities are assumed during this stage, initially they are tolerated rather than accepted. Cass (1984: 156) describes people who tolerate their homosexual identities as follows:

> You feel sure you're a homosexual and you put up with, or tolerate this. You see yourself as a homosexual for now but are not sure about how you will be in the future. You usually take care to put across a heterosexual image. You sometimes mix socially with homosexuals, or would like to do this. You feel a need to meet others like yourself.

Sophie (1985/6) describes this period as the "testing and exploration" phase of lesbian identity formation.

The quality of a person's initial contacts with homosexuals is extremely important (Cass 1979). If initial contacts are negative, further contact with homosexuals may be avoided and non-homosexual perceptions of self will persist, maintained through the strategies of denial, repair, self definition as ambisexual, or temporary identity described earlier. Perceptions of the increased risks of living as a homosexual in a homophobic society, such as blackmail or fear of AIDS, may also encourage individuals to cling to non-homosexual perceptions of self.

Positive contacts with other homosexuals, on the other hand, facilitate homosexual identity formation. Favorable contacts provide lesbians and gay males with the opportunity to obtain information about homosexuality at first hand. Direct positive exposure provides a basis for re-examining and re-evaluating their own ideas about homosexuality and for seeing similarities between themselves and those labeled "homosexual." The meanings attributed to the homosexual label begin to change in a more favorable direction.

Personally meaningful contacts with experienced homosexuals also enable neophytes to see that homosexuality is socially organized and that a group exists to which they may belong, which diminishes feelings of solitariness and alienation. Other homosexuals provide neophytes with role models from whom they learn strategies for stigma management, rationalizations that legitimize homosexuality and neutralize guilt feelings, the range of identities and roles available to homosexuals, and the norms governing homosexual conduct.

Once they adopt homosexual identities, lesbians and gay males are confronted with the issue of stigma and its management. They may adopt one or several stigma-evasion strategies during identity assumption: capitulation, minstrelization (Levine 1987), passing, or group alignment (Humphreys 1972).

Women and men who *capitulate* avoid homosexual activity because they have internalized a stigmatizing view of homosexuality. The persistence of homosexual feelings in the absence of homosexual activity, however, may lead them to experience self-hatred and despair. In *minstrelization*, individuals express their homosexuality along lines etched out by the popular culture. They behave as the wider culture expects them to behave – in highly stereotyped, gender-inappropriate fashions.

Passing as heterosexual is probably the most common stigma-evasion strategy (Humphreys 1972), especially among recently self-defined homosexuals. Women and men who pass as heterosexual define themselves as homosexual, but conceal their sexual preferences and behavior from heterosexuals – family, friends, and colleagues – by careful, even torturous, control of information" (Humphreys 1972: 138). Passers lead "double lives"; they segregate their worlds into heterosexual and homosexual spheres and hope the two never collide.

Group alignment is also adopted commonly by neophyte homosexuals to evade stigma. Men and women who evade stigma through affiliation become actively involved in the homosexual community. The perception of "belonging" to a world of others situated similarly eases the pain of stigma. They look upon other homosexuals as sources of social and emotional support, as well as sexual gratification. Yet an awareness of "belonging" to the homosexual subculture also fosters an awareness of "not belonging," perceptions of being excluded from the worlds of opposite-sex dating, marriage, and parenthood. People may deal with this alienation by *immersing* themselves completely in the homosexual subculture; by *avoiding* heterosexual settings that remind them of their stigma; by *normalizing* their behaviors, that is, minimizing the differences between heterosexuals and homosexuals (Ponse 1978); by *aristocratizing* homosexual behavior, that is, attaching a special significance to homosexual experience (Ponse 1980); or by *nihilizing* heterosexual experience, that is, viewing heterosexual patterns as deviant (Warren 1980).

To recapitulate, positive homosexual experiences facilitate homosexual self-definition, whereas unrewarding experiences reinforce negative attitudes toward homosexuality. Undesirable homosexual experiences may prompt people to reject the identity ("I am really heterosexual"), abandon the behavior ("I want sex with others of the same sex but can get by without it"), or reject both identity and behavior ("I am not homosexual. I can learn to desire the opposite sex").

By the end of the identity assumption stage, people begin to accept themselves as homosexual. Cass (1984: 156) describes *acceptance* of the homosexual identity as follows:

> You are quite sure you are a homosexual and you accept this fairly happily. You are prepared to tell a few people about being a homosexual but you carefully select whom you will tell. You adopt an attitude of fitting in where you live and work. You

can't see any point in confronting people with your homosexuality if it's going to embarrass all concerned.

Sophie (1985/6) also uses the term "identity acceptance" to describe this stage of lesbian identity development.

Stage 4: Commitment

A *commitment* is a feeling of obligation to follow a particular course of action (Theodorson and Theodorson 1969). In the homosexual context, it involves adopting homosexuality as a way of life. For the committed homosexual, "it becomes easier, more attractive, less costly to remain a homosexual" than to try to function as a heterosexual (Plummer 1975: 150). Entering a same-sex love relationship marks the onset of commitment (Coleman 1982; Troiden 1979). The identity assumption and commitment stages described here are incorporated in Minton and McDonald's (1983/4) "universalistic" stage. Following Cass (1979), Sophie (1985/6) labels the fourth stage of lesbian identity formation "identity integration."

The hallmarks of the commitment stage are self-acceptance and comfort with the homosexual identity and role. Commitment has both internal and external dimensions. It is indicated *internally* by the fusion of sexuality and emotionality into a significant whole, a shift in the meanings attached to homosexual identities, a perception of the homosexual identity as a valid self-identity, expressed satisfaction with the homosexual identity, and increased happiness following self-definition as homosexual. It is indicated *externally* by same-sex love relationships, disclosure of the homosexual identity to non-homosexual audiences, and a shift in the kinds of stigma-management strategies.

Internal indicators. The fusion of same-sex sexuality and emotionality into a meaningful whole is one internal measure of a person's commitment to homosexuality as a way of life (Coleman 1982; Troiden 1979; Warren 1974). The same sex is redefined as a legitimate source of love and romance, as well as sexual gratification. Homosexuals themselves see same-sex

romantic preferences as differentiating "true" homosexuals from those who are merely experimenting (Warren 1974).

Another internal measure of commitment to homosexuality as a way of life is reflected by the meanings attached by homosexuals to the homosexual identity. The homosexual subculture encourages both lesbians and gay males (Ponse 1978, 1980; Warren 1974, 1980; Warren and Ponse 1977) to perceive the homosexual identity as an "essential" identity – a state of being and way of life – rather than merely a form of behavior or sexual orientation. Lesbian feminists are especially likely to view lesbianism as all-encompassing: "A lesbian's entire sense of self centers on women. While sexual energies are not discounted, alone they do not create the lesbian feminist" (Faderman 1984/85: 87).

The perception of the homosexual identity as a valid self-identity is also a sign of internal commitment. Homosexual identities and roles are seen as growing out of genuine, deep-seated needs and desires. Homosexual expression is reconceptualized as "natural" and "normal" for the self. Committed homosexuals find the homosexual identity "a more valid expression of the human condition than that afforded by a heterosexual one" (Humphreys 1979: 242).

The degree of satisfaction that people express about their present identities is another measure of internal commitment (Hammersmith and Weinberg 1973). When Bell and Weinberg (1978) asked their sample of homosexuals whether they would remain homosexual even if a magic pill would enable them to become heterosexual, 95 percent of the lesbians and 86 percent of the gay males claimed they would *not* take the magic pill. In addition, 73 percent of the gay males and 84 percent of the lesbians indicated they had "very little or no" regret about their homosexuality. Only 6 percent of the male and 2 percent of the female homosexuals felt "a great deal" of regret. Societal rejection and punitiveness and the inability to have children were the most frequently mentioned sources of regret.

Increased happiness is another indication of an internal commitment to homosexuality. When asked, "At this time would you say you are more, less, or about as happy as you were prior to arriving at a homosexual self-definition?", 91 percent of the gay males I interviewed indicated they were more happy, 8 percent stated they were about as happy, and only one person said he was less happy (Troiden 1979).

External indicators. A same-sex love relationship is one external sign of a commitment to homosexuality as a way of life (Coleman 1982; Troiden 1969; Warren 1974), a concrete manifestation of a synthesis of same-sex emotionality and sexuality into a meaningful whole. Lesbians appear to enter their first same-sex love relationships between the ages of 22 and 23 (Bell and Weinberg 1978; Riddle and Morin 1977), a year or less after they define themselves as lesbians. Gay males typically have their first love affairs between the ages of 21 and 24 (Bell and Weinberg 1978; McDonald 1982; Troiden 1979), roughly two to five years after they define themselves as homosexual. In keeping with their gender-role training, males are much more likely than lesbians to gain sexual experiences with a variety of partners before focusing their attentions on one special person (Troiden 1979). Lesbians are more likely to explore the homosexual community and gain sexual experiences in the context of an emotional relationship with one other woman, or a series of "special" women (Cronin 1974; Smith 1980).

Disclosure of the homosexual identity to heterosexual audiences is another external measure of commitment to homosexuality as a way of life. As mentioned earlier, coming out involves disclosure of the homosexual identity to some members of an expanding series of audiences ranging from self to other homosexuals, to heterosexual friends and/or family, to co-workers, to employers, and to the general public by self-identification as homosexual through the media (Coleman 1982; Hencken and O'Dowd 1977; Lee 1977).

Homosexual identity formation is characterized over time by an increasing desire to disclose the homosexual identity to non-homosexual audiences (Cass 1984). Few people, however, disclose their homosexual identities to everybody in their social environments. Instead, they fluctuate "back and forth in

degrees of openness, depending on personal, social, and professional factors" (de Monteflores and Schultz 1978). Lesbians and gay males appear more likely to come out to siblings, close heterosexual friends, or parents than to co-workers or employers. Fifty percent of the gay males and 62 percent of the lesbians interviewed by Bell and Weinberg (1978) said they had told "some or all" of their siblings about their homosexuality. Regarding disclosure to heterosexual friends, 54 percent of the lesbians and 53 percent of the gay males claimed that "some or most" of their heterosexual friends knew about their homosexuality. Fewer had told their parents about their homosexuality. Forty-two percent of the gay males and 49 percent of the lesbians said they had come out to their mothers, and 37 percent of the females and 31 percent of the males said they had told their fathers.

Bell and Weinberg's (1978) respondents exercised even greater discretion in disclosing their homosexual identities to co-workers and employers. Sixty-two percent of the gay males and 76 percent of the lesbians stated that "few or none" of their co-workers knew they were homosexual, and 85 percent of the lesbians and 71 percent of the gay males claimed that their employers were unaware of their homosexuality. Lesbians and gay males appear reluctant to come out in the workplace for two reasons: fear of endangering job credibility or effectiveness, and fear of job or income loss (Kooden *et al.* 1979; Riddle and Morin 1977).

Those lesbians who disclose their homosexual identities to non-homosexual friends begin to do so at an average age of 28 (Riddle and Morin 1977); gay males begin to disclose their identities between the average ages of 23 and 28 (McDonald 1982; Riddle and Morin 1977). Gay males who disclose their homosexual identities to their parents do so at age 28, on the average; lesbians at an average age of 30 (Riddle and Morin 1977). Those who come out in professional settings do so at even later average ages – 32 for lesbians and 31 for gay males (Riddle and Morin 1977). The AIDS epidemic has increased the stigma attached to homosexuality. As a result, younger (and older) gay males and lesbians may be less willing today than in the past to disclose their homosexual identities to non-homosexual audiences.

A third external indicator of commitment is a shift in stigma management strategies. Covering (Humphreys 1972) and blending appear to replace passing and group alignment as the most common strategies, with a minority opting for conversion (Humphreys 1972).

Women and men who *cover* are ready to admit that they are homosexual (often because it is obvious or known), but nonetheless take great pains to keep their homosexuality from looming large. They manage their homosexuality in ways meant to demonstrate that although they may be homosexual, they are nonetheless respectable. "Imitation of heterosexual marriage, along with other roles and lifestyles designed to elicit praise from the straight segments of society" typifies this form of stigma evasion (Humphreys 1972: 139). Like people who blend, people who cover turn to other homosexuals for social and emotional support as well as sexual gratification, and disclose their homosexual identities selectively to significant heterosexuals.

People who *blend* act in gender-appropriate ways and neither announce nor deny their homosexual identities to non-homosexual others. They perceive their sexual preferences as irrelevant to the kinds of activities they undertake with heterosexuals, and cloak their private lives and sexuality in silence. When quizzed or challenged about their sexual preferences or behavior, they are likely to respond: "What's it to you?" or "It's none of your business." Women and men who blend affiliate with the homosexual subculture and present themselves as homosexual to other gay males and lesbians and to carefully selected non-homosexuals. As used here, blending is similar to Warren's "avoidance without hiding" (1974: 94).

Lesbians and gay males who *convert* acquire an ideology or world view that not only destigmatizes homosexuality but transforms it from a vice to a virtue, from a mark of shame to a mark of pride. People who convert confront rather than evade the homosexual stigma. Formally or informally, they attempt to inform the general public about the realities of homosexuality and the special contribution made to society by homosexuals in hopes of eliminating oppression through education and political change (e.g., equal rights in jobs and housing). A few lesbians and gay males adopt conversionist strategies during the identity assumption stage when they define themselves as homosexual.

Stigma-evasion strategies are situational rather than constant – that is, personal, social, or professional factors may prompt individuals to blend or cover in some situations, disclose their homosexual identity openly in others, and switch to conversationist modes in yet other contexts. Selective and relatively nonselective self-disclosure have important consequences for the self. Identity disclosure enables the homosexual identity to be realized more fully – that is, brought into concrete existence – in a wider range of contexts. A more complete integration between homosexuals' identities and their social worlds is made possible when they can see and present themselves as homosexual and can be viewed as such by others. *Identity synthesis*, associated with identity disclosure, is described by Cass (1984: 156) in the following way:

> You are prepared to tell [almost] *anyone* that you are a homosexual. You are happy about the way you are but feel that being a homosexual is not the most important part of you. You mix socially with homosexuals and heterosexuals [with whom] you are open about your homosexuality.

The passage of time also forges links between many social situations and identities, which accounts partly for the stability of adult identities. By the time individuals reach middle age, the people with whom thy routinely interact have a huge backlog of evidence about what they are like, and should be like, in a variety of roles and situations (Atchley 1982). It becomes increasingly difficult to misrepresent oneself to intimates and co-workers. Moreover, as time passes,

> people tend to conclude that they know themselves as well and probably better than anyone else does or could. This can lead us to assign more weight to what we think about ourselves than to what others say about us. We may also feel that stereotypes about some category we might be assigned to are irrelevant to our own self images. (Atchley 1982: 383)

Commitment to the homosexual identity and

role is a matter of degree. Homosexuals span a continuum from low to high levels of commitment on both internal and external dimensions, which may vary across time and place. For this reason, commitment is always somewhat inconsistent, strengthened or weakened at various points and contexts by personal, social, or professional factors.

CONCLUSIONS

In the final analysis, homosexual identity is emergent – never fully determined in a fixed or absolute sense, but always subject to modification and further change. Homosexual identity formation is continuous, a process of "becoming" that spans a lifetime, a process of "striving but never arriving" (Plummer 1975). The rates of homosexual identity formation, however, may be influenced by a number of factors, which serve as qualifications to the model.

Homosexual events are well defined, clearly recognizable occurrences in the lives of women and men who define themselves as homosexual and adopt homosexuality as a way of life. As indicated earlier, these events (or components of homosexual experience) are often clustered with the various stages. Examples of homosexual events include first awareness of same-sex attraction, first homosexual activity, self-definition as homosexual, first association with other homosexuals, and first same-sex love relationship.

The average ages for the homosexual events reported here were obtained from only a few studies; further replications are necessary. Until more investigations have been conducted, these average ages should be viewed as educated guesses.

Sample characteristics have been shown to influence rates of homosexual identity formation and the reported ages for the homosexual events; the mean ages of respondents in the studies cited here vary, for example. In samples consisting of relatively older lesbians and gay males, the respondents recall that they encountered the various events at relatively higher average ages than younger informants, thus raising the average ages at which the events

seem to occur. Older informants grew up during a time when homosexuality was rarely discussed, and then only in highly stereotypical terms.

Research conducted in the 1970s and 1980s indicates that adolescent lesbians and gay males in the United States may encounter the events and acquire their homosexual identities at earlier ages than did their older counterparts. More specifically, homosexuals under 25 may encounter the various components of homosexual identity at significantly lower ages than those reported here. Increased openness, tolerance, and accurate information about homosexuality in the United States may have made it easier to perceive similarities between self and "homosexuals" (Dank 1971; Remafedi 1987; Troiden 1977, 1979; Troiden and Goode 1980).

On the other hand, the onset of the AIDS epidemic may have the opposite effect on homosexual identity formation; it may delay the process (at least among males) because AIDS has increased the stigma attached to homosexuality. The possibility of contracting AIDS may motivate people defensively to deny their erotic feelings, to delay acting on them, or to express them only in the context of a committed love relationship. In addition, the AIDS crisis may undermine identity integration and a positive sense of homosexual identity. To avoid being seen as potential disease carriers, lesbians and gay males may choose not to disclose their homosexual identities to non-homosexual audiences. Identity fear may replace identity pride; fear of infection may promote erotophobia – the fear of sexual relations – and cause people to avoid homosexual behavior completely or reduce their sexual experimentation.

Gender-inappropriate behavior (Harry 1982), adolescent homosexual arousal and activity, and an absence of heterosexual experiences (Troiden and Goode 1980) may also facilitate progress through the events and stages. Gender-atypical, homosexually active, heterosexually inexperienced lesbians and gay males may experience less identity confusion than other homosexuals to the extent that gender conventions in American society articulate linkages between adult homosexuality and all three of these characteristics. Conversely, gay males and lesbians who are gender-typical, heterosexually active, and homosexually inexperienced may experience more confusion regarding their sexual identities because their characteristics are at variance with prevailing homosexual stereotypes.

Supportive family and friends may also facilitate homosexual identity formation. Individuals may feel more comfortable in acting upon their sexual feelings when they believe that those close to them will accept them as they are. Conversely, lesbians and gay males with nonsupportive families and friends may find it much more difficult to acknowledge and act upon their sexual feelings. Fears of rejection appear to inhibit homosexual identity formation to various degrees.

Educational level and the prevailing atmosphere of the work place may also facilitate or hinder homosexual identity formation. Highly educated lesbians and gay males in homophobic professions may fear that they have more to lose by acknowledging and acting upon their sexual feelings than their less highly educated counterparts. Fears of job or income loss, or concerns about endangering professional credibility, appear to inhibit homosexual identity formation (Kooden *et al.* 1979; Riddle and Morin 1977; Troiden 1977). Less educationally specialized lesbians and gay males and those who work in more supportive occupations may not perceive themselves as occupationally at risk by acting upon and integrating their sexual feelings into their overall lives.

REFERENCES

Atchley, Robert C. (1982), "The Aging Self," *Psychotherapy: Theory, Research, and Practice* 19: 4: 388–96.

Bell, Alan P. and Martin S. Weinberg (1978), *Homosexualities: A Study of Diversity among Men and Women* (New York: Simon & Schuster).

Bell, Alan P., Martin S. Weinberg and Sue Kiefer Hammersmith (1981a). *Sexual Preference: Its Development in Men and Women* (Bloomington: Indiana University Press).

———, (1981b), *Sexual Preference: Its Development in Men and Women: Statistical Appendix* (Bloomington: Indiana University Press).

Blumstein, Philip E. and Pepper Schwartz (1974), "Lesbianism and Bisexuality," in *Sexual Deviance and Sexual Deviants*, ed. Erich Goode and Richard R. Troiden: 278–95 (New York: Morrow).

Califia, Pat (1979), "Lesbian Sexuality," *Journal of Homosexuality* 4: 3: 255–66.

Cass, Vivienne C. (1979), "Homosexual Identity Formation: A Theoretical Model," *Journal of Homosexuality* 4: 3: 219–35.

———, (1983/4), "Homosexual Identity: A Concept in Need of Definition," *Journal of Homosexuality* 9: 2/3: 105–26.

———, (1984), "Homosexual Identity Formation: Testing a Theoretical Mode," *Journal of Sex Research* 20: 2: 143–67.

Coleman, Eli (1982), "Developmental Stages of the Coming-Out Process," in *Homosexuality: Social, Psychological, and Biological Issues*, ed. William Paul, James D. Weinrich, John C. Gonsiorek, and Mary E. Hotvedt: 149–58 (Beverly Hills: Sage).

Cronin, Denise M. (1974), "Coming Out among Lesbians," in *Sexual Deviance and Sexual Deviants*, ed. Erich Goode and Richard R. Troiden: 268–77 (New York: Morrow).

Dank, Barry M. (1971), "Coming Out in the Gay World," *Psychiatry* 34: 2: 180–97.

de Monteflores, Carmen and Stephen J. Schultz (1978), "Coming Out: Similarities and Differences for Lesbians and Gay Men," *Journal of Social Issues* 34: 3: 59–72.

Doyle, James A. (1983), *The Male Experience* (Dubuque, Iowa: Wm. C. Brown).

Faderman, Lillian. (1984/5), "The 'New Gay' Lesbians," *Journal of Homosexuality* 10: 3/4: 85–95.

Gagnon, John H. and William Simon (1973), *Sexual Conduct: The Social Sources of Human Sexuality* (Chicago: Aldine).

Goode, Erich (1984), *Deviant Behavior*, 2nd ed. (Englewood Cliffs, NJ: Prentice-Hall).

Hammersmith, Sue Kiefer and Martin S. Weinberg (1973), "Homosexual Identity, Commitment, Adjustsents, and Significant Others," *Sociometry* 36: 1: 56–78.

Harry, Joseph (1982), *Gay Children Grown Up: Gender Culture and Gender Deviance* (New York: Praeger).

Harry, Joseph and William DeVall (1978), *The Social Organization of Gay Males* (New York: Praeger).

Hencken, Joel D. and William T. O'Dowd (1977), "Coming Out as an Aspect of Identity Formation," *Gai Saber* 1: 1: 18–26.

Humphreys, Laud (1972), *Out of the Closets: The Sociology of Homosexual Liberation* (Englewood Cliffs, NJ: Prentice-Hall).

———, (1979), "Being Odd against All Odds," in *Sociology*, 2nd ed., ed. Ronald C. Federico: 238–42 (Reading, MA: Addison-Wesley).

Kooden, Harold D., Stephen F. Morin, Dorothy I. Riddle, Martin Rogers, Barbara E. Strang, and

Frank Strassburger (1979), *Removing the Stigma: Final Report of the Board of Social and Ethical Responsibility for Psychology's Task Force on the Status of Lesbian and Gay Male Psychologists* (Washington, DC: American Psychological Association).

Lee, John Alan (1977), "Going Public: A Study in the Sociology of Homosexual Liberation," *Journal of Homosexuality* 3: 1: 49–78.

Levine, Martin P. (1987), "Gay Macho: Ethnography of the Homosexual Clones," Doctoral dissertation, New York University.

Lofland, John (1969), *Deviance and Identity* (Englewood Cliffs, NJ: Prentice-Hall).

McCall, George J, and J.L. Simmons (1966), *Identities and Interactions: An Examination of Human Associations in Everyday Life* (New York: Free Press).

McDonald, Gary J. (1982), "Individual Differences in the Coming Out Process for Gay Men: Implications for Theoretical Models," *Journal of Homosexuality* 8: 1: 47–60.

McWhirter, David P. and Andrew M. Mattison (1984), *The Male Couple: How Relationships Develop* (Englewood Cliffs, NJ: Prentice-Hall).

Mills, C. Wright (1940), "Situated Actions and Vocabularies of Motive," *American Sociological Review* 5: 6: 904–13.

Minton, Henry L. and Gary J. McDonald (1983/4), "Homosexual Identity Formation as a Developmental Process," *Journal of Homosexuality* 9: 2/3: 91–104.

Plummer, Kenneth (1975), *Sexual Stigma: An Interactionist Account* (London: Routledge & Kegan Paul).

Ponse, Barbara (1978), *Identities in the Lesbian World: The Social Construction of Self* (Westport: Greenwood Press).

—— (1980). "Lesbians and Their Worlds," in *Homosexual Behavior: A Modern Reappraisal*, ed. Judd Marmor: 157–75 (New York: Basic Books).

—— (1984). "The Problematic Meanings of Lesbian," in *The Sociology of Deviance*, ed. Jack D. Douglas: 25–33 (Newton, MA: Allyn & Bacon).

Reid, John (1973), *The Best Little Boy in the World* (New York: Putnam).

Reinhart, Robert C. (1982), *A History of Shadows* (New York: Avon Books).

Remafedi, Gary (1987), "Male Homosexuality: The Adolescent's Perspective," *Pediatrics* 79: 3: 326–30.

Riddle, Dorothy I. and Stephen F. Morin (1977), "Removing the Stigma: Data from Individuals," *APA Monitor* (November): 16, 28.

Saghir, Marcel T. and Eli Robins (1973), *Male and Female Homosexuality: A Comprehensive Investigation* (Baltimore: Williams & Wilkins).

Schäfer, Siegrid (1976), "Sexual and Social Problems among Lesbians," *Journal of Sex Research* 12: 1: 50–69.

Scott, Marvin B. and Stanford M. Lyman (1968), "Accounts," *American Sociological Review* 33: 1: 46–62.

Simmons, J. L. (1965), "Public Stereotypes of Deviants," *Social Problems* 13: 3: 223–32.

Smith, Karen S. (1980), "Socialization, Identity, and Commitment: The Case of Female Homosexuals," Master's thesis, Miami University.

Sophie, Joan (1985/6), "A Critical Examination of Stage Theories of Lesbian Identity Development," *Journal of Homosexuality* 12: 2: 39–51.

Tavris, Carol and Carole Wade (1984), *The Longest War: Sex Differences in Perspective*, 2nd ed. (New York: Harcourt Brace Jovanovich).

Theodorson, George A. and Achilles G. Theodorson (1969), *A Modern Dictionary of Sociology* (New York: Crowell).

Troiden, Richard R. (1977), "Becoming Homosexual: Research on Acquiring a Gay Identity," Doctoral dissertation, SUNY-Stony Brook.

—— (1979), "Becoming Homosexual: A Model of Gay Identity Acquisition," *Psychiatry* 42: 4: 362–73.

Troiden, Richard R. and Erich Goode (1980), "Variables Related to the Acquisition of a Gay Identity," *Journal of Homosexuality* 5: 4: 383–92.

Warren, Carol A. B. (1974), *Identity and Community in the Gay World* (New York: Wiley).

—— (1980), "Homosexuality and Stigma," in *Homosexual Behavior: A Modern Reappraisal*, ed. Judd Marmor: 123–41 (New York: Basic Books).

Warren, Carol A. B. and Barbara Ponse (1977), "The Existential Self in the Gay World," in *Existential Sociology*, ed. Jack D. Douglas and John M. Johnson: 273–89 (New York: Cambridge University Press).

Weinberg, Martin S. and Colin Williams (1974), *Male Homosexuals: Their Problems and Adaptations* (New York: Oxford University Press).

Weinberg, Thomas S. (1977), "Becoming Homosexual: Self-disclosure, Self-identity, and Self-maintenance," Doctoral dissertation, University of Connecticut.

—— (1978). "On 'Doing' and 'Being' Gay: Sexual Behavior and Homosexual Male Self-Identity," *Journal of Homosexuality* 4: 2: 143–56.

GILBERT HERDT

"Gay and Lesbian Youth, Emergent Identities, and Cultural Scenes at Home and Abroad"

from Gilbert Herdt (ed.), *Gay and Lesbian Youth* (New York: Harrington Park Press, 1989): Introduction

The unprecedented growth of the gay and lesbian community in recent history has transformed our culture and consciousness, creating radically new possibilities for men and women to "come out" and live more openly as homosexuals. This is certainly true of America and Western Europe, where the gay and lesbian population, in hitherto unforeseen ways and in greater numbers, has claimed attention in politics and the media, culture and the arts. Since before the Stonewall riot in New York (1969), the gay perspective had undergone that "significant discontinuity," to use Plummer's (1981) phrase, from being a pathological category to an oppressed minority. Now, gay is identified as more of a social world. Being homosexual – gay or lesbian – now is more understandable, almost recognizable by its positioning within an affluent society, which some call a high culture, one fascinated both with its own hedonism and its "love for human nature" (Sontag 1982). "Gay" has become a symbolic reality, its emergent identities and new cultural scenes have, in this sense, displaced the old, one-dimensional "sexual culture" of homosexuality in the 1960s and 1970s (Altman 1973; 1979), not only by shifting the discourse to incorporate new social issues, but also by extending its cultural meanings to reach abroad, to the urban centers of other countries, even those of the Third World.

And yet for all of this, we[1] had not planned upon or fully anticipated an equally unprecedented consequence of the post-Stonewall struggles to construct a gay culture: the emergence of a generation of teenagers who feel themselves to be homosexual and who thus begin the difficult but affirming process of "coming out."[2] Often, lesbian and gay adolescents were felt not to exist or were ignored as a social problem. Today it is estimated, however, that nearly 3 million of our country's 29 million adolescents are gay.[3] When as a social issue teenage homosexuality was studied in the past, it was sometimes psychologized and pathologized as Martin (1982) suggested, or it was sociologized, as Plummer (1975) showed, with adult subjects' retrospections, substituted for teenagers' or young adults' experience. This problem of retrospective bias and distortion, criticized but still not well appreciated in the literature,[4] is inherent in many adolescent studies (see Boxer and Cohler 1989). Such reductionism and methodological bias presents several formidable roadblocks to understanding gay and lesbian lives: (1) in our post-Stonewall society, gay culture and sexual meanings have changed from a generation ago – this introduces a cohort problem; (2) this generational change is being exacerbated by problems associated with the development of AIDS in a dramatic and deadly way; and (3) the difficulties are even greater when we turn to other cultures, with their own emergent identities as manifested in the lives of homosexual persons. This must include understanding variations in the meaning of "homosexuality" or "gay" and "lesbian" cross-culturally, as well as in the contexts of coming out and being socialized into (largely) urban gay scenes around the world (cf. Blackwood 1986).

The aim here is to address these problems and roadblocks in terms of the words and experiences of adolescents themselves. We use a variety of social science approaches, especially the ethnographic, and the resulting ethnography – as well as the sociology and psychology – are thus meant to redress a gap in the literature. Ours are not only new studies of these young people and their largely untold stories, however; they also represent commentaries on changing relationships across generations in the gay world, itself a part of accelerating social change in the wider society. But the generational problem is most perplexing.

We had not foreseen that the social rights struggles of the 1960s and 1970s – our struggles – might be perceived by youth in a different way, or that, beyond the inheritance of the old stigma surrounding homosexuality, gay youth would also have to contend with the new horrors of AIDS. Nor that, in part because of stigma,[5] and in part due to AIDS, at least as reported in the popular media, teenage gays and lesbians would shun older gays as role models or even as friends.[6] We have the dimming sense that much of post-World-War-II "gay culture" and folklore are not only gone but may soon be lost, and that the same fate may already have befallen the freewheeling "sexual culture" of the American gay scene (Altman 1982), post-Stonewall and pre-AIDS (reviewed in Kotarba and Lang 1986). This is tantamount to suggesting that the knowledge and cultural practices of the gay world, like much of complex and mass culture today, are shifting and ephemeral, having emergent, not fixed, values and meanings. Whether American culture has selected from gay culture its popular tastes and themes (Altman 1982) is arguable. Nonetheless, only now has gay culture begun to institutionalize "socialization" techniques for the transmission of its cultural knowledge to a younger generation. More will be said of this later.

For the present, however, it suffices to note that neither the formal nor informal substance and contemporary changes in gay life are being readily preserved.... What we want, then, is to preserve the "sensibility" of teenage lives today, which, as Sontag (1982) has said in another context, is the most "perishable" aspect of a culture.[7] To be more precise, however, we can refer to three distinctive historical periods of change in these cultural styles: (1) early twentieth century, up to the Gay Liberation movements of the 1960s; (2) the post-Stonewall period after 1969 and up to the early 1980s; and (3) the period following the discovery and objectification of AIDS, c. 1981–2, as a "gay disease" (Feldman and Johnson 1986). Each of these is a distinctive cultural marker, particularly in America, for documenting changes in the sensibilities of gay and lesbian youth.

My concern is to join the recent efforts of those scholars concerned with the perishable sensibilities of gay consciousness and culture in our time by focusing upon gay youth. This must perforce be limited by space, for this "salvage" anthropology and the study of gay teenagers today involves innumerable psychocultural issues that lead, willy-nilly, onto the study of the wider social field of sexuality.[8] My approach here reflects in part the perspective of an anthropologist and the substantive questions of a gender research, which anticipate broader problematics in the field of gender and culture (Herdt 1984; 1987b; 1987c).

PRECONCEPTIONS AND ASSUMPTIONS

In opening the "problem" of teenage gays (and we must constantly strive to say for whom a "problem" is a problem, society or gays), our concern is to confront, on various levels of action and discourse, four fundamental assumptions, or, to use Gadamer's (1965) hermeneutic notion, "presuppositions," regarding homosexuality and adolescence. These are as follows:

1 Gay/lesbian adolescents are subject to the "assumption of heterosexuality," of feeling "guilty until proven innocent" in the social arena, to invert our legal principle.
2 Because they are not heterosexual, these teenagers are, therefore, assumed to be "inverts," according to our cultural presumption of inversion.
3 They are, then, stigmatized as persons, which oppression has real-life consequences for their development and adaptation.
4 Finally, as homosexuals, they are subject to the assumption of homogeneity: the idea that gays and lesbians the *world over* are the same in "coming out" experience, identity, and cultural organization.

Let us review each of these problematics in turn.

The presumption of heterosexuality

The first preconception with which adolescents must contend in social development concerns being straight: the assumption "that parties to any interaction in straight settings are usually presumed to be heterosexual unless demonstrated to be otherwise" (Ponse 1978: 58). Evelyn Hooker (1965) once referred to this as "heterosexual ethnocentricity." We should think long on this stereotype, for if gender theorists are even half-way correct about the power of early experience to shape one's gender identity and even one's world view or sense of existence (Stoller 1968), the influence of an assumed heterosexuality from before puberty must be profound. Whether sexual orientation is caused by cultural or biological factors, alone or interacting, and the extent to which being "gay" is "constructed" or "essential" in the person's development are critical related questions (Hoult 1984), but they do not concern me here. Rather, no matter what the ultimate causes, there will always exist a discordance between the homosexual youths' feeling of being "different" when growing up in a heterosexual environment, and their eventual place in a homosexual world.

The presumption of heterosexuality is identified by many theorists with profound psychosocial problems from the start of adolescent development (Plummer 1981; 1989). Children who manifest nonconformist gender behavior from an early age are, according to some reports, those most susceptible to parental and peer pressure to change their behavior (Green 1987; Whitam 1983), even though they have the greatest likelihood of being gay as adults (Harry 1982). Such findings highlight the widespread significance of the masculine/feminine dichotomy, which itself underlies the heterosexual/homosexual dichotomy (cf. McIntosh 1968). Parker's article on Brazil (1989) and Carrier's on Mexico (1989) suggest similar processes at work in Latin American settings.

A variety of ways of feeling different and becoming self-alienated have been correlated with the heterosexual assumption. Among the most powerful of these factors are early homosexual experiences, early puberty or sexual precosity, and lack of interests of several sorts, such as lack of interest in the opposite sex or in sports. Prior research tends to support these views. Gay men, for instance, do say they feel "very different" from heterosexuals in growing up (based on adult-felt retrospections; see Bell, Weinberg, and Hammersmith 1981). The age of first sexual contact for gays is younger than for heterosexuals (Bell et al. 1981; Roestler and Deisher 1972), although data show that pre-homosexual boys do not develop earlier than heterosexuals (Bell et al. 1981). Harry (1982) has argued that atypical disinterest during adolescence regarding dating and sports reinforce the social alienation of gays. Because heterosexual dating and team sports are two key points of adolescent peer grouping, homosexual youth experience a "major social vacuum" (Harry 1982) in these key domains. They feel unattached, alienated. They are not integrated and thereby sheltered by peer groups or gangs (Lafont 1986). Troiden has touched upon this in his excellent review (1989).

Feeling different and alienated are in turn associated with the earliest aspirations to change identity, which eventually leads to coming out. Both cognition and emotions are involved in such identity change. The very earliest aspect of the process may involve what Weinberg (1983) referred to as the "self-suspicion" of being "different," i.e., of being homosexual. Problems arise here because there is, as Dank (1971) noted in a classic paper, either no "anticipatory socialization" to the gay identity, or else the kind that is inimical as a positive foundation for self-change. Dissonance in cognitions of self and significant others are inevitable, given the presumption of heterosexuality: "Most persons who eventually identify themselves as homosexuals require a change in the meaning of the cognitive category *homosexual* before they can place themselves in the category" (Dank 1971: 189). Stigma is obviously sensed and feared in this (Warren, 1980).

One of the initial responses to feeling different in this way is the decline of self-esteem that accompanies harmful alienation, so that teenagers remain isolated and "closeted" (Minton and McDonald 1983/84). The well known stage models of development emphasize this trend (reviewed in Cass 1984; see also Coleman 1989; Troiden 1989). Another is to displace self-interest from heterosexual dating and sports into intellectual or artistic performance, which effectively promotes compensatory achievement among gay and lesbian youth (Gagnon 1979; Harry 1982). A third possibility is to engage in surreptitious sexual contacts or clandestine same-sex romantic relationships (Jay and Young 1977, reviewed in Cass 1984; Ponse 1978; Warren 1974). Nowadays, the most recent and radical means of dealing with such feelings is for the youth to come out, possibly in the context of a gay or homophile group (Greenberg 1976). Such a coming out group in Chicago is described in Gerstel *et al.* (1989).

The presumption of inversion

Once feelings of being different are converted into self-suspicion, or into what Troiden (1989) calls a "sensitization stage," another preconception emerges. Before the person's full recognition of internalized stigma and externalized oppression, he or she must work through conflicts of reversal in his or her gender behavior and self-strivings. These stem from the stereotype that, not being heterosexual, one must be unnatural, the "invert." Inversion, an old concept, goes back to at least the nineteenth century, and summons up images of the "disease of effeminacy" in males (Foucault 1980). Certainly, Freud's work contributed to the popularization of the idea earlier, which even anthropologists unselfconsciously exported to other cultures (see Herdt 1987b). Lacking what Warren (1974) called "gay knowledge" or what Jay and Young (1977) referred to as the "socializing process" for lesbians, that is, in the absence of explicit knowledge about prevailing positive identities or cultural scenes, the image of inversion, filled with its alienating power of self-preoccupation and psychopathology, comes into play.

First and foremost this is the imagery of the caricature, arising from social stereotypy, secrecy, and guilt, which may produce transitional feelings of existential panic and deterioration of the very foundations of well-being and selfhood. Such images are rooted ultimately in social stigma, to be examined shortly. Their main effect is related to cross-gender behavior: feeling that one is not a normative, heterosexual male or female, one must display attributes of the opposite sex in order to attract attention or to "fit in" – hyperfemininity in males and hypermasculinity in females. Is this different than Sontag's (1982: 105) "camp," the "love of the unnatural," the avant garde sign that "one should either be a work of art or wear a work of art"? I think so.

Youthful gender transformation today seems to be a playful process, at first staged in a political vacuum, but increasingly indicative of a new awareness that will involve manifesting an open gay lifestyle. Troiden (1989) refers in this context to the "minstrelization" of youthful gays whose gender antics poke fun at society. Gender role stereotypy, class consciousness and psychological ghettoization are also involved, as indicated by the strong correlation between class and often anachronistic gender inversion: working-class groups still tend to produce the most exaggerated gender-inverted homosexuals (see Harry 1982; Murray 1984; Read 1980; Parker 1989). Surely the once popular images of the "Drag Show" and "transvestite queen," produced in part for heterosexual audiences and now associated more with small cities in the Midwest, belong here. They seem a mixture of stereotypic inversion and camp protest against stigma, as Esther Newton once argued in *Mother Camp* (1972). Cross-culturally, as Carrier (1980) has shown, the same inversion principle appears elsewhere in what he called sexually restrictive cultures, wherein sexual variations are shunned and those who participate are assigned the inferior status of the dominated. Homophobia, the fear and hatred of homosexuality, is clearly related to this (Weinberg 1972). Page and Yee (1985) have recently shown that negative images of homosexuality among American heterosexuals remain, that stronger reactions are manifested toward males, and the *strongest* of all are expressed toward masculine gay males (Laner and Laner 1979). This confirms a prevailing feeling that gay males are more "visible" in popular culture, and, perhaps, the more despised by heterosexual men for their affluence and for forsaking male privilege.

Not until this phase of inversion of the self is reflected upon can a transformation in gay and lesbian awareness emerge, as hinted by Le Bitoux for the youth of Paris (1989). With such a recognition of a homosexual social world beyond the self, either in gay or lesbian peers, or social groups, or even among supportive heterosexual friends and networks, the restrictive image of the invert seems to recede.

The invert image presses the imagination up against a perceived "natural law," wherein homosexuality goes against "nature," as reflected most radically in the invert's behavior (Ponse 1978; Foucault 1980; cf. Hoffman 1968; Scruton 1986). Here, Ponse reminds us, "homosexuality frequently connotes inversion both in common sense thinking and in scientific theories" (Ponse 1978: 31, n. 14). The recent Supreme Court case (*Bowers v. Hardwick*, 1986) upholding the "unnaturalness" of sodomy in state laws reveals at least one side of public opinion: that the invert is an ogre with the power to subvert those around him, especially the young.[9]

Another expression of the inversion stereotype concerns an exclusionary principle: one can be either homosexual or heterosexual, but not both. During this developmental phase, there is a strong tendency in gender-polarized and restrictive cultures, such as America, to rule out bisexual fantasies or activity (Herdt 1987c). Such a trend runs counter to the surprisingly high rate of bisexuality Kinsey and his colleagues identified in America (cf. Roestler and Deisher 1972). However, we are dealing here not with empirical patterns, but with folk models, ideal types, that are dualistic. This may be, in part, why the Australian Altman (1982: xi) has referred to recent symbolic changes in our culture as a "homosexualization" of America:

> No other country seems as divided around issues of sexuality: the conflict between a repressive puritan heritage and the ethos of contemporary hedonism creates a tension that is reflected in the passion and all too often the violence that surrounds debate over sexuality in America.

According to the prevailing folk ethic, then, someone can be gay or straight but not both,

and the bisexual, so we are told (Paul 1984), experiences the greatest pressures of all: to "come clean" and stop being closeted, by gay friends, or to stop being "adolescent" and hedonistic, to get married and have children, like "normal" straight friends. For some persons, the decision to come out is stymied here: some chose to "pass" as straight, for fear of being "inverted," though passing too, has its cost (Lee 1977). Inversion creeps beneath these images, never too far from what teenagers and even adults have to say about "going" gay.

The recognition of stigma

The third factor of emergent gay experience, beyond the presumptions of heterosexuality and inversion, is the self's confrontation with the social stigma of homosexuality. No matter in what direction the analysis of homosexuality proceeds – whether to culture, the self-concept, theoretical debates between constructionists or essentialists, minority status, sex differences between gays and lesbians in coming out or in passing as heterosexual – there is a profound barrier to always be bargained with: recognition of the stigma and homophobia surrounding homosexuality. Sexism is very related and should be analyzed in parallel fashion. An immense literature now surrounds this aspect of the meaning of homosexuality, and it need not be reviewed again here.[10] That stigma exists in society, in science, and in medical treatment circles regarding homosexuality is a social fact, one that enchants some and disenchants others across these domains. Stigma is the bastard of oppression (Warren 1980). The duality of oppression in social life here concerns domination and heterosexual cooptation (Adam 1978) in socioeconomic roles and institutional homophobia, on the one hand, and internalized stigma, stereotypes, and even self-hatred – internal homophobia (see Savin-Williams 1989) – on the other. De Cecco (1984) reviewed the many shadow-plays of homophobia to find that these remain a powerful force in contemporary society.

A structural sign of this preconception of stigma is the old stereotype that all homosexual youth are deviant and delinquent. Weeks (1985) reminded us that in the nineteenth century, the warnings about prostitution and homosexuality effectively placed gays into deviant subgroups. The psychological theory of a previous generation also equated homosexual activity in adolescence to peripherality and antisocial strivings.[11] Even Erik Erikson's (1968) classic work on identity and youth makes the deviant image essential to and almost obligatory for understanding gay youth. "Negative identity prevails in the delinquent (addictive, homosexual) youth of our larger cities," Erikson (1968: 88) argued, because of hostility to family and culture. Only through complete identification with such deviant subcultures can relief from psychopathology be found for "cliques and ganges of young homosexuals, addicts, and social cynics" (176). These images derived in part from the Freudian framework, of course, which itself makes a fundamental assumption that anything short of heterosexuality and parenthood are suggestive of pathology (see Isay 1986). The Freudian model, simplified and mythologized, has become our folk theory, a piece of popular culture.[12] It is not surprising that such folk theory, which conveniently supports the exploitation and pathologizing of homosexuality more broadly, should have resulted in the initial studies of gay youth being done in bars, among male prostitutes or hustlers, prison inmates, and psychiatric patients. Leznoff and Westley (1956) and Reiss (1961) are social science examples; the novels of Rechy (1963) are cultural counterparts.

Plummer (1975) and Weeks (1985), among others, have shown that many generalized Western biases toward homosexuality rest upon stereotypy and stigma of this sort. Many studies have, of course, since questioned these generalizations on empirical grounds. One need only think of Evelyn Hooker's (1957) groundbreaking study of a non-clinical population's positive mental health for counterfindings thirty years ago. Kinsey and his colleagues (1948) paved the way for these revisions in our views by showing the frequency of homosexual contact in the general population of the United States. Yet his biological assumptions and emphasis upon the "sex act," decontextualized from its personal and symbolic meanings, did not fundamentally alter our conceptions of the homosexual. The many "Kinsey-type" studies to follow (e.g., Bell and Weinberg 1978) further substantiated the "normalcy" of gays, pre- and post-Stonewall. However, these studies have been almost entirely of adults, and, indeed, usually of WASPs. Less effort has been made to show the historical and cultural relationship between the earlier studies and those which followed the momentous events of the 1960s and early 1970s. The many cultural changes that have occurred since then provide a new context for appraisal of stigma, oppression, liberation, and coming out in adolescents and their older gay predecessors.

Such changes have brought positive reinforcements for the coming out process today, with a concomitant decline in psychopathology, at least in certain respects. Secrecy and hiding seem less frequent (Anderson 1987; Troiden 1989); and casual sex contact does not automatically translate into sexual orientation, be it hetero or homosexual (Plummer, 1975). Sexualized contact in the cultural scene of the gay bar used to reign supreme in folklore and American literature on homosexuality (Hoffman 1970), whereas this now seems less so in the fiction of, say, David Leavitt. The overrepresentation of homosexual youth among male hustlers in early studies seems to mirror social stigma here (Roestler and Deisher 1972), whereas hustling is now a very different theme in the literature (Boyer 1989). Lesbians were much more invisible before, whereas now, some new studies are emerging. Where inversion reigned and transvestism as quintessential homosexual cultural style was common (Read 1980), today these seem anachronistic. What seems likely, then, is that stigma and oppression combined to make normative homosexual youth, especially lesbians – the most "invisible" (Ponse 1978) element in the image of the stereotypic "queer" – whom unsympathetic observers interpreted as peripheral "deviants," a token of the homosexuality of the times.[13] The critical papers in both Boyer (1989) and Coleman (1989) on teenage male hustlers and their problems speak to this issue.

Social change in the gay world, which challenges stigma and reconstitutes it, making it "minoritized" (now an oppression), has finally placed the issues of gays and lesbians in their rightful judicial arena and political field: society. Involvement by teens and adults in gay groups illustrates this point about social change. Thus, a shift of participation by gays in homophile groups has occurred over time, for the generalized negative avoidance noted by Sagarin (1969) in the late 1960s, to the more positive findings of Plummer (1975) in the mid 1970s, which confirms the greater openness of the post-Stonewall era (Anderson 1987; Gerstel et al. 1989).

Leading up to and growing out of the events of the Stonewall period was a rapid consolidation of the gay community (Murray 1979). Whereas drinking clubs and bar culture predominated in the lives of gay men following World War II, and may indeed be the main historical foundation for the social formation of the modern gay/lesbian community, other subsequent developments have occurred in urban centers (D'Emilio 1983; Levine 1979). These include gay professional and political action groups, reported upon in a plethora of newly founded gay and lesbian newspapers and related periodicals, some produced by local gay organizations. New gay and lesbian religious groups, such as Catholic Dignity, sprang up (see Humphreys and Miller 1980, for a list of these). Gay merchants and shops emerged and appealed to gay and lesbian clientele, especially in San Francisco and New York. Gay academic unions, social clubs, networks of artists, and special interest groups appeared as never before, providing unprecedented channels of communication and interaction with others, in one's city and elsewhere, too. Many positive signs of cooperation and mutual action existed between homosexual men and women, as anticipated in such manifestos as Altman's classic *Homosexual: Oppression and Liberation* (1973). Class and racial differences seemed less apparent at first than now. The gay world became a satellite culture, Humphreys and Miller (1980) suggested, so that by the late 1970s, the largest dozen American cities had recognizable gay neighborhoods, heavily populated by same-sex couples. And beyond the States, mass tourism

extended this "homosexual geography" to "all large urban centers" throughout the world (Pollak 1986: 54).

What matters here is that this symbolic world, these special interest communal satellites, became more politically empowered in gay and lesbian struggles against stigma and oppression, and this, in turn, provided radically new opportunities for teenagers to reconstruct their social realities along different lines. Gay couples and friends and networks gave added social support to the coming out processes (McWhirter and Mattison 1984). These gay communities became as magnets for hinterland teenagers, whose desire for same-sex led them to the "promised land." New cultural scenes and identities were available for their consumption. Gay bath houses, which at first seemed to be a vanguard of sexual liberation, became in time the very name of consumerism among gays, and some would say an oppression of gays through depersonalized sex (Altman 1981). But these were frequented almost exclusively by adults, not adolescents. Proximity to urban centers was crucial for teens, too, especially in accessing homophile support groups while still living at home and attending high school. Soon, though, some cracks in this fine mirror began to show, cracks that reflect other sociopolitical changes in the mainstream society.

D'Emilio (1983) argued that the Gay Liberation movement had two primary effects in the post-Stonewall period: transformation in the meaning of the coming out process and its association with the emergence of a strong lesbian movement.[14] These changes were part and parcel of the confrontational politics of the 1960s. Their association to "youth protest" (D'Emilio 1983) seems certain.[15] The relationship between such youth sentiment then, and the low-key gay/lesbian teenage activism of today, seems less certain, however. Teenage activists in the 1970s could affirm that:

> The open avowal of one's sexual identity, whether at work, at school, at home, or before television cameras, symbolized the shedding of the self-hatred that gay men and women internalized, and consequently it promised an immediate improvement to one's life.
>
> (D'Emilio 1983: 235)

But today's youth might well not recognize D'Emilio's next sentence, that "to come out of the 'closet' quintessentially expressed the fusion of the personal and the political that the radicalism of the late 1960s exalted" (235). Gone from the cultural scenes of the gay community are the radical politics of then, but such activism seems to have passed in general from the American scene for the time being. We see glimpses of similar sociopolitical change in Mexico (Carrier 1989) and Paris (LeBitoux 1989). While we can therefore agree with Castells (1983), who provides an elegant analysis of the San Francisco history, that "gay culture is inseparable from gay politics" (163), such politics today have a different form than a decade ago.

Some observers suggest that where radical politics are gone, gay as chic, and homosexual as decadent and triumphant consumer capitalism, have emerged in their place (Altman 1982).[16] Perhaps, where the 1950s Mattachine culture of camp sensibility was, as Sontag (1982) suggested, "disengaged, depoliticized – or at least apolitical" (107), the recent less activist gay "community" has undergone successive changes of increasing bourgeois "centrism" and internal factionalism.[17] Gays and lesbians seem more accepted (notwithstanding AIDS) into mainstream Western culture, which is related to their being at the vanguard of middle-class consumerism (Pollak 1986). Yet as presaged in the mid-1970s by Jay and Young (1977), major divisions had already separated lesbians and gay men.

The nature of the homosexual coming out process today inextricably follows upon these changes: class, racial, and sex differences obviously divide America and therefore the homosexual population, with whites generally doing better than blacks, and men generally better than women, as evidenced in the San Francisco gay community (Castells 1983).[18] Gentrification of the inner cities provides a case in point, because this made homosexuals economically useful: former run-down neighborhoods were upgraded through work and investment. Here, gentrification caused gays – mostly gay men – to compete with and displace longstanding inner city minorities. Yet, gays did not in turn create "ghettos" in the same way as other minorities.

They "choose to live together as a cultural community," Castells (1983: 139) argued, New York's Greenwich Village and San Francisco's Castro village being obvious examples. Lesbians, however, did not and do not tend to concentrate in given territories in the same way (Castells 1983; Lockard 1986), which no doubt reflects the lower social status of woman as less privileged persons in a patriarchal culture (reviewed in Blackwood 1986; Kehoe 1986; and Warren 1974). Here, then, we have the conditions for competition between gays and ethnic minorities in gentrification processes, and differential classism and sexism between gays versus lesbians in urban centers, both of which provide conflictual and centripetal structural forces in male and female teenagers' entry into homosexuals worlds.

The assumption of homogeneity

Overcoming presumptions of heterosexuality and inversion are hard; fighting stigma is harder still. But there is embedded in these preconceptions a deeper, more mature and subtle problem, anticipated in the previous section: the view that gay youth are homogeneous, the same kind of persons.

The sources of this assumption are at once simple and complex. By definition homosexuality is one-dimensional: desire for same sex. The multitude of symbolic realities and states of desire present in our own history and in other cultures today are perceived, in Western discourse, to be but one essence or thing, the homosexual. By the end of the nineteenth century, as Foucault (1980) and others have shown, this made homosexuality an objectified and monolithic category, akin to a "species of nature." Of course, this objectification – or "homosexualization," as Altman (1982) referred to it – issues from the preconceptions of inversion and stigma already outlined above. The nature of this discourse frame, however, creates broader difficulties for internal representations of, and relationships between, adult homosexuals within the gay community, on the one hand; and developmental problems for adolescents who are struggling to come out in society at large. The projected homogeneity derives no doubt from the overemphasis in popular culture on sexual practice as the sole defining characteristic of the moral careers and personhood of homosexuals.

"The most striking thing about sociological studies of homosexuality," Altman (1981) wrote, "is that they are obsessed with sex" (45), a reductionism that poses a problem of great import to the gay world. For, paradoxically, it is this very focus on same-sex eroticism that is the rallying point for gay rights activism and resistance to oppression. One cannot easily dismiss the popular stereotypy without undermining the political rhetoric of gays themselves. How are we to turn to the novels of Christopher Isherwood for the larger experience of being homosexual, as Altman might suggest, without finding in them a bedrock of homoeroticism? Moreover, research over the past twenty years or so has tended to emphasize if not homogeneity, then at least vital common concerns (Murray 1984). Thus, it is hard to shake the centrist view, which in one sense or other is so popular, that homosexual desire, in opposition to normative heterosexual desire, unites gays and lesbians in a common culture. The testimonies of young gays in *One Teenager in Ten* (Heron 1983) show such a trend in the American context.

And yet there is strong evidence of several kinds to indicate that inspite of same-sex desire, there is not one, but rather many homosexualities. So much is this the case that some find it difficult to see the common denominators in homosexual orientation development (Bell and Weinberg 1978; Bell *et al.* 1981; Gagnon 1979), and the anthropologist Kenneth Read (1980), in search of a language to characterize this diversity, was forced to refer to the multiple cultural behaviors in a gay bar as "styles." The point reveals a widespread difficulty, as noted in the literature (Murray 1979; 1984): How shall we conceptualize the diversity and uniformity among gays and lesbians? My own deceptive use of such metaphors as "worlds," "communities," "cultures," in regard to gay and lesbian affiliations, is a stop-gap measure that avoids this question.

When it comes to adolescents in our own culture, they are no more clones of each other than the adults. And when teenagers from other cultures are added into the equation, we are indeed confronted with striking diversity. Their social systems and attitudes differ; the symbols they use vary; the contexts and problems to which they must adjust differ even more. Gay youth in other cultures do not necessarily agree on fundamental questions of commitment to and desire for an openly homosexual lifestyle. The sense of gay liberation varies in France and in Mexico, as Le Bitoux (1989) and Carrier (1989) argue, respectively, because what is being liberated and what remains imprisoned in social conventions varies between these two nation-states. Our Western concepts "gay" and "lesbian" may be alien to them, and other, more fluid categories may substitute for them in culture and experience, as Parker (1989) suggests for Brazil. Their responses to parental and peer pressures are quite different from those of Americans, too, and at times, we even search in vain for the center of this "American-ness." Teenagers vary as well with regard to how they handle discrimination, homophobia, and stigma, as Michael Ross (1989) reveals in his four-country study. These teenagers are only beginning to confront the issue of AIDS, if they are aware of it at all (Remafedi 1987b). Furthermore, we can expect that AIDS will impact upon the relationship between older and younger gays across generations (Feldman, 1989). They are not, to sum up, made from the same mold, or molded into the same roles, self-conceptions, and contexts.

Sexual identities and meanings are, like other areas of human life, profoundly shaped by culture and social structure. They are also constructed out of our life histories. Personal and social identities, be they gay or straight or something else, are no different in this regard, as Stoller (1985) suggested in his essay on meanings of the term *homosexuality*. We are forever in danger of forgetting this, because we assume from cultural ideals or political rhetoric that what *seems to be* is. When a homogeneous category such as "gay" or "lesbian" is available for self-identification and social attribution, the temptation to leave the "splitters" of cultural relativism and join the "lumpers" of universalist social classification becomes very great.

A simple illustration shows, however, the fallacy in this tendency to the lumping of universalism. "Female" is a sexual type in morphology, whereas "feminine" is a gender category whose meanings vary enormously (Rosaldo and Lamphere 1973). To say "she is a black female" compresses cultural factors of both the gender- and color-codes of a culture. To add "she is a black feminist" further splits the categorization. And to conclude that "she is a black lesbian," but not a "black feminist lesbian," reveals an enormously complex system of differing identities and cultural scenes to which the person is oriented. Many other examples could be adduced to make the same point in our own culture: gays and lesbians do share things in common, by virtue of their general cultural tradition and their particular sexual orientation, but there are many other ways in which they are also distinct. Deborah Wolf examined such nuances in her important study *The Lesbian Community* (1979), which newer studies have expanded upon (Kehoe 1986).

Now when we turn to the question of cross-cultural variations, the problems multiply because the "surface structures" of shared cultural meanings are no longer constant. This leaves only sexual orientation as a common denominator of homogeneity cross-culturally. Yet, having recognized that sexual identities and meanings are, in certain respects, also culturally constructed, we are left with what would seem to be very little homogeneity – essence – at all (see Blackwood's 1986 critical collection in this regard).

To return to the above example, to say of our "black lesbian" that she is a Brazilian greatly compounds the illustration, and to locate further her relevant identity and contexts of real-life action, we need to know something about her class and education and generation. What is the link between her politics and sexual orientation?[19] This strains the example to the point that we must wonder: In what way is her black lesbian identity like that of an American at all? and is the term "lesbian" her own or was it imposed upon her by outsiders?

These issues in the interpretation of meanings beset the understanding of homosexuality in many times and places. For some, such as the historian John Boswell (1980), "gay" is such a universal category (or perhaps an essence) that he sees as present across the centuries in reference to identities of persons, even in Archaic societies. Many have disagreed with this usage (reviewed in Greenberg and Bystryn 1982; Herdt 1987b; Murray 1984); others are more sympathetic. My point, however, is that the homogenizing of same-sex desire goes too far when it is argued that variations in culture and history are mere accretion or residue in the understanding of such different lives.

The similarities between gays and lesbians who themselves adopt these words as their identities in urban centers around the world, whether Western or Third World, provide new support for the idea of cross-cultural continuities, however. The mere presence of the lexemes "gay/lesbian" is not sufficient to interpret the related identities and meanings as homologous, as Murray (1984) has suggested before. To what extent are Western tourists a primary cause of this increasingly visible gay category abroad, especially in large cities such as Paris, Rome, Hong Kong, and Buenos Aires? We cannot yet be sure, for there are other structural and world system forces at work that clearly are homogenizing the shape of sexual categories around the world (Adam 1987; Ariès 1986; Foucault 1980; Harris 1982; Murray 1984; Weeks 1985). Nonetheless, the local knowledge and symbolic values of homosexually identified persons determine in many ways not only the structural form of their sexual identities and same-sex relationships, but also the cultural content of their sensibilities, or, to return to Sontag's concept, the richness or impoverishment of their consciousness and communicative styles as these are woven into their particular homosexualities.

We must avoid the dangers, both conceptual/ intellectual and political, of assuming too much or too little homogeneity. We cannot settle the matter of whether those homosexuals who themselves self-identify as gay/lesbian are more alike or more different in their essence, their "is-ness" (Plummer 1981), or in their behavior; such closure would, at present, be premature. Indeed, the studies of emergent adolescent identity "gay/lesbian," here and abroad throw into new relief basic questions surrounding assumptions about the "essentialism" and "constructionism" of this subspecies of homosexuality. But to sharpen our analysis, and more fully consider the preconceptions reviewed, let us now highlight the coming out process among this younger generation.

VARIATIONS IN THE COMING OUT PROCESS

Perhaps no aspect of adolescent homosexuality is as weighty or rich in its cultural sensibilities as that of the coming out process, the declaration of one's sexual orientation, across cultures. And, just as well, no other element of the present body of gay and lesbian research is as badly and urgently in need of new models and fresh ideas.[20] We do not know very well whether coming out has changed much over the past few years. For example, shall we consider coming out to mean "out to the self," or only "out to others"? Disclosure may occur to friends but not to family. And the teenager faces the question of whether to come out in high school, to heterosexual peers, and in contexts of work and religion. Here all of the previously mentioned preconceptions historically at play can be understood as they are experienced and practiced in the lives of adolescents and their social worlds.

We can place this coming out discourse in a new light if we think of coming out as a rite of passage in the anthropological sense of the term. Rites of passage, as Van Gennep (1960) argued long ago, typically structure life crisis events among traditional peoples. Their recurrent processes seem to involve (1) separation from the society as a whole; (2) isolation into a special or liminal (from the French word *limin*, for threshold or door) period, with taboos and restrictions of a sacred character; (3) followed by reaggregation or assimilation back into secular society. Life crisis events necessitate ritualization by their effect upon social status changes: from childhood to adulthood, by the onset of puberty, with birth and death and marriage. Each transformation in social state

utilizes ritual process to adjust people's behavior to new and appropriate rights and duties, knowledge and identities, as these refashion social relationships with others. Transition rights also change the persons' interior and exterior, thus linking their psychological states and cultural knowledge to their new moral and sociopolitical responsibilities. Van Gennep himself used a house with many rooms as the key image of society, each room representing a social state or developmental stage, each life transition requiring passage through a threshold, the timeless and formless liminal ritual period, that led onto, and in its turn affected, all the other rooms or social roles. In spite of all the differences ostensibly separating the situation of gay teenagers from those of tribal initiates, such as the Sambia with whom I have worked in New Guinea (Herdt 1981), there are useful parallels to be drawn from the image.

Teenagers today are "betwixt and between" (Turner 1967) different social worlds as never before. For lesbian and gay youth, this inbetweeness is represented by the ordinary heterosexual lifestyles of their parents, on the one hand, and the adult gay and lesbian community, on the other. To feel different and then direct oneself into new contexts opens up basic challenges of the life crisis sort, as suggested by Van Gennep. The closer young people are to puberty, or to separating from their parents' households, the more acutely will they experience their situation as crisis (see Boxer and Cohler 1989). The life crisis, it is true, may begin only in their heads, by the kind of self-suspicion or the cognitive dissonance mentioned earlier. But then, there is real-life action: the exciting and difficult opportunities, or lack of such, to explore, probe, and experiment with new feelings and ideas (Plummer 1989). Thus, more than metaphor are references in the literature, such as Jay and Young's (1977), to the coming out process as a "rite of passage."

Teenagers may at first feel isolated or depressed or worse. They may feel desperate to change their situation (Robertson 1981). Or they may not, in which case they may postpone their developmental change until after high school, or college, until a heterosexual marriage, or to some later point in adulthood (Lee

1977). Whatever the case, youth must deal with the increasing disparity between their own inner desires and desired external objects – romantic partners, new cultural roles – and a working through of the preconceptions that increasingly frustrate and even strangle them: heterosexual ethnocentrism, inversion, stigma, homogeneous cloning. Secrecy is a significant but poorly understood part of this liminal transition (see Martin 1982; Warren 1980). Their eventual changes, as outcome variables, depend upon several factors, including their mental well-being, age, sex, socioeconomic status, ethnicity, urban or rural ambiance, and the degree of support from their familial and cultural systems. We shall touch upon these factors presently.

But to continue on rites of passage, the anthropological analogy would seem to falter in two ways for gay youth. First, they experience the life crisis in isolation, apart from significant others, seemingly not initiated by formal procedures nor as part of an age set or cohort, and even unsupported by the society at large. Second, our society has traditionally suppressed and ignored the social state of being homosexual, especially among adolescents, so that apart from the stigma and being pariah, they have no clear "room" into which they can move and be recognized as esteemed social actors.

To the first objection, it can be argued that social and technological changes have made media and periodical images of the gay world available to many adolescents, even those in rural areas. Gay groups, especially supportive homophile self-help groups (Anderson 1987), today serve essentially as liminal cohorts and contexts for coming out. Other contexts of coming out, such as the armed services, are also available but more problematical, as noted variously by the large social surveys of homosexuality (Bell and Weinberg 1978; Jay and Young 1977).

To the second objection, that our society is a house without room for the homosexual status traditionally, we can offer the signs of some social change. The gay and lesbian world, however oppressed and dehumanized, now presents an alternative social reality for the teenager, in contrast to other normative lifestyles. Society has added a small and perhaps rather poorly furnished back room (some might say a jail cell), but this nevertheless exists, and its existence is surely vital in easing the identity transition process, as Lillian Faderman (1981) argued in writing that those women who come out now are spared some of the painful experiences of those who did so prior to the late 1960s and early 1970s. Political gains of the last two decades have enabled this, and ultimately, political sovereignty rests upon cultural sovereignty. Plummer (1981) also suggested that the existence of this other cultural world, even in the face of stigma, permits young homosexuals now to "rewrite" their personal histories, by "adapting to and creating homosexual meanings … [and then] incorporating these into one's life pattern" (93). The revised cultural context gives expanded personal meaning to the coming out process for young gays.

There is another dimension of contemporary coming out that should be mentioned here: its younger, adolescent age, which links the problems of gay youth to those of adolescence in our mainstream culture. Since the time of Dank's (1971) classic study on coming out, studies have shown that the mean age of coming out has dropped, at least in urban areas. Dank (1971, N = 179, non-random sample) reported a mean age of 19.3 years. Troiden and Goode (1980) more recently reported a mean of 16.3 years for age of first self-definition as homosexual, and Coleman (1982) reported age 15 for males, and age 20 for females coming out. Remafedi (1987a) recently reported a mean age of 14, among gay youth who self-identify as such. Michael Ross (1989) reports on the mean age of realization of coming out in four countries: Sweden (14.1 years), Australia (12.5 years), Finland (13.9 years), and Ireland (15.6 years). The more sexually restrictive the culture, the later age at which one will discover one's own homosexuality. The mean age of becoming homosexually active, however, is much later, between 5 and 7 years later for these countries, respectively. These studies are suggestive but problematic, in that the coming out process is not always defined identically.

Male and female age differences are and always have been significant in coming out

(Troiden 1989), for lesbians have tended to come out later than their male counterparts, although this pattern is changing (see Schneider 1989). This adolescent age range raises adjustment problems that are similar to those of heterosexual teenagers, including the emergence of the sexual (Gagnon 1979) in girls and boys, with its attendant social conflicts. Other issues are separation from home, entry into college or work, and the quest for adult goals. Yet gay youth experience the stigma and burden of coming out on top of all this. The wonder is the relatively good mental health of gays and lesbians (Cohen and Stein, 1986; Gonsiorek 1982).

Ironically, most accounts of normative adolescent development have been conceptualized within the conflict and crisis model (Blos 1962; A. Freud 1958). Empirical studies, such as those by Offer and Offer (1975) and Vaillant (1971), however, increasingly suggest that the conflictual emphasis is inaccurate. Other studies have reported positive relationships with peers and parents among heterosexual teens, though sexuality was not a central issue (Douvan and Adelson 1966; Kandel and Lesser 1972). Nevertheless, a recent commentary suggested that the experience of adolescence is more difficult than ever (Hamburg, Nightingale, and Takanishi 1987). The conflictual nature of the homosexual adolescent's experience is also prominently noted in the literature (Anderson 1987; Boxer and Cohler 1989; Troiden 1979). Surely, cultural and generational changes have influenced this. But precisely how are things more or less conflictual now? What research increasingly suggests is that, as the age of coming out lowers for gay youth, additional developmental age-related pressures may overburden the gay or lesbian teenager. This has greater psychosocial costs, and it raises risk factors, such as suicide, that should be studied more intensively, a later point of discussion.

Very often the question of coming out has been posed as one in which we can infer from the empirical data normative stages of youth identity development among gays and lesbians. The concern here is with charting a territory of homosexual development, in part as counterpoint to that of heterosexuality (Plummer 1981); that is, identity formation as a process. Troiden (1989) reviews and reconsiders important findings from this research genre. He argues, in relation to the decreasing age of coming out, that if it is to emerge, the sense of being gay is "probable" by late adolescence (see Remafedi 1987a). Moreover, once this awareness emerges, he suggests that invariant psychosocial phases, which he labels as sensitivity, individuation, consolidation, and acceptance, occur and must be passed through, on the way to the expression of a mature gay/lesbian identity consonant with the prevailing cultural lifestyle of the local population (Cass 1984; Coleman 1989; Plummer 1981). It is assumed by some (e.g., Silverstein 1981) that these phases will spontaneously emerge at no matter what actual age the person comes out.

To what extent are such identity development stages the same for males and females? Are they universal and applicable to other societies? Tremble and his colleagues (1989) point up differences in the process based on sex, ethnicity, and religious conventions. The majority of our data are on males, however; an unfortunate slant that is to be found throughout the literature. We need more research on younger lesbians. The validity of these stage models in the final analysis is critical, but remains to be fully tested cross-culturally to understand how identity is not only a process, but also a product of particular cultural contexts.

Other contemporary factors of coming out among teenagers are also illuminating: significant life events, contexts, and relationships can be seen as macrolevel factors that influence microfactors, such as sex and class. Of course these cannot be decontextualized from the total sociocultural systems in which they are embedded, but for the sake of heuristic clarity, I shall treat them here as somewhat separate elements of gay youth development.

The sex of the person, as hinted above, has been shown to structure the coming out process in various ways (reviewed in Jay and Young 1977; Ponse 1980). A global dimension of this aspect cross-culturally concerns the subordinate status of females in patriarchal cultures (Faderman 1981; Rubin 1975). A significant empirical difference between males and females has been shown to be how sex versus love enters into their differential coming out processes. Males tend more often to define themselves as gay in contexts of same-sex erotic contact, whereas females experience their lesbian feelings in situations of romantic love and emotional attachment (Ponse 1978; Troiden, 1989). Such a sex difference reminds us of the contrast in moral voices through which females versus males speak (Gilligan 1982). Where females emphasize attachment and personal orientations, males stress independence and positional relationships in public. We can recognize easily how this sex-related difference is structurally based, in the sex roles of our society, in that the normative contexts for exploration of same-sex experience are culturally structured, too. Many of the contexts of sexual exploration listed by Dank (1971), such as the army, public toilets, dormitories, and boy scouts, are available only to males. Females were, as we know, made more invisible in the domestic domain until very recently (Abbott and Love 1972; Kehoe 1986), and Schneider (1989) has documented the consequences of this for young lesbians in narrative accounts. Moreover, the gender roles and life expectations of the sexes are very different, with their reproductive and parenting roles creating contrary developmental and social problems. The pressures on young girls to conform to heterosexual roles are very great (Kehoe 1986), particularly in more traditional societies, such as those of Latin America and Europe, where social roles create quite distinct adaptations in the sexes (Carrier 1980).

Socioeconomic status is another critical, but still largely unknown contributor to the coming out process as a rite of passage. Class is significant in structuring gender codes and roles. The more male/female roles are dichotomized, the greater the tendency of the inversion preconception to manifest itself in cross-gender behavior (Harry 1982; Whitam 1983), a point that Carrier has critically examined (Carrier 1980; 1989). More traditional non-Western polarized societies seem closer to the working class norms of Western culture in this rule-bound restrictiveness (Harry 1985). Both education and class-related attitudes affect the timing of first sexual contact, via attitudes toward sexual activity before adulthood (reviewed in Pollak 1986). Plummer (1989) indicates this to some extent in his article on the relationship between gays and youth culture, showing differential class responses to "punk" styles. The androgyny of punk provides a fluidity which in some ways mediates sex role dichotomies and class barriers.[21] The relationship between urbanized gay gentry and middle- and upper-middle-class consumer norms is well known (Altman 1979; Cassells 1983; Pollak 1986). The large disposable incomes of gay men, which presumably have led to the term "guppy" (gay urban mobile young professional), have been commented upon, as have their professionality and higher education norms (Bell and Weinberg, 1978). One wonders about the representativeness of these samples, however (Carrier 1979).

The impact of the coming out process on education in gay youth is an area that has been neglected. The literature is contradictory on this point: Harry (1982) argued that gay males "compensate for their negative feelings about their homosexuality through the acquisition of higher education" (173). Class is clearly a factor, for in Harry's sample, blue-collar persons tend to feel more guilt than white-collar persons regarding their homosexuality, and guilt makes the engine run, in Harry's view (see also Levitt and Klassen 1974). A West German study (Reichert and Dannecker 1977) seems to support Harry's finding. However, Saghir and Robbins (1973) found, on the other hand, that homosexual men are more likely than heterosexuals to drop out of college before graduation. We may have a cohort effect here: How far these findings apply to gay (and lesbian) teenagers and young adults in the mid-1980s is unclear. Here is an area of research desperately in need of careful study.

The disadvantages of ethnic minorities in coming out today are only very dimly known (Adam 1978). Tremble (1989) shows the effects of coming out in a multicultural context in Canada. One suspects that a greater degree of acceptance of variation in cultural standards and life styles may underlie the response of heterosexual Canadians to gay and lesbian youth there (cf. Soares 1979; Vasquez 1979). By contrast, Gerstell and her colleagues (1989) hint that race is a powerful force for segregation and boundary maintenance in interactions between gay and straight youth in the Chicago area, with blacks being suspected of gay inclinations merely by associating with white teenagers (cf. Vernon 1971). Echoes of this ethnic/class barrier can also be found in Carrier's study (1989). Here is a factor of gay identity construction and maintenance that begs to be studied in multiethnic social fields (see Bass-Hass 1968; Hidalgo and Christensen 1976; and Rich 1979).

The difference between coming out in rural versus urban areas is another, largely unknown, dimension of the total developmental situation, though it has long been believed to influence significantly the age and characteristics of the gay experience in American society. Howard Brown (1976), for instance, provided poignant portraits of "homosexuals in small towns," attempting to counteract the attitude of some gays, to wit: "Let them move to the cities" (p. 89). Silverstein (1981) suggested that males in rural communities can grow up naive of their own eroticism, and thus "be prevented from even knowing that they are gay" (107). They have no label and role for their experience (Troiden and Goode, 1980). The large social surveys done on urbanized adult gay men reveal their attitude about residing in gay urban communities for harmony and protection (Bell and Weinberg, 1978). Now, Lynch (1987) has told us, "non-ghetto" gays have moved back to the suburbs.[22]

The coming out literature generally suggests that youth in close proximity to urban centers have more opportunities for making supportive homosexual contacts, particularly those that derive from the recent appearance of homophile coming out groups (Anderson 1987). Our Chicago study provides a new account of such a group (Gerstell et al. 1989). So much is the situation for gay youth better in the cities that Rose Robertson (1981), in a recent essay on young gays, suggested that those in urban areas are "lucky," and "workers in this field will be aware of the absolute despair of young people in isolated small towns who feel themselves to be

homosexual" (172). Such a dismal picture does seem warranted based upon what is known from America, though Silverstein (1981) provided a more positive report.

The urban scene in other countries tends to be freer and more supportive of the emergence of alternative sexual orientations elsewhere, too. We must take care in interpreting these trends, and in understanding their causes, as indicated above. Not all of these youth selfidentify as gay or homosexual, or the appropriate kindred cultural identity. The presence of Western and local tourists has surely contributed to this trend (Pollak 1986). Yet the studies by Carrier (1989) and Parker (1989), respectively, clearly reveal how local "gay" movements provide their own infrastructural support for the coming out process in teens. How widespread are such local gay support systems? (For reviews see Adam 1987; Lauritsen and Thorstad 1974; and Murray 1984.)

In a short piece on the Sulu Islands near Borneo, Nimmo (1978) reported on a traditional form of male transvestism that was usually indicative of adult homosexuality. Nimmo found that in the process of urbanization, other Sulu males not only did not manifest this form of homosexuality, they even became reluctant to engage in any same-sex contact because of having internalized negative Western stereotypes of "the homosexual" in the cities. Nimmo's paper reminds us that a gloomy and perhaps decadent image of the city, involving crime, pollution, degeneracy, is prevalent in Western mythology, and that the history of Western homosexuality in Western cities is embedded in it (Ariès 1986). One point to draw from such examples is that the phenomenon of gay youth is rapidly changing in our "global village" and that it results from many complex forces that create unusual events and contexts for the affirmation of homosexual desires.

What role does the family system contribute in the process of coming out today? Familial factors of all kinds are always shaped by the broader cultural environment. Attitudes toward homosexuality, and the presence of homophobia within family members, often reflect general social norms and values (see Ross 1989). Yet the importance of parental attitudes, as a directive force in the everyday lives of teenagers, cannot be exaggerated. And here, the preconceptions outlined earlier, particularly the assumption of heterosexuality, still reign. "The grasping at straws by so many parents is significant. It demonstrates the still widely held belief that all young people are heterosexual and can only be corrupted into homosexuality by contact with homosexuals" (Robertson 1981: 174).

Martin (1982) commented in this context on the generalized "pernicious equation of homosexuality and danger to children" (54), a reflection of the stereotypes mentioned above (see Warren 1980). Such attitudes result in prohibitions on contact with gays and lesbians, teenagers or adults. The stigma, however, particularly transfers by association with gay adults, which accounts, in the adolescent experience, for the early and still prevailing distance between gay groups and the individual, as role models (Martin 1982). But there are new signs of hope, as revealed through stories of parents of gays and lesbians, stories which tell of frustration, courage, and the capacity of parents to transcend stereotypes through love of their children (Muller 1987; Rafkin 1987).

Contact with peers is as significant for gay youth as for straight peers, and these peers are less suspect than older gays. Open rebellion against parents is also an option, but one that sometimes creates grave social and financial hardships for youth, who may be forced out of their homes. Extreme emotional responses may accompany this rejection, including suicide. Part of the attraction to present-day peer groups is their fluid, unisex character, which may bewilder parents. The nature of punk culture dovetails with the coming out process, as Plummer (1989) shows emphasizing mutual acceptance by peers: "Where being yourself was acceptable, whether that was gay, straight, bisexual, or cucumber freak," Aaron Fricke wrote (1981: 49). Today, youth gangs are remarkable in how age outweighs gender as the key mode of membership and identification (Lafont 1986). Fluctuations in societal gender roles and norms underlie this androgyny, signaling an overall change in adolescent sensibilities with regard to being lesbian or gay. Indeed,

Ariès (1986: 64) suggested that this is a transcultural trend:

> The unisex fashion is a clear indication of a general change in society. Tolerance of homosexuality is the result of changes in the way the sexes present themselves to the world, in their actions, in their professional lives, in their families, but especially in their function as symbolic figures.

Foucault (1980) would probably have agreed with this summary, though he might have added that it is the product of many structural and infrastructural forces, which include various localized homosexual or gay liberation movements around the world. Or, to cite Parker's perspective from Brazil on the matter, these alternative youth scenes and groups provide "multiple discourses and realities" on society and sexuality for the construction of gay adolescent lives.

A final issue concerns the understanding of social problems among gay youth. Such was the bias of an earlier day that the social problems of gay and lesbian youth were inflated by the stereotyped preconceptions already noted, or else completely ignored and denied. We must make no mistake about it: This is purely a result of homophobic and ghettoization. To take but one example, Berger found, in his study *Gay and Gray* (1982), that "when gerontologists talk about the elderly, they mean heterosexual elderly" (13). The gay and lesbian elderly have been terribly ignored, it is true, because they are structurally invisible (Kehoe 1986); but more significantly because their *existence has been psychologically denied* – in the minds of health care providers, researchers, government agencies, and the public at large. Yet, in his study, Berger (1982) found "striking similarities" between elderly gays and other older Americans, which argues for increased care-giving to the elderly homosexual. The general point could be extended to encompass gay teenage problems of adjustment, grief, depression, drug abuse, school achievement, and so forth. Paradoxically, gays present a "social problem" to society, but when particular social problems are studied, gays are often ignored.

The "problems" of the gay teenager must be understood in this sense. In an unpublished report, Gibson (n.d.) highlighted the issues in understanding gay teenage suicide, which is alarmingly high and must be a cause for great concern. Between 20 and 35 per cent of gay youth have made suicide attempts, the best available statistics show (Gibson: 2). Youthful gays often internalize negative stereotypes and images of themselves. And when you have been told that you are "sick, bad and wrong for being who you are," you begin to believe it, Gibson wrote (5). Peers, older gays, and especially supportive family members can help relieve this terrible pattern.

More than anything else, the impact of AIDS is changing social attitudes regarding homosexuality and gay youth. Much new research is presently underway to understand and fight the disease (Feldman and Johnson 1986). Meanwhile, fear of contagion, hysteria, and hatred have spread. AIDS is creating new and unique problems in society and in the gay world (Herdt 1987a), problems the likes of which we can still only imagine. It will undoubtedly produce far-reaching changes in the nature and meaning of same-sex behavior and relationships. Much has already been demonstrated about the effects of the disease upon the gay population, including the media presentations of it (Baker 1986). AIDS is now a global problem, requiring global solutions and unprecedented international cooperation.

Yet I fear that not enough emphasis has been placed upon our understanding of AIDS risks and prevention in teenagers, a point made clearly in a recent Surgeon General's report. As with fashions and school performance, teenage suicide, and drug use, peer culture can influence sex behavior and awareness of AIDS (Fullilove 1987). We urgently need research on adolescent populations and their perceptions and handling of AIDS. Feldman (1989) shows that American adolescents are still woefully ignorant of what constitutes "safe sex" behavior. Millan and Ross (1987) concluded similarly of Australian youth.

Equally important, AIDS is no doubt affecting the coming out process in ways that are yet unknown. Fear of AIDS has made parental acceptance more complicated than ever (Robinson and Walters 1987). It has changed self-acceptance, too. As one teenager recently told me in our Chicago study: "I never wanted to be gay. Now, with AIDS, I have even less reason to feel positive about that part of myself." We urgently need new studies of this problem.

AIDS has exacerbated an already existing generational difference between older and younger gays. This, too, must be seen in perspective, as but one piece of a larger mosaic of oppression of gays across societies. Berger (1982) noted, for instance, that the invisibility and peripheralization of elderly gays have isolated them from their peers – not just their heterosexual, but also their homosexual counterparts. These older gays are isolated from youth as well. Furthermore, the fear of AIDS contact has seemingly alienated teenagers from younger and middle-aged adults (Feldman 1989), not merely as role models, but just as companions and friends. This is regrettable for many reasons, not the least of which is that older gays and lesbians could help in the reduction of AIDS risks to teens. Let us strive and work for a change in this unfortunate trend. For, as Damien Martin (1982) concluded, "Stigmatization of the gay adolescent has evolved from centuries of misinformation and fear. Education through direct teaching and the example of role models will be the best way to attack discrimination at its root" (63–4).

CONCLUSION

We have just begun to open a new discourse on understanding homosexuality and adolescence. There is so much that remains unknown; we have barely scratched the surface of the sensibilities and culture of these young people. The road to understanding is filled with potholes and intellectual bumps and political landmines. Recent work shows growth, crisis, and change – always the wellsprings of human life – and they have helped to move us beyond what Plummer (1981) referred to as that notorious preoccupation with the childhoods of homosexuals, whose lives seemed to end in their potentiality at age 5. We look forward to this new era of research on gay youth.

NOTES

1 This "we" must stand for the gay and lesbian community, the social science establishment, and – notwithstanding the "bicultural" identity of the gay/social scientist (Murray 1984) – the public gay laity studied mainly by the gay researchers now being studied themselves by (mostly gay and lesbian) historians.

2 Altman 1982: "But at the same time there is a sense in which style and fashion mold behavior, and to this extent the impact of gays is changing American society ... [though] much of what I have to say applies to other Western countries.... the new homosexual affirmation can be found in Sydney, Strasbourg, and even São Paulo, as well as in San Francisco" (xii).

3 Dr. Kenneth Sladkin, Chairman, Section on Adolescent Health, American Academy of Pediatrics. Cited in *Pediatric News* (December 1983): 34.

4 Reviewed in Ross (1980), and recently raised by Risman (1984) in objection to the entire foundation of Joseph Harry's *Gay Children Grown Up* (1982).

5 "The denial of role models is an essential part of the total stigmatization process" (Martin 1982: 55). See also Silverstein (1981).

6 See, for instance, Hippler (1986).

7 Sontag 1982: "The sensibility of an era is not only its most decisive but also its most perishable aspect. One may capture the ideas (intellectual history) and the behavior (social history) of an epoch without ever touching upon the taste which informed those ideas, that behavior" (106).

8 See, for example, Adam 1987; Martin 1982; Plummer 1975, 1981; and, for the longer historical view, see Foucault, 1980.

9 Shepard 1987: "This is why societies like Britain and the USA have had such an exaggerated horror of homosexuality – the sexual invert is assumed to have subversive political attitudes as well, should be banned from high office, and until recently was considered not merely as a potential, but as an actual criminal" (264).

10 See De Cecco's (1984) edited volume on this. What remains obscure, however, are present forms of homophobia among youth.

11 Thus, Ollendorff (1966), in a period work that is typical, stated, "We feel, therefore, that *the occurrence of adolescent homosexuality is a product of a wrong social setting* [italics in original] ... and is a presenting factor of major importance in most psychiatric illnesses" (51).

12 Ann Muller (1987) referred to these Freudian stereotypes as the "trolls of psychiatry" in her narrative account of the parents of gays and lesbians.

13 By contrast, though homosexuality was illegal in Germany after 1871, lesbianism was ignored there and elsewhere, and the Nazis' "counter-revolution" in criminalizing all forms of homosexuality primarily affected males (Herger 1980). Elsewhere, Lauritsen and Thorstad (1974) argued that the homosexual rights movement had the same dual effect upon Germany after the turn of the century, both of which the Nazis were to undo by the late 1930s.

14 D'Emilio (1983): "Gay liberation used the demonstrations of the New Left as recruiting grounds and appropriated the tactics of confrontational politics for its own ends. The ideas that suffused youth protest found their way into gay liberation, where they were modified and adapted to describe the oppression of homosexuals and lesbians. The apocalyptic rhetoric and the sense of impending revolution then made a public avowal of their sexuality seem insignificant" (233).

15 Gays, some commentators (Altman 1982; Ariès 1986) have said, put sex back into polite mixed company, whereas for straights, the themes of the consumer and procreative age still reign. When Michel Foucault visited the West Coast before his death, he is reported to have complained of dining with heterosexual yuppies, who, over dinner, seemed only to discuss their personal computers and their children.

16 No doubt the terrible rise of AIDS during the past several years has had an impact upon these trends, perhaps reversing them. Because the social effects of this are so rapidly unfolding, we cannot be sure of even their near-term outcomes.

17 Steve Murray (personal communication, March 1, 1987) reminded me that the residential North Beach area in San Francisco may have created the early critical mass of gays necessary to mobilize and reject the then prevailing stereotypes of homosexuality.

18 The lesbian and women's culture literature does not emphasize the erotic in the same way as does the gay male scene (cf. Krieger 1982). The lesbian experience seems to emphasize love and attachment to women (Jay and Young 1977) as much as the erotic. And Marg Schneider (personal communication, March 11, 1987) reminded me that feminist issues may ultimately divide gay men from women in ways that transcend the affinities of sexual orientation.

19 Weeks (1987) pointed out that the link between lesbianism as political or sexual identity seems tenuous and more of a choice in longstanding evocative trends in the literature.

20 The existing literature on coming out, so extensive and fruitful, has not been fully tapped for new concepts and syntheses. Troiden's (1989) invaluable review is a marvelous tool in rethink-

ing it. But my suggestion for new research arises mainly from the sense that the problem has been, at once, too broadly and too narrowly defined; broad in the sense that we need more microscopic studies of the full range of homosexualities beyond that of American WASPS (Carrier 1979), and narrow in the sense that the ideas are constrained too much by the folk concepts of Western psychology and sociology, as represented by the primary body of work done in these disciplines in the US. When an anthropology of the coming out process emerges, we shall have passed a critical conceptual roadmark in the understanding of homosexuality for humans, one which could transcend the increasingly threadbare dichotomizing of essentialist/constructionist models.

21 See Fricke's (1981) vignette on the *Rocky Horror Show* film and its cult followers: Here is a common urban gay youth context.

22 Interestingly enough, Lynch's (1987) study of suburban gays (mean age of coming out around 30) suggested that distance from urban areas does indeed postpone the coming out process.

REFERENCES

Abbott, S. and Love, B. (1972), *Sappho Was a Right-on Woman* (New York: Stein & Day).

Adam, B. (1978), *The Survival of Domination* (New York: Elsevier).

Adam, B. (1987), *The Rise of a Gay and Lesbian Movement* (Boston: Twayne).

Altman, D. (1973), *Homosexual: Oppression and Liberation* (New York: Avon Books).

——(1979), *Coming Out in the Seventies* (Sydney: Wild & Woolley).

——(1981), *Coming Out in the Seventies* (Boston: Alyson) (shortened version of 1979 edition).

——(1982) *The Homosexualization of America* (New York: St Martin's Press).

Anderson, D. (1987) "Family and Peer Relations of Gay Adolescents," *Adolescent Psychiatry* 14: 165–78.

Ariès, P. (1986), "Thoughts on the History of Homosexuality," in P. Ariès and A. Bejin (eds), *Western Sexuality* pp. 62–75 (London: Basil Blackwell).

Baker, A. J. (1986), "The Portrayal of AIDS in the Media: An Analysis of Articles in the New York Times," in D. Feldman and T. Johnson (eds), *The Social Dimension of AIDS*: 179–96, (New York: Praeger).

Bass-Hass, R. (1968), "The Lesbian Dyad," *Journal of Sex Research* 4: 108–26.

Bell, A. and Weinberg, M. S. (1978), *Homosexualities: A Study of Diversity among Men and Women* (New York: Simon & Schuster).

Bell, A. P., Weinberg, M. S. and Hammersmith, S.

(1981), *Sexual Preference* (Bloomington: Indiana University Press).

Berger, R. (1982) *Gay and Gray* (Urbana, IL: University of Illinois Press).

Blackwood, E. (1986) "Breaking the Mirror: The Construction of Lesbianism and the Anthropological Discourse on Homosexuality," in E. Blackwood (ed.), *Anthropology and Homosexual Behavior*: 1–17 (New York: The Haworth Press).

Blos, P. (1962), *On Adolescence: A Psychoanalytic Interpretation* (New York: The Free Press-Macmillan).

Boswell, J. (1980), *Christianity, Social Tolerance and Homosexuality* (Chicago: University of Chicago Press).

Brown, H. (1976), *Familiar Faces: Hidden Lives* (New York: Harcourt, Brace, Jovanovich).

Carrier, J. (1979), Review of *Homosexualities: A Study of Diversity among Men and Women*, by A. Bell and M. S. Weinberg, 1978, *Journal of Homosexuality* 4: 296–98.

Carrier, J. (1980), "Homosexual Behavior in Cross-cultural Perspective," in J. Marmor (ed.), *Homosexual Behavior: A Modern Reappraisal*: 100–22 (New York: Basic Books).

Cass, V. (1984), "Homosexual Identity: A Concept in Need of a Definition," *Journal of Homosexuality* 9: 4: 105–26 (New York: The Haworth Press).

Castells, M. (1983), Cultural Identity, Sexual Liberation and Urban Structure: The Gay Community in San Francisco," in *The City and the Grass Roots: A Cross-cultural Theory of Urban Social Movements*: 138–72 (London: Edward Arnold).

Cohen, C. J. and Stein, T. S. (1986), "Reconceptualizing Individual Psychotherapy with Gay Men and Lesbians," in C. J. Cohen and T. S. Stein (eds), *Contemporary Perspectives on Psychotherapy with Lesbians and Gay Men*: 27–54 (New York: Plenum).

Coleman, E. (1982), "Developmental Stages in the Coming Out Process," *Journal of Homosexuality* 7: 2/3: 31–43.

Dank, B. (1971), "Coming Out in the Gay World," *Psychiatry* 34: 180–97.

Darrow, W. W., Gorman, E. M. and Glick, B. P. (1986), "The Social Origins of AIDS: Social Change, Sexual Behavior and Disease Trends," in D. Feldman and T. Johnson (eds), *The Social Dimensions of AIDS*: 95–110 (New York: Praeger).

De Cecco, J. P. (1984), *Bisexual and Homosexual Identities: Critical Theoretical Issues* (New York: The Haworth Press).

De Cecco, J. P. (in press), "Sex and More Sex," in D. McWhirter (ed.), *Homosexuality and Heterosexuality* (New York: Oxford University Press).

D'Emilio, J. (1983), *Sexual Politics, Sexual Communities* (Chicago: University of Chicago Press).

Douvan, E. and Adelson, J. (1966), *The Adolescent Experience* (New York: John C. Wiley & Sons).

Erikson, E. (1968), *Identity, Youth and Crisis* (New York: W. W. Norton).

Faderman, L. (1981), *Surpassing the Love of Men*, (New York: William Morrow).

Feldman, D. A. and Johnson, T. M. (1986), "Introduction," *The Social Dimensions of AIDS: Methods and Theory*: 1–12 (New York: Praeger).

Foucault, M. (1980), *The History of Sexuality* (New York: Pantheon).

Freud, A. (1958), "Adolescence," *Psychoanalytic Study of the Child* 13: 255–78.

Fricke, A. (1981), *Reflections of a Rock Lobster* (Boston: Alyson).

Fullilove, M. (1987, spring), "Teens Rap about Drugs, STDs, and AIDS," *Multicultural Inquiry and Research on AIDS*: 1.

Gadamer, H. G. (1965), *Truth and Method* (New York: Crossroad).

Gagnon, J. (1979), "The Interaction of Gender roles and Sexual Conduct," in H. A. Katchadourian (ed.), *Human Sexuality*: 225–45 (Berkeley: University of California Press.

Gibson, P. (n.d.), "Gay Male and Lesbian Youth Suicide," unpublished manuscript.

Gilligan, C. (1982), *In a Different Voice* (Cambridge, MA: Harvard University Press).

Gonsiorek, J. (ed.), (1982). *Homosexuality: Social, Psychological, and Biological Issues* (Beverly Hills, CA: Sage Publications).

Green, R. (1987), *The "Sissy Boy Syndrome" and the Development of Homosexuality* (New Haven, CT: Yale University Press).

Greenberg, D. and Bystryn, M. (1982), "Christian Intolerance of Homosexuality," *American Journal of Sociology* 88: 515–48.

Greenberg, J. (1976), "A Study of the Self-esteem and Alienation of Male Homosexuals," *The Journal of Psychology* 83: 137–43.

Hamburg, D. A., Nightingale, E. O. and Takanishi, R. (1987), "Facilitating the Transitions of Adolescence," JAMA 257: 3405–6.

Harris, M. (1982), *America Now* (New York: Simon & Schuster).

Harry, J. (1982), *Gay Children Grown Up* (New York: Praeger).

——(1985), "Defeminization and Social Class," *Archives of Sexual Behavior* 14: 1: 1–12.

Herdt, G. (1981), *Guardians of the Flutes: Idioms of Masculinity* (New York: McGraw-Hill).

——(1984), "Ritualized Homosexuality in the Male Cults of Melanesia, 1862–1982: An Introduction," in G. Herdt (ed.), *Ritualized Homosexuality in Melanesia*: 1–81 (Berkeley, CA: University of California Press).

——(1987a, March), "AIDS and Anthropology," *Anthropology Today*.

——(1987b), "Homosexuality," *Encyclopedia of Religion*, vol. 3, Macmillan Religion Encyclopedia, 17 vols (New York: Macmillan).

——(1987c), *Sambia: Ritual and Gender in New Guinea* (New York: Holt, Rinehart, & Winston).

Herger, H. (1980), *The Men with the Pink Triangle*, trans. D. Fernbach (London: Gay Men's Press).

Heron, A. (1983), *One Teenager in Ten: Testimony by Gay and Lesbian Youth* (New York: Warner Books).

Hidalgo, H. A. and Christensen, E. H. (1976), "The Puerto Rican Lesbian and the Puerto Rican Community," *Journal of Homosexuality* 2: 109–21.

Hippler, M. (1986, September 16), "The Problem and Promise of Gay Youth," *The Advocate*, issue 455.

Hoffman, M. (1968), *The Gay World* (New York: Basic Books).

Hoffman, S. (1970), The Cities of Night: John Rechy's City of Night and the American Literature of Homosexuality," in H. M. Ruitenbeek (ed.), *Sexuality and Identity*: 390–402 (New York: Delta).

Hooker, E. (1957), "Adjustment of Male Homosexuals," *Journal Proj. Tech* 21: 18–31.

——(1965), "An Empirical Study of some Relations between Sexual Patterns and Gender Identity in Male Homosexuals," in J. Money (ed.), *Sex Research: New Developments*: 24–52 (New York: Rinehart, & Winston).

Hoult, T. F. (1984), "Human Sexuality in Biological Perspective: Theoretical and Methodological Considerations," *Journal of Homosexuality* 9: 2/3: 137–55.

Humphreys, L. and Miller, B. (1980), "Identities in the Emerging Gay Culture," in J. Marmor (ed.), *Homosexual Behavior*, pp. 142–56 (New York: Basic Books).

Isay, R. A. (1986), "The Development of Sexual Identity in Homosexual Men," *The Psychoan. St. Child* 41: 467–89.

Jay, K. and Young, A. (1977), *The Gay Report*, (New York: Summit).

Kandel, D. and Lesser, G. (1972), *Youth in Two Worlds* (San Francisco: Jossey Bass).

Kehoe, M. (1986), "Lesbians over 65: A Triple Invisible Minority," *Journal of Homosexuality* 12: 3/4: 139–52.

Kinsey, A., Pomeroy, W. B. and Martin, C. E. (1948), *Sexual Behavior in the Human Male* (Philadelphia: W. B. Saunders).

Kotarba, J. A. and Lang, N. G. (1986), "Gay Lifestyle Change and AIDS: Preventive Health Care" in D. A. Feldman and T. A. Johnson (eds), *The Social Dimensions of AIDS*: 127–44 (New York: Praeger.

Krieger, S. (1982), Lesbian Identity and Community: Recent Social Science Literature," *Signs* 8: 91–108.

Lafont, H. (1986), "Changing Sexual Behavior in French Youth Gangs," in P. Ariès and A. Bejin (eds), *Western Sexuality: Practice and Precept in Past and Present Times* (Oxford: Blackwell).

Laner, M. R. and Laner, R. H. (1979), "Personal Style or Sexual Preference? Why Gay Men are Disliked," *Intl. Rev. Mod. Soc.* 9: 215–28.

Lauritsen, J. and Thorstad, D. (1974), *The Early Homosexual Rights Movement* (New York: Times Change Press).

Lee, J. A. (1977), "Going Public: A Study in the Sociology of Homosexual Liberation," *Journal of Homosexuality* 3: 49–78.

Levine, M. (1979), *Gay Men* (New York: Harper & Row).

Levitt, E. and Klassen, A. (1974), "Public Attitudes Toward Homosexuality," *Journal of Homosexuality* 1: 29–43.

Leznoff, M. and Westley, W. (1956), "The Homosexual Community," *Social Problems* 2: 257–63.

Lockard, D. (1986), "The Lesbian Community: An Anthropological Approach," in E. Blackwood (ed.), *Anthropology and Homosexual Behavior*: 83–95 (New York: The Haworth Press).

Lynch, F. R. (1987), "Non-ghetto Gays: A Sociological Study of Suburban Homosexuals," *Journal of Homosexuality* 13: 4: 13–42.

McIntosh, M. (1968), "The Homosexual Role," *Social Problems* 16: 182–92.

McWhirter, D. P. and Mattison, A. (1984), *The Male Couple* (Englewood Cliffs, NJ: Prentice-Hall.

Martin, A. Damien (1982), "Learning to Hide: Socialization of the Gay Adolescent," *Adolescent Psychiatry* 10: 52–65.

Millan, G. and Ross, M. W. (1987), "AIDS and Gay Youth: Attitudes and Lifestyle Modifications in Young Male Homosexuals," *Community Health Studies* 11: 52–3.

Minton, H. and McDonald, G. J. (1983/4), "Homosexual Identity Formation as a Developmental Process," *Journal of Homosexuality* 9: 2/3: 91–104.

Muller, A. (1987), *Parents Matter* (New York: The Naiad Press).

Murray, S. O. (1979), "The Institutional Elaboration of a Quasi-ethnic Community," *Intl. Rev. Mod. Sociol* 9: 165–77.

Murray, S. O. (1984) *Social Theory, Homosexual Realities* (New York: Gai Sabre Books).

Newton, E. (1972), *Mother Camp* (Toronto: Prentice-Hall).

Nimmo, H. (1978), Relativity of Sexual Deviance: A Sulu Example," *University of Oklahoma Papers in Anthropology* 19: 91–7.

Offer, D. and Offer, J. B. (1975), *From Teen-age to Young Manhood: A Psychological Study* (New York: Basic Books).

Ollendorff, R. (1966), *The Juvenile Homosexual Experience and its Effects on Adult Homosexuality* (New York: Julian Press).

Page, S. and Yee, M. (1985), "Conception of Male and Female Homosexual Stereotypes among University Undergraduates," *Journal of Homosexuality* 12: 1: 109–18.

Paul, I. (1983/4) "The Bisexual Identity: An Idea without Social Recognition," *Journal of Homosexuality* 9: 3: 45–63.

Plummer, K. (1975) *Sexual Stigma* (Boston: Routledge & Kegan Paul).

——(1981), "Homosexual Categories: Some Research Problems in the Labelling Perspective of Homosexuality" in K. Plummer (ed.), *The Makings of the Modern Homosexual*: 53–75 (London: Hutchinson).

Pollak, M. (1986), "Male Homosexuality – Or Happiness in the Ghetto," in P. Ariès & Bejin (eds), *Western Sexuality: Practice and Precept in Past and Present Times* (London: Basil Blackwell).

Ponse, B. (1978), *Identities in the Lesbian World: The Social Construction of the Self* (Westport, CT: Greenwood).

——(1980), "Lesbians and their Worlds," in J. Marmor (ed.), *Homosexual Behavior: A Modern Reappraisal*: 157–75 (New York: Basic Books).

Rafkin, L. (1987), *Different Daughters: A Book by Mothers of Lesbians* (Pittsburgh: Cleis).

Read, K. (1980), *Other Voices* (Toronto: Chandler & Sharpe).

Rechy, J. (1963), *City of Night* (New York: Grove).

Reichert, T. and Dannecker, M. (1977), "Male Homosexuality in West Germany," *Journal of Sex Research* 3: 35–53.

Reiss, A. (1961), "The Social Integration of Queers and Peers," *Social Problems* 9: 102–20.

Remafedi, G. (1987a), "Male Homosexuality: The Adolescent's Perspective," *Pediatrics* 79: 326–30.

——(1987b), "Adolescent Homosexuality: Psychosocial and Medical Implications," *Pediatrics* 79: 331–7.

Rich, A. (1979), "Disloyal to Civilization: Feminism, Racism, and Gynephobia," *Chrysalis* 7: 9–27.

Risman, B. J. (1984), Review of *Gay Children Grown Up*, by J. Harry, *Contemporary Sociology* 13: 469–70.

Roberton, R. (1981), "Young Gays," in J. Hart and D. Richardson (eds), *The Theory and Practice of Homosexuality*: 170–6 (London: Routledge & Kegan Paul).

Robinson, B. and Walters, L. (April 1987), "The AIDS Epidemic Hits Home," *Psychology Today*: 48–52.

Roestler, T. and Deisher, R. W. (1972) "Youthful Male Homosexuality," *Journal of American Medical Association* 219: 108–23.

Rosaldo, M. A. and Lamphere, L. (eds) (1973), *Woman, Culture and Society* (Stanford, CA: Stanford University Press).

Ross, M. (1980), "Retrospective Distortion in Homosexual Research," *Archives of Sexual Behavior* 9: 523–31.

Rubin, G. (1975), "The Traffic in Women: Notes on the 'Political Economy' of Sex," in R. R. Reiter (ed.), *Toward an Anthropology of Women*, 157–210 (New York: Monthly Review Press).

Sagarin, E. (1969), *Odd Man In* (Chicago: Quadrangle).

Saghir, M. and Robbins, E. (1973), *Male and Female Homosexuality* (Baltimore: Williams & Williams).

Scruton, R. (1986), *Sexual Desire* (New York: The Free Press).

Shepherd, G. (1987), "Rank, Gender, and Homosexuality: Mombasa as a Key to Understanding Sexual Options," in P. Caplan (ed.), *The Cultural Construction of Sexuality*: 240–70 (London: Tavistock).

Silverstein, C. (1981), *Man to Man: Gay Couples in America* (New York: William Morrow).

Sladkin, K. E. (1983), "Commentary," *Pediatric News* 14: 3–6.

Soares, J. V. (1979), "Black and Gay," in M. Levine (ed.), *Gay Men: The Sociology of Male Homosexuality* (New York: Harper & Row).

Sontag, S. (1982), "Notes on Camp," in *A Susan Sontag Reader* (London: Penguin).

Stoller, R. J. (1968), *Sex and Gender* (New York: Science House).

——(1985), *Presentations of Gender* (New Haven, CT: Yale University Press).

Troiden, R. R. (1979), "Becoming Homosexual: A Model for Gay Identity Acquisition," *Psychiatry*, 42: 362–73.

Troiden, R. R. and Goode, E. (1980), "Variables Related to Acquisition of Gay Identity," *Journal of Homosexuality* 5: 383–92.

Turner, V. (1967), "Les Rites des Passage," in *Forest of Symbols* (Ithaca, NY: Cornell University Press).

Vaillant, G. (1971), "Theoretical Hierarchy of Adaptive Ego Mechanisms," *Archives of General Psychiatry* 24: 107–15.

Van Gennep, A. (1960), *Rites of Passage* (Chicago: University of Chicago Press).

Vasquez, E. (1979), "Homosexuality in the Context of the Mexican-American Culture," in D. Kuhnel (ed.), *Sexual Issues in Social Work: Emerging Concerns in Education and Practice*: 131–47 (Honolulu: University of Hawaii School of Social Work).

Vernon, R. (1971), "Growing up Black and Gay," *Gay Sunshine* 6: 14–17.

Warren, C. (1974), *Identity and Community in the Gay World* (New York: John C. Wiley).

Warren, C. (1980), "Homosexuality and Stigma," in J. Marmor (ed.), *Homosexual Behavior: A Modern Reappraisal*: 123–44 (New York: Basic Books).

Weeks, J. (1985), *Sexuality and its Discontents* (London: Routledge & Kegan Paul).

——(1987), "Questions of Identity," in P. Caplan (ed.), *The Cultural Construction of Sexuality*, pp. 31–51 (New York: Tavistock).

Weinberg, G. (1972), *Society and the Healthy Homosexual* (New York: St Martin's).

Weinberg, T. S. (1983), *Gay Men, Gay Selves* (New York: Irvington).

Whitam, F. L. (1983), "Culturally Invariable Properties of Male Homosexual," *Archives of Sexual Behavior* 12: 207–22.

Wolf, D. G. (1979), *The Lesbian Community* (Berkeley, CA: University of California Press).

SUPPLEMENTAL BIBLIOGRAPHY

All the materials listed below are in:

Gilbert Herdt (ed.), *Gay and Lesbian Youth* (New York: Harrington Press, 1989).

Boxer, Andrew M. and Bertram J. Cohler, "The Life Course and Gay and Lesbian Youth: An Immodest Proposal for the Study of Lives": 315–55.

Boyer, Debra, "Male Prostitution and Homosexual Identity": 151–84.

Carrier, Joseph M., "Gay Liberation and Coming Out in Mexico": 225–52.

Coleman, Eli, "The Development of Male Prostitution Activity Among Gay and Bisexual Adolescents": 131–49.

Feldman, Douglas A., "Gay Youth and AIDS": 185–93.

Gerstel, Camille J., Andrew J. Feraios, and Gilbert Herdt, "Widening Circles: An Ethnographic Profile of a Youth Group": 75–92.

Le Bitoux, Lean and Terrance Brown, "To Be 20 and Homosexual in France Today": 291–7.

Parker, Richard, "Youth, Identity, and Homosexuality: The Changing Shape of Sexual Life in Contemporary Brazil": 269–89.

Plummer, Ken, "Lesbian and Gay Youth in England": 195–223.

Ross, Michael W., "Gay Youth in Four Cultures: A Comparative Study": 299–314.

Savin-Williams, Ritch C., "Parental Influences on the Self-Esteem of Gay and Lesbian Youths: A Reflected Appraisals Model": 93–109.

Schneider, Margaret, "Sappho Was a Right-On Adolescent: Growing Up Lesbian": 111–30.

Tremble, Bob, Margaret Schneider, and Carol Appathurai, "Growing Up Gay or Lesbian in a Multicultural Context": 253–67.

Troiden, Richard R., "The Formation of Homosexual Identities": 43–73.

*L*ooking Out – Institutions and Social Change

INTRODUCTION

The bulk of sociological research in lesbian and gay studies has focused on identity, sexuality, and community. Far less attention has been given to the structure and dynamics of social institutions that shape lesbian and gay lives and to the processes of social change. As the research in Parts 1 and 2 indicates, social psychological perspectives were dominant, and the questions of major concern worked in tandem with the social and political project of gay liberation identity politics and its strong emphasis on coming out and solidarity building.

The materials in Part 3 do a different kind of work and alert researchers to substantive investigations that are long overdue. These articles explore the history and dynamics of lesbian, gay, and AIDS social movements and social institutions; the specific cultural, organizational, and physical threats to gay life; and the multiple ways in which heterosexism is confronted in everyday life and politics. The work these efforts might generate are, as we conceive them, the sociological equivalents to queer theorizing about the construction and reproduction of the hetero/homo binary. They build on lesbian feminist notions of compulsory heterosexuality and they recognize the ways in which the relations of sexuality are deeply embedded in social institutions. The research on social change builds on and contributes importantly to the literature on new social movements.

Part 3 is organized into two sections. The first section, *Creating Social Movements*, focuses on the emergence of lesbian and gay social movements. These movements were founded on the link between identity, sexuality, and politics and reflect multiple efforts to challenge threats from cultural, political, religious, and biological systems. In the 1970s, the impact of other social movements on the language and culture of these post-Stonewall politics was expressed in gay liberation and lesbian feminism. The first selection by Dennis Altman is an early statement of gay politics as identity politics, pointing out the contradictions of a liberation that simultaneously builds gay solidarity but also would "make the homo/hetero distinction irrelevant."

An excerpt from Jeffrey Weeks's book, written almost fifteen years after Altman's, builds on the 1984 work of Rubin (see Part 1) and applies the concepts of choice, relationship, context, and meaning to examine the major controversial issues in radical sexual politics in the United States and Britain. Verta Taylor and Nancy Whittier's research utilizes the notion of collective identity to examine the multiple processes by which lesbian feminist communities sustain a sense of collective identity and to show the continued centrality of feminism for women who identify as lesbian feminists.

AIDS posed a unique, cultural and life-threatening challenge to lesbian and gay life, coming at a time when gays and lesbians were achieving an increasing number of political and legal successes, and when gay lives and communities were growing more visible. Josh Gamson's piece focuses on the AIDS activism of the organization ACT UP and makes sense of its activities, internal struggles, and strategies through the application of Foucauldian insights. Finally, Nancy Stoller discusses lesbians' varied participation in the social movement around AIDS, highlighting the ways in which AIDS has generated conditions for both unity and separation between lesbians and gay men.

Working within and challenging heterosexist institutions has been another important aspect of making social change. For many sociologists, the term "homophobia" is inadequate to serve in the project of dismantling the structural and cultural apparatus of heterosexism and demonstrating the character of resistance by gay men and lesbians. Several articles in the second section of Part 3, *Challenging Institutional Heterosexism*, hinge on the recognition of the "doubled vision" of lesbians and gay men as members of oppressed groups, a vision constructed on an awareness of the power of the ideology of heterosexuality and its structural manifestations coupled with a constantly changing creation of a liveable environment.

Research in the last decade has necessarily had to focus on resistance to old and new forms of oppression. Propelled by a conservative political movement in the 1980s and threatened by feminist critiques of gender relations and the growing political power of the gay/lesbian social movement, religious right groups mounted challenges to what they perceived of as a unitary "gay lifestyle." Among their goals was to cure homosexuality; censor educational materials; allow no legislation in support of gay civil rights; and ban homoerotic art, plays, and other creative work (including AIDS prevention materials). Steven Dubin's chapter examines the acceptability of gay images and charts the changes in representation – from veiled references to explicit – in the context of changing social, political, sexual, and health concerns over the past two decades.

Kath Weston provides a conceptual discussion and empirical analysis of the new ways in which lesbians and gay men claim a historically unique family life and build relationships to sustain both symbolic and material aspects of kinship. The "chosen family" as a major cultural product is one of the primary ways in which lesbians and gay men engage in resistance to dominant institutions (law and religion) that foster invisibility and exclusion. An article by Beth Schneider looks at the workplace as the primary institution in which lesbians and gay men daily confront heterosexism and points to the multi-faceted aspect of that experience.

The paper by Peter Nardi and Ralph Bolton traces the rise of gay-bashing as a form of hate crime; the initial resistance to the inclusion of gays and lesbians as groups that are targeted by hate crimes legislation; and the legal, judicial, and clinical responses to this form of hate violence and defamation. Finally, Canadian sociologist Barry Adam analyzes the resistance to gays in the US military while raising issues about masculinist ideologies and Americanism.

The opportunities for future research in the study of the construction, reproduction, and transformation of heterosexism in major institutions are seemingly enormous. Though many sociologists are now engaged in the study of religious fundamentalism and the political right in the US, many questions remain about the economic and political conditions that foster attacks against lesbians and gays and the context and dynamics of the development of anti-gay ordinances and referenda. Sociologists and sociological work have already been of use in providing evidence to defeat some of these legislative initiatives (see Halley 1989; Rubinstein 1993), and policy-based research is a necessary component of research agendas in the future.

Additionally, increased visibility of lesbians and gay men at work cannot be taken for granted; little is known about how changes at the cultural level affect everyday life, and if they do so, how they are manifest in altered social relationships. If the experience with the military is any indication, conflicts over sexuality occur in all contexts and at many levels of analysis, all of which require systematic attention. An obvious site for systematic study will be the struggles over proposals for gay marriages in legislatures and local communities, and within lesbian and gay communities themselves.

Sociological research on social movements in the near future must face the twin processes of cultural and institutional growth and consolidation within lesbian and gay communities and a decentered identity politics. Most obvious is the long-overdue attention to the symbolic and organizational development of lesbian, gay, and bisexual people of color. Curious in its absence is attention to the cultural aspects of social movement activities such as the Names Project/AIDS Quilt, gay and lesbian film festivals, marches, and choruses, to name just a few. Further, sustained efforts are very much needed to examine the burgeoning gay media and the ways in which we increasingly speak for ourselves.

Sociologists have a crucial intellectual niche to occupy in looking out at the institutions that frame social relations of sexuality and the movements that attempt to challenge them. Through this work and its subsequent engagement with analyses of texts emanating in the humanities, crucial new advancements in queer theorizing and disciplinary transformation are possible.

REFERENCES

Halley, J. (1989), "The Politics of the Closet: Towards Equal Protection for Gay, Lesbian, and Bisexual Individuals," *UCLA Law Review*, 36: 5: 915–76.

Rubinstein, W. (ed.) (1993), *Lesbians, Gay Men, and the Law* (New York: The New Press).

DENNIS ALTMAN

"The End of the Homosexual?"

from *Homosexual: Oppression and Liberation*
(New York: Avon, 1971): Chapter 7

Any movement has a double impact, both on those it represents and on society at large. This is particularly so of a movement like gay liberation which represents a process whereby homosexuals seek to come to terms with themselves and through self-affirmation commence on the path towards human liberation.

The essence of gay liberation is that it enables us to come out. "Out of the closets and into the streets" becomes a liberating process which if not sufficient to overcome oppression – in the short run it may indeed bring oppression more heavily to bear – is certainly a necessary first step. Those who are touched by the new affirmation discover a new perception of how they have been oppressed by society and social norms, and out of this realization comes both peace with oneself and anger at the victimization that we and others have suffered. "I am," wrote Jill Johnston of her new gay consciousness,

> more in sympathy with the black cause than ever before, and in fact with all causes, for it has recently occurred to me that all causes are the same ... and that what we're doing here then is educating all the members of ourselves to certain needs which have gone unheeded or unrecognized or worse damned and vilified and thrust underground so that we can all coexist more happily together.

For the homosexual, the new affirmation involves breaking away from the gay world as it has traditionally existed and transforming the pseudo-community of secrecy and sexual objectification into a genuine community of sister/brotherhood. When a gay group was established at Sydney University, where I teach, I was surprised how strongly its members felt the need to be with other gay people where they could be friendly without this being taken as a prelude to "getting off." Gays are having to create for themselves the very basis of ordinary decent social relationships, for without these we cannot achieve the self-respect necessary to transcend the oppression we have internalized.

But, one might argue, this merely reinforces separatism, exchanging, at best, one sort of gay ghetto for another. In part, this is perfectly true: the price of solidarity, whether for blacks, women or gays, is separation. Against this I can only suggest that my own experience has been that becoming more open about my gayness has enabled me to feel closer to *both* gays and straights. Friendship demands a reciprocity of confidence, and if one is constantly guarding against being "discovered" – which is a real agony for most homosexuals – one is forced into mixing only with others who bear the same stigma and the same need for camouflage.

In coming out, in seeking a gay community, in declaring ourselves as homosexuals, we are sometimes accused of homosexual chauvinism. This charge could mean either that we see homosexuality as inherently superior to heterosexuality, or that we perceive everything through our homosexual status. The former I deny, the latter I admit. It seems a mark of our oppression that each assertion of the validity of homosexuality is regarded as an attack on heterosexuality. Mailer in his "Homosexual Villain" spoke of "many homosexuals [going] to the direction of assuming that there is something intrinsically superior in homosexuality," and more recently the film critic Andrew Sarris has felt the same threat. Equally, many whites perceived "Black Power" as racism in reverse, when in fact it only appeared as such because the whole structure of our culture and our language is so weighted in favor of white supremacy that any attempt to rectify it is seen as a move to create a new dominance/subordination.

But yes, homosexuals are coming to perceive everything in terms of our gayness, because up to now society has structured everything according to a heterosexual norm and expected us to accept it. Such structuring extends from the whole image of the world as presented to us by the advertising agencies to the jokes of my colleagues, in which I am expected to join, about the potential sexual favors of our female students. That I, like the women around, may be repelled by this – or, more honestly, have the same interest in our male students – is ignored. As one boy put it, accepting what people do in bed is the least problem. It's accepting that when we walk down the street we look at others of the same sex that straights find most difficult to accept.

Just as liberals wished to regard blacks as people who happened to be non-white, as if this were an incidental rather like skin color, so liberals would prefer to regard homosexuals as people who happen to be attracted to others of the same sex without recognizing how far that single fact becomes an essential part of their whole being. Now the vision of liberation that I held is precisely one that would make the homo/hetero distinction irrelevant. For that to happen, however, we shall all have to recognize our bisexual potential, and until that is done, homosexuality, like blackness, will remain a major category that defines our lives.

As homosexuals come to accept this, to see that society has so defined us that homosexuality becomes a constant part of us rather than a role we can take up and discard when convenient – most homosexuals still seek to do this, with the result that they lead quite remarkably schizophrenic lives – we come also to see that our oppression *has* made us different from other people and that this has its strengths as well as its weaknesses. "Being a nigger," wrote Goodman,

seems to inspire me to want a more el humanity, wilder, less structured, more and where people have some heart for o and pay attention to distress. That is, my has given energy to my anarchism, utopianism and Gandhianism. There are blacks in this party too.

The homosexual writers with whom I have been predominantly concerned – Baldwin, Genet, Ginsberg, Isherwood, Millett, even John Rechy – would all I think belong to Goodman's party. (And one might add others, for example, W. H. Auden and E. M. Forster.) This is not, emphatically, a plea for homosexual superiority; there are plenty of homosexual villains, real ones, nor are straights excluded from the broader humanity and diversity that Goodman suggests. It *is* to point out that our homosexuality is a crucial part of our identity, not because of anything intrinsic about it but because social oppression has made it so. On one level to love someone of the same sex is remarkably inconsequential – after all, but for some anatomical differences, love for a man or a woman is hardly another order of things – yet society has made of it sometimes portentous, and we must expect homosexuals to accept this importance in stressing their identity.

The liberal hope that homosexuals will come to merge imperceptibly into society *as we know it* – as one conservative homophile spokesman put it on British television, we look forward to the time when straights will invite the homosexual couple next door in for dinner – seems as unlikely as the hope that integration of black and white could be achieved in America without major social change. I have two reasons for saying this: the structure of our society, which seems to produce an unquenchable need for minorities, and the new assertion of identity by homosexuals. Liberals who want to "accept" homosexuals want homosexuals who are exactly like them; they are not very likely to invite homosexuals who insist on, and act out, their homosexuality.

As long as society is based on competitiveness and sexual repression, there will be a need to demarcate it into categories, to maintain socially induced repressions by stigmatizing heavily all those who fall outside the norm. For such purposes the homosexual will remain one of the more attractive minorities. "A minority," says George in Isherwood's *A Single Man*, "is only thought of as a minority when it constitutes some kind of threat to the majority, real or imaginary. And no threat is ever *quite* imaginary." Which is echoed by Goodman (see his essay "Underground Writing 1960" in *Utopian Essays and Practical Proposals*) and Baldwin, who, writing of Gide (in "The Male Prison," *Nobody Knows My Name*), doubts that "at least in the world we know" homosexuality can ever be accepted:

> And one of the reasons for this is that it would rob the normal – who are simply the many – of their very necessary sense of security and order, of their sense perhaps, that the race is and should be devoted to outwitting oblivion – and will surely manage to do so.

Homosexuals can win acceptance as distinct from tolerance only by a transformation of society, one that is based on a "new human" who is able to accept the multi-faceted and varied nature of his/her sexual identity. That such a society can be founded is the gamble upon which gay and women's liberation are based; like all radical movements, they hold to an optimistic view of human nature, above all to its mutability.

Yet such a view becomes realistic precisely because of the impasse to which our present conception of human nature seems to have led. Only recently have we come to realize how much of what we consider normal, especially in family and sex relationships, is in fact learned, and it is the contribution of the gay and women's movements to force a reassessment of what we have grown up believing was part of "human nature." Technological change has both provided the means and the necessity for a large-scale reassessment of the way we order our lives; if, in Baldwin's words, we will "outwit oblivion" – and there is no guarantee of this – we need to unlearn much of what has hitherto been considered natural, including attitudes toward competition and aggression as much as toward sex.

Anthropological evidence suggests that homosexuality is neither alien nor perverse. But beyond this neither history nor anthropology offer much guide to the future, for our society is a qualitatively different one to any ever known, and its potential for transformation correspondingly greater. Under the joint impact of technology and the women's movement, we are divorcing procreation from sex and anatomy from role; the demand to recognize homosexuality as a valid form of human relationship seems a logical extension of this development.

There are of course many within and without the gay movement who question the assumption that the fate of the homosexual depends on revolutionary change, and argue, as did Tom Maurer, the president of the Society for Individual Rights, in his 1969 report, that "SIR is a one-issue organization . . . its position has to be more like the A.C.L.U. [American Civil Liberties Union] than . . . a political club." Tolerance, as I have already suggested, *can* be achieved via liberal means, and within the framework of existing liberal society, and for the achievement of certain very necessary legislative changes Tom Maurer's position makes sense. Acceptance, however, demands a major change in our social framework. Only those who, as in the movement, are prepared to question the basis on which society is organized are likely to fully accept homosexuality as part of the human condition rather than a discrete and foreign phenomenon. It has been said that a liberal is someone who wants to help others; a radical is someone who knows that he/she needs help. The liberal sees homosexuals as a minority to be assisted into a full place in society. The radical sees homosexuality as a component of all people including her/himself.

In several important ways the gay movement does, I believe, contribute to the development of a new woman/man, and gay is indeed good for us all. As the homosexual comes out, he/she leads heterosexuals into a greater acceptance of their own sexuality, in part perhaps because many homosexuals are more aware of sexuality than straights. The other side to homosexual promiscuity – seen in its most extreme form when the hunt for sex becomes an obsession – is that sex *per se* tends to become less immanently important, while the nature of relationships, by contrast, is less taken for granted. It is true that homosexual couples of long standing are rare, but this is in part because a bad homosexual "marriage" is likely to be dissolved far more easily than is a bad straight one. Homosexuals, and especially those not unduly worried by guilt and self-disgust, are often able to approach sex more casually than can heterosexuals and realize that fidelity and love depend on much more than with whom or how one beds. The real infidelity is an existential not a physical one.

More than this, however, the gay contributes to the straight just because we are defined in exclusively sexual terms. Our sense of being different enables us to see the sexual component in much of life that is not immediately obvious, to escape to a limited degree the repressions upon our sexual and erotic impulses. To accept that part of ourselves which is sexual is a necessary stage toward overcoming the repressions and anxieties under which we all labor, which achievement probably means an increase in homosexuality if not in exclusive homosexuality. As is already happening within the women's movement, homosexuality comes to be accepted by a greater number of people as a possibility *for them* – a development which is deplored by the custodians of the old values. In their book *Growing Up Straight*, the Wydens make exactly this point (though not of course, as advocates): "The more acceptable the viewpoints of organized homosexuals become, the more likely that we will see the growth of an ever less covert and more accepted Gay World." Gay liberation liberates straights as much as gays.

Homosexuals too come to see themselves as potential heterosexuals: but this is a lesser revelation. "I think all of us are authorities on the heterosexual problem," wrote Jill Johnston. "Knowledge on the subject is instantly available, in case you've missed out, in every daily newspaper with their front page accounts of the Wars. We are bored with the news from the heterosexual fronts." Exactly. We – even those of us who are behaviorally, on the Kinsey scale, totally homosexual (and how many in fact are?) – know about heterosexuality. Few homosexuals will deny their straight component, and this is an important part of the gay's knowledge of the world under which she/he lives.

Seymour Krim in an *Evergreen* article hailed the blurring of both homo/hetero, female/male distinctions: "Heterosexual love emphasizes basic differences, homosexual love emphasizes basic sameness," he wrote. As the difference dwindles, he sees it easing relations between men and women, now "nervous, cryptic, exasperating psychodrama that has ripped the guts out of practically all of us." I am less sure than he of the first point, for opposites attract within the gay world as much as without, nor are heterosexual couples who mirror-reflect each other uncommon. But his latter point is, I think, important. Warfare between the sexes is an unnecessary product of competitiveness, repression and fear. If accepting homosexuality helps people move closer to an acceptance of their intrinsic erotic and polymorphous natures, it can only ease relations between men and women.

Gay liberation is part of a much wider movement that is challenging the basic cultural norms of our advanced industrial, capitalist and bureaucratic society and bringing about changes in individual consciousness and new identities and life styles. It is a movement that is political, not in the traditional way that we have used that word, but because it challenges the very definitions and demarcations that society has created. In many ways the argument between the "political" and the "cultural" revolutionaries is a false one; gay liberation, like the other sexual liberation movements, is in the long tradition of romantics and existentialists in its insistence that politics and culture merge into one. Unlike liberalism, the movement in America today recognizes no barriers between politics and culture, art and life, public and private. Gay liberation is both an affirmation of the right to live as we choose and an intent to extend that right to others.

In some ways gay liberation is an extension of the Yippie philosophy, "revolution for the hell of it." "What's a revolution if it isn't fun?" said Kate Millett, speaking of her gayness to the Daughters of Bilitis. One of the strengths of gay liberation is that because it is involved in the affirmation of sexuality, it is also involved in an affirmation of eroticism and play, an important antidote to the humorlessness of much of our time. Unlike virtually all other movements, the gay does seem protected by its very being from an over-earnest puritanism.

Which is not to claim perfection for the gay movement, nor to deny the divisions which encumber it and which can be expected to increase as the movement itself increases. Like all movements, it is prone to moments of hyperbole, hysteria and childish feuding; like other groups on the left, it tends to be extra-ordinarily uncritical of its heroes (e.g. the Panthers) while equally intolerant of those whose style is different (e.g. the older homophile groups). As it grows and embraces a wider range of members it is likely to find greater difficulty in reconciling competing life styles and interests. Already, I suspect, the gay movement, albeit smaller than the women's movement, embraces a wider range of persons. I have already stressed that it cuts across racial lines; in class terms too it is less unredeemably middle-class than many women's groups tend to be, and the presence of the street transvestites – for transvestites come disproportionately from lower-class backgrounds – is a welcome contrast to the college kids. As "liberated" homosexuals seek to construct an alternative to the old gay world, it will be just as heterogeneous and varied – even if drugs pose more of a problem than alcohol, petty criminals more than blackmail or Mafia control.

Inasfar, however, as gay liberation involves the construction of a new consciousness, a heightened sense of awareness of our position in society and a comprehension that we are not so much fucked up as fucked over, it is an essential ingredient of the insurgent culture, and one that is likely to have considerable influence on its peers. There are those who would argue that society will be able in time to domesticate the angry gay, to offer him/her sufficient incorporation into the ongoing framework so as to destroy her/his radicalism. I doubt this, as Huey Newton seems to doubt it, because I question whether society as presently instituted could ever offer more than tolerance, and that, as I have sought to show, is not enough. Indeed, homosexual assertion – "Blatant Is Beautiful" –

is likely to outrun society's ability to remove its stigma, at least for some time.

Ultimately, homosexuals are a minority quite unlike any other, for we are a part of all humans – not metaphorically, as the French students might proclaim "nous sommes tous juifs alle-mands" – but actually. Everyone is gay, every-one is straight. This is why the homosexual has been so severely oppressed, for social oppres-sion becomes a means for individual repression, and only when the latter is no longer prescribed will the former be fully overcome. In the long run, then, gay liberation will succeed as its *raison d'être* disappears. We are, I believe, moving towards a far greater acceptance of human sexuality and with that toward both a decrease in the stigma attached to unorthodox sex and a corresponding increase in overt bisexu-ality. To see the total withering away of the distinction between homo- and heterosexual is to be utopian. I suspect, however, it will come before the withering away of the state and may indeed be a necessary prelude to that.

Given that such changes are only embryonic for the moment, it still is not unreasonable to expect a considerable growth in the gay move-ment, both in America and in other "highly developed" Western societies. Indeed the grow-ing tolerance towards homosexuals, by that well-known process of a revolution of rising expectations, is likely to bring a sharp increase in those ready to come out and angry enough to identify with gay liberation. Here the peculiar stigma of homosexuality, its secrecy, becomes crucial. To join a gay group is an act of affirma-tion that is often cathartic in its effect. Whatever the possibilities for individual liberation without full social liberation, and the possibilities are I feel limited, the act of involvement with gay liberation brings with it a new perception of the world that is remarkably radicalizing.

The dilemma remains: any vision of our full liberation involves at the same time an end to our special status and any claims that can be based upon this for an intrinsically gay culture. Those who most clearly perceive this are also likely to be those most involved with the present creation of a gay community. Dotson Rader in his article on gay liberation in *Evergreen*, claimed that homosexuals in the gay liberation movement are now beginning to suspect that in eliminating their status as outlaws they may be delimiting the consciousness (i.e. their positions as rebels) which animates both their extraordinary creativity and their role as a regenerative body.

The price, one suspects, is greater for straights than for gays, given the human misery out of which much of this "extraordinary creativity" has sprung, but the dilemma is a real one. If we finally transcend the divide between hetero- and homosexual, do we also lose our identity?

One hopes that the answer lies in the creation of a new human for whom such distinctions no longer are necessary for the establishment of identity. The creation of this new human demands the acceptance of new definitions of man- and womanhood, such as are being urged by gay and women's liberation. Indeed, the homosexual's very existence is an affront to the way in which society defines roles, sexuality, achievement, and this fact is the essence both of our oppression and of our revolutionary potential. Gay liberation affirms full eroticism and play, and rejects violence; it seeks human diversity and community, and discards the narrow roles that "normality" has prescribed. If these affirmations and objectives can be achieved for us all, Gore Vidal's hope that homosexual will be used only as an adjective to describe behavior rather than a noun to describe a person may be fulfilled, and the homosexual as we know him/her may indeed disappear.

In the attempt to realize this new human, gay liberation as a movement will exhibit all those excesses and mistakes that those who seek liberation are prone to. Gay liberation as a new consciousness, however, can only add to the growth in acceptance of human diversity, of the realization that we all possess far greater potential for love and human relationship than social and cultural structures have allowed us to reveal. "A man's reach must exceed his grasp, or what's a heaven for," wrote Browning. That heaven can be attained is implicit in the challenge of the sexual liberation movements. If man/womankind reaches the point where it is able to dispense with the categories of homo- and heterosexuality, the loss will be well worth the gain.

JEFFREY WEEKS

"The Meaning of Diversity"

from *Sexuality and its Discontents* (London: Routledge, 1985): chapter 9

It is when man is at his most purely moral that he may be most dangerous to the interests, and most callously indifferent to the needs of others. Social systems know no fury like the man of moral absolutism aroused.

(Alvin Gouldner, *For Sociology*)

There is certainly a branch of the sex field that is progressive. Many women, even feminists, even dykes, work in that field. Instead of assuming that sex is guilty until proven innocent these people assume that sex is fundamentally okay until proven bad.

(Gayle Rubin, *Talking Sex*)

EROTIC DIVERSITY

The most intractable problems in contemporary sexual debates stem from the obvious but politically contentious facts of erotic diversity. The early sexologists sought to contain the problem within their proliferating but neatly drawn taxonomies, labellings and definitions, where subtle (and to the untutored eye often imperceptible) distinctions demarcated perversions from perversity, inverts from perverts, abnormalities from anomalies and degeneration from deviation. The categories of the perverse swelled to embrace the marginal and marginalized, despised and despicable sexualities that flourished exotically in the interstices of a normative sexual order (flourished in part *because* of that order) while much effort was steadfastly and self-consciously devoted to the searching out, in the deepest recesses of the human body, blood, chromosomes, genes or psyche, of the aetiologies of these erotic disorders. As each new breakthrough in knowledge occurred – hormones, chromosomes, genetics, the power of

the dynamic unconscious – they were harnessed to the work of bolstering the edifice of sexuality, in all its majestic certainty, and to the provision of a scientific justification for moralistic and medical intervention into people's lives.

But there was always a dangerous gap between the relatively narrow range of theoretical explanations of sexual behaviour and the actuality of an immensely broad range of sexual variations. The sexological descriptions and aetiologies yanked together into broad categories many disparate sexual practices, to create sexual dichotomies which while seeming to help us understand human sexuality actually trapped individuals in mystifying compartments, where morality and theory, fear and hopes were inextricably and dangerously enmeshed. The gap became a void, filled by contending moral and political values.

Kinsey, as ever, was a key figure in transforming this debate. He noted that traditionally there had been a gap between two antagonistic interpretations of sex, the hedonistic, which justifies sex for its immediate, pleasurable return, and the reproductive, where sex is only to be enjoyed in marriage. But Kinsey suggested – coming close, as he rather reluctantly admitted, to Freud's notion of a polymorphous perversity – that there was a third possible interpretation which had hardly figured in either general or scientific discussion: "of sex as a normal biologic function, acceptable in whatever form it is manifested".[1] From our point of view, the *biological* justification is clearly inadequate. But its essential message has become crucial to contemporary controversies. Few mainstream sexologists today – with the exception of conspicuously conservative analysts and psychologists, or openly right-wing moralists – would be easy with the use of a term like "perversion" to describe homosexuality or even the wide range of other sexual practices. For the most authoritative modern study of the subject, that of Robert Stoller, "perversion" is the "erotic form of hatred", defined not so much by the acts (*"the* perversions") but by the content, hostility, while the word "pervert" is cast out of the sexological lexicon virtually completely.[2] Even for the determinists of sociobiology, it is no longer the silent whispers of genetic malfunction that are listened for but the genetic functionalism of the "sexual variations". In part this is a result of theoretical changes, of which Freud and Kinsey are key exponents. In part, it is a result of political pressure. The decision of the American Psychiatric Association to delete homosexuality from its published list of sexual disorders in 1973 was scarcely a cool, scientific decision. It was a response to a political campaign fuelled by the belief that its original inclusion as a disorder was a reflection of an oppressive politico-medical definition of homosexuality as a problem.[3]

Not surprisingly, the retention of the term "perversion" is more clearly now a political stroke and it is as a term of political abuse that it is more commonly used, whether in the insidious tones of the "New Morality", "we hate the perversion but love the pervert", or in the assertions of some moral feminists that "male sexuality" is a perversion.

The speaking perverts, first given a carefully shaded public platform in the volumes of early sexologists, have become highly vocal on their own behalf. They no longer need to ventriloquize through the Latinate and literary prose of a Krafft-Ebing or a Havelock Ellis, or engage in the intricate transference and countertransference of analyst and analysand. They speak for themselves in street politics and lobbying, through pamphlets, journals and books, via the semiotics of highly sexualized settings, with their elaborate codes of keys, colours and clothes, in the popular media, and in the more mundane details of domestic life. There is a new pluralism of sexual styles – styles which have not by any means broken the dominance of the heterosexual norm, but which have thrown its

normalizing claims into some relief. There no longer appears to be a great continent of normality, surrounded by small islands of disorder. Instead we can perceive huge clusters of islands, great and small, which seem in constant motion each to the other, and every one with its peculiar flora and fauna. This is the material basis for our contemporary relativism.

The questions that insistently arise from this ecological chaos go something like this: can each desire be equally valid; should each minute subdivision of desire be the basis of a sexual and possibly social identity; is each political identity of equal weight in the corridors of sexual politics, let alone wider politics? Sex, where is your morality? the moral authoritarian can cry. Sex, where are your subtle distinctions? the weary liberal might whisper.

The inherent difficulty of responding to these interrogations is compounded by the absence of consensus on them within the radical sexual movements themselves. There is little solidarity amongst the sexually oppressed. Lesbians dissociate themselves from the "public sex" of gay men. Gay leaders dissociate themselves from paedophiles. Paedophiles can see little relevance in feminism. And the ranks of feminism are split asunder by divisions on topics such as pornography, sado-masochism and sex itself.

Does pornography constitute an act of violence against women or is it simply a reflection of wider problems? Is inter-generational sex a radical disruption of age expectations or a traditional assault by older people on younger? Is transsexuality a question of control over one's body, or another twist in the medical control of it? Is promiscuity a challenge to sexual repression or a surrender to its consumerized form? Is sado-masochism no more than a ritualized and theatrical enactment of power relations or is it a sinister embrace of socially constructed fantasies? Are butch–fem relations the erotic working through of chosen roles or the replication of oppressive relations? These are not always heated debates in the wider society. They excite enormous controversy in the ranks of the sexually oppressed.[4]

None of the existing discourses of sexual regulation provides an easy passage through these dilemmas. The liberal approach implicitly accepts diversity but flounders in many of the dilemmas it poses. The appeal to the right of free speech might be a useful tool in opposing censorship of erotica, but in practice few liberals would take that right to an absolutist extreme. Historically, there has been liberal acquiescence in the censorship of fascist and communist material, racist literature, horror comics and kiddie-porn. There does not seem any fundamental principles for refusing censorship of the obscene. The same difficulty applies to the question of the "right to privacy". It was not until the 1960s that even the American Civil Liberties Union was prepared to take up the issue of discrimination against homosexuals on these grounds.[5] Many still baulk at the prospect of having to defend *public* forms of homosexual interaction, or paedophilia or sado-masochism. The meaning of free speech and of rights varies, though we speak of them as if they have absolute value.

The historic nature of the categories that liberal arguments depend on, especially the private/public distinction, have been most clearly underlined in the debates surrounding the "Wolfenden" approach in Britain. The two classic propositions on which this approach relies are derived from John Stuart Mill: that no conduct should be interfered with unless it involves harm to others; and that it is not the law's business to enforce morals. The assumption is that intervention should only be contemplated if the harm caused by it will be less than the damage caused by the continuation of a given condition.[6]

But clearly this is a matter for decision-making and calculation. In some cases, as in the British sex-reforms of the 1960s, the operation of what Stuart Hall has called a "double taxonomy" of freedom *and* control[7] becomes apparent as a result of political shifts, where a move towards a greater freedom in the private sphere was balanced by a tightening of control in some aspects of the public sphere. In the Wolfenden approach, the law's role is to hold the ring, to provide the public conditions which would allow the privately contracting citizens ("consenting adults") to decide on their actions ("in private"). But categories, such as "exploitation", "corruption" and "harm", which must

be controlled, and the "vulnerable" or the "young", who must be protected, are obviously flexible and changing ones.

The difficulties with the libertarian response are as acute. Here sex is too often regarded as in itself in opposition to power. As Califia wrote of her book, *Sapphistry*, a controversial look at lesbian sexuality, "This book carries a subversive message. It presents an alternative to conformity."[8] The assumption seems to be that the enactment of an outlawed practice is itself oppositional. What counts is the morality of the act. Charles Shively writes as a gay activist of the merits of "pure sex" and endorses a:

> morality or participants in which being "good" is giving a good blow job or rim job, being "good" is being hot and hard, being "good" is letting it all come out: sweat, shit, piss, spit, cum; being "good" is being able to take it all, take it all the way.[9]

At stake here, clearly, is a politics of romanticism where desire exists to disrupt order, and where disruption and transgression are the keys to pleasure. Much of the iconography and style of the sado-masochist movement is of this type. The lesbian S/M book *Coming to Power* begins deliberately: "This is an outrageous book."[10] The outrage comes from its self-conscious spanning of our usual assumptions about the connections between sex and love, sex and relationships, sex and pleasure; sex and emotions. Developments within capitalism, Tim McCaskell has suggested, have "untangled" the emotions and the erotic: "Where traditionally one need existed, capitalism has produced two. Erotic life and emotional life have come apart. They are now distinct human needs where before they meant the same thing."[11]

There is genuine insight here which underlines the new opportunities for pleasure and self-realization provided by consumer capitalism. But as the Frankfurt Marxists were arguing from the 1930s, the other side of this has been the incorporation of old desires into, and the manufacture of new needs by, consumerism. The selective co-option of the sex radical movements by capitalist society has been widely observed by activists. The aspirations of the gay liberation movement for an alternative sexual-political culture has been answered by the organisation of a huge gay market, with profits to be had in everything from poppers to perfumes, leather accoutrements to orgy houses. The radical transgression implied by the presence of the embryonic S/M subcultures of North America has been paralleled and partly overshadowed by the rise of a sort of leather S/M chic where style obliterates content.[12] The new libertarianism can easily fall into a celebration of the now individual self-realization today. Its opportunities for providing guidelines for *social* change are therefore obviously limited.

The ambiguities of the liberal and libertarian positions inevitably prepare the way for the rise of new certainties. Moral absolutism, as Gouldner suggests, "serves to cut the Gordian knot of indecision".[13] It magically wipes out ignorance and the resultant anxieties, and makes possible the onward march. The decision of the (American) National Organization for Women Convention in October 1980 to sharply distinguish lesbianism from any association with "other issues (i.e. pederasty, pornography, sadomasochism and public sex) which have been mistakenly correlated with Lesbian/Gay rights by some gay organisations and by opponents of Lesbian/Gay rights who seek to confuse the issue"[14] was more than a tactical retreat in the face of a colder climate. It marked the acceptance by a significant body of feminists of a new absolutism which attempts to prescribe appropriate behaviour as the test of legitimate incorporation into the army of the good. The problem with correct ideas is that they can all too readily become correctional ideals. Moral absolutism, Gouldner concludes, "invariably manifests an edge of punitiveness, a readiness to make others suffer. There is, in short, an edge of sadism in moral absolutism."[15] The moral feminism that emerged in the late 1970s has many differences from the old absolutism. On pornography, the most emotive of issues, its ostensible concern has not been, as it was on the moral right, with the effect of explicit sex on the viewer, but its impact on women, and with the power relations inherent in pornography. But on pragmatic politics they have often marched hand in hand with the old morality in favouring censorship, sometimes in tones not

radically dissimilar to traditional ones. "Feminists must demand that society find the abuse of women both immoral *and* illegal."[16] Social purity reformers of the nineteenth century would not have put it very differently. The effect is to support moves to strengthen social authority against sexual dissidents.

The moral absolutists, old and new, have another similarity. In an exact mirror image of the libertarian position, they too concentrate on a morality of acts, where sin or salvation resides in the activity itself. The litany of activities and variations – pornography, promiscuity, paedophilia, sado-masochism – is a checklist of original sin, which does not, in the end, seem very different from the old thesaurus of ecclesiastical anathemas or medical definitions. Political alliances are never neutral. In a context where sex has become a political front line, where moral issues become the displaced arena for arguing about what sort of society we want to live in, then these alignments and divisions are of crucial importance. Their effect in shaping the climate in which the erotic minorities have to live can be decisive. On certain issues many feminists have objectively allied with the Right. Ellen Willis has commented that "as the sexuality debate goes, so goes feminism".[17] Equally, it seems, as feminism goes, so goes sexuality.

The radical pluralist approach is more tentative than the absolutist or libertarian traditions, though it draws inspiration from the sex positive elements of the latter. And it is more decisively aware of the network of power-relations in which sex is embedded than the liberal approach, though being properly aware of the mobilizing force of the discourse of rights and of sexual choice. Its aim is to provide guidelines for decisions rather than new absolute values, but two interrelated elements are crucial: the emphasis on choice and relations rather than acts, and the emphasis on meaning and context rather than external rules of correctness.

Foucault makes a useful distinction between "freedom of sexual *acts*" and "freedom of sexual *choice*". He is against the first, because it might involve endorsement of violent sex-related activities such as rape which should never be acceptable whether between man and woman or man and man. But he is for the second, whether it be "the liberty to manifest that choice or not to manifest it".[18] The implication of this is that the nature of the social relationships in which choice becomes meaningful is of crucial importance. There has long been a weak version of this in the idea that certain types of sexuality (usually homosexuality) become justified only when they are embedded in a "loving relationship". It is in this form that a limited acceptance of non-reproductive sexualities has been incorporated within liberal Christianity. The underlying assumption is that gay sex has to be justified by the relationship it is expressed in.[19] But a stronger version of this position reverses the terms: now we would start with an assumption of the merits of an activity unless the relationship in which it is embedded can be shown to be harmful or oppressive: in Rubin's terms, instead of assuming that sex is guilty until proven innocent we would assume "that sex is fundamentally okay until proven bad". This implies in turn the acceptance of what Foucault calls a "relational right", a claim to break out of the narrow confines of traditional patterns of relationships to invent and explore new forms of communication and involvement.[20]

It is at this point that the second set of elements are important, meaning and context. If we endorse the radical approach that no erotic act has any intrinsic meaning this suggests that, though they may not be the conclusive factors, subjective feelings, intentions and meanings are vital elements in deciding on the merits of an activity. The decisive factor is an awareness of context, of the situation in which choices are made.

Using these criteria – choice, relationship, context and meaning – I want to look more closely at some of the most controversial issues that have riven the world of radical sexual politics in recent years. But rather than simply treating them as unproblematical sexological categories, I want to explore each of them in relationship to the wider issue they most clearly illuminate: the public/private division in relation to gay promiscuity; the question of male power in relation to pornography; intergenerational sex and the issue of consent; and

sado-masochism as a problem of choice. In this way I hope to be able to confront key difficulties in existing approaches. My aim is not to "resolve" intractable problems, rather to indicate the issues that must be confronted in facing sexual diversity.

"PUBLIC SEX" AND THE RIGHT TO PRIVACY

For a long time we have cherished sex as the most private of secrets. We talked about it incessantly but shrouded its details with a discreet veil. For several hundred years now, especially in the Anglo-American heartlands of puritanism, the entrepreneurs of social morality have strenuously engaged in struggles against public manifestations of sexual vice in order to reinforce this private domain. Behind the fights against alcoholism, obscenity, prostitution and homosexuality lay a profound belief that while individual moral reformation was the key to salvation, religious and secular, a cleaning up of public spaces, a remoralization of public life, was a decisive element in encouraging personal change. The moral panics, purity crusades, police interventions and state regulation that punctuate the history of sexuality are the results of such evangelical fervour. Their effects are manifest in the shifting and ambiguous divisions between public and private life that we inhabit today.

Homosexuality has always posed a threat to these distinctions. It does not fit easily into the usual neat divisions between home and family and work. The characteristic forms of picking up, social interaction and erotic relating of most male homosexuals and many lesbians radically cut across conventional forms of courtship and sexual partnership. So it is not surprising that the social regulation of homosexuality often took the form of attempts to outlaw its expression altogether, both in public and private. Unlike prostitution, with which it was often legally linked, it was not the form of its organization but homosexuality as such that was regularly perceived as a threat.[21]

It seems that public displays of gayness still arouse fear and anxiety. The consolidation of lesbian and gay lifestyles within gay communities in recent years has meant that it is more difficult now to attack homosexuality itself. But homosexual practices are much easier to challenge. Significantly, in the trail of the anti-gay backlash that developed in the United States from the late 1970s, alongside the even more predictable accusations of child corruption, it was the "public sex" of homosexuals that was most vociferously excoriated by the Moral Right.[22]

Behind "public sex" lies the threat of rampant promiscuity. Promiscuity implies a frequent change of partners, but it also suggests cruising haunts, meeting places and most insistently during the 1970s the proliferating growth of bath houses, backroom bars, fuck houses, establishments offering varied facilities and degrees of comfort and luxury, but all of them having one purpose: sex, sex for its own sake, sex in isolation, or in couples or in multiples, sex for pleasure, detached from all conventional ties and responsibilities.

Gay men in particular have regularly been attacked for their promiscuity. It has been seen as a fundamental marker dividing lesbians from gay men, while suggesting lines of continuity between homosexual and heterosexual men. Male homosexuality, as the sociobiologists have recently affirmed, is the quintessence of male sexuality. The reality has always been more complex. The various surveys of homosexual behaviour have all suggested that, while gay men might have more partners than heterosexual men, they generally tended to have less frequent sex. Many gay radicals have argued as a result that historically gay men far from being hyperactive have been sexually deprived so that the 1970s celebration of promiscuity was by way of a historic compensation.[23] On the other hand there is no reason to believe that gay men are any less able or willing to form relationships than heterosexual. Spada found that 90 per cent of his respondents preferred sex with affection – but did not regard it as necessary that that affection should be long term.[24] The split between emotional loyalty and casual, but affectionate, sexual ties may be different from conventional modes of behaviour, but it is not in itself a sign of social pathology, more a sign of an alternative way of life.

The deeply rooted injunctions against homosexual sex have had the effect, nevertheless, especially amongst gay men, of focusing attention upon the act of sex itself. The expansion of *public* sex in the 1970s was an expression of an intensified *personal* need, representing, it has been argued, a search for a kind of affirmation of a denied sexuality. Altman saw in the gay bath houses two phenomena: an increased sexual expectation in the light of changes since the 1960s, and the more problematic result of a "commercialization of desire". This suggested a dual impact. On the one hand the new patterns tended to undermine conventional morality, for they were predicated neither on the subordination of women to men (as say in heterosexual brothels) nor on the direct exchange of sex for money (as in prostitution). Instead they relied on a "silent community" of desires, creating a sort of brotherhood of sexual outlaws: "a sort of Whitmanesque democracy, a desire to know and trust other men in a type of brotherhood far removed from the male bondage of rank, hierarchy, and competition that characterises much of the outside world".[25]

On the other hand, the bath houses represented an intricate incorporation of gays into consumer capitalism, with all its ambiguities. At best, there were opportunities as never before: "Imagine, instant sex without any hassle, all for a few dollars." At worst, there was the risk of a commodification of relationships: "It's like going into a candy store and saying 'I'll have this one, and this one and this, and this ...' consumer sex. Sex on the installment plan."[26] Sex was freer than ever, but everywhere it was commoditized and commercialized as never before.

By the turn of the decade every fair-sized American city had its bath house or houses, as did cities across the continent of Europe (with the exception of Britain) and Australasia. Yet already, before the mid-1980s, they were beginning to look like historical accidents, products of a sudden spectacular, but brief breakthrough in the life opportunities of homosexuals rather than of an evolution of new sexual forms. The widespread emergence of AIDS after 1981 posed a major challenge to the easy acceptance of promiscuity. Even if there was nothing in the lifestyle of male gays themselves that produced AIDS, it seemed likely that its spread was facilitated by close sexual contact. The easy solidarity of the baths and similar places ironically began to appear as a source of weakness for the wider gay community. But the challenge posed by the emergence of these commercialized emporia of sex remained. We can observe in operation a series of what can best be described as "consensual communities" whose members know the rules and act according to them. A kind of consent to enter the community operates, least formal but perhaps most rigid in the most public places, say a public square, carefully formalized in terms of entry criteria or membership in the most private, such as a bath house. Within these contexts a consent to "co-presence", in Laud Humphreys' phrase, operates. Such places break with the conventional distinctions between private and public, making nonsense of our usual demarcations. As Humphreys points out, "It is the safeguarded, walled-in, socially invisible variety of sex we have to fear, not that which takes place in public."[27] It is in the home that most sexual abuse of small children takes place and it is relatives or neighbours who are most likely to rape women. Most ostensibly public forms of sex actually involve a redefinition of privacy – a definition based not on received distinctions built around the home/work dichotomy but on a tacit but firm agreement about the conditions for entry and the rules of appropriate behaviour. In this context campaigns for the "right to privacy", as in Toronto in 1981 and 1982 following a series of police raids on gay bath houses,[28] go beyond the traditional implications of that phrase – the rights of individuals in private. Instead they placed on the agenda the question of collective decisions about privacy. Such arguments, of course, do not close the issue, they merely shift its focus. Just as public interest in sexual behaviour cannot in practice stop at the door of the private house (otherwise there would be no social regulation of incest and sexual abuse) so there can be no absolute privacy in "consensual communities". Commercial exploitation, racist exclusions, the subordination of women or of the young and old

are no less important issues when practised amongst the sexually marginal as when displayed by the majority.[29] Nor could acceptance of the conditions of entry involve an abdication of personal responsibility, especially in matters relating to transmittable disease – a topic which became of great importance in the wake of the panic over AIDS. In San Francisco in 1984 the city authorities tried to institute new controls on public bath houses, backed by sections of the gay community. The call for a wider concept of the "right to privacy" does not exclude other criteria of decision-making. But neither is it necessary to wait until all other problems are resolved before confronting the issue.

The point to note is that the demand for the "right to privacy" can transcend its liberal antecedents and become a radical demand for change in the relationship between private and public life. This is the real threat posed by so-called "public sex" – and why it will remain an important issue in debates about sexual choice.

INTER-GENERATIONAL SEX AND CONSENT

If public sex constitutes one area of moral anxiety, another, greater, one, exists around inter-generational sex. Since at least the eighteenth century children's sexuality has been conventionally defined as a taboo area, as childhood began to be more sharply demarcated as an age of innocence and purity to be guarded at all costs from adult corruption. Masturbation in particular became a major topic of moral anxiety, offering the curious spectacle of youthful sex being both denied and described, incited and suppressed. "Corruption of youth" is an ancient charge, but it has developed a new resonance over the past couple of centuries. The real curiosity is that while the actuality is of largely adult male exploitation of young girls, often in and around the home, male homosexuals have frequently been seen as the chief corrupters, to the extent that in some rhetoric "homosexual" and "child molesters" are coequal terms. As late as the 1960s progressive texts on homosexuality were still preoccupied with demonstrating that homosexuals were not, by and large, interested in young people, and even in contemporary moral panics about assaults on children it still seems to be homosexual men who are investigated first. As Daniel Tsang has argued, "the age taboo is much more a proscription against gay behaviour than against heterosexual behaviour".[30] Not surprisingly, given this typical association, homosexuality and inter-generational sex have been intimately linked in the current crisis over sexuality.

Alfred Kinsey was already noting the political pay-off in child-sex panics in the late 1940s. In Britain in the early 1960s Mrs Mary Whitehouse launched her campaigns to clean up TV, the prototype of later evangelical campaigns, on the grounds that children were at risk, and this achieved a strong resonance. Anita Bryant's anti-gay campaign in Florida from 1976 was not accidentally called "Save Our Children, Inc.". Since these pioneering efforts a series of moral panics have swept countries such as the USA, Canada, Britain and France, leading to police harassment of organizations, attacks on publications, arrests of prominent activists, show trials and imprisonments.[31] Each panic shows the typical profile, with the escalation through various stages of media and moral manipulation until the crisis is magically resolved by some symbolic action. The great "kiddie-porn" panic in 1977 in the USA and Britain led to the enactment of legislation in some thirty-five American states and in Britain. The guardians of morality may have given up hope of changing adult behaviour, but they have made a sustained effort to protect our young, whether from promiscuous gays, lesbian parents or perverse pornographers.[32]

From the point of view of moral absolution inter-generational sex poses no problem of interpretation. It is wrong because it breaches the innocence necessary for mature development. The English philosopher Roger Scruton suggested that we are disgusted by it "because we subscribe, in our hearts, to the value of innocence". Prolonged innocence is the prerequisite to total surrender in adult love. Erotic love, he argues, arises from modesty, restraint and chastity. This means "we must not only foster those necessary virtues, but also silence those who teach the language which demeans them".[33] So "intolerance" is not only understandable but virtually necessary – there are no liberal concessions here.

Liberals and radicals on the other hand have found it more difficult to confront the subject. It does not easily fit into the rhetoric of rights – whose rights, and how are they to be expressed: the child's, the adult's? Nor can it be dealt with straightforwardly by the idea of consent. Kinsey argued that in a sense this was a non issue: there was no reason, except our exaggerated fear of sexuality, why a child should be disturbed at seeing the genitalia of others, or at being played with, and it was more likely to be adult reactions that upset the child than the sexual activity itself.[34] This has been echoed by the advocates of inter-generational sex themselves. David Thorstad of the North American Man–Boy Love Association (NAMBLA) argued that "if it feels good, and the boy wants it and enjoys it, then I fail to see why anyone besides the two persons involved should care". Tom O'Carroll, whose *Paedophilia: The Radical Case* is the most sustained advocacy of the subject, suggested that

> The usual mistake is to believe that sexual activity, especially for children, is so alarming and dangerous that participants need to have an absolute, total awareness of every conceivable ramification of taking part before they can be said to consent ... there is no need whatever for a child to know "the consequences" of engaging in harmless sex play, simply because it is exactly that: harmless.[35]

There are two powerful arguments against this. The first, put forward by many feminists, is that young people, especially young girls, do need protection from adult men in an exploitative and patriarchal society, whatever the utopian possibilities that might exist in a different society. The age of consent laws currently in operation may have degrees of absurdity about them (they vary from state to state, country to country, they differentially apply to girls and boys, and they are only selectively operated) but at least they provide a bottom line in the acceptance of appropriate behaviour. This suggests that the real debate should be about the appropriate minimum age for sex rather than doing away with the concept of consent altogether.[36] Secondly, there is the difficult and intricate problem of subjective meaning. The adult is fully aware of the sexual connotations of his actions because he (and it is usually he) lives in a world of heavily sexualized symbols and language. The young person does not. In a recent study of twenty-five boys engaged in homosexual paedophile relations the author, Theo Sandfort, found that "Potentially provocative acts which children make are not necessarily consciously intended to be sexual and are only interpreted by the older persons as having a sexual element."[37] This indicates an inherent and inevitable structural imbalance in awareness of the situation. Against this, it might be argued that it is only the exalted cultural emphasis we place on sex that makes this an issue. That is undoubtedly true, but it does not remove the fact of that ascribed importance. We cannot unilaterally escape the grid of meaning that envelops us.

This is tacitly accepted by paedophile activists themselves who have found it necessary to adopt one or other (and sometimes both) of two types of legitimation. The first, the "Greek love", legitimation basically argues for the pedagogic value of adult–child relations, between males. It suggests – relying on a mythologized version of ancient Greek practices – that in the passage from childhood dependence to adult responsibilities the guidance, sexual and moral, of a caring man is invaluable. This position is obviously paternalistic and is also often antihomosexual; for it is not the gay nature of the relationship that is stressed, but the age divide and the usefulness of the experience for later heterosexual adjustment. The second legitimation relies on the facts of childhood sexuality. O'Carroll carefully assesses the evidence for the existence of childhood sex to argue for the oppressiveness of its denial.[38] But of course an "is" does not necessarily make an "ought", nor does the acceptance of childhood sex play inevitably mean the toleration of adult–child relations.

It is difficult to confront the issue rationally because of the series of myths that shroud the topic. But all the available evidence suggests that the stereotypes of inter-generational sex obscure a complex reality.[39] The adult is usually seen as "a dirty old man", typically "a stranger" to the assaulted child, as "sick" or an "inhuman monster". Little of this seems to be true, at least of those we might describe as the political paedophile. He is scarcely an "old man" (the membership of the English Paedophile Information Exchange, PIE, varied in age from 20 to over 60, with most clustered between 35 and 40); he is more likely to be a professional person than the average member of the population (only 14 per cent of PIE members were blue-collar workers); he is more often than not a friend or relation of the child; and to outward appearances is not a "special type of person" but an apparently healthy and ordinary member of the community. His chief distinguishing characteristic is an intense, but often highly affectionate and even excessively sentimental, regard for young people.[40]

The sexual involvement itself is typically seen as being an assault on extremely young, usually pre-pubertal, people. The members of PIE, which generally is preoccupied with relations with pre-pubertal children, seem chiefly interested in boys between 12 and 14, though heterosexual paedophiles tended to be interested in girls between 8 and 10. This is less startling than the stereotype of babies barely out of the cradle being assaulted but poses nevertheless difficult questions about where protection and care ends and exploitation begins. Most members of NAMBLA, on the other hand, which has attracted obloquy in the USA as great as PIE has attracted in Britain, have a quite different profile. They appear to be chiefly interested in boys between 14 and 19. As Tom Reeves, a prominent spokesman for man/boy love, has put it:

> My own sexuality is as little concerned with children, however, as it is with women. It is self-consciously homosexual, but it is directed at boys at that time in their lives when they cease to be children yet refuse to be men.[41]

Self-identified "boy-lovers" like Reeves scarcely fit into any conceivable picture of a "child molester". They carefully distinguish their own practices from sex between men and girls which "seems to be a reprehensible form of power tripping as it has been reported by women"; and stress the beneficial aspects for adult and young partners of the sexual relationship. When the official age of consent in France is 15 for boys and girls in heterosexual and homosexual relations (compared to 16 for girls in Britain, and 21 for male homosexuals), and when in the 1890s Krafft-Ebing fixed on 14 for the dividing line between sexually mature and immature individuals,[42] the fear that NAMBLA is attempting a corruption of young people seems excessive.

The young people themselves are typically seen as innocent victims. Certainly, many children are cruelly assaulted by adults, but in relations involving self-identified paedophiles or "boy-lovers" there seems to be no evidence of either cruelty or violence. Sandfort found that in his sample the boys overwhelmingly experienced their sexual activities as positive. The most common evaluative terms used were "nice", "happy", "free", "safe", "satisfied", and even "proud" and "strong"; and only minimally were negative terms such as "angry", "sad", "lonely" used. Even when these negative terms were used, it was largely because of the secrecy often necessary and the knowledge of hostile norms and reactions, not because of the sexual contact itself.[43] There is strong evidence that the trauma of public exposure and of parental and police involvement is often greater than the trauma of the sex itself. Moreover, many adult–child relations are initiated by the young person himself. A young member of NAMBLA was asked "You can be desperate for sex at 13?" He replied, "Oh yes".[44] Force seems to be very rare in such relations, and there is little evidence amongst self-declared paedophiles or "boy-lovers" of conscious exploitation of young people.

All this suggests that inter-generational sex is not a unitary category. Brian Taylor has distinguished eight possible categories which pinpoints the existence of "paedophilias" rather than a single "paedophilia". There are the conventional distinctions between "paedophiles" (generally those interested in prepubertal sex partners), "pederasts" (those interested in boys) and "ephobophiles" (those interested in adolescents). But distinctions can

also be made on gender of the older person or the younger person and along lines of homosexuality and heterosexuality. This variety suggests we need to be equally discrete in our responses.[45] There are three continuums of behaviour and attitude which interweave haphazardly. Firstly, there is a continuum of beliefs and attitudes, from the actual violent assaulter at one end to the political paedophile at the other. These can not readily be put in the same class for approval or disapproval. Most people brought before the courts for child abuse are heterosexual men who usually view their girl victims as substitutes for real women. Most activists who court publicity (and risk imprisonment themselves, as happened to Tom O'Carroll of PIE in 1981) have adopted a political identity, which sometimes does not coincide with their actual sexual desires (both NAMBLA and PIE had members interested in older teenagers) but is built around an exaggerated respect for children.[46] It is not obvious that all people involved in inter-generational sex should be treated in the same way by the law or public opinion if intentions or desires are very distinct.

A second continuum is of sexual practices. Some researchers have found coitus rare. It seems that the great majority of heterosexual paedophilia consists of "sex play", such as looking, showing and fondling, and much homosexual involvement seems to be similar. Tom O'Carroll has suggested that these sexual distinctions should be codified, so that intercourse would be prohibited before a certain minimum age of 12.[47] But bisecting these nuances, problematical in themselves, are two other crucial distinctions, between boy partners and girl, and between heterosexual and homosexual relations. There is a strong case for arguing that it is not the sex act in itself which needs to be evaluated, but its context. It is difficult to avoid the justice of the feminist argument that in *our* culture it is going to be very difficult for a relationship between a heterosexual man and a young girl to be anything but exploitative and threatening, whatever the sexual activity. It is the power asymmetry that has effect. There is still a power imbalance between an adult man and a young boy but it does not carry the socio-sexual implications that a heterosexual relation inevitably does. Should these different types of relation carry the same condemnation?

The third continuum covers the age of the young people involved. There is obviously a qualitative difference between a 3-year-old partner and a 14-year-old and it is difficult to see how any sexual order could ever ignore this (even the PIE proposals, which first sparked off the panic about paedophile cradle snatching in Britain, actually proposed a set of protections for very young children). "Sex before eight, or it's too late", the reputed slogan of the American René Guyon Society, founded in 1962 to promote inter-generational sex, is not likely to inspire widespread support, because it imposes sex as an imperative just as now our moral guardians would impose innocence. There is a strong case for finding non-legal means of protecting young children, as Tom O'Carroll has suggested, because it is clear that the law has a damaging and stigmatizing impact.[48] But protection of the very young from unwanted attentions will always be necessary. The difficult question is when does protection become stifling paternalism and "adult oppression". Puberty is one obvious landmark, but the difficulty of simply adopting this as a dividing point is that physiological change does not necessarily coincide with social or subjective changes. It is here that it is inescapably necessary to shift focus, to explore the meanings of the sex play for the young people involved.

Kate Millett has powerfully underlined the difficulties of inter-generational sex when adult/child relations are irreducibly exploitative, and pointed to the problems of a paedophile movement which is arguing for the rights of adults. What is our freedom fight about? she asks. "Is it about the liberation of children or just having sex with them?"[49] If a progressive sexual politics is fundamentally concerned with sexual self-determination then it becomes impossible to ignore the evolving self-awareness of the child. That means discouraging the unwelcome imposition of adult meanings and needs on the child, not simply because they are sexual but because they are external and adult. On the other hand, it does mean providing young people with full access to the means of sexual knowledge and protection as it becomes appropriate. There is

no magic age for this "appropriateness". Each young person will have their own rhythms, needs and time scale. But the starting point can only be the belief that sex in itself is not an evil or dirty experience. It is not sex that is dangerous but the social relations which shape it. In this context the idea of consent takes on a new meaning. There is a tension in consent theory between the political conservatism of most of its adherents, and the radical voluntarism implicit in it.[50] For the idea of consent ultimately challenges all authority in the name of free self-determination. Certain categories of people have always been deemed incapable of full consent or of refusing "consent" – women in marriage, certain children, especially girls, under a certain age, classes of women in rape cases. By extending the idea of consent beyond the narrow limits currently employed in minimum age or age of consent legislation, by making it a positive concept rather than simply a negatively protective or gender-dichotomized one, it may become possible to realize that radical potential again. That would transform the debate about inter-generational sex, shifting the focus away from sex in itself to the forms of power in which it is enmeshed, and the limits these inscribe for the free play of consent.

PORNOGRAPHY AND POWER

"Power" is an amorphous concept. If it is not something that we hold, or a force that is immanent in any particular institution, or the exclusive property of one social class or caste, then its tentacles seem everywhere – and potentially its reality can be found nowhere. The usefulness of "pornography" as an object of feminist anger and evangelical mobilization is that it offers a clear visual target: here, it appears, is the most graphic representation of female sexual exploitation, floating like detritus out of a huge industry of sexual fetishization and commoditization, and providing a searchlight into the heart of male power over women.

It is scarcely surprising, then, that pornography should be a major issue in sexual politics. Long a concern of the moral right, it has become a crucial preoccupation of contemporary feminism. In the United States by the early 1980s the feminist campaigns against pornography were perhaps the best organized and financed in the movement's history and, though they did not have the same salience, there were similarly energetic groupings in countries like Britain and Australia. But at the same time the campaign against pornography seemed to divide the women's movement, for it posed fundamental questions about the nature of female subordination, and hence of the forms of power in contemporary society. Pornography, as Deirdre English has said, "pushes people's buttons. They polarise and go to their corners very fast."[51]

One of the reasons for this is that "pornography" is an exceptionally ambiguous yet emotive term, which takes on different meanings in different discourses. For the traditional moralist pornography is a thing in itself – "explicit sexual images" which incite sexuality in the vulnerable and immature. For the liberal pornography is a movable feast, a product of shifting interpretations of taste and acceptability. For the radical feminist opponent of porn it is a visual demonstration of male power. Yet, as Rosalind Coward has argued, pornography can have no intrinsic meaning, for it is a product of shifting definitions and historically variable codes. It is not an act or a thing but a "regime of representations".[52] These representations do not, however, float free, for they are anchored in concrete forms. Pornography is simultaneously a legal definition, a historically shaped, and changing, product, and a sociological phenomenon, organized into a particular industry in various social locations. It exists as a historical phenomenon because of the regulation and control of what can and cannot be said in relation to sexuality, and thrives on the belief that sex is naughty and dirty, that what is being purveyed is being distributed *because* it is illicit. The institution of pornography results from the designation of certain classes of representation as in some way "objectionable".[53] But what is defined as "objectionable" changes over time, so that the themes of pornography vary, like the technology of representation on which it relies, and the opportunities for production and consumption are variable. There is no doubt that there has been

a vast increase in the pornography industry in recent decades. By the early 1980s it was estimated that in the USA pornography constituted a $5 billion industry, organized in some twenty thousand "adult bookshops" and eight hundred full-time sex cinemas, but it is by no means clear what the real impact of this was. It may even be, as some have argued, that a large part of the pornography and "sex aids" industry was dedicated simply to improving marital sex. Such clear distinctions exist within the pornography industry – for example between heterosexual and gay pornography, between sadistic pornography and kiddie porn – that it is difficult to generalize about markets or impact. Even amongst feminists there is no clear agreement on the merits of pornography. Some feminists have found in a minority of pornography, "a challenge to the puritanical bias of our culture", "a set of models antithetical to those offered by the Catholic Church, romantic fiction, and my mother".[54] Pornography is a complex historical phenomenon and has contradictory effects.

This is not, however, as it appears to the radical feminist opponent of pornography. "When we're talking about pornography," Andrea Dworkin has said, "we are fighting for our lives ... dealing with a life and death situation", for pornography both represents violence against women and *is* violence against women. Pornography is "Material that explicitly represents and describes degrading and abusive sexual behavior so as to endorse and/or recommend the behavior as described". *Simultaneously* it is the reality behind the representation: "I feel my responsibility in this area is to insist on what I know. And what I know is that pornography is reality." At the heart of the feminist anti-porn project, fuelling it and giving it passion, is "female anger" – for pornography is, Brownmiller proposed, "the undiluted essence of anti-female propaganda". Pornography is the theory, said Robin Morgan, and rape is the practice. It is part of the male backlash against women, an expression of male fear at the potential power of women. So pornography itself is not so much about sex as about power and violence. "Erotica is about sexuality", Gloria Steinem wrote, but "pornography is about power and sex as weapon."[55]

Pornography is important, these feminists believe, because it is the distillation of male power over women, the cutting edge which ensures female subordination. It is this which justifies the fervour and moral passion which infuses the anti-porn campaign. At stake is women's survival.

The danger of this position is that it might exaggerate the power of pornography, and elide crucial distinctions which exist within the pornography industry. Violence against women – economic, social, public and domestic, intellectual and sexual – is endemic in our culture and some of this is portrayed in pornographic representations. But not all pornography – perhaps not even the major part – portrays or encourages violence, while the most violent representations themselves may carry their own forms of irony. One of the most notorious images that has recurrently been attacked is of a *Hustler* front cover which shows a woman being pushed through a meat grinder. The image is appallingly distasteful but it is not clear that *Hustler* is either doing this to a victim (it is, after all, a posed picture) or advocating that it should be done. Deirdre English calls it a "self parody ... gross but ... satirical, a self critical joke".[56] Jokes are never neutral, and attempts at a reasoned view of pornography should not lead to the condoning of highly offensive images or humour. But a critique of the form and context in which such representations appear should not, either, lead us to believe that a specific image can in itself, detached from context, harm either the viewer or women as a whole.

The question of "harm" has been a central one in debates on pornography. In effect, moral absolutists have sought to demonstrate that pornography is harmful to the viewer, through a general degeneration of moral susceptibilities, a divorcement of sex from context, and an actual stimulant to sexual violence. Liberals on the other hand have attempted to deflate these claims, or at least demonstrate that they are simply "not proven". Both the USA's President's Commission on Pornography of 1970 and the British Williams Committee Report on Obscenity and Film Censorship of 1978 made great play with weighing the evidence and came out of their deliberations agnostic or downright sceptical of any causal relationship between pornography and sexual harm. This is increasingly a domain of experts who can tease out the implications of contingent relations, statistical analyses and laboratory tests. Anti-porn feminists on the whole have bypassed the debate in favour of a categoric emphasis that pornography must be harmful. But in so doing they shift the terms of the argument to the effects not on the male viewer but on the climate of opinion, in which women live.[57]

It would be foolish to dispute the power of representation. Images help organise the way we can conceive of the external world and can shape our intimate desire. But there is no reason to believe that the effects will be unilinear or uniform. Susan Barrowclough has pointed out that the feminist anti-porn discourse makes three assumptions: that the male viewer's fantasy is the same as the pornographic fantasy; that the pornographic image directly influences behaviour, and that there is an undifferentiated mass of male viewers, all of whom act in the same way and identify with the same point of view.[58] Each of these assumptions is counterable. The huge variety of porn attests to the variety of tastes and desires. Not all men enjoy pornography. And there is very little evidence for any direct correlation between fantasy and behaviour. The shifts in the content of pornography or the changes in its organization and incidence may indicate important changes in the social relations of sexuality, including attitudes towards women. But it is difficult to see how pornography as a contradictory practice could be instrumental in producing these changes.

In the end, for old and new moral absolutists, for left and right, it is difficult to avoid the conclusion that the real objection to pornography is moral, however this is coded. That is fair enough if all that is at stake is a personal position, but it seems a poor ground for making proposals which may have universal effects either through the censoring of pornography, or through a fierce attack on those who consume it, whoever they are and whatever their motives. "We must," wrote Ellen Willis, "also take into account that many women *enjoy* pornography, and that doing so is *not only* an accommodation to sexism, but also a form of resistance to a culture that would allow women no sexual pleasure at all." Pornography, Lisa Orlando has suggested, "may represent women as passive victims, but it also shows us taking and demanding pleasure, aggressive and powerful in a way rarely seen in our culture."[59] Gay men and lesbians, too, have seen in pornography positive aspects which the critics would reject. They argue that gay porn offers images of desire which a hostile society would deny and are therefore real encouragements for a positive sense of self.[60] Just as pornography has to be seen as a contradictory phenomenon, riven by ambiguities, so the response to pornography, the appetite for it, has to be seen as an ambivalent one.

The anti-pornography crusades act on the assumption that it is an undifferentiated male sexuality that constitutes the social problem from which women need to be protected. In the crisis of feminist politics that has been caused by the intractability of female oppression and the rise of the New Right, and in the midst of continuing violence against women, the anti-porn campaigns provide a rallying point. But, the feminist writer B. Ruby Rich has suggested, pornography is really a "soft issue": fear of escalating violence has led to a displacement of anxieties, and produced a will not to see the real dangers. Pornography makes sex explicit; sexism on the whole is not explicit in our culture.[61] It becomes an easy move to reduce sexism to sex, with the result that "In using explicit sex to demonstrate explicit sexism the anti-porn movement locates itself within the discursive framework of pornography itself."[62] It takes for granted the sense of illicitness and a fear-dominated attitude to sex which gives rise to pornography in the first place.

A singular concentration on pornography gives it a political centrality it does not deserve, and in the process the real strategic problems of radical sexual politics are downplayed or ignored. By concentrating on the power of the image in pornography alone the manifold ways in which sexual oppression is produced and reproduced in our culture – in law, medicine, religion, the family, psychiatry – are lost sight of. Ironically, it also means that the pervasive interpretation of sexist imagery throughout the culture, in advertising and the media, even in "romantic fiction", is largely ignored in favour of a dramatic assault on pornography.[63] The sexual oppression and exploitation of women cannot be reduced to pornography, and it is unlikely that a mass assault on the pornography industry will do much to change the position of women.

THE SEXUAL FRINGE AND SEXUAL CHOICE

Our discussions have focused on the effects of power on or in shaping sexuality. The debate on sado-masochism which was stimulated by the emergence of explicit subcultures and activist groupings of gay and lesbian S/Mers in the 1970s[64] takes this a radical step further: to the eroticization of power itself.

Sado-masochism (S/M) places itself at the extreme fringe of acceptable sexuality. "S/M is scary", Pat Califia, one of the leading spokespeople for lesbian sado-masochism, admits. But it is more: it is a "deliberate, premeditated, erotic blasphemy", "a form of sexual extremism and sexual dissent".[65] The style of the statement emphasizes two key characteristics of S/M politics: its subjectivity, with its emphasis on the meaning of the situation as seen by the participants, and its emphasis on choice, on the right to involve yourself in extreme situations to realize pleasure. Subjectivity and choice imply each other, for the argument proposes that S/M is really valid only in consensual situations between equals – knowing your partner's wishes and desires, and responding to them – while choice is crucial to the eroticization of the situation, because for the S/M enthusiast sado-masochism is not about suffering or pain but about the ritualistic eroticization of the wish for suffering and pain, about pleasure as the realization of forbidden fantasies, and about power differences as a signifier of desire:

> We select the most frightening disgusting, or unacceptable activities and transmute them into pleasure. We make use of all the forbidden symbols and all the disowned emotions ... The basic dynamic of S/M is the power dichotomy, not pain. Handcuffs, dog collars, whips, kneeling, being bound, tit clamps, hot wax, enemas, and giving

sexual service are all metaphors for the power imbalance.[66]

Sado-masochism becomes a theatre of sex, where the consenting partners freely engage in extreme activities, from bondage to fist fucking, mixing "shit, and cum and spit and piss with earthiness", all on the borderlines of endurance, to attain an intensified sense of release and pleasure.[67] The political advocates of S/M take many of the beliefs of the early sexologists – that courtship, power, pain and pleasure are intimately connected, as Havelock Ellis for one suggested – and attempt to transform them by taking them from the penumbra of individual pathology and placing them in the glare of publicity as daring acts of transgressive sex.

S/M activists make three distinct claims for their practices: that they provide unique insights into the nature of sexual power, that they are therapeutic and cathartic, and that they show the nature of sex as ritual and play. Let's look at each in turn.

S/M, Califia suggests, is "power without privilege". The dominant roles in sado-masochistic sex are not so much inscribed as won, achieved by performance and trust: "The dominant role in S/M sex is not based on economic control or physical constraint. The only power a top has is temporarily given to her by the bottom." But this intense preoccupation with power differences, the ritual enactment of their erotic possibilities does, S/Mers suggest, provide crucial insights into the nature of power, for it shows the way in which *repressed* sexuality lies behind the formal font of oppressive forces. S/M, Califia suggests: "is more a parody of the hidden sexual nature of fascism than it is a worship or acquiescence to it".[68]

By tearing the veil from the face of authority, S/M reveals the hypocrisy at the heart of our sexual culture – the bulge under the uniform – and therefore contributes to its exposure and to the dissolution of its effects.

But can the enactment of fantasies that arise from a repressive culture ever be free of the taint of that culture? Two Australian feminists, broadly sympathetic to the lesbian S/M grouping Samois, have written:

The main problem for us is when the fantasies and the play involve scenes with highly reactionary political meanings – e.g., nazi uniforms or slave scenes. We wonder if there is a limit to how far the individual context of sexual sex can transform their social meanings.[69]

Perhaps even more powerful critiques of political S/M have come from black lesbians who feel the whole issue an irrelevance when confronted by the real oppression of Third World women, an oppression which has led to the intricate involvement of sexism and racism and its attendant imagery of white master, black slave, which S/M sometimes plays with.[70]

There are effective arguments, the force of which are tacitly acknowledged by S/M activists through their deployment of a second major legitimation – that S/M is intimately therapeutic and cathartic in its effects, that it releases people from the power of violent and potentially asocial fantasies. "A good scene doesn't end with orgasm," Califia argues, "it ends with catharsis."[71] It breaks the spell of a forbidden wish, and allows for release of repression: "Fantasies and urges that are not released in some way are more likely to become obsessions."[72] The living through of fantasies, on the other hand, can produce a new feeling of health and well-being, even states of ecstasy and spiritual transcendence. But, critics have argued, is it really necessary to go to the limits of physical possibility simply because we think we want it? Do we really have to live out each fantasy to be free of it?

This is where the third form of legitimation comes in. S/M, it is proposed, throws new light on to the nature of sexuality itself. Sado-masochism, Ardill and Neumark have suggested,

stands as an explicit example of the political construction of sex – making it clear that the sexual delight caused by a tongue in the ear is as socially constructed as the thrill of being "tickled" by a leather whip or the joy of fingering your lover's black knickers.[73]

It demonstrates that pleasure is not confined to one part of the body, one orifice, or one set of sexual activities, but that we can eroticize diverse practices in highly ritualized situations. The rituals in fact are a key to the heightening of pleasure, and the practices, however diverse and exotic, forbidden and extreme, become "metaphors for abandoning oneself to sexual pleasure".[74]

Sado-masochism itself is a tiny minority activity, and is likely to remain so. The latent imperialism of its claims – that S/Mers have a special insight into the truth of sexuality, that extreme forms of sexuality are peculiarly cathartic or revelationary, or that we must go to the limits to experience heightened pleasures – is never likely to win over the reluctant and the hesitant. Nor are the arguments entirely convincing or consistent. There is an inherent contradiction between the almost Reichian tones of the argument that sexual repression is a key to social authoritarianism and the explicit social constructionism of the case for the eroticization of new parts or regions of the body. The case for S/M oscillates constantly between an essentialization of sex, power and pleasure, and a relativism which suggests that in certain circumstances "anything goes". But there is nevertheless a very important challenge in the politics of sado-masochism: it is the most radical attempt in the field of sexual politics to promote the fundamental purpose of sex as being simply pleasure. Sado-masochism is the quintessence of non-reproductive sex; it "violates the taboo that preserves the mysticism of romantic sex",[75] pleasure becomes its own justification and reward. It is this, rather than the mystical or therapeutic value of S/M, that is the real scandal of sado-masochism.

Sado-masochistic practices dramatize the graphic relationship between context, and choice, subjectivity and consent in the pursuit of pleasure. The starting point of political S/M is the belief that two (or more) people can freely consent to engage in practices which break with conventional restrictions and inhibitions. A contract is voluntarily agreed the sole purpose of which is pleasure. But the condition is equality between contracting partners. It is this condition which, Samois, the Californian-based lesbian S/M grouping, believed made its activities compatible with feminism, while Mark Thompson has spoken of "the responsibility, trust and clarity required for ritualized sex".[76] Only amongst members of the same sexual caste is this possible. The debate that this claim has

sparked off – most vehemently amongst feminists and other sex radicals but extending into the popular media – has had implications wider than the subject of S/M itself. In the wake of its claims other feminists have re-emphasized their claim to a freedom of sexual self-determination and choice, and have tried to break the "sexual silences in feminism" whatever the taboos they violate. "Feminism is a vision of active freedom, of fulfilled desires, or it is nothing", Ellen Willis has stated.[77] That means embracing the range of desires that feminists are beginning to articulate. The S/M debate, by breaking a taboo on what could be said or done, has made it possible to think through again the implications of sexual needs and sexual choice amongst consenting partners.

One implication of this stands out, and that is the way in which traditional definitions of sex have been downgraded in the debates on S/M. It is no longer *the* act and its perversions that is the object of concern but the context and relational forms which allow erotic practices to multiply. In S/M it seems to be the ritual as much as the zone of the body that matters, the eroticization of the situation as much as the orgasm. The whole body becomes a seat of pleasure, and the cultivation of roles and exotic practices the key to the attainment of pleasure. A degenitalization of sex and of pleasure is taking place in these practices which disrupt our expectations about the erotic. In a curious, understated way, in this the extreme of lesbian sado-masochism thus meets up with the extreme of its greatest opponents. They too attempt to minimize the genital nature of sex. They too emphasize the importance of context, if in a differently understood way. The conclusions and prescriptions significantly differ, but both point to the qualitative shift that is taking place in the discussion of the erotic. Increasingly, it is not "sexuality" as ordinarily understood that is the real object of debate, but "the body" with its multitude of possibilities for pleasure – genital and non-genital. Whatever we think of the resulting practices – and surely they are more a question of aesthetics than of morals – it is important to register this profound move in preoccupations and concern. The meaning of sexuality is being transformed – and before our rather startled eyes.

REFUSING TO REFUSE THE BODY

Any progressive approach to the question of sexuality must balance the autonomy of individuals against the necessity of collective endeavour and common cause. But where the exact parameters of the relationship should be is perhaps the most delicate and difficult problem for contemporary sexual politics. Inevitably, as Sue Cartledge has sensitively argued, there is a conflict between "Duty and Desire" in which individual needs can all too readily become twisted and distorted to meet the constraints of obligation – to abstract cause or imagined ideal.[78] But, equally, the celebration of individual desires over all else can lead to the collapse of any collective activity, all social movements and any prospects of real change.

The recent history of sexual politics has seen the development of both tendencies as the utopian hopes of an ultimate resolution of the conflict between duty and desire have receded. The absolutization of individual desires in a moral and political climate where marked social progress seems stymied can easily lead on the one hand to a partial or total retreat into privacy, into the narcissistic celebration of the body beautiful of the "Perrier generation", regardless of the consequences. Sexual liberation becomes merely a synonym for individual self-expression, with scarcely a thought for the social relations in which all action must be embodied. This is the nadir of the libertarianism of the 1960s. On the other hand, a sense of embattlement, of hopes thwarted and "dreams deferred", can as readily involve a search for new absolutes, for unifying norms which govern social movements and activities. Many feminists have found such a norm in the campaigns for sexual separatism, or against pornography where the female principle confronts, in a battle to an ever receding end, the male. Others committed to radical sexual change have sought a governing principle in a new morality or even a socialist eugenics, where the principle of collective need transparently hegemonizes the desires of individuals.[79]

A radical pluralist approach starts with the recognition that certain conflicts of needs, desires and ambitions can never readily be resolved. Its governing principle is that no attempt should be made to reduce human sexual diversity to a uniform form of "correct" behaviour. It does not argue, however, that all forms of sexual behaviour are equally valid, regardless of consequences, nor does it endorse the *laissez-faire* pluralism of the typical liberal approach, which is unable to think through values and distinctions. On the contrary, radical pluralism is sensitive to the workings of power, alive to the struggles needed to change the existing social relations which constrain sexual autonomy, and based upon the "collective self-activity" of those oppressed by the dominant sexual order. The most significant development in sexual politics over the past generation has not been a new volubility of sexual need, nor the new sexual markets, nor the proliferation of sexual styles or practices. It has been the appearance of new sexual-political subjects, constituting new "communities of interest" in political terms who have radically transformed the meaning of sexual politics. The sexually oppressed have spoken more explicitly than ever before on their own behalf: and if there is often confusion and ambiguity and contradictions between different groups, and even within single movements, this seems a small and possibly temporary price to pay for what is ultimately a major transformation of the political scene. There is a new sexual democracy struggling to be born and if its gestation seems over long, with a number of unforeseen complications, there is every indication that the neonate can still grow into a vigorous, healthy maturity.

"Democracy" seems an odd word to apply to the sexual sphere. "Sexuality" as we have seen is a phenomenon which is typically understood as being outside the rules of social organization. We celebrate its unruliness, spontaneity and wilfulness, not its susceptibility to calculation and decision-making. But it is surely a new form of democracy that is called for when we speak of the right to control our bodies, when we claim "our bodies are our own".

The claim to bodily self-determination is an old one, that has roots in a number of different discourses: liberal, Marxist and biological. From liberal roots in the puritan revolution of the seventeenth century we can trace the ideal of "property in one's own person". From the Marxist tradition comes the ideal of a society in which human needs can be satisfied. And from the biological sciences comes an understanding of the body, its capacities and limitations, demarcating the boundaries of individual possibility.[80] None of these traditions, nor the contemporary form of the claim to determination, can resolve the ambivalences within the discourse of choice. If we just look at the claim for a woman's right to choose in relation to abortion we can see that the phrase itself cannot resolve problems: is a woman's right to abortion absolute? Even up to the final month of pregnancy? Whatever the consequences for the potential life or the life of the woman? Saying a woman should choose does not specify under what conditions she can choose and what she should choose. There are ultimately political decisions.

Nevertheless, the concept of the "right to choose" is a powerful mobilizing idea, is still, as Denise Riley argues, the "chief inherited discourse" which fuels any demand for social reform.[81] It has a defensive ring to it against those who would subordinate women to moral control. But it can also have a powerful positive challenge if it is seen as a collective assertion of right in the demand for a new ordering of social possibility.

The willingness to discuss the principles and conditions of sexual behaviour, of what we conventionally designate as "personal life", is what marks the new political movements around sexuality from more orthodox political forms. It does not mean that there will be automatic agreement. On the contrary, conflicts of interpretation, conviction, orientation and behaviour are inevitable if we reject – as I believe we must – any idea of a mystical transcendence of difficulty and difference. The real task is to find mediations for the conflicts that will inexorably arise, to invent procedures for their settlement or discover resources for their acceptance by all parties in a spirit of mutual recognition.

The new sexual-social movements serve to disrupt the private/public dichotomy of liberal politics by their very nature, while specific campaigns (for, say, the rights of gay people at work, for the rights of lesbian parents, against sexual harassment at work) and the cultural politics of feminism and the gay movement can snap traditional distinctions between work and leisure, normal and abnormal sexualities. Feminism and radical sexual politics grow out of a recognition of people's needs and hence can begin to reunite the spheres of personal and political life. They provide a politics of people and not simply for people.

But what is this politics ultimately about? It is not about sexuality as generally understood. The starting points for the political movements around sex were the categorizations of the sexologists, that exotic profusion whose effects have been so defining and limiting. But the movements themselves offered, in Foucault's now famous phrase, a "reverse affirmation", where first homosexuals and then others radically disqualified by the sexual tradition began to demand that their own legitimacy or "naturality" be acknowledged.[82] But though beginning with the categories as they existed, the activities of the new movements gradually evacuated them of any meaning. For the elaborate taxonomies and distinctions existed in the end only to explain the variations in relationship to an assumed norm. Once the norm itself was challenged, then the category of the perverse became redundant, and with them the whole elaborate edifice of "sexuality" – the belief that the erotic is a unified domain, governed by its own laws, organized around a norm and its variations – begins to crumble.

We are left with the body and its potentialities for pleasure. This is a peculiarly ambiguous phrase which states an ambition without specifying its means of attainment. I intend to take it as a metaphor for the subjectivization of erotic pleasure, for the willingness to explore possibilities which may run counter to received definitions but which nevertheless, in context, with full awareness of the needs and limits of the situation, can be affirmed. Many of the new sexual subcultures, implicitly and explicitly, express this attitude. Richard Dyer sees in the subcultures of the gay world a new "body culture" expressed in styles, physical expressiveness and body awareness, that "refuses to refuse the body any more".[83] This surely is the hallmark of the new politics of sexuality, and its organizing principle is the celebration of pleasure. Pleasure, writes Fredric Jameson, "is finally the consent of life in the body, the reconciliation – momentary as it may be – with the necessity of physical existence in a physical world."[84] Pleasure, yes, but not pleasure selfishly attained: pleasure in the context of new codes and of new types of relationships. It is this that makes the new pluralism radical. The new relationships may not yet exist on a large scale. But in the inventiveness of the radical sexual movements in creating new ways of life lies the ultimate challenge to the power of definition hitherto enjoyed by the sexologists and the sexual tradition.

NOTES

1 Kinsey *et al.*, *Sexual Behavior in the Human Male*: 263.

2 Robert J. Stoller, *Perversion: The Erotic Form of Hatred* (London: Quartet Books, 1977) xiii, xii. But see Gayle Rubin, "Thinking Sex" in Carole Vance (ed.), *Pleasure and Danger*: 317.

3 Ronald Bayer, *Homosexuality and American Psychiatry* (New York: Basic Books, 1981).

4 For references on the debates about pornography, inter-generational sex, sado-masochism and promiscuity see below. On transsexuality as a feminist issue see Janice G. Raymond, *The Transsexual Empire* (Boston: Beacon Press, 1979); and a response from a transsexual, Carol Riddell, *Divided Sisterhood: A Critical Review of Janice Raymond's "The Trans-sexual Empire"* (Liverpool: News from Nowhere, 1980).

5 D'Emilio, *Sexual Politics, Sexual Communities*: 213. The original ACLU hostility was on the grounds that homosexuality was not enshrined constitutionally. In 1967 it reversed its position and challenged government regulation of private consensual sexual behaviour on the ground that it infringed the constitutional right of privacy.

6 John Stuart Mill, *On Liberty*; HLA Hart, *Law, Liberty and Morality* (Oxford University Press, 1963).

7 Stuart Hall, "Reformism and the Legislation of Consent", in National Deviancy Conference (ed.), *Permissiveness and Control*: 13–14; Weeks, *Sex, Politics and Society*: ch. 13. Frank Mort, "Sexuality: Regulation and Contestation", in Gay Left Collective (ed.), *Homosexuality: Power and Politics*. On pornography see Rosalind Coward, "Sexual Violence and Sexuality", *Feminist Review* 11 (Summer 1982): 14.

8 Pat Califia, *Sapphistry*, p. xiii.

9 Charles Shively, "Introduction", *Meat: How Men Look, Act, Walk, Talk, Dress, Undress, Taste and Smell* (San Francisco: Gay Sunshine Press, 1980).

10 Samois (ed.), *Coming to Power, Writings and Graphics on Lesbian S/M* (San Francisco: Up Press, 1981): 7.

11 Tim McCaskell, "Untangling Emotions and Eros", *Body Politic* (July/Aug. 1981), p. 22.

12 Tim Carrigan and John Lee, "Male Homosexuals and the Capitalist Market", *Gay Changes* (Australia): 2: 4 (1979): 39–42; Vito Russo, "When it Comes to Gay Money – Gay Lib Takes Care of the Pennies: Will Big Business Take Care of the Pounds?", *Gay News* (England) 212 (April 1981): 16–17; Altman, *The Homosexualization of America*, ch. 3; ZG 2, "Sadomasochism: Its Expression and Style" (London, n.d. [1982]).

13 Alvin Gouldner, *For Sociology* (London: Allen Lane, 1973): 295.

14 *Heresies*, 12: 92.

15 Gouldner, *op. cit.*: 296.

16 Diana E. H. Russell with Laura Lederer, "Questions We Get Asked Most Often", in Laura Lederer (ed.), *Take Back the Night: Women on Pornography* (New York: William Morrow, 1980): 29. See also Irene Diamond, "Pornography and Repression: A Reconsideration", *Signs* 5: 4 (1980).

17 *Diary of a Conference on Sexuality*: 72.

18 Michel Foucault, "Sexual Choice, Sexual Acts", *Salmagundi* 58–9: 12.

19 The earliest coherent advocacy of this was Alastair Heron (ed.), *Towards a Quaker View of Sex: An Essay by a Group of Friends* (London: Friends Home Services Committee, 1963).

20 Deirdre English, Amber Hollibaugh and Gayle Rubin, "Talking Sex", p. 43; Michel Foucault, "Friendship as a Lifestyle: An Interview with Michel Foucault", *Gay Information* (Spring 1981); first published in French in *Le Gai Pied* 25 (April 1981).

21 Weeks, *Sex, Politics and Society*: ch. 6. See especially the discussion of the 1885 Criminal Law Amendment Act (which applied to most of the United Kingdom apart from Scotland) which outlawed all male homosexual activities in *private* as well as in public as part of a measure designed to control prostitution and *public* vice.

22 See, for example, Dennis Altman, "Sex: The New Front Line for Gay Politics", *Gay News* (London) 223 (3–16 September 1981): 22–3 and *Gay Community News* (Melbourne) 3:6 (August 1981): 22–5.

23 Kinsey *et al.*, *Sexual Behavior in the Human Male*: 259; Bell and Weinberg, *Homosexualities*: 69–72; Altman, *The Homosexualization of America*: 174–6; Spada, *The Spada Report*: 63.

24 Spada: 63. See also Joseph Harvey and William B. De Vall, *The Social Organization of Gay Males*: 83; Bell and Weinberg, *Homosexualization*: 219ff.

25 Altman, *The Homosexualization*: 79–80. See also Martin S. Weinberg and Colin J. Williams, "Gay Baths and the Social Organisation of Impersonal Sex", in Martin P. Levine, *Gay Men*; and Edward William Delph, *The Silent Community: Public Homosexual Encounters* (Beverly Hills and London: Sage, 1978).

26 Spada, *The Spada report*: 113, Sylvere Lotringer, "Defunkt Sex", *Semiotext(e): Polysexuality*: 279. Cf. Weinberg and Williams, 179.

27 Laud Humphreys, *Tearoom Trade*: 162. The general discussion is on pp. 154ff.

28 See *Action: A Publication of the Right to Privacy Committee* (Toronto, 1981–2); *Body Politic* (1981–2); and submission of The Right to Privacy Committee to the City of Toronto and Ontario Provincial Legislature 1981 (in my possession; I would like to thank Bob Gallagher for information and documents).

29 See, for example, Daniel Tsang, "Struggling Against Racism", in Tsang (ed.), *The Age Taboo*: 161–2.

30 *Ibid.*: 8. There are plentiful examples of the automatic association made between male homosexuality and child molesting. In the year I write this, 1983, there has been a rich crop of them in Britain, with the low point being reached in the Brighton rape case, August 1983, where a deplorable assault on a young boy led to a rapacious press attack on the local gay community and legal action against members of the Paedophile Information Exchange, who were in no way connected with the case. The moral panic had found its victims; calm was restored; but the three men who actually assaulted the child were never found.

31 Kinsey *et al.*, *Sexual Behavior in the Human Female*: 117, note 16; Mary Whitehouse, *Cleaning-up TV: From Protest to Participation* (London: Blandford Press, 1967), and *A Most Dangerous Woman?* (Tring, Herts: Lion Publishing, 1982); Anita Bryant, *The Anita Bryant Story*. For general commentaries on events see the articles in Tsang, *The Age Taboo*; Altman, *The Homosexualization of America*: 198ff; Mitzel, *The Boston Sex Scandal* (Boston, Glad Day Books, 1980); Tom O'Carroll, *Paedophilia: The Radical Case* (London: Peter Owen, 1980): ch. 12; Ken Plummer, "Images of Paedophilia", in M. Cook and G. D. Wilson (eds), *Love and Attraction: An International Conference* (Oxford: Pergamon, 1979). Major events included the Revere "Sex Scandal" in Boston, the raid on *Body Politic* following its publication of the article "Men Loving Boys Loving Men" in Dec. 1977; the "kiddie porn" panic of 1977; the

trial of Tom O'Carroll and others in England for conspiracy to corrupt public morals in 1981.

32 Pat Califia, "The Age of Consent; An Issue and its Effects on the Gay Movement", *The Advocate* (30 October 1980): 17. See also Florence Rush, "Child Pornography", in Lederer (ed.), *Take Back the Night*: 71–81; Illinois Legislative Investigating Commission, *Sexual Exploitation of Children* (Chicago, The Commission, 1980) (see further references in Tsang: 169–70); and on similar events in Britain Whitehouse, *A Most Dangerous Woman?*: ch. 13, "Kiddie Porn": 146ff.

33 Roger Scruton, *The Times* (London) (13 September 1983).

34 Kinsey *et al.*, *Sexual Behavior in the Human Female*: 121.

35 Interview by Guy Hocquenghem with David Thorstad in *Semiotext(e) Special: Large Type Series: Loving Boys* (Summer 1980): 34; Tom O'Carroll, *Paedophilia*: 153.

36 See, for example, "'Lesbians Rising' Editors Speak Out", in Tsang: 125–32; Stevi Jackson, *Childhood and Sexuality* (Oxford: Basil Blackwell, 1982): ch. 9. See also, Elizabeth Wilson's comments on the debate about proposals to lower the age of consent in England in *What is to be Done about Violence against Women?*: 205.

37 Theo Sandfort, *The Sexual Aspects of Paedophile Relations: The Experience of Twenty-five Boys* (Amsterdam: Pan/Spartacus, 1982): 81.

38 Kenneth Plummer, "The Paedophile's Progress", in Brian Taylor (ed.), *Perspectives on Paedophilia*. See J. Z. Eglinton, *Greek Love* (London: Neville Spearman, 1971): for a classic statement of the first legitimation, and O'Carroll, *Paedophilia*, especially chs 2 and 5 for the second.

39 For an overview of these stereotypes (and the facts which rebut them) to which I am very much indebted, see Plummer, "Images of Paedophilia".

40 Glen D. Wilson and David N. Cox, *The Child-Lovers: A Study of Paedophiles in Society* (London and Boston: Peter Owen, 1983); Peter Righton: ch. 2: "The Adult" in Taylor, *Perspectives in Paedophilia*; Parker Rossman, *Sexual Experiences between Men and Boys* (London: Maurice Temple Smith, 1976).

41 Tom Reeves, "Loving Boys" in Tsang: 27; the age range given on p. 29. On PIE members' interests see Cox and Wilson: ch. II.

42 Krafft-Ebing, *Psychopathia Sexualis*: 552: "By violation of sexually immature individuals, the jurist understands all the possible immoral acts which persons under fourteen years of age that are not comprehended in the term 'rape'."

43 On paedophilia as abuse see Florence Rush, *The Best Kept Secret: Sexual Abuse of Children* (Englewood Cliffs, NJ: Prentice-Hall, 1980);

Robert L. Geiser, *Hidden Victims: The Sexual Abuse of Children* (Boston: Beacon Press, 1979). For alternative opinions: Sandford: 49ff; cf. Morris Fraser: ch. 3, "The Child" and Graham E. Powell and A. J. Chalkley, ch. 4, "The Effects of Paedophile Attention on the Child", in Taylor (ed.), *Perspectives on Paedophilia*.

44 See interview with the then 15-year-old Mark Moffatt in *Semiotext(e)*: 10; cf. Tom Reeves's account of being cruised by two 14-year-olds in Tsang: 30; and O'Carroll: ch. 4, "Paedophilia in Action" in *Paedophilia*.

45 Taylor (ed.) *Perspectives on Paedophilia*, "Introduction", xiii. In the rest of the discussion I shall, however use the term "paedophile" to cover all categories as this is the phrase adopted most widely as a *political* description: "Boy-lover" is specific, but exclusive.

46 On offences see P. H. Gebhard, J. H. Gagnon, W. B. Pomeroy and C. V. Christenson, *Sex Offenders* (New York: Harper & Row, 1965); J. Gagnon, "Female child victims of sex offences", *Social Problems* 13 (1965): 116–92. On identity questions see Plummer, "The Paedophile's Progress."

47 O'Carroll, *Paedophilia*: 120, 118.

48 Ibid.: 6, "Towards More Sensible Laws", which examines various proposals, from Israel to Holland, for minimizing the harmful intervention of the law; compare Speijer Committee, *The Speijer Report*, advice to the Netherlands Council of Health concerning homosexual relations with minors, English Translation (London: Sexual Law Reform Society, n.d.).

49 Interview with Kate Millett by Mark Blasius in *Semiotexte(e) Special*: 38 (also printed in Tsang (ed.)).

50 Carole Pateman, "Women and Consent", *Political Theory* 8: 2 (May 1980): 149–68.

51 Deirdre English *et al.*, "Talking Sex": 51. Laura Lederer (ed.), *Take Back the Night* gives the most comprehensive coverage of the various American campaigns. The most passionate polemics are in Andrea Dworkin, *Pornography: Men Possessing Men* and Susan Griffin, *Pornography and Silence*. For an excellent general critical comment on the feminist politics of pornography see Lesley Steen, "The Body as Evidence: A Critical Review of the Pornography Problematic", *Screen* 23: 5 (Nov./Dec. 1982): 38–60.

52 Rosalind Coward, "Sexual Violence and Sexuality", *Feminist Review* 11: 11.

53 John Ellis, "Pornography", *Screen* (1980): 96. See also Elizabeth Wilson, *What is to be Done About Violence against Women?*: 160.

54 Califia, *Sapphistry*: 15; Lisa Orlando, "'Bad' Girls and 'Good' Politics", *Village Voice Literary Supplement* (Dec. 1982): 1.

55 The quotes are from Elizabeth Wilson, "Interview with Andrea Dworkin", *Feminist Review* 11 (Summer 1982): 26; Helen E. Longino, "Pornography, Oppression and Freedom: A Closer Look", in Lederer (ed.), *Take Back the Night*: 44; "Interview with Andrea Dworkin": 25; Susan Brownmiller, *Against Our Will* (New York: Simon & Schuster, 1975); Robin Morgan, *Going Too Far* (New York: Random House, 1977); Gloria Steinem, "Erotica and Pornography: A Clear and Present Difference", in Lederer (ed.), *Take Back the Night*: 38.

56 Deirdre English *et al.*, "Talking Sex": 38.

57 The absolutist position is expressed clearly in the Longford Committee, *Pornography: The Longford Report* (London: Coronet Books, 1972). "Scientific" evidence supporting it can be found in H. J. Eysenck, *Sex and Personality* (London: Open Books, 1976): 235–6, in H. J. Eysenck and D. K. B. Nias, *Sex, Violence and the Media* (London: Maurice Temple Smith, 1978), while the debate is assessed in Maurice Yaffe and Edward Nelson (eds), *The Influence of Pornography on Behaviour* (London: Academic Press, 1983). The liberal scepticism about such findings is best found in *The Report of the Commission on Obscenity and Pornography* (New York: Random House, 1970): the *Report of the Committee on Obscenity and Film Censorship* and in the liberal-feminist work by Beatrice Faust, *Women, Sex and Pornography* (Harmondsworth: Penguin Books, 1981); the radical feminist rejection of these positions is clearly expressed in Diamond, *op cit.*: 691–7.

58 Susan Barrowclough, "Not a Love Story", *Screen* 23:5 (Nov./Dec. 1982): 32.

59 Ellen Willis, "Who is a Feminist? A Letter to Robin Morgan", *Village Voice Literary Supplement* (December 1982): 17; Lisa Orlando, "'Bad' Girls and 'Good' Politics": 16. Compare Angela Carter, *The Sadeian Woman: An Exercise in Cultural History* (London, Virago, 1979).

60 Gregg Blachford, "Looking at Pornography: Erotica and the Socialist Morality", *Gay Left* 6 (summer 1978): 16–20 and (in a slightly different version) *Screen Education* 29 (winter 1978–9): 21–8; Chris Bearchall, "Art, Trash and Titillation: A Consumer's Guide to Lezzy Smut", *Body Politic* 93 (May 1983): 33; *Diary of a Conference on Sexuality*: 19.

61 B. Ruby Rich, "Anti Porn: Soft Issue, Hard World", *Feminist Review* 13 (spring 1983).

62 Lesley Stern, "The Body as Evidence": 42.

63 On the general point see Coward; on romance see Ann Barr Snitow, "Mass Market Romance: Pornography for Women is Different", *Radical History Review* 20, (spring/summer 1979): 141–63, and Valerie Hey, *The Necessity of Romance* (Canterbury: University of Kent at Canterbury, Women's Studies Occasional Papers, 3 (1983).

64 See Altman, *The Homosexualization of America*: 190ff. Ian Young, John Stoltenberg, Lyn Rosen and Rose Jordan, "Forum on Sado-Masochism", in Karla Jay and Allen Young (eds), *Lavender Culture* (New York: A Jove HBJ Book, 1978); Samois, *What Color is Your Handerkerchief? A Lesbian S/M Sexuality Reader* (Berkeley, CA: Samois, 1979); Samois, *Coming to Power*. Samois, a lesbian and feminist S/M group active between 1979 and 1983, became the most notorious of the political S/M groupings, provoking the reply *Against Sadomasochism* (see note 70 below).

65 Pat Califia, "Unraveling the Sexual Fringe: A Secret Side of Lesbian Sexuality", *The Advocate* (27 Dec. 1979): 19.

66 *Ibid.*: 19–21. See also Califia, *Sapphistry*: 118–32.

67 Mark Thompson, "To the Limits and Beyond", *The Advocate* (8 July 1982): 31. On the theatrical metaphor see Paul Gebhard, "Fetishism and Sado Masochism", in Martin S. Weinberg (ed.), *Sex Research: Studies from the Kinsey Institute* (New York, London, Toronto: Oxford University Press, 1976): 164. For the views of sexologists see Havelock Ellis, *Studies in the Psychology of Sex*, vol. III (Philadelphia: F. A. Davis, 1920): 66–188; Gerald and Caroline Greene, *S-M: The Last Taboo* (New York: Ballantine Books, 1978); T. Weinberg and G. W. Levi Kamel (eds), *S and M Studies in Sadomasochism* (Buffalo, NY: Prometheus Books, 1983).

68 Califia, "Unraveling the Sexual Fringe": 22; *Sapphistry*: 119; "Feminism and Sadomasochism", *Heresies*, 12: 32.

69 Susan Ardill and Nora Neumark, "Putting Sex Back into Lesbianism: Is the Way to a Woman's heart through her Sado-masochism?", *Gay Information* 11 (spring 1981): 11.

70 Karen Sims, "Racism and Sadomasochism: A Conversation with Two Black Lesbians", in Robin Ruth Linden, *Against Sadomasochism: A Radical Feminist Analysis* (East Palo Alto, CA: Frog in the Well, 1982): 99–105.

71 Pat Califia, "Unraveling the Sexual Fringe": 22.

72 Quoted in Mariana Valverde, "Feminism Meets Fist-fucking: Getting Lost in Lesbian S&M", *Body Politic* (Feb. 1982): 43.

73 Ardill and Neumark, *op cit.*: 9.

74 Califia, *Sapphistry*: 10.

75 Califia, "Feminism and Sado Masochism": 32.

76 "Our Statement" in Samois, *What Color is your Handkerchief?*: 2; Mark Thompson, "To the Limits and Beyond": 28.

77 Ellen Willis, *Diary of a Conference on Sexuality*: 72. For a critique of this position from a socialist, not radical, feminist position see: Elizabeth Wilson, "A New Romanticism?", in Eileen Philips (ed.), *The Left and the Erotic* (London: Lawrence & Wishart, 1983): 37–52.

78 Sue Cartledge, "Duty and Desire: Creating a Feminist Morality", in Sue Cartledge and Joanna Ryan (eds), *Sex and Love*: 167.

79 See, for example, David Fernbach, *The Spiral Path: A Gay Contribution to Human Survival* (London: Gay Men's Press, 1981); see my review in *Gay News* (London) (September 1981).

80 I am here following Rosalind Pollack Petchesky, "Reproductive Freedom: Beyond 'A Woman's Right to Choose'", *Signs* 5: 4 (1980): 661–87.

81 Denise Riley, "Feminist Thought and Reproductive Control: The State and the 'Right to Choose'", in The Cambridge Women's Studies Group (eds), *Women in Society: Interdisciplinary Essays* (London: Virago, 1981). See also Michèle Barrett and Mary McIntosh, *The Antisocial Family*: 135–7, who also cite Riley.

82 Michel Foucault, *The History of Sexuality*, 1: 101.

83 Richard Dyer, "Getting Over the Rainbow".

84 Fredric Jameson, "Pleasure: A Political Issue", in *Formations of Pleasure*: 10.

JOSHUA GAMSON

"Silence, Death, and the Invisible Enemy: AIDS Activism and Social Movement 'Newness'"

from *Social Problems* 38: 4 (October 1989): 351–67

Shea Stadium is packed. As the Mets play the Astros, New York AIDS activists scream and shout along with the rest of the fans. Their cheers are somewhat unusual: "ACT UP! Fight back! Fight AIDS!" Their banners, unfurled in front of the three sections they have bought out, shout plays on baseball themes: "No glove, no love," "Don't balk at safer sex," "AIDS is not a ball game." The electronic billboard flashes some of their messages as well. The action gets wide coverage the following day. Later, in a *Newsweek* (1988a) article on the activist group ACT UP, a baseball fan complains, "AIDS is a fearful topic. This is totally inappropriate."

The fan is right, on both counts; in fact, I would suggest, he inadvertently sums up the point of the action. He also calls attention to the oddities: Why fight AIDS at a baseball game? Why mix fear and Americana? Who or what is the target here?

Susan Sontag and others have noted that the AIDS epidemic fits quite smoothly into a history of understanding disease through the "usual script" of the plague metaphor: originating from "outside" plagues are visitations on "them," punishments of both individuals and groups, they become stand-ins for deep fears and tools for bringing judgments about social crisis. "AIDS," Sontag (1988: 89) suggests, "is understood in a premodern way."

Yet the plague of AIDS has brought with it understanding and actions that are hardly "premodern": civil disobedience at the Food and Drug Administration protesting the sluggish drug approval process, guerrilla theater and "die-ins," infiltrations of political events culminating in the unfurling of banners protesting government inaction, media-geared "zaps," illegal drug research and sales, pickets and rallies. AIDS has given rise to a social movement. This is not, in fact, part of the usual script.

Perhaps, then, AIDS can be understood as part of a different script as well. Much has been written in the past decade about "new social movements" (NSMs); perhaps AIDS activism follows an outline particular to contemporary movements. This classification presents its own difficulties: social movements literature has a hard time clarifying exactly what is "new" about contemporary social movements and can, through its fuzziness, easily accommodate yet another social movement without shedding new light.

In this paper, I examine AIDS activism – by which I mean an organized "street" response to the epidemic – through the activities of ACT UP (the AIDS Coalition to Unleash Power), its most widespread and publicly visible direct-action group.

ACT UP, which began in New York, has chapters in Chicago, Boston, Atlanta, Los Angeles, Houston, Rochester, Madison, Nashville, San Francisco, and a number of other cities. The groups are loosely federated under the umbrella of the AIDS Coalition to Network, Organize and Win (ACT NOW). New York is by far the largest ACT UP, with weekly meeting attendance in the hundreds and membership estimated at nearly three thousand, while the others are smaller. San Francisco, with a membership of over seven hundred, averages fifty people at general meetings. My comparisons between ACT UP in San Francisco and chapters in New York and other cities are based on a national conference in Washington, DC, internal publications, informal discussion and interviews, and newspaper reports.

Using data from six months of participant-observation research (September 1988 through February 1989) in San Francisco's ACT UP, coupled with local and national internal documents and newspaper writings about the group, I develop an analysis intended both to sharpen focus on the struggle over the meaning of AIDS and to challenge some of the hazy understandings of social movement newness. The analysis here treats ACT UP not as an exemplar but rather as an anomaly, asking what unique conditions constitutue the case and how the case can aid in a reconstruction of existing theory. Micro- and macro-level analysis are linked through seeking out an "explanation for uniqueness" such that "we are compelled to move into the realm of the 'macro' that shaped the 'micro' that we observe in face-to-face interaction" (Burawoy 1989: 7).

In the first part of the paper I briefly review approaches to contemporary social movements, locating ACT UP within this literature. I then turn to ACT UP's activities and internal obstacles, looking at their response to the plague script, the alternative scripts they propose and their strategies for doing so, and the difficulties they face in this process. I argue that asking "who is the enemy?" provides a fruitful direction for making sense of these dynamics because ACT UP members often have trouble finding their "enemies." The paper continues with an examination of why this may be so, and what light it may shed on contemporary movements. Borrowing from Michel Foucault (1979), I turn to an examination of the forms of domination to which ACT UP members respond. I argue that, in addition to visible targets such as government agencies and drug companies, much of what ACT UP is fighting is abstract, disembodied, invisible: control through the creation of abnormality. Power is maintained less through direct force or institutionalized oppression and more through the delineation of the "normal" and the exclusion of the "abnormal." I suggest that this "normalizing" process, taking prominence in a gradual historical shift, is increasingly unlocked from state oppression in recent decades. State figures and institutions – though certainly still deeply involved in this

domination – are now less apt to continue to the production and dissemination of labels, making the process itself, abstracted, the hazy focus of protest. The paper then traces how responses to normalization play themselves out in ACT UP activities: activities use the labels to dispute the labels, use their abnormality and expressions of gay identity to challenge the process by which this identity was and is defined. Finally, I suggest directions this framework provides for analyzing contemporary movements.

THE THEORETICAL CONTEXT: WHAT'S NEW?

Among the shifts provoked by the rise of massive social movements in the 1960s and 1970s was a rupture in theorizing about social movements. Until that time, the dominant paradigm of collective behavior theory treated non-institutional movements as essentially non-rational or irrational responses by alienated individuals to social strain and breakdown (for example, Smelser 1963). Many 1960s activists did not fit the mold. Neither anomic nor underprivileged nor responding to crises with beliefs "akin to magical beliefs" (Smelser 1963: 8), they in fact came together largely from the middle class, with concrete goals and rational calculations of strategies. The predictions of classical social movements theory regarding who made up social movements and how they operated had broken down (see Cohen 1985; McAdam 1982).

In the last two decades, attempts to retheorize social movements have moved in two major directions. North American resource mobilization theory accounts for large-scale mobilizations by emphasizing rational calculations by actors, focussing on the varying constraints and opportunities in which they operate and the varying resources upon which they draw (see McCarthy and Zald 1977; Oberschall 1973; Tilly 1978; Jenkins 1981). This paradigm, directly challenging the assumptions of collective behavior theory, insists on the rationality of collective action. European theorists on the other hand, have argued that rational-actor models are inappropriately applied to new groups seeking identity and autonomy. The movements of the 1960s and their apparent descendants – the peace movement, for example, or feminist, ecological, or local-autonomy movements – have been taken together by theorists as "new" phenomena to be accounted for; it is their non-rational focus on identity and expression that these theories emphasize as distinctive. They attempt to outline the characteristics shared by contemporary movements and to discern the structural shifts that might account for new dimensions of activity (see Kitschelt 1985; Cohen 1985; Eder 1985; Habermas 1981; Offe 1985 and Touraine 1985).

With some exceptions (see, for example, Doug McAdam's 1982 study of black insurgency), American theory, with its insistence on instrumental rationality, tends to pass over these distinctive characteristics – feminist attention to "consciousness," for example, and black and gay "pride" – to which European theories of "new social movements" (NSMs) direct attention. The European literature, then, in that it attempts to explain these apparently new characteristics found also in AIDS activism, provides the stronger conceptual tools with which to approach ACT UP. Yet what is actually "new" according to European NSM theory is both disputed and unclear. Most agree that a middle-class social base is distinctive (see Eder 1985 and Kreisi 1989); indeed, the fact that NSMs are *not* working-class movements focussed primarily on economic distribution seems to be a characteristic on which there is clarity and agreement. From here, the range of characteristics expands and abstracts; NSMs claim "the sphere of 'political action within civil society' as [their] space" (Offe 1985: 832); they use different tactics from their predecessors (Offe 1985); their conflicts concern not "problems of distribution" but "the grammar of forms of life," arising in "areas of cultural reproduction, social integration and socializing" (Habermas 1981: 33); they "manifest a form of middle-class protest which oscillates from moral crusade to political pressure group to social movement" (Eder 1985: 879); they are "both culturally oriented and involved in structural conflicts" (Touraine 1985: 766), involve a "self-limiting radicalism" that "abandons revolutionary dreams in favor of the idea of structural reform, along with a defense of civil society that does not seek to abolish the autonomous functioning of political and economic systems" (Cohen 1985: 664).

Common to this list is a recognition that the field of operation has shifted, broadly put, to "civil society" and away from the state; that culture has become more of a focal point of activity (through "lifestyle" and "identity" movements, for example); and that this shift has to do with broad changes in the "societal type" to which movements respond and in which they act. Common to the list is also an unclear answer to the question of how new the shift really is; as Jean Cohen (1985: 665) points out, the theme of defending civil society does not in itself imply something new – the question "is whether the theme has been connected to new identities, forms of organization, and scenarios of conflict." New social movement theorists – even those like Touraine and Cohen who address these questions directly – seem to be unclear on what these shifts and changes really are: What exactly is the "cultural field" of "civil society" and what do these movements actually do there? What is it that is different about contemporary society that accounts for the characteristics of new social movements? When and how did these changes take place?

ACT UP AS A NEW SOCIAL MOVEMENT

ACT UP provides an opportunity both to examine some of these issues concretely and to offer new hypotheses. The AIDS activist movement appears to share the most basic characteristics of "new social movements": a (broadly) middle-class membership and a mix of instrumental, expressive and identity-oriented activities. Rather than exclusively orienting itself towards material distribution, ACT UP uses and targets cultural resources as well. What, this examination asks, does ACT UP do on the cultural terrain? What light does their activity shed on the question of "newness"? How can a study of this group contribute to an understanding of shifts in the nature of social movements and in the nature of the social world in which they operate?

The answer begins with the group's overall profile. ACT UP/San Francisco grew out of the 1987 San Francisco AIDS Action Pledge, becoming ACT UP in the fall of that year after New York's ACT UP began to gain recognition. In addition to planned and spontaneous actions, the group meets weekly in a church in the predominantly gay Castro neighborhood. ACT UP/San Francisco is made up almost exclusively of white gay men and lesbians, mostly in their twenties and thirties. The core membership – an informal group of about twenty five activists – draws from both established activists (gay rights, Central American politics, etc.) and those newly politicized by AIDS.[1] Some, but by no means all, of ACT UP's membership has either tested positive for HIV antibodies or been diagnosed with AIDS. As one member said, "I'm here because I'm angry and I'm tired of seeing my friends die." The membership is typically professional and semi-professional: legal and health care professionals, writers, political organizers, students, artists with day jobs. ACT UP/New York and ACT UPs in other cities exhibit similar profiles (Green 1989).

Self-defined in their flyers and media kits as "a nonpartisan group of diverse individuals united in anger and committed to direct action to end the AIDS crisis" (ACT UP 1988a), ACT UP pushes for greater access to treatments and drugs for AIDS-related diseases; culturally sensitive, widely available, and explicit safe-sex education; and well-funded research that is "publicly accountable to the communities most affected" (ACT UP 1988a). Moreover, the group pushes for the participation of people with AIDS (PWAs) in these activities (ACT UP 1989). The idea here is to change the distribution of resources and decision-making power; the principle guiding actions is strategic, aimed at affecting policy changes. "People have been fighting for social justice in this country for centuries," says one member (September 1988). "We're going to get aerosol pentamidine [a treatment drug for pneumocystis pneumonia] a lot quicker than we're going to get social justice."

ACT UP is also often involved in actions, however, whose primary principle is expressive. They focus inward on "building a unified community" (the gay and lesbian community and,

increasingly, a sub-community of PWAs and the HIV-infected), and in the "need to express the anger and rage that is righteous and justified" from the community outward. They organize at times around actions in which AIDS is not the central issue or in which AIDS activism is incorporated into the project of "recreating a movement for gay and lesbian liberation." This orientation towards identity and expression, while not excluding older-style straight action, is one key characteristic cited by students of post-60s social movements.

Most interestingly, though, one hears and sees in ACT UP a constant reference to theater. ACT UP operates largely by staging events and by carefully constructing and publicizing symbols; it attacks the dominant representations of AIDS and of people with AIDS and makes attempts to replace them with alternative representations. At times, ACT UP attacks the representations alone; at times the attack is combined with a direct one on cultural producers and the process of AIDS-image production.

Another action principle weaves through ACT UP. As *Newsweek* (1988a) puts it, ACT UP has often "deliberately trespassed the bounds of good taste": throwing condoms, necking in public places, speaking explicitly and positively about anal sex, "camping it up" for the television cameras. This trespassing or boundary-crossing – and we can include in it the infiltration of public and private spaces (the Republican national convention, for example, where activists posing as participants unfurled banners) – both uses and strikes at the cultural field as well. In this case, rather than reacting to images of AIDS, activists use a more general tactic of disturbing "good taste" and, in a point *Newsweek* quite characteristically misses, calling attention to the connection between cultural definitions and responses to AIDS. Boundary-crossing, along with theatrical and symbolic actions, makes clear that ACT UP operates largely on the cultural field where theorists situate new social movements. It also suggests that an examination of the specific patterns of culturally oriented actions may be especially revealing. By focussing on the cultural activities of AIDS activists as a key *distinctive* element, I by no means want to suggest this activism is primarily cultural. In fact, treatment issues, needle-exchange programs and access to health care, for instance, are all common subjects of action. Pursuing this examination via ACT UP's peculiarities, I hope to generate possibilities for grounding and developing social movement theory.

ACT UP'S INTERNAL OBSTACLES

The examination turns, then, to ACT UP's distinctive characteristics. ACT UP's strong cultural orientation has already been noted. In addition, buried in its various strategies are three fundamental confusions. First, ACT UP's orientation towards theatrics suggests a clear delineation of performer from audience, yet actions are often planned by ACT UP members without an articulation of whom they're meant to influence. If one wants to affect an audience – for example, by invoking a symbol whose meaning is taken for granted and then giving it a different meaning – one clearly needs a conception of who that audience is. In ACT UP planning meetings, there is often an underlying confusion of audiences, and more often the question of audience is simply ignored. When activists in New York infiltrated a Republican women's cocktail party and later unfurled banners ("Lesbians for Bush," read one), the response of the cocktail parties, a defensive singing of "God Bless America" (reported in "Workshop on Creative Actions," ACT NOW Conference, Washington, DC, October 8, 1988), was important not for what it showed about the Republicans' AIDS consciousness, which came as no surprise. Instead, it was important for what it showed the activists about their own power. They were, in effect, their own audience, performing for themselves and making others perform for them. In "brainstorms" for new actions, there is almost never a mention of audience, and action ideas with different audiences proliferate. ACT UP protested Dukakis, for example, with no media coverage, Dukakis nowhere in sight, and no one to witness the protest but passing cars (San Francisco, September 30, 1988). In the meetings I observed, I commonly heard suggestions for actions that bypassed any actual event, heading

straight for the at-home audience through "photo opportunities," mixed in with suggestions for actions that almost no one would see. Much of this confusion is exacerbated by an openness of exchange and decentralized decision-making born of ACT UP's democratic structure (in San Francisco, decisions are made consensually). The loose organizational structure acts against focussed planning and action. I argue, however, that the roots are deeper.

A second point of confusion is that, while ACT UP professes to be inclusive, and ideas are often brought up that target non-gay aspects of AIDS (issues of concern to intravenous drug-users, for example, or access to health care for those who cannot afford it), there are few signs that ACT UP in fact succeeds at including or actively pursues non-gay members. This does not mean that the membership is exclusively gay men; in fact, a good portion of the activists are women.[3] The formation of coalitions is sometimes brought up as a good idea – "we need to join with others in solidarity around common suffering and common enemies," said the keynote speaker at the ACT NOW conference in October 1988 – but generally not effected. Cooperative actions with other groups generate little excitement in San Francisco meetings. Actions are aimed mainly at targets with particular relevance to lesbians and gays; there are few black or Hispanic members, gay or straight. Despite the goal of inclusiveness, ACT UP continues to draw from and recreate the white, middle-class gay and lesbian community.

A third and related problem is perhaps even more fundamental: AIDS politics and gay politics stand in tension, simultaneously associated and dissociated. ACT UP is an AIDS activist organization built and run by gay people. Historically, this is neither surprising nor problematic; among the populations first hit hardest by AIDS, gay people were alone in having an already established tradition and network of political and self-help organizations. Still, this tradition has meant that "AIDS groups have found it very difficult to establish themselves as non-gay, even where they have deliberately presented themselves as such" (Altman 1986–90). AIDS activists find themselves simultaneously attempting to dispel the notion that

AIDS is a gay disease (which it is not) while, through their activity and leadership, treating AIDS as a gay problem (which, among other things, it is).

While this dilemma is in part due to the course the disease itself took, how it plays itself out in ACT UP is instructive. For some, particularly those members who are not newly politicized, ACT UP *is* gay politics, pure and simple, a movement continuous with earlier activism. They emphasize the need for "sex positive" safe-sex education, for example, linking AIDS politics to the sexual liberation of earlier gay politics. The main organizer of a November 1988 election night rally in San Francisco's Castro district for the gay community to "Stand Out and Shout" about results envisioned it as a return to the good old days of gay celebration. In planning speakers for the rally, he and others quickly generated a long list of possibles – from the gay political community. Here, AIDS issues often get buried.

For others, it's important to maintain some separation, albeit a blurry one, between the two sets of issues. In New York, for example, when a newspaper calls ACT UP a "gay organization," ACT UP's media committee sends out a "standard letter" correcting the error ("Media Workshop" at ACT NOW Conference in Washington, DC, October 8, 1988). The ACT UP agenda, when the balance is towards distinctive AIDS politics, often focuses more narrowly on prevention and treatment issues as in, for example, a San Francisco proposal for an "AIDS treatment advocacy project" which argued that "whether it is an entire family with AIDS in Harlem or an HIV + gay man in San Francisco, treatment is ultimately the issue they are most concerned with" (ACT UP 1988b: 1). More commonly, though, ACT UP actions don't fall on one side or the other, but combine an active acceptance of the gay-AIDS connection with an active resistance to that connection.

VISIBLE AND INVISIBLE ENEMIES

Why do these particular confusions occur? They eventually will come to make sense as the particularities of ACT UP's actions are examined. These three confusions within ACT UP, which seem to give its action a somewhat unfocussed character, in fact will prove to be core elements of the group's being. Explaining ACT UP's confusions, and those of social movements like it, hinges on the answer to a pivotal question: Who is the enemy? Asking this question of ACT UP, one often finds that the enemies against which their anger and action are directed are clear, familiar and visible: the state and corporations. At other times, though, the enemy is invisible, abstract, disembodied, ubiquitous: it is the very process of "normalization" through labelling in which everyone except one's own "community" of the de-normalized (and its supporters) is involved. At still other times, intermediate enemies appear, the visible institutions of the less visible process: the media and medical science.

This second enemy forms the basis of my core theoretical claim: that ACT UP is responding to a gradual historical shift towards a form of domination in which power is maintained through a normalizing process in which "the whole indefinite domain of the non-conforming is punishable" (Foucault 1979: 178). Through labelling, or socially organized stigmatization, behaviors and groups are marked as abnormal; in the last two centuries, the norm has largely replaced the threat of violence as a technique of power. As Michel Foucault (1979: 183) argues, individuals are differentiated

> in terms of the following overall rule: that the rule be made to function as a minimum threshold, as an average to be respected or as an optimum towards which one must move. It . . . hierarchizes in terms of values the abilities, the level, the "nature" of individuals. It introduces, through this "value giving" measure, the constraint of conformity that must be achieved. Lastly, it traces the limit that will define difference in relation to all other differences, the external frontier of the abnormal.

In this process, the dominator becomes increasingly abstracted and invisible, while the dominated, embodied and visible (and, importantly, "marked" through stigmatization), becomes the focus of attention. In effect, people dominate themselves; rather than being confronted with a punishment (physical, material) as a mechanism of control, they confront themselves with the threat of being devalued as abnormal.

These ideas are not incompatible with those put forward by the sociology of deviance and discussions of stigmatization (e.g., Lemert 1967; Goffman 1963), which, of course, call attention to the process of labelling and its impact on the "deviant." However, the various forms of labelling theory have also been challenged by collective action since the 1960s. Those theories, by studying how one "becomes deviant," and the defensive reaction of "diviants" to an identity defined for them – the "management of spoiled identities" (Goffman) and "secondary deviation" as a "means of defense" against the "problems created by the societal reaction to primary deviation" (Lemert 1967: 17) – are ill-equipped to explain the organization of the stigmatized into social movements. As John Kitsuse (1980: 5) argues, the accommodative reactions analyzed by deviance sociology (retreat into a subculture, nervously covering up or denying aberrations) do not "account for, nor do they provide for an understanding of, the phenomenal number of self-proclaimed deviant groups that have visibly and vocally entered the politics" of recent decades. Earlier theories are hard-pressed to account for historical change, and for the assertive building of collective movements based on self-definitions that *reject* the dominant definitions. Foucault, on the other hand, treats pressure for conformity not as a given problem for the "deviant" but as a technique of power with a variable history.

Identity strategies are particularly salient and problematic within this domination form. When power is effected through categorization, identity is often built on the very categories it resists. ACT UP's expressive actions, in this light, are part of a continuing process of actively forging a gay identity while challenging the process through which it is formed *for* gay people at a time when the stigma of disease has been linked with the stigma of deviant sexuality. ACT UP members continue to organize around the "deviant" label, attempting to separate label from stigma. Identity-oriented actions accept the labels, and symbolic actions disrupt and resignify them.

Identity actions and representational strategies thus stand in awkward relationship: they are increasingly linked in the attack on the normalization process itself. In a simpler identity politics – in the celebration of gay liberation, for example – labels are important tools for self-understanding. That sort of politics involves what John Kitsuse (1980: 9) calls "tertiary deviation," the "confrontation, assessment, and rejection of the negative identity ... and the transformation of that identity into a positive or viable self-conception." ACT UP members, however, push past this "new deviance" to use stigmas and identity markers as tools against the normalization process. The representation of oneself as abnormal now becomes a tool for disrupting the categorization process; the labels on which group identity is built are used, in a sense, against themselves.

Why, though, is this response to normalizing power coming into its own now? Stigmatization is certainly not new. Foucault, in *Discipline and Punish*, traces a shift in the eighteenth and nineteenth centuries, a shift that takes place primarily in technologies of control: the rise of surveillance techniques and the constitution of the subject by "experts" and scientific discourse. This shift has arguably solidified in this century in Western societies. Yet, while state institutions and actors in the twentieth century certainly have still been involved in the normalization process (as well as in direct repression), they have evidently been less involved in the latter half of this century (or, stated less strongly, less visibly involved). One sees this in the history of civil rights: racism continues while state-sponsored racism and racist policies become less acceptable (see Omi and Winant 1986: 891ff.). Similarly, state definitions of women's "roles" have been liberalized, as the state has withdrawn somewhat from prescribing "normal" female behavior. One sees this as well in the response to AIDS; the federal government, while conservative or split in its policies, has over time become somewhat more liberal in terms of labelling. Public health officials advertise AIDS as an "equal opportunity destroyer"; the Surgeon General warns against treating AIDS as a gay disease and argues in favor of protections against discrimination; the Presidential Commission calls for "the reaffirmation of compassion, justice, and dignity" and indicts, among other things, "a lack of uniform and strong antidiscrimination laws" (Johnson and Murray 1988). State institutions increasingly refuse to "discriminate," that is, to set policies based on social labels. As the state becomes less directly involved in normalization, the process itself necessarily becomes more an independent point of attack by the denormalized and resisted as a process. It is within this overall historical shift in methods of domination, this study proposes, that ACT UP's social movement activity makes sense.

ACT UP AND NORMALIZATION

How does this resistance play itself out? What is the link between enemies and actions? Let's begin with the old forms of domination, which are very much still at work. The state is certainly involved in the domination of people with AIDS, as it is in the repression of sexual minorities. For example, the Federal Food and Drug Administration approves drugs and has been sluggish in approving AIDS-related drugs; it is perceived as allowing bureaucracy to get in the way of saving or prolonging lives (*Newsweek* 1988b). In Ocotber 1988, ACT NOW organized a conference, teach-in, rally, and day of civil disobedience in Washington, DC, to "seize control of the FDA" (Okie 1988; Connolly and Raine 1988). The Reagan and Bush administrations have been notoriously inattentive to the AIDS epidemic. Reagan first mentioned AIDS publicly at a time when over 36,000 people had already been diagnosed and over 20,000 had died from the disease. While subsequently calling AIDS "America's number one health problem," the administration consistently avoided initiating a co-ordinated, adequately financed attack on that problem (see Shilts 1988). Reagan and Bush have become common targets of ACT UP "AIDSgate" signs and T-shirts, of "zaps," of posters charging that "the government has blood on its hands," of disruption and protest during campaign speeches. In this case, specific state institutions and actors are targeted, mostly through conventional protest actions and media-geared actions. In these

cases, it is quite clear who is responsible for needless death and who is controlling resources, and ACT UP functions as a pressure group to protest and effect policy decisions. Here, AIDS politics and gay politics are quite separable and separated.

Similarly, pharmaceutical companies are manifest enemies; they control the price of treatment drugs and make decisions about whether or not to pursue drug development. That drug company decisions are guided by considerations of profit (Eigo *et al*. 1988) is a direct and visible instance of oppression and represents an embodied obstacle to the physical survival of people with AIDS. For example, AZT (azidothymidine, the only drug approved at this writing for treatment of AIDS illnesses) cost $13,000 a year in 1987. Again, ACT UP attacks these targets with pressure tactics: boycotting AZT manufacturer Burroughs-Wellcome, zapping that company and others with civil disobedience actions, publicizing government-drug company relations (Eigo *et al*. 1988). In this example, again, the focus is specifically on issues of relevance to all people with AIDS.

Yet AIDS has also been from the outset a stigma, an illness constructed as a marker of homosexuality, drug abuse, moral deficiencies – stigmas added to those of sexual transmission, terminal disease and, for many, skin color.[4] AIDS has

> come to assume all the features of a traditional morality play: images of cancer and death, of blood and semen, of sex and drugs, of morality and retribution. A whole gallery of folk devils have been introduced – the sex-crazed gay, the dirty drug abuser, the filthy whore, the blood drinking voodoo driven black – side by side with a gallery of "innocents" the hemophiliacs, the blood transfusion "victim," the new born child, even the "heterosexual."
>
> (Plummer 1988: 45)

Associated most commonly with the image of the male homosexual or bisexual AIDS "victim" or "carrier" who is vaguely responsible through deviant behavior for his own demise, AIDS has been appropriated to medicalize moral stances: promiscuity is medically unsafe while monogamy is safe; being a member of certain social groups is dangerous to one's health while being a member of the "general population" is dangerous only when the un-general contaminate it. As Simon Watney (1987: 126) notes, in AIDS "the categories of health and sickness ... meet with those of sex, and the image of homosexuality is reinscribed with connotations of contagion and disease, a subject for medical attention and medical authority."

The construction and reconstruction of boundaries has been, then, an essential aspect of the story of AIDS. The innocent victim is bounded off from the guilty one, pure blood from contaminated, the general population from the AIDS populations, risk groups from those not at risk. Those who span the boundaries arguably become the most threatening: the promiscuous bisexual, the only one who can "account for and absolve the heterosexual majority of any taint of unlawful desire" (Grover 1987: 21) and the prostitute, with her longstanding position as a "vessel" of disease (Grover 1987: 25).

Who achieves this demarcation of boundaries? Who has made AIDS mean what it does? Who is the enemy? Two manifest producers of stigmas appear (in addition to certain public figures who disseminate them): the mass media, on whose television screens and newspaper pages the stigmatized are actually visible, and medical science, which translates the labels into risk-group categories. ACT UP thus challenges the medical establishment, largely by undetermining the expertise claimed by them. Activists keep up to date on and publicize underground and foreign treatments (e.g., Eigo *et al.* 1988), sell illegal treatment drugs publicly, yell the names of known AIDS-illness drugs in front of the FDA ("Show them we know" the organizer calls). They wear lab coats and prepare a "guerilla slide show" in which they plan to slip slides saying "He's lying" and "This is voodoo epidemiology" into an audio-visual presentation by a health commissioner.

ACT UP also sets up challenges to the media. An ongoing San Francisco battle had ACT UP shutting down production and members negotiating with producers over the script of an NBC drama, "Midnight Caller." In that script a bisexual man with AIDS purposely infects others and is shot and killed in the end by one of his female partners. It was objected to by ACT UP members as playing on "the great fear of the "killer queer"[5] and implying that, as an ACT UP representative put it, "basically it's justifiable to kill a person with AIDS" (Ford 1988). A similar response has been discussed for the San Francisco filming of Randy Shilts's *And the Band Played On*, a controversial history of the American AIDS epidemic. The media are usually treated by ACT UP as allies in the public relations operation of garnering coverage. As one New Yorker put it (October 1988), "the media aren't the enemy, the media are manipulated by the enemy, and we can manipulate them too." When actively involved in the labelling of people with AIDS as murderers, however, the media become the enemies to be fought. This ambivalence makes sense: the media, as the institutional mechanism through which normalization is most effectively disseminated, are both a visible enemy and a neccessary link to a more abstract form of domination.[6]

The question of who is behind the generation and acceptance of stigmas, though, for the most part doesn't get asked as activists plan and argue, perhaps because the answer is experienced daily: everyone and no one. No one actually does it and everyone participates in it – your family and your neighbors as well as the blatant bigots far away. It's a process that appears usually as natural, as not-a-process.

PLAYING WITH LABELS, CROSSING THE BOUNDARIES

Fighting this largely hidden process calls for different kinds of strategies, mostly in the realm of symbols. Examining the symbolic maneuverings of ACT UP, we can begin to see how fighting the process calls for particular strategies. ACT UP's general strategy is to take a symbol or phase used to oppress and invert it. For example, ACT UP makes explicit challenges, guided by other AIDS activists and particularly PWAs, on the kind of language used to discuss AIDS. In place of the "AIDS victims" they speak of "people with AIDS" or "people living with AIDS." In place of "risk groups" they insert the category of "risk practices." They talk about blood and semen rather than "bodily fluids" and they challenge the exclusionary use of "general population" (see Grover 1987).

The strategy runs much deeper than speech, however. The visual symbol most widely publicized by American AIDS activists – "SILENCE-=DEATH" written in bold white-on-black letters beneath a pink triangle, the Nazi emblem for homosexuals later co-opted by the gay movement – provides a snapshot look at this process. Here, ACT UP takes a symbol used to mark people for death and reclaims it. They reclaim, in fact, control over defining a cause of death; the banner connects gay action to gay survival, on the one hand, and homophobia to death from AIDS, on the other. ACT UP's common death spectacles repeat the inversion. In AIDS commentary death is used in a number of ways (Gilman 1987); it is either a punishment (the image of the withered, guilty victim), an individual tragedy (the image of the lonely, abandoned dying), or a weapon (the image of the irresponsible "killer queer"). A "die in," in which activists draw police-style chalk outlines around each other's "dead" bodies, gives death another meaning by shifting the responsibility: these are deaths likened to murders, victims not of their own "deviance" but shot down by the people controlling the definition and enforcement of normality. You have told us what our deaths mean, their actions say, now we who are actually dying will show you what they mean.

A similar shift of responsibility takes place around the symbol of blood. In popular discussions blood is talked about in terms of "purity" and a benevolent medical establishment working to keep "bad blood" out of the nation's blood supply. In many ACT UP activists, "blood" is splattered on T-shirts (San Francisco, October 3, 1988) or doctor's uniforms (Washington, DC, October 11, 1988). Members want to shoot it out of squirt guns, blood-balloon it onto buidings, write "test this" with it on walls ("Creative Actions" workshop, Washington, DC, October 8, 1988). Here, on one level, they use the established discourse of purity against its users as an angry weapon: "infected" blood is everywhere. On another level, though, the frame is shifted from purity (in which the blood

supply is "victimized") to crime (in which PWAs are victimized). The blood becomes evidence not of infection, but of murder; the activists are blood-splattered victims, as was made explicit in posters orginally directed at Mayor Koch in New York and later translated into an indictment of the federal government. "The government has blood on its hands" the sign says, "One AIDS death every half hour." Between the two phrases is the print of a large, bloody hand. In a San Francisco rally against Rep. William Dannemeyer's Proposition 102 (October 3, 1988), which would have required by law that doctors report those infected and those "suspected" of infection, require testing at the request of doctors, employers or insurers, and eliminate confidential testing. ACT UP carried a "Dannemeyer Vampire" puppet. The vampire, a big ugly head on a stick, with black cape and blood pouring from its fangs, was stabbed with a stake later in the action. Here, ACT UP activates another popular code in which blood has meaning – the gore of horror movies – and reframes blood testing as blood sucking. It's not the blood itself that's monstrous, but the vampire who would take it. By changing the meaning of blood, ACT UP activists dispute the "ownership" of blood; more importantly, they call attention to the consequences of the labels of "bad" blood and "purity" and implicate those accepting the labels in the continuation of the AIDS epidemic.

Boundary-crossing, though tactically similar, goes on the offensive while inversions are essentially reactive. The spectacle of infiltration and revelation runs through real and fantasized ACT UP actions. Members speak of putting subversive messages in food or in the pockets of suit jackets, of writing messages on lawns with weed killer, of covering the Washington monument with a giant condom, of replacing (heterosexual) bar ashtrays with condom-shaped ashtrays. They place stickers saying "Touched by a person with AIDS" in phone booths and stage a mock presidential inauguration through the San Francisco streets during rush hour (January 1989). The idea, as one activist put it, is to "occupy a space that's not supposed to be yours," to usurp public spaces. San Francisco's underground graffiti group, specializing in "redecorating" targeted spaces, sums up the principle in its humorous acronym. TAN-TRUM: Take Action Now To Really Upset the Masses.

The ideas that charge brainstorming sessions and the eventual choices for visual and theatrical activity at actions are not arbitrary. The selections are revealing. Spaces and objects are chosen that are especially American (that is, middle American – lawns, cocktail parties, baseball games, patriotic symbols, suits) and presumably "safe" from the twin "threats" of homosexuality and disease. ACT UP here seizes control of symbols that traditionally exclude gay people or render them invisible, and take them over, endowing them with messages about AIDS; they reclaim them, as they do the pink triangle, and *make them mean* differently. In so doing, they attempt to expose the system of domination from which they reclaim meanings and implicate the entire system in the spread of AIDS.

It is important to notice that ACT UP's identity-oriented actions often revolve around boundary-crossing and label disruption. These are strategies for which these mostly white, middle-class gay people are particularly equipped, largely because their stigma is often invisible unlike, for example, the stigmatized person of color. They can draw on a knowledge of mainstream culture born of participation rather than exclusion and, thus, a knowledge of how to disrupt it using its own vocabulary. Here the particular cultural resources of ACT UP's membeship become important; they are resources that other movements (and gay people from other races or classes) may not have to the same degree or may not be able to use without considerable risk.

Gay campiness, raunchy safe-sex songs in front of the Department of Health and Human Services, straight-looking men in skirts wearing "Fuck Me Safe" T-shirts (Washington, DC, October 1988), lesbians and gay men staging "kiss-ins," a general outrageousness that "keeps the edge" – these actions simultaneously accept the gay label, build a positive gay identity, challenge the conventional "deviant" label, connect stigmatization to AIDS deaths, and challenge the very process of categorization. This is the power of the pink triangle and

"SILENCE=DEATH"; the building of an identity is linked with the resistance of a stigma as the key to stopping the AIDS epidemic. "We are everywhere," says a sign at a DC ACT NOW rally, a sign common at gay political demonstrations, and the noisy expressions of collective anger and identity add up to the same claim. Here, the gay "we" and the AIDS "we" are melded; the destablizing effect of the suddenly revealed homosexual is joined with the fear that suddenly no space is safe from AIDS. A chant at several San Francisco protests captures the link between asserting an identity and challenging the labels: "We're fags and dykes" the activists chant, "and we're here to stay." Meaning: we are what you say we are, and we're not what you say we are. "We're here," they chant, "We're queer, and we're not going shopping."

What exactly is being challenged in these symbolic inversions? Certainly, in symbols like the Dannemeyer vampire and the bloody hand attributed to the government, the old and consistent enemy, the state, is mixed in; but it isn't exclusive. ACT UP disrupts symbolic representation, heeding the call to "campaign and organize in order to enter the amphitheater of AIDS commentary effectively and unapologetically on our own terms" (Watney 1987: 54). It does so, moreover, often through symbols that are not tied to the state but to "mainstream" American culture. In the case of inversions, AIDS and gay labels are not necessarily linked: any oppressive marker is taken over. In the case of boundary-disruption, AIDS and gay labels are connected; the fear of gay people and the fear of AIDS, now linked in the normalization process, are used to call attention to themselves. In both cases, the *process* of stigmatization, by which symbols become markers of abnormality and the basis for decisions about "correcting" the abnormal, is contested.

STRATEGIES AND OBSTACLES REVISITED

The mix of strategies, then, can be seen in terms of the visibility of enemies. More familiar, instrumental pressure-group strategies attempt to change the distribution of resources by attacking those visibly controlling distribution. Identity-forming strategies are particularly crucial and problematic when the struggle is in part against a society rather than a visible oppressor. Label disruption – contained in identity-forming strategies, and the core of symbolic strategies – is a particular operation on the cultural field. It is made necessary by a form of domination that operates through abstractions, through symbols that mark off the normal. (I am not suggesting, of course, that these are discrete types in concrete actions; actions are always mixed exactly because the forms of domination are simultaneous.)

We can also make sense of ACT UP's internal obstacles through this lens. It's not surprising that the qustion of audience becomes a difficult one to address. First of all, the audience often is the group itself when identity formation becomes a key part of struggle. Yet at the same time, we have seen that identity struggles involve pushing at the very labels on which they're based, and here the audience is the entire society. Actions are thus often founded on a confusion of audiences. More commonly, the question of audience is simply lost because the underlying target of action is the normalization process. While it might be more "rational" for ACT UP activists to try to spell out the particular audience each time they design an action, the struggle in which they are involved makes the particularity of an audience difficult to see. When stigmatization is being protested, the audience is the undifferentiated society – that is, audience and enemy are lumped together, and neither is concretely graspable.

Understanding that ACT UP is attacking this particular form of domination, we can also see why ACT UP is caught between the association and dissociation of AIDS politics from gay politics. Clearly, PWAs and gay people are both subject to the stigmatization process; this process, as it informs and supports reponses to AIDS, has become literally lethal for PWAs, gay and non-gay, and dangerous for those labelled as "risk group" members, gay men (and often by an odd extension, lesbians), drug users, prostitutes, blacks, and Hispanics. Socially organized labels that, before AIDS, were used

to oppress, are joined with the label of "AIDS victim." This form of domination is *experienced* by ACT UP members as a continuous one. AIDS is a gay disease because AIDS has been made to attribute viral disease to sexual deviance. Separating AIDS politics from gay politics would be to give up the fight against normalization.

Yet joining the two politics poses the risk of losing the fight in that it confirms the very connection it attempts to dispel. This is a familiar dilemma, as Steve Epstein (1987: 19) points out, and one that is not at all limited to the gay movement: "How do you protest a socially imposed categorization, except by organizing around the category?" Organizing around a resisted label, in that it involves an initial acceptance of the label (and, in identity-oriented movements, a celebration of it), can tend to reify the label. Identity politics thus contain a danger played out here: "If there is perceived to be such a thing as a 'homosexual person,' then it is only a small step to the conclusion that there is such a thing as a 'homosexual disease,' itself the peculiar consequence of the 'homosexual lifestyle'" (Epstein 1987: 48). The familiarity of the dilemma, though, should not obscure its significance. This is a dilemma attributable neither simply to the random course of AIDS nor to mistakes on the part of activists, but to the form of domination to which social movements respond.

In this light, it's not surprising that ACT UP has difficulty including non-gays and forming coalitions. In some ways, ACT UP is driven towards inclusiveness since AIDS is affecting other populations and since the fight includes more broad-based stuggles over resources. But, as we have seen, resistance to labelling involves accepting the label but redefining it, taking it over. Group identity actions are bound up with this resistance. This drives ACT UP strongly away from inclusiveness. The difficulty in walking these lines – between confirming and rejecting the connection between gay people and AIDS, between including and excluding non-gays – is built into the struggle against normalization in which ACT UP is involved.

BODIES AND THEORIES

I have argued that ACT UP responds to the script of the AIDS plague by undermining that script, resisting the labelling through which contemporary domination is often effectively achieved. This seems to be missed by most observers of AIDS, who interpret the politics of AIDS on the model of conventional politics. Randy Shilt's 1988 best-seller, for example, ignores the development of grassroots AIDS activism even in its updating epilogue. AIDS serves as a particularly vivid case of disputed scripts in American politics in that the epidemic of disease, as others have noted, has occurred simultaneously with an "epidemic of significa-tion". AIDS exists "at a point where many entrenched narratives intersect, each with its own problematic and context in which AIDS acquires meaning" (Treichler 1987: 42, 63). ACT UP illustrates this, treating the struggle over the narratives opened and exposed by AIDS as potentially life-saving.

ACT UP also illustrates major effects of an historical shift. If, as I've proposed in drawing on Foucault, domination has gradually come to operate less in the form of state and institutional oppression and more in the form of disembodied and ubiquitous processes, it is hardly surprising that diseased bodies become a focal point of both oppression and resist-ance. As the enemy becomes increasingly disembodied, the body of the dominated – in this case, primarily the diseased, gay male body – becomes increasingly central. The AIDS epidemic itself fits this process so well as to make it seem almost inevitable: the terror of the disease is that it is an enemy you cannot see, and, like the labels put to use in normalizing power, it is spread invisibly. AIDS activism in part struggles against this disem-bodied type of power by giving that body – its death, its blood, its sexuality – new, resistant meanings. The plague script meets here with the script of new social movements.

But what does this tell us about theorizing new social movements? First, it calls into ques-on the value of "newness" as a reified category analysis. In suggesting that the history of mies and types of domination is central to understanding ACT UP, this study points to a gradual shift rather than a radical break in movement activity; "newness" militates towards a focus on a moment (the 1960s) rather than a history that reaches back into, for example, the eighteenth and nineteenth cen-turies (as in the historical transformation that Foucault describes). It obscures what may be instructive continuities across time. Secondly, this study points towards ways of distinguishing *among* contemporary movements. To assert that ACT UP exemplifies contemporary move-ments would clearly be to overstate the case; rather, this analysis demonstrates the insuffi-ciency of analyzing different movements as like phenomena simply because of a shared cultural and identity focus. Operating on the "cultural field" means something more specific than focussing on problems that "deal directly with private life" (Touraine 1985: 779) or even targeting and using narrative and artistic repre-sentation. ACT UP's cultural strategies reclaim and resignify oppressive markers. Orienting actions towards identity formation means something more specific than "defend[ing] spaces for the creation of new identities and solidarities" (Cohen 1985: 685). Identity asser-tions in ACT UP point up boundaries, using the fear of the abnormal against the fearful. These are specific operations that may be shared by other contemporary social movements – those subject to stigmatization, for example, and which are also in a position to "shock" – and not by others. Stigmatization, moreover, may take different forms and give rise to different types of movement activity. Whether, in Shea Stadium or at the FDA, discerning the types of enemies to whom movements are responding is a task for analysts of social movements as well as for activists within them.

NOTES

1 Unless otherwise noted, quotations and descrip-tions of actions are drawn from the author's field-notes from September 1988 through Jan-uary 1989 (ACT UP weekly general meetings; Media Committee weekly meetings and activ-ities, and other committee meetings; ACT NOW AIDS Activisim Conference October 8–11,

1988, Washington, DC; ACT UP/San Francisco actions). For a sampling of published reporting on ACT UP, see Green 1989, *US News & World Report* 1989; Linebarger 1989; Tuller 1988; Ford 1988; Johnson 1988; Okie 1988; Connolly and Raine 1988; Morgan 1988.

2 By way of comparison, it's important to notice that most AIDS politics does not operate according to this description, but according to a more conventional political model. "Most AIDS politicking," as Dennis Altman (1986: 105) describes it, "has involved the lobbying of federal, state and local governments ... [This] has meant dependence upon professional leaders able to talk the language of politicians and bureaucrats."

3 Why so many women are attracted to the AIDS movement is an interesting question to which I've accumulated only brief, speculative answers: some because their friends are dying, some because of a history of working in health politics through women's health issues. One woman suggested an answer that seems to run deeper than along the lines suggested by this study. Oppression through AIDS, she said, is the most severe end of a spectrum of violence to which "all gay people are subject." For her, while silence might not mean literal death, it would mean a symbolic death (not being allowed to live as "me").

4 The activist response of black communities to AIDS has, though, differed greatly from that in gay communities, and this merits careful examination not allowed for here. The lag in black and Hispanic activism has been attributed by one observer to a combination of lack of material and political resources (minority PWAs are disproportionately lower class or underclass) and "denial" on the part of minority leadership (because of the dangers posed by feeding racism with the stigma of disease, and because of strong anti-gay sentiments in black and Hispanic cultures); see Goldstein 1987.

5 The figure of the irresponsible killer-victim was popularized by Randy Shilts in the character of Gaetan Dugas, an airline steward Shilts labels "Patient Zero." Shilts charges that Dugas knowingly spread the virus through the continent. For a critique of Shilts, see Crimp 1987b.

6 The mass media clearly play a very central and complex role in contemporary activism (see, for example, Gitlin 1980), an examination of which is unfortunately beyond the scope of this paper. It's quite likely that much of the escalation of symbols comes from the need by social movements to compete for attention in an increasingly message-dense environment; this does not explain the content of those symbols, through, nor does it explain why the media at times become explicit enemies.

REFERENCES

ACT UP/San Francisco (1988a), "Our Goals and Demands," informational flyer.

—— (1988b), "The AIDS Treatment Advocacy Project," proposal drafted for ACT NOW Conference. September.

——(1989) "ACT UP PISD Caucus," informational flyer.

Altman, Dennis (1986), *AIDS in the Mind of America*, (Garden City, NY: Anchor Press/Doubleday).

Burawoy, Michael (1989), "The Extended Case Method," unpublished manuscript.

Cohen, Jean L. (1985), "Strategy or Identity: New Theoretical Paradigms and Contemporary Social Movements," *Social Research* 52: 663–716.

Connolly, Mike and George Raine (1988), "50 AIDS Activists Arrested at FDA," *San Francisco Examiner*, October: 11:A1.

Crimp, Douglas, (ed.) (1987a) *AIDS: Cultural Analysis/Cultural Criticism* (Cambridge, MA: MIT Press).

——(1987b), "How to Have Promiscuity in an Epidemic," pp. 237–71 in Douglas Crimp (ed.), *AIDS: Cultural Analysis/Cultural Criticism*, (Cambridge, MA: MIT Press).

Eder, Klaus (1985), "The New Social Movements: Moral Crusades, Political Pressure Groups, or Social Movements," *Social Research* 52: 869–90.

Eigo, Jim, Mark Harrington, Iris Long, Margaret McCarthy, Stephen Spinella, and Rick Sugden (1988), "FDA Action Handbook," unpublished manuscript prepared for October 11 action at the Food and Drug Administration.

Epstein, Steven (1987), "Gay Politics, Ethnic Identity: The Limits of Social Constructionism," *Socialist Review* 17: 9–54.

Ford, Dave (1988), "Midnight Caller Script Provokes Gay Activists' Ire," *San Francisco Sentinel*, October 21: 4–5.

Foucault, Michel (1979), *Discipline and Punish*, (New York: Vintage Books).

Gilman, Sander (1987), "AIDS and Syphilis: The Iconography of Disease," pp. 87–107 in Douglas Crimp (ed.), *AIDS: Cultural Analysis/Cultural Criticism* (Cambridge, MA: MIT Press).

Gitlin, Todd (1980), *The Whole World Is Watching: Mass Media in the Making of the New Left* (Berkeley, CA: University of California Press).

Goffman, Erving (1963), *Stigma: Notes on the Management of Spoiled Identity* (Englewood Cliffs, NJ: Prentice-Hall, Inc.).

Goldstein, Richard (1987) "AIDS and Race," *Village Voice*, March 10: 23–30.

Green, Jesse (1989), "Shticks and Stones," *7 Days*, February 8: 21–6.

Grover, Jan Zita (1987), "AIDS Keywords,"

pp. 17–30 in Douglas Crimp (ed.), *AIDS Cultural Analysis/Cultural Criticism* (Cambridge, MA: MIT Press).

Habermas, Jürgen (1981), "New Social Movements," *Telos* 49: 33–7.

Jenkins, J. Craig (1981) "Sociopolitical Movements," pp. 81–153 in Samuel Long (ed.), *Handbook of Political Behavior* (New York: Plenum Press).

Johnson, Clarence (1988), "Gays Attack KRON Building," *San Francisco Chronicle*, December 12: A2.

Johnson, Diane and John F. Murray (1988), "AIDS without End," *New York Review of Books*, August 18: 57–63.

Kitschelt, Herbert (1985), "New Social Movements in West Germany and the United States," *Political Power and Social Theory* 5: 273–324.

Kitsuse, John I (1980), "Coming Out All Over: Deviants and the Politics of Social Problems," *Social Problems* 28: 1–13.

Kreisi, Hanspeter (1989), "New Social Movements and the New Class in the Netherlands," *American Journal of Sociology* 94: 1078–116.

Lemert, Edwin (1967), *Human Deviance, Social Problems, and Social Control* (Englewood Cliffs, NJ: Prentice-Hall, Inc.).

Linebarger, Charles (1989), "All the Rage: Angry AIDS Activists Pump up the Volume on Deaf Policy-Makers," *San Francisco Sentinel*, February 23: 3–5.

McAdam, Doug (1982), *Political Process and the Development of Black Insurgency 1930–1970* (Chicago: University of Chicago Press).

McCarthy, John and Mayer Zald (1977), "Resource Mobilization and Social Movements: A Partial Theory," *American Journal of Sociology* 82: 1212–40.

Morgan, Thomas (1988), "AIDS Protesters Temper their Tactics as a Way to Reach the Mainstream," *New York Times*, July 22: A12.

Newsweek (1988a) "Acting Up to Fight AIDS," June 6: 42.

———(1988b), "The Drug-approval Dilemma," November 14: 63.

Oberschall, Anthony (1973), *Social Conflict and Social Movements* (Englewood Cliffs, NJ: Prentice-Hall).

Offe, Claus (1985), "The New Social Movements: Challenging the Boundaries of Institutional Politics," *Social Research* 52: 817–68.

Okie, Susan (1988), "AIDS Coalition Targets FDA for Demonstration," *The Washington Post*, October 11: A4.

Omi, Michael, and Howard Winant (1986), *Racial Formation in the United States* (New York: Routledge and Kegan Paul).

Plummer, Ken (1988), "Organizing AIDS," in Peter Aggleton and Hilary Homans (eds), *Social Aspects of AIDS* (London: The Falmer Press).

Shilts, Randy (1988), *And the Band Played On: Politics, People and the AIDS Epidemic* (New York: Penguin Books).

Smelser, Neil (1963), *Theory of Collective Behavior* (New York: The Free Press).

Sontag, Susan (1988) "AIDS and its Metaphors," *New York Review of Books*, October 27: 89–99.

Tilly, Charles (1978), *From Mobilization to Revolution* (Reading, MA: Addison-Wesley).

Touraine, Alain (1985), An Introduction to the Study of Social Movements," *Social Research* 52: 749–87.

Treichler, Paula A. (1987), "AIDS, Homophobia, and Biomedical Discourse: An Epidemic of Signification," pp. 31–70 in Douglas Crimp (ed.), *AIDS: Cultural Analysis/Cultural Criticism* (Cambridge, MA: MIT Press).

Tuller, David (1988), "AIDS Protesters Showing Signs of Movement's New Miltancy," *San Francisco Chronicle*, October 27: A4.

US News and World Report (1989), "The Artists' Diagnosis," March 27: 62–70.

Watney, Simon (1987), *Policing Desire: Pornography, AIDS and the Media* (Minneapolis, MN: University of Minnesota Press).

VERTA TAYLOR and NANCY E. WHITTIER

"Collective Identity in Social Movement Communities: Lesbian Feminist Mobilization"

from Aldon D. Morris and Carol M. Mueller (eds), *Frontiers in Social Movement Theory* (New Haven, CT: Yale University Press, 1992): 104–29

Understanding the relationship between group consciousness and collective action has been a major focus of social science resarch (Morris 1990). The resource mobilization and political process perspectives, in contrast to earlier microlevel analyses, have shifted attention to the macrolevel, de-emphasizing group grievances and focusing instead on the external political processes and internal organizational dynamics that influence the rise and course of movements (Rule and Tilly 1972; Oberschall 1973; McCarthy and Zald 1973, 1977; Gamson 1975; Jenkins and Perrow 1977; Schwartz 1976; Tilly 1978; McAdam 1982; Jenkins 1983; Morris 1984). But the resource mobilization and political process theories cannot explain how structural inequality gets translated into subjectively experienced discontent (Fireman and Gamson 1979; Ferree and Miller 1985; Snow *et al.* 1986; Klandermans 1984; Klandermans and Tarrow 1988). In a recent review of the field, McAdam, McCarthy and Zald (1988) respond by offering the concept of the micromobilization context to characterize the link between the macrolevel and microlevel processes that generate collective action. Drawing from a wide range of research documenting the importance of preexisting group ties for movement formation, they view informal networks held together by strong bonds as the "basic building blocks" of social movements. Still missing, however, is an understanding of the way these networks transform their members into political actors.

European analyses of recent social movements, loosely grouped under the rubric "new social movement theory," suggest that a key concept that allows us to understand this proc-

ess is collective identity (Pizzorno 1978; Boggs 1986; Cohen 1985; Melucci 1985, 1989; Touraine 1985; B. Epstein 1990). Collective identity is the shared definition of a group that derives from members' common interests, experiences, and solidarity. For new social movement theorists, political organizing around a common identity is what distinguishes recent social movements in Europe and the United States from the more class-based movements of the past (Kauffman 1990). It is our view, based on existing scholarship (Fantasia 1988; Mueller 1990; Rupp and Taylor 1990; Whittier 1991), that identity construction processes are crucial to grievance interpretation in all forms of collective action, not just in the so-called new movements. Despite the centrality of collective identity to new social movement theory, no one has dissected the way that constituencies involved in defending their rights develop politicized group identities.

In this chapter, we present a framework for analyzing the construction of collective identity in social movements. The framework is grounded in exploratory research on the contemporary lesbian feminist movement in the United States. Drawing from Gerson and Peiss' (1985) model for analyzing gender relations, we offer a conceptual bridge linking theoretical approaches in the symbolic interactionist tradition with existing theory in social movements. Our aim is to provide a definition of collective identity that is broad enough to encompass mobilizations ranging from those based on race, gender, ethnicity, and sexuality to constituencies organized around more focused visions.

After discussing the data sources, we trace the evolution of lesbian feminism in the early

1970s out of the radical branch of the modern women's movement and analyze lesbian feminism as a social movement community. Substantively, our aim is to demonstrate that lesbian feminist communities sustain a collective identity that encourages women to engage in a wide range of social and political actions that challenge the dominant system. Theoretically, we use this case to present an analytical definition of the concept of collective identity. Finally, we conclude by arguing that the existence of lesbian feminist communities challenges the popular perception that feminists have withdrawn from the battle and the scholarly view that organizing around identity directs attention away from challenges to institutionalized power structures (B. Epstein 1990).

We have used two main sources of data: published primary materials and interviews with participants in lesbian feminist communities. The written sources include books, periodicals, and narratives by community members (Johnston 1973; Koedt *et al.* 1973; Daly 1978; Baetz 1980; Cruikshank 1980; Stanley and Wolfe 1980; Moraga and Anzaldua 1981; Beck 1980; Smith 1983; Daly and Caputi 1987; Frye 1983; Grahn 1984; Johnson 1987) and newsletters, position papers and other documents from lesbian feminist organizations. We have also incorporated secondary data from histories of the women's movement and ethnographies of lesbian communities (Hole and Levine 1971; Barnhart 1975; Ponse 1978; Lewis 1979; Wolf 1979; Krieger 1983; Davis and Kennedy 1986; Lockard 1986; Lord, unpublished; Echols 1989).

In addition, we have conducted twenty-one interviews with lesbian feminists who served as informants about their communities, which included Boston, Provincetown, and the rural Berkshire region of Massachusetts; Portland, Maine; Washington, DC; New York City; Key West and St Petersburg, Florida; Columbus, Yellow Springs, Cleveland, and Cincinnati, Ohio; Minneapolis; Chicago; Denver; Atlanta; and Charlotte, North Carolina. The informants range in age from 21 to 68; sixteen are white, four are black, and one is Hispanic; the majority are from middle-class backgrounds. They are employed as professionals or semi-professionals, small-business owners, students, and blue-collar workers. Interviewees were recruited through snowballing procedures and announcements and notices posted at lesbian events. The in-depth interviews were open-ended and semistructured, lasting from one to three hours, and were tape-recorded and transcribed. The analysis also draws on our experiences as members of the larger community.

Since this work focuses primarily on lesbian feminist activism in the midwestern and eastern regions of the United States, we regard our conclusions as exploratory and generalizable primarily to this sector of the larger lesbian community. It is important to keep in mind that not all lesbians are associated with the communities described here.

THE LESBIAN FEMINIST SOCIAL MOVEMENT COMMUNITY

Analyzing the historical evolution of organizational forms in the American women's movement, Buechler (1990) proposes the concept of a social movement community to expand our understanding of the variety of forms of collective action. Buechler's concept underscores the importance to mobilization of informal networks, decentralized structures, and alternative institutions. But, like most work in the resource mobilization tradition, it overlooks the values and symbolic understandings created by discontented groups in the course of struggling to achieve change (Lofland 1985).

Here it is useful to turn to recent literature on lesbian communities that emphasizes the cultural components of lesbian activism, specifically the development of counter-institutions, a politicized group identity, shared norms, values, and symbolic forms of resistance (Wolf 1979; Krieger 1983; Lockard 1986; Davis and Kennedy 1986; Phelan 1989; Esterberg 1990). From this perspective, we expand on Buechler's model by defining a social movement community as a network of individuals and groups loosely linked through an institutional base, multiple goals and actions, and a collective identity that affirms members' common interests in opposition to dominant groups.

We describe lesbian feminism as a social movement community that operates at the national level through connections among local comunities in the decentralized, segmented, and reticulated structure described by Gerlach and Hine (1970). Like other new social movements, the lesbian feminist movement does not mobilize through formal social movement organizations. Rather, structurally the movement is composed of what Melucci (1989) terms "submerged networks" propelled by constantly shifting forms of resistance that include alternative symbolic systems as well as new forms of political struggle and participation (Emberley and Landry 1989). Although participants use different labels to describe the movement, we are interested here in the segment of the contemporary women's movement characterized as "cultural feminism" (Ferree and Hess 1985; Echols 1989) or "lesbian feminism" (Adam 1987; Phelan 1989). We prefer "lesbian feminism" for three reasons. It is the label most often used in movement writings, although participants also refer to the "women's community," "feminist community," and "lesbian community." Second, it locates the origins of this community in the contemporary women's movement. Finally, the term makes explicit the vital role of lesbians in the women's movement. The term "cultural feminism" erases the participation of lesbians and obscures the fact that a great deal of the current criticism leveled at cultural feminism is, in reality, directed at lesbian feminism.

Scholars have depicted the women's movement that blossomed in the 1960s and 1970s as having two segments, a women's rights or liberal branch and a women's liberation or radical branch (Freeman 1975). The liberal branch consisted primarily of national-level, hierarchically organized, formal organizations like the National Organization for Women (NOW) that used institutionalized legal tactics to pursue equal rights (Gelb and Palley 1982). The radical branch emerged in the late 1960s out of the civil rights and New Left movements and formed a decentralized network of primarily local, autonomous groups lacking formal organization and using flamboyant and disruptive tactics to pursue fundamental transformation of patriarchal structures and values (Hole and Levine 1971; Evans 1979). It is impossible to comprehend contemporary lesbian feminism without locating it in the radical feminist tradition.

Ideologically and strategically, radical feminism opposed liberalism, pursued social transformation through the creation of alternative nonhierarchical institutions and forms of organization intended to prefigure a utopian feminist society, held gender oppression to be primary and the model of all other forms of oppression, and emphasized women's commonality as a sex-class through consciousness-raising. Although it coalesced around common issues such as rape, battering, and abortion, radical feminism was never monolithic (Jaggar and Struhl 1978; Ferree and Hess 1985). By the mid-1970s, radical feminism confronted an increasingly conservative and inhospitable social climate and was fraught with conflict over differences of sexuality, race, and class (Taylor 1989a). Recent scholarship argues that the most important disputes focused on the question of lesbianism (Echols 1989; Ryan 1989).

Conflict between lesbian and heterosexual feminists originated in the early 1970s. Although women who love other women have always been among those who participated in the feminist struggle, it was not until the emergence of the gay liberation movement that lesbians demanded recognition and support from the women's movement. Instead they encountered overt hostility in both the liberal and radical branches. The founder of NOW, Betty Friedan, for example, dismissed lesbianism as the "lavender herring" of the movement. Since charges of lebianism have often been used to discredit women who challenge traditional roles (Rupp 1989; Schneider 1986), feminists sought to avoid public admission that there were, in fact, lesbians in their ranks.

Echols (1989) traces the beginning of lesbian feminism to 1971 with the founding of the Furies in Washington, DC. This was the first separate lesbian feminist group, and others formed shortly after in New York, Boston, Chicago, San Francisco, and other urban localities around the country. The Furies is significant because it included women such as Charlotte Bunch, Rita Mae Brown, and Colletta Reid who, along with Ti-Grace Atkinson, ex-president of the New York Chapter of NOW and founder of the Feminists, articulated the position that would lay the foundation for lesbian feminism (Hole and Levine 1971; Atkinson 1974; Bunch 1986). They advocated lesbian separatism and recast lesbianism as a political strategy that was the logical outcome of feminism, the quintessential expression of the "personal as political." As a result, heterosexual feminists found themselves increasingly on the defensive.

If early radical feminism was driven by the belief that women are more alike than different, then the fissures that beset radical feminism in the mid-1970s were about clarifying the differences – on the basis of race, class, and ethnicity as well as sexual identity – among the "group called women" (Cassell 1977). Recent scholarship argues that such conflict ultimately led to the demise of radical feminism and the rise of what its critics have called "cultural feminism," leaving liberal feminism in control of the women's movement (Echols 1989; Ryan 1989).

We agree with the dominant view that disputes over sexuality, class, and race contributed to the decline of the radical feminist branch of the movement. We do not, however, agree that radical feminism was replaced by a cultural haven for women who have withdrawn from the battle (Snitow, Stansell, and Thompson 1983; Vance 1984; Echols 1989). Rather, we hold that radical feminism gave way to a new cycle of feminist activism sustained by lesbian feminist communities. These communities socialize members into a collective oppositional consciousness that channels women into a variety of actions geared toward personal, social, and political change.

Although no research has been undertaken to document the extent of lesbian communities across the nation, existing work has focused on a number of different localities (e.g. Barnhart's (1975) ethnography of Portland, Wolf's [1979] study of San Francisco, Krieger's [1983] ethnography of a midwestern community, Lockard's [1986] description of a south-western community). White (1980) describes the major trend-setting centers of the gay and lesbian movement as Boston, Washington, San Francisco, and New York. Although our analysis is exploratory and based on only seventeen communities, our data suggest that developments in the major cities are reflected throughout the United States in urban areas as well as in smaller communities with major colleges and universities.

COLLECTIVE IDENTITY: BOUNDARIES, CONSCIOUSNESS, AND NEGOTIATION

The study of identity in sociology has been approached at the individual and systemic levels as well as in both structural and more dynamic social constructionist terms (Weigert et al. 1986). New social movement theorists, in particular Pizzorno (1978), Boggs (1986), Melucci (1985, 1989), Offe (1985), and Touraine (1985), take the politics of personal transformation as one of their central theoretical problematics, which is why these approaches are sometimes referred to as "identity-oriented paradigms" (Cohen 1985). Sometimes labeled postmodernist, new social movement perspectives are social constructionist paradigms (B. Epstein 1990). From this standpoint, collective political actors do not exist *de facto* by virtue of individuals sharing a common structural location; they are created in the course of social movement activity. To understand any politicized identity community, it is necessary to analyze the social and political struggle that created the identity.

In some ways, the most apparent feature of the new movements has been a vision of power as operating at different levels so that collective self-transformation is itself a major strategy of political change. Reviewing work in the new social movement tradition suggests three elements of collective identity. First, individuals see themselves as part of a group when some shared characteristic becomes salient and is defined as important. For Touraine (1985) and Melucci (1989), this sense of "we" is evidence of an increasingly fragmented and pluralistic social reality that is, in part, a result of the new movements. A crucial characteristic of the movements of the 1970s and 1980s has been the advocacy of new group understandings, self-conceptions, ways of thinking, and cultural categories. In Touraine's model, it is an awareness of how the group's interests conflict with the interests of its adversaries, the adoption of a critical picture of the culture as a whole, and the recognition of the broad stakes of the conflict that differentiate contemporary movements from classical ones. Thus, the second component of collective identity is what Cohen (1985) terms "consciousness." Consistent with the vision of the movements themselves, Melucci defines a movement's "cognitive frameworks" broadly to include not only political consciousness and relational networks but its "goals, means, and environment of action" (1989: 35). Finally, for new social movement theorists, the concept of collective identity implies direct opposition to the dominant order. Melucci holds that social movements build "submerged networks" of political culture that are interwoven with everyday life and provide new expressions of identity that challenge dominant representations (1989: 35). In essence, as Pizzorno (1978) suggests, the purposeful and expressive disclosure to others of one's subjective feelings, desires, and experiences – or social identity – for the purpose of gaining recognition and influence is collective action.

Our framework draws from feminist theoretical approaches in the symbolic interactionist tradition (Gerson and Peiss 1985; Margolis 1985; West and Zimmerman 1987; Chafetz 1988). These formulations differ from structural and other social psychological approaches that tend to reify gender as a role category or trait of individuals. Instead, they view gender hierarchy as constantly created through displays and interactions governed by gender-normative behaviour that comes to be perceived as natural and normal. Gerson and Peiss (1985) offer a model for understanding how gender inequality is reproduced and maintained through social interaction. Although they recognize the social change potential for the model, they do not address this aspect systematically.

Building on their work, we propose three factors as analytical tools for understanding the construction of collective identity in social movements. The concept of *boundaries* refers to

the social, psychological, and physical structures that establish differences between a challenging group and dominant groups. *Consciousness* consists of the interpretive frameworks that emerge out of a challenging group's struggle to define and realize its interests. *Negotiation* encompasses the symbols and everyday actions subordinate groups use to resist and restructure existing systems of domination. We offer this scheme as a way of analyzing the creation of collective identity as an ongoing process in all social movements struggling to overturn existing systems of domination.

Boundaries

Boundaries mark the social territories of group relations by highlighting differences between activists and the web of others in the contested social world. Of course, it is usually the dominant group that erects social, political, economic, and cultural boundaries to accentuate the differences between itself and minority populations. Paradoxically, however, for groups organizing to pursue collective ends, the process of asserting "who we are" often involves a kind of reverse affirmation of the characteristics attributed to it by the larger society. Boundary markers are, therefore, central to the formation of collective identity because they promote a heightened awareness of a group's commonalities and frame interaction between members of the in-group and the out-group.

For any subordinate group, the construction of positive identity requires both a withdrawal from the values and structures of the dominant, oppressive society and the creation of new self-affirming values and structures. Newer approaches to the study of ethnic mobilization define ethnicity not in essentialist terms but in relation to socially and politically constructed boundaries that differentiate ethnic populations (Barth 1969; Olzak 1983). This is a useful way of understanding the commonalities that develop among members of any socially recognized group or category organized around a shared characteristic. It underscores the extent to which differentiation and devaluation is a fundamental process in all hierarchical systems and has two advantages over other approaches (Reskin 1988).

First, the concept of boundaries avoids the reification of ascriptive and other differentiating characteristics that are the basis for dominance systems (Reskin 1988); second, it transcends the assumption of group sameness implied by single-factor stratification systems because it allows us to analyze the impact of multiple systems of domination based on race, sex, class, ethnicity, age, sexuality, and other factors (Morris 1990). These distinct hierarchies not only produce differentiation within subordinate groups but affect the permeability of boundaries between the subordinate and dominant groups (Collins 1989; Morris 1990; Zinn 1990).

Boundary markers can vary from geographical, racial, and religious characteristics to more symbolically constructed differences such as social institutions and cultural systems. Our analysis focuses on two types of boundary strategies adopted by lesbian feminists as a means of countering male domination: the creation of separate institutions and the development of a distinct women's culture guided by "female" values.

Alternative institutions were originally conceived by radical feminists both as islands of resistance against patriarchy and as a means to gain power by improving women's lives and enhancing their resources (Taylor 1989a; Echols 1989). Beginning in the early 1970s, radical feminists established separate health centers, rape crisis centers, battered women's shelters, bookstores, publishing and record companies, newspapers, credit unions, and poetry and writing groups. Through the 1980s, feminist institutions proliferated to include recovery groups, business guilds, martial arts groups, restaurants, AIDS projects, spirituality groups, artists' colonies, and groups for women of color, Jewish feminists, disabled women, lesbian mothers, and older women. Some lesbian feminist groups were not entirely autonomous but functioned as separate units or caucuses in existing organizations, such as women's centers and women's studies programs in universities.

As the mass women's movement receded in the 1980s, the liberal branch abandoned protest and unruly tactics in favor of actions geared toward gaining access in the political arena (Rupp and Taylor 1986; Mueller 1987; Echols 1989). An elaborate network of feminist counterinstitutions remained, however, and increasingly were driven by the commitment of lesbian feminists. This is not to say that they were the sole preserve of lesbians. Rather, it is our view that what is described generally as "women's culture" to emphasize its availability to all women has become a predominantly lesbian feminist culture.

A number of national events link local lesbian feminist communities, including the annual five-day Michigan Womyn's Music Festival attended by four thousand to ten thousand women, the National Women's Writers' Conference, and the National Women's Studies Association Conference. In addition, in local and regional events and conferences on the arts, literature, and, in the academic professions, feminist issues proliferated through the 1980s. National newspapers such as *Off Our Backs*, national magazines such as *Outlook*, publishing companies such as Naiad, Persephone, and Kitchen Table Women of Color presses, and a variety of journals and newspapers continue to publicize feminist ideas and activities. In short, throughout the 1980s, as neoconservatism was winning political and intellectual victories, lesbian feminists struggled to build a world apart from male domination.

The second boundary that is central to lesbian feminist identity is the creation of a symbolic system that affirms the culture's idealization of the female and, as a challenge to the misogyny of the dominant society, vilifies the male. Perhaps the strongest thread running through the tapestry of lesbian feminist culture is the belief that women's nature and modes of relating differ fundamentally from men's. For those who hold this position, the set of traits generally perceived as female are egalitarianism, collectivism, an ethic of care, a respect for knowledge derived from experience, pacifism, and cooperation. In contrast, male characteristics are thought to include an emphasis on hierarchy, oppressive individualism, an ethic of individual rights, abstraction, violence, and competition. These gender boundaries are confirmed by a formal body of feminist scholarship (see, e.g., Rich 1976, 1980; Chodorow 1978; Gilligan 1982; Rubin 1984; Collins 1989) as well as in popular writings (see, e.g., Walker 1974; Daly 1978, 1984; Cavin 1985; Dworkin 1981; Johnson 1987). Johnson, for example, characterizes the differences between women and men as based on the contrast between "masculine life-hating values" and "women's life-loving culture" (1987: 226).

Our interviews suggest that the belief that there are fundamental differences between women and men is widely held by individual activists. One lesbian feminist explains that "we've been acculturated into two cultures, the male culture and the female culture. And luckily we've been able to preserve the ways of nurturing by being in this alternative culture."

Because women's standards are deemed superior, it is not surprising that men, including older male children, are often excluded from community events and business establishments. At the Michigan Womyn's Music Festival, for example, male children over the age of 3 are not permitted in the festival area, but must stay at a separate camp. Reversing the common cultural practice of referring to adult women as "girls," it is not unusual for lesbian feminists to refer to men, including gay men, as "boys."

Maintaining an oppositional identity depends upon creating a world apart from the dominant society. The boundaries that are drawn around a group are not entirely a matter of choice. The process of reshaping one's collective world, however, involves the investiture of meaning that goes beyond the objective conditions out of which a group is created. Seen in this way, it is easy to understand how identity politics promotes a kind of cultural endogamy that, paradoxically, erects boundaries within the challenging group, dividing it on the basis of race, class, age, religion, ethnicity, and other factors. When asked to define the lesbian feminist community, one participant highlights this process by stating that "if there is such a thing as a lesboworld, then there are just as many diversities of communities in that world as there are in the heteroworld."

Consciousness

Boundaries locate persons as members of a group, but it is group consciousness that imparts a larger significance to a collectivity. We use the concept of consciousness to refer to the interpretive frameworks that emerge from a group's struggle to define and realize members' common interests in opposition to the dominant order. Although sociologists have focused primarily on class consciousness, Morris (1990) argues that the term *political consciousness* is more useful because it emphasizes that all systems of human domination create opposing interests capable of generating oppositional consciousness. Whatever the term, the important point is that collective actors must attribute their discontent to structural, cultural, or systemic causes rather than to personal failings or individual deviance (Ferree and Miller 1985; Touraine 1985).

Our notion of consciousness builds on the idea of cognitive liberation (McAdam 1982), frames (Snow *et al.* 1986), cognitive frameworks (Melucci 1989), and collective consciousness (Mueller 1987). We see the development of consciousness as an ongoing process in which groups re-evaluate themselves, their subjective experiences, their opportunities, and their shared interests. Consciousness is imparted through a formal body of writings, speeches, and documents. More important, when a movement is successful at creating a collective identity, its interpretive orientations are interwoven with the fabric of everyday life. Consciousness not only provides socially and politically marginalized groups with an understanding of their structural position but establishes new expectations regarding treatment appropriate to their category. Of course, groups can mobilize around a collective consciousness that supports the status quo. Thus, it is only when a group develops an account that challenges dominant understandings that we can use the term *oppositional consciousness* (Morris 1990).

Contemporary lesbian feminist consciousness is not monolithic. But its mainspring is the view that heterosexuality is an institution of patriarchal control and that lesbian relationships are a means of subverting male domination. The relationship between feminism and lesbianism is well summarized by the classic slogan "feminism is the theory and lesbianism is the practice," mentioned by a number of our informants. Arguing that sexism and heterosexism are inextricably intertwined, lesbian feminists in the early 1970s characterized lesbianism as "the rage of all women condensed to the point of explosion" (Radicalesbians 1973: 240) and held that women who choose lesbianism are the vanguard of the women's movement (Birkby *et al.* 1973; Myron and Bunch 1975; Daly 1978, 1984; Frye 1983; Hoagland 1988). The classic rationale for this position, frequently reprinted in newsletters and other lesbian publications, is Ti-Grace Atkinson's analogy: "Can you imagine a Frenchman, serving in the French army from 9 A.M. to 5 P.M., then trotting 'home' to Germany for supper overnight?" (1974: 11).

Despite the common thread running through lesbian feminist consciousness that sexual relationships between women are to be understood in reference to the political structure of male supremacy and male domination, there are two distinct strands of thought about lesbian identity. One position holds that lesbianism is not an essential or biological characteristic but is socially constructed. In a recent analysis of the history of lesbian political consciousness, Phelan (1989) argues that lesbian feminist consciousness emerged and has been driven by a rejection of the liberal view that sexuality is a private or individual matter. A classic exposition of the social constructionist position can be found in Rich's "Compulsory Heterosexuality and Lesbian Existence" (1980), which defines lesbian identity not as sexual but as political. Rich introduces the concept of the "lesbian continuum" to include all women who are woman-identified and who resist patriarchy. By locating lesbianism squarely within the new scholarship on the female world, Rich, like other social constructionists, suggests that sexuality is a matter of choice.

If it is not sexual experience but an emotional and political orientation toward women that defines one as lesbian, then, as the song by Alix Dobkin puts it, "any woman can be a lesbian." Lesbian feminist communities in fact contain women who are oriented toward women emo-

tionally and politically but not sexually. These women are sometimes referred to as "political dykes" or "heterodykes" (Clausen 1990; Smeller, unpublished), and community members think of them as women who "haven't come out yet." Some women who have had both male and female lovers resist being labeled bisexual and cling to a lesbian identity. For example, well-known singer and songwriter Holly Near explains: "I am too closely linked to the political perspective of lesbian feminism . . . it is part of my world view, part of my passion for women and central in my objection to male domination" (1990). The significance of lesbian identity for feminist activists is well summarized by the name of a feminist support group at a major university, Lesbians Who Just Happen to Be Dating Politically-Correct Men.

The second strand of lesbian feminist thought aims to bring sex back into the definition of lesbianism (Treblecot 1979; Califia 1982; Ferguson 1982; Zita 1982; Hollibaugh and Moraga 1983; Rubin 1984; Nestle 1987; Penelope 1990). Criticizing the asexuality of lesbian feminism, Echols suggests that, in contemporary women's communities, "women's sexuality is assumed to be more spiritual than sexual, and considerably less central to their lives than is sexuality to men's" (1984: 60). Putting it more bluntly, sadomasochism advocate Pat Califia characterizes contemporary lesbian feminism as "anti-sex," using the term "vanilla feminism" to dismiss what she charges is a traditionally feminine passive attitude toward sex (1980). These "pro-sex" or "sex radical" writers tend to view sexuality less as a matter of choice and more as an essential characteristic. So, too, do some lesbian separatists, who have little else in common with the sex radicals. Arguing against social constructionism, Penelope (1990) places lesbianism squarely in the sexual arena. She points to the historical presence of women who loved other women sexually and emotionally prior to the nineteenth-century invention of the term *lesbian* and emphasizes that currently there are a variety of ways that women come to call themselves lesbian. In our interviews with lesbian activists, it was not uncommon for women who embraced essentialist notions to engage in biographical reconstruction, reinterpreting all of their prelesbian experiences as evidence of lesbian sexuality.

The emphasis on sexuality calls attention to the unknown numbers of women engaged in same-sex behavior who do not designate themselves lesbian and the enclaves of women who identify as lesbian but have not adopted lesbian feminist ideology and practice. These include lesbians who organize their social lives around gay bars (Nestle 1987), women who remain in the closet, pretending to be heterosexual but having sexual relationships with other women, and women who marry men and have relationships with women on the side. Describing the variousness of the contemporary lesbian experience and the multiple ways women come to call themselves lesbian, one of our interviewees discussed "pc (politically correct) dykes," "heterodykes," "maybelline dykes," "earth crunchy lesbians," "bar dykes," "phys ed dykes," "professional dykes," and "fluffy dykes."

For a large number of women, locating lesbianism in the feminist arena precludes forming meaningful political alliances with gay men. In part, this is because issues of sexual freedom that many feminists have viewed as exploiting women, including pornography, sexual contact between the young and old, and consensual sadomasochism, have been central to the predominantly male gay liberation movement (Adam 1987). Adam, however, suggests that, despite some conflicting interests, the latter part of the 1980s saw growing coalitions between lesbian feminists and gay liberationists surrounding the issue of AIDS. Our data confirm this hypothesis. Yet it is perhaps not coincidental that at a time when lesbian feminist communities serve increasingly as mobilization contexts for the larger lesbian and gay movement, lesbian activists describe a resurgence of lesbian separatism. Calls for more "women only space" pervaded gay and lesbian newsletters by the end of the 1980s (Japenga 1990).

Thus, our analysis suggests that an important element of lesbian feminist consciousness is the re-evaluation of lesbianism as feminism. A number of recent studies, though admittedly based on small samples, confirm that the majority of women who openly embrace a lesbian identity interpret lesbianism within the framework of radical feminist ideology (Kitzinger 1987; Devor 1989; Phelan 1989). Removing lesbian behavior from the deviant clinical realm and placing it in the somewhat more acceptable feminist arena establishes lesbian identity as distinct from gay identity. Yet an increasingly vocal segment of lesbian feminists endorses a more essentialist, or what Steven Epstein (1987) terms "modified social constructionist," explanation of lesbianism. They have undoubtedly been influenced by the identity politics of the liberal branch of the gay liberation movement that has, in recent years, advocated that sexuality is less a matter of choice and more a matter of biology and early socialization.

Highlighting the significance of a dominated group's own explanation of its position for political action, Kitzinger (1987) uses the term *identity accounts* to distinguish the range of group understandings that emerge among oppressed groups to make sense of themselves and their situation. Our findings confirm that these self-understandings not only influence mobilization possibilities and directions but determine the types of individual and collective actions groups pursue to challenge dominant arrangements. In the next section, we examine lesbian feminist practice, emphasizing that it is comprehensible only because it presupposes the existence of a theory of lesbian identity.

Negotiation

Viewing collective identity as the result of repeatedly activated shared definitions, as new social movement theorists do, makes it difficult to distinguish between "doing" and "being," or between social movement organizations and their strategies. Although recent social movement analyses tend to emphasize primarily the political and structural aims of challenging groups, personal transformation and expressive action have been central to most movements (Morris 1984; Fantasia 1988; McNall 1988). The insistence that the construction and expression of a collective vision is politics, or the politicization of the self and daily life, is nevertheless the core of what is "new" about the new social movements (Breines 1982; Melucci 1988; Kauffman 1990). Thus, we propose a framework that recognizes that identity can be a fundamental focus of political work.

Margolis (1985) suggests the concept of negotiation, drawn from the symbolic interactionist tradition, as a way of analyzing the process by which social movements work to change symbolic meanings. Most interactions between dominant and opposing groups reinforce established definitions. Individuals differentiated on the basis of devalued characteristics are continuously responded to in ways that perpetuate their disadvantaged status (Reskin 1988). West and Zimmerman (1987) use the term *identifactory displays* to emphasize, for example, that gender inequality is embedded and reproduced in even the most routine interactions. Similar analyses might be undertaken with regard to class, ethnicity, sexuality, and other sources of stratification. From a social movement standpoint, the concept of negotiations points to the myriad of ways that activists work to resist negative social definitions and demand that others value and treat oppositional groups differently (Goffman 1959).

The analysis of social movement negotiations forces us to recognize that, if not sociologically, then in reality, "doing" and "being" overlap (West and Zimmerman 1987). Yet we need a way to distinguish analytically between the politics of the public sphere, or world transformation directed primarily at the traditional political arena of the state, and the politics of identity, or self-transformation aimed primarily at the individual. We think that the concept of negotiations calls attention to forms of political activism embedded in everyday life that are distinct from those generally analyzed as tactics and strategies in the literature on social movements.

Building on Margolis's (1985) work on gender identity, we suggest two types of negotiation central to the construction of politicized collective identities. First, groups negotiate new ways of thinking and acting in *private* settings with other members of the collectivity, as well as in *public* settings before a larger audience. Second, identity negotiations can be *explicit*, involving open and direct attempts to free the group from dominant representations, or *implicit*, consisting of what Margolis terms a "condensed symbol or display" that undermines the status quo (1985: 340). In this section, we identify actions that lesbian feminist communities engage in to renegotiate the meaning of "woman." Opposition to male domination and the societal devaluation of women is directed both at the rules of daily life and at the institutions that perpetuate them.

In many respects, the phrase "the personal is political," coined by radical feminist Carol Hanisch and elaborated in Kate Millett's *Sexual Politics* (1969), is the hallmark of radical feminism (Echols 1989). Influenced by the civil rights and New Left movements, feminists began in the late 1960s to form consciousness-raising groups designed to reinterpret personal experiences in political terms. Analyzing virtually every aspect of individual and social experience as male-dominated, the groups encouraged participants to challenge prevailing representations of women in every sphere of life as a means of transforming the institutions that produced and disseminated them (Cassell 1977). The politicization of everyday life extended beyond the black power and feminist movements into other movements of the 1960s. In contemporary lesbian feminist communities the valorization of personal experience continues to have a profound impact.

Community members see lesbianism as a strategy for feminist social change that represents what one respondent describes as "an attempt . . . to stop doing what you were taught – hating women." Other women speak of the importance of learning to "value women," becoming "woman-centered," and "giving women energy." Being woman-centered is viewed as challenging conventional expectations that women orient themselves psychologically and socially toward men, compete with other women for male attention, and devalue other women. To make a more complete break with patriarchal identities and ways of life, some women exchange their male-given surnames for woman-centered ones, such as "Sarachild" or "Blackwomyn." Loving and valuing women becomes a means to resist a culture that hates and belittles women. Invoking Alice

Walker's (1974) concept of "womanist," one black woman that we interviewed explained, "My lesbianism has nothing to do with men. It's not about not choosing men, but about choosing women."

At the group level, lesbian feminists structure organizations collectively (Rothschild-Whitt 1979) and attempt to eliminate hierarchy, make decisions by consensus, and form coalitions only with groups that are not, as one activist said, "giving energy to the patriarchy." Demands for societal change seek to replace existing organizational forms and values with ones similar to those implemented in the community (Breines 1982). A worker at a women's festival illustrated the importance of community structure as a model for social change by commenting to women as they left the festival, "You've seen the way the real world can be, and now it's up to you to go out there and change it."

Because a traditionally feminine appearance, demeanor, self-concept, and style of personal relations are thought to be among the mainsprings of women's oppression, lesbian feminist communities have adopted different standards of gender behavior. For example, one of the visions of feminism has been to reconstitute the experience of victimization. Thus, women who have been battered or raped or have experienced incest and other forms of abuse are termed "survivors" to redefine their experiences as resistance to male violence. New recruits to the community are resocialized through participating in a variety of organizations – women's twelve-step programs, battered women's shelters, martial arts groups, incest survivors' groups – that provide not only self-help but also a means for when to renegotiate a lesbian feminist identity. The very name of one such organization in New York City, Identity House, is illustrative. Lesbian mothers organize support groups called "momazonians" or "dykes with tykes" to emphasize that motherhood is a crucial locus of contestation. "Take Back the Night" marches against violence, prochoice demonstrations, participation in spontaneous protests, and feminist music, theater, and dramatic presentations are other examples of public arenas for negotiating new standards of gender behavior.

Essential to contemporary lesbian feminist identity is a distinction between the lesbian who is a staunch feminist activist and the lesbian who is not of the vanguard. Thus, commitment to the politics of direct action distinguishes members of the lesbian feminist community from the larger population of lesbians. One participant illustrates the importance of this distinction, stating that women "who say that they are lesbians and maybe have sexual relationships with women, but don't have the feminist politics" compose a category who "could have been in the community, but they've opted out." Women even choose partners based on political commitment, noting that "sleeping with a woman who is not a feminist just doesn't work for me; there's too much political conflict." The tendency to choose life partners and form other close personal relationships based on shared political assumptions is not, however, unique to lesbian feminism but has been reported in relation to other movements as well (Rupp and Taylor 1986; McAdam 1988). In short, negotiating new gender definitions is central to lesbian feminist collective identity.

Challenging further the notion of femininity as frailty, passivity, and preoccupation with reigning standards of beauty, many women wear clothing that enables freedom of movement, adopt short or simple haircuts, walk with firm self-assured strides, and choose not to shave their legs or wear heavy makeup. Devor (1989) terms this mode of self-presentation "gender blending," arguing that it represents an explicit rejection of the norms of femininity and, by extension, of women's subjugation. By reversing reigning cultural standards of femininity, beauty, and respectability, lesbian feminists strike a blow against female objectification. How central this is to lesbian feminist identity is illustrated by a lesbian support group at a major university with the name Women in Comfortable Shoes.

Because appearance and demeanor are also implicit means of expressing one's opposition, community members' presentation of self is subject to close scrutiny or, to use the vernacular of the activists themselves, is monitored by the "pc police." Women who dress in stereotypically "feminine" ways are often criticized and admit to feeling "politically incorrect." As one respondent commented, "I've always had a lot of guilt feelings about, why don't I just buckle down and put on some blue jeans, and clip my hair short, and not wear makeup, and go aggressively through the world." Some of our interviewees report a return to gendered fashion in contemporary lesbian communities. Women who identify as sex radicals, in particular, have adopted styles of dress traditionally associated with the "sex trade," or prostitution, such as miniskirts, low-cut tops, and fishnet stockings, sometimes combined with more traditionally masculine styles in what is known as a "gender fuck" style of dressing. Suggesting that "the most profound and potentially the most radical politics come directly out of our own identity" (Combahee River Collective 1982), African-American feminists criticize the tendency of many white lesbian feminists to dictate a politics based on hegemonic cultural standards. Some women who are identifiably butch and dress in studded leather clothing and punk and neon haircuts offer class-based motivations for their demeanor, and African-American, Asian-American, and Latina lesbians embrace different cultural styles. In short, the changes in appearance and behavior women undergo as they come out cannot be fully understood as individually chosen but are often the ultimatum of identity communities (Krieger 1982).

We have presented three dimensions for analyzing collective identity in social movements: the concepts of boundaries, consciousness, and negotiation. Although we have treated each as if it were independent, in reality the three interact. Using these factors to analyze lesbian feminist identity suggests three elements that shape the social construction of lesbian feminism. First, lesbian feminist communities draw boundaries that affirm femaleness and separate them from a larger world perceived as hostile. Second, to undermine the dominant view of lesbianism as perversion, lesbian feminists offer identity accounts that politicize sexuality. Finally, by defining lesbians as the vanguard of the women's movement, lesbian feminists valorize personal experience, which, paradoxically, further reifies the boundaries between lesbians and nonlesbians and creates the impression that the differences between women and men and between lesbian and heterosexual feminists are essential.

CONCLUSION

In this chapter, we argue that lesbian feminist consciousness is rooted in a social movement community with ties to but distinguishable from both the gay liberation and the liberal feminist movements. In effect, we are suggesting that, with the absorption of the liberal feminist agenda into the liberal mainstream, the legacy of radical feminism continues in the lesbian feminist community. It is difficult to imagine an argument that would be more controversial in feminist circles, for it confirms the premise that, at least in the contemporary context, lesbianism and feminism are intertwined. This leads to the question posed in a recent speech by feminist philosopher Marilyn Frye (1990), "Do you have to be a lesbian to be a feminist?" It is our view that lesbian communities are a type of social movement abeyance structure that absorbs highly committed feminists whose radical politics have grown increasingly marginal since the mass women's movement has receded (Taylor and Whittier 1992). However insulated, they function to sustain the feminist challenge in a less receptive political climate (Taylor 1989b). Our findings are controversial in another respect. By calling attention to the centrality of feminism for lesbian activism, our study paints a picture of the tenuousness of the coalition between gay men and lesbians in the larger gay and lesbian movement.

Drawing from new data and recent scholarship on lesbian communities, we use this case to illustrate the significance of collective identity for mobilization and to present a framework for analyzing identity processes in social movements. Adapting Gerson and Peiss's (1985) framework, we identify as factors that contribute to the formation of collective identity; (1) the creation of boundaries that insulate and differentiate a category of persons from the dominant society; (2) the development of consciousness that presumes the existence of socially constituted criteria that account for a group's structural position; (3) the valorization of a group's "essential differences" through the politicization of everyday life.

The concept of collective identity is associated primarily with the social movements of the 1970s and 1980s because of their distinctive cultural appearance. It is our hypothesis, however, that collective identity is a significant variable in all social movements, even among the so-called traditional nineteenth-century movements. Thus, we frame our approach broadly to apply to oppositional identities based on class, race, ethnicity, gender, sexuality, and other persistent social cleavages. Certainly any theory derived from a single case is open to criticism. But recent research in the resource mobilization tradition points to the impact that changes in consciousness have on mobilization (Klein 1984; Downey 1986; Mueller 1987; McAdam 1988).

There is a growing realization among scholars of social movements that the theoretical pendulum between classical and contemporary approaches to social movements has swung too far. Social psychological factors that were central to collective behavior theory (Blumer 1946; Smelser 1962; Killian 1964; Turner and Killian 1972) have become the theoretical blind spots of resource mobilization theory. Ignoring the grievances of injustices that mobilize protest movements has, as Klandermans (1986) suggests, stripped social movements of their political significance. In contrast to the structural and organizational emphases of resource mobilization theory, new social movement theory attends to the social psychological and cultural discontent that propels movements. But it provides little understanding of how the injustices that are at the heart of most movements are translated into the everyday lives of collective actors. Our analysis suggests that the study of collective identity, because it highlights the role of meaning and ideology in the mobilization and maintenance of collective action, is an important key to understanding this process.

REFERENCES

Adam, Barry D. (1987), *The Rise of a Gay and Lesbian Movement* (Boston: Twayne).

Atkinson, Ti-Grace, (1974), *Amazon Odyssey* (New York: Link Books).

Baetz, Ruth, (1980), *Lesbian Crossroads* (New York: Morrow).

Barnhart, Elizabeth, (1975), "Friends and Lovers in a Lesbian Counterculture Community," in *Old Family, New Family*, ed. N. Glazer-Malbin (New York: Van Nostrand), 90–115.

Barth, F. (1969), "Introduction," in *Ethnic Groups and Boundaries*, ed. F. Barth (Boston: Little, Brown), 1–38.

Beck, E. T. (1980), *Nice Jewish Girls: A Lesbian Anthology* (Watertown, MA: Persephone).

Birkby, Phyllis, Bertha Harris, Jill Johnston, Esther Newton, and Jane O'Wyatt (1973), *Amazon Expedition: A Lesbian Feminist Anthology* (New York: Times Change Press).

Blumer, Herbert, (1946), "Collective Behavior," in *New Outline of the Principles of Sociology*, ed. A. M. Lee (New York: Barnes and Noble): 170–222.

Boggs, Carl (1986), *Social Movements and Political Power* (Philadelphia: Temple University Press).

Breines, Wini (1982), *Community and Organization in the New Left, 1962–68* (New York: Praeger).

Buechler, Steven M. (1990), *Women's Movements in the United States* (New Brunswick, NJ: Rutgers).

Bunch, Charlotte (1986), "Not for Lesbians Only," in *Feminist Frontiers II*, ed. Laurel Richardson and Verta Taylor (New York: Random House): 452–4.

Califia, Pat (1980), "Feminism vs. Sex: A New Conservative Wave," *Advocate* (February 21).

—— (1982), "Public Sex," *Advocate* (September 30).

Cassell, Joan (1977), *A Group Called Women: Sisterhood and Symbolism in the Feminist Movement* (New York: David McKay).

Cavin, Susan (1985), *Lesbian Origins* (San Francisco: Ism Press).

Chafetz, Janet Saltzman, (1988), *Feminist Sociology* (Itaska, IL: F. E. Peacock).

Chodorow, Nancy (1978), *The Reproduction of Mothering: Psychoanalysis and the Sociology of Gender* (Berkeley: University of California Press).

Clausen, Jan (1990), "My Interesting Condition," *Outlook* 2: 11–21.

Cohen, Jean L. (1985), "Strategy or Identity: New Theoretical Paradigms and Contemporary Social Movements," *Social Research* 52: 663–716.

Collins, Patricia Hill (1989), "The Social Construction of Black Feminist Thought," *Signs* 14:4: 745–73.

Combahee River Collective (1982), "A Black Feminist Statement," in *But Some of Us Are Brave: Black Women's Studies*, ed. Gloria T. Hull, Patricia Bell Scott, and Barbara Smith (Old Westbury, NY: Feminist Press): 13–22.

Cruikshank, Margaret (1980), *The Lesbian Path* (Monterey, CA: Angel Press).

Daly, Mary (1978), *Gyn/Ecology: The Metaethics of Radical Feminism* (Boston: Beacon Press).

—— (1984), *Pure Lust: Elemental Feminist Philosophy* (Boston: Beacon Press).

Daly, Mary and Jane Caputi (1987), *Websters' First New Intergalactic Wickedary of the English Language* (Boston: Beacon Press).

Davis, Madeleine and Elizabeth Laprovsky Kennedy, (1986), "Oral History and the Study of Sexuality in the Lesbian Community," *Feminist Studies* 12: 6–26.

Devor, Holly (1989), *Gender Blending* (Bloomington: Indiana University Press).

Downey, Gary L. (1986), "Ideology and the Clamshell Identity: Organizational Dilemmas in the Anti-Nuclear Power Movement," *Social Problems* 33: 357–73.

Dworkin, Andrea (1981), *Pornography and Silence: Culture's Revenge against Nature* (New York: Harper and Row).

Echols, Alice (1984), "The Taming of the Id: Feminist Sexual Politics, 1968–83," in *Pleasure and Danger: Exploring Female Sexuality*, ed. Carole S. Vance (Boston: Routledge and Kegan Paul), 50–72.

—— (1989), *Daring to Be Bad: Radical Feminism in America, 1967–1975* (Minneapolis: University of Minnesota Press).

Emberley, Julia and Donna Landry (1989), "Coverage of Greenham and Greenham as 'Coverage,'" *Feminist Studies* 15: 485–98.

Epstein, Barbara (1990), "Rethinking Social Movement Theory," *Socialist Review* 20: 35–66.

Epstein, Steven (1987), "Gay Politics, Ethnic Identity: The Limits of Social Constructionism," *Socialist Review* 17: 9–54.

Esterberg, Kristin Gay (1990), "Salience and Solidarity: Identity, Correctness, and Conformity in a Lesbian Community," paper presented at the annual meeting of the American Sociological Association, August 11–15, Washington, DC.

Evans, Sarah (1979) *Personal Politics* (New York: Vintage).

Fantasia, Rick (1988), *Cultures of Solidarity* (Berkeley: University of California Press).

Ferguson, Ann (1982), "Patriarchy, Sexual Identity, and the Sexual Revolution," in *Feminist Theory: A Critique of Ideology*, ed. Nannerl O. Keohane, Michelle Z. Rosaldo, and Barbara L. Gelpi (Chicago: University of Chicago Press): 147–61.

Ferree, Myra Marx and Beth B. Hess (1985), *Controversy and Coalition: The New Feminist Movement* (Boston: Twayne).

Ferree, Myra Marx and Frederick D. Miller (1985), "Mobilization and Meaning: Some Social-Psychological Contributions to the Resource Mobilization Perspective on Social Movements," *Sociological Inquiry* 55: 38–61.

Fireman, Bruce and William Gamson (1979), "Utilitarian Logic in the Resource Mobilization Perspective," in *The Dynamics of Social Movements*, ed. Mayer N. Zald and John D. McCarthy (Cambridge, MA: Winthrop): 8–44.

Freeman, Jo (1975), *The Politics of Women's Liberation* (New York: David McKay).

Frye, Marilyn (1983), *The Politics of Reality: Essays in Feminist Theory* (Trumansburg, NY: Crossing Press).

—— 1990. "Do You Have to Be a Lesbian to Be a Feminist?" *Off Our Backs* 20: 21–3.

Gamson, William A. (1975), *The Strategy of Social Protest* (Homewood, IL: Dorsey Press).

Gelb, Joyce and Marian Lief Palley (1982), *Women and Public Policy* (Princeton: Princeton University Press).

Gerlach, Luther P. and Virginia H. Hine (1970), *People, Power, Change: Movements of Social Transformation* (Indianapolis: Bobbs-Merrill).

Gerson, Judith M. and Kathy Peiss (1985), "Boundaries, Negotiation, Consciousness: Reconceptualizing Gender Relations," *Social Problems* 32: 317–31.

Gilligan, Carol (1982), *In a Different Voice* (Cambridge, MA: Harvard University Press).

Goffman, Erving (1959), *The Presentation of Self in Everyday Life* (Englewood Cliffs, N: Prentice-Hall).

Grahn, Judy (1984), *Another Mother Tongue: Gay Words, Gay Worlds* (Boston: Beacon Press).

Hoagland, Sarah Lucia (1988), *Lesbian Ethics: Toward New Value* (Palo Alto, CA: Institute of Lesbian Studies).

Hole, Judith and Ellen Levine (1971), *Rebirth of Feminism* (New York: Quadrangle).

Hollibaugh, Amber and Cherrie Moraga (1983), "What We're Rollin' Around in Bed With: Sexual Silences in Feminism," in *Powers of Desire*, ed. Ann Snitow, Christine Sansell, and Sharon Thompson (New York: Monthly Review Press): 394–405.

Jaggar, Alison M. and Paula Rothenberg Struhl (1978), *Feminist Frameworks* (New York: McGraw-Hill).

Japenga, Ann (1990), "The Separatist Revival," *Outlook* 2: 78–83.

Jenkins, J. Craig (1983), "Resource Mobilization Theory and the Study of Social Movements," *Annual Review of Sociology* 9: 527–53.

Jenkins, J. Craig and Charles Perrow (1977), "Insurgency of the Powerless: Farm Workers Movement (1946–72)," *American Sociological Review* 42: 249–68.

Johnson, Sonia (1987), *Going Out of Our Minds: The Metaphysics of Liberation* (Freedom, CA: Crossing Press).

Johnston, Jill (1973), *Lesbian Nation: The Feminist Solution* (New York: Simon and Schuster).

Kauffman, L. A. (1990) "The Anti-Politics of Identity," *Socialist Review* 20: 67–80.

Killian, Lewis M. (1964), "Social Movements," in *Handbook of Modern Sociology*, ed. R. E. L. Faris (Chicago: Rand McNally: 426–55.

Kitzinger, Celia (1987), *The Social Construction of Lesbianism* (London: Sage).

Klandermans, Bert (1984), "Mobilization and Participation: Social-Psychological Expansions of Resource Mobilization Theory," *American Sociological Review* 49: 583–600.

—— (1986), "New Social Movements and Resource Mobilization: The European and American Approach," *Journal of Mass Emergencies and Disasters* 4: 13–37.

Klandermans, Bert and Sidney Tarrow (1988), "Mobilization into Social Movements: Synthesizing European and American Approaches," in *From Structure to Action: Comparing Movement Participation across Cultures*, International Social Movement Research, vol. 1, eds Bert Klandermans, Hanspeter Kriesi, and Sidney Tarrow (Greenwich, CT: JAI Press): 1–38.

Klein, Ethel (1984), *Gender Politics* (Cambridge, MA: Harvard University Press).

Koedt, Anne, Ellen Levine and Anita Rapone (1973), *Radical Feminism* (New York: Quadrangle).

Krieger, Susan (1982) "Lesbian Identity and Community: Recent Social Science Literature," *Signs* 8: 91–108.

—— (1983), *The Mirror Dance: Identity in a Women's Community* (Philadelphia: Temple University Press).

Lewis, Sasha Gregory (1979) *Sunday's Women* (Boston: Beacon Press).

Lockard, Denyse (1986), "The Lesbian Community: An Anthropological Approach," in *The Many Faces of Homosexuality*, ed. Evelyn Blackwood (New York: Harrington Park Press), 83–95.

Lofland, John (1979), "White-Hot Mobilization: Strategies of a Millenarian Movement," in *Dynamics of Social Movements*, ed. Mayer N. Zald and John D. McCarthy (Cambridge, MA: Winhrop): 157–66.

—— (1985), "Social Movement Culture," in *Protest*, ed. John Lofland (New Brunswick, NJ: Transaction Books): 219–39.

Lord, Eleanor (unpublished), "Lesbian Lives and the Lesbian Community in Berkshire County," mimeograph.

Margolis, Diane Rothbard (1985), "Redefining the Situation: Negotiations on the Meaning of Woman," *Social Problems* 32: 332–47.

McAdam, Doug (1982) *Political Process and the Development of Black Insurgency, 1930–70* (Chicago: University of Chicago Press).

—— (1988), *Freedom Summer* (New York: Oxford University Press).

McAdam, Doug, John D. McCarthy, and Mayer N. Zald (1988), "Social Movements" in *Handbook of Sociology*, ed. Neil Smelser (Newbury Park, CA: Sage): 695–737.

McCarthy, John D. and Mayer N. Zald (1973), *The Trend of Social Movements in America* (Morristown, NJ: General Learning Press).

—— (1977), "Resource Mobilization and Social Movements: A Partial Theory," *American Journal of Sociology* 82: 1212–41.

McNall, Scott G. (1988), *The Road to Rebellion: Class Formation and Populism, 1865–1900* (Chicago: University of Chicago Press).

Melucci, Alberto (1985), "The Symbolic Challenge of Contemporary Movements," *Social Research* 52: 781–816.

—— (1988), "Getting Involved: Identity and Mobilization in Social Movement," in *From Structure to Action: Comparing Movement Participation across Cultures* (International Social Movement Research, vol. 1, ed. Bert Klaudermans, Hanspeter Kriesi, and Sidney Tarrow (Greenwich, CT: JAI Press): 329–48.

—— (1989), *Nomads of the Present: Social Movements and Individual Needs in Contemporary Society* (Philadephia: Temple University Press).

Millett, Kate (1969), *Sexual Politics* (New York: Ballantine).

Moraga, Cherrie and Gloria Anzaldua (1981), *This Bridge Called My Back: Writings by Radical Women of Color* (Watertown, MA: Persephone).

Morris, Aldon D. (1984), *The Origins of the Civil Rights Movement* (New York: Free Press).

—— (1990), "Consciousness and Collective Action: Towards a Sociology of Consciousness and Domination," paper presented at the annual meeting of the American Sociological Association, August 9–13, San Francisco.

Mueller, Carol McClurg (1987), "Collective Consciousness, Identity Transformation, and the Rise of Women in Public Office in the United States," in *The Women's Movement of the United States and Western Europe*, eds M. F. Katzenstein and C. M. Mueller (Philadelphia: Temple University Press): 89–108.

—— (1990), "Collective Identities and the Mobilization of Women: The American Case, 1960–1970," paper presented at the colloquium on New Social Movements and the End of Ideology, July 16–20, Universidad Internacional Menendez Pelayo.

Myron, Nancy and Charlotte Bunch (1975), *Lesbianism and the Women's Movement* (Baltimore: Diana Press).

Near, Holly (1990), *Fire in the Rain, Singer in the Storm* (New York: Morrow).

Nestle, Joan (1987), *A Restricted Country* (Ithaca, NY: Firebrand Books).

Oberschall, Anthony (1973), *Social Conflict and Social Movements* (Englewood Cliffs, NJ: Prentice-Hall).

Offe, Claus (1985), "New Social Movements: Challenging the Boundaries of Institutional Politics," *Social Research* 52: 817–68.

Olzak, Susan (1983), "Contemporary Ethnic Mobilization," *Annual Review of Sociology* 9: 355–74.

Penelope, Julia (1990), "A Case of Mistaken Identity," *Women's Review of Books* 8: 11–12.

Phelan, Shane (1989), *Identity Politics: Lesbian Feminism and the Limits of Community* (Philadelphia: Temple University Press).

Pizzorno, Alessandro (1978), "Political Science and Collective Identity in Industrial Conflict," in *The Resurgence of Class Conflict in Western Europe since 1968*, eds C. Crouch and A. Pizzorno (New York: Holmes and Meier): 277–98.

Ponse, Barbara (1978), *Identities in the Lesbian World: The Social Construction of Self* (Westport, Conn.: Greenwood Press).

Radicalesbians (1973), "The Woman Identified Woman," in *Radical Feminism*, eds Anne Koedt, Ellen Levine, and Anita Rapone (New York: Quadrangle: 240–5.

Reskin, Barbara (1988), "Bringing the Men Back In: Sex Differentiation and the Devaluation of Women's Work," *Gender & Society* 2: 58–81.

Rich, Adrienne (1976), *Of Woman Born* (New York: Norton).

—— (1980), "Compulsory Heterosexuality and Lesbian Existence," *Signs* 5: 631–60.

Rothschild-Whitt, Joyce (1979), "The Collectivist Organization: An Alternative to Rational-Bureaucratic Models," *American Sociological Review* 44: 509–27.

Rubin, Gayle (1984) "Thinking Sex: Notes for a Radical Theory of the Politics of Sexuality," in *Pleasure and Danger*, ed. Carol S. Vance (Boston: Routledge and Kegan Paul): 267–319.

Rule, James and Charles Tilly (1972) "1830 and the Unnatural History of Revolution," *Journal of Social Issues* 28: 49–76.

Rupp, Leila J. (1989), "Feminism and the Sexual Revolution in the Early Twentieth Century: The Case of Doris Stevens," *Feminist Studies* 51: 289–309.

Rupp, Leila J. and Verta Taylor (1986), "The Women's Movement since 1960: Structure, Strategies, and New Directions," in *American Choices: Social Dilemmas and Public Policy since 1960*, eds Robert H. Bremner, Richard Hopkins, and Gary W. Reichard (Columbus: Ohio State University Press): 75–104.

—— (1990), "Women's Culture and the Persisting Women's Movement," paper presented at the annual meeting of the American Sociological Association, Washington, DC August 12.

Ryan, Barbara (1989), "Ideological Purity and Feminism: The U.S. Women's Movement from 1966 to 1975," *Gender & Society* 3: 239–57.

Schneider, Beth (1986), "I'm Not a Feminist But..." paper presented at the annual meeting of the American Sociological Association, New York, September 2.

Schwartz, Michael (1976), *Radical Protest and Social Structure: The Southern Farmers' Alliance and the One-Crop Tenancy System* (New York: Academic Press).

Smeller, Michelle M. (unpublished), "From Dyke to Doll: The Processual Formation of Sexual Identity," Ohio State University.

Smelser, Neil (1962), *Theory of Collective Behavior* (New York: Free Press).

Smith, Barbara (1983), *Home Girls: A Black Feminist Anthology* (New York: Kitchen Table Women of Color Press).

Snitow, Ann, Christine Stansell, and Sharon Thompson, (1983), *Powers of Desire: The Politics of Sexuality* (New York: Monthly Review Press).

Snow, David A., E. Burke Rochford, Jr. Steven K. Worden, and Robert D. Benford. (1986), "Frame Alignment Processes, Micromobilization, and Movement Participation," *American Sociological Review* 51: 464–81.

Stanley, Julia Penelope and Susan J. Wolfe, (1980), *The Coming Out Stories* (Watertown, MA: Persephone).

Taylor, Verta (1989a), "The Future of Feminism," in *Feminist Frontiers*, ed. Laurel Richardson and Verta Taylor (New York: Random House): 434–51.

—— (1989b), "Social Movement Continuity: The Women's Movement in Abeyance," *American Sociological Review* 54: 761–75.

Taylor, Verta and Nancy Whittier (1992), "The New Feminist Movement," in *Feminist Frontiers: Rethinking Sex, Gender, and Society*, eds Laurel Richardson and Verta Taylor (New York: McGraw-Hill).

Tilly, Charles (1978), *From Mobilization to Revolution* (Reading, MA: Addison-Wesley).

Touraine, Alain (1985), "An Introduction to the Study of Social Movements," *Social Research* 52: 749–87.

Treblecot, Joyce (1979), "Conceiving Women: Notes on the Logic of Feminism," *Sinister Wisdom* 11: 3–50.

Turner, Ralph H. and Lewis M. Killian (1972), *Collective Behavior*, 2nd ed. (Englewood Cliffs, NJ: Prentice-Hall).

Vance, Carole S. (1984), *Pleasure and Danger* (Boston: Routledge and Kegan Paul).

Walker, Alice (1974), *In Search of Our Mothers' Gardens* (New York: Harcourt Brace Jovanovich).

Weigert, Andrew J., J. Smith Teitge, and Dennis W. Teitge (1986), *Society and Identity* (New York:

Cambridge University Press).

West, Candace and Don H. Zimmerman (1987), "Doing Gender," *Gender & Society* 1: 125–51.

White, Edmund (1980), *States of Desire* (New York: E. P. Dutton).

Whittier, Nancy (1991), "Feminists in the Post-Feminist Age: Collective Identity and the Persistence of the Women's Movement," Ph.D. diss., Ohio State University.

Wolf, Deborah Goleman (1979), *The Lesbian Community* (Berkeley: University of California Press).

Zinn, Maxine Baca (1990), "Family, Feminism, and Race in America," *Gender & Society* 4: 68–82.

Zita, Jacquelyn (1982), "Historical Amnesia and the Lesbian Continuum," in *Feminist Theory: A Critique of Ideology,* eds Nannerl O. Keohane, Michelle Z. Rosaldo, and Barbara L. Gelpi (Chicago: University of Chicago Press): 161–76.

NANCY E. STOLLER

"Lesbian Involvement in the AIDS Epidemic: Changing Roles and Generational Differences"

from Beth Schneider and Nancy Stoller, *Women Resisting AIDS: Feminist Strategies of Empowerment* (Philadelphia: Temple University Press, 1995): 270–85

Understanding lesbian involvement in the AIDS epidemic requires analysis beyond the question of ethical choice. Participation in any social movement, including the response to AIDS, is highly determined both by internal movement factors such as recruitment and mobilization techniques,[1] and by external factors such as potential recruits' shared values, sympathy for political goals, and existing organizational memberships. Thus, the values, social location, and occupation of a lesbian significantly affect the possibilities of her involvement in AIDS work. To understand their complex relationship to AIDS, we need to know the dominant networks, cultures, and institutions of North American lesbians when AIDS was first identified in the United States.

FEMINISM

During the 1970s, the combination of the second wave of feminism with the emergence of the gay liberation movement led to a complex flowering of culture and social organization by women. Many of the leadership roles in the women's movement were filled by lesbians (part-time, occasional, emerging, temporary, long-term and otherwise). This was a mutual love affair of lesbians for feminism (the idea that women matter) and of feminism for the essence of the lesbian vision (women are first in time, emotional interest, and political commitment). The slogan that "feminism is the theory and lesbianism the practice" may not be perfectly true, but its emotional validity brought the two movements together. In addition, most feminist organizations during this period attempted to include both heterosexuals and lesbians. On the subject of the body, the motto of feminism was "Our Bodies, Our Selves," which was not just a health slogan but also a call for self-determination, expressed in forms ranging from self-examination to sexual experimentation. Not surprisingly, "political lesbianism" was born in this milieu.

In a concrete sense, what combined aspects of the movements – and especially linked lesbians to feminism – was precisely what had drawn lesbians to work with women and girls throughout the nineteenth and twentieth centuries in the United States. Feminism, and in particular feminist institution building, represented the opportunity to express a lesbian's love of women both at work and in politics, even where the work and politics said "women" and not the subcategory "lesbians." This sort of work-for-women-and-girls provides the opportunity for a universalistic sublimated love, which can exist in a universe parallel to one's private life and particularistic love. With this match, lesbians became the leaders in many of the feminist institutions formed in the 1970s: the women's health movement, with its self-examination and self-help movements, its collectives and health centers; the feminist press; bookstores; restaurants; music. It is through the work of such women that these feminist institutions have survived into the 1980s and 1990s.

In many cases, the language of the movement itself conflated women and lesbians. For example, during the mid-1970s, as lesbian culture went public, it was labeled "women's culture" by its promoters; for example, "women's music," which was really lesbian music, of course, and music for a predominantly white, college-educated audience at that. That this conflation still exists is shown by the fact that Olivia Records, the primary vector for lesbian/women's music, now sells "women's cruises" (no pun acknowledged), which are designed for lesbians, not for "feminists" or women in general.[2]

The feminist movement and the lesbian movement were parallel and interconnecting; they were also linked to other movements and had considerable diversity within them, which is often lost in more superficial reporting.[3] For example, there is a widespread notion that the "women's movement" was white and middle class,[4] but, as I experienced it, it was intentionally cross-class and multiracial. Feminists and lesbians in all segments of the population were active in prison reform and organizing, especially the segment that worked with women; battered women's shelters; antiracist organizing; ethnic liberation struggles; school board fights; and reproductive rights that addressed sterilization abuse.[5]

Despite some invisibility in the eyes of the white Left and to many white gay men, it was during the 1970s that both lesbians and women (at least the feminists in the name of women) "went public."[6] Gaining experience in their own movements, as well as in other struggles, they began to create new sets of institutions for women. As a result, for lesbians, alternative and additional institutions emerged, beyond women's bars and the sports clubs associated with them. Separatist settings and services for women (health clinics, therapy services, restaurants, book stores, retreats, land groups, classes, caucuses) were suddenly everywhere. Women's studies courses and programs were invented. Gay and straight women mingled. Lesbianism was presented as a legitimate option for women; many lesbian-inclined women chose it and did so openly, in ways that their older sisters could not have done so easily.

Feminism helped make this development of women's "spaces" and of lesbian lifestyle and culture possible, because it brought the energies of women of all sexual persuasions together in the name of women, therefore making available many more resources than either straight women or lesbians alone could generate by themselves. Each group had access to different types of resources. In a certain way, the reason why lesbians have led the women's movement and its institutions is that lesbians provide more labor, more focused attention, and less distraction: they are not so torn by the need to return to men. On the other hand, the connection of straight women to men brought a different set of resources, especially financial aid. Since women's salaries ranged from 59 to 63 percent of men's during this period, a woman with a man was almost inevitably in a wealthier household than a woman with a woman.

GAY LIBERATION

The movement for gay liberation, which emerged as a powerful force in 1969 and spread internationally within a few years, further affected lesbian visibility, politics, economics, and culture. While men dominated the movement, women were assertive in many of its political organizations and other institutions. The movement's effects on lesbian-gay solidarity varied by location. In larger urban areas, men dominated the economy and the institutions of the gay community; socializing by men and women was predominantly segregated and reflected different sexual, political, and social values. Lesbian culture, in both its older and its new institutions, was characterized by a more socially critical stance – beyond lesbian/gay assertion. Because women had fewer institutions to call their own, their gathering places continued to be more mixed racially and in terms of class than were male institutions, which, as they multiplied, replicated the class and race character of the larger society more thoroughly than did women's institutions. Lesbians were also just plain worse off economically than gay men; consequently their interests, alliances and culture reflected this difference.

Gay male culture, except for that segment affected by groups such as the Radical Fairies, the Gay Liberation Front, and a few other groups, was more a celebration of male and gay culture without the radicalizing addition of feminism.[7] A major distinction between lesbians and gay men, as articulated in publications and politics of the seventies, was in their differing notions of what sexual freedom meant. In fact, to understand lesbians and the AIDS epidemic, it is important to spend some time looking at these different meanings.

LESBIANS AND GAY MEN: SEXUAL DIFFERENCE IN THE 1970s

Models of sexuality for lesbians which dominated the seventies came from women's socialization and feminism. It has been argued by recent theorists that female development moves in the direction of a relational orientation in contrast to male developmental emphasis on individuation and separation.[8] Gilligan, for example, argued that, within western culture, male moral development has emphasized an ethic of justice, whereas that of women has greater emphasis on caring. Even though some feminist theorists emphasize the role of oppression in developing this orientation in women,[9] it is still true that, regardless of the structural sources, almost all women, including lesbians, have been strongly affected by a pattern of socialization that emphasizes the importance of relationships and networks, as well as caregiving and nurturance. Even though lesbians may have a demonstrated ability to resist certain aspects of female socialization (males as sexual object choices for example), they are not immune from these cultural pressures.

Common wisdom in lesbian culture of the late 1970s and early 1980s asserted that lesbians form couples and model their coupleship on romantic love and enduring relationships. This popular notion was complemented and perhaps strengthened by research on "fusion" in lesbian relationships, which emphasizes the tendency to blur boundaries between self and other and identifies female socialization as a source of this tendency.[10] A second pervasive aspect of female socialization has been the historical and contemporary emphasis on monogamy, tied partly to patriarchal possessiveness but also to the risk of pregnancy and the need for legitimate fathership.

In contrast to these two aspects of female socialization (relatedness and monogamy as values and life orientations), male socialization has emphasized individuation and nonmonogamy. While gay men, like lesbians, challenge traditional sex roles, they are, similarly and simultaneously, drawn to them. Gay male sexuality in the seventies was historically marked by less emphasis on the creation of family or on sexual monogamy. The impact of gay liberation movements on gay male sexuality has been discussed in many venues, primarly because of the belief that patterns of sexuality among gay men have been responsible for the rapid spread of the epidemic.[11] Although a detailed look at this topic is outside the scope of this chapter, gay male and lesbian sexualities and the value systems associated with them were important sources of separation between men and women within the community.

For women who emerged as lesbians in the 1970s, feminism had several sexual messages: communication, equality, androgyny, and nonviolence. Nonmonogamy was not one of the explicit messages of feminism, nor did monogamy suffer a serious critique. Gay liberation provided the opportunity for lesbians to be more "out," while female socialization seemed to ensure that they would move primarily in the directions women are expected to: seeking long-term close relatonships. The critique of male–female sexual relationships led to an emphasis on equality and, for some women (both lesbian and straight), a fear of repeating the same oppressive forms found between men and women in traditional non-feminist couples. This concern and its expression in feminist literature and theory eventually led to the "sex wars" of feminism, in which struggles against sexism, sexual abuse, and oppression were pitted against struggles for freedom to have one's own sex life and to be creative without being censored.[12] Lesbians who were out before the 1970s reacted variously to these messages and conflicts depending on their interest, class, ethnicity, education, and commitment to previous patterns.

Differences within lesbian and feminist communities concerning sexual expression created major divisions which lingered into the 1990s. One strand of feminists gravitated toward a severe critique of power; some became involved in the anti-pornography movement which supported censorship and regulation.[13] Other feminists rallied to protect free speech and self expression as cornerstones of women's right to determine their own sexuality. The conflicts escalated in the late 1970s and early 1980s, especially among the more political and academic segments of the feminist world. Lesbians were actively engaged in this debate. In addition, lesbians involved in femme-butch and the growing S/M community felt attacked by those who emphasized androgyny and equality as the only proper expressions of female sexuality.[14]

The message of gay liberation for men, however, was more one of self-expression of male socialization within the arena of gay sex. This meant multiple partners, self-assertion, and "individuation," or experimentation. Gay male sexuality had involved multiple sex partners before gay liberation; the gay movement, which basically legitimized gay life "as it was," focused on gaining full rights (again, a male theme of justice) for gay men to live their lives – and discover them – as they wished. In the early 1970s, gay male liberation provided a critique of traditional male sexuality. This critique included the presentation of the possibility that gay men might form their own families, whether communal or more nuclear versions. By the end of the decade, more gay men had created families (in some cases linked to lesbians), which included children. However, as the gay movement became institutionalized, it lost much of its radical critique of sexism. There was no movement comparable to feminism to effectively challenge male socialization – although some segments of the gay male community adopted the critique of domination and oppression. They applied this critique to the position of gay male relations as well as to those between gay men and lesbians.

The 1970s saw a rapid increase in public gay male culture, institutions, and political influence (including the first candidate, Harvey Milk, to be elected on a gay rights platform). Within these new institutions, struggles over the appropriate nature of gay male life appeared: What was the meaning and appropriateness of camp? of "super-masculine" behavior? of clone culture? Writers began to speak of gay identity and community replacing homosexual behavior

and populations. Whereas gay men were in some cases able to claim actual locations – the Castro, the Village – for their community centers, lesbians existed more as a relational or fictional community, often on the geographical fringe of gay men's areas, but usually spread more widely and less distinct as a community.

While lesbians were especially connected to the feminist community and institutions, it seems that gay men were more connected to heterosexual life in its more traditional forms, including its "use" of women familially, socially, and economically. Possibly, this lack of challenge by gay men of sexism made it easy for them to appreciate the nurturing they received from lesbians and straight women during the epidemic, but harder to acknowledge women as intellectual equals.

Thus, when the 1970s ended and the AIDS epidemic exploded, most lesbians and gay men were living essentially parallel lives, organized primarily around the separate themes of female values and feminism for the women and masculinity and justice for the men.

THE AIDS EPIDEMIC

Although AIDS has struck men in higher numbers than women, women have been among the ill since the beginning. They have also been involved as caretakers, educators, physicians, public health officials, and community activists. As a diverse social group linked by gender in an epidemic where gender and sexuality are key, women and lesbians in particular have played powerful symbolic, sexual, and social roles.

From the start, lesbians were involved not only in their occupational functions as nurses, activists, social workers, they were also present as women and lesbians, two potential master statuses. Simultaneously active and self-conscious, lesbians were often seen as representing a feminist stance. Their social-psychological backgrounds, the nature of the lesbian–gay community, and the broader social and political context of the early 1980s affected the roles that lesbians could, and did, play in the epidemic. These roles have changed substantially over the first decade of AIDS activism.

The basic arenas of AIDS activity might usefully be sorted into five institutional foci: medical (including research), public health, educational, caring services, and political. As the 1980s began, women in the United States (including lesbians) were occupationally placed in large numbers where they would be likely to encounter men with HIV. In medical settings, they comprised most nurses, as well as a significant proportion of nurses aides, home health workers, medical clerical staff, and an increasing number of physicians. Women also dominated the frontline work force in social work and therapy. They were well represented in public health, especially in health education. Within the lesbian and gay community, many of the service organizations that were cosexual had numerous female staff, because women outnumber men in the helping professions.

The above-noted professional roles, whether in straight or gay institutions, draw on traditional nurturing and service models for female activity. Though some lesbians may have been completely traditional in their attitudes towards their work, most had been recently affected by the enormous changes in lesbian culture and institutions that occurred in the 1970s.

Within these institutions, and especially among activist segments in the political arena, we can delineate four dominant lesbian perspectives in the eighties on whether and how to make AIDS a social priority:

1 Women/lesbians make a distinctive contribution.
2 Equal rights for women/lesbians within the AIDS world.
3 Lesbians and gay men must form coalitions.
4 Lesbians need separatism.

These phrases summarize four approaches, which are best understood as ideal types. I have constructed this typology inductively on the basis of my field research and participation in AIDS work over the past ten years. The typology is complemented and supplemented by the findings of other researchers, although they may not use my language.[15] These perspectives have developed somewhat chronologically during the course of the epidemic, as women have participated in various institutional and social movement responses.[16]

In addition to these four primarily feminist approaches to AIDS, there are the nonfeminist and anti-feminist conservative approaches to AIDS, some of which have specific positions on women and AIDS. Conservative approaches argue, for example, that certain infected adults (such as gay men, prostitutes, drug users, and "the promiscuous") deserve their infection and death. The holder of such a view may argue for quarantine of the "guilty" infected; in California, for example, prostitutes who test positive for HIV become felons instead of the misdemeanants they would be if uninfected. These conservative positions are less common among lesbians who are involved in public responses to AIDS and are therefore not explored in depth in this chapter.

In addition, there are some lesbians who have been called "non-feminists" because they were too "femme," or too "into roles" or "power," or "soft" on pornography. In fact, most of these women did identify as feminists and were critical of those whom they call "lesbian feminists." The sex radicals (as some members of this group call themselves) felt rejected by lesbian separatist and lesbian feminist organizations, many of which were dominated by the philosophy of androgyny and equality. Their interest in AIDS politics and the organizational milieu of AIDS work was fueled by a belief that AIDS organizations would be locations that were more open about sexual diversity. Some were drawn to these gay organizations rather than to the lesbian organizations where they felt invisible or criticized. Strictly speaking, they are feminists, and their activity is included in the discussion of rationales listed below.

Women/lesbians make a distinctive contribution

This approach characterized the first few years of the epidemic and was (and continues to be) most commonly expressed by women working in the medical and caring services. Shorthand versions of this approach are "AIDS needs women" and "To get the best man for the job, call a woman." Distinctive contributionists argue that women have special skills to bring to the AIDS response, which should be brought and taught or shared with "the guys," our gay brothers.

In this model, what do women bring? They bring compassion, women's health movement experience, health skills, nurturing skills; experience with illness; ability to express emotions; relational abilities for organizational growth and change. Many lesbians did bring these skills and styles with them to their work in AIDS. The dominant organizations for the first half of the decade (1981 to 1986) were medical, caring and education organizations. Initially, most of the clients were men. Within these organizations, lesbians played a variety of nurturing and relational roles. In some cases, women acted as leaders; their contribution has generally been underreported and underrated.

The Women's AIDS Network (WAN), located in the San Francisco Bay Area, was founded by a mixed group of lesbians and straight women in 1982 at an early national AIDS conference. Members of the organization, led primarily by lesbians, were overwhelmingly highly educated AIDS professionals:[17] nurses, doctors, therapists, health educators. Similar to the women in Melissa McNeill's study of nineteen prominent lesbian AIDS activists,[18] almost all WAN members arrived with experience in feminism, health organizing, and/or lesbian and gay civil rights work.

They began by giving all they could from what they knew. Such an approach, giving all you've got, is compatible with conservative feminism and with "neo-conservative" or "postmodern" feminism. In fact, some of the lesbians who worked at the San Francisco AIDS Foundation, as either staff or volunteers, are most appropriately described as non-feminists and in some cases hostile to feminists. They saw feminism itself as hostile to gay men (because feminism criticized the men for "camp," or sexual promiscuity) or opposed to individual success. Their involvement was more often a result of connection to the gay male community and less a result of a political analysis. These women were sometimes unsympathetic to their more feminist coworkers, especially when they presented feminist agendas concerning services for women, interpreting such behavior as uncaring toward men.[19]

Most of the lesbians who got involved in AIDS research, service, and policy work in the early years, however, were both feminists and nurturers who saw themselves connected politically and ethically to the various populations at risk for AIDS.

The idea that women have special nurturing skills has frequently been expressed and appreciated in AIDS organizations, including those dominated by men. But the special skills associated with women's organizatonal experience was less acknowledged. This finding held true in McNeill's study as well as in my own research in San Francisco.

Equal rights for women/lesbians within the AIDS world

Soon after women became engaged in the work of the epidemic, a second perspective began to be expressed: that women, as AIDS workers and as people at risk for AIDS, were the victims of sexism and secondary status.

This perspective holds that we need to examine every AIDS response strategy to make certain that women's unique needs are met and that potential oppression and/or exploitation are prevented. Reproductive rights; civil liberties issues; the role of motherhood; HIV and maternal transmission; the scapegoating of prostitutes; equal access of women – and children – to AIDS education, treatment, social services, and food banks – these are all issues addressed by lesbians and straight women in the epidemic. They saw the equal rights approach as necessary because most AIDS policy was being determined by and for men, whether it was set within community based organizations (CBOs) or governmental organizations.

One example of such sexism played out in the San Francisco AIDS Foundation in 1985 and 1986. At that time, I was the coordinator of the women's program and the supervisor of educational materials development and distribution. I had supervised the development of most of the brochures for the foundation which were being distributed nationally: the first HIV test brochures (English and Spanish versions); a multiracial heterosexual brochure (English/

Spanish); "sex, drugs, and AIDS"; a women and AIDS brochure (drafted by the Women's AIDS Networks); and other materials for people with AIDS. The Women's AIDS Network agreed to work jointly with the foundation to produce what would be the first brochure specifically for lesbians. However, when I went to my supervisor, a gay man (and southerner) who was director of the education department, to show him the text and get formal permission for printing, for the first time in my work at the foundation I was told that my brochure would not be approved for printing because, in this case, unlike the others, "Lesbians are not at risk for AIDS." Needless to say, I was shocked by his response. Within a week, WAN was using its contacts within and without the organization to reverse the decision, and eventually (after three months of lobbying), the brochure was published. One rationalization that the director held onto was "Well, lesbians aren't really at risk, but since they are working so hard in AIDS services, they deserve a brochure." Thousands of copies were distributed or sold within the first year. The conflict indicated how invisible lesbians were as women at risk, as activists, and as experts.

In North American AIDS work, championing the equal rights focus for women often means emphasizing class and race issues because most women with HIV are poor and of either African-American or Latino descent. Lesbians, who have often been the primary representatives of straight women as well as themselves, often walked a fine line when they spoke about their own need for visibility. What did it mean to speak for "women" if one were also lesbian? Lesbian networking (through organizations like WAN), as well as direct service by lesbians to women of all sorts, has resulted in a situation in which straight women have increasingly championed lesbian needs as well as their own in terms of HIV/AIDS advocacy. As the international demographic and epidemiological facts have hit home (although slowly) in the United States, heterosexual women are receiving consistently more attention. Lesbians, though, lag far behind. Formal definitions of risk categories for HIV reflect this lesbian invisibility. For example,

until 1993, the US Centers for Disease Control (CDC) excluded any woman from its "lesbian" category if she had sex even once with a man since 1977.

The last two major stances held by lesbians in regard to the epidemic emerged most strongly during the second half of the decade, although, as will be seen, they (like the equal rights approach) also have their roots in feminist activist movements that flourished in the 1970s.

By the middle of the first decade of AIDS, many AIDS organizations had begun to feel the stress of inadequate funding. Additionally, the dream of quick medical solutions and rapid research advances had faded. As a result, direct action tactics became more popular. ACT-UP and its clones were born and spread rapidly throughout the United States and Europe.

Lesbians and gay men must form coalitions

Coalition lesbians argue that lesbians (and for that matter, everyone) should work on improving AIDS policies (even if the particular policy will benefit men primarily) because the public repressive response to the epidemic is a response to communities and populations that include lesbians as well as gay men. Therefore, it is in the interest of women, as well as the most often affected men, to have better AIDS policies.

AIDS is often seen by such women as a "homosexual" issue. They argue that many recent civil rights restrictions are based on homophobia and justified because of AIDS. Furthermore, the concomitant rise in antigay violence and the loss of community leaders, friends, and family through illness and death all affect lesbians as well as gay men. An additional argument is that focusing on AIDS discrimination is the best strategy for ending discrimination against gay people because the two discriminations (AIDS discrimination, and homophobia), as well as the prejudice, stigma and marginalization associated with both, are completely entangled, and there is funding and some political interest in dealing with AIDS discrimination. Therefore, one can reach anti-gay discrimination by working on AIDS.[20]

Many AIDS activist women who share the coalition perspective also view the AIDS epidemic as an opportunity to move toward broader social agendas: national health care, local housing and shelters, effective and humane drug policy, and others. They see these changes as key to improving the role of women and gay people in society.

This approach to AIDS work is often associated with an activist position. McNeill found that, of the half of her sample who were primarily involved in ACT UP and OUT! (the Washington, DC, version of ACT UP), a major appeal was the activism. Many stated positions indicating that they saw AIDS work as a way of approaching the broader society and making changes in it. In my own interviews with lesbian members of ACT UP New York, all stated that they saw their work as part of coalition politics. All were feminists and aligned with the sexual radical side of feminism.

Divisions within the ACT UP organizations of several cities indicate that the definition of coalition politics varies. Whereas some women support the narrow definition of lesbians, gay men, and others working together around AIDS (the initial perspective of ACT UP New York), others are more attuned to the broader critique of society and to the branches of ACT UP that have taken on the wider health issues beyond AIDS.

It is out of the bonds between lesbian and gay male AIDS activists, symbolized in organizations like ACT UP and Queer Nation, that gay antiviolence patrols and queer culture have been formed. This new culture, in which women fill many leadership roles and which is explicitly multicultural, speaks primarily with the voice of the second generation since Stonewall – women and men who have come of age during the 1980s. However, the legacies of racism and sexism have not been overcome in these organizations; they continue to break apart over challenges to the maintenance of white male systems of power.

While these political developments emerged, a previously traveled route was being explored by the "older generation" of lesbians: withdrawal and separatism.

Lesbians need separatism

"AIDS – Later for women!" This last perspective has strong roots in lesbian and feminist separatism. Separatist lesbians holding this perspective argue that both feminist and lesbian health priorities should be focused, not on AIDS, but on other, worse problems affecting women. For example, breast cancer strikes and kills many more women than does AIDS.[21] And our poverty and powerlessness are more serious health problems than HIV disease. This is the perspective presented in Jackie Winnow's speech at the 1988 Lesbians and AIDS conference in San Francisco which was reprinted in Out/Look magazine.[22] Although her comments were directed primarily at lesbians, she argued that all women suffer from the current AIDS funding and organizing focus, due to loss of funds for and diminished attention to women's health issues.

Additionally, some lesbians argue that, even if they themselves see AIDS as a major threat to their communities, this is not the way the average person feels in communities that are not primarily gay-identified, such as African-Americans, Latinos, the homeless, and poor whites. Therefore, AIDS-focused organizing is not an effective way to move toward organizing these communities, including their lesbian members, for survival.

While some lesbians may have stayed "out of AIDS" from the beginning because they were unconnected to gay men, did not see themselves at risk, or just wanted to avoid the whole thing, others who were engaged have left full-time work, some to work in other areas, some to do part-time volunteer activity. Of McNeill's subjects, despite their leadership roles, 25 percent (five) were turning their attention elsewhere. By 1991, fifteen were working primarily on women and AIDS issues, as well as other health issues affecting women and lesbians.[23]

No matter what size or type of AIDS response organization one examines, these four perspectives appear. We are more likely to find the coalitionists in the more radical activist organizations, like the ACT UP chapters, but in three months of visiting with ACT UP New York in 1989, I found that the "distinctive contribution" idea was one of the strongest motivators for highly political women. Their distinctive contribution happened to be their organizing experiences gained in other direct action and civil disobedience movements. Consistently these were identified as feminist organizing "inventions," such as consciousness raising and affinity groups and various techniques to assure participatory democracy.

There is no one predominant lesbian perspective on AIDS. Even within fairly cohesive AIDS organizations with explicit values and priorities concerning the epidemic and women, there is considerable variation.

The priorities of women who have been active in AIDS response organizations have been undergoing considerable change as the organizations, themselves grow, and shrink, and as the nature of the epidemic and the federal, state, and local responses to it have changed. We should expect these transformations in priorities to continue.

GENERATIONAL DIFFERENCES

Of lesbians who got involved in the AIDS epidemic in the first five years, some have stayed within the field, even if they have moved to other organizations (as many gay men have done). They have become career AIDS professionals. A second group has moved into other allied fields (health education, public health, systems management), in some cases with a focus on women. A third group has left AIDS and health altogether, an option that as far as I can tell, is being pursued primarily by those women who were more tangentially or "accidentally" engaged, either because of a single friendship or a coincidence of employment (a lesbian takes a job in a food bank in an AIDS agency, but really wants to be a graphic designer and eventually succeeds at this).

While some have become simultaneous AIDS professionals and direct action activists, this does not seem to be common. McNeill found considerable hostility between the professionals and the activists in her sample. The professionals referred to the activists as irresponsible and ill-informed, while some of the activists thought that the professional women were co-opted. I would argue that, although there may have been the traditional hostility between members of the movement and the institutionalized service sector, there is also a generational split, reflecting major societal change in the last twenty years and its impact on these groups.

The differences between the older lesbians and the younger generation are deep, widespread in the lesbian community, and in many cases quite antagonistic. They affect how and why lesbians do – or don't do – AIDS work. They also affect how lesbians not involved with AIDS view the epidemic, sex (including safe sex), and lesbians who are connected to HIV and AIDS issues. Although the epidemic itself has helped to shape these differences, other social, economic, and cultural factors have also been at work. To explain this, I will conclude with comments on the two generations as they have emerged in this study of women engaged in AIDS activity.

The first group of lesbians (predominantly in their thirties and forties) grew up in the 1960s, where they were influenced both by more traditional female socialization and by the radical activism of the civil rights movement, anti-war demonstrations, and nascent feminism. In the 1970s, when many came of age and came out, feminism was strong, and the opportunity to be "out" relatively easily as a lesbian was new. For many of these women, simply "being" a lesbian and being public about it was a revolutionary sexual step.

The second generation, on the other hand, has come of age – and come out – in the 1980s, a decade marked by explicit sexuality debates, a much greater openness about what would have been called deviant behavior ten years ago, broad female access to education, a deepening depression, and a growing radicalism among both gay men (as the epidemic remains "uncured" and the failed health economy slams into their lives) and other segments of the population. They have less faith in education or government, less of a sense of individual futures, and their sexual radicalness goes beyond being a lesbian. Being able to be a lesbian is more of a given than it was even ten years ago and for many lesbians of the current generation, it is a very limiting identity.

During the 1980s, gay men explored "safe sex" and brought everything from fisting, dildos, and rimming to nipple rings, golden showers, and S/M scenes into public discussion – especially within the gay community, which by now had a shared press read by both men and women. Increasingly, lesbians, especially the younger ones, have sought access to this world of experimentation. Sexual activity that goes far beyond the feminist notions of equality and non-violence have become exciting options to the new generation. While some older feminist lesbians look on in disappointment, younger women (and a few of their older friends) attend Faster Pussycat, the G-Spot and the Ecstacy Lounge, where cruising, S/M, public sex, and such skills as the safe use of dildos, are being (re)introduced to a new generation.

The current generation of AIDS activist lesbians carries a different psychology, culture, politics, and sexuality from those who came to the movement in the early 1980s. The younger activists are connected to the older women by the term *lesbian* and by some similarities of sexual practice. Many, however, see their elders as sexually repressed, conservative and somewhat anti-male.

The two groups may be separated by certain common sources of cross-generational conflict (the inevitable activist mellowing that comes with age and the fact that the older women can be – and in some cases are – the parents of the younger women). But it is the social changes of the 1980s that have provided a different sexual and political framework and have led to a new sexuality and its political expression. The new sexuality includes an even more pointed critique of sexual identities and practices that are organized through the dichotomous categories of male and female. Rebellion by the next generation comes to us all.

NOTES

1 Doug McAdam, John McCarthy, and Mayer Zald, "Social Movements," in *Handbook of Sociology* (New York: Sage, 1988).

2 In 1987 I went on a one-week women's kayak trip, attended by a non-feminist, recently divorced, 53-year-old straight woman who was shocked that everyone but her and the tour guide were lesbians. "What did she expect?" one dyke kayaker asked.

3 See especially Alice Echols, *Daring to Be Bad: Radical Feminism in America, 1967–1975* (Minneapolis: University of Minnesota, 1989), for an excellent analysis of the radical side of 1970s feminism.

4 This approach, which obscures the activity of those who do not command major amounts of resources and media, is repeated in the histories of many movements, where the roles of the poor, the oppressed, and the companions of the powerful are repeatedly denigrated or made invisible because they have produced fewer material records of their role (fewer books, films, newspapers, paintings) which are easily accessible to historians and journalists of dominant classes and races. They are then proclaimed non-existent as activists and creators.

5 B. Epstein, "Lesbians Lead the Movement," *Out/Look* (summer 1988): 27–32.

6 It is interesting that, when straight white men write the history of the 1970s, again and again they record the death of "the movement." What movement do they mean? Perhaps it is "their" movement (the anti-war movement built on the civil rights movement), which was moribund. Of the active movements of the 1970s, which they did not lead, they seem to see little, perhaps because they were not in their center. Feminism, gay rights, movements in Latino and Native American communities, the rise of mass-based anti-nuclear, activism, and environmentalism seem to have passed them by, until they were labeled "identity politics" and somehow defused into "culture" and no longer "real" politics. Defining these movements as being primarily about identity gives the incorrect impression that they are simply about the assertion of community, and not about structural issues at all.

7 John D'Emilio, "The Gay Community after Stonewall," in *Making Trouble* (New York: Routledge, 1992); Estelle Freedman and John D'Emilio, *Intimate Matters: A History of Sexuality in the United States* (New York: Harper & Row, 1988).

8 Carol Gilligan, *In a Different Voice, Psychological Theory and Women's Development* (Cambridge, MA: Harvard University Press, 1982).

9 S. Hoagland, *Lesbian Ethics* (Palo Alto: Institute of Lesbian Studies, 1988).

10 See B. Burch, "Psychological Merger in Lesbian Couples: A Joint Ego Psychological and Systems Approach," *Family Therapy* 9 (1982): 201–77; J. Krestan and C. Bepko, "The Problem of Fusion in the Lesbian Relationship," *Family Process* 19 (1980): 277–89; and S. Smalley,

"Dependency Issues in Lesbian Relationships," *Journal of Homosexuality* 14 (1987): 125–36.

11 Cf. Randy Shilts, *And the Band Played On* (New York: St Martin's, 1987), Larry Kramer, *Faggots* (New York: Random House, 1978) and *Reports from the Holocaust: The Making of an AIDS Activist* (New York: St Martin's, 1989), among other works.

12 See especially A. Snitow, C. Stansell, and S. Thompson (eds), *Powers of Desire: The Politics of Sexuality* (New York: Monthly Review Press, 1983, and Carole S. Vance (ed.) *Pleasure and Danger: Exploring Female Sexuality* (Boston: Routledge, 1984), to get a sense of the nature of these debates.

13 See works by Andrea Dworkin, such as *Pornography: Men Possessing Women* (New York: Perigree, 1981), and Catharine MacKinnon for the detailed expression of this perspective.

14 The best accounts of this conflict and the confusion experienced by femmes and butches of the 1970s and 1980s is found in Joan Nestle's excellent anthology, *The Persistent Desire: A Femme–Butch Reader* (Boston: Alyson, 1992).

15 Cf. Melissa A. McNeill, *Who Are "We"? Exploring Lesbian Involvement in AIDS Work* (Master's Thesis, Smith College School of Social Work, 1991).

16 The alert reader will note the parallelism between my typology and recurrent value constructs concerning appropriate women's roles: traditionalism, liberal feminism, socialist feminism (coalition building), and radical/separatist/lesbian feminism.

17 By this term I mean people who received their primary income from AIDS activities and who met the sociologial definition of a professional, someone whose primary value is in his or her education and received honorific payment.

18 McNeill: 50.

19 Interestingly, in 1992, the notion that lesbians have litle risk from AIDS and are suffering from "virus envy," resurfaced in England, where it is evident in writing by Simon Watney and in the most recent posters from the Terrence Higgins Trust, which proclaim that "Oral sex is very low risk, so throw away those dental dams." Lesbian inventors of the posters claim that safe-sex emphasis for lesbians is part of a combined negative attitude toward sex and a desire by some to be a greater part of the epidemic. See also Watney, *Policing Desire: Pornography, AIDS and the Media* (Minneapolis: University of Minnesota Press, 1987).

20 Interview with Katy Taylor of the New York Human Rights Commission (1989).

21 "About 142,000 American women develop [breast cancer] each year and 43,000 die of it. Only lung cancer causes more cancer deaths among American women." *New York Times* (November 9, 1989): B22, referring to an article in *NEJM* for November 9, 1989.

22 Jackie Winnow, "Lesbians Working on AIDS: Assessing the Impact on Health Care for Women," *Out/Look* 5 (1989): 10–18.

23 McNeill: 55.

BETH E. SCHNEIDER

"Peril and Promise: Lesbians' Workplace Participation"

from Trudi Darty and Sandee Potter (eds), *Women-Identified Women* (Palo Alto: Mayfield Publishers, 1984): 211–30

Lesbians must work.[1] Put most simply, few lesbians will ever have, however briefly, the economic support of another person (man or woman); lesbians are dependent on themselves for subsistence. Thus, a significant portion of the time and energies of most lesbians is devoted to working. Working as a central feature of lesbian existence is, however, rarely acknowledged. As with any significant primary commitment by a woman to job or career, a lesbian's relationship to work is obscured, denied, or trivialized by cultural assumptions concerning heterosexuality.[2]

Moreover, the concept *lesbian* is so identified with sexual behavior and ideas of deviance, particularly in social science literature,[3] that it has been easy to ignore the fact that lesbians spend their time at other than sexual activities; for a lesbian, working is much more likely to be a preoccupation than her sexual or affectional relations. Given the limited research on the sexual behavior of lesbians over the course of their lives, it is no surprise that there is decidedly less known about the working lives and commitments of lesbians.

In asserting the centrality, if not the primacy, of a working life to lesbians, we assume that work provides both a means of economic survival and a source of personal integrity, identity, and strength. While lesbians are certainly not the only women whose identities are at least partially formed by their relationship to work, in a culture defined for women in terms of heterosexual relations and limited control over the conditions of motherhood, most lesbians are likely to have fewer of the commitments and relations considered appropriate and necessary to the prevailing conceptions of women.

On the other hand, work and one's relationship to it is considered a major source of economic and social status, personal validation, and life purpose – certainly for men – in this society.[4] For lesbians then, whose lives will not necessarily provide or include the constraints or the comforts that other women receive ("heterosexual privileges"), working may well take on additional and special meaning. Thus, lesbians' workplace participation is shaped by the possibility of a unique commitment to working, an outsider status by dint of sexual identity, and the set of conditions common to all women workers. The conflicting aspects of these forces define the problematic and often paradoxical context within which lesbians work.

Being a woman worker has many implications for lesbians' material, social, and emotional well-being. Compared to their male counterparts, women employed full-time continue to receive significantly less pay.[5] Most do not have college degrees and enter occupations of traditional female employment where unionization is rare, benefits meager and prestige lacking.[6] Continued employment in female-dominated occupations maintains women's disadvantage relative to men, since it is associated with lower wages; typically, lower wages keep women dependent on men – their husbands (when they have them) or their bosses.[7] In those situations in which women and men are peers at work, status distinctions remain, reflecting the realities of sexism in the workplace and the society.[8] In general then, women are on the lower end of job and authority hierarchies. In addition, basic to the economic realities of all working women is the need to appear (through dress and demeanor) sexually attractive to men, who tend to hold the economic position and power to enforce heterosexual standards and desires.[9]

Thus, as one portion of the female labor force, lesbians are in a relatively powerless and devalued position, located in workplaces occupied but not controlled by women. Herein lies one paradox of a great many lesbians' working lives. The world of women's labor – with its entrenched occupational and job segregation – creates a homosocial female environment, a millieu potentially quite comfortable for lesbians.

But lesbians must also manage their sexual identity difference[10] at work. As women whose sexual, political, and social activities are primarly with other women, lesbians are daily confronted with heterosexual assumptions at work. The nature and extent of heterosexual pressures (over and above those experienced by all women) condition the nature of their social relationships. Two markedly different dynamics simultaneously affect lesbians in their daily interactions at work.

Negative attitudes toward homosexuality are still widespread in the society. The statements and activities of New Right leaders and organizations and the research results of a number of studies on less politicized populations indicate that lesbians and male homosexuals must continue to be cautious in their dealings with the heterosexual world and to be wary of being open about their sexual identity in certain occupations – especially teaching.[11]

Directly related to these public attitudes, employment-related issues and articles tend to predominate in the lesbian and gay press. Either legislative and political efforts toward an end to discrimination are detailed and progress assessed, or some person or persons who have lost their jobs or personal credibility when their sexual identity has become known or suspected are written up. For example, recently readers of both the alternative press and mass media have seen accounts of the anticipated disastrous financial consequences of a publicly revealed lesbian relationship on the women's tennis tour, community censure of public officials who spoke in favor of antidiscrimination laws, lesbian feminists fired or not rehired at academic

jobs, and a purge of suspected lesbians aboard a Navy missile ship, among others.[12]

Nevertheless, there is little systematic evidence that indicates how particular heterosexuals react to lesbians in concrete situations. It is these daily encounters and interactions with heterosexuals that are of crucial concern to lesbians; at work, the disclosure of one's sexual identity might have serious consequences. In a recent study of job discrimination against lesbians, fully 50 percent anticipated discriminaion at work and 2 percent reported losing a job when their sexual identity became known.[13] But in addition, lesbians fear harassment and isolation from interpersonal networks; often they live under pressure or demands to prove they are as good as or better workers than their co-workers.[14]

Whether anyone is fired or legislation is won or lost, the world of work is perceived and experienced by lesbians as troublesome, ambiguous, problematic. And while it is generally assumed that lesbians are more tolerated than gay men and therefore safer at work and elsewhere, a climate of ambivalence and disapproval pervades the world within which lesbians work; most are not likely to feel immediately comfortable about their relationships to co-workers.

Despite these significant disadvantages and potential troubles, a number of studies consistently show that lesbians have stable work histories, are higher achievers than comparable heterosexual women,[15] and have a serious commitment to work, giving it priority because they must support themselves.[16] These findings suggest, but do not describe or document, that lesbians' workplace survival results from a complicated calculation of the degree to which a particular work setting allows them freedom to be open and allows for the negotiation and development of a support network.

At work and elsewhere, lesbians want and have friendships and relationships with other women; while some research suggests that lesbians are no different than single heterosexuals in the extent of their friendship networks, others describe much greater social contacts for lesbians since they must negotiate two possible overlapping worlds (work and social life) and most are free of familial constraints that pull other women away from work relationships.[17] Whatever the extent of their networks, it is these friendships and relationships that are a major source of workplace support – and complication – for lesbians, as well as an important facet of their emotional well-being and job satisfaction.

However, there is virtually no research that systematically explores lesbian work sociability, the creation of a support mechanism there, or the conditions under which lesbians are willing to make their sexual identity known. Most of what is known about these problems is based on findings from research on male homosexuals, and therefore does not take into account the greater importance women as a group, and lesbians specifically, attach to emotional support and relationships.[18] Nevertheless, this research indicates that the more a male is known as a homosexual, the less stressful are his relationships with heterosexuals because he does not anticipate and defend against rejection.[19] But economic success frequently requires denying one's sexual identity: research findings over the last decade are consistent in showing that high-status males are less open than low-status males.[20] A combination of avoidance, information control, and role distance are strategies used by homosexuals to preserve secrecy; the result is often the appearance of being boring, unfriendly, sexless, or heterosexual.[21]

In addition to focusing on men, many of these studies were completed prior to, or at the onset of, the gay liberation movement, which has continued to encourage and emphasize "coming out" for reasons of either political principle and obligation or personal health.[22] Certainly, in the last decade many lesbians have taken extraordinary risks in affirming their sexual identities and defending their political and social communities.[23]

In sum, lesbians' relationship to the world of work is both ordinary and unique. Based on findings from a recent study of 228 lesbian workers, a number of previously unexamined aspects of the conditions of lesbian participation at the workplace are explored here. Following a brief description of the research project from which this data is taken and a discussion of the sample generation and characteristics, four aspects of lesbian existence at work are discussed: (1) making friends, (2) finding a partner, (3) coming out, and (4) being harassed.

RESEARCH METHODS AND SAMPLE

The findings are part of a larger research project on working women (both lesbian and heterosexual) and their perspectives and experiences concerning sociability, sexual relationships, and sexual harassment at the workplace.[24] The project was not explicitly designed to directly examine instances of discrimination against lesbians and cannot adequately address that problem. It was designed to explore some of the more subtle interpersonal terrain that all women are likely to encounter at work, as well as those situations of particular concern to lesbians.

The lesbian sample was gathered with the assistance of twenty-eight contacts who provided me with the names, addresses, and approximate ages of women who they thought were lesbians. The contacts provided 476 names. A self-administered questionnaire with 316 items was mailed to 307 of these contacts during the period between January and March 1980. The letter that accompanied the questionnaire did not assume any knowledge of a particular woman's sexual identity. Eighty-one percent of these women returned the questionnaire, a very high rate of return that seems to reflect significant interest in all the topics covered.

There were 228 women who identified themselves as either lesbian or homosexual or gay in the question asking for current sexual identity. This sample of lesbians ranged in age from 21 to 58 (median = 29.4); 10 percent were women of color (most Afro-American).[25] The sample was unique in that it was not a San Francisco or New York City based population; 55 percent were from New England, 33 percent from Middle Atlantic states and the rest were from other locations east of the Mississippi River.

The lesbians in this study were employed in all kinds of workplaces. More than half (57 percent) were in professional or technical occupational categories (in such jobs as teaching and social work), with the remaining distributed as follows: administrative and managerial (10 percent), clerical (11 percent), craft (7 percent), service (7 percent), operative (5 percent), and sales (2 percent). Sixty-nine percent worked full-time, 20 percent part-time, and the rest were unemployed at the time of the survey. Fifty-two percent were employed in predominantly (55 to 100 percent) female workplaces, 25 percent in workplaces with 80 percent or more females; 10 percent worked in units with 80 percent or more males. While the educational attainment of this group of lesbians was very high for a population of adult women (82 percent were at least college graduates), their median income was $8800 (in 1979). The low income of the total group reflects a combination of its relative youth and the proportion with less than full-time or full-year employment.

Two questions were asked to determine lesbians' openness about themselves at work, a matter of crucial concern to any understanding of daily workplace experiences. The first asked: "How open would you say you are about your lesbianism at your *present* job?" The choices were: "Totally," "Mostly," "Somewhat," "Not at all." The participants varied widely in the extent to which they felt they were open at work: Only 16 percent felt they were totally open, while 55 percent tended to be and 29 percent were closed about who they were at work.

The second question asked the proportion of each woman's co-workers who knew she was a lesbian. Twenty-five percent estimated that *all* their co-workers knew about their sexual identity,[26] half estimated that at least one or "some" knew, and 14 percent stated that "none knew." The remainder simply "didn't know" if anyone knew they were lesbians, a difficult and often anxiety-provoking situation.

MAKING FRIENDS

Most lesbians sampled believed it desirable to integrate their work and social lives in some ways.[27] Thus the distinction between public and private life is not terribly useful in describing their lives, despite its persistence as ideology throughout the culture.[28] For example, only one-third maintained that they kept their social life completely separate from their work life, and 39 percent tried not to discuss personal matters with persons from work. Alternately, 43 percent believed that doing things socially with co-workers makes relationships run more smoothly.

There obviously was variability in beliefs. Lesbians who most consistently and strongly held the view that work and social life should be integrated fell into two categories: those who had to – that is, lesbians in professional employment whose jobs required a certain level of sociability and collegiality, and those who had nothing to lose – women in dead-end jobs with no promise of advancement, those with few or no supervisory responsibilities; and those who were already open with persons from work about their sexual identity.

On the other hand, women who could not or did not believe these spheres could be easily or truly integrated were constrained by powerful forces that limited and denied the possibility of such integration: lesbians in male-dominated workplaces and those in worksites with male supervisors and bosses, in which males bond with each other often to the exclusion and detriment of the females.

The beliefs of the lesbians in the sample were quite consistent with the actual extent of their social contacts with persons from work. Most lesbians (in fact, most women) maintained social ties with at least some persons from work – at the job and outside it. Not surprisingly, 84 percent ate lunch with co-workers, but fewer engaged in social activities outside the work setting. For example, 9 percent visited frequently, 55 percent visited occasionally at each other's homes, 8 percent frequently and 47 percent occasionally went out socially with persons from work.

Two aspects of these findings merit further comment. First, the figures for the lesbians differ by less than 1 percent from those of the heterosexual women workers in the larger research project; if lesbians curtail contact or make certain judgments about co-workers as acquaintances or friends, they may do so for different reasons, but they do so to an extent similar to heterosexual women.

Second, certain conditions determine both lesbians' beliefs about, and the extensiveness of, their social contacts. Those in professional employment have more social ties with persons from work than lesbians in working-class jobs (which as a rule require less sociability); lesbians who are older, who have come to be familiar with a particular job setting over a length of time, and those who are open about their sexual identity are much more likely to maintain social contacts with co-workers than their younger or more closeted counterparts. In this particular study, there were no differences of any significance between lesbians of color and whites with regard to sociability; in fact the lesbians of color had, as a group, more contact with co-workers. This is not surprising in that the networking that produced the original sample reached only as far as a particular group of lesbians of color, who were disproportionately employed in feminist workplaces such as women's centers and women's studies programs, locations that facilitate, however imperfectly, such sociability. Those conditions in which a female culture can develop (granted, often within the limits of a male work world) allow lesbians greater possibilities for being open about their sexual identity with at least some co-workers. Familiar and supportive conditions tend to foster friendships and, as will become clear in the next section, provide the basis upon which more intimate relationships may also develop.

When there is a need to be social, lesbians are; professional jobs require sociability, but very many also require some degree of secrecy as well. This is particularly true for work in traditionally male occupations. In addition, and more important given women's location in the occupational structure, working with children (as teachers, nurses, social workers) can be cause for a relatively closeted existence. In this research, working with children did not seem to influence the extent of lesbian sociability, but it did affect how open they were about themselves at their workplaces. Here lies a classic instance of a highly contradictory situation, one common to many persons in human services and educational institutions. An ideology prevails that encourages (often demands) honesty, trust, and congenial non-alienating working relationships, but a lesbian's ability to actively involve herself in the prescribed ways is often limited or contorted. Frye's description of her experience in a women's studies program captures the essence of the difficulties:

> But in my dealings with my heterosexual women's studies colleagues, I do not take my own advice: I have routinely and habitually muffled or stifled myself on the subject of Lesbianism and heterosexualism ... out of some sort of concern about alienating them.... Much more important to me is a smaller number who are my dependable political coworkers in the university, ... the ones with some commitment to not being homophobic and to trying to be comprehending and supportive of Lesbians and Lesbianism. If I estrange these women, I will lose the only footing I have, politically and personally, in my long-term work-a-day survival in academia. They are important, valuable and respected allies. I am very careful, over-careful, when I talk about heterosexuality with them.[29]

More traditional workplaces provide even fewer possibilities for support than the one described above.

FINDING A PARTNER

In the last section, brief reference is made to lesbians' sexual relationships at work. The typical story of the office affair seems to have little to do with lesbians. It centers on a boss (the powerful person, the man) and his secretary (the powerless person, the woman); the consequences of this double-edged inequality of occupational status and gender are of prime concern. As the story would have it, the powerful one influences the other's (the woman's) career in such a way that she is highly successful ("She slept her way to the top") or her work and career is permanently ruined. It is rarely acknowledged that relationships at work occur between co-workers or between persons of the same gender, or that the consequences may be close to irrelevant – at least with regard to the job. When acknowledged, it seems that heterosexual affairs are more tolerated than are lesbian or homosexual relations.[30]

But the facts tell another story.[31] Twenty-one percent of the lesbians in this study met their current partners at work; overall, 52 percent of the lesbians had had at least one sexual relationship with a person from work during their working lives. This amazingly high proportion makes sense when it is remembered that the vast majority of women (and lesbians) are employed in female-dominated workplaces. Such a work setting is a good location for a lesbian to find a potential lover. But in addition, there have traditionally been few places – other than bars – for lesbians to meet each other socially; most meet, and still meet, through friendship networks (44 percent). While recently the women's and lesbians' communities have provided some alternatives – restaurants, clubs, political activities – employment plays such a significant part in lesbians' lives (and takes such a significant part of their time), that the workplace becomes an important, almost obvious, site for creating and having friendships and more intimate relationships.

Nineteen percent of the currently self-identified lesbians were heterosexual and 9 percent were married at the time of the sexual relationship they reported. This means that 81 percent were lesbians when they entered into at least a somewhat committed (and potentially risky) relationship with a person from work.

The chances that a lesbian will have a relationship with someone at work increase with age. To illustrate, while 79 percent of the sampled lesbians over 40 had had a relationship with someone at work sometime in their lifetime, 59 percent in their thirties and 42 percent in their twenties had had such an involvement. In addition, the longer a woman has identified herself as a lesbian (whatever her age), the more likely she is to have an intimate relationship with a person at work. This certainly suggests that some part of the freedom to pursue an involvement in the work setting is an easiness with oneself as a lesbian and a flexibility and wisdom gained from years of managing the complexities of sexual identity difference at work.

Most of the relationships reported were not brief affairs; 60 percent of the lesbians had been or were currently in a relationship of a year or more duration. Having such a relationship can have many effects, many small and predictable, others large and less controllable. Perhaps most obviously, the longer a relationship lasts, the more likely are some people at work (in addition to friends outside work) to know of the involvement. (In contrast to the heterosexuals in the larger study, lesbians tended to be more secretive about the relationship with people from work.)

Since the "office affair" mythology assumes a heterosexual relationship and the dynamic of superior–subordinate, it is useful to examine who in fact the lesbian workers were involved with. Eighteen percent of the lesbians were involved with a man (most, but not all, were heterosexual at the time); the few self-identified lesbians who were nevertheless involved with a man were almost exclusively involved with their boss in relatively brief affairs. Overall, 75 percent were involved with co-workers, 14 percent with boss or supervisor, 6 percent with subordinates, and 5 percent with customers, clients, and the like. With the female boss still very much a rarity, lesbians are less likely to have the option of a relationship with a woman with institutionalized authority over their working lives. This is in contrast to heterosexual women, whose relationships at work tend to be unequal as a result of the mix of gender and status inequality.

There were only a few consistent and predictable patterns in the effects and consequences of these relationships for the lesbians as a group. Seventy-two percent enjoyed their work more than usual. Some involvements improved relationships with other co-workers (25 percent) while others caused problems with co-workers (35 percent) or trouble with a boss or supervisor (20 percent). Much of the difficulty during the course of the relationship seemed to stem from jealousies, irritation at undone work, or inattention on the part of one or both of the parties to others. Also, the involvements often highlighted the lesbians' sexual identity, forcing them to be less closeted. The data suggest that one of the conflicts a lesbian must face in having a relationship at work is a willingness to either engage in massive secrecy and denial of the situation or become more clear about who she is. Many lesbians (39 percent) reported relief at the end of their involvements in part because hostility or gossip was lessened, in part because the pressures of enforced secrecy were removed.

The effects of being and becoming open about one's sexual identity as a consequence of the relationship are mixed and complicated, and often contradictory. For example, 62 percent of the more open lesbians compared to 19 percent of the more closed ones reported significantly greater friction with co-workers and some (22 percent) felt their chances for advancement were diminished. On the other hand, 31 percent of the more open lesbians reported improvement in workplace relations and improved advancement possibilites (10 percent); they enjoyed their work more than the closed lesbians. It is interesting to note that not one lesbian who was closed about her sexual identity at work believed that her chances for promotion were affected one way or the other by her involvement.

Almost everyone reported suffering the usual kinds of emotional problems at the termination of the relationship, obviously the longer the relationship the more so. The work-related consequences of lesbian involvements with women of similar job status are much simpler and less harmful than those with a superior. Thirteen percent of the lesbians resigned or quit because of the breakup; most of the lesbians who resigned were involved with a boss, rather than a co-worker, some few of whom were women. A very few lesbians (4 percent) reported losing out on some career-related opportunity, such as a promotion or pay increase; none reported gaining any work benefit. In 15 percent of the instances, the other people left the job at the termination of the relationship; in all these cases these were female co-workers.

In general, involvements at work are an integral part of a lesbian's emotional commitments to women. This extension of the prescribed limits of relationships beyond friendship is consistent with most other research on lesbians that similarly shows fluid boundaries between friends and lovers and friendship networks of former lovers.[32]

COMING OUT

Most lesbians are acutely aware that their openness about their lesbianism is not an all-or-nothing phenomenon at work or elsewhere but that it varies depending at the very least on the context and on the particular individuals involved. The lesbians in this study clearly varied in their own sense of how open they *felt* they were at work. As we already saw, being open allowed lesbians greater contact with co-workers, facilitating network-building and support as well as being a basis for (and a possible result of) having a sexual relationship with someone at work.

This study indicates that lesbians tend to be open about their sexual identity when their workplace has a predominance of women and most of their work friends are women, when they have a female boss or supervisor, when they are employed in small workplaces, when they have few supervisory responsibilities, when they have relatively low incomes, and when they are not dealing with children as either students, clients, or patients.

Two aspects of these findings require special comment. First, as noted earlier, the situation of professionally employed lesbians is terribly contradictory. Since the jobs require socializing and contacts with others either at work or in the business or professional communities, lesbians maintain those social contacts; on the other hand, high income professional lesbians are likely to be closeted. The result of this predicament is a well-managed, manicured life delivered to people with whom one is spending a great deal of time.

Second, the influence of gender proportions is crucial. For example, in workplaces that were heavily female-dominated (80 percent or more women as employees), 55 percent of the lesbians were totally or mostly open about their sexual identity. It is worth noting that this still means that 45 percent tended to be somewhat closeted even in these settings. In contrast, in heavily male-dominated workplaces (80 percent or more men as employees), only 10 percent of the lesbians were open.

A workplace with a predominance of women may include other lesbians to whom a lesbian can be open; they may also become friends or lovers. Of the lesbians who met another lesbian at work, almost all (94 percent) did in fact become friends. But even when there are not other lesbians at work, lesbians take certain risks, trusting at least one heterosexual woman to not react negatively to knowledge of her sexual identity. Moreover, most women are not in a structurally powerful position to affect the conditions under which lesbians work. When lesbians do have a female supervisor or boss, they are more often open about their sexual identity than with a male boss. For example, only 21 percent of lesbians with a male boss were open, compared to 47 percent who were open with a female boss. When lesbians were themselves the boss or were self-employed, 88 percent were open about their sexual identity.

How open a lesbian is at her current job is not related to her age or race, or the length of time she has been at that position. However, if she has lost a previous job because she is a lesbian, she is less sociable with people from work at her current job and tends to be more cautious about "coming out" at work. In this study 8 percent of the lesbians reported losing a job when their sexual identity became known and another 2 percent believed (but did no know for certain) they lost a job for this reason. The relatively young age of this sample may account for the lower proportion of job loss than in other studies. Whatever the extent of their openness, 75 percent of all lesbians were concerned that their lesbianism might cause damage to their job or career.

In summary, openness is most likely under conditions that are intimate and safe, free of potentially serious consequences for a lesbian's working life. That is, lesbians are most likely to be open in a small workplace, with a female boss, in a job with relatively little financial or social reward (and possibly few career risks).

The consequences of being open are substantial. Open lesbians have more friends and more social contact at work than closed lesbians; they are more willing to have, and do have, sexual relationships with women from their workplace. In contrast, and almost by definition, lesbians who are closed about their sexual identity at work are more likely to avoid certain situations with co-workers and feel reluctant to talk about their personal life.

While cause and effect is admittedly difficult to disentangle here, open and closed lesbians differ in the extent to which they feel that their sexual identity causes problems in many areas of their life. This research indicates that lesbians who remain closeted at work are obviously more concerned and afraid than open lesbians about losing their jobs. But in addition, closeted lesbians are much more concerned than open ones about losing their friends, harming their relationship with their parents, and, where applicable, harming their lovers' careers or child custody situations. Consistent with this is the finding that openness at work is related to a general freedom to be open elsewhere as well: Lesbians who are open at work are more likely to be open with parents and with both female and male heterosexual friends.

Not surprisingly, closed and open lesbians have uniquely different feelings about their positions at work. Closeted lesbians suffer from a sense of powerlessness and significant strain and anxiety at work, while open lesbians have greater emotional freedom. Eighty-four percent of the closed lesbians in the study felt they had no choice about being closeted; two-thirds felt uncomfortable about that decision, and 39 percent felt that the anxiety about being found out was "paralyzing." A significant 36 percent devoted time and emotion to maintaining a heterosexual front at work.

On the other hand, 94 percent of the open lesbians felt better since coming out, and while the strength of their feelings varied, most felt they were treated with respect because of their candor. Forty percent reported that their work relationships were a lot better than they were before coming out. Disclosure of one's sexual identity at work allows for the possibility of integrating into the workplace with less anxiety about who one is and how one is perceived. But there are some negative consequences to coming out. Twenty-nine percent of the open lesbians sensed that some co-workers avoided them and 25 percent admitted to working harder to keep the respect they had from their peers. While these consequences seem insignificant in contrast to the benefits of disclosure, it is good to remember that coming out often can be a quite limited communication to a quite limited number of persons; thus, protection is built into the very choice of context and relationship.

BEING HARASSED

Eighty-two percent of the lesbians studied experienced sexual approaches at work in the year of the study: that is, 33 percent were sexually propositioned, 34 percent were pinched or grabbed, 54 percent were asked for a date, and 67 percent were joked with about their body or appearance by someone at the workplace.[33] These figures are high for one year; they are however, comparable to those for the heterosexual women in the larger research project who were of similar race and age. Relatively young, unmarried women (this fits the description of most of the lesbians in the study) and those who worked in male-dominated work settings were most often the recipients of these sexual approaches. Ironically enough, the lesbians who tended to be secretive about their sexual identity (therefore presumed to be heterosexual) were more often sexually approached in these particular ways than the more open lesbians. For example, while 32 percent of the more closed lesbians were pinched or grabbed, only 12 percent of the more open were; likewise, 26 percent of the more closed in contrast to 13 percent of the more open were sexually propositioned.

In comments written to the researcher, it became evident that some lesbians were occasionally referring to both women and men in reporting on date requests and jokes, the more prevalent types of interactions. Unfortunately, the data for these experiences did not specify the gender of the initiator, thus making impossible a true profile of all interpersonal dynamics of this sort.

When asked their emotional response to these experiences ("like," "mixed," "dislike"), the great majority (more than 90 percent) reported disliking pinching or grabbing and sexual propositions – whoever initiated them; few lesbians in fact ever reported liking any incident. The one exception was being asked for a date by a co-worker, and even here only 9 percent said they liked this interaction, with 46 percent "mixed." Toleration (mixed feelings) was the main response to jokes and date requests. And in all cases, co-workers were the most tolerated group of initiators; some of these co-workers may well be women. Typically, co-workers do not have the institutionalized authority to affect each other's job or career standing though they may nevertheless make life more difficult in these kinds of ways.

We cannot directly infer from these data the meaning of these experiences to lesbian workers. Unwanted sexual approaches can be seen as harassment explicitly targeted at a lesbian because she is a lesbian or as harassment typically experienced by most working women. These sexual approaches highlight the disadvantages of lesbians in a working environment by emphasizing heterosexual norms of intimacy and behavior and accenting further the outsider position many lesbians feel at work. Research that compares lesbian workers with heterosexual women workers indicates that while lesbians and heterosexuals have a quite similar number of such approaches in their daily lives, these interactions are experienced quite differently. Lesbians are more sensitive to the problem of unwanted sexual approaches and are much more willing than heterosexuals to label behaviors of this type as sexual harassment.[34]

CONCLUSION

This research was an effort using quantitative data to describe the context of daily life at work for lesbians and to understand the sources of lesbian survival at work. It was not a definitive study of the prevalence of lesbian job loss or harassment.

The findings showed fewer difficulties at work than other studies seem to indicate, but like that research, it insufficiently explored the meanings lesbians attach to particular situations. One obvious question that remains is the extent to which a problem or harassment situation at work is attributed specifically to discrimination on the basis of sexual identity rather than understood as a reflection of the general condition of women. In this research (in which all but one of the lesbians indicated that she was a feminist), the interpretation of events is complicated and complex.

Applying a feminist interpretation to certain workplace situations could diminish or exaggerate the extent to which lesbians perceive those instances as resulting from, or in reaction to, their lesbianism. Sexual harassment is a particularly clear case. A lesbian may well wonder why she was hugged by a male co-worker: was it a gesture of friendship, harassment specifically directed to her as a lesbian, or harassment similar to that most women encounter at work? If most lesbians considered the variety of harassing experiences at work discrimination against them as lesbians, the proportion reporting workplace problems would surely increase.

While a more complete picture of workplace problems awaits additional research, these findings underscore some important dimensions of lesbians' workplace participation. First, the experience of lesbians is both similar and different from that of heterosexual women workers. It is similar in (1) the creation of a supportive environment of work friends, (2) the experience of unwanted sexual approaches from various parties with whom they interact, and (3) the use of the workplace to meet sexual partners. It is different in (1) the necessity of strategizing in the face of fear of disclosure and possible job loss, and (2) the meanings attached to interactions and events in the workplace.

While the fear of job or career loss or damage is often uppermost in a recitation of workplace problems, most lesbians do not lose their jobs. Two mutually reinforcing aspects of a strategy seem to account for this general lack of this most serious and negative sanction. First, lesbians tend to remain closeted, keeping their sexual identity secret from most persons at work; at the same time, they create an environment that protects them, emotional ties with a few people who contribute to a sense of a less hostile and alienating work world.

Coming out is clearly a process; within any particular institutional context, such as work, an assessment is made as to the degree to which a lesbian can be open about who she is. The extent of disclosure varies, dependent on the particulars of personnel and place; it changes over time. Certainly few are the lesbians and fewer still the workplaces that can manage or tolerate complete disclosure. At the minimum, lesbians come out when they are ready and conditions are good, meaning in some workplaces and with some people. While the exact process is not detailed here, it is clear that coming out occurs when a woman believes that a person is trustworthy, sensitive, or politically aware. This is an assessment over which a lesbian has some control. When a lesbian is known as such at work, a congenial and supportive relationship has typically preceded disclosure.

The ease with which a lesbian is disclosing about her sexual identity reflects historically specific conditions as well. In this sample of highly politicized lesbian women workers in late 1979, 40 percent felt they were totally or mostly open about being lesbians; 75 percent were concerned that their lesbianism might affect their employment situation. In the current climate of conservatism reflected in recent efforts to defend and preserve the "sanctity of the family,"[35] lesbians are forced to constantly weigh the costs of disclosure. Thus, a combination of forces – personal choice, workplace characteristics, and political concerns – continue to define the options and limitations of the workplace environment.

Finally, female support systems at work – allies and networks – can be seen as an integral part of lesbians' emotional commitments to women. While it is certainly ironic and contradictory to exclaim the virtues of "women's work," with its devalued economic and social worth, those workplaces do provide an easier, more congenial atmosphere than is immediately available in more highly paid, male-segregated locations. Many lesbians know these facts and in decisions regarding work may well take them into account.

While the fear and peril of lesbians' workplace situation cannot be denied or diminished, neither can the challenge. Lesbians' participation and relationship to work is similar to the kind of "double vision" shared by other groups who are outsiders:[36] an acute awareness of the strength and force of an oppressive ideology of heterosexuality and its structural manifestations, coupled with an active accommodation and creation of a livable working environment.

NOTES

1 The only concern of this article is with lesbians in paid employment. Necessarily excluded are volunteer labor in political activities and unpaid labor of household maintenance and child care responsibilities. While there are seventeen lesbians who are working for wages in consciously organized feminist workplaces, and they are included in the discussion, no effort is made to talk about the particular challenges of working in such locations.

2 The socioemotional climate of work is based on strong cultural assumptions of heterosexuality. An ideology of heterosexuality includes the following beliefs: (1) All persons are heterosexual. (2) All intimate relations occur between persons of opposite gender. (3) Heterosexual relationships are better – healthier, more normal – than homosexual relations. With regard to employment, the ideology assumes that every woman is defined by, and in some way is the property of, a man (father, husband, boss); thus, women's work is secondary, since she is, will be, or ought to be supported by a man. See the following for statements concerning the cultural and structural dimensions of heterosexuality; Charlotte Bunch, "Not for Lesbians Only," *Quest: A Feminist Quarterly* 2 (fall 1975): 50–6; Gayle Rubin, "The Traffic in Women: Notes on the 'Political Economy' of Sex," in Rayna Rapp (ed.), *Toward an Anthropology of Women* (New York: Monthly Review Press, 1975): 157–210; Catharine A. MacKinnon, *Sexual Harassment of Working Women: A Case of Sex Discrimination* (New Haven, CT: Yale University Press, 1979); Adrienne Rich, "Compulsory Heterosexuality and Lesbian Existence," *Signs* 5 (4): 631–60; Lisa Leghorn and Katherine Parker, *Women's Worth: Sexual Economics and the World of Women* (Boston: Routledge & Kegan Paul, 1981).

3 See Anabel Faraday, "Liberating Lesbian Research," and Kenneth Plummer, "Homosexual Categories: Some Research Problems in the Labelling Perspective of Homosexuality," in Kenneth Plummer (ed.), *The Making of the Modern Homosexual* (Totowa, NJ: Barnes & Noble Books, 1981).

4 For a review of the literature on the relationship of work to individual wellbeing, see Rosabeth Moss Kanter, *Work and Family in the United States: A Critical Review and Agenda for Research and Policy* (New York: Rusell Sage, 1977).

5 United States Bureau of Labor Statistics, *Perspectives on Working Women: A Databook*, Bulletin 2080 (Washington, DC: US Government Printing Office, 1980).

6 Louise Kapp Howe, *Pink Collar Workers: Inside the World of Women's Work* (New York: G. P. Putnam's, 1977).

7 Heidi Hartman, "Capitalism, Patriarchy, and Job Segregation by Sex," in Zillah Eisenstein (ed.), *Capitalist Patriarchy and the Case for Socialist Feminism* (New York: Monthly Review Press, 1979): 206–47.

8 Neal Gross and Anne Trask, *The Sex Factor and Management of Schools* (New York: John Wiley, 1976); and Rosabeth Moss Kanter, *Men and Women of the Corporation* (New York: Basic Books, 1977).

9 MacKinnon.

10 Throughout this article, sexual identity, rather than sexual orientation or sexual preference, is the term used to describe and distinguish heterosexual and lesbian women. As a construct, sexual identity most adequately describes the process of creating and maintaining an identity as a sexual being. In contrast to sexual orientation, it does not assume an identity determined by the end of childhood; in contrast to sexual preference, it does not narrow the focus to the gender of one's partner or to particular sexual practices. See Plummer (n. 3 above) for a recent discussion of the issues and problems of homosexual categorization in the social sciences.

11 Amber Hollibaugh, "Sexuality and the State: The Defeat of the Briggs Initiative," *Socialist Review* 45 (May–June 1979): 55–72; Linda Gordon and Alan Hunter, "Sex, Family and the New Right," *Radical America* 11 (Nov. 1977–Feb. 1978); George Gallup, "Report on the Summer 1977 Survey of Attitudes Toward Homosexuality," *Boston Globe* (September 10, 1977); Albert Klassen Jr and Eugene Levitt, "Public Attitudes Toward Homosexuality," *Journal of Homosexuality* 1 (1974): 29–43.

12 See any issue of *Gay Community News* and any newsletter of the National Gay Task Force for a more complete sampling of these types of stories; also see Judith McDaniel, "We Were Fired: Lesbian Experiences in Academe," *Sinister Wisdom* 20 (spring 1982): 30–43; and J. R. Roberts, *Black Lesbians* (Tallahassee, FL: Nalad Press, 1981): 74–6.

13 Martin P. Levine and Robin Leonard, "Discrimination Against Lesbians in the Workforce," paper presented at Annual Meetings of the American Sociological Association, September 1982.

14 Sasha Gregory Lewis, *Sunday's Women: A Report on Lesbian Life Today* (Boston: Beacon

Press, 1979); Laud Humphreys, *Out of the Closets: The Sociology of Homosexual Liberation* (Englewood Cliffs, NJ: Prentice-Hall, 1972).

15 Jack Hedblom, "The Female Homosexual: Social and Attitudinal Dimensions," in Joseph McCaffrey (ed.), *The Homosexual Dialectic* (Englewood Cliffs, NJ: Prentice-Hall, 1972); William Simon and John Gagnon, "The Lesbians: A Preliminary Overview," in W. Simon and J. Gagnon (eds), *Sexual Deviance* (New York: Harper & Row, 1967): 247–82.

16 Fred A. Minnegerode and Marcy Adelman, "Adaptations of Aging Homosexual Men and Women," paper presented at Convention of the Gerontological Society, October 1976.

17 For an analysis that suggests a similarity of friendship networks between lesbians and single heterosexual women, see Andrea Oberstone and Harriet Sukoneck, "Psychological Adjustment and Lifestyles of Single Lesbians and Single Heterosexual Women," *Psychology of Women Quarterly* 1 (winter 1976): 172–88; for one that suggests differences between these two groups, see Alan Bell and Martin Weinberg, *Homosexualities: A Study of Diversity Among Men and Women* (New York: Simon and Schuster, 1978).

18 E. M. Ettorre, *Lesbians, Women and Society* (London: Routledge & Kegan Paul, 1980); also see Lewis, and Bell and Weinberg.

19 Martin Weinberg and Colin Williams, *Male Homosexuals: Their Problems and Adaptations* (New York: Oxford University Press, 1974).

20 Joseph Harry, "Costs and Correlates of the Closet," paper presented at annual meeting of the American Sociological Association, September 1982; also, Humphreys.

21 Kenneth Plummer, *Sexual Stigma: An Interactionist Account* (London: Routledge and Kegan Paul, 1977).

22 Karla Jay and Allen Young (eds), *Out of the Closets: Voices of Gay Liberation* (New York: Pyramid Books, 1972); Karla Jay and Allen Young (eds), *Lavender Culture* (New York: Jove Publications, 1978). See particularly, Barbara Grier, "Neither Profit Nor Salvation," in *Lavender Culture*: 412–20.

23 William Paul *et al.* (eds), *Homosexuality: Social, Psychological and Biological Issues* (Beverly Hill, CA: Sage Publications, 1982).

24 For those interested in more detailed statistical and analytical discussion of the findings of this research, see Beth E. Schneider, "Consciousness about Sexual Harassment Among Heterosexual and Lesbian Women Workers," *Journal of Social Issues* 38 (Dec. 1982): 75–97; and Beth E. Schneider, "The Sexualization of the Workplace," Ph.D. dissertation, University of Massachusetts, 1981.

25 It is difficult to assess the accuracy of the proportion of lesbians of color in this sample since the population is unknown. Moreover, because of racism in the feminist and lesbian communities as well as the varying extent to which sexual identity rather than race or class identity is most salient to lesbians of color, many may not be part of lesbian community networks. Thus, the sampling procedures used here – working through contacts (only two of whom were lesbians of color) – likely proved inadequate to reach them.

26 Ninety-four percent of the lesbians who reported that *all* co-workers knew they were lesbians also reported being "totally" or "mostly open" about their sexual identity. They were employed in all occupations, but a disproportionate number were in human service jobs (40 percent), and 27 percent were in explicitly feminist work organizations. Thirty-one percent were self-employed, in a collective, or were the boss or owner of a workplace; of those who worked for someone else, almost all had a woman supervisor.

27 Women workers' beliefs about the integration of their public and private lives were measured using an index composed of four statements. These were: "The best policy to follow is to keep work separate from friendship," "You try to keep your social life completely separate from your work life," "Doing things socially with co-workers makes work relationships run more smoothly," and "You follow the general rule of not discussing personal matters with people from work." The sociability index combined four behaviors to measure the extent of social contact the women had with people at their current jobs. These four were eating lunch together, talking on the phone after work hours, visiting at each other's homes, and going out socially.

28 For a discussion of these issues, see Kanter (n. 4 above) and Lydia Sargent (ed.), *Women and Revolution: A Discussion of the Unhappy Marriage of Marxism and Feminism* (Boston: South End Press, 1981).

29 Marilyn Frye, "Assignment: NWSA-Bloomington-1980: Lesbian Perspectives on Women's Studies," *Sinister Wisdom* 14 (1980): 3–7, esp. 3.

30 For one effort to discuss this distinction, see Richard Zoglin, "The Homosexual Executive," in Martin P. Levine (ed.), *Gay Men: The Sociology of Male Homosexuality* (New York: Harper & Row, 1979): 68–77.

31 The results described here are in response to a series of questions about involvement in sexual relationship at the workplace. The initial item – "Have you *ever* been involved in an intimate sexual relationship with someone from your

workplace?" – was followed by a series of descriptive questions about the relationship.

32. Ettorre; Lewis; Sidney Abbott and Barbara Love, *Sappho Was a Right-On Woman: A Liberated View of Lesbianism* (New York: Stein and Day, 1972); Del Martin and Phyllis Lyon, *Lesbian/ Woman* (San Francisco: Glide Publications, 1972).

33. Sixteen questions measured the frequency of experiences in the last year of: requests for dates, jokes about body or appearance, pinches or grabs, and sexual propositions by four initiators (boss, co-worker, subordinate, and recipient of service). Sixteen additional questions measured levels of dislike of these experiences. In the larger study, there were also questions concerning the general problem of unwanted sexual approaches at work and those behaviors that women most likely define as sexual harassment.

34 Schneider.

35. Zillah Eisenstein, "Antifeminism in the Politics and Election of 1980," *Feminist Studies* 7 (summer 1981): 187–205; Susan Harding, "Family Reform Movements," *Feminist Studies* 7 (spring 1981): 57–75; Rosalind Pollack Petchesky, "Antiabortion, Antifeminism and the Rise of the New Right," *Feminist Studies* 7 (summer 1981): 206–46.

36 See Barry Adam, *The Survival of Domination: Inferiorization and Everyday Life* (New York: Elsevier, 1978); Dorothy E. Smith, "A Sociology for Women," in Julia A. Sherman and Evelyn Torton Beck (eds), *The Prism of Sex: Essays in the Sociology of Knowledge* (Madison: University of Wisconsin Press, 1977); Albert Memmi, *Dominated Man: Notes Toward a Portrait* (Boston: Beacon Press, 1968); Erving Goffman, *Stigma: Notes on the Management of Spoiled Identity* (Englewood Cliffs, NJ: Prentice-Hall, 1963).

KATH WESTON

"Families We Choose"

from *Families We Choose: Gays, Lesbians, and Kinship* (New York: Columbia University Press, 1991): chapter 5

> Friendship is an upstart category, for it to usurp the place of kinship or even intrude upon it is an impertinence.
>
> (Elsie Clews Parsons)

Every Thursday night in the cityscape that framed my experience of "the field," my lover and I had dinner with Liz Andrews. The three of us juggled work schedules, basketball practice, and open-ended interviews around this weekly event. Occasionally these gatherings meant candlelight dinners, but more often Thursday found us savoring our repast in front of the TV. The first few weeks of gourmet meals gave way to everyday fare with a special touch, like avocado in the salad or Italian sausage in the spaghetti sauce.

Responsibility for planning, preparing, and subsidizing the meals rotated along with their location, which alternated between Liz's home and the apartment I shared with my lover. At only one point did this egalitarian division of labor and resources become the subject of conscious evaluation. Liz offered to pay a proportionately greater share of a high-ticket meal, reasoning that she had the largest income. In the ensuing discussion, reluctance to complicate "power dynamics" in the group resolved the issue in favor of maintaining equal contributions.

After supper we might play cards, trade anecdotes about mutual acquaintances, describe recent encounters with heterosexism, discuss world politics or the opening of a new lesbian strip show, exchange recipes, explain how we would reorganize the Forty-Niner offensive line-up, or propose strategies for handling the rising cost of living in San Francisco. Or we might continue watching television, taking advantage of commercial breaks

to debate that perennial enigma: "What *do* heterosexual women see in Tom Selleck, anyway?" While we grew comfortable with argument and with differences in our class backgrounds, age, and experiences, we tended to assume a degree of mutual comprehension as white women who all identified ourselves as lesbians.

After a few months of these dinners we began to apply the terms "family" and "extended family" to one another. Our remarks found a curious counterpart in a series of comments on changes in the behavior of Liz's cat. Once an unsociable creature that took to hiding and growling from the other room when strangers invaded her realm, now she watched silently from beneath the telephone table and even ventured forth to greet her visitors. Not that she does that for everyone, Liz reminded us: clearly we were being taken into an inner circle.

In retrospect, the incipient trust and solidarity imaged in this depiction of a world viewed through cat's eyes appears as one of several elements that combined to make Thursdays feel like family occasions. The centrality of the meal – sharing food on a regular basis in a domestic setting – certainly contributed to our growing sense of relatedness. In the United States, where the household is the normative unit of routinized consumption, many family relationships are also commensal relationships. Although we occupied separate households, we interpreted the option of independent residence as a feature distinguishing gay families from straight, one that qualified "our" kind of family as a creative innovation. In truth, this contrast may have been a bit overdrawn. Moving to the same neighborhood I had prompted the routinization of the weekly dinner meetings, and I personally enjoyed walking over to Liz's apartment when it was her turn to cook. These evening strolls underlined the spatial contiguity of our households while allowing me to avoid the seemingly interminable search for a parking space in San Francisco.

Efforts to encourage a low-key atmosphere framed our interactions during supper as everyday experience rather than a guest–host relationship. It was not uncommon for any one of us to leave immediately following the meal if we were tired or had other things to do. Conversation, while often lively, seldom felt obligatory. Also facilitating the developing family feeling was a sense of time depth that arose after the arrangement had endured several months, a dimension augmented by a ten-year friendship between Liz and myself.

On some occasions other people joined our core group for activities, events, and even Thursday night get-togethers. Once Liz asked two gay male friends to dinner, and another time – with somewhat more anticipation and formality – the group extended an invitation to Liz's parents. When her parents arrived a guest–host relationship prevailed, but Liz, my lover, and I became the collective hosts, preparing and serving the food and making sure that her parents were entertained. One could imagine other possible alignments: for example, Liz and her parents busy in her kitchen while my lover and I waited to be served. The differentiation of activities and space presented a graphic juxtaposition of the family Liz was creating with the family in which she had been raised. By introducing my lover and me to her parents in the context of a Thursday night meal, Liz hoped to bridge these two domains.

About the time that the three of us began to classify ourselves as family, we also began to provide one another with material assistance that went beyond cooking and cleaning up the dinner dishes. When one of us left on vacation, another volunteered to pick up the mail. After Liz injured her foot and decided to stay at her parents' house, I fed the cat. On street cleaning days Liz and my lover moved each other's vehicles. Liz offered me the use of her apartment for interviews or studying while she was at

work. "Emotional support" accompanied this sort of assistance, exemplified by midweek phone calls to discuss problems that could not wait until Thursday. Our joint activities began to expand beyond the kitchen and living room, extending to the beach, the bars, political events, restaurants, a tour of Liz's workplace, and Giants games at Candlestick Park.

Faced with the task of analyzing this type of self-described family relationship among lesbians and gay men, my inclination while yet in the field was to treat it as an instance of what anthropologists in the past have termed "fictive kin." The concept of fictive kin lost credibility with the advent of symbolic anthropology and the realization that all kinship is in some sense fictional – that is, meaningfully constituted rather than "out there" in a positivist sense. Viewed in this light, genes and blood appear as symbols implicated in one culturally specific way of demarcating and calculating relationships. Under the influence of Continental philosophy, literary criticism, and an emerging critique of narrative form in ethnographic writing, anthropological monographs – like the kinship structures they delineated – came up for review as tales and constructions, inevitably value-laden and interpretive accounts (Clifford 1988; Clifford and Marcus 1986; Geertz 1973; Marcus and Fischer 1986; Rabinow 1977). Although the category "fictive kin" has fallen from grace in the social sciences, it retains intuitive validity for many people in the United States when applied to chosen families. From coverage in the popular press to child custody suits and legislative initiatives, phrases such as "pretended family relations" and "so-called family" are recurrently applied to lesbian or gay couples, parents, and families of friends.

The very concept of a substitute or surrogate family suffers from a functionalism that assumes people intrinsically *need* families (whether for psychological support or material assistance). Commentators who dispute the legitimacy of gay families typically set up a hierarchical relationship in which biogenetic ties constitute a primary domain upon which "fictive kin" relations are metaphorically predicated. Within this secondary domain, relationships are said to be "like" family, that is, similar to and probably imitative of the relations presumed to actually comprise kinship. When anthropologists have discussed the institutionalization of "going for sisters" (or brothers, or cousins) among urban blacks in the United States, for example, they have emphasized that such relationships can be "just as real" as blood ties to the persons involved (Kennedy 1980; Liebow 1967; Schneider and Smith 1978; Stack 1974). While framed as a defense of participants' perspectives, this type of argument implicitly takes blood relations as its point of departure. Insofar as analysis becomes circumscribed by the unvoiced question that asks how authentic these "fictive" relations are, it makes little difference that authenticity refers back to a privileged and apparently unified symbolic system rather than an empirically observable universe.

Theoretically I have adopted a very different approach by treating gay kinship ideologies as historical *transformations* rather than derivatives of other sorts of kinship relations. Some might contend that these emergent ideologies represent variations modeled on a more generalized "American kinship" to the extent that they utilize familiar symbols such as blood and love, but this terminology of modeling would prove misleading.[1] As Rayna Rapp has convincingly argued,

> When we assume male-headed, nuclear families to be central units of kinship, and all alternative patterns to be extensions or exceptions, we accept an aspect of cultural hegemony instead of studying it. In the process, we miss the contested domain in which symbolic innovation may occur. Even continuity may be the result of innovation.
>
> (1987: 129)

Gay families do not occupy a subsidiary domain that passively reflects or imitates the primary tenets of a coherent "American kinship system." The historical construction of an ideological contrast between chosen (gay) families and blood (straight) family has not left biologistic and procreative conceptions of kinship untouched. But if coming out has supplied gay families with a specific content (the organizing principle of choice) by exposing the selective aspects of blood relations, it remains to be shown how choice became allied with kinship

and gay identity to produce a discourse on families we choose.

BUILDING GAY FAMILIES

The sign at the 1987 Gay and Lesbian March on Washington read: "Love makes a family – nothing more, nothing less." From the stage, speakers arguing for domestic partner benefits and gay people's right to parent repeatedly invoked love as both the necessary *and the sufficient* criterion for defining kinship. Grounding kinship in love deemphasized distinctions between erotic and non-erotic relations while bringing friends, lovers, and children together under a single concept. As such, love offered a symbol well suited to carry the nuances of identity and unity so central to kinship in the United States, yet circumvent the procreative assumption embedded in symbols like heterosexual intercourse and blood ties.

It has become almost a truism that "family" can mean very different things when complicated (as it always is) by class, race, ethnicity, and gender (Flax 1982; Thorne with Yalom 1982). In her studies of kinship among Japanese-Americans, Sylvia Yanagisako (1978, 1985) has demonstrated how the unit used to calculate relatedness ("families" or "persons") may change, and additional meanings adhere to symbols like love, based on variable definitions of context that invoke racial or cultural identities. Determining who is a relative in a context that an individual perceives as "Japanese" may draw on different meanings and categories than determining relationship in a context defined as "American."

In speaking broadly of "gay families," my objective is not to focus on that most impoverished level of analysis, the least common denominator, or to describe symbolic contrasts in pristine seclusion from social relations. Neither do I mean to imply an absence of differences among lesbians and gay men, or that gay families are constructed in isolation from identities of gender, race, or class. Rather, I have situated chosen families in the specific context of an ideological opposition between families defined as straight and gay – families identified with biology and choice, respectively. On the one hand, this highly generalized opposition oversimplifies the complexities of kinship organization by ignoring other identities while presenting its own categories as timeless and fundamental. On the other hand, the same discourse complicates understandings of kinship in the United States by pairing categories previously believed to be at variance ("gay" and "family").

The families I saw gay men and lesbians creating in the Bay Area tended to have extremely fluid boundaries, not unlike kinship organization among sectors of the African-American, American Indian, and white working class. David Schneider and Raymond Smith (1978: 42) have characterized this type of organization as one that can "create kinship ties out of relationships which are originally ties of friendship." Listen for a moment to Toni Williams's account of the people she called kin:

> In my family, all of us kids are godparents to each others' kids, okay? So we're very connected that way. By when I go to have a kid, I'm not gonna have my sisters as godparents. I'm gonna have people that are around me, that are gay. That are straight. I don't have that many straight friends, but certainly I would integrate them in my life. They would help me. They would babysit my child, or ... like my kitty, I'm not calling up my family and saying, "Hey, Mom, can you watch my cat?" No, I call on my inner family – my community, or whatever – to help me with my life.
>
> So there's definitely a family. And you're building it; it keeps getting bigger and bigger. Next thing you know, you have hundreds of people as your family. Me personally, I might not have a hundred, because I'm more of a loner. I don't have a lot of friends, nor do I *want* that many friends, either. But I see [my lover] as having many, many family members involved in what's going on.

What Toni portrayed was an ego-centered calculus of relations that pictured family members as a cluster surrounding a single individual, rather than taking couples or groups as units of affiliation. This meant that even the most nuclear of couples would construct theoretically distinguishable families, although an area of overlapping membership generally developed. At the same time, chosen families were not restricted to person-to-person ties. Individuals occasionally added entire groups with preexisting, multiplex connections among members. In one such case, a woman reported incorporating a "circle" of her new lover's gay family into her own kinship universe.

In the Bay Area, families we choose resembled networks in the sense that they could cross household lines, and both were based on ties that radiated outward from individuals like spokes on a wheel. However, gay families differed from networks to the extent that they quite consciously incorporated symbolic demonstrations of love, shared history, material or emotional assistance, and other signs of enduring solidarity. Although many gay families included friends, not just any friend would do.[2]

Fluid boundaries and varied membership meant no neatly replicable units, no defined cycles of expansion and contraction, no patterns of dispersal. What might have represented a nightmare to an anthropologist in search of mappable family structures appeared to most participants in a highly positive light as the product of unfettered creativity. The subjective agency implicit in gay kinship surfaced in the very labels developed to describe it: "families *we* choose," "families *we* create." In the language of significant others, significance rested in the eye of the beholder. Participants tended to depict their chosen families as thoroughly individualistic affairs, insofar as each and every ego was left to be the chooser. Paradoxically, the very notion of idiosyncratic choice – originally conceived in opposition to biogenetic givens – lent structural coherence to what people presented as unique renditions of family.

The variety in the composition of families we choose was readily apparent. At one Metropolitican Community Church service, when the time came for communion, the pastor invited congregants to bring along family members. In groups and in couples, with heads bowed and arms linked, people walking to the front of the church displayed ties of kinship and friendship for all to see. On a different occasion, I joined several people preparing for a birthday party in someone's home. When I asked what, if anything, separated those who came early to help decorate from those who arrived after the time officially set for festivities to begin, the host explained that the helpers were family, closer to her than most of the other guests.

Obituaries provide a relatively overlooked, if somber, source of information about notions of kinship. Death notices in the *Bay Area Reporter* (a weekly newspaper distributed in bars and other gay establishments) were sometimes written by lovers, and included references to friends, former lovers, blood or adoptive relatives (usually denominated as "father," "sister," etc.), "community members" present at a death or assisting during an illness, and occasionally co-workers. While I was conducting fieldwork, the *San Francisco Chronicle*, a major citywide daily, instituted a policy of refusing to list gay lovers as survivors, citing complaints from relatives who could lay claim to genealogical or adoptive ties to the deceased. Although the *Chronicle*'s decision denied recognition to gay families, it also testified to the growing impact of a discourse that refused to cede kinship to relations organized through procreation.

By opening the door to the creation of families different in kind and composition, choice assigned kinship to the realm of free will and inclination. In the tradition of Thoreau's *Walden*, each gay man and lesbian became responsible for the exemplary act of creating an ideal environment (cf. Couser 1979). People often presented gay families as a foray into uncharted territory, where the lack of cultural guideposts to mark the journey engendered fear and exhilaration.[3] Indeed, there was a utopian cast to the way many lesbians and gay men talked about the families they were fashioning. Jennifer Bauman maintained that as a gay person, "you're already on the edge, so you've got more room to be whatever you want to be. And to create. There's more space on the edge." What to do with all that "space"? "I create my own traditions," she replied.

"Choice" is an individualistic and, if you will, bourgeois notion that focuses on the subjective power of an "I" to formulate relationships to people and things, untrammeled by worldly constraints. Yet as Karl Marx (1963: 15) pointed out in an often quoted passage from *The 18th Brumaire*, "Men [*sic*] make their own history, but they do not make it just as they please; they do not make it under circumstances chosen by themselves but under circumstances directly

encountered, given and transmitted from the past." Only after coming out to blood relatives emerged as a historical possibility could the element of selection in kinship become isolated in gay experience and subsequently elevated to a constitutive feature of gay families.

Despite the ideological characterization of gay families as freely chosen, in practice the particular choices made yielded families that were far from randomly selected, much less demographically representative. When I asked people who said they had gay families to list the individuals they included under that rubric, their lists were primarily, though not exclusively, composed of other lesbians and gay men. Not surprisingly, the majority of people listed tended to come from the same gender, class, race, and age cohort as the respondent.

Both men and women consistently counted lovers as family, often placing their partners at the head of a list of relatives. A few believed a lover, or a lover plus children, would be essential in order to have gay family, but the vast majority felt that all gay men and lesbians, including those who are single, can create families of their own. The partner of someone already considered family might or might not be included as kin. "Yeah, they're part of the family, but they're like in-laws," laughed one man. "You know, you love them, and yet there isn't that same closeness."

Former lovers presented a particularly interesting case. Their inclusion in families we choose was far from automatic, but most people hoped to stay connected to ex-lovers as friends and family (cf. Becker 1988; Clunis and Green 1988).[4] When former lovers remained estranged, the surprise voiced by friends underscored the power of this ideal. "It's been ten years since you two broke up!" one man exclaimed to another. "Hasn't he gotten over it yet?" Of course, when a breakup involved hard feelings or a property dispute, such continuity was not always realizable. After an initial period of separation, many ex-lovers did in fact re-establish contact, while others continued to strive for this type of reintegration. As Diane Kunin put it, "After you break up, a lot of people sort of become as if they were parents and sisters, and relate to your new lover as if *they* were the in-law." I also learned of several men who had renewed ties after a former lover developed AIDS or ARC (AIDS-Related Complex). This emphasis on making a transition from lover to friend while remaining within the bounds of gay families contrasted with heterosexual partners in the Bay Area, for whom separation or divorce often meant permanent rupture of a kinship tie.

Jo-Ann Krestan and Claudia Bepko (1980: 285) have criticized lesbians' efforts to maintain relationships with former lovers as "triangling," (a no-no in therapeutic circles). They argue that such relationships "tend to be intrusive and involve inappropriate claims." But notions of appropriateness are culturally constituted and contested. What a person expects from an "ex" may not be what they expect from a friend who is also family. In the context of gay kinship, former lovers can be both.

A lover's biological or adoptive relatives might or might not be classified as kin, contingent upon their "rejecting" or "accepting" attitudes. Gina Pellegrini, for example, found refuge at a lover's house after her parents kicked her out of her own home as an adolescent. She was out to her lover's mother before her own parents, and still considered this woman family. Jorge Quintana claimed that his mother adored his ex-lover and vice versa, although Jorge had broken up with this man many years earlier. After years of listening to her father attack homosexuality, remembered Roberta Osabe, "My girlfriend Debi and my father shot pool together. And she whipped his ass! . . . That was his way, I think, of trying to make amends." Jerry Freitag and his partner Kurt had made a point of introducing their parents to one another. "My mother and his mother talk on the phone every once in a while and write letters and stuff. Like my grandmother just died. Kurt's mother was one of the first people to call my mom." For Charlyne Harris, however, calling her ex-lover's mother "family" would have been out of the question. "Her mother didn't like me. Number one, she didn't want her to be *in* a lesbian relationship; number two, she knew that I was black. So I didn't have a lot of good things to say about her mother . . . Pam told me, 'She can't even say your name!'"

In addition to friendships and relationships with lovers or ex-lovers, chosen family might also embrace ties to children or people who shared a residence.[5] *Gay Community News* published a series of letters from gay male prisoners who had united to form "the Del-Ray Family" (only to be separated by the warden). Back in San Francisco, Rose Ellis told me about the apartment she had shared with several friends. One woman in particular, she said, was "like a big sister to me." When this woman died of cancer, the household split up, and "that kind of broke the family thing." In other circumstances, however, hardship drew people together across household lines. Groups organized to assist individuals who were chronically or terminally ill often incorporated love and persisted through time, characteristics some participants took as signs of kinship. Occasionally a person could catch a glimpse of potential family relationships in the making. When I met Harold Sanders he was making plans to live with someone to prepare for the possibility that he might require physical assistance as he moved into his seventies. Harold explained that he would rather choose that person in advance than be forced to settle for "just anyone" in an emergency.

The relative absence of institutionalization or rituals associated with these emergent gay families sometimes raised problems of definition and mutuality: I may count you as a member of my family, but do you number me in yours? In this context offers of assistance, commitment to "working through" conflicts, and a common history measured by months or years, all became confirming signs of kinship. By symbolically testifying to the presence of intangibles such as solidarity and love, these demonstrations operated to persuade and to concretize, to move a relationship toward reciprocity while seeking recognition for a kin tie.

Like their heterosexual counterparts, most gay men and lesbians insisted that family members are people who are "there for you," people you can count on emotionally and materially. "They take care of me," said one man, "I take care of them." According to Rayna Rapp (1982) the "middle class" in the United States tends to share affective support but not material resources within friendships. In the Bay Area, however, lesbians and gay men from all classes and class backgrounds, regularly rendered both sorts of assistance to one another. Many considered this an important way of demarcating friend from family. Diane Kunin, a writer, described family as people who will care for you when you're sick, get you out of jail, help you fix a flat tire, or drive you to the airport. Edith Motzko, who worked as a carpenter, said of a woman she had known ten years, "There's nothing in the world that [she] would ask of me that I wouldn't do for her." Louise Romero joked that a gay friend "only calls me when he wants something: he wants to borrow the truck 'cause he's moving. So I guess that's family!"

Overall, the interface between property relations and kinship relations among lesbians and gay men who called one another family seemed consistent with such relations elsewhere in the society, with the exception of a somewhat greater expectation for financial independence and self-sufficiency on the part of each member of a couple. Individuals distributed their own earnings and resources; where pooling occurred, it usually involved an agreement with a lover or a limited common fund with housemates. Some households divided bills evenly, while others negotiated splits proportionate to income. A person might support a lover for a period of time, but this was not the rule for either men or women. Putting a partner through school or taking time off from wage work for childrearing represented the type of short-term arrangements most commonly associated with substantial financial support.

Across household lines, material aid was less likely to take the form of direct monetary contribution, unless a dependent child was involved. Services exchanged between members of different households who considered themselves kin included everything from walking a dog to preparing meals, running errands, and fixing cars. Lending tools, supplies, videotapes, clothes, books, and almost anything else imaginable was commonplace in some relationships. Many people had extended loans to gay or straight kin at some time. Some had given money to relatives confronted with the high cost of medical care in the United States, and a few

from working-class backgrounds reported contributing to the support of biological or adoptive relatives (either their own or a lover's).

Another frequently cited criterion for separating "just plain" friends from friends who were also family was a shared past. In this case, the years a relationship had persisted could become a measure of closeness, reflecting the presumption that common experiences would lead to common understandings. Jenny Chin explained it this way:

> I have, not blood family, but other kind of family. And I think it really takes a lot to get to that point. Like years. Like five years, ten years, or whatever. I think that we're gonna have to do that to survive. That's just a fact of life. Because the whole fact of being gay, you're estranged from your own family. At a certain level, pretty basic level. Unless you're lucky. There are some exceptions.
> So to survive, you have to have support networks and all that kind of stuff. And if you're settled enough, I think you do get into a ... those people become family. If you kind of settle in together. And your work, and your lives, and your house, and your kids or whatever become very intertwined.

While people sometimes depicted the creation of ties to chosen kin as a search for relationships that could carry the burden of family, there are many conceivable ways to move furniture, solicit advice, reminisce, share affection, or find babysitters for your children. All can be accomplished by calling on relationships understood to be something other than family, or by purchasing services if a person has the necessary funds. But allied to the emphasis on survival in Jenny's account was the notion of a cooperative history that emerged as she bent her litany of years to the task of establishing rather than assuming a solidarity that endures.

Relationships that had weathered conflict, like relationships sustained over miles but especially over time, also testified to attachment. Allusions to disagreements, quarrels, and annoyance were often accompanied by laughter. Charlyne Harris named five lesbians she counted as kin "because if they don't see me within a certain amount of time [they check up on me], and they're always in my business! Sometimes they get mad, too. They're like sisters. I know they care a lot." Another woman chuckled, "I never see these family, so you can tell they're family!" Still others mentioned, as a sign of kinship, hearing from people only when they wanted something. Through reversal and inversion, an ironic humor underscored meanings of intimacy and solidarity carried by the notion of family in the United States (cf. Pratt 1977).

In descriptions of gay families, sentiment and emotion often appeared alongside material aid, conflict resolution, and the narrative encapsulation of a shared past. "Why do you call certain people family?" I asked Frank Maldonado. "Well," he responded,

> Some of my friends I've known for fifteen years. You get attached. You stay in one place long enough, you go through seasons and years together, it's like they're part of you, you're part of them. You have fights, you get over them … It's just unconditional love coming through to people that you didn't grow up with.

Though imaged here as the sole defining feature of kinship, love represents as much the product as the symbolic foundation of gay families. Closely associated with the experience of love were the practices through which people established and confirmed mutual, enduring solidarity.

SUBSTITUTE FOR BIOLOGICAL FAMILY?

Far from viewing families we choose as imitations or derivatives of family ties created elsewhere in their society, many lesbians and gay men alluded to the difficulty and excitement of constructing kinship in the *absence* of what they called "models." Others, however, echoed the viewpoint – popular in this society at large – that chosen families offer substitutes for blood ties lost through outright rejection or the distance introduced into relationships by remaining in the closet.[6] "There will always be an empty place where the blood family should be," one man told me. "But Tim and I fill for each other some of the emptiness of blood family that aren't there." In Louise Romero's opinion,

> A lot of lesbians … I think they're just looking for stuff – maybe the same stuff I am. Like my family ties, before coming out, there was a lot of close-

ness. I could share stuff with my sisters. You used to talk all your deep dark secrets. You can't any more 'cause they think you're weird. Which is true in my case – they really do … I think a lot of women look for that, and you need that.

This theory has a certain appeal, not only becaue it speaks to the strong impact of coming out on lesbian and gay notions of kinship, but also because it is consistent with the elaboration of chosen families in conceptual opposition to biological family. On a practical level, most of the services that chosen kin provide for one another might otherwise be performed by relatives calculated according to blood, adoption, or marriage.

Although gay families are families a person creates in adult life, this theory portrays them primarily as *replacements* for, rather than chronological successors to, the families in which individuals came to adulthood. If chosen families simply represent some form of compensation for rejection by heterosexual relatives, however, gay families should logically focus on the establishment of intergenerational relationships. (Remember that the loss of parents, as opposed to other categories of relatives, was the main concern in deciding whether or not to reveal a gay or lesbian identity to straight family.) But when lesbians and gay men in the Bay Area applied kinship terminology to their chosen families, they usually placed themselves in the relationship of sisters and brothers to one another, regardless of their respective ages. In cases where gay families included children, adults who were chosen kin but not co-parents to a child sometimes characterized themselves as aunts or uncles.

As with any generalization, this one admits exceptions. Margie Jamison, active in organizing a Christian ministry to lesbians and gay men, described her work with PWAs (persons with AIDS) while tears streamed down her face. "When I have held them in my arms and they were dying, it's like my sons. Like my sons." In this case the intergenerational kinship terminology invoked Margie's pastoral role as well as her experience raising two sons from a previous heterosexual marriage. However, the characterization of most ties to chosen kin as peer relationship brings families we choose closer to so-called "fictive kin" relations found elsewhere in the United States than to even a moderately faithful reconstruction of the families in which lesbian- and gay-identified individuals grew up.

Equally significant, the minority of gay people who had been disowned were not the only ones who participated in the elaboration of gay kinship. Many who classified relations with their biological or adoptive relatives as cordial to excellent employed the opposition between gay and straight family. Among those whose relations with their straight families had gradually improved over the years, ties to chosen kin generally had not diminished in importance. If laying claim to a gay family in no way depends upon a break with one's family of origin, the theory of chosen family as a surrogate for kinship lost dissolves. A satisfactory explanation for the historical emergence of gay families requires an understanding of the changing relation of friendship to sexual identity among the large numbers of gay people who flocked to urban areas after World War II.

FRIENDS AND LOVERS

"That's the way one builds a good life: a set of friends." At 64, Harold Sanders had no hesitation about indulging his passion for aphorisms, the turn of phrase stretched backward to gather in experiences of a lifetime. His statement reflected a conviction very widely shared by lesbians and gay men of all ages. People from diverse backgrounds depicted themselves as the beneficiaries of better friendships than heterosexuals, or made a case for the greater significance and respect they believed gay people accord to friendship.[7] Most likely such comments reflected a mixture of observation and self-congratulation, but they also drew attention to the connection many lesbians and gay men made between friendship and sexual identity (as well as race or ethnicity). The same individuals tended to portray heterosexuals as people who place family and friends in an exclusive, even antagonistic, relationship. As a child growing up in a Chinese-American family, said Jenny Chin,

I had a lot drilled into me about your friends are just your friends. *Just* friends. Very minimalizing and discounting [of] friendships. Because family was supposed to be all-important. Everything was done to preserve the family unit. Even if people were killing each other; even if people had twenty-year-old grudges and hadn't spoken.

In contrast, discussions of gay families pictured kinship as an *extension* of friendship, rather than viewing the two as competitors or assimilating friendships to biogenetic relationships regarded as somehow more fundamental. It was not unusual for a gay man or lesbian to speak of another as family in one breath and friend in the next. Yet the solidarity implicit in such statements has not always been a taken-for-granted feature of gay lives. According to John D'Emilio (1983b), recognition of the possibility of establishing non-erotic ties among homosexuals constituted a key historical development that paved the way for the emergence of lesbian and gay "community" – and, I might add, for the later appearance of the ideological opposition between biological family and families we choose.

When Harold Sanders was coming out in the 1930s, particularly in the white and relatively wealthy circles where he traveled, same-sex ties were experiencing a historical devaluation that coincided with a new affirmation of eroticism in relations between women and men embodied in the ideal of companionate marriage. Strong bonds between persons of the same sex became something best left behind with childhood (Pleck and Pleck 1980). By 1982 Lillian Rubin found that two-thirds of the single men in her sample of two hundred could not name a best friend. While the disparagement of same-sex ties may have had a greater impact on men than women, all same-sex relationships became subjected to a higher degree of scrutiny. Today many heterosexuals in the United States are quick to judge certain friendships as "too intense," taking intensity as a sign of homosexuality.[8] According to Lourdes Alcantara, who was born in Peru during the 1950s, such associations are no longer confined to North America.

I read an article in the newspaper, and they present two women hugging like friends in the street. Latin friends, right? And I was in love with this woman. We were lovers. And I was in her house. So I brought the Sunday newspaper to her house, and I took that page out, so her mother didn't see that. And then we were so hot, reading that. But the distortion! They put us like sick people. So to be a lesbian, the description was terrible! Even my girlfriend got upset. She said, "We better be friends, just friends, and get married." And we were 11 years old, 9 years old! God! *Qué* terrible! Can you believe that?

In the United States during the twentieth century, sibling ties and friendship have offered some of the few cultural categories available for making sense of powerful feelings toward a person of the same sex. During high school, Peter Ouillette had what he later identified as a "crush" on another boy. "Absolutely under no circumstances would I think about sex," he said. "It was friendship. But *real close* friendship, that's the way I thought of it. Almost like brothers." Philip Korte remembered thinking, "Wouldn't it be nice to have a big brother. Or wouldn't it be nice to just have a best friend that I could be affectionate with and spend a lot of time with, companionship, those kinds of things. Now I recognize that as gay. But, at the time, what I knew of gay, that didn't fit at all." What did not seem to fit were his fantasies of love and caring for another man, since homosexuality then appeared to him as a matter of sex and sex alone.

Given this alliance between the language of kinship and the language of friendship, which Jonathan Katz (1976) dates to the nineteenth century, one might expect to uncover a direct link between the early interchangeability of these terms and contemporary discourse on gay families. However, historical evidence and day-to-day observation suggest otherwise. By mid-century coming out as a lesbian or gay man entailed learning to discriminate between feelings of erotic and non-erotic love, drawing meaningful contrasts between sexual attraction and friendship. A person could then theoretically sort relationships into two groups: "just friends" (not sexually involved) and "more than friends" (lovers). One day while sitting in a coffeeshop, for example, I overheard a woman in the next booth tell the woman sitting across from her that she was "only" interested in a friendship, since she already had a lover.

Coming-out narratives invoke this distinction when they establish a double time frame, the "before" and "after" of coming out, effectively reinterpreting relationships previously described with the terminology of blood ties as having been "really" erotic all along.

The years following World War II – a watershed period for many groups in the United States – witnessed an unprecedented elaboration of nonerotic solidarities among homosexuals (Bérubé 1989; D'Emilio 1983a, 1983b, 1989b). During the 1950s and 1960s, gay men adapted kinship terminology to the task of distinguishing sexual from non-sexual relationships.[9] At that time the rhetoric of brothers, sisters, and friends applied primarily to nonerotic relationships. In the film version of *The Boys in the Band*, one character quips, "If they're not lovers, they're sisters." This camp usage of "sister" among gay men coexisted with the institutionalization of mentor relationships in which older men introduced younger men to "the life." Normatively, mentor relationships were inter-generational and emphatically nonsexual. Bob Korkowski, who flouted convention by having sex with his mentor, described the experience as "weird, because a mentor is kind of like a father. [It was] like sleeping with your father." This reservation of kinship terminology for nonsexual relations represents a very different usage from its subsequent deployment to construct gay families that could include both lovers and friends.

The contrast between the sexual and the nonsexual was drawn only to be blurred in later years after the possibility of non-erotic ties among gay people because firmly established. By the 1970s both gay men and lesbians had begun to picture friends and lovers as two ends of a single continuum rather than as oppositional categories. "We women been waiting all our lives for our sisters to be our lovers," announced the lyrics of the song *Gay and Proud* (Lempke 1977). The contribution of lesbian-feminism toward codifying this notion of a continuum is evident in Adrienne Rich's (1980) work on "compulsory heterosexuality." Carroll Smith-Rosenberg's (1975) classic article on relations between women in the nineteenth-century United States was also widely read in women's studies classes and cited to buttress the contention that sexual and sisterly relations were semantically separable but overlapping in practice – with little regard for efforts to distinguish precisely these relationships during the intervening decades.

The realignment that linked erotic to non-erotic relations through the device of a continuum was not confined to political activists. As San Francisco moved into the 1980s, "friend" seemed to be overtaking "roommate" in popularity as a euphemistic reference to a lover in situations where lesbians and gay men elected not to reveal their sexual identities. Victoria Vetere's 1982 study of lesbian interpretations of the concepts "lover" and "friend," though based on a small sample, found that most lesbians were uncomfortable with any suggestion of a dichotomy between the two terms. A similar continuity was implicit in coming out stories narrated by women who had first claimed a lesbian identity during the 1970s. One said coming out was epitomized for her by the realization that "oh, wow, then I get to keep all my girlfriends!" Elaine Scavone explained with a laugh, "All of a sudden I felt I could be myself. I could be the way I really want to be with women: I could touch them, I could make friends, I could make my girlfriends and I could go home and kiss them." Although women were sometimes said to be more likely to come out by falling in love with a friend and men through an encounter instrumentally focused on sex, both men and women featured early attractions to friends in their coming out stories.

The category of mentor, which epitomized one type of non-sexual relationship between gay men, appeared to be losing, rather than gaining currency during the same period. In the few cases when the term came up in casual conversation during my fieldwork, its meaning seemed to be changing. One man in his early thirties described himself as a mentor to his *lover*, based on his claim to have been out longer and to know more about what he called "the gay world." Such a statement would have been a *non sequitur* not so many years ago.

Given that any continuum is defined by its poles, these changes did not represent a complete collapse of the categories "lover" and "friend" into one another. The phrases "just friends" and "more than friends" remained in common usage to indicate whether two people had incorporated sex into their relationship. A certain unidirectionality also characterized the enterprise of melding sex and friendship. While a lover ideally should become a friend, many believed that sex could ruin a pre-existing friendship. People who were single seemed as wont as ever to invoke the old gay adage that friends last, while lovers are simply "passing through."

In a 1956 study (reprinted in 1967) Maurice Leznoff and William Westley found that most gay men looked to friends, not lovers, for security in old age. Yet the dictum that friends rather than lovers endure took on a different cast for a later generation that believed lovers should not only double as friends, but continue as friends and kin following a breakup. New contexts can engender novel interpretations of received wisdom.

In retrospect, this shift from contrast to continuum laid the ground for the rise of a family-centered discourse that bridged the erotic and the non-erotic, bringing lovers together with friends under a single construct. But the historical development of friendship ties among persons whose shared "sexual" identity was initially defined solely through their sexuality turned out to be merely an introductory episode in a more lengthy tale of community formation.

FROM FRIENDSHIP TO COMMUNITY

Among lesbians and gay men the term "community" (like coming out) has become as multifaceted in meaning as it is ubiquitous. In context, community can refer to the historical appearance of gay institutions, the totality of self-defined lesbians and gay men, or unity and harmony predicated upon a common sexual identity. Older gay people generally considered the term an anachronism when applied to the period before the late 1960s, since "community" came into popular usage only with the rise of a gay movement."

Often contrasted with "isolation," community subsumed one of the earlier senses of coming out: making a public debut at a gay bar. The area of overlap involved locating other gay people, a project that can remain surprisingly difficult in an era when homosexuality makes headline news. Toni Williams, who had grown up in a large metropolitan area and begun identifying as a lesbian only a few years before I interviewed her, insisted, "I didn't think that there was *nobody* that was going to be like me. But I didn't know *where* to search for that person. I didn't think that there was a community."

Finding community, as one man very eloquently put it, meant discovering "that your story isn't the only one in the world." Such a discovery need not entail meeting other gay people, but rather becoming convinced of their existence. Sean O'Brien, originally from New York City, used to listen to a weekly gay radio show, "a voice coming through a box once a week," which he said helped him "understand myself as part of a community, even though I was not connected with that community." During the 1970s the concept of community came to embody practical wisdom emerging from the bars, friendship networks and a spate of new gay organizations: the knowledge that lesbians and gay men, joining together on the basis of a sexual identity, could create enduring social ties. In the process, sexuality was reconstituted as a ground of common experience rather than a quintessentially personal domain.

From its inception, activists pressed the community concept into the service of an identity politics that cast gays in the part of an ethnic minority and a subculture.[10] Lesbians and gay men represent a constant 10 percent of the population, they contended, a veritable multitude prepared to claim its own distinct history, culture, and institutions. The basis for these arguments was, of course, laid earlier with the recognition that homosexuals could unite through bonds of friendship as well as sex, and elaborated through analogies with identity-based movements organized along racial lines.[11] Many social scientists of the period subscribed to a similar paradigm in their studies of "the gay world."[12] Whether describing an aggregate of persons in ongoing interaction (Evelyn Hooker)

or a "continuing collectivity" of individuals with common interests and activities (William Simon and John Gagnon), they tended to treat homosexuals as a fairly homogeneous group with concrete, if not readily ascertainable, boundaries. More recently Stephen Murray (1979) has used sociological criteria to argue for the validity of applying the community concept to gay men in urban areas of the US and Canada, dubbing them a "quasi-ethnic community."[13]

Deborah Wolf's (1979) ethnography of lesbians (actually lesbian-feminists) in the Bay Area falls prey to many of the same traps that have ensnared other investigators who treat lesbians and/or gay men as members of an integrated subculture. Most studies that set out to explore a "gay world" or "gay lifestyle" not only situate their subjects in a historical vacuum, but assume an amazingly uncomplicated relationship between claiming an identity and feeling a sense of belonging or community. With their presumption of harmonious solidarity and their reduction of varied experience to a single worldview, such approaches have proven far from satisfactory.

Yet the shortcomings of previous research offer no reason to reject the community concept altogether, as Kenneth Read (1980) does in his study of patrons in a gay bar on the West Coast. It is important to understand how gay men and lesbians came to use a category that over time has served as everything from a rallying cry for political unity, to a demographic indicator, to a symbol for a small sector of wealthy white men set apart from the majority of people who call themselves lesbian or gay. Viewed in cultural and historical context, the so-called minority model appears as part of a series of historical struggles to define and dispute the boundaries of communities based on sexual identity, struggles that in turn paved the way for a discourse on gay families. Gay community can best be understood not as a unified subculture, but rather as a category implicated in the ways lesbians and gay men have developed collective identities, organized urban space, and conceptualized their significant relationships.

My interpretation of community departs in several key respects from the long tradition of community studies in the United States (see Hillery 1955). Conrad Arensberg (1954), for example, treats community primarily as a setting in which to conduct sociology, whereas gay communities are only roughly defined spatially and rest on variable interpretations of identity. In the hands of W. Lloyd Warner (1963), community becomes a microcosm of society at large, yet lesbians and gay men have contested and transformed hegemonic understandings of kinship and sexuality. My approach perhaps comes closest to Robert Lynd's and Helen Lynd's (1937) depiction of community as a vantage point from which to view historical events (in their case, the Great Depression), but again I am not concerned with a bounded entity or with community as locale. To comprehend the historical ascendance of a family-centered discourse among lesbians and gay men, my analysis focuses on social movements, and on the meanings of togetherness and identity that have shaped community as a cultural category defined in opposition to equally cultural notions of individualism and selfhood (Varenne 1977).

Although lesbian and gay communities cannot be reduced to a territorial definition, this has not prevented San Francisco from becoming a geographical symbol of homosexuality, renowned here and abroad as the "gay capital" of the United States. With the gay movement came the consolidation of "gay ghettos," neighborhoods featuring a variety of gay-owned businesses and residential concentrations of gay men (Castells 1983). "At some points I have thought, 'Oh, my life is too gay.' I work in a gay environment, I live in a gay neighborhood, most of my friends are gay," remarked Stephen Richter, who rented an apartment in the Castro district. "But I don't know, you go out in the straight world and you can't wait to get home!" Ronnie Walker agreed: "For all the dishing that people do about Castro Street, whenever I go away to middle America, I'm always glad to kneel down and kiss the earth when I get to Castro Street." Others who lived in outlying areas traveled to gay neighborhoods for the express purpose of "feeling the community." Neighborhood had become another marker of the contrast between gay and straight, signifier of belonging, "home," and things held in common.

During the 1980s gay areas of San Francisco did not escape the restructuring of the urban landscape taking place in cities across the United States.[14] On Castro and Polk Streets, many small gay businesses gave way to banks, chain stores, and franchises. Residents fought extension of the downtown financial district into the South of Market region. Even under these economic pressures, however, gay neighborhoods retained enough of their character to contribute materially to the formation of gay identity by offering a place to meet and forge ties to other gay people.

Because gay neighborhoods in San Francisco have been formed and populated principally by men, many lesbians looked to the Bay Area at large as a place to make such connections. John D'Emilio (1989) has pointed out the link between male control of public space and the greater public visibility of gay male (as opposed to lesbian) institutions in the United States. Economic factors are also involved, since rental or ownership in the Bay Area can be prohibitive, and women in general receive lower incomes than men. By the mid-1980s, however, lesbian institutions and residential concentrations had begun to appear in the less expensive Mission and Bernal Heights districts.

"In terms of meeting people," said Sharon Vitrano,

> I feel a bit controlled by [being a lesbian], in that I'd like to at least have the option of living in a small town. One of the reasons that I came out here was that I felt I could meet lesbians in a context that was "normal." Where I could go about my business and meet people that way. I don't like having to hang out with a group of people just because they're gay.

Sharon's juxtaposition of small towns with life in the metropolis echoed the folk wisdom that gay men and lesbians are better off relocating in a big city where they can find others "like" themselves. Almost paradoxically, many people described the urban community they had hoped to discover in terms that incorporated mythical notions of the rural "America" of a bygone era. Expectations of homogeneity based on a common sexual identification lent credence to bids for political power, while depictions of lesbian and gay community as a club or secret society composed of "people who know people" invoked the face-to-face relationships supposed to typify small-town life.

Non-territorial understandings of community that rest on a sense of belonging with one's "own kind" have numerous antecedents in the United States; those most relevant to a gay context include such unlikely compatriots as religion and the tavern. Long before the first gay activists portrayed lesbians and gay men as sisters and brothers, the Puritans elaborated a notion of brotherhood based on the leveling effect of original sin (Bercovitch 1978; Burke 1941). A concept of "beloved community" ushered in the Civil Rights struggle so instrumental to the emergence of later social movements (Evans 1979). On the secular side, community has been symbolically linked to bars, saloons, and neighborhood in the United States since the massive urban immigrations of the late nineteenth century (Kingsdale 1980). During that period, the saloon became a locus for the formation of same-sex (in this case male) solidarity and a proxy for small-town paradise lost. Although lesbians and gay men are now as likely to "find community" through a softball team, a coming-out support group, or the Gay Pride Parade as through a bar, bars remain a central symbol of identity, and almost everyone has a story about a first visit to a gay club (see Achilles 1967).

Among political activists and the bar crowd alike, the notion of community voiced during the 1970s resembled nothing so much as a Jeffersonian version of Victor Turner's (1969) *communitas*: an alternative, non-hierarchical, and undifferentiated experience of harmony and mutuality.[15] Founded on the premise of a shared sexual identity, gay community remained, like friendship, an egalitarian and fundamentally nonerotic concept.

In extending homosexuality beyond the sexual, the notion of identity-based community opened new possibilities for using kinship terminology to imagine lesbians and gay men as members of a unified totality.[16] Identity provided the linking concept that lent power to analogies between gay and consanguineal relations. Wasn't this what families in the United States were all about: identity and likeness mediated by the symbolism of blood ties?

Yet the application of kinship terminology to gay community differed from the subsequent discourse on gay families in that it described *all* lesbians and gay men as kin: no "choice" determined familial relationships. To claim a lesbian or gay identity was sufficient to claim kinship to any and every other gay person. Some people hoped community would replace alienated biological ties (Altman 1979), appealing not to chosen families but to the collectivity: "If I could gain acceptance in the community of lesbians, I would have, I hoped, the loving family I missed" (Larkin 1976: 84).[17] In gay bars across the nation, this was the era of circle dances to the popular music hit, *We Are Family* (Rodgers and Edwards 1979).

While the use of kinship terminology to indicate community membership has fallen into disfavor as the politics of identity have given way to the politics of difference, people still employed it from time to time as a way of hinting at sexual identity. "Don't worry, he's one of the brethren," explained a man I was meeting for lunch when his housemate walked into the room. On another occasion, a woman told me to expect a relatively smooth job interview because the person I would be seeing was "a sister." Marta Rosales, who worked at a hospital, reported one of the nurses asking if a new staff member was "family," and another woman remembered the back door of an East Bay bar being fondly termed the "family entrance." In 1985 a blood drive for persons with AIDS incoporated a unique play on biogenetic notions of kinship and the materialization of identity as shared substance. Leaflets bearing the headline "Our Boys Need Blood" called on lesbians as "blood sisters" to help "our brothers" in a time of need. By all accounts the drive was a great success, and soon became a model for similar events (with similarly styled publicity) across the country.

Tales of "coming home" into community are structured much like the scenes in Victorian novels that depict the recognition of concealed kinship. As metaphor, "home" merges the meanings of coming out and living in a place with a large lesbian and gay population (cf. Dank 1971: 189).

> [Coming out] was like coming home. I can't explain it. It felt so right. It really felt so right. It was like, you know, keeping your eyes shut and looking around a floor full of shoes and when you put your foot into your shoe you know it fits. You don't have to see it, you just know it.

Portrayals of fitting and belonging became a conventional element in coming-out stories with reference to which individuals either equated or distinguished their experiences.

> I've heard of people's experience, like moving from different parts of the country, moving here, and just like going into a women's bar and feeling, oh, wonderful. They've finally found their home, or something like that. The experience that I wanted, but I just haven't had ... I don't feel like I've come home or anything or that I belong here.

Identity and community, so often taken to define the limits of lesbian and gay experience, have become polarized in ways that presuppose culturally specific values of individualism. In the United States, tensions between notions of personhood and collectivity date back to Tocqueville's warnings about a tyranny of the majority. The paradigm that casts lesbians and gay men in the part of a minority (or subculture) interposes community between "the individual" and "society." In this context, it becomes relatively easy to move from a view of community as a comfortable home or unified interest group to a picture of community as a mini-enforcer, mediator of all the conformity and oppression attributed to Society with a capital "S."

By the late 1970s, signs of disenchantment with the unity implicit in the concept of community began to appear: a popular critique of the look-alike styles of "Castro clones"; a resurgence of butch/fem relations among lesbians that flew in the face of feminist prescriptions for androgyny; and a heated debate about sadomasochism (S/M), pedophilia, and other marginalized sexualities. Though some dissenters insisted upon their right to be included in the larger collectivity of lesbians and gay men, others did not experience themselves as community members, much less as agents in community formation. "I was just me, in a gay world," explained Kevin Jones.

During the same period, lesbians and gays of color critiqued the simplistic assumption that mutual understanding would flow from a shared identity. Along with Jewish lesbians and gay men, they drew attention to the racism and anti-Semitism pervading gay communities, and exposed the illusory character of any quest for an encompassing commonality in the face of the crosscutting allegiances produced by an identity politics. Predictably, this recognition of differences, while important and overdue, tended to undermine meanings of harmony and equality carried by "community." Accompanying the positive explorations of what it meant to be black and gay or lesbian and Latina was widespread disillusionment with the failure to attain the unity implicit in the ideal of *communitas*.

DELIBERATING DIFFERENCE

By the 1980s the rhetoric of brotherhood and sisterhood had begun to seem dated and trite. Sherry McCoy and Maureen Hicks (1979: 66), attempting to grapple with "disappointment" and "unrealistic demands" among lesbian-feminists, wrote, "The concept of 'sisterhood' at times seemed to evaporate as we watched."[18] "This newfound reluctance to apply kinship terminology to all other lesbians and gay men extended well beyond activist circles. Many gay men and lesbians began to doubt the existence of "the" community or any single gay "lifestyle." Some abandoned the notion of identity-based communities altogether, attempting to escape social categorization by adopting extreme forms of individualism. "I am who I am," they explained. Others associated community strictly with wealthy white men, who were neither representative of nor identical with the totality of gay people. Along with a recognition of the relative privilege of this sector came the refusal to allow this part to stand for the whole. Seemingly unable to comprehend the inequalities that structure identity-based difference in the United States (white being privileged over Native-American, men over women, and so on), the concept of community lost credibility.

The most popular alternative was to divest community of its egalitarian associations by using it as a proxy for "population." Dissemination of Alfred Kinsey's (1948, 1953) data on the incidence of homosexual sex in the United States had opened the way for picturing an essential 10 per cent who make up the imagined universe ("community") of gay men and lesbians. One indication of the extent of this muddle in the model of community is that, by the time of my fieldwork, most people qualified the term by adding a phrase such as "whatever that means."

The practice of identity politics in the United States has rested upon the cultural configuration of race, ethnicity, class, gender, and sexual identity as categories for organizing subjective experience (Epstein 1987; Omi and Winant 1983). What motivated the transition from "speaking sameness" to a division of community into ever-narrower circumscriptions of identity?[19] In the first place, perceptions of fragmentation represent a view from the top. Attempts to understand the integration of sexuality with other aspects of identity were not experienced as "splits" by those who had never felt included in community from the start. Paradoxically, however, the very process of building gay community contributed to the emergence and timing of this discourse on difference.

John D'Emilio (1989) has argued that the political tactic of coming out to others as a means of establishing gay unity had the contradictory effect of making differences *among* lesbians and gay men more apparent. The distance is considerable from the Chicago of the late 1960s, where Esther Newton (1979) found little social differentiation among gay men and no gay economy to speak of, to the San Francisco of the 1980s, where gay institutions had multiplied and residents were heirs to a social movement for gay pride and liberation. In the Bay Area the sheer size of the relatively "out" gay and lesbian population permitted the recognition and replication of differences found in the society at large.

During the 1980s, categories of identity remained integral to the process of making and breaking social ties among lesbians and gay men. Most gay bars and social or political organizations in San Francisco were segregated by gender. Some of the community institutions that lesbians associated with gay men main-

tained a nominal lesbian presence. A gay theater, for example, included scripts with lesbian characters in its annual repertoire, and the number of women in attendance grew from two or three to a third of the audience when lesbian plays were performed. Yet the most visible gay institutions, businesses, and public rituals (such as Halloween on Castro Street) remained male-owned and male-organized. Even the exceptions seemed to prove the rule. After a crafts fair in the gay South of Market area, the *Bay Area Reporter* published a picture of two women kissing over the caption, "It wasn't all men at the Folsom Street Fair either."

When gay groups in southern California suggested adding a lambda to the rainbow flag, supposedly to represent all gay people, lesbians denounced the addition as a non-inclusive male symbol. At a benefit for the Gay Games sponsored by the Sisters of Perpetual Indulgence (a group of gay men in nun drag), lesbians cheered the women's softball game and martial arts demonstration, but some voiced impatience with "all the boys parading around in their outfits." Disagreements periodically erupted concerning the proportion of men's to women's coverage in newspapers that attempted to serve "the community" as a whole. It was not uncommon for lesbians and gay men to stereotype one another, building on constructions of identity and difference in the wider culture. Jenny Chin, herself Chinese-American, combined notion of gender, sexuality, and racial identity with the image of the Castro clone to portray difference and position herself outside "gay community":

> I would read the *Bay Guardian*, and they'd say "gay rap." And I would take all these buses crosstown, through all these parts of town I'd never been at night, and transfer, and wait on bus corners, and go to this huge room that had like 300 gay men ... These men were very much talking from their hearts, and they were really needing the support, but it's hard for me to identify with all these tall white guys with moustaches talking about how they're being judged because they're not coming well enough, or something like that.

Joan Nestle (in Gottlieb 1986) has condemned the essentialism implicit in generalizations that assert "lesbians do this, gay men do that." When it comes to something like public sex, Nestle points out, some do and some don't. Like other differences, divisions between lesbians and gay men are not absolute, but socially, historically, and interpretively constructed. After a women's musical troupe was asked to play for a gay male swimsuit contest, group members voiced positions ranging from "support our gay brothers," to "porn is porn," to "who cares, let's take the money!" Several lesbians cited their work with AIDS organizations as an experience that had helped them "feel connected" to gay men. Social contexts defined as heterosexual also fostered expectations of solidarity based on sexual identity. At one of our Thursday evening family dinners, Liz told with dismay the story of fighting with a male co-worker at a holiday party given by her employer. "There we were," she explained, "the only two gay people in the place, having it out with each other."

Class differences traced out lines of division within as well as between the men's and women's "communities." Many lesbians attributed the visibility of gay male institutions to the fact that men in general have greater access to money than women. Gay vacation spots at the nearby Russian River proved too expensive for many lesbians (as well as working-class and unemployed gay men), who tended to stay at campgrounds rather than resorts if they visited the area. Popular categories opposed "bikers" to "professionals" and "bar gays" (presumably working-class) to "politicals" (stereotyped as "middle-class"). People described making painful choices regarding employment, based on their perceptions of how out a person could be in a particular type of job. David Lowry, for example, had dropped out of an MBA program to become a waiter after he experienced pressure from corporate employers to be more "discreet" about his sexual identity.

Individuals who had purposefully sought employment in gay businesses reported their surprise at finding the gay employer–employee relationship as marked by conflict and difference as any other (cf. Weston and Rofel 1985). In a dispute between the lesbian owner of an apartment building and one of her lesbian tenants, both sides seemed perplexed to discover that their shared sexual identity could not resolve the issue at hand. The hegemony of a managerial and entrepreneurial class within "the community" was also evident in the relative absence of gay owned and operated discount stores. While merchants encouraged people to "buy gay" and pointed with pride to the proliferation of shops that had made it theoretically possible to live without ever leaving the Castro, only a very small segment of lesbians and gay men could have afforded to do so, even if they were so inclined.

Anyone who visits a variety of lesbian and gay households in the Bay Area will come away with an impression of generational depth. Gay organizations and establishments, however, tended to serve a relatively narrow middle age range. Bowling, for instance, is a sport that many people in the United States pursue into their older years. But gay league nights at bowling alleys across the city found the lanes filled with teams predominantly composed of men in their twenties and thirties. Young lesbians and gay men came to San Francisco expecting to find acceptance and gay mecca but instead experienced trouble getting into bars and often ended up feeling peripheral to "the community" (cf. Hefner and Autin 1978; Heron 1983). Gina Pellegrini had initially gained entrance to one bar with a fake ID, only to encounter hostility from one of the older "regulars":

> I just felt like we all should have been the same no matter [what] – age or not. And she was discriminating against her own quote "kind" unquote. That was very strange to me. I didn't realize that a 15-year-old could be pretty damn much of a pain in the ass when you want to relax and talk to your friends and have a drink.

For their part, older people mentioned ageist door policies at bars, and complained about feeling "other" when surrounded by younger faces at community events.

Racially discriminatory treatment at gay organizations, white beauty standards, ethnic divisions in the crowds at different bars, and racist door policies were other frequently cited reasons for questioning the community concept. Kevin Jones, an African-American man, said that when he first came to San Francisco,

I thought that if I was white, it would be a lot different then. Because it seemed like it was hard for me to talk to people in bars. But it didn't seem like other people were having a hard time talking to each other. It almost seemed like they *knew* each other. And if they didn't know each other, they were gonna go up and talk to each other and meet. But I'd go to the bars, and I could sit there and watch pool, and nobody would ever talk to me. And I couldn't understand that. And I thought, "If I was white, I bet you I would know a lot more of these people."

Something more is involved here than racial identity as a ground for difference and discrimination, or ethnicity as an obstacle to the easy interaction implicit in notions of community. Most people of color claimed membership in communities defined in terms of racial identity, attachments that predated coming out as a lesbian or gay man. Simon Suh, for example, believed that his own coming out was complicated by thinking of gays as "very outside of my own [Korean-American] community." Metaphors like "home" served as well for describing race and ethnicity as sexual identity. Because his best friend was also Latino, Rafael Ortiz explained, "it makes it more like home." This is not to deny divisions of class, language, age, national origin, gender, and so forth that cut across communities organized through categories of race or ethnicity. It is simply to note that many, if not most, lesbians and gay men of color did not experience coming out in terms of any one-to-one correspondence of identity to community.[20]

Whites without a strong ethnic identification often described coming out as a transition from no community *into* community, whereas people of color were more likely to focus on conflicts *between* different identities instead of expressing a sense of relief and arrival. Implicit in the coming out narratives of many white people was the belief that whites lack community, culture and a developed sense of racial identity. As Scott McFarland, a white man, remarked when we were discussing the subject of gay pride day, "There were no other parades that I could march in."

Division of the master trope of community into multiple communi*ties* has forced individuals to make difficult choices between mutually exclusive alternatives, like living in an Asian-American or a gay neighborhood, or working for a gay or an African-American newspaper. Some political activists have endeavored to fabricate a solidarity capable of spanning "the community" without denying differences that divide its members. The general trend, however, has involved building coalitions composed of autonomous groups that invoke more specialized combinations of identities (cf. Reagon 1983).

To avoid prioritizing identities, a person could integrate them – seeking out other gay American Indians, joining a group for lesbians over 40, or hanging out in a bar for gays of color – but this solution is limited in the number of identities and settings it can encompass. A person could move back and forth among communities as an "out" lesbian or gay man, giving up the hope of having all identities accepted in any one context. He or she could pass for heterosexual in situations defined by race or ethnicity, like Kenny Nash, who had decided to remain closeted to other African-Americans. "I didn't want people to think that I'd left the [black] community," he explained, "so that therefore I had no right to speak about things that were of concern to me." Or that person could turn toward a radical individualism which focused on issues of style and railed against conformity, whether it be as a "lesbian for lipstick" or a gay man who objected to uniforms of jeans, keys, and sculptured muscles.

For some, sexual identity had become a minimal defining feature, all "we" have in common. Scott McFarland told the story of getting on the wrong bus when he first arrived in the city during the 1970s, and finding himself on Castro Street:

> It just devastated me. [I thought], this is *it*! This is the dream of all these people like me moving to somewhere [gay] ... Everybody was dressed in these incredibly macho fashions ... These weigh-a-ton shoes. Jeans. The first five years I lived in San Francisco, I refused to wear blue jeans ... It took me years to recover from finding out that gay people weren't like me much at all!

"I knew that I didn't fit into the Castro any more than I fit into my family," another man insisted. Whether that sense of difference was based on categorical understandings of self (mediated by race, age, class, gender) or on tensions between the individual and the social, the result has been a generalized rejection of the unity and above all the sameness implicit in the concept of gay community.

In contrast, the family-centered discourse emerging during this period did not assume identity (in the sense of sameness) based upon sexuality alone. Lesbians and gay men who claimed membership in multiple communities but felt at home in none joined with those who had strategically repositioned themselves outside community in transferring the language of kinship from collective to interpersonal relations. While familial ideologies assumed new prominence in the United States at large during the 1980s, among gay men and lesbians the historical legacy of community-building and subsequent struggles to comprehend relations of difference mediated a shift in focus from friendship to kinship. Meanwhile the possibility of being rejected by blood relatives for a lesbian or gay identity shaped the specific meanings carried by "family" in gay contexts, undermining the permanence culturally attributed to blood ties while highlighting categories of choice and love.

Defined in opposition to biological family, the concept of families we choose proved attractive in part because it reintroduced agency and a subjective sense of making culture into lesbian and gay social organization. The institutionalized gay community of the 1970s, with its shops and bars and associations, by the 1980s could appear as something prefabricated, an entity over and above individuals into which they might or might not fit. Most understood gay families to be customized, individual creations that need not deny conflict or difference. Family also supplied the face-to-face relationships and concrete knowledge of persons promised by the romantic imagery of small-town community (Mannheim 1952). As a successor to non-erotic ties elaborated in terms of community or friendship, chosen families introduced something rather novel into kinship relations in the United States by grouping friends together with lovers and children within a single cultural domain.

NOTES

1 Schneider (1968) represents the classic anthropological text on "American kinship." For a critique of Schneider's account as overly coherent and systematized, as well as insensitive to contextual shifts in meaning, see Yanagisako (1978, 1985). For a discussion of models in culture theory, see Geertz's (1973: 93–4) distinction between "model of" and "model for."

2 Cf. Riley (1988), who found in a small study of eleven lesbians in New York City that those friends characterized as family were "intimate" rather than "social" friends.

3 For a discussion of the theme of uncharted lives in lesbian autobiography, see Cruikshank (1982).

4 In practice this generalization may hold more for lesbians than for gay men, although many gay men also shared the ideal of transforming the formerly erotic tie to an ex-lover into an enduring non-erotic bond.

5 The notion of a substitute family can also be criticized as functionalist in that it assumes all people have a need for family. Social scientists have applied theories of surrogate family to many marginalized groups in the US. See, for example, Vigil (1988) on barrio gangs in southern California.

6 Cf. Hooker (1965) on the importance placed on friendship by gay men of an earlier era.

7 Foucault (in Gallagher and Wilson 1987: 33–4) has speculated that the devaluation of male friendship in eighteenth-century Europe was historically linked to the problematization of sex between men.

8 To my knowledge less is documented concerning lesbian usage of kinship terminology during this period. Among gay men, this application of kinship terminology persists in the form of camp references. In the specialized context of drag balls and competitions, gay male novices enter all-gay "houses" in which "the 'mother' and 'father' supervise the training and activities of their 'children'" (Goldsby 1989: 34–5).

9 For a comprehensive discussion of the development of urban gay communities in the postwar years, see D'Emilio (1983b). On the emergence of a social movement grounded in gay identity, see also Adam (1987).

10 Epstein (1987) explores in more depth the limitations of analogies between ethnicity and gay identity.

11 On the formation of "new types of collective subjectivity" in association with postwar movements that invoked racial identity, see Omi and Winant (1983: 37).

12 See, for example, Hoffman (1968), Hooker (1967), Simon and Gagnon (1967), and Warren (1974).

13 Written before the emergence of discourse on gay families, Murray's piece identified lack of kinship as the major difference distinguishing urban gay communities from urban ethnic communities.

14 On the relation of gentrification to public policy and wider economic trends during the Reagan years, see Harrison and Bluestone (1988).

15 For an application of Turner's concept of *communitas* to feminist and lesbian-feminist organizing before the politics of difference questioned the notion of sisterhood, see Cassell (1977).

16 Cf. Anderson (1983), who has elaborated the notion of imagined community with respect to nation-states.

17 Cf. Lockard (1986: 85), writing about lesbians in Portland: "The Community may be seen as a partial alternative form of family unit for Community members."

18 On the limitations of sisterhood as an all-embracing concept intended to bring women together across lines of race, age, ethnicity, sexual identity, and class, see E. T. Beck (1982), Chrystos (1988), Dill (1983), Fox-Genovese (1979–80), Gibbs and Bennett (1980), hooks (1981), Hull *et al.* (1982), Joseph and Lewis (1981), Macdonald (1983), Moraga and Anzaldúa (1981), and Smith (1983).

19 The term "speaking sameness" comes from Bonnie Zimmerman's (1985) discussion of identity politics among lesbians during the early 1980s.

20 Cf. M. B. Pratt (1984), who very eloquently refutes the notion of home as a space of safety and comfort. For a perceptive commentary on issues raised by Pratt's portrayal of home as a locus of exclusions and oppressions, see Martin and Mohanty (1986).

REFERENCES

Achilles, Nancy (1967), "The Development of the Homosxual Bar as an Institution," in John H. Gagnon and William Simon (eds), *Sexual Deviance*: 228–44 (New York: Harper & Row).

Adam, Barry D. (1987), *The Rise of a Gay and Lesbian Movement* (Boston: Twayne Publishers).

Altman, Dennis (1979), *Coming Out in the Seventies* (Sydney: Wild & Woolley).

Anderson, Benedict (1983), *Imagined Communities: Reflections on the Origin and Spread of Nationalism* (London: Verso).

Arensberg, Conrad M. (1954), "The Community-Study Method," *American Journal of Sociology* 60: 109–24.

Beck, Evelyn Torton (ed.) (1982), *Nice Jewish Girls: A Lesbian Anthology* (Watertown, MA: Persephone Press).

Becker, Carol S. (1988), *Unbroken Ties: Lesbian Ex-Lovers* (Boston: Alyson).

Bercovitch, Sacvan (1978), *The American Jeremiad* (Madison: University of Wisconsin Press).

Bérubé, Allan (1989), "Marching to a Different Drummer: Lesbian and Gay GIs in World War II," in Martin Bauml Duberman, Martha Vicinus, and George Chauncey, Jr (eds), *Hidden From History: Reclaiming the Gay and Lesbian Past*: 383–94 (New York: New American Library).

Burke, Kenneth (1941), *The Philosophy of Literary Form* (Baton Rouge: Louisiana State University Press).

Cassell, Joan (1977), *A Group Called Women: Sisterhood and Symbolism in the Feminist Movement* (New York: David McKay).

Castells, Manuel (1983), *The City and the Grassroots: A Cross-Cultural Theory of Urban Social Movements* (Berkeley: University of California Press).

Chrystos (1988), *Not Vanishing* (Vancouver: Press Gang Publishers).

Clifford, James (1988), *The Predicament of Culture: Twentieth-Century Ethnography, Literature, and Art* (Cambridge: Harvard University Press).

Clifford, James and George E. Marcus (1986), *Writing Culture: The Poetics and Politics of Ethnography* (Berkeley: University of California Press).

Clunis, D. Merilee and G. Dorsey Green (1988), *Lesbian Couples* (Seattle: Seal Press).

Couser, G. Thomas (1979), *American Autobiography: The Prophetic Mode* (Amherst, MA: University of Massachusetts Press).

Cruikshank, Margaret (1982), "Notes on Recent Lesbian Autobiographial Writing," *Journal of Homosexuality* 8:1: 19–26.

Dank, Barry M. (1971), "Coming Out in the Gay World," *Psychiatry* 34: 180–95.

D'Emilio, John (1983a), "Capitalism and Gay Identity," in Ann Snitow, Christine Stansell, and Sharon Thompson (eds), *Powers of Desire: The Politics of Sexuality*: 100–13 (New York: Monthly Review Press).

—— (1983b), *Sexual Politics, Sexual Communities: The Making of a Homosexual Minority in the United States, 1940–1970* (Chicago: University of Chicago Press).

—— (1989), "Gay Politics, Gay Community: San Francisco's Experience," in Martin Bauml Duberman, Martha Vicinus, and George Chauncey Jr (eds), *Hidden From History: Reclaiming the Gay and Lesbian Past*: 456–73 (New York: New American Library).

Dill, Bonnie Thornton (1983), "Race, Class, and Gender: Prospects for an All-Inclusive Siserhood," *Feminist Studies* 9:1: 131–50.

Epstein, Steven (1987), "Gay Politics, Ethnic

Identity: The Limits of Social Constructionism," *Socialist Review* 93/4: 9–54.

Evans, Sara (1979), *Personal Politics: The Roots of Women's Liberation in the Civil Rights Movement and the New Left* (New York: Vintage).

Flax, Jane (1982), "The Family in Contemporary Feminist Thought: A Critical Review," in Jean Bethke Elshtain (ed.), *The Family in Political Thought*: 223–53 (Amherst, MA: University of Massachusetts Press).

Fox-Genovese, Elizabeth (1979/80), "The Personal is Not Political Enough," *Marxist Perspectives* 2:4: 94–113.

Gallagher, Bob and Alexander Wilson (1987), "Sex and the Politics of Identity: An Interview with Michel Foucault," in Mark Thompson (ed.), *Gay Spirit: Myth and Meaning*: 25–35 (New York: St Martin's Press).

Geertz, Clifford (1973), *The Interpretation of Cultures* (New York: Basic Books).

Gibbs, Joan and Sara Bennett (1980), *Top Ranking: A Collection of Articles on Racism and Classism in the Lesbian Community* (New York: Come! Unity Press).

Goldsby, Jackie (1989), "All About Yves," *OUT/LOOK* 2:1: 34–5.

Gottlieb, Amy (1986), "Amy Gottlieb Talks to Joan Nestle," *Rites* (April).

Harrison, Bennett and Barry Bluestone (1988), *The Great U-Turn: Corporate Restructuring and the Polarizing of America* (New York: Basic Books).

Hefner, Keith and Al Autin (eds) (1978), *Growing Up Gay* (Ann Arbor: Youth Liberation Press).

Heron, Ann (ed.) (1983), *One Teenager in Ten: Writings by Gay and Lesbian Youth* (Boston: Alyson).

Hillery, George A. (1955), "Definitions of Community: Areas of Agreement," *Rural Sociology* 20: 111–23.

Hoffman, Martin (1968), *The Gay World: Male Homosexuality and the Social Creation of Evil* (New York: Basic Books).

Hooker, Evelyn (1965), "Male Homosexuals and Their 'Worlds'," in Judd Marmor (ed.), *Sexual Inversion*: 83–107 (New York: Basic Books).

—— (1967), "The Homosexual Community" in John H. Gagnon and William Simon (eds), *Sexual Deviance*: 167–84 (New York: Harper & Row).

hooks, bell (1981), *Ain't I a Woman: Black Women and Feminism* (Boston: South End Press).

Hull, Gloria T., Patricia Bell Scott, and Barbara Smith (eds) (1982), *All the Women Are White, All the Blacks Are Men, But Some of Us Are Brave: Black Women's Studies* (Old Westbury, NY: Feminist Press).

Joseph, Gloria I. and Jill Lewis (1981), *Common Differences: Conflicts in Black and White Feminist Perspectives* (Garden City, NY: Anchor/Doubleday).

Katz, Jonathan (1976), *Gay American History: Lesbians and Gay Men in the USA* (New York: Thomas Y. Crowell).

Kennedy, Theodore R. (1980), *You Gotta Deal With It: Black Family Relations in a Southern Community* (New York: Oxford University Press).

Kingsdale, Jon M. (1980), "The 'Poor Man's Club': Social Functions of the Urban Working-Class Saloon," in Elizabeth H. Pleck and Joseph H. Pleck (eds), *The American Man*: 255–83 (Englewood Cliffs, NJ: Prentice-Hall).

Kinsey, Alfred C., Wardell B. Pomeroy and Clyde E. Martin (1948), *Sexual Behavior in the Human Male* (Philadelphia: W. B. Saunders).

—— (1953), *Sexual Behavior in the Human Female* (Philadelphia: W. B. Saunders).

Krestan, Jo-Ann and Claudia S. Bepko (1980), "The Politics of Fusion in the Lesbian Relationship," *Family Process* 19:3: 277–89.

Larkin, Joan (1976), "Coming Out," *Ms.* 4:9: 72–4, 84–6.

Lempke, Debbie (1977), *Gay and Proud*, performed by the Berkeley Women's Music Collective (Olivia Records, LF915A stereo).

Leznoff, Maurice and William A. Westley (1967), "The Homosexual Community," in John H. Gagnon and William Simon (eds), *Sexual Deviance* 184–96 (New York: Harper & Row).

Liebow, Elliott (1967), *Tally's Corner: A Study of Negro Streetcorner Men* (Boston: Little, Brown & Co.).

Lockard, Denyse (1986), "The Lesbian Community: An Anthropological Approach," in Evelyn Blackwood (ed.), *Anthropology and Homosexual Behavior*: 83–95 (New York: Haworth Press).

Lynd, Robert S. and Helen M. Lynd (1937), *Middletown in Transition* (New York: Harcourt, Brace).

Mannheim, Karl (1952), *Essays on the Sociology of Knowledge* (New York: Oxford University Press).

Marcus, George E. and Michael M. J. Fischer (1986), *Anthropology as Cultural Critique: An Experimental Moment in the Human Sciences* (Chicago: University of Chicago Press).

Martin, Biddy and Chandra Talpade Mohanty (1986), "Feminist Politics: What's Home Got to Do with It?" in Teresa de Lauretis (ed.), *Feminist Studies/Critical Studies*: 191–212 (Bloomington: Indiana University Press).

Marx, Karl (1963), *The 18th Brumaire of Louis Bonaparte* (New York: International Publishers).

McCoy, Sherry and Maureen Hicks (1979), "A Psychological Retrospective on Power in the Contemporary Lesbian-Feminist Community," *Frontiers* 4:3: 65–9.

McDonald, Gary J. (1982), "Individual Differences in the Coming Out Process for Gay Men: Implications for Theoretical Models," *Journal of Homosexuality* 8:1: 47–60.

Moraga, Cherríe and Gloria Anzaldúa (1981), *This Bridge Called My Back: Writings by Radical*

Women of Color (Watertown, MA: Persephone Press).

Murray, Stephen O. (1979), "The Institutional Elaboration of a Quasi-Ethnic Community," *International Review of Modern Sociology* 9: 165–77.

Newton, Esther (1979), *Mother Camp: Female Impersonators in America* (Chicago: University of Chicago Press).

Omi, Michael and Howard Winant (1983), "By the Rivers of Babylon: Race in the United States, Part Two," *Socialist Review* 72: 35–68.

Pleck, Elizabeth H. and Joseph H. Pleck (eds) (1980), *The American Man* (Englewood Cliffs, NJ: Prentice-Hall).

Pratt, Mary Louise (1977), *Toward a Speech Act Theory of Literary Discourse* (Bloomington: Indiana University Press).

Pratt, Minnie Bruce (1984), "Identity: Skin Blood Heart," in Elly Bulkin, Minnie Bruce Pratt, and Barbara Smith (eds), *Yours in Struggle: Three Feminist Perspectives on Anti-Semitism and Racism*: 11–63 (New York: Long Haul Press).

Rabinow, Paul (1977), *Reflections on Fieldwork in Morocco* (Berkeley: University of California Press).

Rapp, Rayna (1987), "Toward a Nuclear Freeze? The Gender Politics of Euro-American Kinship Analysis," in Jane Fishburne Collier and Sylvia Junko Yanagisako (eds), *Gender and Kinship: Essays Toward a Unified Analysis*: 119–31 (Stanford: Stanford University Press).

Read, Kenneth E. (1980), *Other Voices: The Style of a Male Homosexual Tavern* (Novato, CA: Chandler & Sharp).

Reagon, Bernice Johnson (1983), "Coalition Politics: Turning the Century," in Barbara Smith (ed.), *Home Girls: A Black Feminist Anthology*: 356–68 (New York: Kitchen Table: Women of Color Press).

Rich, Adrienne (1980), "Compulsory Heterosexuality and Lesbian Existence," *Signs* 5: 631–60.

Riley, Claire (1988), "American Kinship: A Lesbian Account," *Feminist Studies* 8:2: 75–94.

Rodgers, Nile and Bernard Edwards (1979), *We Are Family*, performed by Sister Sledge (Cotillion Records, SD5209 stereo).

Schneider, David M. (1968), *American Kinship: A Cultural Account* (Englewood Cliffs, NJ: Prentice-Hall).

Schneider, David M. and Raymond T. Smith (1978), *Class Differences in American Kinship* (Ann Arbor: University of Michigan Press).

Simon, William and John H. Gagnon (1967), "The Lesbians: A Preliminary Overview," in John H. Gagnon and William Simon (eds), *Sexual Deviance*: 247–82 (New York: Harper & Row).

Smith, Barbara (ed.) (1983), *Home Girls: A Black Feminist Anthology* (New York: Kitchen Table: Women of Color Press).

Smith-Rosenberg, Carroll (1975), "The Female World of Love and Ritual: Relations Between Women in Nineteenth-Century America," *Signs* 1:1: 1–30.

Stack, Carol B. (1974), *All Our Kin: Strategies for Survival in a Black Community* (New York: Harper & Row).

Thorne, Barrie with Marilyn Yalom (eds) (1982), *Rethinking the Family: Some Feminist Questions* (New York: Longman).

Turner, Victor (1969), *The Ritual Process: Structure and Anti-Structure* (Ithaca: Cornell University Press).

Varenne, Hervé (1977), *Americans Together: Sructured Diversity in a Midwestern Town* (New York: Teachers College Press).

Vigil, James Diego (1988), *Barrio Gangs: Street Life and Identity in Southern California* (Austin: University of Texas Press).

Warner, W. Lloyd *et al.* (1963), *Yankee City* (New Haven: Yale University Press).

Warren, Carol A. B. (1974), *Identity and Community in the Gay World* (New York: Wiley).

Weston, Kathleen M. and Lisa B. Rofel (1985), "Sexuality, Class, and Conflict in a Lesbian Workplace," in Estelle B. Freedman, Barbara C. Gelpi, Susan L. Johnson and Kathleen M. Weston (eds), *The Lesbian Issue: Essays from SIGNS*: 199–222 (Chicago: University of Chicago Press).

Wolf, Deborah Goleman (1979), *The Lesbian Community* (Berkeley: University of California Press).

Yanagisako, Sylvia J. (1978), "Variance in American Kinship: Implications for Cultural Analysis," *American Ethnologist* 5:1: 15–29.

—— (1985), *Transforming the Past: Tradition and Kinship among Japanese Americans* (Stanford: Stanford University Press).

Zimmerman, Bonnie (1985), "The Politics of Transliteration: Lesbian Personal Narratives," in Estelle B. Freedman, Barbara C. Gelpi, Susan L. Johnson, and Kathleen M. Weston (eds), *The Lesbian Issue: Essays from SIGNS*: 27–42 (Chicago: University of Chicago Press).

PETER M. NARDI and RALPH BOLTON

"Gay-Bashing: Violence and Aggression Against Gay Men and Lesbians"

from Ronald Baenninger (ed.), *Targets of Violence and Aggression* (Amsterdam: Elsevier/North Holland, 1991): 349–400

INTRODUCTION

Violence, threats of physical harm, verbal abuse, and other types of aggression directed against individuals because of their sexual orientation or perceived sexual orientation, often referred to collectively as "fag-bashing" or "gay-bashing" are commonplace in contemporary American society. From locker room to board room, from the pulpit to the courts, and from newspaper opinion columns to late-night comedy shows on television, the vilification of gays and lesbians is popular sport. In a recent public service announcement, comedian Bob Hope stated that he had become aware of the seriousness of the problem of attacks on gays and lesbians, which he deplored – after many years of engaging in bigoted humor that was derogatory toward gays. His public service announcement was arranged as a form of penance. The fact is that each year tens of thousands of gay men and lesbians become the victims of aggression and discrimination because of their sexual orientation, while millions of others live with the fear and knowledge that they, too, are at risk of being the targets of hate crimes and of discriminatory actions such as the loss of a job, of housing, and of child custody rights, without legal recourse in many jurisdictions. Indeed, as a report prepared for the US Department of Justice noted, members of the gay minority in the US are more likely than are members of ethnic and religious minorities to be attacked because of their minority status (Finn and McNeil 1987).

Although the focus of this report is on individual gay-bashing, this social phenomenon cannot be understood fully until it is placed in the context of institutionalized gay-bashing which will also be discussed in this chapter and in which even the behavioral sciences themselves have participated, overtly through theorizing that contributes to the stigmatization of homosexuality (deviance theories, for example, and the medicalization of homosexuality) and covertly by failing to acknowledge and examine the problem of anti-gay violence. The theoretical literature produced by specialists on violence and aggression is replete with discussions of the related issues of anti-Semitism and racism, but with almost no attention paid to gay-bashing (cf. Weiner, Zahn, and Sagi 1990). What little work has been done on anti-gay violence and homophobia has generally been reported in non-mainstream journals (e.g., the *Journal of Homosexuality*). Thus, the pervasive homophobic milieu of the society at large and of the academic community itself has resulted in both the neglect and the ghettoization of this important problem.

It needs to be underscored at the outset that aggression and violence against gays and lesbians take many forms from the obvious, such as physical attacks, insults, and vicious jokes, to the subtle but equally pernicious, such as the refusal to recognize the existence and legitimacy of the gay community and gay culture, the re-writing of verse by famous poets to obscure references to same-sex love, and the genocidal failure by the American government to fund AIDS prevention efforts at an adequate level.

Debates within scholarly circles over the causes of variations in sexual orientation continue to rage, with essentialists and social constructionists battling each other in a replay of the nature-versus-nurture controversy that has afflicted the social sciences in many domains of scientific inquiry (Weinrich 1987; Greenberg 1989). However, certain important facts, supported by cross-cultural and cross-historical research by anthropologists and social historians, seem to be beyond reasonable dispute.

The first of these facts is that erotic attraction and sexual behavior between individuals of the same genetic sex are present in most societies in which sexuality has been studied carefully, and, indeed, it is quite possible that homoeroticism is a cultural universal, present to one degree or another in all societies at all times (Blumenfeld and Raymond 1988; Ford and Beach 1951; Herdt 1987a; Whitam 1987). The second fact is that how societies construe homoeroticism varies greatly; in particular, the roles in which homosexual practices are embedded and the practices themselves differ from culture to culture. In some societies in New Guinea and Africa homosexual behavior is not only expected during at least a portion of the life cycle of males, it may be required in ritual contexts of all males (Herdt 1984, 1987b), whereas in others the commitment to and involvement in homosexual behavior is seen as a significant, permanent characteristic of a minority of individuals for whom sexual orientation becomes one component of the personal identity, as is the case in northern European and white American cultures. In still other societies, only some individuals who participate in homosexual activity are thereby defined as "homosexual," such definition depending on the role the individual plays in homosexual encounters (Carrier 1980, 1989). A third compelling fact is that sexual orientation is not a matter of choice for most individuals; instead, it is a given in the same way that skin color and handedness are, though, like the latter, its expression can be facilitated or suppressed.

The fourth fact is that the level of acceptability or unacceptability of homosexual behavior varies tremendously from culture to culture (Carrier 1980; Crapo n.d.; Werner 1979) and even over time within the same culture (Boswell 1980). If one examines this phenomenon at the level of present-day nation states, one can see the sharp contrasts that exist. At one extreme on the acceptability dimension are the Scandi-

navian countries, especially Norway and Denmark. In the former, not only are gays and lesbians guaranteed the same legal rights as other citizens, but in addition Norwegian laws protect them against homophobic attacks (Pedersen 1985). It is illegal to incite animosity or violence against the gay community, and the law has been used to prosecute a radio evangelist for making anti-gay remarks over the public airwaves. Denmark in 1989 became the first country to permit legal marriages between individuals of the same sex.

At the other end of the scale one finds countries such as Iran and Saudi Arabia where homosexual acts are punishable by death (Gmunder and Stamford 1988; IGA 1985). However, the most extreme official persecution of gays in the present century took place in Nazi Germany where thousands of gays, forced to wear a pink triangle, shared the fate of Jews, gypsies, and others who were considered in the Third Reich to be expendable (Heger 1980; Plant 1986; Rector 1981). The gay liberation movement, which had been strong in post-World War I Germany, was destroyed, along with the leading pro-gay institution of the time, the Institute of Sexual Science in Berlin, founded by Magnus Hirschfeld. In addition to being largely ignored by subsequent scholarly research on Nazi genocide, gays who survived concentration camps, in contrast to other survivors of the Holocaust, were never given reparations; they remained the forgotten victims.

Historically, the fate of homosexuals has run parallel to that of Jews in European societies, their oppression waxing and waning in tandem. Both groups served as scapegoats during various periods. Following a period of toleration in the Middle Ages, toward the middle of the twelfth century hostility toward gays increased, and they were subject to the death penalty (Boswell 1980).

ANTI-GAY VIOLENCE AND AGGRESSION IN CONTEMPORARY AMERICA

By contrast with the virulence of anti-gay attacks in the past and in a few cultures today, the present situation for gays and lesbians in the West may seem benign. But the appearances are somewhat deceptive. Laws on the books in some states continue to make felons of those engaging in homosexual acts, and the penalties for consenting homosexual behavior can be as severe as twenty years in prison, although these laws are rarely enforced. They function more as mechanisms of psychological aggression and intimidation. However, violence, threats of physical aggression and verbal abuse are significant risks in the lives of many gays and lesbians.

These dangers are often present even within the families of origin of gays and lesbians. Frequently, gay youths are rejected and abused by parents, siblings and other kin because of their homosexuality. Thus, where other minority youth generally do not face problems with racism and religious intolerance within their own families, for gays and lesbians often abuse begins at home. Many such youths even fear disclosing who they are to parents because of the possibility of rejection. In many cases, aggression against gay youths takes the form of expulsion from the childhood home and a severance of ties and financial support by unsympathetic parents. These young men and women then end up, in many cases, on the streets where they are targets for further violence.

EXAMPLES OF GAY-BASHING

Many cases of gay-bashing that occur today are reminiscent of the worst incidents of racial violence and harassment that were common before the successes of the civil rights movement. A few examples will suffice to illustrate what is often involved in gay-bashing.

Case 1. In 1986, a gay man living in Sacramento walked to the corner store one evening. Two men walking in the opposite direction passed him, and as they did so, he heard one of them mutter, "Too many faggots moving into the neighborhood." He continued on his way, ignoring the comment, until he heard footsteps behind him. As he turned around to look, he was struck on the shoulder by one of the men

and thrown to the ground where he was kicked repeatedly in the face. His attackers retreated shouting, "queer, queer, queer." When he got up, he discovered that he was bleeding and had been stabbed. He managed to crawl to his apartment complex before losing consciousness. He was found by a neighbor who called for medical assistance. His stab wound was one-sixteenth of an inch from a cartoid artery, but he survived. His assailants were never identified.

Case 2. On May 13, 1988 two lesbians were hiking along the Appalachian trail in Pennsylvania when they were shot by an assailant who had been stalking them for a day. The women had camped in a secluded area when the man, hiding in the woods about eighty feet away, opened firm on them. One of the women died at the campsite of back and head wounds; the other walked four miles with wounds in the head, face, upper arm, and neck before she got help. The attorney for the murderer claimed that the women had provoked the attack by performing sexual acts in front of the man. They had made love by the campfire unaware that they were being watched.

Case 3. A fraternity at the University of Vermont used a stamp that read "Drink Beer, Kill Queers" on the hands of students attending a fraternity party, and the same slogan was painted on a fraternity bus during a spring trip to Florida. Sanctions were applied to the fraternity by the university (probation, community service, and attendance at seminars on discrimination) (reported in *The Advocate*, 100, June 7, 1988: 34).

Case 4. Following a series of three gay-bashings in Laguna Beach, California, in August 1988, several shots from a high-powered rifle were fired into an area in which several gay businesses and a gay bar are located. No one was injured and the attackers were not caught (reported by the *Los Angeles Times*, August 14, 1988).

Case 5. A heterosexual male tourist in San Francisco in July, 1987 was stabbed in the face and abdomen. He died two hours later. His attackers had shouted "faggot" and "fruit" at him during the assault, mistakenly identifying him as gay. The police determined that he had done nothing to provoke the attack: He was, in their words, "at the wrong place at the wrong time" (NGLTF 1988).

Case 6. At Columbia University, in October 1988, a football coach filed an official complaint against a male cafeteria worker whom he saw kissing another male friend goodbye. The employee was verbally harassed by members of the football team during "Training Table." Anonymous complaints were also filed by team members, stating, "Get homo's [*sic*] out of the kitchen, you are encouraging AIDS die [*sic*]!" and "Get rid of the fags who serve during Training Table." The attacked employee is heterosexual (NGLTF 1989).

These and many similar incidents, ranging from homicide to verbal insults, represent a category of violence called "hate crimes" which are generating increasing attention and concern among citizens and law enforcement officials. In a report submitted to the US Department of Justice (Finn and McNeil 1987: 1), these incidents have been described as widespread and increasing:

> Bias crimes, or hate violence, are words or actions designed to intimidate an individual because of his or her race, religion, national origin, or sexual preference. Bias crimes range from threatening phone calls to murder. These types of offenses are far more serious than comparable crimes that do not involve prejudice because they are intended to intimidate an entire group. The fear they generate can therefore victimize a whole class of people.

The report concluded that homosexuals were "probably the most frequent victims" of hate violence and bias crimes (Finn and McNeil 1987: 2). Yet, many statutes and policies continue to exclude sexual orientation as a category or motivating factor in bias crime reporting. The reasons for this and the organized responses to it are discussed below.

DEFINITIONS

Gay-bashing involves acts of aggression committed against people because of their actual or perceived sexual orientation. Such acts are in many respects similar to hostile behavior displayed toward members of ethnic, racial, and religious minorities. Beginning in the late 1970s

and early 1980s, a new category of crime was developed, primarily in response to increasing reports of violence committed against racial minorities. This development emphasized the importance of focussing attention on the victims of crimes rather than studying only the characteristics of those committing them. Various terms, including hate violence, bias crime, civil rights violations, human relations incidents, bias-related violence, and several other combinations of these words, have been used to index criminal episodes that fit into this new category.

While a standard definition of this new category does not exist, most definitions of bias crime incorporate several criteria for recognizing a crime as a bias crime. These include the presence of verbal abuse or physical actions, threatened, attempted or carried out, directed against individuals or group, or an attack on their property, motivated, all or in part, by the actual or perceived ethnicity, race, national origin, religion, sex, age, disability, or sexual orientation of the target, with such acts intended to intimidate not just individuals *per se* but the entire group to which the victim is thought to belong. While these elements appear in almost all definitions of bias crimes, controversy typically focuses on which categories should be included. The inclusion of both race and religion is almost universal; some definitions include age, sex and disability; but only a few have included sexual orientation.

The New York State Governor's Task Force on Bias-Related Violence (1988: 2) adopted the following definition:

> An act of bias-related violence is an act or a threatened or attempted act of intimidation, harassment or physical force directed against any person, or group, or their property or advocate, motivated either in whole or in part by hostility to their real or perceived race, ethnic background, national origin, religious belief, sex, age, disability, or sexual orientation, with the intention of deterring the free exercise or enjoyment of any rights or privileges secured by the Constitution or the laws of the United States or the State of New York whether or not performed under color of law.

The Los Angeles County Commission on Human Relations (1989: 5), in its report, Hate Crime in Los Angeles County in 1988, defined hate crimes as "acts directed at an individual, institution, or business expressly because of race, ethnicity, religion, or sexual orientation." The report specifies a number of guidelines to be used in determining if a crime is a hate crime. To be designated as such, the crime "must involve a specific target," "bigotry must be the central motive for the attack"; if graffiti is involved the "graffiti must be racial, ethnic, religious, or homophobic in nature," and, for assaults in which no other motive is present, the assault must be initiated with epithets. Vandalism to organizations as well as threatening phone calls are considered hate crimes, also, when racial, ethnic, religious, or homophobic language is employed as part of the act.

The California Racial, Ethnic, and Religious Crimes Project, according to a report prepared by Abt Associates for the US Department of Justice (Finn and McNeil 1987: 18), defines bias crime as "any act to cause physical injury, emotional suffering, or property damage, which appears to be motivated, all or in part, by race, ethnicity, religion, or sexual orientation." The International Association of Chiefs of Police uses a definition developed by the National Organization of Black Law Enforcement Executives, which focuses on racial and religious incidents: "an act or a threatened or attempted act by any person or group of persons against the person or property of another individual or group which may in any way constitute an expression of racial or religious hostility" (as quoted in Finn and McNeil 1987: 18). This definition, as well as the ones in statutes in Maryland and Pennsylvania, does not include sexual orientation as a motivating factor.

The use of different definitions of bias crime leads to a number of problems, of course. For example, comparing data from different locales is made difficult, and even comparing data for a given locale over time is problematic when changes are made in the criteria for inclusion or exclusion of an event in the records intended to monitor bias-related aggression and violence. Increases or decreases in incidence, under such circumstances may be real or they may be artifacts of changes in data-collection procedures. Work in this area is hampered by divergent definitions and agreement is needed on an "accurate and workable definition of bias crime" (Finn and McNeil 1987: 18). Whether or not to include sexual orientation in the definition continues to be a highly debated issue.

Another important step in arriving at a working definition is to state what is not included as hate violence or bias crime. The Los Angeles County Commission on Human Relations (1989) excludes actions, such as graffiti on freeway overpasses and public phone booths, that are not directed at a specific target; interracial crimes not motivated by race, ethnicity, religion, or sexual orientation; intragroup acts; name calling not accompanied by assault; and rallies and leafletting by hate crime groups.

TYPES AND INCIDENCE OF BIAS CRIMES

During the 1985 hearings on Intro 2, the New York City Council bill to prohibit discrimination in housing, employment, and public acommodations on grounds of sexual orientation, one of the arguments used by the bill's opponents was that data did not exist to prove the need for the bill, i.e., that there was not sufficient evidence available to show that discrimination against gays and lesbians occurs. The same could have been said about anti-gay violence and aggression until very recently – a lack of data. Fortunately, some local governments and gay organizations have begun to remedy this situation by collecting systematic information on this problem. The results of these studies are discussed in this section. Although better data from more localities are definitely needed the pattern that emerges from existing studies indicates the magnitude of the problem of anti-gay violence and aggression.

According to the Los Angeles County Commission on Human Rights (1989, 1990a, 1990b) hate crime in Los Angeles County escalated between 1980 and 1982, levelled off until 1985, increased again in 1986, and then reached record levels between 1987 and 1989. In 1989, there were 167 reported race-based incidents, 125 religion-based incidents, and 86 bias-crime incidents related to sexual orientation. The victims of the racial incidents were as follows: Blacks, 57.5 per cent, Latinos, 13.2 per cent, Asians, 11.3 per cent, Armenians, 6.0 per cent, Arabs, 4.2 per cent, others, 7.8 per cent. Jews were the targets of 88.0 per cent of the incidents based on religious intolerance; Catholics were the victims in 5.6 per cent of the bias crimes based on religious preference.

The bias incidents most frequently cited in the racial and religious categories involved graffiti and hate literature, 32.3 per cent (race) and 56.0 per cent (religion) respectively. (See Table 30.1.) Assaults and attempted assaults were uncommon as bias crimes based on religion, only 8.8 per cent. They were more frequent in the racial category, 31.8 per cent. The pattern is different for crimes related to sexual orientation. Almost two-thirds of the bias crimes related to sexual orientation involved an assault or an attempted assault, whereas graffiti and hate literature accounted for less than one-third of the reported incidents (Los Angeles County Commission on Human Rights 1990a).

In general, shouted epithets and verbal abuse are the single most commonly reported type of incident for all of the categories (race, religion, sexual orientation), but these incidents are typically not recorded in the statistics of bias crimes. What is clear from the comparative data is that

Table 30.1 Hate crime incidents reported in Los Angeles County, 1989 (%)

Racial (N = 167)	
Graffiti/hate literature	32.3
Assault/attempted assault	31.8
Property vandalism	13.2
Criminal threats	11.3
Vandalism plus graffiti	7.2
Other	4.2
Religious (N = 125)	
Graffiti/hate literature	56.0
Criminal threats	15.2
Assault/attempted assault	8.8
Property vandalism	7.2
Vandalism plus graffiti	5.6
Arson	3.2
Other	4.0
Sexual orientation (N = 86)	
Assault/attempted assault	62.8
Graffiti/hate literature	30.2
Property vandalism	2.3
Criminal threats	3.5
Arson	1.2

violent forms of bias crime are more likely to be committed against gay men than against individuals because of race or religion. (In 1989, 93.0 per cent of the victims of the sexual orientation incidents were gay men, and only 7 per cent of the victims were lesbians.) As the Los Angeles County report (1989: 14) noted: "The term [gay bashing] is disturbingly accurate, as the great majority of these incidents involved assaults."

In general, bias crime reporting and investigating began by focusing on violence directed at blacks and Jews. Most of these incidents were committed by individuals and small groups rather than by organized hate groups, such as the Ku Klux Klan and white supremacist groups. The overwhelming majority of those arrested for these crimes are white males between the ages of 16 and 25. In New York City, 70 per cent of arrests for bias crimes between 1980 and 1987 involved persons under 20 years of age (Finn and McNeil 1987).

While most hate crime is committed by people who do not know their victims, in many cases of anti-gay violence the victim knows the assailant. A 1984 survey conducted by NGLTF (reported in NGLTF 1989), found that 34 per cent of gay men and lesbians had been verbally harassed by relatives and 7 per cent had been physically assaulted by family members because of their sexual orientation.

Physical and sexual abuses committed in prisons against people because of their race, ethnicity, religion, or sexual orientation are poorly documented (Governor's Task Force 1988). While there is considerable violence along racial lines, much of that may be related to the disproportionate number of incarcerated minor individuals, rather than to overt racial prejudice (Governor's Task Force 1988). But violence in such settings appears to be especially problematic and severe for gay prisoners. NGLTF (1989: 22) reports that "There are few settings where anti-gay violence is more trivialized than in prisons and jails, and none where it is more inescapable." Wooden and Parker (1982) document some of the types of sexual exploitation that routinely occur in prisons, especially against gay men.

As data collection efforts improve, reports of

hate violence and bias crimes against Hispanics, Southeast Asians, and homosexuals have increased. Racial incidents are more likely to be underreported than religious ones, due to the lack of familiarity with the laws by immigrants and non-English speakers. Sexual orientation cases are also underreported due to the victims' fears of disclosure and to police difficulties in identifying gay men and lesbians.

Although few organizations have kept detailed records on incidents related to gay men and lesbians, the National Gay and Lesbian Task Force (NGLTF) has been documenting such cases since 1982 and has issued reports annually since 1985. The latest is entitled *Anti-Gay Violence, Victimization and Defamation in 1988*. According to NGLTF figures (1989), which in 1988 came from 120 organizations in thirty-eight states and the District of Columbia, 7,248 incidents were reported, a 3 per cent increase over 1987, due primarily to an increase in the number of organizations reporting, especially campus groups and gay churches. The pattern of incidents has remained relatively constant over the past several years. As Table 30.2 shows, the most common type of incident involves verbal harassment or threats of violence, followed by physical assaults.

NGLTF (1989: 8) notes that "these statistics sharply underestimate the actual extent of anti-gay harassment and violence that occurred in the United States in 1988. Anti-gay episodes in the vast majority of US towns and cities,

Table 30.2 Anti-gay incidents reported to NGLTF (%)

	1988 (N = 7248)	1987 (N = 7008)	1986 (N = 4946)
Verbal harassment/ threats of violence	77	78	70
Physical assault	12	12	15
Vandalism	6	5	4
Police abuse (physical/ verbal)	3	3	8
Homicides	1	1	2
Other	1	2	1

and in 12 states ... were not reported to NGLTF in 1988." Furthermore, the majority of the 120 reporting organizations had not systematically collected statistics on anti-gay incidents. In addition, these figures exclude suicides due to anti-gay oppression, reports of discrimination in employment, membership in the armed forces, child custody decisions, housing, and so forth, and cases of harassment and violence that did not appear to be motivated by anti-gay prejudice. In short, as one group indicated to NGLTF (1989: 8), these figures "don't even scratch the surface of the problem."

Other studies of anti-gay hate crimes corroborate these findings and conclusions. In a survey released by NGLTF in 1984 more than 90 per cent of 2,074 people (654 lesbians and 1,420 gay men) in Atlanta, Boston, Dallas, Denver, Los Angeles, Seattle, and St Louis reported having experienced some type of harassment, threat, or assault; more than 30 per cent said they had been threatened with violence; almost 25 per cent of the men and 10 per cent of the women had been physically assaulted; approximately 33 per cent were verbally abused and 7 per cent were physically abused by relatives; and 20 per cent of the women and almost 50 per cent of the men reported they had been threatened, attacked, or harassed in junior or senior high school because they were perceived to be gay or lesbian.

NGLTF (1989) reviewed several other unpublished studies of anti-gay violence conducted in Philadelphia, Washington, DC, and Baltimore in 1988. These studies found that between 9 per cent and 18 per cent of those surveyed had experienced one or more physical assaults because of their sexual orientation. Since several of these studies are based on samples of gay people over time, rather than tabulations of reported bias crime incidents, some trend comparisons can be made. Herek (1989: 950) concluded that these studies "support the hypothesis that victimization is increasing."

Furthermore, NGLTF (1989: 12) reports that the Philadelphia study compared Pennsylvania rates with criminal victimization rates in a Bureau of Justice statistical study and concluded:

When annual rates of criminal violence in the Pennsylvania study are compared with Department of Justice estimates of the number of adult Americans who experienced criminal violence in 1986, gay men in Pennsylvania (excluding Philadelphia) were victimized 9 times more often and Pennsylvania lesbians (excluding Philadelphia) were victimized 7 times more often, than the average rate for the US adult population (i.e., those who live in rural, suburban or urban settings). Gay men and lesbians in Philadelphia only were victimized 10 times and 7 times more, respectively, than the average rates for men and women living in US major cities.

Since the Pennsylvania data are primarily from respondents who are white and above average in affluence and education and since the risk of victimization is greater among minorities and low-income people, these figures are undoubtedly underestimates of the amounts of anti-gay violence and harassment experienced by the gay and lesbian community as a whole.

Another survey of anti-gay violence (Comstock 1989) confirms many of the figures presented above. In that study, questionnaires were distributed to 700 people in gay meeting places and through ads in gay publications, with a 42 per cent response rate (usable questionnaires from 166 gay men and 125 lesbians). The sample was 77 per cent white, 11 per cent black and 8 per cent Hispanic; 39 per cent of the respondents were between 21 and 30 years of age, 39 per cent between 31 and 40, and 17 per cent over 40. Comstock (1989) found that the types of victimization included (1) being chased or followed (32 per cent); (2) objects thrown at them (21 per cent); (3) punched/kicked/hit/beaten (18 per cent); (4) vandalism/arson (16 per cent); (5) robbed (12 per cent); (6) raped (8 per cent); (7) assaulted with weapon (7 per cent); and (8) spit at (7 per cent). While the order was similar for whites and people of color, people of color were more likely than whites to have been chased/followed (43 per cent vs. 29 per cent) or have objects thrown at them (31 per cent vs. 18 per cent).

In the Comstock study, differences by gender were statistically significant: men were more likely than women (1) to have been chased/followed (36 per cent vs. 28 per cent); (2) to have objects thrown at them (2 per cent vs. 14

per cent); (3) to have been punched, kicked, hit or beaten (24 per cent vs. 10 per cent); (4) to have been robbed (19 per cent vs. 2 per cent); (5) to have been raped (10 per cent vs. 5 per cent); and (6) to have been assaulted with a weapon (11 per cent vs. 2 per cent).

Overall, 59 per cent of the respondents reported being victimized in public gay areas (such as gay bars or gay neighborhoods), 31 per cent in public non-gay areas (such as on public transportation or in non-gay neighborhoods), 26 per cent in home settings (parents' or relatives' homes, their own homes), and 25 per cent in schools (high school and college). Men were more likely than women to report victimization in gay public areas (66 per cent vs. 45 per cent), while women were more likely than men to report attacks in public non-gay areas (42 per cent vs. 26 per cent) and in home settings (30 per cent vs. 24 per cent).

While these figures may reflect some increased tendency on the part of individuals who have been victimized in anti-gay attacks to complete a questionnaire on the subject, these numbers are probably closer indicators of the true rate of anti-gay victimization than are those obtained from police records and from the recording of incidents by various agencies. Evidence for this is the finding from Comstock's questionnaire that 73 per cent of the respondents never reported the incident to the police. Most of those not reporting the crime said that they perceived or experienced the police to be anti-gay (67 per cent). And 40 per cent of those not reporting attacks to police said that they feared disclosure of sexual orientation. Of those who did report the incident to the police (and, again, only 27 per cent chose to do so), 51 per cent found the police to be courteous, 67 per cent reported the police to be indifferent, 23 per cent said the police were hostile and 5 per cent said they were abusive (these were not mutually exclusive items).

Herek (1989), too, noted that several surveys of gay-bashing victims discovered that only between 10 and 23 per cent of the victims reported the incident to the police or other agencies. Berrill (1986: 6) concludes that victims of anti-gay violence are less likely than others to report to the police: "Current research indicates that at least three quarters of anti-gay violence victims fail to notify police, while half (52 per cent) of the victims of violent crimes fail to do so." Anderson (1982) describes the results of a 1979 study in Minneapolis in which two-thirds of the lesbians and gay men who were victims of assault took no action in reporting the incident and only 9.3 per cent reported it to the police.

Research by Comstock (1989), NGLTF (1989), and several other unpublished studies (as quoted in NGLTF 1989), all point in similar directions. It is, of course, impossible to get accurate data on crime; all data must depend on what is reported. It is even more difficult to obtain accurate data on gay-related crimes when the fear of reporting such crime may be greater. Furthermore, it is impossible to generate a random sample survey of gay people. Consequently, all findings must be based on those responding to surveys, who are usually middle-class, white, educated, urban, and open about their sexual orientation. Similarly, figures based on data gathered from organizations reporting to a central clearing-house are limited to the number of organizations that choose to record the hate crimes reported to them and then, in turn, choose to report those data to the central agency (in this case, NGLTF).

In short, the numbers presented above should be viewed as relative indicators of what bias crimes are being committed, how frequently, and against whom, rather than as absolute levels. Clearly, though, there is a significant problem of violent crimes being perpetrated against gay men and lesbians because of their sexual orientation. How this problem is being handled by the criminal justice system, the media, and other organizations is the focus of the discussion that follows.

THE CRIMINAL JUSTICE SYSTEM AND GAY-BASHING

From law enforcement practices to the role of the prosecutor's office to the attitudes of the judge to law-makers in state and national government, dealing with bias crimes is generally hampered by prejudice, misinformation, and few guidelines. Of all the groups affected by bias crimes, gay men and lesbians appear to be most vulnerable and ill-treated by the various components of the criminal justice system, largely because of the familiar process known as "blaming the victim."

Police

Many professionals in the law enforcement field do not view bias crimes as a serious problem (Finn and McNeil 1987). In New York State, the response to bias crime "is uneven and inadequate. Few of the 600 police agencies have any awareness of or focused response to bias crimes" (Governor's Task Force 1988: 105). The New York State report continues: "Despite the widespread inability for police agency officials to specify the incidence of bias crime, evidence suggests that it is widespread in the state" (Governor's Task Force 1988: 106).

While some of the perception that bias crime is not a significant problem is due to the fact that many groups fear reporting incidents, ignoring bias crime is also related to the fact that some law enforcement personnel do not take it seriously. Since much hate crime is committed by teenage boys and young adults, it is often considered just an adolescent "prank" or something done by a basically "good kid" (Finn and McNeil 1987; Governor's Task Force 1988). Confusion over the definition and identification of hate crimes is also part of the problem. In addition, some police departments are reluctant to develop a whole new category of crime which will require more paperwork and necessitate the allocation of time and funds to handle, in most instances diverting them from other projects (see Finn and McNeil 1987).

The New York State Governor's Task Force (1988: 134) reported that "Allegations of bias-related violence by police officers were among the most disturbing to come before the Task Force. Many of those incidents marked by the tragedy of death involve law enforcement officers." Public testimony to the Task Force described improper police use of force against blacks, Hispanics, Asians, and gays and lesbians. In this connection it is worth reiterating that Comstock's (1989) study, cited above, found that the most common reason given by respondents for not reporting incidents of gay-bashing to police was a perceived or experienced anti-gay attitude by police. Fear of police abuse was also claimed by 14 per cent of the respondents. Police harassment and abuse accounted for 205 incidents (almost 3 per cent) of the total number of cases reported to NGLTF (1989) for 1988, including such cases as the verbal abuse and clubbing of patrons by police in a Pittsburgh gay bar, police name-calling and striking a suspect perceived to be gay, and security guards yelling "Faggot" and "queer" at protestors in a Massachusetts state senate gallery demonstration.

Prosecutors

Intimidation by some police forces is only the beginning of the problems in the criminal justice system. Prosecutors are also likely to ignore bias crimes or not to see them as a major problem: there is "a low level of awareness of bias crime in many DAs' offices" (Governor's Task Force 1988: 147). Prosecutors who do comprehend the seriousness of such crimes may find their efforts hampered for various reasons. The police, for example, may not gather all the necessary evidence or they may fail to bring cases to be prosecuted; sometimes victims may want to drop the case in order to avoid the risk of public exposure with a trial; plea-bargaining may diminish the civil rights charges in some cases; and smaller cities and towns, especially those without a bias-crime focus in the police force, may not have sufficient resources to allow them to respond to hate crimes (Finn and McNeil 1987).

Judiciary

But even if the police and the district attorney's office are successful in bringing a case to court on a bias-crime charge, problems in the judiciary often change the focus. A typical reaction is to acquit the defendant or to hand down a lenient sentence on the basis of the so-called "homosexual panic" or "gay advance" defense. In these cases, self-defense or temporary insanity is claimed as a result of an actual or perceived sexual advance by the victim (Finn and McNeil 1987). A widely reported example of this phenomenon was the December 1988 sentence hearing of a man convicted of murdering two gay men in Dallas. The defendant was sentenced to thirty years in prison rather than a life sentence as sought by the prosecution. According to an Associated Press report (*Los Angeles Times* 1988), State District Judge Jack Hampton said: "These two guys that got killed wouldn't have been killed if they hadn't been cruising the streets picking up teenage boys." Hampton claimed that the homosexuality of the murder victims entered into his decision to give the killer a lighter sentence. He said he would have given a harsher sentence if the victims had been "a couple of housewives out shopping, not hurting anybody." The Texas Commission on Judicial Conduct is investigating this case.

In another incident in Broward County, Florida, Circuit Judge Daniel Futch jokingly asked the prosecutor when the anti-gay nature of a beating death outside a Ford Lauderdale gay nightclub was brought up. "That's a crime now, to beat up a homosexual?" (as reported in NGLTF 1989: 25). In this and many similar cases, the "homosexual panic" defense is used as a way of shifting responsibility to the victim and away from the defendant. The assumption is "that gay people are sexually aggressive and predatory, and [this] has been used most successfully when the victims are dead and therefore unable to answer the defendant's allegations" (NGLTF 1989: 25). Although NGLTF reports that this type of defense has failed to exonerate defendants in most cases, the fact that it is used speaks to the problems anti-gay violence victims must confront and the prejudices some judges and prosecutors bring to their cases.

The case of the assassination of San Francisco Supervisor Harvey Milk and of Mayor George Moscone in 1978 by Dan White, is perhaps the most famous example of light sentences given to violent offenders when their victims are gay or lesbian. Although this case is better known for its so-called "Twinkie defense," rather than for the use of a "homo-sexual panic" tactic, the outcome, which was a miscarriage of justice, was generally perceived to be heavily influenced by the fact that one of the victims was a gay man (Shilts 1982).

These examples could be multiplied many-fold to illustrate the point that the judicial system has a tendency to treat the perpetrators of anti-gay violence with lenience, which serves to reinforce homophobic ideas that gay-bashing is not a serious crime.

Legislation

Appropriate legislation could help to deter anti-gay violence. However, the same kinds of preju-dices and assumptions that influence police, prosecutors, and judges also are found among legislators, many of whom maintain that exist-ing laws already apply and that newer, more specific ones therefore do not need to be enac-ted. Some object to the special protection nature of bias crime laws, while others are concerned about First Amendment issues related to crimin-alizing verbal harassment (Finn and McNeil 1987).

The central issues that need to be addressed by legislators include raising the charges from misdemeanors to felonies; increasing the penal-ties for convictions; using civil rights injunctions more frequently; mandating bias crime educa-tion, especially targeted to minorities; requiring the collection of bias-crime data; and the most controversial, adding "sexual orientation" as a category in the list of groups included in bias crime bills (see Finn and McNeil 1987; Gover-nor's Task Force 1988). The Governor's Task Force (1988: 218) reported that:

> no single statute in New York State addresses acts of violence which are motivated in whole or in part by prejudice against the victim's race, reli-gion, creed, color, age, disability, national origin, sex or sexual orientation. A number of existing statutes do offer some relief, but only to victims of some types of bias-related violence. Of particular note is omission of anti-gay/lesbian violence from the protection now provided by the existing sta-tutes.

New York is not alone in this regard.

Depending on the state, legislation aimed at bias crimes varies in what is covered, which groups are included, and what kinds of penalties are imposed. Property damage statutes (especially aimed at religious buildings and cemeteries) are in effect in twenty-one states; some states have raised the penalties for assault to a felony if the assault is due to bias (Minnesota, California, and Wisconsin have such laws); some states have statutes forbidding interfering with some-one's civil rights; and a few states require police departments to collect bias-crime data at the local and state level (Connecticut and Minne-sota have such laws). But as of late 1989, only California and the city of Seattle prohibit acts motivated by the sexual orientation of the victim. Leaders of the Republican Party in the New York State Senate – despite the recom-mendation from the governor's Task Force, passage by the State Assembly, and support from Governor Cuomo – blocked the passage of a bias-crime bill which contained "sexual ori-entation" as a category.

According to NGLTF (1989), Michigan's state senate removed a sexual orientation provi-sion from a hate crimes bill although it had been included in the House version of the bill. At the city level, Oklahoma City included sexual ori-entation as a minority group protected from harassment in its bill; Columbus, Ohio, despite the Mayor's request to drop gays from its bill, voted to increase penalties for bias crimes including those based on sexual orientation; and San Francisco, San Diego County, and Montgomery County, Maryland have required data collection on bias crimes including those committed against gays and lesbians.

At the federal level, the Hate Crime Statistics Act (HR, 3193; S.702) which would require the collection of statistics at the federal level on crimes based on race, religion, ethnicity, and "homosexuality or heterosexuality," passed the House of Representatives by a large margin (383–29) in May 1988, but was blocked in the Senate by Jesse Helms, despite passing unan-imously in the Senate Judiciary Committee. The bill, re-introduced in February 1989, passed in the House in June 1989 (386–47) and in Feb-ruary 1990 in the Senate (92–4). At this writing, it is on President Bush's desk awaiting his signature (he backed the bill).

Sexual orientation has also been included in a model hate-crime statute developed by the national Anti-Defamation League of B'nai B'rith. This model proposes enhanced criminal penalties for bias-motivated crimes, a civil cause of action for victims, and mandatory data collection by law enforcement agencies (NGLTF 1989).

The inclusion of "sexual orientation" as a category in bias crime bills has led to the rejection of proposed statutes in many locales. The Governor's Task Force (1988: 219) recognized the greater likelihood of a bias crime act being passed if lesbians and gay men are excluded, but strongly states:

> the Task Force believes that excluding anti-gay/lesbian violence victims from the protection of the Act would be wrong. To do so would give the false impression that such conduct is either condoned by the state or that such acts of bias-related violence do not exist. Neither of these notions is correct.

The New York state bill was defeated because of the sexual orientation provision.

THE CAUSES OF ANTI-GAY AGGRESSION

The deficiencies in the criminal justice system outlined above clearly serve as contributory factors in gay-bashing. If anti-gay crimes tend not to be reported, if the offenders tend not to be apprehended, if legislators have not provided the legal tools for penalizing offenders, and if the sentences meted out to those successfully prosecuted for such offenses tend to be light, then the possibility for deterring individuals who might commit bias crimes is small. But the other causes of anti-gay aggression are complex and legion. Some of the factors responsible for attacks on gays and lesbians are unique to this category of victims, but others are identical to the factors generally implicated in violence and aggression targeted to minorities in general. Most of the theories used to explain racism and religious intolerance can be applied to understanding gay-bashing, but a comprehensive theory of anti-gay aggression must include variables that are specific to this category of victim.

The sociopolitical climate of the 1980s in the United States certainly contributed to the increasing severity of the problem of hate crime in general. The Anti-Defamation League of B'nai B'rith has documented a five-year high in anti-Semitic incidents in 1988, an increase of 19 per cent in vandalism and 41 per cent in harassment over the preceding year (as reported in NGLTF 1989). Other organizations (such as the Center for Democratic Renewal, the National Institute Against Prejudice and Violence and the Southern Poverty Law Center) which monitor racial and religious bias also have reported increases, leading NGLTF (1989: 30) to conclude that "growing reports of hate violence suggest that the pluralistic fabric of our society may be unravelling, a trend that should alarm all those concerned about human and civil rights."

SOCIAL AND CULTURAL CAUSES

Finn and McNeil (1987: 1), in their report for the Department of Justice, suggested that, while some increases in bias-crime statistics are related to more accurate reporting and clearer definitions, the widespread problem is due to "increased economic competition for minorities, visibility of gay men, ethnic neighborhood transition, and a perceived decrease in government efforts to prevent discrimination in education, housing, and employment." The rhetoric of white supremacist groups and the failure of local and national leaders to condemn these groups more strongly also contribute to the increase in bias-motivated incidents.

Los Angeles County's Commission on Human Rights (1989) suggested that the causes of increases in hate crimes include rapid ethnic demographic change, ongoing intergroup tension, international events, and entrenched bigotry in some segments of the population, and the New York State Governor's Task Force (1988) concluded that broad social forces, such as the failure of schools to educate about diversity and anti-bias, the failure of the media to provide accurate portrayals of ethnic and racial groups, and the perpetuation of segregated housing which denies minorities equal access to housing, are responsible for the increase in bias crimes. Many of these factors are relevant to the situation of gay men and lesbians as well as that of other minorities.

Although there have been increases in the 1980s in hate crimes generally, within American society over the past twenty years the acceptability of overt racism and anti-Semitism has declined. A similar magnitude of decline in negative attitudes towards gays and lesbians and in values related to homosexuality is difficult to document. For many of the religious denominations in this country, for example, homosexuality remains a sin. While a few Protestant denominations have been moving toward full equality and acceptance for gays and lesbians, the Catholic church's anti-homosexual stance has become vocally more strident in recent years, with Vatican spokesmen and some leading figures in American Catholicism, such as New York's John Cardinal O'Connor, actively expressing their opposition to the gay subculture.

During the two decades since the Stonewall Rebellion in 1969, the gay rights movement has pushed for equal rights for gays and lesbians. As a result, gays and lesbians have become more visible to the general public, augmenting considerably the awareness of homosexuality as a significant phenomenon in American society that resulted from the research by Kinsey and his associates which demonstrated that homosexual behavior was much more widespread than had been thought previously. The struggle for gay rights brought with it an increase in anti-gay rhetoric on the part of both religious and political leaders, and this rhetoric, too, must be seen as a major contributor to gay-bashing, fueling overt hostility and violence against the gay minority. While various denominations in the past justified discrimination against and hostility toward members of racial and religious outgroups, such as blacks and Jews, citing biblical scriptures to justify bigotry, few do so today. Opposition to homosexuality, however, continues to be based in religious beliefs. There-

fore, some of the same groups that in the past supported civil rights for ethnic groups are strongly opposed to equal rights and protections for gays and lesbians.

Highly visible attacks on gays are made with regularity by influential politicians and political commentators. These attacks by Senators and Congressmen such as Jesse Helms and William Dannemeyer and by political commentators such as Patrick Buchanan continue a long tradition in which gays and lesbians have served as scapegoats and targets of opportunity. An alleged association between homosexuals and communists was stressed during the McCarthy era when gay-bashing in Congress was especially serious, with careers and lives ruined by the attacks during that witch-hunt aimed at ridding American society of undesirables and unpopular beliefs. The second-class status of gays and lesbians persists today inasmuch as laws which prevent them from exercising the same rights as other citizens are still on the books and are often enforced. Discrimination continues with respect to membership in the armed forces, security clearances, immigration and naturalization, child custody and visitation rights, adoption and foster care, housing and public accommodations, marriage, and inheritance (Stoddard et al. 1983). While the civil rights protections of other minorities may have eroded to some degree during the 1980s, the gay minority has still to attain many of the rights and protections guaranteed to members of ethnic and religious minorities.

In one sense, the gay minority's victimization rises and falls along with the victimization of other minorities in response to the increase or decrease in the factors that have an impact on attacks on outgroups generally. However, it is also likely that as other minorities are perceived as less legitimate targets of attack (condemned by opinion molders in the society), gays and lesbians will become more and more the victims of hate crimes. Indeed, with the current changes in Eastern Europe and the Soviet Union and the resultant decline in anti-communism, it is also quite conceivable that intolerance will focus attention more strongly on gays and lesbians.

STEREOTYPING AND THE ROLE OF THE MEDIA

Stereotypes of gay men, and perhaps to a lesser extent of lesbians, play a key role in the etiology of gay-bashing, just as stereotypes of other minority groups are implicated in bias crimes committed against their members. Furthermore, the perpetuation of these stereotypes in the media as well as the media's handling of gay-bashing merit examination as indirect causes of bias crimes. Newspapers, television, and other public forms of communication can provide useful information about bias incidents, yet they can also create images about the groups involved that provoke new incidents.

The Governor's Task Force (1988) studied ten daily newspapers throughout New York State and concluded that the media was not performing a positive function with respect to bias violence. More specifically, the report found that newspaper coverage emphasizes physical violence out of proportion to actual rates; that bias incidents are portrayed as isolated from normal, everyday life; and that violence against some groups is systematically underreported, "particularly true of attacks on gays and on Asians and other ethnic groups with a high proportion of recent immigrants.... No reports of anti-gay violence were found in the sample of newspapers in this study even though gays and lesbians may be the most victimized group in the nation" (Governor's Task Force 1988: 228).

The Task Force saw this in part as a reflection of the underreporting of gay violence to police by the victims and the dependency of media on police reports for information. Also, The Governor's Task Force (1988: 229) concluded,

> The failure of the media to report about anti-gay and anti-lesbian violence on a regular basis may also reflect the continuing reluctance of the media to acknowledge that anti-gay actions are as serious as actions motivated by hatred of a person's race, religion, or ethnicity.
>
> In this respect the media are reflecting what is often considered to be the prevalent social attitudes toward lesbian and gay men. The existence of the gay community was frequently ignored by the media prior to the onset of the AIDS crisis; only in the last few years have the media begun to

acknowledge that a significant minority of Americans face unique concerns related to their sexual orientation. The violence resulting from hostile attitudes toward lesbians and gay men has still failed to attract media interest.

Further findings about media coverage by the Governor's Task Force (1988: 232) include the dependence on official sources for perspectives and viewpoints on the incident; attempts to delegitimate the victims by questioning the honesty of the victim's version and focusing on motives and character; and frequent attempts to deny the bias motivations in the incident by framing it in terms of youthful perpetrators "protecting their turf" or the protection of property.

There has also been an increase in radio and television talk shows which perpetuate "false and sometimes vicious myths that reasonable and sensitive listeners take to be anti-Jewish, anti-Black, anti-gay, and anti other groups" (Governor's Task Force 1988: 235). Coupled with low minority representation among media employees and the almost exclusive use of whites in advertisements, the media rarely portray minorities in everyday life situations, thereby enhancing the out-of-context aspects of bias crimes when they are reported. Defamatory remarks by public figures in the media against lesbians and gay men are not included in the bias incident statistics. Yet, many of these statements can be viewed as the source of subsequent assaults (NGLTF 1989). They are included here as a means of illustrating the context in which gay-bashing incidents occur and to show how they may be related to the violence which occurs soon after they are aired.

The NGLTF report quotes an article in the Boston Gay Community News about Philadelphia city council member Francis Rafferty's statement opposing Gay Pride Month by declaring that gays have nothing to be proud about because they are spreading AIDS. Soon after that, "a Philadelphia gay activist was beaten by two men who began their attack by claiming that 'We're for Rafferty and we're for the majority'" (NGLTF 1989: 28).

The case of Andy Rooney is instructive. Rooney, a CBS commentator, made anti-gay remarks in his syndicated columns and also on a television special in December 1989. Subsequently, he was reported to have made racist remarks as well, which he denied. He was suspended from his job for three months by CBS. Newspaper reports seemed to suggest that the suspension came not because of his admitted inflammatory anti-gay remarks but because of his alleged racist comments. In any case, his early reinstatement following a public outcry in his favor sent a message that both homophobic and racist attacks are acceptable.

Other media incidents reported to NGLTF ranged from a comedy album by Sam Kinison that blames AIDS on gay men having intercourse with monkeys; a song, "Homesick Heroes," on an album by country and western singer Charlie Daniels which encourages punching out "sissy" gays and sending them back "where women are women and men are men"; a radio disc jockey in Connecticut who stated that "fags" should be castrated to prevent AIDS from spreading, followed soon by a gay man with AIDS being chased by teenagers screaming that he didn't deserve to live since the deejay said "queers" spread AIDS; a Miami radio station advertising a nightclub offering special activities including "beating up queers," and an HBO television comedy special which had comedian Damon Wayans talking about gay-bashing as he "wobbled feyly across the stage while rolling his eyes and swishing his wrists" (NGLTF 1989: 29). Although such incidents are not included when defining or recording bias crime incidents, the media are being monitored for anti-gay remarks and stereotyping by various chapters of the Gay and Lesbian Alliance Against Defamation and protests against such incidents are being lodged with media representatives and program sponsors, since their impact on gay-bashing is far from negligible.

Aspects of the widespread stereotype of gay men in American culture may also contribute to gay-bashing. These include the perception of gay men as feminine and weak, as men who engage in unmanly occupations such as hair-dressing, interior decorating and the arts, which are of lesser value to society than stereotypical, straight male occupations. The general tendency of the media is to focus on those segments of the gay community that conform to this pattern.

There is very little effort made to portray gays who do not conform to the swishy stereotype. If gay men are portrayed as feminine and weak, it is natural for gay-bashers to perceive them as easy targets and a safe outlet for thrill-seeking.

In addition to seeing gays and lesbians as cost-free targets, there is a widespread perception that homosexuality is illegal, and, therefore, attacks on gays and lesbians can be justified as attacks on criminals. While homosexual behavior is a felony in some states, this perception persists even in states where homosexuality has been decriminalized for almost two decades. A common misunderstanding of the *Bowers* v. *Hardwick* sodomy case decided by the Supreme Court in 1986 is that the ruling handed down outlawed homosexuality, whereas it simply made it permissible for states to have laws of that type. While that case did not make homosexuality illegal, the fact that it did uphold the rights of states to outlaw homosexual behavior can be interpreted as institutional gay-bashing by giving permission to withhold equal rights, even the right of the gay minority to exist. It is noteworthy that reports of gay-bashings increased significantly in many locales after news of that decision appeared in the media.

Other dimensions of the gay stereotype are also worth mentioning. Gay men are often viewed as hypersexual, their lives being defined by their sexuality. They are seen as highly promiscuous, an image that was exacerbated by AIDS reporting which stressed the number of partners some gay men have. They are seen as incapable of maintaining relationships, and their intimate life is interpreted as involving lots of sex but no love. The image often portrayed is one of well-to-do, self-indulgent hedonists without the responsibilities of mature heterosexual men. Moreover, the belief that gay men recruit new members by seducing young boys is widespread. And long after the psychological professions removed homosexuality from the list of mental illnesses, the stereotype of gays and lesbians as mentally disturbed or sick individuals persists. Some elements of this stereotype gays share with other minorities, e.g., hypersexuality and unstable relationships with blacks, wealth with Jews (see Adam 1978).

While some media producers have made some efforts to portray gays and lesbians in a more positive light (PBS, in particular, in some cities), the efforts are insufficient to eliminate erroneous elements in the popular gay stereotype and to counter the anti-gay material broadcast on radio and television.

Explanations for anti-gay sentiments and gay-bashing need to take into account the negative stereotypes, which are perpetuated by the media, as does the work by Harry (1982: 546) who discusses the concept of "derivative deviance" which he defines as "that subset of all victimizations which is perpetrated upon other presumed deviants who, because of their deviant status, are presumed unable to avail themselves of civil protection." He distinguishes two kinds: cultural derivative deviance and opportunistic derivative deviance. The former occurs when the victim is unknown to the assailant, who relies on stereotypes of appearance and place. This kind of victimization results in assaults and robberies, what Harry (1982) calls "fag-bashing." The latter type occurs when a pre-existing relationship is present and the victim has trustingly shared his or her stigmatized status with the perpetrator. This kind typically leads to incidents of extortion or blackmail.

Harry's (1982) data support the idea that "fag-bashing" is more likely to occur in gay-defined areas and when the person conforms more to cultural stereotypes (39 per cent of the self-defined effeminate men were assaulted versus 22 per cent of the masculine and 17 per cent of the very masculine self-defined men). Similarly for cases of blackmail: the more effeminate and those not attached to a reference group of other gays were more likely successfully extorted. Thus, Harry (1982: 560) concludes that "those who most conform to stereotypes of deviants appear to bear the brunt of the derivative victimization, both cultural and opportunistic."

Although Harry found that marginal gays were more likely to be blackmailed, he was unable to show a significant relationship between those gays unattached to a large gay network and increased assaults, thus contradicting the findings of Miller and Humphreys (1980: 177), whose data suggested that homo-sexual marginals, i.e., those who operate "on the periphery of gay institutions and social networks," are more likely to be victims of violent crimes. Rather, attachment to a visible gay community and participation in activities in gay areas make gay men and lesbians more vulnerable to identification and possible victimization.

Given that most anti-gay incidents are committed by young males, Herek (1984) believes that the pressure among peers to accept masculine gender role traits and to solidify group membership by affirming masculinity through violence should be considered as a possible explanation in our culture. More and more, "sexual orientation is becoming the component defining masculinity" (Franklin 1988: 163). As this happens, heterosexuality becomes increasingly relevant as the core idea of masculinity; the pressure to deemphasize homosexuality and intimacy between men increases; and the devaluing of feminine behaviors in men continues. In such a cultural climate, young males are more likely to target openly gay men, males perceived to be more feminine in appearance and behavior, and anyone else perceived to be non-conforming to gender roles.

Thus, from a sociological perspective, crimes committed against lesbians and gay men are related to cultural stereotyping, opportunities to identify people as stigmatized by seeing them participate in gay contexts, and other social definitions of what constitutes appropriate gender behavior as perceived especially by young males.

ANTI-GAY ATTITUDES AND HOMOPHOBIA

The negative stereotype of gays discussed above tends to be accompanied by anti-gay attitudes on the part of a significant proportion of the American population, and in more extreme cases by homophobia, a concept used to designate irrational fear of and hostility toward homosexuals. Evidence of the magnitude of homophobic attitudes in this society is provided by many studies. Results from a few of these studies can be described here. Inasmuch as young males tend to be the chief perpetrators of anti-gay violence, an understanding of homophobia in that segment of the population is essential. A survey of the attitudes of 2823 junior and senior high school students in twenty school districts in New York State, conducted by the Governor's Task Force (1988) provided data on anti-gay hostility. The report (1988: 97) concluded that:

> One of the most alarming findings in the youth survey is the openness with which the respondents expressed their aversion and hostility toward gays and lesbians ... the students were quite emphatic about their dislike for these groups and frequently made violent, threatening statements. Gays and lesbians, it seems, are perceived as legitimate targets which can be openly attacked.

One of the findings from this survey clearly showed gender differences in attitudes toward gays. While 74 per cent of the boys agreed that it would be "bad" or "very bad" to have gays move into the neighborhood, 48 per cent of the girls checked those attitudes. Overall, between 69 per cent and 91 per cent of the students rejected the idea of having gays as neighbors. Only 12 per cent believed it would be "very good" or "good" to have a gay person move into their neighborhood. For purposes of comparison, 50 per cent to 60 per cent said it would be "very good" or "good" to have neighbors of ethnic and racial minorities (blacks, Hispanics, Asians, Jews). When comments were made on the questionnaires by the students, most were positive about interracial and intercultural interactions. However, when the comments were about gay people, they "were often openly vicious. Emphasis was frequently added to the negative responses and a number of students threatened violence against gays" (Governor's Task Force 1988: 84).

Data from sixty-four higher education campuses in New York State show similar results. In a survey of official representatives of four-year colleges and universities, 20 per cent perceived that gay and lesbian students were rejected by fellow students, 37 per cent felt that they were avoided by others, and 23 per cent believed they were ignored by other students. In other words, 80 per cent reported that they perceived gay and lesbian students as being rejected, avoided, or ignored; the next closest group was black students, perceived to be avoided or ignored by 55 per cent of the administrators. As the Governor's Task Force (1988: 55) stated: "No other group is defined as rejected in institutional authorities' perceptions. This refusal to accept gay and lesbian students leads all too frequently to active rejection ... active rejection of other groups is not normative on campus."

In addition, 35 per cent of these sixty-four administrators report that anti-gay and lesbian incidents have occurred on their campuses, 60 per cent believe there is anti-gay sentiment, and 32 per cent say they have policies against gay bias. The Governor's Task Force (1988: 56) concludes:

> The pattern seems clear. Many campuses in New York experience anti-gay/lesbian incidents and even more have anti-gay/lesbian feelings. In the face of this, most have no organizational support and few have experimented with promising policies to alleviate this problem.

From a psychological viewpoint, the concept of homophobia is given much prominence as a driving force in the development of negative and violent behavior toward homosexuals. Homophobia has generally been perceived as a unidimensional trait of personality, often unrelated to the social context in which prejudicial attitudes (including racism and sexism) develop and are maintained.

In another study (D'Augelli 1989), this one of students at a major university who had applied for the position of resident assistant, all of the subjects indicated that they had heard disparaging remarks made about gays and lesbians, 83 per cent of them indicated that they heard such remarks often, and indeed, most of the subjects admitted that they themselves had made such remarks. Furthermore, the subjects all agreed that harassment of gays and lesbians was likely on their campus, with 52 per cent believing that harassment, threats of violence, or physical attack are "very likely."

Herek (1984) provided a list of factors that correlate with the holding of negative attitudes toward lesbians and gay men; according to his review of the literature, those with more negative attitudes, (1) have had less personal contact with gays and lesbians, (2) have themselves not engaged in homosexual behavior or identified themselves as gay or lesbian, (3) tend to perceive that their peers hold anti-gay attitudes, (4) tend to live in areas of North America where negative attitudes towards gays have been found to be more prevalent, (5) tend to be older and low in educational level, (6) tend to be more religious, to be more frequent churchgoers, and to believe in more conservative religious ideology, (7) tend to hold traditional sex-role attitudes, (8) tend to be more negative about sexuality generally and to express more guilt about sexuality, and (9) tend to score high on authoritarianism and related personality measures.

In Herek's (1984) view, attitudes serve as strategies for meeting a variety of psychological needs in different social contexts. Homophobic attitudes, in particular, can serve various functions for different people. Herek (1984) sees three major needs being met by three types of attitudes: those which categorize reality based on past interactions (experiential), those which are used to cope with conflicts and anxieties by projecting them onto others (defensive), and those used to express abstract ideological concepts which are closely linked to notions of self (symbolic). These explain the variation in findings from studies about attitudes toward homosexuals.

The persistence of anti-gay attitudes and their effects on aggression have been supported in other research. Using male college students, San Miguel and Millham (1976) studied the interactive effects of attitudes, type of contact, perceived similarity, and sexual orientation on aggressive behavior and attitudes. Despite a limited sample and an absence of measures on actual violence, they found that there was significantly more aggression expressed toward homosexuals than heterosexuals. In addition, they (1976: 26) concluded that "homosexuals who are perceived by a heterosexual as personally similar to himself are likely to experience heightened rather than diminished aggressiveness from that person." In addition, aggression was not attenuated among heterosexuals who held prior negative attitudes towards homosexuals even after experiencing a positive cooperative interaction. In short, homosexuals "are subject to higher levels of aggression than are their normative counterparts" (San Miguel and Millham 1976: 26).

Clearly the question of how attitudes toward homosexuality and gays and lesbians are formed and maintained is an important one in understanding anti-gay violence, especially from a psychological perspective. Since many people hold favorable attitudes toward gays and lesbians, even in a social and cultural context less supportive of homosexuals, personality traits and attitude formation become salient variables in explaining bias crimes.

AIDS AND GAY-BASHING

The AIDS epidemic added to the problems confronting the gay community in the 1980s. On top of having to cope with a rising death toll and to make critical changes in patterns of behavior related to HIV transmission, gay men (and lesbians as well) became concerned about the possibility of a backlash and heightened homophobia and anti-gay violence. Originally labelled GRID (Gay-Related Immune Deficiency), AIDS became associated with homosexuality in the US because the first cases were recognized in gay men living in major urban areas, notably in cities with large gay populations (New York, San Francisco, and Los Angeles). The high case fatality rate, ignorance about the etiology and the means of transmission of the disease, failure by the Reagan administration to deal with the epidemic, and sensationalist reporting by the press (when they were not ignoring the epidemic entirely), all helped to generate hysteria, a secondary epidemic sometimes referred to as "AFRAIDS." Political and religious opponents of the gay community were quick to use AIDS as a weapon, blaming AIDS on the sinfulness of gays and citing AIDS as justification for continued oppression of the gay minority (see Lang 1989). To what extent, then, does AIDS serve as a cause of gay-bashing?

NGLTF (1989) reports that 17 per cent of all incidents in their files were classified by local groups as "AIDS-related." Typically this designation refers to incidents involving verbal references to AIDS by assailants or actions directed against persons with AIDS because of their condition. While this percentage has been fairly consistent over the years (15 per cent in 1987; 14 per cent in 1986), it is probably under-estimated since many organizations do not question victims about whether AIDS was a factor in the incident, many victims do not include AIDS as a variable when reporting, and many times it goes unspoken yet may be an underlying motivating factor.

However, AIDS is probably less a direct cause of the aggression than an excuse to allow the assailant to justify committing the hate act. Data from studies completed before AIDS became an issue provide evidence that anti-gay violence (in particular, physical assaults) existed as a serious problem even before the AIDS era. This is not to say that verbal harassment and property vandalism have remained steady, how-ever. Again, problems in wording, categories used, and sampling prevent definitive conclu-sions from being made about rate changes over the years. In their 1969 survey (pre-gay libera-tion) of San Francisco Bay Area homosexuals, Bell and Weinberg (1978) found that 38 per cent of the gay white men, 21 per cent of the gay black men, 2 per cent of the white lesbians, and 5 per cent of the black lesbians reported they had been robbed or assaulted one or more times because of their homosexuality. They also report that 35 per cent of 458 Chicago gay white men in a 1967 pilot study said that they had been assaulted or robbed because of their homosexuality.

Anderson (1982) reports the results of a study conducted in Minneapolis of 289 gay men and lesbians in 1979. About 23 per cent said they had experienced physical assault and almost 6 per cent stated they were raped because of their sexual orientation. In a 1978 study of 1600 gay men (91 per cent white) in Chicago, Harry (1982) found that 27 per cent of those living in a gay neighborhood and 20 per cent of those living in non-gay areas reported that they had been assaulted because of their homosexuality. These pre-AIDS figures, while difficult to compare exactly with the current figures because of the use of different categories of incidents, are not significantly different from the data reported by NGLTF, by Comstock

(1989) and in the summary of unpublished studies analyzed by Herek (1989).

Thus, AIDS may not be a direct cause of violence. However, the AIDS epidemic has cer-tainly made the gay community more visible, and this enhanced visibility could heighten the likelihood of gays and lesbians increasingly becoming targets of bias aggression. A reason-able though untested hypothesis can be advanced to account for the increases in anti-gay aggression of recent years, to wit, that the behaviors are justified by the attackers in terms of AIDS but they are produced by changes taking place in the total configuration of poten-tial minority group targets seen as appropriate by intolerant individuals and by the greater visibility and accessibility of gays and lesbians due to the public attention they attract in their efforts to combat AIDS. As Herek (1989: 951) says,

> Much of the variance in AIDS-related bigotry is explained by antigay attitudes, which presumably predate the epidemic. Thus, AIDS may be less a cause of antigay sentiment than a focal event that crystallizes heterosexuals' preexisting hostility toward gay people.

While AIDS may have contributed in the early years of the epidemic to increased hostility toward gays, it is important to point out that the opposite reaction has also occurred. As *News-week* (March 12, 1990: 21) reported recently, "the devastation AIDS has created has led to greater sympathy in the straight world, and gays' responsible handling of the crisis has led to new respect for the community." Ironically, then, on balance in the long run, AIDS may contribute to a reduction in the incidence of gay-bashing.

RECOMMENDATIONS AND PROPOSALS

In order to reduce anti-gay violence, attention must be paid to a complex set of issues related to hate crime. The first task is to gain acceptance by a variety of constituents for the development of strong bias-crime laws and policies. Second, where not already included, sexual orientation needs to be added as a category of bias crime. Third, comprehensive efforts must be made to reduce homophobia and negative attitudes towards homosexuality. Fourth, educational efforts must be intensified to improve the public's understanding of AIDS. And fifth, the needs of the victims of bias crimes should be addressed through the provisioning of appropriate services, and the treatment of victims by law enforcement agencies and mental health care facilities should be improved.

Legislation

At the top of the list of recommendations is the enactment of the federal Hate Crime Statistics Act which would require the collection of statistics on hate crimes at the national level. States and local communities must also be required to criminalize bias-motivated crimes and upgrade charges from the category of misdemeanor to that of felony. Mandatory data collection at the local and state level is also necessary to insure that hate violence receives the attention it merits. Sexual orientation, of course, must be included as a category in these laws. The enactment of a national law prohibiting discrimination on the basis of sexual orientation in housing, employment, public accommodations, and other aspects of life, and the repeal of sodomy laws in those states where they still exist would further serve to ameliorate the problem of anti-gay aggression.

Victim services

The New York State Governor's Task Force (1983: 3) discusses the "rediscovery" of the victim and points to the need for policy-makers and practitioners "to constantly improve their awareness of victims' needs and [to] pioneer innovative assistance programs." The report further states that some victims' experiences, such as those of the victims of bias-related violence, are so traumatic that special help should be given.

In a survey conducted by the Governor's Task Force (1988) in New York State, 46 per cent of the district attorneys perceived that the

essential services were available and were being delivered to the victims of hate crimes, and 81 per cent agreed that bias-crime victims need special services. Additionally, the Task Force found that stereotypical handling of bias-crime victims existed, that few victim programs actually included any special effort to assist bias-crime victims, and that these individuals, rather than their assailants, were often blamed for the criminal event.

Anderson (1982) delineated some of the unique problems experienced by victims of assaults, especially sexual assaults against gay men, noting that the stages an assault victim goes through parallel those of female rape victims: the set-up (power ploys), the attack, and the aftermath (shock, denial, shame, guilt, self-blame, embarrassment, fear, suspicion, depression, low self-esteem). The content and intensity of such attacks may vary depending on whether the victim is a woman, a gay male, or a straight male perceived to be gay, but, in general, victims of hate crime, and in particular of physical and sexual assaults, must deal with the larger issues of sexual identity and gender in ways that the victims of non-bias-related assaults do not. The special problems raised by gender and sexual orientation must be taken into consideration when exploring ways to create appropriate services for the victims of bias-related violence.

Education and prevention

The primary goal, of course, is to prevent bias crimes rather than to deal with them after they have been committed, and crucial to the achievement of this objective is education on this issue for all segments of society, but most notably for those most closely linked to the problem, and that includes junior high and high school students, college students, police, prosecutors, judges, legislators, mental health personnel, and media professionals. The focus of such educational efforts needs to be on prejudice and the questions of racism, sexism, anti-Semitism, religious intolerance, and homophobia. The enactment and enforcement of effective bias-crime legislation nationwide is likely to depend on massive educational campaigns on these core topics.

Education should also include ways to identify bias crimes, training law enforcement personnel in sensitive methods of interviewing victims, the development of strategies to encourage individuals to report incidents with confidentiality, getting prosecutors and judges away from a "blame-the-victim" mentality, informing people of the seriousness of prejudice-motivated incidents, and aiding law enforcement agencies in working with community-based organizations representing various ethnic, racial, religious, and gay constituencies. Finally, prevention programs, training programs, effectively enacted legislation, and good data collection all require funding and a commitment from the government to support them. Nothing short of this will bring about any change in the widespread and continuing problem of bias-related violence.

Perhaps the most succinct way to end this chapter is to quote from the conclusion of a recent NGLTF (1989: 34) report:

In assessing the impact of anti-gay violence, statistics alone fail to adequately do the job. Statistics do not measure the anguish, suffering, and rage experienced not only by the survivors but by the larger lesbian and gay community. As with other crimes motivated by prejudice, anti-gay attacks are acts of terrorism aimed at discouraging lesbians and gay men from exercising their rights to freedom of speech, association and assembly. On a more basic level, anti-gay violence seeks to deny to lesbians and gay men the essential right to live and love as they choose … The slowness of government on every level to acknowledge and combat anti-gay violence parallels its willful failure to deal with AIDS in the early stages of that epidemic. Some leaders in government, law enforcement, civil rights and religion have begun to address this issue. Their efforts, however, are frequently met by fierce – and often successful – opposition on the part of those who seek to exclude gay men and lesbians from protection in laws and programs aimed at combatting hate violence. The denial of such protections to gay people is a legal and moral disgrace that must be challenged by all people of conscience.

REFERENCES

Adam, B. (1978), *The Survival of Domination* (New York: Elsevier).

Anderson, C. (1982), "Males as Sexual Assault Victims: Multiple Levels of Trauma," *Journal of Homosexuality*, 7:2/3: 145–62.

Bell, A. and Weinberg, M. (1978), *Homosexualities: A Study of Diversity Among Men and Women* (New York: Simon and Schuster).

Berrill, K. (1986), *Anti-Gay Violence: Causes, Consequences, Responses* (Washington, DC: National Gay & Lesbian Task Force).

Blumenfeld, W. J. and Raymond, D. (1988), *Looking at Gay and Lesbian Life* (Boston: Beacon Press).

Boswell, J. (1980), *Christianity, Social Tolerance, and Homosexuality: Gay People in Western Europe from the Beginning of the Christian Era to the Fourteenth Century* (Chicago: The University of Chicago Press).

Carrier, J. M. (1980), "Homosexual Behavior in Cross-cultural Perspective," in *Homosexual Behavior: A Modern Reappraisal*, ed. J. Marmor, pp. 100–22 (New York: Basic Books).

—— (1989), "Sexual Behavior and Spread of AIDS in Mexico," in *The AIDS Pandemic: A Global Emergency*, ed. R. Bolton, pp. 37–50 (New York: Gordon and Breach).

Comstock, G. D. (1989), "Victims of Anti-gay/Lesbian Violence," *Journal of Interpersonal Violence*, 4:1: 101–6.

Crapo, R. H. (n.d.), *Factors in the Cross-cultural Patterning of Homosexuality: A Reappraisal of the Literature*, unpublished manuscript.

Davis, D. L. and Whitten, R. G. (1987), "The Cross-cultural Study of Human Sexuality," *Annual Reviews in Anthropology* 16: 69–98.

D'Augelli, A. R. (1989), "Homophobia in a University Community: Views of Prospective Resident Assistants," *Journal of College Student Development*, 30: 546–52.

Finn, P. and McNeil, T. (1987), *The Response of the Criminal Justice System to Bias Crime: An Exploratory Review*, submitted to US Department of Justice (Cambridge, MA: Abt Associates).

Ford, C. S. and Beach, F. A. (1951), *Patterns of Sexual Behavior* (New York: Harper & Row, Publishers).

Franklin, C. W. (1988), *Men and Society* (Chicago: Nelson-Hall).

Gmunder, B. and Stamford, J. D. (1988), *Spartacus Guide for Gay Men*, 17th ed. (Berlin: Bruno Gmunder Verlag).

Governor's Task Force on Bias-Related Violence (1988), *Final Report* (Albany, NY).

Greenberg, D. (1989), *The Construction of Homosexuality* (Chicago: University of Chicago Press).

Harry, J. (1982), "Derivative Deviance: The Cases of Extortion, Fag-bashing, and Shakedown of Gay

Men," *Criminology* 19:4: 546–64.

Heger, H. (1980), *The Men with the Pink Triangle* (Boston: Alyson Publications, Inc.).

Herdt, G. H. (ed.) (1984), *Ritualized Homosexuality in Melanesia* (Berkeley: University of California Press).

—— (1987a), "Homosexuality," *Encyclopedia of Religion* Vol. 3 (New York: Macmillan).

—— (1987b), *The Sambia: Ritual and Gender in New Guinea* (New York: Holt, Rinehart, & Winston).

Herek, G. (1984), "Beyond 'Homophobia': A Social Psychological Perspective on Attitudes toward Lesbians and Gay Men," *Journal of Homosexuality* 10:1/2: 1–21.

—— (1989), "Hate Crimes against Lesbians and Gay Men," *American Psychologist* 44:6: 948–55.

IGA, International Association of Lesbians/Gay Women and Gay Men (1985), *IGA Pink Book 1985: A Global View of Lesbian and Gay Oppression and Liberation* (Amsterdam: COC-magazine).

Lang, N. G. (1989), "AIDS, Gays and the Ballot Box: The Politics of Disease in Houston, Texas," in *The AIDS Pandemic: A Global Emergency* ed. R. Bolton, pp. 111–17 (New York: Gordon and Breach.

Los Angeles County Commission on Human Relations (1989), *Hate Crime in Los Angeles County 1988* (Los Angeles, CA).

—— (1990a), *Hate Crime in Los Angeles County 1989* (Los Angeles, CA).

—— (1990b), *Hate Crime in the 1980's: A Decade of Bigotry* (Los Angeles, CA).

Los Angeles Times (1988), "Dallas Gay Leader Angry at Judge over his Remarks on Murder Case" December 17.

Miller, B. and Humphreys, L. (1980), "Life-styles and Violence: Homosexual Victims of Assault and Murder," *Qualitative Sociology* 3:3: 169–85.

National Gay & Lesbian Task Force (NGLTF) (1987), *Anti-Gay Violence, Victimization and Defamation in 1986* (Washington, DC: NGLTF).

—— (1988), *Anti-Gay Violence, Victimization and Defamation in 1987* (Washington, DC: NGLTF).

—— (1989), *Anti-Gay Violence, Victimization and Defamation in 1988* (Washington, DC: NGLTF).

Pedersen, L. (1985), "The Anti-discrimination Law: The Experience So Far," In *The IGA Pink Book 1985*, ed. IGA, pp. 117–19 (Amsterdam: COC-magazine).

Plant, R. (1986), *The Pink Triangle: The Nazi War Against Homosexuals* (New York: Henry Holt and Company).

Rector, F. (1981), *The Nazi Extermination of Homosexuals* (New York: Stein and Day).

Renzetti, C. (1988), "Violence in Lesbian Relationships: A Preliminary Analysis of Causal Factors," *Journal of Interpersonal Violence* 3:4: 381–99.

San Miguel, C. and Millham, J. (1976), "The Role of Cognitive and Situational Variables in Aggression toward Homosexuals," *Journal of Homosexuality* 2:1: 11–27.

Shilts, R. (1982), *The Mayor of Castro Street* (New York: St Martin's Press).

Stoddard, T. B., Boggan, E. C., Haft, M. C., Lister, C. and Rupp, J. P. (1983), *The Rights of Gay People: An American Civil Liberties Union Handbook*, Rev. ed. (Toronto: Bantam Books).

Weiner, N. A., Zahn, M. A. and Sagi, R. J. (eds) (1990), *Violence: Patterns, Causes, Public Policy* (San Diego: Harcourt Brace Jovanovich, Publishers).

Weinrich, J. D. (1987), *Sexual Landscapes* (New York: Charles Scribner's Sons).

Werner, D. (1979), "A Cross-cultural Perspective on Theory and Research on Male Homosexuality," *Journal of Homosexuality* 4:4, 345–62.

Whitam, F. L. (1987), "A Cross-cultural Perspective on Homosexuality, Transvestism and Transsexualism," in *Variant Sexuality: Research and Theory*, ed. D. G. Wilson, pp. 176–201 (London: Croom Helm).

Wooden, W. and Parker, J. (1982), *Men Behind Bars: Sexual Exploitation in Prison* (New York: Plenum Press).

STEVEN C. DUBIN

"Gay Images and the Social Construction of Acceptability"

from *Arresting Images: Impolitic Art and Uncivil Actions*
(London: Routledge, 1992): Chapter 7

The road to Selma didn't lead to the right to sodomy.

> (William Dannemeyer, 1991)

We're here! We're Queer!
We're fabulous! Get used to it!

> (Queer Nation protest chant, 1990)

Congressman William Dannemeyer (R-CA) issued a dire warning in 1989. "Currently we are a divided nation," he declared. "Such a division has not existed in America since the Civil War."[1] And what did he cite as the basis of this split: possibly class or race? Religion or ideology? No; these factors were all overshadowed by what the Congressman feared as the gravest social danger of all – homosexuality.

For Dannemeyer and many others, gays are not a benign presence. Instead, openly gay men and women seem to them to challenge biblical authority and undermine traditional morality. Dannemeyer proffered an explicit recommendation to combat this presumed problem: "We must reinstate traditional prohibitions against homosexuality in order to establish a sense of order and decency in our society, to reconnect us with our normative past."[2]

Orthodox religious believers see gays as a threat to the family unit, a judgment that has been corroborated in their minds by the onset of the AIDS epidemic and its initial locus in the gay male community (at least in the US). For particularly spiteful fundamentalists, this is a clear example of divine retribution for a grievous sin. But such beliefs rest atop a more basic presumption: religious traditionalists feel they are forced to give up no less than "natural categories" of masculine and feminine and "normal" sexual behavior if they tolerate homosexuality.

Same-sex relationships are unsettling to a fundamentalist way of thinking to an extent that other subjects can hardly match. In an article which appeared in the *American Family Association Journal*, a critic of popular culture railed against the lack of standards in contemporary culture, and cited the Judeo-Christian tradition of a God that characteristically made distinctions: between light and darkness, the separation of the Sabbath from the secular week, and – by extension – the distinction between male and female.[3] To blend attributes from any of these sets of categories is to challenge the notions of sacred and profane, and to raise basic questions about how reality is socially constructed.[4] Homosexuals defy accepted notions about "proper" affectional choices and sometimes confound gender expectations; their overt presence can disturb other people.

That partially explains the adverse reaction to Madonna's music video of "Justify My Love." One of its most controversial aspects was a scene where the singer kissed an actress sporting a mannish appearance, an act that prompted letter writers to the *Los Angeles Times* to declare. "We used to like her videos, but now yuck, yuck and double yuck!"[5] But it is important to note that the writers in question were two sixth-grade girls. Such a response is somewhat understandable from these youngsters, given the insecurities involved in forming a sexual identity at that age. But the fact that a major newspaper would deem it newsworthy or acceptable to publish such an opinion reveals a great deal about the persistent prejudice against gays in our society, and the resistance to positive depictions of same sex affection.

One of the most effective ways to demean a man in many societies continues to be to question his masculinity, and allude to the possibility that he may be homosexual. This was, of course, a dominant motif in the derisive painting of Mayor Washington in Chicago, and also has surfaced in depictions of despised foreign leaders. In 1986, for example, the *New York Post* once again helped define tabloid journalism by publishing a story based on the report of unnamed informants that Moammar Khadafy was drug-crazed and wore women's clothing, makeup and gilded high heels. The article was accompanied by the rendering of a spit-curled general adorned with lipstick, earrings and beauty marks: "Dressed in drag, Libyan leader Moammar Khadafy *might look like this*."[6] And after Saddam Hussein's troops were routed from Kuwait in 1991, locals added long hair and lipstick to a large portrait of the dictator and then defaced it. All these symbolic representations combined specific targets with broader social anxieties.

Running counter to such images are those generated by gay artists themselves. The types of work gay artists have produced have been affected significantly by larger events. Art from before the Stonewall Rebellion in 1969 (when an angry gay crowd[7] with drag queens in the forefront defiantly battled with police at a Greenwich Village bar) differs markedly from material created afterwards. And then the onset of the AIDS crisis in 1981 radically altered both subject matter and predominant methods of artistic presentation. But whether homosexual content has been disguised or boldly presented in art, other social groups have often rejected the images which express the beliefs and values of this sexual minority.[8]

THROUGH THE VEIL

Living life in the closet makes it more difficult for others to see and understand what goes on inside. Homosexual argot captures an important aspect of this with the phrase "dropping your hairpins," or giving off signals that a savvy recipient can decipher or identify someone as gay. A similar notion is captured in a distinction made by Erving Goffman in this study *Stigma*. Goffman proposed that people with characteristics that their society was likely to stigmatize could face two different predicaments. If the characteristics are overt, the challenge to those who possess them would be to manage the tension that comes from hostility, social discrimination and rejection. But "passing" is a possibility if those characteristics are covert. Here the problem is to manage information and regulate self-disclosure.[9]

Of course these distinctions merge in real-world situations, but they are useful in characterizing certain artists and their output. In general, pre-Stonewall art that deals with homosexual subject matter has a muted quality because artists adopted evasive strategies to avoid controversy. The meaning of their work is only apparent through decoding signals or possibly bringing in supplemental biographical information about their lives. Contrariwise, an overt stance is much more common for post-Stonewall gay artists. The imagery they employ is accessible to larger publics, and they are increasingly likely to conduct their lives in the open. Controversies have also proliferated as a result.

There are striking examples of pre-Stonewall artists whose work broadcasts homoerotic messages which can be unscrambled. The photographer F. Holland Day (1864–1933) is one such case. Day shocked the public with the first image of a male frontal nude displayed in a photo exhibit at the Boston Camera Club in 1898. His dreamy portraits of swarthy, lower-class young men posed with classical accoutrements betray an intense interest in the male physique, in addition to a deep intimacy with his models (some of whom he assisted financially). But his major biographer hedges throughout her book when it comes to confronting Day's homosexuality. She claims "It was a mark of Day's genius that he could disguise in his models a real-life vulgarity,"[10] thereby virtually equating homosexual desire with obscenity. And when she describes his photographic recreation of the passion of St Sebastian (a common homosexual subject), she uncomfortably finds "previously sublimated or disguised ... homoerotic masochistic posturing," instead of the "exalted sainthood" that marked his earlier religious subjects.[11] It is hardly surprising that Day was cautious in his work and circumspect in the conduct of his life when even the opinions of latter-day critics are apt to be value-laden.[12]

F. Holland Day's artistic output also provides interesting antecedents for Robert Mapplethorpe, a photographer whose gay life was markedly open, and for a non-gay photographer, Andres Serrano. Day repeatedly photographed black men, albeit in an overly romanticized manner: his chauffeur was presented as an Ethiopian chief, for example.[13] And his interest in religious themes led a starved and long-haired Day to assume the persona of Jesus and re-enact the crucifixion in 1898. The photographic chronicle of this "historically accurate" recreation provoked a critical outcry, primarily because it recorded an event that had actually taken place, not a scene conjured up in a painter's mind and then transferred by brush to canvas.

There was a tangible reality to the photos that profoundly unsettled viewers. The editors of the *British Journal of Photography* wrote,

> Mr. Holland Day's photos [are] repulsive because we are conscious that the individuality of the originals has not been, cannot be, so completely masked or subdued as to destroy the mental persuasion that we are looking at the image of a man made up to be photographed as the Christian Redeemer, and not at an artist's reverent and mental conception of a suffering Christ.[14]

And another reviewer could have just as easily been writing about Mapplethorpe's sadomasochistic subjects or Serrano's combination of religious icons and bodily products when he drew back from the immediacy and concreteness of the photographic document: "In looking at a photograph you cannot forget that it is a representation of something which existed when it was taken."[15]

This explains in part why photography became such a "hot medium" during the contemporary period as well. We understand intellectually that photographs can seriously mislead; people cannot hold up the Eiffel Tower, notwithstanding conventional tourists' snapshots. Nevertheless, photographs appear to have an immediacy that other artistic media do

not. We tend to assume that if the camera saw it, it existed. We also generally suppose that what the camera produces is less mediated than a painting or a book, which we know has to be explicated or interpreted by the artist.[16] Photographs have a singular ability to strike us viscerally, even more so when they depict unorthodox people or behavior. It's one thing to understand – and perhaps even accept on an abstract level – that homosexuals exist. It's quite another to confront photographic documentation of actual people and authentic acts.

Close scrutiny of the work of photographer Minor White also reveals disguised homosexuality. White worked primarily in the 1940s and 1950s, a time when homosexuality could be a public liability. According to critic Ingrid Sischy, his output can be decoded to reveal a creative life that was stunted by the fear of being exposed as a homosexual. His work is marked by indirect expressions and substitutions, the rocks and cracks in stones standing in for parts of human bodies, for instance. White learned to be cautious early in his career when an exhibition of his work was canceled in San Francisco "on the rounds of taste."[17] "Amputations" was accused of being unpatriotic, a charge that seems frivolous now; the images depicted the horrors of war by focusing on the gashes on the surfaces of rocks, not actual human bodies.

White subsequently depicted the human male torso, but in a "tasteful" manner. Sischy is a harsh commentator. She feels White trivialized his work by deflecting his energy into "a career spent avoiding calling a spade a spade." In the final analysis, she views him as "crippled, rather than inspired, by repression."[18] His tortured writings also expose an archetypically covert, pre-Stonewall, guilty homosexual, during this period when Edward Steichen's *The Family of Man* offered a prototype for the artistic representation of ideal social life.

Concealed references in the work of some visual artists now known to have been homosexual also require unraveling in order to extract their full meaning. Some Charles Demuth (1883–1935) watercolors show sailors with their genitals exposed; yet although there are only men in certain scenes, in others there is ambiguity about the gender of particular partners. But a large proportion of his paintings depict flowers, fruits, and vegetables, subject matter than can invite comparisons with human sexuality without directly portraying it. These latter paintings have been highlighted most commonly in public exhibitions, along with his industrial scenes and "poster portraits," images which primarily use words and numerical references to describe famous personages such as Georgia O'Keefe, Arthur Dove and William Carlos Williams, and the not-so-well-known such as Bert Savoy, a successful female impersonator in the 1920s.[19]

Curatorial decisions have manipulated Demuth's oeuvre: in 1950 officials excluded his painting *A Distinguished Air* from a retrospective at the Museum of Modern Art because they considered its sexual theme too controversial,[20] and the tame scene *From the Kitchen Garden* (1925) adorned the cover of the catalogue for the retrospective mounted by the Whitney Museum in 1987–8. While the full range of his work was displayed in that show, room after room of delicately executed flower paintings dominated. In addition, the small size of most of Demuth's sexually explicit drawings isolated them even more amidst his larger paintings of neutral subject matter.

Marsden Hartley (1877–1943) was another homosexual artist whose subject matter was typically natural, with mountains and seascapes being frequent subjects. Yet other works touchingly record his liaisons with men who met early and tragic deaths. His famous *Portrait of a German Officer* (1914) memorializes his lover Lieutenant von Freyburg who was killed in battle. Executed in what Hartley called "Cosmic" or "Subliminal Cubist" style, the painting contains numerical references to the soldier's age and regiment, and iconic allusions to his uniform such as the Iron Cross, spurs, tassels, and feathers.[21] The work is opaque without this information, looking like a vibrant jumble of colors and shapes.[22]

Hartley also commemorated his relationship with Alty Mason, a Nova Scotia fisherman lost in a boating accident. His initial artistic response came in *Northern Seascape, Off the Banks* (1936), portraying the ocean as the source of the tragedy, but not the victims. It was

two years before he created the poignant family scene *Fisherman's Last Supper* (1938), where Alty and his brother are marked as doomed members of a clan taking their final meal together. This elegiac painting captures a universal feeling of tragedy by placing these men within the familial context that is fated to be irrevocably altered. But Hartley's personal feeling of loss comes out most fully in the portrait of his lost love, *Abelard the Drowned, Master of the Phantom* (1938–9). This painting crackles with a sexual charge when the viewer knows the nature of the link between the artist and his subject. *Abelard* presents the massive dark-complexioned figure in a rather pensive pose, a rose tucked behind his ear as an enigmatic and delicate counterpoint to his thick black hair, eyebrows, mustache, and chest hair.[23]

But perhaps nothing reflects the subterfuge which homosexuals in creative fields felt they had to endure than the role played by Rock Hudson in the film *Pillow Talk* (1959). This comedy with Doris Day represents the zenith of pre-Stonewall self-deception. It is a remarkable document of stereotypes and misconceptions, with masquerade and misrepresentation the primary leitmotifs. Most of the world discovered that Rock Hudson was a homosexual when his imminent death from AIDS was revealed in 1985. But there was little to indicate his furtive life in the portrait by *Saturday Evening Post* photographer Sid Avery in the 1950s: Hudson is shown fresh from a shower, hair tousled, a towel discreetly covering his midsection. As the putative all-American heterosexual, Hudson is presumably arranging yet another female conquest while he chats on the phone.

That's precisely the nature of his on-screen role of Brad Allen, who shares a Manhattan telephone party line with the Doris Day character, Jan Morrow. Brad is a playboy who is constantly making arrangements for liaisons, which ties up the line and enrages Jan. A struggle for control ensues, with Allen accusing Morrow of being a prude and having "bedroom problems." She responds near the film's end that *his* difficulties could not be worked out in a thousand bedrooms.

Morrow realizes Allen is a champion of

insincerity when she repeatedly picks up the receiver to hear him singing a supposedly original love song to different women, while in fact it's the same tune with only the lady's name changed. True to 1950s comedic conventions, Brad falls for his adversary when he actually sees her, and attempts to woo her by manufacturing another persona, "Rex Stetson" the wealthy Texan. Try to visualize the levels of deception here: Hudson the homosexual is playing a heterosexual Don Juan, and his movie character then poses as a sweet, naive out-of-towner in order to make a new conquest. If it sounds complicated, imagine what it must have been like for the star himself to keep these different personalities straight! At one juncture the Rex character arouses Jan's suspicions about his sexual orientation: he eats a snack dip with his pinkie extended in the air, and wants to take the recipe home to his mother, obvious and derogatory gay stereotypes. But this, too, is a pretense: it allows "Rex" to move in for a kiss, the opening he needs to assure Jan he's romantically interested.

Other running gags require Hudson to deny his authentic self. His dual characters require that he segregate his audiences, lest he be revealed to be someone he is not – the ongoing challenge to someone in the closet. In order to maintain the charade, he is forced at one point to duck into an obstetrician's office where he is mistaken for a "pregnant man." In response to what evolves into a running joke, a doctor advises his disbelieving nurse that this patient may have "crossed a new frontier." Sadly, however, Hudson was entrapped in a cycle of denial in order to protect his screen personality, a fabrication that likely would have been subverted – and deemed unmarketable[24] – had he revealed who he truly was during a sexually repressive time.

Playwrights have similarly used artifice in their creations. Both Edward Albee's *Who's Afraid of Virginia Woolf?* and Tennessee Williams's *A Streetcar Named Desire* are widely interpreted as gay-themed dramas encased within heterosexual wrappings; reading the subtext reveals an entirely hidden dimension. But homosexually inclined artists now have many more opportunities to be gay in both their private and public lives than ever before. These opportunities are not limitless, however, for there continues to be pressure to engage in denial and deceit. A case in point: in 1991 a television mini-series entitled *A Season of Giants* purported to tell the stories of Michelangelo and Leonardo da Vinci, both homosexuals. But their sexuality was wildly distorted: Michelangelo had an erotic dream about a Bolognese noblewoman, and Leonardo was presented as asexual.[25]

OUT OF SIGHT, OUT OF MIND

When you review the negative responses to certain art works in the past, it's not difficult to understand why depictions of homosexual behavior or a "gay sensibility" were relatively infrequent or concealed. Take the example of gay writer James Baldwin's *Giovanni's Room* (1956) which chronicled the calamitous liaison between an American bisexual expatriate and an Italian bartender. Baldwin created a novel that would be more palatable to 1950s readers and critics by fashioning the main character as confused rather than resolved about his sexuality (he is engaged to an American girl), and by making him white rather than black (Baldwin himself was black). He was, as one literary historian explains, "playing the game,"[26] a strategy that nevertheless garnered mixed to negative reviews for the book. But his 1962 novel *Another Country*, because it dared to enter the dangerous territories of both homosexuality and interracial relations, occasioned far more serious condemnation.

Community members and politicos swiftly responded when the book was included on the reading list of a Chicago city college. A group called Citizens for Decent Literature and Movies pressured the City Council to take action, whereupon a committee approved a resolution denouncing the novel after a clamorous eight-hour hearing. Although the Council did not have the legal authority to directly enforce the measure, they did have latent power by virtue of their right to confirm all appointments to the school board. Mayor Daley concurred in the Council's judgment, yet the school board was able to resist this official pressure and public opinion: after a two-month battle they voted to keep the book on the reading list, but stipulated that students who objected to it could be assigned another selection.[27]

The tenor of the debate is clearly transmitted by a hateful *Chicago Tribune* editorial that branded Baldwin's work "disgusting" and charged that it contained the "vilest words in the vocabulary." The writers of the piece went on to defend Negro citizens whose integrity they felt had been compromised by the book's portrayal of them as homosexuals, and they finally exploded with the following tirade: "We freely concede that our own book section some years back contained a namby-pamby review of this book by a professor who was moved by the author's 'compassion' for queers and misfits. But such dicta are binding neither on *The Tribune* nor its editor."[28] Impassioned reactions like this probably explain why a publisher decided to deceptively package a contemporaneous novel. Christopher Isherwood's *A Single Man* (1964) was remarkable for its matter-of-fact account of a day in the life of a gay man. When it was issued in paperback in 1968 by Lancer Books, the cover quoted from a review in the homosexual journal *One*, yet it showed a man looking pensively downward, while a woman clings to his shoulder and arm. Because she was pictured in her slip and a robe, they look like a couple facing domestic difficulties. The main theme of a man coping with the death of his male lover was thereby camouflaged.

Another artist encountered difficulties years earlier for work that merely depicted male sexuality, although not with direct homosexual referents. Paul Cadmus first ran foul of the government over his 1934 painting *The Fleet's In!* which depicted drunken sailors carousing with women in New York's Riverside Park. The portrayal infuriated Assistant Secretary of the Navy Henry Latrobe Roosevelt, who had it removed from a show of PWAP art (the Public Works of Art Program, a forerunner of the better-known WPA projects) at Washington's Corcoran Gallery. Cadmus expressed surprise at the response, and disavowed any libelous intent;[29] but the painting was subsequently consigned to Washington's Alibi Club, and not returned to public view until 1981, when an art history professor intervened on its behalf.[30]

Cadmus was warily given another chance when he was commissioned to execute a mural for the Parcel Post Building to Richmond, Virginia, under the auspices of the Treasury Section of Fine Arts in 1939. His subject of *Pocahontas Saving the Life of Captain John Smith* seemed relatively safe – until the design was exhibited at Vassar College. The fact that one of Pocahontas's breasts was fully exposed did not rise any ire. But a warrior's bared buttocks in the center of the mural did provoke a din of protest, as did the rendering of another warrior with an animal skin dangling between his legs. The pelt bore a remarkable resemblance to a set of male genitals because of the way it was positioned. Government officials ordered Cadmus to remove the fox's snout that disconcertingly simulated a penis.[31]

Although these works did not contain explicitly homosexual themes, the tight sailor uniforms in *The Fleet's In!* allowed Cadmus to emphasize the buttocks and prodigious endowments of some of the servicemen. And in *Pocahontas* his foregrounding of masculine anatomy was anathema in a culture accustomed to odalisques, yet not so comfortable with the male body. The homoerotic elements are an easily observed subtext in these paintings, created by an artist who admitted in an interview at age 86 that the Stonewall Rebellion "made him more comfortable about being gay."[32]

An attempt to publicly commemorate that beginning of the modern gay movement also encountered a difficult reception. The sculptor George Segal was commissioned by the Mariposa Foundation (a gay rights and educational organization) to create a statue for Christopher Park, adjacent to the site of the Stonewall Rebellion. He created a life-sized work entitled *Gay Liberation*, featuring a lesbian couple and a gay male couple. The figures touch one another on the leg and the arm in a casual, not erotic manner. But opponents emerged from many directions when the piece was to be erected in 1980. Some thought it was ugly, while others saw it as too large and inappropriate for a small, nineteenth-century public space. Further criticism came from those who feared it would attract hordes of tourists, and some even expressed concern that it would be "an invitation to public sex."[33] Disapproval was also voiced by some members of the gay community, particularly those who felt the work was racist because it featured only white figures. After all these opinions had been aired, it became clear that even in a community with a reputation for an enlightened and tolerant atmosphere, public art proposals can become highly volatile issues.[34]

The sculpture received a brutal reception when it was displayed on the campus of Stanford University in 1984, where an assailant attacked the bronze tableau with a hammer. The act stunned the university community, but also mobilized it in anger. According to one student, "I feel as if we have lost four valuable members of our community." And another sorrowfully stated, "each of us ... who walk past the sculpture every day, feels personally assaulted. The sculpture as it stands now is no longer a monument to gay liberation, but is tangible evidence of the violence perpetrated against gay people."[35]

Gay Liberation likewise elicited mixed responses in Madison, Wisconsin (1986: 91), where another cast of it was shown first at the Madison Art Center and later installed in a public park. Some sympathetic critics nevertheless found it "stiff and static" or commented on its "abject *ordinariness*," but others condemned it as "gay propaganda" and "insulting to straight people."[36] It was vandalized several times by teenagers and young men, while neighborhood residents were quite solicitous of its welfare. Some of them cleaned it when it was blemished by paint, and wrapped the figures in hats and scarves when it was cold.[37] At a hearing held to determine whether to continue to display the work, one local citizen testified to the potential of public art as a catalyst to candid civil dialogue: "It's clearing the air. It's making people who feel compassion and support for homosexuality say their piece. And it's making people who feel the opposite say their piece too."[38]

These varied reactions undermine Hilton Kramer's claim that Segal's work "is inevitably sentimental, condescending and mawkish. The sense of elevation we look for in public sculpture is missing."[39] By viewing Segal's work within a gallery context, this armchair critic failed to understand its impact upon other people.

If the male nude and discreet depictions of gay people can so unnerve some segments of the public, then more candid portrayals – particularly when they appear on mass media such as radio or television, or if produced with government support – carry the potential to cause even greater disturbance. One month prior to the Nelson/Washington incident in Chicago, for example, the New York's State Council on the Arts (NYSCA) was strongly criticized by state legislators for certain grants they had awarded. The subsidies in question primarily dealt with topics related to sexual minorities, as broadcast in the *New York Post* headline of March 16, 1988: "Cuomo Orders 'Drag!' $ Probe." Included in the list of so-called offenders was a photography exhibition of transvestism, a lesbian feminist literary magazine, an archive of lesbian and gay writers and a film of a gay rights march in Washington, DC. But once the critical charge was sounded by the *Post*'s investigation, other projects with strong social and political components were also singled out: grants to a Manhattan tenants' advocacy group and to the production of a film about a Sandinista leader became additional targets.

NYSCA's chairperson Kitty Carlisle Hart was summoned to Albany to face legislators' questions and to defend the agency's grant procedures. The case had already been tried in the pages of the *New York Post*. *Post* writers repeatedly equated support for artistic projects with "promotion" of deviant and "offbeat" behavior. In one editorial, transvestism was characterized as a psychological disorder which now had the imprimatur of the state.[40] Hart successfully vindicated the agency by emphasizing the centrality of social and political issues to many spheres of activity, including the arts. In some ways the defense was made easier because of the absurd and uninformed nature of the charges: the critics failed to realize that the project on transvestites mostly concerned *straight* men; they automatically collapsed all non-conventional gender and sexual behavior into the despised and feared gay category.[41]

When gay characters have appeared on television, even the simplest expressions of same-sex affection have generated problems. After two male characters on the popular series *thirtysomething* were shown lying in bed together – engaging in post-coital chatter, with blankets prudently pulled up to mid-chest – the producers had to pay a large price. Jittery advertisers withdrew more than $1 million worth of support from this episode. They reacted similarly to the tune of $500,000 to a later installment where the two men saw each other at a New Year's Eve party and exchanged a kiss on the cheek. But because of their rarity, such affirmative scenes can assume inordinate importance for gay people. As one activist attested after the first episode,

> I actually cried (I'm a sentimental kind of guy). To see something validated which is very ordinary in my life, which as a kid I never saw validated ... and to know that my parents and young people growing up trying to figure out who they are and what it means to be gay or not to be gay [would also see this] was extremely moving ... Later when I pulled myself together I thought, "My God, I would have this kind of emotional surge from something as cheap and ordinary as that?" Well, yes![42]

The episode with the bedroom scene was one of the few to be excluded from summer reruns, a network choice to avert an additional loss of revenue.[43] And another flap ensued because two female characters on *LA Law* kissed one another. In reaction, Reverend Donald Wildmon pledged to contact the advertisers on that show and to pressure them to disavow their support for portrayals of homosexuality as normal and acceptable.[44]

Although today we tend to think of radio as merely background diversion, this medium has also faced problems when it has presented gay-related material. For example, an incident occurred in Cincinnati in 1981 which was amazingly prescient in respect to later events there. John Zeh, producer of the lesbian and gay program *Gaydreams* on a community radio station, was indicted for distributing obscene material harmful to juveniles. The charges stemmed from a broadcast in which Zeh humorously read a report on sexual lubricants, a broadcast that some children recorded and replayed to their parents. The prosecution was undertaken by Simon Leis, the county prosecutor who had garnered a reputation for his zealous anti-obscenity crusades and anti-gay campaigns. Zeh was exonerated two years later, but only after losing his job and his apartment, and facing the possibility of a lengthy jail term. The court decided that the program was not deliberately aimed at children, and in accord with regulations at that time, everything that was broadcast on the radio did not have to be suitable for children. According to the station manager, "Cincinnati is a conservative town and Zeh was like a college student 'mooning' – like turning your butt to the whole world and saying 'Kiss it.'"[45]

In 1986 the Federal Communications Commission (FCC) targeted Robert Chesley's *Jerker*, a two-man play in which the characters engage in sexual fantasy play over the telephone, for possible obscenity violation. The play had been read over KPFK in Los Angeles, a Pacifica-affiliated, listener-supported station. The Justice Department eventually decided not to prosecute, but only after Pacifica had incurred approximately $100,000 in legal fees to defend itself.

Over time FCC statutes were broadened to allow the agency to regulate not only the constitutionally specific category of obscenity, but also the more indeterminate "indecent." In 1988 regulations also swept aside the notion of a "safe harbor" (when children were presumed to be asleep and any type of programming was permissible), extending the ban of "indecent" language to twenty-four hours.[46] Radio stations feared that material *could* be judged indecent, and they became more cautious in their programming since there were not clear-cut guidelines defining the field.

For example, WBAI, the Pacifica station in New York, had regularly broadcast Allen Ginsberg's *Howl*, a poem that indicted conventional society of the 1950s, and included explicit homosexual references. In 1988 the poem was scheduled to be broadcast as part of a series on censorship entitled *Open Ears/Open Minds*. But the five Pacifica stations opted instead to broadcast an interview with the poet, fearful of possible legal repercussions because of their earlier struggle with the FCC. In that interview Ginsberg accused the FCC of "evasive double-talk," and of creating a chilling effect where stations were censoring themselves, in effect doing the bidding of the government. Ginsberg blasted the FCC as being a "spiritual death squad for literature," quite possibly a reference to the fact that WBAI had also feared broadcasting a reading of James Joyce's *Ulysses* after the FCC enacted its new "decency" clause.[47] In May 1991 the United States Court of Appeals for the District of Columbia struck down the twenty four-hour ban, a ruling upheld in the Supreme Court in March 1992. The FCC was ordered to reinstate a "safe arbor."

DARK STRANGER

If Salman Rushdie was a stranger of the British Commonwealth, photographer Robert Mapplethorpe was his American counterpart. Mapplethorpe left his Catholic home in Queens at age 16 and hardly looked back. An interview with his father published after Mapplethorpe's death goes a long way toward explaining why. The elder Mapplethorpe, a retired electrical engineer, lived in a vastly different world from the one his son gravitated to and eventually embraced. Father and son were strikingly different people, from matters of decorative taste to social beliefs and sexual practices. In 1990 the father, surrounded by the ceramic and plastic ephemera distinctive of lower-middle-class homes, made it clear to a *Washington Post* reporter just how much mutual misunderstanding, incomprehension and distance there had been between him and his son. He had little interest in Robert's photographs, even less tolerance of the homosexuality that was such an important theme in the work, and no concern about the storm of controversy that swirled around the retrospective which toured the country from 1988 through 1990. "I could care less" epitomized his response.[48]

The differences between these two generations of men from the same family almost seem to characterize different species of creatures.[49]

Robert Mapplethorpe, like most openly gay individuals, was forced to refashion a radically new identity for himself. This process requires casting off many elements from the past and embracing new beliefs, values and modes of behavior. But it is doubtful whether this ever entails a total renunciation of one's origins. His life was once summed up as "the middle of a contradiction – part altar boy and part leather bar."[50] Blend this mixture of influences with society's widespread rejection of homosexuality, and you find that gays are generally familiar with the condition of marginality.

But rather than being a negative condition in Mapplethorpe's case, these circumstances nourished his artistic sensibility as he turned his creative eye to the fast-lane gay society of the 1970s and early 1980s in which he was an active participant. Many people judged the images that he brought from there to be documents of exotic specimens engaged in peculiar conduct. Through them he captured a sense of post-Stonewall exuberance that pushed sexual frontiers – before the onset of the AIDS crisis. In the 1990s his sexual photographs, along with his floral images have become elegies to a lost world.

After an art education at Pratt Institute in Brooklyn, Mapplethorpe drifted into New York City's avant-garde punk underground, embodied in his close friend, singer Patti Smith. He spliced this world with another: Times Square, and its commercialized pornography industry. Mapplethorpe frequently cited gay porno as an early source of inspiration, evident by his incorporation of such images into his early collage work. He had his first gallery show of photos in 1976, followed by three more in 1977. His association with well-connected personalities (for example, the collector Sam Wagstaff and John McKendry of the Metropolitan Museum) expedited his successful career as a "bad boy" in the art world. Mapplethorpe quickly became known for his work in three classic genres: male and female nudes, still lifes, and celebrity portraits.

There is a cool, detached formality to Mapplethorpe's images, even when the subject matter is emotionally loaded. He has often been compared to Edward Weston (known for his exquisite work with natural subjects), and to fashion photographers Irving Penn and Richard Avedon. Much of Mapplethorpe's work is sexually charged, and a sense of fragile beauty, the inevitability of mortality, and even innocence runs through various photographs. He anthropomorphized flowers into figures brimming with erotic power: in *Tulips* (1984) two blossoms seem to reach for one another against a stark black background, one yearning with receptivity as the other sensually descends from above. And he also objectified human beings, literally putting them on pedestals or isolating body parts as objects to be admired and desired. The title of the disputed exhibition, *The Perfect Moment* conveys this attempt to capture the apex of beauty before decay commences.

His self-portraits record a similar trajectory, and the contradictory nature of the artist. In 1975 he leaps into the frame, with just his boyish face, outstretched arm, and a sliver of his chest making it into the photo. In 1978 he becomes the Devil incarnate with his leathers and a bullwhip stuck into his rectum, twisting behind as a tail; he bends his upper torso backwards to confront his audience with a threatening stare. In 1980 he could be either the leather-clad smart aleck with a cigarette dangling from his mouth, or the ethereal waif with lipstick pout, mascaraed eyes, and naked, vulnerable torso. In 1983 he again looks menacing in a leather coat and gloves, challenging the viewer with a machine gun and a defiant stare.

But the inevitable entropy had set in by 1988, accelerated by the progress of Mapplethorpe's AIDS. Now the counterpoint to the artist's gaunt face is a skull-topped cane he defiantly grasps in the foreground; both images appear to float in black space.[51] And in another photograph from that same year, only a chipped human skull is pictured. Mapplethorpe died at the age of 42 in 1989, while his retrospective was receiving a positive (and substantial) reception in Chicago. By an odd twist of fate his last portrait assignment was a shot of Surgeon General C. Everett Koop for *Time* magazine. As Dr Koop recalled, "It was a poignant experience to have my picture taken by a man dying of a disease I've spent so much time trying to educate the public about."[52]

THE MEASURE OF THE MAN

Several "generations" of critics arose in response to Mapplethorpe's work. One of the most consistent points of dissension was that his work was over-aestheticized. According to Mapplethorpe, "I don't think there's that much difference between a photograph of a fist up someone's ass as a photograph of carnations in a bowl."[53] But to many critics this became boring and tedious, an approach that was all surface and no substance. In Donald Kuspit's estimation in an article entitled "Aestheticizing the Perverse" there was "a hot emotional point to the cool visual tale Mapplethorpe tells,"[54] but one that largely was glossed over sometimes, in elaborate custom-designed frames incorporating mirrors and expensive fabrics. Some lamented the lack of moral evaluation in this body of work, comparing its "rhetoric of artifice" to Fascist aesthetics.[55] Yet most of these detractors conceded that Mapplethorpe was a serious artist who had earned a place on the contemporary photographic pantheon. By the late 1980s, Mapplethorpe had lost the power to shock most people in the art world. His work became ordinary and acceptable as it became more well-known: "Elegance spoils it as pornography," one critic remarked, "and avidity wrecks it as fashion."[56]

Mapplethorpe was also cited for the possible racist implications of his image-making. As with other images that bring up difficult topics, Mapplethorpe's photographs provoked a variety of reactions. One reviewer indicted him in 1986 for removing his black models to a hermetic environment which cloaked the troubled history of race relations in the US. But another felt that, by placing black men on pedestals and highlighting the sensualness of their skin, Mapplethorpe successfully subverted the racial hierarchy in the studio.[57] This theme was developed by an observer who noted that *Thomas in a Circle* (1987) – where a crouched nude man pushed against the sides of a spherical structure that surrounded him – could be interpreted as a metaphor for a black man struggling to preserve his heritage "in an ever-closing circle of white culture."[58]

More than anything else, the mere fact that

he addressed race was sufficient to cause discomfort. *Thomas and Dovanna* (1987) embodies the prototypical white racist nightmare: a naked, muscular black man dances with a white woman clothed in a white gown, dipping her as she follows his lead. But was the photographer demolishing or confirming the cliché here? Mapplethorpe's regular use of black models, and especially his focus on only certain body parts, most frequently disturbed reviewers. *Man in Polyester Suit* (1980) was routinely reproached for underscoring racial stereotypes of black men as hyper-sexed. The photo presents a black man in a three-piece suit, the image cropped at about mid-chest and above the knee. In startling contrast is his imposing penis, heavily dangling from his unzipped pants. One possible reaction picks up the inherent humor and absurdity of the situation: it could be confronting racist assumptions by exposing them in a comical way. But in accord with another reading this is a racist image itself, reminiscent of a scene in Saul Bellows' *Mr Sammler's Planet*: in that instance the protagonist is confronted by a black mugger in an apartment building vestibule, and is most upset when the man brandishes his penis at him like a weapon. There was more insult than injury in this fictional instance.

The most thorough critique of Mapplethorpe's use of black men was offered by a black gay man, Essex Hemphill. His reaction to this last photo, as well as to other images, was that Mapplethorpe exploited and objectified black men by focusing on body parts, a practice in accord with assessing the work potential of slaves. He accused Mapplethorpe of engaging in a "colonial fantasy" where blacks were available to "service the expectations of white desire."[59] Hemphill's outrage was based on the perception that Mapplethorpe's fetishization of limbs and organs ignored what might be going on in black men's heads. As he argued, "this blindness allows white males to pursue their sexual fantasies about black males without ever actually entering a ghetto, a jail, or a black man's shoes, or a black man's bad day to see if he feels like stripping down for aesthetic and/or erotic reasons."[60]

Non-gay critics took similar affront, faulting Mapplethorpe for equating the desirability and worth of men to the size of their sexual equipment, a process similar to what routinely happens to women. The sexual orientation of a critic only has relevance if it appears to jaundice one's view. Arthur C. Danto cites, for example, "the perfect male nude, viewed from the rear – from its vulnerable side."[61] What an odd comment, given the vulnerability of the naked male both fore and aft, except when considered in the context of the fear of sexual violation through penetration, a fear evidently heightened for this reviewer when he wrote about the depiction of homosexual desire.

But as Hemphills' critique makes clear, opinion in the gay community was divided over Mapplethorpe, as reflected in the response after the gay magazine *The Advocate* posthumously named the photographer "man of the year" in 1990. His memory was feted because of the assault that right-wing critics launched against his work in 1989. Some readers dissented from the editors' judgment in letters published in a subsequent issue, one writer declaring "Mapplethorpe is to art what the Crips and Bloods gangs are to community neighborhoods."[62] This last opinion notwithstanding, while the many critiques of Mapplethorpe's work took issue with certain aspects of it, they also acknowledged its importance and right to exist. A new set of political critics emerged in 1989, however, who vilified Mapplethorpe, questioned the status of his work as art and also challenged its right to receive public funds and to be shown in particular contexts.

THE SOCIAL CONSTRUCTION OF ACCEPTABILITY

In a cynical world we are prone to believe that politicians do not experience moments of epiphany so much as somehow incubate new strategies for self-aggrandizement within their minds. Whatever the case, a critical moment reportedly occurred for Senator Jesse Helms (R-NC) in July, 1989. In a home decorated with religious and nature scenes, Helms showed his wife Dorothy a catalog of *The Perfect Moment*, the touring Robert Mapplethorpe retrospective.

She quickly put it down, and he quoted her crying out in dismay, "Lord have mercy, Jesse, I'm not believing this."[63] Helms himself took special offense at the shot of a small girl who is caught at the instant when she lifted her dress and thereby exposed herself (*Honey*, 1976). He admitted his embarrassment over speaking to a reporter or to his wife about this picture.[64]

There was a great deal that upset the domestic tranquility of the Helms household that day, including the challenge inherent within Mapplethorpe's photographs to at least two important social hierarchies, sexual and racial. Helms directed particular outrage against images that broached both interracial and homoerotic themes: "There's a big difference between 'The Merchant of Venice' and a photograph of two males of different races [in an erotic pose] on a marble table top," he argued.[65] The reaction of the Helmses was important in setting the terms of a prolonged and acrimonious debate, that led to canceled plans at a museum, congressional action, and extended legal battles.

That debate was guided in part by a new generation of cultural critics. Richard Grenier, writing in the *Washington Times*, rekindled Biblical fury by labelling Mapplethorpe "the great catamite." He also fantasized about dousing the body of the late photographer with kerosene and burning it. In the same publication Judith Reisman equated *Honey* with child abuse, and accused Mapplethorpe of "photographically lynching" the man in the polyester suit.[66] But it was Patrick Buchanan who launched the most sustained attack in print, through a series of venomous columns. Buchanan detected a struggle for the soul of America in the battle over the artists. On one side was a small band of arts and gay rights radicals, out of touch with most of society, and suffering from "an infantile disorder."[67] They promoted filth and degradation in the guise of mediocre art, and a lifestyle that was suicidal, witness Mapplethorpe's death from AIDS. In Buchanan's view, the goal of this new *Kulturkampf* was to overturn tradition and create a pagan society.[68] On the other side were the stalwart defenders of the good, the true and the traditional, like himself.

The credentials of these reviewers derived as much or more from their political as their artistic concerns. Yet some well-established art critics sounded a very similar sense of alarm. Hilton Kramer characterized what was actually a "tamer" retrospective at the Whitney in 1988 as "this bizarre exhibition."[69] And adopting the self-appointed role of guardian of standards and the public morals, he joined the fray after *The Perfect Moment* became controversial. Kramer decided what he saw as Mapplethorpe's attempt to "force" the public to accept "loathsome" sexual values by publicly exhibiting images "designed to aggrandize and abet erotic rituals involving coercion, degradation, bloodshed and the infliction of pain."[70] Kramer would have no part of this, and utilized a ploy which almost became *de rigueur* for conservative critics: "I cannot bring myself to describe these pictures in all their gruesome particularities ... [And therefore] [s]hould public funds be used to exhibit pictures which the press even in our liberated era still finds too explicit or repulsive to publish."[71] Making judgments from such an elevated position may shield others from potential harm, but it also short-circuits their opportunity to reach independent conclusions.

The pictures that Kramer referred to most frequently were from the X, Y, and Z portfolios. The Y portfolio contained flower photos, moderating the X portfolio that chronicled sadomasochistic homosexual behavior, and the Z portfolio that featured the sexuality of black men. But at the Hartford, CT Atheneum, for example, viewing these images was strictly a matter of choice. A separate admission was charged for this show at the museum's entrance, and the entire exhibit was in a series of upstairs galleries. There was no chance of accidentally stumbling into it, or glimpsing any of it in passing. In addition, once in the exhibit area a visitor had to stand on a separate line that slowly made its way down the length of the X, Y, Z section, after reading another notice that it contained potentially offensive material. Rows of prints from each series were spread horizontally across library display cases, and the images were much smaller in size than ones on the walls. In other words, everything was done to minimize the shock value of these images, a successful procedure judging by the hushed viewers and their generally serious mien.

The Perfect Moment was scheduled for a tour of seven cities throughout the country.[72] And as the show travelled, there were widely disparate responses to the same material. In Philadelphia and Chicago the show went largely unremarked, beyond generally amiable reviews. Chicagoans were too distracted by the events happening a mile or so south down Michigan Avenue, as veterans and others protested Dread Scott's flag installation. Months later, a commentator deemed the timing of the Mapplethorpe exhibit there to be "the lucky moment."[73] It was also while the show continued to attract record-breaking crowds to Chicago's Museum of Contemporary Art that Mapplethorpe died, an event respectfully noted by the local gay press.[74] The next stop was Washington, DC, and from there on the exhibit took on a controversial aura.

The range of reactions it evoked – from nonchalance to outrage to veneration – demonstrates that art and artists judged to be outlaws at one time and place can flourish at other sites. To claim that Mapplethorpe's photographs were inherently scandalous misses an important point: for controversy to be activated, something must be added from *outside* the objects themselves. This was more likely to occur once the photographs were subject to evaluation by people who were relatively unfamiliar with the contemporary art world, or by those who were automatically repelled by topics like homosexuality. Such opinions were the leavening that caused the conflict to rise. It is foolish to focus exclusively on "inflammatory" cultural artifacts; thorough investigators must expand their view to consider the social circumstances under which definitions of offense emerge.

NOT IN MY BACKYARD

The Corcoran Gallery of Art is the US capital's oldest art museum, located just a couple of blocks from the White House. Engraved over an entrance is the motto "Dedicated to Art." It was not difficult to appreciate the irony of that epigram during the summer of 1989 when the museum canceled the Mapplethorpe exhibit at the eleventh hour. It was a stunning decision, with far-reaching consequences.

The Corcoran had weathered other controversies. In 1851 the founder of the collection shocked his contemporaries by his display of a copy of the nude sculpture *The Greek Slave*, by Hiram Powers. When the original work toured the country a few years earlier, discretion had prevailed: men and women had been admitted separately to view it.[75] As mentioned, government officials removed the Paul Cadmus painting of "sailors and floozies" from an exhibit there in 1934, and five years later another conflict occurred. A searing anti-fascist painting of Mussolini's Italy by Peter Blume was rejected from the Corcoran's Sixteenth Biennial, a move that prompted the American Artists' Congress and other groups to protest. The explanation that the curator offered confirmed the protestors' worst fears: "the *Eternal City* may have been rejected because the jury considered it political propaganda and out of place in an art exhibit."[76] There were also suspicions that the veto was dictated by concern for the sensibilities of foreign diplomats, and so the painting was subsequently exhibited at another locale. And in more recent times, the museum deleted the preface from the catalog of *Recent Graphics from Prague*. Critics of the decision believed that the institution bowed to pressure from the Czech government, which wished to deflect attention away from its repressive policies.[77] But these were all minor brushfires next to the Mapplethorpe firestorm.

On June 12, 1989, Director Christina Orr-Cahall announced that the heated political climate in Washington made it unwise for the Corcoran to go forward with its commitment to host the Mapplethorpe retrospective. Vocal members of Congress were still steaming over government support of Andres Serrano's *Piss Christ*, and the Dread Scott affair a few months earlier was fueling an explosion of official flag-waving that continued for the remainder of the summer.[78] Representative Dick Armey had collected over one hundred signatures on a letter calling for a review of NEA procedures, and copies of *The Perfect Moment* catalog were allegedly circulating in Congress. Orr-Cahall felt that the appearance of such controversial images in close proximity to Capitol Hill could jeopardize the NEA's future. The Corcoran itself was also vulnerable because it has no endowment of its own and is dependent on a federal program for a significant infusion of money.

Orr-Cahall defended her actions by alleging "I don't think there was censorship at all. The [show's catalogue] is out, the exhibit has been seen elsewhere and will be seen elsewhere. I think censorship would have been editing the show."[79] But many people took her to be naive at best, villainous at worst. As Mapplethorpe's dealer Robert Miller declared in a public statement, "When one thinks of the terrors that Washington generates and sends out into the world, the thought that depiction of the naked human body might be disturbing to Washington seems ludicrous."[80] Rather than squelching controversy, the Corcoran's director fanned the flames even higher.

The reaction of the artistic community was swift – and creative. Three days after the cancellation was announced, up to one hundred protestors marched at the Corcoran in a demonstration coordinated by the DC Gay and Lesbian Activist Alliance, the National Gay and Lesbian Task force, and Oppression Under Target (OUT).[81] On 30 June, nine hundred to one thousand demonstrators witnessed an imaginative use of technology when slides of Mapplethorpe's work were projected onto the Corcoran façade. This unconventional extension of the museum's walls enabled images which were not allowed to be seen inside to be shown outside instead.

Artist Lowell Nesbitt decided to withhold a bequest to the museum that would be worth over one million dollars upon his death, and students at Corcoran's school of art demonstrated several times. In one instance, three female students erected an eight-foot papier maché penis on the school's grounds, a figure wrapped in an American flag and holding a bottle of urine and a cross.[82] Their representation thereby managed to incorporate most of the previous major artistic flash points into one site. And another institution, the small, artist-run Washington Project for the Arts (WPA), stepped in as the new sponsor of the exhibit in the District of Columbia. A familiar pattern was established: publicity boosted attendance records to nearly forty times normal.[83]

Artists also boycotted the Corcoran, its reputation now significantly sullied. Annette Lemieux withdrew her solo show, as did six sculptors who had been scheduled for a group exhibition. A third show was also endangered, a joint effort of Soviet and American painters entitled *10 + 10*. The international nature of this exhibit was a source of embarrassment, for it seemed to highlight growing domestic repression at the same time that the Cold War was thawing and the Eastern Bloc was experiencing more freedom. Once the Corcoran earned a reputation as an unpredictable and unreliable institution, negotiations for other future shows were also threatened.

Damage control became the order of the day. One of the ways the museum attempted to redeem itself was via the proposal by an ad hoc curators' group to mount an exhibition on censorship, including work by the artistic gadflies Serrano and Mapplethorpe. One curator contacted the New York-based artists' collective Group Material about assembling such a show, but after considering it the group declined the offer.[84] Finally, after being the target of intense criticism for three months, Orr-Cahall issued an apology on September 18. It was an important gesture, but some artists felt that it did not go far enough. Orr-Cahall expressed regret over offending parts of the art community, but did not appear to acknowledge that the Corcoran had done anything wrong. After several more months of public pummeling, Orr-Cahall tendered her resignation on December 18, 1989. By the next spring *10 + 10* was back on track, opening the possibility of the museum returning to some level of normalcy.

But the costs to the institution had been immense; the Corcoran was in a bureaucratic shambles. Three other major curatorial and administrative positions were vacated within a year of the cancellation. Staff morale in general was low, and the unwieldy character of the board – and its difficulty in reaching a consensus on most matters – was revealed to the general public. Confusion remained over who had authorized the cancellation of the Mapplethorpe exhibit, necessitating an eventual restructuring of governance procedures. In her letter of resignation, Orr-Cahall claimed that her personal feelings were compromised by her responsibilities as an executive.[85] To this day, however, there are many unanswered questions about how the Corcoran decided to abort its own program.

Defenders of that decision had a field day in the press. The "letters to the editor" column of the *Washington Times* was a predictable venue for a well-tuned conservative response: "Billing Mr Mapplethorpe's work as art and demanding federal dollars to pay for it is equivalent to Larry Flynt [editor of *Hustler*] asking the National Institutes of Health for a grant to study female anatomy."[86] But then, the rank and file has such leaders as William F. Buckley as models. Buckley applauded the Corcoran's courage, good sense, and absolute right to say "no" to *The Perfect Moment*, and threw in a jab to Serrano, whom he accused of "the kind of infantile antinomianism that thinks it amusing to paint swastikas on the walls of synagogues."[87] And James J. Kilpatrick joined the chorus: even though he had not heard of Mapplethorpe until the Corcoran cancellation, and apparently had not viewed the images firsthand, he still labelled the work "prurient junk."[88]

Detractors of what the Corcoran did were less certain of how to present their case. It was difficult for many people to get beyond their outrage when the Corcoran claimed it was acting in the best interests of Mapplethorpe, and in the best interests of the arts community. This did not seem to be a benevolent gesture. Most importantly, the incident caught most artists and arts administrators off guard. In the recent past they had not had to dwell on the intersection of artists' rights, public funding and accountability, and legal issues related to free expression, nor had they been pressured to decide where they were prepared to take a stand when these matters became complicated. Confusion now reigned as the attackers held court advantage.

Even important leaders seemed befuddled by what was happening, as reflected in a statement made by National Gallery Director J. Carter Brown: "We have to keep the First Amendment rights apart from any controversy."[89] On the contrary, First Amendment rights were one of the key issues, yet slighted in this circumspect and prudent statement. There was also a conscious reluctance to rally around Mapplethorpe's sado-masochistic imagery; it was simply too difficult for many people to come to terms with, and on short notice. In a lengthy editorial where the *Washington Post* took the Corcoran to task for its bungling performance, there was the denial that homophobia was a pivotal factor in the cancellation scenario.[90] The refusal to acknowledge the possible contribution of such bias in this and many other art controversies was striking. It took an accumulation of many incidents before there began to be a public dialogue on anti-homosexual bias.

Senator Jesse Helms pledged that the cancellation at the Corcoran was not the end of the matter. Beyond the internal consequences for one museum, far-reaching repercussions of this event indeed continued to issue from Congress. Helms sustained the conflict, with the proper use of public funds being the primary question at this juncture. Obscenity had entered into the debate, but initially as a catchphrase, not a legal distinction.

TIGHTENING THE SCREWS

Jesse Helms held the charge against art for five months, in the summer and fall of 1989. His canny tactics kept his opponents dodging punches from several directions. He excelled at turning out memorable quotes: "If someone wants to write ugly nasty things on the men's room wall," he declared in a disparaging tone, "the taxpayers do not provide the crayons."[91] This first principal guided his legislative maneuverings as he attempted to constrict the NEA's operation.

Helms launched a three-pronged assault. His initial maneuver was a "sneak attack," bringing a measure attached to an appropriations bill to voice vote when only a handful of his fellow Senators were present. Known as the Helms Amendment, it barred the use of Federal funds to "promote, disseminate or produce obscene or indecent materials, including but not limited to depictions of sadomasochism, homoeroticism, the exploitation of children, or individuals engaged in sexual acts; or material which denigrates the objects or beliefs of the adherents of a particular religion or nonreligion." It also cut $45,000 from the NEA's appropriation (an amount equal to the support for Serrano and the Mapplethorpe exhibit),[92] and proposed a five-year ban on the supporting institutions, SECCA and ICA. This measure passed the Senate, but a House bill authorized only the $45,000 cut, not the five-year ban nor the ban on obscene art.

Helms deployed another stratagem when a Senate and House Conference Committee was assembled to work out a compromise. The Senator sent committee members a packet of Mapplethorpe photos: the children *Honey* and *Jesse McBride*, as well as the man in the polyester suit and a picture of a penis perched upon a pedestal. On the Helms scale of offensiveness, he rated these a "5" on a scale of from 1 to 10.[93] But after the committee appeared to be leaning toward softening the bill, Helms fortified his approach: he requested that all the pages and the women ("ladies") leave the chamber so that he might show his colleagues the pictures. Helms hoped once again that a first-hand confrontation with the evidence would secure his victory, but he was also vigilant to protect the sensibilities of those who, he believed, might not be sufficiently robust owing to their age or gender to tolerate such a visual assault.

Senator Helms's final tactic was to threaten to bring matters to a voice vote "so that whoever votes against it [the anti-obscenity clause] would be on record as favoring taxpayer funding for pornography."[94] Helms had managed to steer the debate in such a way that pornography – pro or con – was the main issue. It appeared to be a wise move, for it seemed unlikely that any legislator would be willing to face irate constituents after voting for what many members of the general public considered offensive art.

Helm's gambit had a mixed outcome: the conference committee eliminated the five-year ban on SECCA and ICA, although it required the NEA to notify Congress before awarding a grant to either institution.[95] It also prohibited federal funding of art that could be considered obscene, a compromise suggested by Congress-man Sidney Yates (D-IL) in accord with the 1973 Supreme Court decision *Miller* v. *California*. This was a relaxation from the original Helm proposal. *Miller* prescribes that three distinct tests must be met before the designation of obscenity applies; the vague notions of "indecency" and "denigration" were dropped from the bill.

As Andres Serrano joked afterwards, "the [original] wording was 'obscene and indecent.' I always assumed that Mapplethorpe was the obscene one and I was the indecent one. And so when they knocked indecent out of the language, I thought it was okay for me!"[96] Nevertheless, the arts community was not off the hook with this measure, the first content-specific restriction placed upon the NEA. It was not completely clear who would apply the Miller test or where, even though under its principles the notion of "obscene art" is virtually an oxymoron. But the answers to these questions would soon be forthcoming.

"VAS YOU EVER IN SINSINNATI?"[97]

When *The Perfect Moment* moved from Washington, DC to Hartford, Connecticut, it enjoyed a momentary respite from notoriety. The Hartford Atheneum was extremely cautious in its presentation of the show. In addition to logistic considerations already recounted, the museum prohibited admission to anyone under 17 unless accompanied by a parent. It also implemented the separate admission charge to guarantee that no public funds were used to underwrite this show. The Atheneum sponsored public forums to establish a context for understanding Mapplethorpe's photographs, and issued a set of questions and answers with a defensive, apologetic tone that carefully explained the work and the museum's sponsorship of it.[98]

From fifteen to twenty-five demonstrators appeared on opening day, primarily members of the Connecticut Citizens for Decency, an anti-pornography and anti-abortion group. They picketed against the backdrop of two young gay men kissing on the steps, and in front of a crowd that swelled to four times the normal attendance.[99] The large crowds continued and the peacefulness of the sojourn was maintained. It was a welcome lull: the reception in Cincinnati was vastly different.

Cincinnati is an easy and recurrent target of jokes. This is not on the magnitude of New Yorkers dumping on New Jersey, nor Chicagoans chiding Gary, Indiana, yet so-called sophisticates have singled out Cincinnati as an outpost of Philistinism for a long time. As Tom Wolfe wrote, "believe me, you can get all the tubes of Winsor & Newton paint you want in Cincinnati, but the artists keep migrating to New York all the same."[100] The official response to Mapplethorpe guaranteed the continuance of that dubious reputation.

Cincinnati had an inflated ego in the nineteenth century. The "Queen City" was the major cultural center west of New York, and its leaders were convinced it was destined to become even more important as the country expanded. They grossly miscalculated. Post-Civil War growth in cities such as Chicago, Cleveland and St Louis elbowed out this city on the Ohio River, consigning it to a diminished role on the national stage. However, the arts did flourish there, from painting to literature, music to pottery. Many cultural institutions were established with nineteenth-century enthusiasm and wealth, leaving the city with a substantial legacy.[101]

And like practically every other American city, Cincinnati has a heritage of art controversies as well. In the mid-nineteenth century, Hiram Powers' *The Greek Slave* raised eyebrows here, just as it had in Washington, DC with Mr Corcoran's guests. A committee of clergymen was charged with evaluating its suitability for display, and they ultimately gave their assent "since her hands were chained, her undraped condition was beyond her control, and she would not endanger public virtue."[102] The writer Lafcadio Hearn shocked Cincinnati in the latter part of the century with his accounts of the underside of life in the city, his own debauched lifestyle, and even an account of artists using undraped models in their painting studios![103]

In more recent times, a production of *Equus* was reviewed by the police before it was allowed on stage in 1989; the nudity in the play had become a cause for concern. Religious organizations effectively blocked *The Last Temptation of Christ* from being screened until fourteen months after its release,[104] and *Hair*, *Oh! Calcutta*, and the Playboy Channel have all run into opposition. And Cincinnati is also the place where Larry Flynt was convicted on obscenity charges for his magazine *Hustler*.

One of the most extended contemporary disputes centered on a sculptural installation by Andrew Leicester for the main entrance to a riverfront park, proposed as part of the city's 1988 bicentennial celebration. *Bicentennial Gateway* became known as "the flying pigs" because it featured two bronze pairs of the winged creatures atop a group of pillars. The iconography invoked Cincinnati's nineteenth-century nickname, "Porkopolis," but this did not please some citizens, whipped up by local media who knew a good story when they saw one. The panel that approved the design was headed by the Contemporary Art Center's (CAC) Dennis Barrie, and the work was eventually installed after much farcical quarrelling.[105]

The Contemporary Art Center occupies a unique niche in the ecology of arts organizations in Cincinnati. It is the *parvenu* among the stodgy, nineteenth-century dowagers. According to CAC's chief curator Jack Sawyer,

> As a contemporary art museum, our mission is to be an outsider; that's a natural position for us.... We haven't really collected objects, so that baggage is not on us ... We're always seeking out art which doesn't have a place in the culture. For the most part the people on our board are like the three women who founded the place in 1939 [as the Modern Art Society], pulling away from the comfort and security of Cincinnati.[106]

Even its local is distinctive: it is housed above a Walgreen's Drug Store in downtown Cincinnati, part of a mercantile arcade where restaurants and shops link old structures with more modern ones.

Many observers have noted the contradictory character of this city, as has mystery writer Jonathan Valin. In *Day of Wrath*, lead character Harry Stoner confronts an archaic plaster statue of a black jockey on a lawn. He is surprised only by its conspicuousness, for he envisages hidden armies of them "like a race of imprisoned elves, waiting to be returned to daylight ... Racial prejudice didn't die in this city; it just got stored in the basement with the rest of the supplies."[107] This tendency to push difficult matters from public view is most clearly represented by how Cincinnati has opted to regulate sexual information and conduct.

The city has taken advantage of its geographic location to rid itself of the commercial sex industry: there are no X-rated movie theaters, video or bookstores in Cincinnati. Pornographic material is available for sale only across the river in Kentucky. This marks a civic compartmentalizing of desire unmatched in other US cities of this size. Newport, Kentucky, ("Sin City") has been a center of vice serving a tri-state area for decades. But as Eelise LaShay of the Brass Mule and some of her colleagues from other Monmouth Street establishments testified on a Donahue show, police have been cracking down there as well. It seems that the concentration of clubs has made it difficult to attract a diversity of businesses to the area.[108] As a consequence, people are now forced to go to other Kentucky towns to meet their needs for sexual goods and services. The CAC's Sawyer recounted that a co-worker offered the judgment that "New Orleans is dirty and fun and corrupt and Cincinnati is well-organized, clean and boring."

Cincinnati is a prime instance of the nexus of values and power. According to research conducted at the University of Cincinnati's Institute for Policy Research, this city falls "in the center" on important social and economic questions. In other words, for mid-sized cities it is no more liberal or conservative than others on issues such as pornography, censorship or abortion.[109] But values are just one part of the equation. What makes the decisive difference in Cincinnati are seasoned moral crusaders and key government officials who can mobilize against anything that violates their sense of propriety.

Local businessman Charles Keating – later notorious as the head of the insolvent Lincoln Savings and Loan in California – founded Citizens for Decency through Law in 1956.[110] Cincinnati is currently the headquarters of the National Coalition Against Pornography, as well as a local morality organization that spear-

headed the anti-Mapplethorpe campaign, the Citizens for Community Values (CCV). The CCV initiated its campaign against the Mapplethorpe exhibit before it arrived in Cincinnati with a mass-mailing reminiscent of Helm's techniques; in this instance, there were detailed descriptions of seven of the photographs. The CCV's position was that these images were obscene, and anyone displaying them in public should be prosecuted. Eventually the Contemporary Art Center was the target of threatening phone calls, as were board members. And shortly before the opening of the exhibit, the chairman of CAC's board resigned, the bank where he was a vice-president had received calls of protest as well.[111] According to a CCV spokesperson, "Cincinnati is the pinnacle. We enforce the law to the nth degree."[112]

The Mapplethorpe exhibit also provided another opportunity for Simon Leis to exert his authority. An important player in the prosecution of gay broadcaster John Zeh, Leis has been a public official in Cincinnati for twenty years. Leis built his career upon crusading for decency, in the positions of county prosecutor, judge, and in 1990 as sheriff of Hamilton County. In addition, the county prosecutor Arthur Ney was Leis' handpicked successor,[113] and the judge in the case had been Leis' assistant at one time. The judge and the sheriff attended all the same schools, and belonged to the same athletic club.[114] A picture emerged of an old boy's network, a circle of supportive officials sharing the same values and mutually dependent upon one another's support. When CAC's head Dennis Barrie was charged with pandering obscenity, there was an amazing sense of *déjà vu*: the prosecutor and the defense attorney had previously faced off in a case involving the distribution of *Penthouse* magazine. The trial was presided over by Judge F. David J. Albanese, the same man who would handle the Mapplethorpe/Barrie litigation.[15]

THE LONG ARM OF THE LAW

Before 1990, much of Cincinnati's reputation derived from being the corporate headquarters of Procter and Gamble, and from its renowned chili. The Mapplethorpe exhibit amended that, perhaps for ever.

The CAC was determined that the show go on. The gallery was careful to dissociate itself from the public funding debate that had swirled around Serrano and had dominated the Corcoran debate. According to Sawyer, "In one of our private meetings the staff said that it was better that we lose our jobs and the CAC become a store front operation than to back away from showing the photographs – rather than go through what the Corcoran did, because then we couldn't attract anyone worth showing." The retrospective was sponsored in Cincinnati by a grant from a local business, and by increasing the usual admission fee from two to five dollars. The CAC also excluded itself from being a beneficiary of the Cincinnati Institute of Fine Arts, a local umbrella group that raises money to support a myriad of cultural endeavors. Although the CAC had received nearly one quarter of its budget from that source the previous year, it did not wish to hamper the group's fundraising efforts because of the developing controversy in 1990. The CAC posted warning signs about the graphic nature of some of the photographs, and at this site *no one* under the age of 18 was to be admitted.

The CAC attempted to clarify its legal situation on March 27 (before the exhibition opened) by requesting that a jury examine the controversial images and determine whether they were obscene. A judge denied this request ten days later, forcing the CAC to proceed with the exhibit without knowing if it could be held in violation of any criminal statutes. A tense period ensued, with Barrie and the CAC receiving threatening phone calls, and CAC staff fielding and diffusing various rumors. On the evening of April 6, thousands of people lined up for a members-only preview of the show. Their ranks were swelled by a flurry of new affiliates who suspected the exhibit could be shut down by a police raid, and wished to view it before such an action could occur.

The mounting uncertainty over the exhibition's fate was shattered when a showdown occurred on the official opening day, April 7. Nine members of a Hamilton County grand jury were among the first visitors. After their viewing they decided that seven of the photographs were obscene, and charged the CAC and director Dennis Barrie with two misdemeanor counts each of pandering obscenity and illegal use of a child in nudity-related material.[116] Later that afternoon police armed with a search warrant cleared the gallery of visitors in order to videotape the exhibit.

This effort to collect evidence prompted an enraged crowd to shout "Gestapo go home" and "Sieg Heil." This was a highly emotional and hazardous situation, intensified because the enclosed arcade area was jammed with people, and the primary means of entry and egress from the gallery are two escalators connecting the first and second levels. In fact, over two thousand people filled the atrium and snaked in lines onto the sidewalks outside. The county prosecutor had waited until the exhibition opened to the public in order for a crime to be committed. The police chief heralded this as an example of restraint, a demonstration that "there are no raving Neanderthals running amok."[117] Yet Sawyer felt that the police and other pubic officials *were* frighteningly out of control: "We really didn't believe it would come to police action because it was just inconceivable that they would come into an art museum . . . I think if they had brought Dennis [Barrie] out in handcuffs there very well could have been a riot."[118]

Several months of legal wrangling followed, during which time the exhibit was allowed to remain open. *The Perfect Moment* completed its run against a backdrop of city/county jurisdictional disputes, and arguments over what specific charges should be brought (the indictment for the childrens' portraits were later amended to include "a lewd exhibition or graphic focus on the genitals"). By the time the case was eventually heard in September, the tour was completing its two-year journey in Boston. The period leading up to the trial prolonged the agony of the CAC and Barrie, the first US museum director indicted for obscenity in the course of doing his job. As the title of an op-ed piece written by Barrie declaimed, "Pandering? That's Nonsense . . . I'm a museum director."[119]

Not unexpectedly, everyone appeared to have an opinion in this case, views that were aired continuously. A great deal of support for

Barrie and the CAC came from outside Cincinnati. For example, the Art Dealers Association of America took out an ad in support of them in the *New York Times*, and the Association of Art Museum Directors pledged to pay any fine which might be imposed on Barrie. The Coalition of Writers' Organizations also voted its endorsement, as did the College Art Association, which terminated its consideration of Cincinnati as a possible convention site in 1995. But affirmative gestures were also initiated locally, including a resolution passed by the University of Cincinnati's Faculty Senate. The results of a telephone poll of Hamilton County, Ohio residents revealed that 63 per cent of the respondents opposed the prosecution of the arts center,[120] and the art reviewer for *The Cincinnati Enquirer* gave the show a generally favorable assessment.

However, that critic laced his commentary with some value-laden observations which tempered the review's overall impact, remarking on "the sadness of his [Mapplethorpe's] life," and noting "a feeling of self-loathing, a cry of despair" that the photos evoked for him.[121] These comments made it difficult to distinguish a supporter from an opponent. And opponents were legion – and vocal – in Cincinnati. A trio of doctors used their credentials to bulwark their testimony, claiming that the disputed exhibit "forces upon us a bizarre, sexual vision" by presenting "degrading acts that diminish us all." As one of those physicians also asserted authoritatively on television, to people struggling with "addictions" to pornography, seeing the sadomasochistic or homoerotic images in an art museum could give them the green light to engage in similar (destructive) behaviors themselves.[122]

Their collective judgment was bolstered by a retired professor of economics who was also the local coordinator for the American Family Association. He claimed that moral pollution precipitated effects as deleterious as physical pollution, and alleged that mounds of scientific evidence had demonstrated the evils of pornography. In his estimation, "Cincinnati needs an art program which will lift us up instead of drag us down, which promotes the good, the true and the beautiful, instead of the false, the ugly and the depraved."[123] And another professor

sounded the alarm over depictions of unbridled sexual desire and its inevitable connection to social decay: "A society ... which cannot distinguish between liberty and license, is a society that will experience the sexual chaos, the sexual excesses and the decline of family values which so conspicuously mark our age."[124] Many such anxious pronouncements could be recounted, but they were all comically skewered by a local cartoonist: "Jim Borgman's World" presented a scene where all types of people are going about their business on a Cincinnati street in various stages of undress, under signs trumpeting commercial sexual encounters. Two fully dressed women react with shock, one saying to the other "I *told* you that exhibit would undermine our community values, Edna!"[125]

AS SIMPLE AND AMERICAN AS APPLE PIE

Appeals by the defense attorney failed to derail the trial. Not even the argument that some of the contested photos appeared in books in the collection of the county public library was sufficient to cause the judge to dismiss the charges. In fact, three decisions by the judge in the pre-trial stage greatly distressed the defendants and their supporters. First, Judge Albanese ruled that the jury could hear testimony only about the seven allegedly obscene images out of 175 photographs in the retrospective. A key section of the Miller test states that to be judged obscene, "the work, *taken as a whole*, lacks serious literary, artistic, political, or scientific value."[126] The judge took this to mean each photograph as a whole, not the complete exhibition. He rejected the view that there was an integrity to the entire selection or, as the director of the Walker Art Center later testified, that "Pictures speak to each other; they become part of a totality."[127]

Second, Albanese denied a request for adjournment by ruling that the CAC was a gallery rather than a museum. Under Ohio law, museums are allowed to display obscene materials for educational and cultural purposes. But the CAC's rules of incorporation failed to meet this semantic test, and the institution was subject to prosecution.[128] And finally, the judge refused to restrict the juror pool to the city of Cincinnati, which presumably would generate a more liberal panel. He instead ordered that it be drawn from Hamilton County as a whole. These procedural setbacks seemed to bode ill for the CAC and Barrie.

Jury selection also troubled the defense. On the face of it, the jury pool did not offer people who appeared naturally inclined to endorse CAC's point of view. For example, they were generally non-museumgoers: only three of fifty had seen the Mapplethorpe exhibit, and most had not gone to museums aside from school trips. But beyond this, Judge Albanese appeared to favor the prosecution when he allowed the questioning of some women to continue even after they admitted to holding strong religious and moral opinions, and acknowledged that they would have a difficult time examining the evidence. Although they were eventually excluded from the panel, the judge's apparent willingness to consider them as prospects seemed like an ominous sign. In the end, four men and four women were selected. Only one was a resident of the city, and one held a college degree. They were a predominately working-class group, with little interest or experience with art.[129]

The prosecution's case was rudimentary: they presented only three police officers who confirmed that the photos were displayed at CAC. Their supposition was that the photos were prima facie evidence of the CAC's and Barrie's guilt.[130] But the defense was intricate, backed by four days of expert testimony. It was assembled in anticipation of a much more formidable selection of adversaries, so that this turned out to be a lopsided contest.

The CAC compiled a list of over fifty curators who were willing to talk about the merits of Mapplethorpe's work, although Sawyer reports "in the early stages it was unclear as to who was willing to identify themselves with this photographer." CAC officials laid out the "intellectual geography" for the lawyers: "We wanted to make it difficult for anyone with a countervailing view . . . you wanted your own big guns because you assumed they [the prosecution] would have theirs." Well-heeled art professionals presented a crash course in aesthetics, art history and criticism to this relatively unsophisticated audience

of jurors. Defense witnesses were alchemists who recast images of extreme sexual acts into figure studies, and transformed the arc of the urine being directed into a man's mouth into a classical study of symmetry. This was a strategy to deflect attention away from the difficult subject matter of the photographs, onto formalist considerations such as composition. It was well-conceived, and extremely well-executed.

The defense's case was also strengthened by affidavits of support signed by the parents of both of the children whose photos were in dispute. These were important because Ohio law prohibits "any material or performance that shows a minor who is not the person's child or ward in a state of nudity." Not only did the parents verify that the photos had been taken with their permission, but they were also dismayed that religious and political leaders were now presenting them as evidence of visual child abuse. They had never viewed them as anything but innocent and natural portrayals.[131] The little boy Jesse McBride (age 19 the time of the trial) shared his parents' opinions, stating in an interview that "It's [the picture] angelic. It's art."[132] And Jesse contributed a unique display of support: he allowed himself to be re-photographed nude as an adult in the same pose, a portrait which was printed in the *Village Voice*.[133]

The defense did not go completely unchallenged, however. The prosecution called one expert witness to rebut the testimony that championed the photographs as art. That person was the aforementioned Dr Judith Reisman, whose credentials included writing songs for *Captain Kangaroo* and conducting research for the American Family Association. Reisman concentrated on the subject matter of the photos, not their formal qualities. She blasted the anonymity of the sex acts they portrayed, and dismissed the claims for them as art because they failed to express human emotion. Reisman noted that only one even showed a face, for example. Her attack on the childrens' pictures was similarly disparaging; she assessed them as dangerous public displays that legitimized child abuse.[134]

Reisman's criticisms were considered opinion, not the statements of an expert. As such they were not sufficient to sway the jury, whereas the "apple pie" approach of Barrie's attorney H.

Louis Sirkin was apparently more persuasive. Sirkin compared the Miller standard to an apple pie for the jurors. If a recipe called for three ingredients to make an apple pie, he argued, merely one or two of them would not be sufficient to get the desired result. *Mutatis mutandis*, a ruling of obscenity could occur only if all three conditions of Miller were met. After merely two and a half hours of deliberation, the jury obviously accepted the food metaphor and acquitted Barrie and the CAC on all charges. Barrie had faced up to one year in jail and a fine of $2,000, and the CAC could have been fined $10,000.

The verdict was a surprise to many people, supporters and detractors of the Mapplethorpe exhibit alike. Some commentators touted this as a resounding victory for the American justice system and for freedom of artistic expression, in articles with titles such as "Grand Juries" and "Rank-and-File Rebuff to Censorship."[135] But beyond the gloating there was also a sense that a considerable degree of luck had been involved: the prosecution had essentially failed to assemble a plausible case. As one of the jurors stated afterwards, "If the prosecution could have come up with just one credible witness – a sociologist, a psychologist, somebody, anybody – maybe we would have voted differently."[136]

But more importantly, it seems that the victory turned upon an uninformed group of people deferring to expert opinion. The barrage of professional artistic testimony convinced the jurors to put aside their beliefs and acquiesce to what the authorities had to say. It is disquieting to acknowledge that strong class elements were at work here, with elite intellectuals initiating their inexperienced fellows into the workings and understandings of the art world. In important respects the specialists finessed their way through without forthrightly addressing the disturbing nature of the content of these photos.

It was an important victory that marked not only the triumph of these particular defendants, but also underscored the legitimacy of art world participants to decide what could be consecrated as art. Yet while this battle was won, the proponents of free expression had not fully confronted all the issues which Mapplethorpe's photographs raised. They had not decisively won the war.

The impact of the case was felt well beyond the courtroom. Three days after gay rights advocates demonstrated at the outset of the trial, two gay Cincinnatians were arrested for holding hands in a parked car. A month later the charges against the men were dismissed, but gay leaders feared that this was merely the latest incident in what they identify as an ongoing moral crusade against gays in Hamilton County.[137] The Gay and Lesbian March Activists also launched a boycott against Chiquita bananas in response to the Mapplethorpe prosecution. Leaders accused the company's major shareholder of supporting public officials in their campaign against Barrie and the CAC.[138]

The CAC's legal expenses were $350,000. But assistance was forthcoming before and after the trial from many outside sources, and the debt was retired within a year.[139] By then Dennis Barrie was even hailed as a "folk hero" in a local newspaper story.[140] But what is destined to be a legacy of the prosecution is that it opened up a rift in Cincinnati's art community: most of the major arts institutions were not willing to openly support the CAC in its struggle and jeopardize their own situations. The CAC was left in relative isolation, targeted by the collusion of politicians and moral leaders, too controversial to attract many corporate sponsors and separated from its fellow arts organizations by its advocacy of "difficult" work.[141]

Jack Sawyer still vividly recalls the ugliness in the air over the Mapplethorpe exhibit in Cincinnati and the sense of siege and duress the CAC felt for months. He also remembers tuning in a rerun of *To Kill a Mockingbird* on cable television shortly before the police raided the gallery and the additional resolve the movie engendered:

> I watched the film very intently, which had affected me quite strongly when I first saw it when I was very young. And I felt (and I'm sure Dennis did, too) a strong identification with Gregory Peck on his rocking chair out front of the jailhouse, setting himself apart from the people in his community. It made me realize that my only ability to defend what I think is right is with my words and my body, and that every once in a while you may have to lay that on the line. And that is very tonic.

WHAT GOES AROUND . . .

Following the reception Cincinnati accorded the Mapplethorpe exhibit, there was every reason to believe that Boston would follow suit. After all, its reputation as a bluenose burg was earned over decades of campaigning by vigilant anti-obscenity societies and by the activities of watchful public officials. But Mapplethorpe's supporters abandoned the defense and took an impressive proactive stance in Boston. They not only talked about freedom of expression – they asserted it. Boston completed the retrospective's tour, with local groups and institutions offering significant new lessons about the social construction of acceptability.

Adversaries attempted to mobilize public sentiment against this show, but without much success. A thirteen-member coalition of groups calling itself the First Amendment Common Sense Alliance was the primary opponent. But it was unable to convince Boston Mayor Raymond Flynn, the State Attorney General or a municipal magistrate to take action. The State House of Representatives did pass some punitive legislation in a late-night session, only for it to be stalemated in the State Senate.[142] And *The Pilot*, newspaper of the Catholic archdiocese of Boston, ran an editorial, a commentary, and a full-page ad in protest, but the tabloid *Boston Herald* counseled "hands off."[143]

While the opposition was spotty and largely ineffective, supporters were shrewd. The strongest evidence of this was a number of "solidarity shows" installed at other Boston sites. The Museum of Fine Arts presented *Figuring the Body*, an exhibit on the human form; Harvard's Fogg Museum displayed another selection of Mapplethorpe's work; and the Photographic Resource Center assembled *The Emperor's New Clothes: Censorship, Sexuality and the Body Politic*, drawing on images from fashion, art and pornography. In no other city did arts institutions join in common cause like this, and nowhere else did the arts community gain the upper hand and control the terms of the debate. This remarkable closing of artistic ranks was also evident when a *Boston Globe* critic reviewed the retrospective as "A poetic and seductive 'Perfect Moment,'" and characterized

Mapplethorpe as an Apollonian, not a Dionysian.[144]

The local public television affiliate WGBH upped the ante even further. In answer to many conservative critics who sneeringly noted the photos generally had not been printed in newspapers or shown on TV because of their highly charged nature, WGBH broadcast them on the *Ten O'Clock News* the evening before the exhibit opened to the public. Nor did they shy away from presenting the most controversial images, including the man urinating into another's mouth, and the self-portrait with bullwhip. This addressed but did not lay this issue to rest: Rev. Wildmon and at least two other individuals complained to the FCC. Wildmon sent a tape of the broadcast to the FCC and claimed that it contained material that was indecent and obscene. The FCC rejected the indecency complaint on jurisdictional grounds (the broadcast was after 10 p.m.), and felt the obscenity charge was "unsustainable" applying the Miller test.[145]

Finally, a crowd of about two hundred and fifty people demonstrated in support of the exhibit on its opening day, easily overwhelming those who opposed it. This event occurred just two days after the formation of a Queer Nation chapter in Boston, a local branch of the militant direct action group that had been formed in New York City earlier in the summer.[146] The coalescence was fortuitous: Queer Nation had its first opportunity to demonstrate against homophobia in the service of defending the work and reputation of a deceased artist who had been reviled in other locales.

It was a fitting end to a tumultuous circuit through the country, and marked some distinctive changes in the gay community and in the public mood. The Mapplethorpe affair also confirmed two typical features of art controversies. Opposition breeds enormous interest, and *The Perfect Moment* consistently broke attendance records. For example, nearly eighty thousand people viewed it in Cincinnati, a figure larger than the CAC has recorded for most *years*.[147] And controversy adds cachet that also increases a work's market value. Record auction prices followed in the exhibit's wake, a boon to the coffers of the Mapplethorpe estate.

Its commitment to AIDS research and to promoting photography has been unwittingly strengthened by the actions of those who most feverishly oppose Mapplethorpe and his work. These are ironic lessons dating back at least to the time of Nero, lessons which Tacitus observed in his *History*.[148]

A FALSE ALARM

The range of reactions to the work of Rushdie and Mapplethorpe are merely two of the most distinct examples of the social construction of acceptability. The same process occurs with regularity, albeit with less dramatic and sometimes mixed results. A case in point is a mini-controversy which developed over the exhibit *Diamonds Are Forever: Artists and Writers on Baseball*. The show was organized by the New York State Museum and was presented in Chicago in July 1989 as the eighth stop on a ten-city tour. It received a benign reception at every other location, but the director of a Chicago non-profit sports organization singled out an Eric Fischl painting entitled *Boys at Bat* (1979) for criticism. Ziff Sistrunk claimed that the painting "promoted" homosexuality and child molestation. He further asserted that the exhibit underrepresented black contributions to the sport, and he challenged the depictions there were of black players.

The charges seemed absurd. Not only were black baseball players portrayed, but the work of black artists such as Howardena Pindfell and Jacob Lawrence was included. In fact, this exhibit had a better record of racial inclusion than is generally the case. The interpretation of the Fischl painting was similarly preposterous. The work pictures a nude man in a baseball cap in the foreground of a suburban backyard, hitting a baseball. A uniformed boy (8 years old? perhaps 10?) somewhat anxiously looks on, cradling a bat upright in his hand. The quote that the exhibitors chose to accompany it was by Donald Hall about fathers and sons. The painting appears congruent with many of Fischl's works, which are generally expressionistic bourgeois suburban scenes with some nudity. Although some of his work is inlaid with

traces of adolescent sexual fantasy or activity, it is an immense leap to accuse *Boys at Bat* of promoting homosexuality or child molestation. This certainly had not been the interpretation of audiences in other cities.

The ingredients necessary to spark controversy appeared to be in place: sex, race, a city with a past history of artistic turmoil, and a publicly funded and operated exhibit space, the Chicago Cultural Center. An outraged Southside resident wrote to the Commissioner of Cultural Affairs

> The penis oriented "Bat-e" by Margaret Wharton, the gob of sewage of "Rank" by Robert Rauschenberg, as well as the well publised [sic] nude baseball player, and Christ playing baseball [*Untitled*, by Steve Gianakos] ... [demonstrate that] our art is worst [sic] than the bombing by Americans of the two cities in Japan![149]

And Sistrunk shrilly announced: "This picture has nothing to do with baseball. If Mayor Richard J. Daley were alive, this exhibit would be clean. I am prepared to die for this issue."[150] But even the invocation of the late, great Mayor could not ignite the conflict: Sistrunk could hardly mobilize more than fifteen boys for a protest.

A number of factors help to explain why this effort miscarried. First, the campaign's instigator was an unknown leader of an inconsequential group. Sistrunk simply did not have the political capital, nor the financial or membership resources, to conduct a successful campaign. This was an example where certain values might have been compromised, but the sense of outrage could not be coupled with sufficient power to correct the situation. Second, there was civic fatigue. The previous conflicts at the School of the Art Institute had exhausted many segments of the public; another long and divisive battle hardly seemed worth the effort. Public weariness also probably shortcircuited significant official actions or grassroots mobilizing against Mapplethorpe in Boston. People there had the advantage of learning from the turmoil and folly at other locales. Third, there were bigger fish to fry on the national scene. This issue arose at the very moment when Congress was debating how to punish the NEA because of the sponsorship of

Serrano and Mapplethorpe. In fact, Chicago's elder statesman Representative Sidney Yates (a staunch supporter of the NEA) was in the thick of the battle. This quirky interpretation of the Fischl painting did not ring true – or loudly enough to pick up arms over.

Finally, the Cultural Center presented the Fischl painting in such a way as to minimize any potential it might have to shock. It was positioned at the most secluded end of the exhibition hall, on the back side of a partition. It could not be glimpsed from the entrance, nor seen unless a viewer purposely sought it out. And after Sistrunk voiced his concerns, staff posted a sign warning visitors that some works could possibly cause offense. These precautions appeared to be adequate for the material in question, and the exhibit continued without additional problems.

MISREADING METAPHORS

In another Chicago incident seven months earlier, an artist who was presenting male nudes did not fare so well. Joe Ziolkowski ("Joe Z.") participated in a show sponsored by the alumni association of the School of the Art Institute, which was mounted in the lobby of a Loop office building. The show was a mixed-media installation, with pieces dealing with a range of social and political issues from the 1980s, including women's rights, the environment, and US involvement in El Salvador.

Only Joe Z.'s work confronted issues of male intimacy. Two of his photos were included from the *Beyond Boundaries* series, which features nude men suspended by their heels with rope. The photos are inverted when they are hung, so that the figures seem to eerily bob up like human buoys. The artist claims that his images depict loving and caring between men, but that something is always pulling them down.[151] He seeks to explore universal questions regarding power, sexuality, and intimacy – whether the individuals be gay or straight – and does not believe that his work is primarily homoerotic. Yet, within hours of its installation, one of his images prompted complaints from people working in the building. The two men in one of

the photographs were nude, but they were pictured above the waist and were separate from one another; that did not cause any problem. In his second photo, however, two full-length nude men embraced each other, with their genitals touching.

The building's management acceded to their tenants' objections and ordered that either that photo be covered or removed, or the entire show might have to come down. The landlord claimed the right to approve any displays in the building and maintained that the site was a "fishbowl," observable to passers-by on the street as well as anyone entering the lobby. As a consequence, *Beyond Boundaries 3* was covered with paper and a sign was posted next to it, explaining that the action had been taken at the request of the management.

Joe Z. intends his work to stimulate discussion around sexual issues. In this case, however, that potential exchange was quickly truncated. To his mind the disputed image addressed a male issue, not a distinctly gay one. In fact, the only image in his portfolio that he would cite as distinctly homoerotic is one where a solitary man is bent over in what the artist describes as a totally vulnerable position. The man has gone limp, with a "go ahead, do whatever you want to me" air. Otherwise, "I don't see it [my work] as something to get off on."

But as this artist found out, there is something profoundly disquieting about seeing the male sex organ. Joe Z. does not focus on it, but views it just another body part, like a thumb or a toe. If he intended to create eroticism or pornography, he would show the penis erect. This has not been his choice, yet people have balked at both displaying and publishing his work. In this case the repressive action was uncomplicated: the site was private, and individual distaste was easily honored. It was deemed a wise business decision, backed up by a chatty news item in *Crain's Chicago Business*. The incident demonstrated the validity of the real estate maxim "location, location location" in determining if particular images will find comfortable homes in particular settings. But, as we have seen, things get much more complicated when public monies are involved.

Joe Z.'s work has obvious cultural resonance

in the age of AIDS, where intimacy has become suffused with the threat of death. And that is a theme taken up by the 1991 movie *Poison*, written and directed by Todd Haynes. *Poison* interweaves three narratives, entitled "Hero," "Horror," and "Homo." The first tells the story of a 7-year old boy who commits patricide and then mysteriously flies out the window. The second follows a doctor who accidentally drinks a sex drive potion and turns into a leper sex killer; and the third probes one man's obsession for a fellow criminal. It is a pastiche of film styles, drawing as much from investigative documentaries as from B-grade *noir* suspense movies of the 1940s and 1950s. It is also flavored with a generous dash of camp parody. Haynes cites the writings of Jean Genet as an inspiration (most clearly the source for the "Homo" segment) but there are many indications that this is fantasy: poisons were never bathed in such erotic light, nor do reform-schoolboys gambol in such lovely gardens.

It is farfetched (but conceivable) that someone could take this avant-garde movie literally. The Reverend Wildmon, basing his opinion on segments of advance reviews instead of a first-hand viewing, damned the film in successive letters to members of Congress. In the March 15, 1991 version he condemned the film for homoeroticism and explicit scenes of homosexual anal intercourse. His conclusion: *Poison* was pornographic, and should have never received a $25,000 NEA grant for post-production costs.[152] But his judgment differed from the peer panel of professionals which awarded the grant, it clashed with major movie reviewers throughout the country and contradicted the conclusion of jurors at the Sundance Film Festival who awarded it the Grand Jury Prize for best feature film.

This is another example where parable was confused with fact, and where a few elements were isolated from a work of art and required to bear the weight of the whole. All three narratives deal with outcasts, transgression and punishment. In this sense they are profoundly moral. The film is iconoclastic, and more inferential than explicit. The homosexual theme nevertheless set off an alarm for Wildmon.

The attack snapped a period of relative quiescence from attacks on the NEA, and appeared to have the potential to cause major problems for the agency and its chairman John Frohnmayer. The grant was made directly to the artist, not channelled through another institution. And the film-maker had submitted a complete script with his application so that the content was sanctioned in advance. There was evidence that Frohnmayer's conservative enemies regarded this as an opportunity to oust him, knowing that the White House and particularly Chief of Staff John Sununu had no patience for continued strife over the NEA. *Poison* provided another target in a battle which was already over two years old. In this instance the strategy was worked out in advance by Sununu and conservative leaders at a Republican Party breakfast.[153] But before this issue was settled, Sununu was himself under investigation for alleged misuse of funds by appropriating military airplanes and government and corporate vehicles for personal trips.

Frohnmayer came out forcefully for the first time in support of the agency's artistic decisions. At a press conference he prefaced his remarks with a reiteration of his own small town background and commitment to traditional American values. He then stated "I don't suppose most Americans would object to their tax dollars being used for a film [about how] violence is destructive to the family."[154]

He thereby took the most cautious route in mounting his defense. The "Hero" segment does deal with family violence: at the end we discover that the boy murdered his father to stop the man from beating his adulterous wife. But Frohnmayer ran wide around the gay and AIDS themes. While he recognized that *Poison* was explicit at points, it was not "prurient nor obscene."[155] This was another instance where a gay artist found himself under assault for depicting matters that are consequential to his community, yet only begrudgingly was extended support from mainstream individuals.

Gay-themed art has changed dramatically since the closeted, pre-Stonewall days. And as gay artists have become more frank in their work, truthfulness and sincerity have evoked a backlash from some segments of society. It is unlikely that a veiled seduction scene like the one between

Lawrence Olivier and Tony Curtis in the 1960 film *Spartacus* would raise many eyebrows today. Yet it was excised from the original, and finally reinstated when a restored version was released in 1991. For the first time in thirty years viewers could watch the Slave Antoninus attentively wash his master's back as he is questioned about his preferences. In the end, the master Crassus declares his sexual interest via a gustatory analogy: "My taste includes both snails *and* oysters."[156] And once again, we witness the resilience of cultural products.

There has been an enormous amount of social change in the intervening period. Robert Mapplethorpe's work – which freezes the post-Stonewall sense of sexual experimentation and exuberancy in time – would have been inconceivable just a few years earlier.[157] And because of the AIDS epidemic, making similar work now is somewhat improbable. It has been virtually impossible to separate gay life from the epidemic since the early 1980s, when representations of the community and its social, political, sexual, and health concerns became inexorably linked.

NOTES

1 Dannemeyer, William, *Shadow in the Land: Homosexuality in America* (San Francisco: Ignatius Press, 1989): 227.

2 *Ibid.*: 221.

3 Medved, Michael, "Popular Culture and the War against Standards," *American Family Association Journal*, April 1991: 14.

4 One of the cultural outcomes is the development of "camp" within the gay subculture. Esther Newton notes that incongruity is the subject matter of camp, when gays juxtapose otherwise discrepant elements to one another to form something fresh and unexpected. This may include mixing typically masculine and feminine attributes, or objects of high and low status, for example. She intriguingly argues that this penchant for reformulating categories and relationships springs from the ostensible incongruity of two men or two women being together in bed. Once the "natural categories" of heterosexuality and male/female are shattered, the rest of the world is likewise subject to transformation. See *Mother Camp: Female Impersonators in America* (Chicago: University of Chicago Press, 1979): esp. 104–111.

5 Letter to the editor, *Los Angeles Times*, January 12, 1991: F3. Madonna evokes the most contradictory reactions. When ABC's *Nightline* showed the video and interviewed her, the show garnered its second highest rating ever (see James Caryn, "Beneath All That Black Lace Beats the Heart of a Bimbo...," *New York Times*, December 16, 1990: H38. *Forbes* featured her on its cover with the question "America's Smartest Business Woman?" October 1, 1990, while *Outweek*'s adulatory paean trumpeted across its cover "immaculate connection: Madonna and Us" March 20, 1991. And in a particularly contrary op-ed piece, renegade Camille Paglia championed the video "Justify My Love" but also supported the MTV ban of it ("Madonna – Finally, a Real Feminist," *New York Times*, December 14, 1990: A39). Like other commanding cultural figures, Madonna attracts the fears and accolades of various constituencies.

6 Lathem, Niles and Doug Feiden, "Madman Moammar Now a Druggie Drag Queen," *New York Post*, June 17, 1986: 4, emphasis added.

7 *Gay* is an anachronism, for the word replaced *homosexual* in general use only after the political struggles that were spawned by Stonewall. A new quarrel over terminology began in 1990 with younger, more militant men and women embracing *queer* instead of *gay*, a term which they associated with white, middle-class assimilationists. The quote from Queer Nation that introduces this chapter reflects this new activist stance. I will generally use *homosexual* to describe same-sex *behavior*, and *gay* to denote a self-conscious, public presentation and *identification* of self as someone who is primarily attracted to the same sex.

8 It will quickly become apparent that my examples are almost exclusively drawn from gay men's experiences, not lesbians'. Two notes of explanation. The same forces which have blocked opportunities for artistic success for women in general also apply to lesbians. Circumstances are changing, however, and lesbians are making more of an impact. This is particularly the case in some fields like performance art. And lesbian sexuality tends not to call out as fierce a negative response as does male homoeroticism. One of the few controversial incidents directly related to lesbian representations occurred in a show at the New York State Museum in Albany, *The State of Upstate: New York Women Artists* (1989). Julie Zando withdrew a series of videos after museum officials questioned their "appropriateness" in this venue.

9 See Goffman, Erving, *Stigma: Notes on the Management of Spoiled Identity* (Englewood Cliffs, NJ: Prentice-Hall, 1963).

10 Jussim, Estelle, *Slave to Beauty: The Eccentric*

Life and Controversial Career of F. Holland Day, Photographer, Publisher, Aesthete (Boston: David R. Godine, 1981): 168. Jussim claims there is no tangible evidence to document Day's physical relationships, but there are abundant signs on which to base inferences about homosexual conduct.

11 *Ibid.*, 173.

12 The circumspection of biographers and estates in regard to renowned individuals who happen to be homosexual was apparent once again when *Letters From a Life: Selected Letters and Diaries of Benjamin Britten* (Faber and Faber Ltd., and University of California) was published in 1991. Composer Britten was discreet about his relationship with tenor Peter Pears, and extraordinary measures were taken to insure a restricted and "suitable" readership for the details of his life. For example, the price was prohibitive ($125 for the US edition), the two-volume set was shrink-wrapped in plastic within a boxed casing, and few review copies were distributed. See Lebrecht, Norman, "The Secret Life of Benjamin Britten," *Los Angeles Times*, June 20, 1991: F4; and Moor, Paul, "Britten in Love," *The Advocate*, August 13, 1991: 64–5.

13 Jussim,: 107. Later on in his career, Day's portrayal of blacks became less exotic.

14 Quoted in *ibid.*: 134.

15 Quoted in *ibid.*: 135.

16 The relative lack of mediation also characterizes performance art, discussed in the preceding chapter. Such performers are not interpreting someone else's script, they're more frequently presenting their own lives.

17 Sischy, Ingrid, "Photography: White and Black," *The New Yorker*, November 13, 1989: 130.

18 *Ibid.*: 130, 135.

19 See Haskell, Barbara, *Charles Demuth* (New York: Harry N. Abrams, 1987). The poster portraits require substantial decoding to understand the allusions.

20 Cooper, Emmmanuel, *The Sexual Perspective: Homosexuality and Art in the Last 100 Years in the West* (New York: Routledge & Kegan Paul Ltd, 1986): 119.

21 *Ibid.*: 122.

22 Artist Robert Indiana has memorialized the relationship between Hartley and von Freyburg in *The Hartley Elegies*, appropriating much of Hartley's original iconography. Indiana's work became a subject of controversy when it was shown at Bates College in Maine. Gay activists protested that the gallery slighted the relationshp between Indiana's subjects in their presentation of the work, and that they failed to acknowledge that Indiana is gay, and the possible influence of that fact on his choice and execution of his own work (see "Artist, Title, Media, ... and Sexual

Preferences," *New Art Examiner* November 1991: 48.

23 Cooper, *op. cit.*: 125–6. Cooper indicates there was reciprocated sexual interest between the men, citing an autobiographical story by Hartley as evidence. Other commentators overlook this possibility; see, e.g., Scott, Gail R., *Marsden Hartley* (New York: Abbeville Press, 1988).

24 Actor Brad Davis died of AIDS in 1991. After his death his wife released a book prospectus in which he planned to discuss his fears that he would become unemployable in Hollywood if he went public with his health condition.

25 In 1987 researchers discovered that Leonardo had performed his own gender identity sleight of hand when computer imaging revealed that the Mona Lisa was actually a self-portrait; see Schwartz, Lillian, "Leonardo's Mona Lisa," *Art & Antiques* January 1987: 50–5ff.

26 Austen, Roger, *Playing the Game: The Homosexual Novel in America* (Indianapolis: Bobbs-Merrill, 1977).

27 See, for example, Deuel, Peter, "Daley: Council Has Right To Assail Baldwin Book," *Chicago Sun-Times*, January 15, 1965: 1; and "Here Is Text of Resolution by Aldermen," *Chicago Tribune*, January 28, 1965.

28 "Moral Abdication," *Chicago Tribune*, January 30, 1965. Sec. 1: 10.

29 "Art Row In Navy Surprises Painter," *New York Times*, April 20, 1934: 24.

30 Waterman, Daniel, "Bell-Bottom Scandal," *ARTnews*, April 1990: 37.

31 See Marling, Karal Ann, *Wall-to-Wall America: A Cultural History of Post-Office Murals in the Great Depression* (Minneapolis: University of Minnesota Press, 1982): 282–9.

32 Cunningham, Al, "Courage, Canvas, And Cadmus," *The Advocate*, July 31, 1990: 65.

33 Shehadi, Philip, "Community Board Approves Christopher Park Statue," *Gay Community News*, November 1980: 1. See also Hager, Steve, "Gay Sculpture Controversy," *Horizon*, December 1980: 10, 12.

34 Segal has been no stranger to controversy. In 1973 an Israeli foundation commissioned a work from him. But *Abraham and Isaac* was rejected because it might be interpreted as critical of the Jewish state sacrificing its young to wars. Another version of the statue was offered to Kent State University in 1978 to commemorate the slaying of four students during demonstrations in 1970. It, too, was rejected.

35 Quoted in Mehren, Elizabeth, "Damage To Gay Art Shocks Sanford," *Los Angeles Times*, March 12, 1984: Part VI: 1.

36 See Davis, Phil, "Trash or Treasure?" *Isthmus*, August 22, 1986: 26; Kaufman, L. Aaron, "'Gay Liberation': Hardly Either," *OUT!*, June 1986; Waller, Thomas M., "Gay Statue Opposition

Continues," *Wisconsin State Journal*, June 27, 1986: sec. 4, p. 6; and "Sculpture kept in Orton Park," *Wisconsin State Journal*, June 11, 1987.

37 See Dehli, Joyce, "Sculpture of Gay Community Moving On," *Wisconsin State Journal*, December 22, 1990, sec. 1, p. 1.

38 Quoted in Schmeling, Sharon L., "'Gay Lib.' Statue to Stay," *Capitol Times Area News*, June 11, 1987.

39 Kramer, Hilton, "When George Segal Goes Public," *New York Times*, October 19, 1980: D36.

40 "All Dressed Up, Nowhere to Go," *New York Post*, March 17, 1988: 28.

41 As an semi-regular viewer of television talk shows undoubtedly knows, transvestism is primarily an interest of heterosexual, not homosexual, men. The photo exhibit in question was later published in book form: Allen, Mariette Pathy, *Transformations: Crossdressers And Those Who Love Them* (New York: E. P. Dutton, 1989); see it for details.

42 Jim Fouratt interview, August 6, 1990.

43 See Weinstein, Steve, "When Gay Means Loss of Revenue," *Los Angeles Times*, December 22, 1990. F1, 3. It ran without difficulty in England, however: see Kaye, Jeff, "'Banned' Lifts Lid Off Censored Fare," *Los Angeles Times* April 27, 1991: F1, 13. This is somewhat ironic because England has many repressive laws regarding freedom of expression and homosexuality, for instance, the notorious Clause 28, which forbids local government funding of activities believed to "promote homosexuality." Another ABC series, *China Beach*, ran into similar difficulties over an episode dealing with abortion, a program that also became one of the only ones not to be re-broadcast: see Rosenberg, Howard, "Advertisers Cooling Off to Hot Topics," *Los Angeles Times*, July 26, 1990: F1, 11. *thirtysomething*'s producers may have had the last laugh, however. In the last season, the pivotal character Michael resigned his high-level advertising position rather than carry out an order to fire an actor who participated in an anti-war rally and offended his firm's client/sponsor. The episode put individual conscience above success as a "company man."

44 It is notable that this occurred between two women, not two men. As Wildmon stated, "I would imagine it's not as repulsive as seeing two men" (quoted in Enrico, Dottie, "TV Politics And Strange Bedfellows," *New York Newsday*, March 4, 1991: 35. And, it was not clear whether or not these historic kissers actually regarded themselves as lesbians; one stated that she was attracted to men, but considered herself "flexible."

45 Clark, Jil, "Ohio Court Upholds Dismissal of Charges Against Gay Broadcaster," *Gay Community News*, January 22, 1983: 3.

46 The parameters of this time frame changed periodically. It always ended at 6 a.m., but began at 8 p.m., 10 p.m. or midnight in various plans.

47 All the Ginsberg quotes are from the program "Open Ears/Open Minds," broadcast on January 7, 1988 in New York. For a discussion of the Joyce controversy, see Hentoff, Nat, "Saying No to Molly Bloom," *Village Voice*, June 9, 1987: 42.

48 See Masters, Kim, "For the Artist's Father, a Painful Rejection of the Ordinary," *Washington Post*, May 3, 1990: D1, 6. This remarkably sensitive article is suffused with a sense of sorrow and a degree of insight that distinguishes it from most newspaper reporting.

49 That's the image the son of writer Shirley Jackson used to describe his mother and grandmother: "A goldfish giving birth to a porpoise"; see Oppenheimer, Judy, *Private Demons: The Life of Shirley Jackson* (New York: Fawcett Columbine, 1988): 14. Here, however, the respective species seem to be reversed.

50 Dunne, Dominick, "Robert Mapplethorpe's Proud Finale," *Vanity Fair*, February 1989: 132.

51 One critic drew the parallel between the phallic cane and the fist Mapplethorpe had pictured in an earlier image in an instance of "fisting"; he therefore saw this later imagery as unrepentant. See Brenson, Michael, "The Many Roles of Mapplethorpe, Acted Out in Ever-Shifting Images," *New York Times*, July 22, 1989: 11.

52 Miller, Robert, "From the Publisher," *Time*, April 24, 1989: 4.

53 Quoted in Hodges, Parker, "Robert Mapplethorpe, Photographer," *MANhattan Gaze*, December 10, 1979: 5. In an interview given ten years later, Mapplethorpe maintained the same position: "Whether it's a cock or a flower, I'm looking at it in the same way"; see the interview by Chua, Lawrence, "Robert Mapplethorpe," *Flash Art*, January/February 1989: 103.

54 Kuspit, Donald, "Robert Mapplethorpe; Aestheticizing the Perverse," *Artscribe International*, November/December 1988: 65.

55 Ribalta, Jorge, "Decorative Heroism: The Death of Mapplethorpe," *Lapiz*, April 1989.

56 Schjeldahl, Peter, "The Mainstreaming of Mapplethorpe: Taste and Hunger," *7 Days*, August 10, 1988.

57 Rooney, Robert, "The Unambiguous Stare of Mapplethorpe's Lens," *Australian*, February 25, 1986, and Schoofs, Mark, "Robert Mapplethorpe: Exquisite Subversions," *Windy City Times*, March 16, 1989: 28.

58 Langdon, Ann, "Fire and Ice," *The Hartford Advocate*, October 16, 1989: 16.

59 Hemphill, Essex, "The Imperfect Moment," *High Performance* (Summer 1990): 18. Hemphill drew upon the work of Isaac Julien and Kobena Mercer for these quotes.

60 *Ibid.* Dennis Barrie, director of Cincinnati's Contemporary Art Center, offered a different account of black reactions. During a First Amendment colloquium sponsored by The Playboy Foundation and The Nation Institute (New York City, October 24, 1990), Barrie reported that the Mapplethorpe exhibition drew a larger than usual number of blacks to his institution. Based on what black visitors told him, he surmised that "he [Mapplethorpe] glorified and gave great credibility to the black male – in a time when the black male was demeaned in society" (transcript, p. 49).

61 Danto, Arthur, C., "Robert Mapplethorpe," pp. 211–17 in *Encouners & Reflections Art in the Historical Present* (New York: Farrar Straus Giroux, 1990): 216.

62 Letter to the editor, *The Advocate*, January 15, 1991: 13.

63 Quoted in Dowd, Maureen, "Unruffled Helms Basks in Eye of Arts Storm of His Own Making," *New York Times*, July 28, 1989: B6.

64 Also referreed to as "Rosie," this photograph has been one of the most disputed within a notably controversial body of work. When the *New Art Examiner* wished to use it to accompany an article on the difficulties the Mapplethorpe exhibit encountered in Cincinnati, their printer from Pontiac, Illinois, balked. The magazine substituted a photo of this image being projected upon the side of the Corcoran Gallery. NAE's editors previously had been prevented by the printers from running two other photographs: a photo of Lynda Benglis which showed her wearing a dildo, and a Joe Ziolkowski image of two nude men embracing. See Miner, Michael, "A Printer's Perogative," *Chicago Reader*, November 9, 1990: 4.

65 Dowd.

66 Grenier, Richard, "A Burning Issue Lights Artistic Ire," *The Washington Times*, June 28, 1989; and Reisman, Judith, "Promoting Child Abuse as Art," *The Washington Times*, July 7, 1989: F1, 4.

67 Buchanan, Patrick J., "Why Subsidize Defamation," *New York Post*, November 22, 1989: 31.

68 See Buchanan, Patrick J., "Jesse Helms' Valiant War Against Filth In The Arts," *New York Post*, August 2, 1989; "In the New *Kulturkampf*, the First Battles Are Being Fought," *Richmond [VA] Times-Dispatch*, June 19, 1989; and "Artists Seek to Create 'Pagan' Society," *Chicago Sun-Times*, March 23, 1990.

69 Kramer, Hilton, "Mapplethorpe Show at the Whitney: A Big, Glossy, Offensive Exhibit," *The New York Observer*, August 22, 1988: 12.

70 Kramer, Hilton, "Is Art Above the Laws of Decency?", *New York Times*, July 2, 1989: H7.

71 *Ibid.*

72 The tour included Philadelphia, Chicago, Washington, DC, Hartford, CT, Berkeley, CA, Cincinnati and Boston.

73 Miner, Michael, "Mapplethorpe in Chicago: The Lucky Moment," *Chicago Reader*, August 18, 1989: sec. 1: 4.

74 See Schoofs, and the obituary in *Windy City Times*, March 16, 1989: 12.

75 Conroy, Sarah Booth, "A Scandalous Precedent," *Washington Post*, June 18, 1989: F1, 5.

76 Quoted in Whiting, Cecile, *Antifascism in American Art* (New Haven: Yale University, 1989): 55. The painting now hangs in the Museum of Modern Art, New York.

77 Clapp, Jane, *Censorship: A Chronology of Proscribed and Prescribed Art* (Metuchen, NJ: Scarecrow Press, 1972): 361.

78 As heated as the atmosphere was in Washington, there was one potential controversy that fizzled. About two weeks after the Corcoran cancelled the Mapplethorpe retrospective, the June 29 *Washington Times* reported a raid on a homosexual escort service. Officials seized files which reportedly contained the names of Reagan and Bush Administration officials among the clients, and the paper anticipated a large scandal. It never congealed, although it remained a minor story in the news because one of the people named, lobbyist Craig Spence, later committed suicide. See O'Neill, Cliff, "*Washington Times* Alleges 'Nest of Homosexuals' in White House, *Outweek*, July 17, 1989: 16–17; and Randolph, Eleanor, "The Bombshell That Didn't Explode," *Washington Post*, August 1, 1989: D1, 6.

79 Quoted in Kastor, Elizabeth, "Corcoran Cancels Photo Exhibit," *Washington Post*, June 13, 1989: C1.

80 Statement dated June 13, 1989.

81 Kastor, Elizabeth, "Gays, Artists to Protest at Corcoran," *Washington Post*, June 16, 1989: B1, 6; and Hinckle, Doug, "Gay, Arts Communities Join Forces," *Washington Blade*, June 23, 1989: 4.

82 Hinckle, Doug, "Eight-foot Penis at the Corcoran," *Washington Blade*, December 8, 1989: 1; see, also, Kastor, Elizabeth, "Corcoran Students on the March," *Washington Post*, September 21, 1989: C1, 10.

83 Yasui, Todd Allan, "The Mapplethorpe Bonanza," *Washington Post*, August 21, 1989: B7.

84 Somewhat ironically, and apparently unbeknownst to the curator who proffered the suggestion, one of the members of Group Material is married to Serrano.

85 See her letter, reprinted in *New Art Examiner*, January 1990: 7.

86 *The Washington Times*, June 23, 1989.

87 Buckley, William, F., Jr., "The Corcoran Caves In," *Washington Post*, September 22, 1989: A27.

88 Kilpatrick James, J., "The Corcoran's Wise Decision," *Washington Post*, June 19, 1989: A9.

89 Quoted in Kastor, Elizabeth, and Carla Hall, "Mapplethorpe Aftermath," *Washington Post*, June 23, 1989: F6.

90 "...And the Corcoran Mess," *Washington Post*, June 29, 1989: A24.

91 Quoted in Dowd, "Unruffled Helms."

92 In the case of the Mapplethorpe retrospective, the NEA's $30,000 of support supplemented the $180,000 raised from private sources; see Collins, Glenn, "On Helms and Grants With Poison Pills," *New York Times*, August 7, 1989: C11.

93 Swisher, Kara, "Helm's 'Indecent' Sampler," *Washington Post*, August 8, 1989: B2.

94 Quoted in Honan, William H., "Compromise Is Proposed on Helms Amendment," *New York Times*, September 28, 1989: C14.

95 Punitive action was taken against ICA in the next grant-making cycle: two of three of their requests were approved by the peer panels, but overturned by NEA's National Council. According to council member Jacob Nuesner, awarding them at that time "would be tweaking the nose of Congress." See Taylor, Kimberly, "NEA National Council Vetoes ICA Grants," *New Art Examiner*, Summer, 1990: 11.

96 From an interview conducted October 21, 1989.

97 Sign at an anti-censorship rally in Cincinnati. See the photo in the *New York Times*, April 6, 1990: A15 (the phrase intended to feign a German accent, making the implicit link with Nazism).

98 It's difficult to view Mapplethorpe as a provocateur when you examine his own statements regarding his work, for instance, a 1988 interview: "I don't care if somebody just wants to show flowers; I'll just show flowers ... Sometimes they feel they can put certain kinds of pictures in, but can't go any further ... That's all right. I've seen too many artists being so overly sensitive to how their work is represented, and it's so unattractive that I try to avoid it at all costs." See Indiana, Gary, "Robert Mapplethorpe," *Bomb* Winter 1988: 18.

99 McNally, Owen, "Art Exhibit Draws Protestors," *The Hartford Courant*, October 22, 1989: A1, 12; see, also, Merkling, Frank, "Mapplethorpe: A Perfect Moment in Hartford," *The News-Times* [Danbury, Ct], October 27, 1989: 31.

100 Wolfe, Tom, *The Painted Word*, New York: Bantam, 1976: 15.

101 See Vitz, Robert C., *The Queen and the Arts: Cultural Life in Nineteenth-Century Cincinnati* (Kent, Ohio: The Kent State University Press, 1989).

102 Quoted in Clapp, Jane, *Censorship: A Chronology*: 133.

103 See The Federal Writers Project, *Cincinnati: A Guide to the Queen City and Its Neighborhoods* (Cincinnati: The Wiesen-Hart Press, 1943): 73–8.

104 Knippenberg, Jim, "Have the Arts Gone Too Far? Or are We More Conservative?" *The Cincinnati Enquirer*, April 8, 1990: D5.

105 See Lyman, David, "Huffing and Puffing over Four Little Pigs," *New Art Examiner*, October 1988: 43–4. Similar imagery was used one hundred years earlier: when the renowned conductor Theodore Thomas was summoned to Cincinnati to head a proposed music school, *Puck* pictured him directing before an audience of pigs; see Vitz: 106–7.

106 From an interview conducted August 26, 1991. This and all subsequent unattributed quotes are from that interview.

107 Valin, Jonathan, *Day of Wrath* (New York: Congdon and Lattes, Inc., 1982): 23.

108 See transcript no. 3044, "Cleaning Up Sin City," September 28, 1990.

109 Knippenberg: D1.

110 Another Cincinnatian, baseball's Pete Rose, had recently been convicted in a bribery scandal, and Auditor Joseph L. DeCourcy was linked to unscrupulous activities. In some respects we encounter the politics of diversion once again: attempts to divert the public's attention away from official misconduct.

111 See Mannheimer, Steven, "Cincinnati Joins the Censorship Circus," *New Art Examiner*, June 1990: 33–5.

112 Wilkerson, Isabel, "Trouble Right Here in Cincinnati: Furor Over Mapplethorpe Exhibit," *New York Times*, March 29, 1990: A21.

113 Wilkerson, Isabel, "Sheriff: When a Crusade Is a Career," *New York Times*, April 14, 1990: 6.

114 Wilkerson, Isabel, "Focus Is on Judge in Trial of Museum," *New York Times*, October 2, 1990: A16.

115 Kaufman, Ben L., "Familiar Adversaries to Try CAC Case," *The Cincinnati Enquirer*, April 17, 1990: A9, 10.

116 Prendergast, Jane, "Grand Jury: Mapplethorpe Photos Obscene," *The Cincinnati Enquirer*, April 8, 1990: A1.

117 *Ibid.*

118 Sawyer reports having paranoid feelings at the height of the tensions, fearing for example that the Sheriff's office might raid his home for "obscenity" (might he have an old *Playboy* lying around?). But given the collusion between business interests and public officials in Cincinnati, this is surely one of the many

instances where paranoia has a real basis. In August 1991, a dramtic display of corporate and governmental complicity surfaced. Procter & Gamble was the subject of a *Wall Street Journal* story which reported some impending personnel and organizational changes. P & G pressured the Hamilton County prosecutor to invoke an Ohio statute which prohibits the release of confidential information (a felony). The prosecutor then subpoenaed the records of Cincinnati Bell, Inc. for *all* the calls made during a three-and-a-half-month period to the area code where the reporter lived. Officials inspected the phone records of hundreds of thousands of area residents, an act of intimidation which confirmed Cincinnati's image as a "company town." After enormous public outcry, P & G later apologized for its actions.

119 *New York Times*, April 18, 1990: A25.

120 See CAA press release April 9, 1990; Prendergast, Jane, "CAC gets National Support," *The Cincinnati Enquirer*, April 14, 1990: A8; and Geyelin, Milo, "Cincinnati Sends a Warning to Censors," *Wall Street Journal*, October 8, 1990: B1, 3.

121 Findsen, Owen, "'Perfect Moment's' Time Arrives," *The Cincinnati Enquirer*, April 6, 1990: C19.

122 Vester, John W., William J. Gerhardt and Mark Snyder, "Mapplethorpe in Cincinnati," *The Cincinnati Enquirer*, March 24, 1990: 46, and Mark Snyder on *Nightline*, April 10, 1990.

123 Williams, Henry F., "The Upward Path to Greatness, *The Cincinnati Enquirer*, April 6, 1990."

124 Christenson, Reo M., "Cincinnati as the Last Redoubt," *The Cincinnati Enquirer*, April 20, 1990.

125 *The Cincinnati Enquirer*, April 8, 1990.

126 *Three* conditions must be met to satisfy a *legal* definition of obscenity. First, "the average person, applying contemporary community standards, would find that the work, taken as a whole, appeals to the prurient interest [in sex]." Second, "the work depicts or describes, in a patently offensive way, sexual conduct specifically defined by the applicable state [or federal] law." *And* the third condition, as described in the text, emphasis added. See *Final Report of the Attorney General's Commission on Pornogoraphy* (Nashville: Rutledge Hill Press, 1986): 17–18.

127 Quoted in Kaufman, Ben L., "Mapplethorpe Issue before Court," *The Cincinnati Enquirer*, August 21, 1990: A5, 8.

128 Findsen, Owen, "Ruling that CAC is not a Museum Jolts Art World," *The Cincinnati Enquirer*, June 21, 1990.

129 See two articles by Isabel Wilkerson: "Selection of Jury Begins in Ohio-Obscenity Trial," *New York Times*, September 25, 1990: A16, and "Jury Selected in Ohio Obscenity Trial," *New York Times*, September 28, 1990: A10."

130 Jurors did not see the original photos, but "fizzy copies." The homosexual pictures were larger than the originals, and the photos of the two children were smaller. See Merkel, Jayne, "Art on Trial," *Art in America*, December 1990, 78 (12): 46. Such "distortions" can be significant to how an image is received and evaluated; see, for instance, the discussion of Serrano's *Piss Christ*.

131 Span, Paula, "For His Friends, Portraits of Children's Beauty and Innocence," *Washington Post*, May 3, 1990: D1, 12.

132 Hartigan, Patti, "The Picture Of Innocence," *Boston Globe*, August 8, 1990: 40.

133 See Carr, C., "Suffer the Children," *Village Voice*, June 5, 1990: 27.

134 See Harrison, Eric, "Gallery Photos Compared to Child Porn,"*Los Angeles Times*, 5 October, 1990: A27; and Wilkerson, Isabel, "Witness in Obscenity Trial Calls Explicit Photographs Destructive" *New York Times*, October 5, 1990: A20.

135 Quindlen, Anna, *New York Times*, October 25, 1990: A27; and Margolick, David, *New York Times*, October 6, 1990: 5.

136 Quoted in Wilkerson, Isabel, "Obscenity Jurors Were Pulled 2 Ways,"*New York Times*, October 10, 1990: A12.

137 See "I Want To Hold Your Hand," *The Advocate*, December 4, 1990: 8; and Richards, Dell, "Activism Arrests," *The Advocate*, April 4, 1991: 48–9.

138 News item, *The Advocate*, July 3, 1990: 16.

139 CAC's membership swelled during the controversy and then dipped somewhat, later on. Even so, its ranks remained significantly enlarged.

140 Kay, Joe, "Obscenity Case Makes Folk Hero of CAC Director," *The Cincinnati Enquirer*, August 25, 1991: B8. Although the report emphasized the applause that Barrie now garners, Sawyer related an incident from about the same time where someone recognized Barrie on the street and called out "scum."

141 See, for example, Cembalest, Robin, "After the Acquittal," *ARTnews*, February 1991: 31; and Lyman, David, "Post-Mapplethorpe Blues in Cincinnati, *New Art Examiner*, January 1991: 56. But Sawyer reported that some conciliatory gestures were being made a year after the trial, including some degree of cooperation from members of the business community, who were making their own art work available for loans for CAC shows."

142 See Hartigan, Patti, "Mapplethorpe Show to Open amid Controversy," *Boston Globe*,

August 1, 1990: 1, 16; Catalano, Peter, "Mapplethorpe Not Banned in Boston," *Los Angeles Times*, July 30, 1990: F1, 8; and "Mapplethorpe Complaints Denied," *Los Angeles Times*, September 6, 1990: F2. Hartigan reported that among the members of the coalition were representatives from Morality in Media, Citizens for Family First, and the Catholic League for Religious and Civil Rights.

143 Hartigan, Patti, "The Pilot Joins Mapplethorpe Fray," *Boston Globe*, July 27, 1990: 29, 36; and Catalano: F8.

144 Temin, Christine, "A Poetic and Seductive 'Perfect Moment,'" *Boston Globe*, July 31, 1990: 57, 62.

145 See letter from Roy J. Stewart to Donald E. Wildmon, April 26, 1991.

146 See French, Desiree, and Vernon Silver, "Shouting Breaks the Calm at ICA," *Boston Globe*, August 2, 1990; and Longcope, Kay, "Boston Gay Groups vow New Militancy against Hate Crimes," *Boston Globe*, August 2, 1990: 25, 31.

147 Findsen, Owen, "Controversy Brought Crowds," *The Cincinnati Enquirer*, May 26, 1990: A1; and Thomas, Scipio, "Exhibit Leaves; Debate Remains," *The Cincinnati Enquirer*, May 27, 1990: A1, 4.

148 See Jansen, Sue Curry, *Censorship: The Knot that Binds Power and Knowledge* (New York: Oxford University Press, 1991): 41–2.

149 Letter dated July 24, 1989.

150 Quoted in Dawes, K. O., "Picketing Groups Assail and Hail Nude Painting," *Chicago Sun-Times*, July 15, 1989.

151 This and all subsequent unattributed information and quotes derived from an interview conducted February 19, 1991.

152 Wildmon, *The Washington Times* and others also criticized grants to the San Francisco International Lesbian and Gay Film Festival in 1990 and 1991. At about the same time the *Poison* controversy was unfolding, however, John Frohnmayer defended the grants. See "The NEA's Porn Festival," *Richmond Times Dispatch* (editorial), June 24, 12990; "NEA gives Homosexual Film Festival $12,000 Tax Grant," *AFA Journal*, June 1991: 17; and O'Neill, Cliff, "NEA Chief Stands by Film Festival," *Outweek*, May 22, 1991: 19–20.

153 See Parachini, Allan, "Conservative Group Renews Attack on NEA," *Los Angeles Times*, March 27, 1991: F1, 5; and Wilson, Daniel, "Far Right Mounts Anti-NEA Charge," *The Advocate*, May 7, 1991: 52–3. Frohnmayer's tenure outlasted Sununu's, but conservative opponents of the NEA chief were finally able to force his resignation in February 1992, after the Presidential primary campaign heated up.

154 Quoted in Richter, Paul, "The NEA Defends Funding of Controversial Film," *Los Angeles Times*, March 30, 1991: F1. Frohnmayer went on to distill the movie's message as "violence breeds violence, lust breeds destruction, and, in our society, we reap what we sow", quoted in Gamarekian, Barbara, "Frohnmayer Defends Grant for Prize Film," *New York Times*, March 30, 1991: 9.

155 *Ibid.*

156 This is preceded by the following dialogue:

> *Olivier*: Do you eat oysters?
> *Curtis*: When I have them, master.
> O: Do you eat snails?
> C: No, master.
> O: Do you consider the eating of oysters to be moral and the eating of snails to be immoral?
> C: No, master.
> O: Of course not. It is all a matter of taste.
> C: Yes, master.
> O: And taste is not the same as appetite and therefore not a question of morals. Hmmmm?
> C: It could be so argued, master.

157 It is interesting to note that visual media did not predominate in the post-Stonewall, pre-AIDS interregnum. Literary output, however, was impressive: fiction and nonfiction, and particularly "coming out" tales, both male and female.

BARRY D. ADAM

"Anatomy of a Panic: State Voyeurism, Gender Politics, and the Cult of Americanism"

from Wilbur J. Scott and Sandra Carson Stanley (eds), *Gays and Lesbians in the Military: Issues, Concerns and Contrasts* (New York: Aldine de Gruyter, 1994): 103–18

Despite the alarm raised in many quarters of American society over the idea of gays in the military, there is no intrinsic relationship, whether positive or negative, between homosexual relationships and military activity. Yet the American state and its most avid supporters have constructed a fantastic, paranoid vision of their supposed nexus and a complex, multi-million-dollar surveillance apparatus to protect itself from its imaginary demons. A glance through the cross-cultural evidence of homosexuality and the military reveals that societies make diverse connections between the two phenomena, constructing the relationship as positive, irrelevant, or negative.

A dispassionate review of the military position justifying its persecution and purgation of the gay men and lesbians in its ranks shows that the military's claims are fanciful, bizarre, and contradictory. No sense can be made of the debate that has gripped American public discourse over the first half of 1993 by seeing the gays in the military issue as a clash of reason or evidence. The entire paroxysm of public debate around the issue can be made comprehensible only by probing into the psychoemotional underpinnings that charge its trajectory in order to reveal the tangle of gender politics and national identity that impelled it forward.

HOMOSEXUALITY AND THE MILITARY: THE EVIDENCE

What do homosexuality and the military have to do with each other? The answer is entirely dependent on specific cultural constructions of the meanings of both activities. Unlike the hegemonic American version, which has proven so durable that the Clinton administration has been able to make no more than an imperceptible reform to it, many societies around the world and throughout history have, in fact, drawn quite opposite conclusions about the connection between the two. The culturally entrenched answer to this question in American society is to posit the two as diametrically opposed. One is the subversion of the other.

The crux of the issue in the United States is the culturally embedded view that homosexuality represents a feminization of men and that this feminization entails a world of implications debilitating to military effectiveness, namely, all of the traditional traits assigned to the feminine – weakness, submission, passivity, softness, compassion, and peaceableness – all of which detract from military readiness. Seventy years ago, this same semiotic divide underpinned national debates over extending the vote to women. Opponents to women's enfranchisement were deeply convinced at the time that nations would soon be overrun by foreign invaders because the female electorate would choose surrender over violence.[1] Today the same meaning systems fuel debates over gays in the military.

The construction of a "homosexual threat to the military" is a story about the perceived potential emasculation of American masculinity. Certainly, lesbians bear the full brunt of the anti-homosexual policy, but the psychodynamic matrix of the issue revolves around a panic among men. The irony of this cultural axiom of American society is that it depends on a gender discourse with the most tenuous of foundations. An entirely opposite construction of the relationship between homosexuality and the military has occurred in many societies around the world. Homosexuality can just as easily be understood as having a masculinizing effect in males and therefore be not only compatible with but an indispensable asset in military mobilization.[2] Most of these alternative conceptions of same-sex relations fall into some variant of the apprentice or acolyte model of intermale relationship.

In the ancient model, homosexuality is a medium for the transmission of folklore contained by the masculine gender and is a second stage of parenting, which succeeds the mother-child relationship.[3] In this social arrangement, boys are considered to be in need of masculinization, typically during their adolescence, as they leave behind the maternal influence of childhood. This masculinization occurs through the formal linkage of a boy with a man in a sexual relationship, the latter usually selected through kinship obligations or personal qualities valued by the boy's family. This kind of system can be easily adapted to military demands.

Examples can be drawn from Asia, Africa, Europe, Melanesia, and the Middle East. In Japan, the samurai tradition was characterized by intense erotic and emotional relationships between professional soldiers and their acolytes, who themselves eventually became samurai through a lengthy process of care and discipline.[4] The nineteenth-century central African Azande empire (crushed by British imperialism in the late nineteenth century) included a military class with a similar tradition. Evans-Pritchard wrote of the Azande: "Many of the warriors married boys and a commander might have more than one boy wife. When a warrior married a boy, he paid spears, though only a few, to the boy's parents as he would have done had he married their daughter."[5] The ancient Greeks furnish the best-known European example. Harmodius and Aristogeiton were credited in Greek mythology as the pair of lovers who slew a tyrant, thereby ushering in the democratic foundations of Western civilization. The sacred band of Thebes was said to be the most effective fighting force of its day, having been organized so that the younger men fought on the front line while their lovers backed them up. The story of Achilles and Patroclus is familiar to virtually every schoolchild.[6]

In parts of Melanesia, the male lineage was bound together as a cohesive fighting unit through the transmission of semen from older to younger males.[7] The people of the Siwa oasis in the Libyan desert maintained a military caste from ancient times into the twentieth century that functioned as a bachelor society bonded through sexual relationships.[8]

Even in homophobic societies, homosexual people are counted among some of their well-known military leaders. General Gordon, who fell at Khartoum, and Lawrence of Arabia are noteworthy British examples. Though not officially acknowledged, the homosexuality of *Sandinista comandantes* Jaime Wheelock Roman and Dora Marfa Tellez is widely rumored throughout Nicaraguan society. Both had distinguished careers as military leaders in the overthrow of the Somoza dictatorship, which had ruled Nicaragua for two generations. Both subsequently held high office in the revolutionary government which redistributed land to the dispossessed and organized the first democratic political system in the history of the nation.

Today, in comparing the advanced capitalist nations of North America, the European Community, Australia, and Japan,[9] only the United Kingdom and the United States remain mired in premodern policies excluding lesbians and gay men from military service. As Peter Tatchell points out in reviewing the European situation:

> Membership in the armed forces is open to homosexuals in eleven countries – Austria, Belgium, Denmark, Germany, Finland, France, Netherlands, Norway, Spain, Sweden and Switzerland – providing sexual relationships take place outside of barracks during off-duty hours. In the German armed forces, however, homosexuals are barred from officer rank.[10]

For these countries (with the partial exception of Germany), homosexuality has little or no bearing on military matters. In the Netherlands, in fact, lesbian and gay soldiers have an association that is recognized by the defense ministry. These countries continue to participate in the modernizing trend of extending equal rights to all of their citizens regardless of traditionally ascribed attributes or prejudices.

A perusal of the cross-cultural evidence, then, shows that there is no intrinsic or necessary relationship between homosexuality and the military. Cultural representations of the relationship vary widely from the ancient and Melanesian models, which construct same-sex bonding as a military asset to modern conceptions, which find sexual orientation to be an irrelevant consideration in military recruitment. The United States, with the United Kingdom, remains exceptional in its continuing reproduction of homophobic ideology and its attachment to superstitions and paranoid postulations of a fictive connection.

THE SPECTACLE OF A HETEROSEXIST PANIC

One is left then casting about for an explanation of the ferocity and intransigence of the anti-gay ban in the United States. Complicating the picture is the fact that even the most extremist elements of the reactionary right have increasingly conceded the modernist critique. Even Senator Strom Thurmond (R-SC), a leading proponent of the ultraright, allowed for the "dedicated and heroic service by many gays in the ranks of our armed services" in testimony before the Armed Services Committee of the US Congress.[11] Barry Goldwater wrote a widely published essay denouncing the injustice of the ban. The military itself commissioned two inquiries into the anti-gay ban, which concluded that its continuation was irrational and unwarranted. The 1988 report of the Defense Personnel Security Research and Education Center, *Nonconforming Sexual Orientations and Military Suitability*, and the 1989 report, *Preservice Adjustment of Homosexual and Heterosexual Military Accessions*, concluded that "homosexuals show preservice suitability-related adjustment that is as good or better than the average heterosexual."[12] Vice Adm. Joseph Donnell, commander of the Navy Surface Atlantic Fleet, admitted in a leaked memo that "lesbians may be among the Navy's 'top' performers."[13]

Reviews of social science research in the area come to similar conclusions. Gary Melton's 1989 summation of the research literature observed. "The army's self-declared rationale for excluding lesbians and gay men is contradicted by scientific research," and "[t]here is no rational basis for the army's counterproductive exclusion of gay people."[14]

A moment's reflection on the official rationale provided by the US military for maintaining the ban demonstrates its absurd – even bizarre – logical contortions. Gregory Herek, who measures the official position against the social science research, shows that the claims forwarded by the official position are simply groundless.[15] Judith Stiehm, who examined their logical consistency, finds that they rapidly fall apart under scrutiny.[16] The claim that lesbian and gay soldiers pose a security risk lacks any evidence and even worse, contains a self-fulfilling element because the policy creates the very risk of exposure that is posited to be subject to blackmail.

The claim that lifting the ban lacks public acceptability and that no one would want to join the military if gay people were present must face the fact that the potential recruit who avoided the military because of the presence of gay people would then presumably seek employment in a larger society where gay people are present (and not systematically expelled from employment) and where, in at least eleven states,[17] they are protected from workplace discrimination. The claim that lesbian and gay soldiers would destroy unit cohesion and themselves be subject to violence replays the primary argumentation used in 1948 against racial integration in the military.[18] As Stiehm points out, "trust and confidence develop not from homogeneity but shared experience."[19]

And yet lesbians and gay men find themselves yet again in the gays in the military debate, the objects of a heterosexist orgy of sexual paranoia, vilification and manipulation. Gay people confronted a circus-full of generals, senators, religious ideologues, and media commentators, all proud of their ignorance of homosexuality, busily engaged in legislating the meaning and worth of their lives. Like other inferiorized peoples, gay people discover themselves as symbols manipulated in the transmission of the dominant culture. Their "objective" identity lives beyond their control; the image of self, institutionalized by cultural agents, exists alien to their own experience and self-expression. The ongoing, emergent lives of a people are confronted by a "representation" that exists only as an object for the other. The social construction of the gays in the military issue reveals the powerlessness of reason and the weakness of such fundamental tenets of modern civilization as the idea that employment should be a matter of one's competence and not of an ascribed characteristic. The public discourse demonstrates once again, in the words of Eve Sedgwick, "how obtuseness itself arms the powerful against their enemies."[20]

Can one avoid the conclusion then that the gays in the military question is not about gays in the military but about the dynamics and practices of the heterosexist mind?

GAY AND LESBIAN RESPONSES

While the dominant public discourse on the issue is about how the military constructed homosexuality in a manner that successfully fended off the modernizing probe of the Clinton administration, it is worth considering how lesbians and gay men constructed military issues in their press and in their movements. Military concerns have had their place in gay American history and have sparked debates within lesbian and gay communities concerning participation in this agency of the state.

War has had a much more multivalent effect on the development of homosexuality in the United States than the military itself imagines. Allan Bérubé notes that the vast mobilizations of entire generations of young men and women in the national efforts of World Wars I and II served as catalysts in realizing socially repressed desires.[21] At the same time as the military was developing its anti-gay repressive apparatus, military mobilization was moving millions of young people out of small towns and away from parental supervision, into large same-sex environments where personal relationships would be developed anew. Bérubé's meticulous historical account details how many gay Americans served in the military or even discovered their homosexual interests there. The military, as well, taught self-assertion to soldiers, demanding that they put their lives on the line, and then for many gay and lesbian veterans, threw them away, blocked their health and educational benefits, and issued them discharge papers that prevented them from securing employment even after the war.

When black soldiers, after defending their country against fascism, returned to the unemployment and racism of American society immediately after the two world wars, civil disturbances broke out in several major cities. Similarly, gay and lesbian soldiers were among those who took the first steps toward the organization of a modern gay and lesbian civil rights movement in the form of the postwar Veterans' Benevolent Association, which protested against the stigma of the "blue discharge." In Bérubé's words:

> The military, ironically, encouraged gay veterans to assume a stronger gay identity when it began to identify and manage so many people as homosexual persons rather than focus narrowly on the act of sodomy ... Having served their country well in a time of national emergency, gay veterans, especially those who had fought in combat, felt a heightened sense of legitimacy as citizens, entitlement as veterans, and betrayal when denied benefits ... A few began to speak of rights, injustice, discrimination, and persecution as a minority.[22]

In 1966, the small, low-profile homophile organizations that had survived through the 1950s and 1960s organized themselves into a North American Conference of Homophile Organizations, which adopted a resolution protesting the military ban.[23]

When a new wave of more militant organizing occurred in 1969 and the 1970s in the form of gay liberation and lesbian feminism, military issues took another turn. In the midst of the deeply unpopular US war in Vietnam, the movement took little interest in opposing a ban that, in the opinion of many, saved them from being conscripted to do the "dirty work" of forwarding the imperial ambitions of the US elite. This was a time when many heterosexual men feigned homosexuality in an attempt to avoid engagement in a war that they believed to be morally bankrupt. Many gay activists remained suspicious of a state system that issued medals for killing men but expelled them for loving men.

In the post-Vietnam era, the problem of the military ban resurfaced. The gay and lesbian movement faced a dilemma not unlike the black and Latino movements of the day. While many abhorred involvement in the repeated military adventures of the US state, which entailed the suppression of nonwhite peoples overseas, many others joined because of the attractive opportunities offered by the military for educational and social mobility – or because of their belief in the "patriotic" undertakings of the military.

In the more peaceable 1980s when many of the imperial exploits of the US state were subcontracted to a variety of "contras" around the world, a series of lawsuits began to pick away at the military ban. With well over a thousand military people expelled every year for homosexuality over a fifty-year time span, a number of military men and women have been willing to take on the lengthy and expensive proceedings of challenging military practices of withholding diplomas from graduates of the naval academy, refusing re-enlistment to soldiers with distinguished service records, conducting witch-hunts of navy women fingered through rumors and personal vendettas, and denying pension and other benefits to those who had completed tours of duty.

Ultimately gay and lesbian organizations could scarcely ignore institutionalized state predation and terror directed against gay and lesbian people. Could anything be won from the state while it so actively engaged in the reproduction of homophobia within itself?

THE SEX OF THE US STATE

The "problem" of gays in the military, then, has very little to do with the lives and experiences of lesbians and gay men. It is, rather, a projection of a series of fears and anxieties characteristic of the ideologies of dominant classes in general, and more particularly, of gendered, nativist, and heterosexist discourses circulated and reproduced by certain constituencies in American society. State and military homophobia partakes of a general ideology of domination, which assigns similar traits to inferiorized peoples whether they are Jews, women, blacks, or the poor. The gaze of the powerful contains within it a fantasy image of the powerless. They are repeatedly found to be subhuman, impulsive, and instinctual, hypersexual, traitors and conspirators, and over-visible.

The "treason" charge is visible in the security risk claim forwarded by the official justification for the ban on gay people.[24] It surfaced again when the Navy convinced itself, in the absence of any supporting evidence, that a 1987 explosion that occurred in the gun turret of the battleship USS *Iowa* "must have been" the result of a "lover's quarrel" between two sailors.[25] More telling perhaps, is the barely concealed sexual paranoia of the "intimate quarters" claim of the official story.

Sexual paranoia and state voyeurism

The American public has been treated to a range of television clips and magazine stories picturing US senators gazing upon the cramped living quarters of sailors and soldiers and worrying about their "sleeping and showering arrangements." In an article by Charles Moskos, reputedly one of the architects of the so-called "don't ask, don't tell" policy adopted by the state, the punchline narratologically positioned to deliver the knockout blow to convince everyone of the need to ban gay people from the military reads: "Just as most men and women dislike being stripped of all privacy before the opposite sex, so most heterosexual men and women dislike being exposed to homosexuals of their own sex."[26] In testimony before the congressional Armed Services Committee, Indiana Senator Daniel Coats' (R-Ind.) primary concern was what washrooms gay men would use if the ban were lifted.[27]

Gay men began to understand that the army, supposedly unafraid of a host of evil empires from communism to Saddam Hussein, was terrified that gay men might catch a glimpse of their penes! Even though gay men have grown up with, showered with, and – yes – seen the penes of many men throughout their lives in schools, gyms, dormitories, and washrooms, it appears that in the military their gaze is so powerful as to virtually paralyze the phallocratic military machine. So serious is this threat that the military has constructed a massive voyeuristic system to spy upon the sexuality of gay men and lesbians by employing investigators and inquisitors to break into their sleeping quarters at 2 a.m. in the hopes of catching them *in flagrante delicto*, to read their mail and eavesdrop upon their conversations, and to squeeze out stories of sexual acts and contacts from its unsuspecting victims. Here we find an elaborate and expansive state machinery of surveillance organized by heterosexual men in order to gaze upon gay men, their bodies and, most prized of all, their erotic activity, all because gay men might happen to see their penes. The military has invented a real system of sexed desire in order to contain the imagined desires of gay men.[28]

None of this is unprecedented. It parallels racist phantasms about black sexuality. As the move to integrate public transit got under way with Martin Luther King, Jr, a leading Alabama politician charged that the main goal of the NAACP was "to open the bedroom doors of our white women to the Negro Man."[29] While the black civil rights movement worked to secure job rights and equitable treatment, the white opposition agitated itself with anxieties of black sexual predation and miscegenation. And while the gay and lesbian movement seeks fair employment practices in the military, the military is seized by anxieties of gay soldiers sleeping in the next bunk and lesbian sailors watching other women in the showers.

Lesbians and gay men have never been quite sure whether to laugh or cry in the face of heterosexist fantasies that such institutions as the military take so seriously as to inflict them upon gay people themselves. The paranoiac paradoxes of heterosexist phantasms create fertile ground for camp humor. This missive appeared in the gay press in the midst of the military debate:

Why Straight Men Should Not Be in the Military
1 Straight men are constantly flaunting their heterosexuality, and make gay men uncomfortable.
2 Because of fear of being branded gay, straight men refrain from forming truly close relationships with other men. This interferes with the bonding and loyalty essential to military teamwork.
3 Straight men are not used to seeing other men naked, so they are not psychologically equipped to shower with other men.
4 Straight men are militant about converting others to their lifestyles, which includes unwanted pregnancies, disease, and cheap cologne.
5 Straight men never get harassed, so they don't have well-developed defense techniques.[30]

Gender politics

At the heart of the sense of terror among the military in the face of homosexuality is a semiotic chain, which binds aggression, masculinity, and self-esteem into a tightly wound mechanism designed to motivate and discipline the male soldier. This mechanism is a well-honed extreme of a larger social obligation, which threatens men with the loss of male prerogatives should they show signs of or sympathy with things "feminine." In basic training, homophobic and misogynist threats serve as a primary tool of combat preparation. Recruits are assailed with taunts of "little girl" or "faggot" for every sign of failure or weakness in order to forge an identification of violence with basic esteem.

R. Wayne Eisenhart argues that basic training works by fusing military authority and peer dynamics among recruits into a pressure cooker intended to shape every recruit in the image of aggressive masculinity.[31] Every recruit is threatened with psychological annihilation and physical jeopardy; his very being depends on his ability to show violence. The "alternative" is failure and expulsion as a "faggot" or a "girl." The fusion of military effectiveness with masculinity and concomitant demonization of femininity and homosexuality has become so fundamental a part of the military psyche that the prospect of gays in the military stimulates a psychological panic rooted in fears of loss of the self.

The integration of women into the military

has suffered from the same dynamic, proceeding at a snail's pace and resisted by military authorities every step of the way. Once in, women are at an even greater risk of being expelled from the military on the grounds of homosexuality than are men.[32] Lesbianism carries its own set of associated meanings for the male regime ruling the military. Women who show independence, resistance to sexual harassment, or the "masculine" qualities so valued by the military are particularly vulnerable to the charge of lesbianism. Unlike the case of the gay male who is constructed as the nightmare simulacrum of the failed and emasculated soldier, women are caught in the acute contradiction that they are trained in the hypermasculinist ideology of the military as soldiers, at the same time as the same ideology demands their subordination to be seen as "proper" women at all. Not surprisingly the male military has no trouble catching all kinds of putative "lesbians" in its double binds.

The identification of the military task as fundamentally masculine, the manufacture of an anti-sexual male world based on the denigration of women, and the reliance on homophobia as a disciplinary tool all conspire to give the gays in the military issue an emotional charge that surpasses the *prima facie* merits of the issue.

The cult of Americanism

The homophobic psychodynamic is further interlocked with national ideologies. Superpower states such as the United States are clearly gendered as male.[33] National identity and pride are caught up with masculinist ideologies of strength and belligerence. During periods when national populations experience a sense of threat, during wartime or self-doubt following military decline or defeat, conservative forces cast about for "fifth columns," traitors, or sites of moral weakness in an attempt to defend the overweening national ego of the superpower state. There are numerous historical examples where the British, German, and United States governments have launched campaigns of persecution against gay men and lesbians, along with

series of other scapegoats, during times of national crisis or uncertainty.[34] As L. J. Moran contends, in reference to the British state:

> The male body becomes a device through which an idea of the nation is realised ... Thus manliness/nation is represented as order, strength, rationality, the upper part of the body, stiffness, harmony, proportion, stability, unchanging values, timelessness ... It is within the terms of the iconic repertoire set up in the idea of the Mannerstaat, that the homosexual is produced through a particular chain of associations: the emotional, effeminate, weak, subversive, conspiratorial, rebellious, revolutionary, corrosive, dark, dangerous, sensuous, irrational, unstable, and corrupt.[35]

Still, one must ask why the gays in the military question has become so major an issue in American society when it has occasioned only minor comment in other advanced industrial societies. Apart from its commonalities with other imperial nations past and present, American national identity has its exceptional characteristics as well. Despite the widespread acceptance of lesbian and gay recruits into the militaries of its allies (as discussed above), the public debate in the United States has shown no interest in the examples of these nations. Only the Israeli military attracts the attention of American commentators. Like the US military, the Israeli military has been actively and repeatedly belligerent throughout the post-World-War-II period. The lengthy United Nations peacekeeping history of, for example, the Canadian military seem to hold little interest to the primary imperial army of the modern world system.

Unlike those of its allies, the military maintains a particularly central role in the American national imagination as the symbol of US preeminence. Public discourse in the United States rarely questions the right or the consequences of the exertion of US military power around the world.[36] The US military has a special place as a medium through which the United States constructs itself in opposition to a long series of special "enemies." Public opinion polls show a surge of popular support for every act of military aggression such that presidents have learned to dole them out periodically in order to bolster their public profile, whether the target is

Libya, Grenada, Panama or continuing episodic attacks up in Iraq.

Finally, the issue indexes a much deeper divide in American society and must contend with powerful New Right constituencies who identify gay and lesbian rights with the effects of modernization. The United States has a particularly well-established coalition of right-wing constituencies that are able and willing to carry out symbolic crusades against a range of socio-historical symbols associated with securalization, family change, and popular enfranchisement.[37]

Unlike many other countries, then, that now treat military recruitment as "another job," the US military plays a more central role in the nation's self-image and self-esteem, thus raising the stakes for the issue of gays in the military.

THE CLOSET RULE

The denouement of the public debate on gays in the military has been the imposition of a closet rule that supposedly takes away the active persecution and surveillance of homosexual service people but nevertheless removes none of the underlying policy that makes that persecution possible in the first place. The policy mandates the dismissal of anyone who "engages in homosexual conduct," which includes merely saying, or having someone say a person said, that she or he "is homosexual."[38] The "don't ask, don't tell" rule reimposes a primary tool of homophobic assault. As Sedgwick remarks in surveying numerous previous examples of the state practice of the closet rule, "the space for simply existing as a gay person ... is in fact bayonetted through and through, from both sides, by the vectors of a disclosure at once compulsory and forbidden." Lesbians and gay men become obliged to transverse an unknowable minefield, "an excruciating system of double binds, systematically oppressing gay people, identities, and acts by undermining through contradictory constraints on discourse the grounds of their very being."[39]

The US state has adopted the homophobic doctrine propounded by the Vatican in demanding that the sexual and emotional lives of homosexual people be confined to the interior of their minds. The military/church retains control of defining and interpreting the sign system by which "homosexuality" is to be read, while gay people get to be the mice in the cat-and-mouse game of concealment and discovery.

CONCLUSION

The gays in the military issue has been an occasion for the gay and lesbian movement to attempt to disrupt the semiotic chains that continue to bind homosexually interested people. The approach of movement activists has been to attempt to display the masculine soldiers, the patriotic women, and the reasonable and competent people among its ranks. The 1993 March on Washington featured a good deal of flag-waving, the application of basic American values and constitutional rights to citizens who want to love and live with the persons of their choice, and an attack on the popular prejudice that labels gay men and lesbians as the Other, by advancing the truism that gay people are among everyone's family, friends, and neighbors. It is a strategy that is necessary and unavoidable in derailing the ideological ruts and prejudicial precepts that have continued to give warrant to the homophobic regime of violence and exclusion that has assailed lesbians and gay men throughout American history.

On the other hand, the entire gays in the military debate has been framed in a characteristically American way as a question of the rights of individual citizens to be accorded equal opportunity by the US state. What has yet to be considered is a question left over from the days of gay liberation that has become muted in a more conservative era. That question is the relationship of gay men and lesbians as a collectivity to the US state and its foreign policy.

Despite its size and relatively well-developed resources when compared with movements in other countries, the gay and lesbian movement in the United States has been peculiarly insular and myopic in relation to the plight of lesbian and gay men around the world. Despite the recognition of homosexual prisoners of conscience by Amnesty International and the work of the International Lesbian and Gay Association[40] in attempting to rally movement organizations against state and terrorist campaigns of assassination and imprisonment against homosexual people in many countries around the world, US gay and lesbian groups have shown only limited interest in the relationship of US foreign policy to the dilemmas of gay people abroad. The struggle to integrate the US military may indeed one day win a success – but what will be the nature of the ultimate gain?

The struggle to integrate black and Latino people into the US military has resulted in such high-ranking black military officials as Gen. Colin Powell acting as the efficient tool of the Reagan administration in carrying out its policy of torpedoing the Central America peace process in the 1980s. Fortunately, his mission to Costa Rica failed to destroy that peace process and the Costa Rican president went on to win the Nobel peace prize for his work. All the same, throughout the 1980s, the US government carried out a campaign of low-intensity warfare, direct sabotage, and a propaganda barrage against the revolutionary Nicaraguan government eventually succeeding in installing a counter-revolutionary government more to its liking.[41]

While the revolutionary government had introduced anti-sexist education and a new opening for the rights of women and gay people, the succeeding reactionary government of Violeta Chamorro brought in a sweeping criminalization of homosexuality and restoration of Roman Catholic precepts on the status of women. The outstanding question raised by the gays in the military is: will the integration of lesbians and gay men into the US military result in actions that are in the interests of homosexual people outside the United States?

Some four hundred gay men and lesbians "disappeared" during the "dirty war" perpetrated by the Argentine military dictatorship in the 1970s and 1980s with the active support and training of the Pentagon.[42] In both of these examples, and in hundreds of others, lesbians and gay men have made up only a small part of a much larger assault upon the basic living conditions and civil rights of the dispossessed in other countries, such that Edward Herman concludes:

[US foreign policy is] grounded in an ideology that rationalizes the collective interest of the military establishment, the local business and landed elite [in Third World countries], and the multinational corporation – the joint venture partners who require terror to preserve and enlarge their privileges and the already gross levels of inequality prevalent in the Third World.[43]

The gay and lesbian movement, then, finds itself caught in a much wider geopolitical dynamic, which it can scarcely pretend to ignore: While solving one egregious case of heterosexist oppression, it may very well contribute to the reinforcement of a wider regime of repression against gay and non-gay people around the world.

The gays in the military debate then has revealed a larger political dynamic involving state voyeurism, gender politics, and the cult of Americanism. Those who argue the merits of the issue on its face value have been swept aside by larger psychosocial and historical forces reliant on ancient prejudices, conflicting political agendas and entrenched symbol systems. The further development of the issue will depend on the further playing out of this larger historical drama.

NOTES

1 Ramsay Cook and Wendy Mitchinson (eds), *The Proper Sphere* (Toronto: Oxford University Press, 1976).
2 This, of course, raises the question of why the military and masculinity are so closely connected in all of these societies. Female militarism has indeed been a rarity. Apart from the occasional warlike female head of state or leader such as Joan of Arc, it is located most often in the mythology of the Amazons and of the ancient Celtic queen Boadicea.
3 Barry D. Adam, "Age, Structure, and Sexuality," *Journal of Homosexuality* II (1985, 3/4): 22.
4 Saikaku Ihara, *Comrade Loves of the Samurai* (Rutland, VT: Charles E. Tuttle, 1972); *The Great Mirror of Male Love* (Palo Alto, CA: Stanford University Press, 1990).
5 E. E. Evans-Pritchard, *The Azande* (Oxford: Clarendon, 1971): 199.
6 J. Ungaretti, "Pederasty, Heroism, and the Family in Classical Greece," *Journal of Homosexuality* 3 (1978): 291–300; John Boswell, "Battleworn," *New Republic*, May 10, 1993: 15, 17–18.

7 Gilbert Herdt (ed.), *Ritualized Homosexuality in Melanesia* (Berkeley: Univeristy of California Press, 1984).

8 Barry D. Adam, "Siwa Oasis," in *Encyclopedia of Homosexuality*, vol. 2, ed. Wayne Dynes (New York: Garland, 1990): 1198.

9 Stanley Harris, "Military Policies Regarding Homosexual Behavior," *Journal of Homosexuality* 21 (1991, 4): 71.

10 Peter Tatchell, *Europe in the Pink* (London: GMP, 1992): 81–2.

11 Carroll Doherty, "Heated Issue Is Off to Cool Start as Hearings on Gay Ban Begin," *Congressional Quarterly Weekly Report* 51 (1993, 14): 853.

12 Thomas Stoddard, "Lesbian and Gay Rights Litigation before a Hostile Federal Judiciary," *Harvard Civil Rights – Civil Liberties Law Review* 27 (1992, 2): 563.

13 Judith Stiehm, "Managing the Military's Homosexual Exclusion Policy," *University of Miami Law Review* 46 (1992, 3): 694.

14 Gary Melton, "Psychology and Law of Gay Rights," *American Psychologist* 44 (1989): 933–40.

15 Gregory Herek, "Sexual Orientation and Military Service," *American Psychologist* (May 1993): 538–49.

16 Stiehm, "Managing the Military's Policy."

17 Wisconsin, Massachusetts, Connecticut, New Jersey, Hawaii, California, Maine, Minnesota, New Hampshire, Rhode Island, and Vermont.

18 Gary Bass, "Their Words," *New Republic*, February 22, 1993: 15.

19 Stiehm, "Managing the Military's Policy," 693.

20 Eve Sedgwick, *Epistemology of the Closet* (Berkeley: University of California Press, 1990): 7.

21 Allan Bérubé, *Coming Out Under Fire: The History of Gay Men and Women in World War Two* (New York: Free Press, 1990).

22 *Ibid.*: 249.

23 Stuart Timmons, *The Trouble with Harry Hay* (Boston: Allyson, 1990): 221.

24 On the manufacture of "gay treason" by the British state, see Simon Shepherd, "Gay Sex Spy Orgy," in *Coming On Strong*, eds Simon Shepherd and Mick Wallis (London: Unwin Hyman, 1989): 213–30.

25 Randy Shilts, *Conduct Unbecoming: Lesbians and Gays in the US Military – Vietnam to the Persian Gulf* (New York: St Martin's, 1993).

26 Charles Moskos "From Citizens' Army to Social Laboratory," *Wilson Quarterly* 17 (1993: 1): 94.

27 Doherty, "Heated Issue," 853.

28 See Guy Hocquenghem, *Homosexual Desire* (London: Allison & Busby, 1978) for a discussion of state territorializations of desire.

29 Barry D. Adam, *The Survival of Domination* (New York: Elsevier/Greenwood, 1978): 45.

30 Carol Magary, "Why Straight Men Should Not Be in the Military," *Cruise Magazine* (Detroit) 15 (1993, 25): 19.

31 R. Wayne Eisenhart, "You Can't Hack It Little Girl," *Journal of Social Issues* 31 (1975, 4): 13–23.

32 Judith Stiehm, *Arms and the Enlisted Woman* (Philadelphia: Temple University Press, 1989): 129.

33 See Susan Jeffords, *The Remasculinization of America* (Bloomington: Indiana University Press, 1989). This book uses a critical strategy, which is unfortunately common in psychoanalytic and feminist analyses where "authoritarian regimes or homophobic masculinist culture [is] damned on the grounds of being *even more homosexual* than gay male culture" (Sedgwick, *Epistemology of the Closet*, 154). This analytic tactic confuses homosexuality with the repression of homosexuality. See Adam, *Survival of Domination*.

34 Barry D. Adam, *The Rise of a Gay and Lesbian Movement* (Boston: Twayne, 1987): 57–8.

35 L. J. Moran, "The Uses of Homosexuality," *International Journal of the Sociology of Law* 19 (1991): 160–1.

36 Barry D. Adam, "The Imperal Gaze," *Research in Communication* 5: 113–37; Edward Herman and Noam Chomsky, *Manufacturing Consent* (New York: Pantheon, 1988).

37 This thesis is developed in Adam, *Rise of a Movement*: ch. 6.

38 "Text of Pentagon's New Policy Guidelines on Homosexuals in the Military," *New York Times* 142 (July 10, 1993).

39 Sedgwick, *Epistemology*: 70.

40 The International Lesbian and Gay Association Information Secretariat is located at 81 rue Marche au Charbon, B-1000 Brussels 1, Belgium. There is a San Francisco-based ILGA affiliate in the International Gay and Lesbian Human Rights Commission, 520 Castro Street, San Francisco, 94114.

41 Peter Kornbluh, "The US Role in the Counterrevolution," in *Revolution and Counterrevolution in Nicaragua*, ed. Thomas Walker (Boulder, Colo.: Westview, 1991), 323–49; Barry D. Adam, "Nicaragua, the Peace Process, and Television News," *Canadian Journal of Communication* 16 (1991, 1): 19–39; Barry D. Adam, "Television News Constructs the 1990 Nicaragua Election," *Critical Sociology* 17 (1990: 1): 99–109.

42 Carlos Jauregui, *La homosexualidad en la Argentina* (Buenos Aires: Tarso, 1987): 171; Noam Chomsky and Edward Herman, *The Washington Connection and Third World Fascism* (Boston: South End, 1979): 27, 35, 45, 266–71.

43 Edward Herman, *The Real Terror Network* (Montreal: Black Rose, 1982): 84–5.

*L*ooking Ahead – Challenges for Future Research

PART FOUR

INTRODUCTION

Each of the introductions to the sections of the reader and the *Afterword* by Ken Plummer point to significant gaps in the research on lesbian and gay lives and on the institution of heterosexuality. Topics for further research are offered which highlight the comparative underdevelopment of lesbian/gay studies in sociology, even in areas that have had several decades of attention. In this section we look ahead to three very important trends that speak not only to some of the already identified gaps but point the way to the future.

The future in lesbian and gay studies is multidisciplinary and decidedly queer. Part 4, *Looking Ahead*, includes writings by sociologists and also literary critics, political scientists, historians, a poet, and a creative writer. Prominent in this newer work are three major concerns. The first is presented in the section *Globalizing Gay and Lesbian Studies*, and includes writings which illustrate the necessity of internationalizing lesbian and gay studies through investigations that challenge the potential narrowness of work which focuses primarily, if not exclusively, on life in the United States.

The existence of a globally linked South Asian lesbian and gay identity is described in the first piece in an essay by Nayan Shah. Forged, at least in part, out of the experiences of rejection or invisibility of South Asians in Canada, Britain, and North America, a network was built through collective cultural projects, like newsletters and journals, whose aims were to articulate identity and assert a newly defined community.

In "Lesbian and Gay Rights in Europe," Evert van der Veen, Aart Hendriks, and Astrid Mattijssen produce an analysis of the components of various international human rights treaties that could be, or have been, utilized by lesbians and gay men to secure rights. With a focus on Europe, they then evaluate the efforts undertaken by the various and varied social movements there to reform laws dealing with issues such as the right to a family life and freedom of expression. Finally, Dennis Altman raises questions in an excerpt from his book about the parallels and differences among countries throughout the world in their responses to AIDS through community-based organizations. He is attentive to the similarities in response among English-speaking countries where a culture of voluntarism and well-organized gay and lesbian communities prevailed. All of these selections extend our understanding of the constraining and facilitating factors in the mobilization of lesbian and gay communities.

For nearly two decades, women of color have written against the assumption of a unitary subject – women – either explicit or implied in feminist theory and feminist politics. To speak of "woman," they argued, was to privilege white, middle-class women; to privilege gender oppression over all others, was to systematically ignore their daily lived experience in which race, gender, class and sexual oppression intersect. Many of these women were lesbians who also addressed this critique to the post-Stonewall gay liberation movement with its tendency to privilege white, gay men.

In the second section, *Doing Race, Class and Gender*, we offer three essays that build on these initial insights and highlight important omissions or distortions in the work of more contemporary scholars and activists. For example, the first selection is by the black feminist group from Boston, called the Combahee River Collective. Their much reprinted and cited statement discusses the interlocking systems of racial, gender, class, and sexual oppression and demonstrates its applicability in feminist politics. Gloria Anzaldua is a Chicana lesbian who has been exceedingly influential in articulating the position of lesbians of color in Chicano communities and in feminist and gay movements. In "Bridge, Drawbridge, Sandbar or Island," she confronts the difficulties of cross-race interactions and delineates the political and social relationships possible between white lesbians and gay men and people of color in broad-based coalition work.

Tomás Almaguer, relying on the anthropological research on homosexuality and the sex/gender systems of Latin America and Mexico, complicates any simple notion of the "gay man" in his sketch of the US Chicano male and their forms of sexual identity and sexual practice. With so little written by or about Chicano gay men, Almaguer turns to the writings of Cherrie Moraga, a Chicana lesbian writer, to fill in a portrait of the complex social world of Chicanos and Chicanas as they deal with class disadvantage, racism, and homophobia in the multiple communities in which they are participants.

These scholars alert us to the need for race-conscious, sociologically grounded readings of important community issues and political events, such as the problems of child custody or debates about gays in the military. Each demonstrates the importance of not trivializing the politics of race in the movement or the country and of not perpetuating the notion that whiteness is a defining characteristic of homosexuality.

The last section, *Queering the Sociological*, presents four pieces which touch on the challenges posed by queer theory, the links between queer theory and queer politics, and the ways it can be used by sociologists and historians. (For a discussion of the relationship of the sociology of sexuality to queer theory, see the July 1994 issue of the journal *Sociological Theory*, edited by Steven Seidman.) Two articles focus on dynamics and change within lesbian and gay movements. Arlene Stein provides an accounting of the processes through which the connection between lesbianism and feminism became solidified in the 1970s and later became decentered. In providing this analysis, she highlights the complications of boundary-making to socially constructed collective identities and offers some suggestions about the meaning of this transformation for identity-based movements.

Joshua Gamson's work complements Stein's. Working from an empirical analysis of editorials and letters to the editor in a San Francisco gay newspaper concerned with the name of the Freedom Day Parade ("The Year of the Queer"), and issues of bisexuality and transsexuality, Gamson begins to demonstrate how in everyday life queer theory and politics problematize collective identity, thus forcing a consideration of the political desirability of clearly delineated sexual identities.

Two other pieces, by Lisa Duggan and Janice Irvine, look directly at the rhetoric and politics involved in confrontations with organized political opposition. Lisa Duggan's essay has important political implications for the next decade of political battles with Christian coalitions and scared liberals. She attempts to marshall the critical insights of queer theory to develop a new political language and strategy that circumvents some of the limiting assumptions of the rhetoric of gay rights and militant gay nationalism. Focusing on the ways in which the state supports heteronormativity, Duggan turns the opposition argument against them and argues for a public policy that rejects "special rights" for heterosexuals or promotes and enforces heterosexual relations.

Janice Irvine uses the debates surrounding the adoption of the Rainbow curriculum in the New York City public schools to raise questions about the relationship of identity, culture, and sexuality. Central to her discussion is the problem of dealing with an opposition that claims lesbians and gay men are not a cultural group but rather sexual deviants and that pits racial cultures against sexual cultures. Irvine urges the adoption of the intellectual insights of critical race theorists by queer theorists and activists in efforts to counter these arguments.

The articles in Part 4 are here to challenge sociologists to develop exciting and diverse ways to push lesbian and gay studies in theoretically and empirically innovative directions.

NAYAN SHAH

"Sexuality, Identity, and the Uses of History"

from Rakesh Ratti (ed.), *A Lotus of Another Color: An Unfolding of the South Asian Gay and Lesbian Experience* (Boston: Alyson, 1993): 113–32

tri-kon *n.* (*tri* as in *trim*, *kon* as in *cone*) Sanskrit for triangle. Pink triangles were first used in Nazi concentration camps to identify gay prisoners. Today the sign is embraced by gay men and women not only as a reminder of injustices of the past, but also as a symbol of gay pride.

(Savir and Arvind "Our First Time" *Trikon*)[1]

Words invent the world.

(Suniti Namjoshi and
Gillian Hanscombe, *Flesh and Paper*)[2]

In 1986 Savir and Arvind invented the word *trikon* to break silence and to create a sense of identity for themselves. The lead story for the first issue of the *Trikon*[3] newsletter opened with a dictionary-style definition of the new name, a definition which attempted to translate the symbols of North American and European gay politics into a South Asian language. This definition invokes a particular history of oppression and the transformation of that history into a symbol of gay political assertion.

Trikon was one of the first of a half dozen South Asian lesbian and gay newsletters and support groups that emerged after the mid 1980s in North America, Britain, and India. *Anamika* (US) started a year before *Trikon* (US); *Khush Khayal* (Canada), *Shakti Khabar* (UK), *Freedom* (India), *Shamakami* (US) and *Bombay Dost* (India) followed fast on its heels. These newsletters mix politics and desire. They have served as forums for articulating identities, shaping community, and sharing the cultural products of South Asian lesbians and gay men. Following the first issue of *Trikon*, they have presumed the existence of an audience which shares a distinctive yet global identity, a sexual identity which binds the concerns and needs of gay men in Patna with those in Pittsburgh, with

lesbians in London and Lahore. The desire for community has led to the creation of a global South Asian queer identity, an identity that has fought silence and invisibility to emerge.

Silenced in both South Asian patriarchal societies and the white queer communities in North America and Europe, South Asian gays and lesbians have had to invent themselves, often with new words and names of identification. They have appropriated the Hindi and Urdu word *khush*, which means "happy"; some have reconfigured it to mean "gay," while others define it as "ecstatic pleasure." In 1985, a lesbian collective in the United States used the Sanskrit word *anamika*, meaning "nameless," to address the lack of names in South Asian languages for relationships between two women. The *Anamika* newsletter folded in 1987. By the time a new lesbian collective formed in 1990, the editors had created a name for their newsletter which affirmed their relationships – *Shamakami*, which in Bengali means "desiring one's equal." The appropriation of language has been integral to the invention of identity for South Asian men and women who feel marginalized in dominant South Asian societies. They have used language to name themselves and also to address heterosexist oppression.

Many of the essays, stories, poems, and letters that have appeared in these newsletters and other publications have engaged in this politics of assertion. Many self-identified South Asian lesbians and gay men have struggled for representation in both dominant South Asian worlds and dominant white queer worlds. In this struggle they have enlisted history – personal, archaeological, and social – to attain visibility and voice. The uses of history have complicated assumptions about the construction of identities and about the project of reclaiming history.

The formation of South Asian queer communities has inspired me to claim an identity, that of a South Asian gay man living in the United States. The narratives, testimonies, and histories produced by self-identified South Asian lesbians and gay men often resonate with my own struggle for identity and desire for community. These powerful resonances have also generated sharp doubts and raised questions about the nature of identity and the creation of culture and community.

MARKING SEXUAL DIFFERENCES

Identity is about belonging. At its most basic level identity marks what we have in common with some people and what differentiates us from others. Jeffrey Weeks reminds us that

> each of us lives with a variety of potentially contradictory identities ... Behind the quest for identity are different and often conflicting values. By saying who we are, we are also striving to express what we are, what we believe, and what we desire. The problem is that these beliefs, needs, and desires are often patently in conflict, not only between different communities but within individuals themselves.[4]

The cultural production of South Asian lesbians and gay men charts these conflicting identities.

The South Asian queers, like other gays and lesbians in North America and Europe, have used coming out narratives to make sense of their feelings of difference from mainstream society. These narratives follow two general patterns which seek to explain the process of developing a queer identity. The first explains sexual orientation as originating in adolescence with an awareness of attraction to members of the same sex. The second narrative pattern shows desire developing out of politics.

The first set of narratives often dwell on a first crush or sexual experience. Emotional relationships and sexual experiences often drive self-knowledge and the assumption of a gay or lesbian identity. In a typical narrative strategy, Rahul recalls feelings of tenderness for another boy which he now interprets as sexual. He describes his feelings for his classmate Ali Askar at age 9: "I experienced a warm rush through my body and felt an urgent desire to feel his body close to mine. I wasn't even aware that my feelings were sexual at that time." Later, after recounting several high school love affairs with boys, Rahul explains, "I have been gay as long as I can remember. It seems quite immaterial to me to find a reason for homosexuality."[5] Shilpa Mehta experienced a similar sense of same-sex attraction: "Around puberty, I got real conscious that I was attracted to women, not men. Men were my buddies ... [but] It was women I wanted."[6] Shilpa did not act on her desires and have sexual relationships with women until she left Bombay for college in the United States.

In the first set of narratives, both men and women define sexual identities through reflections on their objects of desire. However, women alone seem to participate in the second set of narratives, which describes the movement from political consciousness to sexual identification. Feminism spurs many self-identified lesbians to articulate their sexual desires. Uma, a New Zealander of Indian descent, fashioned a sexual identity after engaging in battles against discrimination and racism in Australia:

> At the university in 1975, I discovered more about sexual discrimination, and felt myself validated at last about this form of oppression ... I could read and find out what women around the world were writing – that women who were fighting against sexism called themselves "feminist." I then became a "black feminist" ... I think that my sexuality came more through my politics than anything else. And, of course, because I am a political person, I made my sexuality a political act and came out as publicly as possible.[7]

Kamini Chaudhary also became aware of lesbian relationships and identities through exploring feminism: "I wonder if I had not heard about lesbianism through the women's/feminist literature I was reading, or if I wasn't close friends with a lesbian couple, would I have discovered that loving a woman can be sexual. Was that what was undiscovered with Nazreen?"[8] Kamini's reflections on her intimate adolescent friendship with Nazreen suggests that "politics" alone does not explicate the difference involved in marking identities. Kamini's choice is one of both pleasure and politics. Kamini and Uma's narratives suggest that sexual identities and expression are a choice – a pleasure choice – not something prescribed by biology and certainly not by the hypothalamus.[9]

Kamini's knowledge of lesbian relationships informs her reflections about the intimacy between women in India:

> I have always loved women. Women friendships in India weren't sexual, but they were like love affairs. Drama, trauma, jealousy, intimacy, hugging, holding, touching, and involvement far more intense and complete that any I have experienced in a friendship or relationship with an American.[10]

While she marks the romance with Indian women as "more intense and complete" than those she experienced with American women, Kamini is able to name friendships between women in India "romances" through a language of lesbian relationships learned in the United States.

In most of these coming out narratives, knowledge of relationships and identities as gay men and lesbians were acquired by South Asians living in North America, Britain, and Australia. Men and women who have never left South Asia have also developed a sensitivity to gay relationships through European publications, American films, and now through newsletters such as *Trikone, Shamakami,* and *Shakti Khabar,* which are distributed through personal networks and subscriptions at college campuses and in major South Asian cities among the English literate middle and elite classes. While sexual experiences may have occurred in Bangladesh or Sri Lanka, the framework to understand and celebrate these experiences as gay and lesbian identities developed in white societies.

These coming-out narratives reveal a shared strategy of reframing the past with present knowledge. Many times these narratives attempt to show a linear progression or the origination of an identity, but often the straight lines tumble into spirals or tangle into webs. In one narrative, memory and desire mix so often with denial and flashes of awareness that the processes of desire and self-understanding can

be read in a number of different ways. A woman recounts:

> I had my first lesbian relationship when I was twelve years old. I had a crush on a girl in my boarding school which developed into a deep emotional involvement. We would spend hours together, kissing and touching, we had no words to describe what was happening but I remember Rita often saying, "We love each other but we're not lesbians, are we?" There were all these negative connotations to lesbianism – that it was bad and wrong and that as long as we weren't lesbians, it was okay.[11]

Even at age 12 there were words to name their experiences, but perhaps no meanings that celebrated and affirmed their affection; "bad" and "wrong" seemed unlikely adjectives to match their delight. Years later, when she left India for studies in the US she became a feminist:

> Suddenly I had a framework to explain a lot of feelings and frustrations I had been experiencing ... I also began to meet women who called themselves lesbians, and it was comforting to find that I was not alone, that I wasn't abnormal or weird or crazy ... the term "lesbian" began to acquire many new dimensions for me. It wasn't just about sleeping with women; it was the way in which I defined myself as a woman in relation to other women.[12]

Lesbianism no longer meant "bad" sexual acts. To identify as a lesbian was an attempt to claim a community, to share needs and values.

RESISTING SILENCE

Despite the affirmation that may develop from a lesbian and gay identity, many self-identified South Asian lesbians and gay men fear rejection from their families. A South African graduate student in New York writes of the alienation he feels from his family:

> I'm an outsider, an outcast in my natural community, a hidden silenced nonperson. To participate in the life of my family, I bury my sexuality, my politics, my anger as deeply as possible; I suspect there is a secret dread in my family that I might ultimately shame them horribly.[13]

This dependence on family and South Asian communities for affirmation has paralyzed many gays and lesbians in South Asian immigrant communities. These communities and families act as a nurturing refuge in environments of racial hostility and cultural misunderstanding. Members of Khush have "discovered that the greatest obstacle to our members' coming out is the fear of losing our ties to our families and communities. We are people whose sense of identity is constructed in a very large part of these institutions."[14]

Lesbians and gay men have felt invisible in the South Asian subcontinent as well. Many have felt as helpless as the poet Suniti Namjoshi: "what could we uncover? / the history not for taking: / the family not for joining: / the cause not for naming."[15] Entangled in the feeling of alienation is an acute sense of bewilderment. How does one justify one's own existence when one cannot summon the history or utter a name that describes one's identity? Names creatively appropriated, such as Khush and Shamakami, are not always enough:

> I know not any word for myself
>> but Khush
>> and even that is a mocking translation
> I cannot envision
>> living in India
>> persevering in my "American" individualism
>> loving a woman
>> building a home with her
>> defying family, friends
>> ignoring disapproval, silence
>> and still speaking, still fighting
>> to prevent silence.[16]

In trying to speak and live, we confront the contradictions of our identities. South Asian heterosexists have often denied the authenticity of queer-identified South Asians by labeling homosexual relationships a white disease, insinuating that our presence in the US or Britain has "contaminated our minds and desires."[17] These heterosexists attempt to use the politics of race to condemn lesbians and gay men. They perceive queer identities as a threat to the cultural integrity of South Asian immigrants. The rhetoric is lethal and well understood by immigrants and their children, who are unceasingly chastised for shedding their "culture" and acquiring the degenerate and destructive values of white societies. The notion of culture here is like a

fossil – solid and petrified. The conservative ideologies of heterosexist South Asians equate queer sexualities with an already well-defined yet adaptable arsenal of "Western evils" – divorce, drinking alcohol, eating meat, or drug abuse. Any unfavorable value is displaced onto a non-South Asian source. Ironically, these heterosexists unquestioningly accept the "Western" notion that heterosexuality is natural, normal, and biologically correct and that homosexuality is unnatural and perverse.

Arvind Kumar, the editor of *Trikone*, has attempted to address this pervasive argument that homosexuality is a "Western disease" and non-existent in South Asia. He writes that "the Trikon Archives are an attempt to prove the perception false. This effort is to validate our existence not only in the minds of others but also our own. We were present in Ancient India. We were there in Moghul India. And we are very much here in South Asia now."[18] *Shakti Khabar* has also solicited references to "homosexuals in the history of the subcontinent, particularly in the various religions, i.e., Sikh, Muslim, Hindu, so that we can prove that homosexuality has nothing to do with the color of one's skin."[19] Both organizations have begun to create archives and libraries as an act of representation, validation, and recovery of the past.

WHATEVER HAPPENED TO THE VEDIC DYKE?

To resolve the conflict between national and racial identity and sexual identity, several South Asian queers have searched for "our very own gay tradition." Shivananda Khan, editor of *Shakti Khabar*, describes the historical presence of homosexuality in South Asia: "Within the history of the subcontinent there has always been homosexuality. Sex between those of the same gender is discussed in many Hindu texts and sex manuals. Homosexual activity was also depicted in religious statues.[20] Subodh Mukherjee of Calcutta explores descriptions of Tantric initiation rites, Hindu festivals and sects which celebrated homosexual acts, the descriptions of sodomy in *Kama Sutra*, the court customs of Babar, and references to women loving women in the *Mahabharata* and *Ramayana*.[21]

Giti Thadani, a lesbian living in New Delhi, has embarked on an archaeological project which substantiates Shivananda's claims. Giti's work began with a study of Sanskrit texts: "I set out to read ancient texts, looking for traces of visions of a feminine world which pre-dated patriarchal society. Then I travelled all over India for three years, taking photographs of sculptures, temples, and vestiges from those times." Her photographs and summaries of her interpretations are frequently published in South Asian queer newsletters. She interprets the texts such as the *Rig Veda* and sculptures which depict sexual acts between women as revelations of a feminine world prior to 1500 BC where sexuality was based on pleasure and fertility.[22]

Giti's analysis begs the question, "So, whatever happened to the Vedic dyke?"[23] Giti claims that Aryan invasions dating to 1500 BC first began to suppress homosexuality through the emerging dominance of patriarchy. Both sexual systems coexisted, despite fluctuations in relative repression and freedom, until British colonialism when the destruction of images of homosexual expression and sexual expression in general became more systematic and blatant. Giti argues that Indian middle-class acceptance of Western "homophobia" has encouraged destruction of ancient temple images.[24]

Subodh Mukherjee also envisions a golden age of sexual tolerance, but he dates the onset of the repression to the thirteenth century during Moghul rule. Since then there has been a gradual erosion of liberal attitudes toward sexuality, "damaging Indian gay culture and forcing it underground." He insists that

> by coming out to society as gays, we will thus be only reviving our ancient and varied culture and freeing it from the shackles of unnatural prudery and nauseating morality ... For our movement to be successful in India, Indian gays must discard disruptive Western models. In light of our own tradition, we must build a new movement for acceptance of gay love by our society.[25]

The irony in Subodh's observations is that while he finds Western models of gay identity disruptive, he still relies on the notion of an "Indian gay" movement which is itself a Western construct.[26]

This concern about reclaiming the past, this search for the Vedic dyke, makes me think about what I consider history. History is about interpreting the past. We are writing history by producing new interpretations of the past and the formation of cultural identities is dynamically related to the project of writing history. The past is not a thing waiting to be discovered and recovered. A "recovered past" cannot secure or fix an identity for eternity. The relationships between identities and histories are fluid and constantly shifting. As Stuart Hall reminds us, "identities are the names we give to the different ways we are positioned by, and position ourselves within, the narratives of the past."[27] Implicit, then, in the writing of history are the politics of knowledge and the politics of position.

The politics of the South Asian gay and lesbian history are refreshingly self-conscious. Shivananda Khan writes that we can use the past to buttress our claims, our identities in the present. We are not then producing a history of Vedic times. We are at best using ancient text and sculpture to shade today's meanings of sexual practices:

> As we, living toward the end of the twentieth century, fight for our rights to be lesbian or gay, we need to reclaim our historical antecedents, to reconstruct our history, to reinvent the social and philosophical basis that preceded our historical times. If we are to reclaim our own invisible history ... then we need to explore our temples, our religious sites, reread our Sanskrit texts, truly explore our history with open eyes to go out here and record our history. We must not leave it to the dominant heterosexuals to construct our own history for us.[28]

This is precisely where Giti's work, and historical narratives like hers, are the most exciting. They reconstruct and revise the master narratives of the past which have sought to erase differences and ignore contested values. The alternative vision they provide can empower us to reclaim and remake both our present world and the understanding of historical contexts which shaped it.

Shivananda, however, goes too far when he interprets Giti Thadani's work as follows: "If we define a lesbian and gay culture as a legitimate space to form same biological gender sexual/emotional relationships that were *socially acceptable* as well as having *high esteem* ... it seems therefore that pre-Aryan India had a strong lesbian and gay culture" (my emphasis). Giti Thadani's work does not prove that same-sex relationships were "socially acceptable" and "highly esteemed" several thousand years ago in some parts of South Asia. The presumption here is that sexuality is a definable and universal activity, ignoring the variety of cultural patterns and meanings.[29] How do we know that a representation of two women embracing meant sex for historical actors? And even if they did refer to sex, does sex have the same meaning as it does for us today?

How does one go about proving that some social practices are acceptable and highly esteemed? What kind of evidence does one need to make those kinds of claims? It is necessary to understand the context, the map of social reality at the time. Trying to reconstruct the context of second-century India is difficult. Yet we can begin by reading legal texts, religious documents, court texts, and even the placement of the sculpture within architectural complexes. These texts, of course, are usually prescriptive; they provide ideals. They cannot be used to understand attitudes, actual behavior, or motives. We can use these texts and materials to speculate about how people lived and thought. Perhaps, though, the only people we will know anything about are the elite men who wrote and were written about, who endowed temples and who designed law. These are the conditions of our knowledge of the past. They influence my own skepticism about how much we can know about ancient India.

While the project of reclaiming and reconstructing the past is critical for present political and cultural struggles, let us not read too much of "us" today into the past. We may trap ourselves in the need of a history to sanction our existence. South Asian lesbians and gay men are present now. On that alone we demand acknowledgment and acceptance.

Sharpening our present political struggles demands an understanding of our current historical context. We can begin by acknowledging

that while there may have been homosexual acts in the past, "what is perhaps relatively new is the idea and development of a "gay relationship." Gay relationships are not limited to "emotional and sexual bonds akin to marriage between heterosexual couples."[30] Over the past several decades, lesbians and gay men have developed a range of social arrangements and relationships, relationships which have, at moments, allowed some women and men to break out of conventional gender relations and identities.

Recovering histories both of the ancient and recent past challenges us all to understand the possibilities of alternative sexualities and social arrangements. Through mobilizing histories, reappropriating languages, and other cultural strategies, we may be able to gain affirmation and support within South Asian immigrant communities for queer desires and relationships. Simultaneously, these cultural strategies may unexpectedly destabilize the self-definitions of South Asian lesbian and gay communities.

DESIRING COMMUNITY

Claims that lesbians and gay men who can trace their origins to the subcontinent share a common social history and identity has shaped the politics of South Asian queer organizations. While social support groups like Khush have a local focus – for gay men in Toronto – the newsletters presume an international audience. Shamakami's editorial mission is typical of this perspective: "While *Shamakami* will be based in the United States of America, it will strive to promote international networking among South Asian feminist lesbians."[31]

Yet, it is the migration from the subcontinent that generated a distinctive South Asian queer identity. The formation of South Asian queer communities has been structured by the post-Stonewall gay liberation movement, experiences of racism, and the development of racial minority identities in North America and Britain. The experiences that spurred the creation of *Shakti* are typical:

The main reason for forming a South Asian lesbian and gay group is because of racism and cultural marginalization. Many white organizations and individuals do not see us as people but as exotic creatures. We want to define our own agenda within a racist climate and not have an agenda imposed by white people.[32]

The social organizations and networks like *Shakti* which emerged in the second half of the 1980s developed a self-conscious policy of developing contact internationally with other South Asian lesbians and gay men. The newsletters consistently provided information, addresses, and frequent news of the other organizations. These groups distribute their newsletters and focus coverage on lesbian and gay experiences and histories on the subcontinent. Increasingly, gay and lesbian organizations drawing their membership from the urban middle class and elite of India have adopted this international South Asian queer identity. In *Bombay Dost*'s first official issue, the editors reprinted a December 1990 article from the *Advocate* which proclaimed Urvashi Vaid, executive director of the National Gay and Lesbian Task Force of the US, "woman of the year." The editors served notice that Urvashi Vaid's "presence alone does a great deal for us here in India."[33]

Despite its fluid application, the construction of this identity has been problematic. In 1989, Khush organized a cultural program called "Salaam Toronto." One of the organizers, Ian Rashid, reflects on the problems of self-representation and coalition building:

As a fledgling organization, Khush had wanted to use Salaam Toronto to introduce ourselves to the larger gay and lesbian and South Asian communities. But in many ways, the event was primarily for Khush. The members of the group, coming from different parts of the world, wanted to reconcile and reclaim our various ties to our notions of South Asia ... Very few of Khush's members are actually South Asian born, the majority coming from East Africa, the Caribbean, Britain, and North America. Constructed around individual memories, mythologies, and histories, Salaam Toronto was trying in some ways to link all of us to a collective sense of source. There seemed a need within Khush to justify the existence of the group beyond our sexual orientation; to develop a sense of collective as opposed to individual identity.[34]

Ian describes a collective identity that is mitigated by individual memories and histories, an identity which must be molded from individual particularities and differences to provide some sense of collective "source." Ian points to how we not only presume community and identity, but also create it. This presumed queer South Asian identity is not singular or static. The organizers of "Salaam Toronto" form a coalition of people with different identities, politics, and positions. The debates, disputes, and labor involved in the process of organizing the event produce new political practices and identities. Since "Salaam Toronto" in 1989, South Asian feminists, lesbians, and gay men in Toronto have organized two other cultural festivals: "Desh/Pradesh 1990" and "Desh/Pradesh 1991." Events such as these are transformative; they can constitute new identities.[35]

LIBERATING IDENTITY POLITICS

Although identity emerges from an awareness of difference, articulating an identity can also serve to mask differences. By presuming a global South Asian queer identity, what do these organizations, newsletters, and individuals lose or deny? What complexities, diversities, and contradictions are tensely bound in this collective identity? The differences in experiences and understanding that Ian describes do more than simply complicate the notion of a global South Asian queer identity, they draw into question the assumption that these "imagined political communities" are ideal democracies.[36] These inequalities – often analyzed through categories of gender, class, and race – within our communities must be addressed.

Some South Asian lesbians have called attention to the way gender inequalities structure organizations like Khush and Trikone, which are dominated by men. Lesbians in North America have often developed their own networks through the newsletters *Shamakami* and *Anamika*, or affiliated themselves with Asian or black lesbians in order to establish more supportive communities. Recently, these structural inequalities have been challenged in the pages of *Trikon*. Mita Radhakrishnan wrote:

You, Trikone men, have to talk about violence against women and what you can do, as gay South Asian males, to stop it. You have to talk about lesbian invisibility. You have to talk about sexism, and how you as males are privileged in comparison to us, your South Asian lesbian sisters ... When you say that women have been "underrepresented in Trikone" you have to realize and take *responsibility* for the fact that "underrepresentation" of women doesn't just "happen" passively. It is the direct result of sexism within the organization and within individual men. Make *the ending of sexism one of Trikone's reasons for being.*[37]

The editor, Arvind Kumar, responded by changing Trikone's editorial statement to include a commitment to "ending sexism and discrimination against women in all forms" and specific encouragement of women to "develop [editorial] policy guidelines and co-edit issues."[38] These changes in policy and purpose pleased Mita Radhakrishnan, and she encouraged the readers of Trikone to "continue the hard but wonderful work of confronting sexism and other oppressions."[39] Although women continue to contribute to Trikone, none of the four issues since Mita's original letter has had a female co-editor.

There has, though, been even less conversation about class differences and inequalities. Often the subjects of South Asian gay and lesbian discourse see themselves as undifferentiated, as profoundly middle-class and educated. There are sometimes nostalgic stories of young men and women having sex with servants in their households in South Asia. Sharmeen Islam relates how she "found women who worked as domestic help in our house to be a lot [more] comfortable with me physically than educated women."[40]

However, once in Britain or the United States, there is less awareness that South Asian lesbians and gay men may experience differences in class positions and origins. An explanation is perhaps that race structures so much of our experience here. In a society where South Asians are rendered either invisible or alien, South Asian queer organizations have developed to create safe spaces. These spaces are defined by race and often displace class differences. Curiously, even racism is not always

acknowledged. Sunil Gupta criticizes *Shakti* for having a curious lack of self-conscious politicization despite the fact that the group itself is defined by race. He writes that "the pain and anger of daily living the race problem has to be recognized."[41]

Race structures organizations and communities not only from the outside but from within as well. Aziz Ahmed sees the presence of racial consciousness within South Asian communities when he notes that every South Asian

wants to be as white as possible, or at least wants to be looked on as being fair. Whiteness has become the criterion for beauty. We are defining ourselves from the perspective of white people. We need to challenge racism not only from white people, but also from our own people.[42]

I share with Sunil Gupta the belief that talking about the "inherent contradictions and subtle differentiations of color and background"[43] within queer communities will help us acknowledge and celebrate differences. We need not fear that differences or a lack of predetermined "unity" will produce irreconcilable divisions. It will help us develop communities which are stronger and more self-affirming. A global South Asian queer identity does not have to presume a singular set of experiences. It can be about building coalitions and networks of support and understanding.

South Asian lesbian and gay newsletters have served as forums for articulating identities, establishing communities, and have demonstrated the necessity of identity politics as an important stage in the liberation process. The gathering of solidarity and support is critical for any struggle. In a 1986 issue of *Anamika*, Anu wrote that the individual strategies "deshi dykes" had developed to deal with the pressures of inhabiting contradictory and fragmentary lives were not enough. "For it seems clear to me that any advance will have to be collectively imagined, if we are to escape the stealthy and fugitive-like existence whereby we only dare come out to the tried-and-trusted few."[44] Forums like *Anamika* provided a safe space where one no longer has to fear judgment or retribution. For many these organizations and networks have transformed their social landscape. Pratibha Parmar recalls that when she first came out living in Britain in 1976 "there were very few South Asian lesbians and gays around. We knew we were around and would travel hundreds of miles to meet. Now [in 1990] we have Shakti, a very strong, over 1,000-member lesbian and gay group with a newsletter, regular meetings, and socials."[45]

However, the practice of everyday life will not automatically be transformed by the existence of safe spaces, no matter how strong. Parents and relatives, employers and strangers, friends and acquaintances may respond to our lives with hostility, misunderstanding, or indifference. But the creation of safe spaces and communities has made a difference. As Ravi relates in a 1987 issue of *Trikone*, "no South Asian will have to embark on this journey of self-discovery and self-affirmation in isolation, but will be able to draw upon a supportive South Asian gay and lesbian *community*."[46] These imagined communities serve a real purpose. They allow us to engage in struggle and self-discovery without feeling alone or alienated.

In inventing identities, creating new subjectivities, and imagining communities, we embark in forms of "empowerment political consciousness."[47] These personal, social and archaeological histories are engaged in the act of self-representation. bell hooks explains that the process of becoming subjects "emerges as one comes to understand how structures of domination work in one's own life, as one develops critical thinking and critical consciousness, as one invents new, alternative habits of being."[48] For South Asian lesbians and gay men, as with other silenced groups, self-representation alone cannot liberate us, but breaking silence is the first step in resisting conventional expectations and challenging domination. In 1991 Jigne Desai of California tantalizes us with the transformations in her own life. She says, "Being Indian and queer, I felt I was the only one. I've always looked at myself as not fitting in. That's changing. Now I'm not afraid to say who I am and what I believe in."[49]

NOTES

1 "Our First Time," *Trikon*, January 1986: 1.
2 Suniti Namjoshi and Gillian Hanscombe, *Flesh and Paper* (Charlottetown, Prince Edward Island: Ragweed Press, 1986): 1.
3 Trikon changed the spelling of its name to Trikone in 1987 in order to be incorporated as a non-profit organization in California (*Trikone* 2: 4 (November 1987): 2. I have used "Trikon" to refer to the newsletter and support group prior to November 1987 and "Trikone" for the November 1987 issue to the present.
4 Jeffrey Weeks, "The Value of Difference," in *Identity: Community, Culture, Difference*, ed. Jonathan Rutherford (London: Lawrence & Wishart, 1990): 88–9.
5 Rahul Mukhopadhyay, "Transplanting Roots from India to America," *Trikone* 4:3 (May, June 1989): 1–2.
6 "Silent No More: A Talk with Shilpa Mehta," *Trikone* 4:2 (March–April, 1989): 3.
7 "Uma," *Connexions*, (Fall 1983): 5. A different version written by Uma, entitled "Don't Open those Lips," was published in the British Asian women's journal, *Mukti* 3 (spring 1985): 7–10.
8 Kamini Chaudhary, "The Scent of Roses: Developing a Sexual Identity," *Trikone* 4:3 (May–June, 1989): 1–2.
9 The latest development in deducing a biological basis for sexuality is Simon LeVay's hypothesis that differences in the structure of the hypothalamus determine sexual object choice. Like straight women, gay men purportedly have a smaller hypothalamus than straight men. Scientists and journalists have speculated that lesbians might have a hypothalamus structure similar to straight men's. LeVay's research follows more than a century of European and American scientific inquiry which has persistently tried to fix a biological cause or measure to putative differences in race, gender, and sexuality. This kind of research has attempted to naturalize social inequalities as the result of differences in human biology and genetics. See Simon LeVay, "A Difference in Hypothalamic Structure between Heterosexual and Homosexual Men," *Science* 253 (August 30, 1991): 956–7, and Ann Gibbons, "The Brain as a Sexual Organ," *Science* 253 (August 30, 1991): 959–60.
10 Kamini Chaudhary: 2.
11 Anonymous, "khayal," *Anamika* 1:2 (March 1986): 9.
12 Ibid.
13 Letter by R.S., "South African, Indian and Gay," *Trikone* 2:4 (November 1987): 2.
14 Ian Rashid, "Out of Home: The Contradictions of Identity: Creating a South Asian Gayness in Toronto," *Rites* 7:3 (July–August 1990): 9.

15 Suniti Namjoshi and Gillian Hanscombe, "Because of India," in *Flesh and Paper* (Charlottetown, Prince Edward Island: Ragweed Press, 1986): 62.

16 A. V., "A Response to 'A Room of One's Own,'" *Shamakami* 2:1 (January 1991), 4–5.

17 "A White Disease," *Shakti Khabar* 3 (August–September 1989): 1.

18 "The Trikon Archives," *Trikon* (March 1986): 7.

19 Shivananda Khan, "Networking in London," *Trikone* 3:4 (July 1988): 4.

20 "A White Disease," *Shakti Khabar*: p. 1.

21 Subodh Mukherjee, "Homosexuality in India: A Personal Quest for Historical Perspective," *Trikone* 5:1 (January–February 1990): 1, 3.

22 Interview with Giti Thadani reprinted from *Lesbia Magazine* (January 1991), in *Shakti Khabar* 14 (June–July 1991): 3.

23 This question is a paraphrase of the question raised by feminist historian Uma Chakravarti, "Whatever Happened to the Vedic *Dasi*? Orientalism, Nationalism and a Script of the Past," in *Recasting Women: Essays in Indian Colonial History*, eds Kumkum Sangari and Sudesh Vaid (New Brunswick, NJ: Rutgers University Press, 1990): 27–87.

24 Shivananda Khan, "Giti Thadani: Sexuality and Gender in Ancient India," *Shakti Khabar* 15 (August–September 1991): 12.

25 Subodh Mukherjee, "Homosexuality in India": 1, 3.

26 Subodh Mukherjee's investigation of ancient sexual practices also relies on the work of Orientalist scholars, particularly the work of French scholar Alain Danielou. Subodh fails to consider the pervasiveness of the assumptions of Orientalist scholars that India was more primitive, sensual, and eroticized than repressed, and that civilized Western Europe may have shaped Danielou's expectations and interpretations of ancient Indian sexuality. For an examination of Orientalism, see Ronald Inden, *Imagining India* (London: Basil Blackwell, 1990).

27 Stuart Hall, "Cultural Identity and Diaspora," in *Identity: Community, Culture, Difference*, ed. Jonathan Rutherford (London: Lawrence & Wishart, 1990): 225.

28 Shivananda Khan, "Giti Thadani," 13.

29 For an elaboration of this argument about sexuality as socially constructed and historically constituted, see David Halperin, "Sex before Sexuality: Pederasty, Politics and Power in Classical Athens," in *Hidden from History: Reclaiming the Gay and Lesbian Past*, ed. Martin Duberman, Martha Vicinus and George Chauncey, Jr (New York: New American Library, 1989), and Jeffrey Weeks, *Sex Politics and Society: The Regulation of Sexuality since 1800* (London: Longman, 1981).

30 "A White Disease," *Shakti Khabar*: 1.

31 "Shamakami Editorial Policy," *Shamakami* 1:1 June 1, 1990: 3.

32 Editor's response to letter from L.N. in *Shakti Khabar* 11 (December 1990–January 1991): 13.

33 "Being Legit: Event or Process!", *Bombay Dost* 1:1 (July–September 1991): 3.

34 Ian Rashid, "Out of Home," *Rites*: 9.

35 Judith Butler writes about how coalitional politics need not assume that "identity" is a premise or "unity" has been reached in advance to proceed with political action. Coalitions then can develop and identities can emerge or dissolve depending on the concrete political practices which constitute them. See Judith Butler, *Gender Trouble: Feminism and the Subversion of Identity* (New York: Routledge, 1990): 14–16.

36 Benedict Anderson, *Imagined Communities: Reflections on the Origin and Spread of Nationalism* (London: Verso, 1983): 15–16.

37 Mita Radhakrishnan, "An Open Letter from a South Asian Lesbian to Trikone Men," *Trikone* 5:3 (May–June 1990): 1–2.

38 "Trikone," *Trikone* 5:3 (May–June 1990): 2.

39 Mita Radhakrishnan, "Letter from Delhi," *Trikone* 5:4 (July–August 1990): 1–2.

40 Aziz Ahmed and Sharmeen Islam, "Breaking the Silence," *Trikone* 3:5 (September 1988): 2.

41 Sunil Gupta, "Correct Singularities," *Gay Times*, (August 1989): 40–41.

42 Aziz Ahmed, "Breaking Silence": 5.

43 Sunil Gupta, "Correct Singularities,": 40–1.

44 Anu, "Notes from an Indian Diary," *Ananika* 1:2 (March 1986): 8.

45 Nelson Carvohlo, "Pratibha Parmar: Fight Back and Struggle (Because You Have To)," *Khush Khayal* 2:2 (June 1990): 7.

46 Ravi, "Bits and Pieces," *Trikon* (September 1987): 7.

47 Pratibha Parmar interview in Lloyd Wong, "Fuck You: This Is Our Home. Claiming South Asian Identity in Britain," *Fuse* (summer 1990): 10.

48 bell hooks, "The Politics of Radical Black Subjectivity," in *Yearning: Race, Gender, and Cultural Politics* (Boston: South End Press, 1990): 15.

49 Jigne Desai interview in "Out in America," *Outweek* 105 (July 3, 1991).

EVERT VAN DER VEEN, AART HENDRIKS, and ASTRID MATTIJSSEN

"Lesbian and Gay Rights in Europe: Homosexuality and the Law[1]"

from Aart Hendriks, Rob Tielman and Evert van der Veen (eds), *The Third Pink Book: A Global View of Lesbian and Gay Liberation and Oppression* (Buffalo, NY: Prometheus, 1993): 225–46

The discussion about lesbian and gay rights is an important although complex one. None of the international human rights treaties explicitly distinguishes the recipients of rights and freedoms on the basis of their sexual orientation. Nor is the word "homosexuality" or "sexual minority" mentioned in any of the existing human rights treaties. This may easily lead to the conclusion that lesbian and gay rights are not recognized by these codes. However, on several occasions authoritative bodies and scholars have interpreted human rights provisions in a way commensurate with the demands formulated by the lesbian and gay movement. Indeed, the international treaties seem to contain even more provisions that may potentially offer lesbians and gay men their warranted legal protection.

In Europe the relationship between homosexuality and the law is an old one. The European lesbian and gay movement has traditionally put a lot of energy into trying to influence the (democratically elected) legislature and to alter the interpretation of the existing laws by the ("independent") judge, first to abolish discriminatory laws and later to find official recognition of their specific interests. For self-evident reasons, the protection and promotion of lesbian and gay rights have always been connected to the domain of human rights law. The specific lesbian and gay interests became known (read: were self-proclaimed) as "lesbian and gay rights," being a broad set of claims on the authorities to protect lesbian and gay interests. To a large extent, lesbian and gay rights fully overlap with the internationally recognized human rights provisions, in spite of the sometimes restrictive interpretation given to these by some authoritative bodies and scholars. Some lesbian and gay rights, however, go a bit further. Lesbians and gay men not only demand equality before the law, but at the same time require safeguards to develop their own lifestyles as well as adequate protection against discrimination and other forms of less favorable treatment. As such, these demands do not conflict with international human rights laws, although they do not as yet enjoy full legal recognition. Insistent efforts on the part of the European lesbian and gay movement resulted in the (sometimes reluctant) official recognition by the major European institutions of the existence of discrimination against lesbians and gay men. In this respect the International Lesbian and Gay Association (ILGA) and its strong European network have been instrumental.

In this article we will examine the relevant provisions of the various human rights treaties that were, or potentially can be, invoked by lesbians and gay men to safeguard their rights and dignity. We shall focus primarily on developments at the supranational European level. To that end, special attention will be paid to the European Commission and Court of Human Rights, both established under the European Convention of Human Rights (ECHR) on the one hand; and, on the other, the statements adopted by the Parliamentary Assembly of the Council of Europe and the European Parliament, the latter being the democratically elected forum affiliated with the European Communities. We aim at evaluating the efforts made by the European lesbian and gay movement to reform the law. Prior to this assessment, we will briefly describe the various patterns of discrimination against lesbians and gay men in Europe in conjunction with the human rights of same-sex lovers under the European legislation.

DISCRIMINATION AGAINST LESBIANS AND GAY MEN

Discrimination against lesbians and gay men is a phenomenon difficult to define. For several reasons, lesbians and gay men are occasionally or systematically less favorably treated if compared with heterosexuals. Thus, the difference in treatment forms the core element of this phenomenon, which arises in very distinct situations. However, different treatment is not automatically worse, and may be perfectly justified. Therefore, besides difference in treatment, discrimination implies that the way people are treated is less favorable for unjustifiable reasons. The core of discrimination is that those who discriminate attribute a negative connotation to such irrelevant criteria as sexual orientation or (sexual) lifestyle.

It has to be noted that non-homosexuals can also be the victims of anti-lesbian or anti-gay discrimination. This is particularly true in cases where they are erroneously looked upon as homosexuals. The parents, children, friends, and relatives of lesbians and gay men may also become the targets of discrimination.

Discrimination against lesbians and gay men finds its "justification" in the persistent negative views many in society hold about homosexuality, which they still consider as sick, sinful, perverse, unnatural, dangerous, contagious for children, shameful to the family, and so on. Whatever the legitimation, it is regarded as inferior to heterosexuality, particularly since lesbian and gay couples cannot procreate "by nature."

Discrimination against lesbians and gay men takes many forms. It may assume the shape of direct and explicit discrimination. This means that one is discriminated against purely for reasons of sexual preference. Forms of direct discrimination range from "bashing" to exclusion from jobs or military service and denial of certain goods and services, and limitations imposed on the freedom of expression and the right to assembly. For example, in Italy (as in many other countries), men risk dishonorable discharge from the armed forces following sexual contact with another male.

Most prevalent, however, is the so-called indirect form of discrimination, whereby lesbians and gay men experience less favorable treatment due to an interwoven network of legal and social rules presented as "objective." These rules are perceived by many, and thus upheld, as the moral foundations of our society. Consequently, efforts to change these rules usually meet with massive opposition. These moral values, deeply embedded in habits and tradition, dominate various gender roles attached to marriage, public health and decency laws and so on. All these "neutral" rules are equally applied to lesbians and gay men, who generally experience them not only as inappropriate but as highly discriminatory. For example, in the Netherlands a lesbian who applied for a job at a public transport company was rejected after a negative evaluation by the company's psychologist. The psychological examination "revealed" that the woman's political ideas on sexuality did not fit the company's employment policy.[2]

What is considered discrimination changes from time to time and from place to place. The mechanisms generally remain the same, but the targets and intensity of discrimination may vary. Twenty years ago, no one in Europe would ever have dreamed of assigning equal parental rights to a lesbian couple with children. Nowadays many Europeans favor this idea. We are aware that our notion of discrimination is culturally biased and may, as a consequence, be somewhat different from those of our readers. As far as possible, we will substantiate our views and indicate why we disapprove of certain forms of unequal treatment, while approving of others.

It should be equally noted that there is no universal standard for lesbian and gay lifestyles, let alone the ways lesbians and gay men organize. We must accept that the struggle against discrimination reflects the variety within the lesbian and gay movement itself and depends equally on such environmental factors as the political climate and the legal system.

HUMAN RIGHTS LAW AND LESBIAN AND GAY RIGHTS

Human rights legislation is supposed to protect individual and collective rights of minority groups of whatever kind. Recognizing that all people have equal rights and dignity forms the core of human rights law.

There are various human rights instruments, each with its own particularities. The most widely accepted human rights standards are laid down in the Universal Declaration of Human Rights (UDHR, 1948), a formally non-binding document almost unanimously adopted by the General Assembly of the United Nations. This declaration, embodying the full range of human rights, is generally considered the "common standard of achievement" for humanity. The rights enumerated in this document became elaborated in the International Covenant on Civil and Political Rights (ICCPR, 1966) and the International Covenant on Economic, Social, and Cultural Rights (ICESR, 1966), being legally binding documents from which ratifying states are not allowed to deviate unless explicitly foreseen by the treaties themselves. The rights enshrined in these three documents, in combination with the optional protocol to the ICCPR, are now generally known as the "International Bill of Human Rights," and recognized by the vast majority of countries.

Additionally, two major human rights treaties were prepared under the auspices of the Council of Europe. These treaties are the ECHR (1950) and the European Social Charter (ESC, 1961). While the ECHR may be said to be a regional "counterbalance" to the ICCPR, the ESC has more in common with the ICESCR. It should be noted that there is no hierarchical stratification among the various international human rights instruments. These systems are, rather, complementary, with regional systems generally elaborating on the universal principles, being more specific and covering more issues.

If the legal protection offered by the rights embodied in these treaties is considered insufficient, there are generally two channels through which adaptation can be sought. First of all, one can strive to formally amend the treaty and/or some of its provisions. This can be accom-plished only by a treaty drafting body, such as the Council of Europe, after which the contracting parties (the countries) still have to accept this amendment. Experience has shown that, instead of amending an existing treaty, it is easier to adopt an additional protocol or to draft an entirely new treaty on a specific issue.

A second channel for seeking legal reform is by way of jurisprudence. By having the body authorized with the binding interpretation of the provisions enshrined in a treaty revise its views, the warranted legal protection may be obtained as well. A way to produce such legal revisions is by preparing test cases. A judgment may then be provoked by bringing a case to court which, in the eyes of the litigants, should lead to legal reform. In this respect, the European human rights protection mechanism, with extensive authority ascribed to the Strasbourg-based European Commission and Court of Human Rights, offers excellent opportunities. Such test cases produce either jurisprudence with which national regulations can be influenced or else they are rejected by the European Human Rights Commission, which exposes the weakness in the protection by human rights law.[3] Both methods, trying to alter the law and producing test cases, have been used extensively by the European lesbian and gay movement.

CAN HUMAN RIGHTS BE INVOKED IN THE FIGHT AGAINST ANTI-LESBIAN AND ANTI-GAY DISCRIMINATION?

Article 2 of the UDHR states that each individual can claim all the rights and freedoms set forth in the declaration without distinction of any kind whatsoever. If the rights contained therein grant people equal protection, then it should logically follow that this also holds true for lesbians and gay men. In other words, they should be able to equally enjoy the rights and freedoms as enshrined in the declaration. However, experience has shown that there are deeply rooted structures discriminating against people on the basis of their sexual orientation. Historical, religious, moral, and other values and traditions are invoked to justify the privileges ascribed to heterosexuals. Most societies seem to be centered on the *assumption of heterosexuality*, that is to say, they implicitly assume that everybody is heterosexual. Complex societal structures, therefore, inhibit lesbians and gay men from enjoying equal, not to mention equally privileged, treatment. What lesbians and gay men consider as their human rights, however, have not always been recognized as such in legislation, jurisprudence, or legal literature.

Lesbian and gay rights are not a deviation from "general" human rights law; the core of lesbian and gay rights is that they demand a broader, less heterosexually biased interpretation of the recognized human rights standards. Therefore, the lesbian and gay movement considers its rights to be part of overall human rights, and it is determined to achieve a more just and fair interpretation of the existing provisions.

The international lesbian and gay movement has been, and still is, striving forcefully to convince the international community that fundamental rights for lesbians and gay men need to be recognized as part of international human rights law.[4] Before we describe these efforts, we will analyze the current status of lesbian and gay demands *vis-à-vis* the human rights treaties currently in force in Europe. We will focus on those fundamental rights that have also been embodied in the ECHR and the ICCPR, aware that some very fundamental lesbian and gay rights will thus fall outside the scope of this study. The following rights will be analyzed:

- the right to respect for private and family life (Article 8 ECHR and Article 17 ICCPR)
- the right to freedom of expression (Article 10 ECHR and Article 19 ICCPR)
- the right to freedom of assembly and association (Article 11 ECHR and Articles 21 and 22 ICCPR)
- the right to marry and to found a family (Article 12 ECHR and Article 12 ICCPR)
- the principle of non-discrimination (Article 14 ECHR and Article 26 ICCPR).

The right to respect for private and family life

As far as gay men are concerned, the right to private life is, as a result of successful litigation, partly recognized by the European Commission and Court. With regard to lesbians, discrimina-

tion in the area of privacy has not yet been petitioned before the Strasbourg court. This is not to say, however, that anti-lesbian discrimination does not exist or that lesbians do not feel a need to enjoy the protection of the right to private life.

The right to lesbian and gay family life, often being perceived as one right, is totally denied.

The right to private life reflects the old liberal idea that the individual should be protected against any undue interferences with his or her private space and autonomy.[5] In addition to the protection of the individual's family life, home and correspondence, this right also protects the individual's particular identity, integrity, autonomy, private communications, and sexuality.[6] In 1976, the commission explicitly stated that one's sexuality forms an important aspect of one's personal life and that undue interferences with this would amount to a violation of Article 8(1) ECHR.[7]

As a result of the famous *Dudgeon* and *Norris* cases,[8] gay men are now also recognized as a group that can, though only to a certain extent, enjoy the right to private life. After the court had stated in the *Dudgeon* case: "[T]here can be no denial that some degree of regulation of homosexual conduct, as indeed of other forms of sexual conduct, by means of criminal law can be justified as 'necessary in a democratic society'";[9] it concluded:

[A]s compared with the era when that legislation was enacted, there is now a better understanding, and in consequence an increased tolerance, of homosexual behavior to the extent that in the great majority of the member States of the Council of Europe it is no longer considered to be necessary or appropriate to treat homosexual practices of the kind now in question as in themselves a matter to which the sanctions of the criminal law should be applied; the Court cannot overlook the marked changes which have occurred in this regard in the domestic laws of the member States.[10]

From the court's final conclusions it can be learned that it wants to depenalize only certain forms of male homosexual behavior, i.e., sexual acts committed in private between consenting males over 21 years of age. Like the minimum age provision,[11] the "privacy" restriction in practice has amounted to a serious limitation of same-sex relationships. In the UK, for example, hotels and prisons are considered public places. Moreover, according to English Sexual Offences Act, as amended in 1967, homosexual acts in private with more than two persons taking part or present is equally forbidden. According to the European Commission, "the existence of this legislation does not constitute an interference with his right to respect for private life or his home."[12]

Over time, this lowered the initial enthusiasm of the lesbian and gay movement over this verdict, now that the European Court and Commission seem to be unwilling either to nullify discriminatory ages of consent or to eradicate the "privacy" restriction. In spite of this, the success of the *Dudgeon* and *Norris* cases inspired several other lesbian and gay groups in countries with a total ban on homosexual acts to file a complaint with the Strasbourg legal organs. In 1990, the European Commission ruled favorably on the admissibility of Alexos Modinos's complaint against Cyprus.[13] UK groups are now considering submission of a similar petition against the authorities of the Island of Man.

The right to lesbian and gay family life is not recognized at all by the European Commission and Court. According to the commission, a family, as referred to in Article 8(1) ECHR, consists of a man and a woman with their possible (biological or adopted) offspring. Lesbian and gay couples do not, according to the commission, qualify as a "family" in the same sense. In the case of a Malaysian–English gay couple the commission reasoned as follows: "Despite the modern evolution of attitudes towards homosexuality, the Commission finds that the applicants' relationship does not fall within the scope of the rights to respect to family life ensured by Article 8."[14] The British government did not, therefore, violate the right to family life by denying the Malaysian partner a work permit in the UK.

Similar problems emerged in the case of an Australian–British lesbian couple in the UK with a child conceived by artificial insemination. After the birth of the child, the Australian mother decided to quit her job in order to devote herself to child-rearing. The fact that she had no income made her lose her work permit. After the mothers had petitioned before the Strasbourg organs, the commission eventually refused to recognize this trio as a family under Article 8, paragraph 1. Thus the protection of family provisions, as enshrined in the British immigration law, was denied to the couple and their child.[15]

In 1992, the commission declined the claim of a Dutch lesbian couple to be granted full parental rights over their son.[16] According to the commission, the right to family life cannot be interpreted in such a broad way.

The commission and court are notably more tolerant and willing to interpret the concept of "family life" far more extensively and autonomously when it concerns other than lesbian or gay issues. Over the years, the following extramarital relationships have become equally recognized as family types: brothers and sisters and other relatives,[17] unmarried heterosexual couples with a common household,[18] polygamous family types,[19] and a parent with a child born outside of marriage or after divorce.[20] In other words, according to the Strasbourg organs, the right to family life envisages the protection of all people bound together by satisfactory true bonds.[21] Apparently, in the view of the commission and the court, lesbians and gay men lack the capacity to establish such bonds.

THE RIGHT TO FREEDOM OF EXPRESSION

Whereas the interpretation of the rights to private life has, reluctantly, found some legitimation in the Strasbourg Commission and Court, this hardly holds true for the right to freedom of expression. The dignity of lesbians and gay men was (and is) definitely at stake now that British local authorities, under Section 28 of the Local Authorities Act, are forbidden to "promote" homosexuality as an accepted form of family life. This type of legislation imposes clear restrictions on the right of lesbians and gay men to express themselves in a positive way. However, the now famous Section 28 has so far never been challenged for review by the Strasbourg organs, probably now that its adversaries anticipate, in line with previous judgments, a very restrictive interpretation by these same organs.

The only positive statement the commission ever made with regard to the expression of homosexuality was when it was petitioned to review the case of a British man imprisoned because of homosexual acts. The applicant alleged that his detention inhibited him from expressing his affection for men. The commission thereby stated "that there may be an issue under Article 10 regarding his . . . claim that the fact of imprisonment denied him the right to express feelings of love for other men."[22] In its report however, the commission came to the conclusion that "the concept of 'expression' in Article 10 concerns *mainly* the expression of opinion and receiving and imparting ideas . . . It does *not* encompass any notion of the physical expression of feelings in the sense submitted by the applicant" (emphasis added).[23]

The right to freedom of expression was of paramount importance in the case of the Belgian teacher Eliane Morissens. Morissens was dismissed after she had openly spoken on television about her experiences as a lesbian and the negative repercussions of her sexual orientation on her professional career. The commission stated that the Belgian state could justifiably restrict Morissens's freedom of expression in view of the special responsibilities her profession imposed upon her for the protection of her school and the persons she had mentioned in the program. The commission concluded that dismissal was a "proportional" measure in such cases.[24]

The UN Committee in Geneva, established under the ICCPR, also did not rule favorably in the complaint submitted in the famous SETA case.[25] In this case, five individuals opposed the ruling of the censor of the Finnish state-controlled broadcasting company on homosexual themes. The committee declared that the state should have some freedom of maneuver, as one could not check the negative impact the promotion of homosexuality by radio and TV broadcasts could have on the public.

The right to freedom of assembly and association

This right assumes that there is also a right to freedom of organization and the right to affiliate oneself with such entities. Consequently there should be a right to found and to become a member of such groups as political parties, trade unions, and lesbian and gay interest groups.[26] Laws prohibiting the establishment of lesbian and gay organizations, such as the Austrian Penal Code,[27] may actually be in defiance of the right to freedom of assembly and association. Cases such as these, however, have never been brought to the attention of the Strasbourg Commission and Court by the lesbian and gay movement.

The right to marry and to found a family

When the texts of the human rights treaties were drafted, probably nobody even thought that the living together of two people of the same sex might be covered by the right to marry. In one of the first cases to challenge the traditional concept of marriage, the so-called *Rees* case,[28] the European Commission and Court, in a unanimous decision, decided that "the right to marry guaranteed by Article 12 refers to the traditional marriage between persons of opposite biological sex. This also appears from the wording of the article which makes it clear that Article 12 is mainly concerned to protect marriage as the basis of the family."[29]

The reluctance of the European Court to recognize same-sex cohabitants as a "family" entitled to marriage did not prevent the lesbian and gay movement from finding alternative ways to obtain the warranted recognition of same-sex relationships. Since October 1, 1989, the Act on Registered Partnership has been in force in Denmark. This law bestows on registered same-sex partnerships most of the rights, privileges, and duties traditionally reserved to heterosexual marriage. Norway and Sweden will probably follow soon. In France, a proposal to recognize the *parténariat civil* is presently under discussion. In July 1991, the *Schwulenverband in Deutschland* (German

Gay Alliance) launched a proposal for the *nichtehelige Partnerschaft* (non-marriage partnership). In the Netherlands, numerous local authorities recently opened their municipal registration and record offices to same-sex partnerships.

In the *Dudgeon* case the European Court clearly indicated that it is willing to adjust its standing jurisprudence in view of "the marked changes that have occurred in this respect in the domestic law of the [Council of Europe] member states."[30] Thus, by pushing for national law reform, the lesbian and gay movement may eventually achieve a readjustment of the European human rights bill along the line of domestic law changes.

As we all know, there is not necessarily a causal relationship between marriage and procreation. Strong evidence exists that the commission and the court, though probably unconsciously, seem to agree with this statement. In the *Marckx* case the court explicitly stated that the concept of family is not necessarily connected to that of marriage.[31] In the so-called *Cossey* case, Judge Martens, in his dissenting opinion, stated that

> it cannot be assumed that the stated purpose of the right to marry (to protect marriage as the basis of the family) can serve as a basis for its delimitation: under Article 12 it would certainly not be permissible for a member State to provide that only those who can prove their ability to procreate are allowed to marry.[32]

Despite the fact that the Strasbourg organs, as discussed above, have in practice also recognized non-traditional heterosexual relationships as "families," including their rights to procreate and custody over children, so far these privileges have systematically been denied to lesbian and gay couples. It seems, however, that in this respect also the lesbian and gay movement is making progress. While in the Netherlands various commissions have recommended considering same-sex social (i.e., non-biological) parents as similar to opposite-sex social parents for full parental rights,[33] in the UK the lesbian and gay movement succeeded in the spring of 1991 in preventing Parliament from adopting a proposal that would almost automatically take away all parental rights from lesbian and gay parents.

THE PRINCIPLE OF NON-DISCRIMINATION

The right to equality and nondiscrimination is enshrined in Article 26 ICCPR. Other universal human rights codes that recognize this principle include the UDHR (Article 2) and the International Covenant on Economic, Social, and Cultural rights (Articles 2 and 3). This principle also inspired the drafting of specific codes, such as the International Convention on the Elimination of All Forms of Racial Discrimination, the Convention on all Forms of Discrimination against Women, and the Declaration on the Elimination of All Forms of Intolerance and of Discrimination based on Religion or Belief. There is no such code on discrimination against homosexuals, however.

The ECHR contains a provision similar to Article 26 of the ICCPR, but, contrary to its ICCPR counterpart and most national constitutional equality provisions,[34] ECHR Article 14 does not have an autonomous status; it only prohibits discrimination with regard to "the enjoyment of the rights and freedoms set forth *in this Convention*" (emphasis added). Therefore, in the legal literature, Article 14 is considered to have an "accessory" or "complementary" character.

Although in neither the universal nor the regional nondiscrimination clauses are homosexuality or sexual preference explicitly mentioned, their scope does not envisage any limitations. The grounds mentioned are not exhaustive, something that is confirmed by the phrase "or other status." This suggests that sexual orientation is also one of the grounds that does not allow any discrimination.

The European Commission in its reports often stresses the broad interpretation that should be given to the anti-discrimination clause.[35] However, none of the gay or lesbian cases brought to the attention of either the European Human Rights Court and Commission or the Human Rights Committee was ever considered favorably. The Strasbourg organs always decided that there were objective and reasonable grounds, serving a legitimate aim, that would justify the different treatment. The major reason still seems to be that the members of these bodies lack the political willingness – and maybe the simple capacity – to discover discriminatory patterns in our society. This should not deter the lesbian and gay movement, however, from consistently addressing these institutions in case malicious governmental practices are being reported in society.

In summary, one can say that as of now the European human rights bodies recognize the right of gay men over 21 to a "private life" to be conducted in private. An absolute prohibition of male homosexuality can, according to the European Commission and Court, not be deemed necessary in a democratic society for the protection of morals and health – hereby justifying states to impose other restrictions on homosexuality. Similar cases involving lesbians have not come up yet. All attempts to get other lesbian and gay demands included in the European human rights code have failed so far. There are, however, good prospects that the commission and court may follow the more enlightened European governments and attach more value in the near future to the recommendations of the European Parliament and the Parliamentary Assembly of the Council of Europe. We will now try to analyze the limited success of the lesbian and gay movement so far.

AN ANALYSIS OF THE REACTION OF THE EUROPEAN JUDICIARY WITH RESPECT TO THE EFFORTS OF THE LESBIAN AND GAY MOVEMENT

Soon after its birth, the European Commission of Human Rights was confronted with a number of cases in which gay men alleged that their fundamental rights had been violated. In the 1950s, the commission received complaints from German civilians, who were charged under Article 175 of the criminal law book. The complainants, claimed that their punishments, based on a general prohibition of homosexuality, conflicted with the guarantees laid down in Articles 8 (respect for private life) and 14 (sex discrimination) of the ECHR. The commission rejected the charges, without argumentation,

and upheld the German government's reasoning that such a prohibition is necessary in view of the "protection of health and morals."[36] The commission also rejected the claim that discrimination on the basis of gender had taken place. In its report it stated that in the underlying case men and women could be treated distinctly, because homosexual men were a larger social and moral threat to society than women.[37]

It took the commission until 1975 to change its negative, almost hostile, attitude toward homosexuality. The commission dealt with two complaints submitted by British citizens against their government. They alleged that the laws in England and Northern Ireland, criminalizing homosexual acts between men, were discriminatory and a unjustifiable infringement on their right to private life.[38] The English case was rejected. In the *Dudgeon* case the commission, and eventually the court, stated that the Northern Irish law was not in accordance with Article 8 (right to private life) of the ECHR as far as it concerned sexual acts between consenting men over 21 years of age and acts committed in private.

In the later *Norris* case[39] the court confirmed this view. Norris complained in 1983 that the Irish Offences against the Person Act (1861) and the Criminal Law Amendment Act (1885) were not in accordance with Article 8. Like the Northern Irish law, the Irish law prohibits "buggery" defined as an "abominable crime ... committed either with mankind or with any animal" (Section 61 Offences against the Person Act). Although these laws had not been applied for several decades, the existence of these laws as such posed a threat and exposed all male homosexuals to criminal prosecution. Therefore, the commission and the court declared that the sole existence of these laws already caused a breach of the right to private life as guaranteed by the ECHR.

Two important conclusions can be drawn from the Strasbourg case law, notably from the development having taken place between the decisions in the cases of the German applicants in the 1950s and the judgments in the corresponding British and Irish cases in the 1970s and 1980s. First, one can observe an increasing willingness by the commission and the court to recognize anti-lesbian and anti-gay discrimination and to give a more ample interpretation of Article 14 ECHR. Second, lesbian and gay rights and the dignity of homosexuals have been recognized with respect to the right to private life.

In the 1950s, gay men were still regarded as posing a moral and social threat to society. In the 1970s, the decade in which lesbian and gay groups were mushrooming all over Europe,[40] the commission took a more differentiated approach. In the case of X, v. *the United Kingdom*, the commission recalled its earlier views; it questioned the state's authority to regulate the private, notably the sexual, life of two consenting adults, considering the societal developments in this area.[41] In the *Dudgeon* case, the commission went even further by stating that beyond doubt the mere existence of a law prohibiting any form of homosexual contact in private was an undue interference with the plaintiff's private life.[42] The court concluded that the moral judgment on male homosexuality in Northern Ireland did not justify such a severe infringement on Dudgeon's private life.[43] These general principles were repeated in the case of Norris, who, unlike Dudgeon, was himself not arrested on the basis of the relevant laws but who claimed that the existence of these laws *threatened* him in the enjoyment of his private life.

Aside from the fact that, in terms of lesbian and gay demands, both the *Dudgeon* and *Norris* cases resulted in positive verdicts, it also makes clear to what extent the Strasbourg organs are willing to approve discrimination against lesbians and gay men. So far the commission has dealt with cases on homosexuality only in the context of the right to individual privacy, as distinct from the right to family life not to mention the right to found a family. The rights of lesbians and gay men as a minority group, with a dignity equal to heterosexuals, are not being recognized. Neither have laws impeding lesbians and gay men in the development and fulfillment of their identities[44] been criticized. The core of the *Dudgeon* and *Norris* cases is that sexuality is an important aspect of one's personality and that the state should not be allowed to interfere, unless there is an objective

and reasonable ground that serves a legitimate aim. This adapted view reflects the general changes of ideas in medicine and social science.[45]

The reluctant recognition of lesbian and gay rights by the European judiciary corresponds, according to Girard,[46] with the interpretation of sexuality in general. Sexuality is considered an important part of private life and the state should provide the conditions for the optimal development of people's sexuality. For a long time, however, sexuality was exclusively seen as a procreational activity. Politicians, health educators, and representatives from many other professions still have great difficulty in recognizing the recreational function of sexuality.[47]

The consequence of this narrow vision is that, as yet, the discussion of equal opportunities for lesbians and gay men is not admissible. In the *Dudgeon* case the court declined to give its opinion concerning the admissibility of different ages of consent for heterosexuals and homosexuals. According to the court, this falls within the jurisdiction of the national legislators.[48]

We can learn from this that the fight for equal opportunities should not be restricted to petitioning the Strasbourg Commission and the Court. This is evident not only from the *Dudgeon* case but also from the other petitions made by lesbians and gay men.[49]

If we compare the view of the European Commission and Court on lesbian and gay rights with the current European legal reality, we cannot but conclude that the ideas of the (majority of the) members of the Strasbourg organs are rather conservative.[50] Total bans on (male) homosexuality in theory still remain in force in the Channel Islands, Cyprus, Ireland, the Island of Man, Gibraltar, and the former Yugoslav republics of Serbia, Bosnia-Herzegovina, and Macedonia. In practice, however, these provisions are hardly ever applied.

The real exceptions in Europe are Romania and most of the former Soviet republics,[51] where homosexuality is not only forbidden but where homosexuals, both male and female, are criminally prosecuted for "committing their sin." It seems, however, that in these countries also law reforms are on the way, partially inspired by the jurisprudence of the Strasbourg organs, anticipating closer collaboration with the EC and the Council of Europe.

The Strasbourg Commission and Court can also be said to uphold a completely outdated definition of the "family," denying same-sex couples the right to form a family unit. This not only strongly contradicts the legal traditions of the more progressive countries of Denmark, the Netherlands, Norway, and Sweden, but is now also undermined by the family policy launched by the EC. The European Parliament, Council, and Commission seem to recognize "new family types" besides the "traditional nuclear family" such as "de facto families," "single-parent families" and "reconstituted families."[52] The EC policy reflects, in our view, a far more contemporary and realistic approach than the philosophy of the Strasbourg organs.

It took the lesbian and gay movement a lot of energy and resources to provoke a favorable judgment by the European Court. One could argue whether or not the strategy followed was efficient and effective in achieving its goals. The progress made can be judged, at best, as moderate. On the one hand, one could say that the recognition of homosexuals as entitled to the right to private life is a first and essential step that should lead to the full and integral recognition of lesbian and gay rights. On the other hand one could also argue that the limited interpretation of this right could endanger the other demands of the lesbian and gay movement (e.g., equality and non-discrimination, and protection of family life). Besides that, the petitions made by self-proclaimed lesbians and gay men made the movement as such more visible, and revealed that patterns of repression of lesbian and gay rights are similar throughout Europe (and throughout the world).

Independent of the outcome of this evaluation, it must be considered a great advantage that the lesbian and gay movement has more diverse aims than legal reform by means of Strasbourg jurisprudence. Many other plans have been set into motion over the past decade. Apart from the European Court and Commission, many other European institutions, such as the European Parliament and the Parliamentary Assembly of the Council of Europe, have been the target of carefully planned lesbian and gay lobbying strategies. Attempts have also been made to draft an additional protocol to the ECHR, spelling out lesbian- and gay-specific rights.

EUROPEAN POLITICS

As a result of the extensive efforts by the lesbian and gay movement, both the Parliamentary Assembly of the Council of Europe and the European Parliament adopted several pro-lesbian and gay measures.

In 1981, without any form of international precedent, the assembly accepted both a resolution and a recommendation concerning anti-lesbian and anti-gay discrimination. Both pronouncements were based on a report prepared by the so-called Committee Voogd.[53] The assembly, recognizing that everybody has the right to sexual self-determination, expressed its concern about the fact that lesbians and gay men frequently are the subject of discrimination, and sometimes even repression. In its recommendation the World Health Organization (WHO) was urged to remove homosexuality from its International Classification of Diseases (ICD).[54] In one of its resolutions, the assembly made an appeal to ban certain forms of discrimination, specifically: exclusion of lesbians and gay men from certain professions, anti-lesbian and anti-gay violence, and the keeping of files on homosexuals by the police.

How successful the efforts by the lesbian and gay movement were, can be seen in the official text of the assembly's recommendations, which repeat almost verbatim the demands put forward by the lesbian and gay lobby. The recommendation and resolution call upon member states to take appropriate measures in order, first, that all laws and practices that criminalize and brand as "sick" homosexual acts between adults be totally banned; second, that the same age of consent apply to both homosexual and heterosexual acts; third, that discrimination in the areas of employment and salary be eliminated; fourth, that medical acts aimed at changing sexual orientation be prohibited; fifth, that custody, visiting rights and accommodation of children by their parents not be restricted solely on the grounds of a parent's sexual preference; and, finally, that effective measures to reduce the danger of rape and violence in prisons be introduced.

Actions of this kind are not unsuccessful. Although the Council of Ministers of the Council of Europe was not at all pleased with these actions by the assembly, national governments did turn their attention to these progressive statements. Probably as a direct result of these pronouncements, France adjusted the differences in ages of consent in 1982. When adopting this legal amendment, the French legislature referred to the Council of Europe's resolutions. The Spanish parliament accepted the resolution and recommendation in 1985.

The ILGA is proposing the adoption of an additional protocol to the ECHR to extend the protection of the rights enshrined in the assembly's document to lesbians and gay men.[55] If this protocol is accepted, which, despite an intensive lobbying campaign, has not happened yet, the European Court and Commission will have to revise their case law, paying more attention to the interests of lesbians and gay men.

The Assembly of the Council of Europe has not been the only object of a lesbian and gay lobby; similar activities have been directed at the European Parliament. Since 1979, the European Parliament has been working on the shaping of a lesbian and gay emancipation policy. Until now, these efforts have not had a big impact on the overall EC, notably as a result of stubborn opposition by the Council of Ministers (being the most powerful institution within the EC). The reluctance of the council finds its legitimation in the fact that the EC treaty does not contain specific references to the protection of human rights. This, however, does not restrain the council from persistently underlining the importance of full recognition of human rights "both as one of the cornerstones of European cooperation and in the relations of the Community with third nations."[56] Indeed, in 1977 the European Parliament, and the European Council and Commission made a joint statement in which they emphasized the importance they attach to the protection of human rights and declared to respect these rights in the exercise of their power.[57]

To illustrate that times are changing, reference should be made to two projects funded by the Commission of the EC. The first project concerns an inventory on the social and legal situation of lesbians and gay men in the EC. This study, presented to EC Commissioner of Social Affairs, Mrs. Vasso Papandreou, in December 1992, may be an important incentive to revitalize the discussion on a European lesbian and gay policy.[58] The second project concerns a visibility study of lesbians in the various EC countries.[59] Moreover, since 1989 the EC has been funding lesbian and gay exchange study programs in the context of the so-called Erasmus program.

The council's reluctance did not deter the European Parliament from adopting progressive statements. The first resolution of the parliament[60] on lesbian and gay issues was based on a report by the Italian member, Vera Squarcialupi, adopted on February 1, 1984.[61] She prepared a document on anti-lesbian and anti-gay discrimination, following two resolutions by the parliament in 1979 and 1982. Her recommendations were approved by the parliament in 1984 and correspond with the assembly's resolution and recommendation. In its own recommendation, the European Parliament also urges its Legal Affairs Committee to look for ways to end the inequality in EC members states' legislation concerning homosexuality. This recommendation has never been effected, however, despite pressure from several parliamentary members.[62] After the Squarcialupi report many other activities touching upon lesbian and gay issues followed.[63] Some members of the European Parliament were actively involved in setting up ILGA's Iceberg Project, and enabled the project to be presented in Strasbourg on the occasion of a parliamentary session there.

One of the most recent victories is the approval of a new recommendation by the Council of Social Affairs on "Protecting the Dignity of Women and Men at Work: A Code of Practice on the Measures to Combat Sexual Harassment."[64] This code also condemns the harassment of lesbians and gay men in the workplace. The inclusion of this explicit condemnation followed a discussion of the issue of harassment at a meeting between EC Commissioner Papandreou and ILGA representatives in December 1990. In 1992, the European Parliament took the decision to report annually on the state of human rights within the European Community. In the first report and motion for a resolution, prepared by reporter Mr Karel de Gucht, there were a number of explicit references to issues highly relevant to the lesbian and gay movement. These reports, which are expected to have an unprecedented influence, may offer new opportunities to the lesbian and gay movement to attain its goals.

The Parliamentary Assembly of the Council of Europe and European Parliament are both very progressive in their statements; however, their influence is limited. The lesbian and gay movement has been effective in influencing both institutions and has been able to open and guard communication channels between the movement and these institutions. This may be very important in view of future, follow-up strategies to be decided upon soon.

going pressure is needed to provoke a more liberal interpretation of the human rights treaties that goes beyond the limits of the right to private life.

The strategy of confronting the Strasbourg organs with test cases has been partially successful. The same can be said of the strategy to effect law reform through pressure at democratic fora, such as the Parliamentary Assembly of the Council of Europe and the European Parliament of the European Community. They have proven to be far more sensitive to the demands of the lesbian and gay movement. Their limited powers, however, have restricted the success of their initiatives.

Especially in view of the process of a unifying Europe, with more powers being given to supranational agencies, the question of continued investment of effort by the lesbian and gay movement in the European institutions becomes an issue of paramount importance. Regular evaluation and innovative lobbying strategies need to receive high priority in the ILGA.

CONCLUSIONS

According to the lesbian and gay movement, their rights enjoy insufficient protection under the recognized human rights codes. This is not so much a result of textual shortcomings of the major treaties, as it is the consequence of the rather conservative interpretation of their provisions given by the authoritative bodies. Both the European Commission and Court of Human Rights as well as the UN Committee for Human Rights has so far only secured for lesbians and gay men limited protection under the right to private life provisions. The committee and the court show a lack of political willingness in guaranteeing lesbians and gay men appropriate legal protection against infringements on their dignity as well as enabling lesbians and gay men to develop a lifestyle that follows from their sexual preference. The European Parliament, the Parliamentary Assembly of the Council of Europe, and ever more European governments seem to disagree with this stubborn rejection of lesbian and gay rights, and are developing, in response, far more progressive policies. On-

NOTES

1 This chapter is an elaboration and update of a 1990 article by E. van der Veen and A. Mattijssen, published in the legal magazine *Ars Aequi* under the title "Homoseksualiteit en mensenrechten" ("Homosexuality and Human Rights"), vol. 39 (September 1990): 535–44.

2 Unless otherwise noted, the examples all come from the compilation of cases by the Iceberg Project (K. Waaldijk *et al.*, "The Tip of an Iceberg: Anti-Lesbian and Anti-Gay Discrimination in Europe, 1980–1990," first draft of report [Utrecht: Gay and Lesbian Studies Department, University of Utrecht, October 7, 1991]), with the exception of the Dutch cases, which come from the Centre Anti-Discrimination Homosexuality (CADH) (E. van der Veen and A. Dercksen, "Onderzoeksverslag deel I" ("Research Report, Part 1") (Utrecht: Gay and Lesbian Studies Department, University of Utrecht, 1989).

3 P. Ashman, "Homosexuality and Human Rights Law," *The Second ILGA Pink Book* (Utrecht: Interfacultaire Werkgroep Homostudies, 1988): 47.

4 P. Ashman, "Background of the Proposal for a Protocol to Amend the European Convention of Human Rights," CSCE Parallel Activities, Study

Conference on the Possibilities of Expanding the European Convention of Human Rights to Eliminate Discrimination Based on Sexual Orientation (Copenhagen: Landforeniging for bösser og lesbiske Forbundet af 1948, 1990).

5 "European Court of Human Rights," *Belgian Linguistic Case* 23, July 1968, series A, no. 6 (1968): 24–5.

6 See M. Novak, "UNO-Pakt über bürgerliche und politische Rechte und Fakultativprotocol" ("UN Agreement on Civil and Political Rights and Optional Protocol"), *CCPR Kommentar* (Kehl/Strasbourg/Arlington: Engel, 1989): 302ff.

7 European Commission of Human Rights, Case 5935/72, *X v. Federal Republic of Germany*, Yearbook XIX (1976): 277ff.

8 European Court of Human Rights, *Dudgeon* case, October 22, 1981, series A, no. 45 (1982, and *Norris* case, October 25, 1988, series A, no. 142 (1988).

9 *Dudgeon*: 20.

10 *Ibid.*: 21.

11 In most European countries the age of consent for heterosexuals ranges from 12 to 18 years.

12 European Commission of Human Rights, Case 10389/93, *Johnson v. UK*, D&R 72 (1986).

13 European Commission of Human Rights, Case 15070/89, *Modinos v. Cyprus*, December 7, 1990, Council of Europe press release.

14 European Commission of Human Rights, Case 9369/81, *X and Y v. UK*, May 3, 1983, D&R 32 (1983): 221.

15 Case 14753/89, *X and Y v. UK*, October 9, 1989 (unpublished).

16 Hoge Raad (Dutch Supreme Court) February 24, 1989, Rek. Nr 737, *Rechtspraak van de Weel* (*Jurisprudence of the Week*), 1989, No. 65.

17 European Court of Human Rights, *Marckx* case, June 13, 1979, series A, no. 31 (1979).

18 European Commission of Human Rights, Cases 7289/75 and 7349/76, *X and Y v. Switzerland*, Yearbook XX (1977): 168ff.

19 European Commission of Human Rights, *Khan v. UK*, Yearbooks X (1967): 478. Cf. "Toelatingsbeleid bij polygame huwelijken" ("Admission Policy in Case of Polygamous Marriages"), with a comment by S. W. E. Rutten, *NJCM Bulletin* 16: 5 (1991): 430–6.

20 *Marckx*.

21 *Ibid.*: 15. Cf. P. van Dijk and G. J. H. van Hoof, *De Europese conventie in theorie en praktijk* (*The European Convention in Theory and Practice*) (Nijmegen: Ars Aequi Libri Rechten van de mens, 1982, 1990).

22 European Commission of Human Rights, Case 7215/72, *X v. UK*, Yearbook XXI (1978): 374.

23 Report of October 12, 1978, D&R 19 (1980).

24 European Commission of Human Rights, Case

11389/85, *Morissens v. Belgium*, May 3, 1988 (unpublished). See also Anonymous, "The Eliane Morissens Affair: A Lost Case," *ILGA Bulletin* 4 (1988): 15.

25 Views of the Human Rights Committee no. 4. 14/61, *Leo. R. Herzberg et al. v. Finland*, Report of the Human Rights Committee 1982, p. 165.

26 Cf. European Commission of Human Rights, case 1038/61, *X v. Belgium*, Yearbook IV (1961): 324: "Their right to set up an association or a trade union."

27 Under Article 221 of the Austrian Penal Code, those who establish or belong to an organization that supports "homosexual lewdness" and causes public offense are liable to six months' imprisonment. See P. Tatchell, *Out in Europe* (London and Glasgow: Channel Four Television Publications, 1990).

28 European Commission of Human Rights, *Rees* case, October 17, 1986, series A, no. 106 (1987): 15–19.

29 *Rees*: 19. Cf. European Commission of Human Rights, Case 7654/76, *Oosterwijck v. Belgium*, Report of March 1, 1979, par. 57: "A marriage requires the existence of a relationship between two persons of the opposite sex."

30 *Dudgeon*: 24.

31 *Marckx*: 14.

32 European Commission of Human Rights, *Cossey* case, September 27, 1990, series A, no. 184 (1990): 18.

33 A. Hendriks and L. Markenstein, "Recht als medicijn" ("Law as Medicine"), in M. Moerings and A. Mattijssen (eds), *Homoseksualiteit en recht* (*Homosexuality and Law*) (Arnhem: Gouda Quint, 1992): 185–214.

34 E.g., Article 6, Belgian Constitution; Article 1, Dutch Constitution; Article 2, French Constitution; Article 3, German Constitution; Article 4, Greek Constitution; Article 40, Irish Constitution; Article 3, Italian Constitution; Article 11, Luxembourg Constitution; Article 13, Portuguese Constitution; Article 14, Spanish Constitution.

35 Among others: *Johnson*, Case 7525/76; *Z. v. UK*, March 3, 1978, D&R 11 (1978); Case 7215/75, *X v. UK*, D&R 11 (1978); Case 9237/81, *B v. UK*, D&R 34 (1983); Case 11716/85, *S v. UK*, May 14, 1986, D&R 37 (1986).

36 European Commission of Human Rights, Case 104/55, *X v. Federal Republic of Germany*, Yearbook I (1955–7): 229.

37 European Commission of Human Rights, Case 167/56, *X v. Federal Republic of Germany*, D&R 1 (1955–7); European Commission of Human Rights, Case 530/59, *X v. Federal Republic of Germany*, Collection of Decisions; Case 5935/72, *X v. Federal Republic of Germany*, D&R 3, p. 46.

38 European Commission of Human Rights, Case 7215/75, *X v. UK*, D&R 11 (1978): 117–32 (cf. n. 8).

39 *Norris*: Ashman, "Homosexuality and Human Rights Law", p. 48.

40 See John Clarke, "The Global Lesbian and Gay Movement: Mass Movement, Grassroots, or by Invitation Only," in Hendriks, Tielman and van der Veen, *The Third Pink Book*: 65–61.

41 European Commission of Human Rights, Case 7215/75, *X v. UK*, D&R 11 (1977), p. 43.

42 *Dudgeon*.

43 *Ibid*.

44 According to the European Commission, in a case considering the right to private life, "the right to establish and develop relationships with other human beings, especially in the emotional field," is conditional to "the development and fulfillment of one's own personality." Case 6959/75, *Brüggeman & Scheuten* v. *Federal Republic of Germany*, Yearbook XIX (1976): 414.

45 In the 1970s, the ideas concerning homosexuality altered in Europe. Homosexuality had long been officially seen as a mental disease and was treated as such. After the 1970s, the central problem was the repression of homosexuality. New psychological therapies were developed which no longer tried to "cure" homosexuality, but aimed instead at making the person accept sexual preference as part of his or her personality. In psychiatry and the other branches of medicine, the illness syndrome was overthrown. The main focus of research shifted to social sciences, where the central theme was repression of homosexuality by society (R. Tielman, *Homoseksualiteit in Nederland: Studie van een emancipatiebeweging* (*Homosexuality in the Netherlands: Study of an Emancipation Movement*) (Amsterdam: Boom, 1982).

46 Ph. Girard, "The Protection of the Rights of Homosexuals under the International Law of Human Rights: European Perspectives," *Canadian Human Rights Yearbook* 3 (1986): 11.

47 A. Hendriks, "Homorechten in de jaren negentig" ("Gay Rights in the Nineties"), in A. Dercksen *et al.* (eds), *Tolerantie onder NAP: 20 essays over homoseksualiteit voor Rob Tielman* (Utrecht: Gay and Lesbian Studies Department, University of Utrecht, 1992); "The Political and Legislative Framework in which Sexual Health Promotion Takes Place," in H. Curtis (ed.), *Promoting Sexual Health* (London: British Medical Association, 1992).

48 *Ibid.*: 18.

49 European Commission of Human Rights, Case 7215/75, *X v. UK*; Case 9237/81, *John Bruce* v. *UK*; Case 9721/82, *Richard Desmond* v. *UK*; Case 11716/85, *Mary X* v. *UK*; Case 12513/86, *X v. UK*; *Johnson*, note 13.

50 A. Hendriks, "Homoseksualiteit in West Europa: een landenoverzicht" ("Homosexuality in Western Europe: An Overview by Country"), unpublished paper, Utrecht, September 1991; "Gay Men and Lesbians in Central and Eastern Europe: A Survey," unpublished paper, Utrecht, September 1991.

51 As of March 1993, Ukraine and the Baltic republics of Latvia and Estonia have repealed the total prohibition on homosexual acts from their Penal Codes.

52 European Parliament, Resolution on Family Policy (83/C 184/116); conclusions of the Council regarding family policy (89/C 277/02): Commission document (COM[89] 363).

53 Parliamentary Assembly of the Council of Europe, Thirty-Third Ordinary Session, Recommendation 924 (1981) of October 1, 1981, and Resolution 756 (1981) of October 1981, on discrimination against homosexuals.

54 Eventually went into effect in late 1991.

55 Draft Protocol of the Convention for the Protection of Human Rights and Fundamental Freedoms concerning the elimination of discrimination based on sexual orientation, Study Conference, Copenhagan, 1990.

56 Conclusions of the Council of Ministers, Luxembourg, June 28–9, 1991, Annex V, in *Europa van Morgen* July 3, 1991).

57 Declaration of April 5, 1977, *Official Journal* (1977), no. C 103/1.

58 P. Ashman *et al.* (eds) *Homosexuality: A Community Issue: Essays on Why and How to Incorporate Lesbian and Gay Rights in the Law and Politics of the European Community* (Dordrecht and Boston: Martinus Nijhoff, 1993). This volume is a document of the European Commission prepared by the European Human Rights Foundation (Belgium); the European University (Italy); and the Gay and Lesbian Studies Department, University of Utrecht (the Netherlands).

59 The "Lesbian Visibility Project" is currently being carried out by the women's group of LBL/ F-48 in Denmark.

60 European Parliament, 1984–5 Debates (doc. no. 1–311, 12), Resolution of March 13, 1984. EP Doc. 1–1072/82, PE 87. 477 def.

61 European Parliament, Documents 1983–4 (doc. no. 1–1358/83), February 13, 1984, PE 87.477 def. Report for the Committee for Social Affairs and Employment about Sexual Discrimination and Labour (Squarcialupi).

62 E.g. MEP Ien van den Heuven made a proposal for EC action with regard to discrimination against lesbians and gay men. EP Debates March 13, 1984, no. 1–311/1, at p. 19; also European Parliament, Documents 1982–3 (doc. no. 1–1072/82) (Van den Heuven). Cf. H. d'Ancona, *Europese Notities, mensen en andere*

minderheden in het Europa van morgen (*European Notes: People and Other Minorities in Tomorrow's Europe*) (Utrecht and Antwerp: Veen, 1989): 88.

63 In a resolution on human rights in the former Soviet Union in 1983, the Soviet government was urged to end the KGB tactic of making dissidents suspicious by accusing them of immorality and homosexuality, and to end the persecution of homosexuals (Resolution on the Human Rights in the Soviet Union, no. 3 161: 67–70, 1983). In 1986, the European Parliament approved a resolution on the rise of racism and fascism in Europe, in which it called for respect for all men and women. Homosexuality was explicitly mentioned (d'Ancona, p. 89). Also in 1986, a resolution by the former member of Parliament Hedy d'Ancona (at present Minister of Welfare, Health, and Cultural Affairs of the Netherlands) on sexual violence against women included a call to extend the word *discrimination* to include sexual preference. Moreover, a call was made to subsidize lesbian self-help groups (Resolution on violence against women, doc. A2-44/86).

64 The Code of Practice was approved on November 27, 1991. Cf. Stonewall Press Release, December 6, 1991.

DENNIS ALTMAN

"The Emergence of a Non-government Response to AIDS"

from *Power and Community: Organizational and Cultural Responses to AIDS* (London: Taylor & Francis, 1994): chapter 2

A number of factors will influence the course of an epidemic, of which the bio-medical are not necessarily the most important. In the case of HIV, its spread was largely related to specific social and cultural patterns: the sexual networks of homosexual men, the availability of needles, the political and economic power relationships of prostitution, the nature of transport routes through areas of high prevalence. Just as the discovery of the virus was possible only because of pre-existing knowledge and assumptions about (retro) viruses, so too the ways in which it spread, and the responses to it, were very much products of particular ideological, political, and social formations, present in the last decades of the twentieth century.

While there were clearly significant differences between the impact of HIV in developed and developing countries, differences linked to the epidemiological patterns found in various societies, AIDS became a reality in a world where global communications had already broken down many of the traditional frontiers and differences between countries. It is perhaps symbolic that the first AIDS cases diagnosed – though almost certainly not the first to exist – were found among homosexual men, for the gay world is a particularly international one, involving rapid mobility and cross-cultural contacts. Without accepting Randy Shilts's rather fanciful concept of "Patient Zero," an airline steward who infected large numbers of homosexual men across North America,[1] there is little doubt that HIV was spread rapidly via international travel, and the common explanation for relatively high infection rates among homosexual men in places as dispersed as San Juan, Sydney and Zurich was their interaction during the early

1980s with American gay men.

It is tempting to postulate two simultaneous epidemics, one in the developed world, beginning in North American gay ghettos and moving from there into injecting drug user and hemophiliac populations, the other, far more generalized, beginning in Central Africa and spreading not into specific communities but into the "general population". While Africa was not necessarily the source – certainly not the only source – this latter pattern was repeated in the Caribbean, South and South-east Asia and the rest of Africa. This has some parallels to early mappings of the epidemic which spoke of Patterns I, II and III based on different epidemiological patterns. Just as these are too simple – in some parts of the world, e.g. Brazil, one could find evidence for all three patterns simultaneously – so too is a divide between the developed and the developing world in terms of the political and social response. Denial and the availability of resources for prevention, care and community organization is not always linked to levels of development or affluence: few societies have been as reluctant to come to terms with the challenge of AIDS as was that very rich country Japan. Community responses were often strongest in countries with relatively few resources, such as Uganda or Zambia.

Nor were social responses to HIV/AIDS necessarily that different across frontiers. Unfortunately denial, ignorance and persecution on the basis of AIDS has been almost universal, and the stigma of the disease has clearly been compounded by its association with already stigmatized forms of sexual (and drug-using) behavior. Almost all societies went through periods in which there were attempts at branding AIDS as a disease imported by foreigners, whether it was Japanese gay bars refusing admission to Westerners, the banning of foreigners (in practice white foreigners) from prostitution complexes in Indonesia, or Indian doctors refusing to treat African students. (Typical of many reactions were the comments of one Indian state health minister that "There is a risk of foreigners giving us this disease called AIDS on a platter".[2]) AIDS panics have taken different forms in different societies, but it would be foolhardy to assume they have been less frequent in societies with greater levels of education and affluence, and an increasingly globalizing media ensured that scare stories, and those portraying AIDS as a disease of "the other," spread rapidly across the world.[3]

Just as the epidemiology of AIDS must be understood within its social context, so too must the community response. The decade in which AIDS was recognized, conceptualized and named was a decade in which the Western world was undergoing the economic rationalizations of Reagan and Thatcher. As Elizabeth Fee and Daniel Fox have written: "Containing health costs had become a major objective of governments in the United States and Western Europe, and these governments were reluctant to recognize, let alone deal with, the potentially devastating costs of coping with a new epidemic."[4] These concerns were reflected in the "structural adjustments" imposed on developing countries by international agencies led by the International Monetary Fund and World Bank which also meant severe reductions in the size of the public sector.

There is considerable literature on the impact of "structural adjustment" on developing countries, and the ways in which it has both increased income gaps within many countries, hastened rapid migration to the shanty towns which now make up the majority of Third World metropolitan areas, and hit women particularly hard.[5] In a 1993 letter to the President of the World Bank, written by the Inter-Church Coalition on Africa, the "single greatest factor" contributing to the poor health of the developing world was identified as the Bank's own emphasis on the diverting of resources to debt servicing and the development of export indus-

tries.[6] Moreover, AIDS developed in a world in which political upheavals, particularly in Eastern Europe and the former Soviet Union, would start to reshape the post-World-War-II map of the world, while destroying public services in places torn by civil strife such as Bosnia and Georgia.

Whether because of "structural adjustments" in South American and Africa, the impact of civil strife and military rule in Burma and Cambodia, or the collapse of communism in Eastern Europe, the spread of the epidemic has often been directly related to larger questions of political economy. One cannot understand, for example, the role of prostitution in Thailand, and the growing importation of young girls into Thai brothels from neighboring Burma and Laos, without understanding the interconnected power of the military and certain government and business interests. The opening up of Vietnam and Cambodia to tourism and the subsequent development of a large sex industry have dramatically increased the risk of spreading HIV infection.[7] The war on drugs, whether in the "golden triangle" of South-east Asia or in South America and US cities, has changed patterns of drug consumption, often increasing rather than decreasing needle use as against inhalation or smoking.

From the former Soviet empire of Eastern Europe and Central Asia come disquieting reports of the spread of HIV as basic services (including blood screening and the availability of disposable syringes) break down, as population mobility and commercial sex increases, and as there are no resources available for prevention or for basic information. As one writer put it: "The Berlin Wall acted as the world's biggest condom."[8] Since its collapse HIV has the potential to spread rapidly in Eastern Europe. In Poland there has been a marked increase in needle use, alongside a shortage of syringes, and stringent Catholic restrictions on providing condoms. Many hospitals in the former Soviet Union lack facilities for proper sterilization, and HIV information is rarely available.[9]

I prefer a formulation which stresses the centrality of political economy to vulnerability to AIDS and its impacts to that which has been framed by Jonathan Mann and adopted by the

Global AIDS Policy Coalition (of which I am a member: this is clearly a friendly disagreement over priorities). In a statement of the Coalition one sentence is central: "The critical relationship between societal discrimination and vulnerability to HIV is the central insight gained from a decade of global work."[10] But "societal discrimination," whether due to difference of gender, class, race, nationality, sexuality or occupation, grows out of the political economy of a given society, namely those arrangements which determine the allocation of resources both nationally and internationally. In a number of cases "development" itself contributes to the conditions making for vulnerability, as when economic changes force many out of rural life, pushing young men to leave their villages for the cities or minefields, and young women into urban factories or "hospitality" work, disrupting families and increasing commercial sex.[11] Political economy, too, helps explain the ways in which AIDS research is both funded and directed. If, as is generally believed, about one-third of all HIV/AIDS research is controlled by the pharmaceutical industry, it becomes important to note that this is essentially an industry dominated by large firms concentrated in half a dozen countries, with development and research led by the United States, Japan and a handful of Western European countries.[12]

If the epidemic developed in a world of structural adjustments and privatization, it also developed in a world in which feminism and gay assertion meant the existence, in at least some places, of existing organizations and communities able to respond to the new crisis. The very idea that community-based organizations should play a leading role in meeting the challenge of a public health crisis is related to a whole series of political and social developments over the past twenty years. The redefinition of public health, sometimes described by the term "the new public health," achieved official status with the adoption in 1986 by an international conference of thirty-eight countries of what has become known as the Ottawa Charter. This declaration is committed to a policy for "health for all," stressing the importance of primary health care, of the promotion of healthy life styles and of prevention and health promotion. Most significant for our purposes, the Ottawa Charter, through its focus on the creation of supportive environments and the "enabling" of communities through development of personal skills and health advocacy, is "in a real sense a challenge to professional practice as it is found throughout the world."[13] As the Charter states:

> Health promotion works through concrete and effective community action in setting priorities, making decisions, planning strategies and implementing them to achieve better health. At the heart of this process is the empowerment of communities, their ownership and control of their own endeavors and destinies.[14]

In a sense AIDS, already developing at the time the Ottawa Charter was adopted, proved an acid test for the principles of "the new public health." (It may also have showed the limits of this new paradigm, particularly in its failure to place respect for basic human rights in a sufficiently central position.) No other disease, Jonathan Mann has claimed, has so revolutionized attitudes to the meaning and provision of health care. The old paradigm, Mann notes:

> focused on discovering the external agents of disease, disability and premature death. Inevitably the emphasis was medical and technological, involving experts and engineers, and for certain purposes this approach was quite effective. However this paradigm envisioned a fundamental dichotomy between individual and social interests; accordingly, and in concert with the spirit of the age, governments were called upon to mediate and to prevent disease through laws and the work of bureaucracies. Attention to behavioral, social and societal considerations was often rudimentary and naive. Public health systems often favored coercion and compulsion without considering their effects on human rights.[15]

Already when AIDS was first conceptualized many of the assumptions of this old paradigm were being challenged. The requirements imposed by a new epidemic, which could not be cured nor prevented through bio-medical means, made new models of public health particularly relevant, as concepts of empowerment and self-esteem came to be central in the development of new strategies for education and intervention. Perhaps most significant, leaders like Mann developed an analysis of human rights as central to any AIDS strategy, not just for moral reasons but also because their abuse made it more difficult to reach and affect those people who were most vulnerable to HIV.[16]

Concern for human rights is a theme which runs through this book. For the moment let me note that there are two basic sorts of rights which have engaged community groups, namely those involving protection against discrimination and those ensuring equal access to information, support and care. The former have received considerable attention, with reference to issues such as travel, compulsory testing, confidentiality etc. The latter is less often discussed under the rubric of human rights, yet it is central: the greatest abuses of human dignity in the current epidemic are found in the extraordinary inequality of resources available to provide both basic information, preventive measures and even palliative care to those with HIV/AIDS. Access to condoms, to clean needles and to basic medical treatment is as essential to empowerment and self-esteem as is protection against discrimination and persecution, and larger concerns such as food and shelter have immediate consequences for HIV care and prevention.[17] All too often, access to such basic services is distorted by patterns of discrimination based on gender, race, sexuality and the larger inequalities of the global political economy.

The "new public health" is built on the interest in "community organizing" that had been growing in most Western countries since the late 1960s (and become a major ingredient of development theory in many Third World countries). The new interest in "community organizing" stemmed both from those with a commitment to grassroots participation *and* from those interested in cutting back the role of the state, leading to sometimes strange alliances (in theory at least) between new right and new left critiques of the state. Particularly in the English-speaking industrialized world, cut-backs, economic rationalization and "de-institutionalization" have been the framework within which conservative governments have seen community organizations as worthy of support. As Rosamund Thorpe suggests,

governments have fostered community organizations as an alternative to more costly direct interventions, while at the same time such organizations develop from the anger of those who find the existing state system is unable to meet their demands.[18] While there may seem to be a division between those who see the voluntary sector as complementary to government, and those who see it as posing a fundamental challenge, by the early 1980s considerable numbers of people had been exposed to the ideas of participatory involvement, community organizing, opposition to large-scale bureaucracy, and the need to transform political consciousness as a means of transforming social structures.[19]

For somewhat different reasons the idea of "community development" was also enthusiastically fostered by various United Nations programs from the 1960s onwards, as a "third way" towards economic development. As J. A. Ponsioen wrote in 1962:

> Community development is not only a method of development ... The ideology of community development rejects the authoritarian way of developing countries – the Soviet approach – and the individualistic way through competition for material welfare – as was the Western approach. The ideology of community development appeals to the citizens of a community to develop their own initiatives.[20]

The influence of concepts of community development would become increasingly significant as international development agencies, both inter-governmental and private, became increasingly concerned with HIV/AIDS from the late 1980s on.

The stress on development would be accompanied by a somewhat belated recognition of the significance of gender, as there came to be a greater understanding of the double impact of HIV on women as both those at greater risk of infection and those on whom the burdens of care most heavily falls. In many developing countries, governments and development agencies have turned to women's organizations in order to develop AIDS-specific programs. But a feminist analysis had already impacted on the response to HIV in the developed world. As Eve K. Sedgwick wrote:

> Feminist perspectives on medicine and health care

issues, on civil disobedience, and on the politics of class and race as well as of sexuality have been centrally enabling for the recent waves of AIDS activism. What this activism returns to the lesbians involved in it may include a more richly pluralized range of imaginings of lines of gender and sexual identification.[21]

THE DEVELOPMENT OF AIDS COMMUNITY ORGANIZATIONS

As AIDS was first identified in the United States (where for a short time, let us remember, it bore the name Gay Related Immune Deficiency) it was here that the first community based responses emerged. I have written elsewhere about the particularly American nature of volunteerism which was expressed in those early groups.[22] The first of them, the Gay Men's Health Crisis (GMHC) was formed by a group of concerned gay men in New York in 1982, and focused originally on research and education. Quickly GMHC found itself having to set up a plethora of direct services for people infected by the virus, and developed a large number of volunteers programs to help people in need of home care and support. One observer, commenting on the rapid development of GMHC into a major agency, quotes Tocqueville's admiration at "the extreme skill with which the inhabitants of the United States succeed in proposing a common objective for the exertions of a great many men and inducing them voluntarily to pursue it."[23] Those who volunteered for AIDS work, however, differed somewhat from what had become the normal profile of American volunteers, particularly in health care, a group described by Diane Johnson in her novel of hospital life as "a corps of candy-stripers and retired people of the upper middle class".[24] As we shall see, they included a large number of people who were politically aware, and would demand a role in managing the epidemic very different from that of the conventional healthcare volunteer.

This development of voluntary organizations providing direct services was soon followed in other American cities, then by comparable organizations in Canada, Australia and northern Europe, often directly inspired by the American model. The New Zealand case, where the original AIDS Support Network was founded by a small group of gay men, including one who had been infected by HIV during his time in the States,[25] was common to a number of countries. In Britain, the Terrence Higgins Trust was founded in 1982 by Higgins's lover and friends after he died of AIDS.[26] In Sweden and Denmark, the existing gay organizations became the central focus for HIV work in their communities, although there have been tensions between RFSL, the major Swedish gay organization, and the far more respectable Noah's Ark, which was established to do AIDS prevention and support in conjunction with the Swedish Red Cross. In a number of cases, such as the Netherlands and Canada's first AIDS organization, AIDS Vancouver, gay doctors played a crucial role. Indeed gay doctors, whether as individuals or through organizations such as the Bay Area Physicians for Human Rights in San Francisco, were critical as mediators between emerging community organizations and biomedical and health authorities, although their role has tended to decline as the organizations have institutionalized their relations with the state. Similarly, the impetus for HIV organizing in some societies has come from nurses, as in Poland where one of Eastern Europe's first AIDS counselling services uses midwifery and nursing students for peer education.[27]

In all of these cases, such organizations could not have existed without the previous decade of organizing among gay men and lesbians which followed the student riots of 1968 in France and other Western countries, and the Stonewall riots in New York in 1969. During the 1970s, there had been a slow institutionalization of the new lesbian/gay consciousness which grew out of these political movements, with the development of a well-organized press, of social and political groups and of a large and visible commercial world.[28] Almost without exception the first AIDS organizations built on this base, and one observer has commented that in Germany "the basic and leading decisions in health politics of how to design the strategies of learning and the protection of blood products were decided mainly in the triangle of state–medical system–gay movement."[29]

Particularly important in these formative years was the gay press, which provided much of the available early information on the epidemic, as well as acting as a vital tool in mobilizing the community. When I lived in San Francisco for a while in 1985, non-gay researchers and educators found in *New York Native* (a gay bi-weekly) an invaluable source of information and ideas; the *Native* became far less influential as it became obsessed with a series of rather strange theories about the cause of the epidemic, but other gay publications, such as *Outrage* (in Australia), *Body Politic* (in Canada) and *Le Gai Pied* (in France)[30] seemed to provide the best explanation for non-specialists of what was painstakingly being reported in the medical press. A handful of gay journalists, such as Nathan Fain, Larry Mass, and Michael Helquist (in the United States) and Adam Carr (in Australia), played an absolutely crucial role in developing the base upon which early communal organizing could take place. Nor has the crucial role of the press been confined to the developed world: in India and Indonesia (and I suspect in some Latin American countries as well) the emergence of a gay press was an integral part of the development of early community HIV work.[31]

Where an organized gay base was lacking it was much more difficult to establish AIDS organizations. Apart from people with hemophilia, who also had pre-existing networks and organizations, other groups in Western countries found responding to the demands of AIDS much more problematic, so that even now there are weak communal structures in countries such as Spain and Italy where the epidemic is primarily found amongst drug-users and their partners. (But even there the gay community was significant. Thus the first community-based organization in Italy, the Associazione Solidieta AIDS of Milan, was founded by gay activists, and the Portuguese group ABRACO has a significant gay membership amongst its Trustees.) While AIDS has gradually opened up space for organization among users, only the Netherlands, with its National Federation of Junkie Unions, had an existing institutional base for work among needle users.[32] Japan stands out as the one country where hemophilia organiza-

tions have been the most effective part of the community sector in influencing governmental responses,[33] although a number of other countries have provision for compensating people with hemophilia who contracted HIV through infected blood products.[34]

One study in the United States suggested that government responses to AIDS were clearly linked to the strength of the gay movement in respective cities.[35] This seems true of the development of both government and non-government responses in most Western countries, and the failure to analyze the relationship between existing gay/lesbian organization and government responses is a weakness of the attempt by Moerkerk to develop a typology of European responses to the epidemic.[36] It is clear, however, that those countries he identifies as making a "pragmatic" response to HIV/AIDS (The Netherlands, Norway, Denmark, and Switzerland) are ones where the gay movement was already institutionalized and recognized to a greater extent than those (such as Sweden, Germany, and Britain) where the response is described as "political," and certainly more so than those where it is typified as "bio-medical" (France, Belgium, Spain, and Italy) or emergent (Eastern Europe). In the latter two cases, the gay movement was weak or non-existent; in the case of the "political response," governments sometimes seemed, as in the case of Sweden, interested in deliberately de-homosexualizing AIDS.[37] At least some areas of what was then West Germany and perhaps Belgium would seem to fit better Moerkerk's idea of the pragmatic, as in both countries there as considerable co-operation between the state and community groups. (It is also true that in Bavaria there was a more traditional public health response summed up by one commentator as "contain-and-control."[38]) The French case is also more complex: it is true that the gay community was far less organized than its Scandinavian or Dutch counterparts, but when Daniel Defert sought to establish AIDES in 1984 he was able to draw on very considerable gay support and personnel. Moerkerk's typology does seem to fit Britain, bearing out the observation of Simon Watney that gay communities were not recognized there as legitimate constituencies as in the United States, Denmark, and The Netherlands.[39]

There was a further common element to those countries where AIDS organizations first developed, and that was a tradition of volunteerism. The willingness of citizens to participate in voluntary work is a particular feature of English-speaking democracies, and is nowhere more marked than in the United States. (Ironically, the emergence of groups such as GMHC and AIDS Project Los Angeles during Reagan's Presidency, caused some embarrassment for an Administration which loudly trumpeted its support for volunteer organizations – while being very unwilling to recognize that the gay community was taking the lead, as when it rejected a nomination of Gay Men's Health Crisis for an award honoring volunteer work.[40]) This tradition is much weaker in most other countries, and is often advanced as a reason for the slowness of AIDS organizations to emerge in countries such as France, despite their comparatively high number of cases. One observer was told in Germany that there was no tradition of volunteering because it was felt that the state should provide, and that volunteer service was "women's work."[41]

Despite this comment, the local branches of Deutsche AIDS Hilfe have, in fact, recruited a considerable number of volunteers. In France, and even more so in the rest of southern Europe, community-based organizations seem much weaker than in countries such as Canada or Australia, with smaller populations and lesser case loads. Nonetheless, by 1990 AIDES, which is by far the largest French group, claimed 1500 volunteers in 31 cities, and performed most of the services associated with AIDS organizations in English-speaking countries. It may be that just as France borrowed enthusiastically from American styles of homosexuality in the 1970s and 1980s, so it has been exposed through the AIDS epidemic to American-style volunteerism.

It would be a mistake to assume that volunteerism is confined to developed Western countries; some very poor countries have a strong tradition of both community organizing and volunteer work. Some African countries have a rich network of local community groups, and groups such as TASO in Uganda, or the Family Health Trust of Zambia, have an extensive volunteer component. AIDS workers from India have told me that contrary to my expectations they could call on a large number of potential volunteers, mainly retired people and students. (In some cases volunteers receive what one organizer referred to in conversation as "incentives" for their work, a recognition that one must have a certain basic standard of resources to be able to "volunteer" anything.) The Duang Prateep Foundation, which operates among slum dwellers in the docks area of Bangkok, is able to draw on a network of mainly student volunteers for a range of education and community services.[42] But it is true that the initiative for many of the groups which are emerging in developing countries clearly come from people who are rather similar in background and commitment to those who founded the first AIDS organizations in the West, and in some cases – for example middle-class Westernized gay men, or professional women working with street kids in places like Brazil, the Philippines, or India – are divided by large gulfs of class, culture and even language from many of the people with whom they seek to work.

Certainly the epidemiology of AIDS was different in most of the developing world: not only in Africa, but also in most of the Caribbean, parts of South America, and in south Asia. The early AIDS organizations in these parts of the world, however, also grew out of existing networks and organizations, and in South America in particular the gay influence was very significant.[43] In countries as dissimilar as Peru, Mexico, and Nicaragua, the gay movement was central to the emergence of AIDS-specific groups (and at least in Nicaragua and Peru lesbians played a central role). In Chile the first HIV organization, the Corporacion Chilena de Prevención del SIDA, was begun by a group of gay men, and in turn gave rise to a specifically gay group which then broke with the Corporación. In Brazil some gay groups joined with social workers, researchers, liberal clergy, and PWAs (People with AIDS) themselves to establish HIV/AIDS organizations.[44] In Malaysia and Singapore, gay men played a crucial role in the first AIDS organizations, and in Malaysia it was the defiantly named Pink

Triangle which has become the country's best known AIDS group. Gay networks were important in the beginnings of AIDS organizing in India, Hong Kong, Japan, Indonesia and the Philippines (where one of the first gay groups took its name from the bar where its members first met to become the Library Foundation). The development of AIDS groups in Eastern Europe and the former Soviet Union appear closely linked to the emergence of gay organizations.[45]

In Africa there was some gay influence, for example through the early support for community-based work in Zimbabwe and South Africa, but there the main push came from those most affected by the new epidemic, usually women, who bore the double burden of direct infection and the responsibility of caring for others. Uganda's first AIDS service organization, The AIDS Support Organization (TASO) was founded by Noreine Kaleeba in 1987 after her husband had died from AIDS, and in its origins brought together people who were themselves infected, or who were living with people who were infected. In South Africa, a black woman activist, Refiloe Serote, was instrumental in the establishment of the Soweto Townships AIDS Project and Alexandra AIDS Action.

In other cases, already existing organizations, whether religious, social or developmental, became the major focus for grass roots AIDS work. This was true, for example, in some parts of Africa and the Pacific where the Red Cross or church groups such as the Salvation Army established AIDS projects. It was equally true in Thailand, the Philippines, and India where existing non-government agencies, some of them already involved in grassroots and community development work, became the focal point for much HIV work. (In both India and the Philippines existing health organizations often took on HIV work, and the Indian community sector is notable for the extent to which organizations are still dominated by doctors.) In some countries it was international NGOs such as the Red Cross which provided the basis for initial AIDS organizing, and which continue to provide the bulk of funding and personnel.

The two major variables in the establishment of AIDS organizations appear to be epidemiological and political. By the former, I mean the extent to which the disease was concentrated in, and identified with, particular groups, and the extent to which such groups had the ability to develop their own organizations. By the latter, I am referring to existing traditions of organizing outside government, to the amount of space available for community mobilization. One would not be surprised to find virtually no AIDS organizations in countries such as China or Iraq where the private sphere is virtually non-existent; equally it is not surprising that they are stronger in Sweden than in Romania, in Nigeria rather than Zaire, not because the incidence of AIDS is higher in the former (it is not) but because there is much more developed tradition of community organizing, and more acceptance of its role by governments.

While it is often assumed that community organizations are most likely to occur in rich industrialized countries, in fact the political system rather than economic affluence seems a more reliable guide to the possibilities for organization. Some countries of Asia and South America have traditions of grassroots and community work, stronger than can be found in some much richer countries of southern Europe. Equally, the prospects for community-based groups seem particularly weak in the countries of the Middle East, where governments even in rich countries such as Saudi Arabia or the Gulf states are particularly inhospitable to them.

In some of those countries with limited political space for political or communal organizing of the Western sort, there is nonetheless a strong basis for community mobilization and education through the institutions of the state or the dominant political party. In a number of developing countries, "mass organizations," often of women, youth, students etc., are the closest structures to community-based organizations, and in some cases they have been mobilized to run AIDS prevention campaigns. Their dependence on governments does, of course, raise questions about their ability to reach people engaging in activities which are officially denied or frowned upon, but in both Vietnam and China there are signs that some far-sighted officials have found way of stretching the limits of what is allowed in the interests of prevention. (In China, for example, there has been a limited amount of outreach to homosexual men in Beijing which involved some tentative attempts at community building, at least until it went beyond what the government could accept.)

In the early developments around AIDS one can see the outlines of a struggle for control, in which medical professionals, government officials, affected communities, and traditional sources of moral authority, particularly churches, vied to be seen as the "experts" on the new disease. How AIDS was conceptualized was an essential tool in a sometimes very bitter struggle: was it to be understood as a primarily biomedical problem, in which case its control should be under that of the medical establishment, or was it rather, as most community-based groups argued, a social and political issue, which required a much greater variety of expertise?

At some level the ways in which an epidemic is conceptualized determines the sort of responses which are possible. If for example it is seen as essentially a foreign import, then screening and quarantine become attractive measures: the Indian minister referred to earlier went on to argue: "This country is not so supine as to just sit and watch... At least we should screen the high-risk group among foreigners, because our women are exposed to them."[46] If, on the other hand, it is understood as the result of private behavior among people, many of whom will have good reason to fear state regulation and control, there is likely to be a very different emphasis on education and grassroots organization.

This point can be illustrated by the sort of comparison already referred to by Moerkerk between the response of countries such as The Netherlands and Norway, which tended to the latter response, and those (also liberal democracies) such as Sweden and Belgium where there was a much stronger emphasis on traditional public health methods of control. Within the United States there are striking differences between cities such as San Francisco, where a pre-existing gay/lesbian political establishment affected the city response, and more conservative jurisdictions such as Miami or Dallas. Here

the human rights dimension becomes crucial: in almost all countries, as we shall see, discrimination and prejudice has made the defense of basic human rights a central issue for AIDS organizations. The extent to which this is supported by governments is a reflection of larger political forces and pre-existing political patterns.

The role of CBOs has been increasingly supported by international agencies, such as the Global Programme On AIDS (GPA) and the United Nations Development Programme (UNDP). They have produced copious documentation arguing for the centrality of the community sector in meeting the challenges of the epidemic, and in providing peer education and on-the-ground support and care. They have been less forthright about the need for CBOs to play a role in policy-making, although without this being recognized the community sector runs the risk of becoming a source of cheap labor carrying out programs which may not be appropriate to the needs of those it represents.

DIFFERENT FORMS OF AIDS ORGANIZATIONS

Governments tend to speak of non-government organizations (NGOs) and community-based organizations (CBOs) without making much distinction. The former term is a much broader one, and one which covers both the sort of grassroots response to AIDS found in GMHC, Pink Triangle, or TASO, as well as the established international agencies such as Red Cross, World Vision, or the Salvation Army. In an early attempt at clarifying these terms Broadhead and O'Malley wrote of

> groups which represent the views of and act on behalf of their own members: peasant movements, trade unions, and feminist organizations, for example. Such bodies are referred to as "people's organizations" to distinguish them from those NGOs which act as intermediaries in the development process rather than as grassroots organizers.[47]

How we conceptualize AIDS organizations – which terms we use – is therefore crucial. For the most part this books speaks of "community-based organizations" (CBOs) rather than "non-government organizations" (NGOs) or "AIDS service organizations" (ASOs). The former is, of course, a much broader grouping, which could be discussed in terms of the work of, say, the Red Cross and Red Crescent, or of already existing development agencies (Oxfam, World Vision etc.) in the HIV field. Many NGOs are international, and it is often difficult to distinguish between the work done as a result of external decisions and that which is driven by indigenous factors. (Using a broad definition of NGOs one estimate claimed that by 1991 there were more than 200 NGOs working on AIDS in Africa and 500 in Latin America.[48]) ASOs is a term used by the World Health Organization's Global Programme on AIDS, and is useful to describe all those organizations other than government which provide services related to HIV. At the same time it implies an emphasis on the provision of efficient services but not necessarily on accountability or representation. In recent years there has been some use of the term GOGs (Groups Outside Government) and, in the United States, PVOs (Private Voluntary Organizations).

With all these terms the emphasis is clearly on groups which are independent of the state and whose membership is by choice rather than ascriptive. If we exclude economic associations, and those which are not controlled by their membership, we further refine the concept to mean "spare time participatory associations," which is the approach adopted by David Sills.[49] A further refinement is to use the term "self-help organization," and Carl Milofsky has recently proposed the term "community self-help organization," to center on groups which "represent attempts to solve social problems through local participation, social action, resource mobilization, and building a sense of community and of geographic identification."[50] The term in much social work literature of self-help groups places the emphasis on the people who are affected, but has connotations of limited and non-political activity, while voluntary organization has similar drawbacks – the emphasis suggests people who offer to assist within existing structures rather than to create forms which allow them to determine their own work. Nonetheless, at least one major national AIDS organization – Deutsche AIDS Hilfe[51] – refers to itself as a self-help group (at least in its English publications), and defines itself as an amalgam of a professional association and a representative body.

A further refinement of this idea comes in the distinction made by Aggleton, Weeks and Taylor-Laybourn between self-help and altruism as competing characteristics of AIDS organizations.[52] There is already a small literature around the concept of "altruism" in AIDS work, with some disagreement about its centrality. While Weeks and Kayal, writing of Britain and the United States respectively, have seen it as a very significant concept, Patton is more critical, stressing the need to "deconstruct the revitalized rhetoric of altruism which reappears in the context of Reaganism after nearly two decades in which new social movements have preached community and self-empowerment. This new, rightist altruism has engendered social policies ... [of] privatization of formerly social welfare practices." This maneuver relies on free market economics that presuppose notions of individualism and competition, an implicit evolutionism which undercuts analyses of systemic disenfranchisement of racial/ethnic minorities, and in the late 1980s equated volunteerism with female leisure activity.[53] Some of this difference, as Weeks points out, is due to the greater strength of a social democratic notion of the state in Britain than in the United States; there is a religious component to Kayal's notions of altruism which is very American in its conception. While Patton's warning seems to me important, it is also true that the amount of volunteer work in AIDS organizations is remarkable, and no less so because there is a complex mix of motivations underlying volunteer involvement.[54]

In general I shall use the term "community-based organization," which is the term adopted by those AIDS organizations with which I am most familiar (although there are some language problems: outside Quebec the term "organisation communautaire" has little meaning in French). Certainly the elements which Milofsky seeks in his "community self-help organisations" are those I will seek to elucidate in the discussion of community-based organizations – except that the rather clinical term "social problem" is barely adequate to encompass the human grief and devastation which the HIV/AIDS epidemic represents to those who are responding to it. In using the term community-based organizations I recognize that this may leave open just which and whose communities are being referred to, and that many of the groups I shall discuss work with, rather than grow organically out of, their communities. For my purposes the basic test is the extent to which the organization has a commitment to the development and the empowerment of the people it claims to represent (and thus some groups may be included which in other senses are more accurately described as NGOs).

Other non-government organizations have developed in response to AIDS, both fund-raising bodies, such as the American Foundation for AIDS Research (AMFAR) or the Japanese AIDS Foundation, and associations of professionals such as the AIDS Society for Asia and the Pacific (ASAP), but these would not normally fit the definition of a CBO. On the other hand we shall be discussing some organizations which did not originate because of HIV, but which have accepted AIDS as one of their central concerns. The clearest example may be the various organizations of people with hemophilia, but there are many other examples, such as the development agency ENDA (Environmental Development Action in the Third World) based in Senegal which lists action against AIDS as one of its ten major development priorities.

It should be noted that in most cases there will be a strong emphasis on volunteerism in these organizations, even if the bulk of work is performed by paid staff. Writing of Indonesia Philip Eldridge has made the point that

> most organizations could not function without paid staff, even though general levels of remuneration in the voluntary sector are generally below what can commonly be obtained in the public or private sectors, with longer and more unpredictable working hours. However, the other dimension of meaning associated with the concept of voluntarism, emphasizing autonomy, free will and creativity remains important to the whole enterprise.[55]

Eldridge suggests implicitly that community organizations exist in a third sector, which is neither that of the state nor of profit-driven enterprise, and this distinction is significant in both developed and developing countries.

Rather than dividing organizations between those in the developed and the developing world – which is an unnecessarily crude and sometimes misleading distinction – it might be useful to think of them as divided between those which are based in communities defined by behavior and those defined by place. The first case includes groups based on identities which are assumed to have a special relationship to HIV/AIDS: people with hemophilia, gay men, injecting drug users, sex workers, street kids. The second involves the more traditional usage of community as related to geography, and will be found where HIV is spread more widely through a particular area without it being particularly linked to any minority behavior or identity. Such places will be found largely in the developing world, although there are some community organizations in ethnic ghetto areas of the United States which would fit this model.

There are further permutations one might suggest: some organizations, such as TASO, were founded by and include many people who are HIV-positive and their families.[56] In many cases existing organizations became *de facto* AIDS organizations, whether these were hemophilia societies, church groups in parts of Africa and the Pacific, or development agencies such as ENDA. This is true for a number of groups working with sex workers, where organizations such as Empower in Thailand or Kabalikat, a health and welfare agency in the Philippines (whose full name means "partner of the Filipino family"), found themselves increasingly involved with AIDS, partly because of the magnitude of the problem and partly because of the availability of HIV-related funding. As HIV impacts more and more on women, one can see an increase in the role of women's organizations in the HIV field. In India many of the small NGOs working on HIV/AIDS grew out of already existing networks of primary health care organizations.[57]

Though useful for analytical purposes, the distinction between AIDS-specific and more general organizations is often blurred. In many cases HIV has been the trigger for community organizing among previously unacknowledged communities, whether these be sex workers, drug users, or gay men (sometimes in alliance with lesbians), and these organizations in turn will develop new forms of community and will make new demands on the political system. The development of gay organizations in a number of Asian cities in the past few years has clearly been assisted by the AIDS epidemic, which has generated both a sense of urgency and some resources for organizing.[58] AIDS is often the impetus for organization among sex workers, as in the case of the group Patita Uddhar Sabha which was set up in 1992 by prostitutes in Delhi's red light area to demand better health facilities and the supply of condoms.[59] Even organizations of positive people are rarely totally exclusive, often allowing participation for lovers, family and friends, giving rise to the phrase "people living with AIDS" (PLWAs).

AIDS AND COMMUNITIES OF IDENTITY

Thinking about community immediately opens up very interesting ways of extending the now well-known distinction between behavior and identity. We are used to recognizing that by no means all men who have sex with men can be thought of as members of the gay community. I would suggest that equally there are some people who do not have sex with their own gender who may well be part of that community: their work, their commitment, their political allegiance binds them to it, even if they would fail a Kinsey scale test on sexual orientation. Such people have played a crucial role in almost every gay-based AIDS organization that has an unresolved contradiction between the fact that they claim a special relationship to the gay (sometimes gay and lesbian) community, while also providing support and services to everyone affected by HIV, irrespective of sexuality.

In the case of other communities of identity there are somewhat different issues. Many people who speak for sex workers or drug users are not so themselves (though they may once have been). Where prostitution and drug use are heavily stigmatized and criminalized it may

indeed be impossible to develop communal organizations; the best one can do is to develop advocacy organizations which will seek to represent them. (Sometimes professional social workers claim to speak on behalf of drug users and sex workers, though in effect retaining a traditional professional–client relationship.) Effective user groups still remain essentially confined to a small number of liberal social democracies, such as The Netherlands, Germany, Australia, and Italy, although there is a small amount of peer-based outreach to drug users in Malaysia, Nepal, Thailand, and Brazil. There is a parallel in some developing countries, where the gay presence in AIDS organizations needs to be played down, so that a group such as Action for AIDS in Singapore is *de facto* a gay organization, but because very few people are prepared to come out as gay must disguise this to some extent.

Whether sex workers and users will generate communities similar to the gay community seems to me an open question. Unless there is a willingness to assert that sex work and drug use are actually desirable it is difficult to see how they can become the basis for a genuine socio-political identity: so far the bulk of self-organization has tended to hover uneasily between an apologetic and a defiant tone, which is not sufficient to produce the basis for a communal identity. Thus a declaration of the European Interest Group of Drug Users in 1992 proclaimed: "As with alcohol, we do not encourage drug use. But if a person uses drugs and faces problems, we urge a non-criminalizing approach, unprejudiced medical and social care, safer use and harm reduction." This is not the language of self-assertion usually associated with successful community organizing.

Yet despite this reservation, it is certainly true that community organizing by and among commercial sex workers has been a feature of HIV/AIDS work in large numbers of countries, often following a model described for Morocco:

> Our point of entry was "Fatima," a prostitute with whom we developed a relationship at our clinic in Casablanca. We gave her condoms to distribute to her colleagues, and some of them began coming to us with her in search of information about AIDS. This led to the creation of peer

IDENTITY + CATEGORISATION — Mobilisation of communities in response to epidemic

education networks which distributed condoms along with information about AIDS and other sexually transmitted diseases. Fatima and several of her fellow prostitutes have made an audio tape in which they speak in their own words about AIDS prevention.[60]

Even though the organization among sex workers in this case originated with an existing agency, the encouragment to the women to develop their own networks and their own means of education, without any pressure to remove them from the sex trade, makes this approach fall clearly within the ambit of community development.

Unlike the more traditional community organization based on place, the development of identity-based CBOs is closely related to larger questions around sexuality (or, in the case of users, drugs). But even the geographic-village, neighborhood-community organization dealing with HIV will find it comes in contact with similar issues. Any attempt at grassroots prevention education means confronting the realities of human behavior which propriety and custom would prefer to ignore. Prostitution, child abuse, homosexuality, and drug use are realities that those working in AIDS constantly face, and in dealing with these realities more conservative community organizations themselves go through cultural and social changes. At the grassroots level many church groups accept, and even encourage, practices such as the use of condoms that their leadership proscribe. At least one Catholic organization in Brazil, Apoio Religioso Contra AIDS, has supported the self-organization of commercial sex workers.

A dialectic process is at work here: communities give rise to organizations, but organizations can also help create communities as HIV/AIDS opens up new possibilities and needs for people to organize around categories such as sexuality, sex work, and drug use. Indeed, the extent to which the early discourse around the epidemic stressed its links to homosexuality ("the gay plague" was a common term in many countries) – even though this was soon not an accurate reflection of the known epidemiology – helped ensure a powerful mobilization in response. There is a certain irony that an epidemic that in some ways has brought an upsurge of homophobia (in its original meaning of "fear and loathing of homosexuality and homosexuals") has also led to the strengthening of gay communities and the recognition of homosexuality as legitimate in many parts of the world.[61] At least in some countries the same is true for drug users and sex workers.

NOTES

1 Shilts, R. (1987), *And the Band Played On* (New York, St Martin's Press).
2 Quoted in Girimaji, P. (1990), "India: Less Complacency Now," in *The Third Epidemic*, a Panos Dossier (London: Panos Institute) 191.
3 See Brown P. (1992), "AIDS in the Media," in Mann, J., Tarantola, D. and Netter, T., *AIDS in the World* (Cambridge, MA: Harvard University Press): especially 721–2.
4 Fee, E. and Fox, D. (1992), "The Contemporary Historiography of AIDS," in Fee, E. and Fox, D. (eds), *AIDS: The Making of a Chronic Disease* (Berkeley: University of California): 2–3.
5 See, for example, Bujra, J. (1990), "Talking Development: Why Woman Must Pay? Gender and the Development Debate in Tanzania," *African Review of Political Economy* 47: 44–63; Ghai, D. (1991), *The IMF and the South: The Social Impact of Crisis and Adjustment* (London: Zed Books); Hellinger, S., Hellinger, D. and O'Regan, F. (1988), *Aid for Just Development* (Boulder and London): 147–50, Lynne, Rienner; Murphy, C. (1990), "Freezing the North–South Bloc(k) after the East–West Thaw," *Socialist Review* (Berkeley), 90: 3: 25–46.
6 Miller, S. K. (1993), "Prescription for the Health of the World?", *New Scientist* (10 July): 8.
7 Strubbe, B. (1993), "Vietnam's Next Battle," *Outrage* (Melbourne) (May): 8–10.
8 McCathie, A. (1993), "The World's Biggest Condom?," *Checkpoint* (Berlin), 6: 17.
9 See the articles collected in AIDS/Link (National Council for International Health), Washington (January/February 1993).
10 Mann, J. (1993), *Global AIDS Policy Coalition: Towards a New Health Strategy* (Cambridge, MA: Harvard University Press).
11 See Miller, N. and Carballo, M. (1989), "AIDS: A Disease of Development?" *AIDS & Society* (October): 1–21; Weeramunda, J. (1990), "Prostitution and AIDS in Sri Lanka," *AIDS & Society* (April): 5.
12 For an introduction to the complex world of multinational pharmaceutical companies see Balance, R., Pogany, J. and Forstner, J. (1992),

The World's Pharmaceutical Industries (Aldershot, Hants: Edward Elgar).

13 Ashton, J. and Seymour, H. (1988), *The New Public Health* (Milton Keynes: Open University Press): 37.

14 Ottawa Charter for Health Promotion WHO, Health & Welfare Canada, Canadian Public Health Association, 1986. Note that the thirty-eight countries represented included both West and East bloc countries, but relatively few developing ones.

15 Mann, J. (1991), "The New Health Care Paradigm," in *Focus: A Guide to AIDS Research and Counselling*, AIDS Health Project, San Francisco, University of California, 6: 3 (February): 1.

16 For an overview of the human rights issues raised by HIV/AIDS, see Hamblin, J. (1991), "The Role of the Law in HIV/AIDS Policy," *AIDS* 5 (suppl. 2): S239–43; Somerville, M. and Orkin, A. (1989), "Human Rights, Discrimination and AIDS," *AIDS* 3 (suppl. 1): S283–87; Tomasevski, K. (1992), "AIDS and Human Rights," in Mann, J., Tarantola, D. and Netter, T. (1992), *AIDS in the World* (Harvard University Press): 538–73.

17 See Hendriks, A. and Leckie, S. (1993), "Housing Rights and Housing Needs in the context of AIDS," *AIDS* 7 (suppl. 1): S271–80.

18 Thorpe, R. and Petruchenia, J. (1985), *Community Work or Social Change: An Australian Perspective* (Sydney: RKI).

19 See, for example, Lees, R. and Mayo, M. (1984), *Community Action for Change* (London: Routledge & Kegan Paul): 11.

20 Ponsioen, J. A. (1962), *Social Welfare Policy: Contribution to Theory* (Mouton's-Gravenhage: Mouton): 52.

21 Sedgwick, E. K. (1990), *Epistemology of the Closet* (San Francisco: University of California Press): 38–9.

22 See Altman, D. (1986), *AIDS and the New Puritanism* (London: Pluto) (also published as *AIDS in the Mind of America* (Doubleday, 1986): especially ch. 4.

23 Kobasa, S. (1991), "AIDS Volunteering," in Nelkin, D., Willis, D. and Parris, S., *A Disease of Society* (New York: Cambridge University Press): 177.

24 Johnson, D. (1990), *Health and Happiness* (New York: Knopf): 5.

25 See Parkinson, P. and Hughes, T. (1987), "The Gay Community and the Response to AIDS in New Zealand," *NZ Medical Journal* 100: 77–9.

26 On the early history of the Trust see Davies, P. M., Hickson, F., Hunt, A., Weatherburn, P. and Project SIGMA (1993), *Sex, Gay Men and AIDS* (London: Falmer Press): 23–5.

27 Interview with Zbigniew Halat (1992), *Global AIDS News* 3: 16–24.

28 See Altman, D. (1982), *The Homosexualization of America* (New York: St Martin's Press): especially ch. 4.

29 Rosenbrock, R. (1992), "AIDS: Questions and Lessons for Public Health" *Wissenschaftszentrum Berlin für Sozialforschung*: 18.

30 For a survey of the role of *Gai Pied*, see Arnal, F. (1989), "Agence en Panne," *Gai Pied* (Paris) 388 (October 5).

31 On India, see Gargan, E. (1991), "Coming Out in India, with a Nod from the Gods," *New York Times* (15 August): A4.

32 See van Wijngaarden, J. K. (1992), "The Netherlands: A Consensual Society," in Kirp, D. and Bayer, R., *AIDS in the Industrialised Democracies* (New Brunswick: Rutgers University Press).

33 See Feldman, E. and Yonemoto, S. (1992), "Japan: AIDS as a 'Non-issue'," in Kirp, D. and Bayer, R., *AIDS in the Industrialised Democracies* (New Brunswick: Rutgers University Press).

34 See Table 9.26 in Mann, J., Tarantola, D. and Netter, T. (1992), *AIDS in the World* (Cambridge, MA: Harvard University Press): 444.

35 Cohen, I. and Elder, A. (1989), "Major Cities and Disease Crises: A Comparative Perspective," *Social Science History* 13: 1: 25–63.

36 Moerkerk, H. with Aggleton, P. (1990), "AIDS Prevention Strategies in Europe," in Aggleton, P., Davies, P. and Hart, G. (eds), *AIDS: Individual, Cultural and Policy Dimensions* (London: Falmer Press): 181–90. A somewhat different typology of European responses is being developed by Patrick Kenis at the European Centre for Social Welfare Policy and Research, Vienna.

37 *Ibid.*: 186. See also Henriksson, B. (1988), *Social Democracy or Societal Control* (Stockholm: Institute for Social Policy): 34–5.

38 Frankenberg, G. (1992), "Germany: the Uneasy Triumph of Pragmatism," in Kirp, D. and Bayer, R., *AIDS in the Industrialised Democracies* (New Brunswick: Rutgers University Press).

39 See, for example, Warney, S. (1989), "Practices of Freedom: 'Citizenship' and the Politics of Identity," in Rutherford, J. (ed.), *Changing Identities* (London: Lawrence & Wishart).

40 See Altman, D. (1986), *AIDS and the New Puritanism* (London: Pluto): 178.

41 Knott, B. (1988), "Volunteerism Strategy Study," report for AFAO (unpublished).

42 See (1992), "Facing up to AIDS in a Bangkok slum" in Lyons, J. (ed.), *Community Responses to HIV and AIDS* (New Delhi, UNDP).

43 See Borges, M. (1992), "Community-based Organisations in the Fight against AIDS," *AIDS & Society* (January/February): 5.

44 Parker, R. (1990), "The Response to AIDS in Brazil," in Misztal, B. and Moss, D. (eds), *Action on AIDS* (New York: Greenwood Press): 67–8.

45 On Russia see Ken, I. (1993), "Sexual Minorities," in Ken, I. and Riordan, J. (eds), *Sex and Russian Society* (Bloomington: Indiana University Press): 104–11.

46 "India: Less Complacency Now".

47 Broadhead, T. and O'Malley, J. (1989), "NGO's and Third World Development: Opportunities and Constraints," paper prepared for Global Programme on AIDS, Geneva, December.

48 Mann, J. Tarantola, D. and Netter, T. (1992), *AIDS in the World* (Cambridge, MA.: Harvard University Press): 306.

49 Sills, D. (ed.) (1968), "Voluntary Associations: Sociological Aspects," *International Encyclopedia of the Social Sciences* (New York: Macmillan).

50 Milofsky, C. (1988), "Structure and Process in Community Self-Help Organizations," in Milofsky, C. (ed.), *Community Organizations* (Oxford: Oxford University Press): 187.

51 Deutsche AIDS-Hilfe (1992), "German AIDS-Help – AIDS Solidarity," Berlin (Roneoed publication].

52 Aggleton, P., Weeks, J. and Taylor-Laybourn, A. (1993), "Voluntary Sector Responses to HIV and AIDS: A Framework for Analysis," in Aggleton, P., Davies, P. and Hart, G. (eds) *AIDS: Facing the Second Decade* (London: Falmer Press): 137.

53 Patton, C. (1990), *Inventing AIDS* (London: Routledge): 140. See Weeks, J. (1989), "AIDS, Altruism and the New Right," in Carter, E. and Watney, S. (eds) *Taking Liberties* (London: Serpent's Tail): 127–32; and Kayal, P. (1993), *Bearing Witness* (Boulder: Westview).

54 See Kayal (see note 53): 130–3.

55 Eldridge, P. (1989), "NGOs in Indonesia," Centre of South-east Asian Studies, Melbourne, Monash University, Working Paper, 55: 3.

56 See Hampton, J. (1991), *Living Positively with AIDS*, rev. ed. (Oxford: Actionaid, AMREF & World in Need).

57 See Nataraj, S. (1992), "Role of NGOs," Seminar, The Monthly Symposium, New Delhi, 338, August.

58 On this see Altman, D. (1991), "Regional Profile: South and East Asia," *World AIDS* (March): 11; Miller, N. (1992), *Out in the World* (New York: Random House), chapters on Japan, Thailand, and Hong Kong.

59 Dhawan, S. and Narula, R. (1992), "Silent Killer," *First City* (Delhi) (November): 37.

60 Interview with Hakima Himmich, (1993) founder of the Moroccan Association against AIDS (ALCS), *Global AIDS News* 2: 22.

61 On homophobia and AIDS see Altman, D. (1988), "Legitimation through Disaster: AIDS and the Gay Movement," in Fee, E. and Fox, D. (eds) *AIDS: The Burdens of History* (San Francisco: University of California Press); Padgug, R. and Oppenheimer, G. (1992), "Riding the Tiger: AIDS and the Gay Community," in Fee, E. and Fox, D. (eds) *AIDS: The Making of a Chronic Disease* (San Francisco: University of California Press); Patton, C. (1990), *Inventing AIDS* (London: Routledge), esp. Ch.5; Watney, S. (1988), "AIDS, 'Moral Panic' Theory and Homophobia," in Aggleton, P. and Homans, H. (1988), *Social Aspects of AIDS* (London: Falmer Press).

THE COMBAHEE RIVER COLLECTIVE

"A Black Feminist Statement"

from Zillah R. Eisenstein (ed.), *Capitalist Patriarchy and the Case for Socialist Feminism* (New York: Monthly Review Press, 1979): 362–72

We are a collective of black feminists who have been meeting together since 1974.[1] During that time we have been involved in the process of defining and clarifying our politics, while at the same time doing political work within our own group and in coalition with other progressive organizations and movements. The most general statement of our politics at the present time would be that we are actively committed to struggling against racial, sexual, heterosexual, and class oppression and see as our particular task the development of integrated analysis and practice based upon the fact that the major systems of oppression are interlocking. The synthesis of these oppressions creates the conditions of our lives. As black women we see black feminism as the logical political movement to combat the manifold and simultaneous oppressions that all women of color face.

We will discuss four major topics in the paper that follows: (1) the genesis of contemporary black feminism; (2) what we believe, i.e., the specific province of our politics; (3) the problems in organizing black feminists, including a brief herstory of our collective; and (4) black feminist issues and practice.

THE GENESIS OF CONTEMPORARY BLACK FEMINISM

Before looking at the recent development of black feminism, we would like to affirm that we find our origins in the historical reality of Afro-American women's continuous life-and-death struggle for survival and liberation. Black women's extremely negative relationship to the American political system (a system of white male rule) has always been determined by our membership in two oppressed racial and sexual castes. As Angela Davis points out in "Reflections on the Black Women's Role in the Community of Slaves,"[2] black women have always embodied, if only in their physical manifestation, an adversary stance to white male rule and have actively resisted its inroads upon them and their communities in both dramatic and subtle ways. There have always been black women activists – some known, like Sojourner Truth, Harriet Tubman, Frances E. W. Harper, Ida B. Wells Barnett, and Mary Church Terrell, and thousands upon thousands unknown – who had a shared awareness of how their sexual identity combined with their racial identity to make their whole life situation and the focus of their political struggles unique. Contemporary black feminism is the outgrowth of countless generations of personal sacrifice, militancy, and work by our mothers and sisters.

A black feminist presence has evolved most obviously in connection with the second wave of the American women's movement beginning in the late 1960s. Black, other Third World, and working women have been involved in the feminist movement from its start, but both outside reactionary forces and racism and elitism within the movement itself have served to obscure our participation. In 1973 black feminists, primarily located in New York, felt the neccessity of forming a separate black feminist group. This became the National Black Feminist Organization (NBFO).

Black feminist politics also have an obvious connection to movements for black liberation, particularly those of the 1960s and 1970s. Many of us were active in those movements (civil rights, black nationalism, the Black Panthers), and all of our lives were greatly affected and changed by their ideology, their goals, and the tactics used to achieve their goals. It was our experience and disillisionment within these liberation movements, as well as experience on the periphery of the white male left, that led to the need to develop a politics that was antiracist, unlike those of white women, and antisexist, unlike those of black and white men.

There is also undeniably a personal genesis for black feminism, that is, the political realization that comes from the seemingly personal experiences of individual black women's lives. Black feminists and many more black women who do not define themselves as feminists have all experienced sexual oppression as a constant factor in our day-to-day existence.

Black feminists often talk about their feelings of craziness before becoming conscious of the concepts of sexual politics, patriarchal rule, and, most importantly, feminism, the political analysis and practice that we women use to struggle against our oppression. The fact that racial politics and indeed racism are pervasive factors in our lives did not allow us, and still does not allow most black women, to look more deeply into our own experiences and define those things that make our lives what they are and our oppression specific to us. In the process of consciousness-raising, actually life-sharing, we began to recognize the commonality of our experiences and, from that sharing and growing consciousness, to build a politics that will change our lives and inevitably end our oppression.

Our development also must be tied to the contemporary economic and political position of black people. The post-World-War-II generation of black youth was the first to be able to minimally partake of certain educational and employment options, previously closed completely to black people. Although our economic position is still at the very bottom of the American capitalist economy, a handful of us have been able to gain certain tools as a result of tokenism in education and employment which potentially enable us to more effectively fight our oppression.

A combined antiracist and antisexist position drew us together initially, and as we developed politically we addressed ourselves to heterosexism and economic oppression under capitalism.

WHAT WE BELIEVE

Above all else, our politics initially sprang from the shared belief that black women are inherently valuable, that our liberation is a necessity not as an adjunct to somebody else's but because of our need as human persons for autonomy. This many seem so obvious as to sound simplistic, but it is apparent that no other ostensibly progressive movement has ever considered our specific oppression a priority or worked seriously for the ending of that oppression. Merely naming the pejorative stereotypes attributed to black women (e.g., mammy, matriarch, Sapphire, whore, bulldagger), let alone cataloguing the cruel, often murderous, treatment we receive, indicates how little value has been placed upon our lives during four centuries of bondage in the Western hemisphere. We realize that the only people who care enough about us to work consistently for our liberation is us. Our politics evolve from a healthy love for ourselves, our sisters and our community which allows us to continue our struggle and work.

This focusing upon our own oppression is embodied in the concept of identity politics. We believe that the most profound and potentially the most radical politics come directly out of our own identity, as opposed to working to end somebody else's oppression. In the case of black women this is a particularly repugnant, dangerous, threatening, and therefore revolutionary concept because it is obvious from looking at all the political movements that have preceded us that anyone is more worthy of liberation than ourselves. We reject pedestals, queenhood, and walking ten paces behind. To be recognized as human, levelly human, is enough.

We believe that sexual politics under patriarchy is as pervasive in black women's lives as are the politics of class and race. We also often find it difficult to separate race from class from sex oppression because in our lives they are most often experienced simultaneously. We know that there is such a thing as racial–sexual oppression which is neither solely racial nor solely sexual, e.g., the history of rape of black women by white men as a weapon of political repression.

Although we are feminists and lesbians, we feel solidarity with progressive black men and do not advocate the fractionalization that white women who are separatists demand. Our situation as black people necessitates that we have solidarity around the fact of race, which white women of course do not need to have with white men, unless it is their negative solidarity as racial oppressors. We struggle together with black men against racism, while we also struggle with black men about sexism.

We realize that the liberation of all oppressed peoples necessitates the destruction of the political-economic systems of capitalism and imperialism as well as patriarchy. We are socialists because we believe the work must be organized for the collective benefit of those who do the work and create the products and not for the profit of the bosses. Material resources must be equally distributed among those who create these resources. We are not convinced, however, that a socialist revolution that is not also a feminist and antiracist revolution will guarantee our liberation. We have arrived at the necessity for developing an understanding of class relationships that takes into account the specific class position of black women who are generally marginal in the labor force, while at this particular time some of us are temporarily viewed as doubly desirable tokens at white-collar and professional levels. We need to articulate the real class situation of persons who are not merely raceless, sexless workers, but for whom racial and sexual oppression are significant determinants in their working economic lives. Although we are in essential agreement with Marx's theory as it applied to the very specific economic relationships he analyzed, we know that this analysis must be extended further in order for us to understand our specific economic situation as black women.

A political contribution which we feel we have already made is the expansion of the feminist principle that the personal is political.

In our consciousness-raising sessions, for example, we have in many ways gone beyond white women's revelations because we are dealing with the implications of race and class as well as sex. Even our black women's style of talking/testifying in black language about what we have experienced has a resonance that is both cultural and political. We have spent a great deal of energy delving into the cultural and experiental nature of our oppression out of necessity because none of these matters have ever been looked at before. No one before has ever examined the multilayered texture of black women's lives.

As we have already stated, we reject the stance of lesbian separatism because it is not a viable political analysis or strategy for us. It leaves out far too much and far too many people particularly black men, women, and children. We have a great deal of criticism and loathing for what men have been socialized to be in this society: what they support, how they act, and how they oppress. But we do not have the misguided notion that it is their maleness, *per se* – i.e., their biological maleness – that makes them what they are. As black women we find any type of biological determination a particularly dangerous and reactionary basis upon which to build a politic. We must also question whether lesbian separatism is an adequate and progressive political analysis and strategy, even for those who practice it, since it so completely denies any but the sexual sources of women's oppression, negating the facts of class and race.

PROBLEMS IN ORGANIZING BLACK FEMINISTS

During our years together as a black feminist collective we have experienced success and defeat, joy and pain, victory and failure. We have found that it is very difficult to organize around black feminist issues, difficult even to announce in certain contexts that we *are* black feminists. We have tried to think about the reasons for our difficulties, particularly since the white women's movement continues to be strong and to grow in many directions. In this section we will discuss some of the general reasons for the organizing problems we face and also talk specifically about the stages in organizing our own collective.

The major source of difficulty in our political work is that we are not just trying to fight oppression on one front or even two, but instead to address a whole range of oppressions. We do not have racial, sexual, heterosexual, or class privilege to rely upon, nor do we have even the minimal access to resources and power that groups who possess any one of these types of privilege have.

The psychological toll of being black women and the difficulties this presents in reaching political consciousness and doing political work can never be underestimated. There is a very low value placed upon black women's psyches in this society, which is both racist and sexist. As an early group member once said. "We are all damaged people merely by virtue of being black women." We are dispossessed psychologically and on every other level, and yet we feel the necessity to struggle to change our condition and the condition of all black women. In "A Black Feminist's Search for Sisterhood," Michele Wallace arrives at this conclusion:

> We exist as women who are black who are feminists, each stranded for the moment, working independently because there is not yet an environment in this society remotely congenial to our struggle – because, being on the bottom, we would have to do what no one else has done: we would have to fight the world.[3]

Wallace is not pessimistic but realistic in her assessment of black feminists' position, particularly in her allusion to the nearly classic isolation most of us face. We might use our position at the bottom, however, to make a clear leap into revolutionary action. If black women were free, it would mean that everyone else would have to be free since our freedom would necessitate the destruction of all the systems of oppression.

Feminism is, nevertheless, very threatening to the majority of black people because it calls into question some of the most basic assumptions about our existence, i.e., that gender should be a determinant of power relationships. Here is the way male and female roles were defined in a black nationalist pamphlet from the early 1970s.

We understand that it is and has been traditional that the man is the head of the house. He is the leader of the house/nation because his knowledge of the world is broader, his awareness is greater, his understanding is fuller and his application of this information is wiser ... After all, it is only reasonable that the man be the head of the house because he is able to defend and protect the development of his home ... Women cannot do the same things as men – they are made by nature to function differently. Equality of men and women is something that cannot happen in the abstract world. Men are not quite equal to other men, i.e., ability, experience, or even understanding. The value of men and women can be seen as in the value of gold and silver – they are not equal but both have great value. We must realize that men and women are a complement to each other because there is no house/family without a man and his wife. Both are essential to the development of any life.[4]

The material conditions of most black women would hardly lead them to upset both economic and sexual arrangements that seem to represent some stability in their own lives. Many black women have a good understanding of both sexism and racism, but because of the everyday constructions of their own lives cannot risk struggling against them both.

The reaction of black men to feminism has been notoriously negative. They are, of course, even more threatened than black women by the possibility that black feminists might organize around our own needs. They realize that they might not only lose valuable and hard-working allies in their struggles but that they might also be forced to change their habitually sexist ways of interacting with and oppressing black women. Accusations that black feminism divides the black struggle are powerful deterrents to the growth of an autonomous black women's movement.

Still, hundreds of women have been active at different times during the three-year existence of our group. And every black women who came, came out of a strongly felt need for some level of possibility that did not previously exist in her life.

When we first started meeting early in 1974 after the NBFO first eastern regional conference, we did not have a strategy for organizing, or even a focus. We just wanted to see what we had. After a period of months of not meeting, we began to meet again late in the year and started doing an intense variety of consciousness-raising. The overwhelming feeling that we had is that after years and years we had finally found each other. Although we were not doing political work as a group, individuals continued their involvement in lesbian politics, sterilization abuse and abortion rights work, Third World Women's International Women's Day activities, and support activity for the trials of Dr. Kenneth Edelin, Joan Little, and Inez Garcia. During our first summer, when membership had dropped off considerably, those of us remaining devoted serious discussion to the possibility of opening a refuge for battered women in a black community. (There was no refuge in Boston at that time.) We also decided around that time to become an independent collective since we had serious disagreements with NBFOs bourgeois-feminist stance and their lack of a clear political focus.

We were also contacted at that time by socialist feminists, with whom we had worked on abortion rights, who wanted to encourage us to attend the National Socialist Feminist Conference in Yellow Springs. One of our members did attend and despite the narrowness of the ideology that was promoted at that particular conference, we became more aware of the need for us to understand our own economic situation and to make our own economic analysis.

In the fall, when some members returned, we experienced several months of comparative inactivity and internal disagreements which were first conceptualized as a lesbian–straight split but which were also the result of class and political differences. During the summer those of us who were still meeting had determined the need to do political work and to move beyond consciousness-raising and serving exclusively as an emotional support group. At the beginning of 1976, when some of the women who had not wanted to do political work and who also had voiced disagreements stopped attending of their own accord, we again looked for a focus. We decided at that time, with the addition of new members, to become a study group. We had always shared our reading with each other, and some of us had written papers on black femi-

nism for group discussion a few months before this decision was made. We began functioning as a study group and also began discussing the possibility of starting a black feminist publication. We had a retreat in the late spring which provided a time for both political discussion and working out interpersonal issues. Currently we are planning to gather together a collection of black feminist writing. We feel that it is absolutely essential to demonstrate the reality of our politics to other black women and believe that we can do this through writing and distributing our work. The fact that individual black feminists are living in isolation all over the country, that our own numbers are small, and that we have some skills in writing, printing, and publishing makes us want to carry out these kinds of projects as a means of organizing black feminists as we continue to do political work in coalition with other groups.

BLACK FEMINIST ISSUES AND PRACTICE

During our time together we have identified and worked on many issues of particular relevance to black women. The inclusiveness of our politics makes us concerned with any situation that impinges upon the lives of women, Third World, and working people. We are of course particularly committed to working on those struggles in which race, sex, and class are simultaneous factors in oppression. We might, for example, become involved in workplace organizing at a factory that employs Third World women or picket a hospital that is cutting back on already inadequate health care to a Third World community, or set up a rape crisis center in a black neighborhood. Organizing around welfare or daycare concerns might also be a focus. The work to be done and the countless issues that this work represents merely reflect the pervasiveness of our oppression.

Issues and projects that collective members have actually worked on are sterilization abuse, abortion rights, battered women, rape, and health care. We have also done many workshops and educationals on black feminism on college campuses, at women's conferences, and most recently for high school women.

One issue that is of major concern to us and that we have begun to publicly address is racism in the white women's movement. As black feminists we are made constantly and painfully aware of how little effort white women have made to understand and combat their racism, which requires among other things that they have a more than superficial comprehension of race, color, and black history and culture. Eliminating racism in the white women's movement is by definition work for white women to do, but we will continue to speak to and demand accountability on this issue.

In the practice of our politics we do not believe that the end always justifies the means. Many reactionary and destructive acts have been done in the name of achieving "correct" political goals. As feminists we do not want to mess over people in the name of politics. We believe in collective process and a nonhierarchical distribution of power within our own group and in our vision of a revolutionary society. We are committed to a continual examination of our politics as they develop through criticism and self-criticism as an essential aspect of our practice. As black feminists and lesbians we know that we have a very definite revolutionary task to perform and we are ready for the lifetime of work and struggle before us.

NOTES

1 This statement is dated April 1977.
2 Angela Y. Davis, "Reflection on the Black Women's Role in the Community of Slaves," *Black Scholar* 4 (December 1971): 2–15.
3 Michele Wallace, "A Black Feminist's Search for Sisterhood," *The Village Voice*, 28 July 1975: 6–7.
4 Mumininas of Committee for Unified Newark, *Mwanamke Mwananchi (The Nationalist Woman)*, Newark, N.J., *c.* 1971: 4–5.

GLORIA ANZALDÚA

"Bridge, Drawbridge, Sandbar or Island: Lesbians-of-Color *Hacienda Alianzas*"

from Lisa Albrecht and Rose M. Brewer (eds), *Bridges of Power: Women's Multicultural Alliances* (Philadelphia: New Society, 1990): 216–31

La gente hablando se entiende
(People understand each other by talking)
                                   (Mexican proverb)

Buenos dias marimachas, lesberadas, tortilleras, patlaches,[1] dykes, bulldaggers, butches, femmes, and good morning to you, too, straight women. This morning when I got up I looked in the mirror to see who I was (my identity keeps changing), and you know how hair looks when you've washed it the night before and then slept on it? Yes, that's how mine looked. Not that I slept that much. I was nervous about making this talk and I usually never get nervous until just before I'm on. I kept thinking, What am I going to tell all those women? How am I going to present and represent myself to them and who, besides myself, am I going to speak to and for? Last night lying in bed in the dorm room I got disgusted with my semiprepared talk so I wrote another one. I threw that out too. Then I skimmed several papers I was working on, looking for ideas. I realized that I couldn't use any of this material and ordered my unconscious to come up with something by morning or else. This morning I walked over here, picking lint off my shirt, feeling wrinkled, and thinking, Here I am, I'm still the poor little Chicanita from the sticks. What makes me think I have anything useful to say about alliances?

Women-of-color such as myself do have some important things to say about alliance and coalition work. The overlapping communities of struggle that a mestiza lesbian finds herself in allows her to play a pivotal role in alliance work. To be part of an alliance or coalition is to be active, an activist. Why do we make alliances and participate in them? We are searching for powerful, meaning-making experiences. To make our lives relevant, to gain political knowledge, to give our lives a sense of involvement, to respond to social oppression and its debilitating effects. Activists are engaged in a political quest. Activists are alienated from the dominant culture but instead of withdrawing we confront, challenge. Being active meets some basic needs: emotional catharsis, gratification, political epiphanies. But those in an alliance group also feel like a family and squabble and fight like this one, complete with favorite (good child) and a scapegoat (bad child).

THE FRACTURE: AT HOMENESS/ESTRANGEMENT

I look around me and I see my *carnalas*, my *hermanas*, the other half and halves, *mita' y mita'* (as queer women are called in South Texas), and I feel a great affinity with everyone. But at the same time I feel (as I've felt at other conferences) like I am doing this alone, I feel a great isolation and separateness and differentness from everyone, even though I have many allies. Yet as soon as I have these thoughts – that I'm in this alone, that I have to stand on the ground of my own being, that I have to create my own separate space – the exact opposite thoughts come to me: that we're all in this together, *juntas*, that the ground of our being is a common ground, *la Tierra*, and that at all times we must stand together despite, or because, of the huge splits that lie between our legs, the faults among feminists are like the fractures in the earth. Earthquake country, these feminisms. Like a fracture in the Earth's crust splitting rock, like a splitting rock itself, the quakes shift different categories of women past each other so that we cease to match, and are forever disaligned – coloured from white, Jewish from colored, lesbian from straight. If we indeed do not have one common ground but only shifting plots, how can we work and live and love together? Then, too, let us not forget *la mierda* between us, a mountain of *caca* that keeps us from "seeing" each other, being with each other.

Being a mestiza queer person, *una de las otras* ("of the others") is having and living in a lot of worlds, some of which overlap. One is immersed in all the worlds at the same time while also traversing from one to the other. The mestiza queer is mobile, constantly on the move, a traveler, *callejera*, a *cortacalles*. Moving at the blink of an eye, from one space, one world to another, each world with its own peculiar and distinct inhabitants, not comfortable in anyone of them, none of them "home," yet none of them "not home" either. I'm flying home to South Texas after this conference, and while I'm there, I'm going to be feeling a lot of the same things that I'm feeling here – a warm sense of being loved and of being at home, accompanied by simultaneous and uncomfortable feeling of no longer fitting, of having lost my home, of being an outsider. My mother, and my sister and my brothers, are going to continue to challenge me and to argue against the part of me that has community with white lesbians, that has community with feminism, that has community with other *mujeres-de-color*, that has a political community. Because I no longer share their world view, I have become a stranger and an exile in my own home. "When are you coming home again, *Prieta*," my mother asks at the end of my visit, of every visit. "Never, Momma."[2] After I first left home and became acquainted with other worlds, the Prieta that returned was different, thus "home" was different too. It could not completely accommodate the new Prieta, and I could barely tolerate it. Though I continue to go home, I no longer fool myself into believing that I am truly "home."

A few days ago in Montreal at the Third International Feminist Book Fair (June 1988), I felt a great kinship with women writers and publishers from all over the world. I felt both at home and homeless in that foreign yet familiar terrain because of its strangeness (strange because I had never been there). At the conference, and most especially at the lesbian reading, I felt very close to some white lesbian separatist friends. Then they would make exclusionary or racist remarks and I would feel my body heating up, I would feel the space between us widening. Though white lesbians say their oppression in a heterosexist, homophobic society is similar to the suffering of racism that people-of-color experience, they *can* escape from the more overt oppressions by hiding from being gay (just as I can). But what I can't hide from is being Chicana – my color and features give me away. Yes, when I go home to put up with a lot of heterosexist bullshit from my family and community, from the whole Chicano nation who want to exclude my feminism, my lesbianism. This I have in common with women-of-all-colors. But what really hurts, however, is to be with people that I love, with you *mujeres-de-todos-colores*, and to *still* feel, after all our dialogues and struggles, that my cultural identity is *still* being pushed off to the side, being minimized by some of my so-called allies who unconciously rank racism a lesser oppression than sexism. Women-of-color feel especially frustrated and depressed when these "allies" participate in alliances dealing with issues of racism or when the theme of the conference we are attending is racism. It is then that white feminists feel they have "dealt" with the issue and can go on to other "more important" matters.

At the Montreal Conference I also felt an empathy with heterosexual women-of-color and with the few men who were there, only to be saddened that they needed to be educated about women-only space. It also made me sad, too, that white lesbians have not accepted the fact that women-of-color have affinities with men in their cultures. White lesbians were unconsciously asking women-of-color to choose between women and men, failing to see that there is more than one way to be oppressed. Not all women experience sexism in the same way, and for women-of-color sexism is not the only oppression. White lesbians forget that they too have felt excluded, that they too have interrupted women-of-color-only space, bringing in their agenda and, in their hunger to belong, pushed ours to the side.

Alliance work is the attempt to shift positions, change positions, reposition ourselves regarding our individual and collective identities. In alliance we are confronted with the problem of how we share or don't share space, how we can position ourselves with individuals or groups who are different from and at odds with each other, how can we reconcile one's love for diverse groups when members of these groups do not love each other, cannot relate to each other, and don't know how to work together.

THE ACTIVIST Y LA TAREA DE ALIANZAS

Alliance-coalition work is marked or signaled by framing metacommunication, "This is alliance work."[3] It occurs in bounded specific contexts defined by the rules and boundaries of that time and space and group. While it professes to do its "work" in the community, its basis is both experiential and theoretical. It has a discourse, a theory that guides it. It stands both inside (the community one is doing the work for) and outside ordinary life (the meeting place, the conference). Ideally one takes alliance work home.

In alliance-coalition work there is an element of role playing, as if one were someone else. Activists possess an unspoken, untalked about ability to recognize the unreality and game-playing quality of their work.[4] We very seriously act/perform as well as play at being an ally. We adopt a role model or self-image and behave as if one *were* that model, the person one is trying to be. Activists picture themselves in a scenario: a female hero venturing out and engaging in nonviolent battles against the corrupt dominant world with the help of their trusted *comadronas*. There are various narratives about working at coalition, about making commitments, setting goals and achieving those goals. An activist possesses, in lesser or greater degree, a self-conscious awareness of her "role" and the nature of alliance work. She is aware that not only is the alliance-coalition group struggling to make specific changes in certain institutions (health care, immigration laws, etc.)

but in doing so the group often engages in fighting cultural paradigms[5] – the entire baggage of beliefs, values and techniques shared by the community. But in spite of all cultural inscriptions to the contrary, the activist with her preconceived self-image, her narrative, and self-reflectivity resists society's "inscribing" cultural norms, practices, and paradigms on her. She elects to be the one "inscribing" herself and her culture. Activists are agents.

IN COLLUSION, IN COALITION, IN COLLISION

For now we women-of-color are doing more solidarity work with each other. Because we occupy the same or similarly oppressed cultural, economic space(s) or share similar oppressions, we can create a solidarity based on a "minority" coalition. We can build alliances around differences, even in groups which are homogenous. Because people-of-color are treated generically by the dominant culture – their seeing and treating us as parts of a whole, rather than just as individuals – this forces us to experience ourselves collectively. I have been held accountable by some white people for Richard Rodriguez's views and have been asked to justify Cesar Chavez's political strategies. In classes and conferences I am often called to speak on issues of race and am thereafter responsible for the whole Chicano/Mexicano race. Yet, were I to hold a white woman responsible for Ronald Reagan's acts, she would be shocked because to herself she is an individual (nor is her being white named because it is taken for granted as the norm).

I think we people-of-color can turn this fusion or confusion of individual/collectivity around and use it as a tool for collective strength and not as an oppressive representation. We can subvert it and use it. It could serve as one base for intimate connection between personal and collective in solidarity work and in alliances across differences. For us the issue of alliances affects every aspect of our lives – personal growth, not just social. We are always working with whitewomen or other groups unlike ourselves toward common and specific goals for the time the work of coalition is in process. Lesbians-of-color have always done this. Judith Moschkovitz wrote: "Alliances are made between people who are different."[6] I would add between people who are different but who have a similar conscience that impels them toward certain actions. Alliances are made between persons whose vague unconscious angers, hopes, guilts, and fears grow out of direct experiences of being either perpetrators or victims of racism and sexism.

Feelings of anger, guilt, and fear rose up nine years ago at Storrs, Connecticut, at the 1981 NWSA Women Respond to Racism Conference, when issues of alliances and racism exploded into the open. Along with many women-of-color I had aspirations, hopes, and visions for multicultural *comunidades*, for communities (in the plural) among all women, of *mundos surdos* (left-handed worlds). Cherríe Moraga and I came bringing an offering, *This Bridge Called My Back: Radical Writings By Radical Women Of Color*; it made its debut at that conference. Some of my aspirations were naive, but without them, I would not have been there nor would I be here now. This vision of *comunidad* is still the carrot that I, the donkey, hunger for and seek at conferences such as this one.

At the 1981 conference we laid bare the splits between whitewomen and women-of-color, white lesbians and lesbians-of-color, separatists and nonseparatists. We risked exposing our true feelings. Anger[7] was the strongest in/visible current at that conference, as it is at this one, though many of us repressed it then and are still repressing it now. Race was the big issue then, as it is now for us. Race, the big difference. When asked what I am, I never say I'm a woman. I say I am a Chicana, a mestiza, a *mexicana*, or I am a woman-of-color – which is different from "woman" (woman always means white-woman). Monique Wittig claims that a lesbian is not a woman because woman exists only in relation to men; woman is part of the category of sex (man and woman) which is a heterosexual construct.[8] Similarly, for me a woman-of-color is not just a "woman"; she carries the markings of her race, she is a gendered racial being – not just a gendered being. However, nonintellectual, working-class women-of-color

do not have the luxury of thinking of such semantic and theoretical nuances, much less exempting themselves from the category "woman." So though I myself see the distinction, I do not push it.

A large part of my identity is cultural. Despite changes in awareness since the early 1980s, racism in the form of, "Your commitment has to be feminism, forget about your race and its struggles, struggle with us not them" is still the biggest deterrent to coalition work between whitewomen and women-of-color. Some white feminists, displacing race and class and highlighting gender, are still trying to force us to choose between being colored or female, only now they've gone underground and use unconscious covert pressures. It's all very subtle. Our white allies or colleagues get a hurt look in their eyes when we bring up their racism in their interactions with us and quickly change the subject. Tired of our own "theme song" (Why aren't you dealing with race and class in your conference, classroom, organization?) and not wanting to hurt them and in retaliation have them turn against us, we drop the subject and, in effect, turn the other cheek. Women-of-color need these and other manipulations named so that we can make our own articulations. Colored and whitewomen doing coalition work together will continue to reflect the dominated/dominator dichotomy *unless* whitewomen have or are dealing with issues of racial domination in a "real" way. It is up to them *how* they will do this.

ESTRANGED STRANGERS: A FORCED BONDING

Alliance stirs up intimacy issues, issues of trust, relapse of trust, intensely emotional issues. "We seem to be more together organizationally and estranged individually."[9] There is always some, no matter how minimal, unease or discomfort between most women-of-color and most white-women. Because they can't ignore our ethnicity, getting our approval and acceptance is their way to try to make themselves more comfortable and lessen their unease. It is a great temptation for us to make whitewomen comfortable. (In the past our lives may have depended on not offending a white person). Some of us get seduced into making a whitewoman an honorary woman-of-color – she wants it so badly. But it makes us fidget, it positions us in a relationship founded on false assumptions. A reversed dependency of them upon us emerges, one that is as unhealthy as our previous reliance on them. There is something parasitic about both of these kinds of dependencies. We need to examine bondings of this sort and to "see through" them to the unconscious motivations. Both white and colored need to look at the history of betrayal, the lies, the secrets and misinformation both have internalized and continue to propagate. We need to ask, Do women-of-color want only patronage from white women? Do white feminists only need and expect acceptance and acknowledgment from women-of-color? Yet there is an inherent potential for achieving results in both personal and political cross-racial alliances. We could stick to each other like Velcro, whose two different sides together form a great bond – the teeth of one fasten onto the fabric of the other half and hold with a strength greater than either half alone.

Though the deepest connections colored dykes have is to their native culture, we also have strong links with other races, including whites. Though right now there is a strong return to nationalist feeling, colored lesbian feminists in our everyday interactions are truly more citizens of the planet. "To be a lesbian is to have a world vision."[10] In a certain sense I share this vision. If we are to create a lesbian culture, it must be a mestiza lesbian culture, one that partakes of all cultures, one that is not just white in style, theory, or direction, that is not just Chicana, not just Black. We each have a choice as to what people, what cultures, and what issues we want to live with and live in and the roles we want to play. The danger is that white lesbians will "claim" us and our culture as their own in the creation of "our" new space.

"CHUSANDO" MOVIDAS/A CHOICE OF MOVES

There are many roles, or ways of being, of acting, and of interacting in the world. For me they boil down to four basic ones: bridge, drawbridge, sandbar, and island. Being a bridge means being a meditator between yourself and your community and white people – lesbians, feminists, white men. You select, consciously or unconsciously, which group to bridge with – or they choose you. Often, the you that's the meditator gets lost in the dichotomies, dualities, or contradicitons you're meditating. You have to be flexible yet maintain your ground, or the pull in different directions will dismember you. It's a tough job, not many people can keep the bridge up.

Being a drawbridge means having the option to take two courses of action. The first is being "up," i.e., withdrawing, pulling back from physically connecting with white people (there can never be a complete disconnection because white culture and its perspectives are inscribed on us/into us). You may choose to pull up the drawbridge or retreat to an island in order to be with your colored *hermanas* in a sort of temporary cultural separatism. Many of us choose to "draw up our own bridges" for short periods of time in order to regroup, recharge our energies, and nourish ourselves before wading back into the frontlines. This is also true for whitewomen. The other option is being "down"– that is, being a bridge. Being "down" may mean a partial loss of self. Being "there" for people *all the time, meditating all the time* means risking being "walked" on, being "used." I and my publishing credentials are often "used" to "colorize" white women's grant proposals, projects, lecture series, and conferences. If I don't cooperate I am letting the whole feminist movement down.

Being an island means there are no causeways, no bridges, maybe no ferries, either, between you and whites. I think that some women-of-color are, in these reactionary times, in these very racist times, choosing to be islands for a little while. These race separatists, small in numbers are disgusted not only with patriarchal culture, but also with white feminism and the white lesbian community. To be an island, you have to reject certain people. Yet being an island cannot be a way of life – there are no life-long islands because no one is totally self-sufficient. Each person depends on others for the food she eats, the clothes on her back, the books she reads, and though these "goods" may be gotten from within the island, sequestering oneself to some private paradise is not an option for poor people, for most people-of-color.

At this point in time, the infrastructures of bridge and drawbridge feel too man-made and steel-like for me. Still liking the drawbridge concept, I sought and found the sandbar, a submerged or partly exposed ridge of sand built by waves offshore from a beach. To me the sandbar feels like a more "natural" bridge (though nature too, some argue, is a cultural construction). There is a particular type of sandbar that connects an island to a mainland – I forget what it is called. For me the important thing is how we shift from bridge to drawbridge to sandbar to island. Being a sandbar means getting a breather from being a perpetual bridge without having to withdraw completely. The high tides and low tides of your life are factors which help decide whether or where you're a sandbar today, tomorrow. It means that your functioning as a "bridge" may be partially underwater, invisible to others, and that you can somehow choose who to allow to "see" your bridge, who you'll allow to walk on your "bridge," that is, who you'll make connections with. A sandbar is more fluid and shifts locations allowing for more mobility and more freedom. Of course there are sandbars called shoals, where boats run amuck. Each option comes with its own dangers.

So what do we, lesbians-of-color, choose to be? Do we continue to function as bridges? Do we opt to be drawbridges or sandbars? Do we isolate ourselves as islands? We may choose different options for different stages of our process. While I have been a persistent bridge, I have often been forced to "draw the bridge," or have been driven to be an island. Now I find myself slowly turning into a sandbar – the thing is that I have a fear of drowning.

Mujeres-de-color, mujeres blancas, ask yourselves what are you now, and is this something that you want to be for the next year or five years or ten? Ask yourself if you want to do alliance-coalition work and if so what kind and with whom. The fact that we are so estranged from whitewomen and other women-of-color makes alliance work that much more imper-

ative. It is sad that though conferences allow for short-term alliances, the potential for achieving some feminists' goals are short-circuited by politically correct "performances" by participants instead of more "real" and honest engagement. Choosing to be a bridge, a drawbridge, and a sandbar allows us to connect, heart to heart, *con corazones abiertos*. Even islands come to NWSA conferences – perhaps they come to find other islands.

TERMS OF ENGAGEMENT

Mujeres-of-color, there are some points to keep in mind when doing coalition work with whitewomen. One is to not be lulled into forgetting that *coalition work attempts to balance power relations and undermine and subvert the system of domination-subordination* that affects even our most unconscious thoughts. We live in a world where whites dominate colored and we participate in such a system every minute of our lives – the subordination/domination dynamic is that insidious. We, too, operate in a racist system whether we are rebelling against it or are colluding with it. The strategies of defense we use against the dominant culture we also knowingly and unknowingly use on each other.[11] Whites of whatever class always have certain privileges over colored people of whatever class, and class oppression operates among us women-of-color as pervasively as among whites.

Keep in mind that if members of coalitions play at the deadly serious and difficult game of making alliances work we have to set up some ground rules and define the terms we use to name the issues. We need to "see through" some common assumptions. One is that there is no such thing as a common ground. As groups and individuals, we all stand on different plots. Sisterhood in the singular was a utopian fantasy invented by whitewomen, one in which we women-of-color were represented by whitewomen, one in which they continued to marginalize us, strip us of *our* individuality. (One must possess a sense of personhood before one can develop a sense of sisterhood.) It seems to me that through extensive coalitions, various *"hermanidades"* may be a created – not one sisterhood but many. We don't all need to come together, *juntas* (total unity may be another utopian myth). Some of us can gather in affinity groups, small grassroots circles and others. All parties involved in coalitions need to recognize the necessity that women-of-color and lesbians define the terms of engagement: that we be listened to, that we articulate who we are, where we have come from (racial past), how we understand oppression to work, how we think we can get out from under, and what strategies we can use in accomplishing the particular tasks we have chosen to perform. When we don't collectively define ourselves and locations, the group will automatically operate under white assumptions, white definitions, white strategies. Formulating a working definition, preferably one subject to change, of alliance/coalition, racism and internalized racism will clear the floor of patriarchal, white, and other kinds of debris and make a clean (well sort of clean) space for us to work in. I've given you my definitions for alliance and coalition. Racism is the subjugation of a cultural group by another for the purpose of gaining economic advantage, of mastering and having power over that group – the result being harm done, consciously or unconsciously, to its members. We need to defy ethnocentrism, the attitude that the whole culture is superior to all others. Ethnocentrism condones racism. Racism is a theory, it is an ideology, it is a violence perpetuated against colored ethnic cultures.

> The intensity of the violence may range from hidden indirect forms of discrimination (housing) through overt forms of ethnocidal practices (enforced schooling, religious harassment) to forms of physical and direct violence culminating in genocide (holocaust) . . . It becomes structurally institutionalized as the basis of hegemony, it turns into systematic racism.[12]

Internalized racism means the introjecting, from the dominant culture, negative images and prejudice against outsider groups such as people-of-color and the projection of prejudice by an oppressed person upon another oppressed person or upon her/himself. It is a type of "dumping."[13] On the phone the other day I was telling my mother that I'd confronted my neighbor – a Black man who "parties" everyday, from morning til night, with a dozen beer-drinking buddies – and demanded that he not intrude on my space with his noise. She said, "No, don't tell them anything, Black men kill. They'll rape you." This is an example of internalized racism, it is not racism. Chicanos as a group do not have the power to subjugate Black people or any other people. Where did my mother learn about Blacks? There are very few Black people in the Rio Grande Valley of South Texas. My mother has internalized racism from the white dominant culture, from watching television and from our own culture which defers to and prefers light-skinned *gueros* and denies the Black blood in our *mestisaje* – which may be both a race and class prejudice, as darker means being more *indio* or *india*, means poorer. Whites are conditioned to be racist, colored are prone to internalize racism and, for both groups, racism and internalized racism appear to be the given, "the way things are." Prejudice is a "stabilized deception of perception."[14] I call this "deception" "selective reality" – the narrow spectrum of reality that human beings choose to perceive and/or what their culture "selects" for them to "see."[15] That which is outside of the range of consensus (white) perception is "blanked-out." Color, race, sexual preferences, and other threatening differences are "unseen" by some whites, certain voices not heard. Such "editing" of reality maintains race, class, and gender oppressions.

Another point to keep in mind is that feminists-of-color threaten the order, coherence, authority, and the concept of white superiorty and this makes some white feminists uncomfortable and assimilated colored women uneasy. Feminists of color, in turn, are made uncomfortable by the knowledge that, by virtue of their color, white feminists have privilege and white feminists often focus on gender issues to the exclusion of racial ones. After centuries of colonization, some whitewomen and women-of-color, when interacting with each other, fall into old and familiar patterns: the former will be inclined to patronize and to "instruct"; the latter to fall into subservience and, consciously or unconsciously, model herself after the whitewoman. The woman-of-color might seek white approval or take in gradations of stances, from meek to hostile, which get her locked into passive-aggressive to violently reactive states.

But how are you to recognize your *aliada*, your ally in a roomful of people? Coalition work is not a sport where members of a particular team go bare-chested or wear T-shirts that say AMIGA (which stands for an actual organization in Texas). It can get confusing unless you can distinguish each other. And once you identify each other, how will you work together?

When calling a foul, do you harangue the other person in a loud voice? Do you take on a *matador* defense – neglect to guard opposing player in favor of taking the limelight to inflate your ego? Will your organization be a collective or a hierarchy? Should your *modus operandi* be hands on or hands off? Will your offensive strategies consist of nudges, bumps, shoves or bombs? You may have to accept that there may be no solutions, resolutions or even agreement *ever*. The terms *solution, resolution*, and *progressing* and *moving forward* are Western dominant cultural concepts. Irresolution and disagreement may be more common in life than resolutions and agreements. Coalition work does not thrive on "figurehead" leaders, on grandstanding, "leadership always makes you master and the others slaves."[16] Instead, coalition work succeeds through collective efforts and individual voices being heard. Once we focus on coalition/alliance we come to the questions, How long should we stay together? Should we form temporary *carnalaship* of extended family which leads to strong familial and tribal affiliation but which work against larger coalitions?

IF YOU WOULD BE MY ALLY

Ideally as allies (all lies), we can have no major lies among us, and we would lay our secrets on the conference table – the ones we've internalized and the ones we propagate. In looking at the motivations of those we are in solidarity with (women-of-color) and those who want to make alliances with us (whitewomen), we not only need to look at who they are, the space(s) they occupy, and how they enter our space and manuever in it, *but* we have to look at our own motivations. Some issues to ponder and questions to ask ourselves: if all political action is founded on subconscious irresolutions and personal conflicts, then we must first look at that baggage we carry with us before sorting though other folks' dirty laundry. Having examined our own motives we can then inquire into the motivations of those who want to be our allies: Do they want us to be like them? Do they want us to hide the parts of ourselves that make them uneasy, i.e., our color, class, and racial identities? If we were to ask white lesbians to leave their whiteness at home, they would be shocked, having assumed that they have deconditioned the negative aspects of being white out of themselves by virtue of being feminist or lesbians. But I see that whiteness bleeds through all the baggage they port around with them and that it even seeps into their bones. Do they want to "take over" and impose their values in order to have power over us? I've had white and colored friends tell me I shouldn't give my energy to male friends, that I shouldn't go to horror movies because of the violence against women in them, that I should only write from the perspective of female characters, that I shouldn't eat meat. I respect women whose values and politics are different from mine, but they do not respect me or give me credit for self-determining my life when they impose trendy politically correct attitudes on me. The assumption they are making in imposing their "political correctness" on me is that I, a woman, a chicana, a lesbian should go to an "outside" authority rather than my own for how to run my life.

When I am asked to leave parts of myself out of the room, out of the kitchen, out of the bed, these people are not getting a whole person. They are only getting a little piece of me. As feminists and lesbians, we need all of us together, *tlan* (from the Nahuatl meaning close together), and each one of us needs all the different aspects and pieces of ourselves to be present and totally engaged in order to survive life in the late twentieth century.

Do they only want those parts of us that they can live with, that are similar to theirs, not different from them? The issue of differences continues to come up over and over again. Are we asked to sit at the table, or be invited to bed, because we bring some color to and look good behind the sheets? Are we there because those who would be our allies happen to have ancestors that were our oppressors and are operating out of a sense of guilt? Does this whitewoman of-color or man-of-color want to be our ally in order to atone for racial guilt or personal guilt? Does this person want to be "seen" and recognized by us? According to Lacan, every human action, even the most altruistic, comes from a desire for recognition by the Other and from a desire for self-recognition in some form.[17] For some, love is the highest and most intense recognition.

Maria Lugones, a Latina philospher, a woman who is at this conference, wrote a paper with a whitewoman, Vicky Spelman, "Have We Got a Theory For You: Feminist Theory, Cultural Imperialism, and the Demand for the Woman's Voice,"[18] in which they posit that the only motivation for alliance work is love and friendship. Nothing else. I have friends that I totally disagree with politically, friends that are not even from the same class, the same race, the same anything, but something keeps us together, keeps us working things out. Perhaps Lugones and Spelman are right. Love and friendship can provide a good basis for alliance work, but there are too many "tensions in alliance groups to dismiss with a light comment that bonds are based on love and friendship. This reminds me of Dill's critique of sisterhood being based on common (white) interests and alikeness."[19] What may be "saving" the colored and white feminist movements may be a combination of all these factors. Certainly the tensions between opposing theories and political stances vitalize the feminist dialogue. But it may only be combined with respect, partial understanding, love, and friendship that keeps us together in the long run. So *mujeres* think about the *carnalas* you want to be in your space, those whose spaces you want to have overlapping yours.

RITUALIZING COALITION AND ALLIANCE BUILDING

Speaking and communicating lay the ground work, but there is a point beyond too much talk that abstracts the experience. What is needed is a symbolic behavior performance made concrete by involving body and emotions with political theories and strategies, rituals that will connect the conscious with the unconscious. Through ritual we can make some deep level changes.

Ritual consecrates the alliance. Breaking bread together, and other group activities that physically and psychically represent the ideals, goals, and attitudes promote a quickening, thickening between us.

Allies, remember that the foreign woman, "the alien," is *nonacayocapo* which in Nahuatl means one who possesses body (flesh) and blood like me. *Aliadas, recuerda que mujer ajena tambien es nonacayocapo, la que la tiene cuerpo y sangre como yo.* Remember that our hearts are full of compassion, not empty. And the spirit dwells strong within. Remember also that the great emptiness, hollowness within the psyches of whitewomen propels them to coalition with colored. Oh, white sister, where is your soul, your spirit? It has run off in shock, *susto*, and you lack shamans and *curanderas* to call it back. *Sin alma no te puedes animarte pa'nada.* Remember that an equally empty and hollow place within us allows that connection, even needs that linkage.

It is important that whitewomen go out on limbs and fight for women-of-color in workplaces, schools, and universities. It is important that women-of-color in positions of power support their disempowered sisters. The liberation of women is the private, individual, and collective responsibility of colored and white men and women. *Aliada por pactos de alianzas,* united by pacts of alliances we may make some changes – in ourselves and in our societies.

After reading this paper consider making some decisions and setting goals to work on yourself, with another, with others of your race, or with a multiracial group as a bridge, drawbridge, sandbar, island, or in a way that works for you. *En fin quiero tocarlas de cerca,* I want to be allied to some of you. I want to touch you, kinswomen, *parientas, compañeras paisanas, carnalas*, comrades, and I want you to touch me so that together, each in our separate ways, we can nourish our struggle and keep alive our visions to recuperate, validate, and transform our histories.

NOTES

Rather than discussing anti-Semitism, a dialogue I choose not to take on in this paper for reasons of length, boundaries of topic, and ignorance on my part of all its subtleties (though I am aware that there is a connection between racism and anti-Semitism I am not sure what it is). I've decided not to take it on nor even make a token mention of it. I realize that this is a form of "If you don't deal with my racism I won't deal with yours," and that pleading ignorance is no excuse.

1 The words *marimachas* and *tortilleras* are derogatory terms that *mujeres* who are lesbians are called. *Patlache* is the Nauhtl term for women who bond and have sex with other women. *Lesberadas* is a term I coined, prompted by the word *desperado*.

2 Gloria Anzaldúa, "Never, Momma," a poem published in *Third Woman* (Fall 1983).

3 The concept of framing metacommunication was articulated by Gregory Bateson in *Steps to an Ecology of Mind* (New York: Ballantine, 1972).

4 *Ibid.*

5 For a definition of cultural paradigms see: T.S. Kuhn, *The Structure of Scientific Revolutions* (Chicago: University of Chicago Press, 1970).

6 Judith Moschkovich.

7 This was documented by Chela Sandoval, "Women Respond to Racism," A Report on the National Women's Studies Association Conference held in Storrs, Connecticut 1981 in *Making Face, Making Soul/Haciendo Caras: Creative and Critical Perspectives by Feminists-Of-Color*, ed. Gloria Anzaldúa (San Francisco: Spinsters/Aunt Lute, 1990). See also Audre Lorde, "The Uses of Anger: Women Responding to Racism," in *Sister Outsider: Essays and Speeches* (Trumansburg, NY: The Crossing Press, 1984): 145–75.

8 Monique Wittig, "One is Not Born A Woman," *Feminist Issues*, (Winter 1981).

9 Lynet Uttal, from commentary notes of her reading of this text, February 1990.

10 Elana Dykewomon, talk given in June, 1988, in Montreal at the Third International Feminist Book Fair for a panel on Lesbian Separatism.

11 See Anzaldúa's "En Raport, In Opposition: Cobrando cuentas a las nuestras," in *Making Face, Making Soul/Haciendo Caras: Creative and Critical Perspectives by Feminists-of-Color*, ed. Gloria Anzaldúa (San Francisco: Spinsters/Aunt Lute, 1990) The essay first appeared in *Sinister Wisdom* 33 (Fall 1987).

12 *Minority Literature in North America: Contemporary Perspectives*, ed. Wolfgang Karrer and Hartmut Lutz, unpublished manuscript.

13 Gail Pheterson defines internalized domination as "the incorporation and acceptance by individuals within a dominant group of prejudices against others." "Alliances Between Women: Overcoming Internalized Oppression and Internalized Domination."

14 Alexander Mitscherlich's definition of prejudice in *Minority Literature in North America: Contemporary Perspectives*, ed. Wolfgang Karrer and Hartmut Lutz: 257.

15 See my introduction to *Making Face, Making Soul/Haciendo Caras* cited above. My rationale for hyphenating *women-of-color*, capitalizing *Racism*, and making *whitewomen* one word is in this introduction.

16 Maria Lucia, Santaella, "On Passion as (?) Phanevou (Maybe or Almost a Phenomenology of Passion)", *Third Woman: Texas and More*, 111: 1 and 2: 107.

17 Jacques Lacan, *Écrits, A Selection*, trans. Alan Sheridan (New York: W. W. Norton, 1977).

18 Maria Lugones and Elizabeth V. Spelman, "Have We Got A Theory for You! Feminist Theory, Cultural Imperialism and the Demand for 'The Woman's Voice'," *Women's Studies Int. Forum*, 6–6 (1983): 573–81. Reprinted in *Making Face, Making Soul/Haciendo Caras: Creative and Critical Perspectives by Feminists-of-Color*, ed. Gloria Anzaldúa (San Francisco: Spinsters/Aunt Lute, 1990).

19 Lynet Uttal, from commentary notes of her reading of this text, February 1990. Uttal refers to Bonnie Thornton Dill "Race, Class, and Gender: Prospects for an All Inclusive Sisterhood," *Feminist Studies* 9 (1983): 131–48.

TOMÁS ALMAGUER

"Chicano Men: A Cartography of Homosexual Identity and Behavior"

from *differences: A Journal of Feminist Cultural Studies* 3: 2 (1991): 75–100

The sexual behavior and sexual identity of Chicano male homosexuals is principally shaped by two distinct sexual systems, each of which attaches different significance and meaning to homosexuality. Both the European-American and Mexican/Latin-American systems have their own unique ensemble of sexual meanings, categories for sexual actors, and scripts that circumscribe sexual behavior. Each system also maps the human body in different ways by placing different values on homosexual erotic zones. The primary socialization of Chicanos into Mexican/Latin-American cultural norms, combined with their simultaneous socialization into the dominant European-American culture, largely structures how they negotiate sexual identity questions and confer meaning to homosexual behavior during adolescence and adulthood. Chicano men who embrace a "gay" identity (based on the European-American sexual system) must reconcile this sexual identity with their primary socialization into a Latino culture that does not recognize such a construction: there is no cultural equivalent to the modern "gay man" in the Mexican/Latin-American sexual system.

How does socialization into these different sexual systems shape the crystallization of their sexual identities and the meaning they give to their homosexuality? Why does only a segment of homosexually active Chicano men identify as "gay"? Do these men primarily consider themselves *Chicano* gay men (who retain primary emphasis on their ethnicity) or *gay* Chicanos (who place primary emphasis on their sexual preference)? How do Chicano homosexuals structure their sexual conduct, especially the sexual roles and relationships into which they

enter? Are they structured along lines of power/dominance firmly rooted in a patriarchal Mexican-culture that privileges men over women and the masculine over the feminine? Or do they reflect the ostensibly more egalitarian sexual norms and practices of the European-American sexual system? These are among the numerous questions that this paper problematizes and explores.

We know little about how Chicano men negotiate and contest a modern gay identity with aspects of Chicano culture drawing upon more Mexican/Latin-American configurations of sexual meaning. Unlike the rich literature on the Chicana/Latina lesbian experience, there is a paucity of writings on Chicano gay men.[1] There does not exist any scholarly literature on this topic other than one unpublished study addressing this issue as a secondary concern (Carrillo and Maiorana). The extant literature consists primarily of semi-autobiographical, literary texts by authors such as John Rechy, Arturo Islas, and Richard Rodriguez.[2] Unlike the writings on Chicana lesbianism, however, these works fail to discuss directly the cultural dissonance that Chicano homosexual men confront in reconciling their primary socialization into Chicano family life with the sexual norms of the dominant culture. They offer little to our understanding of how these men negotiate the different ways these cultural systems stigmatize homosexuality and how they incorporate these messages into their adult sexual practices.

In the absence of such discussion or more direct ethnographic research to draw upon, we must turn elsewhere for insights into the lives of Chicano male homosexuals. One source of such knowledge is the perceptive anthropological research on homosexuality in Mexico and Latin America, which has direct relevance for our understanding of how Chicano men structure and culturally interpret their homosexual experiences. The other, ironically, is the writings of Chicana lesbians who have openly discussed intimate aspects of their sexual behavior and reflected upon sexual identity issues. How they have framed these complex sexual issues has major import for our understanding of Chicano male homosexuality. Thus, the first section of this paper examines certain features of the Mexican/Latin-American sexual system which offer clues to the ensemble of cultural meanings that Chicano homosexuals give to their sexual practices. The second section examines the autobiographical writings of Chicana lesbian writer Cherríe Moraga. I rely upon her candid discussion of her sexual development as ethnographic evidence for further problematizing the Chicano homosexual experience in the United States.

THE CARTOGRAPHY OF DESIRE IN THE MEXICAN/LATIN-AMERICAN SEXUAL SYSTEM

American anthropologists have recently turned their attention to the complex meaning of homosexuality in Mexico and elsewhere in Latin America. Ethnographic research by Joseph M. Carrier, Roger N. Lancaster, Richard Parker, Barry D. Adam, and Clark L. Taylor has documented the inapplicability of Western European and North American categories of sexual meaning in the Latin American context. Since the Mexican/Chicano population in the US shares basic features of these Latin cultural patterns, it is instructive to examine this sexual system closely and to explore its impact on the sexuality of homosexual Chicano men and women.

The rules that define and stigmatize homosexuality in Mexican culture operate under a logic and a discursive practice different from those of the bourgeois sexual system that shaped the emergence of contemporary gay/lesbian identity in the US. Each sexual system confers meaning to homosexuality by giving different weight to the two fundamental features of human sexuality that Freud delineated in the *Three Essays on the Theory of Sexuality*: sexual object choice and sexual aim. The structured meaning of homosexuality in the European–American context rests on the sexual object choice one makes – i.e., the biological sex of the person toward whom sexual activity is directed. The Mexican/Latin-American sexual system, on the other hand, confers meaning to homosexual practices according to sexual aim – i.e., the act one wants to perform with another person (of either biological sex).

The contemporary bourgeois sexual system in the US divides the sexual landscape according to discrete sexual categories and personages defined in terms of sexual preference or object choice: same sex (homosexual), opposite sex (heterosexual), or both (bisexual). Historically, this formulation has carried with it a blanket condemnation of all same-sex behavior. Because it is non-procreative and at odds with a rigid, compulsory heterosexual norm, homosexuality traditionally has been seen as either (1) a sinful transgression against the word of God, (2) a congenital disorder wracking the body, or (3) a psychological pathology gripping the mind. In underscoring object choice as the crucial factor in defining sexuality in the US, anthropologist Roger Lancaster argues that "homosexual desire itself, without any qualifications, stigmatizes one as a homosexual" (116). This stigmatization places the modern gay man at the bottom of the dominant sexual hierarchy. According to Lancaster, "the object choice of the homosexual emarginates him from male power, except insofar as he can serve as a negative example and . . . is positioned outside the operational rules of normative (hetero)sexuality" (123–4).

Unlike the European–American system, the Mexican/Latin-American sexual system is based on a configuration of gender/sex/power that is articulated along the active/passive axis and organized through the scripted sexual role one plays.[3] It highlights sexual aim – the act one wants to perform with the person toward whom sexual activity is directed – and gives only secondary importance to the person's gender or biological sex. According to Lancaster, "it renders certain organs and roles 'active,' other body passages and roles 'passive,' and assigns honor/shame and status/stigma accordingly"

(123). It is the mapping of the body into differentiated erotic zones and the unequal, gender-coded statuses accorded sexual actors that structure homosexual meaning in Latin culture. In the Mexican/Latin-American context there is no cultural equivalent to the modern gay man. Instead of discrete sexual personages differentiated according to sexual preference, we have categories of people defined in terms of the role they play in the homosexual act. The Latin homosexual world is divided into *activos* and *pasivos* (as in Mexico and Brazil) and *machistas* and *cochóns* (in Nicaragua).

Although stigma accompanies homosexual practices in Latin culture, it does not equally adhere to both partners. It is primarily the anal-passive individual (the *cochón* or *pasivo*) who is stigmatized for playing the subservient, feminine role. His partner (the *activo* or *machista*) typically "is not stigmatized at all and, moreover, no clear category exists in the popular language to classify him. For all intents and purposes, he is just a normal ... male" (Lancaster: 113). In fact, Lancaster argues that the active party in a homosexual drama often gains status among his peers in precisely the same way that one derives status from seducing many women (113). This cultural construction confers an inordinate amount of meaning to the anal orifice and to anal penetration. This is in sharp contrast to the way homosexuality is viewed in the US, where the oral orifice structures the meaning of homosexuality in the popular imagination. In this regard, Lancaster suggests that the lexicon of male insult in each context clearly reflects this basic difference in cultural meaning associated with oral/anal sites (111). The most common derisive term used to refer to homosexuals in the US is "cocksucker." Conversely, most Latin American epithets for homosexuals convey the stigma associated with their being anally penetrated.

Consider for a moment the meaning associated with the passive homosexual in Nicaragua, the *cochón*. The term is derived from the word *colchón* or mattress, implying that one man gets on top of another as one would a mattress, and thereby symbolically affirms the former's superior masculine power and male

status over the other, who is feminized and indeed objectified (Lancaster: 112). *Cochón* carried with it a distinct configuration of power, delineated along gender lines that are symbolically affirmed through the sexual role one plays in the homosexual act. Consequently, the meaning of homosexuality in Latin culture is fraught with elements of power/dominance that are not intrinsically accorded homosexual practices in the US. As Lancaster notes,

> The resultant anal emphasis suggests a significant constraint on the nature of homoerotic practices. Unlike oral intercourse, which may lend itself to reciprocal sexual practices, anal intercourse invariably produces an active partner and a passive partner. If oral intercourse suggests the possibility of an equal sign between partners anal intercourse most likely produces an unequal relationship.
>
> (112–13)

Therefore, it is anal passivity alone that is stigmatized and that defines the subordinate status of homosexuals in Latin culture. The stigma conferred to the passive role is fundamentally inscribed in gender-coded terms.

> "To give" (*dar*) is to be masculine, "to receive" (*recibir, aceptar, tomar*) is to be feminine. This holds as the ideal in all spheres of transactions between and within genders. It is symbolized by the popular interpretation of the male sexual organ as active in intercourse and the female sexual organ (or male anus) as passive.
> (Lancaster: 114)

This equation makes homosexuals such as the *pasivo* and *cochón* into feminized men; biological males, but not truly men. In Nicaragua, for example, homosexual behavior renders "one man a machista and the other a cochón. The machista's honor and the cochón's shame are opposite signs of the same coin" (Lancaster: 114).

THE POWER OF MYTH AND MALE CULTURAL FANTASY: MEXICAN FEMALE BETRAYAL AND MALE MASCULINITY

Psychoanalyst Marvin Goldwert argues that this patriarchal cultural equation has special resonance for Mexicans and remains deeply embedded in the Mexican psyche. He claims that it has symbolic roots in cultural myths surrounding the Spanish conquest of Mexico in the sixteenth century. This colonial drama unfolded with the Spanish conquistadores playing the role of active, masculine intruders who raped the passive, feminine Indian civilization. Goldwert suggests that

> there now exists in every Mexican male a culturally stereotyped polarity in which "masculinity" is synonymous with the active/dominant personality and "femininity" is passive/submissive. In mestizo society, the macho ... strove to overcome his sense of Indian femininity by asserting a true Spanish dominance over his women.
>
> (162)

In this formulation, Mexican men are disposed to affirm their otherwise insecure masculinity through the symbolic sexual conquest of women: "Male–female relations in Mexico thus were fit into a stereotypical mold of the dominant/aggressive male and the inferior *mujer abnegada*, the passive, self-sacrificing, dutiful woman" (162).

This gender-coded equation finds its clearest expression in the betrayal of Doña Marina (or *la Malinche*), the Indian woman who facilitated the Spanish conquest of Mexico. In *Labyrinth of Solitude*, Octavio Paz sums up the significance of her betrayal for the Mexican mestizo population in the phrase "los hijos de la chingada" ("the sons of the violated mother").[4] He perceptively notes that the distinction between *el chingón* and *la chingada* is not only a Spanish/Indian configuration but is also fundamentally inscribed in male/female terms. According to Paz, the word *chingar* signifies "doing violence to another,"

> The verb is masculine, active, cruel: it stings, wounds, gashes, stains. And it provokes a bitter, resentful satisfaction. The person who suffers this action is passive, inert and open, in contrast to the active, aggressive and closed person who inflicts it. The *chingón* is the *macho*, the male; he rips open the *chingada*, the female, who is pure passivity, defenseless against the exterior world. The relationship between them is violent and it is determined by the cynical power of the first and the impotence of the second.
>
> (77)

Mexican men often find a tenuous assurance of their masculinity and virility in aggressive manliness and through a rigid gender role socialization that ruthlessly represses their own femininity.[5] Psychoanalyst Santiago Ramirez identifies the Mexican family as the procrustean bedrock upon which this psychic structuring lies. From early childhood, the young Mexican male develops an ambivalence toward women, who are less valued than men in patriarchal Mexican society. This fundamental disdain for that which is feminine later gives way to an outpouring of resentment and humiliation onto one's wife or mistress and women in general (Goldwert: 165). The psychic consequences of this rejection of the feminine are profound. According to Goldwert,

> Identifying with an idealized paternal model and repressing the maternal model of tenderness, the young *macho* worships at the shrine of virility. During childhood the sign of virility for the Mexican male is courage to the point of recklessness, aggressiveness, and unwillingness to run away from a fight or break a deal (*no rejarse*). During adolescence the sign of virility is for the male to talk about or act in the sexual sphere ... From adolescence through his entire life, the Mexican male will measure virility by sexual potential, with physical strength, courage, and audacity as secondary factors.
>
> (166)

This cultural and psychic structure has particular significance for men who engage in homosexual behavior. Paz notes that the active/male and passive/female construction in Mexican culture has direct significance for the way Mexicans view male homosexuality. According to him, "masculine homosexuality is regarded with a certain indulgence insofar as the active agent is concerned. The passive agent is an abject, degraded being. Maculine homosexuality is tolerated, then, on condition that it consists in violating a passive agent" (40). Aggressive, active, and penetrating sexual activity, therefore, becomes the true marker of the Mexican man's tenuous masculinity. It is attained by the negation of all that is feminine within him and by the sexual subjugation of women. But this valorization of hypermasculinity can also be derived by penetrating passive, anal-receptive men as well.

MALE HOMOSEXUAL IDENTITY AND BEHAVIOR IN MEXICO

Some of the most insightful ethnographic research on homosexuality in Mexico has been conducted by anthropologist J. M. Carrier. Like other Latin American specialists exploring this issue, Carrier argues that homosexuality is construed very differently in the US and in Mexico. In the US, even one adult homosexual act or acknowledgment of homosexual desire may threaten a man's gender identity and throw open to question his sexual identity as well. In sharp contrast, a Mexican man's masculine gender and heterosexual identity are not threatened by a homosexual act as long as he plays the inserter's role. Only the male who plays the passive sexual role and exhibits feminine gender characteristics is considered to be truly homosexual and is, therefore, stigmatized. This "bisexual" option, an exemption from stigma for the "masculine" homosexual, can be seen as part of the ensemble of gender privileges and sexual prerogatives accorded Mexican men. Thus it is primarily the passive, effeminate homosexual man who becomes the object of derision and societal contempt in Mexico.

> Effeminate males provide easily identifiable sexual targets for interested males in Mexico ... The beliefs linking effeminate males with homosexuality are culturally transmitted by a vocabulary which provides the appropriate labels, by homosexually oriented jokes and word games and by the mass media. From early childhood on, Mexican males are made aware of the labels used to denote male homosexuals, and the connection is always clearly made that these homosexual males (usually called *putos* or *jotos*) are guilty of unmanly effeminate behavior.
>
> (Carrier, "Mexican Male," 78)

The terms used to refer to homosexual Mexican men are generally coded with gendered meaning drawn from the inferior position of women in patriarchal Mexican society. The most benign of these contemptuous terms is *maricón*, a label that highlights the non-conforming gender attributes of the (feminine) homosexual man. Its semantic equivalent in the US is "sissy" or "fairy" (Carrier, "Cultural Factors," 123–4). Terms such as *joto* or *puto* on the other hand, speak to the passive sexual role

taken by these men rather than merely their gender attributes. They are infinitely more derogatory and vulgar in that they underscore the sexually non-conforming nature of their passive/receptive position in the homosexual act. The invective associated with all these appellations speaks to the way effeminate homosexual men are viewed as having betrayed the Mexican man's prescribed gender and sexual role. Moreover, it may be noted that the Spanish feminine word *puta* refers to a female prostitute while its male form *puto* refers to a passive homosexual, not a male prostitute. It is significant that the cultural equation made between the feminine, anal-receptive homosexual man and the most culturally stigmatized female in Mexican society (the whore) share a common semantic base.[6]

Carrier's research suggests that homosexuality in Mexico is rigidly circumscribed by the prominent role the family plays in structuring homosexual activity. Whereas in the US, at least among most European-Americans, the role of the family as a regulator of the lives of gay men and lesbians has progressively declined, in Mexico the family remains a crucial institution that defines both gender and sexual relations between men and women. The Mexican family remains a bastion of patriarchal privilege for men and a major impediment to women's autonomy outside the private world of the home.

The constraints of family life often prevent homosexual Mexican men from securing unrestricted freedom to stay out late at night, to move out of their family's home before marriage, or to take an apartment with a male lover. Thus their opportunities to make homosexual contacts in other than anonymous locations, such as the balconies of movie theaters or certain parks, are severely constrained (Carrier, "Family Attitudes," 368). This situation creates an atmosphere of social interdiction which may explain why homosexuality in Mexico is typically shrouded in silence. The concealment, suppression, or prevention of any open acknowledgment of homosexual activity underscores the stringency of cultural dictates surrounding gender and sexual norms within Mexican family life. Unlike the generally more egalitarian, permissive family life of white middle-class gay men and lesbians in the US, the Mexican family appears to play a far more important and restrictive role in structuring homosexual behavior among Mexican men "Family Attitudes," 373).

Given these constraints and the particular meanings attached to homosexuality in Mexican culture, same-sex behavior in Mexico typically unfolds in the context of an age-stratified hierarchy that grants privileges to older, more masculine men. According to Carrier, these male homosexual transactions usually follow these basic patterns:

> Some post-pubertal males utilize boys as sexual outlets prior to marriage, and, after marriage, continue to utilize both heterosexual and homosexual outlets. Another pattern is that some males in their first year of sexual activity initiate sexual encounters both with post-pubertal girls, and effeminate boys, they find in their neighborhoods, at schools, at social outings. They continue to utilize both sexual outlets prior to marriage, but discontinue, or only occasionally use, homosexual outlets following marriage. Still another pattern exists where some males utilize both genders as sexual outlets during their first couple of years of sexual activity. They have *novias* and plan to marry, but they also become romantically involved with males prior to marriage. After they marry, they continue to have romantic and sexual relationships with males.
>
> ("Mexican Male," 81)

Carrier's research on mestizo homosexual men in Guadalajara found that the majority of the feminine, passive homosexual males become sexually active prior to puberty; many as young as from the ages of 6 to 9. Most of their homosexual contacts are with post-pubescent cousins, uncles, or neighbors. They may occur quite frequently and extend over a long period or be infrequent and relatively short-lived in duration. These early experiences are generally followed by continued homosexual encounters into adolescence and adulthood. Only a segment of the homosexually active youth, however, develop a preference for the anal receptive, *pasivo* sexual role, and thus come to define their individual sense of gender in a decidedly feminine direction ("Gay Liberation," 228, 231).

It is very significant that, in instances where two masculine, active men enter into a homosexual encounter, the rules that structure gender-coded homosexual relations continue to operate with full force. In these exchanges one of the men – typically he who is defined as being more masculine or powerful – assumes the active, inserter role while the other man is pressed into the passive, anal-receptive role. Moreover, men who may eventually adopt both active and passive features of homosexual behavior typically do not engage in such reciprocal relations with the same person. Instead, they generally only play the active role with one person (who is always viewed as being the more feminine) and are sexually passive with those they deem more masculine than themselves ("Cultural Factors," 120–1).

Although some cognitive dissonance is involved in Mexican male homosexual contacts, it appears to be primarily related to the extent of homosexual involvement and how one sets limits to the sexual exchange. Many of these men, who typically start out playing only the *activo* sexual role and begin meaningful homosexual relations, while adolescents experience some uneasiness over their homosexual activity if they stray from the exclusive inserter role. They often reduce this psychic conflict through increased heterosexual contacts (conquests) or by limiting their homosexuality to only the active sexual role ("Gay Liberation," 250).

In sum, it appears that the major difference between bisexually active men in Mexico and bisexual males in the US is that the former are not stigmatized because they exclusively play the active, masculine, inserter role. Unlike in the North American context, "one drop of homosexuality" does not, *ipso facto*, make a Mexican male a *joto* or a *maricón*. As Carrier's research clearly documents, none of the active inserter participants in homosexual encounters ever considers himself a "homosexual" or to be "gay" ("Mexican Male," 83). What may be called the "bisexual escape hatch" functions to insure that the tenuous masculinity of Mexican men is not compromised through the homosexual act; they remain men, *hombres*, even though they participate in this sexual behavior. Moreover, the Mexican sexual system actually militates against the construction of discernable, discrete "bisexual" or "gay" sexual identities because these identities are shaped by and draw upon a different sexual system and foreign discursive practices. One does not, in other words, become "gay" or "lesbian" identified in Mexico because its sexual system precludes such an identity formation in the first place. These "bourgeois" sexual categories are simply not relevant or germane to the way gender and sexual meanings are conferred in Mexican society.

THE PROBLEMATIC NATURE OF A GAY IDENTITY FOR MEXICAN MEN

Given the contours of the Mexican sexual system, and the central role the Mexican family plays in structuring homosexual behavior, it is not surprising that North American sexual categories, identities, and identity-based social movements have only recenly made their appearance in Mexico. Carrier has documented that the gay liberation movement is a very recent phenomenon in Mexico and one that has confronted formidable obstacles in taking root. For example, there existed as late as 1980 only a very small and submerged gay scene in large cities such as Mexico City, Guadalajara, and Acapulco. There are no distinct "gay neighborhoods" to speak of, and only a few gay bars and discos ("Gay Liberation," 225). Those Mexican men who define their sexual identity as "gay" have clearly adopted North American homosexual patterns, such as incorporating both passive and active sexual roles into their homosexual behavior. This more recent incarnation of the "modern Mexican homosexual" is widely considered to be based on North American sexual scripts, and the "foreign" nature of such sexual practices has caused the men who adopt them to be commonly referred to as *internacionales*.

Gay Mexican males who fall into the *internacionales* category are difficult to assess as a group ... Most of them are masculine rather than feminine and during the early years of their sex lives play only the "activo" sexual role – the "pasivo" sexual role is incorporated later as they become inolved in homosexual encounters. Many "internacionales" state that although they may play both sex roles, they nevertheless retain a strong general preference for one over the other.

("Gay Liberation," 231)

It appears that gay liberation in Mexico is more readily advocated by the new, more masculine homosexual, who can utilize his gender conformity as a legitimating factor for embracing a gay lifestyle. These *macho maricas* (as they are referred to in Argentina (i.e., butch queens)) are most likely to develop a gay identity by "coming out of the closet" and becoming part of "los de Ambiente" (245). The masculine stance of the *internacionales* often places them at odds, however, with the more feminine *joto*, who also seeks self-affirmation and a less stigmatized status. Since these stigmatized, effeminate homosexuals have never thought of themselves as or claimed to be heterosexual, they reportedly experience less cognitive dissonance accepting a "gay" identity and fewer problems in coming out (250).

The recent emergence of this "gay" sexual identity in Mexico has brought with it a number of special problems for the homosexual Mexican man. Carrier argues that an ongoing source of tension within the emergent gay subculture typically crystallizes between

those homosexual males who are open and feminine and those who are not. Public demonstrations of feminine behavior by young gay males who consider it a basic part of their makeup is disturbing to those gay males who prefer to comport themselves in more masculine ways and thus be less obvious in straight settings ... Although attempts have been made in the gay liberation movement to get its more masculine members to view feminine male behavior in a more positive way, they have had little success.

("Gay Liberation," 248)

Despite the incorporation of more bourgeois conceptions of sexuality, the privileging of masculinity among Mexican men – whether heterosexual or homosexual – remains a cornerstone of patriarchal Mexican society, which is very resistant to fundamental redefinition and cultural intrusion from the outside.

IMPLICATIONS FOR CHICANO GAY MEN IN THE US

The emergence of the modern gay identity in the US and its recent appearance in Mexico have implications for Chicano men that have not been fully explored. What is apparent, however, is that Chicanos, as well as other racial minorities, do not negotiate the acceptance of a gay identity in exactly the same way white American men do. The ambivalence of Chicanos *vis-à-vis* a gay sexual identity and their attendant uneasiness with white gay/lesbian culture do not necessarily reflect a denial of homosexuality. Rather, I would argue, the slow pace at which this identity formation has taken root among Chicanos is attributable to cultural and structural factors which differentiate the experiences of the white and non-white populations in the US.

Aside from the crucial differences discussed above in the way homosexuality is culturally constructed in the Mexican/Latin-American and European- or Anglo-American sexual systems, a number of other structural factors also militate against the emergence of a modern gay identity among Chicano men. In this regard, the progressive loosening of familial constraints among white, middle-class homosexual men and women at the end of the nineteenth century, and its acceleration in the post-World-War-II period, structurally positioned the white gay and lesbian population to redefine their primary self-identity in terms of their homosexuality. The shift from a family-based economy to a fully developed wage labor system at the end of the nineteenth century dramatically freed European-American men and women from the previously confining social and economic world of the family. It allowed both white men and the white "new woman" of the period to transgress the stifling gender roles that previously bound them to a compulsory heterosexual norm.[7] Extricating the nuclear family from its traditional role as a primary unit of production enabled homosexually inclined individuals to forge a new sexual identity and to develop a culture and community that were not previously possible. Moreover, the tremendous urban migration ignited (or precipitated) by World War II accelerated this process by drawing thousands of homosexuals into urban settings where the possibilities for same-sex intimacy were greater.

It is very apparent, however, that the gay identity and communities that emerged were overwhelmingly white, middle class, and male-centered. Leading figures of the first homophile organizations in the US, such as the Mattachine Society, and key individuals shaping the newly emergent gay culture were primarily drawn from this segment of the homosexual population. Moreover, the new communities founded in the postwar period were largely populated by white men who had the resources and talents needed to create "gilded" gay ghettos. This fact has given the contemporary gay community – despite its undeniable diversity – a largely white, middle-class, and male form. In other words, the unique class and racial advantages of white gay men provided the foundation upon which they could boldly carve out the new gay identity. Their collective position in the social structure empowered them with the skills and talents needed to create new gay institutions, communities, and a unique sexual subculture.

Despite the intense hostility that, as gay men, they faced during that period, nevertheless, as white gay men, they were in the best position to risk the social ostracism that this process engendered. They were *relatively* better situated than other homosexuals to endure the hazards unleashed by their transgression of gender conventions and traditional heterosexual norms. The diminished importance of ethnic identity among these individuals, due principally to the homogenizing and integrating impact of the dominant racial categories which defined them foremost as white, undoubtedly also facilitated the emergene of gay identity among them. As members of the privileged racial group – and thus no longer viewing themselves primarily as Irish, Italian, Jewish, Catholic, etc. – these middle-class men and women arguably no longer depended solely on their respective cultural groups and families as a line of defense against the dominant group. Although they may have continued to experience intense cultural dissonance leaving behind their ethnicity and their traditional family-based roles, they were now in a position to dare to make such a move.

Chicanos, on the other hand, have never occupied the social space where a gay or lesbian identity can readily become a primary basis of self-identity. This is due, in part, to their structural position at the subordinate ends of both the class and racial hierarchies, and in a context where ethnicity remains a primary basis of group identity and survival. Moreover, Chicano family life requires allegiance to patriarchal gender relations and to a system of sexual meanings that directly militate against the emergence of this alternative basis of self-identity. Furthermore, factors such as gender, geographical settlement, age, nativity, language usage and degree of cultural assimilation further prevent, or at least complicate, the acceptance of a gay or lesbian identity by Chicanos or Chicanas respectively. They are not as free as individuals situated elsewhere in the social structure to redefine their sexual identity in ways that contravene the imperatives of minority family life and its traditional gender expectations. How they come to define their sexual identities as gay, straight, bisexual or, in Mexican/Latin-American terms, as in *activo*, *pasivo*, or *macho marica*, therefore, is not a straightforward or unmediated process. Unfortunately, there are no published studies to date exploring this identity formation process.

However, one study on homosexual Latino/Chicano men was conducted by Hector Carrillo and Horacio Maiorana in the spring of 1989. As part of their ongoing work on AIDS within the San Francisco Bay Area Latino community, these researchers developed a typology capturing the different points in a continuum differentiating the sexual identity of these men. Their preliminary typology is useful in that it delineates the way homosexual Chicanos/Latinos integrate elements of both the North American and Mexican sexual systems into their sexual behavior.

The first two categories of individuals, according to Carrillo and Maiorana, are: (1) working-class Latino men who have adopted an effeminate gender persona and usually play the passive role in homosexual encounters (many of them are drag queens who frequent the Latino gay bars in the Mission District of San Francisco); and (2) Latino men who consider themselves heterosexual or bisexual, but who furtively have sex with other men. They are also primarily working-class and often frequent Latino gay bars in search of discreet sexual encounters. They tend to retain a strong Latino or Chicano ethnic identity and structure their sexuality according to the Mexican sexual system. Although Carrillo and Maiorana do not discuss the issue, it seems likely that these men would primarily seek out other Latino men, rather than European-Americans, as potential partners in their culturally circumscribed homosexual behavior.

I would also suggest from personal observations that these two categories of individuals occasionally enter into sexual relationships with middle-class Latinos and European-American men. In so doing, these working-class Latino men often become the object of the middle-class Latino's or the white man's colonial desires. In one expression of this class-coded lust, the effeminate *pasivo* becomes the boyish, feminized object of the middle-class man's colonial desire. In another, the masculine Mexican/Chicano *activo* becomes the embodiment of a potent ethnic masculinity that titillates the middle-class man who thus enters into a passive sexual role.

Unlike the first two categories of homosexually active Latino men, the other three have integrated several features of the North American sexual system into their sexual behavior. They are more likely to be assimilated into the dominant European-American culture of the US and to come from middle-class backgrounds. They include (3) Latino men who openly consider themselves gay and participate in the emergent gay Latino subculture in the Mission district; (4) Latino men who consider themselves gay but do not participate in the Latino gay subculture, preferring to maintain a primary identity as Latino and only secondarily a gay one; and finally, (5) Latino men who are fully assimilated into the white San Francisco gay male community in the Castro District and retain only a marginal Latino identity.

In contrast to the former two categories, Latino men in the latter three categories are more likely to seek European-American sexual partners and exhibit greater difficulty in reconciling their Latino cultural backgrounds with their gay lifestyle. In my impressionistic observations, these men do not exclusively engage in homosexual behavior that is hierarchically differentiated along the gender-coded lines of the Mexican sexual system. They are more likely to integrate both active and passive sexual roles into their sexuality and to enter into relationships in which the more egalitarian norms of the North American sexual system prevail. We know very little, however, about the actual sexual conduct of these individuals. Research has not yet been conducted on how these men express their sexual desires, how they negotiate their masculinity in light of their homosexuality, and, more generally, how they integrate aspects of the two sexual systems into their everyday sexual conduct.

In the absence of such knowledge, we may seek clues about the social world of Chicano gay men in the perceptive writings of Chicana lesbians. Being the first to shatter the silence on the homosexual experience of the Chicano population, they have candidly documented the perplexing issues Chicanos confront in negotiating the conflicting gender and sexual messages imparted by the coexisting Chicano and European-American cultures. The way in which Chicana lesbians have framed these problems, I believe, is bound to have major significance for the way Chicano men reconcile their homosexual behavior and gay sexual identity within a Chicano cultural context. More than any other lesbian writer's, the extraordinary work of Cherríe Moraga articulates a lucid and complex analysis of the predicament that the middle-class Chicana lesbian and Chicano gay man face in this society. A brief examination of her autobiographical writings offers important insights into the complexities and contradictions that may characterize the experience of homosexuality for all Chicanos and Chicanas in the US.

CHERRÍE MORAGA AND CHICANA LESBIANISM

An essential point of departure in assessing Cherríe Moraga's work is an appreciation of the way Chicano family life severely constrains the Chicana's ability to define her life outside of its stifling gender and sexual prescriptions. As a number of Chicana feminist scholars have clearly documented, Chicano family life remains rigidly structured along patriarchal lines that privilege men over women and children.[8] Any violation of these norms is undertaken at great personal risk because Chicanos draw upon the family to resist racism and the ravages of class inequality. Chicano men and women are drawn together in the face of these onslaughts and are closely bound into a family structure that exaggerates unequal gender roles and suppresses sexual nonconformity.[9] Therefore, any deviation from the sacred link binding husband, wife, and child not only threatens the very existence of *la familia* but also potentially undermines the mainstay of resistance to Anglo racism and class exploitation. "The family, then, becomes all the more ardently protected by oppressed people and the sanctity of this institution is infused like blood into the veins of the Chicano. At all costs, la familia must be preserved," writes Moraga. Thus, "we fight back ... with our families – with our women pregnant, and our men as indispensable heads. We believe the more severely we protect the sex roles within the family, the stronger we will be as a unit in opposition to the anglo threat" (*Loving*: 110).

These cultural prescriptions do not, however, curb the sexually nonconforming behavior of certain Chicanos. As in the case of Mexican homosexual men in Mexico, there exists a modicum of freedom for the Chicano homosexual who retains a masculine gender identity while secretly engaging in the active homosexual role. Moraga has perceptively noted that the Latin cultural norm inflects the sexual behavior of homosexual Chicanos: "Male homosexuality has always been a 'tolerated' aspect of Mexican/Chicano society, as long as it remains 'fringe' ... But lesbianism, in any form, and male homosexuality which openly avows both the sexual and the emotional elements of the bond, challenge the very foundation of la familia" (111). The openly effeminate Chicano gay man's rejection of heterosexuality is typically seen as a fundamental betrayal of Chicano patriarchal cultural norms. He is viewed as having turned his back on the male role that privileges Chicano men and entitles them to sexual access to women, minors, and even other men. Those who reject these male prerogatives are viewed as non-men, as the cultural equivalents of women. Moraga astutely assesses the situation as one in which "the 'faggot' is the object of Chicano/Mexicano's contempt because he is consciously choosing a role his culture tells him to despise. That of a woman" (111).

The constraints that Chicano family life imposed on Moraga herself are candidly discussed in her provocative autobiographical essays "La Güera" and "A Long Line of Vendidas" in *Loving in the War Years*. In recounting her childhood in southern California, Moraga describes how she was routinely required to make her brother's bed, iron his shirts, lend him money, and even serve him cold drinks when his friends came to visit their home. The privileged position of men in the Chicano family places women in a secondary, subordinate status. She resentfully acknowledges that "to this day in my mother's home, my brother and father are waited on, including by me" (90). Chicano men have always thought of themselves as superior to Chicanas, she asserts in unambiguous terms: "I have never met any kind of Latino who ... did not subscribe to the basic belief that men are better" (101). The insidiousness of the patriarchal ideology permeating Chicano family life even shapes the way a mother defines her relationships with her children: "The daughter must constantly earn the mother's love, prove her fidelity to her. The son – he gets her love for free" (102).

Moraga realized early in life that she would find it virtually impossible to attain any meaningful autonomy in that cultural context. It was only in the Anglo world that freedom from oppressive gender and sexual strictures was remotely possible. In order to secure this latitude, she made a necessary choice: to embrace the white world and reject crucial aspects of her Chicana upbringing. In painfully honest terms, she states:

I gradually became anglocized because I thought it was the only option available to me toward gaining autonomy as a person without being sexually stigmatized ... I instinctively made choices which I thought would allow me greater freedom of movement in the future. This meant resisting sex roles as much as I could safely manage and that was far easier in an anglo context than in a Chicano one.

(99)

Born to a Chicana mother and an Anglo father, Moraga discovered that being fair-complexioned facilitated her integration into the Anglo social world and contributed immensely to her academic achievement. "My mother's desire to protect her children from poetry and illiteracy" led to their being "anglocized," she writes; "the more effectively we could pass in the white world, the better guaranteed our future" (51). Consequently her life in southern California during the 1950s and 1960s is described as one in which she "identified with and aspired toward white values" (58). In the process, she "rode the wave of that Southern California privilege as far as conscience would let me" (58).

The price initially exacted by anglicization was estrangement from family and a partial loss of the nurturing and love she found therein. In reflecting on this experience, Moraga acknowledges that "I have had to confront that much of what I value about being Chicana, about my family, has been subverted by anglo culture and my cooperation with it ... I realized the major reason for my total alienation from and fear of my classmates was rooted in class and culture" (54). She poignantly concedes that, in the process, "I had disavowed the language I knew best – ignored the words and rhythms that were closest to me. The sounds of my mother and aunts gossiping – half in English, half in Spanish – while drinking cerveza in the kitchen" (55). What she gained, on the other hand, was the greater autonomy that her middle-class white classmates had in defining their emergent sexuality and in circumventing burdensome gender prescriptions. Her movement into the white world, however, was viewed by Chicanos as a great betrayal. By gaining control of her life, Moraga became one of a "long line of vendidas," traitors or "sell-outs," as self-determined women are seen in the sexist cultural fantasy of patriarchal Chicano society. This is the accusation that "hangs above the heads and beats in the hearts of most Chicanas, seeking to develop our own autonomous sense of ourselves, particularly our sexuality" (103).

Patriarchal Chicano culture, with its deep roots in "the institution of heterosexuality," requires Chicanas to commit themselves to Chicano men and subordinate to them their own sexual desires. "[The Chicano] too, like any other man," Moraga writes, "wants to be able to determine how, when, and with whom his women – mother, wife, and daughter – are sexual" (110–11). But "the Chicana's sexual commitment to the Chicano male [is taken as] proof of her fidelity to her people" (105). "It is no wonder," she adds, that most "Chicanas often divorce ourselves from conscious recognition of our own sexuality" (119). In order to claim the identity of a Chicana lesbian, Moraga had to take "a radical stand in direct contradiction to, and in violation of, the women [sic] I was raised to be" (117); and yet she also drew upon themes and images of her Mexican Catholic backround. Of its impact on her sexuality Moraga writes:

> I always knew that I felt the greatest emotional ties with women, but suddenly I was beginning to consciously identify those feelings as sexual. The more potent my dreams and fantasies became and the more I sensed by own exploding sexual power, the more I *retreated* from my body's messages and into the region of religion. By giving definition and meaning to my desires, religion became the discipline to control my sexuality. Sexual fantasy and rebellion became "impure thoughts" and "sinful acts."
>
> (119)

These "contrary feelings," which initially surfaced around the age of 12, unleashed feelings of guilt and moral transgression. She found it impossible to leave behind the Catholic Church's prohibitions regarding homosexuality, and religious themes found their way into how she initially came to define herself as a sexual subject – in a devil-like form. "I wrote poems describing myself as a centaur: half-animal/half-human, hairy-rumped and cloven-hoofed, como el diablo. The images emerged from a deeply Mexican and Catholic place" (124).

As her earliest sexual feelings were laden with religious images, so too were they shaped by images of herself in a male-like form. This is understandable in light of the fact that only men in Chicano culture are granted sexual subjectivity. Consequently, Moraga instinctively gravitated toward a butch persona and assumed a male-like stance toward other women.

> In the effort to avoid embodying la chingada, I became the chingón. In the effort not to feel fucked, I became the fucker, even with women ... The fact of the matter was that all those power struggles of "having" and "being had" were played out in my own bedroom. And in my psyche, they held a particular Mexican twist.
>
> (126)

In a candid and courageously outspoken conversation with lesbian activist Amber Hollibaugh, Moraga recounts that:

> what turned me on sexually, at a very early age, had to do with the fantasy of capture, taking a woman, and my identification was with the man ... The truth is, I do have some real gut-level misgivings about my sexual connection with capture. It might feel very sexy to imagine "taking" a woman, but it has sometimes occurred at the expense of my feeling, sexually, like I can surrender myself to a woman; that is, always needing to be the one in control, calling the shots. It's a very butch trip and I feel like this can keep me private and protected and can prevent me from fully being able to express myself.
>
> (Moraga and Hollibaugh: 396)

Moraga's adult lesbian sexuality defined itself along the traditional butch/femme lines characteristic of lesbian relationships in the postwar period.[10] It is likely that such an identity formation was also largely an expression of the highly gender-coded sexuality imparted through Chicano family life. In order to define herself as an autonomous sexual subject, she embraced a butch, or more masculine, gender persona, and crystallized a sexual desire for feminine, or femme, lovers. She discusses the significance of this aspect of her sexuality in these terms:

> I feel the way I want a woman can be a very profound experience. Remember I told you how when I looked up at my lover's face when I was making love to her (I was actually just kissing her breast at the moment) ... I could feel and see how deeply every part of her was present? That every pore in her body was entrusting me to handle her,

to take care of her sexual desire. This look on her face is like nothing else. It fills me up. She entrusts me to determine where she'll go sexually. And I honestly feel a power inside me strong enough to heal the deepest wound.

(Moraga and Hollibaugh: 398)

In assuming the butch role, Moraga was not seeking simply to cast herself as a man or merely to mimic the male role in the sexual act. Becoming a butch Chicana lesbian was much more complex than that and carried with it a particular pain and uneasiness:

I think that there is a particular pain attached if you identified yourself as a butch queer from an early age as I did. I didn't really think of myself as female, or male. I thought of myself as this hybrid or somethin. I just kinda thought of myself as this free agent until I got tits. Then I thought, oh no, some problem has occurred here ... For me, the way you conceive of yourself as a woman and the way I am attracted to women sexually reflects that butch/femme exchange – where a woman believes herself so woman that it really makes me want her.

But for me, I feel a lot of pain around the fact that it has been difficult for me to conceive of myself as thoroughly female in that sexual way. So retaining my "butchness" is not exactly my desired goal ... How I fantasize sex roles has been really different for me with different women. I do usually enter into an erotic encounter with a woman from the kind of butch place you described, but I have also felt very ripped off there, finding myself taking all the sexual responsibility. I am seriously attracted to butches sometimes. It's a very different dynamic, where the sexuality may not seem as fluid or comprehensible, but I know there's a huge part of me that wants to be handled in the way I described I can handle another woman. I am very compelled toward that "lover" posture. I have never totally reckoned with being the "beloved" and, frankly, I don't know if it takes a butch or a fem or what to get me there. I know that it's a struggle within me and it scares the shit out of me to look at it so directly. I've done this kind of searching emotionally, but to combine sex with it seems like very dangerous stuff.

(Moraga and Hollibaugh, 400–1)

A crucial dimension of the dissonance Moraga experienced in accepting her lesbian sexuality and reconciling the Anglo and Chicano worlds was the conscious awareness that her sexual desires reflected a deeply felt love for her mother. "In contrast to the seeming lack of feelings I had for my father," she writes, "my longings for my mother and fear of her dying were the most passionate feelings that had ever lived inside of my young heart" (*Loving*: 93). These feelings led her to the realization that both the affective and sexual dimensions of her lesbianism were indelibly shaped by the love for her mother. "When I finally lifted the lid on my lesbianism, a profound connection with mother awakened in me" (52), she recalls. "Yes, this is why I love women. This woman is my mother. There is no love as strong as this, refusing my separation, never settling for a secret that would split us off, always at the last minute, like now, pushing me to [the] brink of revelation, speaking the truth" (102).

THE FINAL FRONTIER: UNMASKING THE CHICANO GAY MAN

Moraga's experience is certainly only one expression of the diverse ways in which Chicana lesbians come to define their sense of gender and experience their homosexuality. But her odyssey reflects and articulates the tortuous and painful path traveled by working-class Chicanas (and Chicanos) who embrace the middle-class Anglo world and its sexual system in order to secure, ironically, the "right to passion expressed in our own cultural tongue and movements" (136). It is apparent from her powerful autobiographical writings, however, how much her adult sexuality was also inevitably shaped by the gender and sexual messages imparted through the Chicano family.

How this complex process of integrating, reconciling, and contesting various features of both Anglo and Chicano cultural life are experienced by Chicano gay men, has yet to be fully explored. Moraga's incisive and extraordinarily frank autobiographical account raises numerous questions about the parallels in the homosexual development of Chicana lesbians and Chicano gay men. How, for example, do Chicano male homosexuals internalize and reconcile the gender-specific prescriptions of Chicano culture? How does this primary socialization impact on the way they define their gender personas and sexual identities? How does socialization into a patriarchal gender system that privileges men over women and the masculine over the feminine structure intimate aspects of their sexual behavior? Do most Chicano gay men invariably organize aspects of their sexuality along the hierarchical lines of dominance/subordination that circumscribe gender roles and relationships in Chicano culture? My impression is that many Chicano gay men share the Chicano heterosexual man's underlying disdain for women and all that is feminine. Although it has not been documented empirically, it is likely that Chicano gay men incorporate and contest crucial features of the Mexican/Latin-American sexual system into their intimate sexual behavior. Despite having accepted a "modern" sexual identity, they are not immune to the hierarchical, gender-coded system of sexual meanings that is part and parcel of this discursive practice.

Until we can answer these questions through ethnographic research on the lives of Chicano gay men, we must continue to develop the type of feminist critique of Chicano male culture that is so powerfully articulated in the work of lesbian authors such as Cherríe Moraga. We are fortunate that courageous voices such as hers have irretrievably shattered the silence on the homosexual experience within the Mexican American community. Her work, and that of other Chicana lesbians, has laid a challenge before Chicano gay men to lift the lid on their homosexual experiences and to leave the closeted space they have been relegated to in Chicano culture. The task confronting us, therefore, is to begin interpreting and redefining what it means to be both Chicano and gay in a cultural setting that has traditionally viewed these categories as a contradiction in terms. This is an area of scholarly research that can no longer be left outside the purview of Chicano Studies, Gay and Lesbian Studies, or even more traditional lines of sociological inquiry.

NOTES

1 See, for example, the writings by Chicana and Latina lesbians in Ramos; Alarcón, Castillo, and Moraga; Moraga and Anzaldúa; and Anzaldúa.

See also the following studies on Latinas: Arguelles and Rich; Espin; and Hidalgo and Hidalgo-Christensen.

2 See Bruce-Novoa's interesting discussion of homosexuality as a theme in the Chicano novel.

3 There is a rich literature documenting the ways in which our sexuality is largely structured through sexual scripts that are culturally defined and individually internalized. See, for example, Gagnon and Simon; Simon and Gagnon; and Plummer. What is being referred to here as the Mexican/Latin-American sexual system is part of the circum-Mediterranean construction of gender and sexual meaning. In this regard, see the introduction and essays in Gilmore. For further discussion of this theme in the Mexican context, see Alonso and Koreck. Their essay, which uses many of the same sources as the present essay, explores male homosexual practices in Mexico in relation to AIDS.

4 For a Chicana feminist critique of Paz's discussion of *la Malinche*, see Alarcón.

5 Chicano machismo may also be seen as "a culturally defined hypermasculine ideal model of manliness through which a Mexican male may measure himself, his sons, and his male relatives and friends against such attributes as courage, dominance, power, aggressiveness, and invulnerability" (Carrier, "Gay Liberation," 228).

6 In "Birth of the Queen," Trumbach has perceptively documented that many of the contemporary terms used to refer to homosexual men in Western Europe and the United States (such as *queen*, *punk*, *gay*, *faggot* and *fairy*) also were at one time the slang term for prostitutes (137). See also Alonso and Koreck: 111–13.

7 For a broad overview of the development of a gay and lesbian identity and community in the United States, see D'Emilio; D'Emilio and Freedman; and Katz. A number of articles in the important anthology edited by Duberman, Vicinus and Chauncey document the white middle-class-centered nature of gay/lesbian identity construction and community formation. In particular see Smith-Rosenberg; Newton; Rupp; and Martin.

8 Some of the very best research in Chicano Studies has been conducted by Chicana feminists who have explored the intersection of class, race, and gender in Chicanas' lives. Some recent examples of this impressive scholarship include Zavella; Segura; Pesquera; and Baca-Zinn.

9 This solidarity is captured in the early Chicano movement poster fittingly entitled "La Familia." It consists of three figures in a symbolic pose: a Mexican woman, with a child in her arms, is embraced by a Mexican man, who is centrally positioned in the Portrait and a head taller. This poster symbolized the patriarchal, male-centered privileging of the heterosexual, nuclear family in

Chicano resistance against white racism. For a provocative discussion of these themes in the Chicano movement see Gutiérrez.

10 For an interesting discussion of the butch/femme formulation among working-class white women at the time, see Davis and Kennedy; and Nestle.

REFERENCES

Adam, Barry D. "Homosexuality without a Gay World: Pasivos y Activos en Nicaragua," *Out/Look* 1: 4 (1989): 74–82.

Alarcón, Norma, "Chicana's Feminist Literature: A Re-vision Through Malintzin/or Malintzin: Putting Flesh Back on the Object," Moraga and Anzaldúa: 182–90.

Alarcón, Norma, Ana Castillo, and Cherríe Moraga (eds), *Third Woman: The Sexuality of Latinas* (Berkeley: Third Woman, 1989).

Alonso, Ana Maria and Maria Teresa Koreck, "Silences: 'Hispanics,' AIDS and Sexual Practices," *differences: A Journal of Feminist Cultural Studies* 1.1 (1989): 101–24.

Anzaldúa, Gloria, *Borderlands/La Frontera: The New Mestiza* (San Francisco: Spinsters, 1987).

Arguelles, Lourdes and B. Ruby Rich, "Homosexuality, Homophobia, and Revolution: Notes Toward an Understanding of the Cuban Lesbian and Gay Male Experience, Part I," *Signs: Journal of Women in Culture and Society* 9 (1984): 683–99.

—— "Homosexuality, Homophobia, and Revolution: Notes Toward an Understanding of the Cuban Lesbian and Gay Male Experience, Part 2," *Signs: Journal of Women in Culture and Society* 11 (1985): 120–36.

Baca-Zinn, Maxine, "Chicano Men and Masculinity," *The Journal of Ethnic Studies* 10.2 (1982): 29–44.

—— "Familism Among Chicanos: A Theoretical Review," *Humboldt Journal of Social Relations* 10.1 (1982–3): 224–38.

Blackwood, Evelyn (ed.), *The Many Faces of Homosexuality: Anthropological Approaches to Homosexual Behavior* (New York: Harrington Park, 1989).

Bruce-Novoa, Juan, "Homosexuality and the Chicano Novel," *Confluencia: Revista Hispanica de Cultura y Literatura* 2.1 (1986): 69–77.

Carrier, Joseph M., "Cultural Factors Affecting Urban Mexican Male Homosexual Behavior," *The Archives of Sexual Behavior: An Interdisciplinary Research Journal* 5.2 (1976): 103–24.

—— "Family Attitudes and Mexican Male Homosexuality," *Urban Life: A Journal of Ethnographic Research* 5.3 (1976): 359–76.

—— "Gay Liberation and Coming Out in Mexico," in Herdt: 225–53.

—— "Mexican Male Bisexuality," *Bisexualities: Theory and Research*, ed. F. Klein and T. Wolf (New York: Haworth, 1985): 75–85.

Carrillo, Hector and Horacio Maiorana, "AIDS Prevention Among Gay Latinos in San Francisco: From Behavior Change to Social Change," unpublished ms, 1989.

Davis, Madeline and Elizabeth Lapovsky Kennedy, "Oral History and the Study of Sexuality in the Lesbian Community: Buffalo, New York, 1940–1960," in Duberman *et al.*: 426–40.

D'Emilio, John, "Capitalism and Gay Identity," in Snitow, Stansell, and Thompson: 100–13.

—— *Sexual Politics, Sexual Communities: The Making of a Homosexual Minority in the United States, 1940–1970* (Chicago: University of Chicago Press, 1983).

D'Emilio, John and Estelle B. Freedman, *Intimate Matters: A History of Sexuality in America* (New York: Harper, 1988).

Duberman, Martin Bauml, Martha Vicinus, and George Chauncey Jr (eds), *Hidden from History: Reclaiming the Gay and Lesbian Past* (New York: NAL, 1989).

Espin, Oliva M. "Cultural and Historical Influences on Sexuality in Hispanic/Latin Women: Implications for Psychotherapy," *Pleasure and Danger: Exploring Female Sexuality*, ed. Carol Vance (London: Routledge, 1984): 149–63.

—— "Issues of Identity in the Psychology of Latina Lesbians," *Lesbian Psychologies*, ed. Boston Lesbian Psychologies Collective (Urban: University of Illinois Press, 1987): 35–55.

Freud, Sigmund, *Three Essays on the Theory of Sexuality* (1905), *The Standard Edition of the Complete Psychological Works of Sigmund Freud*, trans. and ed. James Strachey, Vol. 7 (London: Hogarth, 1953): 123–243.

Gagnon, John H. and William Simon, *Sexual Conduct: The Social Sources of Human Sexuality* (Chicago: Aldine, 1973).

Gilmore, David D. (ed.) *Honor and Shame and the Unity of the Mediterranean*, no. 22 (Washington: American Anthropological Association, 1987).

Goldwert, Marvin "Mexican Machismo: The Flight from Femininity," *Psychoanalytic Review* 72.1 (1985): 161–9.

Gutiérrez, Ramón, "Community, Patriarchy, and Individualism: The Politics of Chicano History and the Dream of Equality," forthcoming in *American Quarterly*.

Herdt, Gilbert (ed.) *Gay and Lesbian Youth* (New York: Haworth, 1989).

Hidalgo, Hilda and Elia Hidalgo-Christensen, "The Puerto Rican Lesbian and the Puerto Rican Community," *Journal of Homosexuality* 2 (1976–77): 109–21.

——— "The Puerto Rican Cultural Response to Female Homosexuality," *The Puerto Rican Woman* ed. Edna Acosta-Belen (New York: Praeger, 1979): 110–23.

Islas, Arturo, *Immigrant Souls* (New York: Morrow, 1990).

——— *The Rain God: A Desert Tale* (Palo Alto: CA: Alexandrian, 1984).

Katz, Jonathan Ned, *Gay/Lesbian Almanac: A New Documentary* (New York: Harper, 1983).

Lancaster, Roger N., "Subject Honor and Object Shame: The Construction of Male Homosexuality and Stigma in Nicaragua," *Ethnology* 27.2 (1987): 111–25.

Martin, Robert K., "Knights-Errant and Gothic Seducers: The Representation of Male Friendship in Mid-Nineteenth Century America," in Duberman *et al.*: 169–82.

Moraga, Cherríe, *Loving in the War Years: Lo que nunca pasó por sus labios* (Boston: South End, 1983).

Moraga, Cherríe and Gloria Anzaldúa (eds), *This Bridge Called My Back: Writings by Radical Women of Color* (Watertown, MA: Persephone, 1981).

Moraga, Cherríe and Amber Hollibaugh, "What We're Rollin Around in Bed With: Sexual Silences in Feminism," in Snitow, Stansell and Thompson: 394–405.

Nestle, Joan, "Butch-Fem Relationships: Sexual Courage in the 1950s," *Heresies* 12 (1981): 21–4.

Newton, Esther, "The Mythic Mannish Lesbian: Radclyffe Hall and the New Woman," in Duberman *et al.*: 281–93.

Parker, Richard, "Youth Identity, and Homosexuality: The Changing Shape of Sexual Life in Contemporary Brazil," in Herdt: 269–89.

Paz, Octavio, *Labyrinth of Solitude: Life and Thought in Mexico* (New York: Grove, 1961).

Pesquera, Beatriz M. "Work and Family: A Comparative Analysis of Professional, Clerical and Blue-Collar Chicana Workers," Ph.D. diss. Univ. of California, Berkeley, 1985.

Plummer, Kenneth, "Symbolic Interaction and Sexual Conduct: An Emergent Perspective," *Human Sexual Relations*, ed. Mike Brake (New York: Pantheon): 1982: 223–44.

Ramos, Juanita (ed.), *Compañeras: Latina Lesbians* (New York: Latina Lesbian History Project, 1987).

Rechy, John, *City of Night* (New York: Grove, 1963).

——— *Numbers* (New York: Grove, 1967).

——— *Rushes* (New York: Grove, 1979).

——— *The Sexual Outlaw* (New York: Grove, 1977).

Rodriguez, Richard, *Hunger of Memory: The Education of Richard Rodriguez, An Autobiography* (Boston: Godine, 1982).

——— "Late Victorians: San Francisco, AIDS, and the Homosexual Stereotype," *Harper's Magazine* (Oct. 1990): 57–66.

——— "Masculinity, Femininity, and Homosexuality: On the Anthropological Interpretation of Sexual Meanings in Brazil," Blackwood: 155–64.

Rupp, Leila J. "Imagine My Surprise: Woman's Relationships in Mid-Twentieth Century America," in Duberman *et al.*: 395–410.

Segura, Denise, "Chicanas and Mexican Immigrant Women in the Labor Market: A Study of Occupational Mobility and Stratification," PhD diss. Univ. of California, Berkeley, 1986.

——— "Chicana and Mexican Immigrant Women at Work: The Impact of Class, Race, and Gender on Occupational Mobility," *Gender & Society* 3.1 (1989): 37–52.

——— "The Interplay of Familism and Patriarchy on Employment Among Chicana and Mexican Women," *Renato Rosaldo Lecture Series 5* (1989): 35–53.

Simon, William and John G. Gagnon, "Sexual Scripts: Permanence and Change," *Archives of Sexual Behavior* 15.2 (1986): 97–120.

Smith-Rosenberg, Carroll, "Discourses of Sexuality and Subjectivity: The New Woman, 1870–1936," in Duberman *et al.*, 264–80.

Snitow, Ann, Christine Stansell, and Sharon Thompson (eds), *Powers of Desire: The Politics of Sexuality* (New York: Monthly Review, 1983).

Taylor, Clark, L., "Mexican Male Homosexual Interaction in Public Contexts," in Blackwood: 117–36.

Trumbach, Randolph, "The Birth of the Queen: Sodomy and the Emergence of Gender Equality in Modern Culture, 1660–1750," in Duberman *et al.*: 129–40.

Zavella, Patricia, *Women's Work and Chicano Families: Cannery Workers of the Santa Clara Valley* (Ithaca: Cornell University Press, 1987).

ARLENE STEIN

"Sisters and Queers: The Decentering of Lesbian Feminism"

from *Socialist Review* 20:1 (January–March 1992): 33–55

Recently, a 44-year-old mother of two boys told me that "in the old days," the 1970s, she could go to a particular place – a café or women's center, for example – to find the lesbian community in her medium-sized town. But by the late 1980s, when she broke up with a long-time lover, she went out searching again for that community and couldn't find it. Another woman I knew expressed fears about the number of lesbian friends she had lost to heterosexual conversions, having become convinced that more and more women were forsaking their lesbianism in exchange for what she saw as the greater public respectability afforded by living with men.

Lesbian feminism emerged out of the most radical sectors of the women's movement in the early 1970s. Young women who "came out through feminism," as the saying went, attempted to broaden the definition of lesbianism, to transform it from a medical condition, or at best, a sexual "preference," into a collective identity which transcended rampant individualism and its excesses as well as compulsory gender and sex roles. It was a movement which spawned the most vibrant and visible lesbian culture that had ever existed in the United States.

But by the mid 1980s, the vision of a Lesbian Nation which would stand apart from the dominant culture, as a sort of haven in a heartless (male/heterosexual) world, began to appear ever more distant. In contrast to the previous decade, lesbian culture and community began to seem placeless. This complaint was common, particularly among women who came of age in the 1970s, when becoming a lesbian meant coming into a community committed to some shared values. Philosopher Janice Raymond sounded the call of alarm in a women's studies journal in 1989:

> We used to talk a lot about lesbianism as a political movement – back in the old days when lesbianism and feminism went together, and one heard the phrase lesbian feminism. Today we hear more about lesbian sadomasochism, lesbians having babies and everything lesbians need to know about sex.[1]

As she and others explained it, the 1980s and 1990s brought a retrenchment from the radical visions of the previous decade. A triumphant conservatism had shattered previously cohesive lesbian communities.

While many of these assertions are unquestionably true, the death-of-community scenario cannot explain the apparent paradox that by 1990, in many urban centers, lesbian influence had become in some respects nowhere and everywhere. Last November, the *San Francisco Examiner* reported on the closing of the last lesbian bar in that city. How strange, the columnist noted, that "more lesbians than ever live in San Francisco but that the last lesbian bar was set to close." Bemoaning the loss of a "home base" for lesbians, the former owner of the bar said: "It's a victim of the lesbian community becoming more diverse. There is an absence of a lesbian community in the presence of a million lesbians."[2]

Reflecting this more decentered sense of community, today's lesbian "movement," if one can call it that, consists of a series of projects, often wildly disparate in approach, many of which incorporate radical and progressive elements. If the corner bar was once the only place in town, by 1990 in cities across the country there were lesbian parenting groups, support groups for women with cancer and other life-threatening diseases, new and often graphic sexual literature for lesbians, organizations for lesbian "career women" and lesbians of color, and mixed organizations where out lesbians played visible roles. What is new, I suggest, is the lack of any fundamental hegemonic logic or center to these projects.[3]

The once clear connection between lesbianism and feminism, in which the former was assumed to grow naturally out of the latter, is not all that clear today. Gone is the ideal of a culturally and ideologically unified Lesbian Nation. A series of challenges, largely from within lesbian communities themselves, have shaken many of the ordering principles of lesbian feminism. In the following, I want to explain this process of decentering. What does it mean? Why did it occur? And what might it tell us about the trajectory of identity-based movements?[4]

IDENTITIES AND MOVEMENTS

All movements engage identities, but in recent years "identity" has become a key term, signifying the sense in which the goal of movements is not only to mobilize identities toward some other end but also to act upon collective identities themselves. In the 1960s and 1970s, in response to the widespread perception of postwar social conformity, "new" social movements politicized many people's concerns with autonomy and subjective identity, arguing for notions of political activity which challenged previously clear-cut distinctions between private and public, personal and political.

Lesbian feminism, and the women's liberation movement in general, drew heavily upon the images and symbols of Black Power, and shared its commitment to authenticity, redefining and affirming the self, and achieving individual recognition via group identification. But when we think of social movements, typically we assume that the formation of such collective identities is relatively unproblematic, that they simply reflect "essential" differences among persons which exist prior to mobilization. We

refer, for example, to a supposedly unified subject such as the women's movement, search for signs of collectivization and unity, and downplay evidence of discontinuities and ruptures.

Instead of assuming that collective identities simply reflect differences among persons that exist prior to mobilization, we need, I think, to look closely at the process by which movements remake identities. For it is through the process of mobilization that a sense of "group-ness" is constructed, and through which individual identities are reshaped.[5] Accordingly, I want to re-read the history of lesbian feminism as a series of identity reconstructions which are partial and strategic.

A social movement organized around sexuality may seem a peculiar site for such an examination, since sexual desires and behavior tend to be viewed as pre-social and unchanging. Over the past two decades, however, a host of scholars have argued against such assumptions, claiming, for example, that homosexuality is socially constructed, "situational, influenced and given meaning and character by its location in time and social space."[6]

Lesbian feminists took this constructionist critique very seriously. Indeed, they literally tried to remake lesbian life in the United States by bringing together disaffected members of the homophile, gay liberation, and feminist movements, as well as unaffiliated women, to form autonomous lesbian organizations that would be part of the larger struggle for social and sexual freedom. Yet in the end, I will argue, the movement failed to see the constructed, indeed fragile, nature of its own collective self-concepts.

SMASHING THE CATEGORIES

To my suggestion that lesbianism is becoming decentered, one could reply that the lesbian-feminist movement, consisting of hundreds of semi-autonomous small-scale efforts nationwide, was never centered. However, while it was never unified, it did have a hegemonic project. It was, firstly, an effort to reconstruct the category "lesbian," to wrest it from the definitions of the medical experts and broaden its meaning. It was, secondly, an attempt to forge a stable collective identity around that category and to develop institutions which would nurture that identity. And thirdly, it sought to use those institutions as a base for the contestation of the dominant sex/gender system.

The medical model of homosexuality, dominant for most of the twentieth century, situated sexual object choice outside of society, declaring it fixed at birth or in early childhood, and deemed it an intractable property of the individual. The "old gay" pre-feminist world, a series of semi-secret subcultures located primarily in urban areas, formed in relation to the hegemonic belief that heterosexuality was natural and homosexuality an aberration. But for 1970s "new lesbians," the pre-feminist world and the conviction that lesbians were failed women was no longer tenable or tolerable. In place of the belief in a lesbian essence or fixed minority identity signified by an inversion of gender, long synonymous with the image of lesbianism in the popular imagination, they substituted the universal possibility of "woman-identified" behavior.[7] As a popular saying went, "feminism is the theory, lesbianism is the practice."

In critic Eve Sedgwick's terms, we see the "re-visioning, in female terms, of same-sex desire"

> as being at the very definitional center of each gender, rather than occupying a cross-gender or luminal position between them. Thus women who loved women were seen as more female ... than those whose desire crossed boundaries of gender. The axis of sexuality, in this view, was not only highly coextensive with the axis of gender but expressive of its most heightened essence.[8]

Through its encounter with feminism, lesbianism straddled what Sedgwick has called "minoritizing" and "universalizing" strategies, between fixing lesbians as a stable minority group and seeking to liberate the "lesbian" in every woman. Feminism provided the ideological glue which wedded these two sometimes contradictory impulses.

The movement could not have emerged without the second-wave feminist insight that gender roles are socially constructed, or without the gay liberationist application of that insight to sexuality. If the "exchange of women" – compulsory heterosexuality – was the bedrock of the sex/gender system, as Gayle Rubin and others argued, then women who made lives with other women were subverting the dominant order.[9] Jill Johnston and others declared that a "conspiracy of silence" insured that for most women "identity was presumed to be heterosexual unless proven otherwise ... There was no lesbian identity. There was lesbian activity." Expressing the feelings of many middle-class women of her generation, Johnston wrote in 1973:

> For most of us the chasm between social validation and private needs was so wide and deep that the society overwhelmed us for any number of significant individual reasons ... We were all heterosexually identified and that's the way we thought of ourselves, even of course when doing otherwise.[10]

If homophobia on the part of heterosexual feminists and in society at large deterred many women from claiming a lesbian identity, collapsing the distinction between identification and desire minimized stigma and broadened the definition of lesbianism, transforming it into "female bonding," a more inclusive category, with which a larger number of middle-class women could identify. Indeed, there was historical precedent for this vision in the "passionate friendships" common among women of the eighteenth and nineteenth centuries.[11]

Lesbianism represented a sense of connectedness based on mutuality and similarity rather than difference. Ultimately, it was more than simply a matter of sex, poet Judy Grahn declared: "Men who are obsessed with sex are convinced that lesbians are obsessed with sex. Actually, like other women, lesbians are obsessed with love and fidelity."[12] The new, broadened definition of lesbianism resonated with many women who had long experienced their sexuality in relational rather than simply erotic terms, and who considered sexuality a relatively non-salient aspect of identity and an insufficient basis upon which to organize a mass movement.

Centering lesbianism upon female relationality and identification, these "new lesbians" challenged medicalized conceptions that focused upon gender-inversion and masculinized sexual desire. They blurred the boundary between gay and straight women and transformed lesbianism into a normative identity which over time came to have as much – and sometimes more – to do with lifestyle preferences (such as choice of dress or leisure pursuits) and ideological proclivities (anti-consumerist, countercultural identifications) as with sexual desires or practices.

This shift in meaning enabled many women who have never considered the possibility of claiming a lesbian lifestyle to leave their husbands and boyfriends – some for political reasons, others in expression of deeply rooted desires, many for both. It allowed many of those who lived primarily closeted lives to come out and declare their lesbianism openly. Never before had so much social space opened up so quickly to middle-class women who dared to defy deeply held social norms about their proper sexual place. As a result, the group of women who called themselves lesbians became increasingly heterogeneous, at least in terms of sexuality.

REMAKING THE SELF

Historically, there have always been women who have had sexual/romantic relationships with other women but have not assumed the label "lesbian." There have also been women whose actual sexual desires and practices don't fit the common social definition of lesbian – women, for example, who identify as lesbian but who are bisexual in orientation and/or practice. There are many possible configurations of the relationship between desire, practice and identity – many more such configurations than there are social categories to describe them.

Yet popular understandings of lesbianism assume a clear-cut relationship between sexual orientation/behavior and sexual identity. Lesbians are assumed to be women who are attracted exclusively to other women, and who claim an identity on the basis of that attraction. But for many women, the relation between sexual orientation, sexual identity, and sexual practice is far from stable or uncomplicated.

Moreover, as I have suggested, such definitions change over time. Particularly before the advent of the lesbian-feminist movement, these definitions were situated primarily within the framework of medical expertise, which fixed lesbianism as a "condition" and made it synonymous with cross-gender, or mannish, attributes. It meant that a woman who took on a lesbian identity needed to overcome extreme social disapproval and formulate a favorable sense of herself which included a "deviant" sexuality.[13] Those who took on this identity during the pre-Stonewall era were more apt to be women who never developed stable identities as heterosexuals.

Often these women either had never had significant sexual and emotional relationships with men, or they related to men only in an effort to hide or deny their lesbianism. One such woman described her coming out in the following terms:

> I fell in love with a woman when I was about fifteen or sixteen. I don't know whether I used the term lesbian then, I knew that I loved women, and that was where I was and where I wanted to be. I didn't fall in love with men."[14]

In sociologist Barbara Ponse's terminology, she would be considered a "primary" lesbian – someone who identified homosexual feelings in herself before she understood their social significance, who did so at a relatively early age, and who experienced homosexuality less as a choice than as a compulsion. If the "old gay" world was comprised largely of women for whom lesbianism was "primary," lesbian feminists claimed that the pool of potential lesbians was much larger. Young lesbians in the early 1970s universalized the critique of compulsory heterosexuality and emphasized the possibility of coming out or "electing" lesbianism, proclaiming that it was the "feminist solution." Not only was the institution of heterosexuality constructed, activists argued, but so too were heterosexual desires. Because they were constructed, they reasoned, such desires could just as easily be reconstructed.

This 52-year-old woman had been married

for twenty-two years. Interviewed in the early-1970s, she described her coming out as follows:

> I began ... to become involved with women's consciousness-raising groups, and I began to hear ... of the idea of women being turned on to each other. It was the first time I heard about it in terms of people that I knew ... I was receptive but had no previous, immediate history. Like there was a part of me that had been thinking about it, and thinking, "Gee, that sounds like intellectually that's a good idea."[15]

The movement thus brought into the fold many "elective" lesbians like this woman, for whom relationships with men were often significant; some were married, some had long-term relationships with men with whom they felt they were in love and to whom they were sexually attracted. Nevertheless, they "discovered" women as sexual and emotional partners at some point, and came to identify as lesbians. Writing of this period several years later, a long-time activist recalled:

> Those of us who were active in 1971 and 72 witnessed the tremendous influx of formerly heterosexual women into the Lesbian Movement. They came by the thousands. Lesbians of this background now compose the very backbone of the Lesbian Movement ... We put the world of men on notice that we were out to give their wives and lovers a CHOICE. We got a bad reputation as "chauvinistic." Lesbian feminism was called an "expansionist philosophy" – meaning that we were out to politically seduce (read: awaken) all women. In the years that have followed, it seems ironic to this old-gay-never-married dyke, that some of the most ardent, anti-straight women ... were 1971's HOUSEWIVES![16]

The distinction Ponse and others have drawn between "primary" and "elective" lesbians – who differ as to their accounts of the origins of their lesbianism, the meaning of lesbian activity and lesbian feelings, and their age of entry into the lesbian community – thus suggests very different paths through which women have arrived at lesbian identity. Drawing upon object-relations psychoanalytic theory, Beverly Burch argues that the "early" or primary lesbian incorporates a greater sense of "differentness" within her sense of self than the "later-developing" or elective lesbian.

"Primary" lesbians generally have to struggle to establish a positive sense of themselves as lesbians during adolescence, when other issues of social identity are being negotiated. Women who come out later in life, on the other hand, may have already negotiated other issues of social identity before they assume a "deviant" sexual identity. They may have established a sense of self as relatively "normal," at least in terms of their sexuality. Taking on a lesbian identity at this stage, says Burch, means coping with somewhat different issues. "It may involve a sense of loss in terms of acceptability and social ease, but losing something one has had is an experience quite different from never having had it."[17]

Moreover, as I have suggested, historical evidence shows these sexual choices to be shaped by class position. Women who joined public lesbian subcultures before Stonewall were more likely to be of working-class origin, due at least in part to the fact that they tended to be less concerned with losing social status. Women encouraged to "elect" lesbianism through exposure to feminism, by contrast, were more likely to come from the middle classes. With time, these and other preexisting, largely unspoken, differences in identity would pose thorny problems for the process of collectivization. Smashing the categories, it turned out, was a much simpler task than remaking the self.

BORDER SKIRMISHES

Twelve hundred women attended the first West Coast Lesbian-Feminist Conference, held in Los Angeles in June 1973. The goal of the conference was to unify lesbian feminists under a common program, but almost immediately the gathering was wracked by internal disagreements over the definition of lesbianism and, by extension, debates over who would be admitted. A male-to-female transsexual guitarist was shouted down by the crowd and prevented from performing. A prominent feminist writer and theorist was criticized for living with a man. Shortly after the conference, one woman's comment was telling: "If there was any point of unity it was that almost all lesbians are conscious of and hopeful for the development and existence of a lesbian-feminist culture movement.[18] But a unified culture and movement implied a consensus on the meaning of lesbianism which did not exist.

During the early 1970s, such debates about who was a lesbian became commonplace throughout the country – at conferences, at women's music festivals, and within local communities. Border skirmishes around transsexualism, lesbians with boy children, bisexuality, and other issues deeply divided many lesbian events and communities. Symptomatic of the difficulty of defining the category "lesbian," they marked a growing preoccupation with fixing boundaries, making membership more exclusive, and hardening the notion of lesbian "difference."

The movement had earlier tried to broaden the base of lesbianism by loosening the boundaries around the group. But smashing some categories entailed the creation of others; identity politics requires defining an identity around which to mobilize. Boundary-setting became a preoccupation of the movement once it was faced with the challenge of insuring commitment and guarding against disaffection from the ranks, particularly in view of the pre-existing differences among women which I earlier identified.

If early lesbian feminism emphasized the fluidity of identity categories and the importance of self-description, with time the definition narrowed: Lesbians were biological women who do not sleep with men and who embrace the lesbian label. If they shared certain values in common, foremost among them was their willingness to make lives apart from men. The growing symbolic importance of the notion of a "women's community" in the mid to late 1970s signified the importance of boundary definition.[19] It centered the movement upon a rejection of men and patriarchal society. It claimed that gender is the primary basis of lesbian identity (and that all other divisions are male-imposed), and argued that power was something imposed from without, by men. If power and hierarchy issues surfaced, members of the "women's community" saw this as the residue of patriarchy and male-identification, something that would fade away with time. If women

within the community developed heterosexual desires, lesbians in the mid to late 1970s tended to see this as a sign that patriarchy had been insufficiently purged.

While the language of the movement was radically constructionist, at least in terms of sexuality, in practice it privileged the "primary" lesbian for whom desire, exclusively lesbian, was congruent with identity. Studying the lesbian community in a medium-sized Southern city in the 1970s, Barbara Ponse described the "biographic norm" of lesbian communities as the "gay trajectory," popularly known as "coming out." Lesbians assumed that this process was unidirectional. In the highly politicized milieu of lesbian communities, one did not come out and then "go back in" without suffering the consequences of such a move. Ponse concluded that the fluidity and changeability of both identity and activity at the level of the individual "may elude classification within the frameworks of the paradigms of the lesbian world, which, like the dominant culture, assume a heterosexual–homosexual dichotomy.[20]

The movement also privileged white, middle-class women, for whom lesbianism represented both a sexual choice and an oppositional identity. But for many women of color, as well as white working-class women, the choices were never so clear and unambivalent. Women of color, in particular, often felt that they were forced to pick and choose among identities. Audre Lorde wrote in 1979: "As a Black lesbian feminist comfortable with the many different ingredients of my identity ... I find I am constantly being encouraged to pluck out some one aspect of myself and present this as the meaningful whole, eclipsing or denying the other parts of self."[21] Many resisted pressures to make lesbianism their "dominant" or "master" identity.

What was problematic, I believe, was not so much that boundary-making took place – for it does in all identity-based movements – but that the discourse of the movement, rooted in notions of authenticity and inclusion, ran so completely counter to it. Lesbian feminism positioned itself as the expression of the aspirations of *all* women. Like other identity-based movements, it promised the realization of individual as well as collective identity, and saw the two as intimately linked. At its best, it provided women with the strength and support to proclaim their desires for one another. It allowed many to withdraw from difficult and often abusive situations and opened up social space never before possible in this country. But at its worst, it hardened the boundaries around lesbian communities, subsumed differences of race, class, and even sexual orientation, and set up rather rigid standards for living one's life.

DILEMMAS OF IDENTITY

All identity-based movements have a tendency to fall into what Alberto Melucci has termed "integralism," the yearning for a totalizing identity, for a "master key which unlocks every door of reality." Integralism, says Melucci, rejects a pluralist and "disenchanted" attitude to life and encourages people to "turn their backs on complexity" and become incapable of recognizing difference.[22] Indeed, the contemporary sociological and historical literature on lesbian-feminist communities of the 1970s is rife with such observations.[23] Sociologist Susan Krieger looked at "the dilemmas of identity" posed by a women's community in the Midwest in the mid 1970s. She found that individuals frequently experienced a loss of self, in which they felt either overwhelmed or abandoned by the community. While noting that "all social groups confront their members with this kind of conflict," Krieger admitted that "in some groups" – namely those in which "the desire for personal affirmation from the group is great, and the complementary desire for assertion of individuality is also strong" – this experience is felt more intensely than in other groups and seems to occur more frequently.[24] Lesbian communities were often characterized by likeness, intimacy, and shared ideological orientation; they were comprised of women who were highly stigmatized. Krieger surmised that all these things contributed to the seeming difficulties their members had with maintaining their individuality amid pressures to merge and to become one with the community. Often this dynamic caused individuals to become more preoccupied with bolstering their own identities than with achieving political goals and led to internal struggles over who really belonged in the community.

While Krieger focused on gender as the primary locus of "likeness" within lesbian-feminist communities, one could also add race, class, and personal style to the mix. In many parts of the country, despite their efforts to free themselves from imposed social roles, subcultures often created new ones, prescribing sexual styles, political ideologies, and even standards of personal appearance which relatively few could successfully meet. This had the effect of excluding many women, particularly working-class women of all races, but also women who for any number of reasons may not have felt at home in the movement's countercultural milieu.

Particularly after the mid 1970s, many lesbian-feminist communities, scattered throughout the nation, became increasing private enclaves. If earlier the movement tried to "smash the categories," substituting for the narrow, overly sexualized definitions of lesbianism a broad, normative definition which welcomed all women into the fold, over time these definitions themselves narrowed and became increasingly prescriptive. It is ironic, perhaps, that the very qualities that were once seen as a boon to the lesbian-feminist movement were coming to be viewed as seeds of its demise. Communities of intimacy, it turned out, were also communities of exclusion.

Individuals troubled by the inability of lesbian feminism to resolve the tension between identity and difference were faced with two basic options: They could reject identity as a basis for politics and strike out on their own, asserting their individual autonomy and personal difference. Or they could reshape identity politics and form new attachments which acknowledged "multiple" allegiances and the partial nature of lesbian identity. Indeed, as I will argue, both trends characterize the current phase of lesbian identity politics.

In the early 1980s, a series of structural and ideological shifts conspired to decenter the lesbian-feminist model of identity. First, the predominantly white and middle-class women who comprised the base of the movement aged, underwent various life-cycle changes, and settled into careers and families of various stripes – often even heterosexual ones. Second, a growing revolt emerged from within: Women of color, working-class women, and sexual minorities, three separate but overlapping groups, asserted their claims on lesbian identity politics. The next section focuses on these shifts, particularly on how sexual difference posed a challenge to lesbian-feminist constructions of identity.

SEX, RACE AND THE DECLINE OF THE MALE THREAT?

From the mid 1970s to the early 1980s, the most visible political campaigns undertaken by the feminist movement were against pornography and sexual violence against women. For many women, straight and gay, pornography symbolized male sexuality and power and the fear that stalked women through the ordinary routines of daily life, representing all that was anathema to the vision of a female sexuality that emphasized relationality and reciprocity rather than power and coercion.

But new voices emerged, charging that the radical feminist vision glossed over the real, persistent differences among women and that it idealized women's sexuality and their relationships with one another. These women argued that all the attention upon sexual danger had minimized the possibility of women's pleasure. Highly polarized battles raged in the pages of feminist publications, as "sex radicals" branded their anti-porn, anti-s/m opponents as "good girls," and came to a head in the unlikely setting of a conference at Barnard College in 1982, when anti-s/m activists picketed a speak-out on "politically incorrect sex."[25]

These political clashes, which have come to be called the "sex debates" or "porn wars," rarely addressed the subject of lesbianism explicitly. But insofar as these debates called into question the normative basis of the lesbian-feminist model of identity, lesbianism was the salient subtext. Lesbian "sex radicals" charged that somewhere in the midst of defining sexuality as male, and lesbianism as a blow against the

patriarchy, desire seemed to drop out of the picture. As the editor of *On Our Backs* magazine, a popularizer of the emergent "pro-sex" lesbian sensibility, brashly claimed:

> The traditional notion of femininity as gentle and nurturing creates the stereotype that lesbianism is just a hand-holding society. "Lesbians don't have sex," the story goes. Or if they do, it is this really tiresome affair – five minutes of cunnilingus on each side, with a little timer nearby, and lots of talking about your feelings and career.[26]

As "pro-sex" lesbians saw it, in all the talk about "woman-identification," the specificity of lesbian existence as a sexual identity seemed to get lost. In response, some tried to reengage with the tradition of pre-Stonewall lesbianism, which they saw as unencumbered by feminist ideological prescriptions and rooted in working-class bar culture and butch–femme roles.[27] A burgeoning sexual literature reasserted the centrality of desire and sexuality in lesbian identity and culture. Rather than making the distinction between male and female sexualities the primary political cleavage (as radical feminists had done), it acknowledged the sexual diversity implicit within the lesbian category and often invoked, symbolically at least, the sexual license of an earlier moment in gay male culture.

For many women, the onset of the AIDS crisis, which occurred nearly simultaneously, made coalition-building with gay men an even more immediate task. Centering post-Stonewall lesbian identity upon the shared rejection of men and patriarchy, lesbians had earlier disengaged from a gay liberation movement that was largely blind to their needs. But the tide of homophobia unleashed by the AIDS crisis affected lesbians as well as gay men and served at times to sharpen the differences between lesbians and heterosexual women. As the withered body of the person with AIDS replaced the once-pervasive image of the all-powerful male oppressor, the sense of male threat which underlay lesbian-feminist politics diminished further.

Lesbians in many urban centers joined the ranks of such predominantly gay male organizations such as ACT UP and Queer Nation, which engaged in public actions across the nation to increase lesbian/gay visibility and puncture the "heterosexual assumption." Others attempted to construct sexualized subcultures which took their cue from an earlier era of gay male sexual experimentation. There were more co-ed gay bars, social events, and institutions. The new identifications between lesbians and gay men extended to personal style as well: clothing, music, and other forms of consumption.

By the late 1980s, even if relatively few women were directly touched by these developments, their effects could be felt in many lesbian communities. The break was largely, though not entirely, generational. An emergent lesbian politics acknowledged the relative autonomy of gender and sexuality, sexism and heterosexism.[28] It suggested that lesbians shared with gay men a sense of "queerness," a non-normative sexuality which transcends the binary distinction homosexual/heterosexual to include all who feel disenfranchised by dominant sexual norms – lesbians and gay men, as well as bisexuals and transsexuals.[29]

As a partial replacement for "lesbian and gay," the term "queer" attempted to separate questions of sexuality from those of gender.[30] But in terms of practice, this separation was incomplete. The new coexistence of gay men and women was often uneasy: ACT UP and Queer Nation chapters in many cities were marred by gender (and racial) conflicts. The new "co-sexual" queer culture could not compensate for real, persistent structural differences in style, ideology, and access to resources among men and women. This recurring problem suggested that while the new queer politics represented the assertion of a sexual difference which could not be assimilated into feminism, neither could gender be completely subsumed under sexuality. Despite their apparent commonalities, lesbians and gay men were often divided along much the same lines as heterosexual women and men.[31]

A less noisy but no less significant challenge to lesbian feminism came through the assertion of racial and ethnic identifications. At conferences and national meetings, women of color argued for the importance of acknowledging the divisions of race and class, which had long been subsumed in the interest of building a unified culture and movement. A series of influential anthologies challenged the feminist belief in the primacy of the sex/gender system, and led to the development of autonomous black, Asian, and Latina lesbian-feminist organizations.[32]

If lesbian feminism often presented itself as a totalizing identity which would subsume differences of race, class, and ethnicity and pose a united front against patriarchal society, these challenges pointed toward an understanding of lesbianism as situated in a web of multiple oppressions and identities. Lesbians of color and lesbian sex radicals questioned the belief that lesbian life could ever stand completely outside of or apart from the structures of the patriarchal culture. They problematized the once uncontested relationship between lesbianism and feminism. And they shifted lesbian politics away from its almost exclusive focus upon the "male threat," toward a more diffuse notion of power and resistance, acknowledging that lesbians necessarily operate in a society marked by inequalities of class and race as well as of gender and sexuality.

SEVENTIES QUESTIONS FOR NINETIES WOMEN

Some might interpret the scenario I have painted, of the increasing spatial and ideological fragmentation of lesbian communities and the currently contested nature of the relationship between feminism and lesbianism, as indicative of a "post-feminist" era. Certainly, the series of cultural shifts I have described break with an earlier moment of lesbian-feminist politics. They result in large part from the difficulties lesbians have faced in mobilizing around a sense of group difference, even as these cultural shifts are made possible by the construction of that very sense of difference.

I have argued that the lesbian-feminist movement found itself torn between two projects: between fixing lesbians as a stable minority group, and seeking to liberate the "lesbian" in every woman. As I suggested earlier, feminism provided the ideological glue which wedded these two sometimes contradictory impulses. It redefined lesbianism in more expansive, universal terms, constructing a lesbian culture founded upon resistance to gender and sexual norms. While it opened up the possibility of lesbian identification to greater numbers of women than ever before, it could ultimately only achieve unity through exclusion, through a gender separatism which hardened the boundaries around it.

Younger women today are trying to carve out lesbian identities at a moment when many of the apparent certainties of the past have eroded – the meaning of lesbianism, the relationship between lesbianism and feminism, and the political potential of identity politics. They recognize that while marginalized groups construct symbolic fictions of their experience as a means of self-validation, and that compulsory heterosexuality necessitates the construction of a lesbian/gay identity, identities are always simultaneously enabling *and* constraining. As one 23-year-old New Yorker recently told me:

> What I am is in many ways contradictory. I don't belong in the straight world, though I'm a white girl ... But I don't really belong in the feminist world because I read lesbian porn and refuse to go by a party line. On the other hand, I think I'm a feminist. It's a set of contradictions.[33]

Even as they integrate feminism into their daily lives, she and others reject the view that lesbianism is *the* feminist act, that any sexual identity is more authentic or unmediated than any other. In this sense, they are in fact "post-feminist," if that term is descriptive of the consciousness of women and men who, while holding their distance from feminist identities or politics, have been profoundly influenced by them. They simultaneously locate themselves inside and outside the dominant culture, and feel a loyalty to a multiplicity of different projects, some of them feminist-oriented, others more queer-identified, many of them incorporating elements of both critiques. And they see themselves, and their lesbianism, as located in a complex world marked by racial, class, and sexual divisions.

Indeed, this indeterminacy is deeply troubling to many women, particularly those who once held out the hope of constructing a lesbian-feminist movement that was culturally and ideologically unified. But I want to suggest that today's more "decentered" movement may present new democratic potential. Many women who felt excluded by an earlier model of identity now feel that they can finally participate in politics on their own terms. As clashes over feminist issues such as abortion, sexual harassment, and pay equity heat up over the coming years, as they are likely to do, lesbians will be on the front lines, as they have always been – only this time they will be out as lesbians. Others will continue to participate in movements which are not necessarily feminist at all, but with greater visibility than ever before.

This suggests that any unified conception of lesbian identity is reductive and ahistorical; collective identity is a production, a process. Stuart Hall's comments on ethnic resistance are relevant here.[34] In any politicization of marginal groups, he says, there are two phases. The first comprises a rediscovery of roots, and implies a preoccupation with identity. Only when this "local" identity is in place can a consideration of more global questions and connections begin. For many lesbians in this country, the first phase of this movement has already occurred. We may now be seeing the arrival of the second.

NOTES

1 Janice Raymond, "Putting the Politics Back into Lesbianism," *Women's Studies International Forum* 12: 2 (1989).
2 *San Francisco Examiner*, November 12, 1991: 3.
3 Howard Winant makes a similar argument about the politics of race in "Postmodern Racial Politics: Difference and Inequality," *Socialist Review* 20: 1 (January–March 1990).
4 These ideas are based on archival research and interviews conducted primarily in the San Francisco Bay Area. Parts of the analysis may not hold true for other parts of the country, particularly non-urban areas, where the pace of a change may be slower.
5 Pierre Bourdieu, "What Makes a Social Class? On the Theoretical and Practical Existence of Groups," *Berkeley Journal of Sociology* XXXII (1987): 13. Also see Scott Lash, *Sociology of Postmodernism* (New York: Routledge, 1990), Sandra Harding's discussion of epistemologies as "justificatory strategies" in "Feminism, Science and the Anti-Enlightenment Critiques," *Feminism/Postmodernism*, ed. Linda Nicholson

(New York: Routledge, 1990): 87.

6 Jonathan Katz, *Gay American History* (New York: Harper and Row, 1976): 7. See also Jeffrey Weeks, "The Development of Sexual Theory and Sexual Politics," in *Human Sexual Relations*, ed. Mike Brake (New York: Pantheon, 1982).

7 Radicalesbians, "The Woman-Identified Woman," reprinted in *For Lesbians Only*, eds, Sarah Hoagland and Julia Penelope (London: Onlywoman Press, 1988); Adrienne Rich, "Compulsory Heterosexuality and Lesbian Existence," *Signs* (summer 1980).

8 Eve Sedgwick, *Epistemology of the Closet* (Berkeley: University of California Press, 1990): 36.

9 Gayle Rubin, "The Traffic in Women," in *Toward an Anthropology of Women*, ed. Rayna Reiter (New York: Monthly Review, 1975).

10 Jill Johnston, *Lesbian Nation: The Feminist Solution* (New York: Simon & Schuster, 1973): 58.

11 See Carole Smith-Rosenberg, *Disorderly Conduct* (New York: Knopf, 1985); "The Female World of Love and Ritual," in *Heritage of Her Own*, eds Nancy F. Cott and Elizabeth Pleck (New York: Simon and Schuster, 1979).

12 Judy Grahn, "Lesbians as Bogeywoman," *Women: A Journal of Liberation* 1:4 (summer 1970): 36.

13 Vivienne C. Cass, "Homosexual Identity Formation: A Theoretical Model," *Journal of Homosexuality* 4:3 (1979).

14 Barbara Ponse, *Identities in the Lesbian World: The Social Construction of Self* (Westport: Greenwood, 1978): 160.

15 *Ibid*: p. 162.

16 *Lesbian Tide* (May–June 1978): 19.

17 Beverly Burch, "Unconscious Bonding in Lesbian Relationships: The Road Not Taken," unpublished dissertation, Institute for Clinical Social Work, Berkeley, CA, 1989: 91.

18 Jeane Cordova, *Lesbian Tide* (May–June 1973).

19 Alice Echols, *Daring to be Bad: Radical Feminism in America 1967–75* (Minneapolis: University of Minnesota Press, 1989); Bonnie Zimmerman, *The Safe Sea of Woman: Lesbian Fiction 1969–1989* (Boston: Beacon Press, 1990).

20 Ponse, *Identities in the Lesbian World*: 139.

21 Audre Lorde, "Age, Race, Class and Sex: Women Redefining Difference," in *Sister Outsider* (Trumansburg: Crossing Press, 1984).

22 Alberto Melucci, *Nomads of the Present: Social Movements and Individual Needs in Contemporary Society* (London: Century Hutchinson, 1989): 209.

23 Iris Young, "The Ideal of Community and the Politics of Difference," in *Feminism/Postmodernism* ed. Linda J. Nicholson (New York: Routledge, 1990); Shane Phelan, *Identity Politics: Lesbian Feminism and the Limits of Community* (Philadelphia: Temple University Press, 1989); Cheryl Cole, "Ethnographic Sub/versions," unpublished dissertation, University of Iowa, 1991.

24 Susan Krieger, *The Mirror Dance: Identity in a Woman's Community* (Philadelphia: Temple University Press, 1983): xv.

25 Carole Vance (ed.), *Pleasure and Danger: Exploring Women's Sexuality* (Boston: Routledge, 1984); B. Ruby Rich, "Feminism and Sexuality in the 1980s," *Feminist Studies* 12:3 (fall 1986).

26 From an interview with Susie Bright (October, 1989).

27 Joan Nestle, "Butch–Fem Relationships," *Heresies* 12 (summer 1981).

28 Julia Creet, "Lesbian Sex/Gay Sex: What's the Difference," *Out/Look: National Lesbian and Gay Quarterly* 11 (winter 1991); Gayle Rubin, "Thinking Sex: Notes for a Radical Theory of the Politics of Sexuality," in Vance, *Pleasure and Danger*.

29 The autonomous bisexual movement suggested a politics along much the same lines, but tended to privilege self-identified bisexuals. See, for example, *Bi Any Other Name: Bisexual People Speak Out* eds Loraine Hutchins and Lani Kaalminanu (Boston: Alyson, 1990).

30 Michael Warner, "Fear of a Queer Planet," *Social Text* 29 (1991); Allan Bérubé and Jeffrey Escoffier, "Queer/Nation," *Out/Look: National Lesbian and Gay Quarterly* 11 (Winter 1991).

31 Dan Levy, "Queer Nation in S.F. Suspends Activities," *San Francisco Chronicle*, (27 December 1991); Michele DeRanleau, "How the Conscience of an Epidemic Unraveled," *San Francisco Examiner* (October 1, 1990).

32 These included *This Bridge Called My Back Writings by Radical Women of Color*, eds Cherrie Moraga and Gloria Anzaldua (Watertown, MA: Persephone Press, 1981); *All the Women are White, All the Blacks are Men, But Some of Us Are Brave*, eds Gloria Hull, Patricia Bell Scott and Barbara Smith (New York: Feminist Press, 1982); *Home Girls: A Black Feminist Anthology*, ed. Barbara Smith (New York: Kitchen Table/Women of Color Press, 1983).

33 From an interview with the author in 1989.

34 Stuart Hall, "Cultural Identity and Cinematic Representation," *Framework* 36 (1989).

LISA DUGGAN

"Queering the State"

from *Social Text* 39 (summer 1994): 1–14

The time has come to think about queering the state.[1]

The year 1994 has set a record for anti-gay initiatives in the United States. At latest count, there are between eighteen and twenty-seven ballot battles gearing up, surpassing the previous record of sixteen in 1993. This rising tide of hate is partly a backlash against an increasing number of gay rights initiatives. Last year sixteen state legislatures took up measures to grant civil rights protection to gay men and lesbians or to repeal anti-sodomy laws (most of these proposals failed). But anti-gay initiatives are also part of a grander scheme to organize a right-wing voting block to take on issues such as abortion rights, school curriculums, and tax policies. This fight will be a daunting challenge to the organized lesbian and gay rights movement: the combined budgets of the six largest gay organizations total only about $12 million, compared to them more than $210 million in the combined budgets of the six largest right-wing religious organizations.[2]

The financial clout and cultural reach of these organizations should not be underestimated. For instance, Focus on the Family, based in Colorado Springs and founded by Dr. James Dobson, formerly a member of the Meese Commission on Pornography, boasts a $90 million annual budget and affiliated Family Councils in thirty states. It distributes the anti-gay video *The Gay Agenda*, publishes nine magazines and supports sixteen hundred radio programs. The Christian Coalition of Chesapeake, Virginia, distributed forty million voter guides in the 1992 elections in its campaign to take over state and local Republican parties. It supports the Christian Broad-casting Network, the Family Channel, and the 700 Club, which reach millions of viewers daily, as well as two newsletters, *Religious Rights Watch* and *Christian American*. The Coalition's leader, Pat Robertson, situates their agenda squarely in the middle of party politics: "We want ... to see a majority of the Republican Party in the hands of pro-family Christians by 1996." Finally, Citizens for Excellence in Education, an arm of the National Association of Christian Educators led by Robert Simonds and located in Costa Mesa, California, distributes the manual, "How to Elect Christians to Public Office," and claims that thirty-five hundred Christians have been elected to school boards through its efforts.

It is clear that the strategies of the religious right go well beyond the simple articulation of homophobic, racist, and anti-feminist sentiments. Their targets are precise and their program well formulated, as is indicated in a statement from a fund-raising letter written by Simonds:

> There are 15,700 school districts in America. When we get an active Christian parent's committee in operation in all districts, we can take complete control ... This would allow us to determine all local policy: select good textbooks, good curriculum programs, superintendents, and principals.[3]

But the challenge is not only organizational and financial. The right-wing anti-gay zealots have mobilized new strategies and new rhetorics that challenge the customary practices, arguments, and slogans of liberal gay rights organizations. Successful opposition to the onslaught on the local, state, and national levels will require more than gearing up another round of the same kind of struggle. The opposition has changed its colors, and so must we.

The crisis specifically challenges those of us who teach and write about queer issues. We have already been faced with the rhetoric of crisis in higher education, mobilized by conservatives – a rhetoric that targets teaching and scholarship in the areas of class, race, gender, and sexuality as "politically correct" and as an effort to split, fragment, and destroy the idea of a common culture transmitted through education. In right-wing attacks on the state of higher education, lesbian and gay teachers and writers are often singled out as scholars of the particularly frivolous and absurd, though we are also often represented as uniquely powerful, able to overwhelm and destroy the very conception of a common culture.

These attacks are now paralleled by similar ones launched in the arena of national politics. Lesbian and gay efforts to secure civil rights protections have quickly become central in public debates of various kinds since the election of Bill Clinton. In conservative attacks on the new administrations, queers are represented as ridiculous, with trivial political concerns, but also as a frightfully controlling presence in national politics. Shrill cries of the dominance of the gay lobby have been mobilized with lightning speed, especially in response to the debates surrounding the military. Local and state initiatives to roll back or prevent anti-discrimination measures pick up and elaborate these themes, as they also try out new strategies and rhetorics.

Even in friendly internal critiques of the state of progressive politics – critiques in which the problem of fragmentation is addressed – gay and lesbian politics are sometimes invoked to represent the narrowing of focus (what could be narrower?) and the neglect of the common interest. In a field of progressive alliances often pejoratively described as a conglomeration of "special interest groups," lesbian and gay organizations seem to represent the most "special" interests of all. In this way we appear, on both the right and the left, as signifiers of the "crisis" of liberal politics itself.[4]

The problem for those of us engaged in queer scholarship and teaching, who have a stake in queer politics, is how to respond to these attacks at a moment when we have unprecedented opportunities (we are present in university curriculums and national politics as never before), yet confront perilous and paralyzing assaults. It is imperative that we respond to these attacks in the public arena from which they are launched. We cannot defend our teaching and scholarship without engaging in public debate and addressing the nature and operations of the state upon which our jobs and futures depend. In other words, the need to turn our attention to state politics is not only theoretical (though it is also that). It is time for queer intellectuals to concentrate on the creative production of strategies at the boundary of queer and nation – strategies specifically for queering the state.[5]

In formulating the terms of address in this situation, we are also now faced with the problem of a gap between the languages of our classrooms and scholarship, and the languages of public debate on the subject of homosexuality.

To illustrate what I mean by a language gap, I will re-create a dialogue between literary critic and founding mother of queer studies, Eve Kosofsky Sedgwick, and a young fact-checker for *Rolling Stone* magazine. Stacey D'Erasmo, friend and editor at the *Voice Literary Supplement*, wrote an article on gay and lesbian studies for *Rolling Stone* in which she initially referred to Sedgwick as "straight" – a mistake she later regretted.[6] When someone's sexual identity is referred to in print, most periodicals will verify it; the article was sent to a fact-checker with no particular expertise in the subject area. The fact-checker called Sedgwick. Imagine now a split screen, with Sedgwick on one side in her office at Duke University, and on the other side, the young fact-checker, chewing gum. The dialogue – which I have re-created in the manner of a docudrama from Stacey's second-hand account – is as follows:

FACT-CHECKER: Professor Sedgwick, the article says here that you're straight – are ya straight?
SEDGWICK: Did Stacey say I'm straight? I didn't tell her that.
FACT-CHECKER: Well, it says here you're straight. Is that true?

SEDGWICK: Well, under some discursive regimes I might be considered queer.
FACT-CHECKER: Right. So you're not straight. Then you're gay?
SEDGWICK: I didn't tell Stacey I was gay.
FACT-CHECKER: Right ... But you just said you were queer ... Isn't that the same as gay?
SEDGWICK: Well, as I began to explain, under some discursive regimes ...
FACT-CHECKER: Look, Professor Sedgwick, you're married, aren't ya? So you're straight.
SEDGWICK: I never told Stacey I was married.

I tell this story not to make fun of Sedgwick, who was attempting to interrupt and resist the imperative to sexual categorization, *nor* to condescend to the fact-checker, whose frustration followed from her attempts to decipher what Sedgwick was saying, but to illustrate the difficulty of communication across the gap between the predominantly constructionist language of queer studies and the essentialist presumptions of public discourse. One might easily imagine other examples. A Nightline panel of queer theorists could be assembled to discuss the new military policy: Judith Butler, D. A. Miller, and Leo Bersani. It is not that these figures would have nothing interesting or useful to say. They would simply have a great deal of trouble making themselves understood (as many of us in the field of queer studies would). The problems are on the levels both of cultural legibility and political palatability. Imagine Bersani: "As I argue, Ted, in my article 'Is the Rectum a Grave?' ..." The ensuing discussion of hetero-masculinity's terror of penetration might put Ted in *his* grave.

Right now, several conflicting languages occupy the centers of public discourse in the US. In conservative politics, the language of morality and "values" predominates. This language assumes the universality and normative superiority of marital heterosexual relationships, and positions homosexuality and bisexuality as immoral and sinful threats to family values. In liberal politics, both gay and gay supportive, the rhetoric of rights and the call for an end to discrimination against a fixed minority population of lesbians, gays, and (sometimes) bisexuals hold sway. More militant gay politics stresses difference over equality and assertion over assimilation but still generally posits a fixed minority political constituency, though this is changing. Queer politics is beginning to develop a strategy of public display and cultural intervention – a strategy positing a shifting, oppositional constituency. This politics is still highly contested and only ambivalently constructionist, however.

The language of queer studies, on the other hand, is overwhelmingly constructionist. Queer studies scholars are engaged in denaturalizing categories of sexual identity and mobilizing various critiques of the political practices referred to under the rubric "identity politics." Three of these critiques might be summarized as follows:

(1) The homosexual/heterosexual polarity is historically recent and culturally specific. The notion that these sexual categories are fixed, mutually exclusive, and mark individual bodies and personalities is a modern Western development. In other times and places, sexual acts between or among persons of the same sex have been organized and understood in dramatically different ways.

(2) The production of a politics from a fixed identity position privileges those for whom that position is the primary or only marked identity. The result for lesbian and gay politics is a tendency to center prosperous white men as the representative homosexuals. (We can see this at work in the military issue.) Though proportionately many more lesbians are discharged than gay men, the issue is nearly always represented as centering on men. Every production of "identity" creates exclusions that reappear at the margins like ghosts to haunt identity-based politics. In lesbian/gay politics, such exclusions have included bisexuals and transgender persons, among others.

(3) Identity politics only replaces closets with ghettos. The closet as a cultural space has been defined and enforced by the existence of the ghetto. In coming out of the closet, identity politics offers us another bounded, fixed space of humiliation and another kind of social isolation. Homosexual desire is localized – projected out and isolated in the community of bodies found in the gay ghetto. In this sense, identity politics lets the larger society off the hook of anxiety about sexual difference.[7]

These critiques are now so well known and widely circulated in queer studies scholarship and classrooms that, in my own course called "Queer Cultures" at Brown University, there are no worse epithets than to accuse someone of "essentialism," or of engaging in identity politics. This identity-bashing is presented as the progressive cutting edge of politics as well as theory – but it can also be framed in ways that are quite reactionary. It can be a way of reinventing the closet, of condescending to lesbian and gay scholars, students, and activists, and of avoiding (if not outright despising) lesbian/gay/queer activism altogether – while posing as politically more progressive than thou. But the critical insights of queer theory might also be mobilized (and, I would argue, *should* be) to forge a political language that can take us beyond the limiting rhetorics of liberal gay rights and of militant nationalism.

When we turn our attention to this project, we run into difficulty the moment we step outside our classrooms, books, journals, and conferences. How do we represent our political concerns in public discourse? In trying to do this, in trying to hold the ground of the fundamental criticism of the very language of current public discourse that queer theory has enabled, in trying to translate our constructionist language into terms that have the power to transform political practices, we are faced with several difficulties.

First, the discussion of the construction of categories of sexual identity resists translation into terms that are culturally legible and thus usable in consequential public debates. To illustrate this difficulty, let's imagine that you are asked to appear on the Oprah Winfrey show to talk about public school curriculums. Guest A says material on gays will influence children to think gay is okay and thus to become disgusting perverts themselves. Guest B, from Parents and Friends of Lesbians and Gays, says that this will not happen because sexual identity is fixed by the age of 3, if not in utero. You are Guest C – what do you say? That "the production of queer sexualities is historically and culturally conditioned," that if gay materials in class are conducive to the production of queer sexualities, you are squarely in favor of their use? The difficulties here on the level of legibility and on the level of political palatability are readily apparent.

Second, the use of constructionist language to discuss homosexuality tends to leave heterosexuality in its naturalized place – it can be taken up by homophobes to feed the fantasy of a world without homosexual bodies and desires. "If history can make them, history can also UNmake them" seems to be the logic here. At a conference in Toronto a decade ago, Dorothy Allison and Esther Newton suggested responding to this danger in constructionist arguments by producing buttons demanding "Deconstruct Heterosexuality First." Of course, we can respond as the button suggests and work to denaturalize heterosexuality (which queer studies is, in fact, doing), but this is unlikely to be received in current public debates without guffaws and disbelief.

The usual response to these difficulties is to resort to what is called "strategic essentialism": the use of essentialist categories and identity politics in public debates because that is all anyone can understand, and we need to be effective in the political arena. I take the concerns that lead to the embrace of strategic essentialism seriously, but I think that it is ultimately an unproductive solution.[8] It allows sexual difference and queer desires to continue to be localized in homosexualized bodies. It consigns us, in the public imagination, to the realms of the particular and the parochial, the defense team for a fixed minority, that most "special" of special interest groups – again, letting everyone else off the hook.

I would argue that we need to find a way to close the language gap in queer studies and queer politics. We need to do this especially with reference to the operations of the state. Though queer politics is presently claiming public and cultural space in imaginative new ways (kiss-ins, for example), the politics of the state are generally being left to lesbian and gay civil rights strategies. These strategies are greatly embattled at present, and there are still many gains to be made through their deployment. But they are increasingly ineffective in the face of new homophobic initiatives; they appear unable to generate new rhetorics and tactics against attacks designed specifically to disable identity-based antidiscrimination policies.[9] We cannot afford to fall back on strategic essentialism (it will not get us out of the trouble we are now in), and we cannot afford to abandon the field.

We do have some precedents. Scholars and activists working on the issues surrounding the AIDS crisis have managed to transport the work of theory into the arena of politics and public policy with astonishing speed and commitment.[10] In the arts the films of Isaac Julien and the Sankofa collective and those of Marlon Riggs (*Tongues United* and *Color Adjustment*, both shown on public television) have brought into public discourse very complex ideas about the construction of racial and sexual identities and their intersections.

I have a modest proposal for attempting this translation in the context of our current political situation. We need to find ways to respond to two developing right-wing strategies: No Promo Homo and No Special Rights.

The No Promo Homo campaigns, designated as such by attorney and activist Nan D. Hunter, attempt to proscribe the public "promotion" of homosexuality, at least when state funds are involved.[11] These campaigns began appearing in 1978 with the Briggs initiative in California. The following list provides a brief history of these efforts:

- The Briggs Initiative (California, 1978) would have permitted the firing of any school employee who engaged in "advocating, soliciting, imposing, encouraging, or promoting of private or public homosexual activity directed at, or likely to come to the attention of, school children and/or other employees."
- The Helms Amendment to the Labor-Health and Human Services Appropriation Act for Fiscal Year 1988 provided the caveat that "none of the funds made available under this Act to the Centers for Disease Control shall be used to provide AIDS education, information, or prevention materials and activities that promote or encourage, directly ["or indirectly" was removed], homosexual activities."
- Britain's Clause 28 of the Local Government Act of 1988 stated that local governments would not be permitted to "promote homosexuality or public material for the promotion of homosexuality" or "promote the teaching ... of the acceptability of homosexuality as a pretended family relationship." Nor could government funding go to private entities engaged in those acts.
- In 1989, in the wake of a conservative outcry over reports that the National Endowment for the Arts had supported an exhibit of Robert Mapplethorpe's photographs, the US Congress enacted legislation prohibiting the NEA from funding "obscene" materials, "including but not limited to, depictions of sadomasochism, homoeroticism, the sexual exploitation of children, or individuals engaged in sex acts."
- The 1992 Oregon ballot initiative, appropriating the basic form of Clause 28, would have required that "state, regional, local governments and their properties and monies shall not be used to promote, encourage, or facilitate homosexuality." This legislation was defeated at the state level, then passed by several localities through ballot initiatives. Another effort to pass similar legislation is expected in 1994.

Interestingly enough, No Promo Homo campaigns concede the privacy arguments advanced by lesbian/gay advocates over the past two decades. There is no attempt to police "private" behavior. Instead, there is an attempt to counter identity claims, and anti-discrimination efforts based on those claims, through the policing of speech, that is, "promotion" and "advocacy." These campaigns deny that lesbian/gay identities are fixed, and posit instead a contagion theory. (This may partly explain the turn to biology as a grounding for identity by some gay rights advocates and their liberal supporters, as a counter to the contagion theory at the heart of conservative strategies.) These strategies also borrow from the anti-abortion movement their focus on restriction through limitation of state funding. In addition to conceding privacy arguments, No Promo Homo campaigns also concede some right of access to "public" space, but only public space that is not supported by a state apparatus or by state revenues. This is an extremely constrained "public," in that state funds and institutions reach broadly into education, cultural, and political life in the US.

The appeal in these campaigns is to some notion of a "neutral" state. The argument being made is "you can do what you want" (the concession to privacy) and "you can be who you are" (the concession to identity), but "you can't spread it around on MY dime." This, of course, is a profoundly false neutrality. Queers are presented as those who wish illegitimately to recruit the state into "promoting" a single minority viewpoint, a parochial "special" interest.

Other campaigns that are not, strictly speaking, No Promo Homo campaigns pick up this theme as well. The Colorado ballot initiative of 1992 called for a ban on anti-discrimination legislation to protect lesbian, gay, and bisexual rights, a variation on the many repeal initiatives which began with Anita Bryant's notorious Save the Children campaign in 1977.[12] Many of the 1994 anti-gay initiatives are straightforward attempts to repeal existing anti-discrimination legislation; others are modeled on the more expansive Colorado effort to pre-empt the anti-discrimination strategy before it is mobilized. The Colorado anti-gay activists circulated the popular and effective slogan, "No Special Rights."

We know who really has the special rights. In fact, the state is deeply involved in regulating and "promoting" heterosexuality. It is queers who have been excluded from the benefits of state support in all kinds of areas, from tax law to education to support for cultural production, and more. As Michael Warner has argued, "The dawning realization that themes of homophobia and heterosexism may be read in almost any document of our culture means that we are only beginning to have an idea how widespread those institutions and accounts are."[13]

I therefore propose that we respond to the No Promo Homo and No Special Rights campaigns *not* with our familiar emphasis on equality (we're just like you and want the same rights) or difference (we're here, we're queer, get used to it) *only*, but with campaigns of our own: NO PROMO HETERO, or *WHOSE* SPECIAL RIGHTS? What I am suggesting in substance is that we look beyond the language of rights claims for a fixed minority and calls for anti-discrimination (rhetorical positioning largely borrowed from the civil rights movement and feminism), and instead borrow from and transform another liberal discourse, that surrounding the effort to disestablish state religion, to separate church and state. We might become the new disestablishmentarians, the state religion we wish to disestablish being the religion of heteronormativity.[14] We might argue that public policy and public institutions may not legitimately compel, promote, or prefer inter-gender relationships over intra-gender attachments. Without appropriating too much of the liberal baggage of the discourse of religious tolerance,

we might borrow from this rhetoric a strategy for reversing the terms of anti-gay propaganda and exposing the myriad ways that state apparatuses promote, encourage, and produce "special rights" for heterosexuality.

A rhetorical move such as this has several advantages. First, it highlights the embeddedness of heteronormativity in a wide range of state policies, institutions, and practices. Tracing out in a concrete way the extent of the state's involvement in promoting heterosexuality would be a useful, though enormous, project. Media materials would be effective here. For instance, under the banner of *WHOSE* SPECIAL RIGHTS? we might use billboards, posters, video, film, and other published material to outline the ways in which heterosexuality is endorsed through state activity (education, tax law, marriage and family life, etc.), specifying the unfair preferences that operate in each area.

Second, such a move may be articulated within a widely understood and accepted liberal discourse (the state may no more establish a state sexuality than a state religion, a heterosexual presumption has no more place in public life than a presumption of Christianity). In other words, it could be framed in terms that are completely understandable within this political culture. Yet, third, its implications are much more radical and far-reaching than the rights claims we are currently forwarding. From marriage to employment and from health care policies to public school curriculums, the aggressive deployment of this argument could transform public debate.

In many ways the religion analogy works better than analogies to liberal discourses surrounding race and gender. For instance, affirmative action strategies, which have had some limited success in relation to gender and race, would never work for us. We need strategies that do not require us to specify who is and is not a "member" of our group. If sexual desire is compared to religion, we can see it as not natural, fixed, or ahistorical, yet not trivial or shallow, as the term "lifestyle choice" implies. Religion is understood as not biological or fixed; for instance, people can and do convert. But it is also understood as a deep commitment. That commitment is seen as highly resistant to coerced conversion and deserving of expression and political protection. That is why an argument for "disestablishment" might work better than calls for an end to discrimination against an identifiable population.

Deconstructing heteronormativity reverses the terms of No Promo Homo and No Special Rights campaigns that try to claim that the lesbian/gay movement is seeking privilege and that call upon the populist disdain for privilege to discredit our political efforts. Instead, we point out on "Larry King Live" who really is trying to maintain privilege. Such a reversal has the potential to expose and disable the conservative rhetoric in ways that anti-discrimination language cannot, stripping it of its phony populist appeal.

As Dorothy Allison and Esther Newton proposed, it is a strategy that in a sense deconstructs heterosexuality first. Rather than relying on the solidification of lesbian and gay identities, it attacks the natural and preferred status of heterosexuality. No Promo Hetero and *Whose Special Rights?* would be, in a sense, tactical reversals (of No Promo Homo and No Special Rights), but ones that work to destabilize heternormativity rather than to naturalize gay identities.

Moreover, this destabilization brackets debates about morality and values. As in the case of religious differences, we do not need to persuade or convert others to our view. We simply argue for "disestablishment" of state endorsement for one view over another. It brackets political differences among progressive activists (liberal assimilationists, militant nationalists, and constructionists) and debates about biology (the gay brain, the lesbian twins): we can agree on this strategic move without having to resolve our differences. And it makes a case for freedom of association (to form relationships) and freedom of speech (acknowledgment or assertion) for everyone, rather than asks for "rights" for a fixed minority. In this way, we can escape being positioned as narrow and parochial. Of course, anti-discrimination efforts work to this end as well, arguing for an end to discrimination based on anyone's sexual preference or orientation. (The success of the anti-Briggs campaign in California was partly owing to such an emphasis on *everybody's* rights.) But this is becoming more difficult to do, as the No Promo Homo and No Special Rights rhetoric becomes more sophisticated at forcing gay rights activists to specify the group they represent. Turning the tables by asking right-wing activists to justify the "special rights" of heterosexuality might help undermine this new rhetoric.

Finally, a disestablishment strategy does not require us to localize or naturalize gendered desire. But the disadvantages of such a strategy mirror the advantages. Because this case is formulated within the terms of liberalism, it may trap us in as many ways as it releases us. For instance, in some ways it seems to construct a zone of liberty in negative relation to the state (it argues about what the state can*not* do). This is not the historical moment when we want to set up a negative relation to state power or slip into limiting forms of libertarianism. The arguments would need to be carefully framed to emphasize that state institutions must be even-handed in the arena of sexuality, not that sexuality should be removed from state action completely. Activists might also make the crucial distinction between state institutions (which must, in some sense, be neutral) and "the public" arena, where explicit advocacy is not only allowable but desirable.[15]

The radical implications of a destabliziling strategy, set in motion as they are by liberal arguments, will not be invisible to our opponents. We might very well still find ourselves beyond the pale of the McNeil-Lehrer Report and the *New York Times*. We might expect a very strong response – perhaps the argument that the state *must* and *should* promote and prefer heterosexuality as the foundation for "the family." This response would be very difficult to reply to, given the powerful valence of "family."[16] But it would usefully put conservatives on the defensive. They would have to acknowledge and defend heterosexual privilege rather than claim we are the ones who want unfair preferences. It would force them back into an old conservative argument, taking the au courant antiprivilege spin off their revamped rhetoric.

No Promo Hetero will probably not be

successful in winning any kind of disestablishment of heteronormativity in the near future. Its success in the short run might be the rhetorical disabling of conservative strategies. But even in the event of this kind of success, it is not a broad solution but only a local tactic embedded in a larger strategy of destabilizing heteronormativity. It is one among many conceivable tactics. It is not meant to replace civil rights strategies, and it would not be appropriate in all situations. There are many problems in legal and state institutions that it could not address (antiprostitution laws, for instance). We have to keep imagining new ways both to respond to attacks and to put our own vision forward.

I have one other suggestion for reconceptualizing our relation to state politics. In presenting our situation in public discourse, we need a less defensive, more politically self-assertive linguistic and conceptual tools to talk about sexual difference. (This is the problem to which a nascent queer politics is now productively addressing itself.) We might begin to think about sexual difference not in terms of naturalized identities but as a form of *dissent*, understood not simply as speech, but as a constellation of nonconforming practices, expressions, and beliefs.[17] Here, again, I am drawing from religion. The right to religious dissent has been understood not solely as the right to belief but as a right to practices expressive of those beliefs. Framing our difference in this way would be useful in several contexts. First, a notion of dissent would present our difference as oppositional, bringing into the frame the illegitimacy of the social and political privilege accorded to heterosexuality. Second, this notion of dissent would join our right to sexual conduct, both desire and expression, our right to a multiplicity of possible shifting identities, and our right to state a viewpoint and promote it, to express ourselves publicly, politically, and culturally. This is useful now because of the move in both mainstream religious organizations and the military to separate "orientation" and "conduct," permitting the former (a concession to anti-discrimination arguments) but not the latter. We need to aggressively rejoin these elements, not cooperate in their separa-

tion. Some notion of "dissent" might work to that end.

Finally, the framework of "dissent" could help us think about a central paradox of sexual difference: it is both malleable – historically, culturally, and in many individual lives – and yet highly resistant to coercive change. This paradox of malleability and resistance is built into the general understanding of how "dissent" works; people change their opinions and practices over time yet will hold to them under torture. This is a paradox that neither notions of identity nor fluidity can quite capture.

Extensive transformation of these strategies will be necessary beyond the terms outlined here if they are actually to be mobilized. If we can use the discourses of religious liberty and religious dissent at all, we must rework them into a dramatically new shape. This has been done before. The US civil rights movement drew on and transformed familiar religious rhetoric, reworking it in light of new political needs and cultural practices to get it to do a kind of cultural work it was never designed to do. The question is: At this historical moment, can we transform *any* liberal rhetoric in the interests ultimately of going beyond liberal categories and solutions? Or, given the difficulty of translating our most radical insights and arguments into effective public discourse, can we afford not to try?

Whether this specific strategy will fly or not, we need to think seriously about how to formulate the insights of queer theory and transport them into public discourse. We need (I emphasize *need* here) to be both transformative AND effective. We need not only to defend ourselves in the university, in the polity, and in the streets but to move our political vision forward beyond the limits of lesbian and gay rights and militant nationalism. We need to do this in a way that allows us to address the general without losing sight of the particular. (We need both to specify our own situation and to reach beyond it.) We need to do this for the defense, promotion, and advocacy not only of our scholarship and teaching, but of our political, personal, and indeed our physical lives.

NOTES

1 I borrow here from Gayle Rubin's prescient opening line to her "Thinking Sex: Notes for a Radical Theory of the Politics of Sexuality," in *Pleasure and Danger: Exploring Female Sexuality*, ed. Carole Vance (New York: Routledge, 1984). The line is: "The time has come to think about sex."

2 Lisa Keen, "Record Number of Ballot Fights Looming for Gays," *Washington Blade* (January 21, 1994); Hastings Wyman, Jr, "Strengthening Gays' Political Response in '94," *Washington Blade* (January 7, 1994); Steven Holmes, "Gay Rights Advocates Brace for Ballot Fights," *New York Times* (January 12, 1994).

3 The data on these organizations is taken from materials presented by a member of People for the American Way at a workshop on the religious right sponsored by the Texas Family Planning Association, December 1993.

4 At an April 1993 conference at the University of Illinois, radical critic Todd Gitlin attacked the emphasis on "difference" in progressive politics, and called for a return to "universalism." This kind of pointing to "fragmentation" as caused by all those "special" and parochial interests, rather than by the false "universalism" of a failing left politics, is common. See Gitlin's article in *The Crisis in Higher Education*, ed. Michael Bérubé and Cary Nelson (New York: Routledge 1995).

5 Michael Warner has called for queer intellectuals to turn their attention to theorizing the social, and for critical theorists of politics and the state to take sexuality seriously as a category of analysis. See his introduction to *Fear of a Queer Planet* (Minneapolis: University of Minnesota Press, 1993).

6 Stacey D'Erasmo, "The Gay Nineties: In Schools across the Country, Gay Studies Is Coming on Strong," *Rolling Stone* (October 3, 1991). The article finally referred to Sedgwick as "a bit of a puzzle – a married woman who describes herself as 'queer'" (87). I thank Stacey for allowing me to repeat this story, and I am grateful to Eve Kosofsky Sedgwick for graciously allowing me to use her name.

7 For a collection of articles in which these arguments are laid out, see Henry Abelove, Michele Aina Barale, and David Halperin (eds), *The Lesbian and Gay Studies Reader* (New York: Routledge, 1993). Their "Suggestions for Further Reading" at the end of the volume are especially helpful for a sense of the development of these arguments over time.

8 Amanda Anderson has outlined this strategy and its limits in the context of feminist politics. See "Cryptonormativism and Double Gestures: The Politics of Poststructuralism," *Cultural Critique* 21 (1992).

9 For a discussion of the ways right-wing strategies have evolved in response to progressive identity politics, see Cindy Patton, "Tremble Hetero Swine!" in *Fear of a Queer Planet*.

10 I am thinking here of the work of Douglas Crimp, Paula Treichler, and Cindy Patton, among many others.

11 Nan D. Hunter, "Identity, Speech, and Equality."

12 The Colorado ban has been declared unconstitutional by the courts, but this decision is presently being appealed.

13 Warner, *Fear of a Queer Planet*: xiii.

14 I borrow the evocative term "heteronormativity" from Michael Warner, *ibid*.

15 For an especially helpful discussion of the importance of this distinction, see Nancy Fraser, "Rethinking the Public Sphere: A Contribution to the Critique of Actually Existing Democracy," *Social Text* 25/6 (1990).

16 I am indebted to Henry Abelove, who pointed out that conservatives would no doubt respond to No Promo Hetero with a defence of "the family."

17 Gayle Rubin has used the terms "sexual dissenters," "erotic dissidents," "sexual dissidents" and "dissident sexuality" in ways similar to my use of "sexual dissent" here. See "The Leather Menace: Comments on Politics and S/M," in *Coming to Power*, ed. Samois (Boston: Alyson Publications, 1981), and "Thinking Sex."

JANICE M. IRVINE

"A Place in the Rainbow: Theorizing Lesbian and Gay Culture"

from *Sociological Theory* 12: 2 (July 1994): 232–48

In 1992, volatile debates about culture rocked New York City after the introduction of a teacher's guide for a multicultural curriculum in the public schools. Known as the Rainbow curriculum, this guide was unremarkable until key actors discovered brief sections alluding to lesbian and gay families.[1] The ensuing controversy generated national publicity and ultimately contributed to the firing of Schools Chancellor Joseph Fernandez. The Rainbow curriculum is of central importance because the debates over culture, which the curriculum did not initiate but certainly underscored in popular consciousness, continue throughout the country.

The controversy over the Rainbow curriculum is of academic interest to sociologists because of the complicated theoretical concerns it raises about culture, identity, and sexuality. Especially at a time when the term *culture* has achieved popular and widespread usage, opposition to the demands by lesbians and gay men for recognition as a cultural group generates questions about authenticity and definition of culture. What or who is entitled to claim cultural status? How are cultural identities constituted? Are they essential or constructed? What is the role of history, of social agents, and of representation in the invention of cultures? Are some cultures more legitimate than others? Do sexual cultures exist? Adequate answers to these questions necessitate theoretical paradigms that speak to the intersections of culture, sexuality, identities, race, ethnicity, and difference.

Debates about culture certainly constitute a trajectory within the classical sociological theories of Marx, Weber, and Durkheim. Throughout the century, and from a variety of theoretical standpoints, sociologists have examined questions concerning (for example) cultural autonomy, coherence, and consensus. Analysis of culture has recently assumed increasing prominence in sociological theorizing (Alexander and Seidman 1990; Hall and Neitz 1993; Munch and Smelser 1992; Wuthnow 1987). The growing recognition in the discipline of the importance of culture is significant because changing demographic and political factors unceasingly place cultural concerns in the foreground as central to social life. Further, a vibrant discourse typically glossed as "multiculturalism" has facilitated the deployment of the term *culture* in an ever-widening sphere. Yet sociologists have played a minimal role in the exciting advances of cultural and sexuality studies, and sociological theory is inadequate to analyze social events such as the Rainbow controversy.

Certain theoretical frameworks in sociology, such as those of deviance and social problems, have proved to be useful tools whereby some scholars and activists study sexual cultures. Certainly social construction theory, which has its primary roots in sociology, has transformed the history of sexuality. Several factors, however, contribute to sociology's paradigmatic limitations in this area. First, there is no tradition within mainstream sociology of broader inquiry into the study of sexuality. Compared, for example, with historians and anthropologists, few sociologists participate in the burgeoning interdisciplinary field of sexuality studies (for important exceptions see Almaguer 1991; Gagnon 1977; Giddens 1992; Humphries 1974; Irvine 1990, 1994; Luker 1975; Murray 1979, 1992; Plummer 1975, 1981; Seidman

1991, 1992; Simon and Gagnon 1973; Stein 1993, as well as a number of works by historical sociologist Jeffrey Weeks (1977, 1981, 1985, 1991). Much of this work is recent. Beyond the absence of a critical canon, this vacuum speaks to a certain illegitimacy within sociology concerning the study of sexuality. This is reinforced materially by the lack of graduate training in the sociology of sexuality and by a dearth of job opportunities for those who might choose to specialize in this area.

Of related concern is sociology's insulation from the interdisciplinary multicultural conversation concerning intersections of race, ethnicity, gender, and sexual identity. Particularly relevant for this paper is the chasm between sociology and lesbian and gay studies. Central to the field of lesbian and gay studies is a range of topics that should hold particular fascination for sociologists: examination of the historical invention of sexual taxonomies and the reciprocal effect of the social organization of sexual communities, as well as inquiry into the origins of sexual cultures, the organization of systems of meaning, and the construction and deconstruction of identities. Whereas lesbians and gay men appear most frequently in sociology as objects of discussion in social problems texts, lesbian and gay studies insist on our subjectivity as social actors and as research agents. Lesbian and gay studies center sexuality as a major social category with important correlates of social organization and behavior rather than relegating it to the status of individual variable.

Using key aspects of the debates about culture that were generated by the Rainbow curriculum, I will highlight how placing lesbian and gay sexual identity in the foreground is essential to this analysis. The application of theoretical perspectives from cultural studies and multicultural studies, in particular lesbian and gay studies and African-American studies, is especially useful in exploring the theoretical implications of pitting racial cultures against sexual cultures, and in the debates over essential and constructed identities. I will examine competing claims about culture by social groups, and will discuss evolving cultural theories among social scientists. To fully contextualize the Rainbow debates, this cultural theory must be located in historical analysis about the invention of racial categories, sexual categories, and the emergence of individual and social identities. The initiative by lesbians and gay men to achieve cultural status in public multicultural education not only is a pivotal moment in lesbian and gay liberation but also affords the opportunity to further elaborate social theories about culture through an examination of a cultural group actively engaged in its continual reinvention.

CULTURES, MULTICULTURALISM, AND SEXUALITY

As the debates over the Rainbow curriculum aptly illustrate, attention to culture, once largely confined within academic discourse, currently occupies a varied and mainstream audience. This shift corresponds to major social changes in structures and consciousness wrought by the many civil rights movements of the last twenty five years. Blacks, members of other racial and ethnic groups, women, lesbians and gay men, and disabled people launched legal and social initiatives not only to end discrimination but also to foster recognition of their distinct cultural identities. The richness of recent multicultural awareness is a legacy of these movements. Similarly, the challenges and conflicts generated by multicultural projects rank among the most volatile theoretical and political debates of the late twentieth century.

Much of the sophisticated and engaging new theoretical literature on culture has emerged from those working within cultural studies and in the various ethnic, women's, and lesbian and gay studies programs, as well as from associated independent scholars and activists. In a dialogue that crosses disciplines and identity groups, this scholarship examines a range of questions about the nature, meaning, and practices of culture that should be of great interest to sociologists. As I have noted, some sociologists have traditionally been concerned with issues of culture, race, and ethnicity. Currently, however, and with important exceptions (see, for example, Alba 1990; Collins 1986, 1990; Hall 1989, 1992a, 1992b; Omi and Winant 1986; Stacey and Thorne 1985; Thompson and Tyagi 1993;

Waters 1990), sociologists have not yet had a strong voice in articulating the "new cultural politics of difference" (West 1993a: 18).[2] The proliferation of cultural studies in the United States, as it entails the theorizing of culture in the deeply political context of day-to-day negotiations of race, ethnicity, gender, and sexuality, has been cross-disciplinary or even antidisciplinary, resulting in a number of independent academic centers of cultural studies (Hall 1992a; Nelson, Treichler, and Grossberg 1992). Sociologists have produced little of this cultural studies scholarship.[3]

As Seidman (1990) has aptly observed, sociological inquiries into culture are not simply theoretical, but are central to negotiations of everyday life. This suggests that sociologists may want to attend to the new discursive formulations deployed by scholars who are theorizing the daily complications of culture and multiculturalism as they are articulated and experienced within existing and contested relations of power.

The educational system has proved to be a central location in which the complexities of culture are manifested daily. Schools have been the site of extensive conflict and debate. This is not surprising because educational institutions are primary vehicles for the transmission of culture (Bourdieu 1968). On all levels of the system, historically marginalized groups have sought to destabilize the hegemonic notion of a homogeneous and inclusive "American culture" (Hu-DeHart 1993: 8) and to gain recognition for their own diverse histories, traditions, and identities. The first disruptions started at the university level in the late 1960s, when student protesters demanded the establishment of ethnic and women's studies programs. Multicultural curricula are now being implemented in primary and secondary schools across the country, in a climate of both enthusiasm and opposition.

In multicultural educational systems, schools become the site not simply for cultural assertion and socialization but also for the active invention of culture. Students do not passively learn about cultures and identities, but participate in ongoing adoption and reformulation of traditional cultural identities, logics, and strategies. As Lubiano suggests, education is a site where "people think themselves into being" (Thompson and Tyagi 1993: xxxi). Representation in multicultural curricula is crucial for the visibility and legitimacy it affords to a cultural group, but also for that group's continual reinvigoration. Increasingly, too, multicultural programs are becoming sites not only for the support of cultural identities, but also for destabilizing discussions of the limitations of identity politics and of reified notions of identity (West 1993a).

This power of multicultural education forms the basis for controversies such as the Rainbow curriculum, where lesbians and gay men seek to be included in public school curricula. The fierce and widely publicized battle waged over this curriculum resonated across the country, becoming a benchmark contest over sexuality education more generally. These cultural debates assumed discursive parameters which were made possible only through the intellectual and political achievements of several decades of lesbian/gay liberation. At a moment during which multicultural education is increasingly prominent, it was inevitable that lesbians and gay men would begin initiatives to secure for their own communities a place in these curricula.

Opposition to the Rainbow curriculum is illustrative both of popular ideas about the nature of culture, and of the varied faces of homophobia. Critics refused to acknowledge that lesbian and gay men constitute a culture, and instead adamantly insisted that homosexuals were deviant, immoral individuals who pose a threat to children. This individualizing strategy supported the contention that lesbians and gay men simply live an aberrant lifestyle rather than constituting a legitimate cultural identity. Culture, in the view of the critics, is a status available only to those born into groups with a history and a shared set of practices. It is an essential and consistent identity. This formulation of culture fostered one of the most pernicious aspects of the Rainbow debates: the pitting of racial groups against lesbians and gay men.[4]

Critics of the idea of a lesbian/gay culture deployed a simple but powerful tactic to argue that it should be excluded from the multicultural curriculum. They compared the allegedly stable and indisputable cultural categories of race and ethnicity with the purportedly ridiculous and fictive notion of lesbian/gay culture. "They want to teach my kid that being gay fits in with being Italian and Puerto Rican!" one parent cried (Tabor 1992). Some African-American critics were incensed by comparisons of lesbian and gay politics and culture to the black civil rights movement. At one community school board meeting, a parent and teacher said:

> Years of being thrown in jail for demonstrating against racism and being sprayed by fire hoses taught me something. I ask you where was the gay community when school children died in Mobile, Alabama? Where was the gay community when many of us were beaten at a lunch counter? Is this the only way we can be included in the curriculum? To allow the gay community to piggyback off our achievement?
>
> (D'Angelo 1992)

For others, the outrage was fueled by the contention that, unlike blacks or (presumably) members of other racial groups, lesbians and gay men have no common cultural symbols or artefacts. Olivia Banks (1993), the chair of the curriculum committee of School Board 29, was vehement during a *60 Minutes* broadcast on the Rainbow curriculum:

> How dare they compare themselves to the blacks, who've had to struggle ... for over 250-some years? They have no special language, no special clothing, no special food, no special dress-wear, so what ... makes them a culture? They don't fit into any definition of what a culture is. They are using the racial issue as a way to open doors. How dare they?

When Ed Bradley suggested that lesbians and gay men have a minority identity, Banks fumed, "You're doing it again. You're ... putting a sexual orientation on the same level of a race, and ... that's unacceptable to this person sitting here."

Much popular opposition to the idea that lesbians and gay men constitute a culture rests on an important subtextual insistence that we are all born with and into culture. In this model, race and ethnicity become the quintessentially authentic cultures. Lingering traces of biologism from the social sciences are entrenched in mainstream thought, and cast race as a fixed

and natural essence. As explanatory systems, these racial beliefs, which fuse physiological and social differences, function as "amateur biology" (Omi and Winant 1986: 62). From this perspective, one's social location in a racial culture is secured at birth, and, as Banks implies above, allows one entry into a stable system of shared language, dress, clothing, and other cultural signifiers.

The conviction that cultural status is biologically and generationally transmitted inevitably excludes lesbians and gay men, who cannot make such claims.[5] As illustrated above, critics greet the suggestion of a lesbian and gay culture not simply with opposition but with the fear that such recognition would somehow diminish their social position or erode whatever legitimacy they have managed to garner from years of civil rights efforts.[6] Ironically, however, the establishment of multicultural education in public schools, and of university programs such as black studies, was itself the outcome of protracted efforts, much like those now undertaken by lesbians and gay men, to transform the educational system into a set of institutions more aware and more responsive to the cultures of ethnic and racial groups (Blassingame 1971; Ford 1973).

This discursive positioning of racial/ethnic cultures against lesbian/gay cultures in such a volatile mainstream debate invites an examination of the important scholarship on both racial and sexual cultures. Ironically, as we shall see, opponents of the Rainbow curriculum are promulgating rigidly essential definitions of race at a moment when theorists are destabilizing those ideas by asserting the socially and historically constructed nature of racial categories. Similarly, lesbian and gay scholarship has detailed the important historical transformation of structures and meaning from homosexuality as an individual, deviant sexual act, to a personal social identity, to a complex and sophisticated cultural group. In many ways, then, social theorists of race and of sexuality have been engaged in parallel endeavors of placing both race and sexual identity in the foreground as social categories while rejecting false universalisms and ahistorical essentialisms. Further, in deconstructing racial and sexual categories, these theorists have been insistent that all cultures are historically contingent and invented, including dominant cultures such as those of whites and heterosexuals.

LESBIAN AND GAY CULTURES, COMMUNITIES, AND IDENTITIES

The Rainbow controversy aptly reveals the binarisms rending contemporary society: the idea of a positive lesbian/gay culture worthy of recognition and respect is coterminous with the specter of the deviant, individual homosexual. Lesbian/gay movements throughout the century have sought to erase the stigma of individual sickness and perversion, institutionalized by law, medicine, and science. As the Rainbow debates indicate, these efforts to transform social meanings from homosexual to gay (Herdt 1992; Weinberg 1972) – that is, from individual, pathological behavior to a rich and distinctive cultural system – have been only partially successful. Rainbow opponents, such as the highly visible right-wing organizer Mary Cummins, were strategically canny in framing the debate as exclusively about the (typically male) sexually deviant individual. Cummins described the curriculum as "aimed at promoting acceptance of sodomy." When questioned by reporter Ed Bradley (1993), she insisted, "What is homosexuality except sodomy? . . . There's no difference. Homosexuals are sodomists."

Cultures emerge in a historical, political, and economic context. Cummins's comment, therefore, and a full understanding of the shift from individual homosexual behavior to gay cultural identity, require an examination of the social production of sexual identities. Proponents of the idea of lesbian/gay culture base their arguments on a body of important historical literature about lesbians and gay men as social actors engaged in the active invention of communities and in the transformation of social meanings of same-sex sexual behavior. The shift from the individual sodomist to the lesbian and gay cultural subject occurred in the context of social, political, and economic changes over the course of many decades, including (as we will see) the intellectual activities of sociologists. In addition, academic research produced by lesbians and gay men concerning their cultural status has been shaped by the evolving theoretical perspectives on the nature and definitions of culture within the social sciences, particularly anthropology.

Our current ideas about sexual identity rest on deep and fundamental changes in the social organization of sexuality that date to the late nineteenth century. Historians cite that period as an era during which dominant sexual meanings shifted from a familial and reproductive orientation to a focus on sexuality as vital to individual happiness and emotional intimacy (D'Emilio and Freedman 1988; Foucault 1978; Weeks 1981). Our modern preoccupation with sexuality as a cornerstone of personality and a prerequisite for fulfillment is a decidedly recent phenomenon. This shift is important in understanding the genuine instability of current notions that there are distinct heterosexual and homosexual persons. The organization of individual identity around sexual feelings and behaviors would have been unthinkable before the last century.

A related historical development in the organization of sexual identities was the emergence of the legal, and particularly the medical, professions as central institutions in the regulation of sexuality. Although homosexual activity was subject to sodomy laws in England before 1885, historians emphasize that those laws were directed against specific acts, not particular categories of people (Weeks 1977, 1981). Acts of sodomy committed between women and men were as vulnerable to prosecution as were those between men and men. Beginning in 1885, however, the laws began to target sexual acts between men; at that time, as a result of new medical discourses, homosexuality was increasingly defined as an internal, individual trait. The idea of a deviant, homosexual person was given a public face, in part, by highly publicized trials such as that of Oscar Wilde at the end of the century.

The invention of medical categories of sexual identities in the late nineteenth century was one artefact of the wider expansion of the emerging cultural authority of the medical profession over issues of health, illness, and (increasingly) sexuality (Irvine 1990; Starr 1982). Physicians were consolidating their power to regulate and define large areas of human experience, even those, as later critics would note, which fell outside the bounds of their training and expertise (Conrad and Schneider 1992; Friedson 1970; Zola 1972). The rise of physicians as the new "moral entrepreneurs" ensured the application of the medical model as the dominant explanatory framework for behavior considered different (Becker 1963). As with sexual identity, the medicalization of "deviance" locates its origins within the individual. As with homosexuality, this medicalization stipulates a cause that is anatomical, physiological, or psychological.

Whereas religion and the law previously had taken note of *acts* of sodomy, the new medical discourse recognized a distinct kind of sexual *person*. Beginning in the 1860s, a variety of terms to describe this new individual emerged, including *invert*, *urning*, and *homosexual*. The year 1892 marks some of the earliest textual appearances of the word *homosexual* (Halperin 1990; Katz 1990). By this time a heterosexual character, variously defined, began to appear in the medical discourse as well (Katz 1990).

Historians have differed on the significance of medical labeling: did it create a subculture that organized around the new concept of homosexual identity, or was medicalization a response to, and an attempt to define and control, pre-existing sexual communities (Chauncey 1982 and 1989; D'Emilio and Freedman 1988; Faderman 1981; Newton 1984; Smith-Rosenberg 1985)? Although evidence indicates that the determinative role of medical literature in shaping homosexual activity and identity was limited, medicalization shifted the locus of moral authority to the medicopsychiatric profession, and much early research focused on descriptive and etiological studies of this new individual. The newly medicalized condition was variously conceptualized as a disease or, as by Havelock Ellis, an anomaly akin to color blindness. Whatever the specific diagnosis, homosexuality was seen as an individual condition, and appropriate interventions were subject to the current theories and treatment modalities of medicine and psychiatry.

One hundred years since their invention, the categories of homosexuality and heterosexuality have achieved the status of assumed knowledge; the idea that there are distinct heterosexual and homosexual persons forms the centerpiece of the sexual wisdom of our society. An important factor in the persistence of ideas about fixed sexual identity derives from the cultural activities of lesbians and gay men themselves: it must be re-emphasized that medical discourse did not create categories of sexuality out of whole cloth, but was partially responding to the nascent social organization of groups of people who were beginning to coalesce and identify around their sexual interests and behaviors. Indeed, the last hundred years have witnessed the rapid and transformative development of social worlds of lesbian and gay men, particularly since World War II (D'Emilio 1983).

The social organization of lesbians and gay men has centered on the shared experience of transgressive sexuality, which has been variously defined throughout the century. Certainly legal sanctions and the medicopsychiatric consensus of homosexual pathology shaped early social networks. The stigma of perversion tainted the collective consciousness, even if some individual members refused to internalize that stigma. Pervasive social attitudes that homosexuals were bizarre, criminal, or sick were reinforced by, and contributed to, a crushing isolation and invisibility. Secrecy was an institutional tyranny rather than an individual prerogative; the closet became "the defining structure for gay oppression in this century" (Sedgwick 1993: 48). In this context, the early lesbian and gay world sought a transformation of social definitions from individual homosexual behavior to a social identity and, significantly, from a "spoiled identity" (Goffman 1963) to one of respect and value. This process much later would prompt lesbians and gay men to seek recognition for their own identities and culture within multicultural curricula such as the Rainbow.

This rearticulation of sociosexual meanings has been a complex process proceeding on many fronts. The political initiatives of the lesbian/gay movement have been pivotal in challenging both individual and institutional structures of oppression (see, for example, D'Emilio 1983; Duberman, Vicinus, and Chauncey 1989; Weeks 1977). These efforts, of course, have been shaped by a range of broader social influences, such as social and demographic changes wrought by World War II, the impact of McCarthyism, the rise of religious fundamentalism, and the emergence of liberation movements organized around race and gender.

Academic research and scholarship also helped create an intellectual climate conducive to the redefinition of sexual meaning systems. For example, Alfred Kinsey's (1948, 1953) research challenged the widespread notion that gay people were a distinct and pathological set of individuals, and suggested that everyone had the "capacity" for homosexuality. Although the gay visibility engendered by the Kinsey reports contributed to a cultural panic that fed McCarthysim, it also helped consolidate a growing 1950s homophile movement (Irvine 1990). New sociological theories also supported the efforts of this movement. In particular, deviance theory, which underwent a radical postwar transformation, provided an intellectual infrastructure for new definitions of sexual identities (see D'Emilio 1983). The work of Erving Goffman (1963), Howard Becker (1963), and Joseph Gusfield (1955), for example, was instrumental in shifting the theoretical view of deviance from that of a quality located within the individual person or act to that of a historically specific status created by social censure.

This sociological deviance theory of the 1960s was in radical opposition to the psychoanalytic discourse on homosexuality. Irving Bieber and Charles Socarides rose to prominence at that time with their oedipal and preoedipal theories of the pathological development of homosexuality. Socarides claimed that psychoanalysis could cure up to 50 per cent of "strongly motivated obligatory homosexuals" (see Bayer 1981: 37). On the other hand, the interactionist model of deviance facilitated a definition of lesbians and gay men simply as rule breakers rather than as essentially flawed individuals. In Becker's terms, lesbians and gay men were "outsiders" who had been labeled deviant.

Becker's observation that the deviant identity becomes the defining one, and therefore that outsiders create distinct social worlds, was particularly relevant to the social organization of lesbians and gay men: this century has witnessed the formation of elaborate collectivities of lesbian and gay life organized around erotic identity. These networks, however, have become increasingly expansive, with sexuality less explicitly in the foreground. With the elaboration of this complex social world has come disagreement about how to characterize it. Is it a lifestyle enclave (Bellah *et al.* 1985), a community (D'Emilio 1983; Kennedy and Davis 1993; Murray 1979), a culture (Altman 1982; Bronski 1984; Ferguson 1990; Herdt 1992; Weeks 1977), an ethnicity (Epstein 1987) or nationalism (Duggan 1992; Newton 1993)?

Yet the idea of culture has gained popular and widespread currency as an often loosely defined signifier of shared identity. Much of the intellectual debate among lesbian and gay scholars has concerned the question of cultural status; the discourse has followed theoretical advances in the social sciences, particularly anthropology and cultural studies, on the definition of culture. Until the late 1950s, behaviorism dominated the social sciences, and culture was defined as patterns of behavior, actions, and customs (D'Andrade 1984; Shweder 1984). This notion still retains popular credibility, as evidenced by Rainbow curriculum opponent Olivia Banks's earlier charge that gay people lack unique food or clothing.

As the behaviorist paradigm eroded across the disciplines, ideas about culture shifted. Anthropologists argued that culture is constituted by shared information, knowledge, or symbols – that is, through Geertz's popular notion of "webs of significance" (Geertz 1973: 5). As we will see, this definition introduced complexity not only for gay people but for other cultural groups as well, because it brought to the foreground problems of cultural unity and of how extensively knowledge and symbols are shared within social groups.

The literature on lesbian and gay social organization, until very recently, addressed these two concepts of culture: that of patterns of behavior and customs, and that of shared symbolic systems. With some exceptions (Browning 1993; Ferguson 1990; Grover 1988), there is consensus that lesbians and gay men constitute a community with a distinct culture. This has been argued on a number of fronts. Murray (1979), for example, examined changes in social science definitions of community, from that of a discrete entity to that of a process, and pointed out the lack of a well-defined and agreed-upon definition. Nevertheless, from his studies of Toronto and San Francisco (Murray 1992), he argued that the gay community meets all of the "modes of social relations" inherent in the various definitions of communities. Historians have detailed the elaborate array of social institutions as evidence of a gay community (D'Emilio 1983; Weeks 1977). These include churches, health and counseling clinics, newspapers and other media, sports teams, theater companies, travel agencies, and much more. As lesbian and gay history becomes more articulated, it is clear that community institutions (for example, the urban lesbian bar before Stonewall) were instrumental in supporting not only relationships but identity (Kennedy and Davis 1993). These studies highlight the important dialectical relationship between community and identity.

In the debate about lesbian/gay culture, it is perhaps less complicated although by no means easy to bring the behavioral aspects of culture into the foreground. Thus, in reply to Banks's remark on the Rainbow curriculum that gay people share no common artefacts, a gay man retorted, "We do have a culture. We do have our own literature. We have our own artworks. We have music that would be identifiable to lesbian and gay people" (Madson 1993: 6). Weeks (1977) has described a substantial gay argot as evidence of a culture; Bronski (1984) has discussed gay male sensibility in movies, theater, opera, and pornography. Altman (1982) noted an issue of the *Soho News* in which quiche and Perrier are designated as "the gay food." Clothing is an important cultural signifier, especially for a group whose members need help in recognizing each other. Kennedy and Davis (1993) have described how lesbians in the 1940s and 1950s learned to dress in ways that would both reinforce their sexual identity and signal it to other lesbians.

It has been possible to identify behavioral signifiers of lesbian/gay culture, but it is more difficult to argue the existence of shared symbolic systems of knowledge or information. Bronski offered perhaps the most comprehensive argument with his early, important formulation of the gay (male) sensibility; this formulation, although historically situated, assumes a somewhat determinist aspect. Some of the new anthropological scholarship is more successful in empirically describing the construction of historically specific lesbian and gay communities, with complex systems of cultural meanings (Kennedy and Davis 1993; Newton 1993). These studies reveal how meaning systems within lesbian/gay communities are located along axes of difference, particularly those of race, class, and gender. Although knowledge and symbols may be shared, such a process is inevitably partial and fragmented.

The inability to conclusively demonstrate shared symbolic systems among lesbians and gay men speaks not to the absence of cultural status but to the inadequacy of theory that totalizes culture. In a discussion of "warring factions" among the organizers of the 1993 lesbian and gay march on Washington, Goldstein stated, "Anyone who knows the gay community is aware that it stands for many things, some quite contradictory" (1993). Cultural theory is increasingly rejecting earlier perspectives that highlighted unity in favor of the recognition of internal contradiction and multiplicity. As Clifford notes, "If 'culture' is not an object to be described, neither is it a unified corpus of symbols and meanings that can be definitively interpreted. Culture is contested, temporal, and emergent" (1986: 19). New theoretical articulations of culture and identity have had important implications for the activism and scholarship of all social groups.

DESTABILIZING THEORY

Contemporary debates about culture and identities, as they are enacted in popular discourse such as that concerning the Rainbow curriculum, are infused with notions such as permanence, tradition, and (often implicitly) the imperative for a biological essence. Racial categories almost uniformly meet such criteria; their allegedly stable boundaries are policed by biological markers. On the other hand, sexual identity (read "homosexuality") is found wanting. Critics charge that at its best, the lesbian/gay community is a random group of individuals who have perversely chosen a deviant lifestyle. At its worst, it is a random group which must seduce vulnerable others in order to perpetuate itself. Not surprisingly, this charge can inspire a strategy on the part of some lesbians and gay men of asserting biological origins for their sexuality in the belief that essentialism is a precondition for legitimacy. Emerging multicultural theoretical and political initiatives problematize all of these areas of assumed knowledge, such as the immutability of culture, the construction and meaning of racial and sexual identities, the stability of social categories, and the nature and politics of difference.

These disruptions of the "common sense" arose from the synergistic power of social construction theory (with roots in symbolic interactionism), poststructuralist theory, cultural studies, and multicultural studies as represented by African-American and ethnic studies, women's studies, and lesbian and gay studies or queer theory. These theories have been both shaped and informed by political movements organized around race, ethnicity, gender, and sexuality.[7] In the briefest summary, these critical theories challenge the idea of fixed or essential social identities and raise a persistent question about the historical and political circumstances under which subjectivities are continually recreated. Identities and social categories are recognized as fluid and unstable, but also as multiple and internally contradictory. Narratives of social location therefore must account for the intersectionality of identities. The impulse to destabilize assumed social knowledge is common to these theories.

Poststructuralism and lesbian/gay studies have not necessarily eliminated earlier ideas about culture, but have enlarged and decentered them. If, as some theorists have suggested (e.g., Alexander 1992), culture is a meaningful set of symbolic patterns that can be read as a text, poststructuralism insists that there will be multiple interpretations of such readings, as of texts. Dimensions of culture, whether values, shared language or slang, geography, subjective beliefs, or symbolic systems are not universal, deterministic, or static. Cultural artifacts, subjectivities, and identities are more fragmented and divided. These theories call into question the nature and meaning of all cultural groups by challenging the authenticity of any one culture, by suggesting that the meaning of culture will vary historically and contextually, and by observing that cultural identifications are multiple and overlapping.

Because the categories of race and sexual identity were so frequently positioned in opposition to each other in mainstream debates over the Rainbow curriculum, it is instructive to recognize scholarship that questions the authenticity of an essentially racial culture and identity. Critical race theorists have deployed the insight that identity does not reflect an essential self in arguing that race and ethnicity are constituted not in biology, but in ongoing social and political processes. This is a powerfully radical theoretical challenge in light of the seemingly very visible and immutable quality of race, as compared with the seeming invisibility of sexual identity. Skin color, Stuart Hall (1989, 1992b) argues, has nothing to do with blackness. "People are all sorts of colors. The question is whether you are *culturally, historically, politically* Black" (1989: 15). Rather than an objective, natural category, race is an unstable "complex of social meanings constantly being transformed by political struggle" (Omi and Winant 1986: 68). Race, then, is an identity that people are not born with but must assume in an ongoing process of identification.

The indeterminacy of biological and the construction of racial identities inform a range of painful narratives by critical race theorists about skin color, passing, and the impact of cruel and oppressive racial meanings generated both by the dominant culture and in communities of color (for some recent examples see Carter 1993; Dent 1992; Loury 1993;

McKnight 1993; Njeri 1993; Russell, Wilson and Hall 1992; for an analysis of the social construction of whiteness, see Frankenberg 1993). The conviction that racial identity is a process, but also (significantly) that it is a choice, is thematic to these accounts. As Carter insists, "Race is a claim. A choice. A decision" (1993: 79). Yet he goes on to acknowledge the impact of external social institutions and meanings: "Oh, it is imposed, too. The society tells us: "You are black because we say so." Skin color is selected as one of many possible characteristics of morphology used for sorting. Never mind the reasons. It is simply so. It is not, however, logically entailed" (1993: 79). These critical theories therefore challenge racial essentialism, emphasize the process of individual identification, and analyze the social, political, and economic process of racial formation (Omi and Winant 1986). They historicize the process by which skin color became the basis for the invention of racial categories, and the ways in which these categories mapped new identities not only for persons of color, but also for whites. Inevitably these theories complicate any simple notions of stable and monolithic racial cultures and communities.

Lesbian and gay studies, informed by social construction theory and most recently by queer theory, have undertaken a similar intellectual project. This field has placed sexuality in the foreground as a category which, like gender and race, must be central to social analyses. Social construction theory, which denies the existence of a natural, biological sexuality, has provided the infrastructure for research on the production, organization, and regulation of sexuality. Constructionists argue that sexual acts, identities, and communities are imbued with meaning through social and historical processes; indeed, sexual desire itself may well be socially constructed (Vance 1991). Lesbian and gay scholarship examines the historical invention of sexual identities and communities, the ways in which power is infused and deployed through sexual categories, and the complicated relationships between sexuality and other social categories such as gender, race, and class. (Although it is impossible to cite all of this scholarship, some important works include Beam 1986; Chauncey

1982; D'Emilio 1983; D'Emilio and Freedman 1988; Duberman *et al.* 1989; Foucault 1978; Hull, Scott and Smith 1982; Jackson 1993; Katz 1976; Kennedy and Davis 1993; Lorde 1988; Peterson 1992; Rubin 1975, 1984; Weeks 1977, 1981, 1985, 1991.)

Queer theory builds on social constructionism to further dismantle sexual identities and categories. Drawing on postmodern critiques, the new theoretical deployment of queerness recognizes the instabilities of traditional oppositions such as lesbian/gay and heterosexual. Queerness is often used as an inclusive signifier for lesbian, gay, bisexual, transgender, drag, straights who pass as gay (Powers 1993), and any permutation of sex/gender dissent (see de Lauretis 1991; Doty 1993; Duggan 1992). It is an encompassing identity that simultaneously challenges and resists the calcification of identities and categories. Also, the use of the term *queer* is not unanimously celebrated; some scholars question the historiographic usefulness of deconstructing a marginal identity at a critical moment of activism and scholarship (Penn 1993).[8] Foremost, however, among the tasks of a queer project are challenges to seemingly stable categories – lesbianism and gayness as well as the dominant heterosexuality.

Together, the overlapping intellectual projects of postmodernism, cultural studies, critical race theories, and lesbian/gay studies and queer theory serve as powerful challenges to traditional notions of culture and identity. Cultures cannot be understood simply as a static and historically consistent aggregate of shared practices or knowledge. Rather, they are dynamic processes which, as Clifford notes, "do not hold still for their portraits" (1986: 10). Further, critical theories emphasize that cultures, as the construction of social categories on the basis of physical characteristics or sexual expression, are products of human agency. Cultures are social inventions, not biological inevitabilities. None is more authentic than another.

These deconstructions, however, do not suggest that cultures are so amorphous and so diffuse that they defy social analysis. Nor do they imply that identities are so fluid as to be easily tried on and shrugged off, thus becoming culturally and individually meaningless. Rather, they insist on a recognition of the paradoxes of culture and identity: we need cultural identities for social location, even while we must maintain continual awareness of their constructed nature; social movements simultaneously challenge and reinforce the importance and meanings of identities. In the women's movement, this dilemma has been articulated by Ann Snitow as the "recurring feminist divide" – that is, the imperative to "build the identity 'woman' and give it solid political meaning and the need to tear down the very category 'woman' and dismantle its all-too-solid history" (1989: 205). Similarly, gay social historian Jeffrey Weeks speaks of sexual identities as "necessary fictions" (1991: viii), a term that neatly encompasses the paradox. Finally, Stuart Hall describes an "ethnicity of the margins, of the periphery" (1992b: 258), which supports the recognition that we all speak from a particular social and historical standpoint without being contained by that position. This recurrent tension demands fuller articulation in both our theories and our politics.

BACK TO THE RAINBOW: SOCIOLOGY AND THEORY

This review of historical and theoretical scholarship on the invention of racial and sexual cultures and identities highlights its centrality to analyses of debates such as those over the Rainbow curriculum. The arguments that only racial/ethnic groups have culture, while lesbians and gay men are aberrant individuals, can be understood only through the theoretical lenses of new African-American scholarship on the social construction of race and of literature by lesbian and gay scholars on the historical invention of culture and sexual identity. These theories suggest that all cultures are constructed and unstable; none have more authenticity than others. In addition, the insights of lesbian and gay theory – that sexuality is a major social category giving rise to structures of inequality and patterns of discrimination and invisibility – are obviously crucial to this analysis.

The enterprises of lesbian and gay studies and of African-American and ethnic studies

concern the invention of racial and sexual cultures. Yet they also address other central aspects of the Rainbow debates, such as the construction of self and identities, the instability, multiplicity, and dynamism of cultures, and the limitations of essentialized identities. Further, any effective analysis of the volatile and often destructive debates about the Rainbow curriculum also must untangle the complicated relations of power and difference in the clash of separate and overlapping cultural identifications. For example, gay people were pitted against people of color; thus, complex permutations of racism and homophobia were triggered. Often silenced in the debate were lesbians and gay men of color.

In this area of power, difference, and multiple identifications, programs such as cultural studies, ethnic studies, women's studies and lesbian and gay studies are developing important theory. Beyond a recognition of the invention of cultures lies its day-to-day working out, the discursive formations (Jackson 1993) in which meanings are constituted through fluid negotiations of race, gender, sexual identity, and other social categories. We need theory that affords an understanding of our structural and interpersonal positions as they are configured through power and difference. Also, scholars and activists are engaged in the complicated practice of theorizing and historicizing cultural identities within a simultaneous awareness of their fragility. These dialogues could be central to sociology.

Several themes raised by current popular debates about culture might concern us as theorists while we develop more fully the idea of culture, and of sexual cultures, as deployed and manifested among people without "inherent" shared identities. As we explore the specific processes by which all cultures are constructed, we must articulate more clearly the complexities of social construction theory and must clarify common misunderstandings.[9] Further questions for sociologists concern the complications inherent in cultures and identities that are constructed around seemingly biological categories such as race, ethnicity, and gender. How can we understand and reconcile the needs of some people, often generated by legal and political strategizing, to more deeply essentialize such categories, even while others, through historical and social research, are demonstrating their radically constructed nature? In these debates, how does scientific inquiry function to reinforce particular ideologies about culture and identity? Can the histories of other oppressed groups seeking to achieve political rights and cultural legitimacy yield insights into recent attempts to biologize sexual identity more fully? Is it inevitable, in a context of deprivation and marginality, that different cultural groups will compete for status and resources? Finally, given that individuals have multiple subject positions, can we more fully develop theories that give voice to intersectional identities (Crenshaw 1992) rather than forcing people to choose one standpoint, such as race, over another, such as sexual identity or gender?

It is reasonable to expect that sociologists, for whom the study of social groups is the central task, would theorize these cultural dilemmas. Yet to do so, sociological theory must be more responsive to the insights of lesbian and gay and other multicultural theorists, placing social categories such as sexuality and race in the foreground in the context of power and difference. In 1992 Richard Perry wrote an article titled "Why Do Multiculturalists Ignore Anthropologists?" His argument, among others, was that anthropologists have much to offer multicultural scholars outside the discipline about the study of cultures. This point is well taken, and certainly can be made about the potential contributions of sociologists as well. On the other hand, an equally pertinent question is "Why have the traditional disciplines, sociology among them, not enthusiastically engaged in the important historical and theoretical work of multicultural groups such as lesbian and gay studies?" Sexuality and culture will continue to be central social issues; as such, they are central to our discipline as well.

NOTES

1 Designed as a guide for teachers, the Rainbow curriculum contained lessons on the artifacts, folk songs and holidays of other cultures. It was based on the premise that children could be taught basic lessons in mathematics, grammar, and reading by using the games, songs, and dances indigenous to a wide range of cultures.

The controversy over the curriculum centered on brief sections, in fact merely six entries in a 443-page document, which discussed lesbian and gay families. One section noted, "The issues surrounding family may be very sensitive for children. Teachers should be aware of varied family structures, including two-parent or single-parent households, gay or lesbian parents, divorced parents, adoptive parents, and guardians or foster parents. Children must be taught to acknowledge the positive aspects of each type of household and the importance of love and care in family living." It went on to say that children growing up in families headed by heterosexuals "may be experiencing contact with lesbians/gays for the first time . . . teachers of first graders have an opportunity to give children a healthy sense of identity at an early age. Classes should include references to lesbians/gay people in all curricular areas. Educators have the potential to help increase the tolerance and acceptance of the lesbian/gay community and to decrease the staggering number of hate crimes perpetrated against them." The curriculum emphasized the recognition of lesbian/gay culture; nowhere was there any mention of sex.

2 Sociological theory has certainly informed cultural studies, particularly in Britain. Sociologist Stuart Hall (1990) describes the formation of the Centre for Cultural Studies at the University of Birmingham by a handful of scholars who were marginal to academic life. He notes how sociologists attacked their work even while these new cultural theorists "raided" sociology and other traditional disciplines for theory, which they then rearticulated. Cultural studies served as a challenge to traditional sociology. As Hall notes, they took the risk of saying to sociologists "that what they say sociology is, is not what it is. We had to teach what we thought a kind of sociology that would be of service to people studying culture would be, something we could not get from self-designated sociologists" (1990: 16).

3 For example, an examination of the list of contributors to the proceedings of a large international conference on cultural studies, held in 1990, reveals very few sociologists. See Grossberg, Nelson and Treichler (1992).

4 This is a complicated dynamic that is impossible to fully explore in this article. Although homophobia in certain communities of color certainly contributed to these tensions and formulations, opponents in certain historically racist, white, working-class sections of Queens and Brooklyn inflamed fears and misunderstandings by distorting the curriculum and appealing to anxi-

eties of racial groups they had previously ignored. In a complicated and often ignored role in the debates were lesbians and gay men of color.

5 Some lesbians and gay men, however, are developing political strategies for legitimacy based on the alleged and unproved biological origins of homosexuality.

6 Not only people of color are voicing this threat. For example, Dolores Ayling of Concerned Parents for Educational Accountability (a religious right group that organized to oppose the curriculum) spoke of the outrage at the fact that sexual orientation is included in the Rainbow curriculum in a way that detracts from the authenticity of race as a cultural category (personal conversation, April 14, 1993). Many of these white advocates had not previously been noted for their vigorous support of communities of color.

7 See J. L. Newton for a discussion of how early feminist politics articulated current postmodernist critiques such as the absence of a "universal humanity," the cultural construction of subjectivity, and the interaction of representation and social relations. See Hall (1992a) for an examination of the role of feminism and critical race theories in shaping cultural studies.

8 This concern about the dismantling of the categories "lesbian" and "gay" echoes those expressed by other scholars regarding postmodern critiques of identity. Some theorists have noted how the critique of stable identities and of authoritative experience has emerged at precisely a moment of increasing subjectivity, visibility, and production of knowledge among historically marginalized groups such as women, lesbians and gay men, and people of color. Similarly, the important recognitions of the limitations of identity politics as an expression of static, homogeneous, and essential self-groupings have been coterminous with a vital activism among such groups. See, for example, de Lauretis (1991).

9 Misconceptions about social construction theory have most typically arisen from its use in the area of sexuality. Expansion and clarification are important because of the widespread relevance of constructionism for theorizing issues of culture and identity. First, the constructionist analysis is often mistakenly glossed as one which insists that individual sexual desires and directions are learned and not inborn. Yet constructionism goes far beyond the familiar nature–nurture debates. Social construction theory does not simply speak about the origins of sexuality, but examines the attribution of meaning to sexual desires, behaviors, and communities. Further, it challenges the notion that there is any historical or cross-cultural consistency to sexual acts, beliefs, or practices. Second, to

suggest that sexuality is socially constructed is not to say that it is "a fluid, changeable process open to intentional redefinition" (Epstein 1987: 22). Social constructionists have not fully theorized the ways in which sexual desires, feelings, and beliefs are mediated by socio-cultural factors and, in many people, result in deeply felt inclinations that may then be socialized into sexual identities. This theoretical gap should not be misconstrued as a suggestion that "constructedness" implies a superficial and easily unlearned sexuality. These misconceptions simply highlight areas in which sociologists might articulate social construction theory more fully, particularly in the relationships among social ideologies, individual desires and experiences, and individual and social identities. See Vance (1991) for an excellent theoretical clarification of social constructionism.

REFERENCES

Alba, Richard D. (1990), *Ethnic Identity: The Transformation of White America* (New Haven: Yale University Press).

Alexander, Jeffrey C. (1992), "The Promise of a Cultural Sociology: Technological Discourse and the Sacred and Profane Information Machine": in *Theory of Culture*, ed. Richard Munch and Neil J. Smelser (Berkeley: University of California Press).

Alexander, Jeffrey C. and Steven Seidman (1990), *Culture and Society: Contemporary Debates* (Cambridge: Cambridge University Press).

Almaguer, Tomás (1991), "Chicano Men. A Cartography of Homosexual Identity and Behavior," *differences* 3: 2: 75–100.

Altman, Dennis (1982), *The Homosexualization of America* (Boston: Beacon).

Banks, Olivia (1993), *The Rainbow Curriculum: 60 Minutes*, April 4.

Bayer, Richard (1981), *Homosexuality and American Psychiatry: The Politics of Diagnosis* (New York: Basic Books).

Beam, Joseph (1986), *In the Life: A Gay Black Anthology* (Boston: Alyson).

Becker, Howard (1963), *Outsiders: Studies in the Sociology of Deviance* (New York: Free Press).

Bellah, Robert N., Richard Madsen, William M. Sullivan, Ann Swidler, and Steven T. Tipton (1985), *Habits of the Heart* (Berkeley: University of California Press).

Blassingame, John (1971), *New Perspectives on Black Studies* (Chicago: University of Illinois Press).

Bourdieu, Pierre (1968), "Outline of a Theory of Art Perception," *International Social Science Journal* 2: 4: 589–612.

Bradley, Ed (1993), *The Rainbow Curriculum: 60 Minutes*, April 4.

Bronski, Michael (1984), *Culture Clash: The Making of Gay Sensibility* (Boston: South End Press).

Browning, Frank (1993), *The Culture of Desire: Paradox and Perversity in Gay Lives Today* (New York: Crown).

Carter, Stephen I. (1993), "The Black Table, the Empty Seat, and the Tie": 55–79 in *Lure and Loathing: Essays on Race, Identity, and the Ambivalence of Assimilation*, ed. Gerald Early (New York: Penguin).

Chauncey, George, Jr (1982), "From Sexual Inversion to Homosexuality: Medicine and the Changing Conceptualization of Female Deviance," *Salmagundi* 58–9: 114–46.

———(1989), "Christian Brotherhood or Sexual Perversion? Homosexual Identities and the Construction of Sexual Boundaries in the World War I Era": 294–317 in *Hidden from History: Reclaiming the Gay and Lesbian Past*, ed. Martin Duberman, Martha Vicinus and George Chauncey Jr (New York: Penguin).

Clifford, James (1986), "Introduction: Partial Truths": 1–26 in *Writing Culture: The Poetics and Politics of Ethnography*, ed. James Clifford and George E. Marcus (Berkeley: University of California Press).

Collins, Patricia Hill (1986), "Learning from the Outsider Within: The Sociological Significance of Black Feminist Thought": *Social Problems* 33: S14–S32.

———(1990), *Black Feminist Thought: Knowledge, Consciousness, and the Politics of Empowerment* (Boston: Unwin Hyman).

Conrad, Peter and Joseph Schneider (1992), *Deviance and Medicalization: From Badness to Sickness* (Philadelphia: Temple University Press).

Crenshaw, Kimberle (1992), "Whose Story Is It, Anyway? Feminist and Antiracist Appropriations of Anita Hill": 402–40 in *Race-ing Justice, En-gendering Power: Essays on Anita Hill, Clarence Thomas, and the Construction of Social Reality*, ed. Toni Morrison (New York: Pantheon).

D'Andrade, Roy G. (1984), "Cultural Meaning Systems": 88–119 in *Culture Theory: Essays on Mind, Self, and Emotion*, ed. Richard A. Shweder and Robert A. LeVine (New York: Cambridge University Press).

D'Angela, Laura (1992), "Repercussions Continue after School Board Vote," *Staten Island Sunday Advance* (September 6).

de Lauretis, Teresa (1991), "Queer Theory: Lesbian and Gay Sexualities," *differences* 3: iii–xviii.

D'Emilio, John (1983), *Sexual Politics, Sexual Communities: The Making of a Homosexual Minority in the United States, 1940–1970* (Chicago: University of Chicago Press).

D'Emilio, John and Estelle Freedman (1988), *Intimate Matters: A History of Sexuality in America* (New York: Harper and Row).

Dent, Gina (1992), *Black Popular Culture* (Seattle: Bay Press).

Doty, Alexander (1993), *Making Things Perfectly Queer: Interpreting Mass Culture* (Minneapolis: University of Minnesota Press).

Duberman, Martin, Martha Vicinus, and George Chauncey Jr (1989), *Hidden from History: Reclaiming the Gay and Lesbian Past* (New York: Penguin Books).

Duggan, Lisa (1992), "Making It Perfectly Queer," *Socialist Review* 22: 11–32.

Epstein, Steven (1987), "Gay Politics, Ethnic Identity: The Limits of Social Constructionism," *Socialist Review* 93–4: 9–54.

Faderman, Lillian (1981), *Surpassing the Love of Men* (New York: Morrow).

Ferguson, Ann (1990), "Is There a Lesbian Culture?": 63–88 in *Lesbian Philosophies and Cultures*, ed. Jeffner Allen (Albany: SUNY Press).

Ford, Nick Aaron (1973), *Black Studies: Threat-or-Challenge* (Port Washington, NY: Kennikat).

Foucault, Michel (1978), *The History of Sexuality: An Introduction*, vol. 1 (New York: Vintage).

Frankenberg, Ruth (1993), *White Women, Race Matters: The Social Construction of Whiteness* (Minneapolis: University of Minnesota Press).

Friedson, Eliot (1970), *Profession of Medicine: A Study of the Sociology of Applied Knowledge* (New York: Harper & Row).

Gagnon, John (1977), *Human Sexualities* (Glenview, IL: Scott Foresman).

Gagnon, John and William Simon (1973), *Sexual Conduct: The Social Sources of Human Sexuality* (Chicago: Aldine).

Geertz, Clifford (1973), *The Interpretation of Cultures* (New York: Basic Books).

Giddens, Anthony (1992), *The Transformation of Intimacy: Sexuality, Love and Eroticism in Modern Societies* (Stanford: Stanford University Press).

Goffman, Erving (1963), *Stigma: Notes on the Management of Spoiled Identity* (New York: Simon and Schuster).

Goldstein, Richard (1993), "Faith, Hope, and Sodomy: Gay Liberation Embarks on a Vision Quest," *Village Voice*, June 29: 21–31.

Grossberg, Lawrence, Cary Nelson and Paula Treichler (eds) (1992), *Cultural Studies* (New York: Routledge).

Grover, Jan Z. (1988), "AIDS: Keywords": 17–30 in *AIDS: Cultural Analysis, Cultural Activism*, ed. Douglas Crimp (Cambridge, MA: MIT Press).

Gusfield, Joseph R. (1955), *Symbolic Crusade* (Urbana: University of Illinois Press).

Hall, John R. and Mary Jo Neitz (1993), *Culture: Sociological Perspectives* (Englewood Cliffs, NJ: Prentice-Hall).

Hall, Stuart (1989), "Ethnicity: Identity and Difference," *Radical America* 23: 9–20.

———(1990), "The Emergence of Cultural Studies and the Crisis of the Humanities," *October* (summer): 11–23.

———(1992a), "Cultural Studies and Its Theoretical Legacies": 277–94 in *Cultural Studies*, ed. Lawrence Grossberg, Cary Nelson and Paula Treichler (New York: Routledge).

———(1992b), "New Ethnicities": 252–9 in *"Race" Culture and Difference*, ed. James Donald and Ali Rattansi (London: Sage).

Halperin, David (1990), *One Hundred Years of Homosexuality* (New York: Routledge).

Herdt, Gilbert (1992), *Gay Culture in America: Essays from the Field* (Boston: Beacon).

Hu-DeHart, Evelyn (1993), "Rethinking America: The Practice and Politics of Multiculturalism in Higher Education": 3–17 in *Beyond a Dream Deferred: Multicultural Education and the Politics of Excellence*, ed. Becky W. Thompson and Sangeeta Tyagi (Minneapolis: University of Minnesota Press).

Hull, Gloria, Patricia Bell Scott and Barbara Smith (1982), *All the Women Are White, All the Blacks Are Men, But Some of Us Are Brave* (Westbury, NY: Feminist Press).

Humphries, Laud (1974), *Tearoom Trade: Impersonal Sex in Public Places* (Chicago: Aldine).

Irvine, Janice M. (1990), *Disorders of Desire: Sex and Gender in Modern America–Sexology* (Philadelphia: Temple University Press).

———(1994), *Sexual Cultures and the Construction of Adolescent Identities* (Philadelphia: Temple University Press).

Jackson, Earl, Jr (1993), "The Responsibility of and to Differences: Theorizing Race and Ethnicity in Lesbian and Gay Studies": 131–61 in *Beyond a Dream: Multicultural Education and the Politics of Excellence*, ed. Becky W. Thompson and Sangeeta Tyagi (Minneapolis: University of Minnesota Press).

Katz, Jonathan (1976), *Gay American History* (New York: Crowell).

———(1990), "The Invention of Heterosexuality," *Socialist Review* 21: 7–34.

Kennedy, Elizabeth Lapovsky and Madeline D. Davis (1993), *Boots of Leather, Slippers of Gold: The History of a Lesbian Community* (New York: Routledge).

Kinsey, Alfred C., Wardell B. Pomeroy, Clyde E. Martin and Paul H. Gebhard (1948), *Sexual Behavior in the Human Male* (Philadelphia: Saunders).

———(1953), *Sexual Behavior in the Human Female* (New York: Pocket Books).

Lorde, Audre (1988), *A Burst of Light* (Ithaca: Firebrand Books).

Loury, Glenn C. (1993), "Free at Last? A Personal Perspective on Race and Identity in America": 1–12 in *Lure and Loathing: Essays on Race, Identity, and the Ambivalence of Assimilation*, ed. Gerald Early (New York: Penguin).

Luker, Kristen (1975), *Taking Chances: Abortion and the Decision Not to Contracept* (Berkeley: University of California Press).

Madson, Ron (1993), *The Rainbow Curriculum: 60 Minutes* (April 4).

McKnight, Reginald (1993), "Confessions of a Wannabe Negro": 95–112 in *Lure and Loathing: Essays on Race, Identity, and the Ambivalence of Assimilation*, ed. Gerald Early (New York: Penguin).

Munch, Richard and Neil J. Smelser (1992), *Theory of Culture* (Berkeley: University of California Press).

Murray, Stephen O. (1979), "The Institutional Elaboration of a Quasi-Ethnic Community," *International Review of Modern Sociology* 9: 165–77.

———(1992), "Components of Gay Community in San Francisco": 107–46 in *Gay Culture in America: Essays from the Field* ed. by Gilbert Herdt (Boston: Beacon).

Nelson, Cary *et al.* (1992), "Cultural Studies: An Introduction: 1–16 in *Cultural Studies*, ed. Lawrence Grossberg, Cary Nelson, Paula Treichler (New York: Routledge).

Newton, Esther (1984), "The Mythic Mannish Lesbian: Radclyffe Hall and the New Woman," *Signs* 9: 556–75.

———(1993), *Cherry Grove: Pleasure Island, Gay and Lesbian USA., 1930s–1980s* (Boston: Beacon).

Njeri, Itabari (1993), "Sushi and Grits: Ethnic Identity and Conflict in a Newly Multicultural America": 13–40 in *Lure and Loathing: Essays on Race, Identity and the Ambivalence of Assimilation*, ed. Gerald Early (New York: Penguin).

Omi, Michael and Howard Winant (1986), *Racial Formation in the United States from the 1960s to the 1980s* (New York: Routledge).

Penn, Donna (1993), "If It Walks like a Dyke, Talks like a Dyke, It Must Be a Dyke?" unpublished paper.

Perry, Richard J. (1992), "Why Do Multiculturalists Ignore Anthropologists?" *Chronicle of Higher Education* March 4: A52.

Peterson, John (1992), "Black Men and Their Same-Sex Desires and Behaviors": 147–64 in *Gay Culture in America: Essays from the Field*, ed. Gilbert Herdt (Boston: Beacon).

Plummer, Kenneth (1975), *Sexual Stigma: An Interactionist Account* (London: Routledge).

———(1981), *The Making of the Modern Homosexual* (London: Hutchinson).

Powers, Ann (1993), "Queer in the Streets, Straight in the Sheets," *Village Voice*, June 29: 24.

Rubin, Gayle (1975), "The Traffic in Women: Notes on the 'Political Economy' of Sex": 157–210 in *Toward an Anthropology of Women*, ed. R. Reiter (New York: Monthly Review Press).

———(1984), "Thinking Sex": 267–319 in *Pleasure and Danger: Exploring Female Sexuality*, ed. Carole S. Vance (Boston: Routledge).

Russell, Kathy, Midge Wilson and Ronald Hall (1992), *The Color Complex: The Politics of Skin Color among African Americans* (New York: Harcourt Brace Jovanovich).

Sedgwick, Eve Kosofsky (1993), "Epistemology of the Closet": 45–61 in *The Lesbian and Gay Studies Reader*, ed. Henry Abelove, Michele Aina Barale and David M. Halperin (New York: Routledge).

Seidman, Steven (1990), "Substantive Debates": 217–35 in *Culture and Society*, ed. Jeffrey Alexander and Steven Seidman (New York: Cambridge University Press).

———(1991), *Romantic Longings: Love in America, 1830–1980* (New York: Routledge).

———(1992), *Embattled Eros: Sexual Politics and Ethics in Contemporary America* (New York: Routledge).

Shweder, Richard A. (1984), "Anthropology's Romantic Rebellion against the Enlightenment, or There's More to Thinking Than Reason and Evidence": 27–66 in *Culture Theory: Essays on Mind, Self, and Emotion*, ed. Richard A. Shweder and Robert A. LeVine (New York: Cambridge University Press).

Simon, William and John Gagnon (1973), *Sexual Conduct* (Chicago: Aldine).

Smith-Rosenberg, Carroll (1985), *Disorderly Conduct: Visions of Gender in Victorian America* (New York: Knopf).

Snitow, Ann (1989), "Pages from a Gender Diary," *Dissent*: 205–24.

Stacey, Judith and Barry Thorne (1985), "The Missing Feminist Revolution in Sociology," *Social Problems* 32: 301–16.

Starr, Paul (1982), *The Social Transformation of American Medicine* (New York: Basic Books).

Stein, Arlene (1993), *Sisters, Sexperts, and Queers* (New York: Plume).

Tabor, Mary W. (1992), "S.I. Drops Gay Issues from Student Guide," *New York Times* (June 9).

Thompson, Becky W. and Sangeeta Tyagi (1993), *Beyond a Dream Deferred: Multicultural Education and the Politics of Excellence* (Minneapolis: University of Minnesota Press).

Vance, Carole S. (1991), "Anthropology Rediscovers Sexuality: A Theoretical Comment," *Social Science and Medicine* 33: 875–84.

Waters, Mary C. (1990), *Ethnic Options: Choosing Identities in America* (Berkeley: University of California Press).

Weeks, Jeffrey (1977), *Coming Out: Homosexual Politics in Britain, from the Nineteenth Century to the Present* (London: Quartet Books).

———(1981), *Sex, Politics and Society: The Regulation of Sexuality since 1800* (London: Longman).

———(1985), *Sexuality and Its Discontents: Meanings, Myths and Modern Sexualities*, (London: Routledge).

———(1991), *Against Nature: Essays in History, Sexuality and Identity* (London: Rivers Oram).

Weinberg, George (1972), *Society and the Healthy Homosexual* (New York: St Martin's).

West, Cornel (1993a), "The New Cultural Politics of Difference": 18–40 in *Beyond a Dream Deferred: Multicultural Education and the Politics of Excellence*, ed. Becky W. Thompson and Sangeeta Tyagi (Minneapolis: University of Minnesota Press).

———(1993b), *Race Matters* (Boston: Beacon).

Wuthnow, Robert (1987), *Meaning and Moral Order Explorations in Cultural Analysis* (Berkeley: University of California Press).

Zola, Irving K. (1972), "Medicine as an Institution of Social Control," *Sociological Review* 20: 487–504.

JOSHUA GAMSON

"Must Identity Movements Self-destruct?
A Queer Dilemma"

from *SOCIAL PROBLEMS*, 42: 3 (August 1995): 390–407

Focused passion and vitriol erupt periodically in the letters columns of San Francisco's lesbian and gay newspapers. When the *San Francisco Bay Times* announced to "the community" that the 1993 Freedom Day Parade would be called "The Year of the Queer," missives fired for weeks. The parade was what it always is: a huge empowerment party. But the letters continue to be telling. "Queer" elicits familiar arguments: over assimilation, over generational differences, over who is considered "us" and who gets to decide.

On this level, it resembles similar arguments in ethnic communities in which "boundaries, identities, and cultures, are negotiated, defined, and produced" (Nagel 1994: 152). Dig deeper into debates over queerness, however, and something more interesting and significant emerges. Queerness in its most distinctive forms shakes the ground on which gay and lesbian politics has been built, taking apart the ideas of a "sexual minority" and a "gay community," indeed of "gay" and "lesbian" and even "man" and "woman."[1] It builds on central difficulties of identity-based organizing: the instability of identities both individual and collective, their made-up yet necessary character. It exaggerates and explodes these troubles, haphazardly attempting to build a politics from the rubble of deconstructed collective categories. This debate, and other related debates in lesbian and gay politics, is not only over the *content* of collective identity (whose definition of "gay" counts?), but over the everyday *viability* and political *usefulness* of sexual identities (is there and should there be such a thing as "gay," "lesbian," "man," "woman"?).

This paper, using internal debates from les-bian and gay politics as illustration, brings to the fore a key dilemma in contemporary identity politics and traces out its implications for social movement theory and research.[2] As I will show in greater detail, in these sorts of debates – which crop up in other communities as well – two different political impulses, and two different forms of organizing, can be seen facing off. The logic and political utility of deconstructing collective categories vie with that of shoring them up; each logic is true, and neither is fully tenable.

On the one hand, lesbians and gay men have made themselves an effective force in the USA over the past several decades largely by giving themselves what civil rights movements had: a public collective identity. Gay and lesbian social movements have built a quasi-ethnicity, complete with its own political and cultural institutions, festivals, neighborhoods, even its own flag. Underlying that ethnicity is typically the notion that what gays and lesbians share – the anchor of minority status and minority rights claims – is the same fixed, natural essence, a self with same-sex desires. The shared oppression, these movements have forcefully claimed, is the denial of the freedoms and opportunities to actualize this self. In this *ethnic/essentialist* politic,[3] clear categories of collective identity are necessary for successful resistance and political gain.

Yet this impulse to build a collective identity with distinct group boundaries has been met by a directly opposing logic, often contained in queer activism (and in the newly anointed "queer theory"): to take apart the identity categories and blur group boundaries. This alternative angle, influenced by academic "constructionist" thinking, holds that sexual identities are historical and social products, not natural or intrapsychic ones. It is socially produced binaries (gay/straight, man/woman) that are the basis of oppression; fluid, unstable experiences of self become fixed primarily in the service of social control. Disrupting those categories, refusing rather than embracing ethnic minority status, is the key to liberation. In this *deconstructionist* politic, clear collective categories are an obstacle to resistance and change.

The challenge for analysts, I argue, is not to determine which position is accurate but to cope with the fact that both logics make sense. Queerness spotlights a dilemma shared by other identity movements (racial, ethnic, and gender movements, for example):[4] Fixed identity categories are both the basis for oppression and the basis for political power. This raises questions for political strategizing and, more importantly for the purposes here, for social movement analysis. If identities are indeed much more unstable, fluid and constructed than movements have tended to assume – if one takes the queer challenge seriously, that is – what happens to identity-based social movements such as gay and lesbian rights? Must sociopolitical struggles articulated through identity eventually undermine themselves?

Social movement theory, a logical place to turn for help in working through the impasse between deconstructive cultural strategies and category-supportive political strategies, is hard pressed in its current state to cope with these questions. The case of queerness, I will argue, calls for a more developed theory of collective identity formation and its relationship to both institutions and meanings, an understanding that *includes the impulse to take apart that identity from within.*

In explicating the queer dilemma and its implications for social movement theory, I first briefly summarize the current state of relevant literature on collective identity. Then, zeroing in on the dilemma, I make use of internal debates, largely as they took place in the letters column of the weekly *San Francisco Bay Times* in 1991, 1992, and 1993. I turn initially to debates within lesbian and gay communities over the use of the word *queer*, using them to highlight the emergence of queer activism, its continuities with earlier lesbian and gay activism, and its links with and parallels to queer theory. Next, I take up debates over the inclusion of transgender and bisexual people – the two groups brought in under an expanded queer umbrella – in lesbian and gay politics. Here I point to a distinctive (although not entirely new) element of queerness, a politic of boundary disruption and category deconstruction, and to the resistance to that politic, made especially visible by the gendered nature of these debates. Finally, in drawing out ramifications for social movement theory, I briefly demonstrate affinities between the queer debates and debates over multiracialism in African American politics, arguing that queerness illuminates the core dilemma for identity movements more generally. I conclude by suggesting ways in which social movement literature can be pushed forward by taking seriously, both as theoretical and empirical fact, the predicament of identity movements.

SOCIAL MOVEMENTS AND COLLECTIVE IDENTITY

Social movements researchers have only recently begun treating collective identity construction[5] as an important and problematic movement activity and a significant subject of study. Before the late 1980s, when rational-actor models came under increased critical scrutiny, "not much direct thought [had] been given to the general sociological problem of what collective identity is and how it is constituted" (Schlesinger 1987: 236). As Alberto Melucci (1989: 73) has argued, social movement models focusing on instrumental action tend to treat collective identity as the nonrational expressive residue of the individual, rational pursuit of political gain. And "even in more sophisticated rational actor models that postulate a *collective* actor making strategic judgments of cost and benefit about collective action," William Gamson points out, "the existence of an *established* collective identity is assumed" (1992: 58, emphasis in original). Identities, in such models, are typically conceived as existing before movements, which then make them visible through organizing and deploy them politically; feminism wields, but does not create, the collective identity of "women."

Melucci and other theorists of "new social movements" argue more strongly that collective identity is not only necessary for successful collective action, but that it is often an end in itself, as the self-conscious reflexivity of many contemporary movements seems to demonstrate.[6] Collective identity, in this model, is conceptualized as "a continual process of recomposition rather than a given," and "as a dynamic, *emergent* aspect of collective action" (Schlesinger 1987: 237, emphasis in original; see also Cohen 1985; Mueller 1992; Kauffman 1990). Research on ethnicity has developed along similar lines, emphasizing, for example, the degree to which "people's conceptions of themselves along ethnic lines, especially their ethnic identity, [are] situational and changeable" (Nagel 1994: 154). "An American Indian might be 'mixed-blood' on the reservation," as Joane Nagel describes one example, "'Pine Ridge' when speaking to someone from another reservation, a 'Sioux' or 'Lakota' when responding to the US census, and 'Native American' when interacting with non-Indians" (1994: 155; see also Padilla 1985; Alba 1990; Waters 1990; Espiritu 1992).

How exactly collective identities emerge and change has been the subject of a growing body of work in the study of social movements. For example, Verta Taylor and Nancy Whittier, analyzing lesbian-feminist communities, point to the creation of politicized identity communities through boundary-construction (establishing "differences between a challenging group and dominant groups"), the development of consciousness (or "interpretive frameworks") and negotiation ("symbols and everyday actions subordinate groups use to resist and restructure existing systems of domination") (1992: 100–111; see also Franzen 1993). Other researchers, working from the similar notion that "the location and meaning of particular ethnic boundaries are continuously negotiated, revised, and revitalized," demonstrate the ways in which collective identity is constructed not only from within, but is also shaped and limited by "political policies and institutions, immigra-

tion policies, by ethnically linked resource policies, and by political access structured along ethnic lines" (Nagel 1994: 152, 157; see also Omi and Winant 1986).

When we turn to the disputes over queerness, it is useful to see them in light of this recent work. We are certainly witnessing a process of boundary-construction and identity negotiation: As contests over membership and over naming, these debates are part of an ongoing project of delineating the "we" whose rights and freedoms are at stake in the movements. Yet as I track through the queer debates, I will demonstrate a movement propensity that current work on collective identity fails to take into account: the drive to blur and deconstruct group categories, and to keep them forever unstable. It is that tendency that poses a significant new push to social movement analysis.

QUEER POLITICS AND QUEER THEORY

Since the late 1980s, "queer" has served to mark first a loose but distinguishable set of political movements and mobilizations, and second a somewhat parallel set of academy-bound intellectual endeavors (now calling itself "queer theory"). Queer politics, although given organized body in the activist group Queer Nation, operates largely through the decentralized, local, and often anti-organizational cultural activism of street postering, parodic and nonconformist self-presentation, and underground alternative magazines ("zines") (Berlant and Freeman 1993; Duggan 1992; Williams 1993);[7] it has defined itself largely against conventional lesbian and gay politics. The emergence of queer politics, although it cannot be treated here in detail, can be traced to the early 1980s backlash against gay and lesbian movement gains, which "punctured illusions of a coming era of tolerance and sexual pluralism"; to the AIDS crisis, which "underscored the limits of a politics of minority rights and inclusion"; and to the eruption of "long-simmering internal differences" around race and sex, and criticism of political organizing as "reflecting a white, middle-class experience or standpoint" (Seidman 1994: 172).[8]

Queer theory, with roots in contructionist history and sociology, feminist theory, and post-structuralist philosophy, took shape through several late 1980s academic conferences and continues to operate primarily in elite academic institutions through highly abstract language; it has defined itself against conventional lesbian and gay studies (Stein and Plummer 1994).[9] Stein and Plummer have recently delineated the major theoretical departures of queer theory: a conceptualization of sexual power as embodied "in different levels of social life, expressed discursively and enforced through boundaries and binary divides"; a problematization of sexual and gender categories, and identities in general; a rejection of civil rights strategies "in favor of a politics of carnival, transgression, and parody, which leads to deconstruction, decentering, revisionist readings, and an anti-assimilationist politics"; and a "willingness to interrogate areas which would not normally be seen as the terrain of sexuality, and conduct queer 'readings' of ostensibly heterosexual or non-sexualized texts" (1994: 181–2).

Through these simultaneous and tenuously linked actions, then, the word "queer," as Steven Epstein puts it, has recently "escaped the bounds of quotation marks" (Epstein 1994: 189; see also Duggan 1992; Warner 1993). Its escape has been marked by quite wrenching controversy within sexual identity-based communities. To understand the uses of "queer" and its links to and departures from lesbian and gay activism it helps to hear these controversies, here presented primarily through the letters column debates over "The Year of the Queer."

My discussion of this and the two debates that follow is based on an analysis of seventy-five letters in the weekly *San Francisco Bay Times*, supplemented by related editorials from national lesbian and gay publications. The letters were clustered: The debates on the word *queer* ran in the *San Francisco Bay Times* from December 1992 through April 1993; the disputes over bisexuality ran from April 1991 through May 1991; clashes over transsexual inclusion ran from October 1992 through December 1992. Although anecdotal evidence suggests that these disputes are widespread, it should be noted that I use them here not to provide conclusive data but to provide a grounded means for conceptualizing the queer challenge.

The controversy over queerness: continuities with existing lesbian and gay activism

In the discussion of the "Year of the Queer" theme for the 1993 lesbian and gay pride celebration, the venom hits first. "All those dumb closeted people who don't like the Q-word," the *Bay Times* quotes Peggy Sue suggesting, "can go fuck themselves and go to somebody else's parade." A man named Patrick argues along the same lines, asserting that the men opposing the theme are "not particularly thrilled with their attraction to other men," are "cranky and upset," yet willing to benefit "from the stuff queer activists do." A few weeks later, a letter writer shoots back that "this new generation assumes we were too busy in the '70s lining up at Macy's to purchase sweaters to find time for the revolution – as if their piercings and tattoos were any cheaper." Another sarcastically asks, "How did you ever miss out on 'Faggot' or 'Cocksucker'?" On this level, the dispute reads like a sibling sandbox spat.

Although the curses fly sometimes within generations, many letter writers frame the differences as generational. The queer linguistic tactic, the attempt to defang, embrace and resignify a stigma term, is loudly rejected by many older gay men and lesbians.[10] "I am sure he isn't old enough to have experienced that feeling of cringing when the word 'queer' was said," says Roy of an earlier letter writer. Another writer asserts that 35 is the age that marks off those accepting the queer label from those rejecting it. Younger people, many point out, can "reclaim" the word only because they have not felt as strongly the sting, ostracism, police batons, and baseball bats that accompanied it one generation earlier. For older people, its oppressive meaning can never be lifted, can never be turned from overpowering to empowering.

Consider "old" as code for "conservative," and the dispute takes on another familiar, overlapping frame: the debate between assimilationists and separatists, with a long history in American homophile, homosexual, lesbian, and gay politics. Internal political struggle over agendas of assimilation (emphasizing sameness) and separation (emphasizing difference) has been present since the inception of these movements, as it has in other movements. The "homophile" movement of the 1950s, for example, began with a Marxist-influenced agenda of sex-class struggle, and was quickly overtaken by accommodationist tactics: gaining expert support; men demonstrating in suits, women in dresses.[11] Queer marks a contemporary anti-assimilationist stance, in opposition to the mainstream inclusionary goals of the dominant gay rights movement.

"They want to work from within," says Peggy Sue elsewhere (Bérubé and Escoffier 1991), "and I just want to crash in from the outside and say, 'Hey! Hello, I'm queer. I can make out with my girlfriend. Ha ha. Live with it. Deal with it.' That kind of stuff." In a zine called *Rant & Rave*, co-editor Miss Rant argues that: "I don't want to be gay, which means assimilationist, normal, homosexual ... I don't want my personality, behavior, beliefs, and desires to be cut up like a pie into neat little categories from which I'm not supposed to stray" (1993: 15). Queer politics, as Michael Warner puts it, "opposes society itself," protesting "not just the normal behavior of the social but the *idea* of normal behavior" (1993: xxvii). It embraces the label of perversity, using it to call attention to the "norm" in *normal*, be it hetero or homo.

Queer thus asserts in-your-face difference, with an edge of defiant separatism: "We're here, we're queer, get used to it," goes the chant. We are different, that is, free from convention, odd and out there and proud of it, and your response is either your problem or your wake-up call. Queer does not so much rebel against outsider status as revel in it.[12] Queer confrontational difference, moreover, is scary, writes Alex Chee (1991), and thus politically useful: "Now that I call myself queer, know myself as a queer, nothing will keep [queer-haters] safe. If I tell them I am queer, they give me room. Politically, I can think of little better. I do not want to be one of them. They only need to give me room."

This goes against the grain of civil rights strategists, of course, for whom at least the appearance of normality is central to gaining political "room." Rights are gained, according to this logic, by demonstrating similarity (to heterosexual people, to other minority groups) in a non-threatening manner. "We are everywhere," goes the refrain from this camp. We are your sons and daughters and co-workers and soldiers, and once you see that lesbians and gays are just like you, you will recognize the injustices to which we are subject. "I am not queer," writes a letter writer named Tony. "I am normal, and if tomorrow I choose to run down the middle of Market Street in a big floppy hat and skirt I will still be normal." In the national gay weekly *10 Percent* – for which *Rant & Rave* can be seen as a proud evil twin – Eric Marcus (1993: 14) writes that "I'd rather emphasize what I have in common with other people than focus on the differences," and "the last thing I want to do is institutionalize that difference by defining myself with a word and a political philosophy that set me outside the mainstream." The point is to be not-different, not-odd, not-scary. "We have a lot going for us," Phyllis Lyon says simply in the *Bay Times*. "Let's not blow it" – blow it, that is, by alienating each other and our straight allies with words like "queer."

Debates over assimilation are hardly new, however; but neither do they exhaust the letters column disputes. The metaphors in queerness are striking. Queer is a "psychic tattoo," says writer Alex Chee, shared by outsiders; those similarly tattooed make up the Queer Nation. "It's the land of lost boys and lost girls," says historian Gerard Koskovich (in Bérubé and Escoffier 1991: 23), "who woke up one day and realized that not to have heterosexual privilege was in fact the highest privilege." A mark on the skin, a land, a nation: These are the metaphors of tribe and family. Queer is being used not just to connote and glorify differentness but to revise the criteria of membership in the family, "to affirm sameness by defining a common identity on the fringes" (Bérubé and Escoffier 1991: 12; see also Duggan 1992).[13]

In the hands of many letter writers, in fact,

queer becomes simply a shorthand for "gay, lesbian, bisexual, and transgender," much like "people of color" becomes an inclusive and difference-erasing shorthand for a long list of ethnic, national, and racial groups. And as some letter writers point out, as a quasi-national shorthand "queer" is just a slight shift in the boundaries of tribal membership with no attendant shifts in power; as some lesbian writers point out, it is as likely to become synonymous with "white gay male" (perhaps now with a nose ring and tattoos) as it is to describe a new community formation. Even in its less nationalist versions, queer can easily be difference without change, can subsume and hide the internal differences it attempts to incorporate. The queer tribe attempts to be a multicultural, multigendered, multisexual, hodge-podge of outsiders; as Steven Seidman points out, it ironically ends up "denying differences by either submerging them in an undifferentiated oppositional mass or by blocking the development of individual and social differences through the disciplining compulsory imperative to remain undifferentiated" (1993: 133). *Queer* as an identity category often restates tensions between sameness and difference in a different language.

Debates over bisexuality and transgender: queer deconstructionist politics

Despite the aura of newness, then, not much appears new in recent queerness debate; the fault lines on which they are built are old ones in lesbian and gay (and other identity-based) movements. Yet letter writers agree on one puzzling point: Right now, it matters what we are called and what we call ourselves. That a word takes so prominent a place is a clue that this is more than another in an ongoing series of tired assimilationist–liberationist debates. The controversy of queerness is not just strategic (what works), nor only a power-struggle (who gets to call the shots); it is those, but not only those. At their most basic, queer controversies are battles over identity and naming (who I am, who we are). Which words capture us and when do words fail us? Words, and the "us" they name, seem to be in critical flux.

But even identity battles are not especially new. In fact, within lesbian-feminist and gay male organizing, the meanings of *lesbian* and *gay* were contested almost as soon as they began to have political currency as quasi-ethnic statuses. Women of color and sex radicals loudly challenged lesbian feminism of the late 1970s, for example, pointing out that the "woman's culture" being advocated (and actively created) was based in white, middle-class experience and promoted a bland, desexualized lesbianism. Working-class lesbians and gay men of color have consistently challenged *gay* as a term reflecting the middle-class, white homosexual men who established its usage (Stein 1992; Phelan 1993; Seidman 1993, 1994; Clarke 1983; Moraga 1983; Reid-Pharr 1993; Hemphill 1991). They have challenged, that is, the definitions.

The ultimate challenge of queerness, however, is not just the questioning of the content of collective identities but the *questioning of the unity, stability, viability, and political utility of sexual identities* – even as they are used and assumed.[14] The radical provocation from queer politics, one which many pushing queerness seem only remotely aware of, is not to resolve that difficulty but to exaggerate and build on it. It is an odd endeavor, much like pulling the rug out from under one's own feet, not knowing how and where one will land.

To zero in on the distinctive deconstructionist politics of queerness, turn again to the letters columns. It is no coincidence that two other major *Bay Times* letters column controversies of the early 1990s concerned bisexual and transgender people, the two groups included in the revised queer category. Indeed, in his anti-queer polemic in the magazine *10 Percent* (a title firmly ethnic/essentialist in its reference to a fixed homosexual population), it is precisely these sorts of people, along with some "queer straights,"[15] from whom Eric Marcus seeks to distinguish himself:

> Queer is not my word because it does not define who I am or represent what I believe in . . . I'm a man who feels sexually attracted to people of the same gender. I don't feel attracted to both genders. I'm not a woman trapped in a man's body, nor a man trapped in a woman's body. I'm not someone who enjoys or feels compelled to dress up in

clothing of the opposite gender. And I'm not a "queer straight," a heterosexual who feels confined by the conventions of straight sexual expression ... I don't want to be grouped under the all-encompassing umbrella of queer ... because we have different lives, face different challenges, and don't necessarily share the same aspirations.

(1993: 14)

The letters columns, written usually from a different political angle (by lesbian separatists, for example), cover similar terrain. "It is not empowering to go to a Queer Nation meeting and see men and women slamming their tongues down each others' throats," says one letter arguing over bisexuals. "Men expect access to women," asserts one from the transgender debate. "Some men decide that they want access to lesbians any way they can and decide they will become lesbians."

Strikingly, nearly all the letters are written by, to, and about women – a point to which I will later return. "A woman's willingness to sleep with men allows her access to jobs, money, power, status," writes one group of women. "This access does not disappear just because a woman sleeps with women 'too' ... That's not bisexuality, that's compulsory heterosexuality." You are not invited; you will leave and betray us. We are already here, other women respond, and it is you who betray us with your backstabbing and your silencing. "Why have so many bisexual women felt compelled to call themselves lesbians for so long? Do you think biphobic attitudes like yours might have something to do with it?" asks a woman named Kristen. "It is our community, too; we've worked in it, we've suffered for it, we belong in it. We will not accept the role of the poor relation." Kristen ends her letter tellingly, deploying a familiar phrase: "We're here. We're queer. Get used to it."[16]

The letters run back and forth similarly over transgender issues, in particular over transsexual lesbians who want to participate in lesbian organizing. "'Transsexuals' don't want to just be lesbians," Bev Jo writes, triggering a massive round of letters, "but insist, with all the arrogance and presumption of power that men have, on going where they are not wanted and trying to destroy lesbian gatherings." There are

surely easier ways to oppress a woman, other women shoot back, than to risk physical pain and social isolation. You are doing exactly what anti-female and anti-gay oppressors do to us, others add. "Must we all bring our birth certificates and two witnesses to women's events in the future?" asks a woman named Karen. "If you feel threatened by the mere existence of a type of person, and wish to exclude them for your comfort, you are a bigot, by every definition of the term."

These "border skirmishes" over membership conditions and group boundaries have histories preceding the letters (Stein 1992; see also Taylor and Whittier 1992), and also reflect the growing power of transgender and bisexual organizing.[17] Although they are partly battles of position, more fundamentally the debates make concrete the anxiety queerness can provoke. They spotlight the possibility that sexual and gender identities are not the solid political ground they have been thought to be – which perhaps accounts for the particularly frantic tone of the letters.

Many arguing for exclusion write like a besieged border patrol. "Live your lives the way you want and spread your hatred of women while you're at it, if you must," writes a participant in the transgender letter spree, "but the fact is we're here, we're dykes and you're not. Deal with it." The Revolting Lesbians argue similarly in their contribution to the *Bay Times* bisexuality debate. "Bisexuals are not lesbians – they are bisexuals. Why isn't that obvious to everyone? Sleeping with women 'too' does not make you a lesbian. We must hang onto the identity and visibility we've struggled so hard to obtain." A letter from a woman named Caryatis sums up the perceived danger of queerness:

This whole transsexual/bisexual assault on lesbian identity has only one end, to render lesbians completely invisible and obsolete. If a woman who sleeps with both females and males is a lesbian; and if a man who submits to surgical procedure to bring his body in line with his acceptance of sex role stereotypes is a lesbian; and if a straight woman whose spiritual bonds are with other females is a lesbian, then what is a female-born female who loves only other females? Soon there will be no logical answer to that question.

Exactly: In lesbian (and gay) politics, as in other identity movements, a logical answer is crucial. An inclusive queerness threatens to turn identity to nonsense, messing with the idea that identities (man, woman, gay, straight) are fixed, natural, core phenomena, and therefore solid political ground. Many arguments in the letters columns, in fact, echo the critiques of identity politics found in queer theory. "There is a growing consciousness that a person's sexual identity (and gender identity) need not be etched in stone," write Andy and Selena in the bisexuality debate, "that it can be fluid rather than static, that one has the right to PLAY with whomever one wishes to play with (as long as it is consensual), that the either/or dichotomy ('you're either gay or straight' is only one example of this) is oppressive no matter who's pushing it." Identities are fluid and changing; binary categories (man/woman, gay/straight) are distortions. "Humans are not organized by nature into distinct groups," Cris writes. "We are placed in any number of continuums. Few people are 100 per cent gay or straight, or totally masculine or feminine." Differences are not distinct, categories are social and historical rather than natural phenomena, selves are ambiguous. "Perhaps it is time the lesbian community re-examined its criteria of what constitutes a woman (or man)," writes Francis. "And does it really matter?" Transsexual performer and writer Kate Bornstein, in a *Bay Times* column triggered by the letters, voices the same basic challenge. Are a woman and a man distinguished by anatomy? "I know several women in San Francisco who have penises," she says. "Many wonderful men in my life have vaginas" (1992: 4). Gender chromosomes, she continues, are known to come in more than two sets ("could this mean there are more than two genders?"); testosterone and estrogen don't answer it ("you could buy your gender over the counter"); neither child-bearing nor sperm capacities nails down the difference ("does a necessary hysterectomy equal a sex change?"). Gender is socially assigned; binary categories (man/woman, gay/straight) are inaccurate and oppressive; nature provides no rock-bottom definitions. The opposite sex, Bornstein proposes, is neither.[18]

Indeed, it is no coincidence that bisexuality, transsexualism, and gender crossing are exactly the kind of boundary-disrupting phenomena embraced by much post-structuralist sexual theory. Sandy Stone, for example, argues that "the transsexual currently occupies a position which is nowhere, which is outside the binary oppositions of gendered discourse" (1991: 295).[19] Steven Seidman suggests that bisexual critiques challenge "sexual object choice as a master category of sexual and social identity" (1993: 123). Judith Butler argues that butch and femme, far from being "copies" of heterosexual roles, put the "very notion of an original or natural identity" into question (1990a: 123). Marjorie Garber writes that "the cultural effect of transvestism is to destabilize all such binaries: not only 'male' and 'female,' but also 'gay' and 'straight,' and 'sex' and 'gender.' This is the sense – the radical sense – in which transvestism is a 'third'" (1992: 133).

The point, often buried in over-abstracted jargon, is well taken: The presence of visibly transgendered people, people who do not quite fit, potentially subverts the notion of two naturally fixed genders; the presence of people with ambiguous sexual desires potentially subverts the notion of naturally fixed sexual orientations. (I say "potentially" because the more common route has continued to be in the other direction: the reification of bisexuality into a third orientation, or the retention of male–female boundaries through the notion of transgendered people as "trapped in the wrong body," which is then fixed.) Genuine inclusion of transgender and bisexual people can require not simply an expansion of an identity but a subversion of it. This is the deepest difficulty queerness raises, and the heat behind the letters: If gay (and man) and lesbian (and woman) are unstable categories, "simultaneously possible and impossible" (Fuss 1989: 102), what happens to sexuality-based politics?

The question is easily answered by those securely on either side of these debates. On the one side, activists and theorists suggest that collective identities with exclusive and secure boundaries are politically effective. Even those agreeing that identities are mainly fictions may take this position, advocating what Gayatri

Spivak has called an "operational essentialism" (cited in Butler 1990b; see also Vance 1988). On the other side, activists and theorists suggest that identity production "is purchased at the price of hierarchy, normalization, and exclusion" and therefore advocate "the deconstruction of a hetero/homo code that structures the 'social text' of daily life" (Seidman 1993: 130).

THE QUEER DILEMMA

The problem, of course, is that both the boundary-strippers and the boundary-defenders are right. The gay and lesbian civil rights strategy, for all its gains, does little to attack the political culture that itself makes the denial of and struggle for civil rights necessary and possible. Marches on Washington, equal protection pursuits, media-image monitoring, and so on, are guided by the attempt to build and prove quasi-national and quasi-ethnic claims. By constructing gays and lesbians as a single community (united by fixed erotic fates), they simplify complex internal differences and complex sexual identities. They also avoid challenging the system of meanings that underlies the political oppression: the division of the world into man/woman and gay/straight. On the contrary, they ratify and reinforce these categories. They therefore build distorted and incomplete political challenges, neglecting the political impact of cultural meanings, and do not do justice to the subversive and liberating aspects of loosened collective boundaries.

Thus the strong claims of queer politics and theory – that this is not how it must be, that political and social organization can and should be more true to the inessential, fluid, and multiply-sited character of sexuality; and that gay-ethnic movements make a serious error in challenging only the idea that homosexuality is unnatural, affirming rather than exposing the root cultural system.

Yet queer theory and politics tend to run past a critique of the particular, concrete forces that make sexual identity, in stabilized and binary form, a basis for discipline, regulation, pleasure, and political empowerment. In the hurry to deconstruct identity, they tend to "slide into viewing identity itself as the fulcrum of domination and its subversion as the center of an anti-identity politic" (Seidman 1993: 132); the politic becomes overwhelmingly cultural, textual, and subjectless. Deconstructive strategies remain quite deaf and blind to the very concrete and violent institutional forms to which the most logical answer is resistance in and through a particular collective identity.

The overarching strategy of cultural deconstruction, the attack on the idea of the normal, does little to touch the institutions that make embracing normality (or building a collective around inverted abnormality) both sensible and dangerous. Mall kiss-ins by San Francisco's Suburban Homosexual Outreach Program (SHOP) and other actions that "mime the privileges of normality" (Berlant and Freeman 1993: 196), "Queer Bart" (Simpson, the popular cartoon character) T-shirts and other actions that "reveal to the consumer desires he/she didn't know he/she had, to make his/her identification with the product 'homosexuality' both an unsettling and a pleasurable experience" (Berlant and Freeman 1993: 208), do very little to take on the more directly political: regulatory institutions such as law and medicine, for example, that continue to create and enforce gay/straight and male/female divisions, often with great physical and psychic violence. They do not do justice to the degree to which closing group boundaries is both a necessary and fulfilling survival strategy.

Interest-group politics on the ethnic model is, quite simply but not without contradictory effects, how the American sociopolitical environment is structured. Official ethnic categories provide "incentives for ethnic group formation and mobilization by designating particular ethnic subpopulations as targets for special treatment"; politically controlled resources are "distributed along ethnic lines"; ethnic groups mean larger voting blocs and greater influence in electoral systems (Nagel 1994: 157–9). Ethnic categories serve, moreover, as the basis for discrimination and repression, both official and informal, and thus as a logical basis for resistance. This is the buried insight of the border-patrolling separatists and the anti-queer pragmatists: that here, in this place, at this time, we need, for our safety and for potential political gains, to construct ourselves as a group whose membership criteria are clear.

The overwhelmingly female participation in the *Bay Times* disputes over bisexuality and transgender inclusion underscores this point. Lesbians are especially threatened by the muddying of male/female and gay/straight categorizations exactly because it is by keeping sexual and gender categories hard and clear that gains are made. Lesbian visibility is more recent and hard won; in struggles against patriarchal control, moreover, lesbianism and feminism have often been strongly linked.[20] Gay men react with less vehemence because of the stronger political position from which they encounter the queer challenge: as men, as gay men with a more established public identity. Just as they are gaining political ground *as lesbians*, lesbians are asked not only to share it but to subvert it, by declaring *woman* and *lesbian* to be unstable, permeable, fluid categories. Similar pitfalls were evident in the 1993 fight over Colorado's Amendment 2, which prohibits "the state or any of its subdivisions from outlawing discrimination against gay men, lesbians, or bisexuals" (Minkowitz 1993). The Colorado solicitor general, as reporter Donna Minkowitz put it, made arguments "that could have appeared in a queercore rant," promoting "a remarkably Foucaultian view of queerness as a contingent category, whose members can slip in and out of its boundaries like subversive fish" (Minkowitz 1993: 27). "We don't have a group that is easily confinable," the solicitor general argued. Here, the fluidity of group boundaries and the provisional nature of collective identity was used to argue that no one should receive legal benefits or state protection – because there is no discernible group to be protected. Although the solicitor-general-as-queer-theorist is a strange twist, the lesson is familiar: As long as membership in this group is unclear, minority status, and therefore rights and protection, are unavailable.

Built into queer debates, then, is a fundamental quandary: In the contemporary American political environment, clear identity categories are both necessary and dangerous distortions, and moves to both fix and unfix

them are reasonable. Although it comes most visibly to the fore in them, this dynamic is hardly unique to lesbian and gay movements. The conflict between a politics of identity-building and identity-blurring has erupted, for example, in recent debates in African-American movements over multiracialism. When a group lobbied the Office of Management and Budget (whose 1977 Statistical Directive recognizes four racial groups), proposing the addition of a "multiracial" classification, they were met with tremendous opposition from those who "see the Multiracial box as a wrecking ball aimed at affirmative action," since it threatens to "undermine the concept of racial classification altogether" (Wright 1994: 47; see also Omi and Winant 1986; Webster 1992; Davis 1991).

As one advocate put it, "Multiracialism has the potential for undermining the very basis for racism, which is its categories" (G. Reginald Daniel, quoted in Wright 1994: 48); as one observer put it, "multiracial people, because they are both unable and unwilling to be ignored, and because many of them refuse to be confined to traditional racial categories, inevitably undermine the entire concept of race as an irreducible difference between peoples" (Wright 1994: 49). Opponents respond vehemently to multiracial organizing, in part because civil rights laws are monitored and enforced through the existing categories. In a debate in *The Black Scholar*, African and Afro-American Studies professor Jon Michael Spencer attacked "the postmodern conspiracy to explode racial identity," arguing that "to relinquish the notion of race – even though it's a cruel hoax – at this particular time is to relinquish our fortress against the powers and principalities that still try to undermine us" (in Wright 1994: 55). Here, in a different form, is the same queer predicament.

CONCLUSION: COLLECTIVE IDENTITY, SOCIAL MOVEMENT THEORY AND THE QUEER DILEMMA

Buried in the letters column controversies over a queer parade theme, and over bisexual and transsexual involvement in lesbian organizations, are fights not only over who belongs but over the possibility and desirability of clear criteria of belonging. Sexuality-based politics thus contains a more general predicament of identity politics, whose workings and implications are not well understood: it is as liberating and sensible to demolish a collective identity as it is to establish one.

Honoring both sets of insights from the queer debates is a tall order. It calls for recognizing that undermining identities is politically damaging in the current time and place, and that promoting them furthers the major cultural support for continued damage. It means reconnecting a critique of identity to the embodied political forces that make collective identity necessary and meaningful, and reconnecting a critique of regulatory institutions to the less tangible categories of meaning that maintain and reproduce them.[21]

The neatest and most true to life means for doing so – the theoretical recognition of paradoxes and dialectics – can satisfy intellectually. Certainly a political structure that directs action towards ethnic interest group claims, and requires therefore solid proofs of authentic ethnic membership (the immutability of sexual orientation, for example), creates paradoxical forms of action for stigmatized groups. In the case of lesbians and gays, for example, gender stereotypes used to stigmatize actors (the gay man as woman, the lesbian as man) have been emphasized in order to undermine them; pejorative labels are emphasized in an effort to get rid of them.[22] But the recognition of paradox, while a significant step, is too often a stopping point of analysis. I want to suggest potentially fruitful paths forward, through research and theorizing that take the queer dilemma to heart.

The recent revival of sociological interest in collective identity has brought important challenges to earlier assumptions that identities were either irrational (and irrelevant) or antecedents to action. Yet, even as theorizing has recognized that collective identities are achieved in and through movement activity, the assumption has remained that the impetus to solidify, mobilize and deploy an identity is the only rational one. The suggestion of most social movement theory, sometimes assumed and sometimes explicit, is that secure boundaries and a clear group identity are achievable, and even more importantly, that "if a group fails in [these], it cannot accomplish any collective action" (Klandermans 1992: 81); without a solid group identity, no claims can be made. These theories have little to say about the queer impulse to blur, deconstruct, and destabilize group categories. Current theories take hold of only one horn of the dilemma: the political utility of solid collective categories.

Serious consideration of queerness as a logic of action can force important revisions in approaches to collective identity formation and deployment and their relationship to political gains. First, it calls attention to the fact that *secure boundaries and stabilized identities are necessary not in general, but in the specific* – a point current social movement theory largely misses. The link between the two logics, the ways in which the American political environment makes stable collective identities both necessary and damaging, is sorely undertheorized and underexamined.

More importantly, accommodating the complexity of queer activism and theory requires sociology to revisit the claim that social movements are engaged in simply constructing collective identities. Queer movements pose the challenge of a form of organizing in which, far from inhibiting accomplishments, the *destabilization of collective identity is itself a goal and accomplishment of collective action*. When this dynamic is taken into account, new questions arise. The question of how collective identities are negotiated, constructed, and stabilized, for example, becomes transformed into a somewhat livelier one: for whom, when, and how are stable collective identities *necessary* for social action and social change? Do some identity movements in fact avoid the tendency to take themselves apart?

Investigating social movements with the queer predicament in mind, moreover, brings attention to repertoires and forms of action that work with the dilemma in different ways. At the heart of the dilemma is the simultaneity of cultural sources of oppression (which make loosening categories a smart strategy) and institutional sources of oppression (which make tightening categories a smart strategy). Are some movements or movement repertoires more able to work with, rather than against, the simultaneity of these systems of oppression? When and how might deconstructive strategies take aim at institutional forms, and when and how can ethnic strategies take aim at cultural categories? Are there times when the strategies are effectively linked, when an ethnic maneuver loosens cultural categories,[23] or when a deconstructionist tactic simultaneously takes aim at regulatory institutions?[24]

Such questions can point the way towards novel understandings and evaluations of social movements in which collective identity is both pillaged and deployed. These questions are not a path out of the dilemma, but a path in. The fact that the predicament may be inescapable is, after all, the point: first to clearly see the horns of the dilemma, and then to search out ways for understanding political actions taking place poised, and sometimes skewered, on those horns.

NOTES

1 Although I am discussing them together because of their joint struggle against the "sex/gender system" (Rubin 1975) on the basis of same-sex desire, lesbians and gay men have long histories of autonomous organizing (Adam 1987; D'Emilio 1983). Gender has been the strongest division historically in movements for gay and lesbian rights and liberation, not surprisingly, given the very different ways in which male homosexuality and lesbianism have been constructed and penalized. This division is taken up explicitly later in the discussion.

2 In this discussion, I am heeding recent calls to bring sociology into contact with queer theory and politics (Seidman 1994). It has taken a bit of time for sociologists and other social scientists to join queer theoretical discussions, which although they emerged primarily from and through humanities scholars, could hardly be "imagined in their present forms, absent the contributions of sociological theory" (Epstein 1994: 2). On the relationship between sociology of sexuality and queer theory, see also Stein and Plummer 1994; Namaste 1994.

3 I borrow this term from Seidman (1993).

4 See, for example, Di Stefano (1990), Bordo (1990), and Davis (1991).

5 Collective identity is variously defined. I am using it here to designate not only a "status – a set of attitudes, commitments, and rules for behavior – that those who assume the identity can be expected to subscribe to," but also "an individual pronouncement of affiliation, of connection with others" (Friedman and McAdam 1992: 157). See also Schlesinger (1987).

6 There is no reason to limit this claim to "identity-based" movements, although identity construction is more visible and salient in such movements. As Taylor and Whittier argue in reviewing existing scholarship, "identity construction processes are crucial to grievance interpretation in all forms of collective action, not just in the so-called new movements" (1992: 105).

7 Queer Nation, formed in 1990, is an offshoot of the AIDS activist organization ACT UP. Queer Nation owes much to ACT UP, in its emergence, its personnel and tactics, which are often to "cross borders, to occupy spaces, and to mime the privileges of normality" (Berlant and Freeman 1993: 195). On similar tactics within ACT UP, see J. Gamson (1989). On Queer Nation specifically and queer politics more generally, see Bérubé and Escoffier (1991); Duggan (1992); Stein (1992); Cunningham (1992); Patton (1993); Browning (1993, especially chapters 2, 3, and 5).

8 See, for example, Rich (1980); Moraga (1983); Hemphill (1991); Clarke (1983); Reid-Pharr (1993).

9 Although social constructionists thought generally informs queer theory, it is important to distinguish different strands of constructionist work and their varying contributions to the development of sexual theory. Much constructionist history and sociology, which concerned "the origin, social meaning, and changing forms of the modern homosexual" and challenged essentialist notions of homosexuality, was also "often tied to a politics of the making of a homosexual minority" (Seidman 1994: 171; see, for examples, D'Emilio 1983; Faderman 1981). Post-structuralist writing on gender and sexuality, although often looking quite similar, tends to "shift the debate somewhat away from explaining the modern homosexual to questions of the operation of the hetero/homosexual binary, from an exclusive preoccupation with homosexuality to a focus on heterosexuality as a social and political organizing principle, and from a politics of minority interest to a politics of knowledge and difference" (Seidman 1994: 192; see also Epstein 1994; Namaste 1994; Warner 1993; Hennessy 1993).

It is this latter strand that has most strongly informed queer theory. Eve Kosofsky Sedgwick's *Epistemology of the Closet*, with its famous assertion that "an understanding of virtually any aspect of modern Western culture must be, not merely incomplete, but damaged in its central substance to the degree that it does not incorporate a critical analysis of modern homo/heterosexual definition" (1990: 1), is now often taken as the founding moment of queer theory; Judith Butler's *Gender Trouble* (1990a) also made a tremendous impact in the field. For further examples of queer theoretical work, see Fuss 1991; de Lauretis 1991; Butler 1993. These theoretical and political developments in the field of lesbian and gay studies also draw from and overlap with similar ones in feminism. See Ingraham (1994), and the essays in Nicholson (1990).

10 Although its most familiar recent usage has been as an anti-gay epithet, the word actually has a long and complex history. Along with *fairy*, for example, *queer* was one of the most common terms used before World War II, "by 'queer' and 'normal' people alike to refer to 'homosexuals.'" In the 1920s and 1930s, "the men who identified themselves as part of a distinct category of men primarily on the basis of their homosexual interest rather than their womanlike gender status usually called themselves queer" (Chauncey 1994: 14, 16). Whether as chosen marker or as epithet, the word has always retained its general connotation of abnormality (Chauncey 1994).

11 On assimilation–separation before Stonewall, see D'Emilio (1983) and Adam (1987). On assimilation–separation after Stonewall, see Epstein (1987).

12 Indeed, the "outlaw" stance may help explain why gender differences are (somewhat) less salient in queer organizing (Duggan 1992). Whereas in ethnic/essentialist lesbian and gay organizations participants are recruited as gay men and lesbian *women*, in queer organizations they are recruited largely as *gender outlaws*.

13 There is no question that part of what has happened with queer activism is simply the construction of a new, if contentious, collective identity: Queer Nation, with its nationalist rhetoric, is one clear example. My point, however (developed here), is not that *queer* indicates a group with no boundaries, but that it indicates a strategy for identity destabilization. This logic is not confined to a particular group formation; although it is considerably stronger in groups identifying as queer, many of which are loose associations that are very intentionally decentralized (Williams 1993), it is also often present in more mainstream organizing, albeit in more occasional and muted form. *Queer* is more useful, I am suggesting, as a description of a particular action logic than as a description of an empirically distinguishable movement form.

14 This questioning is not entirely unique to recent queer politics but has historical ties to early gay liberation calls to "liberate the homosexual in everyone" (Epstein 1987). That the current queer formulations have such affinities with earlier political activity underlines that queerness is less a new historical development than an action impulse that comes to the fore at certain historical moments. There is certainly a difference in degree, however, between the strength of a queer-style politic now and in earlier decades: With a few exceptions, earlier lesbian feminist and gay liberationist discourses rarely questioned "the notion of homosexuality as a universal category of the self and sexual identity" (Seidman 1994: 170).

15 On "queer straights," self-identifying heterosexuals who seek out and participate in lesbian and gay subcultures, see Powers (1993).

16 For more bisexuality debate, see Wilson (1992) and Queen (1992).

17 For articulations of these young movements see, on bisexual organizing, Hutchins and Kaahumanu (1991), and on transgender organizing, Stone (1991).

18 For a more developed version of these arguments, see Bornstein (1994).

19 See also Shapiro (1991), on the ways in which transsexualism is simultaneously subversive and conservative of sex and gender organization.

20 On lesbian feminism, see Phelan (1989), Taylor and Whittier (1992), and Taylor and Rupp (1993).

21 I am indebted here to Steven Seidman's discussion and critique of queer theory and politics, which make some of the points from different directions (Seidman 1993; see also Patton 1993, and Vance 1988). I want to push the discussion towards the ground, however, to open questions for political action and empirical research.

22 On this dynamic, see Weeks (1985, especially chapter 8), Epstein (1987), and J. Gamson (1989).

23 The public pursuit of same-sex marriage and parenting may be an example of this. On the one hand, the call for institutions of "family" to include lesbians and gays – as a recognizably separate species – is quite conservative of existing gender and sexual categories. It often appears as mimicry, and its proponents typically appear as close to "normal" as possible: Bob and Rod Jackson-Paris, for example, a former bodybuilder/model married couple who have been the most publicly available symbol of gay marriage, are both conventionally masculine, "traded vows in a commitment ceremony, share a house in Seattle, and plan to raise children" (Bull 1993: 42).

Yet gay families, in attacking the gender requirements of family forms, attack the cultural grounding of normality at its heart (as the religious right fully recognizes). If and when family institutions, pushed by ethnic/essentialist identity movements, shift to integrate gays and lesbians, the very markers of gay/straight difference start to disintegrate (see Weston 1991). If bodily erotic desire implies nothing in particular about the use of one's body for reproduction, its usefulness as a basis of social categories is largely gutted. In this, the gay family strategy may also be a queer one. To the degree that it succeeds, to the degree that the institution of the family changes, the categories must also lose much of their sense – and their power. This may not be true of all ethnic/essentialist actions.

24 The AIDS activist group ACT UP provides a promising starting point from this direction. Many of ACT UP's tactics have been discursive: meaning deconstruction, boundary crossing, and label disruption (J. Gamson 1989). Yet, for reasons obviously related to the immediacy of AIDS and the visible involvement of medical and state institutions, it has rarely been possible to make the argument that AIDS politics should have as its goal the deconstruction of meanings of sex, sexual identity, and disease. In much queer AIDS activism, the disruption of these meanings takes place through direct targeting of their institutional purveyors: not only media and cultural institutions, but science, medicine, and government (Epstein 1991).

For example, interventions into some spaces (medical conferences as opposed to opera houses) put queerness – its sometimes scary confrontation, its refusal to identify itself as a fixed gay or lesbian subject, its disruption of sex and gender boundaries – to use in ways that clearly mark the dangers of institutional control of sexual categories. Refusing the categories for itself, this strategy names and confronts the agents that fix the categories in dangerous, violent, and deadly ways. To the degree that the strategy succeeds, to the degree that cultural categories become frightening and nonsensical, institutional actors – and not just the vague and ubiquitous purveyors of "normality" – must also be called upon to justify their use of the categories.

REFERENCES

Adam, Barry (1987), *The Rise of a Gay and Lesbian Movement* (Boston: Twayne).

Alba, Richard (1990), *Ethnic Identity: The Transformation of White America* (New Haven: Yale University Press).

Berlant, Lauren and Elizabeth Freeman (1993), "Queer Nationality," in *Fear of a Queer Planet*, ed. Michael Warner: 193–229 (Minneapolis: University of Minnesota Press).

Bérubé, Allan and Jeffrey Escoffier (1991), "Queer/Nation," *Out/Look* (Winter): 12–23.

Bordo, Susan (1990), "Feminism, Postmodernism, and Gender-scepticism," in *Feminism/Postmodernism*, ed. Linda J. Nicholson: 133–56 (New York: Routledge).

Bornstein, Kate (1992), "A Plan for Peace," *San Francisco Bay Times*, December 3: 4.

—— (1994), *Gender Outlaw* (New York: Routledge).

Browning, Frank (1993), *The Culture of Desire* (New York: Vintage).

Bull, Chris (1993), "Till Death Do Us Part," *The Advocate*, November 30: 40–7.

Butler, Judith (1990a), *Gender Trouble: Feminism and the Subversion of Identity* (New York: Routledge).

—— (1990b), "Gender Trouble, Feminist Theory, and Psychoanalytic Discourse," in *Feminism/Postmodernism*, ed. Linda J. Nicholson: 324–40 (New York: Routledge).

——(1993), "Critically Queer," *GLQ* 1: 17–32.

Chauncey, George (1994), *Gay New York* (New York: Basic).

Chee, Alexander (1991), "A Queer Nationalism," *Out/Look* (winter): 15–19.

Clarke, Cheryl (1983), "Lesbianism: An Act of Resistance," in *This Bridge Called My Back*, eds Gloria Anzaldúa and Cherrie Moraga: 128–37 (New York: Kitchen Table Press).

Cohen, Jean (1985), "Strategy or Identity: New Theoretical Paradigms and Contemporary Social Movements," *Social Research* 52: 663–716.

Cunningham, Michael (1992), "If You're Queer and You're not Angry in 1992, You're not Paying Attention," *Mother Jones* (May/June): 60–6.

D'Emilio, John (1983), *Sexual Politics, Sexual Communities: The Making of a Homosexual Minority in the United States, 1940–1970* (Chicago: University of Chicago Press).

Davis, F. James (1991), *Who Is Black? One Nation's Definition* (University Park, PA: Pennsylvania State University Press).

de Lauretis, Teresa (1991), "Queer Theory," *differences* 3 (summer): iii–xviii.

Di Stefano, Christine (1990), "Dilemmas of Difference: Feminism, Modernity, and Postmodernism," in *Feminism/Postmodernism*, ed. Linda J. Nicholson: 63–82 (New York: Routledge).

Duggan, Lisa (1992), "Making it Perfectly Queer," *Socialist Review* 22: 11–32.

Epstein, Steven (1987), "Gay Politics, Ethnic Identity: The Limits of Social Constructionism," *Socialist Review* 93/4: 9–54.

—— (1991), "Democratic Science? AIDS Activism and the Contested Construction of Knowledge," *Socialist Review* 21: 35–64.

—— (1994), "A Queer Encounter: Sociology and

the Study of Sexuality," *Sociological Theory* 12: 188–202.

Espiritu, Yen (1992), *Asian American Panethnicity: Bridging Institutions and Identities* (Philadelphia: Temple University Press).

Faderman, Lillian (1981), *Surpassing the Love of Men* (New York: Morrow).

Franzen, Trisha (1993), "Differences and Identities: Feminism in the Albuquerque Lesbian Community," *Signs* 18: 891–906.

Friedman, Debra and Doug McAdam (1992), "Collective Identity and Activism," in *Frontiers in Social Movement Theory*, eds Aldon Morris and Carol McClurg Mueller: 156–173 (New Haven: Yale University Press).

Fuss, Diana (1989), *Essentially Speaking: Feminism, Nature, and Difference* (New York: Routledge).

——— (1991), *Inside/Out* (New York: Routledge).

Gamson, Josh (1989), "Silence, Death and the Invisible Enemy: AIDS Activism and Social Movement 'newness,'" *Social Problems* 36: 351–67.

Gamson, William A. (1992), "The Social Psychology of Collective Action," in *Frontiers in Social Movement Theory*, eds Aldon Morris and Carol McClurg Mueller: 53–76 (New Haven: Yale University Press).

Garber, Marjorie (1992), *Vested Interests: Cross-Dressing and Cultural Anxiety* (New York: Routledge).

Hemphill, Essex (ed.) (1991), *Brother to Brother* (Boston: Alyson).

Hennessy, Rosemary (1993), "Queer Theory: A Review of the Differences Special Issue and Wittig's 'the Straight mind,'" *Signs* 18: 964–73.

Hutchins, Loraine, and Lani Kaahumanu (eds), (1991), *Bi Any Other Name* (Boston: Alyson).

Ingraham, Chrys (1994), "The Heterosexual Imaginary: Feminist Sociology and Theories of Gender," *Sociological Theory* 12: 203–19.

Kauffman, L. A. (1990), "The Anti-politics of Identity," *Socialist Review* 20: 67–80.

Klandermans, Bert (1992), "The Social Construction of Protest and Multiorganizational Fields," in *Frontiers in Social Movement Theory* eds Aldon Morris and Carol McClurg Mueller: 77–103 (New Haven: Yale University Press).

Marcus, Eric (1993), "What's in a Name," *10 Percent*: 14–15.

Melucci, Alberto (1989), *Nomads of the Present: Social Movements and Individual Needs in Contemporary Society* (Philadelphia: Temple University Press).

Minkowitz, Donna (1993), "Trial by Science," *Village Voice*, November 30: 27–9.

Moraga, Cherrie (1983), *Loving in the War Years* (Boston: South End Press).

Mueller, Carol McClurg (1992), "Building Social Movement Theory," in *Frontiers in Social Movement Theory*, eds Aldon Morris and Carol

McClurg Mueller: 3–25 (New Haven: Yale University Press).

Nagel, Joane (1994), "Constructing Ethnicity: Creating and Recreating Ethnic Identity and Culture," *Social Problems* 41: 152–76.

Namaste, Ki (1994), "The Politics of Inside/out: Queer Theory, Poststructuralism, and a Sociological Approach to Sexuality," *Sociological Theory* 12: 220–31.

Nicholson, Linda (ed.) (1990), *Feminism/Postmodernism* (New York: Routledge).

Omi, Michael, and Howard Winant (1986), *Racial Formation in the United States* (New York: Routledge and Kegan Paul).

Padilla, Felix (1985), *Latino Ethnic Consciousness: The Case of Mexican Americans and Puerto Ricans in Chicago* (Notre Dame: University of Notre Dame Press).

Patton, Cindy (1993), "Tremble, Hetero Swine," in *Fear of a Queer Planet*, ed. Michael Warner: 143–77 (Minneapolis: University of Minnesota Press).

Phelan, Shane (1989), *Identity Politics: Lesbian Feminism and the Limits of Community* (Philadelphia: Temple University Press).

——— (1993), "(Be)coming Out: Lesbian Identity and Politics," *Signs* 18: 765–90.

Powers, Ann (1993), "Queer in the Streets, Straight in the Sheets: Notes on Passing," *Utne Reader* (November/December): 74–80.

Queen, Carol (1992), "Strangers at Home: Bisexuals in the Queer Movement," *Out/Look* (spring): 23, 29–33.

Rant, Miss (1993), "Queer is not a Substitute for Gay," *Rant & Rave* 1: 15.

Reid-Pharr, Robert (1993), "The Spectacle of Blackness," *Radical America* 24: 57–66.

Rich, Adrienne (1980), "Compulsory Heterosexuality and Lesbian Existence," *Signs* 5: 631–60.

Rubin, Gayle (1975), "The Traffic in Women," in *Toward an Anthropology of Women*, ed. Rayna R. Reiter: 157–210 (New York: Monthly Review Press).

Schlesinger, Philip (1987), "On National Identity: Some Conceptions and Misconceptions Criticized," *Social Science Information* 26: 219–64.

Sedgwick, Eve Kosofsky (1990), *Epistemology of the Closet* (Berkeley: University of California Press).

Seidman, Steven (1993), "Identity Politics in a 'Postmodern' Gay Culture: Some Historical and Conceptual Notes" in *Fear of a Queer Planet*, ed. Michael Warner: 105–42 (Minneapolis: University of Minnesota Press).

——— (1994) "Symposium: Queer Theory/Sociology: A Dialogue," *Sociological Theory* 12: 166–77.

Shapiro, Judith (1991), "Transsexualism: Reflections on the Persistence of Gender and the Mutability of Sex," in *Body Guards*, eds Julia Epstein and Kristina Straub: 248–79 (New York: Routledge).

Stein, Arlene (1992), "Sisters and Queers: The Decentering of Lesbian Feminism," *Socialist Review* 22: 33–55.

Stein, Arlene, and Ken Plummer (1994), "'I Can't Even Think Straight': 'Queer' Theory and the Missing Sexual Revolution in Sociology," *Sociological Theory* 12: 178–87.

Stone, Sandy (1991), "The Empire Strikes Back: A Posttranssexual Manifesto," in *Body Guards*, eds Julia Epstein and Kristina Straub: 280–304 (New York: Routledge).

Taylor, Verta and Leila Rupp (1993), "Women's Culture and Lesbian Feminist Activism: A Reconsideration of Cultural Feminism," *Signs* 19: 32–61.

Taylor, Verta, and Nancy Whittier (1992), "Collective Identity in Social Movement Communities," in *Frontiers in Social Movement Theory* eds Aldon Morris and Carol McClurg Mueller: 104–29 (New Haven: Yale University Press).

Vance, Carole S. (1988), "Social Construction Theory: Problems in the History of Sexuality," in *Homosexuality? Which Homosexuality?*, eds Dennis Altman *et al.*: 13–34 (London: GMP Publishers).

Warner, Michael (ed.) (1993), *Fear of a Queer Planet: Queer Politics and Social Theory* (Minneapolis: University of Minnesota Press).

Waters, Mary (1990), *Ethnic Options: Choosing Identities in America* (Berkeley: University of California Press).

Webster, Yehudi (1992), *The Racialization of America* (New York: St Martin's Press).

Weeks, Jeffrey (1985), *Sexuality and Its Discontents* (New York: Routledge).

Weston, Kath (1991), *Families We Choose: Lesbians, Gays, Kinship* (New York: Columbia University Press).

Williams, Andrea (1993), "Queers in the Castro," unpublished paper, Department of Anthropology, Yale University.

Wilson, Ara (1992), "Just Add Water: Searching for the Bisexual Politic," *Out/Look* (spring): 22, 24–8.

Wright, Lawrence (1994), "One Drop of Blood," *The New Yorker*, July 25: 46–55.

KENNETH PLUMMER

Afterword
"The Past, Present, and Futures of the Sociology of Same-sex Relations"[1]

This Afterword aims to locate the past ("Looking" and "Looking In"), the present ("Looking Out") and the potential future ("Looking Ahead") of sociological work around same-sex relations. As other summaries have pointed out (Plummer 1981, 1992; Stein and Plummer 1994), until the 1950s, with notable exceptions from non-sociologists such as Kinsey or Hirschfield, there was a total neglect of same-sex research in the social sciences. Throughout the 1950s and 1960s, studies of "sociological aspects of homosexuality" – usually of the empirical, survey type (Schofield 1965; Westwood 1960) – gradually appeared. From the late 1960s onwards, paralleling the rise of the lesbian and gay movement, a stronger theoretical turn towards "labeling theory" and issues of social constructionism began.

Then, in the 1970s, an interest in gender and power, alongside a more empirical sociology of lesbian and gay lives, emerged. This is largely interrupted by two forces in the 1980s: the specter of HIV/AIDS, which generates its own research momentum and leaves room for little

else to be considered; and the "Foucauldian Deluge" where analyses of discourse overtake the analysis of real world events. With the popularization and ascendancy of lesbian and gay studies beginning in the late 1980s (chronicled in Escoffier 1992), new disciplines come to dominate over sociology, which is itself seen to be in another state of crisis.

"Queer" becomes a key concern from the late 1980s onwards and, with that, a taste for somewhat "wilde" theorizing. By the time the benchmark *Lesbian and Gay Studies Reader* (Abelove *et al.* 1993) is published, only four of its forty-two contributions are written by people who could even be called social scientists: Gayle Rubin, Tomás Almaguer, Stuart Hall, and Esther Newton.

There has been, then, a spectacular rise and fall of sociological analysis around same-sex experience. This Afterword elaborates on this brief historical overview and assesses the impact of sociology on lesbian and gay studies before concluding with some directions for the future.

Nineteenth century	Perversion	Denial
Mid twentieth century	Homosexuality	Liberal research
Mid 1960s to early 1980s	Gay	Labeling theory
1970s–80s	Lesbian and gay lives	Gender theory
1980s	HIV/AIDS, "Foucauldian Deluge"	Survey research, cultural studies, discourse theory
Late 1980s	Queer	Post-structuralism

IN SEARCH OF A SOCIOLOGICAL PAST: FROM SOCIOLOGICAL MYOPIA TO SOCIOLOGICAL FERMENT

For the first hundred years of sociology, the discipline betrayed its conservatism by showing almost no concern for the subject of homosexuality. This history of erasure, denial, ignorance and neglect continues, as evidenced by the relative lack of attention given in contemporary introductory texts to sociology. It is indeed a future topic for gay research to see if any work was actually done in the past and whether it might have become hidden from history. Chauncey's (1994) *Gay New York*, Bérubé's (1991) *Coming Out Under Fire*, Newton's (1993) *Cherry Grove*, D'Emilio's (1983) *Sexual Politics, Sexual Communities*, and Davis and Kennedy's (1993) *Boots of Leather, Slippers of Gold* make it very clear that there were large hidden social worlds of homosexuality throughout the twentieth century: it would be surprising if a few sociologists had not investigated them. There are hints, for instance, that some of the Chicago sociologists of the 1920s and 1930s investigated the homosexual world, but nothing seems to have been published (Murray 1984).

Yet, we could easily write the history of the sociology of homosexuality as if nothing at all happened before the post-World-War-II period. Whilst the public domain was full of discussion of sex, sociologists – true to their frequently conservative biases – remained silent (Seidman 1992, 1994). The earliest self-conscious accounts of modern lesbian and gay experiences start to arrive in the late nineteenth century, but they have little to do with sociology. They emerge at the very moment when the homosexual category was being established alongside the hetero/homo binary split that has organized much of Western twentieth-century thinking (Sedgwick 1991). But sociologists generally had other things on their mind: any notion of these crucial gender and sexual problems seems centrally missing from the writings of Marx, Durkheim or Weber. Only Simmel takes gender as a major focus, but even for him same-sex relationships are beyond the pale. It is important to note that although same-sex experiences may be universal, the term *homosexual* was not inven-

ted until the 1860s and the clear division of the world into a heterosexual–homosexual one is not to be found in all societies. Hence, although this was a time when a consciousness of homosexuality was growing, the newly developing discipline of sociology was very distanced from such changes.

More significantly, the very early homophile rights movement was creating the first wave of "gay liberation." Most conspicuously in Europe, a number of "scientists" and scholars became engaged in attempts to explain and understand the difference that was eventually called homosexuality. Ironically, it has now become increasingly clear that some of these earlier studies of the causes and classifications of "the homosexual" – to be denounced by the 1970s – were in fact done by men (*qua* men) who would, these days, almost certainly be gay-identified (but could not then because the very idea hardly existed). Some of the studies could well be seen as the harbingers of empirical sociology which focused on the experiences of self-classified gay men.

The term "*homosexual*" was coined by K. M. Kertbeny in 1869; Karl Heinrich Ulrichs invented the term "*uranian*," embracing the mistaken idea of a third sex with a woman's mind in a man's body, and vice versa – an idea which misleadingly pervades much contemporary sexology; and Magnus Hirschfield created the Scientific Humanitarian Committee and Institute for Sex Research to study the lives of thousands of "homosexuals" (Lauritsen and Thorstad 1974; Weeks 1990). The work in North America of Kinsey – although not a sociologist but a zoological taxonomer – gave rise to some of the first social findings about homosexual lives in North America, and provided a major impetus for change.

For lesbians the literature was different; it mainly lodged in the Victorian male discourses of law, medicine, and pornography and it was murkier, more hidden, and more stigmatized. Women did not have much of their own discourse on sexuality outside that imposed by men. It was usually very negative and rendered the lesbian into a morbid pathology directly linked to the diseased male homosexual (Faderman 1991; Jeffreys 1990). Nevertheless, several cultural patterns of lesbianism become consolidated in this period: the Bohemian such as George Sand, the middle-class cross-dresser such as Rosa Bonheur, and "romantic friend-ships" (Faderman 1981). It is in literature, however, that the new lesbian started to emerge, as part of the construction of the New Woman, canonically and controversially, as the "mythic mannish lesbian" of *The Well of Loneliness* (Newton 1984; Showalter 1991).

For all their now much considered flaws, these early writings of the modern period start providing an articulation and a coherence to "the homosexual" as a distinctly modern idea. And yet it is hard to find a single sociological voice that addresses such issues. In its first hundred years, the discipline of sociology betrayed its conservative origins and engaged in a systematic neglect of the social relations of sexuality.

The history of the sociology of homosexual-ity is usually seen to start with two major clandestine studies produced in the 1950s. The first clear Anglo-American sightings are from the pseudonymous Donald Webster Cory (1951) in the US and Gordon Westwood (1960) in the UK. Both of them, as sociolo-gists, went on to make further contributions in their real names (i.e., Sagarin [1975] and Schofield [1965]). They were primarily con-cerned with a simple documentation of the social lives of homosexuals and the ways in which discrimination, prejudice and hostility affected their lives. These studies come at a time when the emerging homophile world was also developing its own institutes and maga-zines (see Legg 1994).

At this time a scattering of papers appeared, including Leznoff and Westley's 1956 article "The Homosexual Community" which is gen-erally seen as the first empirical study of a small gay community in a Canadian town. It now has considerable historical value, but it also draws out a key distinction between the overt and the covert. A few years later, in 1961, Albert Reiss published his work on male hustlers and the ways they make sense of their lives having sex with other men. These are amongst the earliest field reports of an empirical sociology (and, of course, North American where such a style of work was popular).

By the 1960s, several papers appeared in North America which applied labeling theory to homosexuality: John Kitsuse's (1962) study of student reactions, Edwin Schur's (1965) account of criminalization and its effects, and John Gagnon and William Simon's 1967 for-mulation of a broader sociological perspective. But it was the neo-functionalist framework established by the English sociologist Mary McIntosh which was to go on to be the single most influential paper from sociology in the whole field. Indeed, "The Homosexual Role" has been reproduced so many times that cutting it from this anthology was seriously considered. But it couldn't be cut – it is simply too important and too influential. McIntosh broke the mold: instead of taking "the homosexual" as a given, she turned it into the very problematic to be examined. Using a Parsonian framework, she started removing homosexuality from the dom-inance of biologists and psychologists who had hitherto seen it as a "condition."

By the early 1970s an exciting moment was reached: it was the time for sociology. A series of important studies started both to document lesbian and gay lives and to develop theoriza-tions around the very notion of "the homo-sexual." The sociology of deviance and most especially "labeling theory" came to dominate this moment. Barry Dank problematized iden-tity and the coming out process; Laud Hum-phreys brought a radical ethnographic turn into sharp focus through his investigation of public sex in "tearooms"; Carol Warren applied the insights of phenomenological interactionism to see the links between community and identity; and my own work charted the general theoret-ical baseline of interactionism as a new approach to homosexuality (Plummer 1975). Major studies appeared from the Kinsey Insti-tute which classified lesbian and gay lives and brought a comparative dimension. Most of this work "looked in" at homosexual life with sociological insights.

To summarize, the sociological achievements of this time, as are evidenced in the articles in this book – and feeding into and from such disciplines as anthropology and history – helped to shape a radical new approach to same-sex relations. Broadly, it worked on both theoretical and empirical levels. Theoretically, sociology

1 problematized the notion of "the homosexual," asking questions about the nature, origins, conditions of application, and impact of the category, thereby setting up what was to become known as the essentialist versus constructionist debate (a debate that appears in sociology long before the popularity of either Foucault or queer theory);
2 turned attention to the societal reactions towards homosexuality (never being happy with the simplistic concept of "homophobia," sociology's more historically grounded comparative analysis culminated in David Greenberg's (1988) massive, important, yet too neglected *The Construction of Homosexuality*;
3 questioned the meanings of sexualities and offered new social metaphors, like "script," in preference to biologically reductive ones like "drive" (especially as developed in the vital work of John Gagnon and William Simon);
4 explored the concept of identity long before it had become fashionable, providing valuable accounts of how identities get assembled;
5 investigated the social organization and meanings of culture and community (Ferguson 1991);
6 identified and challenged a "heterosexual assumption" in much research;
7 inserted a political analysis into much study of sex, broadening the arena of debate beyond gay politics *per se*;
8 connected to social theory, with versions of interactionism dominating this stage of analysis, although there were also attempts to bring in more structural approaches (such as Barry Adam's (1978) neglected study of oppression, *The Survival of Domination* and the Continental European work of Hocquenhem, Mieli, Dannecker and Reiche); and
9 showed a plurality of "homosexualities," as Bell and Weinberg's (1978) book was called, whilst demonstrating "normalization homosexuality," as Gagnon and Simon did.

Empirically, sociology started investigations of

1 the institutions of gay life, especially those connected to sociability (like bars) and sexualities (bathhouses, tearooms, truckers, and public spaces, as well as the whole ecosystem of "getting sex" (see Lee [1978]);
2 the relationships and patterns of gay lives, notably the creation of elementary typologies;
3 the everyday lives of everyday gay and lesbian folk and studies of the ways in which communities and community institutions were generated;

4 the tales of "coming out" in the voices of lesbian and gays;
5 the links between gay and lesbian lives and problems of gender;
6 the social reactions to homosexuals both historically (Greenberg [1988]) and situationally (Plummer [1975]); and
7 methodological issues such as "sampling" gays and lesbians (Plummer 1981).

Despite these achievements, in sheer quantity, sociology did not produce a lot. For most sociologists, lesbian and gay matters could be shunted into a ghetto and ignored. And even when it made the contributions listed above, overwhelmingly sociology brought the now more widely recognized traditional biases of white middle-class men (though in these cases they were usually not heterosexual ones). Curiously, too, lesbianism had been ignored, probably because most feminist sociologists focused attention on women and gender issues. Many of the key contributions to the study of lesbians came from outside of sociology and social science generally.

THE FOUCAULDIAN DELUGE AND THE ARRIVAL OF AIDS

The heyday of sociological research on lesbian and gay issues was probably between the mid 1970s and the early 1980s. But several events turned the attention from this analysis. One was AIDS. Not surprisingly, there was a tremendous shift away from most of the earlier fields of inquiry and an urgent move towards more and more research on aspects of the health crisis. AIDS was studied both as disease and as symbol. Studies of changing sexual behavior were initially brought to the fore; subsequently, studies of social movement change, responses to and adaptations to AIDS, including media responses, all became key areas of investigation. These borrowed from some research areas of sociology like medicine, media, and stigma.

For a while, old and new scholars actually seemed to desert gay and lesbian research as the dire needs of AIDS activism took precedence over all over concerns. Every aspect of the AIDS crisis developed its own literature. From behavioral studies of sex to socio-psychological studies of coping with AIDS; from media analyses to discourse tracts; from histories and politics to poetry and biography, an enormous culture of AIDS research and writing was generated. At the same time, there was the tragic loss of a number of leading gay scholars, including Philip Blumstein, Martin Levine, and Richard Troiden.

Whilst AIDS generated specific kinds of research, the arrival of Michel Foucault (1978) started to herald a distinctive turn towards homosexuality as a discourse. Here a focus shifts from what might be called "real life events" to a preoccupation with the power-language spirals on which social life is constituted. Foucault himself became a major intellectual symbol for the gay intellectual community, not just because of his own theories which came to dominate much "left" discourse in the 1980s but also because his own life history as sex radical came slowly to the fore after his death. James Miller's (1993) hugely polemical *The Passion of Michel Foucault* and David Halperin's (1995) *Saint=Foucault* both highlight how important, yet controversial, his work is. Although Foucault is much discussed in sociology his links to lesbian and gay studies are not often mentioned. Ultimately much of this "deconstructivist turn" may be seen to lead to the queer studies, discussed in the next section.

Curiously, then, despite a flourish of analysis and research using sociology in the early days of lesbian and gay studies, its impact rapidly declined during much of the 1980s: almost all significant sociological work turned its attention to AIDS. And once lesbian and gay studies started to establish itself in the late 1980s, the mantle of influence had passed to humanistic and literary scholars. At any major lesbian and gay academic conference, sociologists were few in number. Yet, sociological insights infuse much work in other disciplines – acknowledged, as in George Chauncey's (1994) *Gay New York*, or unacknowledged, as in Judith Butler's (1990) *Gender Trouble*, a discovery of a dramaturgical/performance theory of gender.

But, in general, with a few major exceptions, there is little innovation and development currently taking place within sociology on same-sex relations. Two exceptions might include the British Sociological Association conference on sexualities in 1994 where a surprising number of papers had aspects of gayness as a focus (see Holland and Weeks 1996); and the emergence of a new cohort of young sociological gay and lesbian scholars in the US.

THE PRESENT AND ITS CONTROVERSIES: SOCIOLOGY IN DECLINE AND QUEERING THE FIELD

There are a number of reasons why sociology seems to be playing a lesser role in lesbian and gay studies. These include tensions that have emerged from four sources: a sociological community that marginalizes lesbian and gay concerns; a lesbian and gay community that militates against the constructionism of most sociological analyses; a generationally based "queer studies" that favors cultural studies over sociological studies; and a number of social movements that see much of sociology as inevitably skewed to white male biases. Sociological work can be situated at the intersection of these tensions; its future will depend in part upon how it handles them.

Most obviously, it remains the case that the sociological community has little room for such study. Indeed, it still marginalizes, minimizes, and minoritizes our work. This is not a matter of overt discrimination since few sociologists, one hopes, would wish to be seen as homophobic or discriminatory. Rather, it is simply that, when sociologists in general study the world, they elect to ignore dimensions that are of direct relevance to lesbian and gay lives. The study of social movements or the study of identities are good examples.

In both of these important, influential and currently fashionable areas, gay and lesbian sociology has contributed much. Arguably our movement is one of the most successful of the new social movements and lesbians and gays have been key protagonists in the emergence of identity politics debates (Phelan 1989). There is a very significant amount of primary material available about the lesbian and gay movements, its schisms and conflicts, its history and rhetorics, and its campaigns and manifestos. Of all contemporary social movements, it may be that the lesbian and gay movement has proved the most successful. Yet to read mainstream social movement texts would lead one to think it didn't exist. The writings of Touraine, Snow, Melucci, and Oberschall do not give even passing reference to Barry Adam's (1987 and revised in 1995) key book on *The Rise of a Lesbian and Gay Movement*; and a brief review of major journals, yearbooks, and textbooks finds almost total neglect.

It doesn't get much better with the fully blossoming "identity studies" literature. For instance, Craig Calhoun's (1994) *Social Theory and the Politics of Identity* treats us largely as if the sociology of lesbian and gay identity added nothing to the debate (there is a brief mention of Diane Fuss), whereas in fact it is not only central to it but it has been so for a very long time. Sociologists of lesbian and gay lives have been debating the politics of identity for the past twenty years. Is this a willful ignorance from major social theorists, or even a latent homophobia? It is certainly very puzzling.

There has also been a long and uneasy relationship between the sociology of lesbian/gay communities and the lesbian/gay communities themselves. Some lesbian and gay sociologists are part of this movement but it often leaves them in a curiously contradictory tension: their theories and their politics often seem ill at ease. Thus community members often believe passionately in a "folk essentialism" – that we are born this way – whilst sociologists much more generally take a constructionist line (see Whisman 1996). The popularity of the work of Simon LeVay, celebrating our shrinking hypothalamus, meets disbelief in sociological circles. It is a tension long recognized and widely discussed, but not one that can be easily resolved. Likewise, movement members may take for granted the power and significance of "Stonewall," whilst for sociologists "Stonewall" is a symbol of a shared collective memory for rewriting history. This does not weaken its importance, but it gives rise to a very different perspective.

In addition, it is apparent that movement members have their own schisms and conflicts, from assimilationists to tribalists, something that sociologists can recognize as driving forces in all social movements. But this recognition makes them "strangers" to some of the movement's activities. At the very least, the sociological imagination has to permit multiple ways of seeing and to acknowledge that every way of seeing is a way of not seeing. This makes the taking of sides in such schisms much harder.

Yet even with an eye for the multiplicity of meanings, sociologists have not been attentive to important differences in identity and community that are shaped by racial, ethnic, and national cultures. The articulation of these issues has occurred primarily within the anthologizing efforts of lesbian and gay people of color, including many poets and authors like Gloria Anzaldúa, Audre Lorde, Barbara Smith, and Cherríe Moraga. Once again, sociologists have not been leading the way. Lesbian and gay sociologists need to see the differences within as much as the differences without (as some of the selections in Part 4 argue).

Equally important these days is the direction lesbian and gay studies is taking into "queer theory" which does not appear to encourage sociology. Until recently, very few sociologists have even recognized the existence of queer theory, although the July 1994 (12:2) issue of *Sociological Theory*, edited by Steven Seidman, presents a symposium around it and might make for some increased awareness. Sociology will be the poorer if it fails to engage with queer theory.

However, there is no automatic or easy affinity between the two. Queer theory may have as much to learn from sociology as sociology has to learn from queer theory. Indeed, this theory often draws from sociology but refuses to acknowledge it. It sometimes fails to recognize that the whole deconstructionist project started intellectually before the lesbian and gay movement. Didn't Mary McIntosh, after all, deconstruct the homosexual in 1967? It refuses to recognize that much of queer theory centers on generation differences. Each new cohort of scholars necessarily needs to rewrite their intellectual and political project. They have to invent their own ideas, languages, concepts, and canons.

Further, a major problem emerges for sociology through what may be termed the over-textualization of lesbian and gay experiences. There are important studies to be done in the empirical world, and an obsession with texts is dangerous indeed. It is time to move beyond the text – and rapidly. Whilst lesbian and gay studies "plays" more and more fancifully with a wide array of poems, novels, and films, relatively little research actually exists on what is going on in lesbian and gay worlds right now. Perhaps because we think we live it, we do not need to research it. But if this is so, sociology as a discipline will have come to an end.

Finally, a tension exists between men and women which has been present since the very interception of lesbian and gay studies. Although we talk of a lesbian *and* gay studies, the idea that these two terms can be happily juxtaposed is a problem. The issues that lesbian and gay men confront in the Western world seem at times to be of such a different order, and indeed seem to be so deeply antagonistic to each other, that enmity rather than collaboration has been the rule of the day. The basis of this hostility is not hard to see: some parts of "modern lesbianisms" have become embedded within the women's movement and in feminism with its analysis of male domination and patriarchy, since their mutual inception. As Celia Kitzinger (1987: 64) has argued, "Central to radical feminism is the belief that patriarchy (not capitalism or sex roles or socialization or individual sexist men) is the root of all forms of oppression; that all men benefit from and maintain it and are, therefore, our political enemies."

In this quote, does "all men" include gay men? For the past twenty years, this argument has been repeated on many occasions, from personal rejections of phallocentric gay men (Stanley 1984); to critiques of the organization of some gay male sexualities into such features as cruising, pornography, and sado-masochism (e.g. Jeffreys 1990); to analyses which suggest that the central organizing force of patriarchy is male sexuality, of which male gay sexuality is a part (MacKinnon 1987). Such arguments led to a lesbian feminist separatism. If it was up to this strand of feminist analysis alone, there would be no contact between gay men and lesbians, especially since many gay men have been neither very supportive of a strong women's movement nor doing analysis with the same depth as feminist research.

THE FUTURE OF SOCIOLOGY IN LESBIAN AND GAY STUDIES

There have been a number of recent discussions of future research directions; the introductions to the various sections of this book provide a number of further suggestions. In addition, a call for work that would link to globalization, heterosexism, postmodernism, and intimate citizenship appeared in Plummer (1992). In a later essay with Arlene Stein (1994), I also suggested three zones for inquiry: to re-read the classics; to reconsider whole fields of sociology in the light of lesbian/gay/queer studies; and to rethink pedagogy. Here are several other areas where sociologists still have important contributions to make:

First, modernizing and postmodernizing homosexuality. This is a long overdue recognition that we need to study how homosexuality is linked to modernity/postmodernity. As Seidman (1994: 166–7) writes, "the standard histories link the rise of the modern social science to social modernization (e.g. industrialism, class conflict, and bureaucracy), but are silent about sexual (and gender) conflicts." Some historical researches (e.g., Chauncey 1994) and some of the new social geography (e.g., Bell and Valentine 1995) have hinted at the varieties of patternings in time and space; Henning Bech in Denmark has developed some key ideas around the city and change; and others are studying same-sex relations in contrasting cultures. But there needs to be a much wider and firmer theoretical confrontation with such concerns. Modern homosexualities mesh with modernity; and as modernity shifts into late modernity or even postmodernity, what is happening to same-gender relations? How are they linked to globalization? The concern here must certainly not simply be from a Western point of view, but from the many conflicting experiences emerging all over the world.

Second, gaying (or queering) of sociology. There is a need to bring mainstream sociologists into an awareness of lesbian and gay concerns so that they may incorporate such understandings in their everyday non-gay research and theory. This would be a major achievement and lead to the weakening of the ghettoization of lesbian and gay research. For example, two possible projects could include: (1) anti-homophobic or anti-heteronormative inquiries into a range of fields (e.g. education, family) alongside a concern over the production, organization, intensification, and destabilization of heterosexuality (see Katz 1995); and (2) the placing of homo/hetero/queer debates at the forefront of classic fields (e.g. social theory and classic texts). For instance, what would happen if Durkheim's *Suicide*, Parks's *The City* or Duneier's *Slim's Table* were given "gay" readings?

Third, broadening the analysis of same-sex relations. Although it has long been a truism that "a homosexual is not a homosexual is not a homosexual," very few sociologists have "stretched" their analyses beyond what could be called "the homosexual." Protestations notwithstanding, the focus has remained "the homosexual." But just as queer theory may have helped broaden and weaken the conventional area of analysis, so there are recent signs that sociologists may be looking at the messiness of the field. How, for instance, do some non-gay men come to have – and have to deal with – an array of gay friends; how do women respond to gay men – the "fag hag" syndrome; how do gay men and lesbians live together; or how do lesbian and gay categories come to no longer matter in relationships? What happens in the gym and amongst the body-builders? And how is gender linked into all this (Connell 1992)?

Fourth, rediscovering ethnography. Ethnography has been rediscovered within cultural studies, but it has a long lineage within sociology. What is odd is just how little the full richness of gay lives and gay communities has not been followed through in sociology. For instance, I do not know of a single published ethnography of any aspect of London's lesbian/gay scene. So many areas here cry out for research. Ethnography has taken a much more reflexive turn recently which will lead to more sophisticated treatments.

Fifth, developing media studies of homosexualities. There is major research to be done on mass media and homosexuality: not the rather obvious reading or rereading of texts where "I Love Lucy" can be read as a sign of lesbian life, as in Doty's (1993) *Making Things Perfectly Queer*, but rather with a sense of media research. How do actual lesbian and gay men come to appropriate non-gay and gay images; how do they really consume and read texts? Just as media studies now show a whole array of negotiated reposes to media images, so we could have studies of lesbian and gay negotiations (and not just those of the "expert" film critics or the expert "queer theorist").

Sixth, stratifying homosexualities. Despite the advent of multiculturalism and some forays into the study of lesbian and gay lives from black, Asian, or Latino perspectives, the major forms of inequality, domination, exploitation, and marginalization around the lesbian and gay communities remain hardly touched (Leong 1995). Research on gay and lesbian issues must consider the intersection of race, class, age, gender, and sexual orientation.

Seventh, analyzing heterosexist practices. Sylvia Walby's (1990) work on patriarchy provides a blueprint for sociological work on heterosexism. By seeing heterosexism as a set of practices, a number of institutional domains, such as families, workplace, religion, politics, media, schools, and of course sexualities, could be evaluated from another perspective.

Eighth, transcending discourse. None of the above suggestions seeks a continuation of the currently fashionable concern with discourse, text, and story. It seems to me that this has become the dominant trend in lesbian and gay studies – and it is a dangerous one. It cuts us off from the study of real-world events and turns out to be a stream of analyses which see only language, rhetorics, and discourse. In a special issue of *Critical Sociology* (20: 3, 1994) which aims to provide a critical gay and lesbian sociology, every article but one has a focus on discourse: the Jeffery Dahmer discourse, the meanings of the AIDS Quilt, the rhetorics of the right, homophobia discourse, hegemonic discourse, and the like. Much of this is valuable work; but it is as if the complex, concrete living social worlds of lesbians and gay men do not exist. Instead, we enter a world where language games are prime.

We are not arguing for a simple minded return to streams of small-scale and useless empirical studies. But we do see the need for social theory to become tempered with the everyday lived lives of lesbian and gay men struggling globally in a culture mediated by strong structures of sexual hatred and forms of domination. It is time for sociology to take a major lead in returning lesbian and gay studies to the empirical world.

NOTE

1   The author is very grateful to Peter Nardi and Beth Schneider for their helpful comments on this afterword. A slightly different version is to be found in Theo Sandfort *et al.*'s *Lesbian and Gay Studies* (forthcoming).

REFERENCES

Abelove, Henry, Barale, M. A. and Halperin, D. M. (eds) (1993), *The Lesbian and Gay Studies Reader* (London: Routledge).

Adam, Barry (1978), *The Survival of Domination* (New York: Elsevier).

——(1995) (2nd ed.), *The Rise of a Lesbian and Gay Movement* (Boston: Twayne).

Bell, Alan and Weinberg, Martin S. (1978), *Homosexualities* (London: Mitchell Beazley).

Bell, David and Valentine, Gill (1995), *Mapping Desire* (London: Routledge).

Bérubé, Allan (1991), *Coming Out Under Fire* (New York: Plume).

Butler, Judith (1990), *Gender Trouble* (London: Routledge).

Calhoun, Craig (ed.) (1994), *Social Theory and the Politics of Identity* (Oxford: Blackwell).

Chauncey, George (1994), *Gay New York* (New York: Basic Books).

Connell, R. W. (1992), "A Very Straight Gay: Masculinity, Homosexual Experience and the Dynamics of Gender," *American Sociological Review* 57: 6.

Cory, Donald Webster (1951), *The Homosexual in America* (New York: Greenberg).

Davis, Madeline and Kennedy, Elizabeth (1993), *Boots of Leather, Slippers of Gold: The History of a Lesbian Community* (London: Routledge).

D'Emilio, John (1983), *Sexual Politics, Sexual Communities* (Chicago: University of Chicago Press).

Doty, Alexander (1993), *Making Things Perfectly Queer* (Minneapolis: University of Minnesota Press).

Escoffier, Jeffrey (1992), "Generations and Paradigms: Mainstreams in Lesbian and Gay Studies," *Journal of Homosexuality* 24:1–2: 7–27.

Faderman, Lillian (1981), *Surpassing the Love of Men* (London: Junction Books).

——(1991), *Odd Girls and Twilight Lovers* (New York: Columbia University Press).

Ferguson, Ann (1991), *Sexual Democracy* (Oxford: Westview).

Foucault, Michel (1978), *The History of Sexuality* (New York: Vintage).

Greenberg, David (1988), *The Construction of Homosexuality* (Chicago: University of Chicago Press).

Halperin, David (1995), *Saint=Foucault: Toward a Gay Hagiography* (Oxford: Oxford University Press).

Holland, Janet and Weeks, Jeffrey (eds) (1996), *Sexual Cultures* (London: Macmillan).

Jeffreys, Sheila (1990), *Anti Climax* (London: Women's Press).

Katz, Jonathan (1995), *The Invention of Heterosexuality* (New York: Dutton).

Kitsuse, John (1962), "Societal Reaction to Deviant Behavior: Problems of Theory and Method," *Social Problems* 9, 247–56.

Kitzinger, Celia (1987), *The Social Construction of Lesbianism* (London: Sage).

Lauritsen, John and Thorstad, D. (1974), *The Early Homosexual Rights Movement (1864–1935)* (New York: Times Change Press).

Lee, John Alan (1978), *Getting Sex* (Toronto: General).

Legg, W. Dorr (1994), *Homophile Studies in Theory and Practice* (San Francisco: ONE Institute/GLB Publishers).

Leong, Russell (1995), *Asian American Sexualities* (London: Routledge).

MacKinnon, Catherine (1987), *Feminism Unmodified* (Cambridge, MA: Harvard University Press).

Miller, James (1993), *The Passion of Michel Foucault* (New York: Simon & Schuster).

Murray, Stephen O. (1984), *Social Theory, Homosexual Realities* (New York: Gai Saber Monograph).

Newton, Esther (1984), "The Mythic Mannish Lesbian," *Signs* 9: 4: 557–75.

——(1993), *Cherry Grove, Fire Island* (Boston: Beacon).

Phelan, Shane (1989), *Identity Politics: Lesbian Feminism and the Limits of Community* (Philadelphia: Temple University Press).

Plummer, Ken (1975), *Sexual Stigma* (London: Routledge).

———(ed.) (1981), *The Making of the Modern Homosexual* (London: Hutchinson).

———(ed.) (1992), *Modern Homosexualities* (London: Routledge).

Sagarin, E. (1975), *Deviants and Deviance: An Introduction to the Study of Devalued People and Behavior* (New York: Praeger).

Schofield, M. (1965), *Sociological Aspects of Homosexuality* (London: Longmans).

Schur, Edwin M. (1965), *Crimes Without Victims* (Englewood Cliffs: Prentice Hall).

Sedgwick, Eve Kosofsky (1991), *Epistemology of the Closet* (London: Harvester Wheatsheaf).

Seidman, Steven (1990), *Romantic Longings* (London: Routledge).

———(1992), *Embattled Eros* (London: Routledge).

———(1994), "Symposium: Queer Theory/ Sociology: A Dialogue." *Sociological Theory* 12: 2, (July): 166–77 (reprinted in *Queer Theory/Sociology* (Cambridge, MA: Blackwell, 1996)).

Showalter, Elaine (1991), *Sexual Anarchy: Gender and Culture at the Fin de Siecle* (London: Bloomsbury).

Stanley, Liz (1984), "'Male Needs' The Problems of Working with Gay Men," in S. Friedman and E. Sarah (eds), *On the Problem of Men* (London: Women's Press).

Stein, Arlene and Plummer Ken (1994), "I Can't Even Think Straight: Queer Theory and the Missing Sexual Revolution in Sociology", *Sociological Theory* 12: 2: 178–87.

Walby, Sylvia (1990), *Theorising Patriarchy* (Oxford: Polity).

Weeks, Jeffrey (1990) (2nd ed.), *Coming Out* (London: Quartet Books).

———(1995), *Invented Moralities* (Oxford: Polity Press).

Westwood, G. (1960), *A Minority: A Report on the Life of the Male Homosexual in Great Britain* (London: Longmans Green).

Whisman, Vera (1996), *Queer by Choice: Lesbians, Gay Men, and the Politics of Identity* (New York: Routledge).

INDEX

Note: page numbers in italics denote figures or tables.